Banning the Watsons   285
KKK Wizard Honored   322
Reflection   353
Towards Enlightenment: Are Schools
    Feng Shui?   373
Bonus Pay   413
2 Nice 2B 4-Gotten   440
Get Away from the Starting Line   506
Jerry! Jerry! Jerry!   518
Most Wired Campuses   540
Merit Pay   570
From Vienna to the Bronx   592
Promising Portrait of Today's Teachers   596

PHOTO-SYNTHESIS

A Teaching Legacy   19
The More Things Change, the More
    They Stay the Same   50
Crime and Punishment   91
Signs of the Times   164
School Uniforms   208
The Sound of Music   244
To Test or Not to Test   265
Twentieth Century Classrooms   324
Philosophy Photos   370
Welcome to School   396
Welcome to School   442
The Sports Gender Gap: Then & Now   494
Computer Use   542
Interview Formats   566

PROFILE IN EDUCATION

Jaime Escalante   28
Carlos Julio Ovando   63
Larry Cuban   107
Jonathan Kozol   156
Jeannie Oakes   188
Lisa Delpit   236
Alfie Kohn   266
Jane Roland Martin   362
Anne Bryant   406
Morris Dees   435
Marian Wright Edelman   502
Christa McAuliffe and Sally Ride—
    Sisters in the Sky   534
Margaret Haley   572

YOU BE THE JUDGE

A Teaching Career   6
Special Needs Students   70
Skilled Teachers Are Best Developed
    Through   113
For-Profit Schools   162
Homework Should Be   205
The Extracurriculum . . .   225
State Standards and Tests   272
School Mascots   328
Teacher- versus Student-Centered
    Approaches to Education   358
"Equity" or "Adequacy"   391
Moral Education and Ethical Lessons   453
Keep Students Together or Mix
    Them Up?   509
Computers—Educational Marvel
    or Menace?   531
Have Public Schools Failed or Served
    Society?   578

YOUR KEY TO *TEACHERS, SCHOOLS, AND SOCIETY*, 6/E

REFLECTION highlights reflection questions.

OLC indicates that you should go to the Online Learning Center for more information or to do an activity. The activity will be found under the appropriate chapter.

OLC indicates that you can go to the Online Learning Center to e-mail your professor the response to a reflection question and/or save your response for your portfolio. This option will be located under the appropriate chapter.

TEACHERS, SCHOOLS, AND SOCIETY

TEACHERS, SCHOOLS, AND SOCIETY

SIXTH EDITION

MYRA POLLACK SADKER

Late Professor, American University

DAVID MILLER SADKER

American University

Boston   Burr Ridge, IL   Dubuque, IA   Madison, WI   New York   San Francisco   St. Louis
Bangkok   Bogotá   Caracas   Kuala Lumpur   Lisbon   London   Madrid   Mexico City
Milan   Montreal   New Delhi   Santiago   Seoul   Singapore   Sydney   Taipei   Toronto

McGraw-Hill Higher Education

A Division of The **McGraw-Hill** *Companies*

TEACHERS, SCHOOLS, AND SOCIETY

Published by McGraw-Hill, a business unit of The McGraw-Hill Companies, Inc., 1221 Avenue of the Americas, New York, NY, 10020.

Some ancillaries, including electronic and print components, may not be available to customers outside the United States.

This book is printed on acid-free paper.

1 2 3 4 5 6 7 8 9 0 DOW/DOW 0 9 8 7 6 5 4 3 2

ISBN   0-07-248491-8 (student edition)
ISBN   0-07-252735-8 (instructor's edition)

Publisher: *Jane Karpacz*
Developmental editor: *Cara Harvey*
Editorial coordinator: *Christina Lembo*
Lead project manager: *Susan Trentacosti*
Production supervisor: *Susanne Riedell*
Senior designer: *Jennifer McQueen*
Media producer: *Lance Gerhart*
Senior supplement producer: *Rose M. Range*
Photo research coordinator: *Jeremy Cheshareck*
Photo researcher: *Feldman & Associates*
Cover and interior design: *Kiera Cunningham*
Typeface: *9/12 Stone Serif*
Compositor: *GAC Indianapolis*
Printer: *R. R. Donnelley & Sons Company*
Cover images: Robin Davies, V.C.L., Carol Kohen, Ross Whitaker © Getty Images. Sharon Hoogstraten. Special thanks to Burr Ridge Middle School, Burr Ridge, IL.

Library of Congress Control Number: 2002100720

www.mhhe.com

ABOUT THE AUTHORS

MYRA SADKER

Dr. Myra Sadker was professor of Education and Dean of the School of Education until 1995. Dr Sadker wrote the first book on gender bias in America's schools in 1973, and became a leading advocate for equal educational opportunities. She died while undergoing treatment for breast cancer in 1995. In her name, Myra Sadker Advocates was established to continue her efforts and create more equitable and effective schools. You are invited to learn more about Myra's contributions and the work of Myra Sadker Advocates by visiting the website established in her name.

www. sadker.org

DAVID SADKER

Dr. David Sadker is a professor at The American University (Washington, DC) and with his late wife, Myra Sadker, gained a national reputation for their work in confronting gender bias and sexual harassment. He has directed more than a dozen federal education grants, and authored five books and more than seventy-five articles in journals such as *Phi Delta Kappan, Harvard Educational Review,* and *Psychology Today.* His research and writing document sex bias from the classroom to the boardroom. The Sadkers' work has been reported in hundreds of newspapers and magazines including *USA Today, USA Weekend, Parade Magazine, Business Week, The Washington Post, The London Times, The New York Times, Time,* and *Newsweek.* They appeared on local and national television and radio shows such as "The Today Show," "Good Morning America," "The Oprah Winfrey Show," "Phil Donahue's The Human Animal," National Public Radio's "All Things Considered," and twice on "Dateline: NBC with Jane Pauley." The Sadkers received the American Educational Research Association's award for the best review of research published in the United States in 1991, their professional service award in 1995, the Eleanor Roosevelt Award from The American Association of University Women in 1995, and the Gender Architect Award from the American Association of Colleges of Teacher Education in 2001. The Sadkers' book, *Failing at Fairness: How Our Schools Cheat Girls,* was published by Touchstone Press in 1995.

BRIEF CONTENTS

Preface xv
A Guided Tour of Your Interactive Text xx

PART 1: TEACHERS AND STUDENTS

1 Becoming a Teacher *4*
2 Student Diversity *37*
3 Teacher Effectiveness *80*
Inter-mission *119*

PART 2: SCHOOLS AND CURRICULUM

4 Schools: Choices and Challenges *134*
5 Life in Schools *175*
6 What Students Are Taught in Schools *218*
7 Controversy Over Who Controls the Curriculum *255*
Inter-mission *294*

PART 3: FOUNDATIONS

8 The History of American Education *304*
9 Philosophy of Education *347*
10 Financing and Governing America's Schools *385*
11 School Law and Ethics *423*
Inter-mission *462*

PART 4: TOMORROW

12 The Struggle for Educational Opportunity *472*
13 Technology in Education *516*
14 Your First Classroom *550*
15 Q and A Guide to Entering the Teaching Profession *585*
Inter-mission *607*

APPENDIXES

1 State Offices for Teacher Certification and Licensure *A–1*
2 Information about the Teacher Competency Exams (Praxis Series) *A–5*
3 A Summary of Selected Reports on Education Reform *A–8*
4 Observation Manual *A–12*

Glossary G–1
Notes N–1
Photo Credits P–1
Index I–1

CONTENTS

Preface xv
A Guided Tour of Your Interactive Text xx

1 TEACHERS AND STUDENTS

1 Becoming a Teacher 4

What Are You Doing for the Rest of Your Life? 5

Do Teachers Like Teaching? 5

Professionalism at the Crossroads 9

From Normal Schools to Board-Certified Teachers 15

Teacher Education Today 18

On Discipline 20

On Competition 20

On Honesty and Dependability 21

On Urban Legends about Teaching 21

Southwest Airlines and Teaching 24

We Like Questions 27

Summary 32

Key Terms and People 34

Discussion Questions and Activities 34

Reel to Real Teaching 35

For Further Reading 36

2 Student Diversity 37

Different Ways of Learning 38

Multiple Intelligences and Emotional Intelligence 43

Cultural Diversity 47

Teaching Them All 48

Culture and Education 101 51

Multicultural Education 54

Bilingual Education 56

Exceptional Learners 64

Exceptional Learners: An Exceptional Struggle for Educational Rights 64

The Gifted and Talented 68

Summary 74

Key Terms and People 76

Discussion Questions and Activities 77

Reel to Real Teaching 78

For Further Reading 78

3 Teacher Effectiveness 80

Are Teachers Born, or Made? 81

The Mysterious Case of Teacher Effectiveness 82

Academic Learning Time 83

Classroom Management 84

The Pedagogical Cycle 90

Clarity and Academic Structure 92

Questioning 93

Student Response 96

Reaction or Productive Feedback 99

Variety in Process and Content 102

Models for Effective Instruction 104

Direct Teaching 104

Cooperative Learning 105

Mastery Learning 106

Problem-Based Learning 108

Effective and Reflective Teaching 109

Summary 114

Key Terms and People 115

Discussion Questions and Activities 116

Reel to Real Teaching 117

For Further Reading 118

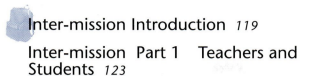

Inter-mission Introduction *119*

Inter-mission Part 1   Teachers and
Students *123*

2 SCHOOLS AND CURRICULUM

4 Schools: Choices and Challenges *134*

A Meeting Here Tonight *135*

The Purposes of School *140*

*Purpose 1: To Transmit Society's Knowledge and Values
(Passing the Cultural Baton) 140*

*Purpose 2: Reconstructing Society (Schools as Tools for
Change) 141*

Public Demands for Schools 144

Where Do You Stand? *145*

Education Reform *148*

Beyond the Neighborhood Public
   School *152*

The Choice Concept 153

Magnet Schools 153

Open Enrollment 153

Vouchers 154

Charter Schools 155

*EMOs (Educational Maintenance Organizations):
Schools for Profit 160*

Is Choice a Good Idea? 163

Home Schools, Home Teachers 166

Summary 170

Key Terms and People 172

Discussion Questions and Activities 172

Reel to Real Teaching 173

For Further Reading 174

5 Life in Schools *175*

Rules, Rituals, and Routines *176*

*"Come Right Up and Get Your New Books":
A Teacher's Perspective 176*

*"Come Right Up and Get Your New Books":
A Student's Perspective 178*

Delay and Social Distraction *179*

Watching the Clock *180*

The Teacher as Gatekeeper *182*

The Other Side of the Tracks *182*

The Power of Elementary Peer Groups *187*

GUEST COLUMN: Haunted by Racist Attitudes 191

High School's Adolescent Society *192*

The Affective Side of School Reform *197*

What Makes a School Effective? *200*

Factor 1: Strong Leadership 201

Factor 2: A Clear School Mission 202

Factor 3: A Safe and Orderly Climate 202

Factor 4: Monitoring Student Progress 203

Factor 5: High Expectations 206

A Note of Caution on Effective Schools Research 207

Beyond Five Factors 210

Summary 212

Key Terms and People 214

Discussion Questions and Activities 215

Reel to Real Teaching 215

For Further Reading 216

6 What Students Are Taught in Schools *218*

What Is a Curriculum? *219*

The Extracurriculum *221*

The Hidden or Implicit Curriculum *225*

The Formal or Explicit Curriculum *226*

The Curriculum Time Machine: A Historical
   Perspective *228*

*Time Capsule 1: The Two Rs in the Seventeenth
Century 228*

Time Capsule 2: Curricula in the Eighteenth Century 228

*Time Capsule 3: A Secularized Curriculum for Students in
the Nineteenth Century 228*

*Time Capsule 4: Progressive Education in the First Half of
the Twentieth Century 229*

Time Capsule 5: Sputnik in Space and Structure in Knowledge, 1940s–1960s 230

Time Capsule 6: Social Concern and Relevance, 1960s–1970s 230

Time Capsule 7: Back to Basics and a Core Curriculum, 1980s–2002 232

The Subjects of the Formal Curriculum 234

Language Arts and English 234

Social Studies 236

Mathematics 238

Science 239

Foreign Languages 240

Technology 241

The Arts 243

Physical Education 243

Health 247

Vocational and Career Education 247

New Directions for the Curriculum 248

Summary 249

Key Terms and People 252

Discussion Questions and Activities 252

Reel to Real Teaching 253

For Further Reading 254

7   Controversy Over Who Controls the Curriculum 255

The Faculty Room 256

Who and What Shape the Curriculum? 257

Teachers 257

Parental and Community Groups 257

Students 257

Administrators 258

The Federal Government 258

The State Government 258

Local Government 259

Colleges and Universities 259

Standardized Tests 259

Education Commissions and Committees 259

Professional Organizations 259

Special Interest Groups 260

Publishers 260

The Standards Movement 260

Tests and Protests 263

Alternatives to High-Stakes Testing 267

The Textbook Shapes the Curriculum 270

Seven Forms of Bias 276

Invisibility 277

Stereotyping 277

Imbalance and Selectivity 278

Unreality 278

Fragmentation and Isolation 278

Linguistic Bias 278

Cosmetic Bias 279

Religious Fundamentalism 279

Censorship and the Curriculum 281

Cultural Literacy or Cultural Imperialism? 284

The Saber-Tooth Curriculum 287

Summary 289

Key Terms and People 291

Discussion Questions and Activities 291

Reel to Real Teaching 292

For Further Reading 293

Inter-mission Part 2   Schools and Curriculum 294

3   FOUNDATIONS

8   The History of American Education 304

Christopher Lamb's Colonial Classroom 305

Colonial New England Education: God's Classrooms 306

A New Nation Shapes Education 309

The Common School Movement 310

Spinsters, Bachelors, and Gender Barriers in Teaching 313

The Secondary School Movement 315

School Reform Efforts 316

John Dewey and Progressive Education 319

The Federal Government 321

The World We Created at Hamilton High:
   A Schoolography 325

A Super School (If You're on the Right Side of the Tracks),
1953–1965 326

Social Unrest Comes to School, 1966–1971 326

The Students' Turn, 1972–1979 326

New Students, Old School, 1980–1985 329

Hall of Fame: Profiles in Education 330

Summary 341

Key Terms and People 343

Discussion Questions and Activities 343

Reel to Real Teaching 344

For Further Reading 345

9   Philosophy of Education 347

Finding Your Philosophy of Education 348

Inventory of Philosophies of Education 350

Interpreting Your Responses 352

Five Philosophies of Education 353

Teacher-Centered Philosophies 354

Essentialism 354

Perenialism 355

Student-Centered Philosophies 359

Progressivism 359

Social Reconstructionism 361

Existentialism 364

Psychological Influences on Education 369

Constructivism 369

Behaviorism 371

Cultural Influences on Education 372

The Three Legendary Figures of Classical
   Western Philosophy 374

Basic Philosophical Issues and Concepts 376

Metaphysics and Epistemology 376

Ethics, Political Philosophy, and Aesthetics 378

Logic 378

Your Turn 378

Summary 379

Key Terms and People 381

Discussion Questions and Activities 382

Reel to Real Teaching 382

For Further Reading 383

**10   Financing and Governing
America's Schools 385**

Follow the Money: Financing
   America's Schools 386

*Why Should Teachers Care Where the Money
Comes from? 386*

The Property Tax: The Road to Unequal Schools 387

Reforming Education Finance 388

The Move toward Adequacy 389

States Finding the Money 391

*The Federal Government's Role in Financing
Education 393*

What the Future May Hold for School
   Finance 394

Accountability 395

Choice Programs 395

Local Fundraising 395

Decaying Infrastructure 398

Governing America's Schools 399

School Governance Quiz 399

The Legal Control of Schools 400

From an Idea to a Reality 401

*State Influence Grows as School Boards Come under
Fire 403*

The School Superintendent and Principal 407

Covert Power in Schools 409

Business and Family 411

Making Schools More Responsive 413

Summary 416

Key Terms and People 419

Discussion Questions and Activities 419

Reel to Real Teaching 421

For Further Reading 422

11 School Law and Ethics *423*

Classroom Law *424*

What Is Your Rights Quotient? *424*

I. Teachers' Rights and Responsibilities *425*

II. Students' Rights and Responsibilities *434*

Teaching and Ethics *445*

Moral Education: Programs That Teach Right from Wrong *447*

Classrooms That Explore Ethical Issues *453*

Summary *456*

Key Terms and People *459*

Discussion Questions and Activities *459*

Reel to Real Teaching *460*

For Further Reading *461*

Inter-mission Part 3   Foundations *462*

4 TOMORROW

12 The Struggle for Educational Opportunity *472*

Educational Opportunity for All *473*

Native Americans: The History of Miseducation *476*

Black Americans: The Struggle for a Chance to Learn *477*

Hispanics: Growing School Impact *481*

Mexican Americans *483*

Puerto Ricans *483*

Cuban Americans *484*

New Immigrants from Latin America *484*

Asian Americans and Pacific Islanders: The Magnitude of Diversity *484*

Chinese Americans *485*

Filipino Americans *485*

Asian Indian Americans *486*

Japanese Americans *486*

Southeast Asian Americans *487*

Arab Americans: Moving Beyond the Stereotype *488*

Women and Education: A History of Sexism *490*

The Impact of Title IX *492*

Our Children, Your Students *492*

Family Patterns *495*

Wage Earners and Parenting *497*

Divorce *498*

Stepfamilies, Interracial Marriages, and Alternative Families *498*

Latchkey Kids *498*

Hidden America: Homeless Families *500*

Children: At Promise or At Risk? *501*

Dropping Out *501*

Sexuality and Teenage Pregnancy *503*

AIDS: HIV Comes to School *503*

Substance Abuse: Drinking, Drugs, and Smoking *504*

Youth Suicide *507*

Gays, Lesbians, and Bisexuals: Our Invisible Students *507*

Tension Point: Are Equity and Excellence Compatible? *508*

Summary *510*

Key Terms and People *512*

Discussion Questions and Activities *512*

Reel to Real Teaching *513*

For Further Reading *514*

13 Technology in Education *516*

The Technology Revolution *517*

Schools.com *520*

It's the Teaching, Not the Technology *524*

The Global Curriculum *529*

The Virtual Teacher *533*

Technology and Equity *538*

The Digital Divide *538*

Is Computer Technology Worth the Effort? *540*

Summary *545*

Key Terms and People 547

Discussion Questions and Activities 547

Reel to Real Teaching 548

For Further Reading 548

14 Your First Classroom 550

Stages of Teacher Development *551*

Your First Year: Induction into the
Profession *552*

Mentors 552

Observation 555

Professional Development Programs 558

Personalizing Schools 560

Finding That First Teaching Position *561*

Résumés, Portfolios, and Interviews 564

Interviewing 564

Teacher Recognition *565*

*The National Board for Professional Teaching
Standards 568*

Merit Pay 569

Career Ladder Programs 570

Educational Associations *571*

Which Teacher's Organization Speaks for You? 573

Professional Associations and Resources 575

American Schools: Better Than We
Think? *577*

Summary 580

Key Terms and People 582

Discussion Questions and Activities 582

Reel to Real Teaching: It's Your Turn 583

For Further Reading 584

15 Q and A Guide to Entering the
Teaching Profession 585

What Are My Chances of Finding a Teaching
Position? *586*

Who Are My Teaching Colleagues? What
Are the Demographics of Today's
Teachers? *587*

What Are My Chances for Earning a Decent
Salary? *587*

Do Private Schools Pay Less than Public
Schools? *588*

How Do I Apply for a Teaching Job? Do I
Need a Résumé or a Portfolio? *589*

What Do I Need in Order to Teach—a License
or Certification? By the Way, What's the
Difference? *590*

Who Awards Licenses, and How Do I Get
One? *591*

What Type of License Do I Need? (You Mean,
There's More than One?) *591*

What Is an Endorsement? *592*

What Is Program Accreditation, and What
Does It Mean in Terms of Getting a
Teacher's License? *593*

What Are "Alternative Routes" to Getting a
Teacher's License? *593*

What Are Teacher Competency Tests? *595*

How Do Teaching Contracts Work? *597*

What Are Some Advantages of Tenure? *597*

What Are Some Disadvantages of
Tenure? *598*

Are Untenured Teachers Protected? *599*

Can Principals Be Tenured? *599*

What Kinds of Educational Careers Are
Available Beyond Classroom
Teaching? *599*

Summary 604

Key Terms and People 606

Inter-mission Part 4   Tomorrow *607*

APPENDIXES

1 State Offices for Teacher
Certification and Licensure *A–1*

2   Information about the Teacher Competency Exams (Praxis Series) *A–5*

3   A Summary of Selected Reports on Education Reform *A–8*

4   Observation Manual *A–12*

Glossary G–1

Notes N–1

Photo Credits P–1

Index I–1

When we were in school, textbooks were generally informative, but uninteresting. We want this text to be both informative and fun, and we worked hard to accomplish this goal. We wrote this book to share with you the excitement we feel about teaching.

Teachers, Schools, and Society is designed for introductory courses in teacher education variously labeled Introduction to Education; Introduction to Teaching, Schools, and Society; or Foundations of Education. Whatever the label, the primary intent of such a course is to provide a sufficiently broad yet detailed exposure to the realities of teaching. The text should help you answer those all-important questions: Do I want to become a teacher? What do I need to become the best teacher possible? What should a professional in the field of education know? To help you answer these questions, we offer a panoramic (and we hope) stimulating view of education.

An Interactive Text

Each edition of *Teachers, Schools, and Society* has broken new ground by creating new features, introducing new topics, and adding new supplements. This edition adds to that rich tradition by creating an even more interactive book for students. The chapters—always lauded for their student-friendly readability—have been revised to encourage more engagement and reflection. Reflection questions have been added to all figures and tables, as well as to many of the boxed features. The Online Learning Center (www.mhhe.com/sadker6e) that was introduced with the previous edition has been revised to be a true extension of the text. Throughout the text, you are directed to the Online Learning Center to complete interactive activities or polls, respond to questions, and to access the online student study guide. See page xx for a tour of the text's features including the Online Learning Center.

Content Coverage

We elected to view the field from several vantage points. In Part One, you will see the world of teachers and students from a new perspective—the teacher's side of the desk. In Part Two, your field of vision will be widened so you can examine the structure, culture, and curriculum of that complex place called school. Part Three then examines the broad forces (historical, philosophical, legal, and financial) that shape the foundations of our educational system. In Part Four, you will have a chance to examine, debate, and speculate about issues and trends, and explore many of the questions students typically bring to this course, often practical and personal questions. Following each of the four parts are *Inter-missions*. The *Inter-missions* offer you the opportunity to develop crucial skills related to the teaching profession and to start your teaching portfolio. The Appendixes contain information about teacher licensing, including relevant addresses; teacher competency exams; and an Observation Manual with guidelines and strategies for collecting important information about teaching as you observe in schools.

Style of Presentation

The trouble with panoramic views is that the observer is often at such a distance from what is being viewed that all richness of detail is lost. Vague outlines devoid of human interaction dominate many survey type texts. We worked hard to personalize this book. At various points throughout the text we replace our wide-angle lens with a more intimate view that captures the human drama as well. For example, in many chapters, we introduce traditionally dry, abstract topics with illustrative scenarios that help personalize and dramatize the topic at hand. The *In the News* feature offers insightful, humorous, and poignant educational news items taken from newspapers, the Internet, and the popular press. *Class Acts* offer personal insights into teaching and schooling. Several "pop" quizzes probe your prior knowledge and beliefs and introduce, even personalize, governance, law, and philosophy. The *Photo-synthesis* feature offers dramatic visual contrasts of pressing educational concerns, while *You Be the Judge* invites you to evaluate different perspectives on relevant educational issues. We hope that these stylistic elements, along with a writing style that is deliberately informal rather than academic, will add spice and human interest to the text.

Inter-missions

The *Inter-missions* feature was introduced in the previous edition, as part-ending activities designed to help you reflect on teaching, build a portfolio, and enhance understanding of the concepts in this text. To make these more practical, the *Inter-missions* are based on the INTASC standards.

New in the Sixth Edition

This sixth edition of *Teachers, Schools, and Society* is designed to improve an already comprehensive text. The entire text was updated and revised to provide the most current coverage possible. Major revision was done in the following areas.

New/Expanded Topics and Issues

Topics receiving increased attention in this edition include philosophy, finance, induction, technology, national standards, and testing. The philosophy chapter has an expanded section on *social reconstructionism* and includes a greater emphasis on female and nonwestern philosophers. The quiz has been revised and shortened, as have the descriptions of the five philosophies. The first chapter, *Becoming a Teacher*, has been rewritten to provide greater focus on the pros and cons of teaching, and to highlight school reform efforts. The chapter also suggests that creating teacher-friendly school climates can be a valuable dimension of school improvement efforts, although it is too rarely a part of the national debate. *Financing and Governing America's Schools* now has an expanded discussion of the legal arguments surrounding educational adequacy.

Multicultural Focus

Multicultural issues, a strong feature in the fifth edition, is further expanded in this sixth edition. Student diversity, which may be the single most critical issue facing our schools in the decades ahead, is a powerful focus, as is the educational history of many ethnic and racial groups. The text also provides several popular theories explaining group differences in academic performance, as well as some practical strategies for nonracist, nonsexist teaching.

Technology

The coverage has been expanded throughout the text, as well as revised in the *Technology in Education* chapter. This chapter has been rewritten to reflect how teacher effectiveness research can be connected to, and enhanced by, technology. We now describe several practical considerations for teachers to consider as they introduce new technology in their classrooms.

Features

The text's features have been revised and expanded. New features include:

- *What Do You Think?* links you to the Online Learning Center where you can take a quick survey or self-inventory. Responses are submitted to a national poll so you can immediately (and confidentially) see where you stand in comparison with your colleagues.

- *Interactive Activities* link you to the Online Learning Center to do a content-related activity.

- *You Be the Judge* is a feature providing two views of relevant, often critical, education issues. The feature invites you to reflect and consider conflicting points of view.

- *Profile in Education* offers brief biographies of leading educators who have made, and continue to make, a difference in the lives of children.

- *Reflection* questions are included throughout the text to engage you in educational issues and ideas. It is one example of the interactive nature of this edition.

- *Frame of Reference* provides research updates, personal anecdotes, critical statistics, and practical advice for new teachers.

- *Reel to Real Teaching,* included at the end of each chapter, describes relevant films and videotapes, and offers strategies for incorporating these media to highlight chapter ideas and concepts.

- *Further Reading* provides selected annotated bibliographies after each chapter.

- *Chapter Summaries* are now organized around focus questions and are more detailed.

- *Key Terms and People* now reference relevant text pages.

You'll find a full listing of the text's features is located on page xx.

Acknowledgments

In March 1995, Myra died undergoing treatment for breast cancer. She worked on this textbook even while undergoing chemotherapy and she was always the major force behind providing a student-friendly introduction to teaching. She will always be the primary author of this book.

 When Phyllis Lerner and I married, she had no idea how cyclical and stressful this literary pregnancy would be. Little sleep, meals at strange hours of the day, personal disputes that erupted from nowhere— but, nine months later, there you are, parents of a new edition. And you look back and wonder: was it worth it?

Rather than have us answer that question, we will leave it to you. We sure hope it was worth it. This book is stronger, more interesting, and more relevant because of Phyllis' efforts. Her decades of practical school experience are reflected on the book's pages. While the *Inter-missions* bear her name and her practical wisdom, all the chapters reflect her comments and contributions. She developed the Annotated Instructor's Edition and updated the Instructor's Manual. She also created and pulled together the *Photo-synthesis* feature and produced the Video Companion. In addition, working with Feldman and Associates, she selected the text photos. And Phyllis was responsible for the backpack design concept used in the book. If you are getting the idea that she is quite creative, you are right. Phyllis took major responsibility for updating the chapters on the *Struggle for Equal Educational Opportunity* and *What Students Are Taught in School*. She has become a major influence and participant in this text, and the book is more multicultural, livelier, and more creative because of her efforts. I was lucky to have her participate. She is lucky that yet another edition is done.

 In this sixth edition, veteran of the classroom and parent-extraordinaire Chris Cozadd was enlisted once again to edit. She edits with precision and tact, a rare combination. But, more important, she reads with intelligence and insight, which creates a more thoughtful and logical book. She has always been a tremendous influence on the book and personal source of encouragement.

 Karen Zittleman is a new and wonderfully talented recruit to this project. She is insightful and wise beyond her years. She had the major responsibility for updating the law chapter, wrote the initial drafts of the vast majority of *Profiles in Education*, found and included the Web links, and constructed the annotated bibliographies included in the *For Further Reading* sections. But the best fun was going to the movies and video store together so we could view and evaluate Hollywood's best efforts and select which to include. When we selected the ones we liked best, it was Karen who wrote the *Reel to Real* features. Whenever a difficult question or a puzzling organizational problem arose, Karen's insight and logic could be relied on to see us through. We were incredibly lucky to have her onboard.

 Jen Engle has been my graduate assistant for several years and this is the second edition that she has tackled. She is an Internet maven, tracking down references in a nanosecond, updating charts, getting permission forms out and signed, and offering content ideas and teaching approaches. She took on the major responsibility for updating Chapter 15, the *Question and Answer* chapter, and wrote many of the accompanying test questions. She has helped enormously. Thanks, Jen!

 Jackie Sadker, one of two extraordinary daughters, did the major revision of the legal arguments discussed in the *Financing and Governing America's Schools* chapter. In previous editions of this book, she has worked on the curriculum chapter, helped with the editing, and indexed the book. Now that she is the editor of her law school newspaper, I find myself seeking her insights and editorial help. The first draft of this book was written before Jackie started elementary school. Now she is a contributor and consultant, and getting ready to graduate from law school. What a kid! Thanks, Jackie.

Sara Kindler helped review and update the technology chapter. While a graduate student at American University, Sara developed strong technology skills, but her skills did not stop there. What became evident in this project are her organizational talents and her strong work effort. Her ideas for reformatting the technology chapter were terrific and, while I am pleased that she is now teaching in the New York area, I hereby formally extend an invitation for her to return to the Washington, DC, area and help with the next edition. Thanks, Sara!

Previous editions were improved by many students and colleagues, who are often in my thoughts. Thanks are extended to Daniel Spiro, Lynette Long, Elizabeth Ihle, Nancy Gorenberg, Elsie Lindemuth, Mary Donald, June Winter, Kirstin Hill, Kate Volker, Ward Davis, Pat Silverthorn, Julia Masterson, Amy Monaghan, Shirley Pollack, and Kathryn McNerney.

Our editor, Cara Harvey, was a constant source of ideas and encouragement, a partner and friend in shaping and revising this text, and a great source of suggestions of just what books we should be reading for enjoyment (if we weren't writing this one). Her energy and abilities made this venture much sweeter. She also whipped the manuscript (and us) into shape. Beth Kaufman, editor on the previous edition, demonstrated her commitment to us and to this edition by her continued involvement and support. Her talent and efforts have strengthened this edition of the text, and her friendship is much appreciated. Jane Karpacz, our publisher at McGraw-Hill, was a lion in getting this book out and gave us all the support we needed to make it a success. I am nominating her for the Publishing Hall of Fame. Wow, were we lucky!

Our thanks to Susan Trentacosti, our project manager, for transforming manuscript into book in record-breaking fashion. We also want to thank the following reviewers of *Teachers, Schools, and Society* for generously sharing with us their experiences in teaching the book:

T. Kaye Abight, *Missouri Southern State College*
Radha Bhatkal, *Castleton State College*
Heather Biola, *Davis and Elkins College*
Les Bolt, *James Madison University*
Joanne Carlson, *College of Saint Mary*
Tonia Causey-Bush, *Texas Tech University*
David Chellevold, *University of Wisconsin–Platteville*
Barbara R. Cole, *McPherson College*
Dr. Frank Dean Cone, *Maple Woods Community College*
Dee Crane, *Siena Heights University*
Barbara J. Davis, *Olivet College*
Leslie J. Davison, *St. Cloud State University*
Paul Dow Dawson, *Edison Community College*
William Dunlap, *University of Wisconsin*

Clayton Dusek, *Baldwin-Wallace College*
Nancy Estes, *Broward Community College*
Allan J. Ten Eyck, *Grand Valley State University*
Robert R. Fortin, *Grand Valley State University*
Teena Gorrow, *Salisbury State University*
Ed Gosnell, *Converse College*
Barbara Graham, *Ball State College*
Katherine K. Gratto, *University of Florida*
Frank Guldbrandsen, *University of Minnesota*
Gale Hairston, *Central Methodist College*
William Hayes, *Roberts Wesleyan College*
Susan Hillman, *St. Joseph College*
Lyle C. Jensen, *Baldwin-Wallace College*
Larry G. Julian, *Brewton-Parker College*
Carolyn J. Kelley, *University of Central Arkansas*
Brad King, *Mid America Nazarene University*
Lawrence Klein, *Christian Heritage College*
Sr. Mary Kremer, *Dominican University*
Dina Laskowski, *Jamestown College*
Barbara J. Lehman, *East Central University*
Phillip C. Matlock, *Columbia State Community College*
Tom Mauhs-Pugh, *Green Mountain College*
Robert W. Meadows, *Saginaw Valley State University*
Shabana Miv, *Indiana University*
Roberta Murata, *University of Nevada–Las Vegas*
Sally S. Naylor, Ph.D., *University of Dubuque*
Chad Osbourne, *Worcester State College*
Thomas M. O'Keefe, *Bucks County Community College*
Dr. Ronald M. Padula, *Delaware County Community College*
Terrell M. Peace, *Huntington College*
Melvin J. Pedras, *University of Idaho*
Gary Railsback, *George Fox University*
Dr. Margaret Reif, *University of St. Thomas*
Susan T. Riggs, *University of Arkansas*
Joseph Sassone, *Pima Community College*
Lynn Stallings, *Kennesaw State University*
Veronica P. Stephen, *Eastern Illinois University*
Menia G. Stone, *University of North Florida*
Martin Tadlock, *Utah State University*
P. Lance Ternasky, *Western Illinois University*
Jeff A. Thomas, *University of Southern Indiana*
Sharon Carter Thomas, *Miami-Dade Community College*
Dan Thompson, *University of Illinois at Urbana-Champaign*
Jane Ward, *Southern Missouri State University*
John Mack Welford, *Roanoke College*
Robert W. Wood, *University of South Dakota*

Finally, I would like to thank my daughters, Robin and Jackie, for their tolerance, insight, and love. When they were in elementary school (during the first edition of this book), they endured the piles of paper, research notes, and drafts that made our house literally a version of the paper chase. At the time of this sixth edition, Jackie is in her last year of law school and Robin, now Dr. Sadker, is practicing internal medicine. The editions that preceded this one all benefited from their ideas and critiques and their growing pains. They are the two most special people in my life, and Myra and I continue to dedicate this book to them.

David M. Sadker

A GUIDED TOUR OF YOUR INTERACTIVE TEXT

If you think that *Teachers, Schools, and Society* was written to introduce you to the world of teaching, you are only half right. This book also reflects our excitement about a life in the classroom and is intended to spark your own fascination about working with children. The basic premise for this text has not changed through all the previous editions: write a book students want to read, not have to read. While we continue to work hard to provide you with information that is both current and concise, we work even harder to create an engaging book—one that will give you a sense of the wonderful possibilities found in a career in the classroom.

To help you determine if teaching is right for you, and to learn more about education in general, you will find Reflection questions throughout this sixth edition. These questions will put you right into the center of these issues, a personal connection that encourages your thoughtful deliberation. While the text has been designed to engage you, we also devised an absorbing "Electronic-option," the Online Learning Center. The Online Learning Center (OLC) is part of the text's website and offers a number of features that respond to different student styles, interests, and experiences. Throughout the text, you will see links to the activities and study resources found on the OLC. Each link includes a brief explanation of what you will find on-line. Now it is time for your first reflection question: How can you discover this wonder trove of electronic treasures? Easy. We have blue "hot link" type whenever there is an Online Learning Center connection. Visit us in our cyber-classroom at www.mhhe.com/sadker6e.

To help you discover and use all of these new interactive opportunities, we have created a key of useful icons. Look for the following as you read this book:

 highlights reflection questions.

 indicates that you should go to the Online Learning Center for more information or to do an activity.

indicates that you can go to the Online Learning Center to e-mail your professor the response to a reflection question and/or save your response for your portfolio.

Now, join us for a tour of the special features of the text.

Class Acts

Each of the four part openers includes a *Class Act*—a story from a current or future teacher about their involvement in education. You can find additional Class Acts on the Online Learning Center submitted by your classmates nationwide. Have you had a teacher who made a difference in your life? We want to hear about that teacher, and perhaps include your story in the next edition of the text. Please submit your own story!

CLASS ACT

Every December I watch *It's a Wonderful Life*. I was 13 years old when I first saw George Bailey scramble down the Main Street of Bedford Falls, waving his arms and screaming at the top of his lungs, rejoicing in the beauty of life, love and friendship. As an adult who savors this film, I feel the bittersweet pang of watching a man who is reborn, glowing in the recognition that he has made a difference in the world. In the final act, as George stands in his living room surrounded by family and friends celebrating his life, I always develop that painful lump in my throat—you know the one. It stings and makes it nearly impossible to swallow. I love this film, and I always want to say that I know a George Bailey. The thing is I do—he's my dad. ❖ My father has been teaching English and Dramatic Arts at the same high school in Massachusetts for the last thirty years. His journey has been one similar to George Bailey's—he has settled down in a small town, a teacher, committed to his family and profession, but at times frustrated. He has seen thousands of students come and go, some moving on to big and exciting things, others staying in the very same town. From time to time growing up, I'd see a glimmer in his eyes wondering, "What if . . . ? What if I'd quit teaching, what if I'd gone off traveling around the world?" These moments of wonder were not full of anger or resentment, only seconds of reflection, and perhaps a little regret for not "doing more with his life." But he always returned to teaching with a positive spirit, endless patience, and astounding energy. ❖ Over the years my dad and I have shared lots of travels together. It was a family joke that no matter where we went, we always ran into one of my father's former students. More often than not the run-in went beyond a courteous hello and how are you. These former students, now adults with children of their own, embrace my dad, literally and figuratively. We could be standing at a light waiting to cross, sitting in a restaurant—we inevitably ran into these joyful faces who recognize the sparkling eyes, full beard and unmistakable energy of my dad. As a younger child I was somewhat bored by the endless stories recounted by these strangers. The older I got, the more I realized that these spontaneous reunions were quite special. These people were paying tribute to someone who touched their lives. It wasn't a grand parade or a front-page article or a million dollar salary bonus. They were simple yet beautifully sincere words—"You inspired me . . . You gave me the courage to try . . . You were the only one who believed in me . . ." ❖ This may sound like a tribute to a father from an adoring daughter, and to some degree it is. But it is also recognition of something more. Just like George Bailey, my dad has a wonderful life. Through teaching he is able to reach that troubled kid who sits in the back making wisecracks and give him a reason to care about school. He has taken the shy girl who doesn't speak, put her up on the stage and helped her find her voice and confidence. He has acted as adviser and inspiration for countless young people, giving them the opportunity to learn, grow and succeed. Although I've never been a student in his class, my dad has inspired me as well. As I begin my pursuit of a Masters in Teaching, I see just how unique my father's gifts are. This year when I watched *It's a Wonderful Life*, I couldn't help but think of my father. I still got that lump in my throat—and loved it.

Amanda Helfen
American University

OLC SUBMIT YOUR OWN CLASS ACT Click on *Class Acts* and submit a *Class Act* about a teacher who has made a difference in your life. Visit the Online Learning Center to read more *Class Acts*.

Chapter Opener

The Chapter Opener page includes Focus Questions and a Chapter Preview to prime you for the content that will follow. At the end of the chapter, the summary will be framed by these very same focus questions. The page also includes an online *What Do You Think?* activity. One such activity might be a quiz that captures your opinion on some of the topics you will soon read about. Answer the questions and then, via the Internet, find out how your peers responded. It's an opportunity to participate in our national survey system and is only one of the activities that you will find on the Online Learning Center.

13 Technology in Education

FOCUS QUESTIONS

1. Has technology changed schools?
2. How does television affect children?
3. Why is computer technology difficult to implement in schools?
4. How can teachers effectively use computers and the Internet?
5. In what ways does global education refocus the curriculum?
6. How is teaching redefined in the virtual high school?
7. Does technology exacerbate racial, class, geographic, and gender divisions?

OLC WHAT DO YOU THINK? How Tech-Savvy Are You? Take this quiz to see how much you know (and don't know).

CHAPTER PREVIEW

In an earlier time, before there were factories, there were cottage industries. People manufactured products, not as a group of workers in a central place but individually, in their houses. Some believe that schools may be retracing these steps—in reverse. Today's factorylike schools may soon be replaced by children learning in their homes. "Cottage schools" may be created as technology brings the teacher, the curriculum, and the library onto our home computer screens. Rather than taking the yellow school bus to a large school building, students are now traveling to school on the Internet.

The Internet can transport students around the world (through virtual field trips) or instantly and inexpensively add millions of books and articles to school libraries. Simulations can bring realism into a classroom, personal tutors can patiently diagnose learning needs, and adaptive technology can help special needs students succeed in school. But not everyone is enamoured with the new technology. Although technological innovation is an attractive, popular (and often expensive) aspect of American culture, history is filled with unmet predictions of technological advances—radio, television, and teaching machines—making schools obsolete. Will computers and technology make an important difference in education or will tomorrow's schools look remarkably similar to schools you attended as a child? The future, if nothing else, is unpredictable. Certainly, the information age has not included everyone. Poorer students and nations, women and non-English speakers have been left behind.

Technology raises other serious concerns for teachers, including the need to monitor inappropriate Internet material and to avoid the health risks associated with computer use. While these pitfalls are real, the potential of technology is

516

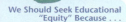

YOU BE THE JUDGE
"EQUITY" OR "ADEQUACY"

We Should Seek Educational "Equity" Because . . .

MONEY TALKS
The gap between wealthy and poor communities makes a mockery of democracy and fairness. Poor students attend schools with leaking roofs and uncertified teachers; wealthy students learn in schools with computers, swimming pools, and well-paid and qualified teachers. No real democracy can ignore such glaring inequities.

EQUALIZING INPUT IS CRUCIAL
Isn't it strange that those who advocate business values like choice and competition ignore the most fundamental business value of all: money. Wealth creates good schools; poverty creates weak ones. Invest money wisely over a period of time, and watch those once poor schools thrive.

EQUITY IS POWERFUL
Democracy and equity are powerful words representing powerful ideals. Adequacy is a feeble word subject to interpretation and compromise. What's adequate? Is it the ability to read at a high school level, or at an eighth grade level? Does an adequate education lead to a minimum wage job? Only "Equity" can serve as a rallying cry.

We Should Seek Educational "Adequacy" Because . . .

MONEY DIVIDES
Robin Hood is dead. Wealthy communities are not going to fund poor ones, happily sending their hard earned dollars to educate someone else's children. The cornerstone of democracy is local control, and trying to redistribute wealth is fundamentally unfair, and smacks of the approach used by Communists (another failed system).

EQUALIZING INPUT IS INEFFECTIVE
We will never make schools more effective by throwing dollars at them. When California moved toward equitable input, the quality of its public schools deteriorated. Our goal is not to increase school budgets and per pupil expenditures, but to increase student achievement.

ADEQUACY IS ATTAINABLE
Equity is a powerful dream, but adequacy is an attainable one. We are unlikely to achieve a completely equitable school system, but we can demand reasonable and reachable educational standards. Moreover, we are on firmer legal footing, since state constitutions guarantee not identical expenditures, but an adequate education for all.

 YOU BE THE JUDGE
Do you believe that adequacy or equity provides the best foundation for reforming schools? Explain. Can these approaches be blended, or are they mutually exclusive?

States Finding the Money
The last fifty years have seen dramatic changes in the centuries-old system of financing schools. We have moved from local communities funding schools through a property tax, to a shared state and local responsibility. (Although you wouldn't know it when listening to political campaign speeches, the federal government is a very junior partner in paying for America's education.) We have already looked at the property tax, the primary revenue source for local communities. As we indicated, it is a flawed system leading to gross inequities in the funding of schools. Let's see what states do to find the dollars they need to fund schools.

391

You Be the Judge

You Be the Judge gives both sides of an argument so you can consider different points of view, and not just ours. Then we ask you to be the judge (law school not required), by responding to the reflection questions following the arguments. You can also do this on the Online Learning Center and either e-mail your response to your instructor, or save your response for your portfolio.

Profile in Education

Teaching is all about people—it's a very human connection. The people we profile are teachers, teacher educators, social activists working for children, and educational researchers. Each was chosen for an important contribution to education. And to follow up the text descriptions, you can visit the Online Learning Center to find out more about the profiled educator. As always, we also invite you to submit your own profiles to be housed on the site.

PROFILE IN EDUCATION   MARIAN WRIGHT EDELMAN

Growing up in South Carolina (vintage 1940s), Marian Wright Edelman learned to counter the summer heat with a swim. African American children were not allowed in the public pool, so Marian and her friends did their summer swimming, diving, and fishing in the creek, despite the fact that it was polluted with hospital sewage. One of her friends decided that the bridge spanning the creek would be a good diving platform, but that decision turned out to be fatal: He broke his neck on impact. His death was one of several tragedies that taught Edelman early lessons on the deadly impact of race segregation. In recalling these tragedies, Edelman says: "You never, ever forget."[1]

Marian Wright Edelman's family provided a refuge from this racial hatred. Her father was a Baptist minister, her mother a devout Sunday schoolteacher, and both instilled a sense of service. Sharing a bed, a meal, or a pair of shoes with foster children or neighbors in need was a common event for Edelman and her four siblings. While public playgrounds were closed to black children, her parents made Shiloh Baptist Church a community resource center for black sports teams, Boys Scouts and Girl Scouts. Edelman learned that "[s]ervice is the rent we pay for living. It is the very purpose of life and not something you do in your spare time."[2]

During the 1960s, Edelman worked as a volunteer at the National Association for the Advancement of Colored People (NAACP), campaigning for passage of the Voting Rights Act as well as finding legal assistance for students jailed during sit-ins and demonstrations. As she sorted through requests for NAACP assistance from poor black citizens, Edelman realized that law could be a vehicle to social justice. She attended Yale University Law School and became the first black woman to pass the bar exam in Mississippi. Although she practiced civil rights law, Edelman's work with poor children helped her to see that they were the most vulnerable and voiceless group in our society. Children "had no one to speak out on their behalf—no one to make sure that there were laws and gov-

ernment policies in place to protect them."[1] During the next four decades, Marian Wright Edelman became their voice.

Edelman founded the Children's Defense Fund (CDF) in 1973, with the mission to "Leave No Child Behind." The CDF works to ensure that every child has a Healthy Start, a Head Start, a Fair Start, a Safe Start, and a Moral Start in life. The CDF strives to protect all children—and particularly children of low-income and minority families—through research, community organization, federal and state government lobbying, and public education. Among those who worked for the CDF was a young Wellesley graduate named Hillary Rodham, who continued to advocate for children's rights later when she became the First Lady and then U.S. Senator from New York.

CDF also sponsors Freedom Schools that recruit college students to serve as mentors to over 12,000 students both after school and during the summer. Edelman understands the lasting influence mentors give students, and she has a message for all teachers:

Teaching is a mission, not just a task or a job. I don't care how fancy the school, how low the student-teacher ratio (which I believe should be lower), how high the pay (which I think should be higher): If children don't feel respected by adults who respect themselves, and don't feel valued, then they lose and all of us lose. Make it a reality that all children, especially poor children, are taught how to read, write, and compute so they can have happy and healthy options in their future. We need to understand and be confident that each of us can make a difference by caring and acting in small as well as big ways.[3]

[1]Marian Wright Edelman, *The Measure of Our Success: A Letter to My Children and Yours* (Boston: Beacon Press, 1992), p. 8. [2]Ibid, p. 6. [3]Marian Wright Edelman, *Lanterns: A Memoir of Mentors* (Boston: Beacon Press, 1999), p. 28; [4]Ibid, p. 22.

REFLECTION
Surf the Children's Defense Fund website at www.childrensdefensefund.org and click on State Data. Compare the social problems and needs of children in your state with national averages. Which statistics surprised you? What responsibilities do you believe teachers have to ensure equal educational opportunity for children in poverty?

 WRITE YOUR OWN PROFILE IN EDUCATION: Click on *Profiles in Education*, write a *Profile in Education* about an educator, and post it on the Online Learning Center. Check out *Profiles in Education* submitted by other future teachers.

To learn more about Marian Wright Edelman, click on *Profiles in Education.*

Photo-synthesis

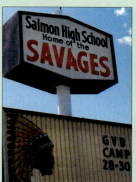

PHOTO-SYNTHESIS | **SIGNS OF THE TIMES**

What does a school's name, mascot, message board, and presentation say about what's happening inside the classroom? What do these school signs tell you? Are there ways to identify a good school by its sign? How would your high school sign fit in the photo gallery?

164

Most of us enjoy "seeing" theoretical concepts come to life. In fact, some people are more visual than verbal and greatly benefit from photographs and illustrations. That's why we developed *Photo-synthesis*—photo collages that encourage analysis. And if you need a thoughtful boost, one or more questions help you focus your inquiry. You can respond to the reflection question on the Online Learning Center and either e-mail your response to your instructor or save your response for your portfolio (or to use for review at a later time).

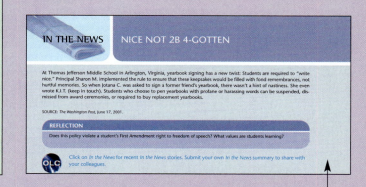

IN THE NEWS | **NICE NOT 2B 4-GOTTEN**

At Thomas Jefferson Middle School in Arlington, Virginia, yearbook signing has a new twist: Students are required to "write nice." Principal Sharon M. implemented the rule to ensure that these keepsakes would be filled with fond remembrances, not hurtful memories. So when Jotana C. was asked to sign a former friend's yearbook, there wasn't a hint of nastiness. She even wrote K.I.T. (keep in touch). Students who choose to pen yearbooks with profane or harassing words can be suspended, dismissed from award ceremonies, or required to buy replacement yearbooks.

SOURCE: *The Washington Post*, June 17, 2001.

REFLECTION

Does this policy violate a student's First Amendment right to freedom of speech? What values are students learning?

Click on *In the News* for recent *In the News* stories. Submit your own *In the News* summary to share with your colleagues.

Frame of Reference

FRAME OF REFERENCE | **BILINGUAL AMNESIA**

"My grandparents picked up English like everyone else back then, in school, where children learned their lessons in English, not ~~ish or Vietnamese.~~"

"If people want to remain immersed in their old culture and old language, they should stay in their own country."

"Bilingual education has given us illiterate youngsters who can do little more than work at Taco Bell."

Sound familiar? After all, many of our ancestors came to America with few resources or funds, but they were a~~ English, pick up American ways, get through school, and succeed against great odds, so why can't today's immigr~~ same? According to Richard Rothstein—author of *The Way We Were?*—we suffer a bad case of national amnesia, a~~ ollection of history differs significantly from actual events. The author believes that some bilingual programs wor~~

These boxes take a closer look at important topics. They provide research updates, further information about a topic, or even suggestions for classroom use.

Interactive Activities

Multiple Intelligences and Emotional Intelligence

~~ puzzled by these contradictions was Harvard professor **Howard Gardner**. Con-
~~ed about the traditional assessment of intelligence, with such a heavy emphasis
~~anguage and mathematical-logical skills, he broadened the concept to define
~~igence as "the capacity to solve problems or to fashion products that are valued
~~ne or more cultural settings."⁵
~~ardner identified eight kinds of intelligence, not all of which are commonly rec-
~~zed in school settings, yet Gardner believes that his theory of **multiple intelli-
~~ces** more accurately captures the diverse nature of human capability. Consider
~~ner's eight intelligences:

~~ogical-mathematical.~~ Skills related to mathematical manipulations and
~~iscerning and solving logical problems (*related careers:* scientist, mathematician)

~~inguistic.~~ Sensitivity to the meanings, sounds, and rhythms of words, as well as
~~ the function of language as a whole (*related careers:* poet, journalist, author)

~~odily-kinesthetic.~~ Ability to excel physically and to handle
~~biects skillf~~lly (*related careers:* athlete, dancer ┌ ~~rgeon~~)

OLC

INTERACTIVE ACTIVITY
MULTIPLE
INTELLIGENCES
Label descriptions of different intelligences.

Interactive Activities are listed in the margin and can be found on the Online Learning Center under the corresponding chapter. The activities are designed to allow you to apply what you are learning in an interactive environment.

In the News

Throughout the chapters you will find brief summaries of education-related news items. We selected these items because we found them funny, poignant, or particularly relevant to the chapter content. The *In the News* items also provide a sense of currency to the issues and topics discussed in the text. To keep them as current as possible, new summaries are regularly added to the Online Learning Center. We also invite you to submit your own summary of a news item that you find interesting. You can respond to the reflection question on the Online Learning Center or e-mail your response to your instructor.

SUMMARY

CHAPTER REVIEW

Go to the Online Learning Center to take a chapter self-quiz, practice with key terms, and review key ideas from the chapter.

1. What are the advantages and disadvantages of being a teacher?

   • In the *You Be the Judge* feature, we consider both advantages and disadvantages of teaching. On the negative side of the ledger, teachers are not paid wonderful salaries, sometimes lack professional respect from others, get bogged down by routine, have inadequate time for contact with other adults, and face frustration when idealistic goals collide with student apathy, parent hostility, and the demands of old-fashioned bureaucratic red tape.

   • On the positive side of the ledger are rising salaries, the growing pride in the profession, the joy of working with children and caring colleagues, and the intellectual stimulation that are so often a part of classroom life, as well as the opportunity to affect the lives of the nation's youth.

2. What are the satisfactions—and complaints—of today's teachers?

   • The vast majority of teachers surveyed indicate that they are satisfied with their jobs, but there are problems. While teachers' salaries have improved, many teachers believe that their pay is still inadequate. Local conditions have a major impact on teacher satisfaction. On the teacher's wish list for job improvement are lighter workloads, more parental support, fewer discipline problems, and greater administration support.

3. Can we consider teaching to be a profession?

   • Some claim teaching has not achieved true professional status and is, at best, a semiprofession. To support their point of view, these critics note the short preparation time needed for becoming a teacher and the employment of teachers with little or no training in programs

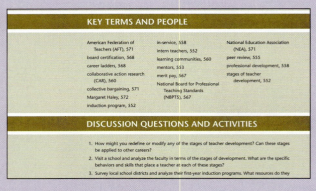

KEY TERMS AND PEOPLE

American Federation of Teachers (AFT), 571
board certification, 568
career ladders, 568
collaborative action research (CAR), 560
collective bargaining, 571
Margaret Haley, 572
induction program, 552

in-service, 558
intern teachers, 552
learning communities, 560
mentors, 553
merit pay, 567
National Board for Professional Teaching Standards (NBPTS), 567

National Education Association (NEA), 571
peer review, 555
professional development, 558
stages of teacher development, 552

DISCUSSION QUESTIONS AND ACTIVITIES

1. How might you redefine or modify any of the stages of teacher development? Can these stages be applied to other careers?

2. Visit a school and analyze the faculty in terms of the stages of development. What are the specific behaviors and skills that place a teacher at each of these stages?

3. Survey local school districts and analyze their first-year induction programs. What resources do they

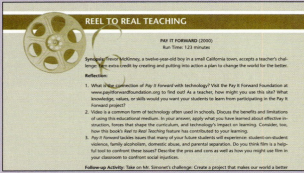

REEL TO REAL TEACHING

PAY IT FORWARD (2000)
Run Time: 123 minutes

Synopsis: Trevor McKinney, a twelve-year-old boy in a small California town, accepts a teacher's challenge: Earn extra credit by creating and putting into action a plan to change the world for the better.

Reflection:

1. What is the connection of *Pay It Forward* with technology? Visit the Pay It Forward Foundation at www.payitforwardfoundation.org to find out! As a teacher, how might you use this site? What knowledge, values, or skills would you want your students to learn from participating in the Pay It Forward project?

2. Video is a common form of technology often used in schools. Discuss the benefits and limitations of using this educational medium. In your answer, apply what you have learned about effective instruction, forces that shape the curriculum, and technology's impact on learning. Consider, too, how this book's *Reel to Real Teaching* feature has contributed to your learning.

3. *Pay It Forward* tackles issues that many of your future students will experience: student-on-student violence, family alcoholism, domestic abuse, and parental separation. Do you think film is a helpful tool to confront these issues? Describe the pros and cons as well as how you might use film in your classroom to confront social injustices.

Follow-up Activity: Take on Mr. Simonet's challenge: Create a project that makes our world a better

FOR FURTHER READING

Cultivating Leadership in Schools: Connecting People, Purpose, and Practice, by Gordon Donaldson, Jr. (2000). Enter the real-life world of decision making by administrators, teachers, parents, and school boards. "See" how interpersonal and intrapersonal skills are the keys to successful leadership.

Equal Resources, Equal Outcomes: The Distribution of School Resources and Student Achievement in California, by Julian R. Betts, Kim S. Rueben, and Anne Danenberg (2000). Debunks the myth that centralized funding of California public schools has equalized spending across districts and demonstrates how inequalities in school resources create inequalities in student achievement.

Equity and Adequacy in Education Finance: Issues and Perspectives, Helen F. Ladd, Rosemary Chalk, and Janet S. Hansen (1999). A timely collection of papers explores such questions as: What do the terms *equity* and *adequacy* in school finance really mean? and What is the impact of court-ordered school finance reform on spending disparities?

Making Money Matter: Financing America's Schools, by Helen F. Ladd and Janet S. Hansen (1999). Details the shifting expectations placed upon public schools in the last half-century and the real diversity that characterizes the existing system of governance and finance for public education. Given this backdrop, the authors discuss ways to break the nexus between student background and achievement.

Partners in Progress: Strengthening the Superintendent-Board Relationship, by Matthew King (1999).

Chapter-Ending Spread

The material at the end of the chapter is designed to structure your review of the content and help you make sure you understand key ideas. Here's what you'll find there:

- A *Chapter Review* link reminds you to go to the Online Learning Center to take a quiz, practice with key terms, and review key ideas from the chapter.

- The *Summary* is organized by the Focus Questions at the start of the chapter. Bullets highlight key ideas.

- *Key Terms and People* will help you identify and remember the critical terminology and influential individuals discussed in the chapter. Page references next to each entry guide you to the place that each is discussed in the chapter.

- The *Discussion Questions and Activities* are designed to promote deeper analysis, further

investigation, and even an evaluation of the controversial issues discussed in the chapter. Also included are the Internet-based *WEB-tivities* you can find on the Online Learning Center.

- *Reel to Real Teaching* summarizes a popular movie, usually available on videotape or DVD, that will add to your appreciation of the information included in this chapter. We believe that Hollywood can actually enhance your education, and movies can both deepen your understanding of the chapter and offer a richer educational context. The *Reel to Real* feature provides questions and follow-up activities that guide you through the movie and the issues described in the text. Go to the Online Learning Center to submit your own review of the movie and read reviews by other students.

- *For Further Reading* includes an annotated list of recent and influential books related to the chapter.

PART 4: TOMORROW

Inter-mission

Here we are, at your final *Inter-mission*. These last applications and reflections are intended to get you ready for—tomorrow.

Applications and Reflections

4:1 ADD A NONTRADITIONAL HERO

Purpose: We know that students need inspiring figures—individuals who serve as role models and motivate students. Your subject matter expertise affords you knowledge of people who might motivate your future students. Although heroes come from all backgrounds, curricular materials do not always reflect diversity. The result is a "disconnect" between the growing diversity of America's students and the curriculum they study. You can tighten this connection by supplementing the curriculum. Can you add to the list of champions in their lives, especially nontraditional individuals (consider ethnicity, race, gender, age, class, lifestyle, and circumstances)? Identifying such heroes has the additional advantage of broadening your own scholarship.

Activity: In a subject area that you will be teaching, select a unique individual or hero who has *made a difference*. Create a billboard, poster, or computer graphic that captures the importance of this person. Make the language, content, and style relevant to the grade level you plan to teach, one that will attract and motivate your students.

Reflection: What has this activity taught you about nontraditional heroes? How might you plan to have your students seek out additional heroes? What criteria might you add to guarantee a good selection? What structure might produce informative research (questions to be covered, length and depth of coverage, assessment)? What format might you create for displaying your students' final products?

> **INTASC PRINCIPLE 1**
> Knowledge of
> Subject Matter

Inter-missions

At the end of each of the four parts of this book you will find an *Inter-missions* section. These sections offer you the opportunity to more carefully consider the ideas that you read about in that part of the text, and to implement some of these activities in the real world. This feature is also your introduction to portfolio development. Whether or not portfolios are used as part of the evaluation process in this course, you will probably find yourself using them in the future. *Inter-missions* are your opportunity to begin building your professional portfolio. In the *Inter-missions* introduction, you will learn what a portfolio is and why it is important. Each section includes several activities you can do to create artifacts for your portfolio. Every activity is keyed to INTASC standards, the very areas that professional educators use to evaluate teachers. These *Inter-missions* offer a tangible way for you to connect with this book. A red OLC icon indicates that a form to be used with the activity is available on the Online Learning Center.

The Online Learning Center

Next, here is a tour of the Online Learning Center located at www.mhhe.com/sadker6e.

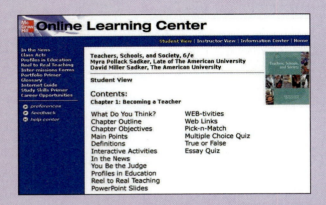

General Resources

- **Activities**
  These activities include archives and updates for *Class Acts, In the News, Profiles in Education, Reel to Real Teaching,* and *Educational Challenge.* You can also make your own submissions here.

- **Resources**
  These resources include an Internet Guide, Portfolio Primer, updated figures and tables, a book glossary, and an interactive map.

Chapter-Specific Resources

- **Online Student Study Guide**
  Each chapter on the Online Learning Center has an online study guide including: outline, objectives, chapter overview, quizzing with feedback, chapter glossary, a key term exercise, Web links, and PowerPoint slides.

- **Activities**
  Go to the specific chapter to find the *What Do You Think?, Interactive Activities,* and *WEB-tivities* listed in the text. You can also access additional resources related to the *In the News* and *Profile in Education* features. Go to the *You Be the Judge* section to submit your response to the reflection question.

Additional Student Supplement: *Making the Grade*

Packaged with your new text is a *Making the Grade* Student CD-ROM. It includes quizzes and feedback for each chapter, as well as a Learning Styles Assessment to help you understand how you learn, and, based on this assessment, how you can use your study time most effectively; an Internet Primer; and a Guide to Electronic Research.

TEACHERS, SCHOOLS, AND SOCIETY

Teachers and Students

CLASS ACT

Every December I watch *It's a Wonderful Life.* I was 13 years old when I first saw George Bailey scramble down the Main Street of Bedford Falls, waving his arms and screaming at the top of his lungs, rejoicing in the beauty of life, love and friendship. As an adult who savors this film, I feel the bittersweet pang of watching a man who is reborn, glowing in the recognition that he has made a difference in the world. In the final act, as George stands in his living room surrounded by family and friends celebrating his life, I always develop that painful lump in my throat—you know the one. It stings and makes it nearly impossible to swallow. I love this film, and I always want to say that I know a George Bailey. The thing is I do—he's my dad. ● My father has been teaching English and Dramatic Arts at the same high school in Massachusetts for the last thirty years. His journey has been one similar to George Bailey's—he has settled down in a small town, a teacher, committed to his family and profession, but at times frustrated. He has seen thousands of students come and go, some moving on to big and exciting things, others staying in the very same town. From time to time growing up, I'd see a glimmer in his eyes wondering, "What if . . . ? What if I'd quit teaching, what if I'd gone off traveling around the world?" These moments of wonder were not full of anger or resentment, only seconds of reflection, and perhaps a little regret for not "doing more with his life." But he always returned to teaching with a positive spirit, endless patience, and astounding energy. ● Over the years my dad and I have shared lots of travels together. It was a family joke that no matter where we went, we always ran into one of my father's former students. More often than not the run-in went beyond a courteous hello and how are you. These former students, now adults with children of their own, embrace my dad, literally and figuratively. We could be standing at a light waiting to cross, sitting in a restaurant—we inevitably ran into these joyful faces who recognize the sparkling eyes, full beard and unmistakable energy of my dad. As a younger child I was somewhat bored by the endless stories recounted by these strangers. The older I got, the more I realized that these spontaneous reunions were quite special. These people were paying tribute to someone who touched their lives. It wasn't a grand parade or a front-page article or a million dollar salary bonus. They were simple yet beautifully sincere words—"You inspired me . . . You gave me the courage to try . . . You were the only one who believed in me . . . " ● This may sound like a tribute to a father from an adoring daughter, and to some degree it is. But it is also recognition of something more. Just like George Bailey, my dad has a wonderful life. Through teaching he is able to reach that troubled kid who sits in the back making wisecracks and give him a reason to care about school. He has taken the shy girl who doesn't speak, put her up on the stage and helped her find her voice and confidence. He has acted as adviser and inspiration for countless young people, giving them the opportunity to learn, grow and succeed. Although I've never been a student in his class, my dad has inspired me as well. As I begin my pursuit of a Masters in Teaching, I see just how unique my father's gifts are. This year when I watched *It's a Wonderful Life,* I couldn't help but think of my father. I still got that lump in my throat—and loved it.

Amanda Helfen
American University

 SUBMIT YOUR OWN CLASS ACT Click on *Class Acts* and submit a *Class Act* about a teacher who has made a difference in your life. Visit the Online Learning Center to read more *Class Acts.*

1 Becoming a Teacher

FOCUS QUESTIONS

1. What are the advantages and disadvantages of being a teacher?
2. What are the satisfactions—and complaints—of today's teachers?
3. Can we consider teaching to be a profession?
4. How has teacher preparation changed over the years?
5. Do educators and the public agree on the most effective way to prepare teachers?
6. What traits and characteristics are needed for successful teaching?
7. Is teaching a "good fit" for you?
8. What steps can you take now on the road to becoming a teacher?

 WHAT DO YOU THINK? Why Do You Want to Be a Teacher? Rate the factors influencing your decision whether to become a teacher, and see how other students have rated these factors.

CHAPTER PREVIEW

This chapter looks at classroom life through the teacher's eyes. You may be thinking: I have spent years in a classroom, watching teachers and what they do. If there is one thing I know, it is teachers and teaching! But during your years in the classroom, you have looked at teaching through "student-colored glasses," a unique but somewhat distorted view, like looking through a telescope from the lens that makes everything tiny instead of large. This chapter offers you a teacher's perspective, a close-up view of the real world of teaching, a telescopic view that enlarges the picture and clarifies the details. We give you an opportunity to consider both the pros and cons of a teaching career, and consider whether you believe that teaching is a true profession. Then we turn to another question that you might very well be contemplating: Will you and teaching be a good match?

We love teaching, but not everything about teaching is wonderful. Many of its shortcomings are related to the not-so-wonderful history of education. In the past, teachers were often considered second-class citizens, pressured to conform to strict moral and social codes while being paid meager wages. Today, teaching and teacher education are undergoing profound changes. In the center of a sometimes stormy national debate on educational reform and renewal, teaching is now center stage, a common topic in the media and in political debates. Teachers' salaries have gone up somewhat, yet the public's expectations of what teachers should accomplish have increased a great deal. Your study of education comes at a propitious time, a period of ferment and change as teachers strive for a more professional, more influential role in U.S. society. What role might you play in tomorrow's classrooms?

The chapter is also about "us." Yes, us. We are now a team, this textbook, the authors and you. When your authors were students, we did not much like our textbooks. They were far from exciting to read. By extension, we feared that we might not like teaching. In the end, we loved teaching—but still hated our textbooks. We want this textbook to be different—to be not only informative, but also enjoyable. This first chapter offers us the opportunity to introduce the textbook, and in a sense, to introduce ourselves.

Welcome to our classroom.

What Are You Doing for the Rest of Your Life?

In a "Peanuts" cartoon, Linus comments that "no problem is so big or complicated that it can't be run away from." Charles Schulz succinctly highlighted a human frailty shared by most of us—the tendency to put aside our problems or critical questions in favor of day-to-day routine. In fact, it is amazing how little care and consideration many of us give to choosing a career. It is always easier to catch a movie, surf the net, or even study for the next exam than it is to reflect on and plan for the future. This may be one reason why questions such as: "What are you going to be when you grow up?" and "What's your next career move?" make so many of us uneasy. The big question facing many readers of this text: Is teaching right for you? For some of you, teaching may become a decades-long career filled with joy and satisfaction. For others, teaching may be limited to only a few years spent in the classroom, one of several careers you explore during your working years. And, still others may reach an equally useful and important realization: Teaching is not the ideal match for your interests or skills. We'd like to help you decide whether you and teaching are a good fit.

Throughout this text, we pose a variety of questions for you to consider. We have devised a feature called *You Be the Judge,* which presents several sides of an issue, and encourages you to sort out where you stand. When the authors have a strong opinion about these or any of the issues in the text, we will not hide it from you. For example, we told you that we love teaching, but there are drawbacks, so you know pretty much where we stand. But our opinion is just our opinion, and we want you to form your own ideas. To that end, we will work hard to be fair, to present more than one side of the issue, and to help you form an independent point of view. *You Be the Judge* is one way that we hope to spark your interest and thinking on these critical issues.

In the first *You Be the Judge,* we highlight the joys and concerns of a career in the classroom. (See pp. 6–8.)

Do Teachers Like Teaching?

In this chapter, the *You Be the Judge* feature helps you focus on the pros and cons of becoming a teacher. You probably noticed that we included comments by teachers

YOU BE THE JUDGE
A TEACHING CAREER

The Good News . . .

YOU ARE NOT WORKING ALONE, STARING AT A COMPUTER SCREEN OR SHUFFLING PAPERS

If you enjoy being in contact with others, particularly young people, teaching could be the right job for you. Almost the entire working day is spent in human interaction. Young people are so often funny, fresh, and spontaneous. Your discussions may range from adding fractions to feeding pet snakes, from an analysis of *The Catcher in the Rye* to advice on applying to colleges. As America's students become increasingly diverse, you will find yourself learning about different cultures and different life experiences. Your life will be enriched by the varied worlds of different children—black, white, Hispanic, Asian, blended—all kinds of children. The children will make you laugh and make you cry, but always they will make you feel needed. "I still can't get used to how much my heart soars with every student's success, and how a piece of my heart is plucked away when any student slips away."[1]

THE SMELL OF THE CHALKBOARD, THE ROAR OF THE CROWD

You spend several days researching and planning your lesson on social protest literature for your eleventh-grade English class. You collect many fine poems and statements to share; you bring your favorite CDs and videos of social protest songs into the classroom; you prepare an excellent PowerPoint presentation to highlight the key labor figures and issues of the time; and you punctuate your lesson with thoughtful discussion questions and creative follow-up activities. Wow, what a lesson! The students are spellbound. They ask many questions and make plans for doing their own research on social protest. One group even decides to meet after school to create an MTV-type video of a social protest song about the destruction of the natural environment. Their animated discussion continues as the bell signals their passage to the next classroom.

When you have taught well, your students will let you know it. On special occasions, they will come up to you after class or at the end of the year to tell you "This class is awesome." At younger grade levels, they may write you notes (often anonymous), thanking you for a good class or a good year.

I'M PROUD TO BE A TEACHER

Although teacher status took a battering in public opinion in the early 1980s, the public is once again acknowledging

The Bad News . . .

STOP THE CROWD—I WANT TO GET AWAY

Right in the middle of a language arts lesson, when fifteen kids have their hands in the air, you may feel like saying, "Stop, everybody. I feel like being alone for the next fifteen minutes. I'm going to Starbucks." For the major part of each day, your job demands that you be involved with people in a fast-paced and intense way—whether you feel like it or not. Researchers report that you will be involved in as many as one thousand verbal exchanges in a single day, almost all of them with children, which could impact behavior beyond school. One kindergarten teacher warned her 40-year-old brother "to be sure and put on his galoshes. Wow! Did he give me a strange look."[2] And as America's classrooms become more multicultural, teacher interactions will become more challenging, as teachers stretch beyond their own background to connect with a diverse student population.

IS ANYBODY THERE?

After teaching your fantastic lesson on social protest literature, you want to share your elation with your colleagues, so you head for the teachers' room and begin to talk about the lesson. But it is hard to capture the magic of what went on in the classroom. You can sense that your description is falling flat. Besides, people are beginning to give you that "What kind of superstar do you think you are?" look. You decide you had better cut your description short and talk about CDF (Casual Dress Friday).

It is rare to have another adult spend even ten minutes observing you at work in your classroom. Once you have obtained tenure, classroom observation becomes incredibly infrequent. Often, the evaluation is little more than perfunctory. Some teachers feel they and their students share a "secret life," off-limits to others. Most of your colleagues will have only a general impression of your teaching competence. The word may leak out—through students, parents, or even the custodian—if you are doing a really fine job; however, on the whole, when you call out, "Hello, I'm here, I'm a teacher. How am I doing?" there will be little cheering from anyone outside your classroom.

I DON'T GET NO RESPECT

While many Americans value teaching, many others don't. One reason for this inconsistency is sexism. Occupations

continued

The Good News . . .

the importance of teachers. By the 1990s, more than a third of students expressed an interest in becoming a teacher, and two-thirds gave their teachers a grade of A or B.[3] When you become a teacher, many people will accord you respect, because they admire teachers. You will be someone whose specialized training and skills are used to benefit others. Mark Twain once wrote, "To be good is noble, but to teach others how to be good is nobler." Which would have summed up this point perfectly, except, being Mark Twain, he added: "—and less trouble."

AS A TEACHER, YOU ARE CONSTANTLY INVOLVED IN INTELLECTUAL MATTERS

You may have become very interested in a particular subject. Perhaps you love a foreign language or mathematics, or maybe you are intrigued by contemporary social issues. If you decide you want to share this excitement and stimulation with others, teaching offers a natural channel for doing so. As one teacher put it: "I want them to be exposed to what I love and what I teach. I want them to know somebody, even if they think I'm crazy, who's genuinely excited about history."[4]

Using your extended vacation times to continue your education can further advance your intellectual stimulation and growth. The Internet is a great source for finding creative teaching ideas, and staying on top of emerging developments in your field. Other helpful sources are journals, weekly educational newspapers, conferences and meetings sponsored by school districts and professional education associations. You have ready access to the intellectual community.

PORTRAIT OF THE TEACHER AS AN ARTIST

You can construct everything from original simulation games to videotapes, from multimedia programs to educational software. Even the development of a superb lesson plan is an exercise in creativity, as you strive to meet the needs of the diverse children who come into your classroom each day. Some people draw clear parallels between teachers and artists and highlight the creativity that is essential to both:

> I love to teach as a painter loves to paint, as a musician loves to play, as a singer loves to sing, as a strong man rejoices to run a race. Teaching is an art—an art so great and so difficult to master that a man [or woman] can spend a long life at it without realizing much more than his [or her] limitations and mistakes, and his [or her] distance from the ideal. But the main aim of my happy days has been to become a good teacher. Just as every architect wishes to be a good architect and every professional poet strives toward perfection.[5]

The Bad News . . .

with large numbers of women generally face prestige problems, and teaching is no exception. (There may come a day when we will not have to mention this issue, but, for the time being, prejudice still exists.) Unfortunately, in our materialistic society, people's work is frequently measured by the size of the paycheck—and most teachers' wallets are modestly endowed. Despite the resurgence of support for teachers, when it comes to the game of impressing people, teachers are still not collecting a large pile of status chips.

THE SAME MATTERS YEAR AFTER YEAR AFTER YEAR

Yes, you will be continually involved in academic subject matter—but the word continually is a double-edged sword. Teaching, like most other jobs, entails a lot of repetition. You may tire of teaching the same subject matter to a new crop of students every September. If this happens, boredom and a feeling that you are getting intellectually stale may replace excitement. For some, working with students who seem unmoved by the ideas that excite you can be frustrating and disillusioning. You may turn to your colleagues for intellectual stimulation, only to find that they are more concerned about the cost of auto repair and TV shows than the latest genetic decoding breakthrough or the intricacies of current government policy.

Since you are just embarking on your teaching career, you may find it difficult to imagine yourself becoming bored with the world of education. However, as you teach class after class on the same subject, interest can wane.

THE BOG OF MINDLESS ROUTINE

Much is said about the creativity of teaching, but, under close inspection, the job breaks down into a lot of mindless routine as well. A large percentage of the day is consumed by clerical work, child control, housekeeping, announcements, and participation in ceremonies. Although there is opportunity for ingenuity and inventiveness, most of the day is spent in the three Rs of ritual, repetition, and routine. As one disgruntled sixth-grade teacher in Los Angeles said,

> Paper work, paper work. The nurse wants the health cards, so you have to stop and get them. Another teacher wants one of your report cards. The principal wants to know how many social science books you have. Somebody else wants to know if you can come to a meeting on such and such a day. Forms to fill out, those crazy forms: Would you please give a breakdown of boys and girls in the class; would you please say how many children you have in reading grade such and such. Forms, messengers—all day long.[6]

continued

The Good News . . .

TO TOUCH A LIFE, TO MAKE A DIFFERENCE

Teaching is more than helping a child master phonics or discover meaning in seemingly lifeless history facts. Each classroom is a composite of the anguish and joy of all its students. You can feel the pain of the child in the fourth seat who always knows the answer, but is too shy to speak. Then there is the rambunctious one who spills all over the classroom in a million random ways, unable to focus on any one task or project. Or that physically unattractive victim, who inspires taunts and abuse from usually well-mannered classmates. You can be the one who makes a difference in their lives:

> Mr. Jacobs won our hearts, because he treated us as though we were already what we could only hope to become. Through his eyes we saw ourselves as capable and decent and destined for greatness. . . . Mr. Jacobs introduced us to ourselves. We learned who we were and what we wanted to be. No longer strangers to ourselves, we felt at home in the world.[7]

BETTER SALARIES, LONGER VACATIONS

In the last two decades, the average teacher salary, adjusted for inflation, rose about 20 percent, from the $30,000 to the $40,000 bracket, though salaries vary enormously from one community to another. The average teacher in South Dakota earns only in the high $20,000 range, while Connecticut teachers average more than $50,000. Additional salary can be earned by working in the summer or accepting extra faculty responsibilities. Occupational benefits, such as health and retirement, are generally excellent. You will enjoy long vacations. A few school districts provide teachers with an opportunity to study, travel, or engage in other forms of professional improvement through an extended leave or sabbatical program. All of these considerations make for a more relaxed and varied lifestyle, one that gives you time for yourself as well as your family. Whether you use your "free time" to be with your family, to travel, or to make extra money, time flexibility is a definite plus.

The Bad News . . .

THE TARNISHED IDEALIST

We all hope to be that special teacher, the one students remember and talk about long after they graduate. But too often, idealistic goals give way to survival—simply making it through from one day to the next. New teachers find themselves judged on their ability to maintain a quiet, orderly room. Idealistic young teachers find the worship of control incompatible with their humanistic goals. Likewise, they feel betrayed if a student naively mistakes their offer of friendship as a sign of weakness or vulnerability. As a result, many learn the trade secret—"don't smile until Christmas" (or Chanukah, Kwanzaa, or Ramadan, depending on your community)"—and adopt it quickly. Even veteran teachers throw up their hands in despair and too often leave teaching. Teacher-student conflict can lead to lost idealism, and worse. Some teachers are concerned with the increase in discipline problems, and a decrease in support from parents and others. How can teachers stay inspired when their classrooms lack basic supplies?[8] Trying to make a difference may result in more frustration than satisfaction.

BUT SALARIES STILL HAVE A LONG WAY TO GO

Although teachers' salaries have improved, they still lag behind what most people would call a good income. Teachers ages 22 to 28 earned an average $7,894 less per year than other college-educated adults of the same age by the late 1990s. The gap was three times greater for teachers 44 to 50, who earned approximately $25,000 less than their counterparts in other occupations.[9] A history teacher says, "It's really difficult to maintain a family . . . I'm not sure I could have done it then except for a wife who's not demanding or pushy. She's completely comfortable with the things we have, and we don't have a great deal."[10] And the following comment comes from a well-to-do suburban community: "You can always tell the difference between the teachers' and the students' parking lots. The students' lot is the one with all the new cars in it."[11] The long vacations are nice—but they are also long periods without income.

YOU BE THE JUDGE

Which of these arguments and issues are most influential in determining if teaching is a good fit for you? Is there a particular point that is most persuasive, pro or con? What does that tell you about yourself? On a scale from 1 to 10, where 10 is "really committed" to teaching, and 1 is "I want no part of that job," what number are you? Remember that number as you read the text and go through this course—and see if you change that rating in the pages and weeks ahead.

themselves revealing their perceptions and feelings about their work. A more structured attempt to assess teachers' views on their careers was carried out by the National Education Association (NEA) and the National Center for Educational Statistics (NCES), part of the U.S. Department of Education. Teachers from around the nation were asked why they decided to become teachers, and why they choose to stay in teaching.[12] Teachers elect a career in the classroom for the intrinsic rewards that make teaching pretty unique, including a desire to work with young people, the significance of education generally, and even the love of a particular subject—not a bad bunch to have as colleagues. And once in the classroom, most teachers report that they like what they are doing.

In the NEA and NCES survey, the vast majority of the teachers, about 80 percent, reported that they were satisfied with their jobs and with their working conditions. Almost 90 percent were satisfied with the intellectual challenge of their work, their job security, and their autonomy in the classroom. The teachers also gave high scores to supervisors, with solid majorities viewing their school principals as supportive and encouraging—leaders who were able to communicate their expectations and to enforce school rules. When asked about the adequacy of resources, such as textbooks, supplies, and copying machines, the majority of teachers agreed that the materials were available as needed. But not everything surveyed was rosy.

High on the teachers' "Top Ten List of Things I'd Like to Change about My Job" was salary, with 55 percent registering their dissatisfaction. Salaries, although better today than they have been historically, are still judged inadequate (Figures 1.1 and 1.2). But salaries are not the only concern. Incremental obstacles pile up and wear down a teacher. Teachers focus their complaints on heavy workloads and extra responsibilities, discipline issues, negative attitudes expressed by students, unresponsive school administrators, and lack of support from parents. Parental support, like most of these factors, varies dramatically from school to school. If you are interested in a teaching position with a high level of parental support and involvement, you would be well advised to begin your search in private schools and at the elementary level.

Despite the common perception that teachers are disillusioned, the majority of teachers report that they love teaching. By 2000, fewer teachers registered complaints than did teachers in the 1980s, and the percentage of new teachers considering another career dropped as well. Yet the rapid turnover of teachers, as well as continuing teacher shortages, underscores the need for greater improvement in the quality of their working lives.

Professionalism at the Crossroads

What noble employment is more valuable to the state than that of the man who instructs the rising generation?

(Cicero)

Education makes a people easy to lead, but difficult to drive; easy to govern but impossible to enslave.

(Lord Brougham)

I shou'd think it as glorius [sic] employment to instruct poor children as to teach the children of the greatest monarch.

(Elizabeth Elstob)

FIGURE 1.1   Teacher Salaries; Beginning and Average Teacher Salary in 1999–2000 Ranked by Average Salary within Region

State	Average Salary	Beginning Salary	State	Average Salary	Beginning Salary
New England			**Southeast**		
Connecticut	$52,410	$30,466	Georgia	$41,122	$30,402
Rhode Island	48,138	27,286	North Carolina	39,404	27,968
Massachusetts	46,955	30,330	Virginia	38,992	26,783
New Hampshire	37,734	24,650	Florida	36,722	25,132
Vermont	36,402	25,791	Alabama	36,689	29,790
Maine	35,561	22,942	Tennessee	36,328	27,228
			Kentucky	36,255	24,753
Mideast			South Carolina	36,081	25,215
New York	$51,020	$31,910	West Virginia	35,011	23,829
New Jersey	50,878	30,480	Arkansas	33,691	22,599
Pennsylvania	48,321	30,185	Louisiana	33,109	25,738
District of Columbia	48,304	30,850	Mississippi	31,897	23,040
Delaware	44,435	30,945			
Maryland	43,720	28,612	**Rocky Mountains**		
			Colorado	$39,073	$24,875
Great Lakes			Idaho	35,155	20,915
Michigan	$48,729	$28,545	Utah	34,946	23,273
Illinois	46,480	30,151	Wyoming	34,188	24,168
Indiana	41,855	26,553	Montana	32,121	20,969
Ohio	41,713	23,597			
Minnesota	40,678	25,666	**Far West**		
Wisconsin	39,897	25,344	California	$47,680	$32,190
			Alaska	46,481	33,676
Plains			Oregon	45,103	29,733
Kansas	$36,282	$25,252	Nevada	43,083	28,734
Iowa	35,678	25,275	Hawaii	41,292	29,204
Missouri	35,660	25,977	Washington	41,047	26,514
Nebraska	33,237	22,923			
North Dakota	29,863	20,422	**Outlying Areas**		
South Dakota	29,072	21,889	Guam	$34,947	$26,917
			Virgin Islands	34,784	22,751
Southwest			Puerto Rico	24,980	18,700
Texas	$37,567	$28,400			
Arizona	34,824	25,613	U.S. Average	$41,820	$27,989
New Mexico	32,713	25,042			
Oklahoma	29,525	24,025			

SOURCE: American Federation of Teachers Survey and Analysis of Teacher Salary Trends, 2000, p. 8.

REFLECTION

How do states and regions differ in teacher salaries? What are some of the reasons for these disparities? Why do you believe that private schools can attract teachers, while generally paying less salary?

The man who can make hard things easy is the educator.

(Ralph Waldo Emerson)

I touch the future; I teach.

(Christa McAuliffe)

Literature, philosophy, and history are replete with such flowery tributes to teaching. In many minds, in some of our greatest minds, teaching is considered the noblest of professions. But the realities of the job do not always mesh with such admirable

FIGURE 1.2   Teacher Salaries

The nation's average teacher salary has climbed steadily since 1985, but when adjusted for inflation, there is little growth in the teachers' pay

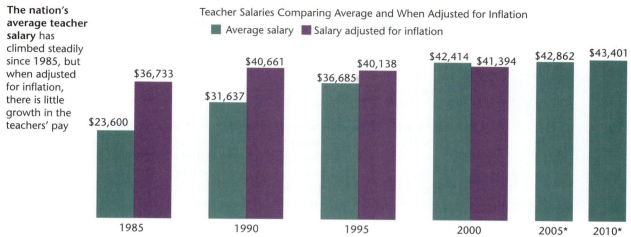

Teacher Salaries Comparing Average and When Adjusted for Inflation

■ Average salary   ■ Salary adjusted for inflation

	1985	1990	1995	2000	2005*	2010*
Average salary	$23,600	$31,637	$36,685	$42,414	$42,862	$43,401
Salary adjusted for inflation	$36,733	$40,661	$40,138	$41,394		

*Projections for moderate growth in salaries.

SOURCE: U.S. Department of Education, National Center for Educational Statistics, Elementary and Secondary Salary Model; National Education Association, Annual Estimates of School Statistics (Latest Edition 2000, Copyright 1999 by the NEA).

REFLECTION

What future developments might increase or decrease projected teacher salaries? Could you create a chart that depicts intrinsic rewards for teachers (satisfaction with working conditions and lifestyle not reflected in salaries)?

appraisals, resulting in a painful clash between noble ideals and practical realities. In the preface to *Goodbye, Mr. Chips*, James Hilton writes that his portrait of the lovable schoolmaster is a "tribute to a great profession." But an article in the *NEA Today*, a teacher's magazine, is entitled: "Are You Treated Like a Professional? Or a Tall Child?" For many teachers, the "Tall Child" analogy is closer to the truth.

The problem is not new. Here's what Ellen Hogan Steele, a teacher who cares passionately about the privilege, responsibility, and dignity of belonging to a profession, said back in the 1970s:

I recall a carpenter—he visited my home to discuss a renovation—talking about a school strike in a neighboring town. Unaware of my occupation he called teachers ignorant, lazy, and lucky to be employed.

"Can you imagine thinking they should make as much as me?" he fumed.

I can imagine that. I presume my work to be as demanding and skilled as that of the carpenters I employ. . . . What do teachers want? This teacher wants to make a reasonable living, to be recognized as a person who performs an essential service, to be considered an expert in my

Collectively, teachers struggle to empower their profession; individually, they struggle to empower their students.

small area of experience, to be occasionally praised when I do well and to be helped to improve when I don't. . . . In short, I want someone to know that I'm alive, and unless they do, I'll keep on kicking.

Says English teacher Carol Davis:

> We're told when to get here, when to leave, what to teach, what to want, what not to want, and how to think. . . . I'm trained in how to teach English, but I'm rarely asked for my opinion. If I were to be "promoted out of my classroom" my opinion would be more respected immediately. The irony would be that I'd no longer be teaching children.[13]

Many teachers feel that the satisfaction they realize inside the classroom is too often jeopardized by forces beyond the classroom: politicians mandating numerous standardized tests, demanding parents offering little support, and textbook publishers determining course content. Teachers desire more autonomy and control over their careers, and like all of us, want to be treated with more respect. Teachers increasingly see themselves as reflective decision makers, selecting objectives and teaching procedures to meet the needs of different learners.[14] They must know their subject matter, learning theory, research on various teaching methodologies, and techniques for curriculum development.[15] Some believe that the problems confronting teachers stem from the more pervasive issue of professional status and competence. Are teachers professionals? What does it take to be a professional, anyway? *Educating a Profession*, a publication of the American Association of Colleges for Teacher Education (AACTE), lists twelve criteria for a **profession**. We have shortened these criteria below, and ask you to consider each one and decide if you believe that teaching meets these criteria. After marking your reactions in the appropriate column, compare your reactions with those of your classmates.

Criteria for a Profession	True for Teaching	Not True for Teaching	Don't Know
1. Professions provide essential services to the individual and society.	_____	_____	_____
2. Each profession is concerned with an identified area of need or function (e.g., maintenance of physical and emotional health).	_____	_____	_____
3. The profession possesses a unique body of knowledge and skills (professional culture).	_____	_____	_____
4. Professional decisions are made in accordance with valid knowledge, principles, and theories.	_____	_____	_____
5. The profession is based on undergirding disciplines from which it builds its own applied knowledge and skills.	_____	_____	_____
6. Professional associations control the actual work and conditions of the profession (e.g., admissions, standards, licensing).	_____	_____	_____
7. There are performance standards for admission to and continuance in the profession.	_____	_____	_____
8. Preparation for and induction into the profession requires a protracted preparation program, usually in a college or university professional school.	_____	_____	_____
9. There is a high level of public trust and confidence in the profession and in the skills and competence of its members.	_____	_____	_____

INTERACTIVE ACTIVITY
IS TEACHING A PROFESSION? Do this exercise online. See how other students responded to each statement.

10. Individual practitioners are characterized by a strong service motivation and lifetime commitment to competence.   _____   _____   _____

11. The profession itself determines individual competence.   _____   _____   _____

12. There is relative freedom from direct or public job supervision of the individual practitioner. The professional accepts this responsibility and is accountable through his or her profession to the society.[16]   _____   _____   _____

Do not be surprised if you find some criteria that do not apply to teaching. In fact, even the occupations that spring to mind when you hear the word *professional*—doctor, lawyer, clergy, college professor—do not completely measure up to all these criteria.

Those who developed these twelve criteria for a profession also listed another twelve criteria that would describe a **semiprofession**. Read these items carefully, and compare them with the characteristics that define a profession. Consider each item separately. Does it accurately describe teaching, or does it sell teaching short? After you have considered all the items and have marked your reactions in the appropriate column, decide whether you think teaching is actually a profession, or whether it would more accurately be termed a semiprofession.

Criteria for a Semi-Profession	True for Teaching	Not True for Teaching	Don't Know
1. Lower in occupational status	_____	_____	_____
2. Shorter training periods	_____	_____	_____
3. Lack of societal acceptance that the nature of the service and/or the level of expertise justifies the autonomy that is granted to the professions	_____	_____	_____
4. A less specialized and less highly developed body of knowledge and skills	_____	_____	_____
5. Markedly less emphasis on theoretical and conceptual bases for practice	_____	_____	_____
6. A tendency for the individual to identify with the employment institution more and with the profession less	_____	_____	_____
7. More subject to administrative and supervisory surveillance and control	_____	_____	_____
8. Less autonomy in professional decision making, with accountability to superiors rather than to the profession	_____	_____	_____
9. Management by persons who have themselves been prepared and served in that semiprofession	_____	_____	_____
10. A preponderance of women	_____	_____	_____
11. Absence of the right of privileged communication between client and professional	_____	_____	_____
12. Little or no involvement in matters of life and death[17]	_____	_____	_____

Where do you place teaching? If you had a tough time deciding, you are not alone. Many people feel that teaching falls somewhere between professional and semiprofessional in status. Perhaps we should think of it as an "emerging" profession.

Teachers work with children only a few hours a day, and some people, not very sympathetic to the demands on teachers, believe that they should be paid pretty much as babysitters. Surprisingly, some teachers see an advantage in that system. Babysitters get about $6.00 an hour, so for a five-hour day, teachers would earn $30 per child. For a class of 25, that would be $750 a day. The school year is 187 days, so that would be $140,250. Summers, weekends, and evenings off. Teachers as babysitters, an idea with some merit!

REFLECTION

What factors do you think should impact a teacher's pay? Class size? Subject area? Grade level?

FIGURE 1.3   New Teacher Satisfaction and Willingness to Enter Teaching Again

SOURCE: Public Agenda Online, April 2000. (See also National Education Association "Status of the American Public School Teacher," 1995–1996 © 1997.)

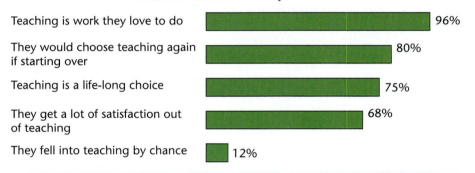

Percent of Teachers Who Say

Teaching is work they love to do — 96%
They would choose teaching again if starting over — 80%
Teaching is a life-long choice — 75%
They get a lot of satisfaction out of teaching — 68%
They fell into teaching by chance — 12%

REFLECTION

Why do you believe that there is a gap between the popular image of disillusioned teachers and the results of this survey? This survey data comes from those who have been teaching for five years or less. Why do you think that the past decade has been marked by an increase in the percentage of teachers who would choose a career in teaching again?

Or perhaps teaching is, and will remain, a "submerged" profession. Either way, teachers find themselves in a career with both potential and frustration. Yet for most new teachers, the potential outweighs the frustration. During their first five years in the classroom, 80 percent report that they would choose teaching again (see Figure 1.3).

Why does all this "profession talk" matter? You may be more concerned with *real* questions: Will I be good at teaching? Do I want to work with children? What age level is best for me? Will the salary be enough to give me the quality of life that I want for myself and my family? You may be thinking, Why should I split hairs over whether I belong to a profession? Who cares? The issue of professionalism may not matter to you now or even during your first year or two of teaching, when classroom survival and performance have top priority. But if you stay in teaching, this idea of professionalism will grow in significance, perhaps becoming one of the most important issues you face. Even now, as a student, you can become more reflective in your views of teaching and learning; you can begin to refine your own professional behaviors and outlooks. Beyond your personal decisions, you will confront a difficult question faced by so many teachers through time: Is teaching a genuine profession? Or does teaching languish in semiprofessional status? The issue remains at a crossroads.

From Normal Schools to Board-Certified Teachers

Basic to any discussion of professionalism is the question of how its members are prepared. As you read this brief history of teacher preparation, think about whether teachers are prepared in a way commensurate with belonging to a profession.

From colonial America into the twentieth century, teacher education scarcely existed. More often than not, teachers in colonial America received no formal preparation at all. Most elementary teachers never even attended a secondary school. Some learned their craft by serving as apprentices to master teachers, a continuation of the medieval guild system. Others were indentured servants paying for their passage to America by teaching for a fixed number of years. Many belonged to the "sink-or-swim" school of teaching, and the education of an untold number of students undoubtedly sank with them.

The smaller number of teachers working at the secondary level—in academies or Latin grammar schools and as private tutors—had usually received some college education, more often in Europe than in America. Some knowledge of the subject matter was considered desirable, but no particular aptitude for teaching or knowledge of teaching skills was considered necessary. Teaching was viewed not as a career but as temporary employment. Many of those who entered teaching, especially at the elementary level, were teenagers who taught for only a year or two. Others were of dubious character, and early records reveal a number of teachers fired for drinking or stealing.

From this humble beginning there slowly emerged a more professional program for teacher education. In 1823, the **Reverend Samuel Hall** established a **normal school** (named for its European counterpart) in Concord, Vermont. This private school provided elementary school graduates with formal training in teaching skills. Reverend Hall's modest normal school marked the beginning of teacher education in America. Sixteen years later, in 1839, **Horace Mann** was instrumental in establishing the first state-supported normal school in Lexington, Massachusetts. Normal schools typically provided a two-year teacher training program, consisting of academic subjects as well as teaching methodology. Some students came directly from elementary school; others had completed a secondary education. Into the 1900s, the normal school was the backbone of teacher education. The lack of rigorous professional training contributed to the less than professional treatment afforded teachers. The following is a teacher contract from the 1920s, a contract that offers a poignant insight into how teachers were seen . . . and treated.

Teaching Contract

Miss _____ agrees:

1. Not to get married. This contract becomes null and void immediately if the teacher marries.

2. Not to keep company with men.

3. To be home between the hours of 8 P.M. and 6 A.M. unless in attendance at a school function.

4. Not to loiter downtown in ice-cream parlors.

5. Not to leave town at any time without the permission of the Chairman of the Trustees.

6. Not to smoke cigarettes. This contract becomes null and void immediately if the teacher is found smoking.

7. Not to drink beer, wine, or whiskey. This contract becomes null and void immediately if the teacher is found drinking beer, wine, or whiskey.

8. Not to ride in a carriage or automobile with any man except her brother or father.

9. Not to dress in bright colors.

10. Not to dye her hair.

11. Not to wear less than two petticoats.

12. Not to wear dresses shorter than two inches above the ankles.

13. To keep the schoolroom clean:

    a. To sweep the classroom floor at least once daily.

    b. To scrub the classroom floor at least once weekly with soap and hot water.

    c. To clean the blackboard at least once daily.

    d. To start the fire at 7 A.M. so that the room will be warm by 8 A.M. when the children arrive.

14. Not to wear face powder, mascara, or to paint the lips.

(Reprinted courtesy of the *Chicago Tribune*, September 28, 1975, Section 1.)

As the contract indicates, by the 1900s, teaching was becoming a female occupation. Both female workers and teaching being held in low regard, the reward for the austere dedication detailed in this contract was an unimpressive $75 a month. But as the twentieth century progressed, professional teacher training gained wider acceptance. Enrollments in elementary schools climbed and secondary education gained in popularity, and so did the demand for more and better-trained teachers. Many private colleges and universities initiated teacher education programs, and normal schools expanded to three- and four-year programs, gradually evolving into state teachers' colleges. Interestingly, as attendance grew, these teachers' colleges expanded their programs and began offering courses and career preparation in fields other than teaching. By the 1950s, many of the state teachers' colleges had evolved into state colleges. In fact, some of today's leading universities were originally chartered as normal schools.

The 1980s marked the beginning of the modern effort to reshape education. A number of education reform reports fanned the flames of controversy regarding professionalism and teacher preparation, including one written by a group of prominent education deans. The **Holmes Group**, named for former Harvard Education Dean Henry H. Holmes, debated the teacher preparation issue for several years before releasing its report, entitled ***Tomorrow's Teachers*** (1986).[18] The same year, the Carnegie Forum also issued a highly publicized report, ***A Nation Prepared***.[19] Both reports called for higher standards and increased professionalism for the nation's teachers. The Carnegie report also called for an end to the undergraduate teaching major, to be replaced by master's-level degrees in teaching. While some universities followed this recommendation and created fiïyear teacher education programs (bachelor's and master's degrees required for teacher education candidates), other colleges continued their undergraduate education programs. Teacher education remains a

FIGURE 1.4   Supporting Teacher Board Certification

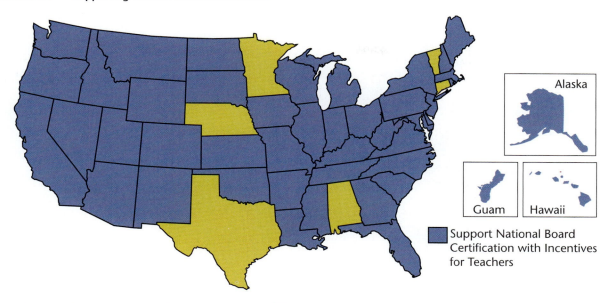

Support National Board Certification with Incentives for Teachers

SOURCE: National Board for Professional Teaching Standards, May 2001.

REFLECTION

Teachers working in most states are given incentives and assistance when they apply for national board certification. Yet the vast majority of local school districts do not provide financial support for this effort. Why are states more likely than local districts to support this effort? How do states and school systems benefit when their teachers become certified? A few years down the road, you may be deciding if you want to apply for board certification. Would state or district assistance influence your decision to seek board certification?

hodgepodge of approaches. Some critics place much of the blame on universities themselves, for failing to adequately fund and support schools of education.[20]

But not all of the attention has been on initial teacher education. In the 1990s, the Carnegie Forum was influential in creating the **National Board for Professional Teaching Standards (NBPTS)**. The goal of the NBPTS is to recognize extraordinary teachers, those whose skills and knowledge indicate their high level of achievement. This is a significant departure from simply licensing new teachers who reach minimal standards. During its first years of operation, the NBPTS developed assessment procedures to identify highly competent teachers, teachers who would be designated **board-certified**. Like medicine, teaching now had not just an entry license—a standard teaching license—but advanced recognition of a higher level of skills and competencies. Thousands of educators annually compile professional portfolios (including videotaped examples of their teaching), and undergo assessment tests and interviews en route to becoming board-certified teachers. As you might imagine, the board assessment is not inexpensive. All this effort is invested in recognizing superior teachers, a concept that was not even considered a decade or two ago.

As teachers aspire to board certification, states and communities are developing ways to recognize their accomplishments. Most states and a few school districts now pay for their teachers to prepare for board certification (Figure 1.4). Many teachers who

How can school districts attract teachers? Offer rewards! (OK, we'll call them incentives.) Maryland is offering signing bonuses for bright college graduates going into teaching, extra pay for teachers working in high poverty areas, reduced tax rate for teachers, and a $5,000 home-buying grant. Check the textbook website at www.mhhe.com/sadker for other examples of how school districts have "sweetened the pot" for teachers.

SOURCE: "Sweetening the Pot," *2000 Editorial Projects in Education,* 19 (18), pp. 28–30, 33–34.

REFLECTION

Would these incentives influence your career decision? If you were asked to design an incentive program, how would you "sweeten the pot"? Some critics point out that these incentives do not attract teachers into high poverty schools, where they are most needed. Could you develop a plan to respond to this need?

OLC Click on *In the News* for recent *In the News* stories. Submit your own *In the News* summary to share with your colleagues.

become board-certified receive stipends or are placed on a higher salary scale. Others are given release time to work with new teachers.[21] Will new responsibilities be found for board-certified teachers? Are we developing a new cadre of educational leaders, "lead" or "principal" teachers? Will board certification evolve into a sort of national merit pay? Or will board certification simply become another failed attempt to transform what some view as a semiprofession into a true profession?[22] These and other pivotal questions will likely be answered during your time as a classroom teacher.

Teacher Education Today

Even as educators strive toward professional status, there is no consensus on how best to prepare teachers. While most of you are enrolled in a typical college or university teacher education program, the current teacher shortage has led many states to explore alternate certification programs, programs that allow individuals with limited training to become teachers quickly. It is possible for people with little or no preparation, and lacking a regular teaching license, to find themselves not just substituting, but staying on as "emergency" teachers for the entire year. Several local as well as national programs "prepare" teachers in only a few weeks, and then they are hired by school districts. Perhaps the best known of these "fast track training" programs is **Teach for America**, in which highly motivated volunteers undergo very brief teacher preparation and begin their careers in some of America's most difficult classrooms. Supporters of the program point out that many of these volunteers become excellent teachers, and that the proportion of teachers of color is higher in Teach for America than in traditional teacher education programs. Moreover, many of the challenging schools where these teachers are assigned have a difficult time finding any teachers, and eagerly welcome these new recruits. Defenders of such fast track training programs argue that "on-the-job-training" is not new, and can be quite effective.

Meet Sarah, Amy and Claudia, representing a three-generation teaching family. Sarah started in 1948 when the average annual salary was under _____. Her daughter Amy, a recently retired principal, began teaching in 1969, when the salaries had climbed to _____. When Claudia entered the field in 1995, the nation's average teaching wage averaged _____. Moving beyond salary, what other differences might have characterized teaching in 1948, 1969, and 1995? If you could interview these three educators, what questions might you ask?

Answers: 1948—$3,000; 1969—$8,626; 1995—$37,704.

SOURCES: American Federation of Teachers www.aft.org/research/survey99/ National Center for Educational Statistics http://nces.ed.gov/pubs2001/digest/dt076.html

Not very long ago, lawyers and doctors were prepared for their professions through similar apprenticeships. But many educators see such programs as the height of irresponsibility, quite the opposite of profession building.[23] Teach for America critics like Linda Darling-Hammond argue that today's classroom challenges require more thorough career preparation, and that even when teachers are in short supply, professional standards must be maintained.[24] How can teaching ever become a profession, critics ask, if it continues to grant "quickie" licenses to those who lack credible training?

Even if there were a consensus on the appropriate length of teacher education programs, what the content should be would spark another debate. As you begin to reflect on teaching, you may also want to consider what skills are most crucial to your teaching success, and the type of classroom climate you want to create. Think of yourself as a consumer of teacher education—because in a very real sense, you are. If you were to design a teacher education program, what would it look like? People hold sharply divided views on how best to prepare teachers. In 1997, Public Agenda, a nonpartisan, nonprofit organization, surveyed 900 education professors from around the nation. Public Agenda then compared their responses not only with those of the public, but also with those of practicing classroom teachers. Public Agenda's poll found dramatic differences on how people envision good teacher training. On the issues below, how do your opinions compare to those of the public, classroom teachers, and education professors?

On Discipline . . .

Are discipline problems a sign of student boredom, or an indicator that firm standards and classroom control are lacking?

The Public Agenda survey indicates that education professors believe that most students arrive at school wanting to learn and that student misbehavior is typically a sign of poor teaching.[25] Professors shy away from advocating punitive measures, and only 30 percent report that their teacher education programs stress skills such as managing a difficult classroom. Education professors stress that good teaching is an effective remedy for student misbehavior.

On the other hand, both the public and classroom teachers indicate that schools should focus more on control and discipline. Teachers indicate that even small behavior problems often lead to bigger ones, and misbehaving students can cause major educational disruptions. That is one reason why so many teachers believe that students caught with drugs or weapons should be permanently removed from school.

REFLECTION

What discipline policies and rules might you create in your classroom? How do you view the relationship between good teaching and student behavior?

On Competition . . .

Should teachers create a more rigorous and competitive learning environment?

Today's schools are being pressed to meet specific standards, resulting in more testing and increased competition. Yet, many education professors have reservations about this trend. Professors report a general aversion to academic competition and external rewards, and you are unlikely to see their cars adorned with bumper stickers such as: "My kid is an honor student at Mia Hamm High School."

Parents surveyed were more supportive of a competitive learning environment, and regale listeners with vivid memories of their own school days, filled with rigorous tests, gobs of homework, and incredibly demanding teachers. (OK, maybe their memories have been colored by time, and their school days were not as challenging as they recall, and they didn't have to walk three miles uphill, in the snow, *to* AND *from* school when they were children. Nevertheless, they remember and value tougher, more demanding schools.) It's not surprising that 70 percent of the public believes that schools need to raise standards and not promote students who do poorly.

REFLECTION

How enthusiastically will you push competition? How do you view the roles of competition versus cooperation in your classroom? Will you sponsor spelling or history "bees," or offer prizes for superior performance in your class? If you are not a fan of high-stakes testing and imposed state standards, how will you feel about devoting class time to prepare students for standards and tests?

On Honesty and Dependability . . .

How much emphasis should teachers place on traditional values, such as punctuality, politeness, and even honesty?

The Public Agenda survey indicates strong support for student behavior that reflects civility and politeness, honesty and punctuality. Professors, teachers, and the public concur that these behaviors lead to more effective learning. They believe that if students were to arrive at school on time and were generally more dependable, for example, academic achievement would improve significantly. The disagreement is on how to accomplish this. Only 8 percent of the professors reported that their programs prepare teachers to handle problems such as cheating. Eighty-five percent of the professors felt that schools are already expected to deal with too many problems (see Figure 1.5).

REFLECTION

Do you believe that a teacher education program should teach strategies for encouraging politeness, honesty and punctuality in students? Or do you feel that this is best left to parents?

On Urban Legends about Teaching . . .

As you can tell, the public does not lack for ideas as to what it takes to make an effective teacher. Sometimes these ideas move from the rational to the extreme: "Teachers are born, not made," or "To be a good teacher, all you really need to know is the subject you are teaching." Like the urban legend of alligators cavorting in the New York City sewer system, these teaching myths have taken on a life of their own. Let's take a brief look at some of the urban legends about teacher education.

Teachers are born, not made: It is certainly true that some students enter a teacher education program with impressive instructional skills, yet training and practice is what is needed to transform a strong teacher into a gifted one. Teaching is far from unique in this. When a group of Olympians and their coaches were asked what it takes to become a champion, none of the answers suggested that they were "born" champions. On the contrary, the athletes credited well-designed practices and good coaching. Accomplished musicians attribute their performance to hours of focused practice, as do master chess players. So too, superior teachers are trained, not born.

All you really need to know is the subject you are teaching: While it is true that subject mastery is critical in effective teaching, research reveals that teachers skilled in **pedagogy**, the art and science of teaching, especially teaching methods and strategies, outperform teachers with superior subject area knowledge.[26]

Teacher education students are less talented than other college majors: This popular canard lives on despite very mixed evidence. On the one hand, education majors are

INTERACTIVE ACTIVITY
WHAT SHOULD TEACHERS LEARN? Create your own teacher education curriculum based on what you think teachers need to know.

FIGURE 1.5   What's Worth Teaching Teachers
These are the qualities education professors believe teacher education programs should impart to their students.

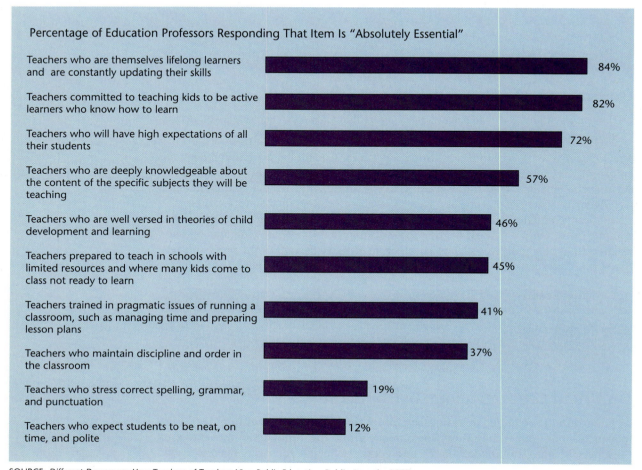

Percentage of Education Professors Responding That Item Is "Absolutely Essential"

Quality	Percentage
Teachers who are themselves lifelong learners and are constantly updating their skills	84%
Teachers committed to teaching kids to be active learners who know how to learn	82%
Teachers who will have high expectations of all their students	72%
Teachers who are deeply knowledgeable about the content of the specific subjects they will be teaching	57%
Teachers who are well versed in theories of child development and learning	46%
Teachers prepared to teach in schools with limited resources and where many kids come to class not ready to learn	45%
Teachers trained in pragmatic issues of running a classroom, such as managing time and preparing lesson plans	41%
Teachers who maintain discipline and order in the classroom	37%
Teachers who stress correct spelling, grammar, and punctuation	19%
Teachers who expect students to be neat, on time, and polite	12%

SOURCE: *Different Drummers: How Teachers of Teachers View Public Education,* Public Agenda, 1997.

REFLECTION

Do you concur with the qualities rated as important—or relatively unimportant—by education professors? Are there areas of disagreement? Can you add a skill that you would like to acquire—one that is missing from this list?

less likely to score in the top 25 percent on the SATs than the general population. On the other hand, adult literacy surveys (see Figure 1.6) show that teachers attain scores similar to those of physicians, writers, engineers, and social workers.[27]

These urban legends aside, it is certainly true that teacher education programs are stronger today than they have been in years. In 1997, 64 percent of teachers gave their own teacher preparation a grade of *A* or *B*. Compare this to 1984, when only 49 percent of teachers awarded such high grades to their programs.[28] (See Figure 1.7.) That's a remarkable—and encouraging—increase.

FIGURE 1.6   **Adult Prose Literacy Scores by Selected Occupations**

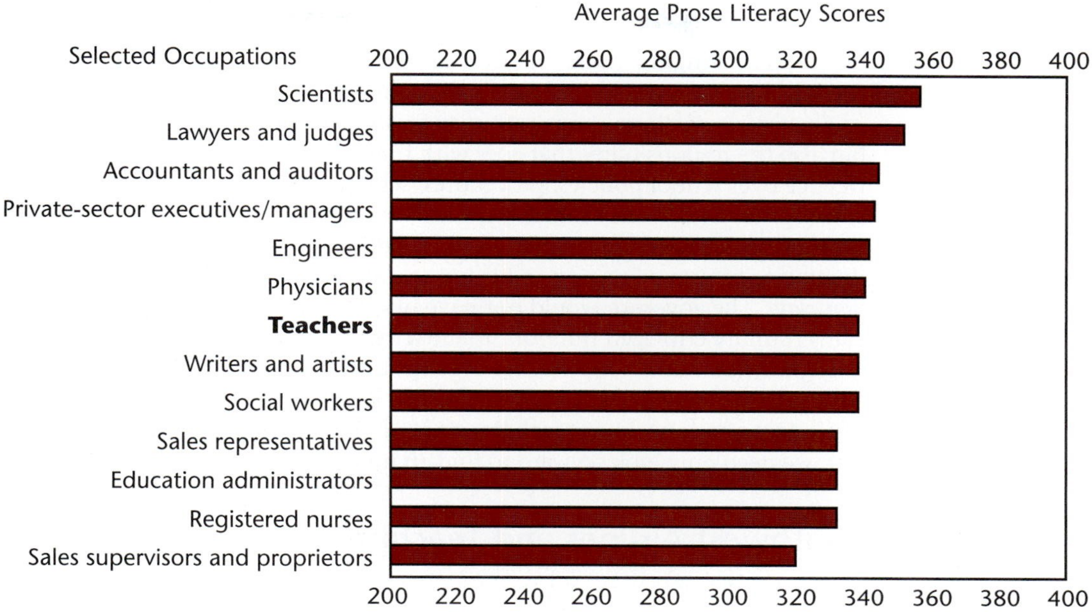

Average Prose Literacy Scores

SOURCE: David C. Berliner, "A Personal Response to Those Who Bash Teacher Education," *Journal of Teacher Education* 51, no. 5, November/December 2000.

REFLECTION

Why is there a popular perception of low teacher competence, despite their strong scores on tests like this one? Which of these occupations that score close to teaching do you find particularly surprising?

What Grade Would You Give the Teacher Education Training You Received?	1997 %	1989 %	1984 %
A and B	64	57	49
A	23	17	14
B	41	40	35
C	25	32	33
D	8	7	10
Fail	2	3	6
Don't know	1	1	2

FIGURE 1.7   Today's teachers give higher marks to their college training than teachers did in the past.

SOURCE: Carol Langdon, The Fourth Phi Delta Kappa Poll of Teachers' Attitudes Toward the Public Schools, *Phi Delta Kappan* 79, no. 3, November 1997.

REFLECTION

How do you explain the improving scores given to teacher education programs?

Why the improvement? Today's teacher preparation programs typically emphasize current research as well as practical classroom skills, often working in close collaboration with local schools. Many teacher education students are studying at the graduate level, bringing more of life's experiences to the classroom than did their predecessors, all signs of positive changes in teacher preparation.

Quality professional preparation suggests not only increased professional status, but also the responsibility that goes with that training. This translates into teacher influence over school policies, procedures, schedules, and curriculum. Yet, teachers are still kept far from policy-making circles. When Andy Baumgartner, National Teacher of the Year in 2000, criticized the lack of significant teacher representation on a commission to reform education in his home state of Georgia, he quickly became *persona non grata*. The governor would not have his photo taken with him, and several politicians roundly criticized him for his audacity.[29]

In the traditional "top-down" organization of schools, teachers find themselves with little influence over education policy, and little say in how schools operate. Yet other organizations do not lack imagination in how they view or treat employees. In fact, we need only look skyward to find an innovative example of employee influence.

Southwest Airlines and Teaching

The first time we flew on Southwest Airlines, we really did not know what to expect. We knew that we paid less for the ticket than other airlines charge, and that made us nervous. We had been advised to eat before the flight, since the airline cuisine consisted of a bag of nuts. Since everything was on a first come, first served basis, we were given firm instructions: "Get to the airport early if you want a good seat." We boarded the plane, found a seat and buckled up.

As we began the takeoff, an amazing sound reverberated through the cabin. It sounded like a whistle, a railroad whistle. Dumbstruck, we wondered: what are they using to power the engines? Is there such a thing as a steam plane? Panic turned to relief as we discovered that the flight attendant was blowing into a toy train whistle. By the time we lifted off, most of the passengers were either laughing or joining the flight attendant with their own versions of train sounds. Once airborne, the flight attendants organized a contest. Each passenger willing to tell a joke on the public address system would receive a $50 voucher. The passengers, by their applause, would choose the best jokester, and that person would receive a $100 voucher (a bit higher than the price of the ticket). Someone would fly for fun *and* profit.

If you have ever flown with Southwest, perhaps you have noticed their flight attendants as they walk through an airport. They are the ones wearing shorts and polo shirts instead of traditional uniforms and suits, strolling about in sneakers instead of wingtips or heels, and smiling, if not laughing. Southwest employees look like they are going on vacation instead of going to work. Not only are they more comfortable than many passengers, they seem happier too! So what's going on at Southwest?

In a book called *Nuts!*, Kevin and Jackie Freiberg write about how Southwest Airline's founders rejected a fundamental tenet in American business, the belief that the customer is always right. At Southwest, there are things more important than the customer, even more important than making money. One of those is the happiness of employees. Yes, employees. Employee happiness creates customer happiness. Southwest prides itself on its egalitarian corporate culture, one in which the head of the company explores options and policies with *all* employees, including those with the lowest paychecks. The president visits employees during meals and at work, seeking their ideas for improvements. Meeting employee needs is a top priority. One thing they need, according to Southwest, are celebrations. Yes, celebrations. Personal and corporate accomplishments and milestones are reasons for employees to be honored and for all involved to celebrate and party. Sound strange? Southwest believes that creating a contented, even joyful workforce does more than improve employee self-esteem and create a caring corporate culture; it also sparks innovative suggestions for improved performance. Celebrations break work routines, a necessary prerequisite for viewing work in a different way, and this leads to new and creative ideas for improving performance. The company's mission is not simply to make money. The kind of motivated employees that the company wants to attract need more than a corporate profit mission to spark their commitment. Southwest's mission is somewhat egalitarian and idealistic: to open air travel to people with limited means. "It is not a job, it is a crusade," is the company motto, a crusade that keeps ticket prices incredibly low.

Have we motivated you to buy some stock? (Don't look for it to be listed under a typical three-letter code like *SWA*. The company is listed under *LUV*.) How does the stock do? Even as many airlines descend into bankruptcy or get "absorbed" in corporate takeovers, Southwest has remained independent and its stock price has soared for three decades. The company may seem iconoclastic, but the bottom line has been all green. Its workforce is considered to be the most efficient in the industry, serving twice the usual number of passengers per employee. Southwest has few delays, and one of the best on-time records of any airline. Its safety procedures are more rigorous than the government requires, and it has been voted the safest airline in the sky. All of this comes from the cheapest airfares around.

Before you run off to buy some *LUV* stock, remember that nothing lasts forever, and despite its remarkable progress, Southwest may very well suffer some reverses in the years ahead. But the first three decades at Southwest have been amazing, and they merit a closer look. What has been the formula for the company's success? Many experts say it is the confidence that the executives placed in Southwest employees. As a result, the company attracted inspired employees and created a model workplace. But before we go any further with our airline industry story, this may be a good time to remind ourselves that we are really interested in teaching and schools (thought we forgot, right?), so let's broaden this discussion and also ask: What traits and characteristics are needed for successful teaching? How do these two sets of characteristics compare?

Here's your challenge: Sort out which of the following job attributes are listed by Southwest, and which have been drawn from the literature on effective teaching. (We did alter a few words to avoid any obvious reference to either occupation.) Put a mark in the appropriate columns to indicate which career attributes you believe are sought by Southwest, and which are drawn from teacher education sources. You certainly can check both columns, if that seems to be appropriate.

The final column is for you. Put a check in the last column if you feel that you are being described by that attribute. After you have marked your columns (but before you race off to apply for a position at either a school or an airline), we will look at the lists, and their meaning.

We are hiring for a new position, and invite you to apply.
To succeed in this career, you should:[30]

	Southwest Airlines	Teacher Education	Does This Describe Me?
1. Have a passion for the job (a purpose you are crazy about)	_____	_____	_____
2. Enjoy and appreciate other people	_____	_____	_____

	Southwest Airlines	Teacher Education	Does This Describe Me?
3. Have a strong work ethic	——	——	——
4. Possess a solid knowledge base	——	——	——
5. Believe in continuous self-improvement	——	——	——
6. Work effectively with people.	——	——	——
7. Be a positive member of the community	——	——	——
8. Successfully respond to people's different needs	——	——	——
9. Develop caring and trusting relationships with people	——	——	——
10. Have a sense of humor	——	——	——
11. Maintain your curiosity in life and work	——	——	——
12. Not take yourself too seriously	——	——	——
13. Not "hide" yourself: Be authentic	——	——	——
14. Dare to be different and experiment	——	——	——
15. Pursue "love" and caring over "techniques"	——	——	——
16. Choose service over self-interest	——	——	——
17. Be committed to unleashing the human spirit, yours and others	——	——	——

INTERACTIVE ACTIVITY
WHAT JOB IS THIS? Match job titles to Education-related job descriptions.

Have you sorted out which items come from teacher education literature, and which from Southwest Airlines? The first item, having a passion for your job, actually appears on both lists. (Did you check both columns?) In fact, the first ten items are tied to teacher effectiveness. In addition to the first statement, items 11 through 17 are from Southwest Airlines. At the core, to be effective and successful in either job requires a passion or spirit as well as strong interpersonal skills.

Why are we drawing this comparison between the attributes needed to be successful at Southwest and at teaching? We are not being paid for the plug, nor do we own stock in Southwest. We make the comparison because we believe that Southwest offers lessons for all of us. Although a stream of headlines and news stories call for improvement in the nation's schools, there is little agreement on just how to accomplish this. While some school critics demand higher standards and more testing, others believe that technology and computers hold the key to more effective schools. Still others believe that increased competition, parent choice and school vouchers will create stronger schools.

If you are not familiar with these arguments and approaches, worry not. In this text, you will learn about all of these and more. You will also learn that few if any of these education critics do what Southwest did: look to career professionals for answers. What would schools be like if teachers were more autonomous, if they were responsible for the curricular, instructional and testing decisions? How could we design schools to be happier places, where learning is a joyful experience? How can we reward teachers for going that extra mile? (These are not rhetorical questions. How do you think schools would be different if communities were committed to making teachers happy, and giving them meaningful decision-making powers?) Although the personal qualities sought by Southwest and by schools are remarkably similar, few headlines or news stories, few pundits or commentators talk about doing in schools

A 1999 poll is one of several reporting that beginning teachers are overwhelmingly happy with their jobs. Do beginning teachers personally enjoy being in the classroom? In the nation's capitol, where the poll was taken, 96 percent of new teachers answered "yes." Only 4 percent said "no." That is an amazingly high satisfaction rate. But all is not *teaching paradise*. New teachers have some major concerns, including difficult students, unfit peers, insufficient resources, and lack of parent involvement.

SOURCE: *The Washington Post,* July 4, 1999.

REFLECTION

What makes the first year of a new job, *any* job, particularly gratifying? What steps might you plan to take to reduce the concerns already identified by these teachers: difficult students, unfit peers, insufficient resources, and lack of parent involvement?

Click on *In the News* for recent *In the News* stories. Submit your own *In the News* summary to share with your colleagues.

what Southwest did in the airline industry: improving the quality of teachers' lives as a starting point to improving the education of students.

This Southwest story tells you something about us, the authors of this book: We love teaching, but want to love it more. We believe that although teaching is a wonderful career, teachers deserve more than they get, both in money and psychic rewards. We have taught in many different settings, from the military to overseas, from elementary school to the university, and while each position gave us joy, we always thought of ways to make those teaching positions better. Like so many careers, teaching has both assets and liabilities, and you would do well to consider both as you look to your own future.

We Like Questions

Education is a dynamic field, rife with controversies, misperceptions, surprises, and constant change. Throughout this book, we will work hard to immerse you in that excitement, and to tweak your interest. (OK, so it's not a Stephen King *Fright Night at the School Prom* novel for that rainy day at the beach. But we do want this text to be more exciting and interesting than most, to mirror the enthusiasm that we feel about education.) Issues discussed in this text may well spark questions. A sage once said that the only dumb question is the one not asked. (While this particular sage might have been overrated, we concur with that premise.) This text is all about answering questions. In fact, at the end of the text, we list a number of questions that students typically ask: How do I get a teacher's license? Where are salaries and working conditions the best? What's on the Praxis exam? We not only ask these questions, we try our best to answer them. What if *your* question is not listed? Responding to your questions is one of the purposes of the website that accompanies this book. (Have you visited the Online Learning Center at www.mhhe.com/sadker6e yet? In addition to attracting and answering student questions, the website is filled with useful Web links, updated news stories, study hints, sample test questions covering each of the chapters in this text, and suggested student activities. We invite you to submit your

JAIME ESCALANTE

Actor James Edwards Olmos with Jaime Escalante

For four years, Jaime Escalante had been struggling to build a strong advanced placement (AP) calculus program at Garfield, a troubled East Los Angeles school with a poor academic history. It had been difficult going, but the program finally blossomed with eighteen students, almost double the number from the year before. Every one of them passed the difficult and prestigious AP examination.

During the summer, however, an unpleasant controversy developed. The Educational Testing Service (ETS), which administers the AP exam, told fourteen of the students that a high correspondence in their answers suggested cheating. They would either have to retake the test or have their scores nullified. Escalante, the students, and others protested. There had been no cheating, they argued. It seemed to be just another example of the experts' underestimating the potential of students who are poor and Latino. But the ETS would not budge, so a retest was arranged. Even after a summer away from the theorems and formulas, all of the students passed the test again, many with higher scores than the first time.

After that, Escalante's calculus program took off, and encouraged other Garfield teachers to add and expand AP classes in history, English, biology, and other subjects. By 1987, Garfield had become known as one of the best public schools in the country.[1]

How does Escalante account for his achievements? He sums up much of his teaching as the pursuit of *ganas*, a Spanish word meaning "the will to succeed."

> Really it's not just the knowledge of math. Because to have knowledge is one thing, and to use that knowledge is another, and to know how to teach or how to motivate these kids is the combination of both. My skills are really to motivate these kids, to make them learn, to give them *ganas*—desire to do something—to make them believe they can learn.[2] Anybody, any kid can learn if he or she has the desire to do it. That's what *ganas* is about. The teacher plays an important role in education—we all remember the first teacher who really touched our lives, or gave us some encouragement, or at least appreciated our best. The teacher gives us the desire to learn, the desire to be Somebody.[3]

Escalante's own life story demonstrates *ganas*. When he immigrated to the United States from Bolivia in 1963, he had already been teaching for eleven years, ever since he was 22 years old, gaining a reputation as one of the finest teachers in La Paz. In Bolivia, he was used to teaching without textbooks or other materials, and the low salary required him to teach three sets of classes a day in order to get by. He brought his unpredictable showmanship to the United States, along with his stern father figure. While "Kimo," as he is nicknamed, can be a charming, colorful character, latecomers and those with incomplete assignments find themselves interrogated, hounded by calls to parents, and threatened with a transfer to a less effective school a very long bus ride away. Whether he has to resort to rewards, taunts, afternoon study sessions, or even mild bribery, Escalante refuses to allow students to give up.

> I use the team approach, I make them believe that we have a team which is going to prepare for the Olympics. And our Olympics is the advanced placement calculus exam. I always talk to them and tell them, "Look, we prepared two years for this competition, and you have to play strong defense. Don't let the test put you down. You're the best." And every time the kids go to take the advanced placement calculus exam, they wear the jacket with a bulldog, which is the school mascot, and the kids go to the testing room yelling "Defense! Defense! Defense!"[4]

Escalante continues:

> The teacher has to have the energy of the hottest volcano, the memory of an elephant, and the diplomacy of an ambassador. . . . Really, a teacher has to possess love and knowledge and then has to use this combined passion to be able to accomplish something.[5]

[1]Jay Mathews, *Escalante: The Best Teacher in America* (New York: Henry Holt, 1988).

[2]Quoted in Anne Meek, "On Creating Ganas: A Conversation with Jaime Escalante," *Educational Leadership* 46, no. 5 (February 1989), pp. 46–47.

[3]Ibid.

[4]Ibid.

[5]Ibid.

SOURCE: Adapted from a profile by Rafael Heller.

questions through the text website, and we will try to answer them. In fact, we like questions so much that we will start the questioning ourselves. The following question is a good one to ask first, because if you are interested in becoming a teacher, there is no time like the present to begin.

What Steps Can I Take between Now and Graduation to Make Myself an Attractive Teaching Candidate?

Become Informed about the Job Market.

Begin gathering current information about the job market and search out those particular content areas and skills that will increase your marketability. This information will help you select appropriate courses and extracurricular activities. Geography plays a role, as some local communities face critical teacher shortages, and others have an ample number. Special education and bilingual skills are often in demand, and demographics plays a big role as well (see Figure 1.8). The nation's growing population of students of color is not matched by an adequate number of teachers of color, so there is a great need to attract African Americans, Hispanics, and Asian Americans into the teaching ranks. There are also too few male candidates for elementary teaching positions, and too few female teachers in physics and technology programs, so gender is yet another consideration. To find out more about the teaching job market, you can check educational associations and state departments of education, many of which are listed in the appendix of this text or found on our website. For example, you can contact the National Education Association at 1201 Sixteenth Street, N.W., Washington, DC 20036, or www.nea.org, and the American Federation of Teachers at 555 New Jersey Avenue, N.W., Washington, DC 20001, or www.aft.org.

For additional sources of information, check with your university's placement office. You may want to begin reading professional education journals that include information about the employment picture. Websites are often the best source of up-to-date information, so you may want to visit sites sponsored by school districts, professional associations, placement services, or your university. You can also visit real sites, such as job fairs sponsored by school districts. Knowledge about the employment picture and the kind of candidate that is in demand can give you a powerful start on your teaching career.

Make Sure Your Coursework Is Planned Carefully.

Your first concern should be to enroll in courses that fulfill your certification and licensure requirements. We will explore certification and licensure in some depth later

29

FIGURE 1.8   **What Administrators Say about the Job Market**

SOURCE: Public Agenda, April 2000.

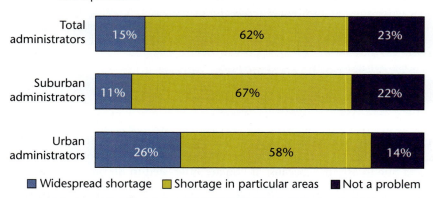

Is your district currently facing a shortage of teachers only in particular areas, is it facing a widespread shortage, or is this not a problem?

	Widespread shortage	Shortage in particular areas	Not a problem
Total administrators	15%	62%	23%
Suburban administrators	11%	67%	22%
Urban administrators	26%	58%	14%

■ Widespread shortage   ■ Shortage in particular areas   ■ Not a problem

REFLECTION

Job market predictions suggest that teachers will have their choice of locales to work. Where would you like to teach? Does the challenge of working in an urban school district, where your skills would be most needed, appeal to you? While rural districts were not surveyed in this study, they typically experience teacher shortages as well. Would you consider teaching in a rural community?

in the text, but for now it is worth remembering that, in addition to earning your degree, you want to leave your program licensed to teach. A second consideration is to make yourself more marketable by going beyond minimum course requirements. For example, technology and special education skills are often in demand by schools, as are elementary teachers with special competence in math or any teacher with a proficiency in a second language. Plan to develop a transcript of courses that will reflect a unique, competent, and relevant academic background. Your transcript will be an important part of your overall candidacy for a teaching position.

Do Not Underestimate the Importance of Extracurricular Activities.

Employers are likely looking for candidates whose background reflects interest and experience in working with children. A day care center or summer camp job may pay less than the local car wash, bank, or restaurant, but these career-related jobs may offer bigger dividends later on. Think about offering your services to a local public school or community youth group. Try to make your volunteer situation parallel the future job you would like to have. You want to build an inventory of relevant skills and experiences as well as personal contacts.

Begin Networking.

Through both your coursework and your extracurricular activities, you will come into contact with teachers, administrators, and other school personnel. You should be aware that these people can function as an informal **network** for information about the local employment picture, as can your professors and even your classmates. Go out of your way to let these people know of your interests, your special skills, and your commitment to teaching. This does not mean that you should become such a nuisance that people will duck behind their desks when they see you coming. It does mean that, at the right times and in the right places, you can let them know what jobs you are looking for and your skills and experiences that qualify you for those jobs.

Begin Collecting Recommendations Now.

Studies reveal that letters of recommendation greatly influence employment decisions. Even if you find it difficult to request such letters, do not wait until you are student teaching to begin collecting them. Extracurricular activities, coursework, part-time employment, and volunteer work can all provide you with valuable recommendations. Your university placement office may be able to begin a **placement folder** for you, maintaining these recommendations and forwarding copies to potential employers at the appropriate time.

Ask for letters of recommendation while you are in a job or course or immediately after leaving it. Professors, teachers, and past employers may move or retire, and, believe it or not, they may even forget you and just how competent and talented you are. You may be asked to help by drafting key points. Anything you can do to lighten the burden will be appreciated. Collecting letters of recommendation should be a continual process, not one that begins in the last semester of your teacher education program.

Develop a Résumé and Portfolio.

Traditionally, a **résumé** has been a central document considered during job applications, typically including a specific career objective and summarizing education, work experience, memberships, awards, and special skills. For example, a résumé might target a social studies teaching position in a particular area as your career objective, and it might report membership in the student NEA, an office held in school government, fluency in Spanish, experience with a student newspaper, honors you have won, and any relevant jobs, such as summer camp counselor or aid in a day care center. Many software packages have résumé templates, there are scores of books and websites devoted to résumé writing, and advisers and counselors at your school should be able to assist.

Today, many colleges and school districts are moving beyond résumés and toward **portfolios**, a more comprehensive reflection of a candidate's skills. If you would like to do something a bit more innovative than simply preparing a dynamite résumé and providing sparkling letters of recommendation, or if your teacher education program is promoting more authentic and creative assessment strategies, then you might want to consider developing a portfolio. This text will help you in that process. You will find, cleverly placed between the major sections of this book, a special feature called *Inter-mission*. The *Inter-mission* will encourage you to reflect on your reading, undertake some interesting observations and activities, and begin collecting relevant materials for your portfolio. Even if you decide not to develop a portfolio, these *Inter-mission* activities will be useful for developing professional materials that you can use in many different ways.

Make Good First, Second, Third, and Fourth Impressions.

In many education courses, you will be asked to participate in local school activities. This participation may take the form of observing or of being a teacher's aide or student teacher. (You may find the Observation Handbook in the appendix of this book particularly useful for school visits.) Recording and thinking about your impressions can be a useful step in deciding on the kind of position you want. In each case, you will be making an impression on the school faculty and administration. Good impressions can lead to future job offers. Poor impressions can result in your name being filed in the *persona non grata* drawer of people's needs.

Consider every visit to a school as an informal interview. Dress and act accordingly. Demonstrate your commitment and enthusiasm in ways that are helpful to school personnel. If you are viewed as a valuable and useful prospective member of the school community, you are a candidate with a head start for a current or future teaching position. Remember, known quantities are nearly always preferred to unknown quantities.

SUMMARY

CHAPTER REVIEW

Go to the Online Learning Center to take a chapter self-quiz, practice with key terms, and review key ideas from the chapter.

1. What are the advantages and disadvantages of being a teacher?

   • In the *You Be the Judge* feature, we consider both advantages and disadvantages of teaching. On the negative side of the ledger, teachers are not paid wonderful salaries, sometimes lack professional respect from others, get bogged down by routine, have inadequate time for contact with other adults, and face frustration when idealistic goals collide with student apathy, parent hostility, and the demands of old-fashioned bureaucratic red tape.

   • On the positive side of the ledger are rising salaries, the growing pride in the profession, the joy of working with children and caring colleagues, and the intellectual stimulation that are so often a part of classroom life, as well as the opportunity to affect the lives of the nation's youth.

2. What are the satisfactions—and complaints—of today's teachers?

   • The vast majority of teachers surveyed indicate that they are satisfied with their jobs, but there are problems. While teachers' salaries have improved, many teachers believe that their pay is still inadequate. Local conditions have a major impact on teacher satisfaction. On the teacher's wish list for job improvement are lighter workloads, more parental support, fewer discipline problems, and greater administration support.

3. Can we consider teaching to be a profession?

   • Some claim teaching has not achieved true professional status and is, at best, a semiprofession. To support their point of view, these critics note the short preparation time needed for becoming a teacher and the employment of teachers with little or no training in programs such as Teach for America. Critics also cite the lack of teacher influence over licensure and curricular standards. Teachers are not even central in determining who is permitted into the field or who should be forced out of teaching due to incompetence.

   • Those who claim that teaching has earned full professional status assert that it is one of the most noble of occupations. Its knowledge and research base is growing, and a number of colleges and universities now require more study (five years) to meet minimum teacher education requirements. In addition, most states now administer qualifying exams, another indication that the entrance standards to teaching are being raised. The development of a National Board for Professional Teaching Standards to identify board-certified teachers, teachers who excel in their professional skills and competencies, represents a new level of professional development.

4. How has teacher preparation changed over the years?

- In colonial times, teachers were treated as meek and docile servants of the public, and teaching was considered only temporary employment. Teachers' conduct both in and out of school was scrutinized closely, and their income was meager.

- In 1823, a private normal school was established to train future teachers. In the 1900s, many private universities established two-year teacher education programs in normal schools. More recent reform reports, including *Tomorrow's Teachers* and *A Nation Prepared*, urge higher standards, increased professionalism for teacher preparation, and recognition of superior performance through board certification.

5. Do educators and the public agree on the most effective way to prepare teachers?

- On a number of key points, teachers, education professors, and the general public differ on what schools should value and emphasize. On discipline, for example, professors relate the student behavior to teaching effectiveness. Reactions from the public and classroom teachers reflect the belief that tough classroom standards and rules are very important, and good behavior is a prerequisite to learning. Classroom teachers and the general public are also more likely than the professors to support ensuring that new teachers instill traditional values, including punctuality, neatness, competition, and tougher promotion standards. What are the important skills for new teachers to master? It is unrealistic to believe that any teacher education program can meet everyone's needs or expectations in this area. Teacher candidates must become active participants in their own professional development, refining their own approach to teaching and exploring resources in addition to those offered by their teacher education program.

6. What traits and characteristics are needed for successful teaching?

- Interpersonal skills are central to successful teaching. Successful teachers enjoy working with children, managing and motivating people, working well with the community, and are often found to have a pretty good sense of humor. A strong work ethic, intellectual curiosity, and a commitment to lifelong learning are also associated with success in the classroom.

- Many of these skills associated with teaching are also useful in other people-oriented occupations. However, while organizations like Southwest Airlines have developed corporate cultures that focus on employee satisfaction and autonomy, schools have yet to mirror that level of confidence in teachers.

7. Is teaching a "good fit" for you?

- In reviewing characteristics and traits related to effective teaching, we ask you to evaluate yourself. How do you rate on these skills and traits? In fact, a major purpose of this text is to help you connect with teaching and assess if teaching is the right career for you.

8. What steps can you take now on the road to becoming a teacher?

- As you explore your potential role in teaching, you will develop questions, invest energy and investigate options. All of these efforts are put to good use in this text through Inter-mission activities, further suggested readings, and online activities. We strive to create a text that is responsive to your interests and needs. As much as possible, we try to anticipate your questions and get you actively involved in this book. You will find typical student questions (and our answers) throughout the text. But we invite you to send additional questions to us, either through email or snail mail. You can email us through the Online Learning Center at www.mhhe.com/sadker6e.

- Even now, there are steps you can take that will help you in the year(s) ahead. If you are not a great planner or organizer, we can help you do a better job as you consider if teaching is right for you. (We can't plan for you or make your decision, but we can help!) If you are pretty sure that teaching is for you, we can help you reach that goal. At the beginning of your program, careful planning and course selection pay dividends. Make certain that you meet with an advisor and check the requirements as you choose your courses. Also, remember that extracurricular activities can be as important as formal coursework. Then there are the job application steps that you can take: prepare your résumé and portfolio, solicit recommendations, and stay informed about the job market. It may be early, but it is not too early.

KEY TERMS AND PEOPLE

A Nation Prepared, 16

board-certified teachers, 17

Holmes Group, 16

Horace Mann, 15

Jaime Escalante, 28

National Board for Professional Teaching Standards (NBPTS), 17

networking, 30

normal school, 15

pedagogy, 21

placement folder, 31

portfolio, 31

profession, 12

résumé, 31

Reverend Samuel Hall, 15

semiprofession, 13

Teach for America, 18

Tomorrow's Teachers, 16

DISCUSSION QUESTIONS AND ACTIVITIES

1. This chapter introduces you to the importance of well-thought-out career decision making. You can read further on this decision-making process in one of the many career books now available. For example, Richard N. Bolles' *What Color Is Your Parachute?* contains many exercises that should help you clarify your commitment to teaching. Or you may want to visit Bolles' website at www.jobhuntersbible.com/. These resources, or a visit to your career center, can help you determine what other careers present viable options for you.

2. Interview teachers at different grade levels to determine what they think are the positive and negative aspects of teaching. Share those interview responses with your classmates.

3. Interview students at various grade levels to determine their perceptions of teachers. Ask them to describe a teacher who has been influential in their lives. Share these interview responses with your classmates.

4. Suppose you could write an open letter to students, telling them about yourself and why you want to teach. What would you want them to know? When you attempt to explain yourself to others, you often gain greater self-knowledge. You might want to share your letter with classmates and to hear what they have to say in their letters. Perhaps your instructor could also try this exercise and share his or her open letter with you.

5. Check out teacher-related websites on the Internet. Schools and school districts, professional teacher organizations, and all sorts of interest groups sponsor not only websites but also listservs, chat groups, and other Internet activities. Seek out opportunities to interview practicing classroom teachers about their own classroom experiences. (Check out our website at www.mhhe.com/sadker6e for related Web links.)

6. Interview some teachers to determine their opinions of whether teaching is—or is not—a profession. Ask some practicing teachers, some preservice teachers, and some retired teachers. Compare and contrast their responses. Summarize your findings. In your opinion, is teaching a profession?

7. Imagine that you are taking part in a career fair. Someone asks why you are exploring teaching. Briefly frame your answer.

WEB-*TIVITIES*

1. The Advantages and Disadvantages of Being a Teacher

2. A Closer Look at Teach for America

3. Why Become a Teacher?

REEL TO REAL TEACHING

Movies with an education theme are a valuable and, yes, fun tool for learning about teachers, schools, and society. The Reel to Real Teaching feature gives you an opportunity to apply your understanding of key concepts explored in each chapter while appreciating the art and power of film. The Reflection provides connections between the chapter, the film, and you, while the Follow-up Activity can build on your understanding of the film. You may also want to visit the website's Critics Corner and share your thoughts with your future colleagues.

STAND AND DELIVER (1988)
Run time: 105 minutes

Synopsis: Convinced that his students have potential, mathematics teacher Jamie Escalante employs unconventional teaching methods to motivate a class of low-achieving inner-city Hispanic students. Escalante teaches his students how to stretch beyond their limited horizons, and how to stand up when the world tries to crush their hopes.

Reflection:

1. Have your teachers ever shared with you their reasons for teaching? Did some teachers tell you through words and others through actions? What were they?

2. Most careers offer both satisfaction and sacrifice. Consider the professional and personal sacrifices made by Escalante. Would you be willing to make the same? Why or why not? You may wish to revisit the You Be the Judge feature in the chapter when contemplating the joys and sacrifices of teaching.

3. Consider how viewing *Stand and Deliver* might influence your answer to the question, "Why teach?"

Follow-up Activity: It's movie night for your campus student education association (e.g., Kappa Delta Pi, Phi Delta Kappa, Student NEA). *Stand and Deliver* is the feature flick and your task is to create a media announcement for the event. Develop a flyer, a newspaper announcement, radio advertisement, a blurb for a website, or create your own idea that really inspires your membership to attend this film.

How do you rate this film? Click on *Reel to Real Teaching* to submit your review of this or another education-related film and read reviews submitted by others.

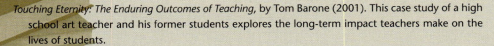

FOR FURTHER READING

Touching Eternity: The Enduring Outcomes of Teaching, by Tom Barone (2001). This case study of a high school art teacher and his former students explores the long-term impact teachers make on the lives of students.

Uncertain Lives: Children of Promise, Teachers of Hope, by Robert Bullough (2001). Presenting the voices of students themselves, Robert Bullough puts a hopeful and ultimately human face on the otherwise grim statistics of disadvantaged, urban school students.

What the Kids Said Today: Using Classroom Conversations to Become a Better Teacher, by Daniel Gartrell (2000). Each story includes an account of a teacher's conversation with children, as well as reflections on how each conversation can help build a stimulating and nurturing classroom.

Among School Teachers, by Joel Westheimer (1998). A compelling account of two middle schools—one urban and one suburban—that attempt to build communities that will foster student growth and learning.

*Primary Teacher's Stress***,** by Geoff Troman and Peter Woods (2001). This book looks at the causes of teacher stress, asks why thousands of teachers are leaving the profession every year due to stress, and suggests ways of coping with and preventing stress.

Goodbye, Mr. Chips, by James Hilton (1986). Generations of boys bid farewell to English schoolmaster Mr. Chipping, remembering this teacher's dedication, inspiration, and generosity of spirit.

Amazing Grace, by Jonathan Kozol (1995). Capturing the consequences of poverty and deprivation in the lives of children in urban America, this book asks questions that are at once political and theological. What is the value of a child's life? How will schools and society help children in need?

Student Diversity

FOCUS QUESTIONS

1. How do cognitive, affective, and physiological factors impact learning?
2. How can teachers respond to different learning styles?
3. What are the classroom implications of Howard Gardner's theory of multiple intelligences?
4. How does emotional intelligence influence teaching and learning?
5. How can teachers meet the diverse needs of an increasingly multicultural student population?
6. What are the different levels of multicultural education?
7. What are the political and instructional issues surrounding bilingual education?
8. How are the needs of special learners met in today's classrooms?

WHAT DO YOU THINK? Different Ways of Learning. Vote on the eight-point proposal presented on page 38 and see what the *Teachers, Schools, and Society* results are.

CHAPTER PREVIEW

At the dawn of the twenty-first century, basic educational concepts are being redefined, re-examined, and expanded. What does "intelligence" really mean? How many kinds of intelligences are there? What is EQ (emotional intelligence quotient), and is it a better predictor of success than IQ (intelligence quotient)? How should classrooms best be organized to meet the needs of different learning styles?

Not only are our basic concepts and assumptions changing; today's students are changing as well. An increasing number of students have their family roots not in Europe or Africa but in Asia and Latin America. As a result of an extraordinary increase in immigration to this country, the native language of well over 30 million Americans is a language other than English, creating a remarkable and formidable challenge for the nation's schools.[1] In many schools, the terms *minority* and *majority* are gaining new meanings as student demographics change.

Another educational transformation is the increasing numbers of school children now identified as exceptional learners—learning and physically disabled, mentally retarded, and emotionally disturbed—all of whom deserve appropriate educational strategies and materials. Gifted and talented students represent another special needs population too often lost in the current educational system.

This chapter will describe the demographic and conceptual changes reshaping America's schools, as well as provide you with insights into and strategies for successful teaching in tomorrow's classrooms.

Different Ways of Learning

Imagine you are on a committee of teachers that has been asked to offer recommendations to the school board regarding academic climates to increase the academic performance of the district's students. It is an awesome responsibility. Here is the first draft of an eight point proposal. Take a moment and indicate your reaction to each of the points.[2]

	Strongly Agree	Agree	Disagree
1. Schools and classrooms should be quiet places to promote thinking and learning.	——	——	——
2. All classrooms and libraries should be well lighted to reduce eye strain.	——	——	——
3. Difficult subjects, such as math, should be offered in the morning, when students are fresh and alert.	——	——	——
4. School thermostats should be set at 68 to 72 degrees Fahrenheit to establish a comfortable learning environment.	——	——	——
5. Eating and drinking in classrooms should be prohibited.	——	——	——
6. Classroom periods should run between forty-five and fifty-five minutes to ensure adequate time to investigate significant issues and practice important skills.	——	——	——
7. Students must be provided with adequate work areas, including chairs and desks, where they can sit quietly for the major part of their learning and study.	——	——	——
8. Emphasis should be placed on reading textbooks and listening to lectures, for this is how students learn best.	——	——	——

You might find that these points seem to make a lot of sense. And, for many students, these eight recommendations may lead to higher academic achievement—for many, but not all. Ironically, for a significant number of students, these recommendations can lead to poorer performance, even academic failure. The reason is that students have different **learning styles**—diverse ways of learning, comprehending, knowing.

Did you notice these different learning styles in your own elementary and secondary school experience? Perhaps you see them now in college or graduate school. Some students do their best work late at night, while others set an early alarm because they are most alert in the morning. Many students seek a quiet place in the library to prepare for finals; others learn best in a crowd of people with a radio blaring; still others study most effectively in a state of perpetual motion, constantly walking in circles to help their concentration. Some students seem unable to study without eating and drinking, simultaneously imbibing calories and knowledge, they all but

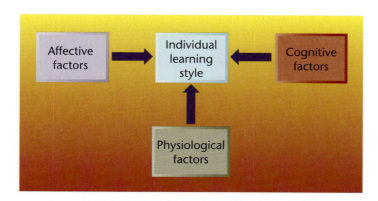

FIGURE 2.1
Factors contributing to learning styles.

REFLECTION

Describe your own learning style by identifying at least one factor under the affective, physi- ological and cognitive domains.

move into the refrigerator when preparing for tests. (These differences really strike home if you and your roommate clash because of conflicting learning styles.)

We are a population of incredibly diverse learners. Intriguing new research focus- ing on the ways students learn suggests that learning styles may be as unique as handwriting. The challenge for educators is to diagnose these styles and to shape in- struction to meet individual student needs.

At least three types of factors—as diagrammed in Figure 2.1—contribute to each student's individual learning style:

1. *Cognitive (information processing).* Individuals have different ways of perceiving, organizing, and retaining information, all components of the **cognitive domain.** Some students prefer to learn by reading and looking at material, while others need to listen and hear information spoken aloud. Still others learn best kinesthetically, by whole body movement and participation. Some learners focus attention narrowly and with great intensity; others pay attention to many things at once. While some learners are quick to respond, others rely on a slower approach.

2. *Affective (attitudes).* Individuals bring different levels of motivation to learning, and the intensity level of this motivation is a critical determinant of learning style. Other aspects of the **affective domain** include attitudes, values and emotions, factors that influence curiosity, the ability to tolerate and overcome frustration, and the willingness to take risks. A fascinating aspect of the affective domain is a concept termed **locus of control.** Some learners attribute success or failure to external factors ("Those problems were confusing," "The teacher didn't review the material well," or "My score was high because I made some lucky guesses"). These learners have an external locus of control. Simply stated, they do not take responsibility for their behavior. Others attribute performance to internal factors ("I didn't study enough" or "I didn't read the directions carefully"). These students have an internal locus of control because they have the sense that they control their fate, that they can improve their performance.

3. *Physiology.* Clearly, a student who is hungry and tired will not learn as effectively as a well-nourished and rested child. Other physiological factors are less obvious. Different body rhythms cause some students to learn better in the day, while others are night owls. Some students can sit still for long periods of time, while others need to get up and move around. Light, sound, and temperature are yet other factors to which students respond differently based on their physiological development.[3]

With this introduction to learning styles, you now know that the committee's eight recommendations will not create a productive learning climate for all students. The following section paraphrases the original recommendations, explodes myths, and provides research concerning diverse learning styles.[4]

**INTERACTIVE ACTIVITY
LEARNING STYLES
ASSESSMENT**
Take a learning styles assessment to determine your own learning style.

Myth	*Fact*
Students learn best in quiet surroundings.	Many students learn best when studying to music or other background noise. Others need so much silence that only ear plugs will suffice.
Students learn best in well-lighted areas.	Some students are actually disturbed by bright light and become hyperactive and less focused in their thinking. For them, dimmer light is more effective.
Difficult subjects are best taught in the morning, when students are most alert.	Peak learning times differ. Some students are at their best in the morning, while others function most effectively in the afternoon or evening.
Room temperature should be maintained at a comfortable 68 to 72 degrees Fahrenheit to promote learning.	Room temperature preferences vary greatly from individual to individual, and no single range pleases all. What chills one learner may provide the perfect climate for another.
Eating or drinking while learning should be prohibited.	Some students learn better and score higher on tests if they are allowed to eat or drink during these times. Banning such activities may penalize these individuals unfairly.
The most appropriate length of time for a class is forty-five to fifty-five minutes.	This period of time may be too long for some and too brief for others. The comfort time zone of the student rather than a predetermined block of hours or minutes is the factor critical to effective learning.
Students should be provided with appropriate work areas, including chairs and desks, where they spend most of their classroom time.	A substantial number of students need to move about to learn. For these learners, sitting at a desk or a computer terminal for long periods of time can actually hinder academic performance.

TEACHING TIPS FOR DIFFERENT LEARNING STYLES

Many educators believe that students have preferred learning styles and that teaching to these preferred styles will increase educational success. Following are three learning styles frequently mentioned in the literature. (Do you recognize yourself in any of these categories?) Since all of these students are typically in class at the same time, as a teacher you will be called on to use a variety of instructional approaches to reach all of them.

VISUAL LEARNERS

About half of the student population learns best by *seeing* information. They are termed visual learners.

Teaching Tips

Textbooks, charts, course outlines, and graphs are useful instructional aids.

Ask these students to write down information, even rewriting or highlighting key points.

Ask students to preview chapters by looking at subheadings and illustrations before they read each chapter.

Seat these students up front, away from windows and doors (to avoid distractions).

Encourage them to ask for comments or directions to be repeated if they did not understand directions the first time.

Use overheads and flip charts.

KINESTHETIC LEARNERS

This is another popular learning style, which is also called *haptic* (Greek for "moving and doing") or *tactile*. These are "hands on" learners, students who learn best by doing.

Teaching Tips

Try to plan for student movement in class presentation, as well as independent study time.

Movement should be planned to avoid distracting others.

Memorizing information can be enhanced if these learners are encouraged to physically move about the room.

Providing students with a colored desk blotter or a colored transparency to read a book is called "color grounding" and can help focus their attention.

Ask them to take notes and encourage them to underline key points as they read.

Encourage them to take frequent but short breaks.

Try to use skits and role-plays to help make instructional points.

AUDITORY LEARNERS

This is a style used less frequently than the previous two. These students learn best by hearing; they can remember the details of conversations and lectures and many have strong language skills.

Teaching Tips

Provide the opportunity for auditory learners to recite the main points of a book or lecture.

Encourage these students to study with a friend, so they can talk through the main points.

Audiotapes of classroom activities can be helpful.

Suggest that they read class notes into a tape.

Encourage them to read the textbook out loud.

It can be helpful for these students to say out loud the meaning of the illustrations and main subject headings, and to recite any new vocabulary words.

Group work can be a useful class activity for auditory learners.

REFLECTION

Choose a subject or topic that you want to teach. Describe three learning activities (visual, kinesthetic, auditory) that you can use to reach students with different learning styles. Which of these learning styles appeals to you? Why?

Myth	*Fact*
Reading a textbook or listening to a lecture is the best way to learn.	Diverse students learn through a variety of modes, not only through reading or listening. While many students rely on these two perceptual modes, they are less effective for others. Some learn best through touch (for example, learning to read by tracing sandpaper letters), while others rely on kinesthetic movement, including creative drama, role-play, and field-based experiences.

Learning style is not the only area undergoing demystification: our understanding of **intelligence** is also being reconstructed. The IQ score, developed early in the twentieth century, is supposed to be a measure of a person's innate intelligence, with a score of 100 defined as normal, or average. The higher the score, the brighter the person. Some of us grew up in communities where IQ was barely mentioned. In many cases this lack of knowledge might have been a blessing. Others of us grew up with "IQ envy," in communities where IQ scores were a big part of our culture. Since the score is considered a fixed, permanent measure of intellect, like a person's physical height, the scores engendered strong feelings. Friends who scored 150 or 160 or higher on an IQ test had a secret weapon, a mysteriously wonderful brain. We were impressed. But then our friend, the "genius," was stumped trying to unpack and plug in a toaster oven or got hopelessly lost trying to follow the simplest driving directions. How could this person have such a high IQ? We may have been equally puzzled when another friend, who scored horribly low on an IQ test, went on to fame and riches (and promptly forgot that we were ever their friends). What is this IQ score supposed to mean?

Some students learn best in cooperative learning situations.

Multiple Intelligences and Emotional Intelligence

INTERACTIVE ACTIVITY
MULTIPLE INTELLIGENCES
Label descriptions of different intelligences.

Also puzzled by these contradictions was Harvard professor **Howard Gardner.** Concerned about the traditional assessment of intelligence, with such a heavy emphasis on language and mathematical-logical skills, he broadened the concept to define *intelligence* as "the capacity to solve problems or to fashion products that are valued in one or more cultural settings."[5]

Gardner identified eight kinds of intelligence, not all of which are commonly recognized in school settings, yet Gardner believes that his theory of **multiple intelligences** more accurately captures the diverse nature of human capability. Consider Gardner's eight intelligences:

1. *Logical-mathematical.* Skills related to mathematical manipulations and discerning and solving logical problems (*related careers:* scientist, mathematician)

2. *Linguistic.* Sensitivity to the meanings, sounds, and rhythms of words, as well as to the function of language as a whole (*related careers:* poet, journalist, author)

3. *Bodily-kinesthetic.* Ability to excel physically and to handle objects skillfully (*related careers:* athlete, dancer, surgeon)

4. *Musical.* Ability to produce pitch and rhythm, as well as to appreciate various forms of musical expression (*related careers:* musician, composer)

5. *Spatial.* Ability to form a mental model of the spatial world and to maneuver and operate using that model (*related careers:* sculptor, navigator, engineer, painter)

6. *Interpersonal.* Ability to analyze and respond to the motivations, moods, and desires of other people (*related careers:* psychology, sales, teaching)

7. *Intrapersonal.* Knowledge of one's feelings, needs, strengths, and weaknesses; ability to use this knowledge to guide behavior (*related benefit:* accurate self-awareness)

8. *Naturalist.* (Gardner's most recently defined intelligence) Ability to discriminate among living things, to classify plants, animals, and minerals; a sensitivity to the natural world (*related careers:* botanist, environmentalist, chef, other science- and even consumer-related careers.)[6]

Gardner and his colleagues continue to conduct research, and this list is still growing. A possible ninth intelligence being explored by Gardner concerns an *existential intelligence*, the human inclination to formulate fundamental questions about who we are, where we come from, why we die, and the like. Gardner believes that we have yet to discover many more intelligences. (Can you can think of some?)

The theory of multiple intelligences goes a long way in explaining why the quality of an individual's performance may vary greatly in different activities, rather than reflect a single standard of performance as indicated by an IQ score. Gardner

The ability to perform intricate and extended physical maneuvers is a distinct form of intelligence.

Giants, Wizards, and Dwarfs was the game to play.

Being left in charge of about eighty children seven to ten years old, while their parents were off doing parent things, I mustered my troops in the church social hall and explained the game. It's a large-scale version of Rock, Paper, and Scissors, and involves some intellectual decision making. But the real purpose of the game is to make a lot of noise and run around chasing people until nobody knows which side you are on or who won.

Organizing a roomful of wired-up grade schoolers into two teams, explaining the rudiments of the game, achieving consensus on group identity—all of this is no mean accomplishment, but we did it with a right good will and were ready to go.

The excitement of the chase had reached a critical mass. I yelled out: "You have to decide *now* which you are—a GIANT, a WIZARD, or a DWARF!"

While the groups huddled in frenzied, whispered consultation, a tug came at my pants leg. A small child stands there looking up, and asks in a small concerned voice, "Where do the Mermaids stand?"

A long pause: A *very* long pause. "Where do the Mermaids stand?" says I.

"Yes. You see, I am a Mermaid."

"There are no such things as Mermaids."

"Oh, yes, I am one!"

She did not relate to being a Giant, a Wizard, or a Dwarf. She knew her category, Mermaid, and was not about to leave the game and go over and stand against the wall where a loser would stand. She intended to participate, wherever Mermaids fit into the scheme of things. Without giving up dignity or identity. She took it for granted that there was a place for Mermaids and that I would know just where.

Well, where DO the Mermaids stand? All the "Mermaids"—all those who are different, who do not fit the norm and who do not accept the available boxes and pigeonholes?

Answer that question and you can build a school, a nation, or a world on it.

What was my answer at the moment? Every once in a while I say the right thing. "The Mermaid stands right here by the King of the Sea!" (Yes, right here by the King's Fool, I thought to myself.)

So we stood there hand in hand, reviewing the troops of Wizards and Giants and Dwarfs as they rolled by in wild disarray. It is not true, by the way, that Mermaids do not exist. I know at least one personally. I have held her hand.

SOURCE: Robert Fulghum, *All I Really Need to Know I Learned in Kindergarten* (New York: Villard Books, 1989), pp. 81–83.

REFLECTION

Was there ever a time when you did not fit neatly into a category—were you ever a mermaid? When and why? How will you make room for mermaids in your class?

also points out that what is considered *intelligence* may differ, depending on cultural values. Thus, in the Pacific Islands, intelligence is the ability to navigate among the islands. For many Muslims, the ability to memorize the Koran is a mark of intelligence. Intelligence in Balinese social life is demonstrated by physical grace.

Gardner's theory has sparked the imaginations of many educators, some of whom are redesigning their curricula to respond to differing student intelligences. Teachers are refining their approaches in response to such questions as[7]

- How can I use music to emphasize key points?
- How can I promote hand and bodily movements and experiences to enhance learning?
- How can I incorporate sharing and interpersonal interactions into my lessons?

The Stuttgart, Arkansas, Junior High School varsity football team all shaved their heads so they could look more like teammate Stuart H., who lost most of his hair while undergoing chemotherapy. The coach explained: *They got together so he wouldn't feel weird, so they would all look weird together.*

SOURCE: *The American School Board Journal,* December 1997.

REFLECTION

Did you ever take risks or make sacrifices for your schoolmates? What can teachers do to foster the flames of compassion?

 Click on *In the News* for recent *In the News* stories. Submit your own *In the News* summary to share with your colleagues.

- How can I encourage students to think more deeply about their feelings and memories?

- How can I use visual organizers and visual aids to promote understanding?

- How can I encourage students to classify and appreciate the world around them?

As instruction undergoes re-examination, so does evaluation. The old pencil-and-paper tests used to assess linguistic, math, and logical intelligences seem much less appropriate for measuring these new areas identified by Gardner.[8] The **portfolio** approach, as found in the *Inter-missions* in this text, is an example of a more comprehensive assessment, which includes student artifacts (papers, projects, videotapes, exhibits) that offer tangible examples of student learning. Some schools ask students to assemble portfolios that reflect progress in Gardner's various intelligences. In other cases, rather than As and Bs or 80s and 90s, schools are using descriptions to report student competence. In music, for example, such descriptions might include "The student often listens to music," "She plays the piano with technical competence," "She is able to compose scores that other students and faculty enjoy," and so on. Whether the school is exploring portfolios, descriptive assessment, or another evaluation method, Gardner's multiple intelligences theory is reshaping many current assessment practices.[9]

While the theory of multiple intelligences raises fundamental questions about instruction and assessment, EQ may be even more revolutionary. **EQ,** or the **emotional intelligence quotient,** is described by **Daniel Goleman** in his book *Emotional Intelligence.* Goleman argues that when it comes to predicting success in life, EQ may be a better predictor than IQ. How does EQ work? The "marshmallow story" may help you understand:

A researcher explains to a 4-year-old that he/she needs to run off to do an errand, but there is a marshmallow for the youngster to enjoy. The youngster can choose to eat the marshmallow immediately. But, if the 4-year-old can wait and *not* eat the marshmallow right away, then an extra marshmallow will be given when the researcher returns. Eat one now, or hold off and get twice the reward.

Like Daniel Goleman, Yale psychologist Peter Salovey works with emotional intelligence issues, and he identifies five elements of emotional intelligence. How would you rate yourself on each of these dimensions?

KNOWING EMOTIONS

The foundation of one's emotional intelligence is self-awareness. A person's ability to recognize a feeling as it happens is the essential first step in understanding the place and power of emotions. People who do not know when they are angry, jealous, or in love are at the mercy of their emotions.

Self-Rating on Knowing My Emotions

Always aware of my emotions__ Usually aware__ Sometimes aware__ Out of touch, clueless.__

MANAGING EMOTIONS

A person who can control and manage emotions can handle bad times as well as the good, shake off depression, bounce back from life's setbacks, and avoid irritability. In one study, up to half of the youngsters who at age 6 were disruptive and unable to get along with others were classified as delinquents by the time they were teenagers.

Self-Rating on Managing My Emotions

Always manage my emotions__ Usually manage__ Sometimes manage__ My emotions manage me.__

MOTIVATING ONESELF

Productive individuals are able to focus energy, confidence, and concentration on achieving a goal and avoid anxiety, anger, and depression. One study of 36,000 people found that "worriers" have poorer academic performance than nonworriers. (A load off your mind, no doubt!)

Self-Rating on Motivation and Focus

Always self-motivated/focused__ Usually self-motivated/ focused__ Sometimes self-motivated/focused__ I can't focus on when I was last focused (and I don't care).__

RECOGNIZING EMOTIONS IN OTHERS

This skill is the core of empathy, the ability to pick up subtle signs of what other people need or want. Such a person always seems to "get it," even before the words are spoken.

Self-Rating on Empathy

Always empathetic__ Usually empathetic__ Sometimes empathetic__ I rarely "get it."__

HANDLING RELATIONSHIPS

People whose EQ is high are the kind of people you want to be around. They are popular, are good leaders, and make you feel comfortable and connected. Children who lack social skills are often distracted from learning, and the dropout rate for children who are rejected by their peers can be two to eight times higher than for children who have friends.

Self-Rating on Relationships

I am rich in friendship and am often asked to lead activities and events.__ I have many friends.__ I have a few friends.__ Actually, I'm pretty desperate for friends.__

RATINGS

Give 4 points for each time you selected the first choice, 3 points for the "usual" or "many" second option, 2 points for the "sometimes" selection, and 1 point for the last choice.

18–20 points: A grade—WOW! Impressive!

14–17 points: B grade—You have considerable skills and talents.

10–13 points: C grade—Feel free to read further on this topic.

5–9 points: D grade—This may be a perfect subject to investigate in greater detail. Do you have a topic for your term project yet?

REFLECTION

Are you satisfied with your rating? If you earned a high rating, to what do you attribute your high EQ? If your rating was lower than you liked, how can you work on increasing your EQ?

What do you think you would have done as a 4-year-old? According to the social scientists who conducted the marshmallow experiment, decisions even at this age foreshadow an emotional disposition characteristic of a successful (or less successful) adult. By the time the children in the study reached high school, the now 14-year-olds were described by teachers and parents in a way that suggested their marshmallow behaviors predicted some significant differences. Students who ten years earlier were able to delay their gratification, to wait a while and garner a second marshmallow, were reported to be better adjusted, more popular, more adventurous, and more confident in adolescence than the group who ten years earlier had gobbled down their marshmallows. The children who gave in to temptation, ate the marshmallow and abandoned their chances for a second one, were more likely to be described as stubborn, easily frustrated, and lonely teenagers. In addition to the differences between the gobblers and waiters as described by parents and teachers, there was also a significant SAT scoring gap. The students who, ten years earlier, could wait for the second marshmallow scored 210 points higher than did the gobblers. Reasoning and control, "the regulation of emotion in a way that enhances living,"[10] might be new, and perhaps better, measures of what we call smart, or intelligent.

Emotional intelligence "is a type of social intelligence that involves the ability to monitor one's own and others' emotions, to discriminate among them, and to use the information to guide one's thinking and actions."[11] Goleman suggests that EQ taps into the heart, as well as the head, and introduces a new gateway for measuring intelligence, for children and adults.[12] By the way, how would you rate your EQ?

Goleman and Gardner are toppling educational traditions, stretching our understanding of what schools are about. In a sense, they are increasing the range and diversity of educational ideas. This chapter is all about diversity. The students you will teach will learn in diverse ways, and a single IQ or even EQ score is unlikely to capture the range of their abilities and skills. But these are not the only differences students bring to school. Let's turn our attention to how cultural, ethnic, and racial diversity is transforming life in the classroom.

INTERACTIVE ACTIVITY
EMOTIONAL INTELLIGENCE QUOTIENT QUIZ
Take an EQ quiz to determine your own emotional intelligence quotient.

Cultural Diversity

America has just experienced the greatest immigration surge in its history. In the past few decades, more immigrants have come to this country than at the beginning of the twentieth century, a time often thought of as the great era of immigration and Americanization. These new Americans have arrived mainly from Latin America and Asia, but also from the Caribbean, the Middle East, Africa, and Eastern Europe. Today, about one in ten Americans is foreign born.

Consider the following:

- By 2012 the west (the geographic area expected to witness the greatest changes) will become "minority majority," with no single racial or ethnic group having a majority.

- The nation has approximately 2.5 million Native Americans, a number that increases to about 4 million when including Americans claiming partial Indian heritage on the census.

- By 2000, the number of Asians, including Asian Indians, in the United States was over 10 million or 3.6 percent of the population.

- About 6 million Americans claimed multiracial heritage with 2 or more races indicated on Census 2000.
- By 2030, the number of U.S. residents who are nonwhite or Hispanic will be about 140 million or about 40 percent of the U.S. population.[13]

Demographic forecasting, the study of people and their vital statistics, provides a fascinating insight into tomorrow's schools. Demographers indicate that at the dawn of the twenty-first century, one out of three Americans will be of color. Some forecast that by 2020 almost half the school population will be from non-European ethnic groups. Demographers draw a portrait of a new generation of students far more diverse—by race, ethnicity, culture, and language—than our country has ever known. You will teach in a nation more diverse and less Eurocentric than the one you grew up in. How will this affect your life in the classroom?

Although the national demographics are powerful, you will not be a national teacher. You will be a local teacher, and the demographic realities you experience will be shaped by where you teach. If you teach in a large, urban school system, you will likely encounter classrooms where the majority of students are of color. In many cities today, students of color already constitute 70 to more than 90 percent of the students. If you decide to start your career in the tony suburbs outside the nation's capital, in Fairfax, Virginia, or Montgomery County, Maryland, for example, you may very well find third- and fourth-generation American children from wealthy homes attending your school, along with students recently arrived in this country—thousands of students speaking more than a hundred different languages. Of course, not every American community is experiencing dynamic population changes. You may find yourself teaching in a very stable school district, one where student demographics have remained basically unchanged for decades. But, even in these communities, changing national demographics will not go unnoticed. As the nation's population changes, so will the nation's culture, politics, and economy. To a degree, we are all part of the national fabric. The challenge for educators is how to prepare all of the nation's students for this more diverse America. (See Figure 2.2.)

Teaching Them All

Imagine this. You have graduated from your teacher preparation program and have signed the contract for your first teaching job, and now you stand before your very first class. As you survey your sixth-grade students, you see fifteen boys and fourteen girls. As you look at your class, you realize that you will be teaching a wonderfully diverse group. Off to the right, near the windows, are half a dozen students eagerly talking in Spanish. Some African American children, comparing their schedules, look to you with curiosity. In the front of the room, several Asian American children are in their seats, looking up to you, awaiting your comments. (You do have a good opening, right?) Several white children and a few students whose backgrounds may reflect more than one racial or ethnic group are looking at the motivational posters you hung just last night. You know from reading student records that six of your students have learning disabilities, and the child in the wheelchair has muscular dystrophy. One of the children has been identified as gifted. About half of your students are from single-parent homes. A third come from middle-class backgrounds, and the remaining children are from working-class or poor families. Whew! The proverbial American melting pot looks more like a tossed salad in your class.

FIGURE 2.2   SAT averages rose for most racial-ethnic groups between 1990 and 2000.

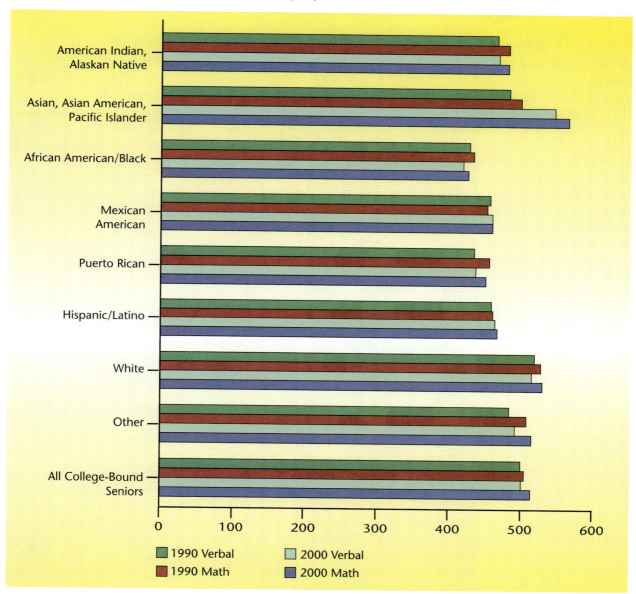

SOURCE: The College Board (2000). *2000 Profile of College Bound Seniors on the SAT.* New York: College Board.

REFLECTION

Why do you believe these scores have improved through the 1990s? Which groups have fared the best? Which groups have not shown significant test score improvement? Do you believe that these scores are a valid indicator of educational quality— or are they given too much weight?

During much of the twentieth century, African American students attended legally segregated schools. Today, while legal segregation has ended, segregation has not. Examine these two photos and suggest similarities and differences between segregation then and now. During the past hundred years, what other ethnic or racial groups might be photographed in much the same way?

You know from your training, reading, and experience that each of these young lives has been shaped, in part, by geography, ethnicity, exceptionality, social class, race, and gender. You understand that these characteristics will influence how these children perceive the world—and how the world views them. You also know that each one is likely to have a learning style as unique as his or her appearance.

How will you meet the needs of these twenty-nine different learners? What strategies and approaches will you use to foster equity and excellence in your classroom?

Culture and Education 101

Before teaching your first class, you may be required, or you may elect, to take courses in special education, gender equity, and multicultural education. Here we offer an introduction, some suggested topics that might be found in a course designed to help you teach diverse learners. We'll call our course "Culture and Education 101." Additional information and strategies for dealing with diversity will be described later in this book.

GENERALIZE, DON'T STEREOTYPE   Although you are the teacher and your students are the "learners," be prepared to do quite a bit of learning yourself. As you assimilate information about your students, their culture, and their experiences, you will need to distinguish between stereotypes and generalizations. While the dangers of stereotyping are common knowledge these days, the usefulness of generalizations is less well known.

Stereotypes are absolute statements applied to all members of a group, statements that ignore individual differences. Stereotypes tend to close off discussion by providing simplistic characterizations. Generalizations offer information about groups that can help you teach more effectively. For instance, a generalization that members of a certain group avoid direct eye contact, while not applying to every group member (that would be a stereotype), is a generalization that teaches us what to expect from many if not most group members. **Generalizations** are flexible insights that provide us with clues about groups, useful information for instructional planning. Generalizations are discussion openers, recognizing that we are all members of many groups: religious, gender, geographic, class, interest, skills, and the like. Look for generalizations about your students' backgrounds that will help you plan for teaching. Avoid stereotypes.

MODEL SKILLS AND BEHAVIORS THAT REFLECT SENSITIVITY   Looking for the first time at ethnically diverse names on a class list, a teacher might blurt out, "I'll never be able to pronounce that one!" or "That's the first time I heard that name." Such comments reflect a lack of cultural understanding and sensitivity, hardly endearing a teacher to a student. Some teachers dig a deeper hole, converting the "unusual" name to an easier to pronounce nickname or unilaterally deciding to Americanize the name, as in "Miguel, do you mind if I call you Mike?" Such names as Tomàs, Twanda, Chu, Ngyuen, or Kenji may take extra effort to learn to pronounce correctly, but it is an effort that demonstrates cultural and personal respect.

Once you have learned about your students and their cultural background, you will have to take the next big step: Ensure that your knowledge is reflected in your behavior. Being responsive to cultural norms is yet another way to demonstrate cultural sensitivity. For instance, one Native American and Asian cultural norm is to shun competition. If you were their teacher, you may want to minimize the practice of

Being a good teacher in the years ahead will almost surely mean dealing with a culturally diverse population.

publicly praising one student's work in front of others, or even providing the stage for such comparisons. You could choose to review student performance through quiet, individual conferences, rather than announcing or posting such grades. Such steps go a long way in promoting effective relationships in and beyond the classroom.

USE CLASSROOM STRATEGIES THAT BUILD ON STUDENT LEARNING STYLES   As was discussed earlier in this chapter, individuals, and even groups, have different, preferred learning styles. If your students are similar to the ones in the class described earlier, they are likely to bring with them an incredible assortment of educational styles and experiences. To get a sense of each student's unique approach to learning, observe each of them doing work and analyze how each approaches the curriculum. Some schools assist you in this effort by providing learning style assessments that you can administer to your students. Use this information and plan a variety of instructional options and teaching strategies that appeal to the different intelligences described by Gardner and others. Give all your students the chance to succeed.

GIVE EQUAL INSTRUCTIONAL ATTENTION   The research on classroom interaction reflects subtle and not so subtle teacher biases. Male students tend to call out more than female students, and, even when males do not call out, teachers tend to call on them more than females. White students also garner more instructional time than students of color. The result is that white males receive more of the most precious items in the teacher's repertoire, time and attention. Even silence is not distributed equally. Teachers give males and perceived high achievers more wait time—more quiet time to respond to questions and to think about their answers. These patterns of bias are usually so subtle that teachers are not aware of them.

To avoid elusive interaction bias, you may want to ask a colleague, friend, or student to carefully and objectively tally the interactions you have with different students. Whom do you talk to the most? Who gets helped or praised the most? How is your wait time distributed?

As I look back over a lifetime of teaching, one special student stands out. Kou was the most memorable student I've ever taught. Short, bandy-legged, and incredibly strong for a 13-year-old, he had come from a rural mountain village deep within Laos to my special-education class in the Santa Barbara suburbs. Although he was no bigger than an American nine-year-old, the hormones of puberty had thrown a dark fuzz over his lip. His voice was deep, a shock coming from that small a body. Often, he wore a bemused expression, compounded of amazement and tolerance for the Americans who were so different from his countrymen in pastoral Laos.

On the playground, Kou was king. He could throw farther, higher, and harder than any other child in school. He was unsurpassed at *hack,* a Laotian game played with the head and feet that seemed like a cross between volleyball and soccer. And in soccer, he was the best. He also carved wonderful wooden tops, which served as trade goods for the American treasures the other boys had.

In the classroom, however, Kou had a problem. The letters, numbers, and words that he painfully memorized one week seemed to vanish during the next.

Although I tried every trick in my teaching bag, nothing seemed to work. With my help, Kou attempted all sorts of experiments designed to help him learn: writing in colored chalk, making clay letters, drawing on the playground. Throughout every effort, he remained cheerful and willing. His attitude seemed to be, "Well, this is how it is in America." But his skills did not improve.

Over time, I noticed that Kou often sang to himself as he worked. "Kou, tell me about your song," I said one day. In his halting English, he told me that the song was about a woman whose man had left her all alone.

"Write it down, Mrs. Nolan," demanded La, his friend. And so our song translation project began. As the class chimed in and squabbled over the meaning of different words, Kou sang, thought, then said the words in his fractured English. I wrote the song down on a sheet of paper. When I was finished, the children all read the song aloud, then sang it with Kou. The next day, my students brought tapes of their native music to school. Suddenly, we had a full-fledged language-experience project underway! As we listened, hummed, and made illustrated booklets about the songs and read them back, the legends and stories of Laos and the Hmong people began to tumble from Kou. For the first time, he had a reason to communicate.

Brief, primitive, and loaded with mistakes, Kou's stories became the foundation for his reading, writing, and language instruction. Never a fan of basal readers, I used this experience as an opportunity to leave the textbooks behind. Kou's quickly improving skills were a source of pride for both of us. When Kou was 15, he left us for junior high. By then he could read at a third-grade level and do survival math. He still had that sweet smile and he still sang softly as he worked. He still longed for the hills of Laos and his old job of herding ducks beside a lake, but he spoke and wrote much better English.

And me? How much I had learned from Kou. Not only did he open the door into a rich and mysterious realm where ghosts walked and crocodiles roamed, but he taught me something about how to be a teacher. From him I learned about the value of starting with a student's interests—and about how powerful a learning tool sharing a culture can be.

SOURCE: Virginia Nolan, "The Song in His Heart," *Instructor* 101, no. 8 (1992), p. 94.

REFLECTION

The section on Multicultural Education lists four levels devised by James Banks. On what level would you place Mrs. Nolan's cultural approach?

Cooperative rather than competitive strategies can also help. Research shows that cooperative learning enhances not only achievement but relationships as well.[14] When students of diverse ethnic and racial backgrounds work cooperatively, they learn to like and respect one another, as well as focus on higher academic goals. Cooperative learning also helps mainstreamed students with disabilities gain social acceptance. But do not expect the magic of cooperative learning without your active participation: Teachers need to monitor the groups, directly teaching social skills.[15]

Similar patterns of bias exist in instructional materials, as some groups receive more attention than others. Students in your class will naturally look for themselves in the curricular materials to see how they are presented. Will they find themselves in the materials that you use or will they be invisible? Are the instructional materials free of stereotypes? Are the views and information presented solely through Euro-centric eyes or are diverse perspectives included?

Because students spend an enormous amount of time working with textbooks and related materials, curricular choices are central to classroom learning. If you were, in fact, enrolled in our fictitious course, "Culture and Education 101," you would un-doubtedly invest a fair amount of time studying curriculum. One of the best-known writers in this area is James Banks, whose useful framework for incorporating multi-cultural concepts in the curriculum is described in the next section.

Multicultural Education

According to **James Banks,** the primary goal of **multicultural education** is to transform the school so that male and female students, exceptional students, and students from diverse cultural, social-class, racial, and ethnic groups experience an equal opportunity to learn.[16] A key assumption of multicultural education is that students are more likely to achieve when the total **classroom climate** is more consistent with their diverse cultures and learning styles.

We have already discussed individual learning styles but have yet to focus on cultural learning styles. Some educators posit that, through **enculturation,** particular groups are likely to exhibit characteristic approaches to learning. For example, based on the groundbreaking work of **Carol Gilligan,** some studies show that women are more likely than men to personalize knowledge; in general, they prefer learning through experience and first-hand observation.[17] Other research suggests that the African American culture emphasizes learning that is aural and participatory. When African American children are required to translate their participatory style onto a written test, they are likely to concentrate on the unaccustomed form of expression, to the detriment of their knowledge of the content.[18] Multicultural educators say that, if we can identify and understand cultural learning styles, we can target curriculum and instruction more appropriately. Further research in cultural and gender learning styles holds the promise of transforming tomorrow's schools.

Multicultural education also seeks to help all students develop more positive atti-tudes toward different racial, ethnic, cultural, and religious groups. According to a 1990s survey of more than one thousand young people between 15 and 24 con-ducted by People for the American Way, about half of the students described the state of race relations in the United States as generally bad. Fifty-five percent of African Americans and whites said they were "uneasy" rather than "comfortable" in dealing with members of the other racial group. However, most respondents felt their atti-tudes toward race relations were healthier than those of their parents.[19]

James Banks notes that one way to achieve more positive attitudes toward differ-ent groups is to integrate the curriculum, to make it more inclusive. He describes four approaches, described below and illustrated in Figure 2.3.[20] (Do you remember any of these approaches in your own schooling?)

1. Multicultural education often begins with the *contributions approach,* in which the study of ethnic heroes (for example, Sacajawea, Rosa Parks, or Booker T. Washington) is included in the curriculum. At this superficial contributions level,

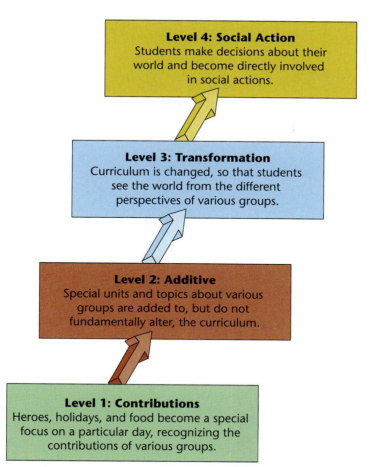

FIGURE 2.3
Banks' approach to multicultural education.

Level 4: Social Action
Students make decisions about their world and become directly involved in social actions.

Level 3: Transformation
Curriculum is changed, so that students see the world from the different perspectives of various groups.

Level 2: Additive
Special units and topics about various groups are added to, but do not fundamentally alter, the curriculum.

Level 1: Contributions
Heroes, holidays, and food become a special focus on a particular day, recognizing the contributions of various groups.

REFLECTION

Think back to your own schooling. At which of Banks's levels would you place your own multicultural education? Provide supporting evidence. As a teacher, which of these levels do you want to reach and teach? Explain.

one might also find "food and festivals" being featured or such holidays as Cinco de Mayo being described or celebrated.

2. In the *additive approach,* a unit or course is incorporated, often but not always during a "special" week or month. February has become the month to study African Americans, while March has been designated "Women's History Month." Although these dedicated weeks and months offer a respite from the typical curricular material, no substantial change is made to the curriculum as a whole.

3. In the *transformation approach,* the entire Eurocentric nature of the curriculum is changed. Students are taught to view events and issues from diverse ethnic and cultural perspectives. For instance, the westward expansion of Europeans can be seen as manifest destiny through the eyes of European descendants, or as an invasion from the east, through the eyes of Native Americans.

Arguing that "love can conquer hate," 14-year-old Aparna Noel Suri, of St. Paul, was chosen as the Most Philosophical Kid in America. Her essay described a neighborhood incident where a black couple faced hateful words from a neighbor by meeting with the neighbors, explaining who they were and why they were different. In the end, the two couples wept and embraced each other.

SOURCE: *Star Tribune* (Minneapolis, MN), May 13, 2001.

REFLECTION

What classroom activities could you undertake to foster the development of emotional intelligence around race and ethnic issues? Why are such efforts rare, and therefore newsworthy?

 Click on *In the News* for recent *In the News* stories. Submit your own *In the News* summary to share with your colleagues.

4. The fourth level, *social action,* goes beyond the transformation approach. Students not only learn to view issues from multiple perspectives but also become directly involved in solving related problems. Rather than political passivity, the typical by-product of many curricular programs, this approach promotes decision making and social action in order to achieve multicultural goals and a more vibrant democracy. (See Chapter 7 for additional multicultural strategies and for a discussion of the debate concerning the place of multiculturalism in the curriculum.)

Bilingual Education

What is going on in America? It is amazing, and disturbing, to ride on a road and see street signs that are printed not only in English but in other languages as well. What's more, even legal documents are now being written in foreign languages. How unnerving to walk down an American street and not understand what people are talking about. Maybe this isn't America. I feel like a stranger in my own land. Why don't they learn to speak English?

Sound like a stroll through today's Miami, or San Diego, or perhaps San Antonio? Good try, but you not only have the wrong city, you are also in the wrong century. Benjamin Franklin expressed this view in the 1750s.[21] He was

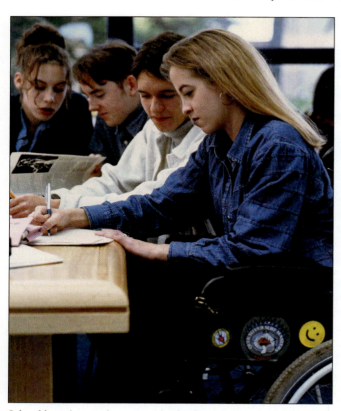

School learning environments in the future must accommodate a wide variety of individual and cultural learning styles.

disgruntled that Philadelphia had printed so many things, including street signs, in another language (German, in this case). Even the *Articles of Confederation* were published in German as well as English, and children were taught in Dutch, Italian, and Polish.

Bilingual education in America is hundreds of years old, hardly a "new" issue. In 1837, Pennsylvania law required that school instruction be given on an equal basis in German as well as English. In fact, that example provides us with a fairly concise definition of **bilingual education,** the use of two languages for instruction. But, almost a century later, as America was being pulled into World War I, foreign languages were seen as unpatriotic. Public pressure routed the German language from the curriculum, although nearly one in four high school students was studying the language at the time. Individual states went even further. Committed to a rapid assimilation of new immigrants, and suspicious of much that was foreign, these states prohibited the teaching of *any* foreign language during the first eight years of schooling. (The Supreme Court found this policy not only xenophobic but unconstitutional as well, in *Meyer* v. *State of Nebraska,* 1923.)[22]

Despite the long history of bilingual education in this country, many school districts never really bought into the concept. In districts without bilingual education, students with a poor command of English had to sink or swim (or perhaps, more accurately, "speak or sink"). Students either learned to speak English as they sat in class—or they failed

In some bilingual education programs, English is learned as a second language, while the student takes other academic work in his or her native language.

school, an approach sometimes referred to as **language submersion.** If submersion was not to their liking, they could choose to leave school. Many did.

Bilingual education had a rebirth in the 1960s, as the Civil Rights movement brought new attention to the struggles of many disenfranchised Americans, including non-English speakers trying to learn in a language they did not understand. And, unlike the 1800s, by the 1960s and 1970s education had become less an option and more a necessity, the threshold to economic success. To respond to this need, Congress passed the **Bilingual Education Act** in 1968. This act provided federal financial incentives, using what some people call "a carrot approach," to encourage schools to initiate bilingual education programs. Not all districts chased the carrot.

From the start, the Bilingual Education Act was fraught with problems. The act lacked concrete recommendations for implementation and did not specify standards. Individual school districts and, in some cases, even individual schools, experimented with different approaches. The result was a patchwork of programs of varying quality, threadbare in spots and peppered with holes where no programs existed at all. In too many cases, the act simply failed to serve the students it was meant to serve.

During the early 1970s, disillusioned parents initiated lawsuits. In 1974, the Supreme Court heard the case of ***Lau v. Nichols.*** This class action lawsuit centered around Kinney Lau and 1,800 other Chinese students from the San Francisco area who were failing their courses because they could not understand English. The Court unanimously affirmed that federally funded schools must "rectify the language deficiency" of these students. Teaching students in a language they did not understand

THE HISTORY OF BILINGUAL EDUCATION IN THE UNITED STATES

1700–1800S: THE PERMISSIVE PERIOD

Linguistic and cultural tolerance maintained the peace in the new nation. Many schools offered content-related classes in languages other than English.

1900–1960S: THE RESTRICTIVE PERIOD

The anti-German hostility during World War I linked foreign languages with alien ideologies. Most states required that all schools teach all content courses in English, and promoted the Americanization of all immigrants.

1950S TO 1980S: THE OPPORTUNIST PERIOD

The Cold War demonstrated that the lack of linguistic ability was a strategic vulnerability, and federal laws were passed to encourage foreign language instruction. The Bilingual Education Act and the *Lau* Supreme Court decisions affirmed the civil rights of language-minority speakers. Schools explored numerous approaches to bilingual education.

1980S TO THE PRESENT: THE DISMISSIVE PERIOD

With the arrival of Presidents Reagan and Bush, an era of antibilingual education re-emerged. Federal support turned into federal hostility, and political movements such as "U.S. English," "English First," and "English Only" sprung up. State actions such as Proposition 227 in California required that English replace any other instructional language used in schools.

SOURCE: Carlos Ovando, "Bilingual Education in the United States: Historical Development and Current Issues." Paper presented at the American Educational Research Association annual convention, Montreal, Canada, April 19–23, 1999.

REFLECTION

Why has teaching in English become a political issue, rather than an educational one? How does conservative political support for English-only courses conflict with conservative goals to enhance the nation's performance in the global economy? Do you believe that bilingual education is a threat to national cohesion and stability?

was not an appropriate education. The Court's decision in *Lau* v. *Nichols* prompted Congress to pass the **Equal Educational Opportunities Act (EEOA).** Under this law, school districts must take positive steps to provide equal education for language-minority students by eliminating language barriers.

Typically in the bilingual approach, **limited English proficiency (LEP)** students learn English as a second language while taking other academic subjects in their native language. The **transitional approach** begins by using the native language as a bridge to English-language instruction. Academic subjects are first taught using the native language, but progressively the students transition to English, to their new language. This is the most widely used approach. The **maintenance,** or **developmental, approach** emphasizes the importance of maintaining both languages. The goal is to create a truly bilingual student, one who acquires English while maintaining competence in the native language. Students are instructed in both languages. **English as a Second Language (ESL)** supplements either the maintenance or transitional

"My grandparents picked up English like everyone else back then, in school, where children learned their lessons in English, not in Spanish or Vietnamese."

"If people want to remain immersed in their old culture and old language, they should stay in their old country."

"Bilingual education has given us illiterate youngsters who can do little more than work at Taco Bell."

Sound familiar? After all, many of our ancestors came to America with few resources or funds, but they were able to learn English, pick up American ways, get through school, and succeed against great odds, so why can't today's immigrants do the same? According to Richard Rothstein—author of *The Way We Were?*—we suffer a bad case of national amnesia, and our recollection of history differs significantly from actual events. The author believes that some bilingual programs work well, and some do not. The key is to find out which are the effective ones and to move the issue of bilingual education out of the political arena and into objective evaluation. Rothstein reminds us that

- *Bilingual education is an American tradition.* In 1837, New York City established bilingual programs for German children, and, throughout the 1800s, Maryland, Colorado, Oregon, Kentucky, Indiana, and Iowa, to name but a few, established their own bilingual programs.

- *Opinions back then were also divided.* Some believed that the programs were essential for academic success, while others thought that they slowed down mastery of English. Then as now, individuals who were being taught in bilingual classrooms—Italian, German, Polish, French, Spanish, and so on—differed as to whether or not bilingual education was a good idea.

- *School performance for immigrants in English immersion programs was horrific.* From 1880 through the 1930s, immigrants were far more likely to drop out of school than to graduate, and they dropped out at much higher percentages than today's students.

- *Non-English-speaking students in New York City early in the twentieth century were 60 percent more likely than English speakers to be labeled "retarded,"* including more than a third of the Italian students.

- In most cases, immigrants to this country never mastered English. In fact, *it was not until the third generation that most immigrant groups became fluent enough in English to excel in school.*

- *As World War I pulled America into the conflict, communities across the nation reacted by eliminating not only bilingual education programs but even the teaching of foreign languages,* the most popular of which was German. It was not until the Supreme Court decision in the 1970s that bilingual education re-emerged as an issue in the nation's schools. And, by then, most Americans had not only forgotten the bilingual education programs of the past, but they had also forgotten what happened to students without them.

SOURCE: Adapted from Richard Rothstein, "Bilingual Education: The Controversy," *Phi Delta Kappan* 79, no. 9 (May 1998), pp. 672–78.

REFLECTION

Why do some Americans believe bilingual education is a relatively recent phenomenon? How are political beliefs reflected in the bilingual debate?

programs by providing special ESL classes for additional instruction in reading and writing English.

Two approaches which cannot truly be considered bilingual, language submersion and immersion, remind us of the "sink or swim" mentality but are used with LEP children nonetheless. Language submersion places students in classes where only English is spoken, and the student either learns English as the academic work progresses, or doesn't. **Immersion** is somewhat less rigid than submersion, because the teacher usually understands the native language and responds in English, sometimes using a "sheltered" or simplified English vocabulary.

Adult Americans who . . .

Speak a language other than English	31,844,979 (about 14 percent)
Speak Spanish	17,345,064
Speak an Asian or Pacific Island language	4,471,621

About half of these Americans report that they do not speak English "very well."

School-age Americans (ages 5–17) who . . .

Speak a language other than English at home	6,322,934 (about 14 percent)
Live in households where everyone speaks a language other than English	4,834,637

SOURCE: U.S. Census Bureau, Language Use, Table 4 (1990). www.census.gov/population/www/socdemo/lang_use.html.

REFLECTION

In what way are these numbers an educational challenge? In what ways are these numbers an educational treasure? As a teacher, how will you meet the needs of limited English speakers?

In schools using one or more of these approaches, problems persist. Consider the following:

> . . . last week I saw an elementary school teacher who was teaching a class of 31 children in the third grade, and the 31 children spoke six languages, *none* of which was English. The teacher had one year of Spanish in her collegiate training.[23]

As schools struggle to meet the needs of LEP students, bilingual education continues to spark political controversy. Millions of students speak hundreds of languages and dialects, including not only Spanish but Hmong, Urdu, Russian, Chinese, Polish, Korean, Tagalog, and Swahili. Misunderstandings are multiplied when language barriers are accompanied by racial and ethnic differences, leading to even greater isolation and segregation for many LEP students. And, while some struggle to make bilingual education work, others believe that it never will.

Opponents of bilingual education point to studies showing that first- and second-generation Hispanic students who attended bilingual programs from the 1970s to the 1990s earned considerably less money than Hispanics who attended "English only" classes. Moreover, Hispanic students who dropped out of bilingual programs were less likely to return and complete high school than were Hispanics who attended English-only programs.[24] LEP parents despair over their children's lack of progress in learning English and graduating from school. The dropout rates for Hispanic students, the largest group of LEP students, hovers around 50 percent.[25] Many parents of students in bilingual programs now oppose these programs, an ironic turnabout, since it was parent protests in the 1960s and 1970s that forced reluctant schools and the federal government to initiate bilingual education. In 1998, more than 60 percent of the voters in California, including a sizable minority of Hispanic voters, supported an initiative to replace most bilingual maintenance programs with a fast-track transition to English. Proposition 227 required that LEP students be provided a year of English immersion instruction and then be shifted into regular classrooms where only English

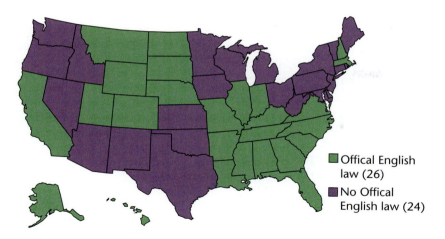

FIGURE 2.4
States with official English laws*

SOURCE: 2000, U.S. ENGLISH, Inc., www.us-english.org/inc/official/states.asp; see also English Plus, http://ourworld.compuserve.com/homepages/JWCRAWFORD/engplus.htm.

Offical English law (26)

No Offical English law (24)

States with Official English Rule and Year Enacted

Alabama	1990	Mississippi	1987
Alaska	1998	Missouri	1998
Arkansas	1987	Montana	1995
California	1986	Nebraska	1920
Colorado	1988	New Hampshire	1995
Florida	1988	North Carolina	1987
Georgia	1986 & 1996	North Dakota	1987
Hawaii*	1978	South Carolina	1987
Illinois	1969	South Dakota	1995
Indiana	1984	Tennessee	1984
Kentucky	1984	Utah	2000
Louisiana*	1811	Virginia	1981 & 1996
Massachusetts	1975	Wyoming	1996

*Hawaii has recognized English and Hawaiian as official languages. An 1811 "enabling act" requires Louisiana to keep records in English. Arizona's 1988 Official English amendment was overturned by the Arizona State Supreme Court in April, 1998.

REFLECTION

Do you see any pattern in which states have passed this law? Does this influence your decision as to where you might want to teach? Do you believe such English Only laws have any practical impact?

is spoken, unless their parents obtain a waiver. Several other states followed suit. The legality of such state laws is in the courts as of this writing.[26]

Many people worry that bilingual education threatens the status of English as the nation's primary vehicle of communication. As a result, an **English-only movement** has emerged (see Figure 2.4). Those who support this movement feel that English is a unifying national bond that preserves our common culture. They believe that English should be the only language used or spoken in public and that the purpose of bilingual education should be to quickly teach English to LEP students. In fact, they assert that bilingual education hurts LEP students, by making them dependent on their native language and discouraging them from learning English.

Bilingual education advocates argue that America is a mosaic of diverse cultures and that diversity should be honored and nurtured. One problem, they point out, is that we simply do not have enough competent bilingual teachers who can respond to the large numbers of LEP children now in our schools.[27] Bilingual advocates oppose the English-only movement, and they feel that it promotes intolerance, will turn back the clock, and may very well be unconstitutional. Education writer James Crawford points out, "It is certainly more respectable to discriminate by language than by race. . . . Most people are not sensitive to language discrimination in this nation, so it is easy to argue that you're doing someone a favor by making them speak English."[28]

Through the 1990s, the opponents of bilingual education gained ground as Congress sharply reduced funding for bilingual education. Moreover, a score of "English-only" bills made their way through various state legislatures and Congress. The future of bilingual education is still being defined.

What does the research say about the effectiveness of bilingual education? Unfortunately, the research is not clear. Educators are just now beginning to analyze long-term data, and they are uncovering some useful findings. In one case, the researchers found that when language-minority students spend more time learning in their native language, they are more likely to achieve at comparable and even higher levels in English.[29] Another study found that the earlier a student starts learning a new language, the more effective that language becomes in an academic setting.[30] Yet another study showed that no single approach holds a monopoly on success, and different approaches to bilingual education can each be effective, suggesting that local school systems should carefully select the programs most appropriate for their communities.[31]

One major bilingual study directed by Virginia Collier and Wayne Thomas evaluated the experiences by 42,000 students over a thirteen-year period. Early findings suggested that the students enrolled in well-implemented bilingual programs actually *outperform* the students in monolingual programs. One successful approach assumed bilingual education to be a two-way street, one in which English speakers and LEP students would learn from each other. In this model, during the Spanish part of the day, the Spanish-speaking students explained the lessons to native-English peers, while, during English instruction, the reverse took place. Collier and Thomas report that, by fourth grade, the students in these two-way classes had actually outperformed the native English speakers who attended English-only classes.[32]

More than two centuries ago, Ben Franklin expressed his fears about the multiple languages heard on America's streets. His concerns have echoed through the centuries, despite a world in which national borders seem to be blurring or even disappearing. In today's global community, Russians and Americans are working together in space, such international organizations as the United Nations and NATO are expanding their membership, and corporations are crossing national boundaries to create global mergers in an international marketplace. Moreover, technological breakthroughs, such as the Internet, have made international communications not just possible but commonplace. However, for most Americans, these international conversations are viable only if the other side speaks English. In this new international era, Americans find themselves locked in a monolingual society. How strange that, instead of viewing those who speak other languages as welcome assets to our nation, some seem eager to erase linguistic diversity.

CARLOS JULIO OVANDO

Why am I not allowed to speak Spanish at school? Why do Mexican students seem ashamed of speaking Spanish? Am I stupid for not learning English quickly so that I can do the assignments? Why are there no teachers who look like me and who share my culture and language? And why did my parents leave the warmth and comfort of Central America for the indifference and coldness of the United States?[1]

It was 1955. Carlos Julio Ovando had emigrated from Nicaragua and was anxious to show his teachers what he knew. But educationally disenfranchised by his linguistic and cultural background, he could not.

The promise of religious freedom and economic stability had motivated the Ovando family's move to Corpus Christi, Texas. In Nicaragua, the Somoza dictatorship opposed the vigorous attempts of Ovando's father, a former priest turned Protestant minister, to convert Catholics. The family was exiled. Yet, their Latin American heritage remained strong. Even after emigrating, Nicaraguan cultural traditions continued in the Ovando home and discussions of spiritual values were central to the family's daily life.

While home was a cultural touchstone for Ovando, school was foreign territory. Unable to understand the lessons in English, he felt abandoned. At age 14, Carlos was placed in the sixth grade and wondered, "Why do teachers show little interest in who I am?" In Nicaragua, the family was entrusted with home life and the school took care of the academic lessons. But school was clearly not working for Carlos.

> I do not recall my parents ever asking to see my report cards or expressing interest in visiting my school to talk to my teachers about my progress. As in the case with many other newly arrived immigrants, it may be that while tacitly interested in my academic well-being, my parents did not know how or were afraid to approach the unfamiliar American schools.[2]

Disconnected from school and doubtful of his own abilities, Ovando was experiencing education that was not so much immersion as submersion, the classic "sink or swim" approach, and Ovando was sinking, looking at America from the bottom of the pool. Ironically, a different kind of pool, a pool hall, provided to be the turning point in his life.

> The turning point in my academic career began when somebody in the church congregation saw me coming out of a pool hall and told my father. Soon after that, in the hope of saving me from sin, my father sent me to a Mennonite high school in northern Indiana.[3]

At the new school, a teacher saw Ovando in an entirely different way. Not so much English challenged, as Spanish blessed. He affirmed Ovando's Latin American roots and championed his native linguistic talent. Spurred by his teacher's encouragement, Ovando rediscovered confidence in his academic abilities. Rather than being punished for speaking Spanish, his language talents were acclaimed. He won honors, including college scholarships. Ovando now reveled in the world of ideas. He taught Spanish in a Midwest high school before going on to college teaching and writing.

His work shows how language is much more than a set of words and grammar rules: It can be a cultural link for students, one that promotes academic achievement. While critics see bilingual education as a threat to national identity, Ovando envisions a society built on the strengths of its diverse population. He challenges teachers to unlock each student's cultural touchstones: "Pedagogy that activates the student voice and embraces the local community provides a much richer environment for student understanding than pedagogy that treats students as if they were empty vessels into which knowledge is to be poured."[4]

[1]Adapted from Carlos J. Ovando and Virginia P. Collier, *Bilingual and ESL Classrooms: Teaching in Multicultural Contexts,* 2nd ed. (Boston: McGraw-Hill, 1998), p. 2.

[2]Ibid, p. 2.

[3]Ibid, p. 3.

[4]Ibid, p. 24.

REFLECTION

How is the history of bilingual education in America re-flected in Ovando's story? What is the downside of pro-moting a monolingual society? How do you explain the popularity of the effort to make English the "official lan-guage" in the United States? Why has the maintenance approach encountered so much difficulty? If you were to teach a student like Ovando, how could you tackle these linguistic and cultural challenges?

WRITE YOUR OWN PROFILE IN EDUCATION:
Click on *Profiles in Education*, write a *Profile in Education* about an educator, and post it on the Online Learning Center. Check out the *Profiles in Education* submitted by other future teachers.

To learn more about Carlos Ovando, click on *Profiles in Education*.

Exceptional Learners

In a typical classroom, a teacher faces students with a great range of abilities, from students reading years behind grade level to students reading years ahead. Both these groups of students are described by the same broad term: **exceptional learners.** In-tegrating exceptional learners into the regular classroom adds further challenge to the job of teaching diverse students.

Typically, exceptional learners are categorized as follows:

- Students with mental retardation
- Students with learning disabilities
- Students with emotional disturbance or behavior disorders
- Students with hearing and language impairments
- Students with visual impairments
- Students with attention deficit hyperactivity disorder
- Students with other health and physical impairments
- Students with severe and multiple disabilities
- Gifted and talented students[33]

Today, children with disabilities constitute approximately 12 percent of the school-age population. Twice as many males as females are identified as disabled. Most students with disabilities who attend public schools are learning disabled (46 percent), another 18 percent have speech and language impairments, and 10 percent are mentally retarded. Almost 90 percent of students receiving special education are considered "mildly handicapped."[34]

We will end this chapter with a close look at issues and developments in teaching exceptional learners, from students with disabilities to gifted and talented learners. Inclusion of each of these populations stretches not only the range of diversity in the classroom but also the range of skills you will need in order to meet the needs of all your students.[35]

Exceptional Learners: An Exceptional Struggle for Educational Rights

Perhaps you have read the book *Karen*. It is the story of a child with cerebral palsy, a child who persevered despite devastating obstacles. A formidable obstacle was an educational system that had no room for children with disabilities. The book was written by Karen's mother, who, like her daughter, refused the rejection of a hostile school and society. She wrote of her attempts to gain educational rights for her daughter and other children with disabilities:

> We constantly sought a remedy for this appalling situation which deprived so many of an education, and eventually we found a few doctors and educators who had made strides in developing valid testing methods for handicapped children. On one occasion, when I voiced a plea for the education of the handicapped, a leading state official retorted, "It would be a waste of the state's money. They'll never get jobs."
>
> We were frequently discouraged and not a little frightened as many of our "learned" men [sic] felt the same way.[36]

Such disparaging attitudes were common in our society for years and resulted in inadequate educational programs for millions of exceptional children. Today, the educational rights of these children have been mandated by courts of law and are being put into practice in classrooms across the nation.

Before the Revolutionary War, the most that was offered to exceptional children was protective care in asylums. The asylums made little effort to help these children develop their physical, intellectual, and social skills. Following the American Revolution, however, the ideals of democracy and the development of human potential swept the nation. Within this humanist social context, procedures were devised for teaching the blind and the deaf. Then, in the early 1800s, attempts were made to educate the "idiotic" and the "insane" children who today would be called "mentally retarded" or "emotionally disturbed."

For many years, the legal system mirrored society's judgment that the best policy toward the disabled was "out of sight, out of mind." The courts typically saw education as a privilege rather than a right, and they ruled that children with disabilities should be excluded from schools. The notion was that the majority of children needed to be protected from those with disabilities: from the disruptions they might precipitate, from the excessive demands they might make, and from the discomfort their presence in classrooms might cause.

The years following World War II brought renewed hope and promise. Such pioneers as Grace Fernald, Marianne Frostig, and Heinz Werner—to name but a few—conducted research, developed programs, and gave new impetus to the field of **special education.** Their work was aided by the emergence of new disciplines, such as psychology, sociology, and social work. Parents also continued their struggle, individually and collectively, to obtain educational opportunities for children with disabilities. They took their cause to both the schools and the courts. Special education has broken away from the isolation and institutionalization so common in the late nineteenth century and has moved to mainstream exceptional children, as much as possible, into typical school settings.

By the 1970s, court decisions and federal law had established five critical principles of special education:

1. **Zero reject.** The principle of zero reject asserts that no child with disabilities may be denied a free, appropriate public education. Representatives of the disabled have asserted that excluding children with disabilities from public schools violates the constitutional interpretation behind the Supreme Court's *Brown v. Board of Education* (1954) decision, which put an end to claims of "separate but equal" schooling. The courts have responded with landmark decisions in Pennsylvania (*Pennsylvania Association for Retarded Children v. Commonwealth*) and in Washington, DC (*Mill v. D.C. Board of Education*) that mandate public schools in

those jurisdictions to provide a free, appropriate education to all children with disabilities. Other federal and state decisions have followed suit.

2. **Nondiscriminatory education.** The principle of nondiscriminatory education, based on the Fifth and Fourteenth Amendments of the U.S. Constitution, mandates that children with disabilities be fairly assessed, so that they can be protected from inappropriate classification and tracking. Much of the court activity in this area has centered on the disproportionate number of children of color assigned to special education classes, a situation that some claim is the result of biased testing. In one case, a court ruled that IQ tests could not be used for placing or tracking students. Other courts have forbidden the use of tests that are culturally biased, and still others have ordered that testing take place in the children's native language.

3. **Appropriate education.** While the principle of zero reject assures that children with disabilities will receive an appropriate public education, it is important to recognize that this principle goes beyond simply allowing children with disabilities to pass through the schoolhouse door. The term "appropriate education" implies that these children have the right to an education involving the accurate diagnosis of individual needs, as well as responsive programs keyed to those needs.

4. **Least-restrictive environment.** The principle of least-restrictive environment protects children with disabilities from being inappropriately segregated from their age-group peers. Court decisions have urged that special classes and separate schools be avoided unless a child's disabilities are such that education in a regular classroom with the aid of special materials and supportive services cannot be achieved.

5. **Procedural due process.** The principle of procedural due process upholds the right of the disabled to protest a school's decisions about their education. Due process entails the right of children with disabilities and their parents to be notified of school actions and decisions; to challenge those decisions before an impartial tribunal, using counsel and expert witnesses; to examine the school records on which a decision is based; and to appeal whatever decision is reached.

These five principles of special education law are encompassed in landmark federal legislation passed in 1975, **Public Law 94-142,** the Education for All Handicapped Children Act. This law offers states financial support to make a free and appropriate public education available to every child with disabilities. It was replaced and expanded in 1991 by the **Individuals with Disabilities Education Act (IDEA),** which not only provided a more sensitive description of the act's purpose but also extended the act's coverage to all disabled learners between the ages of 3 and 21, including individuals with autism or traumatic brain injuries. IDEA also provided for rehabilitation and social work services. IDEA requires that each disabled child "have access to the program best suited to that child's special needs which is as close as possible to a normal child's educational program."[37] Classroom teachers shoulder the responsibilities of monitoring the needs of each child with disabilities placed in their classrooms and of using constructive procedures to meet their needs. The law further states that an **individualized education program (IEP)** be developed to provide a written record of those needs and procedures. The law states that an IEP must be written for each child who receives special education services. The IEP must include:

A statement of the student's current performance, including long-term (annual) goals and short-term objectives

A description of the nature and duration of the instructional services designed to meet the prescribed goals

An overview of the methods of evaluation that will be used to monitor the child's progress and to determine whether the goals and objectives have been met

There is no specific IEP form that must be used, as long as goals, objectives, services, and evaluation are accurately reflected. In fact, hundreds of different IEP forms are currently in use; some run as long as twenty pages; others are only two or three pages. New teachers should learn about their school district's norms and procedures for writing IEPs when they begin teaching. Remember, it is not the format that is important but, rather, whether or not the IEP accurately describes the educational needs and the related remedial plans. While writing these IEPs will undoubtedly consume a great deal of a teacher's time and energy, it often leads to better communication among the school staff, as well as between teachers and parents. Also, the practice of preparing IEPs will likely lead to more effective individualization of instruction for all children, not just those with disabilities.

IDEA has been one of the most thoroughly litigated federal laws in history. Parents whose children qualify for special education services can and do sue the school district if they believe their children's needs are not being met. Local courts agreeing with parents' views have ordered public schools to hire extra teachers or specialized personnel or to spend additional dollars to provide an appropriate education. When judges believe that a school is unable to meet the special needs of a child, even with these additional resources, they can and have ordered the public school to pay the tuition so that the student can attend a private school. The practice of judges ordering public schools to pay the private school tuition of some special needs children is currently being reviewed by the Supreme Court.[38]

There is considerable confusion in identifying learning-disabled (LD) students, in deciding who is entitled to additional resources. Educational literature reflects more

Public Law 94-142 placed students with disabilities into regular classrooms, so that they receive the "least-restrictive" education possible.

than fifty terms to describe students with **learning disabilities.** Some believe that *learning disabled* has become a catchall term for many children whose achievement does not match their potential. Over the past decade, the number of children defined as needing special education services has multiplied, sharply driving up education costs as well.[39] Moreover, there is a disturbing pattern suggesting race bias in special education placement. African American children are almost three times as likely as are white children to be labeled mentally retarded.[40]

Some question the effectiveness of current practices. For instance, many students with mild disabilities attend regular classrooms for part of the day but leave for a period of time to receive special instruction in a resource room. Recently, these "pull-out" programs have been charged with stigmatizing students while failing to improve their academic performance. Many who criticize pulling children out of main-streamed classes for special education are proponents of what is known as the **regular education initiative.** This initiative endorses the placement of special needs children in a regular class from the start and emphasizes close collaboration between the regular classroom teacher and special educators in order to offer special services *within* the regular classroom. By the late 1990s about half of the students with disabilities spent 80 percent or more of the school day in a regular classroom.[41] Debate over the best way to educate students with disabilities is certain to continue. (See Figure 2.5.)[42]

Regular classroom teachers often express concerns about their ability to handle a mainstreamed classroom:

> They want us all to be super teachers, but I've got 33 kids in my class and it's really a job to take care of them without also having to deal with special needs kids too. I'm not complaining really—I wouldn't want to do anything other than what I'm doing—but it is demanding.[43]

Classroom teachers are expected to meet many of society's needs, including the education of special needs students, but are not always given adequate tools to meet those expectations. Frustration is often the result. To succeed with special education students, teachers could benefit from additional time to plan with other professionals, the availability of appropriate curricular materials, perhaps extra classroom assistance, and on-going staff development programs that provide up-to-date instructional strategies. In any case, for **mainstreaming** (also termed **inclusion**) to succeed, teachers must genuinely support the integration of students with disabilities into their classrooms. They must be committed to exploding stereotypes and must recognize the essential value of helping all children learn to understand and accept differences. Although we have emphasized the legal decisions that prompted the mainstreaming movement, inclusion is at its heart a moral issue, one that raises the timeless principles of equality, justice, and the need for all of us to learn to live and grow together—not apart.

The Gifted and Talented

Precocious children are among our most neglected students. They, too, have special needs:

> In Chicago, the school system turned down the request of a 5-year-old boy who wanted to enter school early. While he waits to be allowed to enter kindergarten, the boy spends his time in the public library doing independent research in astronomy and geography. His IQ has been measured at more than 180.

	1989–90	1998–99	Percent Change
Specific Learning Disabilities	2,062,076	2,817,148	36.6%
Speech and Language Impairments	974,256	1,074,548	10.3
Mental Retardation	563,902	611,076	8.4
Emotional Disturbance	381,639	463,262	21.4
Multiple Disabilities	87,957	107,763	22.5
Hearing Impairments	57,906	70,883	22.4
Orthopedic Impairments	48,050	69,495	44.6
Other Health Impairments	52,733	220,831	318.7
Visual Impairments	22,866	26,132	14.3
Autism	NA	53,576	b
Deaf-Blindness	1,633	1,609	−1.5
Traumatic Brain Injury	NA	12,933	
Developmental Delay	NA	11,910	c
All Disabilities	4,253,018	5,541,166	30.3

FIGURE 2.5
Number of students ages 6 through 21 served under IDEA.[a]

SOURCE: U.S. Department of Education, Office of Special Education Programs, Data Analysis System (DANS). 22nd Annual Report to Congress (2000), Table II-2.

[a]Data from 1989–90 through 1993–94 include children with disabilities served under Chapter 1 of ESEA (SOP). Beginning in 1994–95, all services to students with disabilities were provided under IDEA only.

[b]Autism and traumatic brain injury were first required to be reported in 1992–93. The percentage increase for these disability categories between 1992–93 and 1998–99 was 243.9 percent and 226.6 percent, respectively.

[c]Developmental delay was first reported in 1997–98. The percentage increase between the two years was 214.1 percent.

REFLECTION

How do you explain the increases in the special education population? What factors might contribute to the high identification of children in some racial or ethnic groups as needing special education?

In Westchester County, a suburb of New York City, a 2½-year-old boy already emulates the language abilities of his parents. He speaks and reads English, French, Hebrew, Spanish, and Yiddish, and he has mastered some Danish. He is studying music theory and is conducting scientific experiments. The parents, however, are unable to find any educational facility willing and able to educate their young, gifted child. A member of their local school board told them: "It is not the responsibility or function of public schools to deal with such children." As a result, the parents considered moving to Washington state, where there was an experimental preschool program for the gifted.[44]

If you are like most Americans, you may find it difficult to consider gifted and talented children to be in any way disadvantaged. After all, **gifted learners** are the lucky ones who master subject matter with ease. They are the ones who shout out the solution before most of us have a chance to write down the problem. Others may have perfect musical pitch, are athletic superstars, become the class leaders who

YOU BE THE JUDGE

SPECIAL NEEDS STUDENTS

Should Be Mainstreamed Because . . .

WITHOUT INCLUSION, OUR DEMOCRATIC IDEAL IS HOLLOW

Segregating the disabled mirrors the historical segregation of African Americans and other groups, a segregation already rejected by the courts. Separate can never be equal, and all students quickly learn the stigma associated with those in "special" classrooms.

SOCIETY NEEDS THE TALENTS OF ALL ITS CITIZENS

Society needs the skills and economic productivity of all our citizens. Educating the disabled in a segregated setting decreases their opportunity for full and meaningful contributions later in life.

MAINSTREAMING IMPROVES THEIR ACADEMIC AND SOCIAL RELATIONS

Studies indicate that special needs students perform better academically when mainstreamed in regular classes. Not surprisingly, their social adjustment is also improved.

THE NONDISABLED GAIN WHEN SPECIAL NEEDS STUDENTS ARE PRESENT

In our increasingly stratified society, students can spend years in school with peers just like themselves. Inclusion provides an opportunity for children to appreciate and work with people who do not necessarily reflect their own experiences and viewpoints.

Should Not Be Mainstreamed Because . . .

MERELY SITTING IN REGULAR CLASSROOMS DOES NOT GUARANTEE A FITTING EDUCATION

A rallying cry like "democracy" sounds impressive, but we need to ensure that special needs students receive a quality education, and the best place for that is not necessarily in a mainstreamed classroom.

PULL-OUT PROGRAMS CAN OFFER SPECIAL NEEDS STUDENTS THE RESOURCES THEY NEED TO SUCCEED

Pull-out programs for special needs children can offer an adjusted curriculum, special instructional techniques, and smaller class size. Special needs students can soar in classrooms designed to meet their needs, but flounder when they are inappropriately placed in regular classes.

GIFTED AND TALENTED STUDENTS ARE AT PARTICULAR RISK

Gifted and talented students fall within the special needs category, and for them, mainstreaming is a disaster. If the gifted are not challenged, they will be turned off from school, and the gifts of our most able students will be lost to society.

WHEN SPECIAL NEEDS STUDENTS ARE MAINSTREAMED, NONDISABLED STUDENTS SUFFER

As teachers in regular classes adjust learning activities to accommodate the special needs students, other students lose out. The extra time, special curriculum, and attention given to special needs students amount to time and resources taken from others in the class.

SOURCE: Many of these arguments are found in greater detail in Jack L. Nelson, Stuart B. Palonsky, and Kenneth Carlson, *Critical Issues in Education: Dialogue and Dialectics* (New York: McGraw-Hill, 2000), pp. 416–42.

YOU BE THE JUDGE

What training would help you meet the special needs of students mainstreamed into your classroom? Can "separate" ever be "equal"? Whose needs are of most worth, those of special needs students, or of "regular" students? Do their needs actually conflict? As a teacher, would you want special needs children mainstreamed, or pulled out? Imagine yourself the parent of a special needs child. Would you want your child mainstreamed, or pulled out?

inspire us, or demonstrate insights that amaze and inform us. Many exhibit endless curiosity, creativity, and energy. Small wonder that there is relatively little national support for extra funds or programs targeted at these gifted students, the ones who make the rest of us feel somewhat uncomfortable, inadequate, and sometimes just plain envious.

Defining *giftedness,* like defining *learning disabilities,* invites controversy. To some, the traditional definition of *giftedness* includes those with an IQ of 130 or higher; to others, the label *giftedness* is reserved for those with an IQ score of 160 or higher. Still others, such as Gardner and Goleman, have expanded the concept of gifted to include those with special creative or artistic abilities, athletic prowess, interpersonal gifts, or emotional insights.

Education experts Joseph Renzulli and C. H. Smith described the gifted in somewhat traditional terms, as those who demonstrate

1. High ability

2. High creativity

3. High motivation and persistence (the drive to initiate and complete a task)[45]

According to Renzulli and Smith, a child who is better than 85 percent of his or her peers in all three areas, and who exceeds 98 percent in at least one area, can be classified as gifted.

Another researcher, **Robert Sternberg,** has identified three major types of giftedness: analytic, synthetic, and practical. Students who are gifted analytically excel at dissecting problems and understanding their parts. Analytically gifted students usually do well on conventional tests of intelligence. Synthetic giftedness occurs in people who are creative, intuitive, or insightful. Individuals who are practically gifted can go into real-world situations, figure out what needs to be done, and negotiate and work with people to accomplish the task.[46]

Until recently, schools did little to accommodate the special needs of the gifted and talented.

A FEW OF THE PEOPLE IDENTIFIED WITH PHYSICAL, LEARNING AND SPEECH DISABILITIES:
Moses, Demosthenes, Aesop, Cotton Mather, Benjamin Franklin, Clara Barton, Harriet Tubman, Charles Darwin, Jane Addams, Franklin Delano Roosevelt, Congresswoman Carolyn McCarthy, and James Earl Jones.

THE FOLLOWING INDIVIDUALS WERE ASKED TO LEAVE SCHOOL, DROPPED OUT OR FOUND ALTERNATIVES TO THE ADOLESCENT SCHOOL SCENE:
Salvador Dali, Whoopi Goldberg, Beryl Markham, Edgar Allan Poe, George Bernard Shaw, Percy Bysshe Shelley, James Whistler, and Frank Lloyd Wright.

REFLECTION

Do you know accomplished individuals who did not do well in school? How could education respond to the unique needs of these individuals? (You may want to research the learning issues of these well-known people.)

While definitions of *giftedness* vary, only a small percentage of our population possesses this high degree of ability, creativity, motivation, or pragmatic talent, making for a very exclusive club. Exclusivity can invite hostility. Since most people are, by definition, excluded from this highly select group, few believe that the gifted merit any special educational attention. To many Americans, it seems downright undemocratic to provide special services to children who already enjoy an advantage. While many parents of gifted children are strong advocates for their children, some parents of the gifted have shown reluctance to request additional educational programs for their children.

Many gifted students do not make it on their own. Highly talented young people suffer boredom and negative peer pressure when kept in regular classroom settings.[47] Instead of thriving in school, they drop out. The result is that many of our nation's brightest and most competent students are lost to neglect and apathy, and some of our most talented youth have not always succeeded at school.

Even in school districts that recognize the special needs of gifted children, opposition to providing special programs and educational opportunities continues. In some cases, funds are lacking; in others, little interest and commitment to the gifted may be the problem. Some object to special programs for the gifted because they see it as a form of tracking, an undemocratic strategy that separates the gifted from the rest of the population.

Research shows that a significant number of gifted students contemplate suicide. Gifted students may be haunted by a sense of isolation and loneliness, pressure to achieve, and fear of failure.[48] Talent, giftedness, and creativity set adolescents apart at a time when the push is for conformity, for being "normal" and "like everybody else." Gifted students most often talk about their feelings of isolation:

I feel as though I'll never fit in any place, no matter how hard I try.

Basically, the challenge in my schooling has not been academic, but having to conform—to be just like everyone else in order to be accepted.

I hate it when people use you. For example, if you have an incredible vocabulary and someone wants your help writing a speech, and then later they tell you to get lost.[49]

The picture is especially dismal for females and children of color who are identified as gifted, and once identified, are more likely to drop out than gifted white males. Many experts urge the use of multiple criteria for identifying and retaining gifted students, including teacher recommendations and assessments of special talents, so that such programs could be more equitable and inclusive.

Once identified, there is no guarantee that gifted students will find high-quality programs. The regular classroom remains a major instructional resource for gifted students. For instance, a gifted student might spend most of the day in a regular class and be pulled out for a part of the day, perhaps an hour or so, to receive special instruction. Another approach is to set up resource centers within the regular classroom, where gifted students are offered individualized tutoring.[50] At the secondary level, comprehensive high schools have augmented their offerings with challenging courses of study, such as the International Baccalaureate (IB) program, an internationally recognized degree program that includes rigorous science, math, and foreign language requirements. Special high schools, such as the Bronx High School of Science and the North Carolina School for Mathematics and Science, have long and distinguished histories of providing educational opportunities for intellectually gifted students. Other special schools have focused on programs in acting, music, and dance. Yet many believe that we need to do a better job of "gifted inclusion," by designing regular class activities that are more responsive to the needs of the gifted.[51]

Some school districts go beyond their own resources in order to meet the needs of gifted students. For instance, one such program connects gifted high school students with the local college or community college. These students spend part of their day enrolled in college-level courses, being intellectually challenged and receiving college credit while still enrolled in high school. Still other gifted students receive additional instruction through summer camps or even special year-long programs that augment their regular courses. Johns Hopkins University, for example, has been sponsoring the Center for Talented Youth (CTY) in different parts of the nation for several decades.

Many of these college programs are termed **accelerated programs,** for they allow gifted students to skip grades or receive college credit early. **Advanced placement** courses and exams (the APs), provide similar acceleration opportunities, permitting students to graduate before their chronological peers. While many Americans accept the notion of enrichment for the gifted, acceleration runs into stronger opposition. The common belief that the negative social consequences of acceleration outweigh the intellectual benefits represents an obstacle to implementing such programs for the gifted.

Whereas social maladjustment due to acceleration may indeed be a problem for some gifted children, others claim they feel just as comfortable, both academically and socially, with their intellectual peers as they do with their chronological peers. Yet, not accelerating gifted children may lead to boredom, apathy, frustration, and even ridicule. Several studies confirm the value of acceleration, from early admission to elementary school to early admission to college. Grade-accelerated students surpass their classmates in academic achievement and complete higher levels of education. While research suggests that grade acceleration does not cause problems in social and emotional adjustment, cases of students who found acceleration to be a disaster are also plentiful.[52] No single program is likely to meet the needs of all gifted students.

Recognition of the special needs of the gifted has been slow in coming. It is estimated that most school systems provide special gifted services to between 7 and 12 percent of their students. However, with the current trend away from ability grouping, tracking, and special programs, it is possible that fewer resources will be available for the gifted in the years ahead.[53]

The qualities of effective gifted programs include a mastery dimension that allows students to move through the curriculum at their own pace; in-depth and independent learning; field study; and an interdisciplinary dimension that allows for the exploration of theories and issues across the curriculum. Moreover, an important but often overlooked advantage of these programs is the sense of community they offer, the opportunity for gifted students to connect with others like themselves. This is an important step in reducing student anxiety and alienation. When gifted students are placed in appropriate programs, they are often empowered to realize their full potential. One student was relieved to find that "there are lots of people like me and I'm not a weirdo after all." As one 12-year-old girl said,

> My heart is full of gratitude for my teacher who first wanted to have me tested for the gifted program. I'm not trying to brag, but I'm really glad there's a class for people like me. We may seem peculiar or odd, but at least we have fun and we respect each other's talents.[54]

In the final analysis, it is not only the gifted who have suffered from our national neglect and apathy; it is all of us. How many works of art will never be enjoyed? How many medical breakthroughs and how many inventions have been lost because of our insensitivity to the gifted?

These questions of opportunities lost can be broadened to include many of the different student populations discussed in this chapter. How many of these students—because of their race, language, or special needs—have slipped through the educational cracks? How many cultural breakthroughs, intellectual insights, and economic advances have been lost because of inadequate school programs or unresponsive teachers? We will never know the final cost of our neglect, but we can rededicate ourselves to uncovering and nurturing the talents in all our students.

SUMMARY

CHAPTER REVIEW

Go to the Online Learning Center to take a chapter self-quiz, practice with key terms, and review key ideas from the chapter.

1. How do cognitive, affective, and physiological factors impact learning?

   - Individuals exhibit diverse styles of learning that are affected by attitudes, reasoning and physical differences. Cognitive factors impact the way students organize and retain information. Affective factors shape motivation and the ability to handle frustration. Finally, physiological differences influence body needs, from sleep to eating habits to the most comfortable room temperature.

   - Identifying a single optimal educational climate is not possible, since individuals differ so markedly in these three factors. Nonetheless, many schools presume that the ideal learning climate features quiet, well-lighted rooms, with difficult subjects being taught early in the morning in forty- or fifty-minute periods. Such a "one-size-fits-all" model does not work for many students.

2. How can teachers respond to different learning styles?

   - Teachers may need to experiment with the classroom environment, including temperature, lighting, and noise level. Teachers may want to plan activities of varying lengths, to accommodate students with different attention spans or tolerance for sitting quietly.

- Teachers can also offer instructional activities that complement various learning styles, such as visual, kinesthetic, or auditory.

3. What are the classroom implications of Howard Gardner's theory of multiple intelligences?

- Just as some educators challenge the concept of a single appropriate learning style, others challenge the notion of a single type of intelligence. Gardner's theory of multiple intelligences identifies at least eight kinds of intelligence, ranging from the traditional verbal and mathematical to musical, physical, and interpersonal abilities. Teachers can plan their lessons to incorporate and develop these different intelligences described by Gardner (e.g., ask students to re-enact historical events through dance).

4. How does emotional intelligence influence teaching and learning?

- Daniel Goleman advocates that schools concern themselves with emotional as well as intellectual development, for he believes that emotional intelligence may better predict future success than IQ scores.

- Teachers can increase a student's emotional intelligence quotient (EQ) by developing classroom strategies that help students understand their emotions, "read" the emotions of others, and learn how to manage relationships.

5. How can teachers meet the diverse needs of an increasingly multicultural student population?

- Changing patterns of immigration and birth rates have produced increasingly diverse classrooms. Generalized knowledge about different groups can be useful for instructional planning. Stereotypes, however, represent dangerous overstatements about groups and members of groups, and teachers must be wary of the damaging impact such stereotypes can have on both teaching and learning.

- Early in the twenty-first century, one-third of all students will be of color, both enriching and challenging our schools. Teachers of diverse student populations must work to ensure equitable distribution of teacher attention, the accommodation and nurturing of different learning styles, and a curriculum that fairly represents the contributions and experiences of diverse groups.

6. What are the different levels of multicultural education?

- James Banks identifies four levels of multicultural education: contributions, additive, transformation, and social action. While the contributions and additive approaches are more superficial, the transformation and social action approaches hold more promise for ensuring that students of *all* backgrounds experience an equal opportunity to learn.

7. What are the political and instructional issues surrounding bilingual education?

- Educating limited English proficiency (LEP) students has been both an educational and a legal challenge in America since the colonial period. In *Lau v. Nichols* (1974), the Supreme Court ruled that schools were deficient in their treatment of students with limited English proficiency. Congress subsequently passed the Equal Educational Opportunities Act.

- Many districts have redoubled their efforts in bilingual education. Some teach students in their native language only until they learn English (the transitional approach), other schools use both languages in the classroom (the maintenance approach), some supplement with English as a Second Language (ESL) classes, while still others opt for nonbilingual means, such as immersion and "submersion."

- Studies suggest that many bilingual programs fall short of their goals. A political backlash against maintenance programs, and the desire to have all students speak English as soon as possible, has fanned the flames of an "English as the official language" movement in California and elsewhere. The future direction of bilingual education may be as much a political determination as an instructional one.

8. How are the needs of special learners met in today's classrooms?

- Legislation and court decisions have required schools to provide students with appropriate education in the least restrictive environment. The Individuals with Disabilities Education Act (IDEA) guarantees students with disabilities access to public education, and requires that individualized education programs be developed to document the school's efforts in meeting the needs of these students.

- Despite the Individuals with Disabilities Education Act, there are no easy answers to issues such as the identification of special needs children, the best ways to educate these learners, the wisdom of inclusion or mainstreaming, and the training and resources available to teachers.

- Few resources are provided for gifted and talented students in many of the nation's school districts. When their needs are not met, these exceptional learners may become apathetic, bored, and alienated.

- Gifted and talented programs usually promote one of two strategies: enrichment or acceleration. While many people worry that acceleration will lead to social maladjustment, research indicates that acceleration can have a positive impact on gifted students.

KEY TERMS AND PEOPLE

accelerated programs, 73

advanced placement, 73

affective domain, 39

appropriate education, 66

James Banks, 54

bilingual education, 57

Bilingual Education Act, 57

classroom climate, 54

cognitive domain, 39

demographic forecasting, 48

emotional intelligence quotient (EQ), 45

enculturation, 54

English as a Second Language (ESL), 58

English-only movement, 61

Equal Educational Opportunities Act (EEOA), 58

exceptional learners, 64

Howard Gardner, 43

generalizations, 51

gifted learners, 69

Carol Gilligan, 54

Daniel Goleman, 45

immersion, 59

individualized education program (IEP), 66

Individuals with Disabilities Education Act (IDEA), 66

intelligence, 42

language submersion, 57

Lau v. *Nichols*, 57

learning disabilities, 68

learning styles, 38

least-restrictive environment, 66

limited English proficiency (LEP), 58

locus of control, 39

mainstreaming (inclusion), 68

maintenance (developmental) approach, 58

multicultural education, 54

multiple intelligences, 43

nondiscriminatory education, 66

Carlos Julio Ovando, 63

portfolio, 45

procedural due process, 66

Public Law 94-142, 66

regular education initiative, 68

special education, 65

stereotypes, 51

Robert Sternberg, 71

transitional approach, 58

zero reject, 65

DISCUSSION QUESTIONS AND ACTIVITIES

1. How would you characterize your own learning style? Interview other students in your class to determine how they characterize their learning styles. Based on these interviews, what recommendations could you offer your course instructor about how to meet the needs of different students in your class?

2. What is your opinion of Howard Gardner's theory of multiple intelligences? In which of the intelligences do you feel you are the strongest? the weakest?

3. Can you develop additional intelligences beyond the ones Gardner identifies? (This is often best accomplished in groups.)

4. Review Daniel Goleman's book *Emotional Intelligence* and present a summary of Goleman's findings to your classmates.

5. Write a research paper on the education and life experiences of at least one of the recent immigrant groups. If possible, interview students and family members who belong to that group about their experiences.

6. Do you believe that bilingual education should be saved or shelved? Why? If bilingual education is maintained, how can it be made more effective?

7. Given demographic trends, pick a region of the country and a particular community. Develop a scenario of a classroom in that community in the year 2020. Describe the students' characteristics and the teacher's role. Is that classroom likely to be impacted by changing demographics? How will learning styles and the new insights on intelligence be manifested in the way the teacher organizes and instructs the class?

8. Choose a school curriculum and suggest how it can be changed to reflect one of the four approaches to multicultural education described by Banks. Why did you choose the approach you did?

9. Investigate a special education program in a local school. Describe its strengths. What suggestions do you have for improving it?

10. Observe a mainstreamed classroom in a local school and interview the teacher. What is your assessment of the effectiveness of mainstreaming in this classroom?

11. Given budgetary limitations, do you think schools should provide special resources and programs for gifted students? Why or why not?

12. What is your opinion of ability grouping? If you had a gifted daughter or son, would you want your child in a special program? What kind of program?

WEB-*TIVITIES*

1. Multiple Intelligences
2. Multicultural Education
3. Bilingual Education
4. Exceptional Learners

REEL TO REAL TEACHING

CHILDREN OF A LESSER GOD (1986)
Run Time: 119 minutes

Synopsis: Special education instructor Jim Leeds brings his enthusiasm and innovative instruction to a school for deaf students.

Reflection:

1. How does this film redefine traditional notions of intelligence and the idea of one best learning style? Describe scenes in which Jim Leeds integrated the concepts of diverse learning styles, multiple intelligences, and EQ into his teaching.

2. Both Sarah and Jim ask, "If you want to speak to me, learn my language." Connect this statement with issues explored in the chapter for bilingual education. Brainstorm some linguistic and cultural parallels between bilingual and deaf education.

3. Many believe that the Deaf community has developed not only a system of communication (sign language), but also a unique and valuable culture, one that hearing people should learn more about. Using James Banks' four categories of multicultural education, how might you teach hearing students about Deaf culture?

4. Respond to the principal's remark, "No one is trying to change the world around here. We are only trying to help a few deaf kids get along a little better." What biases underlie this view? As a teacher, how might you fully develop the talents of all students in a diverse classroom, including those with special needs?

Follow-up Activities:

1. So, you wanna make a movie? Tap into your linguistic, spatial, and musical intelligences to create a sequel to *Children of a Lesser God.* Tell us about the lives of Sarah and Jim in twenty years. Has technology changed how they communicate with each other? What career choices did they make? Do they have a family?

2. A critical element in the original film was the dynamic between Jim's voice and Sarah's verbal silence. Some critics thought by telling the whole story from a hearing perspective, deafness was earmarked as a weakness to be overcome by Sarah. In *your* sequel, tell the story from Sarah's perspective. Or strike a balance between verbal and nonverbal communication styles.

How do you rate this film? Click on *Reel to Real Teaching* to submit your review of this or another education-related film, and read reviews submitted by others.

FOR FURTHER READING

The Children Are Watching, by Carlos E. Cortés (2000). This book analyzes both entertainment and news media, grappling with issues such as how media frame diversity themes, transmit values concerning diversity, and influence thinking about topics such as race, ethnicity, gender, religion, and sexual orientation.

Crossing Over to Canaan: The Journey of New Teachers in Diverse Classrooms, by Gloria Ladson-Billings (2001). Detailing the struggles and triumphs of eight novice teachers, this book shows how good teachers can use innovation and "teachable moments" to turn cultural differences into academic assets.

Culturally Responsive Teaching: Theory, Research, and Practice, by Geneva Gay (2000). The author discusses the role of teacher expectations and attitudes, formal and informal multicultural curricula, and diverse learning styles in the effort to improve the performance of underachieving students of color.

Latino Students in American Schools, by Guadalupe Valdes (2001). Focusing on the lives and experiences of four Mexican children in an American middle school, Valdes examines the policy and instructional dilemmas surrounding the English language education of immigrant children. Samples of the children's oral and written language as well as an analysis of their classrooms, school, and community are provided.

The Power of the Arts: Creative Strategies for Teaching Exceptional Learners, by Sally Smith (2001). Illustrates how to use the arts to teach academic subjects to children with learning disabilities. Includes step-by-step instructions for arts-based projects that teach science, math, and vocabulary.

3

Teacher Effectiveness

FOCUS QUESTIONS

1. Are teachers born, or made?
2. How is class time organized and what is academic learning time?
3. What classroom management skills foster academic achievement?
4. What are the roles of teachers and students in the pedagogical cycle?
5. How can teachers set a stage for learning?
6. What questioning strategies increase student achievement?
7. How can teachers best tap into the variety of student learning styles?
8. What are the prevailing models of instruction?
9. What are the future directions of effective teaching research?

WHAT DO YOU THINK? Qualities of a Good Teacher. Rate the qualities of a good teacher, and see how other students rated these qualities.

CHAPTER PREVIEW

Albert Einstein believed that they awakened the "joy in creative expression and knowledge." Elbert Hubbard saw them as those who could make "two ideas grow where only one grew before." Gail Godwin surmised that they are "one-fourth preparation and three-fourths theater." Ralph Waldo Emerson believed that they could "make hard things easy." About whom are these talented geniuses talking? You guessed it: teachers. Although these intellectual leaders shared an insight into the importance of teaching, even these artists and scientists could not decide if teaching was an art or a science, a gift or a learned skill. Perhaps it is both.

Some individuals seem to take to teaching quite naturally. With little or no preparation, they come to school with a talent to teach and touch the lives of students. Others bring fewer natural talents to the classroom yet, with preparation and practice, become master teachers, models others try to emulate. Most of us fall in the middle, bringing some skills to teaching but also ready to benefit and grow from teacher preparation and practice teaching.

In this chapter, we present recent research findings on effective instruction, focusing on a core set of skills that comprise good teaching. We also detail the prevailing models of instruction, such as cooperative learning and problem-based learning, classroom approaches that have become particularly popular in recent years. You may draw on these skills and models in your own classroom, selecting those that best fit your subject, students, and purpose.

Are Teachers Born, or Made?

Think about the best teacher you ever had: Try to evoke a clear mental image of what this teacher was like. Here is what some of today's teachers say about their favorite teachers from the past:

> The teacher I remember was charismatic. Going to his class was like attending a Broadway show. But it wasn't just entertainment. He made me understand things. We went step-by-step in such a clear way that I never seemed to get confused—even when we discussed the most difficult subject matter.

> I never watched the clock in my English teacher's class. I never counted how many times she said uh-huh or okay or paused—as I did in some other classes. She made literature come alive—I was always surprised—and sorry—when the bell rang.

> When I had a problem, I felt like I could talk about it with Mrs. Garcia. She was my fifth-grade teacher, and she never made me feel dumb or stupid—even when I had so much trouble with math. After I finished talking to her, I felt as if I could do anything.

> For most of my life, I hated history—endlessly memorizing those facts, figures, dates. I forgot them as soon as the test was over. One year I even threw my history book in the river. But Mr. Cohen taught history in such a way that I could understand the big picture. He asked such interesting, provocative questions—about our past and the lessons it gave for our future.

The debate has been raging for decades: Are teachers born, or made? What do you think?

If you think it is a combination of both, you are in agreement with most people who have seriously considered this question. Some individuals—a rare few—are naturally gifted teachers. Their classrooms are dazzlingly alive. Students are motivated and excited, and their enthusiasm translates into academic achievement. For these truly talented educators, teaching seems to be pure art or magic.

But, behind even the most brilliant teaching performance, there is usually well-practiced skill at work. Look again at those brief descriptions of favorite teachers: Each of them used proven skills—structure, motivation, clarity, high expectations, and effective questioning.

> "We went step-by-step in such a clear way that I never seemed to get confused—even when we discussed the most difficult subject matter." *(structure and clarity)*

> "She made literature come alive." *(motivation)*

> "After I finished talking to her, I felt as if I could do anything." *(high expectations)*

> "He asked such interesting, provocative questions—about our past and the lessons it gave for our future." *(questioning)*

Although there is ample room for natural talent, most teaching is based on "tried and true" skills and models. See Figure 3.1 for a student view of teaching effectiveness. This chapter will introduce you to the research that you can put to work in your classroom.

FIGURE 3.1
Effective teaching through the eyes of students.

REFLECTION

So when you were a kid, how would you have described an effective teacher? Begin to answer the question in the empty writing space.

The Mysterious Case of Teacher Effectiveness

In this chapter, we describe what research tells us about teaching skills and models of instruction that raise student achievement. Some of these research findings may seem like common sense, part of the folk wisdom about teaching. In other cases, the research findings will seem surprisingly counterintuitive, exactly what you thought was not true. Research helps us distinguish between what we "think" will work and what really works. If you decide to teach, it will be your responsibility to keep up with the burgeoning and sometimes shifting **teacher effectiveness** research through conferences, course work, and education journals.[1] For now, let's introduce you to the research on teacher effectiveness.

Academic Learning Time

Research shows that students who spend more time pursuing academic content achieve more. That's the commonsense part, and it's hardly surprising. What is startling is how differently teachers use their classroom time. For example, the classic Beginning Teacher Evaluation Study[2] showed that one teacher in the Los Angeles school system spent 68 minutes a day on reading, whereas another spent 137 minutes; one elementary school teacher spent only 16 minutes per day on mathematics, whereas another spent more than three times that amount. Similarly, **John Goodlad's** comprehensive research study, ***A Place Called School,*** found that some schools devote approximately 65 percent of their time to instruction, whereas others devote almost 90 percent.[3] The variation is enormous.

Although allocating adequate time to academic content is obviously important, making time on the schedule is not enough. How this allocated time is used in the classroom is the real key to student achievement. To analyze the use of classroom time, researchers have developed the following terms: allocated time, engaged time, and academic learning time.

Allocated time is the time a teacher schedules for a subject—for example, thirty minutes a day for math. The more time allocated for a subject, the higher student achievement in that subject is likely to be.

Engaged time is that part of allocated time in which students are actively involved with academic subject matter (intently listening to a lecture, participating in a class discussion, writing an essay, solving math problems). When students daydream, doodle, write notes to each other, talk with their peers about nonacademic topics, or simply wait for instructions, they are not involved in engaged time. When there is more engaged time within allocated time, student achievement increases[4]. As with allocated time, the amount of time students are engaged with the subject matter varies enormously from teacher to teacher and school to school. In some classes, engaged time is 50 percent; in others, it is more than 90 percent.

Academic learning time is engaged time with a high success rate. Many researchers suggest that students should get 70 to 80 percent of the answers right when working with a teacher. When working independently, and without a teacher available to make corrections, the success rate should be even higher if students are to learn effectively. Some teachers are skeptical when they hear these percentages; they think that experiencing difficulty "stretches" students and helps them achieve. However, studies indicate that a high success rate is positively related

Academic learning time is engaged learning time in which students have a high success rate. When working independently, as here, the success rate should be particularly high.

to student achievement. How effectively teachers provide for and manage academic learning time in their classrooms is an important key in determining student achievement.[5]

In the following sections, you will learn about research-based teaching skills that you can use to increase academic learning time and student achievement. Since much time can be frittered away on organizational details and minor student disruptions, we will look first at effective strategies for classroom management. Then we will consider the instructional skills that seem consistently to produce higher academic achievement in students.

Classroom Management

As 10-year-old Lynette approached the room, she could hear the noise of her classmates. So this was going to be her fourth-grade class. Students were running everywhere. Some were drawing on the board; others were playing tag behind the library shelves. A fight seemed to be breaking out in the coat room. "Where is the teacher?" Lynette wondered. School was supposed to have started five minutes ago.

• • •

As Alicia headed to her fourth-grade classroom, she could see a smiling woman with glasses standing in the doorway and greeting students. "Hello, I'm Mrs. Michaelson," she said. "And you are?"

"Alicia Garza."

"I'm so glad you'll be in our class this year. Your seat is in the second row. Go to your desk right now and you'll find a paper you will need to fill out. It's a special interview form—everyone in the class has one—and it will give us a chance to get to know each other better. Be sure to look at the classroom rules posted on the board as you go in. These are very important for all of us, and I want us to discuss these rules this morning."

As Alicia entered the room, she stopped a minute to read the classroom rules:

1. Respect other people's rights and feelings. Avoid teasing and making fun of others.

2. Raise your hand to talk. Also, raise your hand if you need help. Share your time and efforts with others. Listening is as important as speaking.

3. Respect other people's property and places. Move around the room safely, and do not disturb others.

4. If you think of a rule that will help us all live and work together more effectively, please share it with us at any time.

Walking to her desk, Alicia noticed that many students, some unknown and some familiar, were already filling out their forms, and many were quietly giggling as they did so.

"I wonder what's on that form," thought Alicia as she slipped into her seat.

These are two different classrooms on the first day of school—in those first five minutes, it becomes obvious that the students will have two very different educational experiences.

The classroom management approach used by the second grade teacher at Johnson Elementary School was not appreciated by parent Denise W. Her 7-year-old son was confined to a three foot high cardboard cubicle at the back of his class. While the cubicle met the teacher's need to reduce classroom distractions, it also reduced one student's ability to follow instruction. *Now I know why he hates school*, said Ms. W.

SOURCE: The American School Board Journal, February 1998.

REFLECTION

Have you ever experienced or witnessed a teacher's inappropriate attempt to manage behavior? Describe it. Can you recall a particularly wise and effective management strategy? Which image is more powerful and why?

OLC Click on *In the News* for recent *In the News* stories. Submit your own *In the News* summary to share with your colleagues.

Research shows that effective classroom managers are nearly always good planners.[6] They do not enter a room late, after noise and disruption have had a chance to build. They are waiting at the door when the children come in. Starting from the very first day of school, they teach standards or norms of appropriate student behavior, actively and directly. Often they model procedures for getting assistance, leaving the room, going to the pencil sharpener, and the like. The more important rules of classroom behavior are posted, as are the consequences of not following them.[7]

Following are three basic principles for setting expectations, in order to develop a classroom community: (1) rules should be few in number, (2) they should seem fair and reasonable to students, and (3) rules should fit the growth and maturation of the students. Not too long ago (perhaps when you were in school), rules meant obeying the teacher, being quiet, and not misbehaving. As schools have moved away from autocratic teaching styles, student responsibility and ownership of rules (or as one teacher calls them "Habits of Goodness") have become more central.

Student participation in rule formation can be handled in several ways. Some teachers like to develop the list of rules together with their students; other teachers prefer to present a list of established practices and ask students to give specific examples or to provide reasons for having such rules. When rules are easily understood and convey a sense of moral fairness, most students will comply.

Good managers also carefully arrange their classrooms to minimize disturbances, provide students with a sense of confidence and security, and make sure that instruction can proceed efficiently. They set up their rooms according to the following principles:

- *Teachers should be able to see all students at all times*. Student desks should be arranged so the teacher can see everybody from any instructional area. With all students in a direct line of sight, a teacher's nonverbal cues can often short-circuit off-task student behaviors.

INTERACTIVE ACTIVITY CREATE A CLASSROOM
Move classroom furniture around to create your own effectively organized classroom.

- *Teaching materials and supplies should be readily available.* Arranging a "self-help" area so that students have direct access to supplies encourages individual responsibility while freeing up the teacher to focus on instructional activities.

- *High-traffic areas should be free of congestion.* Place student desks away from supply cabinets, pencil sharpeners, and so on. Minor disturbances ripple out, distracting other students from their tasks.

- *Students should be able to see instructional presentations.* Research shows that students who are seated far away from the teacher or the instructional activity are less likely to be involved in class discussions. Good teachers see the entire classroom as their stage, and they intentionally teach from different areas of the class. Placing instructional materials (video monitor, overhead projector, demonstration activity, flip chart, lab station, and the like) in various parts of the room gives each student "the best seat in the house" for at least part of the teaching day.

- *Procedures and routines should be actively taught in the same way that academic content is taught.* Initial planning and organization reduce time wasted on discipline problems and more quickly establish classroom routines and procedures.[8] For students who come from chaotic home environments, these routines offer a sense of stability. Once established, they allow teachers and students more time for academic learning.

The observer walked to the back of the room and sat down. It seemed to him that the classroom was a beehive of activity. A reading group was in progress in the front of the room, while the other children were working with partners on math examples. The classroom was filled with a hum of children working together, and in several languages—but the activity and the noise were organized and not chaotic.

The observer had been in enough schools over the past twenty years to know that this well-managed classroom did not result from magic but that carefully established and maintained procedures were at work. The observer scrutinized the classroom, searching for the procedures that allowed twenty-six students and one teacher to work together so industriously, harmoniously, and effectively.

First he examined the reading group, where the teacher was leading a discussion about the meaning of a story. "Why was Tony worried about the trip he was going to take?" the teacher asked (a few seconds' pause, all the children with eyes on the teacher, several hands raised). "Sean?"

As Sean began his response, the observer's eyes wandered around the rest of the room, where most of the children were busy at work. Two girls, however, were passing notes surreptitiously in the corner of the room.

During a quick sweep of the room, the teacher spotted the misbehavior. The two girls watched the teacher frown and put her finger over her lips. They quickly returned to their work. The exchange had been so rapid and so quiet that the reading group was not interrupted for even a second.

Another student in the math group had his hand raised. The teacher motioned Omar to come to her side.

"Look for the paragraph in your story that tells how Tony felt after his visit to his grandmother," the teacher instructed the reading group. "When you have found it, raise your hands."

While the reading group looked for the appropriate passage, the teacher quietly assisted Omar. In less than a minute, Omar was back at his seat, and the teacher was once again discussing the story with her reading group.

Modern classrooms are complex environments that require carefully planned rules and routines.

At 10:15, the teacher sent the reading group back to their seats and quietly counted down from ten to one. As she approached one, the room became quiet and the students' attention was focused on her. "It is now time for social studies. Before you do anything, listen carefully to *all* my instructions. When I tap the bell on my desk, those working on math should put their papers in their cubbies for now. You may have a chance to finish them later. Then all students should take out their social studies books and turn to page 67. When you hear the sound of the bell, I want you to follow those instructions." After a second's pause, the teacher tapped the bell, and the class was once again a sea of motion, but it was motion that the teacher had organized while the students were now taking responsibility for their own learning.

The observer made some notes on his forms. There was nothing particularly flashy or dramatic about what he had seen. It was not the type of theatrical performance that teachers sometimes put on to dazzle him. But he was satisfied, because he knew he had been witnessing a well-managed classroom.

• • •

Can you remember from your childhood those activity books in which you had to find the five things wrong in a picture? Let us reverse the game: Try rereading this classroom vignette and look for all the things that are *right* with the picture. What could the observer have noted about the teacher's behavior and her procedures that enabled her students to focus on academic content so effectively? Underline four or five examples of what the teacher did well.

In well-managed classes where teachers keep the momentum going, students are more likely to be on task. The teacher in this vignette used several strategies to avoid interruptions and to keep instruction proceeding smoothly.[9] Did you notice that

1. The teacher used a questioning technique known as **group alerting** to keep the reading group involved. By asking questions first and then naming the student to respond, she kept all the students awake and on their toes. If she had said,

"Sean, why did Tony feel concerned about his trip?" the other students in the group would have been less concerned about paying attention and answering the question. Instead, she asked her question first and then called on a student to respond.

2. The teacher seemed to have "eyes in the back of her head." Termed **withitness** by researcher Jacob Kounin, this quality characterizes teachers who are aware of student behavior in all parts of the room at all times. While the teacher was conducting the reading group, she was aware of the students passing notes and the one who needed assistance.

3. The teacher was able to attend to interruptions or behavior problems while continuing the lesson. Kounin calls the ability to do several things at once **overlapping**. The teacher reprimanded the students passing notes and helped another child with a math problem without interrupting the flow of her reading lesson.

4. The teacher managed routine misbehavior using the principle of **least intervention.** Since research shows the time spent disciplining students is negatively related to achievement, teachers should use the simplest intervention that will work. In this case, the teacher did not make a mountain out of a molehill. She intervened quietly and quickly to stop students from passing notes. Her nonverbal cue was all that was necessary, and did not disrupt the students working on math and reading. The teacher might also have used some other effective strategies. She could have praised the students who were attending to their math ("I'm glad to see so many partners working well on their math assignments"). If it had been necessary to say more to the girls passing notes, she should have alerted them to what they *should* be doing, rather than emphasize their misbehavior ("Deanne and U-Mei, please attend to your own work," *not* "Deanne and U-Mei, stop passing notes").

Good classroom management requires constant monitoring of student behavior.

5. The teacher managed the transition from one lesson to the next smoothly and effectively, avoiding a bumpy transition, which Kounin termed **fragmentation**. When students must move from one activity to another, a gap is created in the fabric of instruction. Chaos can result when transitions are not handled competently by the instructor. Did you notice that the teacher gave a clear transition signal, either the countdown or the bell; gave thorough instructions so her students would know exactly what to do next; and made the transition all at once for the entire class? These may seem simple, commonsense behaviors, but countless classes have come apart at the seams because transitions were not handled effectively.

This vignette illustrated routine classroom management and the handling of minor rule infractions. Sometimes teachers, of course, face more serious misbehavior, especially but not exclusively with older students. When students do not obey a simple reminder, the teacher should repeat the warning, clearly stating the appropriate behavior. If this fails, the teacher will need to apply stronger consequences, such as sending the student to the school office or calling the parents. When teachers must apply such consequences, these should immediately follow the inappropriate behavior, should be mildly but not severely unpleasant, and should be as brief as possible.[10] These episodes should communicate the message "I care about you, but I will not tolerate inappropriate behavior."

A child's rage can result from abuse, powerlessness, trauma, and even normal living, events beyond the teacher's power to alter. Nonetheless, teachers must understand and manage student anger and aggression. Several classroom strategies can help:

- *Choice.* Constantly taking away privileges and threatening punishment can cause students to feel intimidated and victimized. Teachers can provide appropriate options to give a student a sense of some control and freedom. Encouraging a student to select a lunch mate or to choose a project topic offers a reasonable decision-making opportunity and can help avoid aggression and rage.

- *Voice.* Listening to young people is one of the most respectful skills a teacher can model. Students who feel they are not heard feel disrespected. Hearing and honoring students' words (and feelings) reduce the likelihood of misbehavior.

- *Responsibility.* Rechanneling student energy and interest into constructive activities and responsibilities can reduce misbehavior. When instruction is meaningful and worthwhile, boredom and fooling around are less likely to occur.[11] When students are empowered, they are less likely to vent rage.[12]

Student misbehavior challenges most new teachers even more than leading instructional lessons. You will have students who will test your patience and others whose stories will tear at your heart. Being observant of student behaviors that might signal a problem is always a good idea. As newspaper stories too frequently remind us, student problems can sometimes explode into tragic violence.

While we can't always detect the signs of danger, we can be on the lookout and can create management plans to handle small distractions as well as major incidents. As researcher David Berliner says, "In short, from the opening bell to the end of the day, the better classroom managers are thinking ahead. While maintaining a pleasant classroom atmosphere, these teachers keep planning how to organize, manage, and control activities to facilitate instruction."[13] Berliner makes an important

Teachers must manage more than thirty major **transitions** every day, from one content area to another, through different instructional activities and through a myriad of routines, including having students line up, collecting papers, distributing texts, and the like. During these transitions, discipline problems occur twice as often as in regular classroom instruction. Classroom management expert **Jacob Kounin** identified five common patterns that can derail classroom management during times of transition:

- **Flip-flops.** In this negative pattern, the teacher terminates one activity, begins a new one, and then flops back to the original activity. For example, in making a transition from math to spelling, the teacher says, "Please open your spelling books to page 29. By the way, how many of you got all the math problems right?"

- **Overdwelling.** This bad habit includes preaching, nagging, and spending more time than necessary to correct an infraction of classroom rules. "Anna, I told you to stop talking. If I've told you once, I've told you 100 times. I told you yesterday and the day before that. The way things are going, I'll be telling it to you all year, and, believe me, I'm getting pretty tired of it. And another thing, young lady . . ."

- **Fragmentation.** In this bumpy transition, the teacher breaks directions into several choppy steps instead of accomplishing the instructions in one fluid unit—for example, "Put away your reading books. You shouldn't have any spelling books on your desk, either. All notes should be off your desk," instead of the simpler and more effective "Clear your desk of all books and papers."

- **Thrusts.** Classroom momentum is interrupted by *non sequitors* and random thoughts that just seem to pop into the teacher's head—for example, the class is busily engaged in independent reading, when their quiet concentration is broken by the teacher, who says, "Where's Roberto? Wasn't he here earlier this morning?"

- **Dangles.** Similar to the thrust, this move involves starting something, only to leave it hanging or dangling—for example, "Richard, would you please read the first paragraph on page 94. Oh, class, did I tell you about the guest speaker we're having today? How could I have forgotten about that?"

SOURCE: Jacob Kounin, *Discipline and Group Management in Classrooms* (New York: Holt, Rinehart & Winston, 1970).

REFLECTION

Since each of the above patterns represents a problem, can you reword the dialogue to produce a more effective transition?

connection between management and instruction. Effective teachers, in addition to being good classroom managers, must also be good organizers of academic content and instruction.

The Pedagogical Cycle

How does one organize classroom life? Researcher **Arno Bellack** analyzed verbal exchanges between teachers and students and offers a fascinating insight into classroom organization, likening these interactions to a pedagogical game.[14] The game is so cyclical and occurs so frequently that many teachers and students do not even know that they are playing. There are four moves:

1. *Structure.* The teacher provides information, provides direction, and introduces the topics.

A time-out area, a visit to the principal, or an hour of detention are typical disciplinary practices in elementary, middle, and high school. What school-based discipline programs can you recall from your K–12 years? Are your recollections influenced by any first-hand experiences?

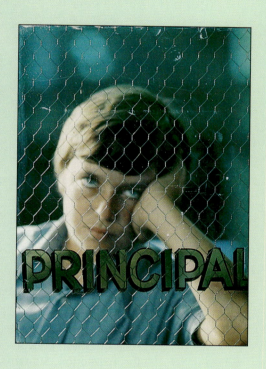

2. *Question.* The teacher asks a question.

3. *Respond.* The student answers the question, or tries to.

4. *React.* The teacher reacts to the student's answer and provides feedback.

These four steps make up a **pedagogical cycle,** diagrammed in Figure 3.2. Teachers initiate about 85 percent of the cycles, which are used over and over again in classroom interaction. When teachers learn to consciously enhance and refine each of the cycle's moves, student achievement is increased.[15]

FIGURE 3.2
Pedagogical cycle and sample classroom dialogue.

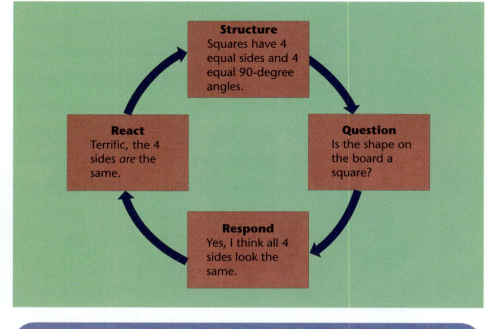

Structure
Squares have 4 equal sides and 4 equal 90-degree angles.

Question
Is the shape on the board a square?

Respond
Yes, I think all 4 sides look the same.

React
Terrific, the 4 sides *are* the same.

REFLECTION

Continue the classroom dialogue around the cycle again. What might the teacher and the student(s) say?

Clarity and Academic Structure

Have you ever been to a class where the teacher is bombarded with questions? "What are we supposed to do?" "Can you explain it again?" "What do you mean?" When such questions are constant, it is a sure sign that the teacher is not setting the stage for instruction. Students need a clear understanding of what they are expected to learn, and they need motivation to learn it.[16] Effective **academic structure** sets the stage for learning and occurs mainly at the beginning of the lesson. Although the specific structure will vary depending on the students' backgrounds and the difficulty of the subject matter, an effective academic structure usually consists of

- *Objectives.* Let the students know the objectives (or purpose) of each lesson. Students, like the teacher, need a road map of where they are going and why.

- *Review.* Help students review prior learning before presenting new information. If there is confusion, reteach.

- *Motivation.* Create an "anticipatory set" that motivates students to attend to the lesson. Consider throwing out an intriguing question, an anecdote, a joke, or a challenging riddle.

- *Transition.* Provide connections to help students integrate old and new information.

- *Clarification.* Break down a large body of information. (This is sometimes called "chunking.") Do not inundate students with too much too fast. This is particularly true for young children and slower learners, although it also applies to older and faster learners.

- *Scaffold.* Step-by-step practice and well-crafted questions support and encourage student understanding.[17]
- *Examples.* Give several examples and illustrations to explain main points and ideas.
- *Directions.* Give directions distinctly and slowly. If students are confused about what they are supposed to do, repeat or break information into small segments.
- *Enthusiasm.* Demonstrate personal enthusiasm for the academic content. Make it clear why the information is interesting and important.
- *Closure.* Close the lesson with a brief review or summary. If students are able to provide the summary, so much the better, for it shows that they have really understood the lesson.

The major activity in academic structuring takes place at the beginning of the lesson, but there may be several points throughout the lesson where substructuring or brief presentations of information are also necessary. Substructures initiate new pedagogical cycles and allow the discussion to continue. A clear summary or review is also important at the close of the lesson.

When teachers generate motivation and provide a clear introduction, all aspects of the lesson will proceed more smoothly.[18] Through effective and clear structure, the stage is set for the remaining steps of the pedagogical cycle.

Questioning

Good questioning is at the very core of good teaching. As John Dewey said,

> To question well is to teach well. In the skillful use of the question more than anything else lies the fine art of teaching; for in it we have the guide to clear and vivid ideas, and the quick spur to imagination, the stimulus to thought, the incentive to action.[19]

Since questioning is key in guiding learning, all students should have equal access to classroom questions and academic interaction, yet sitting in the same classroom taught by the same teacher, students experience significant differences in the number of questions they are asked. Research shows that male students are asked more questions than female students, and white students are asked more questions than non-white students. One of the reasons boys get to answer questions as well as to talk more is that they are assertive in grabbing teacher attention. Boys are more likely than girls to call out the answers to the questions. In addition, when boys call out the answers to questions, teachers are likely to accept their responses. When girls call out the answers, teachers often remind them to raise their hands. Teacher expectations also play a role and are frequently cited as one of the reasons white students (perceived as higher achievers) receive more questions and more active teacher attention than students who are members of other racial and ethnic groups.[20]

If you want all students, not just the quickest and most assertive, to answer questions, establish a protocol for participation. For example, make a rule that students must raise their hands and be called on before they may talk. Too many classes offer variations of the following scene:

TEACHER: How much is 60 + 4 + 12? *(Many students raise their hands—both girls and boys.)*

TONY: *(Shouts out)* 76!

TEACHER: Okay. How much is 50 + 9 + 8?

This scene, repeated again and again in classes across the country, is a typical example of the squeaky wheel—not necessarily the most needy or most deserving—getting the educational oil. Once you make the rule that students should raise their hands before participating, *hold to that rule.*

Many teachers are well-intentioned about having students raise their hands, but, in the rapid pace of classroom interaction, they sometimes forget their own rule. If you hold to that "wait to be recognized" rule, you can make professional decisions about who should answer which questions and why. If you give away this key to classroom participation, you are abandoning an important part of your professional decision making in the classroom.

There is more to managing classroom questions than taking the role of a traffic cop. For instance, you might assign pairs of students to work together (sometimes called "Think-Pair-Share") to develop and record answers and then present them to the class as a whole. Or perhaps teams of four or five students can be established to tackle academic questions on a regular basis. When students are actively involved in either of these approaches, the teacher can move around the room as a facilitator, answering questions, motivating student groups, and assessing how the groups are doing. More important, the students take ownership of the questions, asking sincere questions reflecting their genuine interests.

While the distribution and ownership of questions are important, the type of question asked is also meaningful. This section provides more information about the different levels of classroom questions, as well as strategies for using them fairly and effectively.

Many educators differentiate between factual, lower-order questions and thought-provoking, higher-order questions. Perhaps the most widely used system for determining the intellectual level of questions is Benjamin **Bloom's taxonomy,** which proceeds from the lowest level of questions, knowledge, to the highest level, evaluation.[21]

A **lower-order question** can be answered through memory and recall. For example, "What is the name of the largest Native American nation?" is a lower-order question. Without consulting outside references, one could respond with the correct answer only by remembering previously learned information. (Cherokee for those who do not recall.) Students either know the answer or they don't. Research indicates that 70 to 95 percent of a teacher's questions are lower-order.

A **higher-order question** demands more thought and usually more time before students reach a response. These questions may ask for evaluations, comparisons, causal relationships, problem solving, or divergent, open-ended thinking. Following are examples of higher-order questions:

1. Do you think that William Clinton was an effective president? Why or why not?

2. What similarities in theme emerge in the three Coen movies: *Oh Brother, Where Art Thou, Raising Arizona,* and *Fargo*?

3. Considering changes that have taken place in the past decade, describe the impact of computer technology on campus life.

4. Considering what you have learned in this child care course, if an infant is persistently crying, what are three things you might try to calm the child?

5. What could happen if our shadows came to life?

Although higher-order questions have been shown to produce increased student achievement, most teachers ask very few of them.[22]

**INTERACTIVE ACTIVITY
QUESTIONING LEVELS**
Match questions to the
different questioning
levels.

LEVEL I: KNOWLEDGE

Requires student to recall or recognize information. Student must rely on memory or senses to provide the answer.

Sample Questions

What does "quixotic" mean?

List the first ten presidents of the United States.

LEVEL II: COMPREHENSION

Requires student to go beyond simple recall and demonstrate the ability to mentally arrange and organize information. Student must use previously learned information by putting it in his or her own words and rephrasing it.

Sample Question

In our story, the author discusses why the family left Oklahoma. Can you summarize why in your own words?

LEVEL III: APPLICATION

Requires student to apply previously learned information to answer a problem. At this level the student uses a rule, a definition, a classification system, or directions in solving a problem with specific correct answer.

Sample Questions

Applying the law of supply and demand, solve the following problem. *(applying a rule)*

Identify the proper noun in the following sentences. *(applying a definition)*

Solve the quadratic equation. *(applying a rule)*

LEVEL IV: ANALYSIS

Requires student to use three kinds of cognitive processes: (1) To identify causes, reasons, or motives (when these have not been provided to the student previously), (2) To analyze information to reach a generalization or conclusion, (3) To find evidence to support a specific opinion, event, or situation.

Sample Questions

Why do you think King Lear misjudged his daughter? *(identifying motives)*

What generalizations can you make about the climate of Egypt near the Nile River basin? *(analyze information to reach a conclusion)*

Many historians think that Abraham Lincoln was our finest president. What evidence can you find to support this statement? *(find evidence to support a specific opinion)*

LEVEL V: SYNTHESIS

Requires student to use original and creative thinking: (1) To develop original communications, (2) To make predictions, and (3) To solve problems for which there is no single right answer.

Sample Questions

Write a short story about life on another planet. *(developing an original communication)*

What do you think life would be like if Germany had won World War II? *(making predictions)*

How can our class raise money for the dance festival? *(solving problems for which there is no single right solution)*

LEVEL VI: EVALUATION

Requires student to judge the merits of an aesthetic work, an idea, or the solution to a problem.

Sample Questions

Which U.S. senator do you think is most effective? Support your selection.

Do you think that schools are too hard or not hard enough? Explain your answer.

REFLECTION

Starting with your own sample question at Level I (Knowledge) can you expand your questioning to Level VI (Evaluation)? Or, using Bloom's taxonomy as the content, create a question at each level about this classification system (e.g., Level I; List the six levels of Bloom's Taxonomy).

Many educators think that different questioning levels stimulate different levels of thought. If you ask a fifth-grade student to define an adjective, you are working on lower-level basic skills. If you ask a fifth-grade student to write a short story, making effective use of adjectives, you are working on a higher level of student achievement. Both lower-order and higher-order questions are important and should be matched to appropriate instructional goals:

Ask lower-order questions when students are

- Being introduced to new information
- Working on drill and practice
- Reviewing previously learned information

Ask higher-order questions when students are

- Working on problem-solving skills
- Involved in a creative or affective discussion
- Asked to make judgments about quality, aesthetics, or ethics
- Challenged to manipulate already established information in more sophisticated ways

Student Response

If you were to spend a few minutes in a high school English class, you might hear a classroom discussion go something like this:

TEACHER: Who wrote the poem "Stopping by Woods on a Snowy Evening"? Tomàs?

TOMÀS: Robert Frost.

TEACHER: Good. What action takes place in the poem? Kenisha?

KENISHA: A man stops his sleigh to watch the woods get filled with snow.

TEACHER: Yes. Denise, what thoughts go through the man's mind?

DENISE: He thinks how beautiful the woods are. *(Pauses for a second)*

TEACHER: What else does he think about? Russell?

RUSSELL: He thinks how he would like to stay and watch. *(Pauses for a second)*

TEACHER: Yes—and what else? Rita? *(Waits half a second)* Come on, Rita, you can answer this. *(Waits half a second)* Well, why does he feel he can't stay there indefinitely and watch the woods and the snow?

RITA: He knows he's too busy. He's got too many things to do to stay there for so long.

TEACHER: Good. In the poem's last line, the man says that he has miles to go before he sleeps. What might sleep be a symbol for? Krista?

KRISTA: Well, I think it might be . . . *(Pauses for a second)*

TEACHER: Think, Krista. *(Waits for half a second)* All right then—Eugene? *(Waits again for half a second)* James? *(Waits half a second)* What's the matter with everyone today? Didn't you do the reading?[23]

The teacher is using several instructional skills effectively. His is a well-managed classroom. The students are on task and engaged in a discussion appropriate to the academic content. By asking a series of lower-order questions ("Who wrote the poem?"

"What action takes place in the poem?"), the teacher works with the students to establish an information base. Then the teacher builds to higher-order questions about the poem's theme and meaning.

If you were to give this teacher suggestions on how to improve his questioning techniques, you might point out the difficulty students have in answering the more complex questions. You might also note the lightning pace at which this lesson proceeds. The teacher fires questions so rapidly that the students barely have time to think. This is not so troublesome when they are answering factual questions that require a brief memorized response. However, students begin to flounder when they are required to answer more complex questions with equal speed.

Although it is important to keep classroom discussion moving at a brisk pace, sometimes teachers push forward too rapidly. Slowing down at two key places during classroom discussion can usually improve the effectiveness and equity of classroom responses. In the research on classroom interaction, this slowing down is called **wait time.**[24]

Mary Budd Rowe's research on wait time shows that, after asking a question, teachers typically wait only one second or less for a student response (wait time 1). If the response is not forthcoming in that time, teachers rephrase the question, ask another student to answer it, or answer it themselves. If teachers can learn to increase their wait time from one second to three to five seconds, significant improvements in the quantity and quality of student response usually will take place.

There is another point in classroom discussion when wait time can be increased. After students complete an answer, teachers often begin their reaction or their next question before a second has passed (wait time 2). Once again, it is important for teachers to increase their wait time from one second to three to five seconds. Based on her research, Mary Budd Rowe has determined that increasing the pause after a student gives an answer is equally as important as increasing wait time 1, the pause after the teacher asks a question. When wait time 1 and wait time 2 are increased, classroom interaction is changed in several positive ways.

Teacher questioning patterns have much to do with the learning climate in classrooms.

Changes in Student Behavior

- More students participate in discussion.
- Fewer discipline problems disrupt the class.
- The length of student response increases dramatically.
- Students are more likely to support their statements with evidence.
- Speculative thinking increases.
- There are more student questions and fewer failures to respond.
- Student achievement increases on written tests that measure more complex levels of thinking.

Changes in Teacher Behavior

- Teacher comments are less disjointed and more fluent. Classroom discussion becomes more logical, thoughtful, and coherent.
- Teachers ask more sophisticated, higher-order questions.
- Teachers begin to hold higher expectations for all students.

Research indicates that teachers give more wait time to students for whom they hold higher expectations. A high-achieving student is more likely to get time to think than is a low-achieving student. If we do not expect much from our students, we will not get much. High expectations and longer wait time are positively related to achievement. Researchers suggest that white male students, particularly high achievers, are more likely to be given adequate wait time than are females and students of color. Students who are quiet and reserved or who think more slowly may obtain special benefit from increased wait time. In fact, a key benefit of extended wait time is an increase in the quality of student participation, even from students who were previously silent.

Usually when teachers learn that they are giving students less than a second to think, they are surprised and have every intention of waiting longer, but that is easier said than done! In the hectic arena of the classroom, it is all too easy to slip into split-second question-and-answer patterns.

Sometimes teachers fall into a pattern of quickly repeating every answer that students give. Occasionally this repetition can be helpful—if some students may not have heard it or if an answer merits repetition for emphasis. In most cases, however, this "teacher echo" is counterproductive. Students learn they do not need to listen to one another, because the teacher will repeat the answer anyway. The teacher echo also reduces valuable wait time and cuts down on the pause that allows students to think. Teachers who have worked on increasing wait time offer some useful tips.

Some teachers adopt self-monitoring cues to slow themselves down at the two key wait-time points. For example, one teacher says that he puts his hand behind his back and counts on his fingers for three seconds to slow himself down. Another teacher says that she covers her mouth with her hand (in a thoughtful pose) to keep herself from talking and thereby destroying "the pause that lets them think."

As mentioned previously, wait time is more important in some cases than in others. If you are asking students to repeat previously memorized math facts and you are interested in developing speed, a three- to five-second wait time may be counterproductive. However, if you have asked a higher-order question that calls for a complicated answer, be sure that wait times 1 and 2 are ample. Simply put, students, like the rest of us, need time to think, and some students may need more wait time than others. For example, when a student speaks English as a newly acquired language, additional wait time could help that student accurately translate and respond to the question. And many of us could profit by less impulsive, more thoughtful responses, the kind that can be engendered by a five-second wait time.

When teachers allow more wait time, the results can be surprising. Not only do more students answer questions, there is also an increase in **student-initiated questions.** While many educators believe that questioning is at the heart of learning, students ask remarkably few content-related questions. (Students in the upper grades ask fewer than 15 percent of classroom questions.)[25] Teachers can nourish genuine inquiry and tap student curiosity by encouraging student-initiated questions. As one teacher said, "I never thought Andrea had anything to say. She just used to sit there like a bump on a log. Then I tried calling on her and giving her time to answer. What a difference! Not only does she answer, she asks questions that no one else has thought of."

Reaction or Productive Feedback

"Today," the student teacher said, "we are going to hear the story of *The Three Billy Goats Gruff*." A murmur of anticipation rippled through the kindergarten children comfortably seated on the carpet around the flannel board. This student teacher was a favorite, and the children were particularly happy when she told them flannel-board stories.

"Before we begin the story, I want to make sure we know what all the words mean. Who can tell me what a troll is?"

A 5-year-old nicknamed B.J. raised his hand. "A troll is someone who walks you home from school."

"Okay," the teacher responded, a slightly puzzled look flickering over her face. "Who else can tell me what a troll is?"

Another student chimed in, "A troll is someone with white hair sticking out of his head."

"Okay," the teacher said.

Another student volunteered, "It hides under bridges and waits for you and scares you."

"Uh-huh," said the teacher.

Warming to the topic, another student gleefully recounted, "I saw a green troll named Shrek who lives in the woods."

"Okay," the teacher said.

Wide-eyed, B.J. raised his hand again, "I'm sure glad we had this talk about trolls," he said. "I'm not going home with them from school anymore."

"Okay," the teacher said.

This is a classroom in which several good teaching strategies are in operation. The teacher uses effective academic structure, and the students are on task, interested, and involved in the learning activity. The teacher is asking lower-order questions appropriately, to make sure the students know key vocabulary words before the flannel-board story is told. The problem with this classroom lies in the fourth stage of the pedagogical cycle: This teacher does not provide specific reactions and adequate feedback. Did you notice that the teacher reacted with "uh-huh" or "OK," no matter what kind of answer the students gave? Because of this vague feedback and "OK" teaching style, B.J. was left confused about the difference between a troll and a patrol. This real-life incident may seem amusing, but there was nothing funny to B.J., who was genuinely afraid to leave school with the patrol.

Recently, attention has been directed not only at how teachers ask questions but also at how they respond to student answers. When we analyzed classroom

Quickly mastering names connects you with your students. Some of you will be stellar, able to peg everyone's name from day one. Others may remember only a few names at first, or struggle with pronunciation. Yet, using student names builds your rapport and their self-esteem.

But a popular name today is gone tomorrow and our growing diversity all but ensures that some names on your roster may be unfamiliar. See how the past century has influenced names. Start practicing now with names of children born in 2000!

Most popular names for children born in 1900 (U.S.)				Most popular names for children born in 2000 (U.S.)		
	Male	Female			Male	Female
1.	John	Mary		1.	Jacob	Emily
2.	William	Helen		2.	Michael	Hannah
3.	James	Margaret		3.	Matthew	Madison
4.	George	Anna		4.	Joshua	Ashley
5.	Joseph	Ruth		5.	Christopher	Sarah

In the year 2000, less frequently chosen names (from the bottom of the list) included Zander, Dontae, Kaycee, and Kaylan.

SOURCE: www.ssa.gov/OACT/NOTES/note139/note139.html. The data comes from a sampling of Social Security card applications, depending upon data available at the time.

REFLECTION

Some theorists suggest that we first learn the names we use the most—the students who are discipline problems. What tricks do you possess that will help you to learn every student's name? Trade strategies with classmates.

interaction in more than 100 classrooms in five states, we found that teachers generally use four types of reactions:

1. **Praise.** Positive comments about student work, such as "Excellent, good job."

2. **Acceptance.** Comments such as "Uh-huh" and "OK," which acknowledge that student answers are acceptable. These are not as strong as praise.

3. **Remediation.** Comments that encourage a more accurate student response or encourage students to think more clearly, creatively, or logically. Sample remediation comments include "Try again," "Sharpen your answer," and "Check your addition."

4. **Criticism.** A clear statement that an answer is inaccurate or a behavior is inappropriate. This category includes harsh criticism ("This is a terrible paper"), as well as milder comments that simply indicate an answer is not correct ("Your answer to the third question is wrong.")[26]

Which of these reactions do you think teachers use most frequently? Did you notice that the kindergarten teacher relied heavily on the acceptance, or "okay," reaction? So do most teachers from grade school through graduate school. Our study found that acceptance was the most frequent response, accounting for more than half of all teacher reactions. The second most frequent teacher response was remediation, accounting for one-third of teacher reactions. Used infrequently, praise comprised

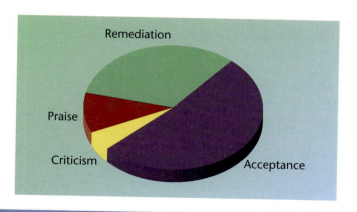

FIGURE 3.3
Teacher reactions.

REFLECTION

Most teacher reactions fall in the acceptance category. Suggest three reasons why this might occur.

only 11 percent of reactions. The rarest response was criticism. In two-thirds of the classrooms observed, teachers never told a student that an answer was incorrect. In the classrooms where criticism did occur, it accounted for only 5 percent of interaction. (See Figure 3.3.)

In *A Place Called School,* John Goodlad writes that "learning is enhanced when students understand what is expected of them, get recognition for their work, learn about their errors, and receive guidance in improving their performances."[27] But many students claim that they are not informed or corrected when they make mistakes. Perhaps this is caused by overreliance on the acceptance response, which is the vaguest kind of feedback that teachers can offer. Since there is more acceptance than praise, criticism, and remediation combined, some educators are beginning to wonder: "Is the 'OK' classroom OK?"

Although the acceptance response is legitimate and often appropriate, it is overused. Since achievement is likely to increase when students get clear, specific **productive feedback** about their answers, it is important for teachers to reduce the "OK" reaction and to be more varied and specific in the feedback they provide. Researcher **Jere Brophy** has done an analysis of praise and student achievement. He found that praise may be particularly important for low-achieving students and those from low socioeconomic backgrounds. Brophy found that it is best when

1. *Praise is contingent upon student performance.* Praise should closely follow student behavior the teacher wants to recognize.

2. *Praise is specific.* When teachers praise, they should clearly indicate what aspect of the student behavior is noteworthy (for instance, creative problem solving or good use of evidence to support an argument).

3. *Praise is sincere.* Praise should reflect the experiences, growth, and development of the individual student. Otherwise, it may be dismissed as being disingenuous.

4. *Praise lets students know about their competence and the importance of their accomplishments*—for instance, "The well-documented review of studies on your website and the connection you made between the two tobacco filters may eventually impact the industry."

5. *Praise attributes success to ability or effort*—for example, "Your analysis of the paintings of the Impressionists is excellent. I'll bet you spent a long time studying their work in the museum" *(attribution to effort).* Or "This story is fantastic. You've got a real flair for creative writing" *(attribution to ability).* When praise is attributed to abilities or effort, students know that successful performance is under their own control.

6. *Praise uses past performance as a context for describing present performance*—for example, "Last week you were really having trouble with your breast stroke kick. Now you've got it together—you've learned to push the water behind you and increase your speed."[28]

Just as students need to know when they are performing well, they need to know when their efforts are inadequate or incorrect. If students do not have information about their weak areas, they will find it difficult to improve.

1. *Corrective feedback is specific and contingent on student performance.* The teacher's comments should closely follow the student behavior the teacher wants to improve.

2. *Critical comments focus on student performance and are not of a personal nature.* All of us find it easier to accept constructive criticism when it is detached from our worth as a person, when it is not personal, hostile, or sarcastic.

3. *Feedback provides a clear blueprint for improvement.* If you merely tell a student that an answer is wrong and nothing more, the student has clear feedback on level of performance but no strategies for improvement. Effective feedback suggests an approach for attaining success, such as "Check your addition," "Use the bold headings as a reading guide when you study for the exams," or "Let's conjugate this verb in both French and English, to see where the error is."

4. *An environment is established that lets the student know it is acceptable to make mistakes.* "We learn from our errors. Hardly any inventions are perfected on the first try."

5. *Corrective feedback relates eventual success to effort.* "Now you have demonstrated the correct sequence in class. Give yourself a solid half-hour tonight working on this, and I bet that you will get most of it correct. I'll check with you tomorrow."

6. *Corrective feedback recognizes when students have made improvements in their performance.* "Last week you were having trouble identifying which of Newton's Laws are applicable in each of these time motion studies. Now you've mastered the skill. You've done a good job."

An "okay classroom" allows student error and misunderstanding to go uncorrected; it lets B.J. think that the patrol will eat him up after school. In classrooms where there is appropriate use of remediation and constructive criticism, students know not only when they have made mistakes but also how to correct them. They also recognize that this process leads to growth and achievement.

Variety in Process and Content

Variety is the spice of life, the saying goes—the spice of lessons also, because variety can enhance both teaching effectiveness and student achievement.[29] Have you ever listened to a lecture for an hour and found your initial interest lapsing into

daydreams? Have you ever watched a class begin a seatwork assignment with active concentration and found, after thirty minutes, that
involvement had turned into passing notes and
throwing paper airplanes? When the teacher
fails to provide sufficient variety, lessons become monotonous and students get off task.

Effective teachers provide **variety** in both
content and process. In elementary school, variety in content can involve moving from one
subject area to another. In secondary instruction, the move might be in the same subject
area, such as the switch from memorizing vocabulary to analyzing symbols in a short story.

As any savvy teacher knows, student interest
can be maintained by moving from one activity
to another during a single lesson. For example,
a 60-minute lesson on the American Revolution

A positive classroom
atmosphere that includes
precise, encouraging
feedback helps motivate
and guide student effort.

might begin with a 10-minute overview providing the structure for the class, then
move into a 15-minute question-and-answer session, then change to a 25-minute
video, and conclude with a 10-minute discussion and closure. Another motivation to
vary content and process in teaching is to accommodate different student learning
styles. Some students might miss what is said in a lecture (not being auditory learners), but easily get it when the teacher shows pictures (because the visual connection
is clear). Gardner's growing inventory of intelligences offers another strong argument
for instructional variety. Following is a sampler of activities teachers can use to maintain student interest by varying the pattern of the lesson.

discussions	student presentations	music activities
lectures	tests	art activities
films, videos, DVDs, PowerPoint	visits to websites	tutoring
	silent reading	spot quizzes
role plays	games	panel discussions
simulations	contests	brainstorming sessions
small-group activities	creative writing	students tutoring one another
software for individuals and groups	theater and drama	
	field trips	cooperative learning activities
guest speakers	boardwork	
independent seatwork	learning centers	debates
guided practice		

Many of the activities listed above can be described as "hands-on" or active learning and can be captivating for students, especially kinesthetic learners, but more is
needed. Variety alone will not produce achievement: Connections must be made, or
variety will be reduced to mere activity. Consider elementary students pasting animal
pictures on charts. The youngsters may be unable to explain what (if anything) they
are learning about animal families. Students in a middle school may be dressing up
for an evening on the Titanic. From the lower to the upper decks, their clothing and

accents change. Yet, if the students have not connected the deck classifications with societal class, the goal is gone. Challenging students with engaging activities is admirable. But the effort must have students' minds as well as their hands on the learning.[30]

Models for Effective Instruction

Part of the challenge for teachers is knowing which model of instruction to choose for particular educational purposes. The following four models differ dramatically from one another, yet each may find a productive use in your classroom.

Direct Teaching

Also called *systematic, active,* or *explicit teaching,* the **direct teaching** model emphasizes the importance of a structured lesson in which presentation of new information is followed by student practice and teacher feedback. In this model, which has emerged from extensive research, the role of the teacher is that of a strong leader, one who structures the classroom and sequences subject matter to reflect a clear academic focus.

Researchers put forward six principles of direct teaching. They say that effective teachers use these principles consistently and systematically:

1. *Daily review.* At the beginning of the lesson, teachers review prior learning. Frequently, teachers focus on assigned homework, clarify points of confusion, and provide extra practice for facts and skills that need more attention.

With direct teaching, teachers carefully explain what students must do to accomplish a task, then present a carefully structured lesson that is usually broken down into small, manageable steps.

2. *New material.* Teachers begin by letting students know the objectives to be attained. New information is broken down into smaller bits and is covered at a brisk pace. Teachers illustrate main points by with concrete examples. Teachers ask questions frequently to check for student understanding and to make sure that students are ready for independent work using new skills and knowledge.

3. *Guided practice.* Students use new skills and knowledge under direct teacher supervision. During guided practice, teachers ask many content questions ("What is the definition of a paragraph?") and many process questions ("How do you locate the topic sentence in a paragraph?"). Teachers check student responses for understanding, offering prompts and providing corrective feedback. Guided practice continues until students answer with approximately 70 to 80 percent accuracy.

4. *Specific feedback.* Correct answers to questions are acknowledged clearly, so that students will understand when their work is accurate. When student answers are hesitant, the teacher provides process feedback ("Yes, Juanita, that's correct because . . . "). Teachers correct inaccurate responses immediately, before errors become habitual. Frequent errors are a sign that students are not ready for independent work, and guided practice should continue.

5. *Independent practice.* Similar to guided practice, except that students work by themselves at their seats or at home. Independent practice continues until responses are assured, quick, and at a level of approximately 95 percent accuracy. Cooperative learning (see the next section) and student tutoring of one another are effective strategies during independent practice.

6. *Weekly and monthly reviews.* Regular reviews offer students the opportunity for more practice, a strategy related to high achievement. Barak Rosenshine, a pioneering researcher in developing the principles of direct teaching, recommends a weekly review every Monday, with a monthly review every fourth Monday.[31]

Direct teaching works well when you are teaching skill subjects, such as grammar or mathematics, or helping students master factual material. The direct teaching model is particularly helpful during the first stages of learning new and complex information, but it is less helpful when imaginative responses and student creativity is called for.

Cooperative Learning

In a classroom using **cooperative learning,** students work on activities in small, heterogeneous groups, and they often receive rewards or recognition based on the overall group performance. Although cooperative learning can be traced back to the 1920s, it seems startling or new because the typical classroom environment is frequently competitive. For example, when grading is done on a curve, one student's success is often detrimental to others. This competitive structure produces clear winners and losers, and only a limited number of *As* are possible. Sometimes classrooms are set up to be less competitive, incorporating independent study or learning contracts. In these cases, students work by themselves to reach individual learning goals. But a cooperative learning structure differs from even these less competitive practices, because students depend on one another and work together to reach shared goals.

According to researchers, cooperative learning groups work best when they meet the following criteria.[32] Groups should be *heterogeneous* and, at least at the beginning, should be *small,* perhaps limited to two to six members. Since face-to-face interaction is important, the groups should be *circular* to permit easy conversation. Positive *interdependence* among group members can be fostered by a *shared group goal, shared division of labor,* and *shared materials,* all contributing to a sense that the group sinks or swims together.

Robert Slavin, a pioneer in cooperative learning techniques, developed student team learning methods in which a team's work is not completed until all students on the team understand the material being studied.[33] Rewards are earned only when the entire team achieves the goals set by the teacher. Students tutor one another, so that everyone can succeed on individual quizzes, and each member of the group is accountable for learning. Since students contribute to their teams by improving prior scores, it does not matter whether the student is a high, average, or low achiever. Increased achievement by an individual student at any level contributes to the overall performance of the group, resulting in equal opportunity for success.

Research shows that cooperative learning promotes both intellectual and emotional growth:

- Students make higher achievement gains; this is especially true for math in the elementary grades.
- Students have higher levels of self-esteem and greater motivation to learn.
- Students have a stronger sense that classmates have positive regard for one another.
- Understanding and cooperation among students from different racial and ethnic backgrounds are enhanced.[34]

In cooperative learning situations, students' individual goals and rewards are tied into group accomplishments.

Yet the practical realities of cooperative learning are not all commendable. Some students, accustomed to starring roles in full class instruction, continue to dominate the small groups. Accurate grading requires an analysis of both the individual and group performance. And, even the most committed practitioners acknowledge that cooperative learning may take more time than direct teaching. Still, as ability grouping becomes more controversial, educators are growing increasingly interested in cooperative learning as a strategy for working successfully with mixed-ability groups and diverse classroom populations.

Mastery Learning

Based on Benjamin Bloom's Learning for Mastery model developed in 1968, **mastery learning** programs are committed to the credo that, given the right tools, all children can learn. Stemming from an individualized reward structure, these programs are in use from early childhood to graduate school.

Mastery learning programs require specific and carefully sequenced learning objectives. The first step is to identify a **behavioral objective,** a specific skill or academic task to be mastered. Students are taught the skill or material in the objective; then they are tested to determine if the objective has been reached. Students who complete the test successfully go on for acceleration or enrichment,

A veteran of the classroom for nearly five decades, Larry Cuban has examined America's schools from varying perspectives. He has been a professor at Stanford University and a teacher in an inner-city social studies classroom. But it was when Cuban was appointed superintendent in Arlington, Virginia, that Sharon Steindam first met him, and discovered some remarkable traits. Steindam, now Assistant Director of the National Study of School Evaluation, was a newly appointed school principal, and quite nervous about being evaluated by the new superintendent. But as she remembers, "He was the only superintendent that I worked for who truly used a variety of information about the school to help him determine how I was doing. He wanted to know why I felt certain students were doing well and others were not. And he was the most human superintendent I ever worked with. He would greet you in the grocery store and ask about your family. Cuban was a true leader, holding high expectations, providing meaningful feedback, and personally engaging."[1]

Cuban has witnessed many exciting efforts to reform and change America's schools. And yet, after sorting out nearly a century of change, he came to a fascinating insight: Teaching remains strikingly similar year in and year out. Despite the efforts of educational reformers to reshape the traditional teacher-centered classrooms of the past, most classrooms function much as they did when he was a child. In *How Teachers Taught: Constancy and Change in American Classrooms, 1890–1980,* Cuban explores why.

Historically, schools have been built around teachers, not students. Not just philosophically, but physically as well. Classrooms featured desks all facing front, bolted to the floor, physically reinforcing the notion that the teacher is the center of instruction. As if the nuts and bolts were not strong enough, the curriculum proved the clincher. To survive instructing very large classes in eight or ten subjects, teachers became dependent on reading and dictating assignments directly from the text. Uniformity and standardization were emphasized, and top-down management was the rule. Principals told teachers what to do, and teachers told students what to do. The organizational climate did not nurture new teaching techniques.

As if all these in-school barriers were not enough to defeat change, teacher training all but guaranteed that the status quo would be maintained. New teachers were brought into the profession through a modeling or an apprenticeship program, doing their student teaching under the tutelage of veteran, often conventional, older teachers. It was a system geared to the passing down of traditional approaches and conservative attitudes from one generation of teachers to the next.

Cuban also believes that the suppression of student-based instruction was no accident. Schools were designed to mold a compliant workforce; student-centered instruction was viewed as rebellious, dangerous, and threatening to educational and economic stability. "Basically, schools reflect the cultural, political, social, and economics status quo in the larger society. The school is not an institution apart—if anything, schools tend not to be at the forefront of change in society."[2]

Since the 1984 publication of *How Teachers Taught,* technology has been hailed for its promise to revolutionize teaching. To Cuban, it is another phony revolution. In studying effective classrooms, he notes that teachers are very concerned with choosing electronic tools that are efficient. Teachers ask: How much time and energy do I have to invest in learning to use the technology versus the return it will have for my students? When students use the technology, will there be disruption? Will it bolster or compromise my authority to maintain order and cultivate learning? Even teachers eager to make use of new technologies face a serious stumbling block, given the pressures to design curriculum around standardized tests. And comprehensive teacher training to use technology effectively is still lacking. Only a small fraction of teachers find the new technologies efficient. The result: "Computers become merely souped-up typewriters and classrooms continue to run much as they did a generation ago."[3]

While Cuban recognizes that classrooms have undergone a few minor reforms—experimenting with online learning, greater informality between teacher and student, and even movable chairs—he concludes that instruction at the dawn of the twenty-first century looks strikingly similar to classroom instruction nearly 100 years ago.

[1]Sharon Steindam, personal communication (June 26, 2001).

[2]Larry Cuban, *How Teachers Taught: Constancy and Change in American Classrooms, 1890–1980* (White Plains, NY: Longman, 1984).

[3]Larry Cuban, *Oversold and Underused: Computers in Classrooms 1980–2000* (Cambridge: Harvard University Press, 2001).

WRITE YOUR OWN PROFILE IN EDUCATION: Click on *Profiles in Education* and write a *Profile in Education* about an educator and post it on the Online Learning Center. Check out the *Profiles in Education* submitted by other future teachers.

To learn more about Larry Cuban, click on *Profiles in Education.*

REFLECTION

Do you agree with Cuban? Think of a few teaching reforms that are currently taking place in a school, district, or state. Which reforms do you think will stick? Why? Which instructional practices have remained constant? What factors contribute to their persistence?

while the students who fail to demonstrate mastery of the objective receive corrective instruction and are retested. The success of mastery learning rests on the *instructional alignment,* which is a close match between what is taught and what is tested.[35]

In mastery learning, students typically work at their own pace, perhaps at a computer terminal or with individualized written materials. The teacher provides assistance and facilitates student efforts, but mastery still remains a student responsibility. Since studies have shown that many students, particularly younger ones, find it hard to take charge of their own instruction, mastery learning programs highlight the role of the teacher as instructional leader, motivator, and guide. Mastery learning is often geared for large groups, and it can benefit from technology, since computers and appropriate software can be particularly effective in self-paced mastery of skills and knowledge.

Studies suggest that mastery learning can be beneficial, particularly for students at the elementary and middle school level, and especially in language arts and social studies classes. In mastery learning:

- Teachers have more positive attitudes toward teaching and higher expectations for their students.

- In general, students have more positive attitudes about learning and their ability to learn.

- Students achieve more and remember what they have learned longer.[36]

Problem-Based Learning

Problem-based learning (PBL) has been more successful in going beyond traditional subject area boundaries. Focusing on authentic or real-life problems is at the heart of PBL, and, as you might imagine, real problems are not bound by a single subject field or even by the school building. This emphasis is apparent in the other terms used to describe PBL: *experience-based education, project-based instruction,* and *anchored instruction* (because it is "anchored" in the real world). In this instructional model, a crucial aspect of the teacher's role is to identify activities that fuel students' interest, such as

- Design a plan for protecting a specific endangered species.
- Formulate solutions that might have kept the United States from plunging into a Civil War.
- How can we stop bullying and harassment in this school?
- How can pollution in a local river or bay or the ocean be checked, or even reversed?
- Develop a set of urban policies to halt the deterioration of a central city.
- How can the racism and sexism in this community be eliminated?

Finding scintillating questions and projects to excite and motivate students is critical, but it is only one aspect of PBL. Other characteristics include

- *Learner cooperation.* Similar to cooperative learning, PBL depends on small groups or pairs of students collaborating as they explore and investigate various issues. This approach de-emphasizes competition. For teachers, the goal is to guide and challenge a dozen such small groups simultaneously.
- *Higher-order thinking.* Exploring real and complex issues requires students to analyze, synthesize, and evaluate material.
- *Cross-disciplinary work.* PBL encourages students to investigate how different academic subjects shed light on each other. In exploring ecological issues, for example, students touch not only on biology and chemistry but also on economics, history, sociology, and political science.
- *Artifacts and exhibits.* Students involved in PBL demonstrate what they learn in a very tangible way. Students may produce a traditional report, or may create a video, a physical model, a computer program, a portfolio of artifacts, or even a presentation, such as a play or a debate. Teachers might organize a class or schoolwide exhibit to share the progress made by PBL students.
- *Authentic learning.* Students pursue an actual unresolved issue. They are expected to define the problem, develop a hypothesis, collect information, analyze that information, and suggest a conclusion, one that might work in the real world. The learning is authentic, not academic, artificial, or hypothetical.

While features of PBL have been around for a long time, in its current form it is both a comprehensive and demanding approach that develops real intellectual skills in students. Moreover, students function as adults in that they explore authentic contemporary issues. Working together, they attempt to solve these problems—in effect, getting a jump on the adult world, even before they are adults.[37]

Effective and Reflective Teaching

"Less is more," is an aphorism attributed to education reformer Ted Sizer. According to Sizer, today's schools are misguided in their emphasis on "covering" material. The goal seems to be teaching and learning a vast body of information, in order to have a sense of accomplishment, or to score well on the ever-growing number of standardized tests. But international tests in science, for example, show that, although U.S. students have studied more science topics than have students in other countries, they

At a middle school in Tennessee, students began collecting paper clips, one for every life destroyed in the Holocaust. It's not easy to appreciate the magnitude of the millions killed in Nazi death camps, so the teacher thought that paper clips could offer the students an insight into the enormity of the atrocity. They were also chosen because during World War II, Norwegians clipped them on their clothing in protest against Nazism. Once the word got out, over 18 million paper clips arrived from around the world, along with an invitation from the Israeli government for a class visit.

SOURCES: *Washington Post,* June 16, 2001, *Seattle Times,* July 10, 2001.

REFLECTION

Check in with the Paper Clip Project at www.marionschools.org/holocaust. Brainstorm with your class several compelling problems related to your subject area and students that could be meaningful social action projects with your class.

Click on *In the News* for recent *In the News* stories. Submit your own *In the News* summary to share with your colleagues.

have not studied them in depth, and their lower test scores reflect this superficiality. In Sizer's vision of effective instruction, good teachers limit the amount of content they introduce but develop it sufficiently for students to gain in-depth understanding.

This direction for teaching and schooling marks a radical departure from the current emphasis on uniform standards, test performance, and competition. In marked contrast to the superficial nature of such test-centered curriculum, Sizer advocates deep teaching. In **deep teaching,** teachers work to organize their content around a limited set of key principles and powerful ideas and then engage students in discussing these concepts. The emphasis is on problem solving and critical thinking, rather than on memorizing.[38]

Deeper teaching of the subject also suggests a deeper understanding of students. **Differentiated instruction** swims against the tide of standardization by organizing instructional activities not around content standards, but in response to individual differences. Teachers are asked to carefully consider each student's needs, learning style, life experience, and readiness to learn. Teachers are trained to develop learning activities that recognize these differences, because students learn best when they make connections between the curriculum and their interests and life experiences.[39]

This vision of deep teaching and differentiated instruction highlights the social nature of learning and of the classroom. As the builder of a classroom **learning community,** the teacher is called on to be a guide or facilitator, skillful in conducting discussions, group work, debates, and dialogues. In this way, the teacher empowers the students to talk with one another and to rehearse the terminology and concepts involved in each discipline. Learning becomes a community effort, not an individual competition.[40]

It is not surprising, therefore, that educators are reconceptualizing schools to create more nurturing learning communities. When learning communities work well, students and teachers get to know each other well and they can develop shared academic goals. Learning communities can be encouraged through several strategies,

The idea of the classroom as a "learning community" conceives of the teacher as someone who helps students activate their prior knowledge of some subject and become intellectually engaged with one another.

including looping and block scheduling. In **looping,** schools "promote" teachers along with their students, a process that allows the teacher an extra year or more to get to know students in depth, to diagnose and meet their learning needs, and to develop more meaningful communication with their parents and families. Looping offers students an increased sense of stability and community. Similarly, **block scheduling** increases teacher-student contact by increasing the length of class periods. The longer periods allow teachers to get to know these students better, while the students benefit from an uninterrupted and in-depth academic study. If you were to teach in a school with block scheduling, you might have 75 students on any given day or in a particular semester, instead of 150.

This notion of a learning community contrasts sharply with many current practices that emphasize state and school-mandated curriculum followed by standardized testing. It points to a more thoughtful classroom, one in which the teacher is the critical decision maker, and a reflective practitioner. Good teachers are expected to continually and intensely analyze their own practices, and to use their analysis to improve performance. "In order to tap the rich potential of our past to inform our judgment, we must move backward, reflect on our experiences, then face each new encounter with a broader repertoire of content-specific information, skills, and techniques."[41] When teachers engage in **reflective teaching,** they ask themselves such questions as

- What teaching strategies did I use today? How effective were they? What might have been even more effective?

- Were my students engaged with the material? What seemed to motivate them the most? If I were to reteach today's class, how could I get even more students involved?

- How did I assess my students' learning today? Would there have been a better way to measure their learning? How well did the students grasp the main points of today's lesson? Do I need to reteach some of these concepts?

WHAT TEACHERS SHOULD KNOW AND BE ABLE TO DO

The National Board for Professional Teaching Standards has described effective teachers with five core propositions.

1. **TEACHERS ARE COMMITTED TO STUDENTS AND THEIR LEARNING**

   Accomplished teachers are dedicated to making knowledge accessible to all students. They act on the belief that all students can learn. They treat students equitably, recognizing the individual differences that distinguish one student from another and take account of these differences in their practice. They adjust their practice based on observation and knowledge of their students' interests, abilities, skills, knowledge, family circumstances, and peer relationships. Equally important, they foster students' self-esteem, motivation, character, civic responsibility, and their respect for individual, cultural, religious, and racial differences.

2. **TEACHERS KNOW THE SUBJECTS THEY TEACH AND HOW TO TEACH THOSE SUBJECTS TO STUDENTS**

   Accomplished teachers have a rich understanding of the subject(s) they teach and appreciate how knowledge in their subject is created, organized, linked to other disciplines and applied to real-world settings. Their instructional repertoire allows them to create multiple paths to the subjects they teach, and they are adept at teaching students how to pose and solve their own problems.

3. **TEACHERS ARE RESPONSIBLE FOR MANAGING AND MONITORING STUDENT LEARNING**

   Accomplished teachers create, enrich, maintain, and alter instructional settings to capture and sustain the interest of their students and to make the most effective use of time. They are as aware of ineffectual or damaging practice as they are devoted to elegant practice. They know how to engage groups of students to ensure a disciplined learning environment, and how to organize instruction to allow the schools' goals for students to be met. They are adept at setting norms for social interaction among students and between students and teachers. Accomplished teachers can assess the progress of individual students as well as that of the class as a whole.

4. **TEACHERS THINK SYSTEMATICALLY ABOUT THEIR PRACTICE AND LEARN FROM EXPERIENCE**

   Accomplished teachers are models of educated persons, exemplifying the virtues they seek to inspire in students—curiosity, tolerance, honesty, fairness, respect for diversity, and appreciation of cultural differences. They draw on their knowledge of human development, subject matter and instruction, and their understanding of their students to make principled judgments about sound practice. Their decisions are grounded not only in the literature, but also in their experience.

5. **TEACHERS ARE MEMBERS OF LEARNING COMMUNITIES**

   Accomplished teachers contribute to the effectiveness of the school by working collaboratively with other professionals on instructional policy, curriculum development, and staff development. They can evaluate school progress and the allocation of school resources in light of their understanding of state and local educational objectives. Accomplished teachers find ways to work collaboratively and creatively with parents, engaging them productively in the work of the school.

SOURCE: www.nbpts.org/standards/five_core.html. Adapted from © 2001, National Board for Professional Teaching Standards.

REFLECTION

Can you demonstrate your understanding of each proposition with a classroom example from your past? If your schooling offers little to brag about (or your memories are faded) let your imagination give credence to the task. Envision an example from the five areas to confirm you comprehend each concept.

- Can I fine-tune tomorrow's or next week's lessons to capitalize on the gains made today?

Going far beyond the rhetorical, these questions are designed to raise consciousness, engender self-scrutiny, and result in effective teaching.[42]

YOU BE THE JUDGE
SKILLED TEACHERS ARE BEST DEVELOPED THROUGH

University Training Because It . . .

CREATES AND PROVIDES SOPHISTICATED KNOWLEDGE
Scholarship is an essential component for producing professionals. If teaching is ever to be seen as a thoughtful and reflective profession, it will be through systematic scholarship available only on university campuses.

PREPARES LEADERS, NOT FOLLOWERS
If teachers are to be more than technicians who carry out the instructions of others, they must be knowledgeable and informed about recent research and current theories. University study provides teachers with this knowledge, so that they understand not only *how* things are done, but *why* they are done as well.

EDUCATES TEACHERS TO EXAMINE CURRENT PRACTICES
Practitioners in the field are interested in staffing schools, not challenging current practices. An emphasis on vocational training and placement creates a climate where teachers are more likely to repeat past errors than explore new approaches.

ATTRACTS TALENTED PEOPLE
If bright and gifted people are to be drawn to this career, teaching must be seen as more than a vocation controlled by others. By producing intellectually active professionals, universities make teaching a more attractive career.

Field-Based Training Because It . . .

IS DESIGNED TO PRODUCE COMPETENT PROFESSIONALS
Producing skilled professionals requires a practical program not found in the university. Only real students with real needs can train real teachers. University courses cannot match real-world preparation.

PROVIDES SKILLED PRACTITIONERS, NOT THEORISTS
The best setting for learning a skill is the place where that skill is used. The best person to teach that skill is a talented artisan. Field-based training matches future teachers with the most appropriate settings and the most competent instructors.

STATE GOVERNMENTS ARE BEST SUITED FOR ORGANIZING TEACHER EDUCATION
Universities often ignore market realities, and so shortages in one teaching field develop, just as there is an oversupply in another. State-run programs could do a better job of matching training programs with job market needs.

PROVIDES SHARPER FOCUS AND FEWER DISTRACTIONS
Teaching, like other careers, takes careful and focused practice. Such focus is difficult to achieve in a university setting where other courses, abstract theories, and campus diversions intrude. Teacher education needs the intensity and focus found only in a field-based environment.

SOURCE: Many of these arguments are found in greater detail in Jack L. Nelson, Stuart B. Palonsky, and Kenneth Carlson, *Critical Issues in Education* (New York: McGraw-Hill, 1990), pp. 232–42.

YOU BE THE JUDGE

Most teacher education programs offer a mix of university and field-based training. Is this the best of both worlds—or the worst? Consider the five core propositions identified by the National Board for Professional Teaching Standards in the Frame of Reference: What Teachers Should Know and Be Able to Do. Would university or field-based training be more effective in acquiring each of these core propositions? Support your answers.

SUMMARY

CHAPTER REVIEW

Go to the Online Learning Center to take a chapter self-quiz, practice with key terms, and review key ideas from the chapter.

1. Are teachers born, or made?
   - While the debate has raged for decades, most people agree that effective teaching can result from natural artistry as well as focused training.

2. How is class time organized and what is academic learning time?
   - A teacher's organization of classroom time influences student achievement.
   - Allocated time is the amount of time a teacher schedules for a particular subject. Engaged time is the amount of allocated time during which the students are actually on task with the subject matter. Academic learning time is engaged time with a high success rate.

3. What classroom management skills foster academic achievement?
   - With good planning, teachers can arrange the classroom to minimize disturbances and establish efficient principles of instruction.
   - Good classroom management can lead to high student achievement. Establishing reasonable rules or standards that are not excessive in number usually means instruction can then proceed smoothly. Even the physical setup of the classroom can help or hinder student achievement.
   - Skills that are necessary for maintaining a well-managed classroom include group alerting, withitness, overlapping, use of the principle of least intervention, and the creation of smooth transitions.

4. What are the roles of teachers and students in the pedagogical cycle?
   - The pedagogical cycle consists of four stages: (1) structure, (2) question, (3) respond, and (4) react.
   - While the student's role is primarily responding, teachers typically are accountable for structuring, questioning, and reacting.

5. How can teachers set a stage for learning?
   - Clear structure gives students a framework understanding what they are expected to learn. Effective teachers introduce the topic and outline the lesson's direction.
   - Most cycles of instruction begin by connecting prior learning to current objectives. Motivating students with a transition to the lesson and then keeping the content clear will help students remain engaged. Effective teachers offer meaningful examples, give accurate directions, display enthusiasm, and present a brief closure to the lesson.

6. What questioning strategies increase student achievement?
   - Questioning is at the very foundation of effective teaching. Bloom's taxonomy provides a useful classification of questions from the lowest level (knowledge) to the highest level (evaluation).
   - Teachers rely most heavily on lower-order questions. While lower-order questions are well-suited for some goals, higher-order questions are associated with higher-order thinking and should also be an important part of classroom instruction.
   - In fact, who is asked the questions is often an indication of teacher expectation. All students should participate and teachers should carefully consider who will be asked to answer questions. Effective teachers use intentional strategies to allocate questions fairly.
   - Teachers need to remember to wait three to five seconds after asking a question (wait time 1) and before reacting to a student answer (wait time 2). Increasing wait time is surprisingly effective in raising the student level of participation (both quality and quantity).

- Teachers also need to be thoughtful in how they react to student comments. Teachers can offer praise, acceptance, remediation, or criticism in responding to the student. Research indicates that teachers use acceptance more than all the other reactions combined, a sign that their reactions may lack precision and perhaps their questions may not be challenging students.

7. How can teachers best tap into the variety of student learning styles?

- Effective teachers provide variety in both content and activity. From discussions and debates to simulations and spot quizzes, teachers increase academic success by responding to the different learning styles in the class.

8. What are the prevailing models of instruction?

- Four models of instruction that can lead to high student achievement include (1) direct teaching, (2) cooperative learning, (3) mastery learning, and (4) problem-based learning.

- The principles of direct teaching include daily review, presentation of new material in a clear manner, guided practice, teacher feedback, independent practice, and weekly and monthly reviews.

- In a cooperative learning classroom, students work in small groups and appraisals often reflect the entire group's performance.

- Mastery learning programs involve specific objectives that must be met, as indicated by assessment. Typically, students work at their own pace, going on to new material only when mastery of previous work has been demonstrated. Teachers often play a central role in content and skill mastery.

- Problem-based learning stimulates students to explore authentic issues. Individually and in small groups, students cross traditional subject boundaries as they investigate real-life problems and demonstrate what they have learned.

9. What are the future directions of effective teaching research?

- The best of today's educators are reflective about their practice. They continually question what they did and how it worked as they take strategic steps to be effective teachers.

- Differential instruction responds to individual student differences, unlike the popular model of standardized instruction and testing.

- Deep teaching promotes meaningful academic development around essential content, teaching less material in greater depth. The prior knowledge a student brings to the lesson must be connected with information gained.

- As learning can be social, teacher expertise can steer the classroom toward a sense of community. Looping and block scheduling increase the time that students and teachers can work together.

KEY TERMS AND PEOPLE

A Place Called School, 83

academic learning time, 83

academic structure, 92

acceptance, 100

allocated time, 83

behavioral objective, 106

Arno Bellack, 90

block scheduling, 111

Bloom's taxonomy, 94

Jere Brophy, 101

clarification, 92

cooperative learning, 105

criticism, 100

Larry Cuban, 107

dangles, 90

deep teaching, 110

differentiated instruction, 110

direct teaching, 104

engaged time, 83

flip-flops, 90

fragmentation, 89, 90

John Goodlad, 83

group alerting, 87

higher-order questions, 94

Jacob Kounin, 90

learning community, 110

least intervention, 88

looping, 111

lower-order questions, 94

mastery learning, 106

motivation, 92

objective, 92

overdwelling, 90

overlapping, 88

pedagogical cycle, 91

praise, 100

problem-based learning, 108

productive feedback, 101

reflective teaching, 111

remediation, 100

Mary Budd Rowe, 97

scaffold, 93

Robert Slavin, 106

student-initiated questions, 99

teacher effectiveness, 83

thrusts, 90

transition, 90, 92

variety, 103

wait time, 97

withitness, 88

DISCUSSION QUESTIONS AND ACTIVITIES

1. Do you think teachers are born, or made? Debate a classmate who holds the opposite point of view. Interview elementary and secondary teachers and ask them what they think about this question. Do some of them say that it is a combination of both? If so, why? Which part is art, which part skill?

2. Observe social studies, language, science, and math classes. What teaching skills seem to be most relevant across all of these academic disciplines?

3. Why do you think there is so much variation in how different teachers and schools use time for learning? Observe in your own college classrooms to determine how much time is wasted. For each class observed, keep a fairly detailed record of how time is lost (students six minutes late, class ends fifteen minutes early, PowerPoint presentation takes 4 minutes to set up, and so on).

4. Research suggests that, in order to achieve, students should be functioning at a very high success rate. Do you agree that this is likely to lead to higher achievement? Or do you think that students need to cope with failure and be "stretched" in order to achieve? Defend your position.

5. Interview teachers at the elementary, secondary, and postsecondary levels, and ask them for strategies they use to involve quieter students in classroom discussion. Share the list of strategies with your classmates.

6. Research suggests that less than 10 percent of classroom questions are higher-order, or thought-provoking, questions. Why do you think this is so? How can increasing wait time help teachers ask more higher-order questions?

7. Why do you think classroom discussion at the elementary and secondary levels proceeds at such a rapid pace? Using a watch with a second hand, calculate wait time 1 and wait time 2 in your college classrooms. Is the time split-second, or do your professors provide three to five seconds of time for thinking?

8. Analyze teacher reactions to student answers in elementary and secondary classrooms where you are an observer and in the college classrooms where you are a student. Are most of these classrooms "okay" classrooms? Why do you think some teacher reactions are vague and diffuse?

9. Think back to your own experiences as an elementary, middle, and high school student. Can you remember a time at each level when you received specific praise concerning an aspect of your performance? How did this make you feel? Describe the incidents to your classmates and compare with their memories. What conclusions can you make about the use of praise in school?

10. Do you think that criticism always has a negative impact? Can you remember any incidents in your own career as a student when criticism was helpful? harmful? Discuss these incidents with your classmates and listen to their descriptions. What generalizations can you make about criticism and its impact on students?

11. Observe in a classroom that is using direct teaching, cooperative learning, mastery learning, or problem-based learning. Discuss these approaches with your classmates. What are their respective benefits? Do there seem to be disadvantages?

12. In small cooperative groups review four key terms: deep teaching, differentiated instruction, learning communities, and reflective teaching. Generate an example of each drawn from an imaginary classroom. Alter the grade level and curriculum area of your classroom. How might deep teaching, differentiated instruction, learning communities, and reflective teaching change?

WEB-*TIVITIES*

1. Classroom Management: What Is in a Name?

2. Cooperative Learning

3. Problem-Based Learning

REEL TO REAL TEACHING

DEAD POETS SOCIETY (1989)
Run Time 128 minutes

Synopsis: "Carpe diem! Seize the day boys, make your lives extraordinary," advises educator John Keating to his class of young men at an all boys boarding school. These words guide his unorthodox lessons that will change their young lives forever.

Reflection:

1. Do John Keating's instructional techniques mirror any of the effective teaching characteristics discussed in this chapter? What additional attributes of an effective teacher did you discover in the film that are not described in this chapter? Is Keating's teaching an art, a skill, or both? Recall scenes from the film to support your answer.

2. Questioning is not just about teachers: Students are also partners in the questioning process. Creating an environment that welcomes student-initiated questions is important to engaged learning time. How did Mr. Keating teach his students to ask questions? How did these questions deepen student understanding?

3. Consider how the character of the student body created a community. How might the story-line change in an all girls school or a historically black school?

Follow-up Activity: You've read about effective questioning and seen "on screen" effective questioning in action. Now take a turn at practicing these techniques. Compose a classroom discussion of *Dead Poet's Society.* Write out a sequence of questions, one each from the six levels of Bloom's taxonomy.

How do you rate this film? Click on *Reel to Real Teaching* to submit your review of this or another education-related film, and read reviews submitted by others.

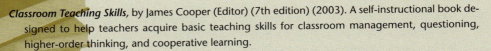

FOR FURTHER READING

Classroom Teaching Skills, by James Cooper (Editor) (7th edition) (2003). A self-instructional book designed to help teachers acquire basic teaching skills for classroom management, questioning, higher-order thinking, and cooperative learning.

Creating High Performance Classroom Groups, by Nina Brown (2000). Offers specific strategies for classroom teachers to design cooperative learning groups in various subjects and grade-levels.

Questioning in the Secondary Classroom, by E. C. Wragg and George Brown (2nd edition) (2001). Explores a variety of questions that teachers can ask, from those requiring simple recall of information to those that stimulate complex reasoning, imagination, and speculation.

Teaching and the Art of Successful Classroom Management: A How-to-Guidebook for Teachers in Secondary Schools, by Harvey Kraut (3rd edition) (2000). A comprehensive and concise guide incorporating the essential features of classroom organization, management, and discipline.

Teaching with Influence, by Peter Hook and Andy Vass (2001). Offers strategies to enhance the personal development and self-esteem of teachers as well as practical ways in which teachers can increase their effectiveness.

Young Investigators: The Project Approach in the Early Years, by July Harris Helm and Lilian Katz (2001). A combination of teacher interviews and accounts of classroom practice demonstrates how children of all abilities may master basic literacy skills through project-based learning.

Inter-mission

by Phyllis Lerner

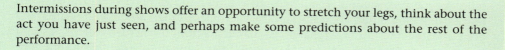

Intermissions during shows offer an opportunity to stretch your legs, think about the act you have just seen, and perhaps make some predictions about the rest of the performance.

Inter-missions in this book will give you a chance to explore your mission as an educator, stretch your teaching "legs," think about what you've already experienced, and make some preparations for your next steps as a teacher.

Welcome to the first ***Inter-mission.***

Inter-missions

The *Inter-missions* are placed after each of the book's four major sections and are designed to help you reflect on and apply the main ideas found in the text. Each *Inter-mission* will include

Applications, which will allow you to actively apply your readings through observations, interviews, and action research

Reflections, which will provide you introspective, developmental tasks to help you think deeply and realistically about education and your place in it

Portfolio artifacts, which will challenge you to collect and manage the necessary items for finding and retaining a teaching position

 indicates that a printable form can be found in the *Inter-mission* section of the Online Learning Center.

Introduction to Portfolios

Our friend Diane was retiring from education after twenty years, with regret but also with exciting plans to begin another career in the Northwest. By moving day, her garage was filled with her teaching career, all boxed up, neatly labeled, and ready for the journey. One box housed her college term papers, and another was marked "master's degree." There was a carton titled "Dinosaurs—grade 4" and another, just as intriguing, inscribed "Science Unit—Diseases." Diane wasn't quite ready to let go of her teaching career or her collection of materials. After all, what would happen if she missed the classroom too much and decided to apply for a teaching job? Still, how much boxed *stuff* could she afford (emotionally, financially, and professionally) to take with her? Diane had a garage filled with boxes—what she needed was a *portfolio*.

A portfolio is a purposeful collection of your work as a teacher. In four places in this book, we have placed *Inter-missions* to help you through the process of creating, collecting, researching, drafting, editing, organizing, and even borrowing the *stuff* that best represents you, your *portfolio*. The text's Online Learning Center (OLC) provides a similar framework for electronic portfolios and links to examples. Click on www.mhhe.com/sadker6e. Starting this procedure *now* will help you improve as a teacher and enhance the quality of your portfolio. (An added advantage may be more space in your garage!)

Building your portfolio can be thought of as a two-part process: creating an extensive *working* portfolio and then selecting just the right items for your *presentation* portfolio. As you visit schools, you'll become a hunter and gatherer of all things, front office paper (you'll find good stuff on the welcome counter, on bulletin boards, and even in dated and discarded materials), handouts from district workshops, student handbooks, and teacher rights and responsibilities manuals. In assembling your portfolio you might also draw on the World Wide Web, library, telephone, and even regular snail mail. During the final *Inter-mission*, you will analyze the contents of your working portfolio, so that you can begin to refine what becomes part of your *presentation portfolio*—what gets boxed and saved, and what should be tossed in the trash! In the end, you want a portfolio that uniquely and accurately represents you as a growing and competent teacher.

Getting Started on Your Portfolio

Portfolios can serve many purposes. Today, they are being used by states for licensure renewal, by school districts for merit pay increases, and by individual schools for hiring new staff. The National Board for Professional Teaching Standards (NBPTS)[1] requires portfolios as part of the rigorous evaluation to reward and recognize high-achieving teachers with board certification. At the classroom level, students collect, build, and store their work portfolios in cubbies or lockers. Teachers are using portfolios as an alternative evaluation method. Parents and teachers may review student portfolios at parent-teacher conferences. Your portfolio will be a tool in your eventual search for a teaching position.

Consider making your portfolio

- Purposeful—based on a sound foundation, such as professional standards
- Selective—choosing only the appropriate materials for a specific purpose or circumstance, such as a job application
- Diverse—going beyond your transcript, student teaching critiques, and letters of recommendation to represent a broad array of teaching talent
- Ongoing—relaying your growth and development over time
- Reflective—both in process and product, demonstrating your thoughtfulness
- Collaborative—resulting from conversations and interaction with others (peers, students, parents, professors, teachers, administrators)[2]

---

[1]National Board for Professional Teaching Standards, *Toward High and Rigorous Standards for the Teaching Profession* (Washington, DC: National Board for Professional Teaching Standards, 1989).
[2]Kenneth Wolf and Mary Dietz, "Teaching Portfolios: Purposes and Possibilities," *Teacher Education Quarterly* (winter 1998), pp. 9–21.

Designate a storage place for your portfolio. A file section in a carton (remember the garage boxes) is the minimalist's marker. Ultimately, you will want an actual presentation portfolio that is both professional and portable.

In the first section, you will want to have an introduction to you—your name and contact information, professional or present career objective, a brief résumé, transcripts, letters of support, and a mission or philosophy statement. Don't panic. We will take you through much of this in the chapters, discussion questions, and activities and during the *Inter-missions*.

INTASC Standards for Licensing Beginning Teachers

Principle 1 Knowledge of Subject Matter

The teacher understands the central concepts, tools of inquiry and structures of the discipline(s) he or she teaches and can create learning experiences that make these aspects of subject matter meaningful to students.

Principle 2 Human Development and Learning

The teacher understands how children learn and develop, and can provide learning opportunities that support their intellectual, social, and personal development.

Principle 3 Diversity in Learning

The teacher understands how students differ in their approaches to learning and creates instructional opportunities that are adapted to diverse learners.

Principle 4 Variety of Instructional Strategies

The teacher understands and uses a variety of instructional strategies to encourage students' development of critical thinking, problem solving, and performance skills.

Principle 5 Motivation and Management

The teacher uses understanding of individual and group motivation and behavior to create a learning environment that encourages positive and social interaction, active engagement in learning, and self-motivation.

Principle 6 Communication Skills

The teacher uses knowledge of effective verbal, nonverbal, and media communication techniques to foster active inquiry, collaboration, and supportive interaction in the classroom.

Principle 7 Instructional Planning Skills

The teacher plans instruction based upon knowledge of subject matter, students, the community, and curriculum goals.

Principle 8 Assessment

The teacher understands and uses formal and informal assessment strategies to evaluate and ensure continuous intellectual, social, and physical development of the learner.

Principle 9 Reflection and Responsibility

The teacher is a reflective practitioner who continually evaluates the effects of her or his choices and actions of others (students, parents, and other professionals in the learning community) and who actively seeks out opportunities to grow professionally.

Principle 10 Relationships and Partnerships

The teacher fosters relationships with school colleagues, parents, and agencies in the larger community to support students' learning and well being.

SOURCE: Adapted from *Model Standards for Beginning Teacher Licensing and Development: A Resource for State Dialogue* developed by the Interstate New Teacher Assessment and Support Consortium (INTASC). Each principle includes knowledge, dispositions, and performance expectations for beginning teachers. INTASC standards in several content areas can also be accessed online at www.ccso.org/intasc.html.

A framework for your portfolio will keep you focused on becoming a teacher and presenting yourself in the job search. We recommend you organize your portfolio to highlight your competency and growth in each of ten areas identified by the Interstate New Teacher Assessment and Support Consortium (INTASC). The standards represent principles for preparing, licensing, and certifying educators.

Note: The Observation Manual in Appendix 4 describes general guidelines and data collection tools for various settings. Consult this appendix before you visit schools to observe or collect data.

Now, it's time for your first *Inter-mission*.

Applications and Reflections

1:1 TEACHER INTERVIEW IN YOUR MAJOR OR FAVORITE SUBJECT AREA

Purpose: Teachers are expected to have knowledge of both the subject(s) they teach and the students they are teaching. Deciding what to teach, and how best to teach it, is a constant responsibility. This activity gives you the opportunity to learn about how teachers go through these tasks and to begin thinking about how you might approach curricular decisions in your major subject area.

INTASC PRINCIPLE 1
Knowledge of Subject Matter

Activity: Interview a teacher in a subject area of special interest to you. Even if you plan to teach in an elementary program, still select the curricular area that you savor. Focus on how the teacher decides what content to teach and how best to teach this content to students. Following are some potential curricular questions to ask (but you are encouraged to develop your own questions as well):

- What factors contributed to your teaching this subject (at this grade level)?
- What do you enjoy most about teaching this curriculum? What do you enjoy least?
- How do you go about selecting what content and skills to teach?
- When do you do your planning? the year before, the night before, as the bell rings?
- Do you integrate other subject areas into your program?
- How do the school district's official curriculum and the textbook shape your decisions?
- Can you make your own decisions as to what topics to teach, or are you confined to the official school curriculum?
- Do professional associations influence your decisions?
- Do parents or students participate in deciding what is taught?
- Are selections made by you alone or with others in your department or grade-level team?
- Do you try to offer different perspectives (multidisciplinary? multifaceted?) on these topics?
- Are there areas of this subject that are controversial? How do you handle these "hot" topics?

OLC

FORM: INTERVIEW QUESTIONS FOR TEACHER INTERVIEW IN YOUR MAJOR OR FAVORITE SUBJECT AREA

Reflection: What advice given by the teacher do you believe may influence your own decisions? How does the teacher's view of the content differ from your own? How will you decide what content to select when you become a teacher? What roles will professional associations, parents, and students play in your decision making? How might you respond to input from others in your department or grade-level team? Why are you interested in this subject area, and how do you anticipate your interest will impact your students and teaching?

1:2 INTERVIEW TEACHERS AT THREE ADJACENT GRADE LEVELS

INTASC PRINCIPLE 2
Human Development and Learning

Purpose: One of the traditional ways we organize schools, by age level, requires teachers to understand the progressive patterns of children's growth, yet children are incredibly different, from day to day and from each other. Educators have been known to ask, "Who is the average 5-year-old? What's a tenth-grader really like?" Many future teachers have a particular age-level interest. They "love the little ones" or are fascinated by "puberty and the middle school mind." Spending time with students may confirm or redirect your plans. Your purposes are to observe students in a similar age group and to distinguish between ages or formulate concepts about age differences.

Activity: Visit three classrooms, at three adjacent grade levels (e.g., third, fourth, and fifth grades). Stay for at least twenty minutes. Whether roll is being taken, homework is being collected, or independent reading is proceeding, you will probably see distinctions between the younger and the older students. Look at their physical sizes and shapes too. Note how the entire group is treated, how small groups operate, and how individuals behave. Watch for evidence of teacher expectations that are especially high or extremely low. Observe the patterns and frequency of routines, instructional time, behavior management, and socialization.

Reflection: How alike were the students at each of the three grade levels? How different were they? Could you determine which students were the youngest or oldest, even at one grade level? What teacher behaviors were cued to the students' levels of development? Was the teacher's use of humor, warmth, or management related to the maturity of the class? Have you selected a particular grade level for your teaching? What growth and development realities are relevant for the grade level of your interest? Why might you be better at a higher grade? Why might you be better at a lower grade? Have you considered teaching a nongraded or combination class (such as a fourth/fifth combo), in a special education program (which could have students from 9 to 14 years old); or with adult vocational learners (from age 17 to 99)?

1:3 MULTIPLE INTELLIGENCE BINGO

INTASC PRINCIPLE 3
Diversity in Learning

Purpose: Students approach learning in different ways. An effective teacher adapts instruction to these diverse learning styles. You have studied the concept of multiple intelligences (MI), and it is time to expand your awareness. While some teachers still tend to focus on the logical and linguistic abilities, others enthusiastically incorporate Gardner's theory into their classrooms. You may even find "MI Schools" that demonstrate MI in action. In this activity, you will be challenged to identify intelligences and to see the theory applied in lessons.

Classroom # _____ Bingo Card		
Intelligence	**Example during Instruction**	**Display or Material Example**
Logical-mathematical		
Linguistic		
Bodily-kinesthetic		
Musical		
Spatial		
Interpersonal		
Intrapersonal		
Naturalist		
Others (your own)		

Activity: Visit two classrooms. Try to include one that your professor recommends as an MI model. Observe in each room for at least forty minutes. Use the following chart to record examples of multiple intelligences. Note both instruction and room displays or materials. Brainstorming with your peers before the observation will help you determine what might constitute evidence of a particular intelligence. See if your observation can fill every slot. Bingo!

FORM: MULTIPLE
INTELLIGENCES BINGO

Reflection: Review your chart and those of your peers. Were any of your classrooms filled with examples of the multiple approaches to learning (any Bingo winners? in how many minutes?)? After your observations, were there any slots that remained empty? What could you do to fill those spaces? Were some classes totally geared to only one or two intelligence areas? Do you suspect that some intelligences are easy and some are always tough to use? How did particular students respond when given an opportunity to explore different intelligences? Were some confident with certain challenges and others withdrawn? How did the class respond, in general, when the lessons involved intelligences other than the logical and linguistic?

1:4 MEMORIES OF A TEACHER

Purpose: Many of us choose education because of a special teacher—someone who may have inspired us to bring a special "style" to the field. This individual was probably good because he or she modeled the best of effective instruction. You may not have been consciously aware of the skills and traits of a really effective teacher, but you knew the class was interesting, challenging, productive, and maybe even arduous. Perhaps you had friends in the class and you accomplished projects in meaningful ways. Possibly you were the star, the standout who could grasp the material and help others understand. You may have been the kid who didn't connect with others, but this teacher made your year better. Whatever the story, we suspect you have one and hope you have many.

INTASC PRINCIPLE 4
Variety of
Instructional
Strategies

Many teachers are purposely effective. They practice the skills and strategies discussed in Chapter 3. Connecting your memories with the research on effective teaching may help you be a more purposeful, and successful, educator.

Activity: Consider one terrific educator from your past. First, brainstorm (freely associate) memories from that class. On the left side of a piece of paper, list each item. See what you can generate at this point without reading farther (it's tempting to peek but worth the effort to wait).

After your first and open response, use the following cues to generate even more memories. Think about the way lessons began, about the subject matter, and about the use of resources or even gimmicks.

- How was the room arranged?
- Where did the teacher "hang out"?
- Do you recall big field trips or perhaps small adventures?
- How were you engaged in academic learning?
- What management techniques or rules do you remember?
- Were transitions from one activity to another handled smoothly?
- What about questioning opportunities and teacher feedback? Did you raise your hand and were you called on? Were others?
- Can you recall anything about tests (their kind, frequency, and resultant anxiety level)?
- Were term papers, major projects, special event days, or assemblies part of the curriculum?
- What else made this teacher the one who made a difference for you?

Reflection: Now, take your brainstormed list of terrific teacher memories and meander back through Chapter 3, "Teacher Effectiveness." Consider each item on your list. What connections can you make between the research on instructional quality and your memorable teacher? What generalizations about effective instruction might you offer following this activity?

1:5 WHY TEACH?

INTASC PRINCIPLE 5
Motivation and
Management

Purpose: People may have already asked you why you are considering teaching. Sometimes they ask with reverent tones, other times with disbelief. (Remember, they are probably sharing something about their own perspective regarding a teaching career.) Analyze your reasons to teach, so that you can provide a good answer to the question and uncover a bit about your own thinking. Besides, in order to discern the various motivations your students bring to the classroom, it's best to understand your own. This examination will contribute to your mission or philosophy statement that belongs in your portfolio.

Activity: Consider the following list of reasons or motivations to teach. Rank them from the most significant to the least significant on the vertical scale that follows. Begin by identifying the one that is *most* important to you—your major reason for teaching—and write that in the first slot. Then select the one that is the *least* important or meaningful to you, and write that by number 12. It will be easiest to work through the list if you apply this strategy, as you will always look for the one that stands out as either the most or least important reason remaining.

Motivating Forces	Rank
Really enjoy and value the subject	1.
Working with youngsters	2.
Salary and benefit package	3.
Job security	4.
Professional fulfillment	5.
Variety of activities	6.
Work and vacation schedules	7.
Collegial rapport	8.
Societal status of education	9.
Stepping stone for _____ (your call)	10.
Job autonomy and control	11.
It's tough and challenging	12.

FORM: WHY TEACH?

Reflection: As you glance at your ranked list, are there any surprises? Are there any motivations missing from the list we presented? Where might you rank these items? What's your answer—why do you want to teach?

1:6 PRINCIPAL INTERVIEW ABOUT THE JOB MARKET AND HIRING PROCEDURES

Purpose: It might be awkward if your first communication with a school administrator was at your job interview. That's not the easiest circumstance for practicing active and effective communication. An informational interview, with a principal, is a great rehearsal for you and could provide timely information on the job market and hiring procedures. It's certainly advice you need and counsel he or she may have.

INTASC PRINCIPLE 6
Communication Skills

Activity: Arrange an interview with a local school administrator (principal, personnel director). Consider going with a small group of peers (visitation team), so that your school leader is not inundated with too many requests. Review the material in the first two chapters that provides information on teacher supply and demand. Develop questions as a visitation team. The following list of suggestions can also provide a framework for your conversation. Don't overstay your welcome—twenty to thirty minutes should be adequate.

- How many and where are the job openings in this area? What are the openings like at particular grade levels or subject areas? What do you anticipate will happen to this pattern in two years? in five years?
- Are new schools being built or others planning to close?
- Are there teachers who move in and out of the system (family leave, special grant projects)?
- What is the diversity breakdown of teachers in the district? How does this compare with the students in this school and districtwide? How do these factors affect screening and hiring?

- In general, what is the application process for this district? Are other staff involved in the procedure and at what point? Do candidates face an individual or a panel interview? Do you require or recommend applicant portfolios?
- If you could describe a perfect candidate, what traits would that teacher possess?
- What other questions should we ask concerning the educational job market and hiring process?

Reflection: Meet with other visitation teams and compare your interviews. Are certain trends evident in your locale? How do these realities influence your own decision making? What questions remain unanswered? Should you schedule a follow-up meeting, phone interview, or Internet conversation? Consider a similar interview during a trip home or while visiting another region of the country. How does all this information affect your teaching plans?

1:7 A MINI-LESSON WITH A MINI-GROUP

INTASC PRINCIPLE 7
Instructional
Planning Skills

Purpose: Planning instruction takes a major portion of a teacher's time and talent. Creating a learning experience in the early part of your program is a chance to begin developing this critical skill. You have read information on effective instruction, and we hope you have observed it in action. The purpose, at this point, is to find your starting line for all the practice and teaching ahead. (Since we recommend working with your classmates, this mini-teaching session could also be a way to review this course's content. There's no better way to acquire new learning than to teach it.)

Activity: Develop and teach a mini-lesson (about five to eight minutes), using content from the text's first section. Work with a small group of peers (five to eight students). Use principles of direct teaching (see pp. 104–105 in Chapter 3) as you include a review or connecting thread for engagement, present material in a clear manner, offer guided practice, model teacher feedback, and set up for independent practice. Your greatest challenge is to make the content of your lesson small enough. Review the summary sections of the text chapters to identify possible lesson topics. Any techniques you use to promote variety in process and content will be appreciated by your "students."

Reflection: You did it. You taught a mini-lesson to your peers, something that many experienced faculty find frightening. What stages did you go through to create your lesson? Did the plan come together? What went well? What did not? Why? How did you adjust—or did you need to—during instruction? Were you working from notes? What evidence do you have that the climate of learning was comfortable and relaxed? (Recall nonverbal clues, such as sweaty palms or sleepy eyelids.) What else do you recall from the actual mini-lesson—or was it an out-of-body experience? Was the content clear? Did your students practice what they learned? Was your feedback effective? Did you spark their interest with independent practice? What's your evidence? If you were to replan this mini-lesson, what changes would you make?

1:8 TUTOR USING EFFECTIVE FEEDBACK

INTASC PRINCIPLE 8
Assessment

Purpose: Assessment is a great deal more than testing and grading. Even the evaluative feedback you give students during one-on-one interactions is considered part of your assessment repertoire. The text covers four feedback reactions to student answers: praise, acceptance, remediation, and criticism (pp. 99–102). Using them effectively and fairly will be one of your toughest challenges.

Feedback (Sample Entries)	Number of Responses
Praise:	
Good job!	II
Acceptance:	
Okay.	IIII
Remediation:	
Now read all the word parts together.	I
Criticism:	
No, that's not the way to pronounce it.	I

Activity: If your program recommends working with a K–12 student, terrific! If not, commit yourself to a tutorial opportunity with a local youngster. Although a "one-shot deal" will accomplish the goals of this activity, an ongoing relationship is an extraordinary chance for you (and a youngster) to learn. Audiotape your session (at least fifteen minutes) with the student. Remember to get permission from the student and faculty coordinator by explaining the purpose of your taping. Listen to your session and code or note the category of your feedback. Review the criteria for each type of feedback and work with a partner if you are unsure about particular comments.

Reflection: What did you notice about yourself and the pattern or frequency of feedback? How did your tutorial session compare with the teacher reaction research (pp. 99–102)? What form did your acceptance comments take (okay, aha, silence)? Did your use of praise represent the attributes identified by Brophy on page 101–102? Was criticism clear when appropriate? Was remediation specific enough to allow the student to improve? How would you assess your use of these skills? What activity can you devise to help you practice and improve your feedback?

1:9 A MINI-CONFERENCE ABOUT YOUR MINI-LESSON

Purpose: Reflection and evaluation of one's *own* work are major responsibilities for good teachers. You won't always have colleagues who can attend your lessons, analyze your teaching, coach you through a crisis, and generate new challenges. There will be many times (almost all the time?) when you must do it yourself. That's the essence of this activity. You will have a chance to analyze your lesson (with a little help from your friends).

Activity: Earlier in this *Inter-mission* (1:7 "A Mini-Lesson with a Mini-Group"), you had the opportunity to teach a brief lesson using content from the text. Gather two or three "students" from the lesson. As a framework for your conversation, discuss three questions: What, in terms of content, did you do? How, in terms of process, did you do it? What, in terms of reflection, were your afterthoughts? - After your investigation, encourage your classmates to offer their concerns or compliments.

Reflection: Frequently, teachers are grateful for the end of a lesson and move quickly to the next one. A little pause for reflection, after a lesson, is a great habit to acquire. What of the content did you recall? What did you remember about the

FORM: TUTOR USING EFFECTIVE FEEDBACK

INTASC PRINCIPLE 9
Reflection and Responsibility

process of instruction? How might you and your peers improve the lesson? How did it feel to have others talking about your teaching? Were you able to stay open to the conversation? Were your "students" able to support their comments and compliments with evidence? What did you learn from others that went beyond your own self-assessment?

1:10 VISIT A STAFF ROOM

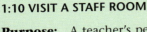
INTASC PRINCIPLE 10
Relationships and
Partnerships

Purpose: A teacher's personal connection with colleagues represents a major dimension of school life. Friendships are often nurtured in small and informal ways: monitoring recess, attending conferences, developing special projects, serving on committees, working on curriculum, and the like. One of the most interesting places to learn about staff relationships and a school's power and social structure is the teachers' lounge. We are not asking you to be an undercover agent and sneak glances at places that are officially off-limits or unofficially verboten. We are suggesting that observing the faculty lounge, with and without teachers, is a chance to bring the anthropologist's skills to a world that is probably rather new for you.

Activity: With permission, visit a staff lounge during a quiet time of day. Make notes regarding the locale, size, and shape of the room; furniture decor, quality, and abundance; equipment access or absence; social atmosphere; and displays on the walls (both aesthetic and informational).

Be a guest in the room during a high use time: before or after school or during recess or faculty lunch.

FORM: QUESTIONS FOR
A VISIT TO A STAFF
ROOM

- How many teachers visit the room compared with the number on staff?
- Are most departments represented or just certain teachers, grade levels, or curricular areas?
- Are there groups of faculty that congregate elsewhere?
- Is there free and open use of space, or do some teachers "possess" a particular chair or table space?
- Are the conversations "kid-" or other-centered? Is there a tone that you would classify as constructive or destructive, on or off task, fun or business?
- Are there categories you could use to describe groups in the room (the women sit around the table, the men at the sofa; the bilingual faculty stay together, the coaches never come in)?

Create a graphic design that illustrates the faculty lounge you visited. Your drawing will help you discuss the *who, what,* and *where* details. List additional observations and include both *factual comments* ("The entire grade-level team can sit comfortably in the lounge") and *color commentary* ("Two subject area cliques seemed visible at every break").

Reflection: Sit with a classmate who visited a different school's lounge. As you share and review your drawings, note similarities and differences. (Try to focus on accurate information rather than artistic talent.) What have you learned from your visit and your colleague's inquiry? What specific observations or inferences can you make about the social fabric and teaching climate of the schools?

Portfolio Artifact Collection

In addition to the activities and reflections (many of which belong in a beginner teacher's box of worthwhile *stuff*), the following collection of important artifacts will contribute to your career decision making. During the four inter-missions, you will be challenged to accumulate items for each of the ten principles.

1:P4 TRICKS OF THE TRADE

Purpose: Through trial and error or painstaking theoretical development, many successful instructional techniques already exist. Teaching methods on questioning strategies, deductive learning, "chunking" or grouping information in a lecture—all will become part of your knowledge base and routine. For the next few years, you may find descriptive handouts and materials everywhere. Many are well worth keeping.

Activity: Start collecting. Strategies are found in the text (e.g., cooperative learning or questioning using the levels of Bloom's Taxonomy in Chapter 3), a peer's graphic organizer during a classroom demonstration, your lesson notes from a method's class, or a conversation held on the Internet. These strategies are an important addition to your repertoire. Duplicate these excerpts (be sure to add the correct date and citation) and place them in your file box under Principle 4. As the years go by, you will upgrade and recreate your methods materials to meet your style and needs.

> **INTASC PRINCIPLE 4**
> Variety of Instructional Strategies

1:P7 MY FIRST LESSON

Purpose: A portfolio allows you to observe your teaching growth over time. When you save selected old lessons (not boxes full in the garage), you are reminded of your professional development and can draw energy from the lessons well learned.

Activity: Collect your lesson plan and the reflections from the earlier *Inter-mission* sections (1:7, 1:9). Develop and date a cover page titled "My *First* Lesson." Briefly include *compliments* and *comments* in a chart. As you expand your knowledge and understanding of teaching, we predict that you'll enjoy looking back (under INTASC Principles 7 and 9) at your early lessons and assessments.

> **INTASC PRINCIPLE 7**
> Instructional Planning Skills

1:P10 SPECIAL EDUCATION SERVICES

Purpose: For many preservice-teachers, the laws and services for students with special needs can be complex and confusing. Gaining a professional understanding of these concerns will help anyone with career plans in education. It might even motivate you to teach children with disabilities. Begin by reviewing the information in the text that covers special education (Chapter 2, pp. 64–68).

Activity: Contact a local school district and identify the director of services for special education. Request a parent information packet that outlines the rights and responsibilities of the district regarding testing, resources, policy, practices, and all other information that would help you understand Public Law 94-142. Scan this material and highlight the key points to promote your understanding and file under Principle 10.

> **INTASC PRINCIPLE 9**
> Reflection and Responsibility

THE LIGHTS HAVE FLICKERED. THIS *INTER-MISSION* IS OVER. IT'S TIME TO OPEN THE NEXT SECTION: "SCHOOLS AND CURRICULUM."

CLASS ACT

As an elementary school teacher, I was particularly eager to find good multicultural books. One day, I planned to read one of the many Juan Bobo stories. Juan Bobo (Simple John) depicts a "noodlehead" who does nothing right. This character is Puerto Rico's favorite fool and simpleton and has been the mainstay for generations. ● Supposedly, Juan Bobo embodies the essence of Puerto Rico—the *jíbaro*—a product of three cultures: Taino Indian, African, and Spaniard. The character stands for the honest and uncorrupted life of the country folks against the pomposity and falsehood of those in the city (i.e., the aristocratic Spaniards and those imitating them). But too often Juan Bobo is instead a mockery of the *jíbaros*—equated with the poor and uneducated country folks. Additionally, Juan Bobo is frequently portrayed as either a person of apparent Black and/or Indian heritage. Among Puerto Ricans, it is highly insulting to be called either *jíbaro* or Juan Bobo. ● As I prepared to read to them, I looked into the face of one of my students—a Latino boy of African heritage. I was transported back to my childhood and saw myself—a little girl of African heritage, also waiting for the teacher to read a story to the class. I recalled painful memories. ● Growing up biracial in Puerto Rico made me aware at a very young age of the deep racism in Latino culture. Although family and friends called me *triguena* (wheat colored), I recall classmates' and even teachers' crueler taunts. ● I glanced at the cover of the book I was about to read. It clearly pictured Juan Bobo as a poor country boy of African heritage. I looked back at the faces of my students—innocent faces reflecting their African and Indian heritage. What was I doing? Persons of African and Indian ancestry are the majority in most Latino countries. Yet the folklore and literature, adults' and children's alike, predominantly present characters of Spanish ancestry. Country folks and Latinos of color disappear or are presented as ignorant and superstitious, as criminals, servants, and buffoons. Those in power are White Latinos. ● Over the years, I have come to an important understanding. Just because a book is "multicultural" doesn't mean it is free of bias. Juan Bobo and other culturally authentic stories have been translated into English and other languages—they can now take their biases across cultures. ● I placed the book down on my lap and told the class: "Today, we are going to do something really special. Books are stories that have been written by authors so others can read and hear them. Today, I am going to tell you a story from my childhood and then, we will tell each other our stories. We are going to write our stories down and publish them so others can read them later." I proceeded: "Once I climbed a tall mountain and thought I had reached the top of the world where the Taino Indian god Yukiyu lives . . ."

Marta I. Cruz-Jansen, Ph.D.
Associate Professor
Multicultural Education
College of Education
Florida Atlantic University

SOURCE: Cruz-Jansen, M.I. (1998, Fall). "Culturally Authentic Bias." *Rethinking Schools*. Vol 13, No 1, p. 5.

SUBMIT YOUR OWN *CLASS ACT:* Click on *Class Acts* and submit a *Class Act* about a teacher who has made a difference in your life. Visit the Online Learning Center to read more *Class Acts.*

4

Schools: Choices and Challenges

FOCUS QUESTIONS

1. What are the various expectations Americans hold for their schools?
2. Should schools transmit the American culture or change it?
3. What school purposes are emphasized by educational reform?
4. How are magnet and charter schools, open enrollment, and vouchers reshaping our concept of the neighborhood public school?
5. Will the business community's for-profit approach to education create more efficient schools?
6. Is school choice a good idea?
7. Why are so many families choosing home schooling?

WHAT DO YOU THINK? What Do You Think Schools and Students Are Like Today? Check off what you think and see how others respond.

CHAPTER PREVIEW

Although most of us take school for granted, the proper role of this institution continues to evoke heated debate. Are schools to prepare students for college, for a vocation, or to achieve high scores on standardized tests? Perhaps schools are really to develop good interpersonal relationships, or develop a national loyalty. Some say many school goals come down to either preparing students to adjust to society or equipping them to change and improve society. Not only do people hold widely divergent views regarding both the goals and the effectiveness of America's schools, but these views seem to vary depending on the times.

   In this chapter, you will have the opportunity to examine some of the major purposes assigned to schools and some of the major criticisms that have been leveled at them. Some believe that America's schools are failing, and reform efforts have led to innovations in how schools are organized, managed, and evaluated. The recent emphasis on standards and tests once again raises the crucial question: What's a school for? The traditional link between a community and its neighborhood school is being strained, if not ruptured. In fact, the "right" to avoid the neighborhood school and choose a school is quickly becoming a major national issue. Competition among schools is being fueled by the business community, which views schools as potential profit centers. And concerned parents, in ever greater numbers, are giving up on schools entirely. The notion of parents educating their own children at home is gaining ground, and in many communities, the family room has become the classroom. Defining the place and purpose of schools has never been more challenging.

A Meeting Here Tonight

Sam Newman has been principal of Monroe High School for just under five years. Becoming principal seemed a natural step to take after teaching and coaching for eight years.

Sam's plans to improve school morale and community relations, as well as to increase faculty involvement in key decisions, pleased the school board enough to give him the principalship over two, more senior candidates. He got off to a good start. He organized rallies, proclaiming, "Monroe is tops!"; he met with parents and teachers in endless meetings; and he created teacher management teams. But all that seems long ago.

Sam now spends his time rushing from one emergency to another. He spends two nights a week trying to complete federal, state, and school district paperwork and one or two more nights attending meetings. During the day, there is an endless parade of students in trouble, teachers with complaints, outraged parents, and, of course, more meetings. Between budgets to balance and supplies to order, Sam rarely has time to think about how to significantly improve education at Monroe.

Today's large, comprehensive high schools reflect the diversity and the conflicting interests of the larger society.

And now, to top it all off, statewide results show that Monroe students have fallen almost a year behind the norm in math and reading. He must have received a hundred calls from angry parents, complaining about higher taxes and inefficient schools, so a meeting has been called to explore solutions to the problem of declining test scores.

On his way to the meeting, Sam detours to the bathroom. As he stares into the mirror to comb his thin, graying hair, he notes sadly the almost complete disappearance of his belt beneath his belly. He once prided himself on staying in shape. Now his shape is mostly round.

But being a principal is not the same as being a coach, and a school is very different from a team. Each passing year has taught him how precious little he knows about schools. He schedules. He budgets. He writes plans. He calms parents. He disciplines students. But, all the while, he realizes that he has little time to shape and direct the school. He is not really leading the school—he is not even sure where to lead it; he is simply trying very hard to keep it afloat. Although he knows more about flowcharts than about philosophy, a line from his college philosophy course sticks in his mind. The line is Santayana's, and it seems to have a lot of meaning for him and for Monroe High School: Fanaticism consists of redoubling one's efforts after having forgotten one's aim.

A quick glance at his watch brings an abrupt end to philosophical speculation. He is already late. He hurries down the hallway to the meeting.

• • •

George Elbright unconsciously tugs at his tie as he mounts the long stairway to Monroe High School. He glances up at the motto, chiseled in stone. "Knowledge Is Power." He thinks back to the first time he read those words, as a 15-year-old freshman. Thirty years later, the memory still makes him perspire and pull at his tie. Funny how schools do that to you.

For George Elbright, Monroe High conjures up memories of hard work, graded homework assignments, and midterms so tough that kids sometimes broke down and cried, unable to go on. And finals! The whole year's work riding on one exam. Tests were rough then, but kids learned. Not like today. Not at all.

And that is why George is back at Monroe High. For years, he watched schools disintegrate, and complained bitterly about the lack of discipline, the growing permissiveness, courses in sex education, drug education, environmental education, and the new teaching methods that sound as if the teachers do not have to teach at all. Finally things were changing. And no wonder. The test scores were in. George Jr. failed the standardized state test. So did many of the students at Monroe. No wonder George Elbright Sr., is about to attend his first parent-teacher meeting in six years.

George reaches into his pocket and pulls out his wrinkled, handwritten list. He has to be clear and forceful. He slowly rehearses his list:

1. Teachers must reassume their responsibility. Skills development, homework, and tests should be the main activities of the classroom. Free-for-all discussion, with the teacher acting as a television talk show host instead of a teacher, has to end. Children have to learn that learning is serious.

2. Students must learn the importance of discipline and respect. Students should speak to adults with respect. We should consider a new dress code or even school uniforms. Sloppy dress and poor manners lead to lazy attitudes and poor work.

3. Kids who do not pass tests should be left back until they do pass them. Too many high school graduates can't read or write well.

4. I am tired of trying to decipher "progress reports" about my child's "social adjustment" and "satisfactory efforts." I want to see report cards with grades and without educational jargon.

5. A school is supposed to teach fundamental skills, and not sex education, human relations, or other frills and electives. It is time that schools get back to the basics.

6. And it is high time that teachers taught kids morality and ethics.

Perhaps it will work; perhaps he can get the school back on the right track. The newspapers are filled with reports that seem to support his point of view. Why, he even read a report that said schools are so weak they jeopardize America's future. At any rate, he has to try for George Jr.'s sake. All the family's hopes are pinned on him. George Jr., would be the first Elbright to make it to college. This is no time for the school to let him down.

• • •

Shirley Weiss sits alone in her classroom, sipping lukewarm coffee from a commuter cup. The evening meeting gives her a chance to stay after school and catch up on her paperwork. She finished grading 15 minutes ago but is determined to wait until the last minute before going down to the auditorium for the meeting. Although anxious to make her position known, she is not anxious to get into one-to-one encounters with angry parents, so she waits.

She is amazed at public reaction to the poor scores on the state's standardized test. Given the teacher cuts and the large size of today's classes, it really isn't all that surprising. Everyone seems to be missing the point entirely. Teenagers today simply aren't contemporary versions of the kids who attended Monroe High ten or twenty years ago. Violence, alienation, racism, sexism, drugs, terrorism—the world is so much more complex. Kids should find out who they are and where they are going. President Jackson's 1830s fight over the National Bank does not exactly speak to them.

That is why Shirley Weiss has restructured her American history course into a contemporary social problems course. Students have to *want* to learn and grow, and that's what her course is all about. And the students do well in her course. They are genuinely interested. They study and they learn. As a matter of fact, if those test makers ever were to leave their air-conditioned, swanky offices and rejoin the real world, they would revise their tests to parallel her authentic assessments, and her kids would soar! The problem is not really with the school or the kids at all! It is with the test makers and the parents who are stuck in the past!

Shirley is good and angry as she pushes back her chair and makes her way down to the auditorium.

• • •

Phil Lambert begins to fidget as he waits for the meeting to begin. His physique and the twenty-five-year-old wooden seat are less than perfect fits.

He has not been back to Monroe since his youngest daughter graduated, almost ten years ago. And he is not overjoyed at being here now. But declining test scores represent a serious problem, not just for Phil but for the entire community.

Phil Lambert, owner of Lambert's Department Store, is also president of the chamber of commerce. Every week, he is involved with enticing professionals, even high-tech firms, and developers to relocate in Monroe. Sooner or later, the talks always turn to the quality of the school system. In a sense, the success of the schools is a barometer of the town's future growth and development. And now the barometer is falling; stormy days are ahead. Declining test scores could cost the town plenty.

But Phil is particularly upset because he has warned people about this problem for years. High school kids are getting into more and more trouble. He has recently been to court three times to deal with teenage shoplifters. And, when kids today apply for work, it is so sad it is almost funny! Wearing baggy jeans and fouling up the application form, they just come off as irresponsible and stupid. For years, Phil has been asking rhetorically, "Didn't you learn *anything* in school?" Now his question is no longer rhetorical.

The schools simply have to get down to business, literally, and begin preparing kids for the real world. Our whole nation is in economic trouble because of weak schools. More courses should be offered, stressing not only the basics but also how to get a job and the importance of the work ethic. Students have to understand that school is not a place where they can come late, dress sloppily, and goof off. Once they understand how serious the real world is, how important getting a job is, they will get serious about their schoolwork.

Lambert checks his cell phone for messages and makes a mental note that the meeting is starting sixteen minutes late. If he were to run the store the way they run the schools, he'd have been bankrupt years ago.

•••

The late start of the meeting gives Mary Jackson a chance to unwind. She has rushed from her job to make the meeting and is beginning to feel the consequences of her long day.

As she gauges the audience, she sees that once again the "haves" outnumber the "have-nots." The middle-class, white, well-dressed parents don't look half as tired as Mary Jackson feels. But they sure do seem worried. For the first time, they are getting a small taste of the problem Mary has been fighting for years. Lower achievement scores are shaking them up. But they could never know the problem as well as Mary does. Even with the drop in scores for white kids, they are still scoring almost two years ahead of the African American students.

Mary has two daughters enrolled in Monroe High. Both are working hard, yet they cannot seem to catch up to the top students. Her kids have never had a nonwhite teacher. And her kids have never gotten into the honors track. Somehow it seems that only white students end up there.

She has tried to make the school aware of the special problems faced by students of color and females by organizing the Parents' Multicultural Task Force. Everyone at Monroe seems sympathetic, from Mr. Newman on down. But nothing has changed, and that makes her feel tired and discouraged—but not tired and discouraged enough to give up.

Mary looks around at the almost completely filled auditorium, spotting precious few black faces in the audience. But Mary would speak for those who could not come, and for those who have given up all hope of changing things. Monroe High should be their stepping-stone up, not an obstacle. Mary would tell them. The past few frustrating years have worn her patience thin.

•••

This was the first time Kay Zittleman ever visited Monroe High, but it all seemed so familiar: unhappy parents gathering to complain about an underperforming school to a very tired-looking principal. This was the kind of scenario that was made-to-order for Unlimited Educational Opportunities, Inc. and their "Horizon" Schools. Kay glanced down to make certain that she had her carton filled with hundreds of multicolored brochures. She knew the plan well. She would let the parents complain, the principal would try to assuage their anxiety, and then she would announce the opening of her company's new charter school. A Horizon Charter School would promise a more focused educational program and guaranteed test score improvements by bringing business efficiency to education. No empty promise: There was a track record. She would explain that over 60 Horizon for-profit schools in other states were already compiling impressive reading and math scores. Horizon uses a Back to Basics curriculum and character education combined with extra time, extra teachers, and laptop computers to achieve its goals. But Kay would have to warn them as well: Although Horizon schools were open to all, it was likely that there would be more applicants than spaces. Kay would alert everyone to the obvious: A lottery system would have to be used to select which students will be admitted.

Kay felt good about the evening meeting, the ability of Horizon to enhance the test scores, and her own decision to leave Wall Street and use her Harvard M.B.A. to promote Unlimited Educational Opportunities. It was looking like another growth year.

●●●

Sam Newman twists the microphone stand to within a few inches of his mouth and prepares to open the meeting. He looks out at the packed auditorium and begins to assess the crowd:

There is Pat Viola, the art teacher. What is she doing here? Art is never assessed on those tests.

Oh, there's Mrs. Jackson, the chair of the Multicultural Task Force. She's not going to pull any punches about those test scores. The black students are two years behind the white students on achievement tests.

And Dr. Sweig, the humanities professor from the university, is here. He's probably going to make his pitch about requiring all students to study the classics. He must have given that "cultural literacy for all" speech a dozen times.

Mrs. Benoit, president of the school board, looks distressed. As long as I can find a solution that pleases everyone and doesn't increase the budget, she'll be satisfied. She needs a magician, not a principal, to run this meeting.

Phil Lambert is here and Shirley Weiss. Isn't that the Elbright kid's father? Wonder what's on their minds?

Sam Newman begins to perspire. He leans forward and announces, "Okay, let's begin."

Good schools depend on strong community support.

The Purposes of School

Sam Newman in the vignette that opens this chapter has a dilemma on his hands. Parents and teachers are pulling him—and trying to pull Monroe High—in different directions. If it is any comfort to Sam—and it probably is not—he is confronting an old question: What is the purpose of a school?

Having spent much of your life as a student, you may find this question too basic, even obvious. Answers come quickly to mind. We go to school to learn things, to earn good grades, to qualify for better jobs, to become a better person—or to please our parents (or even ourselves). But these divergent reasons represent the view only from a student's side of the desk. There are other perspectives, broader views, and more fundamental definitions of the purposes of schools. Although brainstorming all the possible reasons for schools could lead to some creative insights, it may be more practical at this point to focus on two fundamental, yet somewhat antithetical, purposes of schools.

Purpose 1: To Transmit Society's Knowledge and Values (Passing the Cultural Baton)

Society has a vital interest in what schools do and how they do it. Schools reflect and promote society's values. There is a world of knowledge out there, more than any school can possibly hope to teach, so one of the first tasks confronting the school is to *select* what to teach. This selection creates a cultural message. Each country chooses the curriculum to match and advance its own view of history, its own values, its self-interests, and its own culture. In the United States, we learn about U.S. history, often in elementary, middle, and high school, but we learn little about the history, geography, and culture of other countries—or of America's own cultural diversity, for that matter. Even individual states and communities require schools to teach their own state or local history, to advance the dominant "culture" of Illinois or of New York City. By selecting what to teach—and what to omit—schools are making clear decisions as to what is valued, what is worth preserving and passing on.

Literature is a good example of this selection process. American children read works mainly by U.S. and British writers, and only occasionally works by Asian, Latin American, and African authors. This is not because literary genius is confined to the British and U.S. populations; it is because of a selection process, a decision by the keepers of the culture and creators of the curriculum that certain authors are to be taught, talked about, and emulated and others omitted. Similar decisions are made concerning which music should be played, which art viewed, which dances performed, and which historical figures and world events studied. As each nation makes these cultural value decisions, it is the role of the school to transmit these decisions to the next generation.

As society transmits its culture, it also transmits a view of the world. Being American means valuing certain things and judging countries and cultures from that set of values. Democratic countries that practice religious tolerance and respect individual rights are generally viewed more positively by Americans than are societies characterized by opposing norms, standards, and actions—that is, characteristics that do not fit our "American values." Afghani women denied access to schools, hospitals, and jobs by the Taliban conflicted with our cultural and political standards and was repulsive to most Americans. Repression of religious, racial, and ethnic groups usually engenders similar negative feelings. By transmitting culture, schools breathe the breath of cultural eternity into a new generation and mold its view of the world.

The Japanese are quite serious about transmitting a positive image of their culture and history, but World War II is a problem. However, it is not a problem for school children. The Hiroshima memorial explains that "the situation in Pearl Harbor hurtled Japan into the Pacific war." There is no mention of Japan's surprise attack, and no explanation why Japan invaded China four years before Pearl Harbor. China and South Korea have objected to what Japan teaches the young, and have threatened trade sanctions if these inaccuracies are not corrected. They demand a meaningful account of Japan's invasion and occupation of their nations. While many Japanese teachers support such revisions, most school boards are not composed of educators, and it is questionable if any changes will be made.

SOURCE: Kwan Weng Kin, "Teachers Have No Say Over Japan Textbooks," *Straits Times Interactive*, May 21, 2001.

REFLECTION

The Japanese description of World War II is extreme, but not unusual. Most nations paint flattering self-portraits in the school curriculum. Can you identify examples of how the United States glosses over uncomfortable historical events?

Click on *In the News* for recent *In the News* stories. Submit your own *In the News* summary to share with your colleagues.

But this process is limiting as well. In transmitting culture, schools are teaching students to view the world from the wrong end of a telescope, yielding a constricted view that does not allow much deviation or perspective. Cultural transmission may contribute to feelings of cultural superiority, a belief that "we are the best, number one!" Such nationalistic views may decrease tolerance and respect for other cultures and peoples.

Purpose 2: Reconstructing Society (Schools as Tools for Change)

If society were perfect, transmitting the culture from one generation to the next would be all that is required of schools. But our world, our nation, and our communities are far from ideal. Poverty, hunger, injustice, pollution, overpopulation, racism, sexism, and ethical challenges—and, of course, the dark clouds of terrorism, nuclear, chemical, and biological weapons—are societal problems on a depressingly long list. To **reconstructionists,** society is broken, it needs to be fixed, and the school is a perfect tool for making the needed repairs.

Reconstructionists hold a wide spectrum of beliefs. As you might anticipate, there are both liberal and conservative reconstructionists, each pushing schools in different directions. It is not only values that differ; strategies differ as well. At one end are those who believe that students should be made aware of the ills of society; study these critical, if controversial, areas; and equip themselves to confront these issues as they become adults.[1] Other reconstructionists are more action-oriented and believe that schools and students shouldn't wait until the students reach adulthood. They call for a **social action curriculum,** in which students actively involve themselves in eliminating social ills. For example, if a poor neighborhood lacks a day care facility for young children of working parents, the students could petition government officials and private corporations to establish a center.

This idea of students contributing to society is not unique. The Carnegie Foundation for the Advancement of Teaching recommends that every student be required to earn a **service credit,** which might include volunteer work with the poor, elderly, or homeless. The idea behind a service credit includes not only an effort to reduce social ills but also the idea of providing students with a connection to the larger community and of encouraging them to develop a sense of their personal responsibility for improving the social condition.[2] In 1992, Maryland became the first state requiring students to perform community service before they would be granted their high school diploma, and service learning became more popular nationwide throughout the 1990s.[3] In 1999, more than half of students in grades 6 through 12 had participated in service learning, although who participates, and what they do to gain service credits, is somewhat erratic. While 57 percent of girls participated, only 47 percent of boys did. Whites were more likely to participate than African Americans, and African Americans more likely to participate than Hispanics. Participation increases when schools take an active role in setting up the service opportunities, and when they require it for graduation. And student participation increased with the educational level of their parents.[4]

While social democratic reconstructionists are reform-minded, *economic reconstructionists* hold a darker view of society's ills and advocate more drastic, even revolutionary, action. They believe that schools generally teach the poorer classes to accept their lowly stations in life, to be subservient to authority, to unquestioningly follow rules while laboring for the economic benefit of the rich. To economic reconstructionists, schools are currently tools of oppression, not institutions of learning. They believe that students must be introduced to curricula that analyze and reform economic realities. For example, one such curriculum project targets a popular and

Is the business of schools just academic learning, or might the goals include fostering an awareness of the benefits of community service, such as volunteering to tutor others?

HELP WANTED: VOLUNTEERS AGAINST VOLUNTEERING

Not everyone thinks that volunteerism is a good idea. Author Ayn Rand believed that the world should be ruled by self-interest, that the pursuit of one's self-interest is the highest moral principle. In fact, her philosophy portrays altruism as immoral. It is not surprising, therefore, that the Ayn Rand Institute in Marina del Ray, California, was displeased when service credits and community volunteering became a requirement in several high schools. The institute decided to fight fire with fire: They recruited high school volunteers to work against service requirements. The high school volunteers fighting volunteerism can get service credit for their volunteer work. According to the director, volunteering to help others might be problematic, but volunteering in one's self-interest is fine.

SOURCE: *The Washington Post Magazine,* October 4, 1998.

REFLECTION

Do you believe that requiring service credit is a great idea? Are there ways to have students do this type of service without a requirement?

Click on *In the News* for recent *In the News* stories. Submit your own *In the News* summary to share with your colleagues.

highly visible athletic company, one that produces incredibly expensive sport shoes. This company manufactures its products in developing nations, maintaining horrid working conditions. Children in these poor countries are sold into labor bondage by their impoverished families. As young as 6, they work twelve or more hours a day, enduring cruelty and even beatings as they earn only pennies an hour. While the companies defend themselves by saying that they cannot change local conditions, economic reconstructionists believe that companies intentionally select locations because of their cheap labor costs. Economic reconstructionists point out that American children play with products made through the agonizing toil of other children. All the while, the companies profit. Educators who focus on economic reform have developed materials, websites, and social action projects that not only teach children about such exploitation but also provide them with strategies to pressure companies into creating more humane and equitable working conditions.[5]

Perhaps the most noted contemporary economic reconstructionist was **Paulo Freire,** author of ***The Pedagogy of the Oppressed,*** a book about his efforts to educate and liberate poor, illiterate peasants in Brazil.[6] In his book, Freire describes how he taught these workers to read in order to identify problems that were keeping them poor and powerless. From this new awareness, they began to analyze their problems—such as how the lack of sanitation causes illness—and what they could do to solve specific problems and liberate themselves from their oppressive conditions. Freire highlighted the distinction between schools and education. Schools often miseducate and oppress. But true education liberates. Through education, the dispossessed learned to read, to act collectively, to improve their living conditions, and to reconstruct their lives. (See *The Education Hall of Fame* in Chapter 8 for more about Freire.)

Public Demands for Schools

While preserving the status quo and promoting social change represent two fundamental directions available to schools, they are not the only possible expectations. When you think about it, the public holds our schools to a bewildering assortment of tasks and expectations.

John Goodlad, in his massive study ***A Place Called School,*** examined a wide range of documents that tried to define the purposes of schooling over 300 years of history. He and his colleague found four broad goals:

1. *Academic,* including a broad array of knowledge and intellectual skills.
2. *Vocational,* aimed at readiness for the world of work and economic responsibilities.
3. *Social and civic,* including skills and behavior for participating in a complex democratic society.
4. *Personal,* including the development of individual talent and self-expression.[7]

Goodlad included these four goal areas in questionnaires distributed to parents, and he asked them to rate their importance. (See Figure 4.1.) Parents gave "very important" ratings to all four. When Goodlad asked students and teachers to rate the four goal areas, they rated all of them as "very important." When pushed to select one of these four as having top priority, approximately half the teachers and parents selected the intellectual area, while students spread their preferences fairly evenly among all four categories, with high school students giving a slight edge to vocational goals. When it comes to selecting the purpose of schools, both those who are their clients and those who provide their services resist interpreting the purpose of schools narrowly.

What do Americans want from their schools? Evidently, they want it all! As early as 1953, Arthur Bestor wrote, "The idea that the school must undertake to meet every need that some other agency is failing to meet, regardless of the suitability of the schoolroom to the task, is a preposterous delusion that in the end can wreck the educational system."[8]

FIGURE 4.1
Goals of schools.

REFLECTION

Under each goal, list specific efforts a school could make to reach the goal. How would you prioritize these goals? Explain.

Then, in the 1980s, **Ernest Boyer** conducted a major study of secondary education and concluded,

Since the English classical school was founded over 150 years ago, high schools have accumulated purposes like barnacles on a weathered ship. As school population expanded from a tiny urban minority to almost all youth, a coherent purpose was hard to find. The nation piled social policy upon educational policy and all of them on top of the delusion that a single institution can do it all.[9]

Where Do You Stand?

Identifying school goals seems to be everyone's business—parents, teachers, all levels of government, and various professional groups. Over the years, dozens of lists have been published in different reform reports, each enumerating goals for schools. The problem arises when schools cannot fulfill all of these goals, either because there are too many goals or because the purposes actually conflict with one another. It is these smaller pieces that often dominate discussion. Should schools focus on preparing students for college? Should they try to inhibit drug use, or lessen the threat of AIDS? Perhaps schools ought to focus on the economy and train students to become members of a more efficient workforce, one that can successfully compete in the world marketplace.

Look at the following list of school goals. Drawn from a variety of sources, these goals have been advocated singly and in combination by different groups at different times and have been adopted by different schools. In each case, register your own judgment on the values and worth of each goal. When you have completed your responses, we shall discuss the significance of these goals, and you can see how your responses fit into the bigger picture.

Circle the number that best reflects how important you think each school goal is.

1 Very unimportant

2 Unimportant

3 Moderately important

4 Important

5 Very important

	Very Unimportant				Very Important
1. To transmit the nation's cultural heritage, preserving past accomplishments and insights	1	2	3	4	5
2. To encourage students to question current practices and institutions; to promote social change	1	2	3	4	5
3. To prepare competent workers to compete successfully in a technological world economy	1	2	3	4	5
4. To develop healthy citizens aware of nutrition, exercise, and good health habits	1	2	3	4	5
5. To lead the world in creating a peaceful global society, stressing an understanding of other cultures and languages	1	2	3	4	5

INTERACTIVE ACTIVITY
HOW IMPORTANT ARE THESE SCHOOL GOALS? Do this exercise online. See how others responded to each statement.

	Very Unimportant				Very Important
6. To provide a challenging education for America's brightest students	1	2	3	4	5
7. To develop strong self-concept and self-esteem in students	1	2	3	4	5
8. To nurture creative students in developing art, music, and writing	1	2	3	4	5
9. To prevent unwanted pregnancy, AIDS, drugs, addiction, alcoholism	1	2	3	4	5
10. To unite citizens from diverse backgrounds (national origin, race, ethnicity) as a single nation with a unified culture	1	2	3	4	5
11. To provide support to families through after-school child care, nutritional supplements, medical treatment, and so on	1	2	3	4	5
12. To encourage loyal students committed to the United States; to instill patriotism	1	2	3	4	5
13. To teach students our nation's work ethic: punctuality, responsibility, cooperation, self-control, neatness, and so on	1	2	3	4	5
14. To demonstrate academic proficiency through high standardized test scores	1	2	3	4	5
15. To provide a dynamic vehicle for social and economic mobility, a way for the poor to reach their full potential	1	2	3	4	5
16. To prepare educated citizens who can undertake actions that spark change	1	2	3	4	5
17. To ensure the cultural richness and diversity of the United States	1	2	3	4	5
18. To eliminate racism, sexism, homophobia, anti-Semitism, and all forms of discrimination from society	1	2	3	4	5
19. To prepare as many students as possible for college and/or well-paid careers	1	2	3	4	5
20. To provide child care for the nation's children and to free parents to work and/or pursue their interests and activities	1	2	3	4	5

Now, think about your three most valued goals for school and write those goals below:

Three valued goals:

_____, _____, _____

Do your responses to these items and your three priority goal selections cast you as transmitter of culture or as change agent for restructuring society? To help you determine where your beliefs take you, record your scores on the following selected items:

PURPOSE OF SCHOOLS

Transmitting Culture		**Reconstructing Society**	
Focused Item		*Focused Item*	
1	_____	2	_____
3	_____	5	_____
10	_____	9	_____
12	_____	15	_____
13	_____	16	_____
19	_____	18	_____
Total	_____	*Total*	_____

REFLECTION

Do your responses reflect the school experiences you had, or the ones you had hoped for? Which camp are you in: transmitting culture or reconstructing society?

Let's investigate how your choices reflect your values. The current emphasis on standards, tests, and academic performance is reflected in items 1, 13, and especially 14. Are you in agreement with this contemporary educational priority? If you scored high on items 1 and 10, then you value the role schools serve in preparing Americans to adhere to a common set of principles and values. This has been a recurrent theme in schools as each new group of immigrants arrives. Some people called this the melting pot, more formally termed **acculturation,** or **Americanization** (replacing the old culture with the new American one). Others view diversity more as a tossed salad, an analogy that suggests that cultural traditions, practices and identity would be retained in America, and a high score on item 17 reflects a sensitivity to our nation's cultural diversity. Items 2, 17 and 18 suggest a commitment to civil rights and student empowerment, hallmarks of the 1960s and 1970s, and since history often runs in cycles, perhaps these goals will resurface in the not too distant future. Do you like the Horatio Alger folklore: hard work and a little elbow grease, and the poor become wealthy? Agree with this folklore and you probably rated items 15 and 19 pretty high. Take a little time and see where you stand on the other items. And while you look them over, consider item 20, which may seem a bit odd. After all, few people see schools as baby-sitters, but, without this "service," most parents would be overwhelmed. And consider the impact that millions of adolescents would have on the job market. Unemployment would skyrocket and wages would tumble. By minding the children, schools provide parents with time and keep our workforce down to a manageable size.

Ever wonder how schools get their names—and which names are the most popular? The National Education Resource Center researched the most popular proper names for U.S. high schools: Washington, Lincoln, Kennedy, Jefferson, Roosevelt (both Franklin and Teddy), and Wilson. (Presidents do well.) Lee, Edison, and Madison round out the top ten names. (To date, no school has chosen Richard M. Nixon as a namesake.) But proper names are not the most common high school names. Directions dominate: Northeastern, South, and Central High School are right up there. While creativity obviously is not a criterion, politics is. Citizens fight over whether schools should be named after George Washington—who, after all, was a slave holder—and over why so few African Americans, Hispanics, and people of non-European ancestry are honored by having a school named after them. And, considering how many women are educators, it is amazing that so few schools are named to honor women—Eleanor Roosevelt, Amelia Earhart, Christa McAuliffe, and Jacqueline Kennedy are exceptions. Some schools have honored writers (Bret Harte, Walt Whitman, and Mark Twain) or reflect local leaders and culture. (In Las Vegas, you will find schools named Durango, Silverado, and Bonanza, which some complain sound more like casinos than western culture.)

REFLECTION

What choices do you think educators might make if they were responsible for school names? If students were in charge, would schools be named after sports figures or music and media stars? How do our school names reflect the power and culture in a society? What's in a name?

What did your ratings teach you about your values and your view of schools? Were your goals popular during particular periods of our past, or are you more future-oriented? In a later chapter, you will have the opportunity to gain insight into your philosophy of education. You may want to compare your goals for education here with your philosophical preferences as identified in Chapter 9.

Education Reform

Our Nation is at risk. Our once unchallenged prominence in commerce, industry, science, and technological innovation is being overtaken by competitors throughout the world. . . . If an unfriendly foreign power had attempted to impose on America the mediocre educational performance that exists today, we might well have viewed it as an act of war. As it stands, we have allowed this to happen to ourselves. We have even squandered the gains in student achievement made in the wake of the *Sputnik* challenge. Moreover, we have dismantled essential support systems which helped make those gains possible. We have, in effect, been committing an act of unthinking, unilateral educational disarmament.[10]

So began the report of the **National Commission on Excellence in Education,** *A Nation at Risk: The Imperative for Educational Reform,* released in 1983. The report cited declining test scores, the weak performance of U.S. students in comparison with those of other industrialized nations, and the number of functionally illiterate adults. **A Nation at Risk** condemned the "cafeteria-style curriculum." The report called for a more thorough grounding in the "five new basics" of English, mathematics, science, social science, and computer science. It called for greater academic rigor, higher expectations for students, and better-qualified and better-paid teachers.

This report galvanized Americans, moving education to center stage. Remember, in 1983, we were in two wars: the Cold War with the Soviet Union and an economic war with Japan. Our national security was at stake, and poor school performance was putting the nation at risk. With the battle cry sounded, governors, state legislators, and foundations issued a wave of reports (see Appendix 3 for a summary of the salient reform reports). Within the next two years,

- Hundreds of local and state panels were formed.
- More than 40 states increased course requirements for graduation.
- Thirty-three states instituted testing for student promotion or graduation.
- Almost half the states passed legislation to increase qualification standards and pay for teachers.
- Most states increased the length of the school day and/or school year.
- Most states passed laws that required teachers and students to demonstrate computer literacy.[11]

Although state legislatures passed laws, many critics remained skeptical that such changes would truly improve education. They pointed out that these were top-down approaches, dictated from above and far removed from the real world of the classroom.[12] Teachers felt dumped on (*teacher bashing* was the phrase used to protest this), controlled, and regulated by new rules and requirements. Other critics worried that these new regulations might do more harm than good. Increasing student graduation requirements without providing for special programs could hurt racial and ethnic minorities, non-English speakers, females, special education students, and other groups not testing well. Different groups struggled to claim their place on the new list of educational priorities. To be left out of the goals for education reform could be costly, indeed.[13]

The reform reports—and there were many—came in three waves (see Frame of Reference). These **three waves of reform** continue to influence American education today. The first wave of reports came immediately after *A Nation at Risk* and, as previously described, viewed school reform in terms of national defense and economic competition. Corporations complained about the need to teach employees basic reading and math skills, and the military struggled to recruit technically skilled personnel for increasingly sophisticated equipment. Education critics pointed to low scores by American students on international tests, especially in math and science, as they made their case that schools were not meeting the nation's economic and technical needs. By the turn of the century, this first reform wave had trumped many educational issues and topics: It seemed as though everyone was talking about standards, the rapid growth of state tests, and the effort to identify weak performing students, teachers, and schools. While other, smaller waves followed, this first wave never ended. Politicians decried the inadequate performance of public schools, private for-profit companies sprung into existence, saying that their new schools could do a better job, and corporations lamented the fact that their new employees lacked fundamental skills.

Other critics point out that American industry has itself to blame for some of its problems, including many inefficient production practices. Educator Clinton Boutwell, author of *Shell Game: Corporate America's Agenda for Schools,* asserts that,

Wave 1—The goal of the first wave was to raise educational quality by requiring more courses and more testing of student and teacher performance. States were to assume the leadership in improving existing practices and this wave continues to be the strongest.

Wave 2—Again it was state governors who promoted improvement and accountability. Teachers were to be empowered, given more control over their schools. Some of the educational problems confronting children of color and some other students facing educational barriers were also addressed.

Wave 3—In this, the most ambitious wave, reformers called for reformulating our nation of schools. Schools should be seen as more than educational facilities. They should also provide health care, social services, and transportation. In short, the whole array of services needed to bring the child into successful adulthood should be offered at the school: one-stop shopping for educational, social, medical, and other services.

Wave I (began 1982 to present) | Wave II (began 1986) | Wave III (began 1988)
"Raise the Standards" | "Restructure the School" | "Comprehensive Services"

SOURCE: Adapted from Joseph Murphy, "The Educational Movement of the 1980s: A Comprehensive Analysis," in Joseph Murphy (ed.), *The Educational Reform Movement of the 1980s* (Berkeley: McCutchan, 1990).

REFLECTION

Which of these reform waves do you feel would be most effective? Why does the first persist? As familiar as these criticisms have become, they are far from universally accepted. As Educator Larry Cuban has pointed out, "As economic productivity has gone up and down over the last twenty years, the argument has remained the same. But during the last eight years of unparalleled prosperity, nobody has given the public schools an Oscar for outstanding performance. And the reason is that there is no relationship." Researcher Gerald Bracey adds: "If you think about it, the kids who were in high school when *A Nation at Risk* was released became all the dot.com millionaires."[14]

contrary to popular belief, technical and scientific education in America's schools is stronger than ever. Boutwell believes that sinister motives might be at play. Many business leaders complaining about the lack of scientists and engineers are the same executives who fire tens of thousands of scientists and engineers as they downsize the workforce in an effort to increase profits.[15] In fact, the vast majority of new jobs are service-oriented and do not require large numbers of highly educated employees at all.

The second wave of reform, which began in the mid- and late-1980s, was led by educators such as Theodore Sizer, John Goodlad, and Ernest Boyer, rather than by politicians and business leaders. Based on research and school observations, these educators stressed the need for basic reform of school practices. Gerald Grant, for example, in his "schoolography" of Hamilton High, calls for teachers to be given more responsibility to reshape their schools, a process called **empowering teachers. Theodore Sizer** and others see the superficial nature of the curriculum as a central weakness, recommending that students cover fewer topics but study them in greater depth. The second wave of reformers are alarmed at the loss of teacher autonomy in oppressive school climates, bland teaching, and poor academic performance. They emphasize thoughtful changes: reducing bureaucracy; creating a more professionally trained, treated, and salaried corps of teachers; implementing local decision making; strengthening the role of the school principal; and studying subjects in greater depth.

The third wave of reform recognizes that struggling families are unlikely to possess the time and resources required to ensure high-quality education. Underway since the late 1980s and early 1990s, the third wave advocates **full service schools,** providing a network of social services, nutrition, health care, transportation, counseling, and parent education. School boards would be replaced by **children's boards,** made up of professionals and community members who work on the comprehensive needs of children. School policy, focused only on education, would be replaced by **children's policy,** responding to the multiple needs of children. In the late 1990s, full service schools in Florida, New York, and California were operating long hours and providing an array of community services.

> At Intermediate School 218, in the Washington Heights section of New York City, school is open by 7 a.m. for breakfast, sports activities, dance or Latin band practice, all before school "officially" opens. At the school's Family Resource Center, parents receive social services, including immigration, housing, and employment consultations. Social workers, mental health counselors, a health and dental clinic are all on site. After classes end, the building remains open until 10 p.m. for sports, computer lab, music, art, mentoring, English classes, parenting skills, and cultural classes. Intermediate School 218 is a full service school.[16]

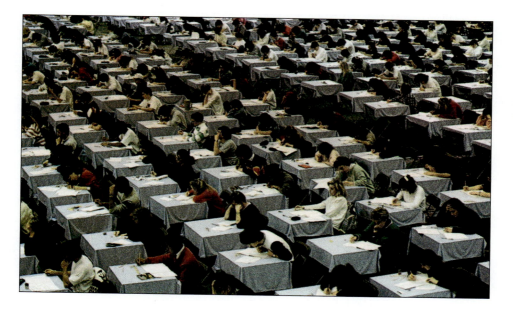

A byproduct of recent calls for educational reform has been an explosion of student (and teacher) testing to ensure that revised school goals are being met.

Beyond the Neighborhood Public School

At the beginning of the chapter, you listened in on the meeting held at Monroe High School. You had the opportunity to hear parents, educators, and business people express their concern, frustration, and disappointment with the test scores at Monroe High. While that meeting was fictional, it offers an insight into the strong feelings and opinions found in communities around the nation, communities disappointed with their public schools. The future of the neighborhood school, for centuries the cornerstone of public education, is now in doubt. Many parents and political leaders, discouraged by the slow pace of educational change, have been experimenting with public schools beyond their neighborhoods, with open enrollments, vouchers, and charter schools, and even with business-sponsored schools designed to make money.[17] Some parents now send their children to these schools created to both educate and turn a profit. Other parents are refocusing their energies on getting their children into private schools. Other parents have given up on all schools, and have joined the growing number of Americans educating their children at home. Many parents are leaving what they consider to be a failing public school monopoly. Let's look at some of these dramatic changes, changes that may well influence where you teach. (See Figure 4.2.)

FIGURE 4.2

Public attitudes: Reforming or replacing public schools.

SOURCE: *The 2000 Phi Delta Kappa/Gallup Poll of the Public's Attitudes Toward the Public Schools*

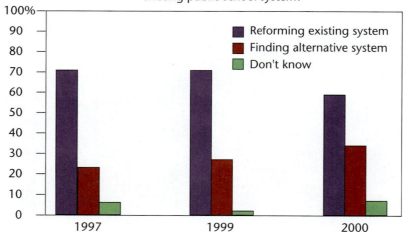

Which approach do you think is preferable— reforming the existing public school system or finding an alternative to the existing public school system?

- Reforming existing system
- Finding alternative system
- Don't know

REFLECTION

Why do you believe that most people prefer to reform the current system rather than find an alternative? Why has support for neighborhood schools declined?

The Choice Concept

In the 1950s, economist **Milton Friedman** suggested that public schools would be more effective if they functioned as a free market, much as private schools do. Friedman believed that public schools were not working well, even back then, because there was no competition, no incentive for them to do their best. Parents were forced to send their children to the neighborhood school, and the neighborhood school had no incentive to compete with other schools or improve. It had a "trapped" clientele. But not everyone was trapped. Because they could afford private school tuition, wealthy parents were able to bail out if the public school was performing poorly. Friedman believed that everyone needed the same freedom to choose what the wealthy enjoyed.

In a 1981 study, **James Coleman** found that private schools were doing a better job of educating students than were the neighborhood public schools. Not only were the students attending independent, often religiously affiliated, private schools better behaved, but they also scored higher on tests. Coleman noted that the private schools enforced more rigorous academic standards and gave teachers and administrators more autonomy. In 1993, another study found that Catholic schools not only were providing particularly effective education for inner-city students of color but also were providing this education at a lower per student cost and in less segregated classrooms than were neighboring public schools.[18] The call for **school choice** was getting louder.

Magnet Schools

Over a quarter century ago, a number of public schools actually began a choice program, although few called it that. In the 1970s, as schools struggled to desegregate, "forced" busing became quite unpopular. But, with neighborhoods so racially segregated, desegregating schools required that students and teachers attend schools outside their local communities. **Magnet schools** were created to draw students, much like a magnet, beyond their neighborhoods. The magnet school "draw" was offering high-quality educational programs, unique programs unavailable in local schools, programs well worth the bus ride.

Today, more than a million students attend several thousand magnet schools. Magnet schools offer unique educational programs in such areas as science and technology, communication skills, career specialties, mathematics and computer science, theater, music, and art. How effective have magnet schools been? After a quarter of a century, the results are mixed. About half of these schools have helped desegregation efforts, but, in hypersegregated cities and other areas, they have had little or no impact on desegregation. In terms of educational quality, some studies suggest that students in magnet schools outperform students in other public schools and in Catholic schools. Research also indicates that those attending career magnet schools that prepare students for the world of work are less likely to be involved in fighting and drinking, and they earn more college credits than their contemporaries in public schools. Although magnet schools cost more than neighborhood public schools, these studies suggest that they may also be more effective.[19]

Open Enrollment

In 1988, Minnesota instituted **open enrollment,** which eliminated the requirement that students must attend the closest public school. Like the magnet schools, open enrollment encouraged parents to choose a school, but it greatly increased the number of schools to choose from. Any public school with available space became eligible. Arkansas, Iowa, Nebraska, and other states soon followed Minnesota's lead and introduced open enrollment legislation. However, even more radical proposals were being launched, proposals threatening to redefine, if not eliminate, the neighborhood school.

Vouchers

The approach that Milton Friedman favored was neither open enrollment nor magnet schools: Friedman proposed that **educational vouchers** be given to parents. The vouchers would function like admission tickets. Parents would "shop" for a school, make their choice, and give the voucher to the school. The school would turn over the voucher to the local or state government, and the government would pay the school a fixed sum for each voucher. Good schools would collect many vouchers and thrive, while poor schools would not attract "customers" and would go out of business. Some voucher plans would give parents the choice of selecting either a public or a private school, while other plans would limit the choice to public schools.

In 1990, Milwaukee became the site of the first publicly financed voucher program. Wisconsin lawmakers approved a plan for Milwaukee students to receive about $3,000 each to attend nonsectarian private schools, then, in 1995, amended the law to allow students to attend religious schools as well. And it is the inclusion of religious schools first in the Milwaukee voucher plan, then in a similar plan in Cleveland, that sparked a heated controversy and a round of lawsuits. The reason that religious schools are so closely involved in the voucher dispute is that they are the prime beneficiaries, receiving upwards of 90 percent of the students using such vouchers. Why is this? Two reasons: First, most private schools are religious schools, and second, most religious schools charge less than the other private schools. Most voucher plans offer modest financial support, usually under $3,000. While a $3,000 voucher covers only a fraction of the cost of a nonsectarian private school, it goes much further in covering the cost of a religious school.[20] Yet, the First Amendment of the Constitution ensures the separation of church and state, and paying for a religious education with taxpayer funds would violate the Constitution—or has all that changed?

In fact, the legal picture, once quite clear, is now somewhat cloudy. In 1971 in **Lemon v. Kurtzman** and in 1973 in the *Nyquist* case, the Supreme Court constructed clear walls limiting the use of public funds to support religious education. What became known as the *Lemon* test provided three criteria to determine the legality of government funds used in religious schools. According to Lemon, the funds (1) must have a secular purpose, (2) must not primarily advance or prohibit religion, and (3) must not result in excessive government entanglement with religion. However, over the past quarter of a century, an increasingly conservative Supreme Court has allowed more public funds to be used in religious settings, particularly when the funds first go to students or parents before being distributed to the religious school. The courts have ruled, for example, that public funds can be used to provide a sign interpreter for a deaf student at a Catholic high school, that a state can give tax deductions to parents who send their children to religious schools, and that religious clubs can use public school facilities to hold their meetings. Future court decisions in this arena are likely.[21]

Religious controversy is one reason for a decline in support of voucher schemes, but it is not the only reason. With the deteriorating state of urban public schools commonplace, voucher supporters targeted these inner-city constituencies as likely allies. But that is not what happened in Detroit and Los Angeles, where voters in the 2000 election rejected a voucher program. Many feared that vouchers, rather than promote healthy competition, would hurt schools by redirecting money from public to private education. The issue is far from resolved. Conservative political foundations have spent millions of dollars on ads promoting the ideas of the small but active pro-voucher Black Alliance for Education, while mainline civil rights groups, like the NAACP, oppose the voucher concept.[22] (See Figure 4.3.)

Charter Schools

Albert Shanker, the late president of the American Federation of Teachers, launched the charter schools movement in a 1988 speech, when he suggested that teachers be empowered in **charter schools,** special schools that focus on student achievement.[23]

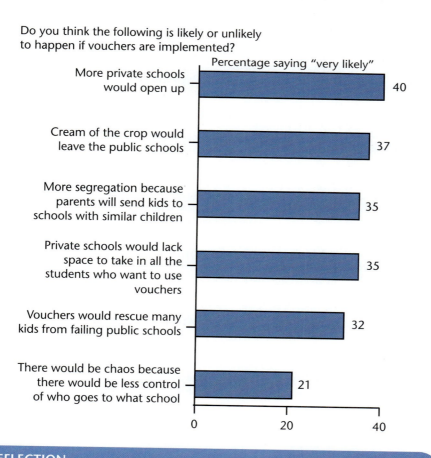

Do you think the following is likely or unlikely to happen if vouchers are implemented?

Percentage saying "very likely"

More private schools would open up — 40

Cream of the crop would leave the public schools — 37

More segregation because parents will send kids to schools with similar children — 35

Private schools would lack space to take in all the students who want to use vouchers — 35

Vouchers would rescue many kids from failing public schools — 32

There would be chaos because there would be less control of who goes to what school — 21

0   20   40

FIGURE 4.3

The public's predictions if vouchers are implemented.

SOURCE: Public Agenda Online, June 1999, *On Thin Ice* (Finding Two).

REFLECTION

Which of these options would you select? Do you believe those answering the question considered that most private schools are religious?

A Harvard graduate and Rhodes scholar, Jonathan Kozol had no idea "what it was like to be a poor kid in America." He quickly learned. In 1964 the Klu Klux Klan in Mississippi murdered three young civil rights workers. The injustice ignited a need to act.

> I'd never been involved with racial issues. I was not particularly political. In fact, I wasn't political at all. But this event had an extraordinary effect. Without thinking it through, I simply got on the subway, which in those days ended in Harvard Square, and went to the other end of the line, which was Roxbury. I volunteered to spend the summer teaching at a black church which had set up a freedom school. When September came, I walked into the Boston school department and said, "I'm going to be a teacher."[1]

He was assigned to the fourth grade of an urban school in Boston, a school so impoverished he didn't have a classroom. Kozol and his disenfranchised students camped out in an auditorium. In an effort to resuscitate their interest in learning, he shared his favorite poetry. And the classroom was transformed. Students recited lines, asked questions, even cried as they identified with the words of Langston Hughes. While the words of the black poet may have inspired students, the author was not on the school's approved reading list. Kozol was fired. He chronicled his first year teaching in *Death at an Early Age* (1967), which alerted the nation to the wrenching injustices found in impoverished schools and the resiliency of their students.

For almost four decades, Kozol's compassionate spirit has given voice to the poor. In his best-selling book, *Savage Inequalities* (1991), he describes life in destitute schools from East St. Louis to the Bronx. Kozol writes of schools so overcrowded that students only get desks when other students are absent. Of students who go for part, most, or all of the

year without textbooks. While decrying this tragedy, Kozol does not find an answer in voucher programs.

> The first time I ever heard vouchers proposed in the U.S. was by Milton Friedman, an economist respected among scholars for some of his pure economics work but better known to some people as the former economic advisor to Augusto Pinochet: the fascist dictator of Chile.
>
> The first time I heard of schools of choice, it was after the Brown decision in the 1950s, when schools in many Southern states set up schools of choice—that was the word. They called them Freedom of Choice Schools as a ploy to avoid desegregation. That's the history.
>
> What have I actually seen? Well, first of all, the idea behind choice (within the district), basically, is that if you let people choose, everybody will get the school they want. Everybody will have an equally free choice; everybody will have equal access. And, those I hear defend choice say it will not increase class or racial segregation. In fact, in virtually every case that I have seen, none of these conditions is met. People very seldom have equal choices, and even when they theoretically have equal choices, they rarely have equal access.
>
> People can't choose things they've never heard of, for example. And lots of the poorest folks in our inner cities are functionally illiterate. I've written a book about that, as some of you know. In many of our inner cities, as many as 30 percent of our adults cannot read well enough to understand the booklets put out by school systems delineating their choices. That's one point.
>
> Even if they can understand and even if the school system is sophisticated enough to print these things in five different languages for all the different ethnic groups in cities like New York or Chicago, there's a larger point that those who hear about new schools, good schools, first are almost always the well connected. They're almost always the people whose friends are in the school system, the people like myself who went to college with the principal or the superintendent or some of the people who run the system. Word of mouth always favors the children of the most wealthy or best educated.
>
> And so, what often happens is that while everybody theoretically has the right to choose any school, the affluent, the savvy, the children of the academics, the children of the lawyers, the children of the doctors, the children of the school superintendent tend to end up in the same three little boutique elementary schools. And I call them boutique schools because they're always charming, and the press loves them, and they always have enough racial integration so it looks okay for the newspaper or the TV camera. But, in fact, they are separated by both race and class, and more and more by class.
>
> What happens is that the poorest of the poor often do not get into these schools or very small numbers get in. Large

numbers of the kids who nobody wants end up concentrated in the schools that no one chooses except by default . . .

Now the dark, terrifying prospect of vouchers or a choice agenda, of a so-called market basis for our public schools, is that rather than encourage a sense of common loyalties among people, choice will particularize loyalties. It will fragmentize ambition, so that the individual parent will be forced to claw and scramble for the good of her kid and her kid only, at whatever cost to everybody else. There will no longer be a sense of "What I choose for my child, I choose for everybody." There's a wonderful quote from John Dewey. He said "What the best and wisest parent wants for his own child, that must the community want for all its children. Any other ideal for our schools is narrow and unlovely. Acted upon, it destroys our democracy."

. . . The best known voucher advocate, John Chubb, of the Brookings Institute, in Washington, says something—I'm paraphrasing him—like this: "Democratic governance of schools is what's wrong with schools. We need a voucher plan in order to break the bonds of democratic education, because it hasn't worked." That's what he says.

When I hear that, I think to myself, "Wait a minute. We've never tried democratic education." We haven't yet given equal, wonderful, innovative, humane schools—at the level of our finest schools—to all our children. . . . I think we should try it first, see how it might work.[2]

[1]Mardell Raney. Interview with Jonathan Kozol. *Technos,* 7 no. 3 (Fall 1998), pp. 4–10.

[2]Reprinted with permission of *Educational Leadership* 50, no. 3 (November 1992), pp. 90–92.

REFLECTION

What American values are reflected—or undermined—in school choice? Is school choice an educational trend or a permanent fixture? Research school choice in your state. Does your state have a voucher system, finance charter schools or support privatization? If your state is experimenting with these options, do you think the public schools are being strengthened, or threatened, by them?

WRITE YOUR OWN PROFILE IN EDUCATION: Click on *Profiles in Education,* write a *Profile in Education* about an educator, and post it on the Online Learning Center. Check out *Profiles in Education* submitted by other future teachers.

To learn more about Jonathan Kozol, click on *Profiles in Education.*

In 1991, Minnesota was the first state to enact charter school legislation. A decade later, nearly two thousand charter schools were in operation. So many created so quickly that some states decided to slow the process down and take a closer look at these schools. Some charters had questionable educational impact, others were drawing few students, and others raised even more serious legal and financial questions. Most charters, however, continued to enjoy public support.[24]

What are these charter schools? The concept is simple. The charter (or contract) represents legal permission from a local or state school board to operate the school, usually for a fixed period of time, perhaps five years, with the right to renew the charter if the school is successful. While charter schools must follow some of the same rules established for other publicly funded schools (for example, health and safety regulations, agreement not to discriminate), charter schools are exempt from many state and local laws and regulations. Charter schools, in effect, "swap" rules and regulations for greater freedom and the promise that they will achieve better results. A charter school typically

- Allows for the creation of a new or the conversion of an existing public school
- Prohibits admission tests
- Is nonsectarian
- Requires a demonstrable improvement in performance
- Can be closed if it does not meet expectations
- Does not need to conform to most state rules and regulations
- Receives funding based on the number of students enrolled

A charter school represents a break with the past, a new way to educate with tax dollars. A charter school might be established to improve academic performance or attendance, to explore a new organizational approach or teaching strategy, or to extend the hours of the school day or the length of the school year. Some charter schools are associated with national programs, such as the International Baccalaureate Degree, while others are independent, meeting local needs. In St. Paul, Minnesota, for example, the City Academy is a year-round charter school serving forty at-risk students. Metro Deaf serves deaf students, while the Teamsters Union and the Minnesota Business Partnership sponsor a vocational and technical school, called Skills for Tomorrow, that uses internship placements to educate students interested in becoming skilled workers. The City on a Hill charter in Boston was created by two veteran teachers committed to providing a more effective education for poor inner-city children.[25] Although charter schools operate differently in different states, the increase in the number of charter schools across the country has been spectacular. Why?

One reason is that charter schools are less controversial than voucher plans. They do not involve religious schools or competition between public and private schools. They appeal to people who support public schools but who have concerns about their quality. The enthusiasm generated by these supporters is contagious, and often translates into a robust educational effort, and a great deal of positive publicity. But is enthusiasm enough for the long haul? Are charters doing as well as some say?

While it is too early to reach a final assessment of charters, some problems are coming to light. Charters were created to experiment, promote innovation, and to trailblaze new educational approaches. This is not happening. Most charters, in fact, are mirroring the most traditional educational practices available. And they are teaching a very select student population. Critics point out that by doing this, they are actually segregating students, creating schools where all the children are similar and

Today, most states have a law allowing public funding for charter schools, which operate outside normal public school channels to satisfy the specific educational goals of the founding group.

share similar goals, a far cry from the inclusive and democratic ideal of public education. Initially advocates proclaimed that the charters would cut the cost of education
by eliminating a "bloated administration," but this has not been the case. Their low
student enrollments and the need to duplicate resources like libraries and computers
has translated into just the opposite, higher administrative costs than public schools.
Added to these financial woes is the fact that many charters are located in inadequate
buildings, either converted facilities or schools built with cheap materials, so we can
include safety concerns to our list.[26] Yet despite these unresolved problems, the charter school movement continues to grow, in no small part because of the ardor of its
advocates. (See Figure 4.4.)

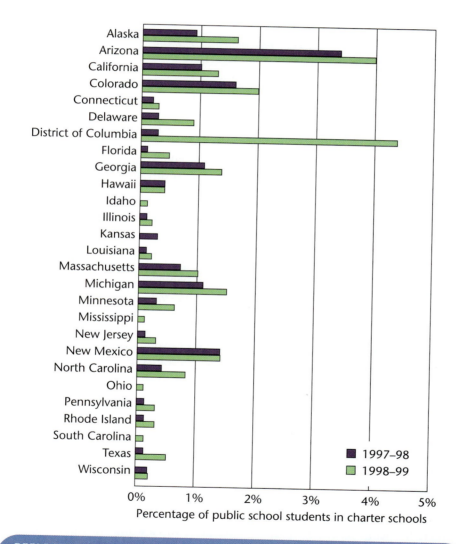

FIGURE 4.4

**Charter school enroll-
ment as a percentage of
public school enrollment,
by state.**

SOURCE: U.S. Department of
Education, National Center for
Education Statistics, Common
Core of Data Survey, The State
of Charter Schools 2000,
Fourth-Year Report.

REFLECTION

Do you see any connections among the states most actively establishing charter schools? Why
is the number of charter schools increasing?

Who are the people who create such schools? Tom Watkins, director of the Detroit Center for Charter Schools, describes three types of charter advocates: reformers, zealots, and entrepreneurs.[27] *Reformers* are those who want to expand public school options and create more teacher- and student-centered institutions. These are the most mainstream advocates, the ones who often engender positive reports in the press. Watkins also describes *zealots,* those who prefer private to public schools, who view teacher unions as the obstacle to change and many of whom are themselves politically quite conservative. The final group consists of *entrepreneurs,* those who view schools as untapped profit centers and charter schools as vehicles for combining business and education. In the next section, we will take a closer look at these educational entrepreneurs.

EMOs (Educational Maintenance Organizations): Schools for Profit

Wall Street calls them **EMOs,** paralleling the HMOs in the health maintenance industry. HMOs are big business, and many on Wall Street are predicting that EMOs will be too. During the past few years, for-profit businesses have contracted with local school districts to provide a wide range of services in an attempt to win a segment of the lucrative education market, a market that exceeds $300 billion a year. Not that the entrance of private companies onto the public educational scene is completely new. For years, school districts have contracted with private businesses to provide school lunches and bus transportation. But, to provide education itself, to be responsible for academic performance, *is* new.

The largest for-profit venture in public schools, the **Edison Schools,** took off after a chance encounter. In 1990, Benno Schmidt, the president of Yale University, was attending a party in the Hamptons, a posh section of Long Island. At that party, Schmidt met Chris Whittle, an entrepreneur who was involved with various education-related projects. Apparently, they hit it off. Whittle offered Schmidt a high salary, reported to be about $1 million a year, to leave Yale and assume leadership of the Edison Schools. Chris Whittle's vision called for creating a model school, one based on proven educational programs, and then franchising the model nationally.

Edison Schools lengthen the school day by one or two hours, while increasing the school year from 180 days to 210 days. In effect, these changes add about two more years of study before graduation. Curricular changes include devoting more school time to math and science, foreign language instruction starting from the early grades, and using proven programs, such as the University of Chicago approach to math and a reading program developed at Johns Hopkins University. Learning contracts are used to increase student accountability. Edison's plan calls for linking each student to the school by a company-provided home computer. The computer offers students a virtual library and gives both parents and students a dedicated communication link to teachers.

The project's start-up costs were enormous, and the franchise idea was not easy to implement. Whittle saw that opening charter schools would be an easier way to disseminate his plan.[28] The charter school movement was a wonderful opportunity for education companies like Edison. The company no longer had to work with entire school districts and school boards to win a contract. Now, Edison could deal directly with parents and neighborhood groups, selling its Edison concept as a charter school. By 2001, more than 100 Edison Schools were up and running with a total student enrollment equivalent to Atlanta or Cincinnati. As Edison schools multiplied, the key question remained unanswered: Are these schools effective? A Columbia University study of Edison found that there was high teacher morale, enthusiasm for the curriculum, and satisfied parents. The American Federation of Teachers and the National Education Association undertook similar studies and found that students at Edison Schools were not doing any better than students at regular public schools, and sometimes, worse. Some Edison employees reported that the company hides its problems from the public and that the needs of special education students, among others, were not being met. Supporters say that with time, the company will thrive, and so will the students. As the enrollments increase, Edison promises its investors that the company will finally turn a profit.[29] While Edison seeks more time to earn a profit and prove its effectiveness, there is some question as to how much time is left. Although a number of public schools have bought into the Edison concept, questions about the financial stability of the Whittle educational empire persist.[30]

Other companies have harbored less grandiose plans than the Edison Schools. Rather than redesigning schools and creating entirely new school programs, these companies have focused on improving school performance through greater efficiency. A pioneer in this effort, **Tesseract** (formerly **Educational Alternatives Incorporated,** or EAI), began contracting with schools as early as 1990. A contract with Miami schools was followed by contracts with schools in Baltimore, Maryland (1992), and Hartford, Connecticut (1994). Tesseract made national news by providing new school managers dedicated to efficiency. The costs of maintenance, supplies, security, transportation, food contracts, and even consultant salaries were scaled back, producing a leaner school budget overall. But student performance did not improve. Tesseract complained that it lacked the power to make real changes, and all of these contracts were eventually terminated. By the late 1990s, the company had changed its name and direction, focusing instead on operating charter schools, turning a profit in the process.[31]

The business community has not been timid about investing in public education. The Edison Project, for example, spent at least $40 million in just the start-up phase, and John Walton, son of Walmart founder Sam Walton, invested heavily in Tesseract, two strong signs indicating the size of the potential profits to be made in the **privatization** of public schools.[32] Private-sector education companies continue to multiply. Advantage Schools, a Boston-based company, focuses on urban school districts, hires nonunion teachers, and promotes direct instruction, a program that relies on intense and frequent teacher-student interactions, and like other private companies, does not have a stellar record with special education students. Sylvan Learning Systems, known for its after-school learning centers, now provides services to several large school districts, including after-school instruction for students who are performing below expectations.[33]

Even Disney entered the school business. In a project called "Celebration," located near Disney World in Florida, Disney joined forces with the Osceola County school district and Stetson University to build and operate a state-of-the-art school. While the school is part of a new residential community "inspired by the main streets of small-town America and reminiscent of Norman Rockwell images,"[34] it was designed to meet the future's demands. Disney donated $11 million for the school itself and another $9 million for the creation of an adjacent academy, where teachers are trained in the techniques and strategies used at Celebration. The school district committed over $15 million to build this "school of tomorrow."

From Mickey Mouse to Thomas Edison, it seems that for-profit companies are anxious to prove their effectiveness, to parents, to educators, and especially, to investors. It is not surprising that these companies are quick to announce even modest gains to prove that their methods work. Opponents are just as eager to question the

YOU BE THE JUDGE
FOR-PROFIT SCHOOLS

Are a Good Idea Because...

COMPETITION LEADS TO BETTER SCHOOLS

For-profit schools will break down the public school monopoly by creating competition and choice. As schools compete, parents (particularly poor parents) will finally have a choice, and not be forced to place their children in the neighborhood school. Just like in business, the weak schools will lose students and declare "bankruptcy." The stronger schools will survive and prosper.

SCHOOLS WILL BE ABLE TO REWARD GOOD TEACHERS, AND REMOVE WEAK ONES

The current public school bureaucracy protects too many incompetent teachers through the tenure system, and does not recognize teaching excellence. Using sound business practices, for-profit schools will reward superior teachers through profit-sharing incentives, retain competent teachers, and terminate ineffective teachers.

BUSINESS EFFICIENCY WILL IMPROVE SCHOOL PERFORMANCE

Education needs the skills and know-how of the business community. For-profit schools will implement the most effective educational strategies in a business culture. The top-heavy management of today's schools will be replaced by only a handful of administrators, and teachers will be driven to greater productivity through the profit incentives.

FOCUSED PROGRAMS AND INVESTOR OVERSIGHT LEAD TO ACADEMIC SUCCESS

For-profit schools will do a better educational job because they provide a focused and proven instructional plan. These schools avoid the public school pitfall of trying to offer "something-for-everyone." And if they falter and profits disappear, investor pressure will put them back on track.

Are a Bad Idea Because...

COMPETITION LEADS TO WEAKER SCHOOLS

Transplanting businesslike competition into the education arena would be a disaster. Competition is not all that business brings: false advertising, "special" promotions, a "feel-good" education—all the hucksterism of the marketplace to mislead students and their parents. Worse yet, the local public school, which holds a community together, will be lost.

TEACHERS WILL LOSE THEIR INFLUENCE AND ACADEMIC FREEDOM

Teachers who speak out against the company, or teach a controversial or politically sensitive topic, will have a brief career. The business community is quite vocal about teachers sharing in the profits, but strangely silent about what will happen during economic hard times.

PROFITS AND EDUCATION DO NOT MIX

For-profit schools are exactly that, "for profit," and when the interests of children and investors clash, investor interests will prevail. If investors demand better returns, if the stock market drops, if the economy enters hard times, the corporate executives will sacrifice educational resources. After all, while students enjoy little leverage, stockholders can fire business executives.

FOCUSED PROGRAMS MEANS KEEPING SOME STUDENTS OUT

Their one-size-fits-all approach practiced by these schools might be good for efficiency, but it is bad for students. The more challenging students, those with special needs, non-native speakers of English, or those who need special counseling, will be left to the underfunded public schools to educate.

YOU BE THE JUDGE

Do you believe that business and schools are a good or a bad match? Explain. Do you believe that profits can be made in schooling the nation's children? As a teacher, would you want to work for a for-profit school?

self-serving reports, and to challenge the ethics of mixing profits with children. The jury is still out on their overall effectiveness. One thing is clear: The years ahead will prove decisive. If successful, for-profits will reshape the nation's educational land-scape, dramatically altering your own working conditions. If they fail, hundreds of millions of dollars invested in this venture will be lost.

Is Choice a Good Idea?

While critics and supporters debate the merits of the various choice plans, you may well want to reflect on the validity of these arguments. To many, choice means com-petition, and to this group, competition is inherently valuable. They point out that wealthy families have always enjoyed educational choices, and now it is time to share this right with poorer Americans. While survey findings have been somewhat incon-sistent, some surveys indicate that a majority of African American favor choice plans, and that the highest support comes from those earning the least.[35] In some, but not all, impoverished neighborhoods—communities where numerous children of color attend some of the poorest public schools—vouchers and charter programs have been applauded. It also appears that choice plans, particularly charter schools and for-profit education companies, may be having a positive influence on public education. Feeling the competition, a number of public schools have adopted some of their ap-proaches and practices, from longer school days to more extensive use of laptop com-puters. So even if the choice plans do not succeed and eventually disappear, they are raising important questions. (See Figure 4.5.) Although we may be several years away from determining the educational effectiveness of for-profits and charter schools, there are those who are sounding the warning bells.

FIGURE 4.5   **Who has your vote?**

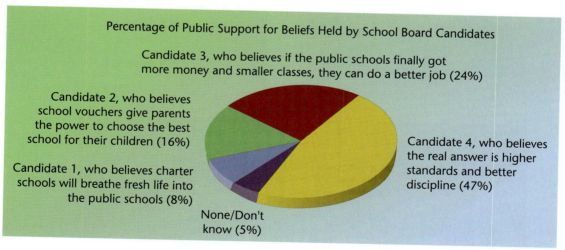

SOURCE: Public Agenda Online, June 1999, *On Thin Ice* (Finding Six).

REFLECTION

Which of these candidates would you vote for—or want to be? What does this graph teach us about the nation's views of pub-lic schools?

What does a school's name, mascot, message board, and presentation say about what's happening inside the classroom? What do these school signs tell you? Are there ways to identify a good school by its sign? How would your high school sign fit in the photo gallery?

Critics fear that increasing competition for limited educational dollars will hurt public education. They argue that all schools would improve if funding were increased, rather than divided. The critics also lament the lost ideals expressed by Thomas Jefferson and Horace Mann, the vision of a democratic nation educated in democratic classrooms being supplanted by "niche" schools serving a narrowly focused clientele. The result, they warn, will be societal fracture.[36] Both the National Education Association (NEA) and the American Federation of Teachers (AFT) have criticized private sector initiatives, warning about "the merchants of greed" and cost-cutting measures that hurt teachers.[37] And while Wall Street sees the economic potential in the HMO-EMO analogy, others are less sanguine about that analogy. Educator Alex Molnar warns,

> The only reason that the health care industry can make a profit is that it has nothing to do with [social] equity. We've got 40 million Americans who on any given day don't have health insurance. Now that's a social catastrophe. The same thing would happen in education. If you cut the schools loose from any concern about equity, you could carve out schools that you could run for a profit. However, it would be at an enormous social cost.[38] (This chapter's *You Be the Judge* feature offers several additional insights into the for-profit school debate, to help you formulate your own conclusions.)

Home Schools, Home Teachers

Thirteen-year old Taylor is working at the kitchen table, sorting out mathematical exponents. At 10, Travis is absorbed in *The Story of Jackie Robinson,* while his brother Henry is practicing Beethoven's Minuet in G on his acoustical guitar. The week before, the brothers had attended a local performance of a musical comedy, attended a seminar on marine life and participated in a lively debate about news reports concerning corporal punishment in Singapore. These boys are part of a growing number of students being educated at home. What makes their story somewhat unusual is that their father is unable to participate in their education as much as he might like, because he must spend time at his own work: teaching English at a local public high school.[39]

Why would a schoolteacher choose to educate his own children outside of school? It is ironic that, while some educators view the world as a classroom, others see education as a cottage industry. Today between half a million and one and a half million children in the United States are believed to participate in **home schooling;** twenty years earlier, only 12,500 students were home schooled.[40] Why the huge increase? Most people credit the explosion in the number of home-schooled children to the growth of fundamentalist Christianity, many of whose adherents choose to educate their children at home. While religious motivation is the reason that most families choose home schooling, it is not the only reason.[41]

Some historical perspective might be helpful. Home schooling is not new; it predates schools and has always been around in one form or another. As recently as the 1970s, "romantic" critics—such as John Holt, Ivan Illich, and Jonathan Kozol—were advocating home schooling as a way to avoid the oppressive, dehumanizing public school practices. It is fascinating that home schooling appeals to liberals, who view schools as too conservative, as well as to conservatives, who view schools as too liberal. But conservatives, liberals, and middle-of-the-roaders can be drawn to home schooling for a number of reasons.

In urban areas, the lack of school safety may motivate some parents to educate their children in the security of their own homes, away from the dangers of guns and violence. Other parents are disenchanted with the quality and lack of responsiveness

HOME-SCHOOL DIVORCE

Sixteen-year-old Jennifer S. and her parents are in court. While Jennifer's parents' traditional Christian beliefs led them to home school their seven children, Jennifer wants out. She has asked the courts to let her attend Virginia's Loudoun Valley High School. Jennifer says that she thrives in competition, appreciates the greater number of course options in school, and believes that her chances to eventually become a doctor will be enhanced if she is allowed to attend a regular high school. Her parents disagree. Their attorney argues that in America, parents have the right to make these kinds of decisions for their children. Jennifer believes that she is old enough to make these decisions herself.

SOURCE: *The Washington Post,* November 15, 1998.

REFLECTION

If you were the judge, would you rule in favor of Jennifer, or her parents? At what age should a child's choice of school replace a parent's choice?

Click on *In the News* for recent *In the News* stories. Submit your own *In the News* summary to share with your colleagues.

of schools, and home schooling provides them with a base from which to launch their ideas about education, and to test their own teaching skills, in an intimate and nurturing environment. Economics can play a role as well. In some two-parent working families, the income earned by one parent is consumed by the high cost of child care. In such cases, one parent can readily give up the "outside" job to become a home teacher—and the family may not lose any real income. But not all home schools are initiated for positive motivations. Sometimes racism, anti-Semitism, or another hateful reason can inspire an ideologue to withdraw his or her children from a public school and initiate home instruction.

Researcher Van Galen divides home schoolers into two groups: ideologues and pedagogues. **Ideologues** are very focused on imparting their values and view the home as their school, a place where they choose the curriculum, create the rules, and enforce the schedules. Van Galen classifies most religiously motivated home schoolers as ideologues. **Pedagogues** are motivated by more humanistic educational goals; they are interested in the process as much as the end product of learning. As a group, they are considered more open to various educational strategies. Pedagogues emphasize intrinsic motivation and experiential activities. While ideologues and pedagogues share a dissatisfaction with schools, they agree on little else.[42]

As home schools' philosophies vary, so does their quality. Some parents are incredibly talented and dedicated teachers, while others are less than competent. Even when parents fall short of teaching excellence, individualized instruction is powerful. This may be one reason home-schooled children generally score quite well on standardized tests, averaging between the sixty-fifth and ninetieth percentiles.[43] A number of home-schooled children have even achieved national acclaim. Grant Colfax was taught by his parents, never attending elementary or secondary school. He won

HOME-SCHOOLED— AND PROUD OF IT

Home schooling was more the norm than the exception in times past. Among wealthier British and U.S. families in the seventeenth and eighteenth centuries, parents and home tutors were the educators of choice. Home-schooling traditions exist in other cultures as well. In many Native American cultures, for example, the elders served—and often still serve—as teachers. Contemporary advocates often dip into the well of history to claim the success of home-schooled people, such as

- Woodrow Wilson
- Margaret Mead
- Florence Nightingale
- John Quincy Adams
- Franklin Roosevelt
- Thomas Edison
- The Wright Brothers

- Andrew Carnegie
- Abraham Lincoln
- Pearl Buck
- Agatha Christie
- Benjamin Franklin
- Sandra Day O'Connor

These success stories indicate that home schooling can be effective. Then again, the student's needs and the teacher's talents—at home or at school—are more important than any list of home-schooled achievers.

SOURCE: R. S. Moore and D. N. Moore, *Better Late Than Early: A New Approach to Your Child's Education* (New York: Reader's Digest Press, 1975); Gary Knowles, James A. Muchmore, and Holly W. Spaulding, "Home Education as an Alternative to Institutionalized Education," *The Education Forum 58* (Spring 1994), pp. 238–43; see also issues of *Growing Without Schooling* magazine; Linda Dobson, *Homeschoolers Success Stories* (Roseville, CA: Prima Publishing, 2000).

REFLECTION

What kind of student is a candidate for home schooling? Would students need a teacher at all? If so, what particular skills would a teacher for the home-schooled need?

admission to Harvard, graduated *magna cum laude,* became a Fulbright scholar, and eventually graduated from Harvard Medical School. His home-schooled brothers enjoyed similar success—all endorsements of home schooling.

Home-schooling critics are more concerned with potential abuses than with success stories, such as that of the Colfax family. Do children educated in isolation from their peers suffer any negative consequences? What is lost by not working and learning with other children of diverse beliefs and backgrounds? Since Americans were originally motivated to build schools in order to promote Americanization, to meld a single nation, it is logical to wonder, will home schooling adversely affect our national cohesion?

Home-schooling families hold different views as to the importance of socialization. Some point out that much of what passes for socialization in school is negative, including everything from unhealthy competition to gang violence. They believe that, in the final analysis, their children come out ahead by remaining at home. Other home-school families believe that socialization is important and create their own social groups, such as book clubs, with like-minded others. Some forge a relationship with local school districts, so that their children, although instructed at home, can participate in district schools' sports and other extracurricular activities. School districts vary in their receptivity to such "dual" enrollments. In Virginia, for example, home schoolers are allowed to participate only unofficially in after-school

Even the decision to have schools reflects a value. In *Deschooling Society,* Ivan Illich likens schools to the church during medieval times.[a] He views schools as institutions that perform a political rather than an educational function. To Illich, the diplomas and degrees issued by schools reflect a certification role rather than an educational one. Schools provide society's "stamp of approval," announcing who shall succeed, who shall be awarded status, and who shall remain in poverty. In addition, by compelling students to attend, by judging and labeling them, by confining them, and by discriminating among them, Illich believes that schools are actually harming children. He would replace our traditional schools with a variety of learning "networks" that would be both lifelong and compulsory. To Illich, the notion of waking up to a world without schools is not an outlandish proposition. It would represent a dream fulfilled.

SOURCE: [a]Ivan Illich, *Deschooling Society* (New York: Harper & Row, 1973).

REFLECTION

How are schools more a political than an educational institution? What would your community be like if it were de-schooled?

---

sports. In Ames, Iowa, on the other hand, home schoolers participate in athletics equally, have access to school textbooks and standardized tests, and may take enrichment classes designed specifically for them. District policies on home schooling vary widely. Some school districts view home schoolers as educational partners; other districts see them as competitors.[44] When seen as competitors, schools do not readily provide assistance. This has led to usually successful litigation by home schoolers to acquire selected school resources and support.[45]

Advances in technology have provided a catalyst for the home-schooling movement, particularly the proliferation of personal computers and increasing access to the Internet. America Online, for example, offers a home-schooling forum, complete with lesson plans, tutoring, legislative updates, and the capability for networking with others interested in group work. In Michigan, the Noah Webster charter school offers a "school-less school," one that connects children and parents to teachers and the curriculum through telephone lines and terminals. Technology is radically altering education, and the school of the future may be less a place than a password onto the information superhighway. In the future, home schooling may be far less exotic and far more prevalent.[46]

This chapter asks the deceptively simple question, What's a school for? This deceptively easy question invites many possible answers. Ivan Illich, for example, questions the role of *any* school. While the elimination of schools is both radical and unlikely, it is evident that schools are undergoing serious transition. The traditional neighborhood school is reshaping itself, moving from a public monopoly into the profit arena, from a single neighborhood institution into the wider community, from the cookie-cutter similarities of the past to different models and approaches. Today's teachers will have the opportunity to choose their future career settings from a greater variety of teaching options than ever existed before.

SUMMARY

CHAPTER REVIEW

Go to the Online Learning Center to take a chapter self-quiz, practice with key terms, and review key ideas from the chapter.

1. What are the various expectations Americans hold for their schools?

   - Since their inception, public schools have tried to meet many divergent needs. Parents, teachers, and students alike expect schools to meet academic, vocational, social, civic, and personal goals. The particulars of these goals are debated constantly, often resulting in bitter disputes. Perhaps nowhere else in our country do personal and societal values conflict so much as when communities examine their schools.

   - People have a myriad of expectations for schools. These include, among others, protecting the national economy and defense, unifying a multicultural society, preparing students for the world of work, improving academic competence, encouraging tolerance for diversity, and providing social and economic mobility.

2. Should schools transmit the American culture or change it?

   - Two fundamental, often opposing, purposes of schools, are (1) to transmit society's knowledge and values, passing on the cultural baton, and (2) to reconstruct society, empowering students to engineer social change as adults—and, sometimes, as students.

   - By choosing what to teach, and what to omit, schools continually make decisions as to what is most worth learning. Over the years, a fairly traditional, Eurocentric cultural legacy has underpinned the school's curriculum and is the focus of the current emphasis on standards and tests.

   - The school goal of reconstructing society envisions a closer connection with the community. From service learning to eliminating economic exploitation, reconstructionists enlist teachers and students in an effort to create a more just society.

3. What school purposes are emphasized by educational reform?

   - While schools have often been the focal point of contention, the 1983 report *A Nation at Risk* triggered a renewed interest in the quality of public schooling. In response to declining test scores and poor student achievement, measured by worldwide standards, the report called for many back-to-basics measures.

   - After *A Nation at Risk,* a deluge of state and foundation reports and recommendations ensued, mostly supporting tighter regulation of schools. These "top-down" reports—the "first wave"—emphasized using schools as tools to transmit rather than reconstruct the culture, and advocated a "back-to-basics" education.

   - A second wave of reports, by Sizer, Goodlad, Boyer, and others, focused on strategies to strengthen the teaching profession and restructure education. These reports and books emerged from lengthy observations and research, and they called for empowering educators at the school level, a bottom-up change.

   - The third wave of reform reports viewed the school as a comprehensive institution providing social, medical, and other services to children. Education would be linked to a broader array of student needs, and the child would be the focus of reform.

   - Of all three waves, the first continues to be the strongest. The current emphasis on tests and standards continues the effort at making schools more accountable for basic skills acquisition, goals similar to those cited in *A Nation at Risk.*

4. How are magnet and charter schools, open enrollment, and vouchers reshaping our concept of the neighborhood public school?

- Conservative economist Milton Friedman believed that competition in American schools would improve them. His idea was to apply the free-market economy to education, with the belief that only the best schools will survive the competition.

- Friedman's original plan included vouchers, which could be used like a ticket for parents to choose a school, rather than send children automatically to the neighborhood school. But using vouchers for private religious schools continues to raise legal challenges about the separation of church and state.

- Open enrollments permit students to attend any public school that has room for them, even if the school is not in their neighborhood.

- Magnet schools are public schools that focus on a special study area, from musical talents to gifted education. Many magnets were formed initially to promote desegregation.

- The charter school movement started in 1991 in Minnesota, and has grown rapidly. By taking out charters (contracts with school boards), new schools are granted a great degree of latitude in what they teach and how they teach it.

5. Will the business community's for-profit approach to education create more efficient schools?

- The creation of for-profit education companies has dramatically altered the educational landscape. Companies such as Edison Schools, Advantage, Sylvan Learning, and Tesseract are being funded by private investors to educate students more effectively and efficiently than private schools, and to turn a profit in the process.

- With over $300 billion invested in public education, these for-profit companies, also called Educational Maintenance Organizations (EMOs), believe that there is a fortune to be made in education. While supporters believe that business efficiency will help schools run smoother, others believe that business will have a negative impact on schools, and that when profits and the needs of children are in conflict, students lose out.

- The charter school movement has given these entrepreneurs a vehicle for combining business and education.

6. Is school choice a good idea?

- Underlying many of these plans, from charter schools to vouchers, is the idea that school choice and competition will lead the nation down the road to better schools. Supporters of choice believe that true reform can occur only at the local, school-district level.

- Advocates believe that choice will break the public school "monopoly" on education, and create more efficient and effective schools. Poor parents will have educational options, as rich ones now enjoy, and incompetent teachers will be removed, rather than protected by tenure.

- But many parents and educators have reservations about these specific options and choice plans in general. They worry about issues ranging from the loss of a teacher's academic freedom to poor business practices such as false advertising. They also lament the segregation of students into highly focused niche schools.

7. Why are so many families choosing home schooling?

- While home schooling is far from a new phenomenon, the number of parents educating their children at home has grown dramatically in recent years.

- Many home-schooling parents do it for religious reasons, (they have been called *ideologues*), while others choose home schooling because they are disappointed with the nature or quality of the school program. (This group has been called *pedagogues*.) Home-schooled children generally outperform students in public schools.

- Technological advances, including the use of the Internet, have opened the possibility of converting education into a "cottage enterprise."

KEY TERMS AND PEOPLE

A Nation at Risk, 148

A Place Called School, 144

acculturation, 147

Americanization, 147

Ernest Boyer, 145

charter schools, 155

children's boards, 151

children's policy, 151

James Coleman, 153

Edison Schools, 160

educational vouchers, 154

EMOs (Educational Mainte-
nance Organizations), 160

empowering teachers, 151

Paulo Freire, 143

Milton Friedman, 153

full service schools, 151

John Goodlad, 144

home schooling, 166

ideologues, 167

Jonathan Kozol, 156

Lemon v. Kurtzman, 154

magnet schools, 153

National Commission on Excellence in Education, 148

open enrollment, 153

pedagogues, 167

*The Pedagogy of the
Oppressed,* 143

privatization, 161

reconstructionists, 141

school choice, 153

service credit, 142

Theodore Sizer, 150

social action curriculum, 141

Tesseract (Educational Alternatives Incorporated), 161

three waves of reform, 149

DISCUSSION QUESTIONS AND ACTIVITIES

1. Discuss your list of school goals that you recorded with your classmates. Which goals seem to be most important to your peers? to your instructor? Which do *you* consider most important? Give reasons for your priorities.

2. Do you believe schools should transmit society's knowledge and values, or do you think schools should prepare students to change society? Find someone of the opposing opinion and hold an informal debate.

3. Summarize the last decade of education reform. Predict what the next big reform report will propose. Consider both concerns and suggestions.

4. If you were charged with writing a national report on education reform, what would *you* advocate?

5. "More testing is good for American education" is a common theme in many reform reports. Do you believe that testing should be emphasized in these reports? Why or why not?

6. Which concerns do you agree with as expressed in *A Nation at Risk?*

7. Imagine you are a school board member and your district is debating whether to move to an open enrollment or to a voucher system. Defend your opinion in a brief memo.

8. If you were to design a magnet school, what would it be like? What students would you recruit? What would you look for in your teaching faculty? Would you have a unique physical plan for your building?

9. Imagine you are a concerned parent and long-time neighborhood activist. As part of a committee petitioning for a charter school, what particular mission or vision would be your goal? Why should your charter be approved?

10. What do you think of private businesses contracting to run schools? What factors would cause you to seek or avoid teaching for a corporation? Would you feel secure in your job, especially if tenure was gone?

11. Collect newspaper, journal, and Internet articles concerning home schools. Decide whether the home schooling described in the articles falls into the "ideologue" or the "pedagogue" category. Are the stories generally objective, or can you detect a bias for or against home schooling?

12. Does your local public school district have an official (or unofficial) policy concerning home schooling? Do home-school students participate in any school activities or receive any school resources? How do you feel about these (un)official policies?

WEB-*TIVITIES*

1. The Purposes of Schools

2. Paulo Freire and Reconstructionism

3. Educational Vouchers and School Choice

4. Educational Maintenance Organizations (EMOs)

5. Home Schools, Home Teachers

REEL TO REAL TEACHING

SCHOOL TIES (1992)
Run Time: 110 minutes

Synopsis: A working-class Jewish quarterback is offered a senior year scholarship to a prestigious New England academy. It's his ticket to an Ivy League education, but there is one condition: The school's administration asks him to hide his religious identity.

Reflection:

1. What is the purpose of education at St. Matthew's Academy, according to the school administration? Teachers? Students? Parents? Alumni? Describe the similarities and differences you discover.
2. Would the school's mission have been different if David Greene were allowed to express his religious identity? How?
3. What characteristics, other than religion, do students formally or informally hide in schools?
4. School choice programs, similar to a private school like St. Matthew's, may be selective about who is admitted to a school. How is a school's purpose reflected in selective inclusion policies?
5. Who should have the final authority to determine a school's purpose? Who had the ultimate authority in *School Ties*?

Follow-up Activity: Using words and pictures, create a school logo that reflects St. Matthew's school mission in *School Ties*. Revisit the *Where Do You Stand* section in the chapter (pages 145–148). What school goals did you mark as very important? Design a logo that reflects these goals.

How do you rate this film? Click on *Reel to Real Teaching* to submit your review of this or another education-related film, and read reviews submitted by others.

Choosing Schools, by Mark Schneider, Melissa Marshall, and Paul Eric Teske (2000). What parents value in education, how satisfied they are with their children's schools, and the impact of choice are analyzed.

The Great School Debate: Choice, Vouchers, and Charters, by Thomas Good and Jennifer Braden (2000). Drawing on a comprehensive research review of vouchers and charter schools, the authors discuss why contemporary choice programs have yet to fulfill the expectations of their advocates.

Inside Charter Schools: The Paradox of Radical Decentralization, by Bruce Fuller (2001). This book takes readers into six strikingly different schools, from an evangelical home-schooling charter in California to a back-to-basics charter in a black neighborhood in Lansing, Michigan.

The Irony of Early School Reform: Educational Innovation in Mid-Nineteenth Century Massachusetts, by Michael B. Katz, 2nd edition (2001). Maps out the origins of school reform and locates the source of educational inequalities and bureaucracies in patterns established in the nineteenth century.

Restructuring the Common Good in Education: Coping with Intractable American Dilemmas, by Larry Cuban and Dorothy Shipps (2000). Explores the long-standing tensions between shared purposes and individual interests in schooling.

Schools for Sale: Why Free Market Policies Won't Improve America's Schools, and What Will, by Ernest R. House (1998). Debunks the myth connecting economic productivity and educational excellence.

Life in Schools

FOCUS QUESTIONS

1. What rituals and routines shape classroom life?
2. How is class time related to student achievement?
3. How does the teacher's gatekeeping function influence classroom roles?
4. What is tracking, and what are its advantages and disadvantages?
5. Why has "detracking" become a popular movement?
6. How do peer groups impact elementary school life?
7. In what ways does the adolescent culture shape teenage perceptions and behaviors?
8. What steps can educators take to create a more supportive school environment?
9. What are the characteristics of effective schools?

WHAT DO YOU THINK? What Was Your School Experience Like?
See how it compares to that of your colleagues.

CHAPTER PREVIEW

School is a culture. Like most cultures, it is filled with its own unique rituals and traditions, and its own set of norms and mores. In school even the familiar, like time, is made new. Forget about nine o'clock, or half past twelve of the outside world. Time is told by subjects ("Let's talk before math") or periods ("I'm going home after seventh period"). Teachers and administrators decide the "what" and "when" of students' lives, organizing the day into blocks of time, from 20 minutes to more than an hour. Students are pinched into passive roles, following schedules created by others, sitting still rather than being active, and responding to teacher questions, but seldom asking any of their own. Such a system challenges both teachers and students, and forces each into confining roles for five or more hours a day. For many, it is an uncomfortable fit.

Life in school—for some, the best time ever; for others, a terribly awkward stage filled with painful memories. Friendships and popularity take on enormous significance during school years. Peer groups create strong subcultures that make winners and losers of us all—at least for a brief time. Adults pick up where children leave off, assigning students to what amounts to an academic caste system through *de facto* tracking or ability grouping. Whenever students are sorted by ability, the ensuing labels (from "gifted" to a seemingly innocuous label such as "robins" for the slowest reading group) can have lasting impact on students' self-image and status, well into adulthood. Students begin to sense who are the "haves" and the "have-nots," and detect how classism and racism influence American life. Finally, adolescents and pre-adolescents are entering the new and confusing world of relationships, romance, and sexuality. While adults may focus on academics in school, many students are most concerned with the social side of school life.

In this chapter we take you beyond academics to the lesser-known three Rs (rules, rituals, and routines). We ask you to analyze the subtle dynamics of classroom communication and the role of peer groups. We also want you to think about some of the political realities of schools, such as ability grouping, and to consider what impact these may have on students. Finally, we look at five factors traditionally associated with effective schools, then take you beyond these factors to explore new arenas of effective schools research.

Rules, Rituals, and Routines

Schools create their own cultures, replete with norms, rituals, and routines. Even simple tasks, like distributing textbooks, are clothed with cultural cues, but they are cues that differ for students and teachers.

"Come Right Up and Get Your New Books": A Teacher's Perspective

Dick Thompson looked at the pile of poetry anthologies stacked on his desk and sighed. Getting texts distributed and starting a new unit always seemed like such a chaotic ordeal, particularly with seventh-graders. But worrying over possible mishaps wouldn't get this poetry unit launched. Besides, his students were getting restless, so he had better get things started.

"Okay, class, quiet down. As you can see, the poetry books we've been waiting for have finally arrived. All right, you can cut out the groans. Give the books a fair trial before you sentence them. I'd like the first person in each row to come up, count out enough books for his or her row, and hand them out."

Six students charged to the front and made a mad grab for the books. In the ensuing melee, one stack of books went crashing to the floor.

"Hey, kids, take it easy and stop the squabbling. There are plenty of books to go around. Since this procedure obviously isn't working, we'll just have to slow down and do things one row at a time. Bob, you hand out the books for row 1 first; then Sally will come up and get the books for row 2. It will take a little longer this way, but I think things will go more smoothly. When you get your texts, write your name and room number in the stamped box inside the cover."

Since the dispensing of books now seemed to be progressing in an orderly fashion, Mr. Thompson turned his attention to the several hands waving in the air.

"Yes, Jessica?"

"I can't fill in my name because my pencil just broke. Can I sharpen it?"

"Go ahead. Jamie?"

"My pencil's broken too. Can I sharpen mine?"

"Yes, but wait until Jessica sits down. Let me remind you that you're supposed to come to class prepared. Now there will be no more at the pencil sharpener today. Scott?"

"Can I use the hall pass?"

"Is this absolutely necessary? All right then [responding to Scott's urgent nod]. Now I think we've had enough distraction for one morning. The period's half over and we still haven't gotten into today's lesson. After you get your book and fill in the appropriate information, turn to the poem on page 3. It's called 'Stopping by Woods on a Snowy Evening,' and it's by Robert Frost, one of America's most famous poets. Yes, Rosa?"

"I didn't get a book."

"Tomàs, didn't you hand out books to your row? Oh, I see. We're one short. Okay, Rosa, go down to the office and tell Mrs. Goldberg that we need one more of the new poetry anthologies. Now, as I was about to say, I'd like you to think about the questions that I've written on the board: How does the speaker in this poem feel as he looks at the snow filling up the deserted woods? Why does he wish to stop, and what makes him realize that he must go on? The speaker says, 'I have miles to go before I sleep.' He may be talking about more than going to bed for the night. What else may 'sleep' mean in this poem? Yes, Timothy, do you have a comment on the poem already?"

What is the hidden curriculum in this teacher-dominated classroom, where teachers actively talk and move about while students passively sit and listen?

"My glasses are being fixed and I can't read the board."

"All right. Take the seat by my desk. You'll see the board from there. April! Maxine! This is not a time for your private chat room. This is a silent reading activity—and I do mean silent. Okay, class, I think most of you have had enough time to read the poem. Who has an answer for the first question? Jordan?"

"Well, I think the guy in this poem really likes nature. He's all alone, and it's private, with no people around to interrupt him, and he thinks the woods and the snow are really beautiful. It's sort of spellbinding."

"Jordan, that's an excellent response. You've captured the mood of this poem. Now for the second question. Maxine?"

"I think he wants to stop because…"

Maxine's answer was cut short by the abrasive ring of the fourth-period bell.

"Class, sit down. I know the bell has rung, but it isn't signaling a fire. You'll have time to make your next class. Since we didn't get as far into our discussion as I had hoped, I want to give you an assignment. For homework, I'd like you to answer the remaining questions. Alice?"

"Is this to hand in?"

"Yes. Any other questions? Okay, you'd better get to your next-period class."

As the last student left, Dick Thompson slumped over his desk and wearily ran his fingers through his hair. As he looked down, he spotted the missing poetry anthology under his desk, a victim of the charge of the book brigade. The whole lesson was a victim of the book brigade. He had been so busy getting the books dispensed and fielding all the interruptions that he had forgotten to give his brief explanation on the differences between prose and poetry. He had even forgotten to give his motivating speech on how interesting the new poetry unit was going to be. Well, no time for a postmortem now. Stampedelike noises outside the door meant the fourth-period class was about to burst in.

"Come Right Up and Get Your New Books": A Student's Perspective

From her vantage point in the fourth seat, fifth row, Maxine eyed the stack of new books on the teacher's desk. She knew they were poetry books because she had flipped through one as she meandered into the room. She didn't care that it wasn't "in" to like poetry; she liked it anyway. At least it was better than the grammar unit they'd just been through. All those sentences to diagram—picking out nouns and pronouns—what a drag that was.

Maxine settled into her seat and began the long wait for her book. Her thoughts wandered: "Mr. Thompson seems like he's in some kind of daze, just staring at the new books like he's zoned out. Wonder what's bugging him. Good enough, the first kids in each row are heading up to get the books. Oh, right, they're getting into a brawl over handing out the stupid books. What a bunch of jerks; they must think they're funny or something. Now it'll be one row at a time and will take forever. I suppose I can start my math homework or write some letters."

Maxine got several of her math problems solved by the time her poetry anthology arrived, along with instructions to read the poem on page 3. She skimmed through the poem and decided she liked it. She understood how Robert Frost felt, watching the snowy woods and wanting to get away from all the hassles. It sure would be nice to read this poem quietly somewhere without listening to kids going on about pencil sharpeners and hall passes and seat changes. All these interruptions made it hard to concentrate.

As she turned around to share her observation about hassles with April Marston, Mr. Thompson's sharp reprimand interrupted her. She fumed to herself, "Private chat room. What's with him? Half the class is talking, and old Eagle Eyes Thompson has to pick on me. And they're all talking about the football game Saturday. At least I was talking about the poem. Oh well, I'd better answer one of those questions on the board and show him that I really am paying attention."

Maxine waved her hand wildly, but Jordan got called for question 1. Maxine shot her hand in the air again for a chance at question 2. When Mr. Thompson called on her, she drew a deep breath and began her response. Once again, she was interrupted in midsentence, this time by the fourth-period bell. Disgruntled, she stuffed her poetry book under her arm and fell into step beside April Marston.

"I really knew the answer to that question," she muttered under her breath. "Now we have to write all the answers out. Boring. Well, next period is science and we're supposed to be giving lab reports. Maybe we'll have a chance to finish the English homework there."

Delay and Social Distraction

You have just read two capsular replays of a seventh-grade English lesson, one from the vantage point of the teacher, the other from the vantage point of a student. Mr. Thompson and Maxine play different roles, which cause them to have very different experiences in this class. In what ways is the same class experienced differently by teacher and student?

One difference you may have detected is that while Mr. Thompson was continually leapfrogging from one minor crisis to the next, Maxine was sitting and waiting. In his perceptive book **Life in Classrooms, Philip W. Jackson** describes how time is spent in elementary school.[1] He suggests that, whereas teachers are typically very busy, students are often caught in patterns of delay that force them to do nothing. Jackson notes that a great deal of teachers' time is spent in noninstructional busywork, such as keeping time and dispensing supplies. In the slice of classroom life you just read, Mr. Thompson spent a substantial part of the class time distributing new texts. Indeed, most teachers spend a good deal of time giving out things: paper, pencils, art materials, science equipment, floppy disks, exam booklets, erasers, happy faces, special privileges—the list goes on and on. The classroom scene described also shows Mr. Thompson greatly involved in timekeeping activities. Within the limits set by school buzzers and bells, he determines when the texts will be distributed, when and for how long the reading activity will take place, and when the class discussion will begin.

What do students do while teachers are busy organizing, structuring, talking, questioning, handing out, collecting, timekeeping, and crisis hopping? According to Jackson's analysis, they do little more than sit and wait.[2] They wait for the materials to be handed out, for the assignment to be given, for the questions to be asked, for the teacher to call on them, for the teacher to react to their response, and for the slower class members to catch up so that the activity can change. They wait in lines to get drinks of water, to get pencils sharpened, to get their turn at the computer, to go to the playground, to get to the bathroom, and to be dismissed from class. If students are to succeed in school, they must be able to cope with continual delay as a standard operating procedure.

One plea that is rarely granted is that of talking to classmates beyond controlled learning activities. Like the character from Greek mythology, Tantalus, who was continually tempted with food and water but was not allowed to eat or drink, students are surrounded by peers and friends but are restrained from communicating with them. In other words, students in the classroom are in the very frustrating position of having to ignore social temptation, of acting as though they are isolated despite the crowd surrounding them. Furthermore, while trying to concentrate on work and to ignore social temptations, students are beset by frequent interruptions—the public address system blaring a message in the middle of an exam, the end-of-class bell interrupting a lively discussion, a teacher's reprimand or a student's question derailing a train of thought during silent reading.

Consider how Maxine in Mr. Thompson's English class had to cope with delay, denial of desire, social distraction, and interruptions. She waited for the delivery of her new text. She waited to be called on by the teacher. Her attempt to concentrate on reading the poem was disturbed by frequent interruptions. Her brief communication with a classmate was interrupted by a reprimand. Her head was filled with ideas and questions. In short, there was a lot she would like to have said, but there was almost no opportunity to say it.

Watching the Clock

Educators concerned about school improvement have called attention to the inefficient use of time in school, claiming that we lose between one-quarter and one-half of the time available for learning through attendance problems, noninstructional activities (such as class changes and assemblies), administrative and organizational activities, and disruptions caused by student misbehavior.[3]

In a classic study of schools, **John Goodlad** found a fair degree of consistency in how time is spent in different activities as children go through the grades. As Figure 5.1 illustrates, about 2 percent of time is spent to social activities, 2 to 5 percent to behavior management, 20 percent to routines, and 75 percent to instruction.

In Goodlad's study, although there was a general consistency in how time was spent at different levels of schooling, one of the most astonishing findings was the enormous variation in the *efficiency* with which different schools used time. When examining the hours per week allocated to subject-matter learning, time ranged from a low of 18.5 hours in one school to a high of 27.5 hours in another. Goodlad was also surprised at the limited amount of time spent on the academic staples, such as reading and writing. He found that only 6 percent of time in elementary school was spent on reading. This dropped to a minuscule 2 percent at the high school level. In contrast, the amount of time students spent listening to teacher lectures and explanations increased from approximately 18 percent in elementary school to more than 25 percent in high school.[4] Many schools have responded by adopting alternative or block scheduling and special focus activities, such as sustained silent reading, to make better use of time in school.

While the business world may suggest "time is money," for educators, time is learning. As one teacher points out,

> Time is the currency of teaching. We barter with time. Every day we make small concessions, small trade-offs, but, in the end, we know it's going to defeat us. After all, how many times are we actually able to cover World War I in our history courses before the year is out? We always laugh a little about that, but the truth is the sense of the clock ticking is one of the most oppressive features of teaching.[5]

There is a limited amount of time set aside for the school day. Research shows that, when more time is allocated to subject-matter learning, student achievement increases.[6] When this valuable resource is spent handing out supplies or reprimanding misbehavior, it is lost for learning. Looked at from this perspective, Mr. Thompson's class was not only frustrating, but it also deprived students of a precious and limited resource—the time to learn.

FIGURE 5.1   School time.

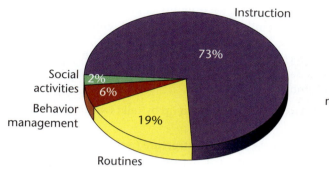

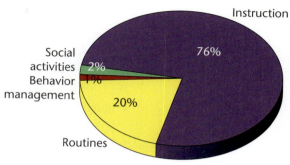

Percentage of elementary school time*

Percentage of high school time*

* Percentages are rounded off and do not necessarily equal 100.

SOURCE: From John Goodlad, *A Place Called School* (New York: McGraw-Hill, 1984).

REFLECTION

About three-fourths of class time is spent in instruction. Does that seem high, low, or about right? The instruction category is quite broad. How might you break it down into more meaningful subcategories?

Part of the hidden curriculum of schools is the "culture of waiting" that accompanies the many transition periods throughout the day. And often, waiting seems to be a gender-segregated activity.

The Teacher as Gatekeeper

Philip Jackson reports that teachers are typically involved in more than one thousand verbal exchanges with their students every day.[7] Count the number of verbal exchanges Mr. Thompson had with his students during our abbreviated classroom scene and you will get some idea of how much and how often teachers talk. One of the functions that keeps teachers busiest is what Philip Jackson terms **gatekeeping.** As gatekeepers, teachers must determine who will talk, when, and for how long, as well as the basic direction of the communication.

In Chapter 3, "Teacher Effectiveness," we presented some of the findings about classroom interaction. Consider what effect these patterns of classroom interaction have on both teachers and students:

- Roughly two-thirds of classroom time is taken up by talk; two-thirds of that talk is by the teacher.[8]
- In the typical "pedagogical cycle," teachers structure (lecture and direct), question, and react to student comments. Teachers initiate about 85 percent of these verbal cycles.[9]
- While questioning signals curiosity, it is the teachers, not the learners, who do the questioning, asking as many as 348 questions a day.[10] The typical student rarely asks a question.[11]
- Most classroom questions require that students use only rote memory.[12]
- Students are not given much time to ask, or even answer, questions. Teachers usually wait less than a second for student comments and answers.[13]
- Teachers interact less and less with students as they go through the grades.[14]

Ironically, while a major goal of education is to increase students' curiosity and quest for knowledge, it is the teachers, not the students, who dominate and manage classroom interaction. Classroom interaction patterns do not train students to be active, inquiring, self-reliant learners. Rather, students are expected to be quiet and passive, to think quickly (and perhaps superficially), to rely on memory, and to be dependent on the teacher. Silent, passive students have less positive attitudes and lower achievement. Perhaps the challenge new teachers should keep before them is finding a way to turn their gatekeeping role into a benefit for students, instead of a hindrance.

The Other Side of the Tracks

We have seen that teachers function as gatekeepers, controlling the amount and flow of student talk in the classroom. Let's step back a moment, and consider an even more basic question: Which students sit (for sit they mainly do) in which classrooms? That very crucial, political decision falls on teachers, counselors, and administrators. Many believe that it is easier for students with similar skills and intellectual abilities to learn together, in **homogeneous** classes. Educators following this belief, screen, sort, and direct students based on their abilities, and as a result, send them down different school paths, profoundly shaping their futures. Students of different abilities (low, middle, and high) are assigned to different "tracks" of courses and programs (vocational, general, college-bound, honors, and AP). **Tracking** is the term given to this

After observing in more than one thousand classrooms, John Goodlad and his team of researchers found that the following patterns characterize most classrooms:

- Much of what happens in class is geared toward maintaining order among twenty to thirty students restrained in a relatively small space.
- Although the classroom is a group setting, each student typically works alone.
- The teacher is the key figure in setting the tone and determining the activities.
- Most of the time, the teacher is in front of the classroom, teaching a whole group of students.
- There is little praise or corrective feedback; classes are emotionally neutral or flat places.
- Students are involved in a limited range of activities—listening to lectures, writing answers to questions, and taking exams.
- A significant number of students are confused by teacher explanations and feel that they do not get enough guidance on how to improve.
- There is a decline in the attractiveness of the learning environment and the quality of instruction as students progress through the grades.

Goodlad concluded that "the emotional tone of the classroom is neither harsh and punitive nor warm and joyful; it might be described most accurately as flat."

SOURCE: John Goodlad, *A Place Called School* (New York: McGraw-Hill, 1984).

REFLECTION

Goodlad's classic study is now two decades old. How many of these findings continue to characterized classroom life?

---

process, and while some teachers believe that tracking makes instruction more manageable, others believe that it is a terribly flawed system.

In the 1960s, sociologist **Talcott Parsons** analyzed school as a social system and concluded that the college selection process begins in elementary school and is virtually sealed by the time students finish junior high.[15] Parsons's analysis has significant implications, for he is suggesting that future roles in adult life are determined by student achievement in elementary school. The labeling system, beginning at an early age, determines who will wear a stethoscope, who will carry a laptop computer, and who will become a low-wage laborer.

Several researchers consider students' social class a critical factor in this selection system. Back in 1929, Robert and Helen Lynd, in their extensive study of Middletown (a small midwestern city), concluded that schools are essentially middle-class institutions that discriminate against lower-class students.[16] Approximately fifteen years later, **W. Lloyd Warner** and his associates at the University of Chicago conducted a series of studies in New England, the deep South, and the Midwest and came to a similar conclusion.

> One group [the lower class] is almost immediately brushed off into a bin labeled "nonreaders, first grade repeaters," or "opportunity class," where they stay for eight or ten years and are then released through a chute to the outside world to become hewers of wood and drawers of water.[17]

The classroom language game, in which teachers talk and students listen, may encourage passivity and boredom.

183

In his classic analysis of class and school achievement, **August Hollingshead** discovered that approximately two-thirds of the students from the two upper social classes but fewer than 15 percent of those from the lower classes were in the college preparatory program.[18] In midwestern communities, **Robert Havinghurst** and associates reported that nearly 90 percent of school dropouts were from lower-class families.[19] The unfortunate tracking by class is one of the oldest of school traditions.

Parents and peers may influence academic choices even more than guidance counselors do.[20] When family and friends encourage children with similar backgrounds to stay together, students of the same race and class typically find themselves on the same school tracks. When school norms and children's culture clash, the result can also lead to racially segregated tracks. For example, some students of color devote time and attention to "stage setting." Stage setting may include checking pencils, rearranging sitting positions, and watching others—all part of a pattern of readiness before work can begin. To a teacher unfamiliar with this learning style, such behavior may be interpreted as inappropriate or as avoidance of work. Some racial and ethnic groups value cooperation and teamwork, yet school norms frequently stress individual, competitive modes of learning. Such cultural clashes work to the detriment of certain groups, relegating them to lower-ability classes and tracks.[21]

Several studies document differences in how students in high-ability and low-ability tracks are treated. In a classic study done in the 1970s, Ray Rist observed a kindergarten class in an all-black urban school. By the eighth day of class, the kindergarten teacher, apparently using such criteria as physical appearance, socioeconomic status, and language usage, had separated her students into groups of "fast learners" and "slow learners." She spent more time with the "fast learners" and gave them more instruction and encouragement. The "slow learners" got more than their fair share of control and ridicule. The children soon began to mirror the teacher's behavior. As the "fast learners" belittled the "slow learners," the low-status children began to exhibit attitudes of self-degradation and hostility toward one another. This teacher's expectations, formed during eight days at the beginning of school, shaped the academic and social treatment of children in her classroom for the entire year and perhaps for years to come. Records of the grouping that had taken place during the first week in kindergarten were passed on to teachers in the upper grades, providing the basis for further differential treatment.[22]

Jeannie Oakes's *Keeping Track* (1985) was a scathing indictment of tracking, adding momentum to the effort to **detrack,** or eliminate tracking practices from the nation's schools. Oakes found that race more than ability determined which students were placed in which tracks, and that the lower-tracked students had fewer learning opportunities.[23] Other studies confirmed that low demands were placed on students in low-ability groups, and teachers expected little from them and offered fewer constructive comments to students in low ability groups. Low tracks suffered from more classroom management problems, and focused more on social rather than academic matters. Over the course of a year, a child in the highest group moved ahead as much as five times more quickly than a child in the lowest group. By the fourth grade, an achievement spread of a full four grades separated children at the top and the bottom of the class, a difference that increased with time.[24] (See Frame of Reference: Tracking and Race.)

"True," tracking advocates argue, "it would appear more democratic to put everyone in the same class, but such idealism is destined to fail." They contend that it is unrealistic to think everyone can or should master the same material or learn it at the same pace. Without tracking we have **heterogeneous,** or mixed ability classes. Tracking advocates are quick to point out that mixed ability classes have their own

THE ANTI-ACHIEVEMENT DILEMMA

Many students avoid academic excellence, because they fear their peers will label them nerds. According to B. Bradford Brown and Laurence Steinberg, who sampled eight thousand high school students in California and Wisconsin, this fear is warranted. Unlike athletes, who are offered adulation, high academic achievers often get resentment instead of respect.[1] To avoid the "nerd" label and the social rejection that comes with it, students learn that they should do well, but not too well. This brain-nerd connection causes students to put the brakes on academic achievement, cut corners, and do only what is necessary to get by. The anti-achievement climate is even stronger for African American students. Signithia Fordham and John Ogbu reported the results of a fascinating ethnographic study in a Washington, DC, high school, where the student population was 99 percent black.[2] They found that the students actively discouraged each other from working to achieve because attaining academic success was seen as "acting white." "Acting white" was understood to include speaking standard English, listening to white music and radio stations, being on time, studying in the library, working hard, and getting good grades. Students who did well in school were called "brainiacs," a term synonymous with jerk. The students who managed to achieve academic success and still avoid the "brainiac" label developed ingenious coping strategies. Some students camouflaged high achievement by "acting crazy," as class clowns or comedians. Others chose friends who would protect them in exchange for help with homework. Female achievers were more likely to hide out, keeping a low profile, so their peers would not know they were smart.

[1] B. Bradford Brown and Laurence Steinberg, "Academic Achievement and Social Acceptance," *The Education Digest* 55 (March 1990), pp. 57–60. Condensed from *National Center on Effective Secondary Schools Newsletter* 4 (fall 1989), pp. 2–4.
[2] Signithia Fordham, *Blacked Out: The Dilemmas of Race, Identity, and Success at Capital High* (Chicago: University of Chicago Press, 1996); Signithia Fordham and John Ogbu, "Black Students' School Success: Coping with the Burden of 'Acting White,'" *Urban Review* 18, no. 3 (1986), pp. 176–205.

REFLECTION

What can teachers do to break the brainiac-jerk association? How can the power of peer pressure be unleashed for success instead of mediocrity or failure? What do you think?

set of problems: In heterogeneous classes, bright students get bored, while slower students have trouble keeping up, and we lose our most talented and our most needy students. Teachers find themselves grading the brighter students on the quality of their work, and the weaker ones on their "effort," which is a big problem (especially with parents!). Teachers get frustrated trying to meet each student's needs, and hardly ever hitting the mark. Putting everyone in the same class simply doesn't work.[25]

Detracking advocates, as you might imagine, offer a different take on the issue. "No sorting system is consistent with equality of opportunity. Worse yet, the tracking system is not based on individual ability. It is badly biased in favor of white middle-class America. We must face the reality that poor children, often children of color, come to school far from being ready to learn. And the school, whose job it is to educate all our children, does little to help. The built-in bias in instruction, counseling, curricular materials, and testing must be overcome. Students get shoveled into second-rate courses that prepare them for fourth-rate jobs. Their track becomes 'a great training robbery,' and the students who are robbed may be ones with great abilities."

While the social pitfalls of tracking have been well documented, its efficacy has not. With little hard evidence supporting tracking, and a growing concern about its negative fallout, it is little wonder that the term "tracking" has fallen out of favor. By the 1990s, only 15 percent of schools had official tracking policies, down from 93 percent in 1965, a quiet but persistent change that has been termed the **unremarked revolution.**[26]

- Minority students are 3 times as likely as white students to be enrolled in low-track math classes and whites are more than 1.5 times more likely to be in high-track classes.
- Schools with predominately poor and minority populations offer fewer advanced and more remedial courses in academic subjects.
- When parents intervene, counselors place middle- and upper-class students with comparably low grades and test scores into higher groups.
- African American and Hispanic students are underrepresented in programs for the gifted.
- Asian students are more likely than Hispanic students to be recommended for advanced classes, even with equivalent test scores.
- Teachers with the least experience and the lowest levels of qualifications are assigned to students in the lowest tracks.
- Students are more likely to "choose" their friends from their ability groups and tracked classes in elementary through high school. The social network and peer status sorting system is linked to the academic sorting system.
- 73 percent of students completing an academic program are white, 10 percent are black, and 7 percent are Hispanic.
- 63 percent of Advanced Placement exam takers are white, 5 percent are black, and 10 percent are Hispanic.

SOURCE: "Race/Ethnicity of Students Taking Advanced Placement Exams, 2000," *The 2000 National Summary Report on Advanced Placement Program* (New York: College Board, 2000); "1994 High School Transcript Study," National Center on Educational Statistics (Washington, DC: U.S. Department of Education, September 1998); Jeannie Oakes, "Ability Grouping and Tracking in Schools," in T. Husen and T. Neville Postlethwaite (eds.), *The International Encyclopedia of Education,* 2nd edition (Tarrytown, NY: Pergamon Press), 1994; Jeannie Oakes, Adam Gamoran, and Reba Page, "Curriculum Differentiation: Opportunities, Outcomes, and Meanings," in Phil Jackson (ed.), *Handbook of Research on Curriculum* (New York: Macmillan, 1992).

REFLECTION

Can a tracking or ability grouping program avoid segregating children by race and ethnicity? How would you create such a program? Why is this so hard?

Most schools today work hard to avoid using the term "tracking." Middle and high schools are taking their cue from elementary schools, where "ability grouping" has been in favor. **Ability grouping** sorts students based on capability, but the groupings may well vary by subject. While tracks suggest permanence, ability grouping is more transitory. One year, a student might find herself in a high-ability math group and a low-ability English group. The following year, that same student might be reassigned to a new set of groups. Today, many middle and high schools talk about "ability grouping," but sometimes it is only the label that has been changed. (You may want to think of school tracking as a take-off on the federal "witness protection program": a reality functioning under an assumed identity.) By seventh grade, two-thirds of all schools have ability grouping in some classes, and about 20 percent have tracking or grouping in every subject.[27] Many educators charge that the United States relies more on tracking than any other nation in the world.[28]

Critics argue that we really can eliminate *de facto* tracking, whatever name it is given. They believe that detracking can work, if it is implemented correctly. Teachers, parents, and students should realize that although students arrive at school from very different backgrounds, learning from each other and together has great advantages. Instruction is best offered through individualized and cooperative learning, rather than the traditional approach of trying to teach all students simultaneously. Alternative assessments work far better than testing everyone with the same test (compare this view to the current emphasis on standardized tests). In fact, detracked schools can be authentic places of learning, academically challenging to all while teaching a living lesson in democracy. What is needed is time, careful planning, and adequate training for teachers so that they can succeed and all students can learn.[29]

As these arguments suggest, tracking is likely to remain an area of controversy in the years ahead, especially for educators who find it "the most professionally divisive issue" in the field.[30] One of the ironies of tracking is that it simply builds on an already divided school culture. What educators do not do to divide students, students often do to themselves.

The Power of Elementary Peer Groups

Educational researcher Raphaela Best wanted to capture a portrait of life in school as a group of elementary school children experienced it. During a multiyear study, she played the role of participant observer, working with children during class time, playing with them at recess, eating lunch with them in the cafeteria, talking with them, observing them, and taking notes. She found that the children "organized their own intense, seething little world with its own frontiers, its own struggles, its own winners and losers. It was a world invisible to outsiders, not apparent to the casual observer,"[31] where the peer group became increasingly important in the children's lives—eventually competing with and even eclipsing parental influence.

In the first grade, when so much about school seems gigantic and fearful, children look to adults for safety: What am I supposed to do in the classroom? Where do I get lunch? How do I find the bus to ride home from school? Both girls and boys look to the teachers and to the principal for answers and for emotional support. In her study, Best found that the children ran to their first-grade teacher not only for this practical information but also for hugs, praise, and general warmth and affection. They climbed onto the teacher's lap and rested, secure, and comforted.

Their relationship to the teacher was far more important than their interactions with one another. For example, when Anne and Matthew were fighting over how to put a puzzle together, the teacher encircled them in her arms and asked, "Can't we find another way to play?" The children nodded affirmatively. "Good! You're so good and I'm so happy with the way you've been playing, but you know that accidents can happen and someone might have to stay out of school. We wouldn't want that to happen, now would we?"[32] Both children solemnly shook their heads and indicated that they would comply with the teacher's request.

By the second grade, the boys had begun to break away from teacher dependence and to place more importance on their peer group. Though loosely structured, this group was largely sex-segregated, with its own leadership hierarchy. In the first grade, the boys and girls had sat side-by-side in the lunchroom, but, by the second grade, the boys had claimed one end of a lunchroom table for themselves. To ensure privacy from the female world, the group's meeting place became the boys' bathroom, where the boys talked about kids at school and decided what to play at recess.

By the third grade, the boys were openly challenging teacher authority. They banded together to organize an all-male club, complete with pecking order, assignments, secrets, and anti-establishment pranks, such as stuffing the locks with paper so the teachers could not get into the building in the morning. Also, by the third grade, the boys' territorial rights had increased, and they had staked out an entirely male lunchroom table for themselves. The playground also became increasingly sex-segregated, as blacktop and grassy areas were reserved for active boys' ball games, and

Jeannie Oakes never dreamed of being a schoolteacher. "It was just too ordinary. The most ambitious girls in high school thought about being teachers. I wanted adventure, unconventionality." So she embraced her passion for reading, earned a degree in American Literature, married, and had children. "It turned out that I was a lot more conventional than I thought I was!" While raising her children at home in the 1960s, Oakes decided that like her high school peers, she would become a teacher for the "same old-fashioned reasons for which women have always taught—I wanted to be with my children when they came home from school every day."[1] But the unconventional spirit in Jeannie Oakes hadn't disappeared. She championed the Civil Rights movement and anti-Vietnam war activities. And she realized that teaching was a vehicle for social justice, that teaching could be far from ordinary.

Her first day in the classroom made a lasting impression. She didn't announce to students they were taking basic English, but recalls how within five minutes they knew and announced, "Oh, we're in the dumb class!" During the seven years Oakes taught middle and high school English in suburban Los Angeles, she struggled to be as good a teacher to low track classes as to the high ones, and was astonished how her own instruction and expectations changed for students placed in honors, average, and basic classes. She also witnessed how tracking dictated disparate lives in schools. "In a very public way, adults make judgments about students' current and future abilities that take on a hierarchical nature: We talk about top groups and bottom groups. And in the culture

of schools, the top group becomes the top kids and the bottom group the bottom kids in a very value-laden and defining way."[2]

Creating innovative classrooms that unlocked successful learning for diverse students became her challenge. Each new school year, Oakes developed new curriculum and instructional strategies, hoping to invigorate enthusiasm for learning in students and fellow teachers. Her calls for change met with administrative resistance and her voice was increasingly silenced. Frustrated and disheartened, she herself became less interested in teaching and more curious about how social differences such as race and class impact success in school. Jeannie Oakes wanted to create better American schools and teachers. Working with John Goodlad, she decided, would help her achieve that goal.

As a doctoral student at UCLA, Oakes researched with Goodlad the varied aspects of life in schools. Oakes specifically explored how tracking and ability grouping limit the school experiences of low-income students and students of color. By demystifying the policies and language of tracking, she wanted to make her findings accessible to teachers. In 1985, her landmark book *Keeping Track: How Schools Structure Inequality* brought the inequities of tracking into the national spotlight, casting a riveting portrayal of how tracking creates segregation within schools and shortchanges quality learning and resources. Yet despite the attention, tracking remains one of the most entrenched school practices, relegating students to separate classrooms based less on ability and more on race and socioeconomic status.

Oakes believes the persistence is rooted in a cultural notion that intelligence is immutable and that there is virtually nothing schools can do to alter a student's fundamental capability. She doesn't buy such a limited view.

> Kindergartners show an enormous interest in learning, and this cuts across socioeconomic, racial, and ethnic lines. But as kids go through school, if they don't have successful experiences, they learn their efforts do not pay off. So by high school, we see disinterest unjustly interpreted by teachers as low ability.[3]

For Oakes, then, the fundamental goal of equalizing opportunity is not simply to detrack but to increase the quality of curriculum and instruction for everybody in schools, so that success is not limited to those in the high track. This requires a powerful shift in conventional norms, one that defines intellectual capacity as not fixed, but learned through interaction, problem solving, and critical thinking.

Oakes recognizes that the process of detracking schools is not easy. School reform efforts are often met with resistance by those who benefit from the current system. This political dimension of inequality cannot be underestimated. Parents of high-achieving students exert considerable pressure to ensure that their children have access to honors and AP classes. Moreover, teachers of high-track students often resist efforts to detrack, enjoying the intellectual challenge and prestige that come from teaching these students. School administrators and teachers who have undertaken detracking efforts often tell her it is their most difficult undertaking—and most rewarding. Jeannie Oakes understands why: "It's about fairness and creating better schools. And getting there is half the fun."[4]

A conventional career, perhaps. But Jeannie Oakes is an unconventional advocate for equity and change.

[1]Carlos Alberto Torres, *Education, Power, and Personal Biography: Dialogues with Critical Educators* (New York: Routledge, 1998), pp. 224–25.

[2]John O'Neill, "On Tracking and Individual Differences: A Conversation with Jeannie Oakes," *Educational Leadership*, 50, no. 2 (October 1992), p. 18.

[3]Ibid, p. 20.

[4]Torres, *Education, Power, and Personal Biography: Dialogues with Critical Educators*, p. 230.

REFLECTION

How has Jeannie Oakes made teaching an act of social justice? Why do you think tracking is a persistent part of school culture? How have you experienced or witnessed the influence of tracking on academic as well as social opportunities in school?

WRITE YOUR OWN PROFILE IN EDUCATION: Click on *Profiles in Education,* write a *Profile in Education* about an educator, and post it on the Online Learning Center. Check out *Profiles in Education* submitted by other future teachers.

To learn more about Jeannie Oakes, click on *Profiles in Education.*

the girls were relegated to the fringe areas, where they stood talking, played hopscotch, and jumped rope. The girls used their time to chat, giggle, and re-create game rules to discourage cut-throat competition. Occasionally, an athletic girl breached the cultural divide and played with the boys, yet her status as tomboy was always a limiting and noninclusive role. A powerful male culture had evolved, with the entitlement and rights of the privileged.

Excluded from this all-male society were not only the girls but also some boys who were considered sissies. For these rejected boys, the consequences of being left out of the **dominant male peer group** were painful and severe. As they progressed through their elementary school years, these excluded male students exhibited an increasing number of social, emotional, and academic problems. Afraid of being teased by the male club, they avoided playing with the girls, even though they might have been very happy doing so. Belonging nowhere, they banded together loosely, not out of liking but out of need.

The girls spent the first few years of school helping the teacher, not switching their allegiance to the peer group until the fourth grade. Throughout their school years, this allegiance was rewarded, in part with good report card grades. Then, instead of joining a club, they formed best-friend relationships, in which pairs of girls pledged devotion to one another. Sometimes fights broke out, when two girls argued over having a third as best friend. In the upper elementary grades, the girls also began to fantasize about the "cute" boys in their class and about what being married and having a family would be like. Being a good student and having a pleasing personality were seen as important, but, by the upper elementary grades, appearance had become the key to social status.

The **gender wall** blocking boys and girls from interacting is stronger than barriers to racial integration; there is more cross-race than cross-sex communication during the elementary school years. When Best asked students why there was not more friendship between boys and girls, they reacted with embarrassment. "Everyone would make fun of you," said one girl. Another commented,

That's what researchers at the University of Michigan wanted to find out as they compared the activities of American 3- to 12-year-olds in 1981 and 1997. Can you identify these changing trends? (In comparing the early 1980s to the late 1990s, indicate whether you believe that children are spending *more* or *less* time in each of the following activities.)

	More	Less
1. Studying	_____	_____
2. Watching television	_____	_____
3. Playing sports	_____	_____
4. Reading	_____	_____
5. Enjoying leisure time	_____	_____
6. Hours in day care	_____	_____
7. Hours in school	_____	_____
8. Involved in religious activities	_____	_____
9. Involved in personal care	_____	_____

Answers: If you said "More" to the following, you are correct: (1) studying, (3) sports, (4) reading, (6) hours in day care, (7) hours in school, (9) involved in personal care. The survey reported "Less" time in the following activities: (2) watching television, (5) enjoying leisure time, and (8) involved in religious activities.

SOURCE: Sandra Hofferth, *America's Children* (Ann Arbor, MI: Institute for Social Research, University of Michigan, 1998).

REFLECTION

Were your perceptions on target—or off? What factors do you see as contributing to these changes? How might this information impact your classroom teaching? Check online for the full findings at www.umich.edu/~newsinfo/Releases/1998/Nov98/r110998b.html.

Social exclusion occurs in mixed sex or same sex peer groups. In either setting, rejection and isolation can be painful.

If you say you like someone, other kids spread it all over the school and that's embarrassing. . . . If you even sit beside a boy in class, other kids say you like him. And they come to you in the bathroom and tease you about liking the boy. Once some of the girls put J. S. and B. B. on the bathroom walls. That was embarrassing.[33]

How children relate to one another is crucial, spilling over into every nuance of school life. For you, as the teacher, a negative peer group dynamic can mean a problem-filled year. For children, the power of the peer group is even more devastating.

"If you hate Graham, sign here." The petition was making the rounds in one fourth-grade classroom not long ago. Fortunately, the teacher intercepted the paper just before it reached Graham's desk. This time, at least, Graham was spared.[34]

In one sense, Graham is not alone. Many children share his predicament. When students respond to questions designed to measure their friendship patterns, 10 percent of them emerge as not being anybody's friend (isolates). About half of these are just ignored. The other half become the victims of active peer group rejection and hostility. In fact, elementary school sociometric measures predict social adjustment better than most other personality and educational tests do.[35] These social preferences can be graphically presented in **sociograms** (see Figure 5.2).

Most friendless children are aware of their problem and report feeling lonely and unsuccessful in relating to others. Children without friends are more likely to experience adjustment problems in later life. Rejection by the child's peer group is a strong indicator of future problems.

GUEST COLUMN: Haunted by Racist Attitudes

As graduation time approaches, I am supposed to get nostalgic about my community and my school. I should be thankful for how they have enriched my life, and I should expect to reminisce later on the "great things" about living here. Frankly, in my case, that will not be possible; I'll be trying to forget the bigotry here. Elementary school fostered my negative first impressions. One kid tried to insult me in the halls by calling me "African." My classmates told me to "go back where you came from." (Obviously they had no idea what country this was, but cultural education is another essay.) Often, I was used as an object in a "cooties" game. I was the contaminated one who had to touch all the other pure white-skinned kids. One day after school I was tied to a tree by some boys. The girls just stood around to laugh. They were the friendly ones because at least they did not inflict bodily pain. Wasn't I the naive buffoon to underestimate the burn of psychological humiliation?

Summer meant parks and recreation day camp, and that was hellish. Each day, I was depantsed by some fifth-grade boys in front of the amused campers. I was too embarrassed to tell my parents, and the counselors paid no attention to the foolish games all little boys play. Adult ignorance was by far the most agonizing injustice. In middle school, I sat in front of a boy who constantly whispered, "You f — nigger, black, disgusting" in my ear. Racism was intolerable. The teacher, I guess, disagreed. At least kids are honest. Isn't it amusing how they are little reflections of a community's attitudes? Today, the same people who tormented me as a child walk down the halls faceless. Once a racist reaches a certain age, he realizes that prejudice is not an outright verbal contract. It is subtle and "understood."

Just yesterday my five-year-old sister came home from her preschool and complained, "A girl said she didn't wanna play with me because I'm black." I said, "That's terrible! Did you tell the teacher?" My sister responded, "My teacher said, 'Just ignore her.'"

Yes, I'll have no trouble trying to forget this place.

Student letter to the school paper[36]

FIGURE 5.2
Sociogram: A teacher's tool.

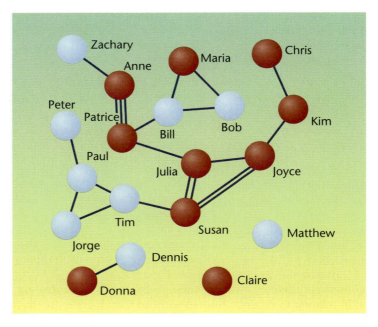

Sociograms provide insights into the social life of a class. In this sociogram, circles represent students, and colors indicate gender. Lines are drawn connecting circles when students interact with one another. Each line reflects a verbal communication: the more lines, the greater number of interactions. In this sociogram it appears that Anne and Patrice are friends; Julia, Susan, and Joyce may form a clique; while Matthew and Claire appear to be isolates. Charting several sociograms of these children over time would confirm or refute these initial perceptions.

REFLECTION

Construct your own sociogram, drawing a circle for each person in your class or in a class that you are observing, or even in a lunchroom or during recess. During a specific period of time, draw a line every time there is an interaction. Can you detect friends, cliques, and isolates? How does class seating impact relationships? What might you do as a teacher to influence these patterns?

The elementary school culture is driven by blatant and subtle peer group dynamics. An insightful teacher can structure a classroom to minimize negative and hurtful interaction and maximize the positive power of peer group relations. For instance, eliminating social cliques and race- and gender-based segregation is a precursor to successful cooperative groups. An "intentional" teacher often assigns students to seats or to group work to counter pupil favoritism and bias. A teacher's perceptiveness and skill in influencing the social side of school can mean a world of difference in the student's environment.

High School's Adolescent Society

Rock singer Frank Zappa said, "High school isn't a time and a place. It's a state of mind." Sociologist James Coleman says that high school is "the closest thing to a real social system that exists in our society, the closest thing to a **closed social system.**" Sociologist Edgar Friedenberg points out that most high schools are so insular that they have their own mechanism for telling time—not by the clock but by periods, as in "I'll meet you for lunch after fourth period." Author Kurt Vonnegut says that "high school is closer to the core of the American experience than anything else I can think of." In his inaugural speech before Congress, President Gerald Ford confided, "I'm here to confess that in my first campaign for president—at my senior class at South High School—I headed the Progressive party ticket and I lost. Maybe that's why I became a Republican." More than forty years later, Gerald Ford still remembered high school. No matter where we go or who we become, we can never entirely run away from high school. It is an experience indelibly imprinted on our mind.[37]

More than 13 million students arrive at twenty thousand public high schools every day. These schools run the gamut from decaying buildings plagued by vandalism and drugs to orderly, congenial places with educators who hold positive expectations and high standards for their students. They vary in size from fifty to five thousand students, who spend days divided into either six or seven 50-minute periods or perhaps fewer, longer blocks of time.

In his book *Is There Life After High School?* Ralph Keyes stirs up the pot of high school memories and draws a very lively picture of what life was like during that time and in that place and state of mind. In researching his book, he asked many people, both the famous and the obscure, about their high school experiences. He was amazed at the vividness and detail with which their memories came pouring out—particularly about the status system, that pattern of social reward and recognition that can be so intensely painful or exhilarating. High school was remembered as a caste system of "innies" and "outies," a minutely detailed social register in which one's popularity or lack of it was continually analyzed and contemplated. In **The Adolescent Society,** James Coleman notes that a high school "has little material reward to dispense, so that its system of reward is reflected almost directly in the distribution of status. Those who are popular hold the highest status."[38]

In a major study conducted almost a quarter of a century after Coleman wrote *The Adolescent Society,* John Goodlad reached a similar conclusion; the junior and senior high school students he researched were preoccupied not with academics but, rather, with athletics, popularity, and physical appearance. Only 14 percent of the junior high and 7 percent of the senior high students said that "smart students were the most popular." Thirty-seven percent of the junior high students said that the "good-looking" students and 23 percent said the athletes were the most popular. (See Figure 5.3.) In senior high, 74 percent of the students said that the most popular kids were "good-looking" and "athletes."[39]

When junior and senior high school students were asked to identify the one best thing about their school, they usually said, "My friends." Sports activities ranked second. "Nothing" ranked higher than "classes I'm taking" and "teachers." In some secondary schools, peer group interests bubbled so close to the surface that they actually pushed attention to academic subjects aside and almost took over the classroom. When asked to describe her school, one high school junior said,

> The classes are okay, I guess. Most of the time I find them pretty boring, but then I suppose that's the way school classes are supposed to be. What I like most about the place is the chance to be with my friends. It's nice to be a part of a group. I don't mean one of the clubs or groups the school runs. They're for the grinds. But an informal group of your own friends is great.[40]

Most informal groups are rigidly homogeneous, as becomes apparent in the seating arrangements of the secondary school cafeteria. A student in one high school described the cafeteria's social geography like this: "Behind you are the jocks; over on

OLC

INTERACTIVE ACTIVITY
HOW COOL ARE YOU?
Test how much of today's slang you understand.

FIGURE 5.3
Middle schoolers' self-perception.

SOURCE: Roper Youth Report, Question 22, Self-Perception, 1999.

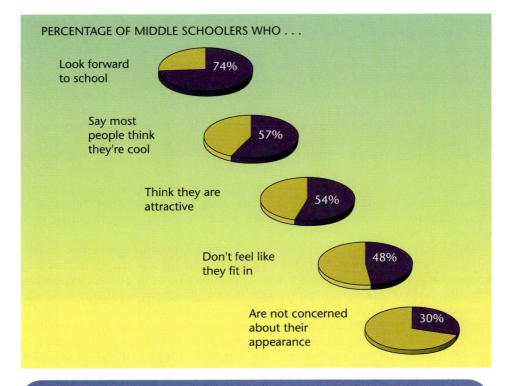

PERCENTAGE OF MIDDLE SCHOOLERS WHO . . .

Look forward to school   74%

Say most people think they're cool   57%

Think they are attractive   54%

Don't feel like they fit in   48%

Are not concerned about their appearance   30%

REFLECTION

Why are peer group opinions such a powerful influence on how adolescents view themselves?

the side of the room are the greasers, and in front of you are the preppies—white preppies, black preppies, Chinese preppies, preppies of all kinds. The preppies are the in group this year; jocks of course are always in and greasers are always out."[41]

In some cases, entire sections of the school are staked out by special groups. In a suburban high school near Chicago, the vice principal easily identified the school's different cliques. The "scums" were the group of students who partied all the time and were rebelling against their parents. Next to the cafeteria was "Jock Hall," where the male athletes and their popular girlfriends could be found. Close to the library was the book foyer, where the bright kids got together.[42]

Perhaps high school students flock to others most like themselves because making their way in the adolescent society is so difficult. David Owen is an author who wanted to find out what life in high school was like in the 1980s. Although he had attended high school from 1969 to 1973, he returned undercover, almost a decade later. Posing as a student who had just moved into the area, he enrolled in what he calls a typical American high school, approximately two hours out of New York City. During his experience, he was struck by the power of the peer group and how socially ill at ease most adolescents are. He likened adolescents to adults who are visiting a foreign country and a strange culture. Experimenting with new behavior, they are terrified of being noticed doing something stupid:

At Northgate High School near Pittsburgh, integrity and honesty pay off in unusual ways. Students who pledge not to smoke or damage the fixtures will be issued magnetized cards that admit them to an *honors bathroom.* Smoke free lavatories are predicted to be the in thing, according to senior Rob S. *Most kids will want to be there,* he says. *I don't think the honors bathroom kids will be nerds.*

SOURCE: *Newsweek,* October 19, 1998.

REFLECTION

What values are evident in "honors" bathrooms in schools or "executive" bathrooms in corporation? What is your reaction to these practices?

Click on *In the News* for recent *In the News* stories. Submit your own *In the News* summary to share with your colleagues.

Relationships among teenagers are founded on awkwardness more than most of them realize. When a typical high school student looks around at his classmates, he sees little but coolness and confidence, people who fit in better than he does. That was certainly the way I thought of my old high school classmates much of the time; no matter how well adjusted I happened to feel at any particular moment, other people seemed to be doing better. At Bingham, though, I saw another picture. Everyone seemed so shy. The kids hadn't learned the nearly unconscious social habits that adults use constantly to ease their way through the world. When kids bumped into each other in the halls, they almost never uttered the little automatic apologies—"Oops," "Sorry"—that adults use all the time. They just kept plowing right ahead, pretending they hadn't noticed. One day, when I was hurrying to my history class, I realized I was on a direct collision course with a girl coming the other way. Each of us made a little sidestep, but in the same direction. Just before we bumped, an expression of absolute horror spread across the girl's face. She looked as though she were staring down the barrel of a gun. The bubble of coolness had been burst. She probably brooded about it for the rest of the day. . . . Being an adolescent is a full-time job, an all-out war against the appearance of awkwardness. No one is more attentive to nuance than a seventeen-year-old. . . . When a kid in my class came to school one day in a funny-looking pair of shoes that one of his friends eventually laughed at, I could see by his face that he was thinking, "Well, that does it, there goes the rest of my life."[43]

The memory of high school rejection is powerful, even for generations of the rich and famous. Actress Mia Farrow recalls a high school dance at which every girl was on the dance floor except her. Cartoonist Charles Schulz never forgot the day the yearbook staff rejected his cartoon, and actress Eva Marie Saint recalls the time she did not get a part in the class play. No matter where we were in the high school system, few of us have egos so strong or skins so tough that we fail to get a psychological lift when we learn that beautiful actress Ali McGraw never had a date during high school, that actor Gregory Peck was regarded as least likely to succeed, that singer John Denver was called "four-eyes," or that no one wanted to eat lunch with former Secretary of State Henry Kissinger.[44]

INTERACTIVE ACTIVITY
THE POPULAR CROWD?
Match celebrities with their high school profiles.

For those who remember jockeying unsuccessfully for a place within the inner circle of the high school social register, it may be comforting to learn that the tables do turn. No study shows any correlation between high status in high school and later achievement as an adult. Those who are voted king and queen of the prom or most likely to succeed do not appear to do any better or any worse in adult life than those whose yearbook description is less illustrious. What works in that very insular adolescent environment is not necessarily what works in the outside world. One researcher speculates that it is those on the "second tier," those in the group just below the top, who are most likely to succeed after high school. He says, "I think the rest of our lives are spent making up for what we did or did not do in high school."[45]

Most students know the feeling of being judged and found wanting by high school peers, and some spend the rest of their lives trying to compensate or get even. Comedian Mel Brooks sums it up well:

> Thank God for the athletes and their rejection. Without them there would have been no emotional need and . . . I'd be a crackerjack salesman in the garment district.[46]

For some students, the impact of rejection does not lead to such positive outcomes. These students struggle to break through clique walls that are invisible but impervious. As one student stated: "I've never really been part of any group. I suppose I don't have anything to offer."[47]

Being part of a group continues to be a challenge for today's adolescents. While historically, entire communities participated in child care, and extended families guided and monitored children, today this social fabric of adult supervision has disappeared. With increased mobility, the generations have been separated, and traditional child care is gone. Two-parent wage earners provide less supervision, and the absence of widespread quality day care has added to the stress of growing up in America. These societal shifts demand a restructuring of the nation's approach to raising children—but that has not happened. In this social vacuum adolescents have created their own, separate culture.

Peer groups appear to be homogeneous and, more than anything else, tend to define the quality of students' school life.

In *A Tribe Apart: A Journey Into the Heart of American Adolescence* (1999), Patricia Hersch shares the story of three years she spent with seventh through twelfth graders in suburban Reston, Virginia.[48] What Hersch discovered was troubling: the development of a more isolated, intense, and perilous adolescent culture, where drugs, alienation, and violence represent ongoing threats. It is a teenage society unknown to many parents. Today's teenagers are less likely to form the tight teenage cliques that adults remember from their own childhood. Contemporary adolescent friendships appear to be more fluid: teenagers may have one group of friends in a drama club, another from math class, and a third set from sports activities. Today cross-gender friendships are also more common as boys and girls do a better job of developing relationships without the need for a romantic attachment.

But even as the number of friendships grows, the quality of adolescent relationships remains a problem (Figure 5.4). Today's teenagers, both girls and boys, report that although they have many friends, they lack intimate, close friends. Teenagers say that there is no one that they can really confide in, no one with whom to share their deepest thoughts. In the midst of a crowd, they feel alone. It is a disturbing admission, and some educators believe that schools can and should do something about it.

The Affective Side of School Reform

The message to children in this period of standards, testing, and competition, is that the school is a place of academics, and that the non-academic needs of students receive low priority. Students get this message. Students report that when they are feeling sad or depressed, overwhelmingly they turn for help to friends (77 percent) or family (63 percent); far less frequently do they seek out educators (33 percent).[49] Yet many teachers despair over the unmet **affective student needs** of today's children.[50] As a kindergarten teacher from an urban school system points out,

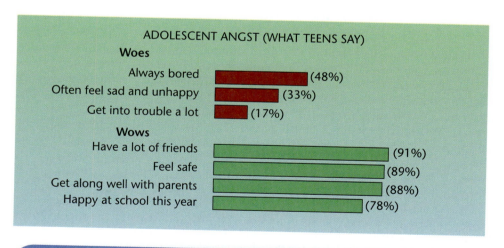

FIGURE 5.4
Adolescent angst (What teens say).

SOURCE: *Are We Preparing Students for the 21st Century? Metropolitan Life Survey of The American Teacher* (2000), p. 46

REFLECTION

Where would you be on this graph? Why the contradiction between the high number of negatives and positives? How can you organize your class so that more students are actively and happily involved in learning?

The difficult part of teaching is not the academics. The difficult part is dealing with the great numbers of kids who come from emotionally, physically, socially, and financially stressed homes. Nearly all of my kindergarten kids come from single-parent families. Most of the moms really care for their kids but are young, uneducated, and financially strained. Children who have had no breakfast, or who are fearful of what their mom's boyfriend will do to them—or their moms—are not very good listeners or cooperative partners with their teachers or their peers. We are raising a generation of emotionally stunted and troubled youth who will in turn raise a generation of the same. What is the future of this country when we have so many needy youngsters?[51]

Those who teach in urban settings warn us that the future of poor and minority children is at risk. But all is not well in suburbia, either. Consider this comment from a teacher in suburban New Jersey: "In the large, efficient suburb where I teach the pressure is on kids from kindergarten to high school to get good grades, bring up the test scores, and be the best on the test."[52] Another teacher says that there is such pressure to get high test scores that students are rushed from one workbook to another. There is no time for anything not directly related to cognitive achievement. "We feel guilty," she says, "doing an art lesson or having a wonderful discussion."[53]

In another study, **Frances Ianni** describes the affluent lifestyle in the suburb of Sheffield (name fictitious), a place where families keep well-manicured lawns and push their children to succeed. Students are groomed to be good at everything—athletics, social skills, academic achievement. "People in Sheffield will tell you," Ianni says, "that the two things you never ask at a cocktail party are a family's income and the Scholastic Assessment Test scores of their children."[54] Virginia English teacher Patrick Welsh tells of teenagers who take the SATs four or five times, pushed on by their parents' promises of new cars if they score well:

> I've had kids in class with their fingernails bitten to the quick and looking miserable, feeling they have to get As, and their parents going to the point of rewriting their papers for them. Every fall T.C. is gripped by "Ivy League Fever." Sweatshirts marked "Harvard" or "Princeton" start appearing. . . . I got so fed up, that one day in class I horrified everybody by saying I have yet to see anybody wearing an Ivy League sweatshirt get into an Ivy League school. The sweatshirts went back to the drawer after that.[55]

Pushed beyond their abilities and alienated from family, friends, and community, some teenagers develop a "delusion of uniqueness," a sense that "no one knows how I feel, no one else faces these problems, no one cares about me." When children feel cut off from what Urie Bronfenbrenner calls "the four worlds of childhood"—family, friends, school, and work—the situation can become serious and even life-threatening.[56] Sara Lawrence Lightfoot describes the following incident that took place in an elite school in a wealthy suburb in the Midwest:

> A student with a history of depression . . . had been seeing a local psychiatrist for several years. For the last few months, however, she had discontinued her psychotherapy and seemed to be showing steady improvement. Since September, her life had been invigorated by her work on *Godspell*—a student production that consumed her energies and provided her with an instant group of friends. After *Godspell,* her spirits and enthusiasm declined noticeably. In her distress, she reached out to a teacher who had given her special tutorial support in the past, and the school machinery was set in motion. A meeting was scheduled for the following day to review her case. That night, after a visit to her psychiatrist, she killed herself.

> The day after, the school buzzed with rumors as students passed on the gruesome news—their faces showing fear and intrigue. . . . But I heard only one teacher speak of it openly and explicitly in class—the drama teacher who had produced *Godspell.* Her words brought tears and looks of terror in the eyes of her students.

"We've lost a student today who was with us yesterday. We've got to decide where our priorities are. How important are your gold chains, your pretty clothes, your cars? . . . Where were we when she needed us? Foolish old woman that I am, I ask you this because I respect you. . . . While you still feel, damn it, feel . . . reach out to each other."[57]

This "reaching out" is what Ianni recommends in her **youth charter** network. "Communities," she says, "can create youth charters that encourage youngsters to move from dependence to independence, from the ethnocentrism of early adolescence to the social competence of young adulthood." She urges the community to move from benign neglect or outrage at the young to an organized system of positive involvement and guidance.[58] Many other child advocates are calling for a coordinated system of school-based social services to replace the existing maze of bureaucratic agencies.[59]

Alfie Kohn is one educator who claims that the social and affective sides of school must become an explicit part of the formal curriculum: "It is possible to integrate prosocial lessons into the regular curriculum. . . . Indeed to study literature or history by grappling with moral or social dilemmas is to invite a deeper engagement with these subjects." According to Kohn, such schools as the California-based Child Development Project, a long-term effort in prosocial education, teach children to take responsibility and care for one another.[60]

While most reform reports emphasize increased academic achievement, only a few recognize the social and emotional needs of children. The Carnegie Council on Adolescent Development report, ***Turning Points: Preparing American Youth for the 21st Century,*** warned that one in four adolescents were in serious jeopardy. Their basic human needs—caring relationships with adults, guidance in facing sometimes overwhelming biological and psychological changes, the security of belonging to constructive peer groups, and the perception of future opportunity—went unmet at this critical stage of life. Millions of these young adolescents will never reach their full potential.[61] Pointing to a society dangerous to adolescent health—one of drug abuse, poor school performance, alienation, and sexual promiscuity—the report called for comprehensive middle school reform to help protect these youngsters.

Middle-grade schools—junior high, intermediate or middle schools—are potentially society's most powerful force to recapture millions of youth adrift. Yet all too often they exacerbate the problems youth face. A volatile mismatch exists between the organization and curriculum of middle-grade schools and the intellectual, emotional, and interpersonal needs of young adolescents.[62]

Describing the trauma students face when they shift from a neighborhood elementary school, where they spent most of the school day with one or two teachers who knew them well, to a larger, colder institution, where they move through six or seven different classes daily, the Carnegie report made the following recommendations:

- Divide large schools into smaller "communities" for learning.
- Create a core curriculum.
- Eliminate tracking.
- Emphasize cooperative learning.
- Develop stronger partnerships between schools and communities.
- Assign teams of teachers and students, with an adult adviser for each student.
- Emphasize the link between education and good health.
- Strengthen teacher preparation for dealing with the adolescent age group.

Imagine life in a school that implements these recommendations. You would see a smaller middle school or high school, one emphasizing community activities and moving away from an atmosphere that produces "large-school alienation." Health issues would become more central, linking diet and exercise more directly to education, enhancing the longevity and quality of students' lives well into adulthood. But, to create such a caring and healthful school, teacher education itself would need to be changed. As you examine your own teacher education program, can you identify ways that these recommendations are being promoted? How does your teacher education program prepare you to develop school-community partnerships, promote cooperative learning, and respond more effectively to the needs of adolescents? Significant changes in many teacher education programs across the nation will need to be made if the recommendations of the Carnegie report are to be implemented.

What Makes a School Effective?

The Carnegie Council's *Turning Points* recommendations were designed to create more sensitive and humane school climates. While some educators continue to be concerned with the personal, social, and psychological world of children, in recent years, the press, public and politicians have focused almost exclusively on standards, test scores and replacing curricular choices with required courses. While we believe you should become familiar with the current research on effective schools, we want to share our concerns as well. We are not comfortable with the current push toward more tests and increased academic stress. We believe that the current movement takes too narrow a view of education, overlooking students' personal needs and individual differences and strengths. We lament that loss. There are many exciting ways to view and measure school life, but too often these days, it comes down to test scores. As we review the salient issues in school effectiveness studies, let's keep in mind that these studies often emphasize academics to the exclusion of other important aspects of a child's life.[63]

The challenge facing teachers and school administrators in the years ahead may well be the thoughtful integration of the research on effective schools and effective teaching with the research on the social and psychological needs of children. How can we improve schools so that they enhance both psychological well-being and academic success? This will not be easy.

Consider the following situation: Two schools are located in the same neighborhood. They are approximately the same size, and the student populations they serve are similar in all characteristics, including socioeconomic level, racial, and gender composition, achievement scores on school entry, and parental education and occupation. However, in one school, the students have high dropout rates and low scores on national achievement tests. In the other school, the students' test scores are at or above the national average, and the students are more likely to stay in school. Why should such differences emerge?

Puzzled by situations such as this, researchers attempted to determine what factors have made some schools more effective in encouraging student achievement. As early as 1971, George Weber studied four schools that seemed successful in teaching reading.[64] Through research such as his, the more effective schools have been identified as those in which achievement, especially for students of color and of poverty, is at a uniformly successful level of mastery. One of the best-known studies, conducted

INTERACTIVE ACTIVITY

WHAT MAKES SCHOOLS EFFECTIVE? Rate what you think makes schools effective. Compare your responses to those of your colleagues.

by Ronald Edmonds and his colleagues, concluded that, in an effective school, students with a working-class background score as high as middle-class students on tests of basic skills.[65] Other groups around the country, from the Connecticut School Effectiveness Project to the Alaska Effective Schooling program, have conducted research to figure out what makes good schools work. In study after study, researchers have found a common set of characteristics, which has resulted in a **five-factor theory of effective schools.**[66] Researchers say that effective schools are able, by means of the five characteristics, to reduce the harmful effects of poor socioeconomic background. Let's start with these classic five factors, and then move on to some more recent studies.

Factor 1: Strong Leadership

In her book ***The Good High School,*** Sara Lawrence Lightfoot drew portraits of six effective schools.[67] Two, George Washington Carver High School in Atlanta and John F. Kennedy High School in the Bronx, were inner-city schools. Highland Park High School near Chicago and Brookline High School in Brookline, Massachusetts, were upper middle-class and suburban. St. Paul's High School in Concord, New Hampshire, and Milton Academy near Boston were elite preparatory schools. Despite the tremendous difference in the styles and textures of these six schools, ranging from the pastoral setting of St. Paul's to inner-city Atlanta, they all were characterized by strong, inspired leaders, such as Robert Mastruzzi, principal of John F. Kennedy High School.

When Robert Mastruzzi started working at Kennedy, the building was not yet completed. Walls were being built around him as he sat in his unfinished office and contemplated the challenge of not only his first principalship but also the opening of a new school. During his years as principal of John F. Kennedy, his leadership style has been collaborative, actively seeking faculty participation. Not only does he want his staff to participate in decision making, but he gives them the opportunity to try new things—and even the right to fail. For example, one teacher made an error about the precautions necessary for holding a rock concert (800 adolescents had shown up, many high or inebriated). Mastruzzi realized that the teacher had learned a great deal from the experience, and he let her try again. The second concert was a great success. "He sees failure as an opportunity for change," the teacher said. Still other teachers describe him with superlatives, such as "he is the lifeblood of this organism" and "the greatest human being I have ever known."[68]

Mastruzzi seems to embody the characteristics of effective leaders in good schools. Researchers say that students make significant achievement gains in schools in which principals

- Articulate a clear school mission
- Are a visible presence in classrooms and hallways
- Hold high expectations for teachers and students
- Spend a major portion of the day working with teachers to improve instruction
- Are actively involved in diagnosing instructional problems
- Create a positive school climate[69]

Factor 2: A Clear School Mission

A day in the life of a principal can be spent trying to keep small incidents from becoming major crises. But the research is clear: In effective schools, good principals somehow find time to develop a vision of what that school should be and to share that vision with all members of the educational community. Successful principals can articulate a specific school mission, and they stress innovation and improvement. In contrast, less effective principals are vague about their goals and focus on maintaining the status quo. They make such comments as, "We have a good school and a good faculty, and I want to keep it that way."[70]

It is essential that the principal share his or her vision, so that teachers understand the school's goals and all work together for achievement. Unfortunately, when teachers are polled, more than 75 percent say that they have either no contact or infrequent contact with one another during the school day. In less effective schools, teachers lack a common understanding of the school's mission, and they function as individuals charting their own separate courses.

The need for the principal to share his or her vision extends not only to teachers but to parents as well. When teachers work cooperatively and parents are connected with the school's mission, the children are more likely to achieve academic success.

Factor 3: A Safe and Orderly Climate

Certainly before students can learn or teachers can teach, schools must be safe. An unsafe school is, by definition, ineffective. Despite the attention-grabbing headlines and the disturbing incidents of student shootings, schools today are safer than they have been in years. (See Figure 5.5.) Nearly all public school teachers (99 percent) and most students (92 percent) report feeling safe in schools.[71] Yet the image of unsafe

A positive, energizing school atmosphere characterized by accepting relationships between students and faculty often begins and ends with the principal.

schools persists, and for more than two decades, opinion polls have shown that the public considers lack of discipline to be among the most serious problems facing schools.[72]

The vast majority of schools provide safe learning environments. This is accomplished by more than metal detectors and school guards. Safe schools focus on academic achievement, the school mission, involving families and communities in school activities, and creating an environment where teachers, students and staff are treated with respect. Student problems are identified early, before they deteriorate into violence. School psychologists, special education programs, family social workers, and schoolwide programs increase communication and reduce school tension.

In some of America's most distressed neighborhoods, safe schools provide a much needed neighborhood refuge. Sara Lawrence Lightfoot tells of the long distances that urban students travel to reach John F. Kennedy High School in the Bronx. One girl, who did not have money to buy a winter coat or glasses to see the chalkboard, rode the subway 1 hour and 40 minutes each way to get to school. She never missed a day, because for her school was a refuge—a place of hope where she could learn in safety.[73]

Factor 4: Monitoring Student Progress

As the researcher walked through the halls of a school we will call Clearview Elementary School, she noted attractive displays of student work mounted on bulletin boards and walls. Also posted were profiles clearly documenting class and school progress toward meeting academic goals. Students had a clear sense of how they were doing in their studies; they kept progress charts in their notebooks. During teacher interviews, the faculty talked about the individual strengths and weaknesses of their students. Teachers referred to student folders that contained thorough records of student scores on standardized tests, as well as samples of classwork, homework, and performance on weekly tests.

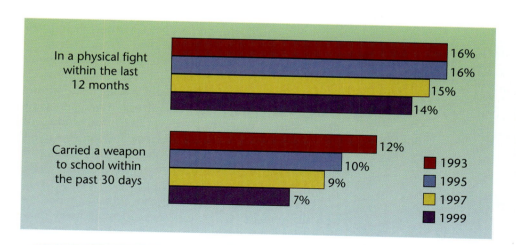

FIGURE 5.5
School-related violence: On the decrease

SOURCE: U.S. Department of Health and Human Services, Public Health Service, Centers for Disease Control and Prevention, National Center for Health Statistics. National Health Interview Survey— Youth Risk Behavior Survey, 1993, 1995, 1997, and 1999.

REFLECTION

How do you explain the popular perception of a more violent society contrasted with these statistics reflecting a decrease in school violence?

SCHOOL UNIFORMS AND SCHOOL SAFETY

In 1994, Long Beach, California became the first school district to require school uniforms for elementary and middle school students. Eagle Pass, Texas did them one better, requiring such uniforms for high schoolers as well. Baltimore, Chicago, Miami and Phoenix now allow individual schools to require uniforms. Why this growing popularity? Many parents and educators believe that a connection exists between safety and dress. Long Beach educators assert that gang clothing and designer sports clothes led to violence, fights, and overall delinquency. After the school uniform policy was initiated, school crime dropped by 76 percent, assaults dropped by 85 percent, and weapons offenses dropped by 83 percent. Meanwhile, attendance figures hit 94 percent, an all-time high. Parents supported the change, reporting that uniforms save them both money and time.

But not everyone agrees that uniforms are the reason for these encouraging figures. Critics indicate that dropping crime figures nationally are at least partially responsible for these positive changes. Educator Ray Rist believes that treating students in a special way affects their behavior. He believes it is not the uniforms, but the special attention that they are receiving that is responsible for the improved behavior. While some students like the uniform requirements, others do not. *I think it's stupid,* says ninth grader Jamie P., *What does school have to do with uniforms?*

SOURCE: *Teacher Magazine on the Web,* March 1998.

REFLECTION

Do you believe that uniforms reduce violence? Support your position.

Click on *In the News* for recent *In the News* stories. Submit your own *In the News* summary to share with your colleagues.

Good schools have safe environments.

A visit to Foggy Bottom Elementary, another fictitious school with a revealing name, disclosed striking differences. Bulletin boards and walls were attractive, but few student papers were posted, and there was no charting of progress toward academic goals. Interviews with students showed that they had only a vague idea of how they were doing and of ways to improve their academic performance. Teachers also seemed unclear about individual student progress. When pressed for more information, one teacher sent the researcher to the guidance office, saying, "I think they keep some records like the California Achievement Tests. Maybe they can give you what you're looking for."

Following the visit, the researcher wrote her report: "A very likely reason that Clearview students achieve more than Foggy Bottom students is that one school carefully monitors student progress and communicates this information to students and parents. The other school does not."

Effective schools carefully monitor and assess student progress in a variety of ways:

YOU BE THE JUDGE
HOMEWORK SHOULD BE

A Major Part of a Student's Life Because...

THERE IS TOO MUCH MATERIAL TO BE MASTERED ONLY DURING SCHOOL TIME

Given demands on students to learn more and to increase their test scores, much study and learning needs to take place at home. After all, students are in school for just five hours of a 24-hour day.

IT BRINGS PARENTS INTO THE LEARNING PROCESS

School cannot accomplish its goals alone. Students achieve much more when academics are reinforced at home. By providing guidance and monitoring homework, parents demonstrate their support of learning, becoming true partners with teachers. Closing the school-home gap fosters competent and attentive students.

MANY STUDENTS DO NOT USE THEIR TIME WISELY

The average student comes home from school, talks on the phone with friends, "hangs out" at the mall, watches television for hours, and then plays a computer game or two before going to bed. Homework at least gives students something meaningful to do with their time.

Limited and Brief Because...

TOO MUCH STRESS IS PLACED ON STUDENTS AS IT IS

Schools have been taken over by this growing obsession with tests. The last thing we need to do is extend this angst to home life. Besides, homework is mostly busywork, unrelated to real learning.

IT FAVORS SOME STUDENTS AND PENALIZES OTHERS

Some children have highly educated parents, home computers, and the resources needed to produce quality homework. Other students have poor and uneducated parents, who may not even speak English, and who may be working two or more jobs. All too often homework is simply a measure of family resources.

MANY STUDENTS DO NOT HAVE THE LUXURY OF EXTRA TIME

Many students go directly from school to their part-time job. Their families may need the money. Other students must care for younger siblings at home while parents are at work. Increasing homework would place an enormous burden on these families.

OLC

YOU BE THE JUDGE

Will you be assigning homework? If so, how much do you think is appropriate, and how will homework factor into your assessment of student work? Do you have a plan to handle differences in family resources?

- **Norm-referenced tests** compare individual students with others in a nation-wide norm group (e.g., the SAT or ACT).
- **Objective-referenced tests** measure whether a student has mastered a designated body of knowledge (e.g., state assessment tests used to determine who has "mastered" the material).

Other measures may be less formal. Teacher-made tests are an important (and often overlooked) measure of student progress. Some teachers ask students to track their own progress in reaching course objectives as a way of helping them assume more responsibility for their own learning.[74] Homework is another strategy to monitor students. Researcher Herbert Walberg and colleagues found that homework increases student achievement scores from the 50th to the 60th percentile. When homework is graded and commented on, achievement is increased from the 50th to

1800–1900	Memorization is the mark of an educated person, and homework consumes many hours
1900–1940	Homework is considered a form of child labor, and a health risk; memorization and homework are de-emphasized
1940–1957	Creative, individualized assignments usher in a more humane return to homework
1957–1967	The launch of *Sputnik* sparks increased homework, especially in math and science
1968–1982	Social concerns and civil rights take precedence over academics and homework
1982–present	*A Nation at Risk* reports that homework is an effective counter to falling test scores, and homework increases dramatically, despite the concern of many parents

SOURCE: Laurel Graeber, "More Work, Less Play," in Education Life, *The New York Times,* January 3, 1999.

REFLECTION

Where do you predict the homework pendulum will be during your time in the classroom? Do you have a preference?

Check the textbook website www.mhhe.com/sadker6e for suggestions about assigning effective homework. You may also want to refer to the U. S. Department of Education's "Helping Your Students with Homework" at www.ed.gov/pubs/HelpingStudents/ or visit some school district sites to see their homework policies.

nearly the 80th percentile. Although these findings suggest that graded homework is an important ingredient in student achievement,[75] how much homework to assign, and what kinds of homework tasks are most effective, continue to be points of contention. (See the *You Be the Judge* feature in this chapter.)

Factor 5: High Expectations

The teachers were excited. A group of their students had received extraordinary scores on a test that predicted intellectual achievement during the coming year. Just as the teachers had expected, these children attained outstanding academic gains that year.

Now for the rest of the story: The teachers had been duped. The students identified as gifted had been selected at random. However, eight months later, these randomly selected children did show significantly greater gains in total IQ than did another group of children, the control group.

In their highly influential 1969 publication, ***Pygmalion in the Classroom,*** researchers **Robert Rosenthal** and **Lenore Jacobson** discussed this experiment and the power of teacher expectations in shaping student achievement. They popularized the term **self-fulfilling prophecy** and revealed that students may learn as much—or as little—as teachers expect.[76] Although methodological criticisms of the original Rosenthal and Jacobson study abound, those who report on effective schools say that there is now extensive evidence showing that high teacher expectations do, in fact, produce high student achievement, and low expectations produce low achievement.[77]

Too often, teacher expectations have a negative impact. An inaccurate judgment about a student can be made because of error, unconscious prejudice, or stereotype. For example, good-looking, well-dressed students are frequently thought to be smarter than their less attractive peers. Often, male students are thought to be brighter in math, science, and technology, while girls are given the edge in language skills. Students of color are sometimes perceived as less capable or intelligent. A poor performance on a single standardized test (perhaps due to illness or an "off" day) can cause teachers to hold an inaccurate assessment of a student's ability for months and even years. Even a casual comment in the teachers' lounge can shape the expectations of other teachers.

When teachers hold low expectations for certain students, their treatment of these students often differs in unconscious and subtle ways. Typically, they offer such students

- Fewer opportunities to respond
- Less praise
- Less challenging work
- Fewer nonverbal signs (eye contact, smiles, positive regard)

In effective schools, teachers hold high expectations that students can learn, and they translate these expectations into teaching behaviors. They set objectives, work toward mastery of those objectives, spend more time on instruction, and actively monitor student progress. They are convinced that students can succeed.

Finally, in effective schools, teachers hold high expectations for themselves. They believe that they can deliver high-quality instruction. In *The Good High School,* Sara Lawrence Lightfoot reported that this sense of teacher efficacy and power was prevalent at Brookline High. "Star" teachers were respected as models to be emulated. Always striving for excellence, these teachers felt that, no matter how well a class went, next time it could be better.

A Note of Caution on Effective Schools Research

Although the research on what makes schools effective has had a direct impact on national reform movements, it has limitations.[78] First, there is disagreement over the definition of an effective school. Researchers use varying descriptions, ranging from "schools with high academic achievement" to schools that foster "personal growth, creativity, and positive self-concept." Although the five factors we have described are helpful, they do not really provide a prescription for developing successful schools.

Another problem is that much of the research has been conducted in elementary schools. Although some researchers suggest applicability to secondary and even higher education, caution must be used in carrying the effective-schools findings to higher levels of education. The generalizability of the research is also limited, since

Many schools, public and private, have opted for official uniforms. Even when dress remains a student choice, peer pressure may create "unofficial" uniforms. Based on the appearance of these students, what assumptions might you make about their schools?

Sixty percent of middle and high school students believe that they will achieve their life goals, but only 19 percent of their teachers agree. Almost three out of four students believe that they will go to college, while their teachers believe that fewer than one in three will make it.

SOURCE: "Extra Credit," *The Washington Post,* October 10, 2000, p. A11.

REFLECTION

How do you explain the "Expectation Gap"? As a student, did you ever experience this gap?

 Click on *In the News* for recent *In the News* stories. Submit your own *In the News* summary to share with your colleagues.

several of the studies were conducted in inner-city schools and tied closely to the achievement of lower-order skills in math and science. If one wanted to develop a school that nurtures creativity rather than basic skills, another set of characteristics might be more appropriate.

Beyond Five Factors

New effective-schools findings offer us insights beyond these original five factors of effective schooling:

- *Early start.* The concept that there is a particular age for children to begin school needs to be rethought. The earlier schools start working with children, the better children do. High-quality programs during the first three years of life include parent training, special screening services, and appropriate learning opportunities for children. While such programs are rare, those that are in operation have significantly raised IQ points and have enhanced language skills. It is estimated that $1 spent in an early intervention program saves school districts $7 in special programs and services later in life.

- *Focus on reading and math.* Children not reading at grade level by the end of the first grade face a one-in-eight chance of ever catching up. In math, students who do not master basic concepts find themselves playing catch-up through-out their school years. Effective schools identify and correct such deficiencies early, before student performance deteriorates.

- *Smaller schools.* Students in small schools learn more, are more likely to pass their courses, are less prone to resort to violence, and are more likely to attend college than those attending large schools. Disadvantaged students in small schools outperform their peers in larger schools, as achievement differences for the rich and poor are less extreme. Many large schools have responded to these findings by reorganizing themselves into smaller units, into schools within schools. Research suggests that small schools are more effective at every educational level, but they may be most important for older students.

It is more difficult to find a teaching position in Connecticut than in most places. Tough standards include entrance exams and video "shakedown" exercises, all designed to select the best teachers for Connecticut's classes. And this may be one important reason why the state's students are doing so well. Connecticut ranks first on several critical measures of student performance (see the figure). While many credit Connecticut's academic success to its wealth and high level of parent education, student scores have been on the rise, while state wealth and parental education remain unchanged. So what's happening in Connecticut?

Many attribute Connecticut's success to the years of effort improving many of the school effectiveness factors discussed in this chapter: high expectations, hard work, high standards, close monitoring of student progress, and a string of talented educational leaders.

For the classroom teacher, the state's commitment is evident. Each new teacher is assigned a mentor, and then undergoes continual testing. If a problem is uncovered, in a classroom or a school, extra resources are devoted to remedy it. Rather than threaten to withhold diplomas from students or punish teachers in "failing schools," the state provides additional help for students and teachers. Teachers also get the message when their salary checks arrive: Connecticut pays the highest teacher salaries in the nation.

Scores and a Success Story

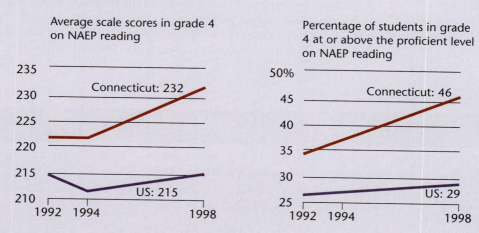

Average scale scores in grade 4 on NAEP reading

Percentage of students in grade 4 at or above the proficient level on NAEP reading

SOURCE: Jay Mathews, "Connecticut's Education Success Story," *The Washington Post,* July 18, 2000, p. A11; National Center for Educational Statistics.

REFLECTION

Before you run off to apply for a teaching job in Connecticut, tell us what factors would draw you to that state, and what might keep you away. While all this sounds grand, Connecticut's test scores are still being used to measure school effectiveness. Can you create your own nontest indicators of school effectiveness? How do you explain the public's fixation on test scores?

- *Smaller classes.* Although the research on class size is less powerful than the research on school size, studies indicate that smaller classes are associated with increased student learning, especially in the earlier grades. Children in classes of fifteen outperform students in classes of twenty-five, even when the larger classes have a teacher's aide present.

- *Increased learning time.* While not an amazing insight, research tells us what we already suspect: more study results in more learning. Longer school days, longer school years, more efficient use of school time, and more graded homework are all proven methods of enhancing academic learning time and student performance.

- *Assessment.* Investing time is useful, but assessing how effectively the time is spent is also important. Testing student performance has been tied to greater achievement, and some districts have gone so far as to pay teachers incentives for improvements in student test scores.

- *Teacher training.* Researcher Linda Darling-Hammond reports that the best way to improve school effectiveness is by investing in teacher training. Stronger teacher skills and qualifications lead to greater student learning. Conversely, students pay an academic price when they are taught by unqualified and uncertified teachers.

- *And what about technology?* School districts that are hesitant to spend funds on teacher training, class size reductions, or early childhood education programs nevertheless are quick to invest significant sums in computers and upgraded technology. Research says very little about the impact of technology on school effectiveness and student performance. Studies are few, sometimes contradictory, and long-term results are still unknown. It is a sad commentary that the glamour of cyberspace is more persuasive than decades of research.[79]

SUMMARY

CHAPTER REVIEW

Go to the Online Learning Center to take a chapter self-quiz, practice with key terms, and review key ideas from the chapter.

1. What rituals and routines shape classroom life?

- Typically, teachers are enormously busy, instructing, monitoring, distributing material, evaluating student work, organizing class activities.

- Students spend much of their time sitting still and waiting. Many students must manage their energy and curiosity by denying their needs, becoming involved in distractions, and sometimes by daydreaming.

2. How is class time related to student achievement?

- John Goodlad and others have documented startlingly inefficient use of time in many classrooms. While some teachers use time efficiently and well, others lose much instructional time in issues ranging from managing student behavior to administrative routines.

- Teachers who can efficiently organize classroom activities and manage students are able to invest more time teaching. In those classrooms, students learn more.

3. How does the teacher's gatekeeping function influence classroom roles?

- Researcher Ned Flanders found that two-thirds of the classroom time is talk; two-thirds of that talk is from the teacher.

- In the "pedagogical cycle," teachers structure (lecture and direct), question, and react to student comments, and initiate about 85 percent of these verbal cycles.

- Research shows that most questions are asked by the teacher and require only rote memory.

- Ironically, while a major goal of education is to increase students' curiosity and quest for knowledge, it is the teachers, not the students, who dominate and manage classroom interaction.

4. What is tracking, and what are its advantages and disadvantages?

- Being tracked into slower classes has a negative impact on students' self-esteem and achievement, and results in fewer opportunities to learn, and a growing achievement gap between students in the highest tracks and those in the lowest ones.

- Researchers such as Jeannie Oakes have found a disproportionate impact on poor children and students of color. These students are more likely to find themselves labeled as slow learners even when their achievement levels are strong. For reasons such as these, it is not surprising that tracking has acquired an "undemocratic" aura.

- Yet many teachers and parents believe that some sort of grouping is necessary. Teaching gifted students along with weaker ones will meet no one's objectives, and serve to frustrate everyone.

- Tracking must be reformed to avoid racism and classism, but advocates argue that tracking is inevitable and can be productive.

5. Why has "detracking" become a popular movement?

- Opposition to tracking grew with recognition that African American and Hispanic students were being underrepresented in programs for the gifted, and teachers with the least experience and the lowest levels of qualifications were being assigned to students in the lowest tracks.

- Supporters of detracking call for more individualization of instruction, more authentic learning, and less reliance on a "one size fits all" view of learning, teaching, and evaluating.

- By 2000, only a small number of schools continued to use the term "tracking," although many continued the practice under names such as "ability grouping."

6. How do peer groups impact elementary school life?

- Beginning in elementary school, peer pressure wields great power in children's lives. Young children's peer groups are rigidly segregated by a gender wall, with boys tending to form hierarchic societies and girls usually forming pairs of best friends. Those left out may develop adjustment problems and emotional difficulties.

- Compared to children in the early 1980s, in the late 1990s, elementary children spent more time studying, playing sports, reading, in day care, in school, and involved in personal care, while spending less time watching television, enjoying leisure time, or in religious activities.

7. In what ways does the adolescent culture shape teenage perceptions and behaviors?

- Sociologist James Coleman described the intensity of the adolescent society, perhaps the closest thing to a "closed social system." Students seek and value peer status as a mark of their own worth.

- Authors such as Ralph Keyes suggest that high school's social status system may very well have a lifelong impact. Students who are socially frustrated in high school may be particularly motivated to succeed as adults.

- In *A Tribe Apart: A Journey Into the Heart of American Adolescence* (1999), Patricia Hersch provides insight into contemporary adolescent culture, and the lack of community or parental monitoring. As a result, today's teenagers are more isolated, intense, and at risk than ever before.

8. What steps can educators take to create a more supportive school environment?

- Concerned by the apathy, alienation, and sometimes violent nature associated with adolescents, leaders like Frances Ianni have called for schools to nurture many of the at-risk children by providing "affective" or emotional and psychological support and resources.

- Ianni advocates youth charters, a coordinated network of school and community services to provide students with the resources that they may not be getting at home.

- The Carnegie Foundation in its report *Turning Points: Preparing Youth for the 21st Century,* also suggests that schools implement more humane and caring structural changes, such as detracking, cooperative learning, and creating smaller school units that can promote a sense of community.

9. What are the characteristics of effective schools?

- Researchers such as Ron Edmonds have set forth a "five-factor theory" of effective schools. These factors can be summed up as (1) strong administrative leadership, (2) clear school goals shared by faculty and administration, (3) a safe and orderly school climate, (4) frequent monitoring and assessment of student progress, and (5) high expectations for student performance.

- Not all educators or parents view the five factors in the same light. For instance, in monitoring student progress, some advocate the use of norm-referenced tests, while others rely more on objective-referenced tests, currently so popular with the state standards and testing movement. Whether to assign homework, and how much to assign, is another point of contention.

- Some limitations on research findings on the five factors include: (1) differences on the definitions of an effective school; (2) overemphasis on urban and elementary schools; (3) the lack of a strong blueprint for developing effective schools.

- Beyond these traditional five factors, newer research connects effective schools with early intervention programs, an emphasis on reading and math, smaller schools, smaller classes, increased learning time, assessment of student progress, and expanded teacher training. To date, there is little evidence connecting technology with school effectiveness.

- Some believe that the long-term reform effort of Connecticut offers a vivid example of an effective schools success story, achieving many of the factors reported in the research.

KEY TERMS AND PEOPLE

ability grouping, 186

The Adolescent Society, 193

affective student needs, 197

closed social system, 192

detrack, 184

dominant male peer group, 189

five-factor theory of effective schools, 201

gatekeeping, 182

gender wall, 189

The Good High School, 201

John Goodlad, 180

Robert Havinghurst, 184

heterogeneous, 184

August Hollingshead, 184

homogeneous, 182

Frances Ianni, 198

Philip W. Jackson, 179

Lenore Jacobson, 207

Life in Classrooms, 179

norm-referenced tests, 205

Jeannie Oakes, 184, 188

objective-referenced tests, 205

Talcott Parsons, 183

Pygmalion in the Classroom, 207

Robert Rosenthal, 207

self-fulfilling prophecy, 207

sociograms, 191

tracking, 182

Turning Points: Preparing American Youth for the 21st Century, 199

unremarked revolution, 185

W. Lloyd Warner, 183

youth charter, 199

DISCUSSION QUESTIONS AND ACTIVITIES

1. Observe in a local elementary school. What are the rules and regulations that students must follow? Do they seem reasonable or arbitrary? Do students seem to spend a large amount of time waiting? Observe one student over a 40-minute period and determine what portion of those 40 minutes she or he spends just waiting.

2. Visit several classrooms and calculate what percentage of the time is spent on noninstructional activity—administrative duties, student reprimands, and the like. Share what you find with your classmates.

3. Do you think that tracking is a valid method for enhancing student performance? Or do you think it is a mechanism for perpetuating inequality of opportunity based on social class, race, or sex? Debate someone in your class who holds an opposing point of view.

4. We have noted the vividness and detail with which many people recall their high school years. Try to answer the following:

   • Who was voted most likely to succeed in your high school class? (Do you know what he or she is doing today?)

   • What was your happiest moment in high school? your worst?

   • Name five people who were part of the "in crowd" in your class. What were the "innies" in your high school like?

   • Is there any academic experience in high school that you remember vividly? If so, what was it?

5. Visit a school and observe student interactions in informal settings. (A shopping mall might work as well.) Do you notice any cliques? Describe them.

6. Research the issue of adolescent alienation. Make some recommendations on how secondary schools could get students to become more involved in academic and extracurricular activities.

7. Read the 1989 report *Turning Points: Preparing American Youth for the 21st Century.* Compare this with the 1983 report *A Nation at Risk.*

8. Based on the characteristics of effective schools, would you consider your elementary, middle, and high schools effective? If not, why? Share your responses with your classmates.

WEB-*TIVITIES*

1. The Anti-Achievement Dilemma

2. Preventing School Violence

3. Monitoring Student Progress

4. Gender Equity: The Work of Myra Sadker

REEL TO REAL TEACHING

ELECTION (1999)
Run Time: 103 minutes

Synopsis: This satirical comedy takes an uncommon look at ambition, ethics, the power of peer groups, and the hidden curriculum of student elections. Jim McAllister is a popular teacher and student government adviser, but he will risk his reputation and career to stop the school's consummate overachiever from winning the school's election. As campaign fever sets in, both teachers and students blur the lines of right and wrong.

Reflection:

1. What purpose(s) did the election have for Tracy Flick? Paul Metzler? Tammy Metzler? Mr. McAllister?
2. Do you agree with Tammy Metzler that student government should be abolished? Can student government ever help create effective schools?
3. Some believe that school elections actually hurt democratic principles, teaching students to vote on popularity rather than substance, and to not expect any real change after the elections. Do student elections actually do more harm than good?
4. Recall your own experiences with high school student elections. Did you run for an office? Why or why not? In your high school, what was the social status of students serving in student government?
5. How were race, gender, and socioeconomic status represented in *Election*? In your own high school elections?
6. What personal boundaries will you establish with your students? Are teacher-student friendships appropriate? Teacher-student sexual relationships? How might the grade level of students influence your answers?

Follow-up Activity: You are Mr. McAllister's successor as student council adviser at George Washington Carver High. After this major election foul-up, it is up to you to spark participation, confidence, and enthusiasm for student government. You must propose election guidelines: Who is eligible to run for office? What power (if any) will each elected position wield? What are acceptable campaign platforms? Are candidates allowed to spend money? Where and when are candidates permitted to campaign? How will ballots be collected and counted? Visit www.mockelection.com for real student election ideas.

 How do you rate this film? Click on *Reel to Real Teaching* to submit your review of this or another education-related film, and read reviews submitted by others.

FOR FURTHER READING

Becoming Good American Schools, by Jeannie Oakes, Karen H. Quartz, Martin Lipton, and Steve Ryan (1999). Tells the story of fifteen schools working to create caring, socially just, and academically rigorous climates.

Bullying, by Sharon Sharp, David Thompson, and Tiny Aroda (2001). An overview of research describing the causes of bullying coupled with practical strategies to prevent harassment in schools.

Caring Classrooms/Intelligent Schools: The Social Emotional Education of Young Children, by Jonathan Cohen (Editor) (2001). A collection of essays on the development of emotional intelligence and social competence. Includes practical strategies and curriculum for affective education.

Children's Peer Relations, by Phillip Slee and Ken Rigby (Editors) (1999). Relationships between peer status and gender, ethnicity, disability, illness, and loneliness are examined.

Class Dismissed: A Year in the Life of an American High School, A Glimpse into the Heart of a Nation, by Meredith Maran (2000). Examines with incredible detail academic tracking, school safety, peer relationship, and the everyday trials of being a teenager—and a teacher—in today's high school.

Ordinary Resurrections, by Jonathan Kozol (2000). Life in and out of schools in a South Bronx neighborhood is described through the resilient, spirited voices of students battling poverty and through the eyes of teachers trying to create protective and stimulating classrooms.

Prom Night: Youth, Schools, and Popular Culture, by Amy L. Best (2000). An analysis of proms as places where students work to understand authority, social class, gender norms, and multicultural schooling.

Tracking Inequality, by Samuel Lucas (1999). Calling the end of formal tracking policies the "unremarked revolution," the author describes how detracking reinforces persistent inequalities in schools.

6

What Students Are Taught in Schools

FOCUS QUESTIONS

1. What curriculum is taught in schools?
2. What is the place of the extracurriculum in school life?
3. How do the formal and the hidden curriculum differ?
4. How do social forces shape curriculum development over time?
5. What are contemporary subject matter trends and tension points?
6. What current curriculum directions may impact you?

WHAT DO YOU THINK? What Books Did You Read in High School English? Compare what you read to what others read for a larger view of the high school canon.

CHAPTER PREVIEW

What did you learn in school today? This is a time-honored question asked by parents, and avoided by children. What children learn varies, depending on whether they are more alert to the formal curriculum, made up of objectives and textbook assignments, or to the hidden curriculum, which emerges from the social side of school. And let's not forget the third curriculum, the one we call the extra-curriculum, the clubs, activities, and sports that influence learning.

This chapter will provide a brief profile of what is taught in today's elementary and secondary schools. Using time capsules, you will go back through time to gain historical perspective on the issues and controversies that have marked curriculum from the Puritans' two Rs (reading and religion) to the current debate over national curriculum standards. What children learn in school also shifts with changing cultural and political values. The chapter explores the curriculum pendulum, which swings between progressive and traditional educational approaches. And, you will see the impact of this movement on the major content areas of instruction.

What Is a Curriculum?

As soon as she opened the door, Mary Jean knew she would like the teachers' room. There was the good smell of strong coffee, and, although it was early, groups of teachers were already clustered about the room, talking about their work and their lives.

As Mary Jean filled her mug and reluctantly turned away from the muffins, she scanned the room. There they were, Mr. Battersea and Mrs. Schwartz, sitting at a round table in the corner.

"I hope I'm not late," Mary Jean apologized as she slipped into the remaining seat at the table. "Is it after eight?"

"Oh no, you're right on time," said Mr. Battersea. "We've been here for a while. We get here early to plan for the day. As soon as you start teaching, those college days of sleeping late are over. So enjoy it while you can."

"He's so lively in the morning," Mrs. Schwartz grimaced. "Personally, I hate the morning. Maybe after I finish this cup of coffee I'll be more coherent." Then she gave Mary Jean a broad wink. "Just kidding. I gripe about the mornings as a matter of principle. I've gotten used to the early hours—well, almost used to them. You said that you needed to conduct an interview for your Introduction to Education class. How can we help you?"

Mary Jean pulled out the sheet her professor had distributed in class. "It says here I'm supposed to ask two teachers at the school where I'm observing to give me their definition of curriculum. So I guess that's the big question. What's a **curriculum?**"

"Kind of a big, broad topic, isn't it?" Mr. Battersea looked puzzled.

"I know. Our professor said you might feel that it was a very general question. But that was the idea. We are all supposed to get different reactions from the teachers in class and then compare them."

"I like that idea," said Mrs. Schwartz, looking a little more lively as she drained the mug. "In fact, I'd like to be a fly on the wall and listen in on your class discussion. I'll try to answer your question. A curriculum. . . . Hmm. . . . What is a curriculum? Well, . . . obviously, it's what kids learn in school. It's the goals and objectives our country sets for the different grade levels, and we certainly set an awful lot of them. Sometimes we add new objectives of our own, and we'll often decide, based on the needs of our own students, which to emphasize and what our priorities should be. The curriculum gets pushed and pulled in different directions. Traditional teachers want it to transmit the culture, and they focus on the past. The progressivists want to prepare students for tomorrow's new challenges. Sometimes these two approaches—preserving the past, anticipating the future—come into conflict."

Carol Schwartz glanced at Mary Jean, who was scribbling furiously. "Got all that? Then, a curriculum is also the textbooks that are selected. Students are working with texts of one kind or another throughout the day, so what a text emphasizes becomes an important part of the curriculum. What we teachers do in class—our own interests and specialties—that becomes the curriculum too. For example, I love to travel. Every summer I go to a different country, and then all during the year I take some time to talk with the children about that place. Sometimes I'll bring in food or show them postcards and videos. I guess that becomes the curriculum too. A curriculum is simply what students learn from their teachers and textbooks in their classrooms."

Jim Battersea broke in, "Carol, I think you've made some great points for Mary Jean, but for me the curriculum is more than what is taught in classrooms. It's everything kids learn in school. For example, we have a drama group that's putting on a reggae version of Shakespeare's *A Midsummer Night's Dream.*" Mary Jean stopped writing and stared at Mr. Battersea. "Oh, I know it sounds weird," he grinned, "but the kids are doing a great job, and the drama teacher is very creative. Kids who are participating in that play are learning a tremendous amount—music, theater, Shakespeare. Other students participate in band, in chorus, in sports. There are several computer clubs. We even have a Special Friends Club that some students use for their service requirement. The students work with kids who have disabilities—take them bowling, play with them during lunch, tutor them. Children learn a lot through these experiences. I think extracurricular activities are an important part of what students learn in school."

"You're right, Jim. I was thinking about the formal academic curriculum. And what children learn in school is broader than that. I also remember one of my education professors talking about a hidden curriculum. I wasn't quite sure what he meant at the time, but, over the years I've been teaching, I've grown more and more aware of just how powerful this hidden curriculum is."

"I couldn't agree with you more." Jim Battersea leaned forward. "What Carol and I are talking about, Mary Jean, is all that subtle, incidental learning that occurs as children interact with each other, with the teacher, with all the different sides and angles of this thing we call school. For example, those kids in the drama club are learning so much more than Shakespeare. How does it feel to be on stage in front of 500 people? Are they nervous? How do they handle stage fright? What do they do if they forget their lines? Can they improvise? Do they help each other and cooperate, or do they compete? And think what a tremendous amount students learn about themselves and human nature when they work with kids with disabilities in the Special Friends Club. This hidden curriculum is an undercurrent of the formal class structure too. What do kids learn when they're playing a game in class and no one chooses them for the team? What do they take away if a teacher treats them unfairly or explodes in anger? Or think of all a youngster will learn from that teacher who sits down to talk with him or her about hobbies, goals, and problems."

"I know just what you're talking about." Mary Jean put down her pencil. "Like right now. I've learned a lot more than formal definitions of the curriculum. I know what the teachers' room is like early in the morning. I know how early you get here, and that you take time out of your busy schedules to talk with someone who wants to be a teacher. I've learned about curriculum and about teaching as well."

●●●

In 1962, highly regarded educator **Hilda Taba** said, "Learning in school differs from learning in life in that it is formally organized. It is the special function of the school to arrange the experiences of children and youth so that desirable learning takes place. If the curriculum is to be a plan for learning, its content and learning experiences need to be organized so that they serve the educational objectives."[1] Today, most educators regard the **formal curriculum** as the organization of intended outcomes for which the school takes responsibility.

In *A Place Called School,* one of the most important and influential studies of school life, **John Goodlad** refers to an explicit and an implicit curriculum.[2] The **explicit curriculum** is reflected in curriculum guides, courses offered, syllabi describing courses, tests given, materials used, and teachers' statements of what they want students to learn. When you study algebra or U.S. history, you are studying the explicit curriculum. But there are other curriculums as well. The **implicit,** or **hidden, curriculum** emerges incidentally from the interaction between the students and the physical, social, and interpersonal environments of the school. The third curriculum has been called the **extracurriculum** and includes student activities, such as sports, clubs, governance, and the student newspaper. Before we look at the formal, or explicit, curriculum of elementary and secondary schools, perhaps we should examine these powerful, less formal, curricula first.

The Extracurriculum

"The Battle of Waterloo was won on the playing fields of Eton," said the Duke of Wellington, perhaps becoming the first to highlight the importance of extracurricular activities. Students seem to agree. In the early 1990s, 83 percent of all high school seniors participated in at least one extracurricular activity, with students from smaller schools and with stronger academic records most likely to be involved.[3] Varsity sports attracted the most students, with 44 percent of the high school boys and 28 percent of the high school girls participating. Students who participate in athletics typically learn leadership, teamwork, persistence, diligence, and fair play. Twenty-eight percent of students were involved with music and drama, developing their creativity and talents. Academic clubs were the third most popular activity, with about one-quarter of all students taking part by senior year, rates that have not changed since the early 1970s. Academic clubs—science, languages, computers, debate—enhance not only academic learning but social skills as well. Nationwide programs, such as Odyssey of the Mind and Future Bowl, promote cross-curricular interests and creative problem-solving skills. Advocates see these activities as so important that they refer to them not as the extracurriculum but as the *cocurriculum.*

Advocates proclaim the value of the extracurriculum to life both during and far beyond the high school years. Researchers Allyce Holland and Thomas Andre found that

- Extracurricular activities enhance student self-esteem and encourage civic participation.
- The extracurriculum, especially athletics, improves race relations.

Sports and varsity athletics comprise an important and influential part of school life.

Female athletic participation has been associated with healthier lifestyles, including lower incidences of breast cancer,[1] reduced rates of teen pregnancy, lower usage of drugs, and higher graduation rates.[2] While the percentage of girls participating in sports grew dramatically after Congress passed Title IX (1972), a law prohibiting gender discrimination, this increase has slowed in recent years. If the current trend continues, it will take high schools until the year 2033 to achieve gender parity in their sports programs.[3]

[1]J. Raloff, "Exercising Reduces Breast Cancer Risk," *Science News* 149, no. 14 (1 October 1994), p. 215.
[2]Feminist Majority Foundation, *Empowering Women in Sports* (Washington, DC: Feminist Majority Foundation, 1995); *Research Report: Health Risks and the Teen Athlete* (2001), www.womenssportsfoundation.org.
[3]Women's Sports Foundation. East Meadow, NY. Based on information in *Women's Sports Facts,* 1989, updated July 1995.

REFLECTION

Consider your own high school athletic program. Were there inequities between male and female programs? Are you a staunch advocate of varsity sports in schools? For whom? Why or why not?

- Participating students have higher SAT scores and grades.
- Involvement in the extracurriculum is related to high career aspirations, especially for boys from poor backgrounds.[4]

Not everyone is so sanguine about the extracurriculum. The underrepresentation of low socioeconomic students is evident in many programs, as are gender differences in the performing arts, school government and literary activities, which are populated by significantly more females.[5] More skeptical than others about any real benefit to students, researcher B. Bradford Brown concludes that the best we can say "is that the effects of extracurricular participation on secondary school students' personal development and academic achievement are probably positive, but very modest, and are definitely different among students with different social or intellectual backgrounds."[6]

If you think back to your own high school days, you may remember both high- and low-profile students: the extracurricular superstar so involved in everything from the student council to the yearbook that she walked around with a little calendar in her backpack to keep activities straight; the nominal participants, involved in a few activities (this is where most students fall); and the nonparticipants, those who were alienated and excluded from the extracurricular side of school.

High-profile students have a complex network of reasons for participating. For some, there is genuine interest and enjoyment. Others see the extracurriculum as a path to social success. One study found that only 16 percent of students surveyed said getting good grades increases status among peers. However, 56 percent of students said that extracurricular activities can lead to popularity.[7] Other calculating students base their choice of activities not on their own interests but, rather, with an eye to the interests of admissions officers, who select the chosen few for the nation's most prestigious colleges and universities.

Is the school's soccer team washing cars to raise money for a homeless shelter? Are the students in Spanish 3 tutoring children at the elementary school? Directing adolescent time and energy to benefit others can help students connect with each other and the real meaning of civic duty. Since many consider service such a worthy cause, it is frequently a requirement for graduation.

What works? When schools invest their resources to develop and schedule community service projects, student participation rates surge.

Who cares? About half of U.S. secondary students participate in service activities, and about half of those students are involved on a regular basis. Participants in extracurricular programs (student government and other school activities) and students who work for pay outside school are the most likely to contribute their time. The busiest young people are the most likely to be involved!

SOURCE: *The Condition of Education 1998,* Indicator 25: Community Service Participation of Students in Grades 6–12. U.S. Department of Education.

REFLECTION

Two questions are considered in this Frame of Reference. If you are (or have been) involved in any service project, *what has worked* to motivate you? How are you like (or unlike) a student *who cares?*

Controversies about the extracurriculum often focus on its uneasy relationship with the academic side of school. For example, the current emphasis on a rigorous academic curriculum has spilled over in the form of policies that bar students from extracurricular participation if they fail a course. In Texas and other states, "no pass, no play" rules deny students in poor academic standing the right to participate in varsity sports. In some communities, budget tightening has led to "pay to play" rules, in which a fee is required for sports participation, posing a serious problem for low-income families and students.

Such policies raise puzzling questions and issues. Should academic performance and financial constraints be factors in deciding who participates in extracurricular activities? If the extracurriculum is a vital part of the learning offered in school, should any students be denied access? According to data from the longitudinal study *High School and Beyond,* African American and Latino males are most likely to be affected by these policies, since one-third fail to maintain a 2.0 grade point average.[8] Since the top academic students, more likely to be wealthy and white, already dominate the extracurriculum, will "pay to play" regulations make this curriculum even more exclusive, driving deeper divisions between the haves and have-nots and further segregating racial and ethnic groups?

An ongoing concern is that, to many, the extracurriculum means only one thing—varsity sports. (See Figure 6.1.) On any autumn Friday evening or Saturday afternoon in thousands of towns across the United States, entire communities—accompanied by bands, parades, and pep rallies—cheer the hometown football team with a level of adulation that can only be dreamed of by academic stars. For small town or large city athletes, the media hype and possibility of multimillion-dollar contracts can lead hopeful high school athletes down a treacherous road. While more than 5 million students across the nation play interscholastic varsity sports, 49 out of 50 will never make a college team. For every 100 male college athletes, only 1 will play professional sports. Many critics worry that the tail is wagging the dog in a system in which athletics get the resources, the hope, and the attention, while academics slide into the shadows.

Michael K., a senior at Westchester High School in Los Angeles, has earned the right to wear a football letter on his school jacket. He chose instead to wear the academic letter. The school awards letters to students with a 3.5 or higher GPA. *I worked harder for the academic jacket than the one for football,* he explained.

SOURCE: *The American School Board Journal,* August 1998.

REFLECTION

At your schools, were students honored for success in all areas of the curriculum? In general, how did you, other students, and faculty respond to these tributes?

 Click on *In the News* for recent *In the News* stories. Submit your own *In the News* summary to share with your colleagues.

FIGURE 6.1
High school seniors attitudes and aspirations.

SOURCE: University of Michigan, Institute for Social Research. Monitoring the Future Survey: 1998.

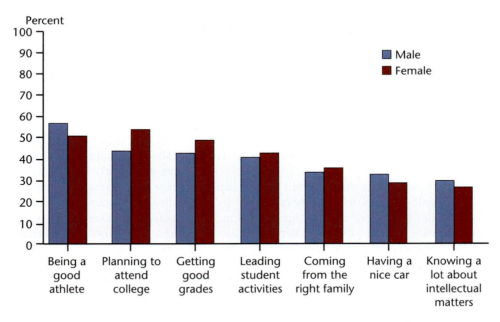

What Is Important to High School Seniors?

REFLECTION

How might these student priorities influence your teaching? How would you explain the gender gap?

YOU BE THE JUDGE
THE EXTRACURRICULUM...

Strengthens Education Because It . . .

BEATS THE STREETS
Students need meaningful activities and a place to spend their time and energy. After-school programs, sponsored by caring adults, keep students out of trouble.

IS A POSITIVE SOCIAL SCENE
Interpersonal and intrapersonal skills, developed in extracurricular activities, provide the real foundation of successful adulthood. Students, especially those with unstable home lives, need the caring relationships found in after-school activities.

PROVIDES SKILLS FOR A LIFETIME
Academics alone don't do enough to support well-rounded individuals. Especially for students whose skills and talents lie outside the formal curriculum, extracurricular activities may keep some students in school.

FURNISHES CAREER OPPORTUNITIES
After-school programs are a place to see the rewards of persistent effort and build a disciplined work ethic. Students' experiences in music, technology or service clubs can lead to part-time employment and valuable careers.

DIMINISHES SOME INEQUITIES
For families with minimal resources, after-school programs may be the only chance some students get to visit a theater, play on a team, or rewire a computer.

Weakens Education Because It . . .

TAKES TIME OFF THE TASK
Students need to focus on their schoolwork. That's what a school is for! Too many distractions from studying put students' academic potential at risk.

IS A PROBLEMATIC SOCIAL SCENE
The social scene students experience in extracurriculars is bleary. Between the cliques and the clubs, students learn who's in and who's out. Team rituals create environments that promote negative behaviors like drinking and bullying.

ADDS A COSTLY FRILL
When dollars are at a premium, every penny needs to be put into the academic arena. Squandering resources on coaches, equipment, and travel means taking money away from what students really deserve: the best education.

CAN BE A CAREER CRUSHER
Athletic success misleads players into believing that college scholarships and professional sports are within their grasp. The demanding and singular focus of activities such as sports takes students away from everything else schools have to offer. Students' dreams get crushed.

SPOTLIGHTS ECONOMIC DIFFERENCES
Poorer students who cannot afford extracurricular fees (pay to play) are denied educational opportunities.

OLC YOU BE THE JUDGE

What do you believe is the best extracurricular program for students? What's the worst? Why? What interests and skills do you possess that make you a valuable sponsor, coach or advisor to the extracurricular world?

The Hidden or Implicit Curriculum

While the relationship between the formal curriculum and the extracurriculum is occasionally controversial, they have one thing in common: Both have goals and methods that are explicit and intentional. Although the hidden curriculum is absent from the official school catalog, it still teaches powerful lessons.

225

Jules Henry is an anthropologist who has analyzed the hidden curriculum of the elementary school and has studied the values and behavior it teaches. He concludes that students are capable of learning many things at one time and that the school teaches far more than academic content. The hidden curriculum consists of implicit learnings that are not always intended. For example, Henry described a fourth-grade classroom in which a spelling bee was taking place. Team members were chosen by two team captains. When a student spelled a word correctly on the board, a "hit" was scored. When three spelling errors were made, the team was "out." Students cheered or groaned, depending on the outcome for their team. According to Henry, these students were learning about more than spelling. They were learning about winning and losing, competition, and the feelings that accompany success and failure. If they were chosen early for a team, they learned about group support and recognition. If they were chosen late, they learned about embarrassment and rejection. Some of the more thoughtful students also learned about the absurdity of a spelling lesson being taught as a baseball game.[9]

Here is another example. The formal academic curriculum stresses the importance of preparing students to become active citizens in a democracy. Courses in government, civics, and history are offered to meet this goal. In the extracurriculum, elections to student government schoolwide and to offices in individual classes and clubs supposedly promote democratic participation. But the subtle and powerful message of the hidden curriculum may lead to some very different learning, learning entirely opposite to that which is intended. As they are run in most schools, elections may teach students that, rather than "selecting the best person for the job," they are merely casting a vote in a popularity contest or that the candidate with the best posters, rather than the best platform, is most likely to win. They may be learning that it does not matter if the winner has intelligent positions on issues, or the snazziest posters, or the most friends, because nothing changes, anyway. Perhaps the fact that a large segment of the adult electorate fails to vote in national elections is a testament to the power of the hidden curriculum.

The Formal or Explicit Curriculum

You will find striking similarities in the courses of study across the 50 states, in what is called the formal curriculum. National curriculum standards, already developed for math, science, social studies, geography, history, and the performing arts, will continue to make state curricula increasingly similar in the coming years.

Although many of you left high school just a few years ago, the curriculum you knew has changed even in that short span of time, responding to new needs and new perspectives. To see how social forces change the curriculum, we have created a curriculum time machine. Because Chapter 8, "The History of American Education," offers you a look at U.S. schooling from colonial times through the progressive era, this time machine will only briefly review this period, while emphasizing curricular issues from the 1950s to the present (see Figure 6.2). In fact, we will even begin to explore the future, setting the context for what and how you will teach.

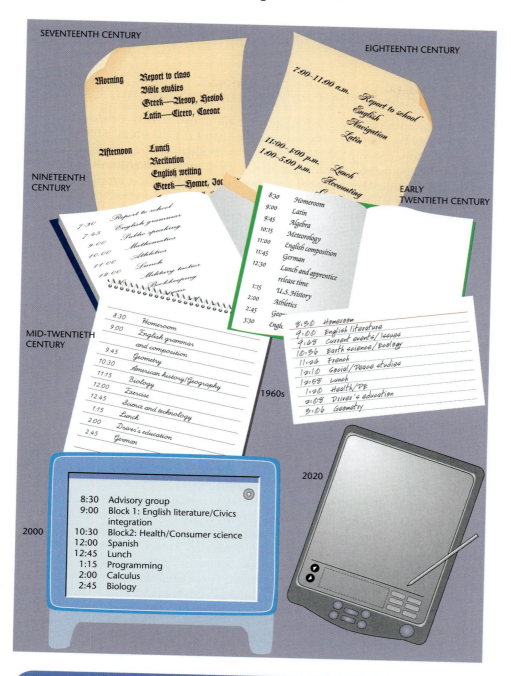

FIGURE 6.2
Student class schedules throughout time.

SEVENTEENTH CENTURY

Morning	Report to class
	Bible studies
	Greek—Aesop, Hesiod
	Latin—Cicero, Caesar
Afternoon	Lunch
	Recitation
	English writing
	Greek—Homer, Iso...

EIGHTEENTH CENTURY

7:00–11:00 a.m.	Report to school
	English
	Navigation
	Latin
11:00–1:00 p.m.	Lunch
1:00–5:00 p.m.	Accounting

NINETEENTH CENTURY

7:30	Report to school
7:45	English grammar
9:00	Public speaking
10:00	Mathematics
11:00	Athletics
12:00	Lunch
	Military tactics
	Bookkeeping

EARLY TWENTIETH CENTURY

8:30	Homeroom
9:00	Latin
9:45	Algebra
10:15	Meteorology
11:00	English composition
11:45	German
12:30	Lunch and apprentice release time
1:15	U.S. History
2:00	Athletics
2:45	Geo...
3:30	Engli...

MID-TWENTIETH CENTURY

8:30	Homeroom
9:00	English grammar and composition
9:45	Geometry
10:30	American history/Geography
11:15	Biology
12:00	Exercise
12:45	Science and technology
1:15	Lunch
2:00	Driver's education
2:45	German

1960s

8:30	Homeroom
9:00	English literature
9:48	Current events/Issues
10:36	Earth science/Ecology
11:24	French
12:10	Social/Peace studies
12:58	Lunch
1:20	Health/PE
2:08	Driver's education
3:06	Geometry

2000

8:30	Advisory group
9:00	Block 1: English literature/Civics integration
10:30	Block2: Health/Consumer science
12:00	Spanish
12:45	Lunch
1:15	Programming
2:00	Calculus
2:45	Biology

2020

REFLECTION

In the space provided, create a student schedule for the year 2020.

The Curriculum Time Machine: A Historical Perspective

Time Capsule 1: The Two Rs in the Seventeenth Century

In the seventeenth century, religion underlay all human activity. Reading the Scriptures provided the route to salvation, and the "two *Rs*" curriculum, a blend of reading and religion, prevailed. A white elementary student in those times would have acquired the rudiments of reading and religion from the **hornbook,** parchment attached to a paddle-shaped board and covered with a piece of transparent horn. If you were a white student toward the end of the century, you would be treated to a fear-inspiring dose of Puritan morality from America's first basal reader, ***The New England Primer.*** After elementary school, you would put away your hornbook if you were female. Secondary schooling was not offered to girls, while African Americans and Native Americans were routinely denied any formal education. If you were male and financially well off, you might go to the **Latin grammar school.** There you would learn Latin, Greek, and more Latin. If you grew weary of conjugating Latin verbs and translating Greek, you could always get a change of pace by reading the Bible and other religious texts.

Time Capsule 2: Curricula in the Eighteenth Century

The 1700s saw an upsurge in trade and commerce; the boundaries of the frontier stretched westward. These were changing times, with great faith in the progress and potential of humanity, dreams of fortunes to be made, and a growing commitment to life in the present instead of salvation after death. The shift from the spiritual to the secular began to free the curriculum from the tight bonds of religion. White elementary students still worked with *The New England Primer.* Studies focused on reading, religion, and morality, although writing and arithmetic were beginning to get more attention.

For white secondary students, there were some new alternatives to the Latin grammar school. At the **English grammar school,** you could learn vocational skills, such as surveying, bookkeeping, accounting, and navigating. By the middle of the century, you could attend the **academy.** Academies were a blend of the Latin and the English schools, and they housed two different courses of study. You could choose either the traditional Latin curriculum or the English course of study, which included English grammar, some history, and foreign languages. The academy broke with tradition in another way, for its doors were open to women as well as men, though the color barriers remained, denying education to Native Americans and African Americans.

Time Capsule 3: A Secularized Curriculum for Students in the Nineteenth Century

The forces of nationalism, democratization, and industrial development spread across the land. As a result, universal literacy, vocational competence, and preparation for citizenship became curricular aims.

As an elementary school student, you would have traded in your *New England Primer* for McGuffey's readers. The course of study expanded to include writing, arithmetic, spelling, geography, and good behavior. As a secondary student, you would probably be enrolled in the academy, which by the middle of the century had become the dominant form of secondary school in America. You could choose either the Latin curriculum, which continued to focus on Latin, Greek, and arithmetic, or the expanding English curriculum, which included English grammar, public speaking, geography, history, and sometimes science, geometry, algebra, and a modern language—a long way from the two Rs of the 1600s!

Time Capsule 4: Progressive Education in the First Half of the Twentieth Century

Migration changed our agrarian nation into a primarily urban one. New and diverse waves of immigrants (Irish, Polish, German, Jewish, Italian, Slovak, Greek, and Finnish) poured ashore; the schools were expected to Americanize them into a homogeneous and productive workforce. New educational philosophies were being explored, such as the progressive movement with John Dewey as its chief spokesperson.

As an elementary student, you would have time for creative expression in the form of drawing, painting, music, dance, and craftwork. Moreover, the rigid distinctions that had separated content fields were breaking down. Rather than studying history, geography, and civics, you would face an integrated course called *social studies*. *Language arts* encompassed reading, writing, speaking, and listening.

As a secondary student, you might attend the **junior high school,** which grew in popularity during the 1920s. Here a core curriculum stressed the integration of various subject areas, studying topics from "conservation in the development of American civilization" to "how I can use my spare time." During this period, high school changed from a college-oriented institution organized to meet the needs of the elite to a secondary school for most white Americans. By 1918, vocational courses, such as typing, stenography, bookkeeping, domestic science, and industrial arts, had joined the curriculum.

Immigrant children such as these were expected to be "Americanized" by the schools of the late nineteenth and early twentieth centuries.

Time Capsule 5: *Sputnik* in Space and Structure in Knowledge, 1940s–1960s

After World War II, the vocational and service-oriented courses of progressivism became known as **life-adjustment education.** As a student, you might have enrolled in such courses as "developing an effective personality" or "common learning," in which you would have studied your own social and personal problems. In the 1950s, the life-adjustment curriculum was ridiculed as anti-intellectual and undemocratic, and progressive education was under attack from many sides.

In 1957, the iciest of Cold War fears seemed to be realized, with the launching of the Soviet *Sputnik,* the first artificial satellite. The schools were made the scapegoat for the U.S. failure in the race for space. *Life* magazine urged an end to the "carnival" in the schools; Congress passed the National Defense Education Act (NDEA) and appropriated nearly a billion dollars for programs in science, math, modern languages, and guidance. Academicians and the lay public alike decried the schools' lack of intellectual rigor.

As students after *Sputnik,* you and your classmates would have studied a foreign language and enrolled in rigorous math and science courses. Prestigious academics became involved in curriculum development, particularly in math and science. One of these scholars was **Jerome Bruner,** a Harvard psychologist, who served as secretary of a conference of scholars, scientists, and educators at Woods Hole, Massachusetts. Bruner's report on this conference, **The Process of Education** (1960), had a major impact on curriculum. Translated into twenty languages and read by educators worldwide, this report put forward the premise that "any subject can be taught effectively in some intellectually honest form to any child at any stage of development."[10] Bruner conceptualized a discipline not as a collection of facts but, rather, in terms of its structure—the principles and methods of inquiry most central to its study. Bruner believed that if students could learn these methods of inquiry, they could then study a field at different levels of sophistication. He envisioned the curriculum as a spiral in which students would return to the principles at the heart of the discipline and study them in progressively more complex and advanced forms. In terms of teacher training, Bruner advocated the **discovery method,** in which teachers would assist students in uncovering meanings for themselves. The result of this curriculum revolution was an array of discipline-oriented curricula, particularly in science and math.

Time Capsule 6: Social Concern and Relevance, 1960s–1970s

During the late 1960s and early 1970s, Cold War competition seemed less pressing, as racial strife and the war in Vietnam tore at the very fabric of our society. As a student of the times, you might have thought that the discipline-oriented curricula of the past decade were out of touch with the needs of disadvantaged children and alienated youth, the movement for civil rights, and the devastation of war overseas.

Once again, school curricula became the object of critical scrutiny, and once again they were found lacking—this time by critics who have been variously labeled the "radical," "compassionate," or **"romantic" critics.** Whatever their label, these critics were concerned about the irrelevance of curricula that emphasized academics at the expense of social reality.

New courses and topics burgeoned, spinning the curriculum into new areas. You would probably have found yourself studying an array of issues from multicultural curricula to your own attitudes and values. As you read about these curricular topics, consider how your own education may have been influenced by the social concerns of this era.

WOMEN'S STUDIES AND MULTICULTURAL CURRICULA During the 1970s, curriculum developers began to design lessons, units, even entire programs, around the needs and contributions of women. These **women's studies** programs generally focused on patterns of sex bias and sought to compensate for the omissions of history and literature books, in which women and their contributions were systematically ignored. Responding to a similar exclusion of racial and ethnic groups, educational institutions developed a **multicultural approach** to the curriculum, particularly incorporated in social studies, language arts, and humanities.

INDIVIDUALIZED EDUCATION PROGRAMS FOR CHILDREN WITH DISABILITIES Public Law 94-142, the 1975 Education for All Handicapped Children Act, mandated an **individualized education program (IEP)** for each child who is eligible for special education. The IEP consists of (1) assessment of the child's present achievement levels, (2) identification of goals and of the services needed to achieve those goals, and (3) systematic progress checks to see if the goals are being met or if they need to be revised. PL 94-142, renamed the Individuals with Disabilities Education Act (1990), remains controversial, as educators debate spiraling costs, accurate identification, and the impact of mainstreaming.

SOCIAL ISSUES: DEATH, WAR AND PEACE, THE ENVIRONMENT During the 1970s, some educators, psychologists, and parents opened up the curriculum to formerly taboo subjects, such as death and dying:

> There is a need for guidance and knowledge about dying, grief, and bereavement [so that each child develops] an acceptance of death as a fact of life.[11]

Educators, also responding to the pervasive impact of violence and war, developed a peace curriculum through which students could analyze the conditions of peace, the causes of war, and the mechanisms for the nonviolent resolution of conflict. Courses in **peace studies** were first instituted in the 1960s, and, by 1974, twenty-nine colleges and universities had instituted either a certificate or an academic major in peace studies. In some cases, elements from these courses filtered down to secondary and elementary schools.

The 1970s ushered in an invigorated concern for the environment. Programs in ecology and **environmental education** stressed our planet's delicate environmental balance, and they continue to influence today's curricular materials.

Today's recycling efforts have their roots in the environmental education programs that emerged in the 1970s.

THE OPEN CLASSROOM In 1967, a Parliamentary commission in Great Britain encouraged English primary schools to adopt a child-centered approach called the **open classroom.** Based on the work of Swiss child psychologist Jean Piaget, the open classroom created **interest,** or **learning centers.** Children were encouraged to select activities they wished to pursue in these learning centers.

Classrooms in the 1970s were exciting places, with students discussing topics ranging from war to changing sex roles; learning about the culture and heritage of various ethnic groups; studying sexuality, peace, drug, and consumer education; and moving freely from one interest center to another within the classroom. However, even as these innovations were occurring, newspaper editorials and articles in professional journals reflected a disenchantment with schools. The comments went something like this: "National tests show that our students are having trouble with reading, writing, and math. In view of this, what business do schools have dabbling in all these curricular frills? It's time to get back to the basics."

Time Capsule 7: Back to Basics and a Core Curriculum, 1980s–2002

There was no unifying manifesto for those who advocated **"back to basics."** The meaning of this movement varied from one individual and school to another. In the early 1980s, a composite of what many back-to-basics advocates wanted schools to do looked something like this:

1. Devote most of the elementary school day to reading, writing, and arithmetic.
2. Place heavy secondary school emphasis on English, science, math, and history.
3. Give teachers more disciplinary latitude, including the authority to use corporal punishment.
4. Use instructional procedures that stress drill, homework, and frequent testing.
5. Adopt textbooks that reflect patriotism and reject those that challenge traditional values.
6. Eliminate electives, frills, and innovations, such as peace education programs.
7. Test, test, and test. Tie student promotion from grade to grade and graduation from high school to demonstrated proficiency on specific examinations. Issue traditional report cards frequently to communicate and monitor student progress.[12]

The conservative *National Review* summed it up this way: "Clay modeling, weaving, doll construction, flute practice, volleyball, sex education, laments about racism, and other weighty matters should take place on private time." The public defined *back to basics* more succinctly as attention to the traditional subject areas of reading, writing, and arithmetic.[13]

The issue of declining test scores gave the movement its major impetus. Between 1952 and 1982, student scores dropped 50 points on the verbal part of the SAT and almost 30 points on the mathematics part. Many researchers focused with alarm on the burgeoning number of electives as a cause for achievement decline. Philip Cusick found a mushrooming curriculum at the high schools he studied. For example, one high school had thirty-one separate courses in English; another had twenty-seven. There was a proliferation of easy electives, such as "girl talk," "what's happening?" "personal relations," and "trouble shooter." Also, activities that used to be extracurricular—yearbook, student council, newspaper, band, glee club—were often given academic credit.[14] Sara Lawrence Lightfoot, in her study *The Good High School,* also found a bewildering array of electives. One of the schools she visited had a 188-page catalog with more than 500 course descriptions. Career courses alone took up 23 pages.[15]

Even though the proliferation of electives may reflect academic richness, there is no doubt that students began to avoid the more rigorous courses. A U.S. Department of Education study showed that, between 1964 and 1980, students flocked from academic study to "personal service and social development" courses. In the 1960s, 12 percent of high school students were enrolled in these more open-ended electives. By the 1970s, enrollment had skyrocketed to 42 percent.

When faced with the question of whether to tilt in the direction of student choice or of a curricular core, most reform reports opted for the latter. For example, the National Commission on Excellence in Education report, *A Nation at Risk* (1983), called for new basics—four years of English, three years of mathematics, three years of science, three years of social studies, and one-half year of computer science.

In his book **High School** (1983), **Ernest Boyer** also called for a **core curriculum,** with the proportion of required courses increased from one-half to two-thirds of the total number of units necessary to graduate. He said that this core should include literature, history, math, science, foreign languages, the arts, civics, non-Western studies, technology, the meaning of work, and health. He advocated the abolition of the three traditional high school tracks (academic, general, and vocational), calling instead for the integration of all students into one track, with a pattern of electives radiating from the center of a common core of learning. Boyer also advocated a service requirement, which would involve students in volunteer work in their communities.[16]

Influential in the reform movement, John Goodlad's *A Place Called School* also recommended a core but stated that a common set of topics should not form the basis of the core. Rather, the core should comprise "a common set of concepts, principles, skills and ways of knowing."[17] Theodore Sizer's *Horace's Compromise* (1984) fueled the movement to reform public schools; it, too, emphasized the process of knowing. Arguing that less is more, Sizer believed that only certain essentials, such as literacy, numeric ability, and civic understanding, should be mandated.[18]

The reform report that placed the most stringent emphasis on core requirements was developed by philosopher and educator **Mortimer Adler,** in his controversial **The Paideia Proposal.** Adler advocated a required course of study that was the same for every child through the first twelve years of schooling. The only choice was the selection of which second language to study. Adler thought that electives only allow students "to voluntarily downgrade their own education."[19]

E. D. Hirsch, Jr., brought the issue of a core curriculum into the national spotlight with his best-selling **Cultural Literacy** (1987). According to Hirsch, the core cultural milestones can be identified. He extracted these markers and compiled them as lists of what literate Americans know.[20] "When the schools of the nation cease to transmit effectively the literate language and culture, the unity and effectiveness of the nation will necessarily decline."[21]

The emphasis on a more rigorous core curriculum inevitably led to a growing standards movement across the nation. By the second Bush administration, states and the national government promoted standards and curricular alignment for each discipline, testing students, schools, and teachers. If state-mandated standards were not being met, "failing" schools would be closed and students transferred to other schools. The curriculum had become a state-regulated and tested vehicle to ensure that a fixed body of skills and knowledge were attained by all students.

Minneapolis teenage students are sleeping about an hour later these days. Sleep authorities suggest that adolescent bodies can't manage early morning wake-up calls. The school district changed the 7:15 A.M. high school start time to 8:30 A.M. Middle schoolers don't start school until 9:40 A.M. What are the results of letting students sleep later? According to researchers at the University of Minnesota, these students are sleeping more, earning better grades, and experiencing less depression. And one more advantage: They are less likely to oversleep and miss school.

SOURCE: *The Startribune.com,* November 1998, *The Washington Post,* August 29, 2001.

REFLECTION

Minneapolis was one of the first districts to alter times to meet teenage body clocks but the research and time changes haven't stopped. We discovered that adolescents really love to discuss this issue! Visit an online teen chat room (or sit and talk with some young people *live*) and ask about school starting times. What can you uncover about their preferences?

OLC Click on *In the News* for recent *In the News* stories. Submit your own *In the News* summary to share with your colleagues.

The Subjects of the Formal Curriculum

In the following sections, we offer a synopsis of what is taught in the formal curriculum in today's schools. We also summarize current tension points and trends that may shape what is taught in the schools of tomorrow.

Language Arts and English

TOPICS Language arts programs emphasize literacy development which includes reading, writing, speaking, listening, viewing, and media study. In elementary school, the language arts curriculum addresses the essentials of how to use language—reading, grammar, spelling, speaking, handwriting, composition, capitalization, punctuation, word processing, peer editing, and research skills. At the secondary level, language arts instruction (or simply, English class) shifts the focus to literature, and senior high school students read both classics and contemporary works by such authors as Shakespeare, Whitman, Austen, and Tan.

TENSION POINTS AND TRENDS Approximately five percent of adults in the United States are functionally illiterate. A disappointing statistic.[22] Adult illiteracy underscores the importance of the debate over whether to use the phonics or the whole language approach to reading instruction. **Phonics** consists of breaking down words into the smallest phonetic units—phonemes—and stringing them together to form words, independent of the words' meaning. **Basal readers,** which taught fundamental reading skills and dominated reading instruction in the 1950s and 1960s, relied on phonics. Some remember phonics as "sounding out the letters to build a

COMMERCIALIZING SCHOOLS: A HIDDEN CURRICULUM

The Center for Commercial-Free Public Education is concerned about marketing products to captive student audiences. Here are some examples of their concern:

- Exxon teaches children that the *Valdez* oil spill was an example of environmental protection.
- In Colorado, Burger King and 7-Up advertise on school buses.
- A Texas school roof is painted with a Dr. Pepper logo to capture the attention of passengers flying overhead.
- McDonald's teaches about deforestation, but fails to include the negative impact of cattle ranching on the rain forest.
- Clairol distributes free shampoo to students leaving school, along with a survey asking if they had a bad hair day.
- Advertising dollars projected well into the millions makes Coke-free (and Pepsi-free) schools unacceptable to Oakland, California school officials.

SOURCE: *Educational Leadership,* October 1998; *San Francisco Chronicle,* June 6, 2001.

REFLECTION

Do you have any examples of school commercialization in your experience? Is this one of the *costs* of doing education today?

Click on *In the News* for recent *In the News* stories. Submit your own *In the News* summary to share with your colleagues.

word." The **whole language** movement condemned phonics as denying students the pleasure of reading for content and meaning. But some children who seemed slow or even unable to grasp the fundamentals of reading through the whole language approach soared to the top of their reading group when they used packaged phonics programs. Some individual teachers work to incorporate principles of both phonics and whole language into their language arts instruction.[23]

Poor writing performance also remains a concern. According to the **National Assessment of Educational Progress (NAEP),** American students' reading skills have improved over the past three decades, while their writing skills have stagnated or declined.[24] A recent "snapshot of student writing" study collected the best writing samples of 2,200 fourth- and eighth-graders. Analysis showed that most students do not write at any length and do not write analytical or research papers, and that only 1 percent revise students' work.[25]

The increased use of technology may reverse this trend. With the advent of computers and word processing, editing is simpler. Computer tools that facilitate spelling and grammar have also redefined the use of technical skills. As students become more involved with email and Internet exchanges, time devoted to writing may increase, and perhaps their writing skills will improve as well.

Another trend worth noting is that, during the past century, the list of authors taught in English classes has become increasingly American. In 1907, nine of the forty most frequently assigned authors were American; by the end of the century, twenty-nine of the forty were American.[26] The inclusion of literature by women and non-Western writers is on the increase, and some argue that such changes will be at the expense of "classic" literature, sometimes referred to as the **canon.**

Teaching is a Delpit family tradition. As a child in Baton Rouge, Louisiana, Lisa Delpit played school as soon as she learned something new, eager to share her latest idea or fact with friends. Lisa didn't have to look far to find educational role models: her mother was a high school teacher; her father was a restaurant owner who donated meals to local elementary schools for children who couldn't afford lunch. So it was much to Delpit's surprise that her family discouraged her from pursuing a teaching career. Impressed with her academic talent, they wanted her to forge new opportunities for

young black women, opportunities beyond "just being a teacher." But Lisa Delpit felt a calling to enrich the lives of students, especially those of color.

Delpit is an ardent supporter of public schools, where she believes an appreciation of diversity should be commonplace. But it is not. Too often American education fails to include, or even see, the vision of those outside the white mainstream culture. Even in the most diverse classrooms, Delpit often witnesses a prevailing tunnel vision—the richness of a multicultural lens obscured by calls for uniform standards based on traditional Eurocentric ideas. The perspectives and needs of students of color are sidelined. Delpit shares her insights:

> I have come to understand that power plays a critical role in our society and in our educational system. The worldviews of those with privileged positions are taken as the only reality. . . . It is others who determine how students of color should act, how they are to be judged. When one "we" gets to determine the standards for all "wes," then some "wes" are in trouble![1]

Delpit has felt this cultural tension in her own language arts classrooms. In her teacher training, she embraced the ideas that open, progressive classrooms are the most humanizing environments, that children should be in control of their own learning, and that students will learn to read and write when they are ready. Determined to use all she had learned to benefit children of color, she accepted a teaching position in inner-city Philadelphia. She put her whole-language teaching approach into action. Little attention was given to basic

In San Francisco, two school board members proposed a curriculum that would mandate that seven authors of a ten-author syllabus must be people of color. This ambitious proposal was eventually tabled in favor of one that requires that four of the ten be minority authors. To respond to the public demands for diversity and the classics in the curriculum, the California Department of Education currently offers 2,700 recommended K–12 titles.[27] Some complain that political correctness is becoming a threat to academic excellence, while others argue that it is time to recognize that great writers come in all colors and both genders.[28]

Social Studies

TOPICS Social studies curricula draw on the disciplines of history, government, geography, economics, sociology, anthropology, and psychology. History remains paramount, yet it has become the battleground for curriculum wars between multiculturalists and advocates of a core curriculum (see Chapter 7). While the curriculum battle still rages, history teaching has moved from a narrow emphasis on political and economic landmarks toward a broader perspective of social life and daily human struggles.[29]

writing skills, like grammar, punctuation, and paragraph structure. Students instead learned to write in meaningful contexts related to their lives and culture.

Delpit knew her students were fluent. In their stories, in jump rope chants on the playground, and in their classroom discussions, she heard their verbal creativity. But they were failing academically, fluent in a language often met with silence in schools. "Whether it is known as Ebonics, jive, or street talk, it is the language spoken by many of our African American children. It is the language through which they first encountered love, nurturance and joy and one that does not lead to success in schools or society."[2]

Lisa Delpit was in a quandary. While she believed in a whole-language approach that embraced diversity, her students were struggling, unable to grasp the language skills they needed, the keys to the language of the mainstream culture. She believes that mainstream ways of speaking and writing represent a language of power that *all* students need to master for success in the larger society. Like a captain who realized that she was sailing in the wrong direction, she charted a new instructional voyage, one that used more traditional methodology. Students diagrammed sentences, learned grammar rules, and memorized verbs. And their performance improved.

But Delpit's traditional approach does not suffer from cultural amnesia. In *Other People's Children,* she shares a vision of classrooms where teachers let the voices of all students come alive and transform the traditional canon to include the knowledge of our multicultural world. For Lisa Delpit, basic skills free students to hear how the language of their culture shapes their thinking, to understand the social realities of their lives, and to become intelligent caretakers of the future. It is a language arts curriculum for all students, including "other people's children."

[1] Lisa Delpit, *Other People's Children: Cultural Conflict in the Classroom* (1995), p. xv.

[2] Lisa Delpit, "Ebonics and Culturally Responsive Schools," *Rethinking Schools* 12 (Fall 1997).

REFLECTION

What images does the phrase "other people's children" evoke in your mind? What is the opposite of "otherness"? How has the school curriculum, both formal and hidden, shaped your definitions? How would you define Delpit's phrase "the language of power"? Other than language arts, choose a content area discussed in this chapter. What is its language of power?

Write Your Own *Profile in Education:* Click on *Profiles in Education,* write a *Profile in Education* about an educator, and post it on the Online Learning Center. Check out *Profiles in Education* submitted by other future teachers.

To learn more about Lisa Delpit, click on *Profiles in Education.*

The early elementary school social studies program emphasizes self, family, and community. Upper elementary school students begin the study of history, geography, and civics. At the high school level, the focus is on U.S. history and government, but a wide array of electives, such as economics, sociology, law, world history, anthropology, and current events, may be offered.

TENSION POINTS AND TRENDS Civics is seen as a course to acquaint a diverse student population with the democratic tradition. In a 1998 NAEP, when twelfth graders were asked to list two ways the American system of government is designed to prevent "absolute arbitrary power," 43 percent could not provide either a partial or acceptable answer. Almost three-quarters of fourth graders and slightly more than half of eighth graders were in civics classes where the Internet was never or hardly ever used.[30]

At all levels of instruction, there is insufficient attention to international topics, and students are often shockingly ignorant of the history, politics, and geography of other nations. Many high school graduates have never studied world history, while still others have studied it for a year or less.[31] One out of three students cannot locate France on a map, and one out of five cannot even locate the United States.[32]

The 1990s revealed some promising developments in geography studies, particularly due to the efforts of the National Geographic Society. The number of college students choosing to major in geography rose 47 percent from the mid-1980s to the mid-1990s. The Advanced Placement exams include geography, enabling students to obtain college credit for this content area.[33]

Mathematics

TOPICS The National Council of Teachers of Mathematics (NCTM) issued groundbreaking curriculum and evaluation standards in 1989 that were widely accepted by teachers. These standards emphasized problem solving, reasoning, technology, communication, and the real-life application of mathematical concepts. Year 2000 revisions stressed increased attention to basic skills yet managed to reinforce the hands-on experiences that help students understand math principles.[34]

The NCTM Standards (2000) identified nine mathematical skill areas: numbers and operations, algebra, geometry, measurement, data analysis and probability, problem solving, reasoning and proof, communication, connections and representations. Goals for the skill areas are identified at each of four grade-clusters (covering prekindergarten through grade 12).[35]

TENSION POINTS AND TRENDS According to the NAEP, average mathematics performance improved between 1973 and 1996 for students at ages 9 and 13, while achievement recently increased for 17-year-olds.[36] International assessments suggest that Americans' mathematics skills do not compare favorably with those of students from other countries. A 1998 international study found that American seniors did not measure up to students in less developed nations in either general or advanced math knowledge.[37] In secondary school, white males typically outperform others in math, posing a challenge for educators who would like to see all students do well in math.

In 2000, the NCTM published Principles and Standards for School Mathematics, which included a continued plea to eliminate ability grouping and tracking to ensure

A major focus of current curriculum reform is how to improve girls' mathematics test scores.

mathematical thinking and problem solving for all. The report spoke to the need for students to see real-world applications of math and emphasized the use of technology and computer graphics.[38]

Science

TOPICS Like mathematics, science was organized into standards that appear at each stage of the K–12 curriculum. Science as inquiry, physical science, life science, earth and space science, technology, personal and social perspective, and the history and nature of the field, are unified by the concepts and process of instruction.[39]

TENSION POINTS AND TRENDS Differences in science course enrollment and achievement are evident by locale, gender, race, ethnicity and age (Figure 6.3). Not surprisingly, higher levels of parent education are associated with higher student performance.[40] According to the 1999 NAEP, eighth- and twelfth-grade science performance remained unchanged for thirty years, while fourth-graders' performance improved. Only 9 percent of the twelfth graders could demonstrate advanced scientific procedures. Fully 41 percent of the high school seniors reported never working on homework for their science classes.[41] Equally alarming was students' performance on a rigorous 1997 NAEP exam of basic science knowledge. Half of the fourth-graders proved unable to identify the Atlantic and Pacific Oceans on a map, and many eighth-graders did not know how many days it takes the earth to circle the sun.[42] Try your hand at the sample problem in Figure 6.4.

In June 1998, the American Association for the Advancement of Science (AAAS) released the *Blueprints of Reform,* a study outlining necessary changes within schools, curricula, funding, and communities to enable American students to graduate from high school literate in math, science, and technology.[43] The AAAS standards emphasize learning through investigation and higher-order thinking, instead of rote

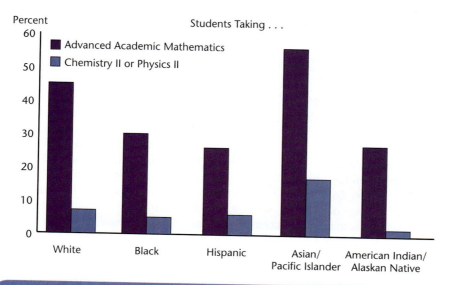

FIGURE 6.3

Coursetaking in mathematics and science.

SOURCE: U.S. Department of Education, NCES. 1998 National Assessment of Educational Progress (NAEP) High School Transcript Study, Indicator 17.

REFLECTION

Which elements in this figure could you have predicted? Which surprised you?

FIGURE 6.4
Sample problem on the NAEP test of basic science knowledge.

SOURCE: National Assessment of Educational Progress

You stand on the end of a boat dock and toss a small stone out into a pond of still water. Ripples form on the surface of the water. Which drawing shows what you will see when you look down at the water? (X marks where the stone enters the water.)

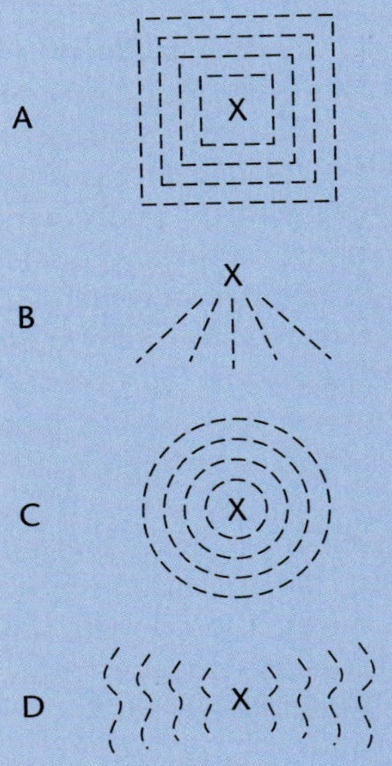

A

B

C

D

REFLECTION

Two in five fourth graders didn't know the answer was C. How did you do?

memorization. The report urges that the number of concepts taught be reduced and deeper understanding of key scientific principles be encouraged. As did the mathematics standards, the science standards define a basic level of core knowledge for all students, regardless of background, ability level, or future aspirations. The proponents of "more is better" often come into conflict with those who believe "less can be more significant."[44] And still others wonder about the potential of computers to significantly enhance science education. A challenge to the successful implementation of new science standards will be the schools' ability to provide students with costly technological resources and equipment.[45]

Foreign Languages

TOPICS In 1915, 36 percent of all high school students studied a foreign language. By 1980, this percentage had been slashed by more than half, and only 5 percent of high school students continued their study of a foreign language for more than two years.

Today, the foreign language taught most often is Spanish, followed by French and German. The middle school curriculum includes grammar, vocabulary development, pronunciation, simple conversation, and appreciation of cultural diversity. In senior high school, the curriculum focus switches to conversational fluency, with expanded emphasis on the worldwide culture.

TENSION POINTS AND TRENDS In a world where 2,700 languages are spoken, only 15 percent of its people are native English speakers. The language with the most speakers is Chinese, and Hindustani comes in second. The United States is one of the most monolingual of all the developed countries. On the bright side, English has become the most common second language in the world—the language of business, science, and diplomacy.

This nation's geographic isolation has historically fueled our linguistic isolation, yet even that is changing as multilingual indicators appear at ATMs and telephone information services. As world travel and communication become commonplace, English language speakers will need to learn other languages to interact globally. Recently, many high schools and colleges have re-established foreign language requirements, and enrollment in these courses is climbing once again. Private school students, perhaps responding to this requirement, are almost twice as likely (55.1 percent) as their public school counterparts (27.6 percent) to be enrolled in a foreign

A pop TV cooking competition (Iron Chef) has set the stage for a similar challenge among science teachers at the San Francisco Exploratorium. The teacher-scientists get a "secret ingredient" (film canister, bar of soap) that must be used to concoct an educational experiment. A potpourri of results is archived on the Iron Science Teacher website: www.exploratorium.edu/iron_science.

SOURCE: *Wired News*, 2:00 A.M. PDT, July 16, 2001.

REFLECTION

Journey to the Exploratorium site and scan several Iron Teacher experiments. How might you recreate this challenge in your subject or grade level area?

Click on *In the News* for recent *In the News* stories. Submit your own *In the News* summary to share with your colleagues.

---

language.[46] Further, educators are calling for earlier emphasis on the study of foreign language—by the fourth grade and even before—and for blocks of time longer than forty or fifty minutes a day for the study of language.[47]

Technology

TOPICS As computers flood American life, from the online trading of securities to cyber-dating, their use in the classroom continues to grow dramatically. Several states require computer literacy course work from kindergarten through twelfth grade. Often taught by teacher-specialists in computer labs, students learn sequenced skills, which may begin with technology games and keyboarding and move to website development and software design. Other states integrate computers into subject area fields. Reading instruction, in the elementary grades, makes up the majority of technology time.[48] In high schools, computers are used primarily for word processing and computer literacy training. Schools continue to position themselves for the information age, as expensive upgrades run up budget costs. While solid research on academic effectiveness continues to evade most researchers, the "technological draw" of the computer age appears irresistible.

TENSION POINTS AND TRENDS In 1998, the NCES released *Technology @ Your Fingertips,* a step-by-step guide for schools, detailing the process of acquiring computers, training users, obtaining technological support, and securing financial assistance. Federal encouragement and local financial support has led to skyrocketing Internet access, with 98 percent of schools reporting that they were online by 2000.[49] Progress at the classroom level has been less impressive. Despite the e-rate, which makes Internet connections available at greatly reduced costs, many classrooms continue to lack meaningful technological capabilities, with only 40 percent of high poverty classrooms online in 2000.[50] Wealth and poverty often determine the dividing line between the technological *haves,* and *have-nots,* a cruel reality that has been termed the **digital divide.** Less attention has been given to the evolving **learning divide,**

FIGURE 6.5
Internet use: Purpose and location.

SOURCE: U.S. Department of Commerce, Bureau of the Census. December and October Current Population Surveys, 1998.

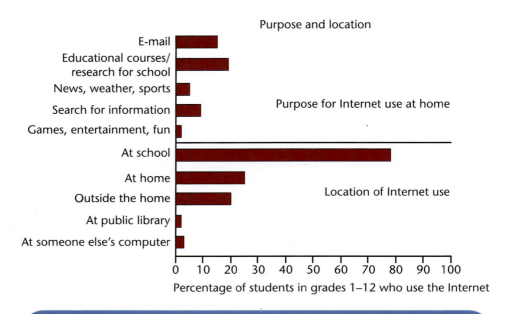

Purpose and location

Purpose for Internet use at home

Location of Internet use

Percentage of students in grades 1–12 who use the Internet

REFLECTION

How does your use of the Internet compare to the patterns of use shown above?

FIGURE 6.6
Computer comparisons in mathematics and writing.

SOURCE: National Center for Education Statistics, National Assessment of Educational Progress (NAEP), Long-Term Trend Assessment (1996, 1999)

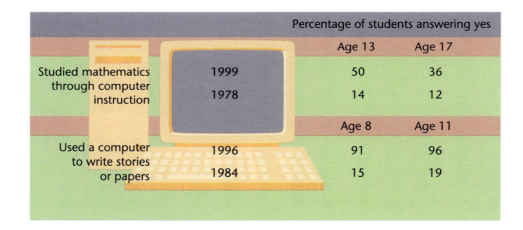

		Percentage of students answering yes	
		Age 13	Age 17
Studied mathematics through computer instruction	1999	50	36
	1978	14	12
		Age 8	Age 11
Used a computer to write stories or papers	1996	91	96
	1984	15	19

REFLECTION

Where does your experience fit in the computer instruction percentages?

which emerges when educators, often in poorer communities, lack training and skills needed to use technology wisely and efficiently.[51] But even the growing access to school technology can create new problems, such as the unauthorized access to school information by outsiders. Today, schools are adding a new item to their budgets: the cost of technological security and additional legal fees.[52]

While the focus is on providing students with access to computers and the Internet, few are asking what happens when schools finally do get hooked up electronically. (See Figure 6.5.) While some studies suggest that student computer use is correlated to a rise in standardized test scores, that increase occurs only when teachers are well trained and comfortable with the technology.[53] All too often, teachers are unfamiliar with computer skills and have not received adequate training on how to integrate technology into the standard curriculum, seriously compromising the vast resources offered by computers.

The Arts

TOPICS Visual arts, dance, theater, and music constitute the four comprehensive arts, but three out of four students receive no instruction in theater or dance.[54] The goals of the arts program include developing the ability to create art forms, understanding art as a cultural phenomenon, and developing aesthetic appreciation and perception. In elementary school, regular classroom teachers do most of the instruction in these areas. Children color, paint, and use materials to explore creatively and to use the elements of design (shading, size, and shape). In music, children learn sight reading and sing traditional childhood favorites, patriotic songs, and music from other lands. Drama and dance provide students with the opportunity to develop movement and related skills. In secondary school, the arts curriculum typically expands to include technical and graphic arts, design, crafts, theater, dance, film, photography, ceramics, sculpture, orchestra, band, chorus, and more specialized music courses.

TENSION POINTS AND TRENDS Many educators consider the arts to be shamefully neglected—the last to be included and the first to be cut when the budget ax falls. The current emphasis on test score performance and core requirements has further diminished arts in schools. One study found that elementary schools commit only 4 percent of their school week to art instruction. Only 25 percent of that time is provided by trained art teachers. Further, some charge that there is too much emphasis on students' acquiring technical and performance skills, rather than gaining greater appreciation of aesthetics and human creativity.

In 1994, a panel of thirty-eight artists, educators, and business representatives approved new, voluntary standards for the arts curriculum that call for more ambitious and sequential instruction. The standards specified that, by high school graduation, students should have a basic level of competency in each of the four arts disciplines—dance, music, theater, and visual arts.[55] This Arts Education Consensus Project was the nation's most significant attempt to assess the arts with both qualitative and quantitative measures.[56]

Physical Education

TOPICS Research shows that physical education provides lifelong health dividends. High-quality programs emphasize not only physical competence, enjoyment and lifetime activity but also social and psychological development, including leadership, teamwork, and cooperation. In the past few decades, there has been a shift away from competitive skill development to fitness and well-being through recreational and individual sports and well-rounded conditioning.

Across the nation, music programs range from grandiose spectacles to the sounds of silence. How does a school's music program amplify its culture?

Public schools are getting serious about student backpacks.

- At North Carroll High School in Hampstead, MD, students may take backpacks to and from school but not to and from class. Teachers were having difficulty navigating the halls around the bulging packs, and administrators complained that food hidden in the packs was adding to the rodent problem.
- Other schools were instituting backpack lessons out of a concern that the weighty packs were contributing to back and neck problems. Keep both shoulder straps on at all times or use a wheelie.
- Cumberland and neighboring Robeson County (NC) require that student backpacks be clear or transparent mesh to protect against drugs and weapons being brought to school.

SOURCES: *The American School Board Journal,* November 1998; *Back Pack Troubles from Back-to-School Backpacks* Lesson Tutor Online (March 29, 2001), www.lessontutor.com/ssl.html; Fayetteville (NC) *Observer-Times* (August 15, 1999).

REFLECTION

Teachers have been known to take home as much work as will fit in the trunk of their car. What are you using to tote your schoolwork around? How would you cope with these backpack challenges?

Click on *In the News* for recent *In the News* stories. Submit your own *In the News* summary to share with your colleagues.

Elementary programs are structured around skill improvement; too frequently through games. Classes vary from little more than teacher-monitored recess to well-sequenced motor development instruction. Middle school programs are often the first time students have certified PE specialists, have a course of study, and "dress out" for class. By high school, the curriculum is governed by electives from aerobics and basketball to soccer and yoga.

TENSION POINTS AND TRENDS According to the President's Council on Physical Fitness and Sports, our children are not physically fit. Thirteen percent of 6- to 11-year-olds and 14 percent of adolescents are overweight.[57] The trends toward decreased childhood fitness and increased body fat are attributed primarily to high-fat diets and a lack of physical activity. Physical education classes account for less than 100 minutes of children's physical activity per week.[58] Illinois is the only state that retains daily physical education for all K–12 students, with Alabama and Wisconsin being lone partners in a K–8 daily requirement.[59] At the beginning of the twenty-first century, only 29 percent of ninth through twelfth graders participated in daily school physical education.[60]

Although in 1972 Title IX required physical education classes to be coeducational, many programs have remained silently gender-segregated.[61] Research shows that gender bias persists even in coed classes. By high school, boys are twice as likely as girls to be enrolled in physical education.[62]

Health

TOPICS Years ago, health education meant little more than learning about the four basic food groups and routine dental care. A film on sex education at the high school level might "round out" the health program. However, we know that healthy children learn better across the curriculum. Today, many schools incorporate health education into both the elementary and secondary curricula. Areas for instruction include tobacco use; dietary patterns that contribute to disease; sedentary lifestyle; sexual behaviors that result in HIV infection, other STDs and unintended pregnancy; alcohol and other drug use; and behaviors that result in unintentional and intentional injuries.[63]

TENSION POINTS AND TRENDS The same factors that put the health of our students at risk also create the public controversy that puts their health education classes at risk, especially in the areas of sex education, teen pregnancy, and AIDS and substance abuse prevention. Of adolescents aged 10–17, 25 percent are at high risk for premature illness or death, and another 25 percent are at moderate risk. When parents are unaware or incapable of dealing with these pressing health concerns, school programs may be the only valid source of information and understanding.[64] In fact, support for health and sex education programs is at an all-time high. Over 90 percent of adults favor such programs in high school, and over 80 percent support these programs at the middle school.[65]

Vocational and Career Education

TOPICS Career education occurs informally in elementary school, with individual lessons on different occupations. At the secondary level, the **vocational education** curriculum is clearly targeted to careers with course titles such as cosmetology, auto body repair, vocational printing, and meal management. Tech prep classes teach students word processing, systems administration, Web page design, and even financial portfolio management. Computer-related vocational education also attracts many college-bound students seeking to gain a technical edge. While overall vocational coursetaking (which includes family and consumer sciences) declined between 1982 and 1998, occupationally specific enrollments remained steady.[66]

Despite the common belief that vocational education constitutes a discrete academic track for low-ability students who plan to work full-time after high school, a recent survey revealed that vocational education plays a much broader role. More than 97 percent of high school students take at least one vocational education course before graduation. Nearly half of all vocational education classes are taken by students who plan to attend a four-year or community college after high school.[67]

TENSION POINTS AND TRENDS Critics point to statistics showing that students who graduate from vocational programs do not have an advantage in the job market, because vocational classes are often inadequate and irrelevant. Programs that lack modern equipment and well-trained staff cannot prepare students for high-tech fields. And the skills needed for low-paying jobs, such as work in fast-food restaurants, are better learned on the job than in school. Other opponents charge that a vocational curriculum tracks students into worthless nonacademic courses and should be abolished.

INTERACTIVE ACTIVITY
CREATE A CLASS SCHEDULE. What do you think your students' week should consist of?

In 1990, Congress passed the **Carl D. Perkins Vocational and Applied Technology Act** (amended in 1998), signaling a shift from the traditional job-skills orientation of vocational education to a broader integration with academic instruction. Proponents of this approach argue that higher-order thinking skills should be emphasized in all vocational courses in order to adequately prepare students for today's job market. The original Perkins Act also channeled federal funds to school districts with the highest proportions of poor students, promoted nonsexist career choices, assisted displaced homemakers as they re-entered the job market, and offered support for post–high school vocational training programs. However, in 1998 Congress backed away from such specific programs and allowed states to make more of these decisions. Critics charge that certain groups, especially women, lost out as states took over these efforts.[68] High school career majors and charter or magnet career academies are giving vocational development programs new momentum.[69]

New Directions for the Curriculum

Technological developments have shifted the focus of the U.S. economy from the production of goods (industrial) to information processing (postindustrial), as new careers in technology, computers, and communications emerge. This accelerated rate of change is also impacting the school curriculum. The tremendous knowledge explosion has produced more information than schools can teach, and many believe that schools need to turn away from the traditional curriculum and emphasize the thinking skills needed in the new information society.

What are these more relevant thinking skills? One of the pioneering works, *Teaching for Thinking: Theory and Application,* identified "thinking operations," **critical thinking skills,** that should be taught directly: comparing, interpreting, observing, summarizing, classifying, decision making, creating, and criticizing. *Teaching for Thinking* incorporates these critical thinking skills into such subjects as mathematics and history, in which teachers ask higher-order questions that prompt students to

Curriculum can use activities that are innately interesting to foster a variety of learning activities. Here, students performing in this play might incorporate literature and history lessons, artistic expression, and social learnings among others.

analyze and evaluate data. Research indicates that not only do students learn critical thinking skills in such programs, but their knowledge of the content also increases when they apply these skills in the classroom.[70]

Teaching for Thinking is just one of several approaches. David Perkins of Harvard University's Project Zero emphasizes thinking frames, so that students develop a framework for acquiring information, internalizing practices, and transferring information.[71] Another approach, developed by Robert Marzano and his colleagues, stresses **metacognition** which enables students to monitor and control their commitment, attitudes, and attention during the learning process. Important traits for creative thinking include the ability to push one's own limits, the willingness to look at situations in new ways, and an ability to focus intensely on tasks. If these behaviors can be taught to students, they will become independent learners for the rest of their lives. Some educators are confident that these critical thinking skills are useful beyond the schoolhouse walls. **Critical pedagogy** is the term given to applying such analytic tools to society at large, and merges teaching and learning with social improvement. The purpose of critical pedagogy is for students and teachers to work on authentic social challenges such as eliminating pollution in a local lake or promoting consumer education in a poor community. Critical pedagogy connects schooling with actions to enhance the quality of life.[72]

As you have read about today's curriculum and how it has changed during the past decades, you may have felt a sense of déjà vu, with many recurring themes. There seems to be a timeless struggle among educators who hold differing visions of what schools should do. While other professions demonstrate steady, long-term progress, researcher Robert Slavin says that "education resembles such fields as fashion and design, in which change mirrors shifts in taste and social climate and is not usually thought of as true progress."[73] Many educators yearn for a more stable time when the radical curricular swing will be fine-tuned, so that innovation will depend more on research about what works than on the politics of who is in power. Only then can we best meet the needs of our students.

SUMMARY

1. What curriculum is taught in schools?

- There are various forms of curricula in schools. One, the explicit or formal curriculum, includes syllabi describing courses, tests, curricular materials, and subject area standards and objectives.

- The explicit curriculum has two functions. One function is to preserve and transmit to students the culture and traditions of the past. The other is to anticipate the knowledge, skills, and abilities that today's students will need in order to function effectively in tomorrow's society. Sometimes these two functions of preserving and anticipating clash.

- The extracurriculum, or cocurriculum, includes student activities such as sports, clubs, student government, and school newspaper.

- The implicit, or hidden, curriculum, emerges incidentally from the interaction between the students and the physical, social, and interpersonal environments of the school.

CHAPTER REVIEW

Go to the Online Learning Center to take a chapter self-quiz, practice with key terms, and review key ideas from the chapter.

2. What is the place of the extracurriculum in school life?

- Although a voluntary part of school life, the extracurriculum has become a central part in the culture of American schooling, with 80 percent of all students participating in such activities as athletics, musical groups, and academic clubs.

- Proponents of the extracurriculum argue that it encourages student self-esteem and civic participation, improves race relations, and raises children's aspirations, as well as their SAT scores. Many remain skeptical, however, seeing extracurricular activities as having very little, if any, positive effect on achievement and personal development.

- When the formal curriculum and the extracurriculum clash, controversy develops. Some states have instituted "no pass, no play" rules, excluding low-achieving students from participating in varsity sports. Since these rules tend to affect minority students disproportionately, many people see these rules as making the extracurriculum exclusive and discriminatory. Others criticize the degree to which schools pour resources and attention into athletics, when that support could be going toward academics.

3. How do the formal and the hidden curriculum differ?

- School subjects are taught in the formal or explicit curriculum, which is constantly undergoing scrutiny and revision. Test scores report student progress—or lack of progress—in the formal curriculum.

- In addition to planned and intentional lessons, schools teach a hidden or implicit curriculum. Subtle messages that students receive from teachers and other students unofficially teach norms, mores, and the culture of the school.

- The hidden curriculum can reinforce formal learnings, or contradict them.

4. How do social forces shape curriculum development over time?

- Seventeenth-century schools taught a "two Rs" curriculum, emphasizing reading and religion. The only secondary schooling available was the Latin grammar school, which was open only to white male students who could afford the cost.

- The eighteenth-century curriculum shifted toward the secular. The English grammar school and the academy became options for secondary schooling. White girls were allowed to attend the academy.

- As a result of nationalism, democratization, and industrial development, the curriculum in the nineteenth century moved toward universal literacy, vocational competence, and preparation for citizenship. Elementary school studies included writing, arithmetic, spelling, geography, and good behavior. The academy was the dominant form of nineteenth-century secondary schooling until the last quarter of the century, when the academy gave way to tax-supported public high schools.

- In the first half of the twentieth century, the curriculum was influenced by John Dewey and the progressive movement. Creative expression, social skills, and a more integrated study of subject areas were stressed. The junior high concept became popular during the 1920s. The mission of high schools was to meet the needs of all the students, not only the college-bound. By 1918, vocational course work had become an important part of the curriculum.

- In 1957, the Soviets launched *Sputnik*, and the poor performance of American schools was blamed for the country's defeat in the race for space. As a result, the curriculum was revised, and toughened, particularly in math and science.

- The curriculum in the late 1960s and the 1970s focused on social issues, with particular emphasis on the needs and contributions of women and minorities. Public Law 94-142, the Education for All Handicapped Children Act (later renamed the Individuals with Disabilities

Education Act), required an individualized education program for each special needs child. Other issues emphasized in the curriculum were peace studies, ecology, and the secular presentation of topics relating to death.

- Popular in the 1970s, open classrooms were divided into flexible areas called interest, or learning, centers. Children were encouraged to explore the classroom and choose activities they wished to pursue.

- The curriculum of the 1980s and 1990s was marked by the back-to-basics movement. Triggered by the problem of declining test scores, this movement stressed achievement in the traditional subject-matter areas, cultural literacy, and an increased emphasis on required courses and a core curriculum.

- Today there is growing emphasis on subject area standards and testing as a way of improving school and student performance.

5. What are contemporary subject matter trends and tension points?

- National standards have already been developed for math, science, geography, and other subject areas. The scope of these changes, as well as tension points, are reviewed in this chapter.

- Although poor student writing performance remains a problem in language arts and English programs, there has been an improvement in student scores on reading tests. However, not everyone is in agreement on the best approach to reading instruction. While some advocate a phonics approach, others support whole language instruction. Many teachers incorporate elements of both in their teaching.

- The question of which authors are read and studied, and which are omitted, is a persistent problem in English courses. The emphasis on the traditional canon of literature in recent years may come at the expense of women and non-western authors in many current literature programs.

- Educators and special interest groups debate the depth versus breadth of subject matter in several subject areas, including the social studies. Social studies curriculum has been criticized for lacking international perspective and doing a poor job in preparing students for their civic responsibilities.

- Math is an area where U.S. students have not performed well compared to students in other nations; the standards movement is intended to rectify such poor student performance. The national math standards describe the concepts students should master beginning in the primary grades and going through senior high school. The standards emphasize both an understanding of critical math concepts and their application to real world situations.

- U.S. students lag behind others in their foreign language instruction and skills. The nation's geographic isolation has added to this problem. A number of educators are calling for more rigorous foreign language instruction beginning at earlier ages.

- Technology and computer instruction continue to appeal to educators and the public. However, the digital divide remains as wealth and poverty create a gap between the technological *haves,* and *have-nots,* a gap that impacts computer literacy for students.

- The fine arts receive little emphasis in most schools, with three out of four students received neither theater nor dance instruction.

- The current emphasis in physical education is to promote lifelong health benefits and enjoyment, yet fewer than one in three high school students participates in daily physical education programs.

- Health and sex education programs are receiving more public support today than they have in the past, in part due to the health threats confronting today's students.

6. What current curriculum directions may impact you?

- In your time, the knowledge explosion has produced more information than teachers can cover and students can learn. Some educators now focus on the process of learning and thinking, including metacognition. Critical pedagogy marries critical thinking skills with analysis of, and work on, social challenges.

- Robert Slavin is among those who believe that education is like "fashion and design," a mirror of changing styles, tastes, and public opinion. He looks to a time when the curriculum will emerge from research and reasoning, not from popular opinion.

KEY TERMS AND PEOPLE

academy, 228

Mortimer Adler, 233

"back to basics", 232

basal readers, 234

Ernest Boyer, 233

Jerome Bruner, 230

canon, 235

career education, 247

core curriculum, 233

critical pedagogy, 249

critical thinking skills, 248

Cultural Literacy, 233

curriculum, 219

Lisa Delpit, 236

digital divide, 241

discovery method, 230

English grammar school, 228

environmental education, 231

extracurriculum, 221

formal or explicit curriculum, 220

John Goodlad, 220

Jules Henry, 226

High School, 233

E. D. Hirsch, Jr., 233

hornbook, 228

implicit or hidden curriculum, 220

individualized education program (IEP), 231

interest (learning) centers, 232

junior high school, 229

Latin grammar school, 228

learning divide, 241

life-adjustment education, 230

metacognition, 249

multicultural approach, 231

National Assessment of Educational Progress (NAEP), 235

The New England Primer, 228

open classroom, 232

The Paideia Proposal, 233

peace studies, 231

Carl D. Perkins Vocational and Applied Technology Act, 248

phonics, 234

A Place Called School, 220

The Process of Education, 230

romantic critics, 230

Sputnik, 230

Hilda Taba, 220

vocational education, 247

whole language, 235

women's studies, 231

DISCUSSION QUESTIONS AND ACTIVITIES

1. For some students, the hidden curriculum and the extracurriculum are most central to their school experience. Define the roles of these unofficial curriculum experiences in your own education. If you were placed in charge of a school today, how would you change these hidden and extracurricular experiences? How might your changes be evident in elementary, middle, and high schools? Why?

2. Discuss your reactions to the current curriculum with your classmates. Were there any topics you studied that you now see as irrelevant? What subjects should be taught differently? Are there any subjects that are not included in the curriculum but that should be?

3. If you were given the job of developing a core curriculum for elementary school, what would it look like? What would you include in a core curriculum for middle and secondary school? for post-secondary education?

4. Reconsider your high school curriculum experience. Estimate the proportion of required courses versus electives. Did students perceive the electives as an opportunity to explore areas of interest or to avoid more rigorous courses? If you were in charge of a school's offerings, would you increase or decrease electives? Why? What particular electives would you want to design and teach?

5. "Critical thinking has always been a silent partner in the curriculum." Do you agree or disagree?

6. Consider past and present curricular developments and think about the changes in contemporary society. Then, with the help of your instructor and classmates, predict what the school curriculum may be like in the year 2020.

WEB-*TIVITIES*

1. The Formal or Explicit Curriculum
2. The Curriculum Time Machine
3. New Directions for the Curriculum

REEL TO REAL TEACHING

MR. HOLLAND'S OPUS (1995)
Run Time: 142 minutes

Synopsis: Glenn Holland is an aspiring composer who takes a teaching job to support his family. As the years unfold, the joy of sharing his passion for music with his students becomes his new definition of success.

MUSIC OF THE HEART (1999)
Run Time: 124 minutes

Synopsis: This is a true story of Roberta Guaspari and her fight against the board of education. Her effort to teach music to underprivileged students in East Harlem involved an innovative violin program.

Reflection:

1. *Mr. Holland's Opus* chronicles a 30-year teaching career. What changes in the music curriculum did you observe? In Mr. Holland's instructional style? What personal and institutional factors influenced these changes?

2. How did gender, race, and socioeconomic status influence the curriculum, teaching and efforts to save music education in *Music of the Heart?* In *Mr. Holland's Opus?*

3. How did the arts influence the education and life experiences of Gertrude and Sadler in *Mr. Holland's Opus?* Guadalupe and Naeem Adisa in *Music of the Heart?* What role did the fine arts play in your elementary and secondary education? In your life? Do your experiences parallel those of the films' characters?

4. Consider Mr. Holland's comment: "The day they cut the football budget in this state, that will be the end of Western Civilization as we know it!" Why do you think extracurricular athletics are often given priority in school budgets over music, art, and even physical education?

Follow-up Activity: It's time to take a stand! You are a colleague of Mr. Holland at John F. Kennedy High or Ms. Guaspari in East Harlem (or choose any school where the fine arts are targeted for elimination).* The local school board is holding finance hearings and you decide to share your opinion. In 500 words or less, create talking points. Use scenes from the films, information from the chapter, and your own life experiences as supporting evidence.

*If you feel strongly for or against another course potentially threatened by budget cuts (sign language, computer animation, child care) use your example for the position paper.

How do you rate this film? Click on *Reel to Real Teaching* to submit your review of this or another education-related film, and read reviews submitted by others.

FOR FURTHER READING

Critical Pedagogy: Notes from the Real World, by Joan Wink (1999). Personal stories about real teachers and students bring the complex theories of critical pedagogy and literacy into today's classroom. Lessons and activities model social justice practices in action.

Developing Personal, Social and Moral Education through Physical Education, by Anthony Laker (2001). Provides practical suggestions for teaching about culture, cooperation, spirituality, and emotional development in the physical education classroom. Activities that focus on fitness and lifetime sports are emphasized.

Global Perspectives for Educators, by Carlos Diaz, Byron Massialas, and John Xanthopoulos (1999). Definitions and purposes of global education are advanced. Lessons are designed to analyze global issues, such as the environment, public health, and technology.

Inquiry-Based English Instruction: Engaging Students in Life and Literature, by Richard Beach and Jamie Myers (2001). Demonstrates ways of engaging students in critical literacy projects that examine how social worlds are portrayed in literature and the media.

Issues in Social Studies: Voices from the Classroom, by Cameron White (2000). Trends in social studies content, such as multicultural education, citizenship, and social justice, are explored. Emphasizes strategies to create reflective students.

Radical Equations: Organizing Math Literacy in America's Schools, by Robert Moses and Charles Cobb (2001). Chronicles the success of the Algebra Project, a civil rights program in schools. Founded on the belief that math literacy is a prerequisite for full citizenship in society, the Project works with parents, teachers, and students to foster achievement for all students, especially those of color.

Science Teaching/Science Learning: Constructivist Learning in Urban Classrooms, by Elnora Harcombe (2001). Demonstrates that when teaching combines constructivist learning theories with science content, teachers are empowered to ignite curiosity and deep understanding in students.

Young People's Views on Sex Education: Education, Attitudes, and Behavior, by Lynda Measor, Katrina Miller, and Coralie Tiffin (2000). Describes how adolescents' views and values toward sex education impact a school's policy and teaching of sex education.

Controversy over Who Controls the Curriculum

7

FOCUS QUESTIONS

1. What forces shape the school curriculum?
2. How does the standards movement influence what is taught in school?
3. Why are some protesting the growing emphasis on high-stakes testing?
4. How do textbook publishers and state adoption committees "drive" the curriculum?
5. What are the seven forms of bias in instructional materials?
6. How do religious differences impact school curricular materials?
7. Why are school books so frequently the targets of censorship?
8. Should the curriculum focus on teaching a core knowledge, or focus on the demands of a changing world?

WHAT DO YOU THINK? The Cheating Problem. Answer the online poll and see where your responses fall in relation to those of your colleagues.

CHAPTER PREVIEW

"We shape our buildings and afterwards our buildings shape us," said Winston Churchill. Had the noted statesman been a noted educator, he might have re-phrased this epigram, substituting curriculum for buildings, for what children learn in school today will affect the kind of adults they will become and the kind of society they will eventually create. In fact, it is the power of curriculum to shape students and, ultimately, society that takes curriculum development out of the realms of philosophy and education and into the political arena.

In buildings from the little red schoolhouse to the White House, adults (and occasionally their charges) discuss what is supposed to be learned in school. Two trends are pushing all schools toward a similar curriculum: the indomitable textbook and the recent emphasis on state standards and testing. While the current standards movement stresses the importance of students doing well on high-risk tests, it is teachers and schools that are also feeling the pressure to "perform." Protests (perhaps better titled "anti-tests") have been growing against the increasing influence of standardized tests in determining how teach-ers and students invest their time.

Many believe that even before the emergence of this new "unofficial national curriculum," we already had a de facto national curriculum: the textbook. For decades, states have indicated what they want in school textbooks and publishers have happily produced just the books that the market demanded. However, they were not always the best texts for students. Texts have been criticized for avoiding difficult topics, providing superficial information, including biased portrayals, and underestimating the intelligence of students. Yet these books continue to influence many teachers' daily activities. And if all that were not enough, the continuing threat of censorship makes the teacher's role in selecting materials to supplement textbooks a constant challenge.

Who and what shapes the curriculum? Let's find out.

The Faculty Room

A casual conversation in the faculty room opens this chapter door on the teacher's role in curricular decisions:

JO: Were you at yesterday's faculty meeting? The sales reps from the publishing company showed their new textbook series.

MAYA: No, I had an emergency dentist appointment—a root canal. That was painful enough! What's the new series like?

JO: Fabulous. It must be worth big money—superslick covers, beautiful photos, and graphics. And talk about supplementary materials. They have everything! It's got a website, which they promise to update regularly, that includes practical student projects. They went online for us yesterday, and it looks great. The objectives are totally spelled out, and there's a step-by-step teacher's guide saying exactly how to cover each objective. There are discussion questions after reading assignments and a student workbook with activities for the kids to do after we've finished the reading. They even have huge banks of test questions for weekly tests and unit exams on CD-ROM.

MAYA: What's got you so excited?

JO: Excited? The prep time alone is endless. Anything that saves me hours, I'm for. And these books look like a time-saving resource.

MAYA: Jo, we've been through so many TGIF afternoons—you know I need more "quality and quantity" time in my life. But some of these new comprehensive textbook systems make me nervous.

JO: What do you mean?

MAYA: I'm not so sure the people in slick offices (who do the slick covers) know what's best for our kids. What makes them so smart that they can determine what we should tell our students? I know my kids! What kind of expertise do they have to tell us how to teach? When was the last time those textbook writers were in a classroom, anyway? I'm a professional, and I am not ready to relinquish my control over what and how I teach.

JO: Sounds like you. But they can save you a lot of grief. You don't want to step on anyone's toes, or get the "Parents for an American Curriculum" breathing down your neck. Those textbooks sidestep a lot of those controversies for you.

MAYA: The other day I was talking with Jena, the new teacher who works across the hall from me. She just graduated from college a few years ago, and she has some terrific ideas. She's using an individualized reading program, and she's really got the kids into it. Instead of the basal reading selections, she's got the class reading everything from Judy Blume to Tolkien. And the kids are loving it. It's a tremendous success. But, instead of being psyched, she's in panic mode—afraid she's harming her students' reading development, because she's not following the official basal reader or the new state standards. The upcoming state reading assessment worries her. If her kids don't do well on that state exam, she's toast.

JO: You're kidding!

MAYA: I wish I were.

Who and What Shape the Curriculum?

From state standards to parental expectations, the curriculum is shaped by a pressure cooker of different interest groups (See Figure 7.1). Everyone from the president of the United States to a single parent can impact what is taught in your classroom. Here is a brief tour of some of the hands in the curricular pie.

Teachers

Teachers develop curriculum both formally and informally. They may serve on textbook selection committees that determine what texts the school will purchase, or they may actually work on writing a district's curriculum. In a less formal but no less powerful way, classroom teachers interpret and adapt whatever official text or curriculum guide has been assigned, stressing certain points in a text while giving scant attention to others; supplementing with teacher-made materials or directing students to the Internet.

Parental and Community Groups

Parents can be quite forceful in impacting the curriculum. They might advocate for more rigorous academic courses, concerned about poor student performance on standardized tests, or they may desire more practical vocational training, such as an increase in computer science courses. While local communities differ, parents often make their voices felt. Banning certain books or videos from the curriculum is also commonplace. In more conservative communities, religious fundamentalists have objected to the absence of Christian values, while liberal communities have objected to books that use racial, ethnic or gender slurs, and stereotypes.

Students

During the 1960s and 1970s, students demanded curricular relevance and sought more relevant curriculum. Although students have not seemed particularly interested in influencing curriculum policy recently, they have been active in protests against standardized testing. Typically, students are given some freedom to select topics for independent projects, research papers, book reviews, and even authentic learning.

Administrators

Principals, in their role as instructional leaders, can wield substantial influence in shaping the curriculum. For example, a principal announces at a faculty meeting that the school's scores on the state standardized test in mathematics were disappointing, and this year's priority is to raise those scores. The result might well be a math curriculum that "teaches to the test." Sometimes central-office personnel, such as a language arts coordinator or a social studies supervisor, might create a new or revised school or district curriculum.

The Federal Government

The federal government influences the curriculum by sponsoring school-related legislation and by promoting national education goals, state standards and testing. For example, the Elementary and Secondary Education Act (ESEA) of 1965 influenced the curriculum in various ways, including developing programs for children from low-income families. The 2001 ESEA reauthorization provided more federal funding, but also increased student testing and school accountability.

The State Government

States are now assuming a stronger leadership role in education, and their interest in curriculum matters has sharpened through the creation of state standards, curriculum guides and frameworks for all state schools to follow. Politics often play a big role in these state decisions. In more conservative states, the role of religion and the treatment of evolution versus creationism are hot-button issues. In more liberal states, instructional materials are expected to include ethnic and racial diversity and to reflect the experiences and contributions of women.

FIGURE 7.1
A pressure cooker of groups shaping the curriculum.

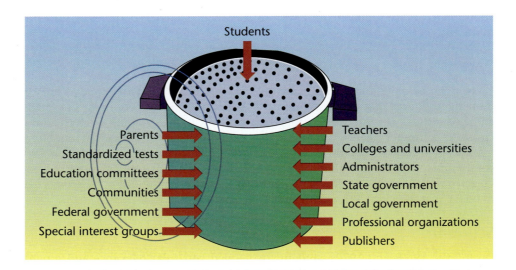

REFLECTION

What groups today exert the most influence? Do you see all these groups as a mark of democratic participation, or an inappropriate intrusion in curricular decision making?

Local Government

Local school boards, composed of elected or appointed citizens, make a variety of curriculum decisions, requiring courses from AIDS education to technology. Some educators and citizens feel that local school boards should have a strong voice in the curriculum, because they are closest to the needs of the local community and have a clear sense of the abilities and interests of the students. Others feel that school board members lack the training and broad perspective needed to maintain a flexible curriculum in touch with national issues.

Colleges and Universities

Institutions of higher learning influence curricula through their entrance requirements, which spell out courses students must take to gain admittance. Many secondary schools base their academic curricula on these college and university stipulations. During the 1990s, increased student enrollment in foreign language, advanced math and science courses reflected changes in college admissions requirements. As A. Bartlett Giamatti noted when he was president of Yale University,

> The high schools in this country are always at the mercy of the colleges. The colleges change their requirements and their admissions criteria and the high schools . . . are constantly trying to catch up with what the colleges are thinking. When the colleges don't seem to know what they think over a period of time, it's no wonder that this oscillation takes place all the way through the system.[1]

Standardized Tests

The results of state and national tests, from the state subject matter tests needed for graduation to the SATs, influence what is taught in the school. If students perform poorly in one or more areas of these standardized tests, public pressure may push school officials to strengthen the curriculum in these weak spots.

Schools of education are not immune from the current focus on test performance. Because an increasing number of states are requiring new teachers to take qualifying tests, such as the National Teacher Exam (NTE, Praxis series), these tests influence what is covered in teacher education programs. For example, if Benjamin Bloom's Taxonomy of Educational Objectives is emphasized on such tests, teacher education colleges will teach more about Bloom in their own programs.

Education Commissions and Committees

From time to time in the history of U.S. education, various committees, usually on a national level, have been called upon to study an aspect of education. Their reports often draw national attention and influence elementary and secondary curricula. The 1983 report, *A Nation at Risk,* and the National Education Summit in 1989 led to a more uniform core of courses, and a program for testing student progress.

Professional Organizations

Many professional organizations such as the National Education Association (NEA), the American Federation of Teachers (AFT), the National Association for the Education of Young Children (NAEYC), and numerous subject area associations (teacher groups in English, math, science, and the like)—publish journals and hold conferences that emphasize curriculum needs and developments. Their programs and materials may focus on teaching with technology, multicultural education, or authentic learning. Teachers, inspired by these presentations, might choose to modify their curriculum and implement new approaches and ideas.

Special Interest Groups

Major business and professional organizations—from labor unions to media conglomerates—have educational outreach programs, replete with curricular materials and instant lesson plans. These "how to" pieces range from using a daily newspaper for social studies to bringing the Olympics to your gymnasium. They are often so current and well-framed that they are easily added to a teacher's agenda, and may become part of the formal curriculum. Sometimes, citizens' groups with wholesome names can have quite partisan purposes. For example, a group called Citizens for Excellence in Education or Family Friendly Libraries can exert strong pressures for or against bilingual education, the teaching of evolution, Ebonics (black English), whole language instruction, or multiculturalism.

Publishers

The major goal of textbook publishers is—not surprisingly—to sell books. That is why textbooks are attractively packaged and chock full of terms and names, but unfortunately, do less well in providing depth or conflicting points of view. Textbooks come to market meeting the demands not of scholars, but of purchasers. Today's increasing emphasis on state standards and high-stakes tests are also influencing publishers.

The Standards Movement

During the 1990s, an educational movement gained tremendous public and political support, eventually reaching virtually every school district in every state: The national standards movement was born. The groundswell of support was easy to understand: After all, who could be against standards, a code word for increasing the educational quality? (See Figure 7.2.)

The standards issue originated in the first Bush administration, was nurtured through the Clinton presidency, and was given even greater prominence during the second Bush presidency. In September of 1989, the senior Bush called the nation's governors together to meet in Charlottesville, Virginia, for the first ever "National Education Summit." Out of this highly publicized meeting came a set of educational goals, goals that were supposed to be reached within the decade. (In fact, many of these goals were actually written before or after the Charlottesville meeting.[2]) The result of that effort, "Education 2000" (modified slightly under the Clinton administration and renamed Goals 2000), was a list of worthy, and in some cases, unrealistically optimistic goals. Not surprisingly, the nation missed reaching any of the goals set out in Charlottesville. The first goal, "All children will start school ready to learn," is a case in point. By the end of the 1990s, only half of the nation's youth were enrolled in preschool. And many of those programs were of poor quality. "We will be first in the world in math and science by the year 2000," was another ambitious goal, one that also missed the mark: Our high school students still rank near the bottom on international comparisons in math and science (although not all educators believe that these tests are appropriate yardsticks of student performance). But

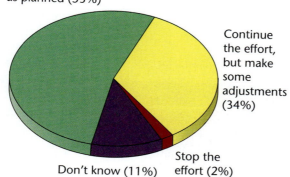

When it comes to your school district's
effort toward higher academic standards,
do you think the school district should:

Continue the effort
as planned (53%)

Continue
the effort,
but make
some
adjustments
(34%)

Don't know (11%)   Stop the
effort (2%)

FIGURE 7.2
No desire to turn back.

SOURCE: Parents who are
aware of standards effort,
Public Agenda September
2000.

REFLECTION

How would you answer the question? Where exactly on the pie would you place your opinion?

these goals did focus public attention on schools, raised the quality of many programs, and encouraged students to enroll in more challenging courses. In retrospect, these national goals developed during the Education Summit were a transition between the call for more rigorous schools found in *A Nation at Risk* (1983), and today's emphasis on state standards and testing.

While the national goals were never attained, they did put the nation on a course of self-examination, and developing standards of learning dominated much of the education literature of the 1990s. The National Education Standards and Improvement Council was formed to harness the ideas of experts in mathematics, history, English, physical education, and other fields. The federal government funded organizations like the National Council for Geographic Education, the National Council of Teachers of Mathematics, and the National Academy of Sciences, and educators and content area experts worked to develop content standards. **Content standards** detailed precisely what students should know and be able to do in each subject at each grade level. States echoed the call for better schools by adopting and adapting many of these content area standards, and in some cases, developing their own. This step was crucial, for in the end the states have the major responsibility for creating the school curriculum.

Professional education associations got into the standards business as well, creating standards for teachers, counselors and others. In this text, we employ the *Intermission* activities to familiarize you with the INTASC teaching standards that you are expected to reach. Business leaders and citizen groups also developed standards for students that mirrored their priorities. And the federal government, which funded standards development, sometimes rejected what the scholars presented. The first conflict was in history.

STANDARDS NEEDED FOR THE STANDARDS

It is becoming clear that there is a gap between adult and student standards. The adults at the Milwaukee school system placed an ad in a local newspaper entitled: "High Standards Start Here." The ad explained that the system had rigourous [sic] standards and tough proficiencey [sic] exams. Meanwhile, other school districts are requiring that sixth-graders be able to examine "maps that diffuse ideas across regions of the globe," while seventh-graders "describe ways in which people of a nation borrow and loan cultural characteristics."

SOURCE: *The American School Board Journal,* June 1997; *The Washington Post,* June 12, 2001.

REFLECTION

While standards receive a great deal of positive attention, hypocrisy is rarely mentioned. Would you support efforts to establish adult literacy and numeracy standards? Should adults be expected to meet the standards they establish for children?

Click on *In the News* for recent *In the News* stories. Submit your own *In the News* summary to share with your colleagues.

When the content standards in history were presented, dissatisfied political leaders rejected them. Conservative commentators argued that the standards developed by history scholars slighted white men and maligned business leaders. The critics were led by Lynne Cheney, a former official in the first Bush administration, who characterized the new standards as "a warped view of American history."[3] No such outburst had accompanied the publication of the national standards for mathematics five years earlier. Forty-one states quickly adopted the mathematics standards, and math textbooks were modified accordingly. For mathematics, a national curriculum began to take shape.[4] Why was the process of adopting standards relatively easy for math but difficult for history? The basic reason is that mathematics raises fewer values questions, while other disciplines, such as history, live and breathe values. Here are just some of the questions raised by history standards:

- Should traditional heroes, sometimes called "DWM" (dead white males)—such as Washington, Jefferson, and other revered Americans—be the focus of the curriculum, or should the experiences and contributions of other groups, women and people of color, be researched and included?

- Should history continue to emphasize European roots, or should Afrocentric issues be included? What about the views of other groups? For instance, should schools teach a penetrating view of European settlement of the Americas as seen through the eyes of Native Americans and Mexican Americans?

- Should U.S. history tell only a story of victors and triumphs, or should it also relate varied views of social, cultural, and economic issues?

The new history standards did not please those with traditional Eurocentric values, both because of what the standards omitted—for example, such familiar names as Daniel Webster, Paul Revere, and the Wright brothers—and because of what they included. Myra Colby Bradwell, for example, was included. Who was she? She was the first woman who took her bid to be admitted to the Illinois bar all the way to the

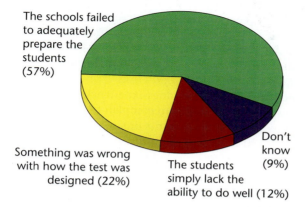

If you heard that many students in your school district did poorly on a standardized test, which of the following would be your most likely reaction?

The schools failed to adequately prepare the students (57%)

Something was wrong with how the test was designed (22%)

The students simply lack the ability to do well (12%)

Don't know (9%)

FIGURE 7.3
When students do poorly.

SOURCE: Public Agenda, September 2000.

REFLECTION

Do you believe that schools have more to lose or to gain in the testing culture? Why is the public so ready to equate test scores with school performance?

Supreme Court. The Civil War received a different perspective as well, going beyond a chronology of battles to include an account of Northern riots by poor laborers who were being drafted for the deadliest war in American history, while rich men simply paid $300 and avoided the draft. It is clear that, whatever the standards, some Americans will be offended.[5] Political pressure resulted in the final adoption of more traditional history standards, and some suggest that over time, such pressure will create remarkably similar standards in all states.[6]

By 2000, progress was being made, and teachers reported that the standards movement was having a positive impact, promoting higher expectations for student performance and creating a more demanding curriculum.[7] (See Figure 7.3.) The second Bush administration passed legislation that required states to complete their work in creating science and history standards, and begin to implement annual testing for grades 3 through 8 in reading and math. The Bush approach was simple: Put the spotlight on school performance and student scores, work to improve performance in low achieving schools while rewarding schools that demonstrate test score improvements. If necessary, punish schools that are unable to raise test scores. The focus now was on **performance standards,** assessing how well students meet the content standards. While content standards initially proved to be quite popular, federally required performance standards mandated testing, and possible punishments for schools that could not achieve passing grades. The standards movement began to cast an ominous shadow, as teachers, principals, parents, and students felt the burden of high-stakes test pressure. Problems and protests soon developed.

Tests and Protests

One educator reported on the experience in a New York City middle school where the principal asked teachers to spend fifteen minutes a day having the students practice answering multiple-choice math questions in preparation for the state-mandated test.

One teacher protested, explaining she taught Italian and English, not math. But the principal insisted, and she followed his directive. As you might suspect, the plan failed, and in the end, fewer than one in four New York City middle schoolers passed the exam. While the importance of the test dominated the formal curriculum, the lessons learned through the hidden curriculum were no less powerful. This educator's students learned that test scores mattered more than English or Italian, and that teachers did not make the key instructional decisions. In fact, once the test was over, one-third of the students in her class stopped attending school, skipping the last five weeks of the school year.[8]

Inner-city schools weren't the only ones experiencing testing woes; rural communities and wealthy suburbs had their own complaints. In Scarsdale, New York, an upscale, college-oriented community, parents organized a boycott of the eighth-grade standardized tests. Of 290 eighth-graders, only 95 showed up for the exam.[9] Nor was Scarsdale alone, as protests were reported in other communities as well.[10] Why the protests? These communities were concerned over the negative impact created by the test culture. "Real learning" was taking a backseat to "test learning": challenging curricular material was being replaced by material that would be tested, individualized student learning projects were disappearing, and class time was devoted to training students to test well. Schools were investing resources on programs that helped students learn how to "psych out" multiple-choice exams. In one school, for example, students were taught to cheer "Three in a row? No, No, No!" The cheer was a reminder that if students answered "c" three times in a row, probably at least one of those answers is wrong since the test maker is unlikely to construct three questions in a row with the same answer letter.[11]

Not surprisingly, in a national study, nearly seven in ten teachers reported feeling test-stress, and two out of three believed that preparing for the test took time from teaching important but non-tested topics.[12] Fourth-grade veteran teachers were requesting transfers, saying that they could not stand the pressure of administering the high-stakes elementary exams, and teachers recognized for excellence were leaving public schools, feeling their talents were better utilized in private schools where test preparation did not rule the curriculum.[13]

If all that were not enough, the tests themselves are often flawed. Test bias remains a constant problem as race, culture, and gender issues compromise many national, one-size-fits-all tests. As an example, the Scholastic Assessment Test (SAT) and PSAT (a test similar to the SAT, but given a year earlier and frequently used in awarding scholarships), are standardized tests that have been used for decades to determine not only college admissions, but financial aid packages as well. Yet a 1990 New York lawsuit, referred to as the Walker case (after Judge Walker), determined that these exams consistently discriminated against females. This test bias resulted in far more college scholarships being awarded to males than females. There is no reason to believe that such biases will disappear with the creation of high-stakes performance standards.

But even if test bias could be eliminated, other fundamental problems persist. Critics point out the inequity in applying the same set of standards to all students, those in well-funded posh schools along with students trying to learn in underfunded and ill-equipped schools. Since students do not receive equal educations, holding identical expectations for all students places the poorer ones at a disadvantage. Pointing out that students learn and test differently, these critics want these individual differences addressed. As a result of their concerns, a third kind of standard has emerged, one called an **opportunity-to-learn standard.** Opportunity-to-learn standards focus on creating a level playing field for all students, recognizing different individual learning styles and the need for adequate educational resources. Opportunity-to-learn standards

As national, state, and district decision makers require more testing, for students and even their teachers, many have protested or boycotted these exams. What perspectives on curriculum do you think the protesters hold? Explain your convictions on testing. What policies would cause you to *take to the streets*?

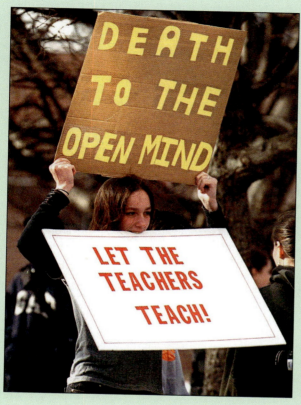

investigate such issues as: Are students given an opportunity to relearn the standard if they fail the test? Are students given adequate resources to achieve the standards at their own pace? Is there adequate time to learn the standards, and adequate time to be tested on the standards? Are the teachers receiving quality in-service training? Does the school have adequate technological resources?

High-stakes tests have also led to highly visible foul-ups, as Minnesota lawyer Martin Swaden discovered. When his daughter failed the state math test by a single answer, Swaden requested to see the exam so that he could help his daughter correct her errors and pass the test next time around. It took a threatened lawsuit before he was able to meet with a state official to examine the answers. Together they made an amazing discovery: six of the sixty-eight answers were keyed incorrectly, not only for his daughter, but for all the students in Minnesota. Jobs had been lost, summers ruined, the joy of graduation turned to humiliation for those students who were misidentified as having failed. Suits followed, but the damage was done, and the

One day in 1967, fifth-grader Alfie Kohn received a class assignment. As expected, he wrote his name and the date at the top of the paper. The title he chose, though, was unanticipated: "Busywork." He doesn't remember the announced purpose of the assignment. He does remember that it was busywork. Over three decades later, Alfie Kohn still discriminates between genuine learning and mindless school routine. As a teacher, researcher, and journalist, his work carries a common theme: Educational excellence comes from personalized learning, from recognizing the uniqueness of each student, not from a lockstep curriculum. As a teacher, he remembers:

> I lovingly polished lectures, reading lists, and tests. I treated the students as interchangeable receptacles—rows of wide-open bird beaks waiting for worms.
>
> Finally I realized I was denying students the joy of exploring topics and uncovering truths on their own.[1]

In his own education, Kohn adopted this personalized approach to learning. As an undergraduate at Brown University, he created an interdisciplinary major, and dubbed it normativism. He again took an unbeaten path at the University of Chicago, writing his graduate thesis on humor. "Learning was meaningful because I started with the question and then drew from whatever fields were useful in exploring it, rather than being confined to the methods and topics of a particular discipline."[2] When he visits classrooms today, Kohn is

often disheartened. Rarely does he witness such engaged learning. Instead, he sees students usually learning just to pass a test.

Kohn challenges today's popular clamor for higher standards and increased testing. "Standardized testing has swelled and mutated, like a creature in one of those old horror movies, to the point that it now threatens to swallow our schools whole."[3] He passionately warns educators, policymakers, and parents that raising standardized test scores is completely different from helping students to learn. And the pressurized culture of testing exacts a high cost. Every hour spent on such exam preparation is an hour not spent helping students to think creatively, to tackle controversial issues, and to love learning.

Common standards often begin with "all students will be able to . . ." and Kohn sees a harmful message in such wording: Individual differences don't exist or are unimportant. Often justified in the name of accountability or rigor, standards turn schools into fact factories. Students may recite Civil War battles, distinguish between phloem and xylem, and memorize prime numbers in hopes of meeting predetermined standards of excellence. Will they? Kohn doesn't think so.

With a focus on standards of outcome rather than standards of opportunity, real barriers to achievement—racism, poverty, low teacher salaries, language differences, inadequate facilities—are lost in the sea of testing. "[A]ll students deserve a quality education. But declaring that everyone must reach the same level is naïve at best, cynical at worst, in light of wildly unequal resources."[4] Equally troublesome is testing's unbalanced reward system. As a bonus for good scores, more money is often given to successful schools and less to those already deprived. Callous is how he describes such a retreat from fairness and the implication that teachers and students need only be bribed or threatened in order to achieve.

Alfie Kohn also knows that change in schools can be slow. Standardized curriculum and testing are fueled by concerns of competition in our global economy and reinforced by a tradition of teacher-centered instruction. "I am not a utopian. I am as aware as anyone of the difficulties of creating schools that are genuinely concerned about learning and about meeting children's needs, but that causes me to redouble my efforts rather than throw up my hands."[5]

[1] Jay Matthews, "Education's Different Drummer," *The Washington Post* (January 9, 2001), p. A10.

[2] Ibid.

[3] Alfie Kohn, "Standardized Testing and Its Victims," *Education Week* (September 27, 2000).

[4] Alfie Kohn, "One-Size-Fits-All Education Doesn't Work," *Boston Globe* (June 10, 2001), p. C8.

[5] Jay Matthews, "Education's Different Drummer."

testing company argued that it was not liable for "emotional damages." Unfortunately, such stories are far from isolated, as the crush of millions of new tests has
overwhelmed the handful of testing companies. Test materials have been delivered
late, or with missing pages, or errors have been found in scoring. Raters complained
that they are given inadequate training and little time to grade essays, and at nine
dollars an hour, many doubt the accuracy of their ratings. Political pressure and the
rapid growth in tests have resulted in massive errors, and many question the wisdom
of rewarding and punishing students, teachers, and schools based on the flawed history of the testing industry.[14]

Critics protest class time being spent on test preparation, the stress and inequities
of high-stakes tests, and the elimination of subjects from the curriculum that are not
being tested. Many business leaders were influential in establishing the standards and
testing movement, and critics argue that the heavy emphasis on standards and high-
stakes testing amounts to little more than teaching the young "to accept their place
in a society dominated by corporate forces."[15] Edward B. Fiske speaks for many educators in his criticism of standardized tests: "They measure the wrong things in the
wrong way for the wrong reasons."[16]

The National Commission on Testing and Public Policy estimated that well over
100 million annual tests were given to elementary and secondary students a little
over a decade ago, a number that has risen dramatically since that original estimate.[17]
In an extreme case, all students in Newark, New Jersey, including first-graders, were
tested nine times a year.[18] In fact, by law, almost all school districts require regularly
scheduled achievement tests, starting in the first grade. Children not yet in the first
grade are not immune from the testing craze: About half of all 4- and 5-year-olds are
tested to determine kindergarten and prekindergarten placement.[19] More and more,
it is not only students who are tested but educators and schools as well. Beginning
teachers are expected to take the Praxis or a state test (see Chapter 15 and Appendix 2), and teachers, principals, and superintendents may have their job security determined by how well or poorly their students score on standardized tests.

Alternatives to High-Stakes Testing

But even as the tests and protests threaten the standards movement, some educators
are working to create tests that more accurately and humanely assess learning. One
recent reform is the creation of tests grounded more firmly in classroom performance. These are often referred to as forms of alternative, performance-based, or authentic assessment—implying that tests are truer when based on what students

EXAMINATION GRADUATION QUESTIONS OF SALINE COUNTY, KANSAS
APRIL 13, 1895

Reading and Penmanship—The Examination will be oral and the Penmanship of Applicants will be graded from the manuscripts.

GRAMMAR (Time, one hour)
1. Give nine rules for the use of Capital Letters.
2. Name the Parts of Speech and define those that have no modifications.
3. Define Verse, Stanza, and Paragraph.
4. What are the Principal Parts of a verb? Give Principal Parts of do, lie, lay, and run.
5. Define Case. Illustrate each Case.
6. What is Punctuation? Give rules for principal marks of Punctuation.
7–10. Write a composition of about 150 words and show therein that you understand the practical use of the rules of grammar.

ARITHMETIC (Time, 1½ hours)
1. Name and define the Fundamental Rules of Arithmetic.
2. A wagon box is 2 ft. deep, 10 feet long, and 3 ft. wide. How many bushels of wheat will it hold?
3. If a load of wheat weighs 3,942 lbs., what is it worth at 50 cents per bushel, deducting 1,050 lbs. for tare?
4. District No. 33 has a valuation of $35,000. What is the necessary levy to carry on a school seven months at $50 per month, and have $104 for incidentals?
5. Find cost of 6,720 lbs. coal at $6.00 per ton.
6. Find the interest of $512.60 for 8 months and 18 days at 7 percent.
7. What is the cost of 40 boards 12 inches wide and 16 ft. long at $20 per in.?
8. Find bank discount on $300 for 90 days (no grace) at 10 percent.
9. What is the cost of a square farm at $15 per acre, the distance around which is 640 rods?
10. Write a Bank Check, a Promissory Note, and a Receipt.

U.S. HISTORY (Time, 45 minutes)
1. Give the epochs into which U.S. History is divided.
2. Give an account of the discovery of America by Columbus.
3. Relate the causes and results of the Revolutionary War.
4. Show the territorial growth of the United States.
5. Tell what you can of the history of Kansas.
6. Describe three of the most prominent battles of the Rebellion.
7. Who were the following: Morse, Whitney, Fulton, Bell, Lincoln, Penn, and Howe?
8. Name events connected with the following dates: 1607, 1620, 1800, 1849, and 1865.

ORTHOGRAPHY (Time, one hour)
1. What is meant by the following: Alphabet, phonetic, orthography, etymology, syllabication?
2. What are elementary sounds? How classified?
3. What are the following, and give examples of each: Trigraph, subvocals, diphthong, cognate letters, linguals?
4. Give four substitutes for caret "u".
5. Give two rules for spelling words with final "e". Name two exceptions under each rule.
6. Give two uses of silent letters in spelling. Illustrate each.
7. Define the following prefixes and use in connection with a word: Bi, dis, mis, pre, semi, post, non, inter, mono, super.
8. Mark diacritically and divide into syllables the following, and name the sign that indicates the sound: card, ball, mercy, sir, odd, cell, rise, blood, fare, last.

9. Use the following correctly in sentences: Cite, site, sight, fane, fain, feign, vane, vain, vein, raze, raise, rays.
10. Write 10 words frequently mispronounced and indicate pronunciation by use of diacritical marks and by syllabication.

GEOGRAPHY (Time, one hour)
1. What is climate? Upon what does climate depend?
2. How do you account for the extremes of climate in Kansas?
3. Of what use are rivers? Of what use is the ocean?
4. Describe the mountains of N.A.
5. Name and describe the following: Monrovia, Odessa, Denver, Manitoba, Heela, Yukon, St. Helena, Juan Fernandez, Aspinwall, and Orinoco.
6. Name and locate the principal trade centers of the U.S.
7. Name all the republics of Europe and give capital of each.
8. Why is the Atlantic Coast colder than the Pacific in the same latitude?
9. Describe the process by which the water of the ocean returns to the sources of rivers.
10. Describe the movements of the earth. Give inclination of the earth.

PHYSIOLOGY (Time, 45 minutes)
1. Where are the saliva, gastric juice, and bile secreted? What is the use of each in digestion?
2. How does nutrition reach the circulation?
3. What is the function of the liver? Of the kidneys?
4. How would you stop the flow of blood from an artery in case of laceration?
5. Give some general directions that you think would be beneficial to preserve the human body in a state of health.

SOURCE: Tana Thomson, "105-year-old Saline County Test in Nation's Spotlight." *The Salina Journal*, 9 July 2000.

REFLECTION

What's the appeal of standards and tests, now and in the past? You may not have done particularly well in answering these questions. Is poor performance on this exam an indication that your education is lacking? Or is poor performance simply a reminder that times have changed, and we now have different educational priorities? What does such a change in priorities say about how today's curriculum may be viewed a hundred years down the road? Could you be taught to improve your score on this test? Would that constitute education, or test preparation?

actually do in school. **Authentic assessment** represents actual performance, encourages students to reflect on their own work, and is integrated into the student's whole learning process. Such tests usually require students to synthesize knowledge from different areas and actively use that knowledge. The student might demonstrate what has been learned through a portfolio (like the ones we encourage you to develop in the *Inter-missions* found in this text), or a journal, or by undergoing an interview, conducting an experiment, or giving a presentation. Whatever the form, an authentic assessment offers a focused and intense insight into what the student has learned, and requires evidence quite different from what is required by responding to questions on a typical high-stakes test.[20] Teaching to an authentic test is encouraged, for in such a test the student must actually perform what he or she is expected to know. Comparisons are often made with sports, in which participants are expected to demonstrate in a game what they have learned in practice. A tennis player works on her backhand, so that she can demonstrate mastery of it in a game; similarly, when students know that they will be called on to demonstrate and use their knowledge, they are more motivated to practice their academic skills. Many states are exploring authentic methods of assessment, especially the writing sample.[21] While this can be an effective means of judging children's writing, critics caution against evaluating a timed writing sample, since such a sample does not allow students time to demonstrate the mastery of the writing process, including revising and editing.

Some of the best examples of authentic assessment come from the Coalition of Essential Schools, led by prominent educator Theodore Sizer. The coalition encourages schools to define their own model for successful reform, guided by nine basic principles that emphasize the personalization of learning. These principles include the requirement that students complete "exhibitions," tasks that call on them to exhibit their knowledge concretely. The high school curriculum is structured around these demanding, creative tasks, which may include:

- Completing a federal Internal Revenue Service Form 1040 for a family whose records you receive, working with other students in a group to ensure that everyone's IRS forms are correct, and auditing a return filed by a student in a different group
- Designing a nutritious and attractive lunch menu for the cafeteria within a specified budget and defending your definitions of nutritious and attractive
- Designing and building a wind instrument from metal pipes, then composing and performing a piece of music for that instrument
- Defining one human emotion in an essay, through examples from literature and history, and in at least three other ways (through drawing, painting, or sculpture; through film, photographs, or video; through music; through pantomime or dance; or through a story or play that you create)[22]

The future of testing in the United States promises to shape education in many ways. As standards and tests become commonplace, some believe that learning will be improved; others fear that true education and learning will be sacrificed. The persistence of traditional, standardized testing may prompt continued emphasis on the memorization of discrete facts, while reducing the teacher's role as an educational decision maker. On the other hand, an increase in authentic testing may contribute to a greater classroom focus on critical thinking and personal development. The jury is still out, but the era of high-stakes testing—and protesting—is here.

The Textbook Shapes the Curriculum

While some argue that the development of standards may lead to a national curriculum, other believe that we already have a *de facto* national curriculum: the textbook.[23] Students spend from 70 to 95 percent of classroom time using textbooks, and teachers base more than 70 percent of their instructional decisions on them. Given this heavy reliance on texts, there is no doubt that they have a major practical influence on what is taught in schools.

Before 1850, textbooks were made up of whatever educational materials children had in their homes. Students took these textbooks to school, and instruction was based on them. Picture yourself trying to teach a class with the wide array of random materials children have in their homes. Although today we might use these personal resources to supplement instruction, back then it was difficult to teach with such disparate materials. In fact, despairing teachers appealed for common texts, so that all students could use the same materials. Local legislators responded by requiring schools to select appropriate books, and then parents were required to buy them. When families moved, they often had to buy new books. Concerned about the costly burden this lack of consistency placed on families, legislators mandated commonly used textbooks across larger geographic areas.

Today, the process of textbook development and adoption has come under intense criticism. One of its chief critics, Harriet Tyson Bernstein, says,

> Imagine a public policy system that is perfectly designed to produce textbooks that confuse, mislead, and profoundly bore students, while at the same time making all the adults in the process look good, not only in their own eyes, but in the eyes of others. Although there are some good textbooks on the market, publishers and editors are virtually compelled by public policies and practices to create textbooks that confuse students with non sequitors, that mislead them with misinformation, and that profoundly bore them with pointedly arid writing.
>
> None of the adults in this very complex system intends this outcome. To the contrary, each of them wants to produce good effects, and each public policy regulation or conventional practice was intended to make some improvement or prevent some abuse. But the cumulative effects of well-intentioned and seemingly reasonable state and local regulations are textbooks that squander the intellectual capital of our youth.[24]

Here's how the system works and why Bernstein and other opponents are so angry. In 1900, when our current textbook system was designed, twenty-two states enacted laws that put in place a centralized adoption system. More than twenty states, located mainly in the South and the West, are **textbook adoption states.** (These states are indicated in Figure 7.4.)

FIGURE 7.4
Textbook adoption states. While some school districts are free to choose any text, others are limited to state-approved textbooks.

SOURCE: Publishers Resource Group, Inc. Austin, Texas, 2001.

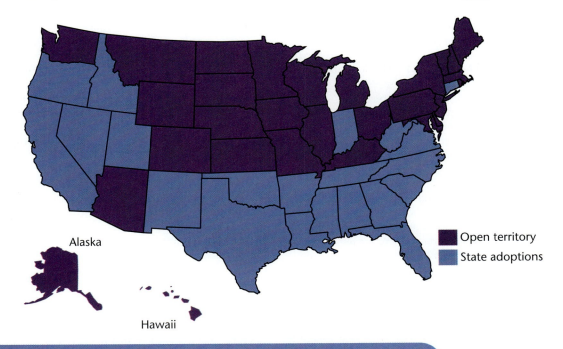

Alaska

Hawaii

■ Open territory
■ State adoptions

REFLECTION

What patterns do you notice in the states that require texts be selected from an approved list? Would such state adoption procedures be a factor in deciding where you might teach? Visit the site for updates at www.prgaustin.com/as/inas.html.

YOU BE THE JUDGE
STATE STANDARDS AND TESTS

Are Desirable Because . . .

SCHOOLS AND EDUCATORS ARE NOT BEING HELD ACCOUNTABLE FOR STUDENT FAILURE

"If they don't want to learn, we can't make them," has been the modus operandi of educators. As a result, we have high school graduates who cannot read or write, and college graduates who do little better. Standards and tests will finally hold educators accountable. We will be able to see what students know, and how well they know it. We can reward successful schools, help troubled schools, and finally close failing schools.

THEY MAKE US EDUCATIONALLY AND ECONOMICALLY COMPETITIVE

Many of today's high school graduates must be retrained in basic literacy skills by the corporations that hire them, because they are unable to do the work that is required. This is a sign that schools are failing. This sort of educational inefficiency leads to technically incompetent workers, and weakens our ability to compete in world markets. We must have standards and tests to educate a first class labor force and maintain our standard of living.

TEACHERS WORK COLLABORATIVELY RATHER THAN IN ISOLATION

A common set of standards promotes cooperation. Teachers and principals will work together to identify problems, develop instructional solutions, and collaborate as a professional team working to ensure that all the standards are met.

THEY WILL BIND THE NATION

National standards offer a unifying experience, as children learn about our common heritage. Without such standards, we become dangerously pluralistic and suffer the risk of becoming not one nation but several. There are already examples of countries that have lost this common thread and whose cultures have disintegrated.

LOCAL PAROCHIALISM WILL BE ELIMINATED

National standards will bring new insights and diverse points of view to the nation's children. Rather than being held hostage to the desires and views of local school boards, students will be able to consider broader perspectives. National standards can end debilitating local parochialism and broaden students' horizons.

Are a Mistake Because . . .

HIGH-STAKES TESTS REPRESENT A TERRIBLE ACCOUNTABILITY

Taking time from studies to prepare for a high-stakes test is not an effective demonstration of educational progress or school accountability. In fact, schools simply replace real learning with test preparation programs. One test is a terribly unreliable way to assess a person's knowledge, and flies in the face of all that we have learned about multiple intelligences, individual differences, and authentic assessment.

NATIONAL STANDARDS AND TESTS ARE A STEP BACKWARD FOR MANY STUDENTS AND SCHOOLS

National standards represent a step down for the nation's strongest school districts. The nation's best schools are well beyond such standards, yet must invest time and resources preparing for the state tests. Our schools prepare very competent scientists and engineers, many of whom are the first to be "downsized" by the same business executives who complain about educational quality. In fact, given our service economy, we may be overeducating our workforce.

TEACHERS WORK IN ISOLATION RATHER THAN COLLABORATIVELY

The pressure of tests and standards will drive teachers away from cooperative planning on educational goals, and into the trap of drilling their students to ensure that their class does well. Teachers will become competitors in a survival of the fittest scenario.

NATIONAL STANDARDS WILL DIVIDE THE NATION

We simply cannot agree on a single set of standards, on which facts to remember (and which to forget). What is important to one group of Americans may be unimportant or offensive to another. The effort to create unifying standards and tests will divide our people.

CENTRAL CONTROL OF OUR LIVES WILL GROW

The authors of the Constitution had it right, local communities and individuals know their children best, and they hold the practical wisdom that made this nation great. All we need is faith in the common sense of Americans, because they do know what's best for their children.

Are Desirable Because . . .

NATIONAL TESTS WILL GIVE US CRITICAL INFORMATION AND DIRECTION

Standardized tests will enable us to compare student performance, and to understand what it takes to earn an "A" in one school, versus an "A" in another. We will discover who is really learning, and who is not. Finally, we will be able to make sense out of what is going on in almost 100,000 school buildings.

Are a Mistake Because . . .

NATIONAL TESTS WILL HURT EDUCATION

High-stakes tests hurt students who are bright, but simply don't test well. Such standardized tests encourage a school curriculum based on test preparation, drive away talented teachers, increase pressure to cheat, and create the kind of boring, predictable, "one-size-fits-all" curriculum that is a disservice to a true democracy.

YOU BE THE JUDGE

Where do you stand on the standards and the testing issue? Can you separate standards from testing? How might you determine if standards are being met—without using a standardized test? Some educators assert that test development should precede standards development. Do you agree or disagree? Why?

Under a state adoption system, local school districts typically select their texts from an official, state-approved list. Those in favor of statewide adoption claim that this process results in the selection of higher-quality texts. This system creates a common, statewide curriculum, which unites educators and makes school life easier for students who move to different schools within the state. State adoptions also save time and work for educators at the local level, and, because of the large numbers of books purchased, the per book cost is kept low.

Criticism of statewide adoptions focuses on what has been called the **Texas and California effect,** which might more accurately be termed the "Four States Effect" (including Florida and North Carolina). Together these four states exert an enormous influence on what is included—or omitted—from the texts. These states draw up plans for what they would like to see in a textbook, and the publishers design books to meet the states' "wish list." These four populous states account for almost a third of the more than $3 billion in annual textbook sales.[25] As you can well imagine, a publisher's dream is to be selected as one of the few approved sources of textbooks, especially in populous states such as these. Because major publishers design their books to meet these state adoption standards, the leading texts available to all states are the ones designed for the adoption states.

Criticism of textbook adoption does not stop with the influence of large states. Many textbook evaluators have limited training for their role. Often, severe time constraints hamper careful decision making. Reviewing large numbers of books in brief periods of time, harried committee members sometimes flip through a book to determine its merit. Publishers are well aware of this "flip phenomenon" and make sure that their books have "eye appeal." Teachers and administrators asked to select a textbook, whether from a state-approved list or not, can be influenced by the cosmetics—the cover, the graphics, the headings, the design. While visual attractiveness can enhance learning, it is no substitute for well-written and accurate content.

Frequently, adoption committees are given criteria sheets to assist them in determining textbook quality. Some criteria sheets are incredibly brief and general; others, in a well-intentioned attempt to be comprehensive, are long and unwieldy, too cumbersome to be used efficiently.[26]

David B., a member of the Texas State Board of Education, objected to the content in an algebra textbook. When his objection was considered inadequate, he pointed out that the book also had manufacturing defects, additional grounds for rejection. He demonstrated the manufacturing defects by ripping the book apart.

SOURCE: *The American School Board Journal,* January 1998.

REFLECTION

How would you feel about serving on a textbook review board? Do you believe that teachers should play the significant role on such boards or should community members, parents and others be included?

Click on *In the News* for recent *In the News* stories. Submit your own *In the News* summary to share with your colleagues.

Criteria sheets often include information on the books' readability, yet another problematic area. By sampling several passages, **readability formulas** assess word difficulty and sentence length to determine the reading skill level for the book. Initially, the use of readability formulas seemed a promising development. What could be more reasonable than making sure the books' reading level was grade-appropriate? But readability formulas have created their own problems. Readability levels vary widely from passage to passage, so it is possible to find eleventh-, eighth-, seventh-, and fourth-grade passages in a single book designated as fifth-grade level. Worse yet, the different readability formulas give different results. For one text, the Spache readability formula indicated a 3.1 grade level, the Dale-Chall 4.2, and the Gunning 4.0, and the Fry put the text at the seventh-grade (7.0) level.[27]

Since some states will buy texts only if they have a specified reading level, publishers are under pressure to develop books that meet this criterion. Often, authors avoid difficult words and long sentences, so that, for example, esophagus becomes food tube and protoplasm becomes stuff. The result, according to former secretary of education Terrell Bell and other critics, is the **dumbing down** of the textbook. Ironically, readability formulas may make books harder, not easier, to read. When authors simplify vocabulary, they replace precise and clear terminology with simple, vague, even ambiguous words. When authors shorten sentences, they often leave out the connective issue—and, but, therefore—words that clarify the relationships between events and ideas. Shortening sentences to make reading simple can make understanding challenging ideas even more difficult.

Writing to the readability level not only hurts comprehension but "squeezes the juice out of some very fine tales."[28] For example, the following is one such distorted reading text version of "The Tortoise and the Hare":

Rabbit said, "I can run. I can run fast." "You can't run fast," Turtle said. "Look Rabbit. See the park. You and I will run. We'll run to the park."

Rabbit said, "I want to stop. I'll stop here. I can run, but Turtle can't. I can get to the park fast." Turtle said, "I can't run fast. But I will not stop. Rabbit can't see me. I'll get to the park."[29]

In this textbook version, the characterization is gone. So is the moral. So is the enjoyment.

As textbooks skim over content, simply to cover it, the student loses information necessary for comprehension. Critics charge that texts typically include too many subjects and gloss over them to such a degree that students do not really understand what is going on. Students are as frustrated by this **mentioning phenomenon** as the adult critics; they say,

> Sometimes they just mention a person's name and then don't talk about them anymore in the whole book.

> They should talk more about each topic. For the War of 1812 there should be more information about the fighters and the treaties. What did the Treaty of Ghent contain? Who wrote it?[30]

One reason for the mentioning phenomenon is the knowledge explosion. But another cause can be traced to the adoption process. In their quest for higher scores on standardized tests, many states have called for aligning the curriculum in textbooks with what is on standardized tests. Adoption committees have delineated in minute detail all the names, dates, and places they want included, and what skills they want students to attain. Frequently, in-depth analysis and clarifying examples are lost in favor of mentioning lots of names, places, and dates. As one disgruntled critic concludes, "Adoption states, special interest groups, and readability formulas have all contributed to produce textbooks designed by a committee, written by a committee, and selected by a committee to please all and offend none."[31]

Researchers have also found that basal readers and other texts, in attempting to be inoffensive to potential purchasers, include only a limited range of story types, often devoid of interpersonal and internal conflict.[32] In their efforts to satisfy local and regional groups, some companies even publish alternative versions of the same book. For example, in some texts, Thanksgiving is truly a "movable feast": if you grew up in Massachusetts, your social studies book may have told you that the first Thanksgiving took place in Plymouth; if you went to school in Virginia, you may have learned that this great celebration occurred in Jamestown.

The lack of depth that characterizes U.S. texts does not keep them immune from errors, as a parent in Pennsylvania discovered. He was working with his daughter on a homework assignment when he found an error in her middle school science text, a best seller. By the time he was done analyzing the text, over 200 errors were documented. Worse yet, Prentice Hall, the publisher, was slow to correct any of them.[33] Nor was this an isolated incident. Another study found science textbooks that had Newton's first law of physics wrong, another had the wrong formula for finding the volume of a sphere, and the wrong definition for absolute zero. One text had a picture of singer Linda Ronstadt labeled as a silicon crystal.[34] Eventually the publishers set up a website (www.publishers.org) so that people could quickly communicate the errors as they found them.

Today's trend is a comprehensive textbook package, with a highly sophisticated instructional design, student materials, classroom visuals, and even website support. Obviously, there are positive elements in these comprehensive, commercially developed textbook systems. If you recall from the conversation in the faculty room at the start of this chapter, comprehensive packages can save overburdened teachers (especially new teachers) a great deal of time, which the teachers can then devote to individualized instruction, as well as a variety of classroom management duties. Some teachers enjoy this "freedom" from making curricular choices. Researcher Allan

Odden has found that, the "more programs are ready made," the less teachers are worn out, reinforcing his belief that packages are more effective than teacher- or school-devised programs.[35]

For schools using these large-scale, often multiple-grade, curricular programs, critics fear that teachers could be reduced to mere technicians. When teachers execute someone else's instructional goals and ideas, teacher autonomy and creativity are lost.[36] "Instead of professional teachers who care about what they do and why they do it, we may have only alienated executors of someone else's plans."[37] If teachers are reduced to curricular technicians, they become increasingly expendable. After all, anyone can administer "foolproof" materials, can't they? Eventually, the "technician" teacher may lose the ability to adapt these materials to the diagnosed needs, abilities, and interests of his or her own students.

"Knowledge is power," the saying goes, and in the final analysis the degree of power and talent you exert as an architect of the curriculum will depend on your own knowledge and skills. If you are supposed to teach a unit on the Civil War but you know little about it, it will be all you can do to implement commercially prepared materials. If you are to teach a unit on poetry but avoided literature classes in college, you will be at the mercy of whatever the publishers or the test makers tell you to do and say. If your knowledge of science is limited to that terrible memory of when you tried to dissect a frog, you may gratefully follow to the last dot on the i whatever instructions are in the teacher's manual (and beg for the science specialist to come in and do it for you). Your own knowledge about content and teaching skills is a classroom asset, giving you the power to put into action one of the most creative functions of teaching: shaping what your students learn in school.

But even when you have a solid intellectual handle on a topic, other challenges emerge. One such continual challenge is the subtle bias that permeates textbooks. Although women and people of color are included more frequently than in the past, they still suffer from tokenism, and American society as a whole is presented in an unrealistic, even idealized manner. What does this bias look like? Glad you asked, because it is an important question, one we explore in the next section.

Seven Forms of Bias

Many Americans are passionate about how various groups are portrayed in textbooks. In the 1970s and 1980s, textbook companies and professional associations, such as the American Psychological Association, issued guidelines for nonracist and nonsexist books; as a result, textbooks became more balanced in their description of underrepresented groups. Today, educators work to detect underrepresentation of those groups, not only in the texts but also in other resources, including the Internet, computer simulations, field trip experiences, guest lecturers, video and fine arts productions, and the extra handouts that so many use to compensate for less than satisfying resources. Moreover, today we have a better understanding of the various manifestations of bias.

Following is a description of **seven forms of bias,** which can be used to assess instructional materials.[38] Although this approach has been used to identify bias against females and various racial and ethnic groups, it can also help identify bias against the elderly, people with disabilities, limited and non-English speakers, gays and lesbians, and other groups.

Invisibility

Perhaps the most fundamental form of bias in instructional materials is the complete or relative exclusion of a particular group or groups from representation in text narrative and/or illustrations. Research suggests, for example, that textbooks published prior to the 1960s largely omitted any consideration of African Americans within contemporary society and, indeed, rendered them relatively invisible in references to the United States after Reconstruction. Latinos, Asian Americans, and Native Americans were largely absent from most resources as well. Many studies indicate that women, who constitute more than 51 percent of the U.S. population, represent approximately 30 percent of the persons or characters referred to throughout the textbooks in most subject areas.

Stereotyping

By assigning rigid roles or characteristics to all members of a group, individual attributes and differences are denied. While stereotypes can be positive, they are more often negative. Some typical stereotypes include

- African Americans as servants, manual workers, professional athletes, troublemakers
- Asian Americans as laundry workers, cooks, or scientists
- Mexican Americans as non-English speakers or migrant workers
- Middle-class Americans in the dominant culture (white Anglo-Saxon-Protestant) as successful in their professional and personal lives
- Native Americans as "blood-thirsty savages" or "noble sons and daughters of the earth"
- Men in traditional occupational roles (rarely as husbands and fathers) and as strong and assertive
- Women as passive and dependent and defined in terms of their home and family roles

Teachers serving on textbook adoption committees apply specific criteria to determine text suitability for their curriculum.

Imbalance and Selectivity

Curriculum may perpetuate bias by presenting only one interpretation of an issue, a situation, or a group of people. These imbalanced accounts simplify and distort complex issues by omitting different perspectives. Examples include

- The origins of European settlers in the New World are emphasized, while the origins and heritage of other racial and ethnic groups are omitted.
- The history of the relations between Native Americans and the federal government is described in terms of treaties and "protection," omitting broken treaties and progressive government appropriation of Native American lands.
- Sources say that women were "given" the vote but omit the physical abuse and sacrifices suffered by the leaders of the suffrage movement who "won" the vote.
- Literature is drawn primarily from European male authors.
- Math and science courses reference only European discoveries and formulas.

Unreality

Many researchers have noted the tendency of instructional materials to ignore facts that are unpleasant or that indicate negative positions or actions by individual leaders, or the nation as a whole. By ignoring the existence of prejudice, racism, discrimination, exploitation, oppression, sexism, and intergroup conflict and bias, we deny children the information they need to recognize, understand, and perhaps some day conquer the problems that plague society. Examples of unreality may be found in programs that portray

- People of color and women as having economic and political equality with white males
- Technology as the resolution of all our persistent social problems

Fragmentation and Isolation

Bias through fragmentation or isolation primarily takes two forms. First, content regarding certain groups may be physically or visually fragmented and delivered separately (for example, a chapter on "Bootleggers, Suffragettes, and Other Diversions"), or even in boxes at the side of the page (for example, "Ten Black Achievers in Science"). Second, racial and ethnic group members may be depicted as interacting only with persons like themselves, isolated from other cultural communities. Fragmentation and isolation ignore dynamic group relationships and suggest that nondominant groups are peripheral members of society.

Linguistic Bias

Language is a powerful conveyor of bias in instructional materials, in both blatant and subtle forms. The dominant language is inherently discriminatory, and can reflect bias against particular races or cultures, gender, accents, age (dis)ability, and sexual orientation. For example:

- Native Americans are frequently referred to as "roaming," "wandering," or "roving" across the land. These terms might be used to apply to buffalo or wolves; they suggest a merely physical relationship to the land, rather than a social or purposeful relation. Such language implicitly justifies the seizure of native lands by "more goal-directed" white Americans, who "traveled" or "settled" their way westward.

- Such words as *forefathers, mankind,* and *businessman* deny the contributions and existence of females.

The insistence that we live in an English only, monolingual society creates bias against non-English speakers in this country and abroad. An imbalance of word order ("boys and girls") and a lack of parallel terms ("girls and young men") are also forms of linguistic bias.

INTERACTIVE ACTIVITY
WHAT IS THE BIAS? Match scenarios with the bias being displayed.

Cosmetic Bias

Cosmetic bias offers the appearance of an up-to-date, well-balanced curriculum. The problem is that, beyond the superficial appearance, bias persists. Cosmetic bias emerges in a science textbook that features a glossy pullout of female scientists but includes precious little narrative of the scientific contributions of women. A music book with an eye-catching, multiethnic cover that projects a world of diverse songs and symphonies belies the traditional white male composers lurking behind the cover. This "illusion of equity" is really a marketing strategy directed at potential purchasers who *flip* the pages and might be lured into purchasing books that appear to be current, diverse, and balanced.

Religious Fundamentalism

Some parents and educators argue that publishers have not gone far enough in producing nonsexist, multicultural books, but others believe that the publishers have gone much too far. While censorship attacks can originate from either liberals or conservatives, since the 1980s, they have been much more likely to come from conservative quarters. One such conservative group is Christian fundamentalists. **Christian, Bible,** or **religious fundamentalists** (sometimes called the **religious right**), generally believe in a strict interpretation of the Bible and advocate a conservative social agenda. Such issues as abortion and evolution can spark a strong reaction from these groups.

> Pressures from the politically organized religious Right have made it risky for publishers to discuss evolution. If evolution is discussed at all, it is often confined to a chapter in the book. Students are conducted on a forced march through the phyla, and given no understanding of the overarching theory (evolution) that gives taxonomy life and meaning. Touchy subjects like dinosaurs, the fossil record, genetics, natural selection, or even the scientific meanings of the words "theory" and "belief" are treated skimpily or vaguely in order to avoid the ire of the Bible fundamentalists.[39]

Here are two examples of the nature of these controversies.

Case 1. A 1986 case in eastern Tennessee made headlines when a group of fundamentalist Christian families objected to a series of Holt, Rinehart & Winston readers. They objected to an illustration in a first-grade reader showing a kitchen scene with a girl reading while a boy cooks (he is making toast). The plaintiffs argued that "the religion of John Dewey is planted in the first graders [sic] mind that there are no God-given roles for different sexes.[40] The plaintiffs also objected to *The Diary of Anne Frank,* which was cited as being antireligion in its acceptance of diversity in religious belief and practice. Consider the following passage:

ANNE: (Softly) I wish you had a religion, Peter.

PETER: No, thanks! Not me.

ANNE: Oh, I don't mean you have to be Orthodox . . . or believe in heaven and hell and purgatory and things . . . I just mean some religion . . . it doesn't matter what. Just to believe in something! When I think of all that's out there . . . the trees . . . the flowers . . . and seagulls . . . when I think of the dearness of you, Peter . . . and the goodness of the people we know . . . Mr. Kraler, Miep, Dirk, the vegetable man, all risking their lives for us everyday. . . . When I think of these good things, I'm not afraid anymore.[41]

It is not only Anne Frank or nontraditional gender roles that capture attention. Other categories called "offensive" included "futuristic supernaturalism, one-world government, situation ethics or values clarification, humanistic moral absolutes, pacifism, rebellion against parents or self-authority, role reversal, role elimination, animals are equal to humans, the skeptic's view of religion contrasting belief in the supernatural with science, false views of death and related themes, magic, other religions, evolution, godless supernaturalism . . . and specific humanistic themes."[42]

Case 2. During the spring of 1988, an assignment from Robert Marzano's *Tactics for Thinking* unleashed a storm of controversy in southern Indiana. Protesters charged that the following exercise could induce a self-hypnotic trance:

Have students focus their attention on some stimulus (e.g., a spot on the wall). Explain to them that you want them to focus all of their energy for about a minute and ask them to be aware of what it is like when they are really trying to attend to something.[43]

Many community members were persuaded that the book was brainwashing children into believing in a one-world government and religion. In Battle Ground, Washington, a group of citizens claimed that *Tactics for Thinking* was teaching the occult. Thomas McDaniel, dean of Converse College, reported that, in one county, *St. George and the Dragon, Puss in Boots,* and *Sylvester and the Magic Pebble* were dropped from the reading curriculum. Parents objected because they were about magic.[44] In at least a dozen other states, there were protests against these and other books connected with the New Age movement or secular humanism.

Scenes like this one involving overt religious prayer have been banned from the school curriculum. Should the study of religion as a vital social force also be banned or watered down because it is politically dangerous?

It is hard to define what conservative religious leaders call the **New Age movement** and **secular humanism.** Humanists define themselves as living ethically without recourse to organized religions, or necessarily to a supernatural being. Christian fundamentalists and other opponents contend that "secular humanists" are anti-religion, deny God, a creator, or any divinity by promoting global education, the occult, values clarification, Eastern mysticism, and a belief in a one-world government. Critics charge that secular humanists are *pseudoreligious,* and promote "agnosticism, various forms of feminism, environmentalism, political liberalism and conservatism, various ethnic or sexual identities . . ."[45]

To respond to this perceived secular threat, several public school systems have developed programs that not only teach, but also promote basic Christian beliefs. Many of these public schools are found in the southeastern region of the country, an area that lacks a strong tradition of separating religious teachings from public education. For example, in the 2000 academic year, a Virginia public school system used the following exam questions:

1. List six proofs that the Bible is God's word.

2. God is supreme ruler and has given man free choice. This shows that God is:

   A. Omniscient   B. Good   C. Sovereign   D. Merciful[46]

By no means is such inappropriate instruction confined to one region of the country. In Belridge, California, for example, the public school system was forced to abandon its Christian education program as a result of a suit by the American Civil Liberties Union. In 1999, Belridge was using textbooks that described non-Christian religions as "cults," taught that God helped Columbus discover America, that Native American accomplishments were "worthless" since they had no knowledge of the "true" God, and asked students to punctuate a sentence that read: "The Hebrew people often grumbled and complained." Clearly the separation of church and state is an ongoing challenge.[47]

While many people are disturbed by these unconstitutional school practices that promote religious beliefs, teachers can overreact. Many teachers shy away from teaching about religion at all for fear that the topic should not be taught in public schools.[48] Actually, teaching *about* different religions is important, but *promoting* or *disparaging* religious beliefs is inappropriate. Although states frequently require that students be taught about the world's great religions by the time they reach the tenth grade, what is taught is less than adequate. Religious topics taught during the elementary years are often quite superficial, while the high school courses rarely cover religious issues beyond the Civil War.[49] Religious ignorance and bigotry are at least partially responsible for the increasing number of censorship attacks on books used in public schools, attacks that can tie a school system into knots and pose a genuine threat to academic freedom.[50]

Censorship and the Curriculum

Ruth Sherman lived just outside New York City, in a Long Island neighborhood known for its Italian community and easy commute to the city. Although she traveled only a short distance to P.S. 75, where she taught third grade, she might as well have been teaching in another country. P.S. 75 was in the Bushwick section of Brooklyn, a graffiti-filled neighborhood populated by poor black and Hispanic families living in the midst of a rampant drug culture. "Why there?" her friends asked her. "Because I want 'to turn things around,'" she responded. She was that kind of teacher. But, in just three months, it was Ruth Sherman, and not her students, who was turned around.

Her problems started in September, although she did not learn about it until later, when she assigned a book called *Nappy Hair,* by African American author Carolivia Herron. Her students loved the book, about a little black girl with "the nappiest, fuzziest, the most screwed up, squeezed up, knotted hair," and clamored for copies to take with them. By Thanksgiving, the parents in Ruth Sherman's class had also discovered the book, which they considered racially insulting. At a parents' meeting, she was confronted by fifty parents (most of them parents of children not in her class), who shouted racial epithets and eventually threatened her. The superintendent sent Ruth home, for her own protection. A review of the book followed. The review brought only praise for a book that promoted positive images for children and presented stories that appealed to them. Within a few days, the superintendent wrote her a letter, commending her performance, inviting her back to the school, and promising security escorts to protect her. But, by then, it was too late. Ruth Sherman, the teacher who wanted to make a difference, did not want to work in a climate that required "escorts" to ensure her safety. She transferred to another school.[51]

This incident occurred in 1998 in New York, but it could occur anywhere at anytime. Nearly everyone—teachers, parents, the general public, and various special interest groups—wants some say as to what is and is not in the school curriculum. No matter what content is found in a particular textbook or course of study, someone is likely to consider it too conservative or too liberal, too traditional or too avant-garde, racist, sexist, anti-Semitic, violent, un-Christian, or pornographic. When this happens, pressure to **censor** the offending materials soon follows. Religious conservatives are often a major source of censorship attempts; however, as the New York case illustrates, censorship can emanate from almost any quarter, liberal or conservative.[52]

There is no such thing as a totally safe, acceptable, uncontroversial book or curriculum. Each of the following has been subjected to censorship at one time or another:

- Mary Rodgers's *Freaky Friday:* "Makes fun of parents and parental responsibility"
- George Eliot's *Silas Marner:* "You can't prove what that dirty old man is doing with that child between chapters"
- Plato's *Republic:* "This book is un-Christian"
- Jules Verne's *Around the World in Eighty Days:* "Very unfavorable to Mormons"
- William Shakespeare's *Macbeth:* "Too violent for children"
- Fyodor Dostoyevsky's *Crime and Punishment:* "Serves as a poor model for young people"
- Herman Melville's *Moby Dick:* "Contains homosexuality"
- Anne Frank's *Diary of a Young Girl:* "Obscene and blasphemous"
- E. B. White's *Charlotte's Web:* "Morbid picture of death"
- Robert Louis Stevenson's *Treasure Island:* "You know what men are like and what they do when they've been away from women that long"
- J. R. R. Tolkien's *The Hobbit:* "Subversive elements"
- Roald Dahl's *Charlie and the Chocolate Factory:* "Racist"

- William Steig's *Sylvester and the Magic Pebble:* "Anti-police" (one of the police officers is drawn as a pig)
- *Webster's Dictionary:* "Contains sexually explicit definitions"[53]

According to the American Library Association, between 1990–1999, there were 5,718 challenges reported.[54] But the incidences of **self-censorship,** which some term **stealth censorship,** is considered much higher.[55] Stealth censorship occurs when educators or parents quietly remove a book from a library shelf or a course of study in response to an informal complaint—or in order to avoid controversy. Teachers practice the same sort of self-censorship when they choose not to teach a topic or not to discuss a difficult issue. Numbers on the frequency of self-censorship are impossible to obtain. Tallying up the number of books that were officially removed or placed on restricted-access shelves in libraries is far easier.[56] The most frequently challenged books in 2000 were:

- *Harry Potter* series, J. K. Rowling (occult/Satanism and anti-family themes)
- *The Chocolate War,* Robert Cormier (violence, offensive language, and being unsuited to age group)
- *Alice* series, Phyllis Reynolds Naylor (sexual content and being unsuited to age group)
- *Killing Mr. Griffin,* Lois Duncan (violence and sexual content)
- *Of Mice and Men,* John Steinbeck (using offensive language, racism, violence, and being unsuited to age group)
- *I Know Why the Caged Bird Sings,* Maya Angelou (sexual content, racism, offensive language, violence, unsuited to age group)
- *Fallen Angels,* Walter Dean Myers (offensive language, racism, violence, unsuited to age group)
- *Scary Stories* series, Alvin Schwartz (violence, unsuited to age group, and occult themes)
- *The Terrorist,* Caroline Cooney (violence, unsuited to age group and occult themes)
- *The Giver,* Lois Lowry (being sexually explicit, occult themes, and violence)[57]

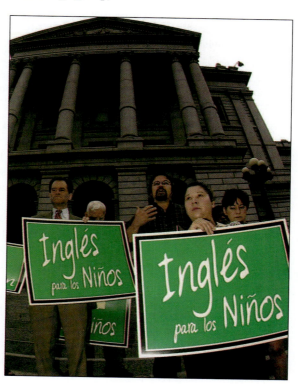

In a multicultural society, to what extent should vocal community groups concerned about a particular issue (sex, religion, abortion, politics) be allowed to influence the school curriculum?

At the heart of the case against censorship is the First Amendment, which guarantees freedom of speech and of the press. Those who oppose censorship say that our purpose as educators is not to indoctrinate children but to expose them to a variety of views and perspectives. The case for censorship (or, perhaps in a more politically correct phrase, *mature judgment and selection*) is that adults have the right and obligation to protect children from harmful influences. But "harmful influences" are in the eye of the be-holder. For instance, challenges to books that include homosexuality have become commonplace. Critics say that these books promote homosexuality, and that is not ac-ceptable in school. Others believe that such books teach tolerance of sexual differ-ences, and serve a positive purpose for both heterosexual and homosexual students. Moreover, they argue, reading about different sexual orientations is a far cry from pro-moting any particular sexual outlook.[58]

The censorship controversy is symbolic of how politicized the curriculum debate has become. What knowledge should be taught, and what information is better kept from impressionable young minds? And who gets to decide? These questions are both political and legal. From the classroom to the courtroom, each side makes a com-pelling case for its own point of view.

Cultural Literacy or Cultural Imperialism?

Both George Orwell and Aldous Huxley were pessimists about the future. "What Or-well feared were those who would ban books," writes author Neil Postman. "What Huxley feared was that there would be no one who wanted to read one."[59] Perhaps neither of them imagined that the great debate would revolve around neither fear nor apathy but, rather, deciding which books are most worth reading.

Proponents of **core knowledge,** also called **cultural literacy,** argue for a com-mon course of study for all students, one that ensures that an educated person knows the basics of our society. Novelist and teacher John Barth laments what ensues with-out core knowledge:

> In the same way you can't take for granted that a high school senior or a freshman in col-lege really understands that the Vietnam War came after World War II, you can't take for granted that any one book is common knowledge even among a group of liberal arts or writing majors at a pretty good university.[60]

Allan Bloom's *The Closing of the American Mind* (1987) was one of several books that sounded the call for a curricular canon. A canon is a term with religious roots, referring to a list of books officially accepted by the church or a religious hier-archy. A **curricular canon** applies this notion to schools by defining the most use-ful and valued books in our culture. Those who support a curricular canon believe that all students should share a common knowledge of our history and the central figures of our culture, an appreciation of the great works of art and music and, par-ticularly, the great works of literature. A shared understanding of our civilization is a way to bind our diverse people.

Allan Bloom, professor of social thought at the University of Chicago, took aim at the university curriculum as a series of often unrelated courses lacking a vision of what an educated individual should know, a canonless curriculum. He claimed that his university students were ignorant of music and literature, and charged that too many students graduate with a degree but without an education.[61] One of the criti-cisms of Bloom's vision was that his canon consisted almost exclusively of white, male, European culture. Critics charged that the canons were loaded with "dead white males."

Book banning is alive and well in Nebo School District, Utah. Officials there banned "The Watsons Go to Birmingham—1963" when two parents complained about the violence and swearing in the book. The book tells about the civil rights fight in the 1960s, including the church bombing that took the lives of four African American girls. Neither the powerful story nor the fact that the book won a Newbery Award for children's literature could save it. The teacher, who spent $160 of her own money to buy copies for her students, donated the books elsewhere.

SOURCE: *The Washington Post,* June 12, 2001.

REFLECTION

Would you use or avoid books that employed violence or swearing? Does the quality and message of a story justify disturbing scenes and words in a book?

 Click on *In the News* for recent *In the News* stories. Submit your own *In the News* summary to share with your colleagues.

E. D. Hirsch, Jr., in his book ***Cultural Literacy,*** was more successful than Bloom in including the contributions of various ethnic and racial groups, as well as women. This is a rarity among core curriculum proponents. In fact, Hirsch believes that it is the poorer children and children of color who will most benefit from a cultural literacy curriculum. He points out that children from impoverished homes are less likely to become culturally literate. A core curriculum will teach them the names, dates, places, events, and quotes that every literate American needs to know in order to succeed. In 1991, Hirsch published the first volume of the core knowledge series, *What Your First Grader Needs to Know.* Other grades followed in these mass-marketed books directed not only at educators but at parents as well.[62]

Not everyone is enamored with the core curriculum idea. A number of educators wonder who gets included in this core, and, just as interesting, who gets to choose? Are Hirsch, Bloom, and others to be members of a very select committee, perhaps a blue-ribbon committee of "Very Smart People"? Why are so many of these curricular canons so white, so male, so Eurocentric, and so exclusionary?

Many call for a more inclusive telling of the American story, one that weaves the contributions of many groups and of women as well as of white males into the textbook tapestry of the American experience. Those who support **multicultural education** say that students of color and females will achieve more, will like learning better, and will have higher self-esteem if they are reflected in the pages of their textbooks. And let's not forget white male students. When they read about people other than themselves in the curriculum, they are more likely to honor and appreciate their diverse peers. Educator and author James Banks calls for increased cultural pluralism:

> People of color, women, and other marginalized groups are demanding that their voices, visions, and perspectives be included in the curriculum. They ask that the debt Western civilization owes to Africa, Asia, and indigenous America be acknowledged. . . . However, these groups must acknowledge that they do not want to eliminate Aristotle and Shakespeare, or Western civilization, from the school curriculum. To reject the West would be to reject important aspects of their own cultural heritages, experiences, and identities.[63]

INTERACTIVE ACTIVITY
DO YOU KNOW THE "BASICS"? See how you do on this hypothetical quiz created to test your cultural literacy. Get a firsthand feel for the testing issue.

Some opponents of cultural literacy take a more radical approach. They believe that an ethnocentric school curriculum is fine, as long as the focus for black children is Africa. **Afrocentrists** argue that African American children have been dislocated—first by their ancestors' removal from Africa and today by a school that devalues their history and culture. Their ideas have led to innovations, such as the African American immersion schools.

A is for Armstrong, B is for Banneker, C is for Carver. For children at Victor Berger Elementary School, African American culture is the foundation of all instruction.

The first graders are learning to count from 1 to 10 in Swahili as well as English. They know that the colors of the African American flag are red, black, and green just as surely as they know the American flag is red, white, and blue. And at art time, the children identify the pipe cleaner spiders they are making not as the itsy-bitsy spider in the well-known song but as the clever Anansi of African folk tales.[64]

Critics claim that an Afrocentric curriculum has no place in a public school, where common American values and culture should be taught. They worry about the disuniting of American school and society. Should there also be a curriculum that is centered on Asia or Latin America? Should these be further divided into separate strands for children from Vietnam or Nicaragua? As noted historian Arthur Schlesinger wonders,

What good will it do young black Americans to take African names, wear African costumes, and replicate African rituals, to learn by music and mantras, rhythm and rapping? . . . Will such training help them understand democracy better? Help them fit better into American life? . . . The best way to keep a people down is to deny them the means of improvement or achievement and cut them off from the opportunities of the national life.[65]

What balance should schools seek between teaching a common core curriculum that binds all Americans together and teaching a curriculum that celebrates the many cultures that have been brought to the United States?

Advocates of a core curriculum claim that it will empower the poor and the disadvantaged. Opponents say it will rob them of the chance to see their experiences reflected in history and literature. What some call *cultural literacy* others see as *cultural imperialism*. "Whose knowledge is of most worth?" is the question of the day. And, as America becomes a nation of growing diversity, the argument will continue to drive the debate about what is core, what is fair, and what should be in the curriculum.

The Saber-Tooth Curriculum

How can the curriculum prepare for tomorrow while preserving the past? Here is how curriculum scholar Michael Apple puts it:

> The curriculum must simultaneously be both conservative and critical. It must preserve the ideals that have guided discourse in the U.S. for centuries: a faith in the American people, a commitment to expanding equality, and a commitment to diversity and liberty. Yet it must also empower individuals to question the ethics of their institutions and to criticize them when they fail to meet these ideals.[66]

Unless we carefully consider what a school is for and what kind of curriculum can meet those goals, we might end up with a "saber-tooth curriculum." Since many of you may never have read this classic satire on Paleolithic curriculum written by Abner Peddiwell, known in real life as Harold Benjamin, we will summarize the story of **The Saber-Tooth Curriculum** for you here. This clever parody reveals the flaws of a saber-tooth curriculum. Are there any positive aspects of this kind of curriculum?

• • •

New-Fist was a brilliant educator and thinker of prehistoric times. He watched the children of his tribe playing with bones, sticks, and brightly colored pebbles, and he speculated on what these youngsters might learn that would help the tribe derive more food, shelter, clothing, security, and, in short, a better life.

Eventually, he determined that in order to obtain food and shelter, the people of his tribe must learn to fish with their bare hands and to club and skin little woolly horses; and in order to live in safety, they must learn to drive away the saber-tooth

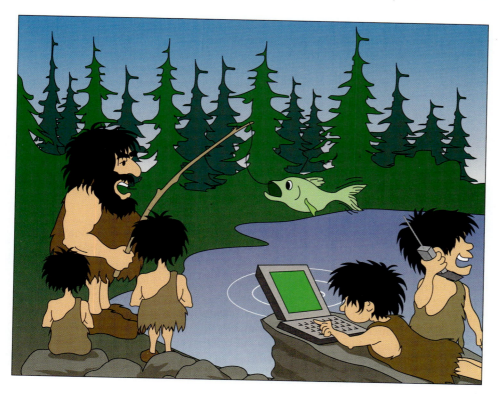

tigers with fire. So New-Fist developed the first curriculum. It consisted of three basic subjects: (1) "Fish-Grabbing-with-the-Bare-Hands," (2) "Woolly-Horse-Clubbing," and (3) "Saber-Tooth-Tiger-Scaring-with-Fire."

New-Fist taught the children these subjects, and they enjoyed these purposeful activities more than playing with colored pebbles. The years went by, and by the time New-Fist was called by the Great Mystery to the Land of the Setting Sun, all the tribe's children had been systematically schooled in these three skills; the tribe was prosperous and secure.

All would have been well and the story might have ended here had it not been for an unforeseen change—the beginning of the New Ice Age, which sent a great glacier sliding down upon the tribe. The glacier so muddied the waters of the creeks that it was impossible for people to catch fish with their bare hands. Also, the melted water of the glacier made the ground marshy, and the little woolly horses left for higher and drier land. They were replaced by shy and speedy antelopes with such a scent for danger that no one could get close enough to club them. And finally, as if these disruptions were not enough, the increasing dampness of the air caused the saber-tooth tigers to contract pneumonia and die. The tigers, however, were replaced by an even greater danger: ferocious glacial bears, who showed no fear of fire. Prosperity and security became distant memories for the suffering tribe.

Fortunately, a new breed of brilliant educators emerged. One tribesman, his stomach rumbling with hunger, grew frustrated with fruitless fish-grabbing in cloudy waters. He fashioned a crude net and in one hour caught more fish than the whole tribe could have caught had they fish-grabbed for an entire day. Another tribesman fashioned a snare with which he could trap the swift antelope, and a third dug a pit that captured and secured the ferocious bears.

As a result of these new inventions, the tribe again became happy and prosperous. Some radicals even began to criticize the school's curriculum and urged that net-making, snare-setting, and pit-digging were indispensable to modern life and should be taught in the schools. But the wise old men who controlled the schools objected:

> With all the intricate details of fish-grabbing, horse-clubbing, and tiger-scaring—the standard cultural subjects—the school curriculum is too crowded now. We can't add these fads and frills of net-making, antelope-snaring, and—of all things—bear-killing. Why, at the very thought, the body of the great New-Fist, founder of our Paleolithic educational system, would turn over in its burial cairn. What we need to do is to give our young people a more thorough grounding in the fundamentals. . . . The essence of true education is timelessness. It is something that endures through changing conditions like a solid rock standing squarely and firmly in the middle of a raging torrent. You must know that there are some eternal verities, and the saber-tooth curriculum is one of them.[67]

• • •

The Saber-Tooth Curriculum was written in 1939, but it has meaning today. Clearly, educators need to avoid a curriculum out of touch with the reality of today's students and thoughtlessly programmed for obsolescence. No educator worth his or her salt wants to be caught waving unnecessary firebrands at tigers long extinct. Today's debate over curricula for various ethnic groups versus a common, Eurocentric core is related to issues raised in *The Saber-Tooth Curriculum*. Is Latin a "saber-tooth" subject? What about the ancient history of the Romans and Greeks? Should these topics make way for subjects more relevant, useful, or culturally inclusive? If we omit these, do we lose an important part of the nation's cultural heritage? Is there room for everything? If not, how do we establish priorities? These are the kinds of questions thoughtful teachers face on a daily basis.

SUMMARY

1. What forces shape the school curriculum?

   • Many different groups can influence the curriculum. These include publishers, teachers, students, parents, administrators, the federal, state, and local governments, colleges and universities, national tests, education commissions and committees, professional organizations, and special interest groups.

   • In recent years, the move toward subject matter standards and statewide testing has added another powerful force influencing what is taught in schools.

2. How does the standards movement influence what is taught in school?

   • The effort to create subject matter standards or content standards gained momentum throughout the 1990s. The federal government initiated the trend with The National Education Summit held in Charlottesville. The first Bush administration championed the development of standards; the Clinton and second Bush administration continued this effort.

   • The progress in standards development has been uneven. In mathematics, national standards were quickly developed. But in more value-laden disciplines like history, arguments and disagreements erupted over what should be included.

   • Most Americans believe that the use of national standards will enhance the level of learning. However, at the beginning of the twenty-first century, concern arose regarding performance standards. Performance standards measure student's mastery in statewide testing.

3. Why are some protesting the growing emphasis on high-stakes testing?

   • Schools and students that score poorly on performance tests would receive extra resources, but if low test scores continue, penalties would follow, perhaps resulting in the closing of "failing schools."

   • Many schools and teachers "teach to the test," at the cost of curricular topics which are not tested. Some schools even teach strategies and tricks to increase test scores. In response, groups of students, teachers, and parents have protested and even boycotted some of these exams.

   • Others protest the lack of opportunity-to-learn standards. These critics argue that performance standards would cause damage if student and school differences are not recognized. They believe that students learn in different ways, and even test differently. Since some schools enjoy superior facilities and resources, while other schools have few resources, poorer schools must be given the resources to compete with wealthy schools.

   • Standardized tests are fraught with problems. Test bias, errors in grading, faulty or confusing test questions, not to mention the costs of such exams, all compromise test effectiveness and bring into question the use of high-stakes tests.

   • Some educators prefer authentic assessment, in which students' actual performance is evaluated, rather than their responses to a paper-and-pencil exam. An authentic assessment demands that students synthesize what they have learned in various areas to complete a challenging, often creative, task. Accomplishing something *real* is motivating for students, and perhaps more relevant than most high-stakes tests. Educator Theodore Sizer has developed many examples of authentic assessment tasks, which he refers to as "exhibitions."

4. How do textbook publishers and state adoption committees "drive" the curriculum?

   • More than twenty states, mainly located in the South and West, are textbook adoption states. In this centralized adoption system, local school districts must select their texts from an official, state-approved list.

CHAPTER REVIEW
Go to the Online Learning Center to take a chapter self-quiz, practice with key terms, and review key ideas from the chapter.

- Those who are in favor of the state adoption system believe that this process leads to the selection of higher-quality texts and creates a common, statewide curriculum. Those who criticize the state adoption system claim that large, populous states (California, Texas, Florida, and North Carolina) exert unfair influence over textbook development.
- Under pressure to publish books that have appropriate readability levels, publishers and authors "dumb down" textbooks. Substituting simplified, shorter words and phrases for more complex ones may result in books in which sophisticated ideas are simplified into meaningless ones. Critics of textbooks cite the "mentioning phenomenon" as another problem. They claim that the books are peppered with too many subjects so that each one is barely discussed, giving students little depth or context.
- The growth of comprehensive textbook packages, complete with student materials, classroom displays, websites, and the like, make the teacher's task easier. But such programs also detract from a teacher's role in curricular development.

5. What are the seven forms of bias in instructional materials?

- Seven forms of bias can characterize textbooks: invisibility, stereotyping, imbalance and selectivity, unreality, fragmentation and isolation, linguistic bias, and cosmetic bias. These forms of bias can work against a group's race, ethnicity, gender, age, or (dis)ability.
- Teachers can alert students to these types of bias, and prepare them to detect and evaluate books accordingly and provide supplementary materials that provide more accurate and equitable information.

6. How do religious differences impact school curricular materials?

- Controversies over religious fundamentalism and secular humanism have characterized textbook adoption in recent years. In some communities, these controversies have led to book banning and censorship.
- Teachers do not always appreciate the difference between teaching about religion and promoting a religious belief. As a result, some teachers promote their beliefs, while many others avoid the topic entirely.

7. Why are schoolbooks so frequently the targets of censorship?

- Censorship can emanate from the political left or right. Liberals argue against books that defame or omit certain racial, ethnic, or other groups. Conservatives, particularly religious fundamentalists, target books and ideas that conflict with their values. The censors have targeted even some of the most popular books, from Shakespeare to the Harry Potter series.
- The courts have ruled that adults do have the right to select appropriate material for schools. However, the line between "selecting" and "censoring" unpopular ideas is not always clear.
- Many teachers, fearful of censorship attacks, follow a path of stealth or self-censorship, avoiding books and topics that could be controversial. Unfortunately, such self-censorship denies students information and learning.

8. Should the curriculum focus on teaching a core knowledge or focus on the demands of a changing world?

- Proponents of a core curriculum and cultural literacy, such as E. D. Hirsch, feel that it will benefit the disadvantaged and transmit the culture essential for well-educated citizens.
- Multiculturalists, such as James Banks, argue that most examples of cultural literacy minimize the roles, experiences, and contributions of women and people of color.
- When developing curricula, it is useful to keep in mind the lessons learned from the satire of *The Saber-Tooth Curriculum*. A curriculum must include objectives and activities that teach students how to preserve the past, but not be limited by it. Students also need to function effectively in the present, and prepare for the future, and the curriculum should be responsive to these changes.

KEY TERMS AND PEOPLE

Afrocentrists, 286

authentic assessment, 269

Allan Bloom, 284

censor, 282

Christian, Bible, or religious fundamentalists, 279

The Closing of the American Mind, 284

content standards, 261

core knowledge, 284

cultural literacy, 284

Cultural Literacy, 285

curricular canon, 284

dumbing down, 274

E. D. Hirsch, Jr., 285

Alfie Kohn, 266

mentioning phenomenon, 275

multicultural education, 285

New Age movement, 281

opportunity-to-learn standard, 264

performance standards, 263

readability formulas, 274

religious right, 279

The Saber-Tooth Curriculum, 287

secular humanism, 281

self-censorship, 283

seven forms of bias, 276

stealth censorship, 283

Texas and California effect, 273

textbook adoption states, 271

DISCUSSION QUESTIONS AND ACTIVITIES

1. This chapter presents an overview of the various groups and forces that influence what children are taught in schools. In your opinion, which of these groups and forces have the most influence on curricula? Why?

2. What subject areas spark the greatest debate and controversy over creating a single, national curriculum? Are there strategies to help reach a consensus on these issues? How might a national history curriculum written today differ from one written a century from now? A century ago? Why?

3. Do you believe that children's educational materials should be censored? Are there any benefits to censorship? Any dangers? What kinds of materials would you refuse to let elementary school students read? Middle or high school students? Postsecondary students?

4. Are you in favor of a comprehensive textbook system, or do you think this inhibits teachers from pursuing one of the important professional aspects of their work?

5. Collect textbooks from your local elementary and secondary schools and analyze them according to the following criteria:

   • Do they include instructional objectives? Do these require students to use both recall of factual information and analytical and creative thinking skills?

   • Were readability formulas used in the preparation of the textbooks? If so, did this appear to have a negative or positive impact on the quality of the writing?

   • Are underrepresented group members included in the textbooks' narrative and illustrations? Are individuals with disabilities included?

   • When various individuals are included, are they portrayed in a balanced or a stereotyped manner?

6. Is American society best characterized as a melting pot? A salad? A stew? Stir-fry in a sauce? Why? Is there another metaphor that better captures the nature of American society?

7. Consider the materials and textbooks used on your campus in your major courses. Do you think a traditional or a multicultural perspective is reflected?

8. Support the statement "Standardized testing is good for U.S. education." Then refute it.

9. Do we have a saber-tooth curriculum today? Through satire, Abner Peddiwell made a persuasive case against the saber-tooth curriculum. Can you write a satire in defense of today's curriculum?

10. Your course instructor probably used this textbook as a framework for curriculum development in this course. How has this text served as a foundation for content, testing, discussion, and activities?

 ONLINE WEB-*TIVITIES*

1. Censorship and the Curriculum

2. The Textbook Shapes the Curriculum

3. Is the United States Going Test Crazy?

4. The Teacher as the Curriculum Developer

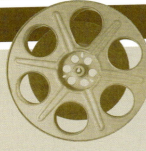

REEL TO REAL TEACHING

INHERIT THE WIND (1960)
Run Time: 127 minutes

Synopsis: A small Tennessee town gained national attention in 1925 when a biology teacher was arrested for violating state law by teaching Darwin's theory of evolution. The explosive battle between science and religion continues to this day.

Reflection:

1. Bertram Cates is the character of what real life person? What happened to his teaching career following the trial? Who do Henry Drummond and Matthew Harrison Brady represent in real life?

2. Who should control what is taught in schools? Government? School boards? Teachers? Parents? Why?

3. In which court was Bertram Cates tried: a court of law or the court of public opinion? Who won the trial? Support your answer with specific quotes and scenes from the film.

4. Should there be a difference between the type of control exerted by state legislatures over what teachers can teach in public elementary and secondary schools as opposed to what professors teach in publicly supported universities? Why or why not?

5. Research recent attempts to ban the teaching of evolution. Who or what sparked the debate? What were the outcomes? Why is evolution still considered a controversial theory?

6. Where do professional teaching associations stand on the issues of teaching religion versus teaching about religion, teaching evolution versus teaching creationism? You may want to start with the National Science Teachers Association, National Council for Social Studies, American Federation of Teachers, and National Education Association.

7. Explain the meaning of the phrase "inherit the wind."

Follow-up Activity: Create your own *You Be the Judge: Voices of Human Origin.* Develop arguments for and against the question "Should alternative theories of human origin be taught along with evolution?" After presenting 5–6 well-supported points on both sides of the issue, you be the judge and hand down a definitive ruling.

 How do you rate this film? Click on *Reel to Real Teaching* to submit your review of this or another education-related film, and read reviews submitted by others.

FOR FURTHER READING

The Case Against Standardized Testing: Raising Scores, Ruining Schools, by Alfie Kohn (2000). Argues that standardized tests undermine quality learning and reflect the interests of politicians and business leaders rather than students and educators.

Caught in the Middle: Nonstandard Kids and a Killing Curriculum, by Susan Ohanian (2001). Describes how curriculum standards impart a singular definition of success that fails many students. The lives of eight students who "think outside the box" are detailed.

The Competent Classroom, by Allison Zmuda and Mary Tomalino (2001). Describes the cross-disciplinary approach of two teachers working to align curriculum, assessment, and performance standards in their classrooms.

Protecting the Right to Learn: Power, Politics, and Public Schools, by James Daly, Patricia Schall, and Rosemary Skeele (2001). Investigates how censorship stifles the ability of schools and teachers to educate students in meaningful ways through a case study of one school district embroiled in a legal battle over control of the curriculum.

Standards in the Classroom: How Teachers and Students Negotiate Learning, by John Kordalewski (2000). Explores how teachers and students, rather than political rhetoric, can collaborate to create standards in the classrooms that empower students with critical thinking skills.

The Way We Were? The Myths and Realities of America's Student Achievement, by Richard Rothstein, (1998). An analysis of student achievement across several decades debunks the myth that American students are learning less. Instead, their continued progress and achievements are revealed.

Why Fly That Way? by Kathy Greeley (2000). Teachers share their concerns about the current overemphasis on standardized testing and a back-to-basics approach to instruction.

Inter-mission

It's been four chapters since your first Inter-mission. To refresh your memory, here you will find a series of application and reflection tasks that parallels the INTASC (Interstate New Teacher Assessment and Support Consortium) principles. (See page 00 to review these). Tackling these tasks will lead to a firmer understanding of Part 2, and some of these efforts may become part of your growing portfolio collection.

Applications and Reflections

2:1 CURRICULUM AND THE GENERATION GAP

INTASC PRINCIPLE 1
Knowledge of Subject Matter

Purpose: The purpose of this activity is to informally acquire information regarding curriculum *changes* in your favorite subject or major field. Some teachers construct lessons that easily blend new content with time-tested approaches and strategies. Others are devastated when there is any change in the curriculum, such as a new textbook or new state standards. Since curricular knowledge is ever changing and ever challenging, you will spend many of your teaching days in the *en garde* (or ready) position.

Activity: You're going to facilitate a *generation gap* conversation. Find two people (teachers or family or community members) who are from a different generation than you. Ask them about *your major* or *favorite subject area* during their years of schooling. Develop leading questions to see *what* they were taught and *how* it differed from your program.

Dig into your own experience to help generate questions. If you sang a song about the state capitals, in alphabetical order, when you took social studies, turn that into curriculum questions: "Did you have to memorize the states and their capitals? How did that assignment connect with other content in the class?"

Reflection: How have things changed? How are they the same? With the information explosion, has the coverage of subjects exploded as well? in what ways? What do you think is driving what we teach and how we include new concepts and content? Can you make any predictions about the curriculum you will be covering and testing when you begin teaching?

2:2 SCOPING SCHOOL CULTURE

INTASC PRINCIPLE 2
Human Development and Learning

Purpose: Have you ever wanted to "stop the world" and, rather than get off, take the time to really observe people's behavior? Here's your chance. Your inherent curiosity, coupled with some directed observations, can offer a rich opportunity to study the growth and development of students.

Activity: Visit an elementary, middle, or high school campus, preferably one that you anticipate will be different from your own experience. Set yourself up to the side of the major thoroughfares with notepad, laptop, or sketchbook and make "notes." Consider three public and informal spaces: cafeteria, hallways, open space quad, blacktop/field, or "recess" areas.

- What does the "scene" look like? How are individuals and groups dressed? What else do you see?

- Focus on students and their body language. What's the composition of groups, pairs, or individuals? Who's talking, touching, or teasing? Describe the behavior.

- Focus on staff or faculty in the area. What are their roles? Are they detached, integrated, or "in charge"? Describe their actions.

- What noise is evident—music, varied languages, general chatter, or the "sounds of silence"?

- Compare and contrast these areas: cafeteria, hallways, open spaces. (Are various cliques entitled to special spots or activities? Is studying more evident in one section?

- What other behaviors, in general, do you observe?

Reflection: Check in with classmates who scoped out different schools and compare notes. Did the students' behavior appear to vary by such factors as gender, race, physical size, language fluency, and clothing? What insights did you have about this student body and individual pupils? How did their use of time and space in the halls, cafeteria, and open areas interest and inform you? What insights about student and teacher behavior might you draw from your observations? How might these observations help you understand human development?

2:3 CURRICULUM BIAS BUSTERS

Purpose: The way curricular materials portray different groups can promote either knowledge or stereotypes. In this activity, you will practice examining materials for bias. As a teacher, you must recognize bias, so that you can select good resources or adapt materials to serve multiple perspectives.

Activity: Review the seven forms of bias discussed in Chapter 7. Borrow a K–12 textbook (appropriate for your subject major or grade level) from your college's curriculum resource center, a local school, or a teaching friend. Look for an example of each form of bias, but here's the trick: Your illustration can be either positive (for example, overcoming gender *invisibility*) or negative (for instance, reinforcing a racial *stereotype*).

Reflection: Selecting examples was intended to help you clarify your understanding of these forms of bias. Do several forms of bias appear in the same example? Why might this be the case? For each negative selection, how might you overcome this bias with your students?

FORM: SCOPING
SCHOOL CULTURE

INTASC PRINCIPLE 3
Diversity in Learning

FORM: BIAS BUSTERS

Bias Busters			
Book Title/Author/Reference Information:			
Brief description of text:			
Type of Bias	**+ or −**	**Page #**	**Example**
1. Invisibility			
2. Stereotyping			
3. Imbalance and selectivity			
4. Unreality			
5. Fragmentation and isolation			
6. Linguistic bias			
7. Cosmetic bias			

2:4 TIME CAPSULE

INTASC PRINCIPLE 4
Variety of Instructional Strategies

Purpose: Good teachers want students to think critically, solve problems, and develop skills, and good teachers have purposeful ways of making this happen in classrooms. One strategy is to use a wide variety of materials (such as videotapes, comic strips, theater costumes) to promote instruction. A beginning teacher wrote, "I found that the path of least resistance was just to teach from books, notes—it took effort to use technology, hands-on artifacts, and so on, but it was very effective." Successfully incorporating teaching aids is indicative of a high-performing teacher.

Activity: Imagine you are creating a time capsule of the critical teaching aids for your classroom. Use a student backpack—a symbolic capsule of our times. What items would you pack inside to share with the generation of teachers one century from now? What symbols must be included that represent our curriculum? What educational minutia are a "must have"? Draw, video, list, or actually pack the items in your capsule.

Reflection: Spend "show-and-tell" time with classmates by sharing your backpack time capsule. What teaching aids in your bag of tricks are memorable? What items did you overlook or leave out?

2:5 RULES AND REGULATIONS: A SAMPLER

INTASC PRINCIPLE 5
Motivation and Management

Purpose: Most teachers struggle to balance motivating students with managing them. Sometimes, in an attempt to keep it "all together and in control" teachers overregulate a class. At other times, they wait too long to rein in exuberant students. Start to consider behavior techniques right along with your study of schools, because, as a prospective teacher, you need to begin figuring out how you will manage a classroom.

Activity: Gather at least four samples of school and class rules. You could use technology to collect regulations, policies, and practices. At a low-tech level, use a copying machine to duplicate examples from a local school, a peer's portfolio, or a management course. You might photograph or videotape posted class (or library, cafeteria, or office) rules. Surfing the Internet could connect you with teachers who would share their standards or rules. Students online might also add to your file. There are also websites on student behavior and management that you will find useful.

Reflection: Consider your collection and what you might do during the first week of school to balance motivation and management. Which of these rules and approaches appeal to you? How will you implement your own management plan? Will you post rules or create them with your class? Will you avoid the topic until a need arises? Will you rely on the grade level or department rules, or will you distinguish yourself with personal policy and practice? How do you anticipate that you will manage management?

2:6 A PUBLIC SERVICE ANNOUNCEMENT FOR YOUR NATIONAL EDUCATION GOALS

Purpose: Standards and goals provide direction for schools and educators. Your ability to formulate and express your own education goals can guide your formal application for a teaching position. Communicating your goals clearly and concisely will let you practice verbal language skills, a foundation of effective instruction.

INTASC PRINCIPLE 6 Communication Skills

Activity: Develop a public service announcement (PSA) supporting your own national goals, ones you feel strongly about. Think of it as a radio spot (thirty to forty-five seconds long) that tells the listening public just what *they* need to know. Write it, edit it, and practice it with a stop watch. Rewrite, edit again, and rehearse until it's right. You may not always be able to practice and tighten your lessons this thoroughly, but the strategies you use to develop and refine your PSA are a necessary part of your communication repertoire.

Deliver your PSAs in small groups during a class session, maybe as a series of "commercial breaks."

Reflection: How were your peers' messages similar or different? Which PSAs appealed to you the most? Why? If you were given a second chance, how would you redo your PSA? Sometimes, negative media attention surrounds education, and it is tough to let the public know about the positive things that occur. Developing PSAs is probably a useful device. What topic would you choose for your next one?

2:7 STORY STARTERS

Purpose: Chapter 5, "Life in Schools," detailed several factors of effective schools: strong leadership, a clear school mission, a safe and orderly climate, the monitoring of student progress, and high expectations. These characteristics are also evident in successful classrooms. Your purpose is to do the good, conscious planning that can make instruction effective in five classroom scenarios.

INTASC PRINCIPLE 7 Instructional Planning Skills

Activity: To help you make this school-classroom connection, we have given you some *story starters*. It's your job to finish the following scenarios so they illustrate the connection between the five factors and student achievement. In keeping with Rosenthal and Jacobson's study, we hold high expectations for your ability to finish these stories with endings that promote student achievement. It's like making your own happy endings. Working in teaching teams or small groups might assist you in being both creative and on target.

1. The principal at your new school is an experienced educator and a true model of effective leadership. First-year teachers are required to submit sample lesson plans. You have a meeting with the principal this week, and you pack your old lesson plan file to take with you. What happens? (Remember—knowing what you've studied about effective schools, create a positive ending to our story starter, one that promotes student achievement.)

2. You have just accepted a job at a school that has revised and simplified its mission statement. One aspect of a school mission is a phrase that adorns the school's letterhead and is emblazoned across the cafeteria wall, such as *Every student's a winner.* At back-to-school night, in just two weeks, you are to share this mission with parents. What happens?

3. You join a high school faculty and hear that many of the teachers tend to avoid conflict with students by avoiding disciplining or managing them outside of the classroom. You are assigned to cover your department wing during nutrition break. Many kids start snacking near their lockers, a breach of policy. What happens?

4. You are trying to give your students meaningful homework and monitor it for accuracy. You know that you must provide feedback on their assignments that is informative and timely. In your first month of instruction, you sometimes grade papers, have partners edit assignments, and keep accurate records on all their efforts. What else do you do, and what happens? (Hey, it's your story. Make it a good one!)

5. You have a student in your class who is unlike anyone you've ever encountered. Thinking of the numerous possibilities, describe this student (in imaginative detail) and determine how your expectations will encourage this student's academic achievement. What will you think, say, and do? What happens? (Is there a movie script offer in your future?)

Reflection: Did you find some story starters easy to finish, others harder? Why? What did you learn about the connection between effective schools and student achievement? What factors do you suspect will carry over to your own teaching? Why?

2:8 MEMOIRS OF A TIME-TESTED STUDENT

Purpose: National, state, and district tests are a huge part of school culture, yet few teachers analyze their own role in the current testing climate. This activity will help you define that role.

Activity: Think about the quizzes and tests you took as a student. Either through your own journal entry or a conversation with a partner (live, taped, or via an Internet chat room), consider the following questions as you review and ponder your experiences with test taking:

- What's an early memory of a "big deal" test? sharpening your number 2 pencil? unsealing special pamphlets in elementary school? being tucked in a cardboard "cubby" for privacy? proctors milling through rows, looking for cheating? a just-for-you test accommodating special needs? the President's Council on Physical Fitness twelve-minute run? taking a review course for the PSATs and SATs? Try to recall the good, the bad, and the ugly.

- Consider thoughts from your classmates and see if more recollections are sparked.

- On one side of the *You Be the Judge* sheet, brainstorm things that teachers can do to ensure a positive climate for student testing. On the other side, list actions teachers should definitely avoid.

You Be the Judge: Testing "Do's and Don'ts"	
What Teachers SHOULD Do . . .	**What Teacher Should NOT Do . . .**
1. Describe the purpose of the test*	1. Leave the room*
2.	2.
3.	3.
etc.	etc.

*Sample items.

OLC

FORM: YOU BE THE JUDGE: "TESTING DO'S AND DON'TS"

Reflection: Looking back, would you rate your teachers as helpful, or not so helpful, when it comes to administering quizzes and tests? Are there any teacher actions you would replicate in terms of test-giving style?

2:9 REFLECTIONS OF A HIGH SCHOOL YEARBOOK

Purpose: Part 2 of this text looked at all aspects of the school scene, from the student role to a teacher's reality. While you may have shifted perspective as you walked away from your high school graduation ceremony, the purpose of this activity is to look back and assess some of your choices and actions. Your high school yearbook symbolizes a snapshot of your school and a view of yourself in the social system. What does it show you about your school, yourself, and others?

INTASC PRINCIPLE 9
Reflection and Responsibility

Activity: Dig out your high school yearbook or see if it is posted on the Internet. Many schools now have their own web pages. Look at it carefully. Ponder the following points for later reflection:

- Find yourself. How often and where are you? What is the caption under your senior photo? Did you get caught in candid shots? Are you with clubs, in activities, and in teams? Are you surrounded by your friends or often on your own? Which images recall emotions: pride, embarrassment, sadness? Did your school have an FTA (Future Teachers of America) organization? Were you pictured with them? How does being a future teacher or a member of that club look today? Were your curricular strengths evident by achievements, awards, and participation? (You were an officer for the Model UN and you're now a social studies major; you belonged to the Storyteller Society and you want to be an elementary teacher; you lettered in many sports and plan to teach physical education.) In what ways are you the same or different today?

- Find your friends. In what ways were you similar or different from them? When and where do they appear?

- Find lesser-known faces. Stop and really stare at students you may have walked by for years. What of their stories do you suspect or know? What groups were they in? What labels described their lives?

- Who is invisible or missing? Are there students who appear only in their "mug shot" and never as part of the campus culture? Do female or male students, from varied racial and ethnic groups, dominate particular activities or campus locales?

- What about the faculty and administration? Are they a part of or apart from your yearbook? How and where do you imagine yourself in the *teaching* section of the annual?

Reflection: What do you notice, about your school and yourself, as you reflect on the yearbook? How does it compare with the student cultures described in your text? How would you write or edit it today? Would you want to teach there, at a similar, or at a very different site? What *stories* from your yearbook pages would be valuable to share with classmates?

2:10 SUPPORT STAFF INTERVIEW

INTASC PRINCIPLE 10
Relationships and
Partnerships

Purpose: When you have a teaching job, you become part of a learning community. Knowing about the roles and responsibilities of support personnel will enhance your understanding of the way schools work. Nonteaching employees contribute significantly to a well-functioning school. Bus drivers, clerical personnel, media and custodial staff, instructional aides, playground and lunch supervisors, resource specialists, medical and psychological professionals, and security and safety personnel all do their part. They befriend alienated kids, clean up after trashy nutrition breaks, reset chairs in an auditorium as many as eight times a day, frisk students with clothes baggy enough to cover goods and evils, know most students' names when they step up to the office counter, make lunchrooms smell like fresh cookies (maybe not quite often enough), find media materials with the leanest of hints from teachers and students, toss balls in one direction and *bench* students in another, and provide one-on-one practice for the most unique of tasks and talents. And these support personnel have their own special view of students, schools, and teachers. Fostering relationships with these colleagues is a way to create a valuable extension of your classroom community.

Activity: Try to schedule a 20-minute interview with one of the nonteaching employees at a local school. Spend the time asking your interviewee about his or her job. What's a day in the life of_____ like? What are his or her reasons for working at a school? What are the benefits and drawbacks? How do students and teachers impact the employee's work? How do teachers *support* the support personnel?

Reflection: Exchange interview reflections with classmates. What information was confirmed by your interview? What new information have you gathered about the job and/or the personnel? How might this interview affect your rapport and behavior with support staff?

Portfolio Artifact Collection

2:P1 WHAT'S UP TO STANDARD?

Purpose: As you enter teaching, make sure you are knowledgeable about the current standards in your field. Many professional associations have developed national curriculum standards and program goals. Groups from AAHPERD (American Alliance for Health, Physical Education, Recreation and Dance) to NCTE (National Council of Teachers of English) have promoted their frameworks and subject-matter expertise.

Activity: Collect the most recent professional curriculum standards in your major or high interest field.

2:P3 CLIPPINGS FILE ON MULTICULTURALISM

Purpose: Education is *In the News;* just like the clippings you will find throughout this text, news accounts can grab our interests or reinforce our anxieties. Start a multicultural news file to expand your understanding of diversity. Be on the alert for ways you might incorporate what you learn into your teaching.

Activity: Your clippings file on multicultural education may collect topics from Afrocentrism to Zen Buddhism. The coverage might provide stories of intolerance or inspiration. Read them and highlight comments that are significant. Be sure to log the source and date on each article.

THIS *INTER-MISSION* IS FINISHED. STRETCH YOUR BODY A BIT; THEN SETTLE IN FOR PART 3: "FOUNDATIONS."

INTASC PRINCIPLE 1
Knowledge of Subject Matter

INTASC PRINCIPLE 3
Diversity in Learning

3

Foundations

CLASS ACT

A chilly morning in early September 1952. My parents walked me down the dirt road to the state highway, where the No. 3 school bus passed by our farm. I boarded the faded yellow bus with no idea where I was going. Half an hour later, I was deposited in front of an old brick building: Dardanelle Elementary School. ● I walked into a school that had been constructed in 1869, and had once housed both elementary and secondary students. Now grades one through six filled the school. Greeting me at the schoolhouse door, the principal escorted me to my first grade class. Stepping inside the classroom, it seemed as if I had entered the nineteenth century. The two-seat student desks were bolted to the floor, facing the teacher's desk that rested upon a wooden platform. A cracked chalkboard stood behind the teacher's desk. My assigned seat was next to a "town girl" on the first row. ● After printing her name on the chalkboard, Mrs. "T" began the year-long process of teaching academic skills to students who had had no preparation for the first grade. We had no preschool, no kindergarten, and no educational television in those days. It was Mrs. T's job to fill our minds with basic academic knowledge. For seven hours each day, she lectured, recited, dictated, directed, questioned, and criticized. If we broke any of her many rules, we could expect a tongue-lashing or a public spanking, for physical punishment was not unusual back then. ● Though she was a harsh taskmaster, Mrs. T proved an effective teacher. Using textbooks from the 1930s, she taught us how to read, write, and cipher. Our favorite class was spelling, because the textbooks were new, and it was also our last class of the day. At three o'clock every afternoon, the dismissal bell freed us. Mrs. T, who had been a member of the Woman's Army Corps during World War II, was a warrior on the educational front lines in 1952. This massive wave of children, which we now call the "baby boom," would strain the resources of America's educational system. It was left to the well-educated but ill-paid American teachers to cope with this flood of students. Mrs. T created a nineteenth-century style classroom climate to allow her to cope with thirty illiterate, rambunctious children, who came from the county seat, outlying hamlets, and scattered rural farms. She narrowed the curriculum to four essential subjects—reading, writing, spelling, and mathematics. Teaching the essential subject in time-honored fashion, she tolerated no "misbehavior" and ruled her classroom with an iron hand. ● In retrospect, I admire Mrs. T's accomplishments during the 1952–1953 school year. In one year, she taught us the basic academic skills we needed for success in the upper grades. Most of her students not only completed high school, but they also finished college. Several even managed to earn post-graduate degrees. However, her harsh classroom climate left its mark. Today, when I walk into a classroom, I feel the old fear that I experienced in her class fifty years ago. Mrs. T taught me about the lifelong influence that a powerful first grade teacher can have. And she taught me something about myself as well: my personal commitment to create a classroom without fear.

John Solomon Otto
American University

SUBMIT YOUR OWN *CLASS ACT:* Click on *Class Acts* and submit a *Class Act* about a teacher who has made a difference in your life. Visit the Online Learning Center to read more *Class Acts*.

8 The History of American Education

FOCUS QUESTIONS

1. What was the nature and purpose of colonial education?
2. How did the Common School Movement influence the idea of universal education?
3. How did teaching become a "gendered" career?
4. How did secondary schools evolve?
5. How have twentieth century school reform efforts influenced schools?
6. What were the main tenets of the Progressive Education movement?
7. What role has the federal government played in American education?
8. Who are some of the key individuals who have helped fashion today's schools?

WHAT DO YOU THINK? **How Much Do You Already Know about the History of Education?** Before reading the chapter, take a quiz that includes some "basics" and fun facts.

CHAPTER PREVIEW

Understanding the history of America's schools offers you perspective—a sense of your place in your new profession. Your classroom is a living tribute to past achievements and sacrifices.

In this chapter, we will trace American education from colonial times to the present. Education during the colonial period was intended to further religious goals and was offered primarily to white males—typically, wealthy white males. For females and children of color, education was difficult to attain, and, even when available, the education was often inferior. Over time, educational exclusivity diminished, but, even today, wealth, race, and gender continue to impact educational quality. To a great extent, the story of American education is a battle to open the schoolhouse door to more and more of our citizens. In this chapter, we share the story of the struggle to have America honor its commitment to equality. Later in this book, in Chapter 12 "The Struggle for Educational Opportunity," we will offer additional insights into the effort to open the schoolhouse door.

The complex network of expectations surrounding today's schools is the product of a society that has been evolving for over three centuries. Individuals, groups, and the government all have contributed to making public schools more accessible. Benjamin Franklin, Horace Mann, Emma Hart Willard, and Mary McLeod Bethune, for example, fought to free America from historical biases. New federal laws were designed to create more equitable and effective educational opportunities. Today, the federal focus is to increase school competition, identify failing schools, and either "fix" them or replace them. But the notion of competition and standards is only the most recent chapter in the story of our nation's schools. In the colonial era, the goals were simpler: to teach the Scriptures and to develop a religious community. We will begin by looking into the classroom of Christopher Lamb, a New England teacher in one of the earliest American schools, over three centuries ago.

Christopher Lamb's Colonial Classroom

The frigid wintry wind knifed through Christopher Lamb's coat, chilling him to the bone as he walked in the predawn darkness. The single bucket of firewood that he lugged, intended to keep his seventeenth-century New England schoolroom warm all day, would clearly not do the job. Once the fire was started, Christopher focused on his other teaching tasks: carrying in a bucket of water for the class, sweeping the floor, and mending the ever so fragile pen points for the students. More than an hour after Christopher's predawn activities had begun, Margaret, the first student, arrived. Although Margaret, like most girls, would stay in school for only a year or two, Christopher believed that she should learn to read the Bible, so that she could be a better wife and mother. With any luck, she might even learn to write her name before she left school. But that was really not all that important for girls. As other students trickled in, they were directed to either the boys' bench or the girls' bench, where, in turn, they read their Testament aloud.

Those who read the Scriptures without error took their place at the table and wrote on their slates. Christopher was amazed at how poorly some students read, tripping over every other word, whereas others read quite fluently. The last student to finish, Benjamin, slowly rose from the bench, cringing. Christopher called out, "Lazy pupil," and a chorus of children's voices chimed in: "Lazy pupil. Lazy pupil. Lazy pupil." Benjamin, if not totally inured to the taunts, was no longer crushed by them, either. He slowly made his way to the end of the student line.

After the recitation and writing lessons, all the children were lined up and examined, to make certain they had washed and combed. A psalm was sung, and Mr. Lamb exhorted the students to walk in God's footsteps. For ten minutes, the class and teacher knelt in prayer. Each student then recited the day's biblical lesson. Those who had memorized their lessons received an *O*, written on their hand, a mark of excellence. Those who failed to recite their lessons correctly after three attempts once again were called "lazy pupil" by the entire class, and this time their names were written down. If by the end of the day they had finally learned the lesson, their names were erased from the list, and all the children called out "Diligent!" to those students.

Christopher Lamb had been an apprentice teacher for five years before accepting this position. He rejected the rod approach used so frequently by his master teacher. Using the children to provide rewards and punishments was far more effective than welts and bruises, marks left by a teacher's rod. Yes, Christopher was somewhat unorthodox, perhaps even a bit revolutionary, but the challenges of contemporary seventeenth-century society demanded forward-thinking educators, such as Christopher Lamb.

Colonial New England Education: God's Classrooms

One of the striking differences between Christopher Lamb's colonial classroom and today's typical public school is the role of religion in education. The religious fervor that drove the Puritans to America also drove them to provide religious education for their young, making New England the cradle of American education. In Christopher Lamb's time, school was meant to save souls. Education provided a path to heaven, and reading, writing, and moral development all revolved around the Bible.

Early colonial education, both in New England and in other colonies, often began in the home. (Today's home schooling movement is not a *new* approach.) The family was the major educational resource for youngsters, and the first lessons typically focused on reading. Values, manners, social graces, and even vocational skills were taught by parents and grandparents. Home instruction eventually became more specialized, and some women began to devote their time to teaching, converting their homes into schools. These "dames" taught reading, writing, and computation, and their homes became known as **dame schools.** A "dame," or well-respected woman with an interest in education, became (for a fee) the community's teacher.

An **apprenticeship** program rounded out a child's colonial education. While boys, sometimes as young as 7 years of age, were sent to live with masters who taught them a trade, girls typically learned homemaking skills from their mothers. Apprenticeship programs for boys involved not only learning skilled crafts but also managing farms and shops. Many colonies required that masters teach reading and writing as well as vocational skills. The masters served **_in loco parentis_**—that is, in place of the child's parent. The competencies of the masters guiding apprentices varied greatly, as did the talents of family members, dames, ministers, and others fulfilling the teaching role. Not surprisingly, this educational hodgepodge did not always lead to a well-educated citizenry; a more formal structure was needed.

Twenty-two years after arriving in the New World, the Puritans living in the Commonwealth of Massachusetts passed a law requiring that parents and masters of apprentices be checked periodically to ensure that children were being taught properly. Five years later, in 1647, Massachusetts took even more rigorous

Recitation lesson in a colonial classroom.

measures to ensure the education of its children. The Massachusetts Law of 1647, more commonly known as the **Old Deluder Satan Law**—the Puritans' attempt to thwart Satan's trickery with Scripture-reading citizens—required that

- Every town of 50 households must appoint and pay a teacher of reading and writing.
- Every town of 100 households must provide a (Latin) grammar school to prepare youths for the university, under a penalty of £5 for failure to do so.[1]

By 1680, such laws had spread throughout most of New England. The settlement patterns of the Puritans, who lived in towns and communities rather than scattered throughout the countryside, made establishing schools relatively uncomplicated. After learning to read and write, most girls returned home to practice the art of housekeeping. Boys who could afford to pay for their education went on to a **Latin grammar school.** In 1635, only fifteen years after arriving in America's wilderness, the Puritans established their first Latin grammar school in Boston. The Boston Latin Grammar School was not unlike a "prep" school for boys and was similar to the classical schools of Europe. The Boston Latin Grammar School was a rather exclusive school for boys of wealth, charging tuition to teach boys between the ages of 7 and 14.

Many consider the Boston Latin Grammar School to be the first step on the road to creating the American high school, although the school's curriculum reflected European roots. Students were expected to read and recite (in Latin, of course) the works of Cicero, Ovid, and Erasmus. In Greek, they read the works of Socrates and Homer. (Back to basics in colonial times meant back to the glory of Rome and Greece.) By the eighteenth century, the grammar school had incorporated mathematics, science, and modern languages. Classes started at 7 A.M., recessed at 11 A.M., and picked up from 1 P.M. until 5 P.M. Graduates were expected to go on to college and become colonial leaders, especially ministers.

Within a year of the founding of the Boston Latin Grammar School, Harvard College was established specifically to prepare ministers. Founded in 1636, Harvard was the first college in America, the jewel in the Puritans' religious and educational crown.[2]

For attendance at exclusive schools, such as Boston Latin Grammar, or at college, wealth was critical. The least desirable educational and apprenticeship opportunities were left to the poor. Some civic-minded communities made basic education in reading and writing more available to the poor, but only to families who would publicly admit their poverty by signing a "Pauper's Oath." Broadcasting one's poverty was no less offensive in colonial times than today, and many chose to have their children remain illiterate rather than sign such a public admission. The result was that most poor children remained outside the educational system.

Blacks, in America since 1619, and Native Americans were typically denied educational opportunities. In rare cases, religious groups, such as the Quakers, created special schools for children of color.[3] But these were the exceptions. Through racism and slavery, whites denied formal schooling to most Native Americans and blacks; they also eventually passed laws prohibiting their education. (See Chapter 12, "The Struggle for Educational Opportunity," for a more complete review of these issues.) Girls did not fare much better. After they had learned the rudiments of reading and writing, girls were taught the tasks related to their future roles as mother and wife. They were taught various handicrafts. Girls memorized the alphabet and then learned to stitch and display their accomplishments. They also learned to reproduce and attractively display religious sayings, on the road to becoming good Christian wives and mothers. As much as we value these beautiful samplers today, they are a sad reminder of a time when they marked the academic finish line for girls, the diploma of a second-rate education, a depressing denial of equal educational rights.

Location greatly influenced educational opportunities. The northern colonies were settled by Puritans who lived in towns and communities relatively close to one another. Their religious fervor and proximity made the creation of community schools dedicated to teaching the Bible a predictable development.

In the middle colonies, the range of European religious and ethnic groups (Puritans, Catholics, Mennonites, the Dutch, and Swedes) created, if not a melting pot, a limited tolerance for diversity.[4] Various religious groups established schools, and apprenticeships groomed youngsters for a variety of careers, including teaching. In the middle colonies, the development of commerce and mercantile demands promoted the formation of private schools devoted to job training. By the 1700s, private teachers and night schools were functioning in Philadelphia and New York, teaching accounting, navigation, French, and Spanish.

The first city in North America was St. Augustine, Florida, where there is evidence that the Spanish settlers established schools. In terms of education, the southern English colonies trailed behind. The rural, sparsely populated southern colonies developed an educational system that was responsive to plantation society. Wealthy plantation owners took tutors into their homes to teach their children not only basic academic skills but also the social graces appropriate to their station in life. Plantation owners' children learned the proper way to entertain guests and "manage" slaves, using such texts as *The Complete Gentleman*. Wealthy young men seeking higher education were sent to Europe. Girls made do with just an introduction to academics and a greater focus on their social responsibilities. Poor white children might have had rudimentary home instruction in reading, writing, and computation. Black children made do with little if any instruction and, as time went by, encountered laws that actually prohibited their education entirely.[5]

Education has come a long way from colonial days and from Christopher Lamb's class—or has it? Consider the following:

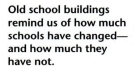

Old school buildings remind us of how much schools have changed—and how much they have not.

THE DEVELOPMENT OF COLONIAL HIGHER EDUCATION

Many of today's colleges and universities began as small, religiously sponsored institutions founded to train the clergy. The first fifteen institutions of higher education established in the colonies were all affiliated with a religious denomination.

Year	Institution	Year	Institution
1636	Harvard University	1769	Dartmouth University
1693	College of William and Mary	1782	Washington College
1701	Yale University	1782	Washington and Lee University
1746	Princeton University	1783	Hampton-Sidney College
1754	King's College (Columbia University)	1783	Transylvania College
1755	University of Pennsylvania	1783	Dickinson College
1765	Brown University	1784	St. John's College
1766	Queen's College (Rutgers University)		

REFLECTION

What religious artifacts, if any, exist on these campuses today? Do you know when your campus was founded? Did that period influence the culture of your college?

1. The colonial experience established many of today's educational norms:
   - Local control of schools
   - Compulsory education
   - Tax-supported schools
   - State standards for teaching and schools

2. The colonial experience highlighted many of the persistent tension points challenging schools today:
   - What is the role of religion in the classroom?
   - How can we equalize the quality of education in various communities?
   - How can the barriers of racism, sexism, religious intolerance, and classism be eliminated, so that all children receive equal educational opportunity?
   - How can we prepare the most competent teachers?

A New Nation Shapes Education

The ideas that led to the American Revolution revolutionized our schools. European beliefs and practices, which had pervaded America's schools, were gradually abandoned as the new national character was formed. None of these beliefs had been more firmly adhered to than the integration of the state and religion.

In sixteenth- and seventeenth-century England, the Puritans' desire to reform the Church of England was viewed as treason. The Puritans encountered both religious

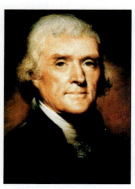

In addition to serving two terms as president, Thomas Jefferson was the colonial era's most eloquent spokesperson for education and was the founder of the University of Virginia.

and political opposition, and they looked to the New World as an escape from persecution. However, they came to America *not* to establish religious freedom, as our history books sometimes suggest, but to establish their own church as supreme, both religiously and politically. The Puritans were neither tolerant of other religions nor interested in separating religion and politics. Nonconformers, such as the Quakers, were vigorously persecuted. The purpose of the Massachusetts colony was to establish the "true" religion of the Puritans, to create a "new Israel" in America. Schools were simply an extension of the religious state, designed to teach the young to read and understand the Bible and to do honorable battle with Satan.

During the 1700s, American education was reconstructed to meet broader, nonsectarian goals. Such leaders as **Thomas Jefferson** wanted to go beyond educating a small elite class or providing only religious instruction. Jefferson maintained that education should be more widely available to white children from all economic and social classes. Public citizens began to question the usefulness of rudimentary skills taught in a school year of just three or four months. They questioned the value of mastering Greek and Latin classics in the Latin grammar schools, when practical skills were in short supply in the New World.

In 1749, **Benjamin Franklin** penned *Proposals Relating to the Youth of Pennsylvania,* suggesting a new kind of secondary school to replace the Latin grammar school—the **academy.** Two years later, the **Franklin Academy** was established, free of religious influence and offering a variety of practical subjects, including mathematics, astronomy, athletics, navigation, dramatics, and bookkeeping. Students were able to choose some of their courses, thus setting the precedent for elective courses and programs at the secondary level. In the late 1700s, it was the Franklin Academy and not the Boston Latin Grammar School that was considered the most important secondary school in America.[6]

The Franklin Academy accepted both girls and boys who could afford the tuition, and the practical curriculum became an attractive innovation. Franklin's Academy sparked the establishment of six thousand academies in the century that followed, including Phillips Academy at Andover, Massachusetts (1778), and Phillips Exeter Academy in Exeter, New Hampshire (1783). The original Franklin Academy eventually became the University of Pennsylvania.

Jefferson's commitment to educating all white Americans, rich and poor, at government expense, and Franklin's commitment to a practical program of nonsectarian study offering elective courses severed American educational thought from its European roots. Many years passed before these ideas became widely established practices, but the pattern for innovation and a truly American approach to education was taking shape.

The Common School Movement

During the early decades of the nineteenth century, education was often viewed as a luxury. However, even parents who could afford such a luxury had limited choices. The town schools still existed in Massachusetts, and some charity schools served the poor and orphans. Dame schools varied in quality. In some areas, religious schools of one denomination prevailed, while, in rural areas and the South, few schools existed at all. The United States was a patchwork quilt of schools, tied together by the reality that money was needed to attain a decent education.

A rich variety of textbooks, media, library books, and computer software provide today's teachers with curricular resources unimaginable just a few years ago. As a teacher, you will come across references to some of the limited but influential curriculum materials of the past. Here is a brief profile of the best-known instructional materials from yesterday's schools.

HORNBOOK

The most common teaching device in colonial schools, the **hornbook** consisted of an alphabet sheet covered by a thin, transparent sheet made from a cow's horn. The alphabet and the horn covering were tacked to a paddle-shaped piece of wood and often hung by a leather strap around the student's neck. Originating in medieval Europe, the hornbook provided colonial children with their introduction to the alphabet and reading.

NEW ENGLAND PRIMER

The first real textbook, the ***New England Primer*** was a tiny 2½- by 4½-inch book containing 50 to 100 pages of alphabet, words, and small verses accompanied by woodcut illustrations. First published in 1690, it was virtually the only reading text used in colonial schools until about 1800. The *Primer* reflected the religious orientation of colonial schools. A typical verse was

> In Adam's Fall
> We sinned all.
> Thy Life to mend,
> This Book attend
> The idle fool
> Is whipt at School.

AMERICAN SPELLING BOOK

The task undertaken by Noah Webster was to define and nourish the new American culture. His ***American Spelling Book*** replaced the *New England Primer* as the most common elementary textbook. The book contained the alphabet, syllables, consonants, rules for speaking, readings, short stories, and moral advice. The bulk of the book was taken up by lists of words. Royalty income from the sale of millions of copies of this book supported Webster in his other efforts to standardize the American language, including his best-known work, which is still used today, the *American Dictionary*.

MCGUFFEY READERS

William Holmes McGuffey was a minister, professor, and college president who believed that clean living, hard work, and literacy were the virtues to instill in children. He wrote a series of readers that emphasized the work ethic, patriotism, heroism, and morality. It is estimated that more than 100 million copies of McGuffey Readers educated several generations of Americans between 1836 and 1920. **McGuffey Readers** are noteworthy because they were geared for different grade levels and paved the way for graded elementary schools.

REFLECTION

Can you detect the morals and traditional values being promoted in today's texts? Can you cite any examples?

During the early decades of the nineteenth century, the democratic ideal became popular as many "common people"—immigrants, small farmers, and urban laborers—demanded greater participation in the democracy. With the election of Andrew Jackson in 1828, the voices of many poor white people were heard, particularly their demands for educational access. Many more decades would pass before additional voices—particularly those of people of color—would also be heard.

Horace Mann became the nation's leading advocate for the establishment of a **common school** open to all. Today we know this common school as the public **elementary school.** Historians consider Horace Mann to be the outstanding proponent of education for the common person (the common school movement), and he is often referred to as "the father of the public school." (More about Mann appears in The Education Hall of Fame, later in this chapter.) Mann helped create the Massachusetts State Board of Education and in 1837 became its secretary, a position similar to today's state superintendent of schools. In this role, Mann began an effort to reform education, believing that public education should serve both practical and idealistic goals. In practical terms, both business and industry would benefit from educated workers, resulting in a more productive economy. In idealistic terms, public schools should help us identify and nurture the talents in poor as well as wealthy children, and schools should ameliorate social disharmony.[7] Mann decried the rifts between rich and poor, Calvinists and religious reformers, new Irish immigrants and native workers. A common school instilling common and humane moral values could reduce such social disharmony (a popular belief today as well). Mann attempted to promote such values, but he encountered strong opposition when the values he selected revealed a distinct religious bias, one that offended Calvinists, atheists, Jews, Catholics, and others. His moral program to create a common set of beliefs had the opposite impact, igniting a dispute over the role of religion in school.

The idea of public education is so commonplace today that it seems difficult to imagine another system. But Horace Mann, along with such allies as Henry Barnard of Connecticut, fought a long and difficult battle to win the acceptance of public elementary schools. The opposition was powerful. Business interests predicted disaster if their labor pool of children were taken away. Concerned taxpayers protested the additional tax monies needed to support public education. There was also the competition. Private schools and religious groups sponsoring their own schools protested the establishment of free schools. Americans wondered what would become of a nation in which everyone received an elementary education. Would this not produce

Contributing to the school reforms of the nineteenth century were the poor physical conditions that characterized most U.S. schools.

overeducated citizens, questioning authority and promoting self-interest? The opposition to public elementary schools was often fierce, but Horace Mann and his allies prevailed.

As he fought for public schools for all, Mann also waged a battle for high-quality schools. He continually attempted to build new and better schools, which was a problem, since so many Massachusetts schools were in deplorable condition. By publicly disseminating information about which communities had well-built or poorly built schools, he applied public pressure on districts to improve their school buildings. He worked for effective teacher training programs as well and promoted more stringent teacher licensing procedures. As a result of his efforts, several **normal schools** were founded in Massachusetts, schools devoted to preparing teachers in pedagogy, the best ways to teach children. He also championed newer teaching methods designed to improve and modernize classroom instruction. He opposed the routine practice of corporal punishment and sought ways to positively motivate students to learn. Mann emphasized practical subjects useful to children and to adult society, rather than the mastery of Greek and Latin. Mann saw education as a great investment, for individuals and for the country, and he worked for many years to make free public education a reality. He worked for the abolition of slavery, promoted women's educational and economic rights, and even fought alongside the temperance movement to limit the negative impact of alcohol. He was not only a committed educator but a committed reformer as well.

By the time of the Civil War, this radical notion of the public elementary school had become widespread and widely accepted. Educational historian Lawrence Cremin summarized the advance of the common school movement in his book *The Transformation of the School:*

> A majority of the states had established public school systems, and a good half of the nation's children were already getting some formal education. Elementary schools were becoming widely available; in some states, like Massachusetts, New York, and Pennsylvania, the notion of free public education was slowly expanding to include secondary schools; and in a few, like Michigan and Wisconsin, the public school system was already capped by a state university. There were, of course, significant variations from state to state and from region to region. New England, long a pioneer in public education, also had an established tradition of private education, and private schools continued to flourish there. The Midwest, on the other hand, sent a far greater proportion of its school children to public institutions. The southern states, with the exception of North Carolina, tended to lag behind, and did not generally establish popular schooling until after the Civil War.[8]

Spinsters, Bachelors, and Gender Barriers in Teaching

Textbooks typically explore history's "big picture," focusing on how schools developed or how national reform movements grew. But too often this approach misses the personal, often moving, stories in history. One poignant thread of stories in our nation's history concerns how gender and sexuality have been used to short-circuit the contributions of both women and men in education. While some teachers have courageously fought such confining social conventions, many others have been victimized. Their stories are worth remembering.

Although today's popular perception is that teaching is predominantly a female career, in fact, men dominated teaching well into the mid-nineteenth century. Teaching was a **gendered career**, and it was gendered "male." Although a few women taught at home in *dame schools,* the first women to become teachers in regular school settings, earning a public salary, were viewed as gender trespassers, "unsexed" by their ambition, and considered masculine. Concerned by this negative characterization, early feminists such as Catherine Beecher implored female teachers to accentuate their feminine traits, highlight their domestic skills, and continue their preparation for marriage.[9] Despite the national reluctance to allow women into the workforce, and despite the perception that teachers should be male, the demand for more and inexpensive teachers created by common schools made the hiring of women teachers inevitable.

By the early part of the twentieth century, women constituted upwards of 90 percent of teachers. But not all women were equally welcome. School districts preferred "spinsters," women unmarried and unlikely to marry. Such women would not suffer the dual loyalties inherent in "serving" both husband and employer. Unmarried women were hired so frequently in the late nineteenth and early twentieth century that teaching and spinsterhood became synonymous. Cartoonists, authors, and reporters made the spinster school teacher a cultural icon. Boarding and rooming houses, and eventually small apartments, sometimes called *teacherages,* were built to provide accommodations for this new class of workers. Teaching was gendered again, but now it was gendered "female."

As women came to dominate teaching, the gender tables were turned, and a new concern arose: the fear that female teachers were "feminizing" boys. There were demands to bring men back to teaching, and to halt the "feminization" of young schoolboys. President Theodore Roosevelt added a touch of racism to the debate, arguing that since so many white women were choosing teaching over motherhood, they were committing "race suicide," and the continuance of the white race was in jeopardy.[10] School districts responded by actively recruiting male teachers, and male educators carved out their own niches in school systems. Administration, coaching, vocational education, and certain high school departments, specifically science and math, became male bastions.

For women, teaching meant economic and financial liberation. But not without cost. The dedicated teaching *spinsters* of the nineteenth century became the object of ridicule in the twentieth century. Women choosing teaching over motherhood were considered unnatural by a mostly male cadre of psychologists, physicians, and authors. Articles and books began to appear early in the twentieth century arguing that being unmarried caused women to be spiteful, hateful, and disgusting. The eminent psychologist G. Stanley Hall wrote an article entitled "Certain Degenerative Tendencies among Teachers," explaining why unmarried women were frustrated, bitter, and otherwise unpleasant. Political opinions parading as research soon appeared claiming that as many as half of all single teachers were lesbians. Stage shows and movies picked up the theme, portraying lesbian relationships in and beyond school settings. The National Education Association reacted by campaigning for school districts to drop their ban against hiring married women. But when the depression hit in the 1930s, the idea of hiring wives and creating two-income families was anathema: the scarce jobs were to be funneled to women living alone or to men, the family "breadwinners." It was not until the end of World War II that most school districts even employed married women.

Men who remained in teaching also paid a price. Conventional wisdom early in the twentieth century held that effeminate men were gay men, and that gay men were naturally drawn to teaching. Worse yet, gay men were considered to be a teaching time bomb, since they would be poor role models for children. All male teachers became suspect, and few were drawn to teaching. School districts avoided hiring men who did not possess a clearly masculine demeanor. (Married men with children were preferred.) The Cold War and the accompanying McCarthy anti-Communist scare of the 1950s declared war on liberal ideas and unconventional choices: Homosexuality was seen as a threat to America. "There was a list of about twenty-one things that you could be fired for. The first was to be a card-carrying Communist, and the second was to be a homosexual."[11] Single teachers declared their "healthy" heterosexuality, and gay teachers stayed hidden. During this time, the number of married teachers doubled.

While recent years have witnessed a loosening of gender straightjackets, sex stereotypes, myths, and bigotry against gays continue to restrict and confine both women and men. Men drawn to teaching young children and women seeking leadership roles confront both barriers and social sanctions. Gay and lesbian teachers (and students) frequently endure hurtful comments and discriminatory treatment. As long as these gender and sexual barriers persist, we are all the poorer.

The Secondary School Movement

With Mann's success in promoting public elementary schools, more and more citizens were given a basic education. In 1880, almost 10 million Americans were enrolled in elementary schools, and, at the upper levels of schooling, both private and public universities were established. But the gap between the elementary schools and the universities remained wide.

Massachusetts, the site of the first tax-supported elementary schools and the first college in America, was the site of the first free **secondary school.** Established in Boston in 1821, the **English Classical School** enrolled 176 students (all boys); shortly thereafter, 76 students dropped out. The notion of a public high school was slow to take root. It was not until 1852 that Boston was able to maintain a similar school for girls. The name of the boys' school was changed to The English High School and, even more simply, Boys' High School, to emphasize the more practical nature of the curriculum.

As secondary schools spread, they generally took the form of private, tuition-charging academies. Citizens did not view the secondary schools as we do today, as a free and natural extension of elementary education.[12] On the eve of the Civil War, over a quarter of a million secondary students were enrolled in six thousand

Almost from their inception, high schools in the United States have been viewed as a means of enculturating immigrant students into the mainstream of American life.

tuition-charging private academies. The curricula of these academies varied widely, some focusing on college preparation and others providing a general curriculum for students who would not continue their studies. For those wanting to attend college, these academies were a critical link. In academies founded for females or in coeducational academies, "normal" courses were often popular. The normal course prepared academy graduates for teaching careers in the common schools. A few academies provided military programs of study.

A major stumbling block to the creation of free high schools was public resistance to paying additional school taxes (sound familiar?). But, in a series of court cases, especially the **Kalamazoo, Michigan, case** in 1874, the courts ruled that taxes could be used to support secondary schools. In Michigan, citizens already had access to free elementary schools and a state-supported university. The courts saw a lack of rationality in not providing a bridge between the two. The idea of public high school slowly took hold.

During the last half of the nineteenth century, the nation moved from agrarian to industrial, from mostly rural to urban, and people viewed the elementary school as inadequate to meet the needs of a more sophisticated and industrialized society. More parents viewed the high school as an important stepping-stone to better jobs. With the gradual decrease in demand for teenage workers, high school attendance grew. Half a century earlier, the public elementary school had reflected the growing dreams and aspirations of Americans and their changing economy. Now the public high school was the benchmark of these changes.

The high school developed in a uniquely American way. As a school for students with various social class, ethnic, and religious backgrounds, the American secondary school was a radical departure from the rigid tracking system of Europe. Relatively early in a European student's career, the limits of secondary education were set, with class status and wealth often primary factors. In the United States, although the high school served the dual purposes of vocational and college preparation, this rigid European tracking system was less pronounced, and early decisions did not predetermine a child's destiny. The high school became a continuation of elementary education, a path to public higher education, and an affirmation of democracy.

While the high school grew in popularity, it soon became clear that it did not meet the needs of all its students, especially the younger ones. The **junior high school,** first established in 1909 in Columbus, Ohio, included grades 7, 8, and 9, and was designed to meet the unique needs of preadolescents. More individualized instruction, a strong emphasis on guidance and counseling, and a core curriculum were designed to respond to the academic, physiological, social, and psychological characteristics of preadolescents. The junior high school concept was further refined in the **middle school,** which included grades 5–8. Created in 1950, the middle school was built on the experiences of the junior high school, while stressing team teaching, interdisciplinary learning, de-emphasizing the senior high school's heavy emphasis on both subject matter mastery and competitive sports. During the last decades of the twentieth century, middle schools were rapidly replacing junior high schools.[13]

School Reform Efforts

In 1890, the United States was a vibrant nation undergoing a profound transformation. Vast new industries were taking shape; giant corporations were formed; labor was restive; massive numbers of immigrants were arriving; population was on the

THE DEVELOPMENT OF AMERICAN SCHOOLS

ELEMENTARY SCHOOLS

Dame schools (1600s)

These private schools taught by women in their homes offered child care for working parents willing to pay a fee. The dames who taught here received meager wages, and the quality of instruction varied greatly.

Local schools (1600s–1800s)

First started in towns and later expanded to include larger districts, these schools were open to those who could afford to pay. Found generally in New England, these schools taught basic skills and religion.

Itinerant schools (1700s) and tutors (1600s–1900s)

Rural America could not support schools and full-time teachers. As a result, in sparsely populated New England, itinerant teachers carried schooling from village to village; they lived in people's homes and provided instruction. In the South, private tutors taught the rich. Traveling teachers and tutors, usually working for a fee and room and board, took varying levels of education to small towns and wealthy populations.

Private schools (1700s–1800s)

Private schools, often located in the middle colonies, offered a variety of special studies. These schools constituted a true free market, as parents paid for the kind of private school they desired. As you might imagine, both the curricula and the quality of these schools varied greatly.

Common schools (1830–present)

The common school was a radical departure from earlier ones in several ways. First, it was free. Parents did not have to pay tuition or fees. Second, it was open to all social classes. Previously, schools usually taught either middle-class or upper-class children. Horace Mann's common school was intended to bring democracy to the classroom. By the mid-nineteenth century, kindergarten was added. In the past few decades, many common schools, now called *elementary schools,* have added Head Start and other prekindergarten programs.

SECONDARY SCHOOLS

Latin grammar schools (1600s–1700s)

These schools prepared wealthy men for college and emphasized a classical curriculum, including Latin and some Greek. From European roots, the curriculum in these schools reflected the belief that the pinnacle of civilization was reached in the Roman Empire.

English grammar schools (1700s)

These private schools moved away from the classical Latin tradition to more practical studies. These schools were viewed not as preparation for college but as preparation for business careers and as a means of instilling social graces. Some of these schools set a precedent by admitting white girls, thus paving the way for the widespread acceptance of females in other schools.

Academies (1700s–1800s)

The academies were a combination of the Latin and English grammar schools. These schools taught English, not Latin. Practical courses were taught, but history and the classics were also included. Some academies emphasized college preparation, while others prepared students to enter business and vocations.

High schools (1800s–present)

These secondary schools differed from their predecessors in that they were free; they were governed not by private boards but by the public. The high school can be viewed as an extension of the common school movement to the secondary level. High schools were open to all social classes and provided both precollege and career education.

Junior high schools (1909–present) and middle schools (1950s–present)

Junior high schools (grades 7–9) and middle schools (grades 5–8) were designed to meet the unique needs of preadolescents and to prepare them for the high school experience.

REFLECTION

If you were responsible for creating a new school based on contemporary needs, what kind of school would you create?

---

upsurge; and traditional patterns of life were changing. In fact, these descriptions parallel changes much later, at the close of the twentieth century. How would education generally, and the new high schools specifically, respond to these changes?

In 1892, the National Education Association (NEA), one of the oldest teacher organizations, established the **Committee of Ten** to develop a national policy for high schools.[14] Chaired by Charles Eliot, president of Harvard University, the committee was composed, for the most part, of college presidents and professors who wanted to bring consistency and order to the high school curriculum. This committee of college professors viewed high schools in terms of preparing intellectually gifted students (typically, white males) for college. The Committee of Ten did not envision today's high school, one that serves all our youth. Nonetheless, many of the committee's recommendations have been influential in the development of secondary education. In 1893, the committee recommended the following:

- A series of traditional and classical courses should be taught sequentially.
- High schools should offer fewer electives.
- Each course lasting for one year and meeting four or five times weekly should be awarded a **Carnegie unit.** Carnegie units would be used in evaluating student progress.
- Students performing exceptionally well could begin college early.

A generation later, in 1918, the NEA once again convened a group to evaluate the high school. Unlike the Committee of Ten, this committee consisted of representatives from the newly emerging profession of education. Education professors, high school principals, the U.S. commissioner of education, and other educators focused concern not on the elite moving on to college but on the majority of students for whom high school would be the final level of education. This committee asked the question, What can high school do to improve the daily lives of citizens in an industrial democracy? This committee's report, ***Cardinal Principles of Secondary Education,*** identified seven goals for high school: (1) health, (2) worthy home membership, (3) command of fundamental academic skills, (4) vocation, (5) citizenship, (6) worthy use of leisure time, and (7) ethical character. The high school was seen as a socializing agency to improve all aspects of a citizen's life.

Since the publication of the *Cardinal Principles* in 1918, not a decade has passed without a committee or commission reporting on reforms needed to improve U.S. schools. During the 1930s, the Progressive Education Association (PEA) provided suggestions to promote social adjustment as well as individual growth. Similar findings reported in the 1940s and 1950s noticeably influenced the evolution of our high schools. More electives were added to the high school curriculum. Guidance counselors were added to the staff. Vocational programs were expanded. The result was the formation of a new, comprehensive institution.

In time, the United States has come full circle, echoing the original call for intellectual rigor first voiced by the Committee of Ten in 1893. In 1983, the federal government's National Commission on Educational Excellence issued ***A Nation at Risk: The Imperative for Educational Reform,*** maintaining that mediocrity, not excellence, characterized U.S. schools. The commission declared that the inadequate rigor of U.S. education had put the nation at risk, losing ground to other nations in commerce, industry, science, and technology. The commission called for fewer electives and a greater emphasis on academic subjects.

Reports on the status of education and recommendations for school reform have become a U.S. tradition. These reports have underscored a built-in dichotomy in public education, a conflict between intellectual excellence and basic education for the masses, between college preparation and vocational training, between student-centered education and subject specialization. Some of the reports have called for more focus on the student, on programs to enhance the student's entrance into society and the workplace. Others have cited the need for more emphasis on academic and intellectual concerns, as well as for programs to enhance the student's preparation for college. This dichotomy has been and continues to be an integral feature of American education. Regardless of the particular reforms advocated, all the reports, from the 1890s to the present, have had a common theme: a faith in education. The reports have differed on solutions but have concurred on the central role of the school in maintaining a vibrant democracy.

John Dewey and Progressive Education

John Dewey was possibly the most influential educator of the twentieth century—and probably the most controversial one. Some saw him as a savior of U.S. schools; others accused him of nearly destroying them. Rather than become engrossed in the heated controversy surrounding Dewey, however, let us look at *progressivism,* the movement with which he is closely associated, and later in this text, explore the philosophy behind progressivism.

As early as 1875, Francis Parker, superintendent of schools in Quincy, Massachusetts, introduced the concepts of progressivism in his schools and by 1896, John Dewey had established his famous **laboratory school** at the University of Chicago. But it was not until the 1920s and 1930s that the progressive education movement became more widely known. During the 1920s and 1930s, the Dalton and Walden schools in New York, the Beaver Country Day School in Massachusetts, the Oak Lane Country Day School in Pennsylvania, and laboratory schools at Columbia and Ohio State universities began to challenge traditional practices. The progressive education approach soon spread to suburban and city public school systems across the country. Various school systems adapted or modified progressive education, but certain basic features remained constant, and elements of progressive education can still be found in many schools.

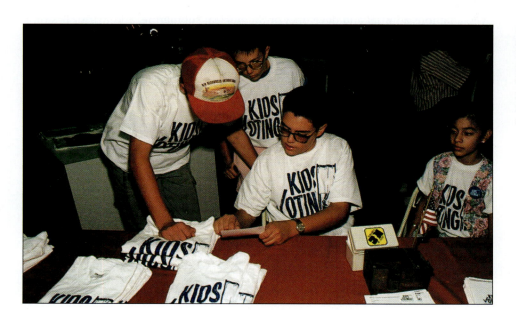

Progressive educators, such as John Dewey, believed that participation in democratic decision making developed rational problem-solving abilities and social skills.

Progressive education included several components. First, it broadened the school program to include health concerns, family and community life issues, and a concern for vocational education. Second, progressivism applied new research in psychology and the social sciences to classroom practices. Third, progressivism emphasized a more democratic educational approach, accepting the interests and needs of an increasingly diverse student body.

This model of education assumed that students learn best when their learning follows their interests. Passively listening to the teacher, according to the progressive movement, is not the most effective learning strategy. The role of the teacher is to identify student needs and interests and provide an educational environment that builds on them. In fact, progressive education shares some characteristics with problem-based and authentic learning, popular innovations in some of today's schools.

Although not involved in all the progressive education programs, John Dewey, in many minds, is the personification of progressive education, as well as its most notable advocate. (See "The Education Hall of Fame" later in this chapter for a description of Dewey and his achievements.) In no small part, this is due to the tens of thousands of pages that Dewey wrote during his long life. (Dewey was born on the eve of the Civil War in 1859 and died during the Korean War in the early 1950s.) Toward the end of Dewey's life, both he and progressive education came under strong attack.

The criticism of Dewey and progressive education originated with far-right political groups, for it was the era of Senator Joseph McCarthy and his extremist campaign against communism. While McCarthy's hunt for communists was primarily directed at the government and the military, educators were not immune. Some viewed progressive education as an atheistic, un-American force that had all but destroyed the nation's schools. Because students were allowed to explore and question, many critics were able to cite examples of how traditional values were not being taught. Although these critics were generally ignorant of Dewey's ideas and progressive practices, a second group was more responsible in its critique.

This second wave of criticism came not from the radical right but from individuals who felt that the school curriculum was not academically sound. Hyman Rickover, a famous admiral and developer of the nuclear submarine, and Arthur Bestor, a liberal arts professor, were among the foremost critics decrying the ills of progressive education. They called for an end to "student-centered" and "life-adjustment" subjects and a return to a more rigorous study of traditional courses. While the arguments raged, the launching of *Sputnik* by the Soviet Union in 1957 put at least a temporary closure on the debate. The United States was involved in a space race with the Soviets, a race to educate scientists and engineers, a race toward the first moon landing. Those arguing for a more rigorous, science- and math-focused curriculum won the day. Although many still argued vociferously over the benefits and shortcomings of progressive education, traditionalists were setting the direction for the nation's curriculum.

Before leaving progressive education, however, it will be beneficial to examine one of the most famous studies of the progressive movement. The Progressive Education Association, formed in 1919, initiated a study during the 1930s that compared almost three thousand graduates of progressive and of traditional schools as they made their way through college. The study, called the **Eight-Year Study,** was intended to determine which educational approach was more effective. The results indicated that graduates of progressive schools:

1. Earned a slightly higher grade point average
2. Earned higher grades in all fields except foreign languages
3. Tended to specialize in the same fields as more traditional students
4. Received slightly more academic honors
5. Were judged to be more objective and more precise thinkers
6. Were judged to possess higher intellectual curiosity and greater drive

The Federal Government

As World War II drew to a close, the United States found itself the most powerful nation on earth. For the remainder of the twentieth century, the United States reconstructed a war-ravaged global economy while confronting world communism. In fact, the United States viewed education as an important tool in accomplishing these strategic goals. When the Soviets launched *Sputnik,* for example, the government enlisted the nation's schools in meeting this new challenge. Consequently, Congress passed the **National Defense Education Act (NDEA)** in 1958 to enhance "the security of the nation" and to develop "the mental resources and technical skills of its young men and women." The NDEA supported the improvement of instruction and curriculum development, funded teacher training programs, and provided loans and scholarships for college students that allowed them to major in subjects deemed important to the national defense (such as teaching). However, looking back in history, it is not at all clear how the federal government was legally able to do this. After all, the framers of the Constitution made their intentions clear: Education was to be a state responsibility, and the federal government was not to be involved. How did the NDEA and other federal acts come to pass?

Many people are unaware that the responsibility for educating Americans is not even mentioned in the Constitution. Under the **Tenth Amendment,** any area not specifically stated in the Constitution as a federal responsibility is automatically assigned to the states. Why was education a nontopic? Some historians believe that, since the individual colonies had already established disparate educational systems, the framers of the Constitution did not want to create dissension by forcing the states to accept a single educational system. Other analysts believe that education was deliberately omitted from the Constitution because Americans feared control of the schools by a central government, any central government, as had been the case in Europe. They saw central control as a possible threat to their freedom. Still others suggest that the framers of the Constitution, in their haste, bartering, and bickering, simply forgot about education (what a depressing thought!). Whatever the reason, distinct colonial practices continued, as each state created its own educational structure—its own approach for preparing teachers and funding schools.

Over time, however, the federal government discovered ways to influence education. As early as the revolutionary period, the new nation passed the **Land Ordinance Act** of 1785 and the **Northwest Ordinance** of 1787. These acts required townships in the newly settled territories bounded by the Ohio and Mississippi rivers and the Great Lakes to reserve a section of land for educational purposes. The ordinances contained a much-quoted sentence underscoring the new nation's faith in education: "Religion, morality, and knowledge being necessary to good government and the happiness of mankind, schools and the means of education shall forever be encouraged."

School board member Roberta W. is trying to change the name of Nathan Bedford Forrest middle school in Gadsden, Alabama. Named for the Confederate general who went on to become the first grand wizard of the Ku Klux Klan, Ms. Roberta W. feels the time to change the name is long overdue. Her request to explore a new name was defeated when no one seconded her motion.

SOURCE: *The American School Board Journal,* April 1998.

REFLECTION

Is it fair to apply contemporary values to historical figures? It is a "cop out" if we avoid including such figures?

OLC Click on *In the News* for recent *In the News* stories. Submit your own *In the News* summary to share with your colleagues.

The federal government also exerted its influence through targeted funding, or **categorical grants.** By using federal dollars for specific programs, the government was able to create new colleges and universities, to promote agricultural and industrial research efforts, and to provide schools for Native Americans and other groups. During the Great Depression of the 1930s, the federal government became even more directly involved with education, constructing schools, providing free lunches for poor children, instituting part-time work programs for high school and college students, and offering educational programs to older Americans. With unemployment, hunger, and desperation rampant in the 1930s, states welcomed these federal efforts. More and more Americans were coming to realize that some educational challenges were beyond the resources of the states.

The Supreme Court decision in *Brown v. Board of Education of Topeka,* followed by the 1964 Civil Rights Act, made it possible for students of all races, cultures, and disabling conditions to receive a desegregated education.

The following is a partial list of legislation indicating the long history of federal involvement in education.

1. *Land Ordinance Act* and *Northwest Ordinance* (1785 and 1787). These two ordinances provided for the establishment of public education in the territory between the Appalachian Mountains and the Mississippi River. In these new territories, 1 square mile out of every 36 was reserved for support of public education, and new states formed from these territories were encouraged to establish "schools and the means for education."

2. *Morrill Land Grant College Acts* (1862 and 1890). These acts established sixty-nine institutions of higher education in the various states, some of which are among today's great state universities. These acts were also called simply the *Land-Grant College Acts,* since public land was donated to establish these colleges.

3. *Smith-Hughes Act* (1917). This act provided funds for teacher training and program development in vocational education at the high school level.

4. *Servicemen's Readjustment Act* (G.I. Bill of Rights, 1944). This act paid veterans' tuition and living expenses for a specific number of months, depending on the length of their military service.

5. *National Defense Education Act* (1958). In response to the Soviet launching of *Sputnik,* the NDEA provided substantial funds for a variety of educational activities, including student loans, the education of school counselors, and the strengthening of instructional programs in science, mathematics, and foreign languages.

6. *Elementary and Secondary Education Act* (1965). This law provided financial assistance to school districts with low-income families, to improve libraries and instructional materials, and to promote educational innovations and research. In the 1970s, this legislation was expanded to include funding for bilingual and Native American education, drug education, and school lunch and breakfast programs.

7. *Project Head Start* (1964–1965). This act provides medical, social, nutritional, and educational services for low income children 3 to 6 years of age.

8. *Bilingual Education Act* (1968). In response to the needs of the significant number of non-English-speaking students, Congress authorized funds to provide relevant instruction to these students. The primary focus was to assist non-English speakers, particularly Spanish-speaking students, almost 70 percent of whom were failing to graduate from high school. Although many other languages besides Spanish are included in this act, a relatively limited percentage of non-English-speaking students participate in these programs, due to funding shortfalls.

9. *Title IX of the Education Amendments* (1972). This regulation prohibits discrimination on the basis of sex. The regulation is comprehensive and protects the rights of both males and females from preschool through graduate school, in sports, financial aid, employment, counseling, school regulations and policies, admissions, and other areas. Title IX enforcement has been lax and many schools violate one or more parts of the regulation.

10. *Individuals with Disabilities Education Act* (1975, 1991). This act provides financial assistance to local school districts to provide free and appropriate education for the nation's 8 million children with disabilities who are between 3 and 21 years of age.

11. *No Child Left Behind Act* (2001). This act revises the Elementary and Secondary Education Act (ESEA, 1965) and calls for state standards in grades 3–8, and annual testing of math and reading. Schools that test poorly may receive additional funds for improvement, but also face the possibility of being closed. Parents are given greater freedom to select schools, with increased federal support for charter schools. The act also attempts to improve teacher quality, assist students with limited English skills, and encourage tutoring and supplemental educational services, even when carried out by private and religious organizations.

REFLECTION

Current federal initiatives promote standards and testing. How is this a departure from the general history of federal legislation?

For over one hundred years, many classrooms have looked strikingly similar. What does each of these rooms say about the roles of teachers and students? How would you describe the aesthetic of these spaces? Design the classroom you would like to have when you begin teaching.

Court action also provided an avenue for federal involvement in schools, as in the landmark ***Brown v. Board of Education of Topeka*** (1954). In this case, the U.S. Supreme Court ruled that separating children "from others of similar age and qualifications solely because of their race generates a feeling of inferiority as to their status in the community that may affect their hearts and minds in a way unlikely to ever be undone." By the 1970s, courts had ruled that discrimination based on gender or directed at students with disabilities was a violation of the U.S. Constitution.

As the twentieth century drew to a close, more conservative administrations reduced federal financial support of education, but not federal influence. Through presidential and congressional leadership, the U.S. government continues to help shape the nation's schools by promoting increased school standards and student testing.

The World We Created at Hamilton High: A Schoolography

In 1988, Gerald Grant published a fascinating book describing life at Hamilton High School (real school, fictitious name) from the 1950s to the 1980s. Like a biography that helps us understand the forces shaping and directing individual lives, *The World We Created at Hamilton High* may be thought of as a "schoolography," offering powerful insights into the forces that have shaped today's schools. The events at Hamilton probably mirror many of the developments in the life of the school you attended, or the one in which you will be teaching. The biography of Hamilton High offers a microcosm of the roots of and reasons behind the current demand for educational reform.[15]

A Super School (If You're on the Right Side of the Tracks), 1953–1965

In 1953, Hamilton High opened its doors to students growing up in one of the new suburban developments, a prototype of those that were sprouting up all across post-war America. Carefully coifed girls in sweaters and skirts and neatly dressed boys with crewcuts and baggy khakis relished their new school, with its tennis courts, modern design, and strong academic offerings. The social life of the Northern, all-white, middle-class school was driven by fraternities and sororities that prohibited or limited the membership of Catholics and Jews. The principal, a former coach, did not provide instructional leadership but certainly did run a tight ship. The purpose of the school was college preparation, and an evaluation of Hamilton written in 1960 reported that a "strong, almost pathological resistance to taking noncollege preparation courses exists in this school community." While letters in the school paper debated whether school spirit was dwindling and what would happen if girls were allowed to wear miniskirts, the school board was approving a desegregation plan that would bring the "southern problem" to Hamilton and open a second, more volatile chapter of the school's history.

Social Unrest Comes to School, 1966–1971

Northern desegregation was as difficult as southern desegregation, with white teachers unprepared to teach black students and both black and white students encountering the reality of racism. SAT scores fell, racial incidents and conflicts rose, and white families began leaving the neighborhood. The proportion of African American students in the school system jumped from 15 to 33 percent. As racial confrontations grew, Hamilton was forced to close several times because of bomb threats and the cloud of threatened violence. Fear gripped the school, teachers became physically ill trying to survive the tension, and several principals, unable to control or eliminate the problems, came and went during this period. By the fall of 1971, more than 70 percent of the teachers who had taught at Hamilton in 1966 had left the school.

The Students' Turn, 1972–1979

The old world of fraternities, sororities, and a social structure that was discriminatingly clear disintegrated in the race riots of the 1960s and split the faculty: some were sympathetic to the curricular change and goals of the student protests; others opposed such changes. The administration used uneven standards of discipline, with white children penalized less harshly than black children. There was a lack of trust between the old and the young, parents and the school, and even between the students and administration at all levels as protests over the Vietnam War and the draft grew more intense. As America's social fabric unraveled, the Supreme Court handed down influential decisions awarding greater liberties to students, including grievance procedures and due process rights. Many teachers and administrators were unclear about what constituted legal or illegal discipline. As a result, they found it legally smarter not to discipline students. An abyss was created, with power unclear and the rules in limbo.

From this maelstrom, student leaders (with some faculty supporters) emerged, and student demands began to reshape the world at Hamilton. While teachers and the administration tolerated student infractions of the rules (for fear of being drowned in

SEVENTEENTH CENTURY

Informal family education, apprenticeships, dame schools, tutors

1635	Boston Latin Grammar School
1636	Harvard College
1647	Old Deluder Satan Law
1687–1890	*New England Primer* published

EIGHTEENTH CENTURY

Development of a national interest in education, state responsibility for education, growth in secondary education

1740	South Carolina denies education to blacks.
1751	Opening of the Franklin Academy in Philadelphia
1783	Noah Webster's *American Spelling Book*
1785, 1787	Land Ordinance Act, Northwest Ordinance

NINETEENTH CENTURY

Increasing role of public secondary schools, increased but segregated education for women and minorities, attention to the field of education and teacher preparation

1821	Emma Willard's Troy Female Seminary opens, first endowed secondary school for girls.
1821	First public high school opens in Boston.
1823	First (private) normal school opens in Vermont.
1827	Massachusetts requires public high schools.
1837	Horace Mann becomes secretary of board of education in Massachusetts.
1839	First public normal school in Lexington, Massachusetts
1855	First kindergarten (German language) in United States
1862	Morrill Land Grant College Act
1874	*Kalamazoo case* (legalizes taxes for high schools)

1896	*Plessy v. Ferguson* Supreme Court decision supporting racially separate but equal schools

TWENTIETH CENTURY

Increasing federal support for educational rights of under-achieving students; increased federal funding of specific (categorical) education programs

1909	First junior high school in Columbus, Ohio
1919	Progressive education programs
1932	New Deal education programs
1944	G.I. Bill of Rights
1950	First middle school in Bay City, Michigan
1954	*Brown v. Board of Education of Topeka* Supreme Court decision outlawing racial segregation in schools
1957	*Sputnik* leads to increased federal education funds.
1958	National Defense Education Act funds science, math, and foreign language programs.
1964–1965	Job Corps and Head Start are funded.
1972	Title IX prohibits sex discrimination in schools.
1975	Public Law 94-142, Education for All Handicapped Children Act (renamed Individuals with Disabilities Education Act, 1991), is passed.
1979	Cabinet-level Department of Education is established.
1990– present	Increased public school diversity and competition through charter schools, for profit companies, open enrollment and technological options. Promotion of educational goals, standards and testing.
2001	Passage of No Child Left Behind Act.

SOURCE: Compiled from Edward King, *Salient Dates in American Education, 1635–1964* (New York: Harper & Row, 1966); National Center for Education Statistics, U.S. Department of Education, *Digest of Education Statistics, 1994.*

REFLECTION

What milestones do you believe may occur in the years ahead?

litigation), students suffered no such inhibitions. They flexed their legal muscles by bringing suits against parents, guardians, and teachers. In class, students felt free to play their radios—that is, when they attended; most students reported that they regularly skipped classes. Drinking and gambling became a part of the school parking-lot landscape, and the students even published an underground newspaper that kept

YOU BE THE JUDGE
SCHOOL MASCOTS

Should Change with the Times Because . . .

MASCOT NAMES CAN BE HURTFUL
A pep rally featuring chanting "Indians" shaking rubber tomahawks trivializes meaningful rituals and cultural differences. Names such as the "Lady Bucks" or "Tigerettes" perpetuate an image of female inferiority and the second-class status of their sports.

MASCOT NAMES PROMOTE VIOLENCE
Stands filled with "Pirates" wielding sabers and chanting insults bring us all closer to potential violence and injury. Mascots should build a positive climate, not a destructive one.

WE SHOULD SET AN EXAMPLE FOR STUDENTS
We must teach by example, and changing offensive mascot names gives us that opportunity. By adopting names like "Freedom" or "Liberty," we teach our children how names can model our historical best, not our historical bigotries, and how adults can learn from past mistakes.

Should Not Change over Time Because . . .

IT'S JUST A NAME
There are more important issues to address than changing names of athletic teams. Exaggerated complaints about mascot names consume hours of school board meetings, and only show how political correctness is driving the times.

MASCOT NAMES BUILD SCHOOL SPIRIT
Proud mascot names like the "Patriots" highlight courage and bravery. Mascot names instill school spirit, a trait sorely needed by today's young people.

TRADITION MATTERS
Some things really do need to stay the same. Building a positive and stable school community is hard enough with people constantly moving and families splitting. School mascot names provide stability, and do not mindlessly mirror every passing fad.

YOU BE THE JUDGE

You and your classmates may want to share your own experiences on this hot-button issue. Should any mascot names be changed? Which names and why (or why not)? Brainstorm positive team names and mascots. (Prepare yourself. This may be more challenging than you think. Students and Teachers Advocating Respect (STAR) is dedicated to understanding mascot names. Founded by educator Christine Rose from Fairfield, Connecticut; visit their website at groups.yahoo.com/group/STAR2.)

them up-to-date on their legal rights, as well as strategies for cutting classes without being caught—not that the classes themselves were difficult or demanding. In fact, course requirements were reduced significantly. Electives were the choice of the day. Some students were revitalized by the new curriculum, but others took easy classes (called "gut" courses) and graduated from Hamilton without much to show for their high school years.

In 1978, a new principal came to the high school, a veteran educator considered tough enough to handle the problems. A uniform discipline code for blacks and whites was established, administrators were taught to back up teachers in their discipline efforts, and the avalanche of easy courses was replaced by a more demanding curriculum. Student suspensions soared. That year, thirty seniors who had cut too many classes were prohibited from participating in graduation. Ever so slowly, adult authority was re-established, and Hamilton's experiment in rule by students came to an end.

New Students, Old School, 1980–1985

Racial desegregation and student protests radically changed Hamilton during the 1970s; the enrollment of students with disabilities sparked the school's second transformation. Although a new federal law (PL 94-142) required that special education students be mainstreamed and taught in regular classes, the teachers were unprepared to respond to their needs, and a number of Hamilton's students were hostile to the new arrivals. Students with disabilities were mainstreamed—and taunted. Mentally retarded, emotionally disturbed, and physically disabled students both experienced and caused frustration when placed in regular classrooms.

During these years, immigrants from Southeast Asia were introduced to Hamilton through the English as a Second Language (ESL) program. Tension between the newly arrived Vietnamese and Cambodian students and African Americans at Hamilton led to fights. While Hamilton searched for peace and consensus with its new student populations, some students escaped from reality through drug use. By 1984, a third of Hamilton's students were experimenting with drugs, typically marijuana. However, an increase in adult authority had checked the escalation of black-white tensions and had increased academic demands. The decline in national test scores at Hamilton had stabilized, and "white flight" had ceased. The school was settling down, but Hamilton was not a particularly inspiring or dynamic institution. The academic star of the 1950s had become an academic has-been of the 1980s. Many people were disappointed in their school.

The disappointment at Hamilton High has been felt in other communities. In 1983, *A Nation at Risk* was published, and it initiated a national evaluation of schools. How effective is our educational system? Is it accomplishing its goals? (These and other questions were considered in Chapter 4, "Schools: Choices and Challenges.")

While Grant's account of Hamilton High ends in 1985, schoolog021aphies continue. If you were to author the most recent period of school history, what title and description might you give to this latest, and as yet unwritten chapter, of *The World We Created at Hamilton High?*

INTERACTIVE ACTIVITY
WHEN DID THAT HAPPEN? Place important educational events on a timeline to test your knowledge.

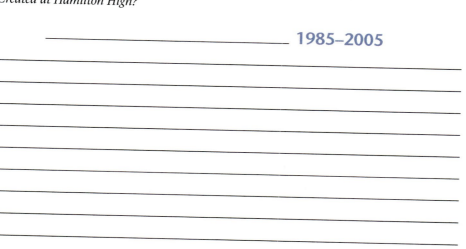

1985–2005

Hall of Fame: Profiles in Education

A "hall of fame" recognizes individuals for significant contributions to a field. Football, baseball, rock and roll, and country music all have halls of fame to recognize outstanding individuals. We think education is no less important and merits its own forum for recognition. In fact, Emporia State University in Kansas is currently developing a Teachers' Hall of Fame. Following are the nominations we would offer to honor educators who we believe should be in a hall of fame.

Obviously, not all influential educators have been included in these brief profiles, but it is important to begin recognizing significant educational contributions. Indirectly or directly, these individuals have influenced your life as a student and will influence your career as a teacher.

For his pioneering work in identifying developmental stages of learning and his support of universal education—

Comenius, born Jan Komensky (1592–1670). A teacher and administrator in Poland and the Netherlands, Comenius's educational ideas were revolutionary for his day. Abandoning the notion that children were inherently bad and needed corporal punishment to encourage learning, Comenius attempted to identify the developmental stages of learners and to match instruction to these stages. He approached learning in a logical way and emphasized teaching general principles before details, using concrete examples before abstract ideas, sequencing ideas in a logical progression, and including practical applications of what is taught. He believed that education should be built on the natural laws of human development and that caring teachers should gently guide children's learning. Comenius supported universal education, and his ideas were later developed by Rousseau, by Pestalozzi, and, nearly 400 years later, by the progressive education movement in the United States.

For his work in distinguishing schooling from education and for his concern with the stages of development—

Jean-Jacques Rousseau (1712–1778). French philosopher Rousseau viewed humans as fundamentally good in their free and natural state but corrupted as a result of societal institutions, such as schools. Like Comenius, he saw children as developing through stages and believed that the child's interests and needs should be the focus of a curriculum. In *Emile,* a novel he wrote in 1762, Rousseau described his educational philosophy by telling the story of young Emile's education, from infancy to adulthood. Emile's education took place on a country estate, under the guidance of a tutor and away from the corrupt influences of society. The early learnings came through Emile's senses and not through books or the words of the teacher. The senses, which Rousseau referred to as the *first teachers,* are more efficient and desirable than learning in the schoolroom. Nature and related sciences were acquired through careful observation of the environment. Only after Emile reached age 15 was he introduced to the corrupt influences of society to learn about government, economics, business, and the arts. Rousseau emphasized the senses over formalized teaching found in books and classrooms, nature over society, and the instincts of the learner over the adult-developed curriculum of school. Rousseau's visionary education for Emile can be contrasted with the sexist education he prescribed for Sophie, the book's female character. Sophie's education amounted to little more than obedience school, because Rousseau expected women to be totally subservient to men. (This terribly restricted view of the role of women is an indication that even members of the Education Hall of Fame have their limitations.)

Rousseau was a pioneer of the contemporary deschooling movement, as he separated the institution of the school from the process of learning. His work led to the child study movement and served as a catalyst for progressive education. Rousseau's romantic view of education influenced many later reformers, including Pestalozzi.

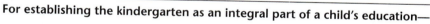

For his recognition of the special needs of the disadvantaged and his work in curricular development—

Johann Heinrich Pestalozzi (1746–1827). Swiss educator Pestalozzi read, agreed with, and built on Rousseau's ideas. Rather than abandoning schools, Pestalozzi attempted to reform them. He established an educational institute at Burgdorf to educate children, as well as to train teachers in more effective instructional strategies.

He identified two levels of effective teaching. At the first level, teachers were taught to alleviate the special problems of poor students. Psychological, emotional, and physical needs should be remediated by caring teachers. In fact, the school environment should resemble a secure and loving home, contributing to the emotional health of the child. At the second level, teachers should focus on teaching students to learn through the senses, beginning with concrete items and moving to more abstract ideas, starting with the learner's most immediate surroundings and gradually moving to more complex and abstract topics.

Pestalozzi's ideas are seen today in programs focused on the special needs of the disadvantaged student. His curricular ideas emerge in today's expanding-horizons social studies curriculum, where children learn first about their family, then their community, their state, and eventually the national and world community. Pestalozzi's ideas influenced Horace Mann and other U.S. educators committed to developing more effective school practices.

For establishing the kindergarten as an integral part of a child's education—

Friedrich Froebel (1782–1852). Froebel frequently reflected on his own childhood. Froebel's mother died when he was only 9 months old. In his recollections, he developed a deep sense of the importance of early childhood and of the critical role played by teachers of the young. Although he worked as a forester, chemist's assistant, and museum curator, he eventually found his true vocation as an educator. He attended Pestalozzi's institute and extended Pestalozzi's ideas. He saw nature as a prime source of learning and believed that schools should provide a warm and supportive environment for children.

In 1837 Froebel founded the first **kindergarten** ("child's garden") to "cultivate" the child's development and socialization. Games provided cooperative activities for socialization and physical development, and such materials as sand and clay were used to stimulate the child's imagination. Like Pestalozzi, Froebel believed in the importance of establishing an emotionally secure environment for children. Going beyond Pestalozzi, Froebel saw the teacher as a moral and cultural model for children, a model worthy of emulation (how different from the earlier view of the teacher as disciplinarian).

In the nineteenth century, as German immigrants came to the United States, they brought with them the idea of kindergarten education. Margaretta Schurz established a German-language kindergarten in Wisconsin in 1855. The first English-language kindergarten and training school for kindergarten teachers were begun in Boston in 1860 by Elizabeth Peabody.

For his contributions to moral development in education and for his creation of a structured methodology of instruction—

Johann Herbart (1776–1841). German philosopher Herbart believed that the primary goal of education is moral education, the development of good people. He believed that through education, individuals can be taught such values as action based on personal conviction, concern for the social welfare of others, and the positive and negative consequences associated with one's behavior. Herbart believed that the development of cognitive powers and knowledge would lead naturally to moral and ethical behavior, the fundamental goal of education.

Herbart believed in the coordinated and logical development of all areas of the curriculum. He was concerned with relating history to geography and both of these to literature—in short, in clearly presenting to students the relationships among various subjects. Herbart's careful and organized approach to the curriculum led to the development of structured teaching. His methodology included preparing students for learning (readiness), helping students form connections by relating new material to previously learned information, using examples to increase understanding, and teaching students how to apply information.

Herbart's concern for moral education paved the way for contemporary educators to explore the relationship between values and knowledge, between a well-educated scientist or artist and a moral, ethical adult. His structured approach to curriculum encouraged careful lesson planning—that is, the development of a prearranged order of presenting information. Teachers who spend time classifying what they will be teaching and writing lesson plans are involved in the kinds of activities suggested by Herbart.

For opening the door of higher education to women and for promoting professional teacher preparation—

Emma Hart Willard (1787–1870). The sixteenth of seventeen children on a farm in Connecticut, Willard was fortunate enough to be born of well-educated and progressive parents who nurtured new ideas. At a time when it was believed that women could not learn complex subjects, Willard committed her life to opening higher education to women. In her own education, she pursued as rigorous an academic program as was permitted women at the time. She had mastered geometry on her own by the age of 12. At 17, she began her career in teaching. In 1814, she opened the Middlebury Female Seminary. In reality, the seminary offered a college-level program, but the term *college* was avoided and *seminary* was used so as not to offend the public. Although she herself was denied the right to attend classes at nearby Middlebury College, she learned college-level material on her own and incorporated this curriculum into the subjects she taught her female students at the seminary.

She put forth her views on opening higher education to women in a pamphlet entitled *An Address to the Public; Particularly to the Members of the Legislature of New York, Proposing a Plan for Improving Female Education* (1819). The pamphlet, written and funded by Willard, won favorable responses from Thomas Jefferson, John Adams, and James Monroe, but not the money she sought from the New York State Legislature to open an institution of higher learning for women. Eventually, with local support, she opened the Troy Female Seminary, establishing a rigorous course of study for women, more rigorous than the curriculum found in many men's colleges. Moreover, the seminary was devoted to preparing professional teachers, thus providing a teacher education program years before the first normal (teacher training) school was founded. To disseminate her ideas and curriculum, Willard wrote a number of textbooks, especially in geography, history, and astronomy. In 1837, she formed the Willard Association for the Mutual Improvement of Female Teachers, the first organization to focus public attention on the need for well-prepared and trained teachers.

Emma Hart Willard was a pioneer in the struggle for women's intellectual and legal rights. She wrote and lectured in support of the property rights of married women and other financial reforms, and she dedicated her life to promoting the intellectual and educational freedom of women. Her efforts promoted the recognition of teaching as a profession and the creation of teacher education programs. In the years that followed, colleges, graduate schools, and the professions opened their doors to women. It was Emma Hart Willard's commitment to providing educational opportunities for women that has shaped the past two centuries of progress, not only for women but for all Americans.

For establishing free public schools and expanding the opportunities of poor as well as wealthy Americans, and for his visions of the central role of education in improving the quality of American life—

Horace Mann (1796–1859). Perhaps the most critical factor in shaping the life of Horace Mann was not what he was given but what he was denied. Although he proved to be an able and gifted student, he was not afforded very much in the way of formal schooling. Forced to learn on his own, he acquired an education and was eventually admitted to Brown University. Before him was a career in law as well as a career in politics, but neither influenced his life as much as his struggle to gain an education. He worked to ensure that others would not be denied educational opportunities. That struggle directed his life and altered the history of U.S. education.

As an educator and a member of the Massachusetts House of Representatives, he worked to improve the quality of education. Corporal punishment, floggings, and unsafe and unsanitary school buildings were all denounced by Mann in speeches, letters, and his lobbying efforts before the state legislature and the U.S. Congress. Of the numerous challenges Mann confronted, he was probably most violently denounced for his efforts to remove religious instruction from schools. He also worked to lengthen the school term; to increase teacher salaries; and, by establishing the first public normal school in 1839, to prepare better teachers. He organized school libraries and encouraged the writing of textbooks that included practical social problems. Mann's efforts resulted in the establishment of the Massachusetts Board of Education, and he became the board's first secretary of education, a position equivalent to a state superintendent of schools.

Of the many achievements attributed to Mann, he is probably best remembered for his leadership in the common school movement, the movement to establish free, publicly supported schools for all Americans. He viewed ignorance as bondage and education as a passport to a promising future. Through education, the disadvantaged could lift themselves out of poverty, blacks could achieve freedom, and children with disabilities could learn to be productive members of society. Mann's credo was that social mobility and the improvement of society could be attained through a free education for all.

However, Mann's fervor was not confined to establishing quality public education. As a member of Congress, he denounced slavery, child labor, worker exploitation, workplace hazards, and the dangers of slum life. Later, as president of Antioch College, he provoked further controversy by admitting women and minority members as students. In the 1850s, this was not only a radical move; for many, it suggested the imminent collapse of higher education. Mann did more than verbalize the importance of freedom and education; his life and actions were a commitment to these principles. The fruits of Mann's efforts are found in our public school system; the education of minorities, the poor, and women; and efforts to provide well-trained teachers working in well-equipped classrooms.

For her integrity and bravery in bringing education to African American girls—

Prudence Crandall (1803–1889). Born of Quaker parents, Prudence Crandall received her education at a school in Providence, Rhode Island, founded by an active abolitionist, Moses Brown. Her upbringing within Quaker circles, in which discussions of abolition were common, may have inspired her interest in racial equality, an interest that led her to acts of personal courage as she strove to promote education among people of all colors.

After graduating from the Brown Seminary around 1830, Crandall taught briefly in Plainfield, Connecticut, before founding her own school for girls in the neighboring town of Canterbury. However, her decision to admit a black girl, Sarah Harris, daughter of a neighboring farmer, caused outrage. While African Americans in Connecticut were free, a large segment of the white population within Canterbury supported the efforts of the American Colonization Society to deport all freed blacks to Africa, believing them to be inherently inferior. Many were adamant that anything but the most basic education for African Americans would lead to discontent and might encourage interracial marriage. The townspeople voiced fears that Crandall's school would lead to the devaluation of local property by attracting a large number of blacks to the area. Prudence Crandall was pressured by the local population to expel Sarah Harris. However, she was determined to defy their wishes. When the wife of a prominent local clergyman suggested that, if Harris remained, the school "could not be sustained," Crandall replied, "Then it might sink then, for I should not turn her out."

When other parents withdrew their children, Crandall advertised for pupils in *The Liberator,* the newspaper of abolitionist William Lloyd Garrison. A month later, the school reopened with a student body comprising fifteen black girls. However, the townspeople made life difficult for Crandall and her students. Supplies were hard to obtain, and Crandall and her pupils faced verbal harassment, as well as being pelted with chicken heads, manure, and other objects. Nonetheless, they persisted.

In 1833, only one month after Crandall had opened her doors to African American girls, the Connecticut legislature passed the notorious "Black Law." This law forbade the founding of schools for the education of African Americans from other states without the permission of local authorities. Crandall was arrested and tried. At her trial, her counsel advised the jury, "You may find that she has violated an act of the State Legislature, but if you also find her protected by higher power, it will be your duty to acquit." Her conviction was later overturned on appeal, but vandalism and arson continued. When a gang stormed the school building with clubs and iron bars, smashing windows and rendering the downstairs area uninhabitable, the school finally was forced to close.

Prudence Crandall's interest in education, racial equality, and women's rights continued throughout her life. Several of her students continued her work, including her first African American student, Sarah Harris, who taught black pupils in Louisiana for many years.[16]

For her work in identifying the educational potential of young children and crafting an environment in which the young could learn—

Maria Montessori (1870–1952). Montessori was no follower of tradition, in her private life or in her professional activities. Shattering sex-role stereotypes, she attended a technical school and then a medical school, becoming the first female physician in Italy. Her work brought her in contact with children regarded as mentally handicapped and brain-damaged, but her educational activities with these children indicated that they were far more capable than many believed. By 1908, Montessori had established a children's school called the Casa dei Bambini, designed to provide an education for disadvantaged children from the slums of Rome.

Montessori's view of children differed from the views held by her contemporaries. Her observations led her to conclude that children have an inner need to work at tasks that interest them. Given the right materials and tasks, children need not be rewarded and punished by the teacher. In fact, she believed that children prefer work to play and are capable of sustained periods of concentration. Young children need a carefully prepared environment in order to learn.

Montessori's curriculum reflected this specially prepared environment. Children learned practical skills, including setting a table, washing dishes, buttoning clothing, and displaying basic manners. They learned formal skills, such as reading, writing, and arithmetic. Special materials included movable sandpaper letters to teach the alphabet and colored rods to teach counting. The children developed motor skills as well as intellectual skills in a carefully developed sequence. The Montessori teacher worked with each student individually, rather than with the class as a whole, to accomplish these goals.

The impact of Montessori's methods continues to this day. Throughout the United States, early childhood education programs use Montessori-like materials. A number of early childhood institutions are called **Montessori schools** and adhere to the approach she developed almost a century ago. Although originally intended for disadvantaged students, Montessori's concept of carefully preparing an environment and program to teach the very young is used today with children from all social classes.

For his work in developing progressive education, for incorporating democratic practices in the educational process—

John Dewey (1859–1952). John Dewey's long life began before the Civil War and ended during the Korean War. During his 93 years, he became quite possibly the most influential educator of the twentieth century. Dewey was a professor at both the University of Chicago and Columbia University, as well as a prolific writer whose ideas and approach to education created innovations and provoked controversies that continue to this day.

Dewey's educational philosophy has been referred to as *progressivism, pragmatism,* and *experimentalism.* Dewey believed that the purpose of education is to assist the growth of individuals, to help children understand and control their environment. Knowledge is not an inert body of facts to be committed to memory; rather, it consists of experiences that should be used to help solve present problems. Dewey believed that the school should be organized around the needs and interests of the child. The learner's interests serve as a springboard to understanding and mastering contemporary issues. For example, a school store might be used to teach mathematics. Students involved in the store operation would learn mathematics by working with money and making change. Dewey was committed to child-centered education, to learning by doing, and to the importance of experience. Classrooms became laboratories in which students could experiment with life and learn to work together.

Dewey's philosophy was founded on a commitment to democratic education. The student should be free to explore and test all ideas and values. Basic American beliefs and institutions should be investigated and restructured when necessary. Education consists of change and of reconstructing experiences. Children, like adults, should learn how to structure their lives and develop self-discipline. Autocratic governments and authoritarian schools are disservices to democracy, for students should participate in shaping their education. Not only should school be a preparation for democracy, but also it should be a democracy. Students should continue this process and shape their world as adults.

The disciples of Dewey's philosophy became a powerful force in education. They founded the Progressive Education Association, which influenced education well into the 1950s. Today, Dewey's writings and ideas continue to motivate and intrigue educators, and there still exist educational monuments to Dewey, both in a variety of school practices and in professional organizations, such as the John Dewey Society. Dewey's philosophy helped open schools to innovation and integrated education with the outside world.

For her contributions in moving a people from intellectual slavery to education—

Mary McLeod Bethune (1875–1955). The first child of her family not born in slavery, Bethune rose from a field hand, picking cotton, to an unofficial presidential adviser. The last of seventeen children born to South Carolina sharecroppers, she filled the breaks in her fieldwork with reading and studying. She was committed to meeting the critical need of providing education to the newly freed African Americans, and, when a Colorado seamstress offered to pay the cost of educating one black girl at Scotia Seminary in Concord, New Hampshire, she was selected. Bethune's plans to become an African missionary changed as she became more deeply involved in the need to educate newly liberated American blacks.

With $1.50, five students, and a rented cottage near the Daytona Beach city dump in Florida, Bethune founded a school that eventually became Bethune-Cookman College. As a national leader, she created a number of black civic and welfare organizations, serving as a member of the Hoover Commission on Child Welfare, and acting as an adviser to President Franklin D. Roosevelt.

Mary McLeod Bethune demonstrated commitment and effort in establishing a black college against overwhelming odds and by rising from poverty to become a national voice for African Americans.

For his creation of a theory of cognitive development—

Jean Piaget (1896–1980). As a student at the University of Paris, Swiss psychologist Piaget met and began working for Alfred Binet, who developed the first intelligence test (a version of which we know today as the Stanford-Binet IQ test). Binet was involved in standardizing children's answers to various questions on this new test, and he enlisted Jean Piaget to assist. Piaget not only followed Binet's instructions, but he went beyond them. He not only recorded children's answers but also probed students for the reasons behind their answers. From the children's responses, Piaget observed that children at different age levels see the world in different ways. From these initial observations, he conceptualized his theory of cognitive, or mental, development, which has influenced the way educators have viewed children ever since.

Piaget's theory outlines four stages of cognitive development. From infancy to 2 years of age, the child functions at the *sensorimotor stage.* At this initial level, infants explore and learn about their environment through their senses—using their eyes, hands, and even mouths. From 2 to 7 years of age, children enter the *preoperational stage* and begin to organize and understand their environment through language and concepts. At the third stage, *concrete operations,* occurring between the ages of 7 and 11, children learn to develop and use more sophisticated concepts and mental operations. Children at this stage can understand numbers and some processes and relationships. The final stage, *formal operations,* begins between 11 and 15 and continues through adulthood. This stage represents the highest level of mental development, the level of adult abstract thinking.

Piaget's theory suggests that teachers should recognize the abilities and limits at each stage and provide appropriate learning activities. Children should be encouraged to develop the skills and mental operations relevant to their mental stage and should be prepared to grow toward the next stage. Teachers, from early childhood through secondary school, need to develop appropriate educational environments and work with students individually according to their own levels of readiness.

Piaget revealed the interactive nature of the learning process and the importance of relating the learner's needs to educational activities. His work led to increased attention to early childhood education and the critical learning that occurs during these early years.

For his contributions in establishing a technology of teaching—

Burrhus Frederick (B. F.) Skinner (1904–1990). When poet Robert Frost received a copy of young B. F. Skinner's work, he encouraged the author to continue writing. But Skinner's years of serious writing in New York's Greenwich Village were unproductive. As Skinner explained, "I discovered the unhappy fact that I had nothing to say, and went to graduate study in psychology, hoping to remedy that short-coming."

Skinner received his doctorate from Harvard, where he eventually returned to teach. He found himself attracted to the work of John B. Watson, and Skinner's ideas became quite controversial. One critic described him as "the man you love to hate."

Skinner's notoriety stemmed from his belief that organisms, including humans, are entirely the products of their environment; engineer the environment, and you can engineer human behavior. Skinner's view of human behavior (called **behaviorism**) irked individuals who see it as a way of controlling people and enslaving the human spirit. Skinner's response was that he did not create these principles but simply discovered them and that a constructive environment can "push human achievement to its limits."

Skinner's early work included the training of animals. During World War II, in a secret project, Skinner trained, or conditioned, pigeons to pilot missiles and torpedoes. The pigeons were so highly trained that they were capable of guiding a missile right down the smokestack of an enemy ship.

Skinner believed that children could be conditioned to acquire desirable skills and behaviors. By breaking down learning into small, simple steps and rewarding children after the completion of each step, learning mastery is achieved. By combining many of these steps, complex behaviors can be learned efficiently. To advance his ideas, he developed the "teaching machine," a device that used these principles of step-by-step instruction requiring and rewarding student responses. This approach laid the foundation for the later development of behavior modification and computer-assisted instruction.

Skinner's creative productivity resulted in both inventions and numerous publications. The "Skinner box" enabled researchers to observe, analyze, and condition pigeons and other animals to master tasks, while teaching machines translated these learning principles into human education. Skinner's books, including *Walden Two*, *The Technology of Teaching*, and *Beyond Freedom and Dignity*, spread his ideas on the importance of environment and behaviorism to educators, psychologists, and the general public. He provided guiding principles about the technology of learning, principles that can be used to unleash or to shackle human potential.

For her creative approaches placing children at the center of the curriculum—

Sylvia Ashton-Warner (1908–1984). Sylvia Ashton-Warner began her school career in her mother's New Zealand classroom, where rote memorization constituted the main avenue for learning. The teaching strategies that Ashton-Warner later devised, with their emphasis on child-centered learning and creativity in the classroom, stand in opposition to this early experience.

Ashton-Warner was a flamboyant and eccentric personality; throughout her life, she considered herself to be an artist rather than a teacher. She focused on painting, music, and writing. Her fascination with creativity was apparent in the remote New Zealand classrooms, where she encouraged self-expression among the native Maori children. As a teacher, she infuriated authorities with her absenteeism and unpredictability, and in official ratings she was never estimated as above average in her abilities. However, during the peak years of her teaching career, between 1950 and 1952, she developed innovative teaching techniques that influenced teachers around the world and especially in the United States.

Realizing that certain words were especially significant to individual pupils because of their life experiences, Ashton-Warner developed her "key vocabulary" system for teaching reading to young children. Words drawn from children's conversations were written on cards. Using these words, children learned to read. Ashton-Warner asserted that the key to making this approach effective lay in choosing words that had personal meaning to the individual child: "Pleasant words won't do. Respectable words won't do. They must be words organically tied up, organically born from the dynamic life itself. They must be words that are already part of the child's being."

Bringing meaning to children was at the center of Ashton-Warner's philosophy. This belief provided the foundation of several reading approaches and teaching strategies used throughout the United States. Her work brought meaning to reading for millions of children. In her best-selling book, *Teacher,* she provided many future teachers with important and useful insights. Her emphasis on key vocabulary, individualized reading, and meaningful learning is evident in classrooms today in America and abroad.

For his work in identifying the crippling effects of racism on all American children and in formulating community action to overcome the educational, psychological, and economic impacts of racism—

Kenneth Clark (1914–). Born in the Panama Canal Zone, Clark was influenced by a forceful mother, who relocated the family to New York City when Clark was 5 years of age in order to provide better educational opportunities for her children. Working as a seamstress in a New York sweatshop, she helped organize the International Ladies' Garment Workers Union. Clark attributes the lessons he learned concerning the importance of "people doing things together to help themselves" to his mother.

Clark attended schools in Harlem, where he witnessed an integrated community become all black and felt the growing impact of racism. He attended Howard University and received his doctorate from Columbia University, but his concern with the educational plight of African Americans generally, and the Harlem community in particular, was always central in his professional efforts.

Clark participated in the landmark study of racial segregation undertaken by Gunnar Myrdal, which resulted in the publication of *An American Dilemma* in 1944. In his own work, he investigated the impact of segregated schools in New York City, concluding that black students receive an education inferior to that of whites. To counter this problem, he established several community self-help projects to assist children with psychological and educational problems. One of those programs, called HARYOU (Harlem Youth Opportunities Unlimited), was designed to prevent school dropouts, delinquency, and unemployment. His efforts served as a catalyst for government action, with both New York City and the federal government providing funds to enhance educational opportunities for minority students.

Kenneth Clark was the first African American appointed to a faculty position at the City College of New York. In books such as *Prejudice and Your Child,* he analyzed the impact of racism on both whites and blacks. The Supreme Court, in its 1954 *Brown* decision, cited Clark's work as psychological evidence for the need to desegregate U.S. schools. His psychological studies and community efforts represented pioneering achievements in desegregating U.S. schools and enhancing U.S. education. As Clark noted decades ago, "A racist system inevitably destroys and damages human beings; it brutalizes and dehumanizes blacks and whites alike."

For his contribution in establishing an American school of cognitive psychology and for his insights in shaping the school curriculum—

Jerome Bruner (1915–). As a graduate student in psychology at Harvard, Jerome Bruner found himself deeply involved in the study of animal perceptions and learning. Psychology was then a new field, and U.S. psychologists, heavily influenced by the behaviorist tradition, turned a deaf ear to studying anything as "unscientific" as human thinking and learning. But Bruner's involvement in World War II altered the direction of his efforts and helped initiate an American school of cognitive psychology, a movement to study human behavior.

During the war, Bruner worked in General Eisenhower's headquarters, studying psychological warfare. His doctoral dissertation concerned Nazi propaganda techniques. After the war, he published works showing how human needs affect perception. For example, poor children are more likely to overestimate the value of coins than are richer children. Adult values and needs affect the way they see the world as well, and realities that do not conform to these needs and beliefs are mentally altered. Bruner showed that human behavior can be observed, analyzed, and understood in an objective way. By 1960, he had helped found Harvard University's Center for Cognitive Studies. Bruner helped legitimize the systematic, objective, and scientific study of human learning and thinking.

Bruner's thoughtful and practical approach to issues was applied to the study of the school curriculum. He was a leader of the Woods Hole conference, a summit of scientists, educators, and scholars interested in reforming education. (The conference followed the Soviet success in launching *Sputnik*.) His report on the conference was published in ***The Process of Education*** (1960), hailed as a practical and readable analysis of curriculum needs. The Process of Education has been translated into twenty-two languages and is studied by teachers around the world. In his book, Bruner argued that schools should not focus on facts but should attempt to teach the "structure," the general nature, of a subject. He also stressed the need for developing intuition and insights as a legitimate problem-solving technique. Finally, in his best-known quotation from *The Process of Education,* Bruner stated, "Any subject can be taught effectively in some intellectually honest form to any child at any stage of development." Bruner has cogently argued for more problem solving and direct involvement in the process of education for all learners, from young children to adults.

For his global effort to mobilize education in the cause of social justice—

Paulo Reglus Neves Freire (1921–1997). Abandoning a career in the law, Brazilian-born Freire committed himself to the education of the poor and politically oppressed. His efforts moved literacy from an educational tool to a political instrument.

Freire denounced teacher-centered classrooms. He believed that instructor domination denied the legitimacy of student experiences and treated students as secondary objects in the learning process. He termed such instruction "banking" education, since the students become little more than passive targets of the teacher's comments. Freire championed a *critical pedagogy,* one that places the student at the center of the learning process. In Freire's pedagogy, student dialogues, knowledge, and skills are shared cooperatively, legitimizing the experiences of the poor. Students are taught how to generate their own questions, focus on their own social problems, and develop strategies to live more fruitful and satisfying lives. Teachers are not passive bystanders or the only source of classroom wisdom. Freire believed that teachers should facilitate and inspire, that teachers should "live part of their dreams within their educational space." Rather than unhappy witnesses to social injustice, teachers should be advocates for the poor and agents for social change. Freire's best known work, ***Pedagogy of the Oppressed,*** illustrated how education could transform society.

Freire's approach obviously threatened the social order of many repressive governments, and he faced constant intimidation and threats. Following the military overthrow of the Brazilian government in 1964, Freire was jailed for "subversive" activities and later exiled. In the late 1960s, while studying in America, Freire witnessed racial unrest and the antiwar protests. These events convinced Freire that political oppression is present in "developed nations" as well as third world countries, that economic privilege does not guarantee political advantage, and that the pedagogy of the oppressed has worldwide significance.

INTERACTIVE ACTIVITY
WHO AM I? Using hints, determine the identity of famous educational figures.

SUMMARY

1. What was the nature and purpose of colonial education?

   - In early colonial days, most education took place in the home through dame schools, in the church, and through apprentice programs, with instruction dominated by religious teachings.

   - In 1647, Massachusetts passed the "Old Deluder Satan Law," requiring that every town of 50 households appoint and pay a teacher of reading and writing, and every town of 100 households provide a Latin grammar school. This law offered a model for other communities and made the establishment of schools a practical reality.

   - Colonial Latin grammar schools prepared white boys for a university education. In the 1700s, academies were established; they were more secular and practical in their curriculum and were open to girls.

   - Thomas Jefferson and Benjamin Franklin viewed the new nation's schools as a continuation of democratic principles and as a break from classist European traditions. They advocated for schools that would serve all the people, and identify a natural aristocracy, the talented and gifted from all classes. Racial mores continued to prevent African Americans from entering school.

   - Slowly, an American curriculum developed, and schools progressed from the rudimentary hornbook to the *McGuffey Reader.*

   - While today's public school systems hardly resemble their colonial origins, many of our current controversies are rooted in the past. We continue to dispute the role of religion in schools, local control and state standards, and inequities in educational opportunities for women, people of color, and the poor.

   - The Constitution has helped determine the shape of modern education in several ways. By omitting any mention of education as a federal responsibility, the Constitution left schooling to the states. Each state government set up its own policy, practice, and means of funding schools.

2. How did the Common School Movement influence the idea of universal education?

   - During the nineteenth century, public support grew for the concept of universal education, and the belief that schools should serve the poor as well as the wealthy.

   - As leader of the common school movement, Horace Mann is sometimes called the father of the public school. Mann fought for the establishment not only of the common school, today's elementary school, but for quality teacher education through normal schools.

   - By the Civil War, the concept of the elementary public school had become widely accepted.

3. How did teaching become a "gendered" career?

   - Teaching was initially "gendered" male well into the nineteenth century. The advent of the common school created a demand for a large number of inexpensive teachers, and women were recruited to teaching. From the late nineteenth century until today, teaching positions were dominated by women, and teaching was gendered a "female" career.

   - At first women entering teaching were considered masculine, abandoning marriage for careers. Soon "spinsters" were considered quite desirable as teachers because of their dedication. Later, their single status was considered "unnatural" and charges of lesbianism emerged.

   - Men who stayed in teaching were under suspicion of being effeminate or gay.

   - Men and women carved out their own educational enclaves. Women dominated elementary teaching, and men dominated leadership positions, an informal segregation that continues today.

CHAPTER REVIEW

Go to the Online Learning Center to take a quiz, practice with key terms, and review key ideas from the chapter.

4. How did secondary schools evolve?

- Public high schools caught on much more slowly than elementary schools. The first publicly supported secondary school was the English Classical School in Boston. As the country moved from agrarian to industrial and from rural to urban, support of public funding of high schools slowly grew.

- The Kalamazoo case (1874) created the legal basis for high school funding. Eventually, high schools came to represent democratic ideals of equal opportunity; later, many believed that education could be a panacea for societal problems.

- Early in the twentieth century junior high schools developed, and later middle schools. Both were designed to meet the special needs of preadolescents.

5. How have twentieth century school reform efforts influenced schools?

- From the Committee of Ten in 1892 to the 1989 National Education Summit, waves of educational reform have become part of the American landscape. While reform movements have not reached a consensus as to the best educational system for the nation, one idea remains key: Schools should have a central role in maintaining a vibrant democracy.

6. What were the main tenets of the Progressive Education movement?

- Progressivism, with John Dewey as its most notable advocate, had a significant impact on education in the twentieth century. Its emphasis on learning by doing and shaping curricula around children's interests has influenced many educators to this day.

- Dewey and progressivism have come under frequent attack, however, first by extremists of the 1950s, who saw progressivism as communistic and contrary to American values. Later, in the wake of the Soviet *Sputnik* launching, progressivism was blamed for causing U.S. students to lag behind in important subjects.

- While progressivism has ceased to be the organized educational movement it once was, many of its ideas continue to be debated and re-examined.

7. What role has the federal government played in American education?

- While the Constitution leaves the responsibility for schooling to the states, the federal government has played an increasing role in education over the past century. National programs have included targeted funds for federal priorities, such as enhanced teacher training and science and math instruction through the National Defense Education Act

- Legislation and court action have also been used to promote federal priorities. Such strategies have been used to fight segregation and other forms of discrimination in the schools. From the 1980s into 2000, more conservative forces decreased federal funding, but increased federal support for school standards and student testing.

8. Who are some of the key individuals who have helped fashion today's schools?

- Each of the chapters in this text highlights a significant educator through the *Profile in Education* feature. In this chapter, seventeen noted educators from sixteenth century Comenius to twentieth century Paulo Freire are profiled.

KEY TERMS AND PEOPLE

KEY TERMS

academy, 310

American Spelling Book, 311

apprenticeship, 306

behaviorism, 337

Brown v. Board of Education of Topeka, 325

Cardinal Principles of Secondary Education, 318

Carnegie unit, 318

categorical grants, 322

Committee of Ten, 317

common school, 312

dame schools, 306

Eight-Year Study, 320

elementary school, 312

English Classical School, 315

Franklin Academy, 310

gendered career, 313

hornbook, 311

in loco parentis, 306

junior high schools, 316

Kalamazoo, Michigan, case, 316

kindergarten, 331

laboratory school, 319

Land Ordinance Act, 321

Latin grammar school, 307

McGuffey Readers, 311

middle schools, 316

Montessori schools, 335

A Nation at Risk: The Imperative for Educational Reform, 318

National Defense Education Act (NDEA), 321

New England Primer, 311

normal schools, 313

Northwest Ordinance, 321

Old Deluder Satan Law, 307

Pedagogy of the Oppressed, 340

The Process of Education, 340

progressive education, 320

secondary school, 315

Tenth Amendment, 321

KEY PEOPLE

Sylvia Ashton-Warner, 338

Mary McLeod Bethune, 336

Jerome Bruner, 339

Kenneth Clark, 339

Comenius, 330

Prudence Crandall, 334

John Dewey, 319, 335

Benjamin Franklin, 310

Paulo Reglus Neves Freire, 340

Friedrich Froebel, 331

Johann Herbart, 332

Thomas Jefferson, 310

Horace Mann, 333

Maria Montessori, 335

Johann Heinrich Pestalozzi, 331

Jean Piaget, 337

Jean-Jacques Rousseau, 330

Burrhus Frederick (B. F.) Skinner, 337

Emma Hart Willard, 332

DISCUSSION QUESTIONS AND ACTIVITIES

1. In the colonial period, a number of factors influenced the kind of education you might receive. Describe how the following factors influenced educational opportunities:
   - Geography
   - Wealth
   - Race/ethnicity
   - Gender

2. Identify current educational practices that are similar to or had their roots in the colonial period. What colonial educational practices are no longer with us?

3. Contrast the Latin grammar school with the Franklin Academy.

4. "The United States was founded on a commitment to the importance of education, yet it failed to develop a national strategy for shaping education." Support both parts of this statement.

5. Identify the arguments against Horace Mann's state-supported elementary schools.

6. How has "gendering" teaching hurt students?

7. In what ways were U.S. secondary schools different from European high schools?

8. "New England, more than any other region, was the birthplace of educational innovation." Support this statement, using examples from elementary, secondary, and postsecondary education.

9. Compare the report of the Committee of Ten (1893) with the reports on the status of education issued during the 1980s.

10. Progressive education has sparked adamant critics and fervent supporters. Offer several arguments supporting the tenets of progressivism, as well as arguments against this movement.

11. If you were asked to design a role for the federal government in education, would your plan differ from the role provided in the U.S. Constitution? How?

12. Can you relate any of the stages of Grant's Hamilton High to your own high school? How would you describe the most recent chapter in the life of your high school, from 1985 to the present?

13. What characteristics do members of the Education Hall of Fame share? Whom would you add to the roster of this hall of fame?

14. Identify the contributions made by the following educators, whom some might consider candidates for the hall of fame: Septima Poinsette Clark, Madeline C. Hunter, Charlotte Hawkins Brown, Johnetta Cole, Joyce Ladner, Henri Mann.

15. Some teacher preparation programs do not consider or discuss the history of education, while other programs devote courses reviewing and analyzing educational history. Set up a debate (or use another *academic controversy* strategy) arguing the pros and cons of the following proposition. Resolved: Teacher preparation programs should focus on current issues and not consider the history of education.

WEB-*TIVITIES*

1. Historical Events and Trends: Shaping American Education

2. American Schools of the Past: A Day in the Life

3. Early Textbooks

4. The Education Hall of Fame

5. American Schools: What's in a Name?

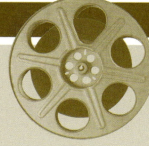

REEL TO REAL TEACHING

You can find a wealth of classic movies with an education twist. Watch one of the four oldies but goodies described here, or visit the classics section of your local video store and check out a film "new" to you.

BLACKBOARD JUNGLE (1955)
Run Time: 101 minutes

Synopsis: The story of an idealistic teacher on his first job in a tough, urban, all male high school. A shocking film for its time, *Blackboard Jungle* was banned in some cities for its multiracial content and fear that it would spark violence.

THE MIRACLE WORKER (1962)
Run Time: 107 minutes

Synopsis: The true story of Anne Sullivan's devotion to teaching Helen Keller, a girl whose childhood illness caused her to become blind and deaf, how to communicate.

TO KILL A MOCKINGBIRD (1962)
Run Time: 129 minutes

Synopsis: Atticus Finch, a lawyer and single parent in a small Southern town during the Great Depression, defends an African American man wrongfully accused of raping a white woman. During the trial, his children and the community learn lessons of racial and disability tolerance.

TO SIR, WITH LOVE (1967)
Run Time: 105 minutes

Synopsis: Unable to find work as an engineer, an African American engineer accepts a teaching job in the slums of London. To motivate his rebellious students, he rejects traditional textbooks and lectures, and endeavors to earn their trust through unorthodox instruction.

Reflection:

1. Does the film you viewed remind you of a current issue? Which one(s)? Describe the similarities and differences.
2. What elements of effective teaching did you observe in the film? Is good teaching in the 1950s and 1960s still considered good teaching today?
3. Would you like to teach in the school depicted in the film? Why or why not?

Follow-up Activity: If there were an Education History Movie Hall of Fame, which classic film would you honor? Visit the *Reel to Real Teaching* on our website and post your nomination. Tell us why this film is a timeless winner!

 How do you rate these films? Click on *Reel to Real Teaching* to submit your review of these or other education-related films, and read reviews submitted by others.

FOR FURTHER READING

The American School 1642–2000, by Joel Spring (2000). A critical analysis of the economic, political, and multicultural forces that have shaped education from colonial times to the present.

Cultural History and Education, by Thomas Popkewitz, Barry Franklin, and Miguel Pereyra (2001). Traces historical changes in the definitions of student, teacher, school, and community across Europe, Latin America, and North America.

Lessons of a Century: A Nation's Schools Come of Age, by *Education Week* (2000). From curriculum to instruction to governance and student life, the trends and personalities that have shaped American education are retold through narratives and photographs.

Pedagogies of Resistance: Women Educator Activists, 1880–1960, by Margaret Smith Crocco, Petra Munro, and Kathleen Weiler (1999). Chronicles the lives of women who resisted conventional gender roles to make education and society more equitable.

The White Architects of Black Education: Ideology and Power in America, 1865–1954, by William H. Watkins (2001). Describes how corporate power and private wealth shaped unequal race relations and structured segregated education.

Women and Teacher Training Colleges, 1900–1960, by Elizabeth Edwards (2000). Details the roles of women in building three teacher training colleges: Homerton, Avery Hill, and Bishop Otter.

Philosophy of Education

9

FOCUS QUESTIONS

1. What is a philosophy of education, and why should it be important to you?
2. How do teacher-centered philosophies of education differ from student-centered philosophies of education?
3. What are some major philosophies of education in the United States today?
4. How are these philosophies reflected in school practices?
5. What are some of the psychological and cultural factors influencing education?
6. What were the contributions of Socrates, Plato, and Aristotle to Western philosophy, and how is their legacy reflected in education today?
7. How do metaphysics, epistemology, ethics, political philosophy, aesthetics, and logic factor into a philosophy of education?

WHAT DO YOU THINK? What Is Your Philosophy of Education? Take an electronic version of the quiz on page 350. Then, submit your responses to see how they compare to those of your colleagues.

CHAPTER PREVIEW

The root for the word **philosophy** is made up of two Greek words: *philo*, meaning "love," and *sophos*, meaning "wisdom." For thousands of years, philosophers have been wrestling with fundamental questions: What is most real—the physical world or the realm of mind and spirit? What is the basis of human knowledge? What is the nature of the just society? Educators must take stances on such questions before they can determine what and how students should be taught.

Since educators do not always agree on the answers to these questions, different philosophies of education have emerged. Although there are some similarities, there are also profound differences in the way leading educators define the purpose of education, the role of the teacher, the nature of the curriculum and assessment, and the method of instruction.

This chapter is intended to start you on a path of thoughtfully considering your values and beliefs. Five influential philosophies will be described, and you will see how each can shape classroom life. We invite you to consider how psychological and cultural beliefs can also affect schools. We revisit the roots of Western philosophy with three ancient Greeks as our guides: Socrates, Plato, and Aristotle. Finally, we briefly examine the building blocks of philosophy, the divisions within philosophy that focus on questions pertinent to educators (what is of worth? how do we know what we know?). The ideas in this chapter will spark some very basic questions about your role in the classroom, and the school's role in society. Your answers to these questions will help you frame your philosophy of education.

Finding Your Philosophy of Education

What is a philosophy of education? Do you have one? Do you think it matters? If you are like most people, you probably have not given much thought to philosophy, in education or elsewhere. Being a practical person, you may be more concerned with other questions: Will I enjoy teaching? Will I be good at it? How will I handle discipline problems? Believe it or not, underlying the answers to these practical questions *is* your philosophy of education.

At this point, your philosophy may still be taking shape (not a bad thing). Your beliefs may reflect an amalgam of different philosophies. Unfortunately, they may also be filled with inconsistencies. In order to help you shape a coherent and useful educational philosophy, you must consider some basic—and very important—questions, such as:

What is the purpose of education?

What content and skills should schools teach?

How should schools teach this content?

What are the proper roles for teachers and students?

Still not sure what a philosophy of education is all about, or how it shapes classroom and school life? Let's listen to some teachers discussing the direction a new charter school should take. You'll see that each teacher has very clear ideas about what schools are for, what students should learn, and how teachers should teach.

Hear that noise coming from the faculty room down the hall? Your potential colleagues sometimes get a bit loud as they debate the possible directions for the new charter school. As you listen in, try to sort out which of these educational directions appeals to you.

JACKIE POLLACK: I am so excited! This new charter school can be just what we need, a chance to reestablish a positive reputation for the quality of public education! Let's face it, we are competing in a global economy, against nations whose students outscore ours on all the standardized tests that matter. It's embarrassing. If we can create a rigorous school (I'd prefer to call it an "Academy") with tough standards and a real commitment to learning, then look out! We'll make those "preppie" kids from Country Day School sorry they ever opted out of the public school system. I'd love to see a school with a strict code of conduct and core courses, like literature, history, math, and science, without those silly electives like "mass media." I would love to see our students wear uniforms and enroll in courses at the Advanced Placement level. What a great school not only for kids to learn, but for us to teach! It's all about rigorous standards.

ROBIN MILLER: Jackie, you and I both would like to teach in a more rigorous school, one with a tougher curriculum. But I am getting tired of standards and testing. I'll tell you a secret: I don't much care whether South Korean kids score better than Americans on some silly short answer test. I'm interested in a school committed to learning, not testing or competing. The new school should replace these boring textbooks with Great Books, books that intrigue, entice, and teach. Kids thirst for meaningful ideas. The school I envision would focus on classic works of literature and art. We would teach through intellectual questioning, a "Socratic dialogue." What exciting discussions we could have about *The Old Man and the Sea,* Plato's *Republic* and Homer's *Iliad.* Maybe we can re-invent the all-but-extinct American student: One who knows not only how to read, but a student who actually *wants* to read, *enjoys* reading and best of all, knows how to *think.* Jackie, I like the name you came up with—"Academy"—but I want our new charter school to create great minds, not just great test scores.

MARK WASHINGTON: I agree with Robin that we need to move beyond today's tyranny of testing, but Hemingway and Homer are not the answers. Problem is, we have more relevant issues and skills to deal with, issues never dreamed of in Plato's or Shakespeare's day. Our job as teachers is to make certain that our students can do well in the real world. We must be practical. Let me give you an example: When I was in eighth grade, my class took a three-week trip around the Midwestern states by train. Most of the semester was spent planning this trip. We worked together, researching different areas of the region and deciding where to go. We learned how to read train schedules and maps because we had to. We had to be organized and run meetings effectively. Math, history, geography, writing . . . talk about an integrated curriculum! We learned by doing. I still remember that trip and what went into it as a high point in my life. I want all students to have that kind of intense experience, to learn how to solve real world problems, not just answer test questions or discuss books.

TED GOODHEART: I want students to do more than simply fit into society; I want them to leave the world a better place than they found it. Behind our community's pretty façade are people in pain. We need to educate kids to care more about these people than we did. One out of six children is born into poverty here. One out of six! I want to teach kids to make a difference, and not let books and homework insulate them from real world concerns. The new charter school must equip children to tackle issues like poverty, violence, pollution, bigotry, and injustice. We need to prepare students with both a social conscience and the political skills needed to improve our society. I want to teach students whose actions will make me, and all of us, proud. Teaching in a socially responsible charter school would be my dream.

ALICIA CAMUS: Everyone in this room has been trying to design a charter school backwards, thinking mostly about what we teachers think. Here's a revolutionary idea: Let's build an education around the students. Why not have the students decide what they will learn? Students must assume primary responsibility for their own learning. I would like our charter school staffed by teachers who are skilled in facilitating and counseling children to reach their personal goals. Believe it or not, I trust students, and I would give every child (even the youngest or least able) an equal voice in decision making. It's not enough to slowly reform education; we need to rebuild it from the center, from where the students are.

As you might have suspected, these teachers are not only discussing different approaches to a proposed charter school, they are also shedding light on five major educational philosophies. Do any of these diverse views sound attractive to you? Do any sound particularly unappealing? If so, note which of these teachers you thought reflected your own beliefs, and which were really off the mark. If you found that you had strong opinions—pro or con—about one or more of these teachers' positions, then you are beginning to get in touch with your educational philosophy. Let's leave the faculty room conversation, and take a closer, more orderly look at your own philosophical leanings. The following inventory can help you sort out tenets of your educational philosophy.

Inventory of Philosophies of Education

As you read through each of the following statements about schools and teaching, decide how strongly you agree or disagree. In a bit, we will help you interpret your results. Write your response to the left of each statement, using the following scale:

5   Agree strongly

4   Agree

3   Neither agree nor disagree

2   Disagree

1   Disagree strongly

_____   1. A school curriculum should include a common body of information that all students should know.

_____   2. The school curriculum should focus on the great ideas that have survived through time.

_____   3. The gap between the real world and schools should be bridged through field trips, internships, and adult mentors.

_____   4. Schools should prepare students for analyzing and solving the social problems they will face beyond the classroom.

_____   5. Each student should determine his or her individual curriculum, and teachers should guide and help them.

_____ 6. Students should not be promoted from one grade to the next until they have read and mastered certain key material.

_____ 7. Schools, above all, should develop students' abilities to think deeply, analytically, and creatively, rather than focus on transient concerns like social skills and current trends.

_____ 8. Whether inside or outside the classroom, teachers must stress the relevance of what students are learning to real and current events.

_____ 9. Education should enable students to recognize injustices in society, and schools should promote projects to redress social inequities.

_____ 10. Students who do not want to study much should not be required to do so.

_____ 11. Teachers and schools should emphasize academic rigor, discipline, hard work, and respect for authority.

_____ 12. Education is not primarily about workers and the world economic competition; learning should be appreciated for its own sake, and students should enjoy reading, learning, and discussing intriguing ideas.

_____ 13. The school curriculum should be designed by teachers to respond to the experiences and needs of the students.

_____ 14. Schools should promote positive group relationships by teaching about different ethnic and racial groups.

_____ 15. The purpose of school is to help students understand themselves, appreciate their distinctive talents and insights, and find their own unique place in the world.

_____ 16. For the United States to be competitive economically in the world marketplace, schools must bolster their academic requirements in order to train more competent workers.

_____ 17. Teachers ought to teach from the classics, because important insights related to many of today's challenges and concerns are found in these Great Books.

_____ 18. Since students learn effectively through social interaction, schools should plan for substantial social interaction in their curricula.

_____ 19. Students should be taught how to be politically literate, and learn how to improve the quality of life for all people.

_____ 20. The central role of the school is to provide students with options and choices. The student must decide what and how to learn.

_____ 21. Schools must provide students with a firm grasp of basic facts regarding the books, people, and events that have shaped the nation's heritage.

_____ 22. The teacher's main goal is to help students unlock the insights learned over time, so they can gain wisdom from the great thinkers of the past.

_____ 23. Students should be active participants in the learning process, involved in democratic class decision making and reflective thinking.

_____ 24. Teaching should mean more than simply transmitting the Great Books, which are replete with biases and prejudices. Rather, schools need to identify a new list of Great Books more appropriate for today's world, and prepare students to create a better society than their ancestors did.

_____ 25. Effective teachers help students to discover and develop their personal values, even when those values conflict with traditional ones.

_____ 26. Teachers should help students constantly reexamine their beliefs. In history, for example, students should learn about those who have been historically omitted: the poor, the non-European, women, and people of color.

_____ 27. Frequent objective testing is the best way to determine what students know. Rewarding students when they learn, even when they learn small things, is the key to successful teaching.

_____ 28. Education should be a responsibility of the family and community, rather than delegated to formal and impersonal institutions, such as schools.

Interpreting Your Responses

Write your responses to statements 1 through 25 in the columns below, tally up your score in each column. (We will return to items 26 to 28 in a bit.) Each column is labeled with a philosophy and the name of the teacher who represented that view in this chapter's opening scenario (the charter school discussion). The highest possible score in any one column is 25, and the lowest possible score is 5. Scores in the 20s indicate strong agreement, and scores below 10 indicate disagreement with the tenets of a particular philosophy.

A	B	C	D	E
			Social	
Essentialism (Jackie)	Perennialism (Robin)	Progressivism (Mark)	Reconstructionism (Ted)	Existentialism (Alicia)
1. _____	2. _____	3. _____	4. _____	5. _____
6. _____	7. _____	8. _____	9. _____	10. _____
11. _____	12. _____	13. _____	14. _____	15. _____
16. _____	17. _____	18. _____	19. _____	20. _____
21. _____	22. _____	23. _____	24. _____	25. _____
Scores _____	_____	_____	_____	_____

INTERACTIVE ACTIVITY
WHERE DO YOU STAND ON THE PHILOSOPHY SPECTRUM? Note where you think your philosophy of education falls, and compare where you stand to where your colleagues do.

Your scores in columns A through E, respectively, represent how much you agree or disagree with the beliefs of five major educational philosophies: essentialism, perennialism, progressivism, social reconstructionism, and existentialism. Check back to see if your scores reflect your initial reactions to these teachers' points of view. For example, if you agreed with Jackie's proposal to create an "Academy," then you probably agreed with a number of the statements associated with essentialist education, and your score in this column may be fairly high.

Compare your five scores. What is your highest? What is your lowest? Which three statements best reflect your views on education? Are they congruent and mutually supporting? Looking at the statements that you least support, what do these statements tell you about your values? You may notice that your philosophical leanings, as identified by your responses to statements in the inventory, reflect your general outlook on life. For example, your responses may indicate whether you generally trust people to do the right thing, or if you believe that individuals need supervision. How have your culture, religion, upbringing, and political beliefs shaped your responses to the items in this inventory? How have your own education and life experiences influenced your philosophical beliefs?

Now that you have begun to examine varying beliefs about education, you may even want to lay claim to a philosophical label. But what do these philosophical labels mean? In the following pages we will introduce you to all five of these educational philosophies, and look at their impact in the classroom.

Five Philosophies of Education

Essentialism, perennialism, progressivism, social reconstructionism, and existentialism. Taken together, these five schools of thought do not exhaust the list of possible educational philosophies you may consider, but they present strong frameworks for you to refine your own educational philosophy. We can place these five philosophies on a continuum, from teacher-centered (some would say "authoritarian"), to student-centered (some would characterize as "permissive").

Are you politically conservative or liberal? (Great, now we are bringing politics into this discussion.) Actually, your political stance is one predictor of your educational philosophy. Conservatives often champion teacher-centered philosophies and practices that emphasize the values and knowledge that have survived through time, while liberals find student-centered approaches more to their liking. (See Figure 9.1).

Let's begin our discussion with the teacher-centered philosophies, for they have exerted significant influence on American education during the past two decades.

FIGURE 9.1   Teacher- and student-centered philosophies of education.

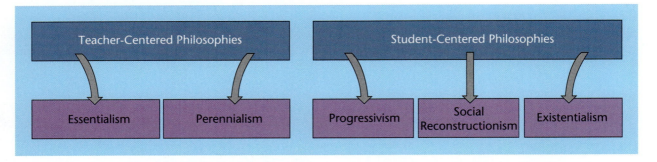

Teacher–Centered Philosophies

Traditionally, **teacher-centered philosophies** emphasize the importance of transferring knowledge, information, and skills from the older (presumably wiser) generation to the younger one. The teacher's role is to instill respect for authority, perseverance, duty, consideration, and practicality. When students demonstrate through tests and writings that they are competent in academic subjects and traditional skills, and through their actions that they have disciplined minds and adhere to traditional morals and behavior, then both the school and the teacher have been successful. (If you recall from Chapter 4, "Schools: Choices and Challenges," these philosophies view the primary purpose of schools as "passing the cultural baton.") The major teacher-centered philosophies of education are essentialism and perennialism.

Essentialism

Essentialism strives to teach students the accumulated knowledge of our civilization through core courses in the traditional academic disciplines. Essentialists aim to instill students with the "essentials" of academic knowledge, patriotism, and character development. This traditional or **back-to-basics** approach is meant to train the mind, promote reasoning, and ensure a common culture among all Americans.

American educator **William Bagley** popularized the term *essentialism* in the 1930s,[1] and essentialism has been a dominant influence in American education since World War II. Factors such as the launching of *Sputnik* in 1957, the 1983 report *A Nation at Risk,* intense global economic competition and increased immigration into the United States have all kept essentialism at center stage. Some educators refer to the present period as **neoessentialism** because of the increased core graduation requirements, stronger standards and more testing of both students and teachers.

Whether they call themselves essentialists or neoessentialists, educators in this camp are concerned that the influx of immigrants threatens American culture. In response, they call for rigorous schools teaching a single, unifying body of knowledge for all Americans. One of the leading essentialists, **E. D. Hirsch, Jr.**, authored *Cultural Literacy: What Every American Needs To Know,* and *The Schools We Need and Why We Don't Have Them.* Hirsch provides lists of people, events, literature, historical facts, scientific breakthroughs and the like, lists that specify what students at every grade level should know to be "culturally literate."

Most of you reading this chapter have been educated in essentialist schools. You were probably required to take many courses in English, history, math, and science, but were able to enroll in only a few electives. Such a program would be typical in an essentialist school.

THE ESSENTIALIST CLASSROOM Essentialists urge that traditional disciplines such as math, science, history, foreign language, and literature form the foundation of the curriculum, which is referred to as the **core curriculum**. Essentialists frown upon electives that "water-down" academic content. Elementary students receive instruction in skills such as writing, reading, measuring, and computing. Even when studying art and music, subjects most often associated with the development of creativity, students master a body of information and basic techniques, gradually moving to more complex skills and detailed knowledge. Only by mastering the required material are students promoted to the next higher level.

Essentialists maintain that classrooms should be oriented around the teacher, who should serve as an intellectual and moral role model for the students. The teachers or administrators decide what is most important for the students to learn and place little emphasis on student interests, particularly when such interests divert time and attention from the academic curriculum. Essentialist teachers rely on achievement test scores to evaluate progress. Essentialists expect that students will leave school possessing not only basic skills and an extensive body of knowledge, but also disciplined, practical minds, capable of applying schoolhouse lessons in the real world.

ESSENTIALISM IN ACTION: THE COALITION OF ESSENTIAL SCHOOLS The **Coalition of Essential Schools**, headed by Theodore Sizer, offers several tangible examples of essentialism in action. The 200 coalition schools pledge to promote intellectual rigor, test students for mastery of information and skills, have teachers and students work closely together, and develop strong thinking skills across subjects. But is the Coalition of Essential Schools purely essentialist? Not entirely. Coalition schools recognize and promote individual student differences, a clear departure from a strict essentialist interpretation. In fact, schools in the coalition do not share a fixed core curriculum, but each school continually analyzes and can alter core contents. The coalition also stresses "less is more," since Sizer believes that teachers and students should focus on fewer topics, but go into them more deeply. In fact, these essential schools also incorporate components of perennialism, which happens to be the next teacher-centered philosophy that we will discuss.

Perennialism

Perennialism is a cousin to essentialism. Both advocate teacher-centered classrooms. Both tolerate little flexibility in the curriculum. Both implement rigorous standards. Both aim to sharpen students' intellectual powers and enhance their moral qualities. So what are the differences?

Perennialists organize their schools around books, ideas and concepts, and criticize essentialists for the vast amount of factual information they require students to absorb in their push for "cultural literacy." Perennial means "everlasting"—a perennialist education focuses on enduring themes and questions that span the ages. Perennialists recommend that students learn directly from the **Great Books**—works by history's finest thinkers and writers, books as meaningful today as when they were first written.

Perennialists believe that the goal of education should be to develop rational thought and to discipline minds to think rigorously. Perennialists see education as a sorting mechanism, a way to identify and prepare the intellectually gifted for leadership, while providing vocational training for the rest of society. They lament the change in universities over the centuries, from institutions where a few gifted students (and teachers) rigorously pursued truth for its own sake, to a glorified training ground for future careers.

Those of you who received a religious education might recognize the perennialist philosophy. Many parochial schools reflect the perennialist tradition with a curriculum that focuses on analyzing great religious books (such as the *Bible, Talmud,* or *Koran*), discerning moral truths, and honoring these moral values. In the classroom description that follows, we will concentrate on secular perennialism as formulated in the twentieth-century United States by such individuals as Robert Hutchins and Mortimer Adler.

THE PERENNIALIST CLASSROOM As in an essentialist classroom, students in a perennialist classroom spend considerable time and energy mastering the three "Rs," reading, 'riting and 'rithmetic. Greatest importance is placed on reading, the key to unlocking the enduring ideas found in the Great Books. Special attention is given to teaching values and character training, often through discussion about the underlying values and moral principles in a story. (Former Secretary of Education Bill Bennett wrote a collection of such stories in 1993, entitled *Book of Virtues*.) High school marks an increase in academic rigor as more challenging books are explored, including works of Darwin, Homer, and Shakespeare. Few elective choices are allowed. In an extreme example, in his *Paideia Proposal,* published in 1982, **Mortimer Adler** proposed a single elementary and secondary curriculum for all students, with no curricular electives except in the choice of a second language.

Electives are not the only things perennialists go without. You find few if any textbooks in a perennialist class. **Robert Hutchins**, who as president of the University of Chicago introduced the Great Books program, once opined that textbooks "have probably done as much to degrade the American intelligence as any single force."[2] Because perennialist teachers see themselves as discussion seminar leaders and facilitators, lectures are rare. Current concerns like multiculturalism, gender stereotypes, or computer technology would find no place in a perennialist curriculum.

While critics chastise perennialists for the lack of women, people of color, and non-Western ideas in the Great Books they teach, perennialists are unmoved by such criticism. To them, "training the mind" is ageless, beyond demographic concerns and transient trends. As Mortimer Adler wrote,

> The Great Books of ancient and medieval as well as modern times are a repository of knowledge and wisdom, a tradition of culture which must initiate each generation.[3]

PERENNIALISM IN ACTION: ST. JOHN'S COLLEGE The best-known example of perennialist education today takes place at a private institution unaffiliated with any religion: St. John's College, founded in 1784 in Annapolis, Maryland (www.sjcsf.edu). St.

ESSENTIALISTS AND PERENNIALISTS: DIFFERENT CORE CURRICULA

While both essentialism and perennialism promote a conservative, status quo approach to education and schools, these teacher-centered philosophies draw their curricula from different sources. The first column includes excerpts from essentialists' *List* (we included a few of the words and phrases under the letter "c"); the second column provides selections from the perennialists' *Great Books* curriculum. Remember, these are only a few suggestions from very long lists!

The List

centigrade
center of gravity
cerebellum
carry coals to Newcastle
capital expenditure
Cèzanne
Canberra
Cain and Abel
Caesar Augustus
Candide
Calvary
cast pearls before swine
Cascade Mountains
cadre
catharsis
carbon dioxide
carte blanche
Caruso, Enrico
cathode ray tube

Great Books

Aristotle, *Sense and Sensible*
The Bible
Geoffrey Chaucer, *Canterbury Tales*
Charles Darwin, *On the Origin of Species*
Charles Dickens, *Oliver Twist*
F. Scott Fitzgerald, *The Great Gatsby*
Homer, *The Iliad*
Henry James, *In the Cage*
James Joyce, *Ulysses*
The Koran
Thomas Mann, *Death in Venice*
Karl Marx, *Das Kapital*
Herman Melville, *Moby Dick*
George Orwell, *Animal Farm*
Thomas Paine, *Common Sense*
Plato, *Charmides*
Jonathan Swift, *Gulliver's Travels*
Virginia Woolf, *Night and Day*
Leo Tolstoy, *War and Peace*

REFLECTION

How many of these names and terms can you identify? Does this list make you feel culturally literate—or illiterate? Do you believe that lists like this one should be important? Why or why not?

John's College adopted the Great Books as a core curriculum in 1937 and assigns readings in the fields of literature, philosophy and theology, history and the social sciences, mathematics and natural science, and music. Students write extensively and attend seminars twice weekly to discuss assigned readings. They also complete a number of laboratory experiences and tutorials in language, mathematics, and music, guided by the faculty, who are called *tutors*. Seniors take oral examinations at the beginning and end of their senior year and write a final essay that must be approved before they are allowed to graduate.

Although grades are given in order to facilitate admission to graduate programs, students receive their grades only upon request and are expected to learn only for learning's sake. Since the St. John's experience thrives best in a small-group atmosphere, the college established a second campus in 1964 in Santa Fe, New Mexico to handle additional enrollment.

YOU BE THE JUDGE

TEACHER- VERSUS STUDENT-CENTERED APPROACHES TO EDUCATION

Teacher-Centered Approaches Are Best Because . . .

AFTER CENTURIES OF EXPERIENCE, WE KNOW WHAT TO TEACH

From Plato to Orwell, great writers and thinkers of the past light our way into the future. We must pass our cherished cultural legacy onto the next generation.

TEACHERS MUST SELECT WHAT IS WORTH KNOWING

The knowledge explosion showers us with mountains of new, complex information on a daily basis. Selecting what students should learn is a daunting challenge. Teachers, not students, are trained and best equipped to determine what is of value. To ask students to choose what they should learn would be the height of irresponsibility.

SCHOOLS MUST BE INSULATED FROM EXTERNAL DISTRACTIONS

Students can be easily distracted by the "excitement" of contemporary events. While academic and rigorous school-based learning may be less flashy and less appealing, in the long run, it is far more valuable. Once schoolwork has been mastered, students will be well prepared to leave the sanctuary of learning and confront the outside world.

WE ARE FALLING BEHIND OTHER NATIONS

U.S. student performance on international tests lags behind that of students from other nations. We have grown "educationally soft," lacking the challenging teacher-centered curriculums that other nations use. Only by creating a tough and demanding curriculum can we hope to compete with other nations.

COMPETITION AND REWARDS ARE IMPORTANT FOR MOTIVATING LEARNERS

Most people want and need to be recognized for their effort. Students are motivated to earn good report card grades and academic honors, to "ace" the SATs and be admitted to a prestigious college. Competition to earn high grades is the engine that drives successful school performance. Competition and rewards also drive the nation's productive workforce.

Student-Centered Approaches Are Best Because . . .

GENUINE LEARNING ORIGINATES WITH THE LEARNER

People learn best what they want to learn, what they feel they should or need to learn. Students find lessons imposed "from above" to be mostly irrelevant, and the lessons are quickly forgotten.

THEY BEST PREPARE STUDENTS FOR THE INFORMATION AGE

The knowledge explosion is actually a powerful argument for student-directed learning. Teachers can't possibly teach everything. We must equip students with research skills, then fan the flames of curiosity so they will want to learn for themselves. Then students can navigate the information age, finding and evaluating new information.

EDUCATION IS A VITAL AND ORGANIC PART OF SOCIETY

The most important lessons of life are found not on the pages of books or behind the walls of a school, but in the real world. Students need to work and learn directly in the community, from cleaning up the environment to reducing violence. Social action projects and service learning can offer a beacon of hope for the community, while building compassionate values within our students.

MULTIPLE CHOICE TESTS ARE NOT AN OLYMPIC EVENT

Education is not a competition, and academic tests are not a new Olympic event where youngsters have to get the highest score to please the cheering crowd. National success will come from living up to our beliefs, not "beating" the children of some other nation on a multiple choice test.

MEANINGFUL REWARDS DO NOT COME FROM ACADEMIC COMPETITIONS

Grades, funny stickers, and social approval are poor sources of motivation. Authentic learning rests on a more solid foundation: intrinsic motivation. Real success comes from an inner drive, not from artificial rewards. Schools need to develop students' inner motivation and stress student cooperation, not competition.

Teacher-Centered Approaches Are Best Because . . .

DISCIPLINED MINDS, RESPECTFUL CITIZENS
Students who listen thoughtfully and participate respectfully in classroom discussions learn several important lessons. For one, they learn the worth and wisdom of Western culture. They also learn to appreciate and to honor those who brought them this heritage, the guardians of their freedom and culture: their teachers.

Student-Centered Approaches Are Best Because . . .

HUMAN DIGNITY IS LEARNED IN DEMOCRATIC CLASSROOMS
Democracy is learned through experience, not books. Students flourish when they are respected; they are stifled when they are told what and how to think. As students manage their own learning, they master the most important lesson any school can teach: the importance of the individual's ideas.

OLC

YOU BE THE JUDGE

Do you find yourself influenced more by the arguments supporting teacher-centered approaches, or those advocating student-centered approaches? Are there elements of each that you find appealing? How will your classroom practices reflect your philosophy?

Student-Centered Philosophies

Student-centered philosophies are less authoritarian, less concerned with the past and "training the mind," and more focused on individual needs, contemporary relevance, and preparing students for a changing future. Progressivism, social reconstructionism, and existentialism place the learner at the center of the educational process: Students and teachers work together on determining what should be learned and how best to learn it. School is not seen as an institution that controls and directs youth, or works to preserve and transmit the core culture, but as an institution that works with youth to improve society or help students realize their individuality.

Progressivism

Progressivism organizes schools around the concerns, curiosity, and real-world experiences of students. The progressive teacher facilitates learning by helping students formulate meaningful questions and devise strategies to answer those questions. Answers are not drawn from lists or even Great Books; they are discovered through real world experience. Progressivism is the educational application of a philosophy called pragmatism. According to **pragmatism**, the way to determine if an idea has merit is simple: test it. If the idea works in the real world, then it has merit. Both pragmatism and progressivism originated in America, the home of a very practical and pragmatic people. John Dewey refined and applied pragmatism to education, establishing what became known as progressivism.

John Dewey was a reformer with a background in philosophy and psychology who taught that people learn best through social interaction in the real world. Dewey believed that because social learning had meaning, it endured. Book learning, on the other hand, was no substitute for actually doing things. Progressivists do not believe that the mind can be disciplined through reading Great Books, rather that the mind should be trained to analyze experience thoughtfully and draw conclusions objectively.

Dewey saw education as an opportunity to learn how to apply previous experiences in new ways. Dewey believed that students, facing an ever-changing world, should master the scientific method: (1) Become aware of a problem; (2) define it; (3) propose various hypotheses to solve it; (4) examine the consequences of each hypothesis in the light of previous experience; and (5) test the most likely solution. (For a biography of John Dewey, see the Hall of Fame: Profiles in Education in Chapter 8.)

Dewey regarded democracy and freedom as far superior to the political ideas of earlier times. Dewey saw traditional, autocratic, teacher-centered schools as the antithesis of democratic ideals. He viewed progressive schools as a working model of democracy. Dewey wrote:

> To imposition from above is opposed expression and cultivation of individuality; to external discipline is opposed free activity; to learning from texts and teachers, learning through experience; to acquisition of isolated skills and techniques by drill is opposed acquisition of them as means of attaining ends which make direct vital appeal; to preparation for a more or less remote future is opposed making the most of the opportunities of present life; to statistics and materials is opposed acquaintance with a changing world.[4]

THE PROGRESSIVE CLASSROOM   Walk into a progressivist classroom, and you will not find a teacher standing at the front of the room talking to rows of seated students. Rather, you will likely see children working in small groups, moving about and talking freely. Some children might be discussing a science experiment, while another group works on a model volcano, and a third prepares for a presentation. Interest centers would be located throughout the room, filled with books, materials, software, and projects designed to attract student interest on a wide array of topics. Finally you notice the teacher, walking around the room, bending over to talk with individual students and small groups, asking questions and making suggestions. You sense that the last thing on her mind is the standardized state test scheduled for next week.[5]

Progressivists build the curriculum around the experiences, interests, and abilities of students, and encourage students to work together cooperatively. Teachers feel no compulsion to focus their students' attention on one discrete discipline at a time, and students integrate several subjects in their studies. Thought-provoking activities augment reading, and a game like Monopoly might be used to illustrate the principles of capitalism versus socialism. Computer simulations, field trips, and interactive websites on the Internet offer realistic learning challenges for students, and build on students' multiple intelligences.

PROGRESSIVISM IN ACTION: THE LABORATORY SCHOOL   In 1896, while a professor at the University of Chicago, Dewey founded the Laboratory School as a testing ground for his educational ideas. Dewey's writings and his work with the **Laboratory School** set the stage for the progressive education movement. Based on the view that educators, like scientists, need a place to test their ideas, Dewey's Laboratory School eventually became the most famous experimental school in the history of U.S. education, a place where thousands observed Dewey's innovations in school design, methods, and curriculum. Although the school remained under Dewey's control for only eight years and never enrolled more than 140 students (ages 3 to 13) in a single year, its influence was enormous.

Dewey designed the Lab School with only one classroom but with several facilities for experiential learning: a science laboratory, an art room, a woodworking shop, and a kitchen. Children were likely to make their own weights and measures in the laboratory, illustrate their own stories in the art room, build a boat in the shop, and learn chemistry in the kitchen. They were unlikely to learn through isolated exercises or drills, which, according to Dewey, students consider irrelevant. Since Dewey believed that students learn from social interaction, the school used many group methods such as cooperative model-making, field trips, role playing, and dramatizations. Dewey maintained that group techniques make the students better citizens, developing, for example, their willingness to share responsibilities.

Children in the Laboratory School were not promoted from one grade to another after mastering certain material. Rather, they were grouped according to their individual interests and abilities. For all its child-centered orientation, however, the Laboratory School remained hierarchical in the sense that the students were never given a role comparable to that of the staff in determining the school's educational practices.

Social Reconstructionism

Social reconstructionism encourages schools, teachers, and students to focus their studies and energies on alleviating pervasive social inequities, and as the name implies, reconstruct society into a new and more just social order. Although social reconstructionists agree with progressivists that schools should concentrate on the needs of students, they split from progressivism in the 1920s after growing impatient with the slow pace of change in schools and in society. **George Counts**, a student of Dewey, published his classic book, *Dare the Schools Build a New Social Order?*, in which he outlined a more ambitious, and clearly more radical, approach to education. Counts's book, written in 1932, was no doubt influenced by the human cost of the Great Depression. He proposed that schools focus on reforming society, an idea that caught the imagination and sparked the ideals of educators both in this country and abroad.

Social challenges and problems provide a natural (and moral) direction for curricular and instructional activities. Racism, sexism, environmental pollution, homelessness, poverty, substance abuse, homophobia, AIDS and violence are rooted in misinformation and thrive in ignorance. Therefore, social reconstructionists believe that school is the ideal place to begin ameliorating social problems. The teacher's role is to explore social problems, suggest alternate perpectives, and facilitate student analysis of these problems. While convincing, cajoling, or moralizing about the importance of addressing human tragedy would be a natural teacher response, such adult-led decision making flies in the face of reconstructionist philosophy. A social reconstructionist teacher must model democratic principles. Students and teachers are expected to live and learn in a democratic culture; the students themselves must select educational objectives and social priorities.

THE SOCIAL RECONSTRUCTIONIST CLASSROOM A social reconstructionist teacher creates lessons that both intellectually inform and emotionally stir students about the inequities that surround them. A class might read a book and visit a photojournalist's exhibit portraying violent acts of racism. If the book, exhibit and the class discussion that follows move the students, the class might choose to pursue a long-term project to investigate the problem. One group of students might analyze news coverage of racial and ethnic groups in the community. Another student group might conduct a survey analyzing community perceptions of racial groups and race relations. Students might visit city hall and examine arrest and trial records in order to determine the

"Domephobia," the fear of things domestic, is Jane Roland Martin's word for gender bias in schools and in society. She coined the term when she compared the distinct educations Jean-Jacques Rousseau designed for his fictitious students Emile and Sophie. Martin was frustrated that while the boy, Emile, was said to revel in intellectual exploration, Sophie was to receive second-rate training—to be a wife and mother.

Martin deplores the disconnect between intellectual development and the development of abilities to love and care for a family. She recognizes that today's schools continue to craft different expectations for males and females. In fact, she knows this inequity firsthand. Teaching philosophy at the University of Massachusetts at Boston for over thirty years, Martin found herself fighting to have her intellectual voice heard in a traditional male discipline. Her experience of bias fueled her anger that equal opportunity education is still so far from reality.

Yet, Jane Roland Martin knows "women are barometers of change." Feminism today, like Sophie's education 300 years ago, gives men and women a special gift—a new perspective on gender roles. At the dawn of a new millennium, women's roles at work and in the family are indeed changing. Not only are women wives and mothers, they are corporate CEOs, medal-winning soccer players, and Supreme Court justices. Yet even as society may champion the greater earning power and talents of women, we are seeing a backlash against the more liberated roles of women. The trouble? The changes have cast as fiction the rosy Norman Rockwell portrait of the American family: More than half of all mothers work outside the home and single-parent homes number 1 in 5. These numbers stir concern that day care is bad, working mothers are neglectful and the well-being of the nation's children is threatened.

What society may see as problematic, Jane Roland Martin envisions as opportunity. Historically the physical, emotional, and social needs of children have been met by family, primarily mothers. Today, women are drawn by economic need and personal desire to enter the workforce. Martin sees these changes as a defining moment for schools, a chance to recreate within schools the nurturing tasks traditionally performed at home.

Martin's critics say no, schools should focus only on intellectual development. Not Martin. A social reconstructionist, she challenges schools to open their doors to what she calls the 3Cs—caring , concern, and connection. As more children are cared for outside the home, she fears the 3C curriculum is in danger of being lost. And American society has paid a heavy price for ignoring such domestic needs. Social inequalities continue and children are often the victims. Martin has an antidote: transform schoolhouses into "schoolhomes."

The schoolhome is far different from traditional "factory-model schooling which views children as raw material, teachers as workers who process their students before sending them on to the next station on the assembly line, [and] curriculum as the machinery that forges America's young into marketable products."[1] Instead, Martin's schoolhome focuses on students' individual emotional and cognitive needs. It embraces the experience of all learners and welcomes racial, cultural, and gender diversity. Martin's vision of schools reflects her vision of American society as everyone's home:

> Instead of focusing our gaze on abstract norms, standardized tests, generalized rates of success and uniform outcomes, the ideas of the schoolhome direct action to actual educational practice. Of course a schoolhome will teach the 3Rs. But it will give equal emphasis to the 3Cs—not by designating formal courses in these but by being a domestic environment characterized by safety, security, nurturance and love. In the schoolhome, mind and body, thought and action, reason and emotion are all educated.[2]

The schoolhome will incorporate the 3Cs into our very definition of what it means for males and females to be educated. Creating such nurturing and equitable schools will require "acts of both great and small, strategic and utterly outrageous. The cause demands no less, not one whit less."[3]

[1]Jane Roland Martin. *The Schoolhome: Rethinking Schools for Changing Families* (Cambridge, MA: Harvard University Press, 1992), p. 41.

[2]Jane Roland Martin. "Women, School, and Cultural Wealth." In Connie Titone and Karen Maloney (eds.). *Thinking Through Our Mothers: Women's Philosophies of Education* (Upper Saddle River, NJ: Merrill, 1999), pp.161–62.

[3]Jane Roland Martin. *Coming of Age in Academe: Rekindling Women's Hopes and Reforming the Academy* (New York: Routlege, 2000), p. 182.

REFLECTION

Do you agree with Jane Roland Martin that the 3Cs should be an integral part of the curriculum? Explain. Describe what a 3C curriculum might look like in schools today.

WRITE YOUR OWN *PROFILE IN EDUCATION*: Click on *Profiles in Education*, write a *Profile in Education* about an educator, and post it on the Online Learning Center. Check out *Profiles in Education* submitted by other future teachers.

To learn more about Jane Roland Martin, click on *Profiles in Education*.

role race plays in differential application of the law. Students might examine government records for information about housing patterns, income levels, graduation rates and other relevant statistics. The teacher's role would be as facilitator: assisting students in focusing their questions, developing a strategy, helping to organize visits, and ensuring that the data collected and analyzed meet standards of objectivity. Throughout, the teacher would be instructing students on research techniques, statistical evaluation, writing skills, and public communications.

In a social reconstructionist class, a research project is more than an academic exercise; the class is engaged in a genuine effort to improve society. In this case, the class might arrange to meet with political leaders, encouraging them to create programs or legislation to respond to issues the students uncovered. The students might seek a *pro bono* attorney to initiate legal action to remedy a social injustice they unmasked. Or perhaps the students might take their findings directly to the media by holding a press conference. They might also create a Web page to share their findings and research methods with students in other parts of the country, or other parts of the world. How would the teacher decide if the students have met the educational goals? In this example, an objective, well-prepared report would be one criterion, and reducing or eliminating a racist community practice would be a second measure of success.

SOCIAL RECONSTRUCTIONISM IN ACTION: PAULO FREIRE **Paulo Freire** believed that schools were just another institution perpetuating social inequities while serving the interests of the dominant group. Like social reconstructionism itself, Freire's beliefs grew during the Great Depression of the 1930s, when he experienced hunger and poverty firsthand. Influenced by Marxist and neo-Marxist ideas, Freire accused schools of perpetuating the status quo views of the rich and powerful "for the purpose of keeping the masses submerged and content in a culture of silence."[6] Schools were endorsing **social Darwinism,** the idea that society is an ingenious "sorting" system, one in which the more talented rise to the top, while those less deserving find themselves at the bottom of the social and economic pecking order. The conclusion: Those with money deserve it, those without money deserve their lot in life, and poverty is a normal, preordained part of reality.

Freire rejected this conclusion. He did not believe that schools should be viewed as "banks," where the privileged deposit ideas like social Darwinism to be spoon fed into the limited minds of the dispossessed. He envisioned schools as a place where the poor can acquire the skills to regain control of their lives and influence the social and economic forces that locked them in poverty in the first place. Freire engaged the poor as equal partners in dialogues that explored their economic and social problems

TABLE 9.1   Five philosophies of education.

	Underlying Basis: Metaphysics	Underlying Basis: Epistemology	Focus of Curriculum	Sample Classroom Activity	Role of Teacher	Goals for Students	Educational Leaders
Teacher-Centered Philosophies							
Essentialism	The physical world is the basis of reality	We learn through reasoning, primarily empirical reasoning	Core curriculum of traditional academic topics and traditional American virtues	Teacher focuses on "essential" information or the development of particular skills	Model of academic and moral virtue; center of classroom	To become culturally literate individuals, model citizens educated to compete in the world	William Bagley, E. D. Hirsch, Jr., William Bennett
Perennialism	The realm of thought and spirit rooted in the physical world; all human beings are by nature rational animals	We learn through reasoning—particularly through creative, deep, and logical analysis	Core curriculum analyzing enduring ideas found in Great Books	Socratic dialogue analyzing a philosophical issue or the meaning of a great work of literature	Scholarly role model; philosophically oriented, helps students seek the truth for themselves	To increase their intellectual powers and to appreciate learning for its own sake	Robert Hutchins, Mortimer Adler
Student-Centered Philosophies							
Progressivism	The physical world is the basis of reality; the world inevitably progresses over time	We learn best from meaningful life experiences, social interaction, and scientific experimentation	Flexible; integrated study of academic subjects around the needs, and experiences of students	Learning by doing—for example, students plan a field trip to learn about history, geography, and natural science	Guide and integrate learning activities so that students can find meaning	To become intelligent problem solvers, socially aware citizens who are prepared to live comfortably in the world	John Dewey, Nel Noddings

and possible solutions. Freire believed in **praxis,** the doctrine that when actions are based on sound theory and values, they can make a real difference in the world. (It is no accident that the term praxis is also the name given to the teacher competency tests required by many states.) Freire's ideas took hold not only in his native Brazil, but in poor areas around the globe. As poor farm workers became literate and aware, they organized for their self-improvement, and began to work for change. It is not surprising that the autocratic leaders of his country eventually forced him into exile, for he had turned schooling into a liberating force. (For a biography of Paulo Freire, see the Hall of Fame: Profiles in Education in Chapter 8.)

Existentialism

Existentialism, the final student-centered philosophy we will discuss, places the highest degree of importance on student perceptions, decisions, and actions. **Existentialism** rejects the existence of any source of objective, authoritative truth other

TABLE 9.1   *(concluded)*

	Underlying Basis: Metaphysics	Underlying Basis: Epistemology	Focus of Curriculum	Sample Classroom Activity	Role of Teacher	Goals for Students	Educational Leaders
Student-Centered Philosophies (concluded)							
Social Reconstructionism	The physical world is the basis of reality; world progresses, but slowly	We learn best from meaningful social experiences that improve society	Focus on social, political, and economic needs; integrated study of academic subjects around socially meaningful actions	Learning by reconstructing society—for example, students work to remove health hazards in a building housing the poor	Provide authentic learning activities that both instruct students and improve society	To become intelligent problem solvers, to enjoy learning, to live comfortably in the world while also helping reshape it	George S. Counts, John Brameld, Jane Roland Martin
Existentialism	Reality is individually determined; people shape their innermost nature in accordance with their free will	Each individual determines learning strategies; learning engages emotional as well as intellectual faculties	Each student determines the pace and direction of his or her own learning	Students choose their preferred medium—such as poetry, prose, or painting—and evaluate their own performance	One who seeks to relate to each student honestly; skilled at creating a free, open, and stimulating environment	To accept personal responsibility; to understand deeply and be at peace with one's own unique individuality	A. S. Neill, Maxine Greene

REFLECTION

How many of these philosophies have you experienced in your own education? Describe the circumstances. Would you like to encounter others as a student? a teacher? Explain.

than the individual. Individuals are responsible for determining for themselves what is true or false, right or wrong, beautiful or ugly. In short, it is up to the student to make all relevant educational decisions, and to evaluate those decisions.

Noted philosopher **Jean-Paul Sartre**'s (1905–1980) classic formulation of existentialism is "existence precedes essence." What does this mean? One interpretation goes as follows: We did not ask to be born into this world; so we "exist" before we are anything. We also are powerless at the other end of the life cycle, when we die. In between those two uncontrollable events, we shape our essence.

Existentialists believe that each person needs to define life's meaning. To become an authentic individual, one who values and practices free choice, we must struggle free of the influences of our parents, teachers, schools, religion, and culture. Existentialists believe education should be about helping each of us answer the fundamental questions: Why am I here? What is my purpose?

William Bagley (1874–1946) *Essentialism* Bagley believed that the major role of the school is to produce a literate, intelligent electorate; argued against electives while stressing thinking skills to help students apply their academic knowledge.

Robert M. Hutchins (1899–1979) *Perennialism* During the sixteen years he served as president of the University of Chicago, Hutchins abolished fraternities, football, and compulsory attendance, and introduced the Great Books program.

John Dewey (1859–1952) *Progressivism* A founder of progressivism, Dewey not only worked to democratize schools, he also fought for women's suffrage and the right of teachers to form unions.

George S. Counts (1907–1974) *Social Reconstructionism* Counts viewed education as an important tool to counter social injustices, and, if educators questioned their own power to make critical decisions, Counts's plea was to "Just do it!"

A. S. Neill (1883–1973) *Existentialism* Neill's attitude toward education stemmed from his own problems as a student, problems which fueled his creation of Summerhill, a school that encouraged youngsters to make their own decisions about what and when to learn.

REFLECTION

The ideas of Dewey and Counts were particularly popular in the 1930s, 1960s, and 1970s, while the teacher-centered philosophies were popular in the other decades of the twentieth century. Existentialism drew a few influential supporters, but never many adherents. How did historical events during the twentieth century influence which of these voices were heard?

E. D. Hirsch, Jr. (1928–) *Essentialism* He established the Core Knowledge Foundation to develop a prescribed curriculum in subject areas, including technology. Visit your local bookstore and browse through his books delineating what educated people should know.

Mortimer Adler (1902–2001) *Perennialism* He renewed interest in perennialism with the publication of *The Paideia Proposal* (1982). Adler advocated that all students be educated in the classics and that education be a lifelong venture.

Nel Noddings (1929–) *Progressivism* She believes that an ethic of care can best be cultivated when the curriculum is centered around the interests of students. Schools are challenged to nourish the physical, spiritual, occupational, and intellectual development of each child.

bell hooks (1952–) *Social Reconstructionism* Her theory of education, *engaged pedagogy*, helps students and teachers develop a critical consciousness of race, gender, and class biases. A prolific writer, her books include *Ain't I a Woman: Black Women and Feminism* (1981) and *Teaching to Transgress: Education as the Practice of Freedom* (1994).

Maxine Greene (1917–) *Existentialism* She believes that it is crucial for students and teachers to create meaning in their lives. Greene sees the humanities and the arts as catalysts for moving people to critical awareness and conscious engagement with the world.

REFLECTION

How do these spokespersons reflect current political trends? Which voices are being heard in public policy circles today, and which are not? Why is this the case?

THE EXISTENTIALIST CLASSROOM Existentialism in the classroom is a powerful rejection of traditional, and particularly essentialist thinking. In the existentialist classroom, subject matter takes second place to helping the students understand and appreciate themselves as unique individuals. The teacher's role is to help students define their own essence by exposing them to various paths they may take in life and by creating an environment in which they can freely choose their way. Existentialism, more than other educational philosophies, affords students great latitude in their choice of subject matter and activity.

The existentialist curriculum often emphasizes the humanities as a means of providing students with vicarious experiences that will help unleash their creativity and self-expression. For example, existentialists focus on the actions of historical individuals, each of whom provides a model for the students to explore. Math and the natural sciences may be de-emphasized because their subject matter is less fruitful for promoting self-awareness. Career education is regarded more as a means of teaching students about their potential than of teaching a livelihood. In art, existentialism encourages individual creativity and imagination more than it does the imitation of established models.

Existentialist learning is self-paced, self-directed, and includes a great deal of individual contact with the teacher. Honest interpersonal relationships are emphasized; roles and "official" status de-emphasized. According to philosopher Maxine Greene, teachers themselves must be deeply involved in their own learning and questioning: "Only a teacher in search of his freedom can inspire a student to search for his own." Greene asserts that education should move teachers and students to "wide awakeness," the ability to discover their own truths.[7]

Although elements of existentialism occasionally appear in public schools, this philosophy has not been widely disseminated. In an age of high-stakes tests and standards, only a few schools, mostly private, implement existentialist ideas. Even Summerhill, the well-known existentialist school founded in England by **A. S. Neill** in 1921, struggles to persevere with its unusual educational approach.

EXISTENTIALISM IN ACTION: THE SUDBURY VALLEY SCHOOL Visit Sudbury Valley School just outside of Boston, Massachusetts, look around, look closely, and you still may not see the school. The large building nestled next to a fishing pond on a ten-acre campus looks more like a mansion than a school. Walk inside, and you will find students and adults doing pretty much as they please. Not a "class" in sight. Some people are talking, some playing, some reading. A group is building a bookcase over there, a student is working on the computer in the corner, another is taking a nap on a chair. All ages mix freely, with no discernable grade level for any activity. In fact, it is even difficult to locate the teachers. If there is a curriculum, it is difficult to detect. Instead, the school offers a wide variety of educational options, including field trips to Boston, New York, and the nearby mountains and seacoast, and the use of facilities that include a laboratory, a woodworking shop, a computer room, a kitchen, a darkroom, an art room, and several music rooms.

Sudbury Valley provides a setting, an opportunity, but each student must decide what to do with that opportunity. Students are trusted to make their own decisions about learning. The school's purpose is to build on the students' natural curiosity, based on the belief that authentic learning takes place only when students initiate it. The school operates on the premise that all its students are creative, and each should be helped to discover and nurture his or her individual talents.

Sudbury Valley is fully accredited, and the majority of Sudbury Valley's graduates have continued on to college. The school accepts anyone from 4-year-olds to adults and charges low tuition, so as not to exclude anyone. Evaluations or grades are given only on request. A high school diploma is awarded to those who complete relevant requirements, which mainly focus on the ability to be a responsible member of the community at large.

Psychological Influences on Education

While essentialism, perennialism, progressivism, social reconstructionism, and existentialism are influential philosophies of education, they are far from the only forces shaping today's schools. Teachers who take their profession seriously pay attention to work in other fields, such as psychology, and may modify their teaching based on models proposed there. The following descriptions offer a glimpse into some of these forces guiding current school practices.

Constructivism

Constructivism, like existentialism, puts the learner at the center of the educational stage. **Constructivism** asserts that knowledge cannot be handed from one person to another (from a teacher to a learner), but must be *constructed* by each learner through interpreting and reinterpreting a constant flow of information. Constructivists believe that people continually try to make sense and bring order to the world.

Built on the work of Swiss and Russian psychologists, Jean Piaget and Lev Vygotsky, constructivism reflects the cognitive psychologists' view that the essence of learning is the constant effort to assimilate new information. Let's take a brief spin in your car to see how this works. You are driving happily along the highway and don't you know it—you hear an odd noise. No, it's not your passenger, it is coming from the engine. Just before panic sets in, you remember that your friend Karen mentioned that the air pressure looked low in your left front tire. You suspect that is causing the noise. You are doing just what a constructivist would expect you to do: looking for a pattern, a meaning to explain the noise. You step out of the car, look at the tires, but they all seem just fine. Now you need to figure out another explanation for the noise, another meaning. You open the hood, look around the engine, and find the fan belt waving wildly, hitting everything in sight. You back off, relieved that you have "learned" what is making the noise. You have reconstructed your thoughts based on new information. Next time you hear that noise, you might look first for that pesky fan belt. If that is not the problem, you will start the process again, and build more knowledge about what could go wrong in your car.

In a constructivist classroom, the teacher builds knowledge in much the same way, gauging a student's prior knowledge and understanding, then carefully orchestrating cues, penetrating questions, and instructional activities that challenge and extend a student's insight. Teachers can use **scaffolding,** that is, questions, clues or suggestions that help a student link prior knowledge to the new information. The educational challenges facing students in a constructivist classroom could be creating a new way to handle a math problem, letting go of an unfounded bias about an ethnic group, or discovering why women's contributions seem all but absent in a history textbook. In a constructivist classroom, students and teachers constantly challenge their own assumptions. (If you check back to the philosophy inventory, see how you responded to item 26, which captured this aspect of constructivism.)

Each of these photographs reflects a major tenet of the five educational philosophies described in this chapter. See if you can match the picture with the philosophy it best represents.

A

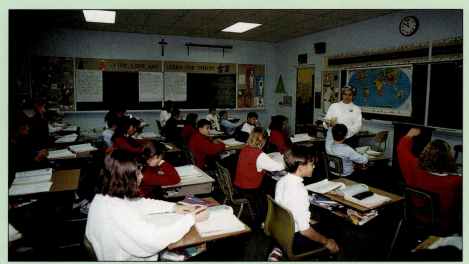

B

While constructivism runs counter to the current emphasis on uniform standards and testing, it is enjoying popularity, especially among school reformers. Perhaps part of the reason for its growing acceptance is that constructivism dovetails with authentic learning, critical thinking, individualized instruction, and project-based learning, ideas popular in reform circles.

C

E

D

Behaviorism

In stark contrast to both existentialism and constructivism, **behaviorism** is derived from the belief that free will is an illusion, and that human beings are shaped entirely by their environment. Alter a person's environment, and you will alter his or her thoughts, feelings, and behavior. People act in response to physical stimuli. We learn, for instance, to avoid overexposure to heat through the impulses of pain our nerves

INTERACTIVE ACTIVITY
WHAT PHILOSOPHY OR
APPROACH IS THIS? Read
scenarios and match the
philosophy or approach
being exhibited.

send to our brain. More complex learning, such as understanding the material in this chapter, is also determined by stimuli, such as the educational support you have received from your professor or parents and the comfort of the chair in which you sit when reading this chapter.

Harvard professor **B. F. Skinner** became the leading advocate of behaviorism, and he did much to popularize the use of positive reinforcement to promote desired learning. (For a biography of B. F. Skinner, see the Hall of Fame: Profiles in Education in Chapter 8.) Behaviorists urge teachers to use a system of reinforcement to encourage desired behaviors, to connect learning with pleasure and reward (a smile, special privilege, or good grades). In a program termed **behavior modification**, extrinsic rewards are gradually lessened as the student acquires and masters the targeted behavior. By association, the desired behavior now produces its own reward (self-satisfaction). This process may take minutes, weeks, or years, depending on the complexity of the learning desired and on the past environment of the learner. The teacher's goal is to move the learner from extrinsic to intrinsic rewards. (If you check the inventory at the chapter's opening, behaviorism was represented by statement 27. How did you respond?)

Behavior modification is perhaps most commonly used to manage student behavior. One well-known program is **assertive discipline**, developed by Lee and Marlene Canter. "The key to assertive discipline is catching students being good, recognizing and supporting them when they behave appropriately, and letting them know you like it, day in and day out."[8]

Critics of behaviorism decry behaviorists' disbelief in the autonomy of the individual. They ask, Are people little more than selfish "reward machines"? Can clever forces manipulate populations through clever social engineering? Are educators qualified to exert such total control of students? Those who defend behaviorism point to its striking successes. Behaviorism's influence is apparent in the joy on students' faces as they receive visual and auditory rewards via their computer monitor, or in the classroom down the hall where special needs learners make significant progress in a behaviorist-designed curriculum.

Cultural Influences on Education

Most of the ideas and philosophies discussed in this chapter are drawn from Western culture. As a nation, we rarely identify or reflect on the ideas that derive from many parts of Asia, Africa, and Latin America. We are guilty of **ethnocentrism**, the tendency to view one's own culture as superior to others, and (perhaps worse) a failure to consider other cultures at all. Let's broaden our view, and examine education as practiced in other cultures.

In much of the West, society's needs dictate educational practices, with statewide standards, national goals, and high-stakes testing. In the rest of the world, that is to say, in most of the world, the child's education is primarily a concern of the family, not the society. A child's vocational interests, for example, might mirror the occupation of a parent or be built around the unique interest or talent of the child, rather than respond to the broader employment market or societal priorities. Family and community are foremost; the nation is a weaker influence.

In Western society, formal schools, formal certification and degrees are valued; in other societies, more credence is placed on actual knowledge and mastery rather than educational documentation. The notion of *teachers* and *nonteachers* is foreign in many

TOWARDS ENLIGHTENMENT: ARE SCHOOLS *FENG SHUI?*

Dècor makes a difference, at least that's what some researchers say about the link between school architecture and student achievement. As classroom daylight increases, so does student performance in math and reading. In windowless classrooms (typical of the energy efficient 70s and security conscious 90s) students experience a kind of jet lag, which contributes to a lag in academic success.

SOURCE: *The New York Times,* August 5, 2001.

REFLECTION

Feng shui is the ancient art and science of design and placement. How does your college classroom use daylight, windows, and other architectural features to promote or inhibit learning?

Click on *In the News* for recent *In the News* stories. Submit your own *In the News* summary to share with your colleagues.

cultures, since all adults and even older children participate in educating the young. Children learn adult roles through observation, conversation, assisting and imitating, all the while absorbing moral, intellectual, and vocational lessons. This shared educational responsibility is called **informal education**.[9] (What does calling this practice "informal education" reveal about Western values and assumptions? Would someone in a culture practicing this integrated education call it "informal education"?) In the process, adults also learn a great deal about the children in the community. Strong bonds are forged between the generations. (As you probably already concluded, item 28 on our opening inventory describes informal education. You might want to check your answer to that statement.)

Oral traditions enjoy particular prominence in many parts of the world, even in literate societies where reading and writing are commonplace and valued. In the **oral tradition**, spoken language becomes a primary method for instruction: Word problems teach reasoning skills; proverbs instill wisdom; and stories, anecdotes, and rhymes teach lessons about nature, history, religion, and social customs. The oral tradition refines communication and analytical skills, and reinforces human connections and moral values. Not infrequently, religious and moral lessons were passed on initially through oral communication, only later to be written. In fact, the word Qur'an (Koran) is often translated as "the Recitation."

The practices and beliefs of peoples in other parts of the world offer useful insights for enhancing—or questioning—our own educational practices, but they are insights too rarely considered, much less implemented. Perhaps this will change in the years ahead as immigration continues to bring these ideas to our communities, while technological advances bring all world cultures closer together. For now, however, our education philosophies are rooted in the ideas and thoughts of Western thinkers. Let's visit some of these powerful thinkers and their influential, enduring contributions.

The Three Legendary Figures of Classical Western Philosophy

To understand Western philosophy, we must look back to the birthplace of Western philosophy—ancient Greece. Specifically, we must begin with a trio of philosopher-teachers: Socrates, Plato, and Aristotle. Together they laid the foundation for most of Western philosophy. It is likely that you are familiar with at least their names. Let's review their lasting contributions to the world of philosophy.

The name of **Socrates** is practically synonymous with wisdom and the philosophical life. Socrates (469–399 B.C.E.) was a teacher without a school. He walked about Athens, engaging people in provocative dialogues about questions of ultimate significance. Socrates is hailed as an exemplar of human virtue whose goal was to help others find the truths that lie within their own minds. In that regard, he described himself as a "midwife"; today we call his approach the **Socratic method**. By repeatedly questioning, disproving, and testing the thoughts of his pupils on such questions as the nature of "love" or "the good," he helped his students reach deeper, clearer ideas.

Socrates's method did not just promote intellectual insights in his students; it also challenged the conventional ideas and traditions of his time. Socrates offended many powerful people and was eventually charged with corrupting the youth of Athens. Even in this, Socrates provides a lesson for today's teachers: challenges to popular convention may lead to community opposition and sanctions. (Luckily, sanctions today are less severe than those meted out to Socrates, who was condemned to death for his "impiety.")

We know about Socrates and his teachings through the writings of his disciples, one of whom was **Plato** (427–347 B.C.E.). Plato's writing is renowned for its depth, beauty and clarity. His most famous works were dialogues, conversations between two or more people, that present and critique various philosophical viewpoints. Plato's dialogues feature Socrates questioning and challenging others and presenting his own philosophy. After Socrates was put to death, Plato became disillusioned with Athenian democracy and left the city for many years. Later, he returned to Athens and founded **The Academy**, considered by some to be the world's first university.

Plato held that a realm of eternally existing "ideas" or "forms" underlies the physical world. In Plato's philosophy, the human soul has three parts: intellect, spirit, and appetite (basic animal desires). Plato believed that these faculties interact to determine human behavior. Plato urged that the intellect, the highest faculty, be trained to control the other two. For a look at Plato's famous "Parable of the Cave," from *The Republic*, setting out his political philosophy (he envisioned a class of philosopher-kings that would rule over the warriors and the common people) visit the Online Learning Center.

Just as Plato studied under Socrates, **Aristotle** (384–322 B.C.E.) studied under Plato. Aristotle entered Plato's Academy at age 18 and stayed for twenty years. In 342 B.C.E., Aristotle went to northern Greece and, for several years, tutored a young boy named Alexander, later known as Alexander the Great. After educating Alexander, Aristotle returned to Athens to set up his own school, the **Lyceum**, adjacent to Plato's Academy.

The depth and breadth of Aristotle's ideas were unsurpassed in ancient Western civilization. In addition to tackling philosophical questions, Aristotle wrote influential works on biology, physics, astronomy, mathematics, psychology, and literary

TEACHER: Today we will try to understand what we mean by the concepts of right and wrong. What are examples of conduct you consider wrong or immoral?

STUDENT: Lying is wrong.

TEACHER: But what if you were living in Germany around 1940 and you were harboring in your house a certain Jewish man named Nathan Cohen, who was wanted by the Nazis? If asked by a Nazi if you knew the whereabouts of that Mr. Cohen, wouldn't it be acceptable, even obligatory, to lie?

STUDENT: I suppose so.

TEACHER: So could you rephrase what you meant when you said that lying is wrong or immoral?

STUDENT: I think what I meant is that it is usually wrong to lie. But it is true that there are times when lying is acceptable, because the overall effects of the lie are good. Look at how much your Mr. Cohen was helped; the lie about where he was may have saved his life.

TEACHER: So you are saying that it is okay to lie, as long as the consequences of the lie are positive. But consider this hypothetical situation: I am a business tycoon who makes millions of dollars selling diamonds to investors. I sell only to very rich people who can afford to lose the money they invest in my diamonds. I tell my customers that my diamonds are worth $10,000 each, but they really are fakes, worth only $2,000 each. Rather than keeping the profits myself, I give all the money to the poor, helping them obtain the food and shelter they need to live. If you look at the obvious consequences of my business—the rich get slightly poorer and the needy are helped out immensely—you may conclude that my business has a generally positive effect on society. And, yet, because the business is based on fraud, I find it immoral. Do you agree?

STUDENT: Yes, I find it immoral. I suppose I was wrong in saying that whenever a lie has generally good results it is morally acceptable. In your diamond example, unlike the Nazi example, the lie was directed at innocent people and the harm done to them was significant. I want to change my earlier statement that a lie is acceptable whenever it has generally good results. What I want to say now is that you should never lie to innocent people if that would cause them significant harm.

As is typical of Socrates' dialogue, this one could go on indefinitely, because there is no simple, "correct" solution to the issues being discussed—the meaning of right and wrong and, more specifically, the contours of when a lie is morally acceptable. By asking questions, the teacher is trying to get the student to clarify and rethink his or her own ideas, to come eventually to a deep and clear understanding of philosophical concepts, such as right and wrong.

REFLECTION

Have you ever experienced the Socratic Dialogue as a student? What were your reactions? Would you like to develop this teaching technique? Why or why not?

criticism. Aristotle placed more importance on the physical world than did Plato. Aristotle's teachings can, in fact, be regarded as a synthesis of Plato's belief in the universal, spiritual forms, and a scientist's belief that each animal, vegetable, and mineral we observe is undeniably real.

Aristotle also won renown for his ethical and political theories. He wrote that the highest good for people is a virtuous life, fully governed by the faculty of reason, with which all other faculties are in harmony. Aristotle promoted the doctrine of the **Golden Mean,** or the notion that virtue lies in a middle ground between two extremes. Courage, for example, is bordered on the one side by cowardice and on the other side by foolhardiness.

- **Socrates.** His philosophical lifestyle; the Socratic method, in which students are provocatively questioned so that they can rethink what they believe; his noble death
- **Plato.** Discussions of philosophy through eloquent dialogues; the theory of "forms," or "ideas," that exist in an eternal, transcendent realm; a vision of utopia, where an elite group of philosopher-kings rules over other members of society
- **Aristotle.** The breadth of his knowledge; the synthesis of Plato's belief in the eternal "forms" and a scientist's belief in the "real" world that we can see, touch, or smell; the theory of the Golden Mean (everything in moderation)

REFLECTION

How might your current classroom instruction change if your education professor was Dr. Socrates, Plato, or Aristotle? Detail aspects of a "typical" lesson.

Many of the ideas first formulated by Socrates, Plato, and Aristotle have long been integrated into Western culture and education.

Basic Philosophical Issues and Concepts

Philosophy has many subdivisions that are of particular significance to educators: metaphysics, epistemology, ethics, political philosophy, aesthetics, and logic. (See Figure 9.2.) These fields are where key educational questions are raised, including: How do we know what we know? What is of value? What is education's role in society? As you ponder these questions, you should find elements of your philosophy of education coming into sharper focus.

Metaphysics and Epistemology

Metaphysics deals with the origin and structure of reality. Metaphysicians ask: What really is the nature of the world in which we live? **Epistemology** examines the nature and origin of human knowledge. Epistemologists are interested in how we use our minds to distinguish valid from illusory paths to true knowledge. It may be easiest to remember the scope of these closely related disciplines by considering that epistemology and metaphysics address, respectively, *how* we know (epistemology) *what* we know (metaphysics) about reality.

IS REALITY COMPOSED SOLELY OF MATTER? One of the most basic metaphysical issues is whether anything exists other than the material realm that we experience with our senses. Many philosophers assert the existence only of the physical, affirming fundamentally the existence of matter, a philosophy called **materialism**. By emphasizing in their curriculum the study of nature through scientific observation, modern public schools clearly deem that the material world is real and important. Other philosophers contend that the physical realm is but an illusion. They point out that matter is known only through the mind. This philosophy is called spiritualism or **idealism**. Educators responding to ideals might focus on students' relationships

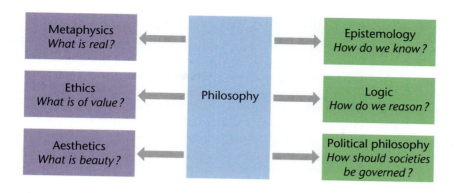

FIGURE 9.2
Branches of philosophy.

with each other or with a more spiritual world. A third group of philosophers asserts that reality is composed of both materialism and idealism, body and mind, a belief associated with French philosopher Renè Descartes and called **Cartesian dualism**.

IS REALITY CHARACTERIZED BY CHANGE AND PROGRESS? Metaphysicians question whether nature is constantly improving through time. The belief that progress is inevitable is widely held in the United States. On the other hand, some philosophers hold that change is illusory and that a foundation of timeless, static content underlies all reality. Still others believe that change is cyclical, swinging widely from one side of center to the opposing side.

Teachers who believe in the inevitability of progress seek new approaches to teaching and new subjects to be taught, thereby "keeping up with the times." Other teachers, less enamored with change, pay little heed to current trends and technologies. They may prefer to teach everlasting, timeless truths discovered by great thinkers, such as Plato and Aristotle. Finally, some teachers suggest that, with change such a constant, it is pointless to try to keep pace. They choose to ignore these cycles and to simply select the teaching methods they find most comfortable.

WHAT IS THE BASIS OF OUR KNOWLEDGE? Empiricism holds that sensory experience (seeing, hearing, touching, and so on) is the source of knowledge. Empiricists assert that we experience the external world by sensory perception; then, through reflection, we conceptualize ideas that help us interpret that world. For example, because we have seen the sun rise every day, we can formulate the belief that it will rise again tomorrow. The empiricist doctrine that knowledge is gained most reliably through scientific experimentation may be the most widely held belief in Western culture. People want to hear the latest research or be shown documentation that something is true. Teachers expect students to present evidence before drawing conclusions. Even children demand of one another, "Prove it."

Rationalism emphasizes the power of reason—in particular, logic—to derive true statements about the world, even when such realities are not detected by the senses. Rationalists point out that the field of mathematics has generated considerable knowledge that is not based on our senses. For example, we can reason that 7 cubed equals 343 without having to count 7 times 7 times 7 objects to verify our conclusion experientially. Whereas educational empiricists would support hands-on learning activities as the primary source for discovery and validation of information, rationalists would encourage schools to place a greater emphasis on teaching mathematics, as well as such nonempirical disciplines as philosophy and logic.

Ethics, Political Philosophy, and Aesthetics

Whereas metaphysics focuses on what "is," ethics, political philosophy, and aesthetics are concerned with what "ought to be." In these disciplines, philosophers grapple with the issue of what we should value. As you read on, consider the place of ethics, political philosophy, and aesthetics in the classroom.

Ethics is the study of what is "good" or "bad" in human behavior, thoughts, and feelings. It asks, What is the good life? and How should we treat each other? (What should schools teach children about what is "good" and what is "bad"?)

Political philosophy analyzes how past and present societies are arranged and governed and proposes ways to create better societies in the future. (How might schools engage in an objective evaluation of current governments, including our own?)

Aesthetics probes the nature of beauty. It asks, What is beauty? Is beauty solely in the eyes of the beholder? Or are some objects, people, and works (music, art, literature) objectively more beautiful than others? (How can teachers help students understand how their personal experiences, peer group values, and cultural and ethnic history shape their standards of what is beautiful?)

Logic

Logic is the branch of philosophy that deals with reasoning. Logic focuses on how to move from a set of assumptions to valid conclusions and examines the rules of inference that enable us to frame our propositions and arguments. While epistemology defines reasoning as one way to gain knowledge, logic defines the rules of reasoning.

Schools teach children to reason both deductively and inductively. When teaching **deductive reasoning**, teachers present their students with a general rule and then help them identify particular examples and applications of the rule. Inductive reasoning works in the opposite manner. When teaching **inductive reasoning**, teachers help their students draw tentative generalizations after having observed specific instances of a phenomenon.

A teacher who explains the commutative property of addition ($a + b = b + a$) and then has the student work out specific examples of this rule (such as $3 + 2 = 2 + 3$) is teaching deductive reasoning. Contrast this with a teacher who begins a lesson by stating a series of addition problems of the form $3 + 2 = 5$ and $2 + 3 = 5$, then asks, "What do you notice about these examples?" If students can draw a generalization about the commutative property of addition, they are reasoning inductively. While math is a natural field to isolate examples of deductive and inductive reasoning, logic equips students to think more precisely in virtually any field.

Your Turn

[I]n modern times there are opposing views about the practice of education. There is no general agreement about what the young should learn either in relation to virtue or in relation to the best life; nor is it clear whether their education ought to be directed more towards the intellect than towards the character of the soul. . . . [A]nd it is not certain whether training should be directed at things useful in life, or at those conducive to virtue, or at nonessentials. . . . And there is no agreement as to what in fact does tend towards virtue. Men [sic] do not all prize most highly the same virtue, so naturally they differ also about the proper training for it.[10]

Aristotle

More than 2,300 years later, we still find that reasonable people can come to entirely different points of view on all kinds of issues in education. (Remember the charter school discussion in the faculty room at the beginning of the chapter?) If everyone agreed on what should be taught, and how to teach it, there might be just one philosophy of education. But it is not so simple.

Rereading the inventory statements at the beginning of this chapter can help you determine if one of the five major philosophies speaks for you. You may be more eclectic in your outlook, picking and choosing elements from different philosophies. Your responsibility as an educator is to wrestle with tough questions, to bring your values to the surface and to forge a coherent philosophy of education.

You might say a clear philosophy of education is to a teacher what a blueprint is to a builder—a plan of action; reassurance that the parts will fit together in a constructive way. With a clear philosophy of education, you will not ricochet from one teaching method to another, and will not confuse students, parents and administrators with conflicting messages about the role of students and teacher in the classroom. If you have a well-honed philosophy of education, you will be better able to assess whether you will find a comfortable fit in a school and a community. Simply put, a philosophy brings purpose and coherence to your work in the classroom.

SUMMARY

1. What is a philosophy of education, and why should it be important to you?

   • Behind every school and every teacher is a set of related beliefs—a philosophy of education—that influences what and how students are taught. A philosophy of education represents answers to questions about the purpose of schooling, a teacher's role, and what should be taught and by what methods.

2. How do teacher-centered philosophies of education differ from student-centered philosophies of education?

   • Teacher-centered philosophies tend to be more authoritarian and conservative, and emphasize the values and knowledge that have survived through time. The major teacher-centered philosophies of education are essentialism and perennialism.

   • Student-centered philosophies are more focused on individual needs, contemporary relevance, and preparing students for a changing future. School is seen as an institution that works with youth to improve society or help students realize their individuality. Progressivism, social reconstructionism, and existentialism place the learner at the center of the educational process: Students and teachers work together on determining what should be learned and how best to learn it.

3. What are some major philosophies of education in the United States today?

   • Essentialism focuses on teaching the essential elements of academic and moral knowledge. Essentialists urge that schools get back to the basics; they believe in a strong core curriculum and high academic standards.

   • Perennialism focuses on the universal truths that have withstood the test of time. Perennialists urge that students read the Great Books and develop their understanding of the philosophical concepts that underlie human knowledge.

CHAPTER REVIEW

Go to the Online Learning Center to take a quiz, practice with key terms, and review key ideas from the chapter.

- Progressivism is based largely on the belief that lessons must be relevant to the students in order for them to learn. The curriculum of a progressivist school is built around the personal experiences, interests, and needs of the students.

- Social reconstructionists separated from progressivism because they desired more direct and immediate attention to societal ills. They are interested in combining study and social action, and believe that education can and should go hand in hand with ameliorating social problems.

- Existentialism is derived from a powerful belief in human free will, and the need for individuals to shape their own futures. Students in existentialist classrooms control their own education. Students are encouraged to understand and appreciate their uniqueness and to assume responsibility for their actions.

4. How are these philosophies reflected in school practices?

- Essentialism and perennialism give teachers the power to choose the curriculum, organize the school day, and construct classroom activities. The curriculum reinforces a predominantly Western heritage while viewing the students as vessels to be filled and disciplined in the proven strategies of the past. Essentialists focus on cultural literacy, while perennialists work from the Great Books.

- Progressivism, social reconstructionism, and existentialism view the learner as the central focus of classroom activities. Working with student interests and needs, teachers serve as guides and facilitators in assisting students to reach their goals. The emphasis is on the future, and on preparing students to be independent-thinking adults. Progressivists strive for relevant, hands-on learning. Social reconstructionists want students to actively work to improve society. Existentialists give students complete freedom, and complete responsibility, with regard to their education.

5. What are some of the psychological and cultural factors influencing education?

- Constructivism has its roots in cognitive psychology, and is based on the idea that people construct their understanding of the world. Constructivist teachers gauge a student's prior knowledge, then carefully orchestrate cues, classroom activities, and penetrating questions to push students to higher levels of understanding.

- B. F. Skinner advocated behaviorism as an effective teaching strategy. According to Skinner, rewards motivate students to learn material even if they do not fully understand why it will have value in their futures. Behavior modification is a system of gradually lessening extrinsic rewards.

- The practices and beliefs of peoples in other parts of the world, such as informal and oral education, offer useful insights for enhancing our own educational practices, but they are insights too rarely considered, much less implemented.

6. What were the contributions of Socrates, Plato, and Aristotle to Western philosophy, and how are their legacies reflected in education today?

- Socrates, Plato, and Aristotle are the three most legendary ancient Greek philosophers. Socrates is hailed today as the personification of wisdom and the philosophical life. He gave rise to what is now called the Socratic method, in which the teacher repeatedly questions students to help them clarify their own deepest thoughts.

- Plato, Socrates's pupil, crafted eloquent dialogues that present different philosophical positions on a number of profound questions. Plato believed that a realm of externally existing "ideas," or "forms," underlies the physical world.

- Aristotle, Plato's pupil, was remarkable for the breadth as well as the depth of his knowledge. He provided a synthesis of Plato's belief in the universal, spiritual forms and a scientist's belief in the physical world we observe through our senses. He taught that the virtuous life consists of controlling desires by reason and by choosing the moderate path between extremes.

7. How do metaphysics, epistemology, ethics, political philosophy, aesthetics, and logic factor into a philosophy of education?

- Metaphysics deals with the nature of reality, its origin, and its structure. Metaphysical beliefs are reflected in curricular choices: Should we study the natural world, or focus on spiritual or ideal forms?

- Epistemology examines the nature and origin of human knowledge. Epistemological beliefs influence teaching methods. "How we know" is closely related to how we learn and therefore, how we should teach.

- Ethics is the study of what is "good" or "bad" in human behavior, thoughts, and feelings. What should we teach about "good" and "bad," and should we teach that directly, or by modeling?

- Political philosophy analyzes how past and present societies are arranged and governed and proposes ways to create better societies in the future. How will a classroom be organized, and what will that say about who wields power? How will social institutions and national governments be analyzed?

- Aesthetics is concerned with the nature of beauty. What is of worth? What works are deemed of value to be studied or emulated?

KEY TERMS AND PEOPLE

KEY TERMS

The Academy, 374

aesthetics, 378

assertive discipline, 372

back-to-basics, 354

behavior modification, 372

behaviorism, 371

Cartesian dualism, 377

Coalition of Essential
Schools, 355

constructivism, 369

core curriculum, 355

deductive reasoning, 378

empiricism, 377

epistemology, 376

essentialism, 354

ethics, 378

ethnocentrism, 372

existentialism, 364

Golden Mean, 375

Great Books, 356

idealism, 376

inductive reasoning, 378

informal education, 373

Laboratory School, 360

logic, 378

Lyceum, 374

materialism, 376

metaphysics, 376

neoessentialism, 354

oral tradition, 373

Paideia Proposal, 356

perennialists, 356

philosophy, 347

political philosophy, 378

pragmatism, 359

praxis, 364

progressivism, 359

rationalism, 377

scaffolding, 369

social Darwinism, 363

social reconstructionism, 361

Socratic method , 374

student-centered
philosophies, 359

teacher-centered
philosophies, 354

KEY PEOPLE

Mortimer Adler, 356, 367

Aristotle, 374

William Bagley, 354, 366

George Counts, 361

John Dewey, 359, 366

Paulo Freire, 363

Maxine Greene, 367

E. D. Hirsch, Jr., 355, 367

bell hooks, 367

Robert Hutchins, 356, 366

Jane Roland Martin, 362

A. S. Neill, 366, 368

Nel Noddings, 367

Plato, 374

Jean-Paul Sartre, 365

B. F. Skinner, 372

Socrates, 374

DISCUSSION QUESTIONS AND ACTIVITIES

1. Consider a teacher who had an impact on you and describe that teacher's philosophy of education.

2. Suppose that you are a student who must choose one of five schools to attend. Each reflects one of the five major philosophies. Which would you choose and why? Which school would you choose to work in as a teacher? Why?

3. Interview a teacher who has been teaching for several years. Find out what that teacher's philosophy was when he or she started teaching and what it is today. Is there a difference? If so, try to find out why.

4. If you could meet a philosopher discussed in this chapter, who would it be and what questions would you ask? What answers might you anticipate?

5. Reread the five statements by the teachers in the faculty room at the beginning of the chapter. In what areas do you think these teachers could agree? In what areas are their philosophies distinct and different? What do you predict will be the result of their meeting?

6. Which of the statements by the five teachers do you agree with most? Are there elements of each teacher's philosophy that could combine to form your own philosophy of education?

7. How would you describe your own philosophy of education? Imagine you are a teacher. Create a 3-minute speech that you would give to parents on back-to-school night that outlines your philosophy of education and identifies how it would be evident in the classroom.

8. The key terms and people in this chapter could be dramatically expanded by including Far Eastern and Middle Eastern philosophy. Consider the following additions: Buddhism, Confucius, Hinduism, Islam, Jainism, Judaism, Mohammed, Shinto, Taoism, Zen Buddhism. Research and briefly describe each of these. What has been (or might be) the impact of these religions, principles, and individuals on our present school philosophy?

WEB-*TIVITIES*

1. What Is Your Philosophy of Education?

2. Philosophies of Education

3. Progressivism and Dewey's Laboratory School

4. Existentialism

5. Behaviorism

REEL TO REAL TEACHING

QUIZ SHOW (1992)
Run Time: 130 minutes

Synopsis: By giving answers to the players they wanted to win, the producers of the popular 1950s game show *Twenty-One* had their trump card for capturing huge audience ratings. Charles Van Doren, college professor and scion of a great literary family, was the "perfect" game show contestant. The fact that the handsome and genteel Van Doren was prepared to participate in the cheating was an extra benefit. Based on a true story, the film probes the fault lines between knowledge, privilege, and scandal, and raises serious questions about what is most worth knowing.

Reflection:

1. What hooks you into a good game show or causes you to quickly flip channels? How is your educational philosophy reflected in your passion (or distaste) for game shows?
2. Which educational philosophy is best represented in *Quiz Show*? What elements of the classroom are seen on the game show stage?
3. How did factors such as race, religion, gender, and socioeconomic class determine who knew the answers on *Twenty-One*? Compare how these same factors shape how we define who is intelligent in schools.
4. After the scandal, Charles Van Doren noted that he believed the difference between good and evil was "not cut and dried." How is this statement revealed in the motives of the *Twenty-One* producers? Contestant Herb Stempel? Charles Van Doren? What power did each have? What power did each believe he had? How is this "winning at all costs" attitude reflected in schools and the testing culture?
5. What accounts for the popularity of quiz shows in the 1950s? Today? Consider the events, people, and values of each time period. How do game shows reflect American society and the value it places on knowledge?

Follow-up Activity: It's Game Night at your school. Choose a subject area and design your own "quiz show" based on one of the five philosophies discussed in the chapter. How will you define winning? How will the host, contestants, questions/answers, interactions, seating arrangements, and prizes reflect the key principles of the philosophy? Consider the many variables, such as the "facts"; the roles of gender, race, and class; and political motivations, among other things, that go into creating a "quiz show."

How do you rate this film? Click on *Reel to Real Teaching* to submit your review of this or another education-related film, and read reviews submitted by others.

FOR FURTHER READING

Approaches to Teaching, by Gary Fenstermacher and Jonas Soltis (3rd ed., 1998). Through an interactive, case studies approach, the authors explore the strengths and weaknesses of various philosophical perspectives. Readers are challenged to critically assess their own philosophical positions on education and to unpack the meaning of teaching.

Children as Philosophers, by Joanna Haynes and Tony Brown (2001). This book was written with the belief that philosophy can assist with children's thinking, speaking, and listening skills as well as provide a stimulus and structure for moral inquiry.

Democratic Education, by Amy Gutmann (1999). Who should have the authority to shape the education of citizens in a democracy? In searching for the answers, Gutman explores a wide range of issues, from the democratic case against book banning to the role of teachers' unions in education.

Historical and Philosophical Foundations of Education: A Biographical Introduction (2nd ed., 1997). A comprehensive account of the competing schools of educational philosophy and their applications to schooling. This book provides thumbnail sketches of significant figures and guides readers in investigating their own philosophies.

A Light in Dark Times: Maxine Greene and the Unfinished Conversation, by William Ayers and Janet Miller, eds. (1998). A collection of Maxine Greene's essays on a broad array of educational topics, including the arts, literature, diversity, school reform, women's studies, and civil rights.

Philosophy of Education, by Paul Hist and Patricia White (1998). A critical review of how feminist theory, critical theory, phenomenology, and Marxism have influenced schools.

Women's Philosophies of Education: Thinking Through Our Mothers, by Catherine Titone and Karen Maloney (1999). This work presents the educational philosophies of seven women from various times, cultures, and classes whose ideas have influenced educational thinking in the United States.

Financing and Governing America's Schools

10

FOCUS QUESTIONS

1. Why do teachers need to know about finance and governance?
2. How is the property tax connected to unequal educational funding?
3. What is the distinction between educational equity and educational adequacy?
4. What are the sources of state revenues?
5. How does the federal government influence education?
6. What current trends are shaping educational finance?
7. How do school boards and superintendents work together to manage schools?
8. What is the "hidden" government of schools?
9. How does the business community influence school culture?
10. How are schools being made more responsive to teachers and the community?

WHAT DO YOU THINK? What Costs More? Try your hand at ranking the cost of several items on a state education budget.

CHAPTER PREVIEW

Do you know who pays for U.S. schools, and how? You might be surprised. In this chapter we introduce you to the decentralized, politically charged systems of school funding and school governance in the United States. You will become familiar with the sources of financial inequity in schooling, and, more important, learn how reformers are pursuing strategies to keep effective education within the reach of all, not just the very wealthy. Both the formal structure of power in school governance (school boards, school superintendents, and the like) and the informal, hidden government will impact your life in the classroom. By understanding the mechanics behind school finance and governance, you will be more empowered as a classroom teacher, and better able to influence decisions that shape the education of our nation's children.

Local and state governments have long grappled with the difficult proposition of raising enough public funds to adequately support education while dodging taxpayer ire over high taxes. But raising enough money is only part of the challenge. The growing gap between the haves and the have-nots, a consequence of America's great range of wealth and poverty, is painfully evident in the kinds of schools the nation provides its children. Students in wealthy neighborhoods attend modern, well-equipped schools; poorer children make their way to decaying, ill-equipped school buildings in impoverished communities. Courts have forged solutions aimed at reducing these glaring disparities and bringing a measure of fairness to education. Equalizing school funding is no easy task, and equalizing financial inputs does not necessarily equalize educational outcomes. Many states are now focusing on guaranteeing that every student receives an adequate and appropriate education.

Day-to-day classroom life is influenced not only by economic issues but also by the ways in which schools are governed. While you may be somewhat familiar with school boards, superintendents, and principals, you may be surprised at the influence wielded by school secretaries, parents, and the business community. In this chapter, you will learn how schools are managed, officially and unofficially. Your knowledge of educational decision making can be a powerful ally in shaping a successful teaching career.

Follow the Money: Financing America's Schools

Why Should Teachers Care Where the Money Comes from?

Why should a teacher be concerned much about school finance? (Put another way, why should I want to read this chapter?) Doesn't a teacher's responsibility pretty much start and end at the classroom door?

Sounds reasonable, but here is where the authors jump in. We believe that it is unwise, and even dangerous, for teachers to invest their time and talent in a career where the key decisions are considered beyond their knowledge or influence. Educational finance may well determine not just the quality of life you experience as a teacher, but the very futures of the students you teach. Common sense tells us that the amount of money spent in a school is directly related to how well students learn, but not everyone agrees. What is the wisest way to invest educational dollars—and who should decide?

In the Watergate scandal that toppled Richard Nixon from the presidency, the *Washington Post* reporters who broke the story were given invaluable advice from a strange and still anonymous source: "Deep Throat." Deep Throat advised the reporters to "Follow the money." He explained that in politics, the money trail reveals what is happening and who is benefiting. Money is the key to what is happening in schools as well.

We believe that teachers should be major participants in financial and governance policy decisions. The current trend toward testing teachers and developing school standards is an example of what happens when teachers are left out of policy circles. The emphasis on standards and testing too often casts the teacher in the role of a technician, implementing other people's goals with the resources other people decide they should have. And in the end, other people evaluate how well teachers (and students) perform. We believe that this system serves neither teachers nor students well. We see teachers as advocates for children, children who themselves are excluded from policy decisions. Teachers and students find themselves the victims of raising educational expectations but limited educational resources. Teachers should have a voice, and be a voice for children as well. Consider this chapter a step in that direction, and a primer on both the economics and governance of schools.

The Property Tax: The Road to Unequal Schools

> The method of financing public schools . . . can be fairly described as chaotic and unjust.
>
> *Supreme Court Justice Potter Stewart*

To someone from another country, the way the United States funds its schools must seem bizarre, and certainly unfair. Unlike many other nations, which use a centralized funding system, we have a very decentralized system. In fact, we have three levels of government—local, state, and federal—all raising and distributing funds. Currently, the local and state governments share the biggest burden of funding schools, with the federal government responsible for just 6 to 8 percent of the total. What a tangled web we weave when fifty states, fifteen thousand local governments, and one enormous federal government become involved in funding and managing 90,000 schools.

How did this financial hodgepodge begin? In colonial America, schools were the concern of local communities. Then, at the birth of our nation, the Constitution did not designate a federal role in education, effectively leaving it the responsibility of the states. "Local control" of schools became a well-established tradition, one that still holds sway today.

In the agrarian society of colonial times, wealth was measured by the size of people's farms. So to raise money for schools, colonial towns and districts assessed a **property tax.** Although today only 2 percent of Americans still work the land, the

Steadily increasing property taxes have led to taxpayer revolts in such states as California, Texas, and Massachusetts, where voters have passed propositions limiting such taxes.

property tax continues to be the major source of school revenue. Today's property taxes are levied on real estate (homes and businesses) and sometimes personal property (cars and boats). Whether a school district will find itself rich in resources, or scrambling to make ends meet, depends largely on the wealth of the community being taxed. Not surprisingly, a tax on a Beverly Hills mansion raises many more thousands of dollars than a tax on a house in South Central Los Angeles. Communities blessed with valuable real estate can easily raise funds for their schools. Impoverished communities are not so fortunate. Urban areas struggle the most, suffering not only from lower property values, but also the need to use those limited resources to fund more police officers, hospitals, subways, and other services than their suburban counterparts, a phenomenon known as **municipal overburden.**[1]

Reforming Education Finance

Unequal school funding results in stark differences, sometimes in close quarters. In 1968, 48-year-old sheetmetal worker Demetrio Rodriguez looked with despair at his children's school in a poor Latino section of San Antonio, Texas. Not only did Edgewood Elementary School lack adequate books and air conditioning, the top two floors were condemned and barely half the teachers were certified.[2] Ten minutes away, in affluent Alamo Heights, children were taught by certified teachers, in comfortable surroundings with ample materials. The educational cards were stacked against Rodriguez and his neighbors: even though Edgewood residents paid one of the highest tax rates on their property of any Texas community, the property itself was not worth much. Edgewood raised only $37 per student; Alamo Heights raised $412 per student. Rodriguez went to court, claiming that the system violated the U.S. Constitution's guarantee for equal protection under the law.

In a landmark decision, *San Antonio v. Rodriguez* (1973), the Supreme Court ruled against Rodriguez, deferring to the long history of local communities funding neighborhood schools. The Court declared that education was not a "fundamental right" under the U.S. Constitution, and that preserving local control was a legitimate reason to use the property tax system. While the Court recognized that educational funding through the property tax was a seriously flawed system, it was left up to the states to change it. It took sixteen more years before the Texas Supreme Court would act on the Rodriguez case. By the mid-1980s, Edgewood had neither typewriters nor a playground, but affluent Alamo Heights had computers and a swimming pool. Throughout Texas, per-pupil expenditures ranged from $2,112 in the poorest community to $19,333 in the wealthiest. In *Edgewood v. Kirby* (1989) the Texas Supreme Court issued a unanimous decision that such differences violated the Texas constitution, and ordered Texas to devise a fairer plan.

Reformers had more courtroom success under state constitutions' equal protection clauses. The California Supreme Court, in *Serrano v. Priest* (1971), struck down the state's financing system as unconstitutional. The court, faced with the glaring differences between Beverly Hills spending $1,232 per student, and nearby Baldwin Park spending only $577 a student, declared that education was a fundamental right under the California constitution and that the property tax system violated equal protection of that right. The court found that heavy reliance on the local property tax "makes the quality of a child's education a function of the wealth of his parents and neighbors. . . . Districts with small tax bases simply cannot levy taxes at a rate sufficient to produce the revenue that more affluent districts produce with a minimum effort." The *Serrano v. Priest* decision ushered in both a wave of litigation in other states

FIGURE 10.1   The public education dollar: Where the money comes from.

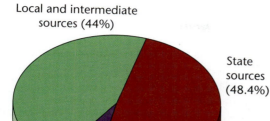

Local and intermediate sources (44%)

State sources (48.4%)

Federal sources (6.8%)

SOURCE: *Digest of Education Statistics,* National Center for Educational Statistics, U.S. Department of Education (2000), Table 158.

REFLECTION

Is the proportion of revenue spent by local, state, and federal governments on education different from your initial perceptions? If you were able to suggest changes in this pie graph, what would they be? Why?

FIGURE 10.2   The public education dollar: Where the money goes.

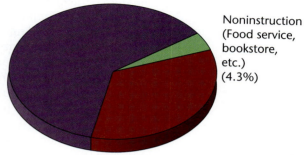

Instruction (teacher salaries, textbooks, etc.) (61.7%)

Noninstruction (Food service, bookstore, etc.) (4.3%)

Support services (school maintenance, nurses, administration, library, etc.) (34%)

SOURCE: U.S. Department of Education, National Center for Education Statistics, Common Core of Data (CCD). "National Public Education Financial Survey" 1998–99.

REFLECTION

Does the distribution of educational funds surprise you? Are there changes that you would suggest?

and an increase in the state share of school funding.[3] (See Figures 10.1 and 10.2.) **Robin Hood reformers,** as they were called, won a victory as they took funds from wealthy districts and redistributed the monies to the poorer districts, much like the Robin Hood hero of Sherwood Forest fame. States have used different programs to try to equalize funding. In the **foundation program,** the state provides funds to ensure that each student receives a minimal or "foundation" level of educational services. Unfortunately, the established minimum is frequently far below actual expenditures. Another approach is the **guaranteed tax base program,** which adds state funds to poorer districts, helping to reduce economic inequities.

The Serrano victory in California was short-lived. Many voters feared tax increases, and wealthy voters revolted as their tax dollars were transported from their own children's schools to faraway poor schools. **Proposition 13** was passed to limit the property tax. With decreased tax revenue, California saw its schools go into a rapid decline. California schools were finally becoming equal, but equally bad.

The Move toward Adequacy

In New Jersey, the state constitution promises citizens a "thorough and efficient" education. But in cities such as Camden, school buildings were in disrepair and student academic performance was dismal.[4] It was not much of a stretch to realize that a "thorough and efficient" education was not happening in Camden. The state court agreed that more funds were needed to remedy the situation. In **Abbott v. Burke** (1990, 1998), the court identified 28 failing districts (known as "Abbott districts") and mandated that significantly greater funds be spent to transform their students into "productive members of society."[3] For decades, New Jersey courts tangled with a legislature that was dominated by wealthy interests and those supporting local government rights, culminating in a one-day court ordered school shutdown throughout the state. Bullied into submission, the legislature finally raised funding to the poorest districts. Through state redistribution of funds, Camden received tens of millions of dollars in additional aid. Yet the extra dollars did not translate into significant improvement in academic performance. One of the pervasive and troubling problems in education finance is that increased funding can make a difference, but it does not always make a difference. One lesson from New Jersey is that if there is no coherent statewide educational improvement plan in place, and if the courts and the legislature are not in agreement, increased funding may not be enough to turn a failing school district into a successful one. Sherwood Forest was quite a bit easier for Robin Hood than New Jersey.

Trying to level the financial playing field is not enough: More money might very well be critical, but money alone does not guarantee a better education. If a school district uses money unwisely, or if the problems call for more than a financial infusion, educational progress is negligible. As we saw in the *Abbott* cases, a new line of litigation has emerged, recognizing the important difference between **financial input** (per-pupil expenditures) and **educational outcome** (student achievement). Now the legal action focuses on a word that sounds less powerful than equity, but holds great promise: adequacy. **Adequate education** is guaranteed in many state constitutions.[4] Some constitutions call for an "efficient" or "thorough education" or the need for the schools to be "free and uniform." Whatever the term or phrase, the bottom line is the same: If students are attending **failing schools,** they are not receiving their constitutionally guaranteed adequate education.[5]

Cases have been filed in state courts across the country, with mixed results. In Kentucky, an activist court looked beyond the financial disparities between school districts and considered how well the state was educating its students. The verdict: not well at all. The court ruled that the state's "entire system of common schools was infirm."[6] The court defined an "efficient" education as one that provides students with oral and written communications skills; knowledge of economics, history, and social systems; and sufficient preparation for academic and career success. To meet these goals, the state legislature enacted the Kentucky Education Reform Act in 1990, launching a new curriculum, statewide performance tests, preschool programs for at-risk students, multiple grades in the same class, and economic incentives for educational progress. Kentucky's experience demonstrated how courts and the legislature working together can reshape schools.

Other states, such as New York, have taken a minimalist approach, requiring schools to be funded at a level that is truly minimally adequate—apparently, the New York constitution entitles students to desks and pencils, but not up-to-date science textbooks.[7] And some state courts, such as in Rhode Island, have refused to become involved in education financing at all. (If you want to learn more about relevant court cases in specific states—including those that you may be considering for a teaching position—visit the Online Learning Center at www.mhhe.com/sadker6e.)

YOU BE THE JUDGE
"EQUITY" OR "ADEQUACY"

We Should Seek Educational "Equity" Because . . .

MONEY TALKS

The gap between wealthy and poor communities makes a mockery of democracy and fairness. Poor students attend schools with leaking roofs and uncertified teachers; wealthy students learn in schools with computers, swimming pools, and well-paid and qualified teachers. No real democracy can ignore such glaring inequities.

EQUALIZING INPUT IS CRUCIAL

Isn't it strange that those who advocate business values like choice and competition ignore the most fundamental business value of all: money. Wealth creates good schools; poverty creates weak ones. Invest money wisely over a period of time, and watch those once poor schools thrive.

EQUITY IS POWERFUL

Democracy and equity are powerful words representing powerful ideals. Adequacy is a feeble word subject to interpretation and compromise. What's adequate? Is it the ability to read at a high school level, or at an eighth grade level? Does an adequate education lead to a minimum wage job? Only "Equity" can serve as a rallying cry.

We Should Seek Educational "Adequacy" Because . . .

MONEY DIVIDES

Robin Hood is dead. Wealthy communities are not going to fund poor ones, happily sending their hard earned dollars to educate someone else's children. The cornerstone of democracy is local control, and trying to redistribute wealth is fundamentally unfair, and smacks of the approach used by Communists (another failed system).

EQUALIZING INPUT IS INEFFECTIVE

We will never make schools more effective by throwing dollars at them. When California moved toward equitable input, the quality of its public schools deteriorated. Our goal is not to increase school budgets and per pupil expenditures, but to increase student achievement.

ADEQUACY IS ATTAINABLE

Equity is a powerful dream, but adequacy is an attainable one. We are unlikely to achieve a completely equitable school system, but we can demand reasonable and reachable educational standards. Moreover, we are on firmer legal footing, since state constitutions guarantee not identical expenditures, but an adequate education for all.

YOU BE THE JUDGE

Do you believe that adequacy or equity provides the best foundation for reforming schools? Explain. Can these approaches be blended, or are they mutually exclusive?

States Finding the Money

The last fifty years have seen dramatic changes in the centuries-old system of financing schools. We have moved from local communities funding schools through a property tax, to a shared state and local responsibility. (Although you wouldn't know it when listening to political campaign speeches, the federal government is a very junior partner in paying for America's education.) We have already looked at the property tax, the primary revenue source for local communities. As we indicated, it is a flawed system leading to gross inequities in the funding of schools. Let's see what states do to find the dollars they need to fund schools.

Let's assume that you have been asked by your (choose one or more of the following): (a) education professor, (b) teacher association, (c) favorite political candidate, or (d) spouse, to "follow the money" and find out how states raise their educational funds. States have a dizzying number of budget items to fund. But for our purposes, the basic question is: Where do we find the money for our schools?

At the state level, a common revenue source is the **sales tax,** which is simply a charge added to all sales. Consumers pay a few extra pennies for small purchases or a few extra dollars for large purchases. The sales tax accounts for 30 percent of the typical state's income.[8] More than forty states use a sales tax, usually collecting between 2 percent and 8 percent of the item's value. A problem with the sales tax is that some people may choose to avoid paying the tax by taking their business to a neighboring state with a lower tax rate. And the tax is regressive: poor families must spend most of their income purchasing necessities, and end up feeling the impact of the tax much more than wealthy people.

Another popular option is the **personal income tax,** used in more than forty states. The personal income tax brings in more than 25 percent of state revenues.[9] Like the federal income tax, the personal income tax is collected through payroll deductions, even before a worker receives his or her paycheck. The tax is a percentage of income, typically above a particular threshold of income, so how each state determines these percentages in the end will resolve how equally, or unequally, the tax burden falls on the poor, the middle class, and the rich.

In a relatively new funding source, state lotteries, poorer people once again bear the greatest burden. **State lotteries** offer holders of winning tickets the chance to collect millions in prize money. But there are few winners and a disproportionate percentage of the poor purchase these long-shot lottery tickets. Roughly two-thirds of the states now have lotteries, and nearly half of those claim to dedicate at least a portion of the revenues to education. In reality, however, most states use lottery revenues to supplement, not fund, parts of an established education budget.[10]

Other common state sources of funding include: **excise taxes** (on tobacco, gasoline, and liquor, sometimes known as **sin tax); severance tax** (based on the state's mineral wealth); **motor vehicle license fee;** and **estate** or **gift taxes.**

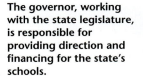

The governor, working with the state legislature, is responsible for providing direction and financing for the state's schools.

Your brief course in "State Finance 101" is over. You can see some of the limits of state revenue sources. For extra credit, can you devise an entirely new scheme to raise state funds?

The Federal Government's Role in Financing Education

At this point, some of you might be thinking: Even if every state provided every school district with adequate funding and a great education plan, the economic gaps among the states would still be enormous. If you thought about that, congratulations, you have put your finger on a systemic problem. For instance, in Connecticut, students throughout the state typically receive far more education dollars than students in Mississippi, regardless of what finance plans each of those states use. (See Frame of Reference: State Education Spending.) While we have been discussing *intrastate* equity, we have yet to explore *interstate* equity. Because of the Constitution, this is a problem the United States seems unable to correct.

If the Constitution had assigned education as a federal responsibility, we might expect to see the federal government close the economic gap between states. U.S. schools might be centrally financed and governed; or at the very least, the Supreme Court might rule funding inequities among states unconstitutional. But this is not the case. The Supreme Court has ruled that education is not a "fundamental right" under the U.S. Constitution, and has left education to the states. Accordingly, the federal government's role in the financing of education is relatively small. In fact, the federal government typically pays only 6 to 8 percent of the nation's educational costs.

However, the federal government still manages to influence schools. How does it do this? One way has been through **categorical grants**—funds directed at specific categories and targeted educational needs. Categorical grants have provided funding for preschool programs for poor children, library construction, acquisition of new technology, educational opportunities for veterans, the training of teachers and administrators, educational research, lunches for low-income youth, and loans to college students. By targeting funds into these categories, federal aid, although limited, has had a significant impact on schools.

More recently, there has been a shift away from categorical grants to "block grants." The obligations, rules, and even competition associated with seeking federal dollars were greatly reduced in the 1980s and 1990s. States were awarded **block grants,** lump sums of money, and were given great latitude in how to spend this money. As a result, there were educational winners and losers in the quest for federal dollars:

> *Winners.* Under the block grant system, more funds went to purchase instructional materials, including computers. Many rural communities that lacked the resources even to apply—much less compete—for federal dollars, received federal support. The paperwork for all districts was reduced.

> *Losers.* Desegregation efforts were cut by two-thirds under the block grant approach. Programs for disadvantaged and urban students, women's equity, and many other targeted programs were reduced or eliminated. Long-range programs lost support, and accountability for how the funds were spent was greatly weakened.[11]

In 1979, President Jimmy Carter established the **United States Department of Education,** raising federal involvement in education to cabinet status. The Department of Education influences schools by conducting research, publishing

STATE EDUCATION SPENDING (PER PUPIL)

States Spending Most per Pupil				States Spending Least per Pupil		
Rank	State	Dollars($)		Rank	State	Dollars($)
1	NJ	9,643		42	OK	5,033
2	CT	8,904		43	NM	5,005
3	NY	8,852		44	TN	4,937
4	DC	8,393		45	AL	4,849
5	AK	8,271		46	ID	4,721
6	RI	7,928		47	AR	4,708
7	MA	7,778		48	SD	4,669
8	DE	7,420		49	AZ	4,595
9	PA	7,209		50	MS	4,288
10	WI	7,123		51	UT	3,969

Source: Children in the States, 2001. www.childrensdefense.org/states/2001_intro_main.htm.

REFLECTION

Do your teaching plans include any of the states at the top or bottom of this list? Will this spending information influence your decision on where to teach? For more information on how different states respond to the needs of children, visit www.childrensdefense.org/statesdata.htm.

information, proposing legislation, and disbursing targeted, if limited, federal funds. Expenditures for the Department of Education are dwarfed by other federal priorities. (See Figure 10.3.)

Although the federal government's financial role is limited, the federal government can exert tremendous influence on our schools through federal laws and court actions. For example, the 1954 Brown decision desegregated schools, and civil rights laws have increased educational opportunities for students of color, limited speakers of English, females, and others. (You will read about these laws and court cases, and more, in Chapter 11, "School Law and Ethics.")

What the Future May Hold for School Finance

Today, we are in a period of shifting governmental responsibility for the financing of schools. Reformers are focusing less on financial inequity and more on educational inadequacy. What are some other trends in educational finance, and what issues are likely to surface in the years ahead?

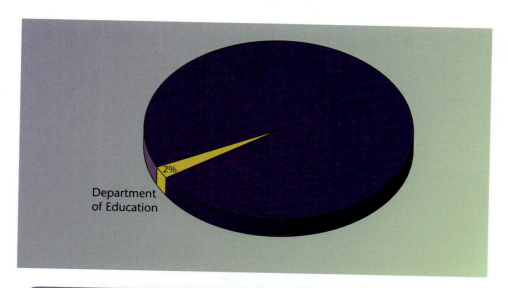

2%

Department
of Education

FIGURE 10.3
Federal budget. Within the federal budget, education expenditures remain quite small.

SOURCE: Federal Role in Education, U.S. Department of Education (2001). www.ed.gov/offices/OUS/fedrole.html

REFLECTION

Can you think of an area of the Federal budget that receives fewer dollars than education?

Accountability

The public wants to see academic progress for their tax dollars—in short, **accountability.** Students will be tested, and so will educators. Graduation will be based less on time spent in school and more on proven performance. Teachers may find tenure more difficult to obtain. Schools will be required to identify specific goals, such as minimum achievement levels on standardized tests, and will be held responsible for reaching these goals.

Choice Programs

The neighborhood school, long a mainstay of public education, may be radically reshaped (or even eliminated) in the years ahead. As discussed in Chapter 4, "Schools: Choices and Challenges," many reformers are promoting a business culture and the value of competition as the keys to school improvement. Choice programs, charter schools, and vouchers are front burner issues in education. The idea is to rescue students from failing schools by giving parents a choice of schools, and letting the best schools win, and the others, close their doors.

Local Fundraising

Wealthier school districts are developing creative strategies to ensure that their schools are not endangered by Robin Hood redistribution plans. Through Parent Teacher Association donations, online fundraisers, cooperative agreements with local businesses, and tax-sheltered private educational foundations, additional dollars are collected for advanced science equipment, computers, special devices for disabled

Students and staff arrive to very different school buildings. What attitudes might develop as a result of learning in these dissimilar facilities? What physical improvements would you make to the dilapidated school building? List the physical characteristics of a school building that you believe are needed to ensure an "adequate education."

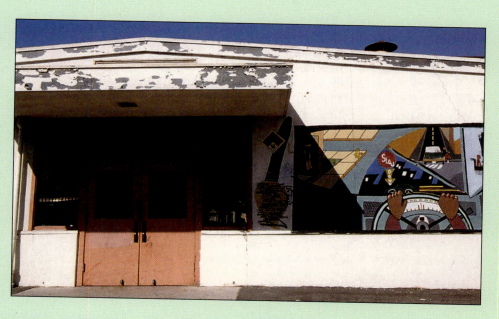

397

students, and college scholarships. Wealthy communities defend such practices as a way to prevent parents from fleeing "to private school if they don't perceive the public education to be excellent."[12]

Decaying Infrastructure

Here we are in the twenty-first century, using schools that were built in the nineteenth. When local governments need to replace these aging buildings, they usually resort to issuing bonds. A **bond** is a certificate of debt issued by a government guaranteeing payment of the original investment plus interest by a specified future date. Bonds give the local communities the money they need to build the schools and fifteen to twenty years to pay off the debt.

But for most schools, repair not replacement is the remedy for antiquated buildings. While keeping schools current means new wiring and electrical outlets for computer and Internet installation, teachers and principals give higher priority to "adequate" heating, lighting, acoustics, ventilation, and air conditioning. The Department of Education estimates that 25,000 schools need major repairs, at an estimated cost of over $112 billion.[13] One piece of good news: Polls indicate that the public recognizes the financial need of our schools suggesting that local bonds will be approved. (See Figure 10.4 below.)

FIGURE 10.4
Public opinion about government spending on education.

SOURCE: Greenberg-Quinlan Research, Inc./The Tarrance Group (commissioned by the National Education Association), 2000.

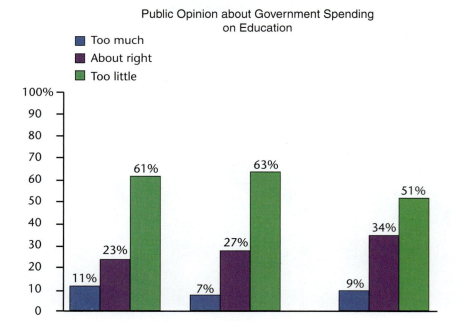

REFLECTION

While most taxpayers are resistant to government expenditures, education is an exception. Why? How might these opinions impact future education funding?

Governing America's Schools

School Governance Quiz

The following quiz should help you focus on how schools are governed. If you are puzzled at some of these questions, fear not; the remainder of the chapter is organized around a discussion of these questions and their answers.

1. Most school board members are (choose only one)
   a. Conservative, white, male, and middle or upper class.
   b. Liberal, middle-class women, about half of whom have been or are teachers.
   c. Middle of the road politically, about evenly divided between men and women, and representing all socioeconomic classes.
   d. So diverse politically, economically, and socially that it is impossible to make generalizations.

2. State school boards and chief state school officers are
   a. Elected by the people.
   b. Elected by the people's representatives.
   c. Appointed by the governor.
   d. Appointed by officials other than the governor.
   e. All of the above.
   f. None of the above.

INTERACTIVE ACTIVITY
SCHOOL GOVERNANCE QUIZ: Take an electronic version of this quiz.

3. During the past two decades, control and influence over education have increased at the
   a. Federal level.
   b. State level.
   c. Local level.

4. Local school district superintendents are (you may choose more than one):
   a. Often mediating conflicts.
   b. Civil service–type administrators.
   c. Elected officials.
   d. Sometimes powerless figureheads.

5. Who might be considered part of the "hidden school government" (you may choose more than one):
   a. The school principal.
   b. The state school superintendent.
   c. The U.S. secretary of education.
   d. The school secretary.
   e. Parents.
   f. The Teacher Arbitration and Labor Relations Board.

6. The influence of the business community in U.S. schools can best be characterized as
   a. Virtually nonexistent.
   b. Felt only in vocational and commercial programs.

    c. Extensive and growing.

    d. A recent phenomenon.

7. In most schools, teachers are expected to

    a. Design the policies guiding their schools.

    b. Collaborate with principals and district officials to create policies to suit their schools.

    c. Comply with policies made by principals and by district and state officials.

    d. Comply with policies that seem appropriate and change those that do not.

School Governance Answer Key

1. a   2. e   3. b   4. a, b, d   5. d, e   6. c   7. c

> *0 to 1 wrong:* You receive the Horace Mann Award.
>
> *2 wrong:* You may want to run for school board.
>
> *3 wrong:* Read the rest of the chapter carefully.
>
> *4 or more wrong:* Take detailed notes on this part of the chapter; become a frequent visitor to the text Web page; find a friend to quiz you.

The Legal Control of Schools

The following sections review and discuss the quiz you have just taken, beginning with the first two questions:

1. Most school board members are . . . *conservative, white, male, and middle or upper class.*

2. School boards and chief state school officers are . . . *elected by the people, elected by the people's representatives, appointed by the governor, or appointed by officials other than the governor.*

There is great diversity in school governance. In some states, school boards and chief state school officials are elected; in others, they are appointed. Depending on the state, chief state school officers may be called superintendent, commissioner, or secretary. Although some say that "variety is the spice of life," you are probably thinking, How did this strange system get started (and will I ever sort it out)?

By the time the Constitution was written, control of schools by local communities was well established. The Constitution recognized and reaffirmed the states' responsibilities in this area under the **Tenth Amendment:** "The powers not delegated to the United States by the Constitution [as education is not], nor prohibited by it to the States, are reserved to the states, respectively, or to the people."

Today, the United States is unusual in this respect. Whereas most nations have a national ministry of education, which determines what and how children are taught in all parts of those nations, in the United States the legal responsibility for public education resides within each of the fifty states, the District of Columbia, and several U.S. territories. Since few governors or state legislators possess special expertise in education, state governments have delegated much of their authority to state boards of education, state superintendents, and departments of education, and finally to local governments. Probably the best way for you to learn how school boards, superintendents, and the entire governance structure works, is to consider a specific example.

From an Idea to a Reality

A state-level policy decision usually begins when someone, a legislator, school board member, superintendent, or a citizens' group suggests a new educational program, such as the need to improve student writing skills or the desire to limit class size. For our example, let's assume that the testing craze has led to a new policy in your state: All new candidates for a teaching license must take a course in "Instructional Strategies for Improving Student Test Performance."

Perhaps you're wondering, Who thinks up these policies? Policy suggestions originate from all kinds of sources: professional educators, school board members, state legislators, superintendents, state and federal court decisions, federal laws or initiatives, special interest groups, and the general public. In short, the role of the state school board is to consider recommendations for educational policy and to vote for or against their implementation.

Policy implementation is the responsibility of the chief state school officer and the state department of education. The chief state school officer is given different titles in different states (superintendent, director, commissioner, or secretary of education) and is usually the executive head of the state department of education. Together, the superintendent and the state department enforce state laws, evaluate teachers and schools, plan for future educational developments, and provide training and information to educators throughout the state. In our example, the superintendent would inform all school districts in the state of the new course requirement. If you were to apply for a teacher's license in the state, someone in the state department of education would review your transcript to make certain that you had successfully completed the new course on improving test scores. If this and other requirements were met, you would be issued your teacher's license.

What about a job? States issue teacher's licenses, but the hiring and firing of teachers is done by local education districts. The nearly fifteen thousand school districts across the country are the most visible agency of educational governance—the ones you read about most often in your local newspaper. These districts are actually agencies of state rather than local governments, but they exercise control over such local matters as recruitment of school staff, curriculum formulation, and budgets—including teacher salaries and school building programs.

Most local school districts look something like the state government, but on a smaller scale. They have a school board, a superintendent, and an education office that, like the state department of education, helps administer the schools. Most local **school boards** are elected, although a few local communities appoint them. Each local board then hires a local superintendent to provide educational leadership within the community. Thus, in any given state, educational governance involves not only a state superintendent with a department of education and a statewide board but also local school boards and local superintendents. In many instances, local administrators and board members influence education more than do their counterparts at the state level. In practice, each state is unique in the way it delegates and administers its educational program. Figure 10.5 shows an example of a state school system's structure. And the main agents of school governance are described in the following paragraphs.

STATE BOARD OF EDUCATION The **state board of education** is responsible for formulating educational policy. The members are usually appointed by the governor, but sometimes they are chosen in a statewide election.

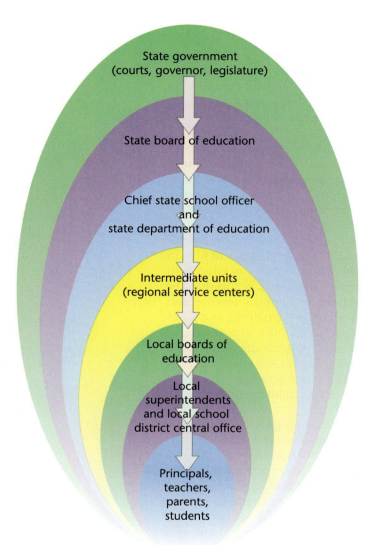

FIGURE 10.5
Structure of a typical state school system.

REFLECTION

What are some of the difficulties in these many levels of governance? Do you favor elected or appointed school boards? Why?

CHIEF STATE SCHOOL OFFICER Called *superintendent, commissioner, secretary of education, or director of instruction,* the **chief state school officer** is responsible for overseeing, regulating, and planning school activities, as well as implementing the policies of the board of education. The state superintendent is usually selected by the board of education but sometimes campaigns for the position in an election.

STATE DEPARTMENT OF EDUCATION The **state department of education** performs the administrative tasks needed to implement state policy. This includes licensing teachers, testing student progress, providing information and training to teachers, distributing state and federal funds, seeing that local school systems comply with state laws, and conducting educational research and development. The state superintendent usually manages state department of education activities.

SCHOOL DISTRICTS—LOCAL SCHOOL BOARDS AND SUPERINTENDENTS All states except Hawaii have delegated much of the responsibility for local school operations to local school districts. (Hawaii treats the entire state as a single school district.) School districts vary in size from those serving only a few students to those with more than a million. Sometimes, local school districts are grouped into intermediate units as a way to simplify management. Most local school districts mirror the state organization, with a local school board, **superintendent,** and office of education. Local school districts may be responsible for school construction, taxing, budgeting, the hiring of school personnel, curriculum decisions, local school policy, and the education of students. Although school districts operate at the local level, their authority derives from the state, and they must operate within the rules and regulations specified by the state. (The *Frame of Reference:* Who Controls What? Levels of Educational Power summarizes the relationships between state and local control of schools.)

STATE GOVERNMENTS

- Levy taxes
- License teachers and other educators
- Set standards for school attendance, safety, etc.
- Outline minimum curricular and graduation standards (sometimes including specific textbooks to be used and competency tests for student graduation and teacher certification)
- Regulate the nature and size of local school districts

LOCAL SCHOOL DISTRICTS

- Implement state regulations and policies
- Create and implement local policies and practices for effective school administration
- Hire school personnel
- Provide needed funds and build appropriate facilities
- Fix salaries and working conditions
- Translate community needs into educational practice
- Initiate additional curriculum, licensing, or other requirements beyond state requirements
- Create current and long-range plans for the school district

REFLECTION

As a classroom teacher, offer some examples of the issues that would lead you to deal with state government. Which issues would send you down a path to the local government?

State Influence Grows as School Boards Come under Fire

3. During the past two decades, control and influence over education have increased at the . . . *state level.*

Forged in the hamlets of colonial New England, for centuries school boards have been a symbol of small-town democracy, representing the public's interest in shaping the policies and practices of their local schools. School board meetings evoke the essence of Americana—the kind painted by Norman Rockwell and made into a Frank Capra movie starring Jimmy Stewart as the beleaguered, but triumphant, school board president. Therefore, it was a great shock to many during the 1990s when America's school boards came under intensive scrutiny and criticism. School boards' inability to improve student performance or to innovate led many to believe that they were unresponsive and entrenched bureaucracies. Courts and public frustration forced state governments to center stage. (See *Frame of Reference:* Everything You Always Wanted to Know About School Boards But Never Thought to Ask.)

Part of the problem is that there is little consensus on how school boards should operate.[14] Most school board members view themselves as **trustee representatives,** selected to serve because of their educational expertise and good judgment, and independent of ever-changing popular opinions. But others, including many voters, see school board members as **delegate representatives,** responsible for implementing the will of the public (or being voted out of office if they do not). The type of elections used to select school board members can shape the kind of school

INTERACTIVE ACTIVITY
WHO IS IN CONTROL?
Test your knowledge of who controls different aspects of the school.

FRAME OF REFERENCE

EVERYTHING YOU ALWAYS WANTED TO KNOW ABOUT . . .

. . . SCHOOL BOARDS BUT NEVER THOUGHT TO ASK

- The first school board was established in 1721 in Boston.
- In the United States, there are almost 15,000 school boards in charge of 47 million students in 91,000 schools.
- Three-quarters of the school districts are small, with fewer than 2,500 students in each.
- Just 1 percent of the school districts in urban areas enroll 23 percent of all students in the United States.
- Eighty-five percent of local school boards are elected.
- School board members are typically white (81.3 percent), male (54.1 percent), financially secure (two-thirds earn more than $60,000 and almost half earn over $80,000).
- School boards hire superintendents who look much like themselves (96 percent of the superintendents are white, 88 percent are male, 95 percent are married).

SOURCE: Data compiled from Digest of Education Statistics, 2000; Educational Vital Signs, 1998; Characteristics of the 100 Largest Public Elementary and Secondary School Districts in U.S.: 1998–1999. NCES; C. Emily Feistritzer, "A Profile of School Board Presidents," in Patricia First and Herbert Walberg (eds.), *School Boards: Changing Local Control* (Berkeley: McCutchan, 1992); Jesse L. Freeman, Kenneth E. Underwood, and Jim C. Fortune, "What Boards Value," *American School Board Journal* 178 (January 1991), pp. 32–37.

REFLECTION

Can you think of other public institutions that are governed by a group similar to a school board? How does the school board in your community compare to the demographics of the typical board? To the demographics of your community?

board that will emerge. When school boards are selected through "at-large" elections, in which the entire school district votes for all the members of the school board, the school board is expected to represent the interests of the entire community—in line with the notion of trustee representatives. But some school districts do not have at-large elections, instead choosing to have smaller geographic areas vote. In this type of election each of these smaller neighborhoods selects a board member to represent its interests (delegate representation).

While it might appear that at-large elections are less partisan, they do have serious drawbacks. Districtwide, at-large elections typically result in more elite, politically conservative and upper class individuals being elected to school boards. After all, it is the well-established individual who is likely to have the financial resources and educational and business background needed to win a big, districtwide election. Poorer citizens, people of color, and women are less likely to find themselves on school boards selected through at-large elections. Unfortunately, many citizens feel disenfranchised when it comes to school board elections.

Other criticisms of school boards run deeper than criticism of the method of election. The Twentieth Century Fund and the Danforth Foundation conducted an intensive study of school boards, and recommended a total overhaul of the system, charging that

- School boards have become *immersed in administrative details,* at the expense of more important and appropriate policy issues. One study of West Virginia school boards showed that only 3 percent of all decisions made concerned policy.

Superintendents (mostly white males) along with members of state and local boards of education comprise the official governance system of schools.

- School boards are *not representing local communities,* but only special interest groups. Elections to the school board receive little public support. In a New York City school board election, for instance, only 7 percent of the voters participated.

- The *politics of local school board elections* have a negative impact on attracting and retaining superintendents and lead to conflict with state education agencies.

- The composition of the boards is *not representative,* with individuals of color, women, the poor, and the young unrepresented or underrepresented.

- School boards have been in the *backseat when it comes to educational change and reform.* As a matter of fact, many school boards do not support current educational reform proposals, and members have lagged behind public opinion on such issues as school choice and educational vouchers.

- The education of children goes beyond school issues to include health, social, and nutritional concerns. School boards are *too limited in scope* to respond to all the contemporary concerns of children.

- If schools continue to be *financed less from local funds and more from* state funds, local boards could become less influential.

- Many of the new reforms call for *new governance organizations,* site-based management, or choice programs that relegate the school board to a less important, perhaps even unnecessary, role.[15]

While these criticisms suggest a dismal future for school boards, preparing their obituary may be premature. School boards have endured a long time and may be around long after many of the reform recommendations are forgotten.

However, school board practices need to be improved. Board membership should be more representative of the communities they serve, including younger members, women, people of color, and less affluent individuals. Board responsibilities could be expanded to include nutrition, preschool programs, health care, welfare benefits, and

"Because they care about children and believe that all children can achieve. Most of [them] . . . serve with little or no remuneration. When you think of it, they are the one group who often makes a decision based on the needs of all children."[1]

Who are these community-oriented individuals? While few people consider them in this light, Anne Bryant, executive director of the National School Board Association (NSBA), is quick to underscore the service and commitment of the nation's school board members. Bryant believes that the strength of local school board leadership arises from school board members' capacity to represent the diversity of students and communities. The National School Board Association (NSBA) is a federation of 53 state and territorial organizations, representing 14,500 school districts, and almost 100,000 school board members. At the helm is Anne Bryant.

Bryant has long held a passion for public education, a commitment cultivated as a student teacher. Tapping into the intellectual curiosity of her students was a welcomed challenge. School bureaucracies and traditional teacher-centered instruction were not. Seeking to understand the political, economic, and social forces that shape education, Bryant became a student once again, pursuing graduate studies at the University of Massachusetts at Amherst. She wanted to unleash learning from the politics she believed stifled it. "With a doctorate in education, I felt prepared to reinvigorate life into teaching and learning and to lead schools in excellence and equity."[2]

Today Bryant is a seasoned school association executive. Prior to leading the NSBA, she served as executive director of the American Association of University Women (AAUW), a national organization advancing equity for women and girls in education, the workplace, and the family. With the release of AAUW's *How Schools Shortchange Girls* (1992), she brought attention to the academic, physical, and emotional losses females encounter in school. Bryant soon experienced the wrath of disgruntled constituents. Regressive political forces, ultraconservative parents, and sometimes even very traditional faculty and students denounced Bryant's call for gender equity, claiming that equal educational opportunities for females come at the expense of males. Bryant stood her ground.

As executive director of NSBA, Bryant understands such attacks, and appreciates how politics, special interests, and intensely traditional beliefs can derail school boards from meeting the contemporary needs of students. "My message is simple: Stop the power plays and personal vendettas and concentrate on improving student achievement."[3] While the national conversation about student achievement often focuses narrowly on students' abilities to perform well on standardized tests, Bryant contends that school boards must work to define achievement in ways that are meaningful to the communities they represent.

> Demands on students are increasing as never before. The changing character of society and today's technology-based economy are driving new questions about what students should know and be able to do when they graduate. Expectations are rising, not just for students but for schools and communities too. If we want students to succeed, school boards need to take action.[4]

Local governance of public education is, according to Bryant, a cornerstone of democracy. Yet, she believes that school boards are too often unrecognized partners in educational reform. As a link between the public and schools, she sees local boards uniquely positioned to lead efforts aimed to improve education. At the forefront of the NSBA's mission, then, is working with local boards to forge new partnerships with parents, teachers, and businesses. When tackling issues from school choice to school safety, building repairs to technology, Bryant encourages board members to imagine their entire community supporting the needs of students and to then make that vision a reality. And her message to board members is constant: Serving public schools is an honorable calling.

[1]Anne Bryant. Personal communication. (July 10, 2001).

[2]Anne Bryant. Personal communication (July 16, 2001).

[3]Jay Matthews. The Freedom Choice. *Washington Post* 10 July 2001. Online at www.washingtonpost.com

[4]Anne Bryant. Technology on Board. *Technos Quarterly* 7 (Fall 1998), pp. 26–29.

Write Your Own *Profile in Education:* Click on *Profiles in Education,* write a *Profile in Education* about an educator, and post it on the Online Learning Center. Check out *Profiles in Education* submitted by other future teachers.

To learn more about Anne Bryant, click on *Profiles in Education.*

other issues influencing the well-being of children. Perhaps school boards could benefit from a name change, such as Children's Education and Development Boards, to better reflect their broader responsibilities. Some educators suggest that we need to re-think how we currently select our boards, depending less on elections and more on appointments of nonpolitical educators. Too often, school board membership is seen as a political stepping-stone to higher office, or as a way of paying back political debts, instead of as an educational responsibility.

Finally, the relationship between school boards and superintendents needs to be improved. In regard to the official organization of a school district, the school board formulates policy and hires the superintendent to manage the day-to-day school district activities. So much for the official version. The unofficial version can be quite different.

The School Superintendent and Principal

4. Local school district superintendents are: *often mediating conflicts, civil service–type administrators, and sometimes powerless figureheads.*

The first superintendents were hired to relieve school boards of their growing administrative obligations. The year was 1837, and these new superintendents worked in Buffalo and Louisville. As the nineteenth century progressed, more communities followed this example. Superintendents were expected to supervise and hire teachers, examine students, and buy supplies, which had become too burdensome for the school boards themselves. Superintendents also kept school records, developed examinations, chose textbooks, and trained teachers.

By the twentieth century, the superintendent's role had changed from the board's administrative employee to its most knowledgeable educational expert—from helper to chief executive officer. Today, the superintendent is the most powerful education officer in the school district, responsible for budgets, buildings, new programs, daily operations, long-term goals, short-term results, and recruiting, hiring, demoting, and firing personnel. When things are going well, the superintendent enjoys great popularity. But, when things are going poorly, or school board members are not pleased, or local community groups are angry, or teacher organizations turn militant, or . . . you get the picture. When there is a problem, it is usually the head of the system, the superintendent, who gets fired. The superintendent lives and works in a fishbowl, trying to please various groups while managing the school district. It is a very insecure existence of sidestepping controversies, pleasing school board members, responding to critics, juggling many different roles and goals, and living with conflict. In 1998, only three of forty superintendents in Westchester County, just north of New York City, had served more than eight years.[16]

One need not look hard for the reasons for this turnover. Successful superintendents must win and maintain public support and financing for their schools. This involves forming political coalitions to back their programs and to ward off attacks from those more concerned with rising taxes than with the school budget. In an era in which most citizens in many communities do not have children in schools, this becomes a real test of political acumen. Superintendents find themselves serving on a number of civic committees, speaking to community groups, and being the public relations spokesperson for the school district.

School superintendents who survive and thrive are the politically savvy administrators who can "read" their school board. In *The School Managers: Power and Conflict in American Public Education,* Donald McCarty and Charles Ramsey provide a useful classification system that matches school board types with different superintendent styles.[17]

School boards in communities that are . . .	*Prefer superintendent style that is . . .*
Dominated: School boards run by a few local elite who dominate community and school policies	*Functionary:* Follows wishes of the board
Factional: Divided community, competing factions	*Political:* Balances often opposing concerns, avoids appearance of favoritism
Pluralistic: Competition among interest groups	*Adviser:* Moves cautiously as advisor among shifting community coalitions
Inert: No visible power structure, little interest in schools	*Decision maker:* Board relies on superintendent for leadership and decision making

Some of the new superintendents appointed in the late 1990s and early 2000s have been political, military and business leaders, known for their organizational and coalition-building skills. Seattle chose John Sanford, a three-star general; in New York, Harold Levy, an attorney for Citigroup, became school chancellor; federal prosecutor and Rhodes scholar Alan Bersin took the leadership role in San Diego; and in Los Angeles, former Colorado Governor Roy Romer was chosen for the top position. Typically, these noneducators have appointed a capable and experienced educator as their deputy responsible for curricular and instructional issues, while they invest their talents in setting goals, providing a vision and direction for change, finding additional resources, and building support both within and beyond the schools system.[18]

An effective superintendent must be an effective manager. For large school districts that employ thousands of professionals and serve tens of thousands of students, management is a challenge. Superintendents have been terminated when textbooks or teacher paychecks arrive late. In more than one district, the superintendent's choice of school day closings proved unpopular, and resulted in the selection of a new superintendent. Some school districts have adopted performance-based contracts that link superintendent compensation directly to student performance.[19]

While the superintendent is the district's educational leader, the principal is the school's educational leader. Teachers are much more likely to interact with the school principal than with a school superintendent. Like superintendents, principals report a great deal of job pressure, which is one reason why the $60,000 to $80,000 annual salaries have not been enough to attract a sufficient candidate pool. Accountability and testing pressures, inadequate pay, continuing bad press and increasing demands on a principal's time all discourage potential candidates. Even at the elementary level, where many consider the stress most tolerable, a typical elementary principal supervises 30 teachers, 14 other staff members, 425 students, and works an average of nine or ten hours a day, 54 hours or more a week.[20] Amazingly, 20 percent of principals report spending five to ten hours a week in efforts aimed at a single purpose: avoiding lawsuits.[21]

Not only is there a shortage of candidates for principal positions, there is a disturbing racial and ethnic imbalance as well. African American, Hispanic and Asian Americans combined account for only 15 percent of elementary principals, although these ethnic and racial populations are rapidly becoming the majority of the nation's students.[22] Perhaps one of the few bright spots is the increase in the number of females as principals, now over 40 percent. (Figure 10.6 provides insight into elementary principal demographics.)

Covert Power in Schools

5. Who might be considered part of the "hidden school government" . . . *the school secretary and parents.*

So you think that the school principal is the only one responsible for school personnel decisions, including hiring and firing. Think again. Parents, vocal individuals, the school secretary, and community groups have **covert power** and can bring

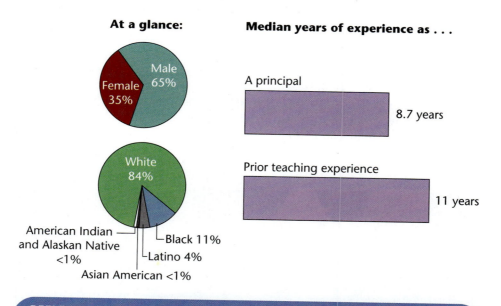

At a glance:

Male 65%
Female 35%

White 84%
American Indian and Alaskan Native <1%
Black 11%
Latino 4%
Asian American <1%

Median years of experience as . . .

A principal
8.7 years

Prior teaching experience
11 years

FIGURE 10.6
Elementary and secondary school principals.

SOURCE: National Center for Educational Statistics, "Principals in Public and Private Elementary and Secondary Schools, by Selected Characteristics, 1993–94," *Digest of Educational Statistics 2000* (Washington, DC: U.S. Department of Education, 2000).

REFLECTION

What are the potential challenges for schools with white principals and a majority of students of color?

significant pressure to bear on which teachers stay in a school, and which leave. These unofficial but highly involved persons and groups constitute the **hidden government** of schools.

The concept of hidden government is not unique to schools. In fact, most of our institutions, including the White House, have developed their own unique forms of hidden government. There, decision making is often influenced more by old colleagues back home (the "kitchen cabinet") than by the president's official advisers and cabinet members.

How does hidden government operate in schools? Following are some examples.

EXAMPLE 1 A first-year teacher in a New England junior high school spent long hours after school, preparing lessons and working with his students. Admirable as all this appeared, the school secretary, Ms. Hand, advised the teacher not to work with female students after school hours, because "You may get your fingers burned." The teacher smiled, ignored the secretary's advice, and continued providing students with after-school help.

Within a week, the principal called the teacher in for a conference and suggested that the teacher provide extra help to students only if both male and female students were present. The teacher objected to the advice and to the secretary's complaining to the principal. The principal responded, "You're new here, and I can understand your concern. But what you have to learn is that Ms. Hand is more than a secretary. She knows this school better than I do. Follow her advice and you'll do just fine."

Lesson: You can't always tell which people hold the real power by their official position.

Lesson: The school secretary is often the eyes and ears of the principal. In some cases, the secretary manages the day-to-day operations of the school.

EXAMPLE 2 A young teacher in an elementary school in the Midwest was called into the principal's office for a conference. The principal evaluated her teaching as above average but suggested that she maintain greater discipline. Her classroom was simply too noisy, and the students' chairs were too often left in disarray. The conference was over in ten minutes.

The teacher was offended. She did not feel her classroom was too noisy, and the chairs were always arranged in a neat circle. Moreover, the principal had visited her class for only five minutes, and during that time the students had said hardly a word.

The school secretary holds a position that can exert significant covert power in his or her pivotal role as the principal's "eyes and ears."

The next day, in the teacher's lounge, all became clear when she discussed the conference with another teacher. The teacher nodded, smiled, and explained:

"Mr. Richards."

"The custodian?"

"Yup. He slowly sweeps the halls and listens for noisy classrooms. Then he tells the principal. He also hates it when the chairs are in a circle, since it makes sweeping harder. Nice straight rows are much easier. Just make sure your classroom is quiet when he's in the halls and have your students put the chairs in neat, straight rows at the end of the day. That's the ticket for getting a good evaluation!"

Lesson: School custodians are often a source of information for principals and of supplies for teachers. They make very helpful allies and powerful adversaries.

EXAMPLE 3 An elementary school teacher in a rural southern community was put in charge of the class play. Rehearsals were under way when the teacher received a note to stop by the principal's office at 3:00 P.M.

The principal had received a call from a parent who was quite disappointed at the small part her daughter had received in the play. The principal wanted the teacher to consider giving the child a larger part. "After all," he explained, "her mother is influential in the PTA, and her father is one of the town's most successful businessmen. It's silly for you to alienate them. Give her a bigger part. Life will be easier for both of us, and we may be able to get her parents' support for the next school bond issue. That would mean a raise for all of us."

Lesson: Parents can also be influential in school decisions by applying pressure on principals, school boards, and community groups. When you decide to make a stand in the face of parental pressure, choose a significant issue and be able to substantiate your facts.

Business and Family

6. The influence of the business community in U.S. schools can best be characterized as . . . *extensive and growing.*

Corporate America is increasingly involved in school activities, and many companies have formalized this association through **educational partnerships.** It is true that most schools have traditionally emphasized values held dear by the business community: hard work, competition, dependability, punctuality, neatness, conformity, and loyalty.[23] So intertwined have business values and school practices become that educators have adopted the business vocabulary. An education leader is called a *superintendent,* the same title originally given to a factory supervisor. A school building, like a factory, has been called a *plant. Quality control, accountability, management design*, and *efficiency* have also been expropriated from business and applied to education. School superintendents are frequently evaluated by their cost-effectiveness and management skills, and some even come from the business sector. Business leaders, like IBM's Louis Gerstner, have brought national attention to schools, claiming that the future of the business community lies in a well-educated workforce. The business community has "adopted" schools, started special technology programs, put commercial ads in school buildings, created charter schools to prepare workers for certain careers, established companies to compete with public schools, and has organized campaigns calling for tougher school standards and more testing. Many educators are wary about the motivations and tactics of the business community, claiming that preparing a dutiful workforce and selling (sometimes unhealthy)

Competition and other business-oriented values have become so familiar and pervasive in our schools that we have become inured to them.

When parents work with the school to make sure homework is completed, student achievement increases.

products is not the purpose of a public school. But whether we are comfortable or uncomfortable with this trend, "The most far-reaching initiative in education to emerge in recent years is the growing corporate interest in public schools."[24]

Beyond the growing influence of business in schools, schools themselves are reaching out to families, trying to create more effective home-school partnerships. Children spend 87 percent of their time outside of school, mostly under the influence of their parents. There is great disparity in how families invest their time in academic efforts such as homework. Educators are partnering with families to improve this picture:

Governor Jeb Bush of Florida decided to give teachers and schools millions of dollars in "bonus pay" as a reward for high scores on standardized tests. But when two middle schools offered the cash bonuses directly to high scoring students, as much as $150 per student, the governor objected. The chair of the school board argued that if adults get bonuses, so should children. Florida Congressman Jim Davis characterized the episode as "a new and inevitable low in testing run amok."

SOURCE: "Cash for Success," *The Washington Post*, August 21, 2001.

REFLECTION

If businesses pay bonuses for productivity, do you think that schools should as well? Would you steer the bonuses to administrators, teachers, or students? Why?

Click on *In the News* for recent *In the News* stories. Submit your own *In the News* summary to share with your colleagues.

- Arizona teachers have organized a basic skills package, published in English, Spanish, and Navajo, to assist parents in working with children.

- Missouri funds an ambitious program called Parents as First Teachers. The program includes seminars about the language development of children, home visits by teachers, parental instruction on activities to promote hand-eye coordination, and the testing of children's vision, hearing, speech, and motor development. Missouri saw this funding as an investment in the future and a preventive measure to avoid the high cost of remedial programs for these children in later years.

- District hot lines for homework, family websites, college information guides, practice tests and parent-teacher email represent a growing technological link to enhance home-school partnerships.[25]

Making Schools More Responsive

7. In most schools, teachers are expected to . . . comply with policies made by principals and by district and state officials.

While parents, community groups, and the business sector carve out their roles in schools, teachers traditionally have been omitted from meaningful involvement in school governance. To get a sense of what that might feel like, imagine that you are the senior faculty member at Someplace High School. Having taught there for thirty years, you know the school like the back of your hand. You are regarded as an excellent teacher, an expert at judging the needs of your students. Should you participate in making decisions affecting the management of your school?

To get a sense of how little say teachers have once they leave their own classrooms, let's join the first faculty meeting of the fall at Someplace High. The principal, Mr. Will E. Tell, is discussing the new teacher assessment forms with the faculty:

413

MR. TELL: If you all look in your folders, you'll see the criteria on which you will be assessed when I observe in your classrooms. Look these forms over carefully, and let me know if you have any questions. I'll be scheduling my school observation visits with you shortly. Another issue I wanted to raise with you concerns our need to develop better relations with the community. I've passed around a sign-up sheet for a committee to turn around the low attendance at parent conferences. What I have in mind is a car wash or a bake sale or another fund-raising activity to bring the community together. Ms. Johnson, you have a question?

MS. JOHNSON: Yes, Mr. Tell. I thought that we were going to talk about setting up a better school website, one that can pull parents into school conferences and activities, assist students with their homework, have links to resources, and address special interest topics for teachers and parents. We all indicated at last year's faculty meeting that this should be a top priority.

MR. TELL: You're absolutely right, Louise, and I'm glad you raised the topic. That was going to be our first order of business, but I'm happy to report that the district office called yesterday and has promised us website support by the second semester. I'll be getting out my first newsletter to the faculty in a few weeks, and I'll be sure to include that information. I'll also be announcing the in-service training sessions for the fall semester. I heard some interesting speakers at the national convention I attended, and I think I'm going to be able to get some of them to come to our district. Before we end the meeting, I want to introduce our new faculty member. I hired Ms. Wetherby over the summer, and she'll join the teachers in our English department. I know you'll all do everything you can to make sure that Ms. Wetherby feels welcome. Now, if there are no further topics for discussion, let's all get back to our classrooms. Tomorrow the kids arrive. It's time for a new year.

From listening in on this faculty meeting, you can tell that many of the most crucial decisions were made by others. Whether a teacher will be assigned to advanced placement literature classes or remedial English is a decision usually made by the

Teachers, who know more than most people in the educational chain about the needs and interests of individual students, have often been excluded from school management and policy-making.

principal. Teachers, as a rule, do not participate in hiring new teachers, in developing criteria by which their teaching will be evaluated, in setting graduation requirements, or in scheduling classes.

Objection to top-down decision making by principals and school district authorities prompted a broad movement to give teachers a greater role in school governance.[26] You may hear such terms as *participatory management, shared leadership, teacher empowerment,* and *faculty-led renewal.* During the 1990s, two of the most widely adopted reforms were the related actions of moving decision-making authority to individual schools (known as **site-based,** or **school-based, management**) and dispersing the authority more broadly within schools (known as **collaborative decision making**). Large urban school systems, such as those in Chicago, Miami, Los Angeles, and San Diego, led the trend of adopting school-based management, while such states as Colorado, Kentucky, North Carolina, and Texas made collaborative decision making mandatory at every school.[27]

Today, all over the country, various visions and versions of school-based management and teacher empowerment are influencing how schools are governed. In Montgomery County, Maryland, for example, quality management councils composed of the principal, peer-elected teachers, and representatives appointed by the principal have jurisdiction over everything from ordering supplies and making curricular decisions to hiring new staff. Not all teachers are enamored with this, as one pointed out: "This may really help us. It may really hurt us. Especially if it turns out to be just another meeting you've got to go to."[28]

Caution is appropriate, since the success enjoyed by site-based approaches varies from community to community. In Dade County, Florida, site-based management was credited with decreasing teacher turnover and lowering student absences. But, in Los Angeles, a similar plan led to power struggles, conflict, and complaints of ineffectiveness. In Minneapolis, site teams have increased the sense of teacher professionalism and accountability, but measurable gains in student performance have been more elusive.

While there is a general consensus that teacher morale and parent involvement have increased at many schools that have made these changes, the impact on student achievement has been more difficult to discern. In order for school-based management to be truly effective, most experts suggest that it be part of a broader strategy for improving education. One parent involved in school governance summarized the situation this way: "Site-based management is an innovation, yet it is trying to fit into an administration and a school board that were made 92 years ago. It doesn't fit together . . . we need to look at a new system."[29]

As smaller and more responsive schools gain in popularity, educators are reconsidering school district size. For most of the last century, small rural districts have merged into larger ones, a trend called **consolidation.** (See Frame of Reference: Consolidation in Action.) Larger districts were considered more cost-effective because they lowered the per pupil expenses of many services, from preparing food to building maintenance, and bigger school districts were able to offer more courses, extracurricular activities, and sports programs.[30]

But today, larger school districts also means larger schools, more red tape, greater student alienation and increased tension, and less parent-teacher involvement. Very large districts, such as New York City, have moved away from consolidation by creating subdistricts, smaller units to help avoid some of the problems of bigness, a process called **decentralization.** While consolidation has been a fact of life in U.S. education for over a century, its benefits are now being reconsidered.[31]

The following numbers show the dramatic reduction in the number of school districts as smaller ones consolidate. Still, 75 percent of the remaining districts are fairly small, servicing fewer than 2,500 students each.

School Year	Number of Public School Districts
1929–1930	119,001
1939–1940	117,108
1949–1950	83,718
1959–1960	40,520
1970–1971	17,995
1980–1981	15,912
1989–1990	15,367
1998–1999	14,566

SOURCE: *Digest of Education Statistics 2000,* U.S. Department of Education, National Center for Education Statistics.

REFLECTION

While district size is difficult for a student to gauge, school size is far easier. In your opinion, what is the "ideal" size for a high school? What was the size of your high school? How does your experience influence the notion of an "ideal" size?

SUMMARY

CHAPTER REVIEW

Go to the Online Learning Center to take a quiz, practice with key terms, and review key ideas from the chapter.

1. Why do teachers need to know about finance and governance?

   • While issues of finance and governance at first may appear to be beyond the interest of classroom teachers, in fact such issues often directly influence the quality of life in the classroom.

   • Teachers should become more involved in finance and governance policies, so that they can influence the direction of schools, take an active role in their own profession, and be a voice for the children they teach. Unfortunately, the insights of students and teachers are not heard in policy circles.

2. How is the property tax connected to unequal educational funding?

   • Local communities generally fund their schools through a property tax, which many people consider outdated and unfair. Since some areas are wealthier than others, some school districts generate more than enough money for schools, while others must struggle to keep schools open.

   • Municipal overburden refers to the additional revenues needed by cities to respond to numerous social needs.

   • Robin Hood laws built on the California *Serrano* decision, and attempted to equalize educational funding between wealthy and poor communities. Resistance to these attempts led to passage of laws such as Proposition 13, which limited property taxes and lowered the quality of education in many communities.

- Although the Supreme Court recognized that financing schools through the property tax is a flawed system, it did not rule the process unconstitutional. It has been left up to states to address the financial inequities brought about by relying on the property tax to finance our schools.

3. What is the distinction between educational *equity* and educational *adequacy*?

- Resistance to funding equalization plans arose through court decisions such as *Abbott v. Burke* in New Jersey. When courts directed that funds from wealthier districts be moved to poorer ones, opposition to educational equity plans grew.

- Citizens objected to the loss of local control, and wealthy and influential communities voiced their opposition to the transfer of local funds to other communities.

- Increased funding did not always lead to higher educational scores. Courts began to differentiate between financial input and educational outcome.

- Several state court decisions have cited state constitutional language guaranteeing adequate or efficient education. Many, but not all states, are now focusing on the educational skills of graduates, rather than per pupil expenditures, as the yardstick for fairness in education.

4. What are the sources of state revenues?

- The most common state sources of school funding are property tax, sales tax, personal income tax, state lotteries, and other taxes. Funding is especially difficult for poorer communities and states, where even high tax rates do not raise enough money for the schools.

- Many of the state sources of revenue are regressive, putting most of the burden on the poorest citizens.

- States have experimented with different funding methods, such as foundation programs and a guaranteed tax base for all districts, in order to help poorer communities fund schools. None has proved very successful.

5. How does the federal government influence education?

- According to the Tenth Amendment of the U.S. Constitution, education is the responsibility of the states. Still, the federal government exercises great influence through court actions, categorical grants, and specific programs sponsored by the U.S. Department of Education.

- Federal monies provide between 6 and 8 percent of K–12 educational costs, much of which is in block grants. Most Americans believe that all levels of government underfund education.

6. What current trends are shaping educational finance?

- School financing in the future will be influenced by demands tying school performance to funding levels (accountability), the popularity of choice programs, the great need for repairing deteriorating school buildings (infrastructure), and the continuing effort of wealthy communities to retain their tax revenues in their own community to ensure superior public schools.

7. How do school boards and superintendents work together to manage schools?

- At the state level, the legislature, state board of education, state superintendent, and state department of education provide the policy and administration of schools. The state also delegates some of its power to local school boards and superintendents, who administer individual school districts.

- The board of education at both the state and local levels is responsible for formulating educational policy. The chief state school officer, often called the superintendent, is responsible for implementing the policies of the state board of education, just as the local superintendent implements the policies of the local board of education.

- School boards can act as trustee representatives, serving the interests of the entire community, or representative delegates, serving the interests of their neighborhoods. School board members are typically white, male, conservative, and economically well-off.

- School boards vary in the way they operate, and the kind of superintendent they prefer. Boards range from dominating educational decisions to passive acceptance. Successful superintendents can "read" their school board, and manage bureaucracies.

- Several large school districts are turning to former lawyers, business executives, political leaders and even military officers to lead their school districts.

- School principals also confront stressful job pressures, which contributes to the shortage of candidates for this position. Most principals are male and white, although the number of female principals has been increasing.

8. What is the "hidden" government of schools?

- Parents, school secretaries, and custodians can be influential in a teacher's success. They are part of the hidden government of schools.

9. How does the business community influence school culture?

- The business community has had a significant impact on schools. Certain business-oriented values, such as competitiveness and punctuality, are part of the school culture. Moreover, many businesses are becoming directly involved in schools, donating products, dollars, and volunteers to work with students.

- The business community has been demanding higher standards and testing to prepare a more effective workforce.

- Some question the growing business influence and commercialism in the nation's schools. Critics argue that the purpose of schooling should be more than providing workers for corporate America.

- In addition to the growing business influence, parents and civic groups are also involved in school partnerships. Many schools are working to create better home and school partnerships.

10. How are schools being made more responsive to teachers and the community?

- Traditionally, teachers have not had a significant role in school governance. However, the recent trends of school-based management, also called site-based management, and collaborative decision making, may provide teachers with a more influential position in school governance.

- The size, culture, and history of individual school districts influence the effectiveness of these programs, and teacher participation in school policy appears more effective in some districts than others.

- Consolidation has decreased the number of school districts while increasing the average size of schools.

- Supporters of consolidation believe that it increases educational opportunities and efficiency by absorbing small school districts with limited educational resources and electives into larger districts.

- Those who oppose consolidation claim that it increases alienation and red tape. As a result, many larger school districts have reorganized themselves into smaller, decentralized administrative units.

KEY TERMS AND PEOPLE

Abbott v. Burke, 390

accountability, 395

adequate education, 390

block grants, 393

bond, 398

Anne Bryant, 406

categorical grants, 393

chief state school officer, 402

collaborative decision making, 415

consolidation, 415

covert power, 409

decentralization, 415

delegate representative, 403

Edgewood v. Kirby, 388

educational outcome, 390

educational partnerships, 411

estate (or gift) taxes, 392

excise taxes, 392

failing schools, 390

financial input, 390

foundation program, 389

guaranteed tax base program, 389

hidden government, 410

motor vehicle license fee, 392

municipal overburden, 388

personal income tax, 392

property tax, 387

Proposition 13, 389

Robin Hood reformers, 389

sales tax, 392

San Antonio v. Rodriguez, 388

school boards, 401

Serrano v. Priest, 388

severance tax, 392

sin tax, 392

site-based (school-based) management, 415

state board of education, 401

state department of education, 402

state lotteries, 392

superintendent, 402

Tenth Amendment, 400

trustee representative, 403

United States Department of Education, 393

DISCUSSION QUESTIONS AND ACTIVITIES

1. Why has state support for local school systems grown?

2. Briefly describe the major sources of state and local funds for schools.

3. What are the typical programs for state distribution of education funds?

4. Create a plan for (a) raising funds for education and (b) distributing funds equitably to all school districts within a state.

5. How can the differences in state wealth be dealt with to ensure that all students, regardless of the state they live in, benefit from equal educational expenditures?

6. If you were a state judge, would you focus more on financial resources (input) or educational output?

7. What is your opinion of the "adequacy" argument? Do you have any reservations about this approach? Do you believe that educational expenditures and educational quality are directly related? Support your position.

8. If educational vouchers were applied only to public schools, what would be the result?

9. Contrast the *Serrano* and *Rodriguez* court decisions.

10. If you were a superintendent of schools, what steps would you take to avoid taxpayer opposition to increasing school funding levels?

11. Research the average costs of educating a student in a local district. Discuss with classmates as you compare district programs, tax base, facilities, and student achievement.

12. Why does a high property tax rate not always result in a well-funded school program?

13. You are the chief financial officer of a school district with a 3 percent increase for next year's budget. Determine what percentage of your total monies will be spent on the following sample categories:

teachers' raises

new buildings and facilities

expand technology, including computers

long-delayed capital expenses for a gymnasium and the heating/cooling system

new hires to lower class size

YOU DECIDE

In what way would you divide (starting with 100 percent) your new monies? How would you defend your choices? (Use your imagination and the information in this chapter.)

14. Can you create job incentives that would entice qualified individuals to seek careers as principals and superintendents?

15. Which of the four types of school boards would you prefer to serve on, or work for? Why? Which of the four types of school superintendents would you prefer to be, or to work for? Why?

16. Have you had any personal experience in an organization that had both a formal and a "hidden" government? Explain how these governments operated.

17. Identify both the advantages and the disadvantages of the unusual U.S. form of local control over schools.

18. Based on your own experiences in school, can you recall examples of how business values were taught to you? Do you feel that this is a positive or a negative aspect of public education? Why?

19. If you had the power to reorganize the governance structure of public education, what changes would you make?

20. Someone once said, "What is good for General Motors is good for the country." If we were to paraphrase this statement to apply to U.S. schools, would you agree or disagree? Why?

21. Support or refute the following statement: "The least critical expertise needed by school super-intendents is knowledge about teaching, learning, and children."

22. Describe the advantages and disadvantages of (a) increasing state influence on education and (b) decreasing federal influence on education.

23. If you were responsible for creating school partnerships, what businesses, community groups, or other organizations would you seek out to contribute to the educational process? Why?

24. Why was the twentieth century marked by school consolidation? What problems did consolidation bring?

25. Identify at least five powers that states have to influence education.

26. Find a school that has implemented site-based management or collaborative decision-making. Interview a teacher to find out what the effects have been for teachers.

WEB-*TIVITIES*

1. States to the Rescue

2. The Federal Government's Role in Financing Education

3. The Legal Control of Schools

4. Superintendents

5. School Boards Under Fire

6. The Business of America Is Business

7. Trends in School Governance: Educational Partnerships

REEL TO REAL TEACHING

OCTOBER SKY (1999)
Run Time: 108 minutes

Synopsis: The true story of Homer Hickam, a high school student seemingly destined to repeat his father's harsh life in the West Virginia coal mines, until the Soviet launch of *Sputnik* in 1957 sparks his own scientific aspirations. With the encouragement of a science teacher, Homer and his fellow "Rocket Boys" venture to launch their own homemade rockets.

Reflection:

1. This chapter emphasizes the financing and governing of schools. How did these two factors shape students' lives in Coalwood? Give examples from the film. How did your schooling reflect educational governance and financing?

2. Consider how inequitable funding is related to geography. How does school finance impact educational opportunities in rural, suburban, and urban schools?

3. *October Sky* is set in the late 1950s, prior to many of the landmark legal rulings on educational funding discussed in this chapter. How might these court decisions have altered educational opportunities at Coalwood High?

4. What student expectations are revealed in the principal's comment to Ms. Riley: "Our job is to give these kids an education, not false hopes. Once in a while a lucky one gets out on a football scholarship. The rest work in the mines."

5. What academic and social purposes do events such as science fairs, spelling bees, and music festivals play in schools and communities? How do these differ in wealthy and poor schools? Interview classmates who attended rural, suburban, and urban schools to learn about these differences.

Follow-up Activity: *October Sky* is a "coming of age" film. Homer Hickam wrestles with accepting life in the mines and pursuing his own dreams. It is a common theme not only in film, but also in life. Interview older friends or family members about whether they were ever expected to "follow in the footsteps" of others. How did they feel about it? Why did they choose to follow tradition or make a new path? Was their decision influenced by a pivotal schooling experience, a motivating teacher, or inspiring hero? What do they think now of the decisions they made then? Capture their stories by audiotaping, video recording, or taking notes on the interviews.

 How do you rate this film? Click on *Reel to Real Teaching* to submit your review of this or another education-related film, and read reviews submitted by others.

FOR FURTHER READING

Cultivating Leadership in Schools: Connecting People, Purpose, and Practice, by Gordon Donaldson, Jr. (2000). Enter the real-life world of decision making by administrators, teachers, parents, and school boards. "See" how interpersonal and intrapersonal skills are the keys to successful leadership.

Equal Resources, Equal Outcomes: The Distribution of School Resources and Student Achievement in California, by Julian R. Betts, Kim S. Rueben, and Anne Danenberg (2000). Debunks the myth that centralized funding of California public schools has equalized spending across districts and demonstrates how inequalities in school resources create inequalities in student achievement.

Equity and Adequacy in Education Finance: Issues and Perspectives, Helen F. Ladd, Rosemary Chalk, and Janet S. Hansen (1999). A timely collection of papers explores such questions as: What do the terms *equity* and *adequacy* in school finance really mean? and What is the impact of court-ordered school finance reform on spending disparities?

Making Money Matter: Financing America's Schools, by Helen F. Ladd and Janet S. Hansen (1999). Details the shifting expectations placed upon public schools in the last half-century and the real diversity that characterizes the existing system of governance and finance for public education. Given this backdrop, the authors discuss ways to break the nexus between student background and achievement.

Partners in Progress: Strengthening the Superintendent-Board Relationship, by Matthew King (1999). Shows how superintendents and board members can work together to improve communication and achievement within the entire school community.

Principles of Power: Women Superintendents and the Riddle of the Heart, by C. Cryss Brunner (2000). Shares perspectives from twelve successful women superintendents and puts them in a cultural context that highlights methods for success.

Rethinking Leadership: A Collection of Articles, by Thomas Sergiovanni (2000). Explores the developmental stages of leadership, defines the moral requirements of educational leaders and stresses the importance of building democratic, learner-centered communities.

FOCUS QUESTIONS

1. What are your legal rights and responsibilities as a teacher?
2. What legal rights do students enjoy (and do they have legal responsibilities)?
3. What are today's main approaches to moral education?

WHAT DO YOU THINK? **What Is Your Rights Quotient?** Take an electronic version of the quiz on page 425.

CHAPTER PREVIEW

An honors student sues the school district after being randomly stripped searched.

A teacher is reprimanded for allowing a first grader to read a Bible story to the class.

A school puts the senior yearbook on its Web page and finds that it has helped pedophiles identify potential targets.

A student complains that peer grading of assignments is a violation of privacy.

A homosexual student sues a school district for discrimination.

Lawyers and judges are more and more becoming a part of school life. In this chapter, you will have the opportunity to respond to actual legal situations that have confronted teachers and students. (Get ready to determine your RQ—Rights Quotient.) Also included are some pragmatic steps for your legal self defense, steps that you can take to avoid potential problems. But, beyond the nitty-gritty of these legal case studies, we will ask more penetrating questions about right and wrong, questions that go beyond the law, such as: How should teachers deal with ethical issues that emerge in the classroom? Should teachers take positions on moral issues? Or should they play a more neutral role? We will offer some suggestions for ways teachers can organize their classrooms, and themselves, to handle these important but difficult ethical dilemmas.

Classroom Law

You have probably heard it before: the United States is a litigious society. "Take them to court," "I'll sue," and "Have your lawyer call my lawyer" are phrases that have worked their way into the American lexicon. And actions match words. People sue companies. Companies sue people. Governments sue companies. Companies and people sue governments. We tend to seek redress in the courts for all kinds of problems, from divorce to physical injury, from protecting our beliefs to complying (or not complying) with laws.

Today, parents sue teachers. Students sue teachers. Teachers sue schools. Despite the growing importance and influence of school-related law, many educators are still unaware of their basic legal rights and responsibilities. This can be a costly professional blind spot.[1]

What rights do you have in the classroom? Consider this exchange between a college professor and a former associate superintendent of public instruction for California:

SUPERINTENDENT: "Teaching is a privilege, not a right. If one wants this privilege, he or she has to give up some rights."

PROFESSOR: "Just what constitutional rights do people have to give up in order to enter teaching?"

SUPERINTENDENT: "Any right their community wants them to give up."[2]

Although such simplistic attitudes still exist, recent years have seen extraordinary changes in the legal rights of both teachers and students. Once the victims of arbitrary school rules and regulations, today's teachers and students can institute legal action if they believe that their constitutional rights are being threatened. In an increasing number of cases, the courts are finding school administrators guilty of violating the rights of both teachers and students.

As a classroom teacher, what can you legally say and do? Can you let your students log freely onto the Internet? What disciplinary methods are acceptable? How does your role as teacher limit your personal life? Knowing the answers to these questions *before* you step into a classroom can help you avoid costly mistakes.

While teachers would like to know definitively what is legal and what is not, courts often set forth standards with such terms as "reasonable care" or "appropriately under the circumstances." Courts try to balance legitimate concerns that can be raised on both sides of an issue and to keep their options open. Staying legally up-to-date is an ongoing professional task.

What Is Your Rights Quotient?

The following case studies focus on court cases or federal law.[3] The vignettes are divided into two parts: teachers' rights and students' rights. In each case, an issue is identified, a situation is described, and you are asked to select an appropriate (legal) response. After your selection, the correct response and relevant court decisions or laws are described. Keep track of your rights and wrongs; a scoring system at the conclusion will help you determine your RQ (rights quotient). Good luck!

Federal, state, and local governments all have a voice in education, although they don't necessarily speak in unison. To help you navigate the legal landscape, here's a brief look at how the different branches and levels of government influence school law.

THE U.S. CONSTITUTION

While the Constitution does not mention education, it does guarantee to individuals basic rights, rights that are of concern in schools. Three Constitutional Amendments are of special interest to teachers and students.

- **First Amendment** protects freedom of religion and speech. An important part of this Amendment is the **establishment clause**, which prohibits government (including school) advancement of religion.
- Fourth Amendment protects basic privacy and security.
- Fourteenth Amendment protects right to due process.

FEDERAL LAWS

Many federal laws influence education. The Civil Rights Act of 1964 bars discrimination on the basis of race, color, or national origin. Title IX prohibits discrimination on the basis of sex. The Individuals with Disabilities Act expands educational opportunities to persons with disabilities. By funding certain programs, and withholding funds from others, from elementary school through college, the federal government exerts a significant influence on education.

STATE AND LOCAL LAWS

State constitutions as well as state and local laws influence education, so there are significant local differences throughout the nation. State and local laws (also known as statutes) often deal with school financing, collective bargaining, teacher certification, and compulsory attendance.

THE COURTS

A dual judicial system of state and federal courts exists in the United States. State courts initially hear most legal issues in education. Only cases challenging the U.S. Constitution or federal laws are heard in federal courts, including the U.S. Supreme Court.

SOURCE: Michael LaMorte, *School Law: Cases and Concepts* (Needham Heights: Allyn & Bacon, 1999).

REFLECTION

What are the advantages and disadvantages of these different government jurisdictions determining school law? Offer at least two benefits and drawbacks of this system.

I. Teachers' Rights and Responsibilities

Issue

Applying for a position

Situation 1

You did it! You finished student teaching (you were great!) and the school district you most want to teach in has called you for an interview. Mr. Thomas, from the personnel office, seems impressed with your credentials and the interview is going well. He explains that the school district is very committed to its teachers and invests a great deal of resources in training. He wants to make certain that this investment makes sense, so he asks you for your long-range plans with such questions as: "Do you see yourself teaching in this system for a long time?" and "Are you planning to get married or have children in the near future?"

_____ You answer the questions realizing that the district is entitled to know about your long-range plans.

_____ You avoid answering the questions. You think it's none of his business, but you are worried that you won't get the position.

Federal and State Laws, Court Decisions   Not too long ago, school districts regularly gave hiring and promotion consideration to marital status and parenthood. For women these were critical factors in being offered a job, and the "right" answer was: "No, I am not going to get married or have children." For male candidates, the question was less important and rarely asked. Now a variety of federal and state laws and court decisions make such inquiries illegal. Generally, interview questions must be related to the job requirements. Questions about race, creed, marital status, sex, religion, age, national origin, and physical or other disabilities and even a request for photographs along with an application are generally illegal. **Title IX of the Education Amendments (1972)** and **Title VII of the Civil Rights Act (1964)** are two federal laws that prohibit many of these practices. In situation 1, the questions are inappropriate and illegal, and you need not answer them. You may wish to notify the school district or even the Office for Civil Rights in order to stop the school district from asking such discriminatory questions in the future. The challenge, of course, is how you could answer such questions without ruining your chances for being offered a position—that is, if you still want the job.[4]

Issue	*Situation 2*
Sexual harassment	After surviving the gender discriminatory interview, you are offered a teaching position and decide to take it. After all, you like the community and the children, and with any luck you will never run into Mr. Thomas (the interviewer) again. You are very excited as you prepare for your first day. You are up an hour early, rehearsing your opening remarks. You enter the school, feeling hopeful and optimistic. Then it's your worst nightmare. You meet the new principal, Mr. Thomas, recently transferred from the personnel office. You spend the next year dodging his lewd comments, his unwanted touches, and his incessant propositions. At the end of the year, you find yourself in counseling and worried about your job. You decide that

_____ Your initial instincts were right. You should never have taken this job. Quit before things get worse.

_____ Enough is enough. You sue the district for damages.

Court Decision   Anita Hill's charges against Supreme Court nominee Clarence Thomas, as well as similar charges against former President Clinton, a stream of Senators, and other officials have awakened millions of Americans to the issue of sexual harassment. The principal's behavior, both verbal and physical, is clearly an example of this problem. The Supreme Court ruled that victims of sexual harassment are also victims of sex discrimination and can recover monetary damages. Keeping a record of the principal's behavior and having witnesses will strengthen your case. You certainly can sue, and, if you are successful, you may be awarded significant monetary damages. You can also file a grievance with the Office for Civil Rights, without even having a lawyer. This grievance will launch an investigation of the school's practices.

(Unlike adult cases, students who are victims of sexual harassment do not fare as well. The court has created very high standards before a school district can be held financially accountable.[5])

Issue

Personal lifestyle

Situation 3

After your first few months, your reputation is established: You are known as a creative and effective teacher and are well liked by students and colleagues (isn't that wonderful!). But your life outside the classroom is not appreciated by school officials. You are single and living with your "significant other." Several school officials have strong feelings about this and believe that you are a poor role model for the students. The school system publicly announces that your cohabitation is having a negative influence on your elementary-age students and suspends you.

_____ You are the victim of an illegal action and should sue to be reinstated.

_____ The school board is within its rights in dismissing you and removing a bad role model from the classroom.

Court Decision   This case hinges on the question of how much personal freedom an individual abandons when assuming the position of a teacher and becoming a role model for students. Although court decisions have varied, the following general standard should be kept in mind: Does your behavior significantly disrupt the educational process or erode your credibility with students, colleagues, or the community? If the school district can demonstrate that you have disrupted education or have lost credibility, then you may be fired.

In the case outlined here, the teacher sued the school district (*Thompson v. Southwest School District*). The court indicated that, until the school district took action to suspend the teacher on grounds of immorality, the public was generally unaware of the teacher's cohabitation with her boyfriend. The court decided that it was unfair of the board of education to make the issue public in order to gain community support for its position. Furthermore, the court ruled that the teacher's behavior had not interfered with her effectiveness in the classroom. With neither a loss of credibility nor a significant disruption of the educational process, the board lost its case and the teacher kept her job.

What if the teacher's "significant other" was of the same sex? Whether gay and lesbian teachers need legal protection from dismissal based on sexual orientation is a divisive and unsettled debate. Eleven states (California, Connecticut, Hawaii, Maine, Massachusetts, Minnesota, New Hampshire, New Jersey, Rhode Island, Vermont, and Wisconsin) and more than 160 cities and counties prohibit sexual orientation discrimination in employment. Even in places without specific laws protecting gay and lesbian teachers, it is unlikely that they can be dismissed without direct evidence showing that a homosexual lifestyle negatively impacts their teaching.

Court decisions regarding the personal lifestyles of teachers have differed from state to state. Driving while intoxicated or smoking marijuana was found to be grounds for dismissal in one state but not in another, depending on whether the behavior resulted in "substantial disruption" of the educational process. On the other hand, an attempt to dismiss a teacher because she did not attend church was not upheld by the court. In fact, the teacher in this case actually won financial damages against the school district.

What about your personal appearance? What can a school district legally require in terms of personal grooming and dress codes for teachers? Courts have not been consistent in their decisions, although the courts may uphold the legality of dress codes for teachers if the dress requirements are reasonable and related to legitimate educational concerns.[6]

Issue	**Situation 4**
Teachers' academic freedom	As a social studies teacher, you are concerned about your students' apparent insensitivity to racism in the United States. You have found a very effective simulation game that evokes strong student feelings on racial issues, but the school board is concerned by this activity and has asked you to stop using the game. The board expressed its concern over your discussion of controversial issues. Committed to your beliefs, you persist; at the end of the year, you find that your teaching contract is not renewed.

_____ Since you think your academic freedom has been violated, you decide to sue to get your job back.

_____ You realize that the school board is well within its rights to determine curriculum, that you were warned, and that now you must pay the price for your indiscretion.

Court Decision   The right to **academic freedom** (that is, to teach without coercion, censorship, or other restrictive interference) is not absolute. The courts will balance your right to academic freedom with the school system's interests in its students' learning appropriate subject matter in an environment conducive to learning. Courts look at such factors as whether your learning activities and materials are inappropriate, irrelevant to the subjects to be covered under the syllabus, obscene, or substantially disruptive of school discipline. In the case of the simulation game

Academic freedom protects a teacher's right to teach about sensitive issues, such as AIDS or other sex education topics, as long as the topic is relevant to the course, is not treated in an obscene manner, and is not disruptive of school discipline.

involving racial issues, the activity appears to be appropriate, relevant, and neither obscene nor disruptive. If you were to sue on the grounds of academic freedom, you would probably get your job back.[7]

Issue	**Situation 5**
Legal liability (negligence)	You are assigned to cafeteria duty. Things are pretty quiet, and you take the opportunity to call a guest speaker and confirm a visit to your class. While you are gone from the cafeteria, a student slips on some spilled milk and breaks his arm. His parents hold you liable for their son's injury and sue you for damages.

INTERACTIVE ACTIVITY
WHAT CAN A TEACHER BE FIRED FOR? Test your knowledge of teachers' rights.

———— You will probably win, since you did not cause the fall and were on educational business when the accident occurred.

———— The student's parents will win, since you left your assigned post.

———— The student who spilled the milk is solely responsible for the accident.

———— No one will win, because the courts long ago ruled that there is no use crying over spilled milk. (You knew that was coming, right?)

Court Decision   In recent years, litigation against teachers has increased dramatically. The public concern over the quality of education, the bureaucratic and impersonal nature of many school systems, and the generally litigious nature of our society have all contributed to this rising tide of lawsuits. Negligence suits against teachers are common. In the cafeteria example, you would be in considerable jeopardy in a legal action. A teacher who is not present at his or her assigned duty might be charged with negligence, unless the absence is "reasonable." The courts are very strict about what is "reasonable" (leaving your post to put out a fire is reasonable, but going to the telephone to make a call is unlikely to be viewed as reasonable). It is a good practice to stay in your classroom or assigned area of responsibility unless there is an emergency.

Teacher liability is an area of considerable concern to many teachers. Courts generally use two standards in determining negligence: (1) whether a reasonable person with similar training would act in the same way and (2) whether or not the teacher could have foreseen the possibility of an injury. Following are some common terms and typical situations related to teacher liability:

- *Misfeasance.* Failure to conduct in an appropriate manner an act that might otherwise have been lawfully performed; for example, unintentionally using too much force in breaking up a fight is **misfeasance.**

- *Nonfeasance.* Failure to perform an act that one has a duty to perform; for example, the cafeteria situation is **nonfeasance,** since the teacher did not supervise an assigned area of responsibility.

- *Malfeasance.* An act that cannot be done lawfully regardless of how it is performed; for example, starting a fistfight or bringing marijuana to school is **malfeasance.**

- *Educational malpractice.* Although liability litigation usually involves physical injury to students because of what a teacher did or failed to do, a new line of litigation, called **educational malpractice,** is concerned with "academic damage." Some students and parents have sued school districts for failing to provide an adequate education. Many courts have rejected these cases, point-ing out that many factors affect learning and that failure to learn cannot be blamed solely on the school system.

Issue	*Situation 6*
Teachers' freedom of speech	As a teacher in a small school district, you are quite upset with the way the school board and the superintendent are spending school funds. You are particularly troubled with all the money being spent on high school athletics, since these expenditures have cut into your proposed salary raise. To protest the expenditures, you write a lengthy letter to the local newspaper, criticizing the superintendent and the school board. After the letter is published, you find that the figures you cited in the letter were inaccurate.

The following week, you are called into the superin-tendent's office and fired for breaking several school rules. You have failed to communicate your complaints to your superiors and you have caused harm to the school system by spreading false and malicious statements. In addition, the superintendent points out that your acceptance of a teaching position obligated you to refrain from publicizing critical statements about the school. The superintendent says although no one can stop you from making public statements, the school system certainly does not "have to pay you for the privilege." You decide to

_____ Go to court to win back your position.

_____ Chalk it up to experience, look for a new position, and make certain that you do not publish false statements and break school rules in the future.

Court Decision   This situation is based on a suit instigated by a teacher named Mar-vin Pickering. After balancing the teacher's interests, as a citizen, in commenting on is-sues of public concern against the school's interests in efficiently providing public services, the Supreme Court ruled in favor of the teacher. It found that the disciplined operation of the school system was not seriously damaged by Pickering's letter and that the misstatements in the letter were not made knowingly or recklessly. Moreover, there was no special need for confidentiality on the issue of school budgets. Hence, con-cluded the Court, prohibiting Pickering from making his statements was an infringe-ment of his First Amendment right to freedom of speech. You, too, would probably win in court if you were to issue public statements on matters of public concern, unless your statements were intentionally or recklessly inaccurate, disclosed confidential ma-terial, or hampered either school discipline or your performance of duties.[8]

Issue	*Situation 7*
Copying published material	You read a fascinating two-page article in a national magazine, and, since the article concerns an issue your class is discussing, you duplicate the article and distribute it to your students. This is the only article you have distributed in class, and you do not bother to ask either the author or the magazine for permission to reprint it. You have

——— Violated the copyright law, and you are liable to legal action.

——— Not violated any copyright law.

Federal Law   Initially, as copiers became commonplace in staff rooms, teachers could reproduce articles, poems, book excerpts, or whatever they pleased with virtually no fear of legal repercussions. But, in January 1976, Congress passed the **Copyright Act** (PL 94-553) and teachers' rights to freely reproduce and distribute published works were greatly curtailed. Under this law, in order to use a published work in class, teachers must write to the publisher or author of the work and obtain written permission. This sometimes requires the payment of a permission fee, something that teachers on a limited budget are usually unwilling to do. Under certain circumstances, however, teachers may still reproduce published material without written permission or payment. This is called **fair use**, a legal principle that allows the limited use of copyrighted materials. Teachers must observe three criteria in selecting the material: brevity, spontaneity, and cumulative effect.

1. *Brevity.* A work can be reproduced if it is not overly long. It is always wise to contact publishers directly, but typical limits might include the following criteria. Poems or excerpts from poems must be no longer than 250 words. Articles, stories, and essays of less than 2,500 words may be reproduced in complete form. Excerpts of any prose work (such as a book or an article) may be reproduced only up to 1,000 words or 10 percent of the work, whichever is less. Only one illustration (photo, drawing, diagram) may be reproduced from the same book or journal. The brevity criterion limits the length of the material that a teacher can reproduce and distribute from a single work. If you were the teacher in this example and you reproduced only a two-page article, you probably would not have violated the criterion of brevity.

2. *Spontaneity.* If a teacher has an inspiration to use a published work and there is simply not enough time to write for and receive written permission, then the teacher may reproduce and distribute the work. The teacher in our vignette has met this criterion so is acting within the law. If the teacher wishes to distribute the same article during the next semester or the next year, written permission would be required, since ample time exists to request such permission.

3. *Cumulative effect.* The total number of works reproduced without permission for class distribution must not exceed nine instances per class per semester. Within this limit, only one complete piece or two excerpts from the same author may be reproduced, and only three pieces from the same book or magazine. Cumulative effect limits the number of articles, poems, excerpts, and so on that can be reproduced, even if the criteria of spontaneity and brevity are met. The teacher in our vignette has not reproduced other works and therefore has met this criterion also.

Under the fair use principle, single copies of printed material may be copied for your personal use. Thus, if you want a single copy for planning a lesson, that is not a problem. Whenever multiple copies are made for classroom use, each copy must include a notice of copyright.

What about videotapes, computer software, and mixed media? Without a license or permission, educational institutions may not keep copyrighted videotapes (for example, from a television show) for more than forty-five days. The tape should not be shown more than once to students during this period, and then it must be erased. The growing use of computers prompted the amendment of the Copyright Act in 1990 to prohibit the copying of software for commercial gain. In 1998, Congress further amended the Copyright Act and passed the Digital Millennium Copyright Act to protect the vast amount of material published on the World Wide Web. Text, graphics, multimedia materials, and even e-mail are copyright protected, and teachers must follow fair use guidelines when using information obtained from the Internet and gleaned from e-mail attachments. With so much information at our fingertips, both teachers and students need to be aware that all work posted on the Internet is copyright protected, whether or not a specific notice is included. It is always advisable to check with your local school district officials to determine school policy and procedures.[9]

Issue	*Situation 8*
Labor rights	Salary negotiations have been going badly in your school district, and at a mass meeting teachers finally vote to strike. You honor the strike and stay home, refusing to teach until an adequate salary increase is provided. During the first week of the strike, you receive a letter from the school board, stating that you will be suspended for fifteen days without pay at the end of the school year, owing to your participation in the strike. You decide

_____ To fight this illegal, unjust, and costly suspension.

_____ To accept the suspension as a legal action of the school board.

Court Decision   In a number of cases, courts have recognized the right of teachers to organize; to join professional organizations, such as the NEA (National Education Association) and the AFT (American Federation of Teachers); and to bargain collectively for improved working conditions. You cannot legally be penalized for these activities. On the other hand, courts have upheld teachers' right to strike in only about half the states. (In some states, the courts have determined that teachers provide a

Although many states have laws prohibiting teachers from striking, most communities choose not to penalize striking teachers.

Strikes are legal for K–12 educators in Alaska, California, Colorado, Hawaii, Illinois, Louisiana, Minnesota, Montana, North Dakota, Oregon, Pennsylvania, and, in very limited cases, Wisconsin.

SOURCE: National Education Association, *Collective Bargaining Laws for Public Sector Education Employees* (Washington, DC: NEA, October 2001).

REFLECTION

Can you offer any generalizations about the states that permit K-12 teachers to strike? What specific circumstance would cause you to strike?

vital public service and cannot strike.) You need to understand your state laws to know if you are breaking the law by honoring the strike. The school board may be within its rights to suspend, fine, or even fire you for striking.

Although about half of the states have laws that prohibit strikes, many communities choose not to prosecute striking teachers. Conversely, even though membership in teacher organizations and the right to collective bargaining have been upheld by the courts, some communities and school boards are adamantly opposed to such organizations and refuse to hire or to renew contracts of teachers who are active in them. Such bias is clearly illegal; nevertheless, it is very difficult to prove in court and, consequently, it is very difficult to stop.

In summary, law and reality do not always coincide. Legally speaking, teachers may be prohibited from striking by state law but are rarely prosecuted or penalized. In some communities, however, active involvement in teacher organizations may result in discriminatory school board actions. If you choose to strike, do so with the realization that such activity makes you liable to legal sanctions.[10]

Issue	Situation 9
Internet censorship	You have found a terrific website, one that really communicates recent changes and unique insights about the economics topic your class is studying. You give out the website address, and some students log on in class, while several others tell you that they will follow up at home. The next day, the principal calls you into her office to tell you that she has gotten several parent complaints about the website. It seems that a number of the items on the site are controversial, and some of the topics discussed have upset them. You thank her, go back to your classroom, and recheck the site. Now you see the problem. There is slick advertising, directing site visitors to free games and prizes. There are links to information forms with personal questions about beliefs and finances. And, you find a story about money management and family decision-making ideas that probably conflicts with the more traditional views of your students' parents. While none of the sites are pornographic, vulgar, or age-inappropriate, some of the positions taken are well out of the mainstream.

_____ You decide that the principal is right and that students should not have unfettered access to the Internet. You take responsibility for inappropriately directing your students to this controversial site, offer an apology, and eliminate it from the curriculum.

_____ You decide to resist, believing that the website has good information and that your students should have access.

Court Decision   In 1997, the Supreme Court struck down the federal Communications Decency Act, an attempt by Congress to make it a crime to transmit on the Internet indecent material to anyone under 18. The high court found such a law a clear violation of the First Amendment. But what can legally be put on the Internet, and what schools choose to allow into their buildings and curricular assignments, are entirely different issues. Many schools have implemented technological measures to ensure that vulgar or pornographic materials are not accessible in school, a position that seems entirely within their legal rights.

The courts have ruled that educators can restrict vulgar, age-inappropriate, and educationally unsuitable materials from the school. Thus, if the website that you assigned reflects any of these characteristics, an apology and withdrawal is called for. The courts have also ruled that controversial materials expressing unpopular ideas are not grounds for censoring material, so merely upsetting parents, the principal's concern, is not grounds for removing site access.

In this instance, the school would be wise to formulate appropriate Internet guidelines for all teachers. The guidelines should allow teachers to assign unpopular and controversial ideas. While legitimate educational concerns may be given as a reason for censoring the Internet, disagreeing with ideas is not reason enough.[11]

II. Students' Rights and Responsibilities

Issue	*Situation 10*
Student records	You are a high school teacher who has decided to stay after school and review your students' personnel folders. You believe that learning more about your students will make you a more effective teacher. As you finish reviewing some of the folders, Phyllis, a 16-year-old student of yours, walks in and asks to see her folder. Since you have several sensitive comments recorded in the folder, you refuse. Within the hour, the student's parents call and ask if they can see the folder. At this point, you

_____ Explain that the information is confidential and sensitive and cannot be shared with nonprofessional personnel.

_____ Explain that the parents can see the folder and describe the procedure for doing so.

Federal Law   The Family Rights and Privacy Act, commonly referred to as the **Buckley Amendment** (1974), allows parents and guardians access to their children's educational records. The amendment also requires that school districts inform parents of this right and establish a procedure for providing educational records on request. Moreover, written parental permission is needed before these records can be shared with anyone other than professionals connected with either the school the

"...UNTIL JUSTICE ROLLS DOWN LIKE WATERS AND RIGHTEOUSNESS LIKE A MIGHTY STREAM

MARTIN LUTHER KING JR

"Flight delayed." For most, those two words evoke frustration and impatience. But for Morris Dees, a delayed flight was a life-changing event. At the airport bookstore, he bought a used copy of Clarence Darrow's *The Story of My Life.* While he had long admired Darrow for his defense of John Scopes in the famous "Monkey Trial" (see *Reel to Real Teaching* at the end of Chapter 7), Dees had not known of Darrow's decision to leave the security and success of corporate litigation to practice civil rights law. Darrow's choice inspired Dees. "[A]ll the pulls and tugs of my conscience found a singular peace. It did not matter what my neighbors would think or the judges, the bankers, or even my friends. I had found an opportunity to return to my roots, to fight for racial equality."[1] He sold the profitable book company that he had started with a friend, and began to practice civil rights law full time.

Dees had earned a law degree from the University of Alabama, and had become quite successful, both at his small law firm and at his book company, Fuller & Dees, which became one of the country's largest publishing houses. The company was based in Montgomery, Alabama. While Dees turned profits, Martin Luther King, Jr. was in the same city, focused on turning hearts. As Dees points out, back then, he didn't pay much attention to King. "The Movement happened all around me, but I was oblivious, too caught up in the finesse of business . . . until [that] stormy night in 1967 at a Cincinnati airport."[2]

Not that Dees was new to the racial struggle of the South. Growing up in Alabama, Morris Dees worked with black laborers in the cotton fields his father owned, an unusual partnership in the deeply segregated South of the 1940s. As he worked alongside them, he learned about the scars of prejudice, both physical and emotional. The seeds of his career in civil rights advocacy were sown on those Alabama cotton fields, but needed time to take root.

In 1969, Dees sued the YMCA. Fifteen years after *Brown v. Board of Education,* the YMCA still refused to admit African American youth to its summer camp. Dees filed a class action suit to stop the YMCA's policy of racial discrimination. The suit

was a long shot. Private organizations were considered beyond the scope of civil rights law—the business and social stalwarts untouchable. Morris Dees didn't flinch, and because of *Smith v. YMCA,* the Montgomery YMCA was forced to desegregate.

Lawyer Joe Levin, another Alabamian, followed *Smith vs. YMCA* closely, impressed with the imagination and dogged determination of Dees. In 1971, the two joined forces to create a small civil rights firm, the Southern Poverty Law Center (SPLC). Today the SPLC is a national nonprofit organization known for its legal victories against white supremacist groups, tracking of hate groups, and sponsorship of the Civil Rights Memorial.

Dees' call for justice and understanding can be heard in the classroom as well. Dees has created Teaching Tolerance, a collaboration between the SPLC and teachers across the country. The project features a magazine, videos, and curriculum to help teachers and students collectively tackle issues of racial, religious, class, and gender bias.

After completing a study that showed an increase of hate websites, Dees realized that "[h]ate has a new home. The Internet. We need to recapture the wonder of the Internet and use it to spread fairness."[3] Dees and Teaching Tolerance created Tolerance.org, an interactive site of antibias lessons and classroom activities. After more than thirty years of litigation and education, Morris Dees has adopted this latest tool in his quest for social justice. "To everything there is a season. There *will* be a season of justice."[4]

[1]Morris Dees, *A Season for Justice: The Life and Times of Civil Rights Lawyer Morris Dees* (New York: Charles Scribner, 1991).

[2]Ibid.

[3]Morris Dees, "About Tolerance.org," www.tolerance.org (July 29, 2001).

[4]Dees, *A Season for Justice.*

REFLECTION

Will you choose to confront discriminatory attitudes and behavior in your classroom? In yourself? (Yes, we all have biases.) How? Take a tour of http://tolerance.org. Submit an original antibias teaching idea to Tolerance.org.

WRITE YOUR OWN *PROFILE IN EDUCATION:* Click on *Profiles in Education,* write a *Profile in Education* about an educator, and post it on the Online Learning Center. Check out *Profiles in Education* submitted by other future teachers.

To learn more about Morris Dees, click on *Profiles in Education.*

student attends or another school in which the student seeks to enroll, health or safety officials, or persons reviewing the student's financial aid applications. If the student has reached 18 years of age, he or she must be allowed to see the folder and is responsible for granting permission for others to review the folder.

Under this law, you should have chosen the second option, for it is the parents' right to see this information.[12]

Issue	Situation 11
Distribution of scholarships	As a secondary teacher, you are concerned with the manner in which scholarships and other financial awards (donated by the local booster club and neighborhood businesses) are distributed at graduation. You notice that nearly all the awards are going to boys. You mention this to the principal, who explains that this has been the case for as long as anyone can remember. The groups donating the scholarship funds use such categories as leadership skills and sports abilities in choosing the recipients. The principal says that, although this is not exactly equitable, it is realistic, because future financial burdens hit males more than females. You decide that

_____ It is an unfortunate but realistic policy.

_____ It is unfair, unreasonable, and unrealistic. You file a complaint with the Office for Civil Rights.

Federal Law   Title IX prohibits using sex as a criterion by which to grant awards, scholarships, or financial aid. Scholarships and aid must be awarded by objective criteria fairly applied without regard to sex. If it turns out that the most qualified students in a given year are predominantly or entirely of one sex, that is acceptable, as long as the procedures and criteria have been fairly applied. But sex itself should not be a criterion; this example is a violation of Title IX and should be corrected.[13]

Issue	Situation 12
Suspension and discipline	You are teaching a difficult class, and one student is the primary source of trouble. After a string of disorderly episodes on this student's part, the floppy disks for the entire class mysteriously disappear. You have put up with more than enough, and you send the student to the principal's office to be suspended. The principal backs you up, and the student is told not to return to school for a week. This action is

_____ Legal and appropriate (and probably long overdue!).

_____ Illegal.

Court Decision   Although troublesome and disorderly students can be disciplined, suspension from school represents a serious penalty, one that should not be taken lightly. In such cases, the Supreme Court has ruled (_Goss v. Lopez_) that teachers and administrators are required to follow certain procedures in order to guarantee the student's **due process** rights granted by the Fourteenth Amendment. In this case, the student must be informed of the rule that has been broken and of the evidence. The

Corporal punishment, the physical discipline of students, is deplored by most educators, yet it remains legal in twenty-three states. Such punishment is restricted in six states and it is outlawed in twenty-one states.

Illegal		Restricted	Legal	
California	Montana	Alaska	Alabama	Mississippi
Connecticut	Nebraska	New Hampshire	Arizona	Missouri
District of Columbia	Nevada	New York	Arkansas	New Mexico
Hawaii	New Jersey	Rhode Island	Colorado	North Carolina
Illinois	North Dakota	South Dakota	Delaware	Ohio
Iowa	Oregon	Utah	Florida	Oklahoma
Maine	Vermont		Georgia	Pennsylvania
Maryland	Virginia		Idaho	South Carolina
Massachusetts	Washington		Indiana	Tennessee
Michigan	West Virginia		Kansas	Texas
Minnesota	Wisconsin		Kentucky	Wyoming
			Louisiana	

The Children's Defense Fund estimates that a public school student is physically punished every 10 seconds.

SOURCE: *Child,* September 1997; Children's Defense Fund, "Moments in America for Children," *Children's Defense Fund Online,* May 2001; Louis Fischer, David Schimmel, and Cynthia Kelly, *Teachers and the Law* (New York: Longman, 1999).

REFLECTION

Knowing whether corporal punishment is legal in your state and in your school is only part of the issue; sorting out your philosophy on this issue is more to the point. As a teacher, would you use physical punishment against a student? Explain your reasoning.

student is also entitled to tell his or her side of the story in self-defense. For suspensions in excess of ten days, the school must initiate more formal procedures. School officials can be held personally liable for damages if they violate a student's clearly established constitutional rights (*Wood v. Strickland*).

If you look back at this vignette, you will notice that you do not know for sure that this student is responsible for the missing floppy disks, nor is the student given the opportunity for self-defense. If you selected "illegal," you chose the correct response.

Many schools have adopted zero-tolerance policies in an attempt to create safe schools. A **zero-tolerance policy** typically sets out predetermined consequences or punishment for specific offenses, regardless of the circumstances or disciplinary history of the student involved. In 1994, Congress enacted the **Gun-Free Schools Act.** Under this law, schools can lose federal funds if they do not have a zero-tolerance policy mandating one-year expulsions for students bringing firearms to schools. Nine out of ten schools report zero-tolerance policies for firearms. Many schools have zero-tolerance policies covering possession of alcohol, drugs, and tobacco, as well as incidents of violence. Courts have generally ruled that students' constitutional right to due process is not violated by zero-tolerance policies.

Zero tolerance sends a powerful message to the school community that violent, aggressive behavior is not acceptable. However opponents point out that zero-tolerance policies are inherently unfair and can backfire. For example, one six-year-old was expelled for bringing a weapon into school. His grandmother had placed a "weapon" in his lunch sack— a plastic knife for spreading peanut butter. The American Bar Association has denounced zero-tolerance policies that mandate expulsion or referral to juvenile court for minor offenses that do not compromise school safety.

While considering discipline, let us look at the legality of **corporal punishment.** In *Ingraham v. Wright* (1977), the Supreme Court ruled that physical punishment may be authorized by the states. The Court ruled that the corporal punishment should be "reasonable and not excessive," and such factors as the seriousness of the student offense, the age and physical condition of the student, and the force and attitude of the person administering the punishment should be considered. Although the courts have legalized corporal punishment, many states and school districts do not believe in it and have prohibited the physical punishment of students; other districts and states provide very specific guidelines for its practice. You should be familiar with the procedures and norms in your district before you even consider this disciplinary strategy.[14]

Issue	*Situation 13*
Freedom of speech	During your homeroom period, you notice that several of your more politically active students are wearing t-shirts with a red line drawn through "www." You call them to your desk and ask them about it. They explain that they are protesting censorship, the new school board policy that limits student access on the Internet. You tell them that you share their concern but that wearing the t-shirts is specifically forbidden by school rules. You explain that you will let it go this time, since they are not disturbing the class routine, but that if they wear them again, they will be suspended.
	Sure enough, the next day the same students arrive at school still wearing the t-shirts, and you send them to the principal's office. The students tell the principal that, although they understand the rule, they refuse to obey it. The principal, explaining that school rules are made to be followed, suspends them. The principal's action is

_____ Legally justified, since the students were given every opportunity to understand and obey the school rule.

_____ Illegal, since the students have the right to wear t-shirts if they so desire.

Court Decision   In December 1965, three students in Des Moines, Iowa, demonstrated their opposition to the Vietnam War by wearing black arm bands to school. The principal informed them that they were breaking a school rule and asked that they remove the arm bands. They refused and were suspended.

The students' parents sued the school system, and the case finally reached the Supreme Court. In the landmark *Tinker* case, the Court ruled that the students were entitled to wear the arm bands, as long as the students did not substantially disrupt the operation of the school or deny other students the opportunity to learn. Since there was no disruption, the Court ruled that the school system could not prohibit students from wearing the arm bands or engaging in other forms of free speech. The school system in this vignette acted illegally; it could not prevent students from wearing the protest t-shirts. Does *Tinker* apply in cyberspace? Probably. Although the courts have not definitely resolved the issue, early "cyberTinker" decisions support First Amendment rights. One of the first lawsuits arose after a Missouri high school suspended a student for creating an Internet homepage that criticized his school administration. The student, Brandon Buessink, created the homepage outside of school on his home computer. The website caused no documented disturbance at this school and a federal district court reversed the suspension, citing the principal's simple dislike of the content as "unreasonable justification for limiting it."[15]

The issue of allegedly "obscene" speech has been considered by the Supreme Court. In a 1986 decision (*Bethel School District v. Fraser*), the Court evaluated the First Amendment rights of a high school senior, Matthew Fraser. Fraser presented a speech at a school assembly that contained numerous sexual innuendoes, though no explicit, profane language. After Fraser was suspended for his speech and told that he was no longer eligible to speak at his class's graduation, his father sued the school district. The Court upheld the suspension on the grounds that the language in the speech was indecent and offensive and that minors should not be exposed to such language. Obscene speech posted on the Internet from a student's home computer is also not constitutionally protected. A Pennsylvania district court upheld the suspension of a middle school student for posting inflammatory and perverse comments about his principal and algebra teacher.[16]

Courts have upheld students' freedom of speech in a number of cases, so long as the protests were not disruptive of other students' right to learn and were not obscene.

At Thomas Jefferson Middle School in Arlington, Virginia, yearbook signing has a new twist: Students are required to "write nice." Principal Sharon M. implemented the rule to ensure that these keepsakes would be filled with fond remembrances, not hurtful memories. So when Jotana C. was asked to sign a former friend's yearbook, there wasn't a hint of nastiness. She even wrote K.I.T. (keep in touch). Students who choose to pen yearbooks with profane or harassing words can be suspended, dismissed from award ceremonies, or required to buy replacement yearbooks.

SOURCE: *The Washington Post*, June 17, 2001.

REFLECTION

Does this policy violate a student's First Amendment right to freedom of speech? What values are students learning?

 Click on *In the News* for recent *In the News* stories. Submit your own *In the News* summary to share with your colleagues.

Issue	Situation 14
School prayer	A student on your team objects to the daily prayer recitation. You are sensitive to the student's feelings, and you make certain that the prayer is nondenominational. Moreover, you tell the student that he may stand or sit silently without reciting the prayer. If the student likes, he may even leave the gym while the prayer is being recited. As a teacher, you have

_____ Broken the law.

_____ Demonstrated sensitivity to individual needs and not violated the law.

Court Decision   You were sensitive but not sensitive enough—you violated the law. As a result of leaving the gym, the student might be subjected to embarrassment, ostracism, or some other form of social stigma. The Supreme Court has ruled that educators must be completely neutral with regard to religion and may neither encourage nor discourage prayer. The Court has ruled that the separation of church and state prevents educators from promoting religious activities, but not necessarily students. For example, students may engage in private prayer and religious discussion during school, and form religious clubs on school property if other, nonreligious clubs are given space in school. "Official" prayers are not permitted, even at graduation ceremonies (where they frequently are heard despite the law). It remains unclear if it is legal for a student giving a graduation speech to use that speech as a platform for prayer. However, the Court has declared that student-led public prayers at athletic events constitute school sponsorship of religion, a violation of the establishment clause of the First Amendment. Finally, the legality of observing a moment of silence in schools varies by state, and educators are encouraged to check their school policies.[17]

Issue   ***Situation 15***

Search and seizure   The drug problem in your school is spreading, and it is clear
                     that strong action is needed. School authorities order a
                     search of all student lockers, which lasts for several hours.
                     Trained police dogs are brought in, and each classroom is
                     searched for drugs. The dogs sniff suspiciously at several
                     students, who are taken to the locker rooms and strip-
                     searched.

_____ School authorities are well within their rights to conduct these searches.

_____ Searching the lockers is legal, but strip-searching is inappropriate and illegal.

_____ No searches are called for, and all of these activities present illegal and
unconstitutional violation of student rights.

Court Decision   Courts have ruled that school authorities have fewer restrictions
than do the police in search-and-seizure activities. Courts have indicated that school
property (such as lockers or cars parked in the school lot) are actually the responsibility of the school. Moreover, the school has a parentlike responsibility (termed *in
loco parentis*) to protect children and to respond to reasonable concerns about their
health and safety. Even random drug testing of student athletes is permissible.

In situation 15, the search of lockers is legal. However, using police dogs to sniff
students (rather than things) is allowable only if the dogs are reliable and the student
is a reasonable suspect. The strip-search is illegal.

The second choice is the correct response. Although school personnel have great
latitude in conducting school search and seizures, educators should be familiar with
proper legal procedures and should think carefully about the related ethical issues.[18]

Student locker searches
for contraband items
are permissible since
schools have parentlike
responsibility for the
safety of their students.

How might these students (and their teachers) feel as they begin the school day? How do search and seizure responsibilities in schools contrast with those for the general public?

Issue

Freedom of
the press

Situation 16

The Argus is the official student newspaper, written by
students as part of a journalism course, but it has run afoul of
school administrators. First the student newspaper ran a story
critical of the school administration. In the next edition, the
paper included a supplement on contraception and abortion.
With their patience worn thin, school administrators closed
the publication for the remainder of the school year.

_____ Closing the student newspaper is a legal action.

_____ Closing the student newspaper is an illegal action.

Court Decision   In 1988, a relatively conservative Supreme Court ruled in the
Hazelwood case that student newspapers may be censored under certain circumstances.
The Court held that student newspapers written as part of a school journalism course

should be viewed as part of the official school curriculum. School administrators, according to the Court, can readily censor such a paper. In situation 16, since the publication is part of a journalism course, closing the school newspaper would be legal.

On the other hand, if the newspaper were financed by the students and not associated with an official school course, the students would enjoy a greater degree of freedom. Additional grounds for censoring a school newspaper include obscenity, psychological harm, and disruption of school activities.[19]

Issue	***Situation 17***
HIV-infected students	As you enter school one morning, you are met by a group of angry parents. They have found out that Randy, one of your students, is HIV positive, and hence can transmit the AIDS-related virus to others. There is no cure for AIDS, and there is no compromise in the voices of the parents confronting you. Either Randy goes, or they will keep their children at home. You listen sympathetically, but find your mind wandering to your own contact with Randy. You worry that you, too, may be at risk. In this case, you decide

_____ It's better to be safe than sorry, so you ask Randy to return home while you arrange a meeting with the principal to discuss Randy's case. There is no cure for AIDS and no reason to put every child's life in jeopardy.

_____ It's probably okay for Randy to attend school, so you check with your principal and try to calm the parents down.

Court Decision   In a case very similar to this situation, Randy, a hemophiliac, and his brothers were denied access to De Soto County Schools in Florida when they tested positive for the HIV virus. The court determined that the boys' loss of their education was more harmful than the remote chance of other students' contracting AIDS. In fact, in this 1987 case, Randy's parents won an out-of-court settlement in excess of $1 million for the pain the school system inflicted on the family. In another case, the court determined that HIV-infected students are protected under PL 94-142, the Individuals with Disabilities Education Act. Clearly, medical guidelines direct the court. If some AIDS children present more of a public risk (for example, because of biting behavior, open sores, and fighting), more restrictive school environments may be required. To date, however, HIV-infected students and teachers are not viewed as a significant risk to the health of the rest of the population and cannot be denied their educational rights.[20]

Issue	***Situation 18***
Sexual harassment	One of your favorite students appears particularly upset. You are concerned, so you go over to Pat and put your arm around him. Pat stiffens his shoulder and pushes you away. He is obviously distressed about something. The next day, you offer to take Pat to a local fast-food restaurant after school, to cheer him up with a hot fudge sundae. He refuses to go but thanks you for the gesture. A few weeks later, the principal calls you into her office to explain that you have been charged with sexual harassment.

_____ You decide not to respond to the principal until you seek legal advice.

_____ You decide to apologize, realizing that you have overstepped the boundaries of propriety.

Court Decision　In *Franklin v. Gwinnett* (1992), the Supreme Court extended the reach of Title IX, allowing students to sue a school district for monetary damages in cases of sexual harassment. The Gwinnett County case involved a Georgia high school student who was sexually harassed and abused by a teacher, a case much more serious than the pat on the back and offer of a hot fudge sundae described in the vignette above. In Georgia, the teacher's behavior was extreme and the school district's response inadequate. The school district was instructed to pay damages to the student—establishing a precedent.

However, just a few years later the Court made collecting personal damages from school districts more difficult. The Court ruled that the school district had to show "deliberate indifference" to complaints about teacher and peer sexual harassment before the district would be forced to pay damages [*Gebser v. Lago Independent School District* (1998) and *Davis v. Monroe County Board of Education* (1999)]. In fact, just notifying the principal when sexual harassment occurred was insufficient, according to the Court. More powerful officials would need to know and not act on this information before damages could be collected—clearly, an extremely difficult standard. The school district could suffer Title IX penalties (lose federal funds), and the individual accused of harassment could be forced to pay personal damages, but the school district, the place where large funds are available, could not be sued.[21]

Teachers have both a legal and ethical responsibility to prevent and respond to harassment. Sexual harassment is a pervasive, harrowing part of everyday school life for both males and females. (See Figure 11.1.) Four out of five students report being harassed at school. Harassment ranges from sexual comments and gestures, to inappropriate touching, to rape and the consequences are troubling. Students fear attending school, withdraw from friends and activities, and suffer sleep and eating difficulties.

FIGURE 11.1
Who Harasses Whom?

SOURCE: Harris Interactive, *Bullying, Teasing and Sexual Harassment in School.* Commissioned by AAUW Educational Foundation (Washington, DC: American Association of University Women, 2001), p. 14.

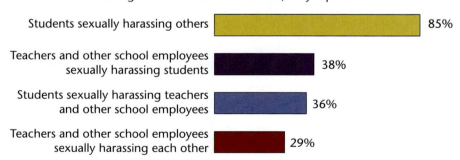

When students were asked for their perceptions of who is harassing whom in their own schools, they report:

Students sexually harassing others — 85%

Teachers and other school employees sexually harassing students — 38%

Students sexually harassing teachers and other school employees — 36%

Teachers and other school employees sexually harassing each other — 29%

REFLECTION

Girls' and boys' assessments of their school climate generally mirror their personal experiences, with one exception. Students perceive that teachers and other school adults harass students more than they personally have experienced. What reasons might you offer for this discrepancy? As a teacher, if you observed each of these four kinds of harassment, how would you respond?

Title IX protections against sexual harassment also apply to gay and lesbian students. Hostility and ridicule toward homosexual students may be actionable in court if they are sufficiently severe and pervasive. For example, a gay student in Wisconsin was awarded a $900,000 judgment when his school district failed to end the violence he endured at the hands of classmates from grades 7 through 11.[22]

Sexual harassment complaints against teachers have been increasing. Teachers need to realize that **sexual harassment** laws protect individuals not only from extreme actions, as in the Georgia case, but from offensive words and inappropriate touching. The mild scenario of comforting words, touching, and an offer of ice cream can indeed lead to problems. While the teacher's intention might have been pure and caring, the student's perception might have been quite different. The threat of the legal broadside that can result from this gap between teacher intentions and student perceptions has sent a chill through many school faculties. Teachers now openly express their fears about the dangers of reaching out to students, and some teachers are vowing never to touch a student or be alone in a room with a student, no matter how honorable the intention. Many teachers lament the current situation, recalling earlier times, when a teacher's kindness and closeness fostered a caring educational climate, rather than a legal case.[23] In the above situation, the first course of action would be the most prudent, to seek legal advice.

Scoring

To determine your RQ (Rights Quotient), the following scoring guide may be useful:

15 to 18 correct:	Legal eagle
13 or 14 correct:	Lawyer-in-training
11 or 12 correct:	Paralegal
9 or 10 correct:	Law student
8 or fewer correct:	Could benefit from an LSAT prep course

This brief review of the legal realities that surround today's classroom is not meant to be definitive. These situations are intended to highlight the rapid growth and changing nature of school law and the importance of this law to teachers. It will be your responsibility to become informed, and stay current, on legal decisions that influence your actions inside and outside your classroom. Ignorance of the law, to paraphrase a popular saying, is no defense. More positively, knowledge of fundamental legal principles allows you to practice "preventive law"—that is, to avoid or resolve potential legal conflicts so that you can attend to your major responsibility: teaching.

Teaching and Ethics

Sam, the new student, seems so awkward in school, and he is often late. You have asked him more than once why he can't get to class on time, but he is barely audible as he mumbles, "I dunno." What's more, his behavior is strange. He seems to have an aversion to chairs, and, whenever possible, he prefers to stand in the back of the room alone. His clothes are not the neatest or cleanest, which is unusual in your class, where most of the children come from middle-class homes and dress fairly well. You have never seen Sam laugh or even smile. Every day, even on the hot ones, he wears a long-sleeve shirt. What is that all about? What a puzzle.

Then, one day, Sam arrives in class with some bruises on his face, and you begin to suspect that there is more to this story. You ask Sam, who shrugs it off and says that he fell and bruised his face. But you are not so sure. You begin to put the puzzle pieces

The courts are constantly asked to draw the line between a teacher's personal freedom and the community's right to establish teacher behavior standards. Historically, the scales have tilted toward the community, and teachers have been fired for wearing lipstick, joining a certain church, or getting married. Today's courts make more deliberate efforts to balance personal liberty and community standards. Although each case must be judged on its own merits, some trends do emerge. The courts have ruled that the community has the right to fire a teacher for

- Making public homosexual advances to nonstudents
- Incorporating sexual issues into lessons and ignoring the approved syllabus
- Inciting violent protest among students
- Engaging in sex with students
- Encouraging students to attend certain religious meetings
- Allowing students to drink alcohol
- Drinking excessively
- Using profanity and abusive language toward students
- Having a sex-change operation
- Stealing school property (even if it is returned later)
- Not living within his or her district if that is listed as a condition of employment

On the other hand, courts have ruled that teachers should not be fired for

- Smoking of marijuana
- Private homosexual behavior
- Obesity (unless it inhibits teaching performance)
- Adultery
- Use of vulgar language outside of school
- AIDS or disability

Why are teachers dismissed in some cases and not in others? Often, the standard the courts use is whether the behavior under question reduces teacher effectiveness. Public behavior, or behavior that becomes public, may compromise a teacher's effectiveness. In such cases, the courts find it reasonable and legal to terminate the teacher. If the behavior remains private, if the teacher shows discretion, the teacher's "right to privacy" often prevails.

SOURCE: These examples have been adapted from Louis Fischer, David Schimmel, and Cynthia Kelly, *Teachers and the Law* (New York: Longman, 1999).

REFLECTION

Courts have disagreed on whether the following three situations constitute grounds for dismissal of a teacher. If you were the judge, how would you rule on the following issues?
- Unwed cohabitation
- Unwed parenthood
- Conviction for shoplifting

together: quiet . . . standing rather than sitting . . . wearing long-sleeve shirts all the time . . . late . . . no smiles . . . no real friends . . . and now bruises. You arrive at a frightening thought: Could Sam be an abused child? How horrible! Now, what do you do?

In this case, you are confronting both an ethical dilemma and a legal challenge. Maybe you should speak to Sam's parents. Or should you press Sam for more information?

Checking with other teachers makes sense, to see how they would handle the problem. Or perhaps it is time to go to the administration and let them find out what is going on.

Wait a second. What if you are wrong? Sam says he fell down and bruised himself. Maybe that is all it is. You should not go around accusing people without real evidence. Are you responsible for Sam's family situation? Is that a private concern rather than your business? Maybe the prudent course of action would be to monitor the situation for now and keep your suspicions to yourself. What would you do?

The ethical issue is pressing. If Sam is being injured, if his safety is in jeopardy, then waiting could be costly. Many would find that the most ethical course to follow would be to share your concerns with an appropriate person in your school, perhaps a school psychologist, counselor, or administrator, or to notify Child Protective Services, a report which can be confidential. The potential for injury is simply too great to remain silent. Sharing your concern is not the same as making an accusation of child abuse, which may be false. By bringing the situation to the school's attention, you start the wheels in motion to uncover facts.

The American Humane Institute states that very few child abuse reports come from educators, yet it is the ethical responsibility of teachers to report the abusive treatment of children. Fortunately, as far as suspicion of child abuse is concerned, this ethical responsibility is reinforced by the law. Every state requires that teachers report "suspected" cases of abuse, and failure to report such cases can result in the loss of a teacher's license. Most of these laws also protect teachers from any legal liability for reporting such cases.

As a teacher, you may well encounter child abuse. In the last twenty years, reports of child maltreatment grew from 416,033 to almost 3 million, although as many as two-thirds of these reports are never investigated.[24]

Child abuse and neglect include a range of mistreatment, such as the following:

- Physical abuse, evidenced by cuts, welts, burns, and bruises
- Sexual molestation and exploitation
- Neglect: medical, educational, or physical
- Emotional abuse

It may be helpful to remember that child abuse and neglect often originate with adults who were themselves abused as children.[25] Parents who hold unrealistic expectations for their children or who are under a great deal of financial or psychological stress are also more likely to become abusers. Abuse and neglect rarely occur as a result of intentional actions. Rather, they usually represent moments of misplaced outrage or a lack of resources or knowledge about how to care for children.

Some citizens believe that the most important issues that face U.S. schools are the ethical ones like how adults treat children. They believe that, beyond adhering to the law, teachers will need to teach more enduring and pervasive moral lessons. (See Figure 11.2.) Yet, while the public applauds moral lessons they are concerned about promoting a narrow set of beliefs.[26] So, how do schools respond to the public's demand for ethical, but not parochial, education?

Moral Education: Programs That Teach Right from Wrong

During the American colonial experience, schools transmitted a common set of values, an approach called **traditional inculcation.** Back then (and in many places today) it was the Protestant ethic: diligence, hard work, punctuality, neatness,

The following summaries highlight the critical cases that have defined the boundaries of civil rights and liberties in American schools. You may not agree with all the decisions, and the current, more conservative Supreme Court may modify some of these rulings. But, for now, they are the law of the land.

TEACHERS' RIGHTS

Freedom of Association

Shelton v. Tucker, 364 U.S. 479 (1960)

A statute required all teachers in public schools to list all of the organizations they had belonged to or had contributed to during the preceding five years. The Court held that, under the First Amendment, teachers could *not* be required to comply, as a condition of employment. The state has a right to request information relevant only to teachers' fitness and competence.

Freedom of Speech

Pickering v. Board of Education, 391 U.S. 563 (1968)

A teacher's letter to the newspaper, a letter that criticized the school board, contained some false statements made because of incomplete research. The teacher was fired. The Court determined that the teacher's letter neither seriously damaged the disciplined operation of the school, disclosed confidential information, nor contained any misstatements that were made knowingly or recklessly. Under the First Amendment, a teacher has the same rights as all other citizens to comment on issues of legitimate public concern, such as a school board's decisions in allocating funds. (See situation 6.)

Separation of Church and State

Engel v. Vitale, 370 U.S. 421 (1962)

A local school board instructed that a prayer composed by the New York Board of Regents be recited aloud every day by each class. The prayer was nondenominational and voluntary. Students who did not want to recite the prayer were permitted to remain silent or leave the classroom while the prayer was said. The Supreme Court held that the New York statute authorizing the prayer in school violated the First Amendment, particularly the establishment clause, and that official, organized prayer in school is not permitted. (See situation 14.)

Wallace v. Jaffree, 472 U.S. 38 (1985)

Lee v. Weisman, 505 U.S. 577 (1992)

Alabama enacted a law that authorized a 1-minute period of silence in all public schools for meditation or voluntary prayer. The Supreme Court held that the Alabama law violated the establishment clause. To determine whether the Alabama law was constitutional, the Court applied the three-part test established in 1971 in *Lemon v. Kurtzman,* 403 U.S. 602 (1971): did the policy (1) have a secular purpose, (2) have a primarily secular effect, and (3) avoid excessive government entanglement with religion? In *Wallace,* the statute was found to have a religious rather than a secular purpose and was thus ruled unconstitutional, even

though prayer was not required during the moment of silence. In *Weisman,* the court declared prayer led by school personnel at public school graduation to violate the establishment clause. However, Federal Courts are again reviewing the observance of a moment of silence.

McCollum v. Board of Education, 333 U.S. 203 (1948);

Board of Education of the Westside Community Schools v. Mergens, 496 U.S. 226 (1990);

Good News Club v. Milford Central Schools, 99 U.S. 2036 (2001)

An Illinois school district allowed privately employed religious teachers to hold weekly religious classes on public premises. The students who chose not to attend these classes in religious instruction pursued their secular studies in other classrooms in the building. In this 1948 case, the Court ruled that a program allowing religious instruction inside public schools during the school day was unconstitutional, because it violated the establishment clause. However, in 1990, the Court modified this somewhat by allowing the use of school facilities by student organizations after school hours if other student clubs had similar access. In *Milford,* the Court allowed adult-led religious organizations the use of school facilities, further lowering the figurative wall of separation between church and state.

Stone v. Graham, 449 U.S. 39 (1980)

A Kentucky statute required the posting of a copy of the Ten Commandments, purchased with private contributions, on the wall of each public classroom in the state. Despite the fact that the copies of the Ten Commandments were purchased with private funds and had a notation describing them as secular, the statute requiring that they be posted in every public school classroom was declared unconstitutional. Under the three-part *Lemon* test, the Court concluded that the statute requiring posting of the Ten Commandments failed under part 1 of the test in that it lacked a secular purpose. Merely stating that the Ten Commandments are secular does not make them so.

STUDENTS' RIGHTS

Freedom of Speech (Symbolic)

Tinker v. Des Moines Independent Community School District, 393 U.S. 503 (1969)

Unless there is substantial disruption in the school caused by student protest, the school board cannot deprive the students of their First Amendment right to freedom of speech. Students do not shed their constitutional rights at the school door. (See situation 13.)

West Virginia State Board of Education v. Barnette, 319 U.S. 624 (1943)

A compulsory flag-salute statute in the public school regulations required all students and teachers to salute the U.S. flag every day. Two Jehovah's Witness students refused to salute the flag, because doing so would be contrary to their religious beliefs, and they were not permitted to attend the public schools. The Court determined that students cannot be compelled to pledge allegiance to the flag in public schools, a right protected by the First Amendment.

Freedom of Speech (Verbal)

Bethel School District v. Fraser, 478 U.S. 675 (1986) The Supreme Court, balancing the student's freedom to advocate controversial ideas with the school's interests in setting the boundaries of socially appropriate behavior, found that the First Amendment does not prevent school authorities from disciplining students for speech that is lewd and offensive. (See situation 12.)

Freedom of the Press

Hazelwood School District v. Kuhlmeir, 108 U.S. 562 (1988) Two articles about divorce and teenage pregnancy that were written in the student paper were deleted by the principal. The Supreme Court held that, since the student paper was school-sponsored and school-funded and was part of the school's journalism class, the school principal had the right to control its content. (See situation 16.) On the other hand, the courts have ruled that school authorities may not censor student newspapers produced at the students' own expense and those produced off school property, papers not part of any school's curriculum.

Freedom of Access to the Printed Word

Board of Education, Island Trees Union Free School District No. 26 v. Pico, 457 U.S. 853 (1982) A school board decided to remove nine books from the school library because the board members felt the books were objectionable and improper for students. The court ruled that school boards may not suppress ideas by removing books from a school library based on their feelings that the material contains controversial or unpopular viewpoints.

Right to Due Process

Goss v. Lopez, 419 U.S. 565 (1975) Several high school students were disciplined by being suspended from school for ten days. The Supreme Court held that before a principal can suspend a student, he or she must present the student with the charges and provide the student with a hearing or an opportunity to present a defense against the charges. The due process Court procedures mandated as a result of this decision can be compared to the "Miranda rights" mandated in criminal cases. (See situation 12.)

Ingraham v. Wright, 430 U.S. 651 (1977) Florida statute allowed corporal punishment. Two students were punished by being hit with a flat wooden paddle and later sued the schools. The Supreme Court held that corporal punishment, such as the paddling, is not cruel and unusual punishment and does not necessarily deprive the student of his or her rights. (See the description following situation 11.)

Separation of Church and State

Santa Fe Independent School District v. Doe, 99 U.S. 62 (2000) In a 6–3 ruling, the Supreme Court held that student-led prayer at football games violated the U.S. Constitution's prohibition against a government establishment of religion. The majority said the Texas school district's authorization of a student vote on whether to have an invocation before games and the election of a student speaker amounted to government sponsorship of prayer. (See situation 14.)

Sexual Harassment

Franklin v. Gwinnett County Public Schools, 503 U.S. 60 (1992) The *Franklin* case involved a Georgia high school student who alleged that a teacher-coach engaged in behavior toward her ranging from unwelcome verbal advances to pressured sexual intercourse on school grounds. The Court ruled that "victims of sexual harassment and other forms of sex discrimination in schools may sue for monetary damages" under Title IX of the Education Amendments of 1972.

Gebser v. Lago Vista Independent School District, 96 U.S. 1866 (1998) The Court limited the circumstances under which a school district can be held liable for monetary damages for a teacher's sexual harassment of a student. The court ruled 5–4 that a district cannot be held liable under Title IX unless a district official with the authority to take corrective action had actual knowledge of teacher misconduct and was deliberately indifferent to it. (See situation 18.)

Davis v. Monroe County Board of Education, 97 U.S. 843 (1999) In a 5–4 ruling, the Court held that districts may be found liable under Title IX only when they are "deliberately indifferent" to information about peer harassment at school and when the harassment is so "severe, pervasive, and objectively offensive" that it bars the victim's access to an educational program or benefit.

Note: The section on legal landmarks was written by Nancy Gorenberg and Karen Zittleman.

REFLECTION

After a test, a teacher asks students to exchange papers and grade each other's exam. How do you feel about this request? Do you think that this violates the Buckley Amendment, protecting student privacy, or is it a responsible and time-saving device for the teacher? Now, try your skills at legal research. Look up Falvo v. Owasso Independent School District (99 U.S. 5130) and see how the Supreme Court ruled.

 INTERACTIVE ACTIVITY PRACTICE WITH COURT CASES. Match names of court cases with their description.

Children who suffer physical abuse may

- Exhibit signs of frequent injury—burns, black eyes, and other bruises
- Refuse to change into gym clothes; wear long-sleeves even in very warm weather
- Not want to sit down
- Show unusually aggressive or unusually withdrawn behavior
- Not show emotion—no joy, pain, or anger
- Be frequently absent or tardy
- Be unusually eager to please
- Complain about pain, beating, or other abusive treatment
- Show a significant change in school attitude, behavior, or achievement

Children who suffer sexual abuse may

- Complain of pain or itching in the genital area
- Exhibit unusual odors or signs of trauma in the genital area
- Wear bloody, torn, or stained undergarments
- Create stories or drawings of an unusually sexual nature
- Exhibit unusually sophisticated knowledge of sexual behavior
- Have difficulty sitting or walking
- Talk about sexual involvement with an adult
- Try to run away from home
- Be extremely mature or seductive in dress and behavior
- Exhibit symptoms of sexually transmitted diseases
- Become pregnant

SOURCE: Childhelp USA, *Combating Child Abuse Across America* (Washington, DC, 1998).

REFLECTION

If one of your students showed warning signs of abuse, whom in your school would you approach first? How would you phrase your concern?

FIGURE 11.2
The dishonor role.

SOURCE: "Rutgers Study Finds Extensive Cheating," *Baltimore Sun,* April 29, 2001, p. 15B.

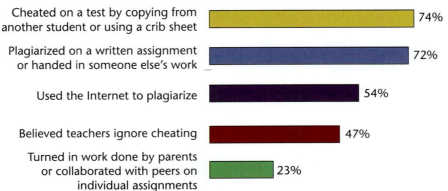

Percentage of Students Polled Admitting They . . .

Cheated on a test by copying from another student or using a crib sheet — 74%

Plagiarized on a written assignment or handed in someone else's work — 72%

Used the Internet to plagiarize — 54%

Believed teachers ignore cheating — 47%

Turned in work done by parents or collaborated with peers on individual assignments — 23%

REFLECTION

This is from a recent study of 4,500 students in twenty-five high schools. Is cheating an acceptable norm in American schools? Why or why not? As a teacher, how might you approach the cheating dilemma?

conformity, and respect for authority. Those few individuals who received a college education during the eighteenth and nineteenth centuries received, above all, an experience in character development. The most important course in the college curriculum was moral philosophy, required of all students and often taught by the college president. Even those receiving a minimal education got a heavy dose of morality, perhaps illustrated best by McGuffey Readers, replete with tales and poems of moral elevation. The tremendous influx of immigrants in the early part of the twentieth century prompted a resurgence of this traditional approach in order to "meld" these new Americans by teaching core U.S. values.

During the social and political uncertainty of the 1960s and 1970s, a more analytical and individual approach to moral education became popular. This **individual analysis** method emphasized the decision-making process of students and avoided prescribing a fixed set of beliefs or values. Students were encouraged to consider the moral implications of past and present events and to formulate a set of values based on their analyses. Today's schools can choose from several different approaches to moral education, ranging from student decision-making to the more traditional paths. Four of the most widely known are (1) values clarification, (2) character education, (3) moral stages of development, and (4) comprehensive values education.

VALUES CLARIFICATION   The controversial **values clarification** program is designed to help students develop and eventually act on their values. Students might be asked to describe their preferences (select the ten things you most enjoy doing), analyze behavior (when did you last do each of these activities?), analyze reasons (what appeals to you about each of these activities?), and develop action plans (how can you schedule more time to do what you enjoy?). Students begin to bring their private values into a public light, where they can be analyzed, evaluated and eventually put into action.

Critics charge that values clarification is itself valueless. In this approach, all values are treated equally, and there is no guarantee that good and constructive values will be promoted or that negative ones will be condemned. If, for example, a student decides that anti-Semitism or fascism is a preferred value, values clarification might do little to contradict this view. This "value neutral" stance is troubling to some and has led to the barring of values clarification in several school districts.

CHARACTER EDUCATION Character education programs—currently legislated in seventeen states[27]—assume that there are core attributes of a moral individual that children should be directly taught in school. (To see if your state requires character education, visit www.character.org.) While still a form of moral inculcation, character education programs are less didactic and more analytic than some of the more traditional approaches.[28] What values are promoted? Core values include trustworthiness, respect, responsibility, fairness, caring, and good citizenship, and are encouraged through the school culture, conduct codes, curriculum, and community service.[29] Younger students may be asked to find examples of these qualities in literature and history, while older students may consider these values through ethical reasoning exercises. Some character education programs include training in conflict resolution to develop problem-solving skills and respect. School districts using character education report a drop in discipline problems and enhanced student responsibility.

Not everyone is enamored with character education. Opponents view this approach as superficial, artificially forcing a diverse student population into a simplistic and narrow set of unexamined values that does not really alter behaviors. They point out that when adults promote one set of values but do not always live up to it, it is the dissonance that becomes the lesson. The real challenge, according to these critics, is changing the behavior of those who influence children.[30]

Other critics believe that character education is little more than the old-fashioned "fix-the-kids" approach, a return to the past conservative, religious agenda that simply rewards students who do what adults desire. Who selects the values or the way the values are taught are issues at the heart of the concerns expressed by these critics. Although character education attempts to walk a middle ground, not all Americans find the values or the approach appropriate.[31]

MORAL STAGES OF DEVELOPMENT Based on the work of Jean Piaget, the psychologist who identified stages of intellectual development (see "The Hall of Fame" in Chapter 8), a schema proposed by **Lawrence Kohlberg** identifies **moral stages of development.** The earliest stages focus on simple rewards and punishments. Young children are taught "right" and "wrong" by learning to avoid physical punishment and to strive for rewards. Most adults function at a middle, or conventional, stage, in which they obey society's laws, even laws that may be unjust. At the highest level, individuals act on principles, such as civil rights or pacifism, that may violate conventional laws. Kohlberg believes that teachers can facilitate student growth to higher stages of morality. In Kohlberg's curriculum, students are encouraged to analyze moral dilemmas presented in brief scenarios. For example, one such scenario might tell the story of someone breaking into a store and stealing, and the question is posed: isn't stealing always wrong, or could it ever be justified? What if the person was stealing medicine needed to save a life; would that justify the theft? The teacher's role in this curriculum is to help students move to higher stages of moral development.

Detractors express concern that traditional (what Kohlberg calls "conventional") values are attacked. Kohlberg pushes toward higher levels of moral development, principled beliefs that may run counter to current law. Other critics point out that Kohlberg's theory was developed on an all-male population and that females may go through different stages of moral reasoning. Harvard professor **Carol Gilligan,** for example, found that women and men react differently when responding to moral dilemmas. While males seem to strongly value those who follow the rules and laws, females value relationships and caring. Kohlberg rated males as reaching a higher level of moral development than females, because the scales he developed were male-oriented. Finally, Kohlberg's stages are intellectually based. Some critics believe that behavior, not intellect, is the real measure of one's morality.

COMPREHENSIVE VALUES EDUCATION Now that we have reviewed three approaches to teaching about values and ethics, it is worth noting that some teachers "mix and match," creating what might be considered a hybrid or fourth approach. Howard Kirschenbaum suggests that both values clarification and traditional inculcation have important lessons for children. In his approach, **comprehensive values education,** traditional values such as honesty, caring, and responsibility are taught and demonstrated directly. However, since other values are less straightforward, such as favoring or rejecting the death penalty, students are taught the analytical skills that will help them make wise decisions. There is an appropriate place in the school curriculum for each approach, Kirschenbaum insists, and many teachers instinctively apply multiple approaches.[32]

YOU BE THE JUDGE

MORAL EDUCATION AND ETHICAL LESSONS

Are Best Taught by Instilling American Values Through Character Education Because . . .

OUR YOUTH ARE BEING CORRUPTED BY THE MEDIA

Television, music, and videos bombard children with commercialism, violence, and sex. Schools must be proactive in helping families instill the moral attitudes and values needed to counteract our lax social mores.

CHILDREN ARE UNABLE TO MAKE THEIR OWN MORAL CHOICES

Throughout history, educators have recognized that children have "impressionable" minds. Without moral training at a young age, as Theodore Roosevelt once noted, they can quickly become "a menace to society."

SHARED VALUES AFFIRM A NATIONAL IDENTITY

Americans believe in a common code of values to teach our children: respect, patriotism, tolerance, and responsibility. Our national fabric is built on such values, and our nation's future depends on them.

Should Help Students Develop Their Own Values Because . . .

SOCIETAL INDIFFERENCE IS CORRUPTING OUR YOUTH

Traditional character education adopts a "blame the media" approach while neglecting real social needs. By ignoring poverty, racism, and sexism, traditionalists inculcate their own rosy picture of America, overlooking genuine if unattractive social injustices.

CHILDREN MUST LEARN TO MAKE MEANINGFUL MORAL CHOICES

Through character indoctrination, students are manipulated to adopt a narrow set of values. Far better is for teachers to help students become reflective thinkers, active citizens ready to work for social justice.

INDIVIDUAL VALUES HONOR DIVERSITY

In a nation of people with diverse cultural backgrounds, indoctrinating one set of fixed values is undemocratic and unwise. Respect for different cultural values will help create a safe and fair society marked by tolerance.

YOU BE THE JUDGE

What role should character education play in public schools? Examine textbooks and curriculum used in a local school to determine the major values being taught to students. Are students expected to accept the values or to critically examine them? Which strategy do you support?

Classrooms That Explore Ethical Issues

For many educators and parents, concerns about values are daily events, too important to be left solely to a specific program or curriculum. How should teachers handle matters of ethics that appear on a daily basis? Consider that as a teacher, you find

A student complains that her Vietnamese culture is being demeaned by the Christian and Western classroom activities.

A student is upset because his e-mail has been opened and read by classmates.

Your best student, the one you just recommended for a special award, is looking at a crib sheet during an examination.

CODE OF ETHICS AND BILL OF RIGHTS

NATIONAL EDUCATION ASSOCIATION CODE OF ETHICS

Preamble

The educator, believing in the worth and dignity of each human being, recognizes the supreme importance of the pursuit of truth, devotion to excellence, and the nurturing of democratic principles. Essential to these goals is the protection of freedom to learn and to teach and the guarantee of equal educational opportunity for all. The educator accepts the responsibility to adhere to the highest ethical standards.

The educator recognizes the magnitude of the responsibility inherent in the teaching process. The desire for the respect and confidence of one's colleagues, of students, of parents, and of the members of the community provides the incentive to attain and maintain the highest possible degree of ethical conduct. The Code of Ethics of the Education Profession indicates the aspiration of all educators and provides standards by which to judge conduct. The remedies specified by the NEA and/or its affiliates for the violation of any provision of this Code shall be exclusive and no such provision shall be enforceable in any form other than one specifically designated by the NEA or its affiliates.

Principle I—Commitment to the Student

The educator strives to help each student realize his or her potential as a worthy and effective member of society. The educator therefore works to stimulate the spirit of inquiry, the acquisition of knowledge and understanding, and the thoughtful formulation of worthy goals.

In fulfillment of the obligation to the student, the educator—

1. Shall not unreasonably restrain the student from independent action in the pursuit of learning.
2. Shall not unreasonably deny the student access to varying points of view.
3. Shall not deliberately suppress or distort subject matter relevant to the student's progress.
4. Shall make reasonable effort to protect the student from conditions harmful to learning or to health and safety.
5. Shall not intentionally expose the student to embarrassment or disparagement.
6. Shall not on the basis of race, color, creed, sex, national origin, marital status, political or religious beliefs, family, social or cultural background, or sexual orientation, unfairly:
   a. Exclude any student from participation in any program;
   b. Deny benefits to any student;
   c. Grant any advantage to any student.
7. Shall not use professional relationships with students for private advantage.
8. Shall not disclose information about students obtained in the course of professional service, unless disclosure serves a compelling professional purpose or is required by law.

Principle II—Commitment to the Profession

The education profession is vested by the public with a trust and responsibility requiring the highest ideals of professional service.

In the belief that the quality of the services of the education profession directly influences the nation and its citizens, the educator shall exert every effort to raise professional standards, to promote a climate that encourages the exercise of professional judgment, to achieve conditions which attract persons worthy of the trust to careers in education, and to assist in preventing the practice of the profession by unqualified persons.

In fulfillment of the obligation to the profession the educator—

1. Shall not in an application for a professional position deliberately make a false statement or fail to disclose a material fact related to competency and qualifications.
2. Shall not misrepresent his/her professional qualifications.
3. Shall not assist entry into the profession of a person known to be unqualified in respect to character, education, or other relevant attribute.
4. Shall not knowingly make a false statement concerning the qualifications of a candidate for a professional position.
5. Shall not assist a noneducator in the unauthorized practice of teaching.
6. Shall not disclose information about colleagues obtained in the course of professional service unless disclosure serves a compelling professional purpose or is required by law.
7. Shall not knowingly make false or malicious statements about a colleague.
8. Shall not accept any gratuity, gift, or favor that might impair or appear to influence professional decisions or actions.

AMERICAN FEDERATION OF TEACHERS BILL OF RIGHTS

The teacher is entitled to a life of dignity equal to the high standard of service that is justly demanded of that profession. Therefore, we hold these truths to be self-evident:

I. Teachers have the right to think freely and to express themselves openly and without fear. This includes the right to hold views contrary to the majority.
II. They shall be entitled to the free exercise of their religion. No restraint shall be put upon them in the manner, time or place of their worship.

III. They shall have the right to take part in social, civil, and political affairs. They shall have the right, outside the classroom, to participate in political campaigns and to hold office. They may assemble peaceably and may petition any government agency, including their employers, for a redress of grievances. They shall have the same freedom in all things as other citizens.

IV. The right of teachers to live in places of their own choosing, to be free of restraints in their mode of living and the use of their leisure time shall not be abridged.

V. Teaching is a profession, the right to practice which is not subject to the surrender of other human rights. No one shall be deprived of professional status, or the right to practice it, or the practice thereof in any particular position, without due process of law.

VI. The right of teachers to be secure in their jobs, free from political influence or public clamor, shall be established by law. The right to teach after qualification in the manner prescribed by law is a property right, based upon the inalienable rights to life, liberty, and the pursuit of happiness.

VII. In all cases affecting the teacher's employment or professional status a full hearing by an impartial tribunal shall be afforded with the right to full judicial review. No teacher shall be deprived of employment or professional status but for specific causes established by the law having a clear relation to the competence or qualification to teach, proved by the weight of the evidence. In all such cases the teacher shall enjoy the right to a speedy and public trial, to be informed of the nature and cause of the accusation, to be confronted with the accusing witnesses, to subpoena witnesses and papers, and to the assistance of counsel. No teacher shall be called upon to answer any charge affecting his employment or professional status but upon probable cause, supported by oath or affirmation.

VIII. It shall be the duty of the employer to provide culturally adequate salaries, security in illness and adequate retirement income. The teacher has the right to such a salary as will: a) Afford a family standard of living comparable to that enjoyed by other professional people in the community; b) To make possible freely chosen professional study; c) Afford the opportunity for leisure and recreation common to our heritage.

IX. Teachers shall not be required under penalty of reduction of salary to pursue studies beyond those required to obtain professional status. After serving a reasonable probationary period a teacher shall be entitled to permanent tenure terminable only for just cause. They shall be free as in other professions in the use of their own time. They shall not be required to perform extracurricular work against their will or without added compensation.

X. To equip people for modern life requires the most advanced educational methods. Therefore, the teacher is entitled to good classrooms, adequate teaching materials, teachable class size and administrative protection and assistance in maintaining discipline.

XI. These rights are based upon the proposition that the culture of a people can rise only as its teachers improve. A teaching force accorded the highest possible professional dignity is the surest guarantee that blessings of liberty will be preserved. Therefore, the possession of these rights imposes the challenge to be worthy of their enjoyment.

XII. Since teachers must be free in order to teach freedom, the right to be members of organizations of their own choosing must be guaranteed. In all matters pertaining to their salaries and working conditions they shall be entitled to bargain collectively through representatives of their own choosing. They are entitled to have the schools administered by superintendents, boards or committees which function in a democratic manner.

REFLECTION

How do these two statements reflect the somewhat different philosophies of these organizations? Do you feel more comfortable with one or the other of these positions? Would you add or delete any items from the lists?

How are teachers to navigate this tricky moral minefield? Educators have offered several recommendations, summarized below:

The Setting

Climate. Create an environment that respects and encourages diverse points of view and that promotes the sharing of diverse opinions, by both the teachers and the students.

School and class rules. Requiring that students unquestioningly follow rules does not lead to democratic values. School and class rules need to be explained to students, and the reasons behind them understood. Many teachers go further and ask students to participate in formulating the rules they will live by.

Parents and community. Citizens and community leaders should participate with the school in developing mission statements and ethical codes of responsibility. One way to encourage such cooperation is to plan joint efforts that tie the family and civic organizations into school-sponsored programs. The key is to reinforce ethical lessons in the school, the home, and the community.

The Teacher

Model. You need to demonstrate the ethical lessons you teach. Teacher behavior should reflect such values as tolerance, compassion, forgiveness, and open-mindedness. (Values are often *caught not taught.*)

Interpersonal skills. You need effective communication skills to encourage students to share their concerns. A critical component of interpersonal skills is empathy—the ability to see problems from more than one point of view, including through the eyes of students.

Commitment. It takes determination and courage on your part to confront ethical dilemmas, rather than to take the easier path of indifference or even inattention.

Reflection skills. To unravel moral questions, you must know how to analyze a dilemma objectively and how to evaluate its essential components. Teachers with effective and deliberate reasoning skills are best suited for this challenge.

Personal opinions. You should not promote or indoctrinate students with your personal points of view, nor should you shy away from showing students that you have strong beliefs. The key is to create a classroom in which individuals can freely agree or disagree, as they see fit.[33]

While laws direct us to what we can and cannot do, moral guidelines direct us in what we should and should not do. Professional associations have also suggested ethical guidelines for educators. (See the *Frame of Reference:* Code of Ethics and Bill of Rights.) Moral issues will continue to be a major concern in the years ahead, in many ways a measure of the quality of our culture. Indeed, even as our society grows in wealth and makes great scientific strides and technological breakthroughs, the final measure of our worth may not be our materialistic accomplishments but, rather, the way we treat each other.

SUMMARY

1. What are your legal rights and responsibilities as a teacher?
   - When applying for a teaching position, you should be familiar with Title IX of the Education Amendments and Title VII of the Civil Rights Act. You do not have to answer questions an interviewer may ask that are unrelated to the job requirements, and you are protected from words and behaviors that can be considered sexual harassment.

- Court decisions indicate that a teacher enjoys job security as long as the teacher's behavior and personal life do not disrupt or interfere with teaching effectiveness.

- The courts hold that the teacher's right to academic freedom is not absolute. Academic freedom does not protect teachers who use obscene, irrelevant, inappropriate, or disruptive materials or instruction.

- When determining whether a teacher has been negligent in a situation, the courts judge whether a reasonable person with similar training would act in the same way and whether the teacher could have foreseen the possibility of injury. A teacher may be liable for misfeasance (failure to act appropriately), nonfeasance (failure to do a duty), or malfeasance (acting unlawfully). However, educational malpractice is not yet an established legal precedent.

- As stated by the Supreme Court in *Pickering v. Board of Education,* teachers are protected under the First Amendment to exercise freedom of speech and to publicly express themselves, unless their statements are malicious, are intentionally inaccurate, disclose confidential material, or hamper teaching performance.

- Teachers must be sure to comply with Public Law 94-553 (the Copyright Act) when distributing copies of other people's works in the classroom, observing the three criteria of brevity, spontaneity, and cumulative effect. This law also applies to computer software and material posted on the Internet (Digital Millennium Copyright Act).

- While information in the Internet enjoys First Amendment protection, teachers may legally choose to limit student access to material that is vulgar or educationally inappropriate.

2. What legal rights do students enjoy (and do they have legal responsibilities)?

- Under the Buckley Amendment (the Family Rights and Privacy Act), parents and guardians have the right to see their child's educational record. On reaching 18 years of age, the student is allowed to see the record, and he or she becomes responsible for providing permission for others to see it.

- Under Title IX, awards, financial aid, and scholarships may not be distributed with sex as a criterion. Title IX also protects students and teachers from sexual harassment.

- Students have constitutionally protected rights to due process before they can be disciplined or suspended from school. Although corporal punishment is rarely used, courts have upheld the school's authority to administer it as long as it is reasonable and not excessive.

- The Gun-Free School Act mandates a one-year expulsion for students bringing firearms to school. It is an example of a zero-tolerance policy, some of which when carried to extreme, can harshly punish students for relatively minor infractions.

- In *Tinker v. Des Moines Independent Community School District,* students were successful in protecting their First Amendment right to freedom of speech. As long as students do not disrupt the operation of the school or deny other students the opportunity to learn, they have the right to freedom of speech within the schools. Early "cyberTinker" cases have extended this right to the Internet.

- Schools must be neutral with regard to religion. Thus, school prayer is not permitted under the doctrine of separation of church and state. The legality of a "moment of silence" varies from state to state.

- Students in schools enjoy a lower level of protection from search and seizure than typical citizens. The school's *in loco parentis* responsibility allows it to search school lockers and cars in school parking lots and submit student athletes to random drug testing.

CHAPTER REVIEW

Go to the Online Learning Center to take a quiz, practice with key terms, and review key ideas from the chapter.

- Students, like teachers, enjoy the right to freedom of the press. However, student publications can be censored if they are an integral part of the school curriculum, such as part of a course, or if they are obscene, psychologically damaging, or disruptive.

- Children with the HIV virus, like others who confront medical challenges, have their student status protected under the Individuals with Disabilities Education Act.

- The following suggestions for teachers are derived from court decisions and are intended to serve as a basic guide:

  - Read school safety rules, regulations and handbooks
  - Respect student confidentiality in records and forms
  - Notify parents if curriculum materials might be objectionable
  - Exercise forethought (due care) by anticipating accidents
  - Report suspected incidents of child abuse
  - Know and follow due process when penalizing students
  - Keep your meetings with students public
  - Separate your personal and professional life
  - Avoid offensive, sexual, and off-color comments
  - Know and follow district policies regarding corporal punishment
  - Seek medical assistance for student injuries or illness
  - Avoid touching students
  - Follow copyright laws

3. What are today's main approaches to moral education?

   - Teachers have an ethical responsibility to safeguard the health and well-being of students. From detecting and reporting suspected cases of child abuse to helping students make ethical judgments, society expects teachers to provide a moral education to students.

   - The public strongly supports moral and ethical education in schools, but rejects the notion of promoting a particular or narrow set of beliefs.

   - The traditional approach to values education was inculcation, where traditional values were imparted in a didactic style.

   - Another approach to ethical education assumes values are best learned through personal reflection and individual analysis, and promotes a strategy called values clarification.

   - Character education promotes a core set of values, including respect, responsibility, citizenship, caring, and fairness. This approach is popular in about seventeen states.

   - Educators such as Lawrence Kohlberg and Carol Gilligan have attempted to map moral stages of development and build curricular materials based on these stages.

   - Comprehensive values education is an attempt to combine both traditional and analytical approaches by directly teaching some values, like honesty and caring, while encouraging students to analyze their own positions on more controversial issues, like the death penalty.

   - Whatever program is taught, and even if no formal program is taught, what teachers do and say provides a model for students, serving as an "informal" curriculum on ethical behavior.

KEY TERMS AND PEOPLE

academic freedom, 428

Buckley Amendment, 434

character education, 451

child abuse, 447

comprehensive values
education, 452

Copyright Act, 431

corporal punishment, 438

Morris Dees, 435

due process, 436

educational malpractice, 429

establishment clause, 425

fair use, 431

First Amendment, 425

Carol Gilligan, 452

Gun-Free Schools Act, 437

in loco parentis, 441

individual analysis, 451

Lawrence Kohlberg, 452

malfeasance, 429

misfeasance, 429

moral stages of
development, 452

nonfeasance, 429

sexual harassment, 445

Title IX of the Education
Amendments (1972), 426

Title VII of the Civil Rights Act
(1964), 426

traditional inculcation, 447

U.S. Supreme Court cases
Engel v. Vitale, 448
*Franklin v. Gwinnett County
Public Schools,* 449
Goss v. Lopez, 449
*Hazelwood School District v.
Kuhlmeir,* 449
Lee v. Weisman, 448
*Pickering v. Board of
Education,* 448
*Tinker v. Des Moines Indepen-
dent Community School
District,* 448

values clarification, 451

zero-tolerance policy, 437

DISCUSSION QUESTIONS AND ACTIVITIES

1. If you were to suggest a law to improve education, what would that law be? Would you make it federal, state, or local? Why?

2. Distinguish among malfeasance, misfeasance, and nonfeasance. Give an example of each.

3. What are the legal factors you should keep in mind if you are about to discipline a student?

4. Define and evaluate the concept of "educational malpractice."

5. What kinds of questions are employers prohibited from asking during an interview?

6. Outline the limits of academic freedom.

7. What do you think are the most critical consequences of teacher strikes? If your teacher association called for a strike, would you join the picket line or teach your classes? Defend your point of view.

8. "The *Tinker* decision sent a strong message that students do not abandon their constitutional rights at the schoolhouse door." Do you agree or disagree with this statement? Support your position with specific examples.

9. The role of religion and prayer in schools has always been controversial, and teachers are advised to neither *encourage* nor *discourage* religious observances. As a teacher, what religious celebrations or practices might you encounter in your class? How would you respond to these issues while maintaining your neutrality?

10. In each of the following cases, indicate if there are grounds for dismissing a teacher:

   • Being identified as a homosexual

   • Publicly criticizing the school system

   • Hitting a student

- Photocopying material without permission
- Striking
- Carrying the HIV virus
- Sexually harassing a student

11. Construct an argument to support the principle that students and their property should not be searched without the students' consent.

12. "The Buckley Amendment increased the access to, but decreased the value of, student records." Explain.

13. What are some of the physical indications of child abuse? What is the teacher's role in preventing such abuse and neglect?

14. Which of the paths to moral education (values clarification, moral development, character education, or comprehensive values education) appeals to you most? Why?

15. Describe some steps you might explore to promote ethical student behavior in your classroom.

16. Review with an ethical eye the legal situations described in this chapter. How do ethical considerations reinforce (or weaken) the legal arguments?

WEB-*TIVITIES*

1. Teachers' and Students' Rights and Responsibilities
2. Students' Rights: Title IX and Sexual Harassment
3. Values Clarification
4. Character Education
5 Classrooms that Explore Ethical Issues

REEL TO REAL TEACHING

FINDING FORRESTER (2000)
Run Time: 133 minutes

Synopsis: *Finding Forrester* is a telling portrayal of ethics and expectations as an African American teen writing prodigy and star athlete finds a mentor in a reclusive author.

Reflection:

1. What expectations did William Forrester, Dr. Crawford, and Clarie hold for Jamal? What social factors influenced these expectations? Did they change throughout the film. Why or why not?
2. How would you describe a successful student? An athlete? Did you picture this student as male or female? As a person of color or white? Now imagine that your successful student (and successful athlete) is the opposite sex or another race. Did your description change? What values are embedded in your answer?
3. As a teacher, how will you confront cheating and plagiarism in your classroom?
4. What lessons in character did Forrester and Jamal learn from each other?

Follow-up Activity: As part of a character education program, create an Honor Code to help students learn about academic integrity. You may want to consider the following questions: Is your Code a teacher's solo creation or a teacher-student partnership? What aspects of school life (such as bullying,

lying, and punctuality) are included in the Code? Who will enforce the Code, and what are the rewards and punishments? What values will students learn from following (or breaking) the Honor Code?

 How do you rate this film? Click on *Reel to Real Teaching* to submit your review of this or another education-related film, and read the reviews submitted by others.

FOR FURTHER READING

Cultivating Heart and Character, by Tony Devine, Joon Ho Seuk, and Andrew Wilson (2000). Provides a wealth of practical strategies to implement a holistic education in character and emotional intelligence.

Education in the Moral Domain, by Larry P. Nucci (2001). Provides lessons and practical strategies for teachers to foster an environment that will encourage children to develop as thoughtful, caring, reflective individuals. Also argues that teaching morality is neither about religious ideals nor is it at odds with First Amendment protections.

Protecting the Right to Teach and Learn, by James Daly, Patricia Schall, and Rosemary Skeele (2001). Explores the legal and pedagogical implications of academic freedom in the face of political and religious challenges to what is taught in schools.

School Law and the Public Schools: A Practical Guide for Educational Leaders, by Nathan Essex (1999). Summarizes educational laws and their impact on the organization of schools and daily classroom practices. Policy guidelines for issues such as school prayer, disability, sexual harassment, and freedom of speech are featured.

School Law: Cases and Concepts, by Michael LaMorte (1999). Designed for educators with little background in school law, this book provides an overview of the nation's legal structure. Details opinions and dissents on landmark cases include those on First Amendment protections, school finance, desegregation, and privacy.

We the Students: Supreme Court Decisions for and about Students, Jamin Raskin (2000). A critical look at how significant court decisions impact the daily school experience of students. Each case is followed by questions designed to help readers apply their understanding of constitutional law to everyday school practices and to clarify their own values.

Inter-mission

Four more chapters have slipped by since your last *Inter-mission.* You are probably ready to stretch your teaching legs and re-examine your educational mission. Now is the right time to walk through the foundations of education.

Applications and Reflections

3:1 SELF-FULFILLING PROPHECY

INTASC PRINCIPLE 1
Knowledge of
Subject Matter

Purpose: Someday, at the end of your career in education, you will no doubt recall your early hopes and dreams. Will you have realized your goals? Project yourself into the future, and imagine you have accomplished all that you set out to do. An orientation toward the future can help you attain your goals.

Activity: Time flies: your own offspring have chosen to be teachers and they open *Teachers, Schools, and Society* (12th edition!) to the history chapter and begin reading the profiles in the "Hall of Fame." And **you are there.** Why? Let's find out. Write yourself into The Education Hall of Fame by following the format in Chapter 8. Provide a graphic image, a statement of significant contribution, and about 250 words that detail your accomplishments in education. Be sure to include your subject-matter expertise in this essay as a major factor in your achievement.

Reflection: The activity should help you define your professional direction and goals. What actions might help you reach your long-time goals? What intermediate steps might you need to make in the future? Are there mentors and professional relationships that might help support your success? Keep this Hall of Fame entry in your portfolio. You could even seal and date it in an envelope to be opened when you teach your first class of students, receive your doctorate in education, are named U.S. Secretary of Education, or attend your retirement dinner.

3:2 MONEY MATTERS

INTASC PRINCIPLE 2
Human
Development and
Learning

Purpose: Most state offices of education work to equalize per-pupil expenditures. Still, children live with very different financial realities at home and at school. A family's income influences a student's physical, social, emotional, moral, and cognitive growth. To better understand and meet the needs of your learners, consider how economics has impacted you and your education.

Activity: Under each developmental area, list ways that your education was helped and/or hindered by money. Money is frequently a culturally taboo topic of conversation; therefore, you may want to keep this activity as a private journal entry or a draft chart you share selectively with a peer.

Developmental Areas and Socioeconomic Class

Physical (such as size, shape, fitness, health, medical resources):

Social (such as autonomy, civility, relationships):

Emotional (such as expressiveness, empathy, motivation):

Moral (such as ethics, honesty, good will):

Cognitive (such as intellectual resources, academic services, inherent abilities):

Reflection: Consider how your childhood's financial security (or lack thereof) contributed to your educational reality. How was your growth and development distinguished by economic class? How might your life have been different if you were raised with a very different financial base?

3:3 MOVIE CLASSICS

Purpose: The philosophies of education are captured not just in this section of the book but in classic films that portray the "good old days" of school. In those movies, you can see many diverse approaches to teaching. Watching will help you consider or reconsider your philosophical preferences.

Activity: As a preview, scan the major philosophies of education (essentialism, perennialism, progressivism, existentialism, social reconstructionism). Then, watch a classic movie. *Goodbye Mr. Chips, Up the Down Staircase, The Prime of Miss Jean Brodie, To Kill a Mockingbird, The Corn Is Green* and *They Call Me Mr. Tibbs* are some masterpieces that have much to say about teaching. As you watch (with or without popcorn), attend to the various techniques the teachers use to meet the needs of the learners. Can you match the theories of philosophy to the cast of characters? Take notes and try to capture the indicators of educational philosophy that appear in the film.

Reflection: Pull your notes together and develop a statement of philosophy that represents the teacher or another important educator in the film. Limit yourself to about 200 words. (That's almost the number of words describing this activity.)

3:4 THE GREAT LECTURE THEORY OF LEARNING

Purpose: Most of us have attended, even been moved by, a great lecture, yet, when we learn about strategies for classroom instruction, the lecture is often relegated to the least effective method or, simply, disparaged. Lecturing is not inherently evil. While it can be tiresome and boring, it can also be motivating, filled with information, clearly understood, and easily recalled. There are reasons that great lecturers are great, and, the sooner you figure out some of the reasons, the sooner you will be able to give terrific lectures yourself.

Activity: Check around the campus with friends and acquaintances to find out which professors give great lectures. Choose one and ask permission to attend a class. (Or, if necessary, check into television courses, videotapes from a distance learning course, or satellite seminar series.) Take notes, not on the specific information the speaker imparts, but on presentation and style. Ask some of the following questions about technique:

- What pulled you into the lecture? (a great story? a provocative question?)
- How did you know where the lecture was going? (Was the purpose or objective stated or implied?)
- How did the speaker use presentation or communication skills?

  Facial expressions?

  Gestures?

  Eye contact?

  Voice?

  Movement?

Interaction with the "audience"?

Other skills?

- What technical aids or materials (videotapes, Power Point presentation) promoted your understanding and interest?

- Did the speaker use vivid examples, stories, metaphors, or role-play to enhance your comprehension?

- How might you assess the speaker's expertise in the lecture's content?

Reflection: All in all, was this lecturer worthy of his or her reputation? Why? How are you when it comes to public speaking? What's your comfort zone? Given what you know about yourself, which of the observed lecturer's strengths might be strengths of yours as well? Which might you want to add to your repertoire?

3:5 WHAT YOU SEE AND WHAT YOU GET

Purpose: The philosophy of a classroom can be seen, felt, and heard, yet future teachers sometimes have a difficult time "getting" it, even when examples of educational philosophy surround us. This activity will help you connect with specific clues that signal a teacher's philosophy.

INTASC PRINCIPLE 5
Motivation and Management

Activity: As you attend classes, record observations on a chart similar to the one that follows. Gather at least three different observations.

Indicators of Educational Philosophy
Course: _____
Room arrangement:
Teacher-student interactions:
Student-initiated actions:
Instructional grouping and organization (full class, individuals/groups, centers/stations):
Instructional resources:
Other:

Reflection: What classroom indicators have you observed? What do these indicators suggest about the philosophy of your teachers, classes, program, or institution? What do your notes tell you about how faculty members manage instruction and motivate learning? Which elements do you want to include in your teaching? Which would you prefer to omit or avoid?

3:6 A PASSION PLAY

Purpose: Teachers may be valued not only by how they teach students but also by how well they communicate clearly with faculty, administrators, parents, and members of the community. Refining and declaring your opinions will allow you to practice professional communication skills.

Activity: Ethical issues can inspire passion in teachers. Taking a strong stand on an ethical concern can, in fact, empower you in your work. Write a letter or e-mail that states your educational opinion and requests a course of action. Limiting yourself to 350 words will help you clarify your thoughts and make your point. Mix and match ideas from the following columns, use real-life situations, or invent your own details.

Mix and Match List	
Letter To	**Education Concern**
President of the United States	Taxes
Newspaper editor (school or local)	Technology
Chief school officer	Laws
Teachers' union leadership	Elections
School district board	Safety
State board of education	Violence
College board of trustees	Curriculum (explicit, informal, hidden)
Your family	EMOs
Family of a student or a peer	Ethics
Faculty, friend or foe	Lotteries
Mentor	Inequalities
Radio or television station	Charter schools
Internet site	Textbooks

Don't even think about sending your letter or e-mail until you reread it, edit it, and reflect on it. (You might want to ask someone to read it and offer suggestions.) When it is *just right* (and especially if it has been drawn from an authentic circumstance), consider submitting it as a model of your advocacy. You may also want to save it in your portfolio as an indication of your current communication skills.

Reflection: What writing techniques and skills created a strong and concise statement? Were there research elements (perhaps from the text) that provided support for your opinion? How did your most recent copy change from your first draft? What did the rewriting, editing, and peer review teach you about your communication skills?

3:7 A REAL IN-SERVICE PROGRAM

Purpose: Several districts and states, along with independent schools, are instituting a service obligation with high school graduation requirements. The intent is to instill a contributory ethic in students. While an ongoing service requirement may be one way to meet this principled goal, you, as a teacher can help by integrating this "service ethic" into your lessons.

Activity: Recall a lesson or unit you have seen. Brainstorm (alone or with others) how you might add a service component. Briefly outline the lesson or unit and then describe, in about 150 words, how you would integrate the service project or activity.

Service Integration Ideas	
Lesson	**Sample Service Component**
Language arts	Read with special population students, children, or seniors
Science	Assist with student health appraisal
Math	Be a homework helper, one on one, with a student
Social studies	Work on a student or teacher rights campaign
Technology	Teach computer skills at a local shelter
Physical education	Referee or supervise a children's sport event or recess
Health	Bring the Great American Smoke Out to a local school
Vocational and career	Review career materials, for bias, at a school job fair
Foreign language	Assist bilingual parents with school visits and conferences
Arts	Volunteer with children in theater, art, dance, or music

Reflection: This reflection might be better called a projection. Project yourself into the future, actually teaching your lesson and including your ethical service component. What goals do you hope to accomplish? Good lesson planning always carries with it the need to respond to unanticipated challenges. What might (and probably will) happen that causes you to monitor and adjust? What solutions might you propose?

3:8 ASSESSING THE ASSESSOR

Purpose: With all the attention being given to the performance of American students on national and local tests, it makes sense for you to explore the promise and problems of districtwide evaluation.

Activity: Invite a school district administrator with assessment responsibilities to your class or study group for one hour. (Create a class chat room on your department's web site if that is more viable). Prepare a series of questions regarding districtwide assessment. Ask your guest to describe the district's history and current evaluation procedures. Then, use the following questions (or your own) to expand your guest's commentary.

- What are the purposes behind these tests?
- What policies and procedures work effectively?
- What benefits have resulted from testing?

- What is the biggest problem you face?
- What role does the public (parents, media, chamber of commerce) play?
- Do special interest groups interfere, or do they support assessments?
- How do these tests affect the teacher?

Reflection: Assessment issues vary among states, districts, schools, courses, and teachers, and they seem to change often. What have you learned? What information surprised you? What do you still have on your "need to know" list?

3:9 MAG OF THE MONTH

Purpose: While the Internet represents ready sources of information, not all of the information on the Internet is of high quality. Professional journals and magazines often include the best writing in our field. Journal articles are submitted and reviewed by educational experts, selected for their high standards of excellence. To be a reflective and responsible teacher, you will need to keep current by reading one or more professional journals.

Activity: Pick a journal or an educational magazine that is new to you. Try one at your professor's suggestion or use sources listed in the endnotes of this text. Spend at least one hour studying the literature. Harvest a sense of what this journal offers by analyzing its intended audience, format, content, style, policy, and readability.

Reflection: If you were marketing this journal to your peers, what sales points would you include? What are its weaknesses? If you could read only one journal a month, would this be it? Why or why not?

3:10 GET ON BOARD

Purpose: One seemingly distant group, the school board, influences every teaching day. As an elected agency of the community, school boards hold regular meetings, usually open to visitors. Because their norms and procedures vary, you have to see one to understand one. The purpose of this activity is to better understand how school boards function and how they might impact your life in the classroom.

Activity: Attend a school board meeting or watch one on television (many are broadcast by local cable networks). Imagine you are covering the meeting for your district's teacher association. Note what is going on. Try to grasp the formal curriculum (old and new business and procedures). Look also at the hidden curriculum, the cultural cues and the nonverbal signals, that tell you what else is going on. Write your notes into a column for your professional colleagues. Limit your final draft to a page.

Reflection: What were your personal and professional impressions of the meeting? What rituals and routines did you observe? How were your assumptions about school boards and meetings altered by your attendance? Were underlying politics evident? How were attendees treated? Did any of the school board's decisions directly impact district teachers? How? Based on your observation of the school board meeting, would you consider teaching in this district? Would you consider running for a school board position? Why or why not?

Portfolio Artifact Collections

3:P2 CHARTS OF CHANGE

Purpose: Talented teachers consider the growth and development of their students. Growth and development charts, from infancy through adulthood, can often be found in child development and psychology texts, journals, and Internet resources. Keeping a copy of selected charts in your portfolio collection will make the information accessible.

Activity: Collect at least three growth and development charts that display information about students. Look for height and weight scales across various racial and ethnic groups, gender differences in children's decision making, fitness at various ages, the use of free time by children and adolescents, homework recommendations for particular grade levels, and cognitive development. Be sure to note where you found each chart for later reference and updating.

INTASC PRINCIPLE 2
Human Development and Learning

3:P5 PHILOSOPHY STATEMENT

Purpose: This is the time to begin writing your philosophy of education statement. It will help promote your own philosophical clarity, give you a foundation for career development, and contribute to positive job interviews. Your statement should be stored in your portfolio, revised throughout your preservice program, and eventually submitted as part of a teaching application or presentation portfolio.

Activity: Your teacher education program may have specific criteria for the format, style, and content of your philosophy of education. In general, your draft statement would be one page long, written in the first person, accurate in representing who you are, and correct regarding spelling and grammar. We offer the following phrases as possible opening lines:

INTASC PRINCIPLE 5
Motivation and Management

- I am convinced that teachers make a contribution to student achievement in specific ways. I intend to . . .
- Teachers are responsible for creating a learning environment that includes "the basics" of instruction. My version of "the basics" means . . .
- My core beliefs about education will be evident with students as I . . .
- Different students learn differently. I plan to meet the individual needs of my learners by . . .
- I have been inspired by meaningful educators. Their strengths will travel with me to the classroom when . . .
- I believe the goals of education are . . .

YOUR THIRD *INTER-MISSION* IS OVER. IT'S TIME FOR "TOMORROW."

CLASS ACT

At this time of year, graduates may feel a little lost. We have been students for SO long, and now suddenly things are changing. At such time of transition, we need a larger purpose to guide us—why have we chosen these careers as educators? It certainly wasn't for the money! I would like to share some words that I have turned to for a sense of purpose. ● Over thirty years ago, W.E.B. DuBois, the great African American writer and activist, said from his death bed: "One thing alone I charge you: As you live, believe in life! Always human beings will live and progress to greater, broader, and fuller life. The only possible death is to lose belief in this truth . . ." ● Despite all the injustice he experienced, DuBois died believing that the future will be ever brighter. In our line of work, it is not always easy to believe in progress. Apparently, DuBois never tried to get licensed at the New York City Board of Ed.! I have had many discussions with other students, wondering how to tackle problems such as glaring educational inequity based on race and class, negative or indifferent attitudes toward bilingual and special education, international disparities in the quality of education, and a general lack of respect in this country for the work that we do. What impact can I have as one individual educator? True, one person alone cannot change society. But each of us does have the power to change other people, and collectively we are an impressive force. For example, think of a teacher or family member who has passed on a legacy to you. ● I am imagining two people up here with me: my mother's mother and my father's father. My grandmother, Mercy Oduro, was a West African woman who touched hundreds as a teacher and headmistress of an elementary school. It's a testament to her life's work that, although she died six years ago, I am still called "Teacher Mercy's granddaughter" when I go back to Ghana. To me, she has passed on a flair for celebration and an unshakeable belief in her students, and I will pass these on to my own students. ● My American grandfather, William Steel, 83 years old, is a retired teacher, but STILL tutoring daily at his local school. His legacy is so strong that on his eightieth birthday he got letters from people he taught over fifty years ago, acknowledging his influence on them. To me, he has passed on a fantastic curiosity about the world and a playful sense of humor, and I will pass these on when I teach. ● Imagine now that all the people we will reach ARE crowded in this room today—hundreds, thousands of them. In each of these people there is a piece of one of us, continuing the legacy of those who came before. Look around. Can you see the ocean of possibility flowing from us here today? Together, how can we NOT create DuBois' vision of greater, broader, and fuller life? Let me tell you, we are powerful: We are educators.

Melissa Steel
Teachers College Graduation Speech
Columbia University

SUBMIT YOUR OWN *CLASS ACT*: Click on *Class Acts* and submit a *Class Act* about a teacher who has made a difference in your life. Visit the Online Learning Center to read more *Class Acts*.

12

The Struggle for Educational Opportunity

FOCUS QUESTIONS

1. How do deficit, expectation, and cultural difference theory explain disparate academic performance among various racial, ethnic, and cultural groups?
2. What major developments have marked the educational history of Native Americans, Hispanics, African Americans, Asian Americans/Pacific Islanders, and Arab Americans?
3. What educational barriers and breakthroughs have girls and women experienced?
4. What classroom strategies are appropriate for teaching culturally diverse learners?
5. What impact do changing family patterns and economic issues have on children and schools?
6. How can educators respond to social issues that place children at risk?

WHAT DO YOU THINK? Estimate the social, racial, and ethnic backgrounds of today's students.

CHAPTER PREVIEW

Have you ever felt the cold slap of rejection because of race, religion, color, sex, language, national origin, social class, sexual orientation, or physical or learning disability? Have you ever denied a family history that included divorce, suicide, or abuse? Frequently, the dominant culture has little tolerance for those who are in any way "different." As most of us know from personal experience, when you happen to be the one who is outside—the one who is deprived even briefly of the benefits, privileges, and status of the inside group—the feeling of being labeled "less worthy" can be more than painful.

Ideally, education should be for all children. In reality, education has repeatedly labeled, tracked, and excluded students who are in any way different. These children have met prejudicial treatment early, right at the schoolhouse door.

This chapter will review the major developments that have pried open the school door and have brought these once excluded learners into the educational mainstream. At times, breaking down the barriers of bias and discrimination has overwhelmed those who have struggled to cope with federal regulations and court decisions. Most have persisted.

Intersecting with racism and sexism, considerable economic and social problems engulf our children and our schools. The recent past has not been kind to children, who now make up the poorest segment of society. Their survival and educational achievements are threatened by poverty, changing family patterns, substance abuse, depression, and even suicide. We will identify strategies that help keep the school door open for these troubled students as well.

Student diversity continues to increase dramatically. Teachers, schools, and society must respond, so that both equity and excellence can be achieved and maintained.

Educational Opportunity for All

"Welcome to class," says the professor as you take your seat. "I want you to respond to the following case study. Now it is, of course, fictional, but suspend belief, read the parable and tell me what you think."

As a student in this class, you think this sounds kind of interesting (and a good grade in this course would be really nice). So you settle down and read the brief story:

> You are a white person and are visited by an official who explains that a mistake has been made, and you were actually born to black parents who live far from where you grew up. The error has to be rectified. At midnight, you will become black, acquiring a darker skin, and body and facial features that reflect your African heritage. Your knowledge and ideas, your "inside," however, will remain the same.
>
> Now this is an unusual and rare problem, the official explains, but the error was not yours, and the organization that he represents is ready and able to offer you appropriate recompense. His records indicate that you are scheduled to live another 50 years.
>
> How much financial recompense would you request?

You look around and see your classmates settle into the task—considering what the possible compensation should be, each from their own unique perspective of race and ethnicity. You wonder: How much money will your white classmates ask for? How do the students of color respond to this controversial, some would say offensive, class exercise? Now the BIG question: How much money would *you* ask for?

While the parable is not true, the scenario is. Professor Andrew Hacker at Cornell put this question to white students in his class, and asked them to come up with a settlement figure: How much money would they want to offset the "error"? If you are wondering what figure Hacker's students came up with, most felt that a reasonable payment for the "mistake" would be fifty million dollars, a million dollars "for each coming black year."

The book that described this activity, *Two Nations: Black, White, Separate, Hostile, Unequal* (1992), received a great deal of media coverage in the 1990s, but we believed that it also left many questions unanswered.[1] What if Professor Hacker had continued the experiment with other groups? How much money would an Hispanic American, African American, and Asian American request if a mistake were made and they had to live the rest of their lives as a member of another race or culture? Would they request less compensation for the "administrative" blunder? The same fifty million? Would they want more money?

Certainly, just posing the problem underscores the American tendency to look to the courts to fix any "mistake," no matter how bizarre. And of course, in this story, money is the all-American panacea, a salve for any social injury. But despite these confounding issues, the parable is fascinating, and the questions it raises are intriguing.

Why did Professor Hacker construct this strange story, and how did he interpret the payment? He believed that the story unmasks America's hidden racism. Professor Hacker considers white privilege to be so commonplace that most of us are no longer able to "see" it. He uses the parable because it makes the hidden advantage of being white visible again. In Hacker's estimation, the fifty million dollars that his students thought "fair" represents the value that white people place on the color of their own skin.

How do you interpret the story? Would you seek a legal settlement and monetary damages? (Here's an idea, perhaps you might feel privileged to experience more than one culture or one race in a single lifetime.) Or like Hacker, do you believe that some races and cultures are more valued in America? And perhaps a more basic question: Do you feel that just going through this exercise is an appropriate classroom activity? Or do you believe that it is too problematic?

When it comes to education, are certain groups more valued? If we ask Americans directly about race and schooling, how do you think they would respond? (And how would you respond?) Well, in fact, that's a question that the Gallup organization asked in 1978, and again in 2001.[2] In 1978, 80 percent of the public believed that the schooling opportunities for all American children, regardless of race or ethnicity, were equal. In 2001, that figure was 79 percent, virtually unchanged. But while most believe that educational opportunity is equal, they do not accept the notion that all students are achieving equally. Almost half said that whites are achieving at a higher rate than African Americans or Hispanics. Why this difference, and what should be done about it? Fifty-five percent surveyed said that while the achievement gap is not the fault of the schools, it is up to schools to close the gap.

The challenge we as educators face is figuring out exactly how this should be done. A number of theories have emerged to explain why some groups soar in school, while others flounder. Some of the explanations are fatalistic, others more hopeful. One argument would go something like this: Certain students do poorly in school because of their cultural, social, or linguistic backgrounds. The values, language patterns, and behaviors that these children learn at home do not mesh with the culture of U.S. schools, putting these students at a disadvantage. This explanation is known as the **deficit theory**. (Before the 1960s, the deficit theory held that genetic and IQ deficiencies of certain groups, especially people of color, were the root cause of academic underachievement. Deficit theory proponents today steer clear of such claims.)

Here's a second view: Some children do poorly because their teachers do not expect much of kids from certain racial and ethnic groups. As a result, they teach these students differently, the students' academic performance suffers, and the entire cycle becomes a self-fulfilling prophecy. This is called the **expectation theory**, which was first made popular by Rosenthal and Jacobson (their classic study is mentioned in Chapter 3, "Teacher Effectiveness"). Expectation theory holds that academic performance can be improved if teacher behavior is modified.

A third explanation argues for better cross-cultural understanding. **Cultural difference theory** asserts that academic problems can be overcome if educators study and mediate the cultural gap separating school and home. Let's consider one case in point, and then see how cultural difference theory works:

> Polynesian children in a Hawaiian village are performing poorly on the school reading tests. They seem unresponsive to the extra time and effort made by teachers to improve their reading performance. Why is this happening, and how can the situation be improved?

In this example, educators studied the Polynesian culture and discovered that older children, rather than adults, play a major role in educating the young. Accordingly, the school established a peer learning center, providing the opportunity for older children to teach younger ones. By recognizing and adopting cultural traditions, the school was able to dramatically improve students' reading scores.[3]

Creating effective classrooms for all children takes a deliberate and thoughtful process. In the first part of this chapter we continue on the road to bridging the cultural, racial, and ethnic divide, and creating a classroom climate that recognizes and honors differences. So you may better appreciate where your students are coming from, we provide brief histories of the U.S. experiences of several nondominant cultures and immigrant groups.

But race, culture and ethnicity are only some of the issues that teachers should consider in their classrooms. Gender is another. Does gender influence teaching—and achievement? You bet it does. How can teachers ensure that both girls and boys are treated fairly? In this chapter, we offer several specific suggestions for nonsexist, nonracist teaching.

As the chapter draws to an end, we will examine barriers to equal opportunity that come from social realities. In today's America, girls and boys from all racial, ethnic, and cultural backgrounds struggle with issues ranging from substance abuse to AIDS, from homophobia to teen pregnancy, from homelessness to being home alone. These issues are all part of today's social fabric, and they all have implications for your classroom. In fact, if the diverse characteristics of today's children were merged into your classroom of thirty students:[4]

19 would be white.

17 will be living with their two biological or adoptive parents.

15 will live in a single-parent family at some point in childhood.

12 will never complete a single year of college.

10 were born to unmarried parents.

10 will be poor at some point in childhood.

10 are a year or more behind in school.

8 live with only one parent.

6 were born poor.

6 were born to a mother who did not graduate from high school.

6 would be Hispanic.

6 live in a family receiving food stamps.

6 have a foreign-born mother.

5 are poor today.

5 would be African American.

4 have no health insurance.

4 live with a working relative but are poor nonetheless.

4 were born to a teenage mother.

4 speak a language at home other than English.

4 will never graduate from high school.

3 might be questioning their heterosexuality or believing that they are gay, lesbian, bisexual, or transgendered.

3 have a disability.

2 live at less than half the poverty level.

2 have difficulty speaking English.

1 would be an Asian American.

1 might be Native American.

1 lives with neither parent.

Several might be biracial or bicultural.

And, for every 35 classrooms, 1 student will be killed by gunfire before age 20.

Native Americans: The History of Miseducation

In the beginning, God gave to every people a cup of clay, and from this cup they drank their life. They all dipped in the water, but their cups were different. Our cup is broken now. It has passed away.

Digger Indian proverb

Over the centuries, the impact of white people on the tribal life of Native Americans has been one of conquest and the attempted and often successful destruction of tradition and culture.[5] The early attempt of whites to provide their own brand of education for Native Americans was carried out by church missionary societies. They operated schools for Native Americans, although the tribes themselves provided most of the resources for their own education. Many Native Americans responded enthusiastically to the white approach to their education—as long as this approach did not attempt to eradicate their cultures. The missionaries, however, often saw their goal as one of "civilizing" and Christianizing the tribes. They ignored or actively suppressed the languages of their pupils and tried to teach exclusively in English.[6]

Indian boarding schools were established to assimilate young Native Americans into the dominant European-American values: veneration of property, individual competition, European-style domesticity, toil, and European standards of dress.

Despite such adverse conditions, Native Americans achieved some extraordinary educational accomplishments. For example, in 1822, **Sequoyah** invented a Cherokee syllabary. This permitted the Cherokee language to be written; books were published in Cherokee; Cherokee schools became bilingual; and the Cherokee nation wrote, edited, and published the *Cherokee Phoenix*, a bilingual weekly newspaper. There have been many other Native American achievements in education, accomplishments that rejected white attempts to deny tribal heritages and languages. However, as federal interventions became more systematic, the tribes' control over their own education diminished.

After the Civil War, the federal government, through the **Bureau of Indian Affairs (BIA)**, dominated the education of Native Americans. Education became a tool of conquest, and the reservations saw more and more white superintendents, farm agents, teachers, inspectors, and missionaries. The largest of the tribes, the Navajos, despite their years of resistance, were assigned to a reservation. The treaty with the Navajos promised that schools would be built to educate their children. In 1892, almost twenty years after the treaty was signed, only seventy-five students attended the one and only school on the reservation. This represented less than 0.5 percent of the Navajo population.

Many Native Americans refused to send their children to reservation schools. Arrest and kidnapping were common practices in forcing Native American children to attend. Rations were often withheld from parents as a means of compelling them to send their children to school.

After 1920, there was an increase in political and legal activity as Native Americans fought for tribal and educational rights. In two instances, Native Americans challenged the federal government for violating treaties, including failure to provide adequate education. The federal courts were not responsive. Greater gains at the state level were made, and in several court cases Native Americans won the right to attend public schools.[7]

Over half of the 2 million Native Americans in this country do not live on reservations, and their youngsters have become invisible children of color in urban centers. As the students have been desegregated across neighborhoods, they have lost their "critical mass," which is often associated with higher achievement.[8]

The recent decades have witnessed continued activity by Native Americans to win control of the reservations, including the schools. The tribes feel strongly that such control will maintain cultural identity, as well as increase the academic achievement of their children. More than 85 percent of Indian children are educated in public schools. Most other Native youth are clustered in programs under the advisory of the Bureau of Indian Affairs or private schools.

Black Americans: The Struggle for a Chance to Learn

Much of the history of African American education in the United States has been one of denial. The first law prohibiting slaves the opportunity for education was passed in South Carolina in 1740. During the next hundred years, many states passed similar and even stronger compulsory-ignorance laws. For example, an 1823 Mississippi law prohibited six or more Negroes from gathering for educational purposes. In Louisiana, an 1830 law imposed a prison sentence on anyone caught teaching a slave to read or write. However, because education has always been integral to African Americans' struggle for equal opportunity, they risked the penalties of these laws and even the dangers of violence for a chance to learn. They formed clandestine schools throughout most large cities and towns of the South. Suzie King Taylor described what it was like to attend one of those secret schools in Savannah, Georgia:

> We went every day about nine o'clock with our books wrapped in paper to prevent the police or white persons from seeing them. We went in, one at a time, through the gate, into the yard to the L Kitchen which was the schoolroom.[9]

The Civil War brought an end to policies of compulsory ignorance and an affirmation of black people's belief in the power of education. Most of the schooling of African Americans immediately following the Civil War was carried out by philanthropic societies. These associations worked with the Freedmen's Bureau, a federal agency established to provide various services, including the establishment of schools. School staffs were usually a mixture of instructors from the North, blacks of Caribbean island heritage, and formerly enslaved literate blacks.

Many white Southerners responded to the education of blacks with fear and anger. Sometimes there was terrorism against black schools. In the end, however, politics replaced violence as the principal means of denying blacks equal educational opportunity. As conservatives began regaining political power, state after state passed laws that explicitly provided for segregated schools. With the 1896 **Plessy v. Ferguson** Supreme Court decision, segregation became a legally sanctioned part of the American way of life. In this landmark case, the Court developed the doctrine of **separate but equal.** Separate but equal initially legalized separate railway passenger cars for black and white Americans. But this doctrine that was immediately used to justify a legally segregated school system, which in many states lasted for more than half a century.

"Separate but equal" was not equal. In 1907, Mississippi spent $5.02 for the education of each white child but only $1.10 for each black child. In 1924, the state paid more than $1 million to transport whites long distances to schools. No money was spent for blacks, and for them a daily walk of more than twelve miles was not out of

The famous Tuskegee Normal School founded by Booker T. Washington became a national symbol for the educational aspirations of African Americans.

the question. Attending schools without enough books, seats, space, equipment, or facilities taught African American children the harsh reality of "separate but unequal." In the South, a dual school system based on race was in existence. This was ***de jure* segregation**—that is, segregation by law or by official action.

In the North, school assignments were based on both race and residence. ***De facto*** (unofficial) **segregation** occurred as the result of segregated residential patterns, patterns that were often prompted by discriminatory real estate practices. As housing patterns changed, attendance zones were often redrawn to ensure the separation of white and black children in schools. Even in schools that were not entirely segregated, black children were routinely placed in special classes or separate academic tracks, counseled into low-status careers, and barred from extracurricular activities. Whatever the obstacle, however, African Americans continued their struggle for access to quality education. As W.E.B. DuBois noted: "Probably never in the world have so many oppressed people tried in every possible way to educate themselves."[10]

Political gains by blacks followed their participation in World War II and the New Deal policies of Franklin Roosevelt. In May 1954, the Supreme Court handed down a ground-breaking decision. In the case of ***Brown v. Board of Education of Topeka*** (Kansas), the Court unanimously ruled that "in the field of public education the doctrine of 'separate but equal' has no place. Separate educational facilities are inherently unequal." In indicating how quickly the **desegregation** of Southern schools was to take place, the Court used the phrase "with all deliberate speed." In effect, the Court established a vague timetable, one without a deadline of any kind, so yet another generation of black children experienced segregated education. Ten years after *Brown*, almost 91 percent of all African American children in the South still attended all-black schools.

In 1964, Congress moved boldly to eradicate racial segregation and discrimination in schools by passing the **Civil Rights Act**, including two titles of particular importance to schools. **Title IV** gave the U.S. Commissioner of Education the power to help desegregate and the U.S. Attorney General the power to initiate law suits to force school desegregation. **Title VI** prohibited the distribution of federal funds to schools with racially discriminatory programs of any kind. Together, these two titles produced more desegregation in their first four years than the Supreme Court's decision in *Brown* had produced during the preceding decade.

During the late 1960s and early 1970s, the courts became the primary battleground in the African American communities' fight for equal educational opportunity. The Supreme Court handed down a series of decisions indicating its impatience

Scenes like this one became commonplace all across America in the years following the landmark *Brown v. Board of Education of Topeka* decision in 1954 and the passage of the Civil Rights Act in 1964.

with the slow pace of desegregation. The Court also began attacking *de facto* segregation stemming from racially imbalanced neighborhoods. In Charlotte-Mecklenburg County, North Carolina, a U.S. district judge ordered extensive **busing** of pupils to achieve integration. In addition to busing, the courts later supported such devices as racial quotas and school pairing in attempts to eradicate school segregation in both the North and the South.

School districts began to experiment with other remedies more acceptable to school families. Typically, these procedures involved more freedom of choice and greater emphasis on improved instruction. Such remedies included magnet schools, choice plans, and voluntary metropolitan desegregation arrangements.

As schools became more racially balanced, students discovered a new barrier to equality. Although in the same school building, black and white students found themselves separated by race, a phenomenon called **second-generation segregation**. Tracking was a common method for second-generation segregation, but not the only one. While whites pursued certain extracurricular activities, blacks gravitated to others. Territoriality developed as areas of school buildings became informally segregated, and African American students also found themselves being treated differently.[11] As the famous Kerner Commission warned back in the 1960s: "Our nation is moving toward two societies, one black, one white—separate and unequal." The commission charged that white society must assume responsibility for the black ghetto. "White institutions created it, white institutions maintain it, and white society condones it."[12]

In the 1980s and 1990s, a more conservative Supreme Court retreated from civil rights initiatives, such as desegregation and affirmative action. In the 1996 **Hopwood v. State of Texas** decision, a federal court eliminated racial set-asides in law school admissions as the path to student diversity, a decision that influenced admissions policies for other schools.[13] By the beginning of the twenty-first century, it became fashionable to bad-mouth America's efforts to desegregate.

Harvard professor Gary Orfield reported in **Schools More Separate: Consequences of a Decade of Resegregation** (2001), that although schools were likely to be our first major institutions to experience nonwhite majorities, they are becoming increasingly segregated. Seventy percent of the nation's African American students were in predominantly segregated schools by the end of the 1990s, up from 63 percent in 1980. The report showed a dramatic rise in Latino segregation. Orfield found that white students remain the most segregated of all races in their schools. On average, whites attend schools where less than 20 percent of the students are from all of the other racial and ethnic groups combined as schools "resegregate." (See Figure 12.1.)[14] Resegregated schools of color, on the other hand, are typically located in "islands of poverty," lacking academic resources, with predictably dismal results.

Evidence suggests that there were clear educational benefits in desegregated schools. Blacks attending schools with whites during the 1970s and 1980s posted achievement gains, improved their graduation rates, and were more likely to continue their education.[15] Today, however, the nation is moving in the opposite direction, and the gains made by African Americans and Hispanics in the 70s and 80s ceased or went into reverse in the 1990s.[16] Yet as noted child psychiatrist James Comer points out,

> Past and present policies which made it extremely difficult for black Americans to achieve at the level of their ability are like dropping the baton. And black America is not another team in competition with white America. Black Americans are part of America's team. If America keeps running without the baton, no matter how fast or how far, we're going to lose.[17]

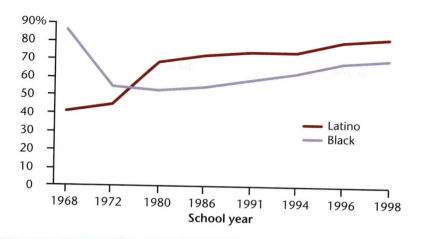

FIGURE 12.1
Students in *de facto* minority schools.

SOURCE: Darryl Fears, "Schools' Racial Isolation Growing," *The Washington Post*, July 18, 2001, p. A3.

REFLECTION

Do you believe that desegregation of America's schools will ever be possible? Is desegregation important? Explain your position.

Magnet schools can offer students exceptional educational opportunities and often attract culturally diverse learners.

Hispanics: Growing School Impact

More than 35 million Hispanics live in the United States, including Puerto Rico, up over 75 percent since 1980. Over two-thirds of Hispanics living in the United States are U.S.-born citizens and constitute 13 percent of the nation's population. Because many Latinos immigrated to the United States to escape economic and political repression, not all of them entered the country legally. Consequently, their numbers may be underestimated. Ongoing legal and illegal immigration, together with high birth rates for young families in their childbearing years, have made Hispanics the youngest and fastest-growing school-age population in the United States. By the year 2030, Hispanic children will represent one-fourth of the total school-age population.[18]

Hispanics consist of several subgroups, which share some characteristics, such as language, but differ in others, such as race, location, age, income, and educational attainment. The three largest Hispanic subgroups are Mexican Americans, Puerto Ricans, and Cuban Americans. There is also significant representation from other Latin American and Caribbean countries, such as the Dominican Republic, El Salvador, Nicaragua, and Honduras.[19] (See Figure 12.2.) In contrast to these new immigrants, many from war-torn or poverty-stricken countries, there is also an "old" population of Mexican and Spanish descent living in the Southwest with a longer history on this continent than those who trace their ancestors to the New England colonies.

FIGURE 12.2
U.S. Hispanic subgroups.

SOURCE: The Hispanic Population Census 2000 Brief, May 2001.

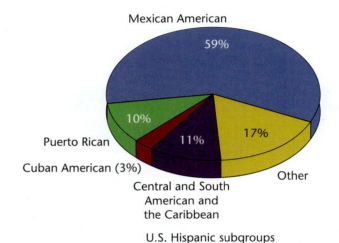

U.S. Hispanic subgroups

REFLECTION

While many refer to Hispanics as a homogeneous community, they are not. What distinctions can you make for each of these segments? What similarities have you observed or studied?

By 2030, Hispanic children will comprise one quarter of the total school-age population.

Latino children confront numerous educational barriers. As early as kindergarten, Hispanic students are less able than their white peers to identify colors, recognize letters, count to fifty, or write their first name. Over a third of Hispanics drop out of school, a number more than twice as high as African Americans and more than three times as high for non-Hispanic whites.[20]

Mexican Americans

At the end of the United States' war with Mexico (1846–1848), the Mexicans who decided to stay in the new U.S. territories were guaranteed full citizenship. By 1900, approximately 200,000 Mexican Americans were living in the Southwest, having built the cities of Los Angeles, San Diego, Tucson, Albuquerque, Dallas, and San Antonio. The devices that were used to deny educational opportunity to Mexican Americans were similar to those imposed on African Americans. By 1920, a pattern of separate and unequal Mexican American schools had emerged throughout the Southwest. With the passage of Civil Rights legislation in the 1960s, Crystal City, Texas, became the flashpoint of the Chicano Movement. The Chicano students walked out of school, protesting inferior facilities and demanding bilingual/bicultural education.[21]

In the late 1960s, Cesar Chavez led the fight of migrant Mexican American laborers to organize themselves into a union and to demand a more responsive education that included culture-free IQ tests, instruction in Spanish, smaller classes, and greater cultural representation in the curriculum.

Then, as now, significant numbers of Mexican American families migrated once or twice a year, exploited as a source of cheap labor in rural, agricultural communities. With constant transitions, children's learning suffered. One superintendent in Texas, reflecting deeply engrained prejudice, argued that education was actually dangerous for Mexican Americans:

> Most of our Mexicans are of the lower class. They transplant onions, harvest them, etc. The less they know about everything else, the better contented they are . . . so you see it is up to the white population to keep the Mexican on his knees in an onion patch . . . . This does not mix well with education.[22]

Today, more than one in four public schools enroll migrant students, mostly Mexican Americans. The greatest numbers are in rural sections of California, Texas, and North Carolina.[23]

Puerto Ricans

During the nineteenth century, many of the Puerto Ricans in the United States were highly respected political exiles striving for the independence of their homeland. But all that changed in 1898, when Puerto Rico was acquired from Spain and became a territory of the United States. Citizenship, through the Jones Act in 1917, provided free movement between the continent and the island. Migration to the mainland peaked during the 1950s, with the majority of Puerto Ricans settling in New York City. By 1974, there were more than a quarter of a million Puerto Rican students in the New York City public schools. Currently, while 3.4 million Puerto Ricans live within the fifty states, nearly 4 million live in Puerto Rico.[24] The frequent passage between the island and the United States, as families search for a better economic life, makes schooling all the more difficult for Puerto Rican children.

Cuban Americans

Following the Castro-led revolution in the 1950s, Cuban immigration to the United States increased significantly. During the 1960s, Cubans who settled in the United States were primarily well-educated, professional, and middle- and upper-class. By 1980, 800,000 Cubans—10 percent of the population of Cuba—were living in the United States. For the most part, Cubans settled in Miami and other locations in southern Florida, but there are also sizable populations in New York, Philadelphia, Chicago, Milwaukee, and Indianapolis. Cubans, considered one of the most highly educated people in American immigration history, tend to be more prosperous and more conservative than most of the other Latino groups.[25]

In the second immigration wave, during the 1980s, there were many more black and poor Cubans, who have not been accepted as readily into communities in the United States.

New Immigrants from Latin America

Since the 1960s, 34 percent of the nation's new immigrants, legal and illegal, have come from Latin America, mainly Mexico, El Salvador, Guatemala, and Nicaragua. For example, after the Sandinista revolution in the 1980s, 200,000 Nicaraguans fled to the United States. Half a million Salvadorans arrived in the 1980s; over half settled in Los Angeles, making it the second-largest Salvadoran city. These more recent arrivals augment the extensive diversity of Hispanic Americans.

Many of the Latin American immigrants survived war, torture, and terrorism in their homelands of El Salvador, Guatemala, and Nicaragua. Those children brought both physical and psychological scars into the schools of their new land. Mental health professionals noted that symptoms of trauma and stress plague many of these children, including depression, nightmares, insomnia, and guilt. In El Salvador, there were "countless situations where children were in the classroom and their teacher was killed." An education advocate from New York City counseled an 8-year-old girl who "saw her father put up against the wall and shot by government troops."[26] Psychological scars, poverty, and limited ability to speak English present enormous educational obstacles for generations of Latino immigrants.

Asian Americans and Pacific Islanders: The Magnitude of Diversity

As the largest and most culturally diverse group to legally enter our nation since the 1970s, Asian Americans and Pacific Islanders account for 9 million Americans, or approximately 4 percent of the population. Demographers predict that this figure will have increased several fold by the year 2050.[27] Asian Americans come from areas as diverse as China, India, and Vietnam. Pacific Islanders are from Guam, Samoa, Tonga, and countless other islands spread across an area larger than the North American continent.

As a group these Americans have attained a high degree of educational and economic success. Despite outstanding accomplishments, the statistics hide problems that many of the new immigrants from Southeast Asia and the Pacific Islands face. Cultural conflict, patterns of discrimination, and lower educational achievement are all concealed by the title "model minority." This section will describe the differing experiences of four of the largest Asian immigrant groups—Chinese, Filipinos, Asian Indians, and Japanese—as well as problems faced by refugees from Southeast Asia.[28]

Frequently, Asian Americans see education as a way to regain status that was lost when their families immigrated to the United States. Education is also viewed as a means of gaining acceptance in U.S. society. These two powerful motivators have driven many to succeed in school, giving rise to the stereotype of the **model minority**. However, as with many stereotypes, there is some truth and a good deal of misconception in this image. In kindergarten, Asian American children are already outscoring their peers in both reading and math.[29] Forty-two percent of Asian American/Pacific Islanders graduate from college with a degree. One year after graduation, they have the highest starting salary of any other racial or ethnic group.[30] These successes also mask problems. Diversity within the Asian community is often overlooked. Fewer than half of Vietnamese and Samoan Americans graduate from high school. Asian New Wavers reflect the current countercultural pattern, with baggy pants, combat boots and dyed hair, challenging the "model minority" notion.[31]

Chinese Americans

When the Chinese first began immigrating to the West Coast in the 1850s, they were mostly young, unmarried men who left China, a country ravaged by famine and political turmoil, to seek their fortune in the "Golden Mountains" across the Pacific and then take their wealth back to their homeland. The California gold mines were largely depleted by the time they arrived, and, after the completion of the transcontinental railroad signaled a loss of jobs for Chinese laborers, many found that the hope of taking fortunes home to their families in China was an impossible dream.

By 1880, approximately 106,000 Chinese had immigrated to the United States, fueling a vicious reaction: "The Chinese must go." With the passage of the Immigration Act of 1882, along with a series of similar bills, further Chinese immigration was blocked. The Chinese already in this country responded to increasing physical violence by moving eastward and consolidating into ghettos called *Chinatowns*. Inhabited largely by male immigrants, these ghettos offered a grim and sometimes violent lifestyle, one with widespread prostitution and gambling. Chinatowns, vestiges of century-old ghettos, can still be found in many of America's cities.

In 1949, the institution of a Communist government in mainland China caused Congress to reverse more than a century of immigration quotas, naturalization, and antimiscengenation laws and grant refugee status to five thousand highly educated Chinese in the United States. Despite facing active prejudice and discrimination, Chinese Americans today have achieved a higher median income and educational level than that of white Americans.

Filipino Americans

After the 1898 Spanish-American War, the United States acquired the Philippines. Filipinos, viewed as low-cost labor, were recruited to work in the fields of Hawaii and the U.S. mainland. Thousands left the poverty of their islands to seek economic security.

With a scarcity of women (in 1930, the male–female ratio was 143 to 1) and the mobility of their work on farms and as fieldhands, the Filipinos had difficulty establishing cohesive communities. Like other Asian immigrants, they came with the goal of taking their earnings back to their homeland; like other Asian immigrants, most found this an impossible dream.

By the 1920s Filipinos were immigrating in greater numbers, and fear of the "yellow peril" became pervasive. Riots erupted, especially in California, where most of the Filipinos had settled. Because of their unique legal status (the United States had annexed the Philippines in 1898), Filipinos were not excluded as aliens under the Immigration Act of 1924. However, the Tydings-McDuffie Act of 1934 was a victory for those who wanted the Filipinos excluded from the United States. Promising independence to the Philippines, this act limited immigration to the United States to fifty per year.

All that changed in 1965, when a new immigration act allowed a significant increase in Filipino immigration. Between 1970 and 1980, the Filipino population in the United States more than doubled. The earlier presence of the U.S. military in Manila generated an educated elite who spoke English, studied the American school curriculum, and moved to the United States with professional skills, seeking jobs commensurate with their training.[32] Concentrated in urban areas of the West Coast, Filipinos are the second-largest Asian American ethnic group in the United States.

Asian Indian Americans

Traders from India arrived in New England in the 1880s, bartering silks and spices. Intellectuals Henry David Thoreau, Ralph Waldo Emerson, and E. M. Forester (Passage to India) gravitated to the culture, religion, and philosophy of the Eastern purveyors. On the West Coast, Indians from Punjab migrated to escape British exploitation, which had forced farmers to raise commercial rather than food crops. With farming conditions in California similar to those in India, Punjabees became successful growers and landowners. They were destined to lose their lands, however, and even their leasing rights, under the California Alien Land Law, which recalled the ownership of land held by Indians and Japanese.

In addition to legal restrictions, Indian laborers were attacked by racist mobs in Bellingham, Washington, in 1907, triggering other riots and expulsions throughout the Pacific region. U.S. government support for British colonial rule in India became the rationale to further restrict Indian immigration. It was not until 1946 that a law allowing Indian naturalization and immigration was passed.

During the 1980s and 1990s, tens of thousands of Indians arrived in America. Most Indians are extremely well educated, and many are professionals. More than 85 percent have graduated from high school, over 65 percent have college degrees, and 43 percent have graduate or professional degrees. Their educational and income levels are the highest of any group in the United States, including other Asians.[33]

Japanese Americans

Only when the Japanese government legalized emigration in 1886 did the Japanese come to the United States in significant numbers. For example, in 1870, records show only fifty Japanese in the United States, but, by 1920, the number had increased to more than 110,000.

With the immigration of the Chinese halted by various exclusion acts, Japanese immigrants filled the need for cheap labor. Like the Chinese, the early Japanese immigrants were males who hoped to return to their homeland with fortunes they earned in the United States. For most, this remained an unfulfilled dream.

Few women were among the early Japanese immigrants. However, the practice of "picture brides," the arrangement of marriages by the exchange of photographs, established Japanese families in the United States. Many researchers suggest that the strong Japanese family structure, maintained in the early system of picture brides, is key to the achievement of Japanese Americans today.

Praised for their willingness to work when they first arrived in California, the Japanese began to make other farmers nervous with their great success in agriculture and truck farming. Anti-Japanese feelings became prevalent along the West Coast. Such slogans as "Japs must go" and warnings of a new "yellow peril" were frequent. In 1924, Congress passed an immigration bill that halted Japanese immigration to the United States.

After Japan's attack on Pearl Harbor on December 7, 1941, fear and prejudice about the "threat" from Japanese Americans were rampant. On February 19, 1942, President Franklin Roosevelt issued Executive Order No. 9006, which declared the West Coast a "military area" and established federal "relocation" camps. Approximately 110,000 Japanese, more than two-thirds of whom were U.S. citizens, were removed from their homes in the "military area" and were forced into ten **internment camps** in California, Idaho, Utah, Arizona, Wyoming, Colorado, and Arkansas. Located in geographically barren areas, guarded by soldiers and barbed wire, these internment camps made it very difficult for the Japanese people to keep their traditions and cultural heritage alive. Almost half a century later, the U.S. government officially acknowledged this wrong and offered a symbolic payment ($20,000 in reparations) to its victims.

Despite severe discrimination in the past, today's Japanese Americans enjoy both a high median family income and educational attainment. Their success is at least partially due to traditional values, a heritage some fear may be weakened by increasing assimilation.

Southeast Asian Americans

Before 1975, the United States saw only small numbers of immigrants from Southeast Asia, including Vietnam, Laos, and Kampuchea/Cambodia. Their arrival in greater numbers was related directly to the end of the Vietnam War and resulting Communist rule.

Asian Americans and Pacific Islanders are the most culturally diverse group to enter the United States since the 1970s.

The refugees came from all strata of society. Some were wealthy; others were poverty stricken. Some were widely traveled and sophisticated; others were farmers and fishing people who had never before left their small villages. Most came as part of a family, and almost half were under age 18 at the time of their arrival. Refugee camps were established to dispense food, clothing, medical assistance, and temporary housing, as well as to provide an introduction to U.S. culture and to the English language.

INTERACTIVE ACTIVITY
MULTICULTURAL LITERACY. Match multicultural terms with their descriptions.

By December 1975, the last refugee camp had closed and the U.S. government had resettled large numbers of Southeast Asians across the nation without too high a concentration in any one location. This dispersal was well intentioned but often left the refugees feeling lonely and isolated. In fact, many moved from original areas of settlement to cities where large numbers of Asian Americans were already located.

A second wave of Southeast Asian refugees followed in the years after 1975. Cambodians and Laotians migrated to escape poverty, starvation, and political repression in their homelands. Many tried to escape in small fishing boats not meant for travel across rough ocean seas. Called *boat people* by the press, almost half of them, according to the estimates, died before they reached the shores of the United States.

Similar to war refugees from Latin America, these children brought memories of terrible tragedy to school. For example, a teacher in San Francisco was playing hangman during a language arts lesson. As the class was laughing and shouting out letters, she was shocked to see one child, a newcomer, in tears. The girl spoke so little English she could not explain the problem. Finally, another child translated. The game had triggered a traumatic memory. In Cambodia, the girl had watched the hanging of her father.[34] April 30, 2000, marked the 25th anniversary of the fall of Saigon. Since 1975, more than 1.4 million Southeast Asians have resettled in the United States. Their struggle to find a place in this society remains conflicted as most Americans associate Vietnam with war.

Arab Americans: Moving Beyond the Stereotype

Misunderstanding and intolerance have been all-too-common facts of life for three million Americans of Arab descent. Arab Americans' quality of life is often influenced by events taking place in other parts of the world. The Gulf War against Iraq, assaults on the terrorist camps in Taliban-ruled Afghanistan, the September 11, 2001 attacks on the World Trade Center and the Pentagon, and the continuing conflict between Israelis and Palestinians create tension and anxiety for Americans of Arab descent. While these news events are troubling enough, media portrayals can exacerbate the problem. Books and movies depict a strange melange of offensive Arab caricatures: greedy billionaires, corrupt sheiks, immoral terrorists, suave oil cartel magnates, and even romantic, if ignorant, camel-riding Bedouins. Nor are children's books immune from such characterizations. Caroline Cooney's *The Terrorist* (1999), a popular book for children in grades 5 through 10, is the fictional tale of an American teenager who tries to find the Arab terrorist responsible for her younger brother's death. It is not surprising that polls taken as far back as the 1980s reveal that most Americans perceive Arabs as anti-American, warlike, anti-Christian, and cunning.[35] The challenge to educators could not be clearer. Students and teachers need to learn about Arab Americans, as well as the Arab world.

The first wave of Arab immigrants, mostly from Syria and Lebanon, came to America at the end of the nineteenth century, for the same reasons that have driven so many immigrants: political freedom and economic opportunity. Toledo, Ohio, and Detroit, Michigan, became important centers of Arab immigration, and business became the economic mainstay of this first wave. Other waves of immigration followed, one just after World War II, and the third as a result of the Palestinian-Israeli conflict. Arabs arrived from over a score of countries, typically settling in major urban centers.

Many Americans confuse Arabs and Moslems, mistaking Islam, a religion, with Arabs, a cultural group. While Islam is the predominant religion of the Middle East, and most Arabs living there are Moslems, there are also millions of Christian Arabs (as well as those who are Jewish or Druse). In the United States, the vast majority of the three million Arab Americans are Christian. And, in contrast, the majority of America's eight million Moslems are not Arab. While Arabs practice different religions, they do share the same language and culture, a culture that is at times in conflict with western values.[36]

Such differences can create friction, in and beyond school. For example, Arabs enjoy close social proximity, and members of the same sex often walk arm-in-arm or hold hands, behaviors at odds with American practice. Features of the Arabic language, including loudness and intonation, may be perceived in America as too loud, and even rude. While punctuality is considered a courtesy in the United States, being late is not considered a sign of disrespect in Arab culture. In addition to these cultural disconnects, more profound differences emerge, such as the disparity between the role of women in Arab society and the role of women in Western society. Many Arab nations cast women in an inferior position, denying them education, inheritance, and power. Saudi Arabia, for example, still forbids women to drive, prohibits coeducation, and requires that women wear veils in public. Arranged marriages and polygamy are practiced in several Arab nations. While the birth of a son is celebrated in conventional Arab families, the birth of a daughter may be met with silence.[37] Yet, change is also sweeping part of the Arab world. Several Arab states have opened schools and the workplace to women, with dramatic results.

Today, students of Arab heritage can be found in all fifty states, and as a group, do well in American schools. The proportion of Arab Americans who attend college is higher than the national average and Arab Americans earn postgraduate degrees at a rate nearly double the national average. Yet they still face challenges. They learn from textbooks that have little if anything to say about their history or experiences. American teachers lack basic information about Arab culture, which may present problems. For example, a traditional Arab student may be troubled or confused in an American school where women can be both teachers and principals. In a similar way, an American teacher who criticizes an Arab student in public may have unintentionally erected a wall of hard feelings. Arabs put a lot of emphasis on personal and family honor, and public ridicule is a serious matter.

If the Arab student happens to be of the Moslem faith, additional issues emerge. Moslems discover that while schools typically celebrate Christmas, they ignore Moslem holidays. For instance, during Ramadan, Moslems fast for a month during daylight hours, yet few schools recognize this observance, much less make provision for it. In terms of dietary restrictions, school cafeterias serve, but do not always label, pork products, a food Moslems are prohibited from eating. Clearly, Arab and Moslem American students are all but invisible in the official and hidden curriculum of most American schools. Teacher training, curricular revision, and a greater understanding of these cultural and religious issues are needed if equal educational opportunities are to become a reality for these Americans.

Women and Education: A History of Sexism

The peopling of America is a story of voluntary immigration and forced migration. The story of women's struggle for educational opportunity may be just as hard to uncover but equally important to reclaim.

For almost two centuries, girls were barred from America's schools.[38] Although a woman gave the first plot of ground for a free school in New England, female children were not allowed to attend the school. In 1687, the town council of Farmington, Connecticut, voted money for a school "where all children shall learn to read and write English." However, the council quickly qualified this statement by explaining that "all children" meant "all males." In fact, the education of America's girls was so limited that fewer than a third of the women in colonial America could even sign their names. For centuries, women fought to open the schoolhouse door.

In colonial America, secondary schools, called female seminaries, appealed to families financially able to educate their daughters beyond elementary school. In New York, Emma Hart Willard struggled to establish the Troy Female Seminary, while, in Massachusetts, Mary Lyon created Mount Holyoke, a seminary that eventually became a noted women's college. Religious observance was an important part of seminary life in institutions such as Mount Holyoke. Self-denial and strict discipline were considered important elements of molding devout wives and Christian mothers. By the 1850s, with help from Quakers, such as Harriet Beecher Stowe, Myrtilla Miner established the Miner Normal School for Colored Girls in the nation's capital, providing new educational opportunities for African American women. While these seminaries sometimes offered superior educations, they were also trapped in a paradox they could never fully resolve: They were educating girls for a world not ready to accept educated women. Seminaries sometimes went to extraordinary lengths to reconcile this conflict. Emma Willard's Troy Female Seminary was devoted to "professionalizing motherhood" (and who could not support motherhood?). But, en route to reshaping motherhood, seminaries reshaped teaching.

For the teaching profession, seminaries became the source of new ideas and new recruits. Seminary leaders, such as Emma Hart Willard and Catherine Beecher, wrote textbooks on how to teach and on how to teach more humanely than was the practice at the time. They denounced corporal punishment and promoted more cooperative educational practices. Since school was seen as an extension of the home and another arena for raising children, seminary graduates were allowed to become teachers—at least until they decided to marry. Over 80 percent of the graduates of Troy Female Seminary and Mount Holyoke became teachers. Female teachers were particularly attractive to school districts—not just because of their teaching effectiveness but also because they were typically paid one-third to one-half of the salary paid to male teachers.

By the end of the Civil War, a number of colleges and universities, especially tax-supported ones, were desperate for dollars. Institutions of higher learning experienced a serious student shortage due to Civil War casualties, and women became the source of much-needed tuition dollars.

Female funding did not buy on-campus equality. Women often faced separate courses and hostility from male students and professors. At state universities, male students would stamp their feet in protest when a woman entered a classroom.

In *Sex in Education* (1873), Dr. Edward Clarke, a member of Harvard's medical faculty, argued that women attending high school and college were at risk because the blood destined for the development and health of their ovaries would be redirected to their brains. The stress of study was no laughing matter. Too much education would leave women with "monstrous brains and puny bodies . . . flowing thought and constipated bowels." Clarke recommended that females be provided with a less demanding education, easier courses, no competition, and "rest" periods, so that their reproductive organs could develop. He maintained that allowing girls to attend such places as Harvard would pose a serious health threat to the women themselves, with sterility and hysteria potential outcomes.

M. Carey Thomas, future president of Bryn Mawr and one of the first women to earn a Ph.D. in the United States, wrote in her diary about the profound fears she experienced as she was studying: "I remember often praying about it, and begging God that if it were true that because I was a girl, I could not successfully master Greek and go to college, and understand things, to kill me for it."[39] In 1895, the faculty of the University of Virginia concluded that "women were often physically unsexed by the strains of study." Parents, fearing for the health of their daughters, often placed them in less demanding programs reserved for females, or kept them out of advanced education entirely. Even today, the echoes of Clarke's warning resonate, as some people still see well-educated women as less attractive, view advanced education as "too stressful" for females, or believe that education is more important for males than for females.

In the twentieth century, women won greater access to educational programs at all levels, although well into the 1970s gender-segregated programs were the rule. Even when females attended the same schools as males, they often received a less valuable education. Commercial courses prepared girls to become secretaries, while vocational

Historically, low teacher salaries can be traced back to the late nineteenth century, when communities found that they could hire capable women teachers for approximately 60 percent of what men teachers were paid.

programs channeled them into cosmetology and other low-paying occupations. After World War II, it was not unusual for a university to require a married woman to submit a letter from her husband, granting her permission to enroll in courses before she would be admitted. By the 1970s, with the passage of Title IX of the Education Amendments of 1972, females saw significant progress toward gaining access to educational programs, but not equality.

The Impact of Title IX

Title IX of the 1972 Education Amendments Act specifically prohibits many forms of **sex discrimination** in education. The opening section of Title IX states

> No person in the United States shall, on the basis of sex, be excluded from participation in, be denied the benefits of, or be subjected to discrimination under any education program or activity receiving federal financial assistance.

Every public school and most of the nation's colleges and universities are covered under Title IX, which prohibits discrimination in school admissions, in counseling and guidance, in competitive athletics, in student rules and regulations, and in access to programs and courses, including vocational education and physical education. Title IX also applies to sex discrimination in employment practices, including interviewing and recruitment, hiring and promotion, compensation, job assignments, and fringe benefits.

Although enforcement of the law remains sporadic, there is still cause for optimism. As teachers begin challenging **sex-role stereotyping** for girls who think that only boys can be doctors and for boys who hate poetry and ballet, they will be advancing gender equity and equality of opportunity for all our children.

In *Backlash*, Susan Faludi documents the negative impact on women resulting from the conservative political gains of the 1980s and 1990s. Most of the educational programs designed to assist girls and women have been eliminated. In certain areas, such as engineering, physics, chemistry, and computer science, few women can be found. In nursing, teaching, library science, and social work, few men can be found. A "glass wall" still keeps women from the most lucrative careers and keeps men from entering traditionally female jobs. Even in careers in which tremendous progress has been made, such as medicine and law, a second generation of bias persists. In both professions, women find themselves channeled into the least prestigious, least profitable areas.

A newly visible cadre of equity advocates decry the focus on females as they claim that the real victims of sexism are males. Males' lower grades, higher presence in special education, and problematic behavior are in need of a teacher's primary attention. For both boys and girls, gender bias continues to be documented in curricular materials, staffing patterns, and teaching behaviors. Given the powerful and painful history of sexism in U.S. schools, it is surprising that so many Americans are unaware of the past efforts to achieve gender equity or of the subtle (and not so subtle) barriers that still exist.[40]

INTERACTIVE ACTIVITY
EDUCATIONAL OPPORTUNITY TIMELINE. Test your knowledge of the chronology of events related to educational opportunity.

Our Children, Your Students

Today, children are the poorest group in our society, and current programs and policies are woefully inadequate to meet their growing needs. Stanford's Michael Kirst sums it up this way:

Johnny can't read because he needs glasses and breakfast and encouragement from his absent father. Maria doesn't pay attention in class because she doesn't understand English very well and she's worried about her father's drinking and she's tired from trying to sleep in her car. Dick is flunking because he's frequently absent. His mother doesn't get him to school because she's depressed because she lost her job. She missed too much work because she was sick and could not afford medical care.[41]

American children living in poor families are among the poorest in all industrial nations. Most parents of poor children work, but they don't earn enough to provide their families with basic necessities—adequate food, shelter, child care, and health care. Children, with little voice and no votes, are among the first to lose services.

Before Title IX, only girls took home economics and only boys took shop. During the past decades, the barriers of sexism have steadily eroded.

Title IX, passed in 1972, requires comparable athletic experiences for females and males. What differences and similarities can you observe over time? What sport experiences did you have in school as a participant or an observer?

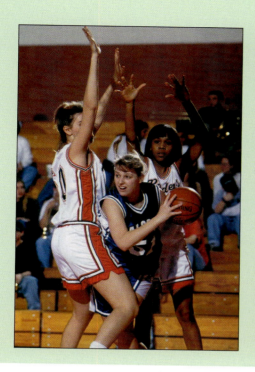
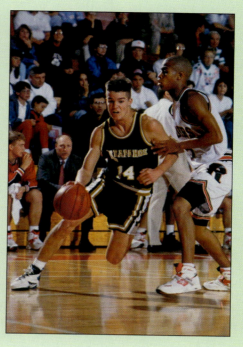

Nearly 11 million children under age 18 have no medical coverage.[42] When children are poor, they are more likely to drop out of school and be involved in violent crime, early sexual activity, and drugs. In short, poverty puts children at risk.

Children living today in the wealthiest American families are easily the most affluent in the world but they too may be plagued by stress, fast-paced lifestyles, new family structures, and predicaments rarely mentioned or even acknowledged just a few decades ago.

Family Patterns

Not too many years ago, the Andersons of *Father Knows Best* lived through weekly, if minor, crises on television; Dick and Jane lived trouble-free lives with their parents and pets in America's textbooks; and most real families contained a father, mother, and three children confronting life's trials and tribulations as a family unit. But today's family bears little resemblance to these images. In fact, just over half of American "families" have no children under 18 at home, and one-fourth of all households are people living alone.[43]

Leave It to Beaver may live in rerun land forever, but Beaver Cleaver resolves the bumps and bruises of childhood in a way that by today's standards appears half a step from a fairy tale. Only fifty years ago, a single-parent family meant one thing: a premature death. Out-of-wedlock children and pregnant, unmarried teenagers were hidden from the public's attention. Divorce was rare. Mothers stayed at home and fathers went to work.

CLASSROOM ORGANIZATION

- *Segregation.* Avoid segregated seating patterns or activities. Sometimes teachers segregate: "Let's have a spelling bee—boys against the girls!" Other times, students segregate themselves. Gender, race, or ethnic groups that are isolated alter the dynamics of the classroom and create barriers to effective communication among students, as well as obstacles to equitable teaching. If necessary, you will need to move students around to create a more integrated class. Knowledgeable teachers know there are times when children need to be in same language, gender, or similar clusters. If there are only two or three students of a certain group in a class, separating them can actually increase the sense of isolation. Diversity and good judgment are both important as teachers group and organize students.

- *Mobility.* Students sitting in the front row and middle seats receive the majority of the teacher's attention. This is because the closer you get to students, the more likely you are to call on them. If you move around the room, you will get different students involved. By the way, students are mobile too. You may want to change their seats on a regular basis to disperse classroom participation more equally.

- *Cooperative education.* Collaboration, rather than individual competition, is a social norm for many groups, including African Americans, Native Americans, and females. When cooperation is less valued, research suggests, inequities emerge, especially when students choose their own partnerships. For instance, in cooperative learning groups, girls tend to assist both other girls and boys, while boys are more likely to help only other boys. Boys get help from everyone in the group, but girls must make do with less support. In addition, some students (usually boys) may dominate the group, while others (usually girls) are quiet. It is a good idea to monitor your groups, in order to intervene and stop these inequitable patterns.

- *Displays.* Check your bulletin boards, your displays, and your textbooks. Are women and other underrepresented groups evident? Should you find resources to supplement materials and create a more equitable classroom climate? Do you remember the phrase "If the walls could speak"? In a sense they do. What messages are the classroom walls and curriculum sending to your students?

CULTURAL CUES

- *Eye contact.* Teachers sometimes assume that children's nonverbal messages are identical to their own. But many factors can change the meaning of "eye" messages. A teacher's respectfully stated request to "Look at me when I am talking to you" anticipates a student will feel comfortable with the request. In fact, many Asian American, Pacific Islander, and Native American children lower their eyes as a sign of respect. For other children, lowered eyes is a sign of submission or shame, rather than respect. Consider the background of your students. Even silent eyes speak many languages.

- *Touching and personal space.* Our personal cultural history contributes to how "touchy" we are and how we reach out and touch others. Many Southeast Asians feel it is spiritually improper to be touched on the head. A similar touch, on an African American child's head, may be perceived as demeaning, rather than kind. Getting close or even "right up in someone's face" can be threatening, or caring. Some teachers, worried that any touch may be misconstrued as sexual harassment, avoid touching students at all, yet we know that touch which supports learning can be a powerful and positive force.

  Teachers need to be conscious and culturally sensitive when being near or touching students. Let students know you will respect their nonverbal comfort zones. In fact, many teachers "read the need" of a child, observing students' use of touch and space.

- *Teacher-family relationships.* Students, depending on their heritage, view teachers with varied degrees of attachment. Hispanics may include the teacher as an extension of family, with high expectations for contact and closeness. Asian Americans may seem more formal, or even distant, evidencing respect for adults and the teacher's role. Parents from certain cultural groups may see the teacher's job as independent of parental influence, so conferences or phone calls may appear unwanted or awkward. Wealthy parents may treat teachers as subordinates, part of a hardworking staff that serves their child's interests. The teacher's goal is to expand relationship skills and relate effectively with diverse student families and cultures.

INTERACTION STRATEGIES

- *Calling on and questioning students.* Do not rely on the "quickest hand in the West," which is usually attached to a male. Relying on the first hand raised will skew the pattern of classroom participation. Be aware that some students will feel intimidated anytime they are called on. Whether it is a lack of English language skill, a personal power strategy to shun the teacher's control or even a sign of respect, some students work to escape teacher contact. Asking a teacher for help can suggest a lack of understanding and may be avoided by Asian American and Native American children.

Develop other strategies for student participation besides hand raising—for example, writing each student's name on a card and using the cards to select students. Or set an expectation for full participation, and then call on students who don't raise their hands. Instead of a few students "carrying" the class, all students will be pulled into the learning process.

- *Wait time 1.* Wait time can be a big help in promoting equitable participation. Giving yourself 3 to 5 seconds before you call on a student allows more time to deliberately and thoughtfully choose which student to call on. The extra wait time also allows you more time to develop an answer. Research indicates that many females, students of color, and limited English speakers particularly benefit from this strategy.

- *Wait time 2.* Give yourself more wait time *after* a student speaks, as well. Research shows that boys get more precise feedback than girls do. Waiting will give you the opportunity to think about the strengths and weaknesses of a student's answer, to be more specific in your reaction, and to provide all students with more specific feedback as well.

- *Assigning tasks.* Too often teachers stereotype classroom activities. Boys (especially bigger boys) are asked to tackle physical jobs or mechanical skills while girls are assigned to grade papers.

- *Discipline.* Boys are reprimanded more often (one study shows that they receive eight to ten times as many control messages as girls do) and are punished more harshly. Not only do teachers punish boys more, but they also talk to them more, listen to them more, and give them more active teaching attention.

REFLECTION

Why are these equitable instructional skills so often missed by teachers? What steps can you take to ensure that you will use them? (Here's a hint . . . these tips are not meant to be a teacher's secret. Explaining to your students why you are committed to equitable teaching skills can spark their interest and help.)

Beaver Cleaver's family structure represents fewer than 6 percent of U.S. families. Generally, our families are getting smaller, older, and more diverse. While Americans still prefer marriage, the past twenty-five years have seen the number of unmarried opposite and same sex partners living together increase from 2 to 5.5 million. Since live-in relationships generally last about eighteen months, the arrival and rearing of children mean less stability for everyone.[44] Approximately 13 million children—one in five—live in single-parent families. The divorced mom often struggles with a severe loss of income. Research shows that children from single-parent families are less likely to achieve and more than twice as likely to drop out of school.[45]

Wage Earners and Parenting

In 1960, 39 percent of married women with children between the ages of 6 and 17 worked outside the home; this number had increased to 78 percent by the late 1990s. The rise in salaried employment for married women with children under 6 has been even more striking, jumping from 19 percent in 1960 to 65 percent in 1997.[46] The costs of this social change are not being managed by employers but rather by working couples who are juggling both work and home life. In one major study, women placed a hold on their career (describing it as a "job") following their first child. Two-thirds of the males waited until their career was successfully in place before scaling back work commitments.[47]

The school participation of mothers in two-parent families is similar to that of single parents, male or female. The reservoir of volunteers for a variety of school functions has been greatly reduced, while the need for child care has increased

significantly.[48] (As Figure 12.3 indicates, about two-thirds of America's families have both or only parent(s) working outside the home.)

Divorce

Although today divorce is common (more than a million children experience divorce each year), it is hardly routine.[49] The underlying stress can increase a child's anguish. Children who have experienced divorce may exhibit a variety of problem behaviors. Symptoms from depression to aggression diminish school performance. Children often go through a classic mourning process similar to that experienced after a death in the family. However, most children are resilient and can rebound from the trauma of divorce, with 80 to 90 percent recovering in about a year. Teachers should give children the chance to express their feelings about divorce and let them know they are not alone in their experience.[50]

Stay-at-home moms, working dads and two children populate television reruns like *Leave It to Beaver,* but no longer reflect most of today's families.

Stepfamilies, Interracial Marriages, and Alternative Families

By the turn of the twenty-first century, more Americans were living in stepfamilies than nuclear families, including about half of our children. **Stepfamilies** are created when divorced or widowed parents remarry, and most do. Stepfamilies consist of biological and legal relationships with stepparents, stepsiblings, multiple sets of grandparents, and what often becomes a confusing array of relatives from old and new relationships.[51]

Other families are combined, not by remarriage, but through cross-cultural and racial unions. It was only in 1967 that the Supreme Court overruled antimiscegenation laws, which had banned **interracial marriage.** Interracial unions are a small yet rapidly growing portion of today's households.[52] The children of interracial marriages do not fit neatly into today's labels. Is the child of an African American and an Asian American to be categorized as African American, Asian American, "blended," or "other"?

Alternative families include family lifestyles other than a married male and female living with their children. Alternative families can consist of single moms or dads with children; biological parents who are not married; relatives or friends acting as child guardians; same-sex couples sharing parenting roles; nonmarried couples living as families; serial relationships with continually changing partners. Yet, the conventional family stereotype still permeates the school curriculum, and children in nontraditional families may feel discomfort about their "abnormal" lifestyle. Clearly, many schools have a way to go before they successfully integrate all family structures into school life.

Latchkey Kids

Jennifer unlocked her door quickly, raced inside, and shut it loudly behind her. She fastened the lock, threw the bolt, dropped her books on the floor, and made her way to the kitchen for her usual snack. Within a few minutes Jennifer was ensconced on the sofa, the

Rank	State	Percentage		Rank	State	Percentage
1	Iowa	83.2		26	South Carolina	68.1
2	North Dakota	83.0		27	Washington	67.5
3	South Dakota	79.4		28	Massachusetts	67.3
4	Vermont	79.0		29	Oregon	67.3
5	Nebraska	78.7		30	Michigan	67.2
6	Wisconsin	77.6		31	Georgia	66.9
7	Missouri	76.9		32	Ohio	66.9
8	Kansas	76.4		33	Illinois	66.6
9	Minnesota	76.1		34	Alabama	66.5
10	Connecticut	75.4		35	Florida	66.3
11	Maryland	73.8		36	Mississippi	65.9
12	Montana	73.7		37	Utah	65.0
13	Wyoming	72.7		38	Oklahoma	64.7
14	New Hampshire	72.6		39	New Jersey	64.7
15	Colorado	72.5		40	Pennsylvania	64.6
16	North Carolina	72.4		41	Delaware	63.6
17	Maine	72.2		42	Alaska	63.4
18	Hawaii	71.7		43	Texas	62.9
19	Indiana	71.6		44	Kentucky	61.4
20	Virginia	71.4		45	Louisiana	61.3
21	Nevada	70.0		46	District of Columbia	61.0
22	Idaho	69.8		47	Arizona	60.1
23	Arkansas	69.4		48	New York	59.4
24	Rhode Island	69.3		49	New Mexico	59.1
25	Tennessee	68.9		50	California	56.3
				51	West Virginia	54.6

National average: 66%

FIGURE 12.3

Percentage of school-age children with both or only parent(s) working.

SOURCE: "24-Month Average April 1996 through March 1998," based on the the CPS, Bureau of Labor Statistics.

REFLECTION

In this chart, what states or rankings differ from your perceptions? Suggest some reasons that might account for the variance between your assumptions and these statistics.

television on and her stuffed animals clutched firmly in her hand. She decided to do her homework later. Her parents would be home then, and she tried not to spend too much time thinking about being lonely. She turned her attention to the television, to spend the next few hours watching talk shows.

Jennifer is a latchkey kid—left to care for herself after school. While we do not know the precise number of latchkey children in America, most agree that there are at least five million, and some believe that the actual number is closer to twice that estimate. Lynette Long and Thomas Long coined the term **latchkey** (sometimes called **self-care**) **kids** to describe these children, who carry a key on a cord or chain around their necks, a key to unlock their home door. Coming from single-parent homes or families with two working parents, they are products of new economic and social realities in the United States. With few extended family units (grandparents and other relatives living with or near parents) and a shortage of affordable, convenient, high-quality child care facilities, many children are simply left on their own. Latchkey kids are found in all racial and socioeconomic groups. The more educated the parents, the

The problems faced by latchkey children cannot be attributed to low socioeconomic or educational levels of the parents as is the case with many other student problems.

more likely they are to have a latchkey child. Although the average latchkey child is left alone two and a half hours per day, a significant number are alone much longer, more than thirty-six hours per week. Over twenty-five of those hours are spent watching television with the leftover time parceled into studies or play.[53]

Hidden America: Homeless Families

In Washington, D.C., a 3-year-old girl and her 5-year-old brother spend their nights with their mother, assigned to a cubicle in a school gym. The mother lost her job because of unreliable child care. Unable to meet her rent payments, she lost her apartment. Now the family is awakened at 5:30 a.m. in order to catch the 7:00 a.m. bus to a welfare hotel where breakfast is served. After breakfast, it is another bus ride to drop the 5-year-old off at a Head Start program, then back to the welfare hotel for lunch. Another bus takes them to pick up the boy from day care and then transports them to dinner back at the hotel. The final bus ride takes them to their cubicle in the gym. The 3-year-old misses her after-noon nap on a daily basis. The mother does not have the time or means to look for a job.

The cycle continues.[54]

America's homeless are urban and rural, and of every racial and ethnic back-ground; and present schools across the nation with a host of problems. Homeless children may be tested, counseled, assigned to a class, and then leave. They lack even rudimentary facilities for study. Many arrive at school hungry and tired. Some school districts require proof of residency or birth certificates, frequently denying education to the homeless. Add to this equation the drugs, crimes, violence, and prostitution sometimes found in shelters, and it is clear that these children are struggling uphill, against overwhelming odds, in order to get an education. Many give up.

Unfortunately, there has not been much of a national response. In 1987, Congress passed the **McKinney Homeless Assistance Act**, providing the homeless with emergency food services, adult literacy programs, job training, and other assistance. In 1990, the act was amended to underscore the importance of education and to

WHAT TEACHERS NEED TO KNOW ABOUT THE EDUCATION OF HOMELESS CHILDREN

- No one needs a permanent address to enroll a child in school.
- The child may remain at the same school he or she attended before becoming homeless or may enroll at the school serving the attendance area where he or she is receiving temporary shelter.
- The homeless child cannot be denied school enrollment just because school records or other enrollment documentation are not immediately available.
- The child has the right to participate in all extracurricular activities and all federal, state, or local programs for which the child is eligible, including food programs; before- and after-school care; vocational education; Title I; and other programs for gifted, talented, and disadvantaged learners.
- The child cannot be isolated or separated from the mainstream school environment solely due to homelessness.

SOURCE: Adapted from the National Law Center on Homelessness & Poverty Fact Sheet: *What You Should Know About the Education of Homeless Children* (1998).

REFLECTION

Recall your earliest encounters with homelessness. How have those images changed and how have they remained the same? What would you do or say if you ran into the parent of one of your homeless students?

facilitate the public school enrollment of homeless children. For example, the requirement of furnishing proof of immunization, a simple task for most families, was often enough to keep a homeless child out of school. The amended act reduced or eliminated many such barriers.[55] Despite this progress, funding remains inadequate to meet the educational needs of the nation's homeless children.

Children: At Promise or At Risk?

It was not too long ago that family life was captured by simplistic TV images, with problems easily solved in fewer than thirty, almost commercial free, minutes. In the mid-1900s, teachers were concerned about students talking out of turn, chewing gum, making noise, running in the halls, cutting in line, and violating dress codes. Half a century later, teachers' top student concerns reflect the devastating changes in the lives of their pupils: drug and alcohol abuse, pregnancy, suicide, rape, robbery, and assault.

Dropping Out

Lamar was finishing junior high school with resignation and despair. He had just managed to squeak through Beaton Junior High with poor grades and no understanding of how this frustrating experience would help him. He wasn't good at schoolwork and felt that the classes he had to sit through were a waste of time.

Lamar's father had left school after eighth grade to go to work. Although he did not make much money, he had a car and seemed to be getting along okay. Lamar's mother had left high school when she became pregnant and had never returned. Neither of Lamar's

Growing up in South Carolina (vintage 1940s), Marian Wright Edelman learned to counter the summer heat with a swim. African American children were not allowed in the public pool, so Marian and her friends did their summer swimming, diving, and fishing in the creek, despite the fact that it was polluted with hospital sewage. One of her friends decided that the bridge spanning the creek would be a good diving platform, but that decision turned out to be fatal: He broke his neck on impact. His death was one of several tragedies that taught Edelman early lessons on the deadly impact of race segregation. In recalling these tragedies, Edelman says: "You never, ever forget."[1]

Marian Wright Edelman's family provided a refuge from this racial hatred. Her father was a Baptist minister, her mother a devout Sunday schoolteacher, and both instilled a sense of service. Sharing a bed, a meal, or a pair of shoes with foster children or neighbors in need was a common event for Edelman and her four siblings. While public playgrounds were closed to black children, her parents made Shiloh Baptist Church a community resource center for black sports teams, Boys Scouts and Girl Scouts. Edelman learned that "[s]ervice is the rent we pay for living. It is the very purpose of life and not something you do in your spare time."[2]

During the 1960s, Edelman worked as a volunteer at the National Association for the Advancement of Colored People (NAACP), campaigning for passage of the Voting Rights Act as well as finding legal assistance for students jailed during sit-ins and demonstrations. As she sorted through requests for NAACP assistance from poor black citizens, Edelman realized that law could be a vehicle to social justice. She attended Yale University Law School and became the first black woman to pass the bar exam in Mississippi. Although she practiced civil rights law, Edelman' s work with poor children helped her to see that they were the most vulnerable and voiceless group in our society. Children "had no one to speak out on their behalf—no one to make sure that there were laws and gov-

ernment policies in place to protect them."[3] During the next four decades, Marian Wright Edelman became their voice.

Edelman founded the Children's Defense Fund (CDF) in 1973, with the mission to "Leave No Child Behind." The CDF works to ensure that every child has a Healthy Start, a Head Start, a Fair Start, a Safe Start, and a Moral Start in life. The CDF strives to protect all children—and particularly children of low-income and minority families—through research, community organization, federal and state government lobbying, and public education. Among those who worked for the CDF was a young Wellesley graduate named Hillary Rodham, who continued to advocate for children's rights later when she became the First Lady and then U.S. Senator from New York.

CDF also sponsors Freedom Schools that recruit college students to serve as mentors to over 12,000 students both after school and during the summer. Edelman understands the lasting influence mentors give students, and she has a message for all teachers:

> Teaching is a mission, not just a task or a job. I don't care how fancy the school, how low the student-teacher ratio (which I believe should be lower), how high the pay (which I think should be higher): If children don't feel respected by adults who respect themselves, and don't feel valued, then they lose and all of us lose. Make it a reality that all children, especially poor children, are taught how to read, write, and compute so they can have happy and healthy options in their future. We need to understand and be confident that each of us can make a difference by caring and acting in small as well as big ways."[4]

[1]Marian Wright Edelman, *The Measure of Our Success: A Letter to My Children and Yours* (Boston: Beacon Press, 1992), p. 8; [2]Ibid, p. 6; [3]Marian Wright Edelman, *Lanterns: A Memoir of Mentors* (Boston: Beacon Press, 1999), p. 28; [4]Ibid, p. 22.

REFLECTION

Surf the Children's Defense Fund website at www.childrensdefensefund.org and click on State Data. Compare the social problems and needs of children in your state with national averages. Which statistics surprised you? What responsibilities do you believe teachers have to ensure equal educational opportunity for children in poverty?

WRITE YOUR OWN *PROFILE IN EDUCATION:*
Click on *Profiles in Education,* write a *Profile in Education* about an educator, and post it on the Online Learning Center. Check out *Profiles in Education* submitted by other future teachers.

To learn more about Marian Wright Edelman, click on *Profiles in Education.*

parents thought school was critical, although both wanted Lamar to finish. But Lamar's patience was wearing thin. He wanted to end these long, boring days, get a job, and get a car. He'd had enough of school.

Lamar is a good candidate to join the nation's dropouts. Students indicate that they drop out of school for a variety of reasons: poor grades, teenage pregnancy, "school was not for me," "school was too dangerous," "couldn't get along with teachers," "didn't get into the desired program," and "was expelled or suspended."[56] Although the United States has made progress toward universal education, we still fall short of that goal. In 1950, just over half of 25 to 29-year-olds completed high school. The investments made in education during the 1970s bore fruit, and by the mid-1980s, high school completion rates had grown to over 86 percent. However, the rate has not improved since then.[57]

Today, roughly one out of every nine students does not graduate from high school. This represents not only a loss of human potential but also increased future costs in welfare, unemployment benefits, and potential criminal activity. Teachers can encourage youngsters to stay in school through one-on-one instruction, mentoring and tutoring, more relevant curricular materials, early intervention and counseling, and advocacy programs.[58]

Sexuality and Teenage Pregnancy

Who can blame today's adolescents for being confused about society's view of sexuality? They are bombarded with sexually suggestive advertising for clothes, drinks, sports, and cars. The media are filled with sexuality, both real-life and made-for-TV stories, yet parents and teachers rarely talk with (or listen to) kids. This puts schools in a difficult position, likely to offend one group or another and trying to walk the fine line between teaching and preaching.

Preaching morality while teaching sex education can be a dangerous mixture. Research indicates that U.S. teenagers receive the message that premarital sex is wrong yet the use of contraception at first intercourse has risen from 48 percent to 78 percent since 1980.[59]

Where are students getting their sex education? Teens rely on peer networks to explain sexuality and relationships. While two out of three public school districts require sex education, only 14 percent include both abstinence and contraception, and few reflect cultural and linguistic differences among students.[60] As one young woman said, "When you're in sex education class, they just tell you what goes on inside your body. They don't tell you what goes *on*."[61]

AIDS: HIV Comes to School

For many communities, decades of opposition to sex education were unceremoniously cast aside with the emergence of the medical nightmare AIDS. Sexually active children represent a major at-risk population for the disease, and sex education has become a prime weapon against the spread of the virus. In the early 1990s, the House Select Committee on Children, Youth, and Families estimated that forty thousand teens each year contract the HIV virus.[62] A decade of very public attention resulted in a decline in AIDS incidence and deaths in 1996. The largest diagnosed

When families are headed by young mothers, they are six times as likely to be in poverty.

- Almost 1 million teenage women (11 percent) of those aged 15–19 become pregnant each year.
- One in five sexually active teen women becomes pregnant.
- Fifty percent of adolescents who have a baby become pregnant again within two years.
- Teenage mothers and their babies are more likely to suffer medical complications and have higher mortality rates than mothers over 20.
- Teen mothers are much more likely to come from low-income families (83 percent).
- The children of adolescent mothers are at increased risk for being a teen parent themselves.
- While 20 percent of the recent decline in teen pregnancy is due to abstinence, 80 percent is due to more effective use of contraceptives.
- About one in five infants born to unmarried minors are fathered by men five or more years older than the mother.

SOURCE: Alan Guttmacher Institute, *Issues in Brief* (2001); reports from the National Center for Health Statistics; reports from the U.S. Bureau of the Census; Children's Defense Fund, *A Vision for America's Future* (Washington, DC: Children's Defense Fund, 1998); L. D. Lindberg et al., "Age Differences Between Minors Who Give Birth and Their Adult Partners," *Family Planning Perspectives*, 1997, 29(2): 61–66. www.agi-usa.org/pubs/fb_teen_sex.html; *"With One Voice: America's Adults and Teens Sound Off about Teen Pregnancy,"* National Campaign to Prevent Teen Pregnancy (2001). www.teenpregnancy.org/april2001.

REFLECTION

The National Campaign to Prevent Teen Pregnancy asked one thousand youth the primary reason for the decline in teen pregnancy over the last decade. Can you predict their top four answers? See how you did.

(Reflection answer: Worry about AIDS/STD (38 percent); More birth control available (24 percent); More attention to the issue (15 percent); More parental involvement (9 percent); Changing morals and values, fewer teens having sex, the improved economy and welfare reform combined for 14 percent.)

population with AIDS in 1998 was men who had sex with men. But, even in this group, AIDS incidence and death are on the decline. The greatest decline is evident in younger children, following efforts to reduce perinatal transmission for pregnant HIV-infected women and their children.[63]

Throughout the 1990s, AIDS-related sex education was an accepted part of some school programs, a controversial part of others, and something that was avoided in still other communities. To many, but not all Americans, the threat of this nearly always fatal disease was horrific enough to eliminate reservations concerning sex education programs in the schools.

Substance Abuse: Drinking, Drugs, and Smoking

"I know personally kids who drink whole bottles of liquor on the weekends by themselves."

"You won't see the drug culture here unless you know what to look for. You'll get a lot of parent and school denial, but the reputation of this school is 'cocaine heaven.'"

"On an average week, I gross over $2,000 dealing drugs at this school."

These statements from high school students add a personal dimension to official reports indicating that the United States has the highest rate of teenage drug use of any industrialized nation in the world. **Substance abuse** ranges from alcohol and

The widespread publicity surrounding Ryan White, a young AIDS victim who led a courageous fight to open school doors to young AIDS patients, did much to relieve the ignorance that surrounds this deadly disease.

The United States has the highest rate of teenage drug use of any industrialized nation in the world.

chewing tobacco to inhalants, cocaine and LSD. Sixty percent of high school students and 30 percent of middle schoolers say drugs are used, kept and sold in their schools.[64]

Alcohol abuse represents by far the most widespread form of substance abuse. In 2000, one-third of all high school seniors reported being drunk in the preceding month.[65] Justice Department figures show that alcohol or drug use is associated with more unplanned pregnancies, more sexually transmitted diseases, and more HIV infection than is any other single factor.[66] The more teenagers drink, the more likely they are to be involved in violent crime, such as murder, rape, or robbery, either as victim or perpetrator.

The year 2000 National Education Goal that pledged America's schools would be "safe, disciplined, and alcohol and drug-free" has now been deemed a complete failure. Among students who have: *ever* tried cigarettes, 85.7 percent, 2.1 million, are still smoking in the twelfth grade; *ever* been drunk, 83.3 percent, 2.1 million, are still getting drunk in twelfth grade; *ever* tried marijuana, 76.4 percent, 1.4 million, are still using it in twelfth grade.

SOURCE: Press Release: *Malignant Neglect: Substance Abuse and America's Schools*, 5 September 2001. www.casacolumbia.org/newsletter1457/newsletter_show.htm?doc_id=80623.

REFLECTION

Calling it *malignant neglect*, The Center for Addiction and Substance Abuse faults teachers, administrators, parents, communities, and students themselves for widespread substance abuse in schools. What steps could you take (as student, parent, teacher, or administrator) to keep young people from starting to smoke, drink, or use drugs?

Click on *In the News* for recent *In the News* stories. Submit your own *In the News* summary to share with your colleagues.

Substance abusers suffer significant school problems. Marijuana users are twice as likely as nonusers to average *D*s and *F*s. A Philadelphia study showed that four out of five dropouts were regular drug users. Unfortunately, many parents and educators are unaware of the extent of the problem. In an Emory University study, although 3 percent of parents said that their children had used marijuana in the past month, 28 percent of those children reported that they had actually taken the drug.[67] "It's normal denial and suburban American dream denial. This isn't supposed to happen here."[68]

Cigarette smoking provides a window on teen substance abuse. Consider the following:

- Teenagers who smoke are more likely to get poor grades, drink alcohol, fight, get drunk, and try marijuana than are nonsmokers.

- Teens who smoke hang out with friends after school, while nonsmokers are more apt to be involved in school sports and activities.

- Almost a third of teens who smoke report doing no homework, compared with 8 percent of their nonsmoking peers.

- Perceptions on smoke-free campuses vary greatly. While most teachers and administrators say their schools are smoke-free, most students do not agree.

- Although teens understand that smoking is bad for their health, nearly one-fourth admit they cannot quit because they are addicted. According to the Center for Disease Control, less than 5 percent of schools nationwide are implementing effective prevention programs.[69]

Youth Suicide

A closely knit New Jersey community across the Hudson River from Manhattan was viewed as a model town. The high school frequently won the state football championship, the police department won awards for its youth-assistance programs, and the town was known for the beauty of its parks and safety of its streets. On an early Wednesday morning in March, the citizens of Bergenfield woke up to discover that four of their teenagers had locked themselves in a garage, turned on a car engine, and left a note requesting that they be buried together. The group suicide brought the total of teen suicides in Bergenfield to eight that year.

In the past twenty-five years, while the general incidence of suicide has decreased, the rate for those between the ages of 15 and 24 has tripled. Suicide is the third most common cause of death among adolescents, and many health specialists suspect it is seriously underreported. Every day five or six adolescents (mostly males) will take their own lives. Particularly at risk are teens questioning their sexuality and girls who have been physically or sexually abused.[70]

What should teachers look for? Depression often precedes suicide attempts. Manifestations include persistent sadness, boredom or low energy, loss of interests in favorite pastimes, irritability, physical complaints and illness, serious changes in sleeping and eating, and school avoidance or poor performance.[71] Impulsivity, which accounts for about one-fourth of all adolescent suicides, is particularly difficult for adults to deal with, since it may cause students to commit suicide in response to their first bout with depression. To date, teachers and parents have not done well in preventing youth depression and suicide.

Gays, Lesbians, and Bisexuals: Our Invisible Students

When I was 11, I started smoking dope, drinking alcohol, and snorting speed every day to make me feel better and forget I was gay. I would party with friends but get more and more depressed as the night would go on. They would always make antigay remarks and harass gay men while I would just stand there. Late at night after they went home, I would go down to the river and dive in—hoping I would hit my head on a rock and drown.[72]

Fear and intolerance toward homosexuals, labeled **homophobia**, characterize the culture of secondary schools and cause depression and suicidal feelings. Some schools have a climate that is actively hostile: Students and even faculty make jokes about "faggots," "dykes," "gays," and "queers," and antigay graffiti cover bathroom walls and school desks. At times, verbal abuse turns physical, as in the case of a black male student in Ohio who was dragged into a bathroom stall. There eight boys called him a faggot, bashed his head against a toilet, and threatened to kill him. As punishment, the eight boys were given demerits for the incident.[73]

Because homophobia is so prevalent and so virulent, most lesbian and gay students go into hiding and try to pass as "straight." Afraid to let other students, faculty, or even their families know, too many become painfully isolated.

The National Education Association (NEA) adopted a resolution advocating equal opportunity for students and staff regardless of sexual orientation and encouraging schools to provide counseling by trained personnel. It developed training materials and workshops on "Affording Equal Opportunity to Gay and Lesbian Students Through Teaching and Counseling." School districts have also responded. San Diego, Cincinnati, and St. Paul have issued antiharassment measures and policies designed to protect homosexual students.[74] These are steps, but much more must be done.

STUDENT SEXUAL DIVERSITY GUIDELINES FOR TEACHERS

- Confront directly school incidents of antilesbian and antigay prejudice.

  Name it: "That is homophobic harassment (or an appropriate age-level alternative)."
  Claim it: "That is not okay in our room (or school) because it is disrespectful."
  Stop it: "It cannot happen again. If it does (state the consequences)."

- Accurately portray and openly acknowledge the roles and contributions of gay, lesbian, and bisexual people.
- Include gay, lesbian, and bisexual concerns in prevention programs (pregnancy, dropout, suicide).

If a student comes to you to discuss gay, lesbian, bisexual or transgendered concerns,

- Be aware of your own feelings. Avoid making negative judgments that may cause the student even more pain.
- Use the terms the student uses. Say "homosexual" if that is the term used, or "queer," "lesbian," or "bisexual" if the student chooses these terms.
- Respect confidentiality. Let the student know you appreciate his or her trust.
- Be aware that the student may be feeling grief and emotional pain.
- Remember that gay and bisexual male students are particularly in need of information concerning protection from AIDS.

SOURCE: Adapted from *Affording Equal Opportunity to Gay and Lesbian Students Through Teaching and Counseling* (Washington, DC: National Education Association, 2000); "When Kids Don't Have a Straight Answer," *NEA Today Online:* Health (March 2001), www.nea.org/neatoday/0103/health.html.

REFLECTION

It has been said that the most powerful contribution to prejudice is not made by the oppressor, but by those who apathetically stand by. Try to recall a time when you said or did nothing about a bigoted or homophobic remark. What could you say *next time* that would identify you as an educator-advocate for gay, lesbian, bisexual, and transgendered students?

Tension Point: Are Equity and Excellence Compatible?

When 6000 young people are killed every year with a gun, when 5000 young people commit suicide every year, when over a million young people run away from home every year, when almost half a million young people drop out of school every year, and when hundreds of thousands of young people get into drugs and alcohol and tobacco and just mess up their lives, can we truly say we are a child-centered society . . . ?

Richard Riley, former U.S. Secretary of Education
The Washington Post, July 23, 1998

While not denying the importance of meeting these pressing social needs, critics question whether this is a proper role for schools. If schools are dispensing social services, at what cost? Promoting cultural sensitivity and responding to social problems are investments not devoted to raising school standards and student achievement.

Equity proponents counter that, without equity, without attending to these basic social needs, America can never be a truly great nation. Without equity and social justice, excellence becomes a hollow goal.

YOU BE THE JUDGE
KEEP STUDENTS TOGETHER OR MIX THEM UP?

Teaching Kids in Segregated Settings . . .

BY GENDER, CAN FOCUS ON ACADEMIC NEEDS

Same gender classes help students focus on academics, not on each other. Girls can get extra encouragement in math and science; boys can get special assistance in reading and language arts.

BY COMMUNITY, PROMOTES RACIAL AND ETHNIC PRIDE

Let's eliminate the alienation caused by busing students out of their neighborhood. Students feel accepted and take pride in local schools, where they can study with friends, and learn from a curriculum that reflects and honors their heritage.

BY CIRCUMSTANCE, OFFERS PREGNANT MINORS A SAFE PLACE TO LEARN

Special facilities and separate programs can bring young women closer for needed encouragement, shielded from the judgment of their nonpregnant peers. And well-designed child care classes can prepare these women for parenthood.

BY NEED, OFFERS AN EDUCATIONAL HOME FOR THE HOMELESS

Special schools can help homeless students cope with their unique personal and academic circumstances. Being with homeless students protects them from comparisons and ridicule that might exist elsewhere.

Teaching Kids Together . . .

PROMOTES GENDER EQUALITY

Learning and succeeding together in the classroom prepares boys and girls to live and work together as adults. Equitable instruction and curriculum will teach students how to eliminate traditional gender barriers in society.

FOSTERS CULTURAL AND RACIAL UNDERSTANDING

We must not allow our nation to be fractured along racial, ethnic, and class lines. Integrating children of different backgrounds mirrors our ideal of a democratic society. Cross-cultural classrooms enrich the learning experience.

GIVES TEEN MOTHERS A REALISTIC SCHOOL EXPERIENCE

Pregnant teens deserve the genuine academic challenges of a regular school program. Modifications might be necessary in a physical education class; otherwise, pregnant teens should learn to participate on equal footing with their peers.

GIVES THE HOMELESS HOPE FOR THE FUTURE

Attending a regular school gives homeless students insight into more secure lifestyles. Clothing drives or free tickets to school events can help needy youngsters feel part of the school community.

YOU BE THE JUDGE

Do you believe equal educational opportunity is best achieved in separate or integrated classrooms? Is your position consistent or does it vary depending upon the identified group? Extend this *You Be the Judge* feature by developing the arguments for either integrating or separating two other groups discussed in this chapter (or identify new groups).

Are equity and excellence compatible? Should investments in equity be made, even at the possible cost of diverting resources from academic excellence? The basic question may be, Can education be excellent if it is not excellent for all?

SUMMARY

CHAPTER REVIEW

Go to the Online Learning Center to take a quiz, practice with key terms, and review key ideas from the chapter.

1. How do deficit, expectation, and cultural difference theory explain disparate academic performance among various racial, ethnic, and cultural groups?

   • Some people believe that being white has a number of very real, but often invisible, privileges. When it comes to school, however, most Americans believe that schools offer equitable educational opportunities to all children. Yet, both educators and the public agree that some groups perform well in school, and some do not.

   • Various reasons are offered for these academic gaps. Deficit theory argues that poor academic performance is a result of the mismatch between group values and school norms. Expectation theory asserts that teachers' lower expectations of some groups becomes a self-fulfilling prophecy. Cultural difference theory states that better understanding and communication between home life and school life can lead to academic success.

2. What major developments have marked the educational history of Native Americans, Hispanics, African Americans, Asian Americans/Pacific Islanders, and Arab Americans?

   • For centuries, the impact of white people on Native Americans has been one of territorial conquest and attempts to diminish the Indian culture, often through schooling.

   • Today, less than half of the 2 million Native Americans in this country live on reservations.

   • The education of African Americans during the colonial period was sometimes illegal, and, when schools were provided, they were inadequate and underfunded.

   • The doctrine of "separate but equal" *(Plessy v. Ferguson)* legalized segregated schools, but, in 1954 *(Brown v. Board of Education of Topeka),* "separate but equal" was declared unconstitutional. The Civil Rights Act of 1964 was passed in an effort to eliminate continuing discrimination and promote the desegregation of schools.

   • A second-generation of segregation now persists, due in large part to racially segregated neighborhoods. African American children are often assigned to special education programs and tracked into less challenging academic areas.

   • While there has been considerable improvement, African American students still have lower test scores and higher dropout rates than do white students.

   • There are more than 35 million Hispanics (or Latinos) living in the United States today. The nation's Latinos comprise several major groups, including Mexicans, Puerto Ricans, and Cubans. Hispanic immigration from Central America, including Nicaragua and El Salvador, is increasing.

   • Students from poverty-stricken countries must overcome psychological trauma, poverty, and language barriers to succeed in the United States. The Hispanic dropout statistics are even higher than those of African Americans.

   • Asian is a broad label assigned to several billion people from a score of nations. Asian Americans and Pacific Islanders, especially more recent immigrants from nations in Southeast Asia, must overcome trauma and adjust to a new culture and language, not unlike many Hispanics.

   • Other Asian Americans, such as the Chinese and Asian Indians, are stereotyped as model minorities, a label that often masks the impact of prejudice on these children.

   • Misunderstanding and intolerance have been all-too-common facts of life for three million Americans of Arab descent. Many Americans confuse Arabs and Moslems, mistaking Islam, a religion, with Arabs, a cultural group.

   • Although students of Arab heritage do well in American schools, teacher training, curricular revision, and a greater understanding of these cultural and religious issues are needed if equal educational opportunities are to become a reality for Arab Americans.

3. What educational barriers and breakthroughs have girls and women experienced?

- For much of this nation's history, females were denied access to schools. Once admitted they were often segregated into gender-restricted programs and careers.

- Today, researchers find subtle bias in classroom interactions, curriculum materials, and enrollment patterns. Some instructional areas, such as computer technology and vocational programs, remain gender segregated.

- Title IX of the 1972 Educational Amendments Act prohibits sex discrimination in schools that receive federal financial assistance. Progress toward gender equity is evident by increased female participation in athletics and improved test scores in math and science. Compliance with Title IX remains erratic.

4. What classroom strategies are appropriate for teaching culturally diverse learners?

- Teachers can create more equitable classrooms through a variety of instructional techniques: ensuring that seating and grouping patterns are not segregated by gender, race or language, varying learning activities, increasing wait-time, using space and eye contact in a culturally sensitive manner, and using materials to meet individual students needs and interests.

5. What impact do changing family patterns and economic issues have on children and schools?

- Nearly one in six U.S. children lives in poverty, a condition that frequently short-circuits their educational promise.

- The traditional family unit of the past has undergone a radical transformation. Divorce, remarriage, wage earning, parenting, and alternative relationships have restructured the family and the home-school connection.

- Latchkey children are those who are left home alone for a significant portion of the day. Latchkey children are found throughout society; the more educated the parent, the more likely there is a latchkey child at home. After-school programs attempt to provide a meaningful (and safe) alternative to being home alone.

- Passage of the 1987 McKinney Homeless Assistance Act, amended in 1990, was intended to lessen the impact of homelessness on Americans. This law protects the rights of children who have no permanent address to attend school and receive all necessary services and opportunities.

6. How can educators respond to social issues that place children at risk?

- Today, just over 86 percent of students complete high school. Poor students, urban students, and students of color are more likely to drop out than are others. Reasons for dropping out range from lack of motivation to teenage pregnancy.

- The mixed messages sent to students in our society have contributed to an alarmingly high rate of teenage pregnancy. Almost one in nine teenage girls becomes pregnant and many are destined for an early end to their educational careers, and ultimately poverty.

- Current school responses vary according to community norms. In some communities, sex education is a major emphasis; in others, it is minor or missing entirely.

- Fear of AIDS has served as a catalyst for establishing sex education programs, in hopes of reducing this deadly disease. The courts, contending that AIDS is a disability, do not allow schools to discriminate against students or teachers with HIV.

- Although substance abuse by teens has generally declined since the 1970s, reports in recent years suggest drug use (especially of alcohol) may again be on the rise. Statistics on the extent of the problem are difficult to quantify and interpret, but, clearly, substance abuse has a devastating impact on the education and health of those involved.

- While the general incidence of suicide has decreased, the youth rate has tripled in the last quarter century , and warning signs are difficult to detect.

- Gay, lesbian, and bisexual youth are more likely to commit suicide than are heterosexual youngsters.
- Guidelines for teachers include taking an active role in recognizing and confronting homophobia across the school culture.
- An ongoing debate exists over whether equity and excellence in education are compatible. Some claim that efforts for equity drain resources from educational programs and subvert academic excellence. We believe that education cannot be excellent unless it is excellent for all.

KEY TERMS AND PEOPLE

alternative families, 498

Brown v. Board of Education of Topeka, 479

Bureau of Indian Affairs (BIA) , 477

busing, 480

Civil Rights Act, 479

cultural difference theory, 475

de facto segregation, 479

de jure segregation, 479

deficit theory, 474

desegregation, 479

expectation theory, 474

Marian Wright Edelman, 502

homophobia, 507

Hopwood v. State of Texas, 480

internment camps, 487

interracial marriage, 498

latchkey (self-care) kids, 499

McKinney Homeless Assistance Act, 500

model minority, 485

Plessy v. Ferguson, 478

Schools More Separate: Consequences of a Decade of Resegregation, 480

second-generation segregation, 480

separate but equal, 478

Sequoyah, 477

sex discrimination, 492

sex-role stereotyping, 492

stepfamilies, 498

substance abuse, 504

Title IV, 479

Title VI, 479

Title IX, 492

DISCUSSION QUESTIONS AND ACTIVITIES

1. Select one of the groups discussed in this chapter for further reading and research. Analyze historical and contemporary educational developments that have affected this group, and discuss your findings with other members of your class.

2. Do research on a group not discussed in this chapter that faces discrimination. Discuss your findings with other members of your class.

3. Observe a classroom, noting how many times teachers call on girls and boys. Compare the amount of attention boys and girls get to their representation in the classroom. Do boys or girls get more than their fair share of teacher attention?

4. How do you react to the various issues raised in this chapter? On a separate sheet of paper complete the following sentences as honestly as you can. If you wish, share your responses with your classmates.

   - To me, the phrase *invisible race privilege* means . . .
   - A great example of expectation theory is . . .

- When I hear the stories about blatant racial discrimination in education, I . . .

- I think the most important thing educators can do to achieve equal educational opportunity for all students is to . . .

- If I were to teach in a school that in my opinion used culturally biased testing practices to track Spanish-speaking children into special education classes, I . . .

- If a boy were to bring a favorite doll to "Show and Tell" in my first-grade classroom and the other kids laughed at him, I . . .

- If there were no information about members of groups of color in the social studies book assigned for my class, I . . .

5. How do the following impact students?

- Poverty

- High divorce rates

- Single-parent families

- Alternative families

- Parental income

6. What can schools do to address each of the issues discussed in question #5?

7. What are some of the major barriers limiting the education of homeless children?

8. Research some school-based programs used to prevent students from dropping out or using drugs. What alternatives might you suggest?

9. Predict the hazards that a school might encounter if it were to implement a curriculum that includes sexuality, teenage pregnancy, and AIDS.

10. What can schools and society do to reduce teenage suicide?

11. Identify at least one teacher intervention for each of the following groups: latchkey kids, homelessness, dropouts, drug use, teenage pregnancy, carriers of HIV, gay and lesbian students.

12. Do you think equity and excellence in the field of education are compatible? Why or why not?

WEB-*TIVITIES*

1. Today's Students: Patterns of Diversity

2. Native American Education Today

3. Black Americans and Desegregation

4. Hidden America: Homeless Families

5. Children: At Promise or At Risk?

REEL TO REAL TEACHING

REMEMBER THE TITANS (2000)
Run Time: 114 minutes

Synopsis: A high school football coach and team find themselves fighting for stakes much higher than the State Championship when a 1971 court order forces three segregated high schools in Virginia to combine their student bodies and faculties.

GIRLFIGHT (2000)
Run Time: 110 minutes

Synopsis: A high school rite of passage story about a quick-tempered Latina who finds discipline, self-respect, and love in the most unlikely place—a boxing ring.

Reflection:

1. In *Remember the Titans,* Coach Boone defends his harsh training regimen to Coach Yoast: "I don't give a damn how sensitive these kids are, especially the young black kids. You ain't doing these kids a favor by patronizing them. You are crippling them, crippling them for life." How did you react to this statement? How is expectation theory reflected in Coach Boone's comment? Describe a coaching style that could serve as a metaphor for your chosen teaching style. Directed intensity and caring compassion are just two examples to get you started.

2. As Diana trained to box in *Girlfight,* a male gym member commented, "This equality crap has gone too far." What is your reaction to this statement? Are there boundaries that should not be broken, like females in a boxing ring? In 2001, Ashley Martin became the first woman to score in a NCAA Division I football game, kicking three extra points. Should women play football? What are your limits to racial and gender equality in athletics, classrooms, and careers? What's "too far?"

3. Even some great films contain exaggerated stereotypes. In *Remember the Titans,* Nikki turns down Cheryl's request to play because "I just did my nails." In *Girlfight,* Diana's father quipped, "Would it kill you to wear a skirt once in a while?" We collected at least ten other "over the top" comments. Which others come to your mind? Did these statements challenge or reinforce bias?

Follow-up Activity: In both films, high school students struggled for athletic opportunities. Race, ethnicity, and gender struggles continue to create barriers across the curriculum and students are disadvantaged by many additional factors discussed in the chapter. Is there an opportunity for you to struggle through a barrier in your world? Attend an athletic event, academic lecture or committee meeting that is outside your typical pattern or comfort zone. Are you the only *male or female* in the stands, the only *nonmajor* in the hall, the only *straight* person in the room? Are you ready to teach students that are like and unlike you? What's your evidence?

How do you rate these films? Click on *Reel to Real Teaching* to submit your review of these or another education-related film, and read reviews submitted by others.

FOR FURTHER READING

Asian-American Education: Prospects and Challenges, by Clara Park and Marilyn MeiYing Chi (1999). Written for educators of all grade levels, this book details the educational and sociocultural needs of Cambodian, Chinese, Filipino, Hmong, Japanese, Korean, and Vietnamese American students in U.S. public schools.

Because of the Kids: Facing Racial and Cultural Differences in Schools, by Jennifer Obidah and Karen Manheim Teel (2001). Presents the difficulties and importance of collaborations between teachers from different racial and cultural backgrounds, as well as insights into how race and culture evolve in teacher-student interactions.

Boys, Girls, and Achievement: Addressing Classroom Issues, by Becky Francis (2000). Explores how adolescents construct their gender identities, the relationship between achievement and gender, and how both teachers and students experience gender bias in schools.

Brown v. Board of Education: A Civil Rights Milestone and Its Troubled Legacy, by James T. Patterson (2001). Details the racial segregation in schools that prompted this legal landmark, the debates surrounding the Supreme Court's decision, and the unfinished business of truly democratizing our educational system.

Class Dismissed: A Year in the Life of an African American High School, A Glimpse into the Heart of a Nation, by Meredith Maran (2001). The seniors of Berkeley High are white, black, Latino, Asian, and multiracial children of judges and carpenters, software consultants and garbage collectors, housewives and housekeepers. Some are Harvard bound; others are illiterate. The lives of three Berkeley High students are chronicled, capturing their success and struggles.

Gay Parents/Straight Schools: Building Communication and Trust, by Virginia Casper and Steven Schultz (1999). Openly addresses the specific educational realities and needs of lesbian- and gay-headed families. Explores why gayness is often perceived as a threat, especially to the education of young children, when it has such potential to enrich the worldviews of both children and adults.

Ordinary Resurrections: Children in the Years of Hope, by Jonathan Kozol (2001). Kozol offers a hopeful vision of life in the South Bronx. Poverty and depravation are viewed through the eyes of the children who live there, and an admiring portrait is painted of the teachers, priests, parents, and grandparents who strive against all odds to ensure that these children grow up with a strong sense of hope and pride.

The Public Assault on America's Children: Poverty, Violence, and Juvenile Injustice by Valerie Polakow (2001). Through personal narratives and national statistics, the violence, educational neglect, poverty and social disregard that shape the lives of poor children are detailed.

We Can't Teach What We Don't Know: White Teachers, Multiracial Schools, by Gary Howard (1999). From his twenty-five years of experience as a multicultural educator, the author looks into the mirror of his own racial identity to discover what it means to be a culturally competent white teacher in racially diverse schools.

13 Technology in Education

FOCUS QUESTIONS

1. Has technology changed schools?
2. How does television affect children?
3. Why is computer technology difficult to implement in schools?
4. How can teachers effectively use computers and the Internet?
5. In what ways does global education refocus the curriculum?
6. How is teaching redefined in the virtual high school?
7. Does technology exacerbate racial, class, geographic, and gender divisions?

WHAT DO YOU THINK? How Tech-Savvy Are You? Take this quiz to see how much you know (and don't know).

CHAPTER PREVIEW

CHAPTER FOCUS
This chapter explores how technology has previously, and is currently, modifying classroom life. We review the impact on schools, our teaching procedures and the way we are digitally divided. Whether or not it revolutionizes education, technology is likely to play a role in the lives of your students and tomorrow's teachers. For a chapter outline, see the IM.

In an earlier time, before there were factories, there were cottage industries. People manufactured products, not as a group of workers in a central place but individually, in their houses. Some believe that schools may be retracing these steps—in reverse. Today's factorylike schools may soon be replaced by children learning in their homes. "Cottage schools" may be created as technology brings the teacher, the curriculum, and the library onto our home computer screens. Rather than taking the yellow school bus to a large school building, students are now traveling to school on the Internet.

The Internet can transport students around the world (through virtual field trips) or instantly and inexpensively add millions of books and articles to school libraries. Simulations can bring realism into a classroom, personal tutors can patiently diagnose learning needs, and adaptive technology can help special needs students succeed in school. But not everyone is enamoured with the new technology. Although technological innovation is an attractive, popular (and often expensive) aspect of American culture, history is filled with unmet predictions of technological advances—radio, television, and teaching machines—making schools obsolete. Will computers and technology make an important difference in education or will tomorrow's schools look remarkably similar to schools you attended as a child? The future, if nothing else, is unpredictable. Certainly, the information age has not included everyone. Poorer students and nations, women and non-English speakers have been left behind.

Technology raises other serious concerns for teachers, including the need to monitor inappropriate Internet material and to avoid the health risks associated with computer use. While these pitfalls are real, the potential of technology is also real but must be considered within the context of what we know about effective teaching. In this chapter, we explore how technology can be used with multiple intelligences, problem-based and cooperative learning, and direct and deep teaching. Whether or not it revolutionizes education, technology is likely to play a role in your classroom. We will explore how technology is currently modifying classroom life and how it may impact your teaching.

The Technology Revolution

In the twentieth century, education was forever changed. Human beings serving as teachers, the core of schooling for centuries if not millennia, were made technologically obsolete. The new invention was used at home and then in the more affluent schools. Eventually, all schools were connected. Slowly but surely, the classroom teacher was replaced. These new machines took students where they had never been before, did things no human could do, and shared an unlimited reservoir of information. Clearly, this technological breakthrough had potential to teach more effectively at a far lower cost than human teachers. Predictions varied from the replacement of all teachers to the replacement of most teachers. Some even predicted the replacement of schools themselves.

Sound familiar? While today's computer revolution has sparked these sorts of predictions, the machine described above is not a computer. These predictions were made in the 1950s about television. The popular perception back then was that educational television would reshape the classroom. If predictions about classroom innovations were exaggerated, predictions about television's impact on America were not. Television has reshaped America's cultural landscape.

Many of today's homes have multiple television sets, tied into satellite dishes, antennae, and cables, pulling hundreds of stations into our lives for an average of six hours a day. Some families turn on television sets in the morning and turn them off in the evening, imitating the waking and sleeping of another family member. Television has reduced our time for sleep, social gatherings, leisure activities, and even conversations with each other. By the time the average student has reached 18 years of age, he or she will have attended eleven thousand hours of school—and watched fifteen thousand hours of television. To ignore the impact of this medium is to ignore a major educational influence on children.

Television is not only a force; it is also a target. Television has been blamed for an array of crises and behavior problems, from a lack of school discipline to student passivity, from a decline in standardized test scores to an increase in family tensions and violence. It is unlikely that television, or any single factor, is responsible for all of society's ills. On the other hand, television does present a bizarre and disturbing view of the world. By the time the average child reaches age 15, he or she will have seen thirteen thousand murders on television, and television violence can influence behavior. Longitudinal data collected on television viewing and violence since 1960 present overwhelming evidence that higher levels of viewing violence on television correlate with increased aggressive behavior, in both children and adults.[1]

Television, our national storyteller, presents an image that is not only violent but distorted.[2] If television programs are to be believed, we are a nation destined for extinction. Less than 1 percent of television characters have children under 6. This is

Four sixth-grade girls attacked their teacher in a Brooklyn classroom after she refused to let them watch the *Jerry Springer Show*.

SOURCE: *New York Daily News*, May 30, 1998.

REFLECTION

What rules or guidelines might you create concerning television use in your classroom?

Click on *In the News* for recent *In the News* stories. Submit your own *In the News* summary to share with your colleagues.

surprising, because, according to TV plot lines, caring for children is a snap. In almost half of the television families with young children, child care concerns are never mentioned, yet children are magically cared for anyway. Although two-thirds of the nation's mothers work for pay, only one-third of television's mothers do. America's population is 51 percent female, but not on television, where some calamity has evidently reduced females to less than half the population.

Family life is not the only subject suitable for television "make-overs," as ethnicity and race are jumbled as well. In televisionland, Asian Americans are servants, villains, detectives, and karate experts. Native Americans are presented without tribal distinctions and are often characterized as lazy, alcoholic, and humorless. African American criminals are a mainstay of many police and adventure shows, offset by a growing number of African American police officers. Characters in children's afterschool programs are overwhelmingly white. It is not surprising, therefore, that research indicates that television viewers have a garbled world view, overestimating the percentage of the world population that is white and wealthy and underestimating the number of Americans living in poverty.

A distorted world scene is only part of the cost paid by the television audience; unregulated viewing robs children of both play and study time while teaching some abhorrent attitudes and behaviors. According to studies in the 1990s by the American Psychological Association and by Stanford University, television increases prejudice, obesity, aggressive behavior, and even drinking. For high school students, each hour of daily television watching corresponds to a 9 percent greater risk of alcohol consumption during the following 18 months. If music videos are watched, the drinking risk rises 31 percent.[3]

Children are more susceptible to, less knowledgeable about, and more naïve about the techniques and products promoted on television than are adults. Bombarded by twenty thousand TV commercials a year, children often have trouble distinguishing advertisements from the programs themselves.[4]

Some believe that the case against television may be both too convenient and overstated. Researchers Daniel Anderson and Patricia Collins found that television's impact depends greatly on who is watching and their general viewing habits, and that many of the bad practices and negative behaviors promoted by television can be prevented by attentive adults. [5] According to the American Psychological Association, when teachers and parents regulate television viewing, children improve their vocabulary, cognitive, and social skills.[6]

At its best, television can promote constructive values and teach useful skills and information. The Children's Television Workshop (CTW), for example, developed *Sesame Street*. To capture children's attention and promote early learning skills, **educational television programming** uses brief, engaging episodes, a lesson learned from commercials. Research indicates that viewing *Sesame Street* increases children's verbal IQ test scores, creates more positive attitudes toward school, and promotes better performance in the first grade.[7] Mister Rogers' Neighborhood viewers have greater persistence and more positive interpersonal realationships. While not everyone is a fan of these shows, research suggests that well-crafted television programs can result in greater educational achievement.

Television is now a part of school life as well. Cable television stations, including A&E, C-Span, CNN, The History Channel, Bravo, The Learning Channel, and The Discovery Channel, join noncable Public Broadcasting to bring high-quality movies and plays, exciting biographies, historical re-enactments, and breaking news stories directly into the curriculum. Monthly television guides written specifically for teachers alert them to upcoming programs of special educational interest. The growing number of videotapes and videodiscs offers teachers a library of rich television resources. Advocates point out that television can be a valuable learning resource, a real asset to classroom instruction. Critics charge that watching television is an unproductive use of class time, an activity that at best should be used as an instructional supplement, to be viewed at home or in the school's media resource room.

Channel One takes the controversy over television in schools to another level. *Channel One* is piped into thousands of high schools and junior high schools across the nation by Whittle Communications. Participating schools receive several tangible benefits: programming, television monitors, and a satellite dish are provided at no charge. When all are in place, students get to watch ten minutes of news each day. And the cost? The children must also watch two minutes of commercials with each newscast. Studies suggest that students who watch *Channel One* do slightly better on a current events test than do their nonviewing counterparts. Many students and teachers in *Channel One* schools report that they are satisfied with the program.[8]

Many researchers and educators are less pleased with *Channel One*, arguing that schools are not the place to be selling things to children. They estimate that *Channel One* costs the public almost two billion dollars a year, while the *Channel One* commercials alone cost students over 300 million dollars of lost instructional time, while offering content of questionable educational value. [9]

Satellites and cables have transformed television into a global phenomenon while also creating the information highway for computers to travel. Like television half a century earlier, computers are today's technological wonder predicted to change schools forever. Television and computers are not unique in this regard. Consider the following soothsayers:

"The motion picture is destined to revolutionize our educational system, and . . . in a few years it will supplant largely, if not entirely, the use of textbooks."

Thomas Edison

"The time may come when a portable radio receiver will be as common in the classroom as is a blackboard."

William Levenson, director of Cleveland Public School's radio station

"With the help of teaching machines and programmed instruction, students can learn twice as much in the same time and with the same effort as in a standard classroom."

B. F. Skinner[10]

Computer technology is only the most recent milestone along a path that has witnessed many innovations, including the chalkboard. With the introduction of the chalkboard, teachers wondered, Could they learn to use this new chalk technology efficiently and how would this fresh innovation affect the curriculum? As is common with novel technologies, chalkboards first collected dust as they went unused in classrooms. Over time, instruction manuals and teacher training programs gave teachers the practical advice and confidence to move the chalkboard to center stage in the teaching-learning process. Similar histories surround duplicating machines, the overhead projector, videotapes, television, and foreign language labs. Technological change includes even the modest highlighter that you use to underline the scintillating sentences and important information in this text. But highlighters get little attention, while computers are all the rage.

It is helpful to remember that chalkboards, highlighters, and silicon chips are all part of ongoing technological change. Given the number of technological advances, it is reasonable to ask why today's schools look so remarkably similar to the schools of a century ago. Why has technology had such a modest impact on education? Will computers be the technological breakthrough, the magic bullet that finally revolutionizes education? The next sections, while skillfully sidestepping this question, attempt to capture some of the excitement, controversy, and captivating applications surrounding computers in the classroom.

Schools.com

Bringing schools into the computer age has been expensive. Recognizing the sizable costs required to bring computer technology to students, Congress passed the Telecommunications Reform Act (1996), establishing a discounted school cost, or

Technological breakthroughs in satellite communications and increasing international trade suggest that global education will become a reality in the years ahead.

E-Rate (education rate), for using the Internet and access increased dramatically (see Figure 13.1). Although very few schools were online during the 1980s, according to the National Center for Education Statistics (NCES), virtually all schools were online by 2000. Wiring schools has proved to be just one of many major costs: hardware and software purchases were at the center of school budget debates for most of the 1990s.

While keeping schools flush with the latest technologies has been a monumental challenge, plugging in teachers has been no less daunting. While educational technology advocates encourage teachers to move from the "sage on the stage" to the "guide on the side," teachers initially were slow to apply for cyber-citizenship.[11] Teachers can teach effectively, even inspirationally, without computers. Long-time teachers unfamiliar with incorporating computer technology into their lessons can be wary of the investment of time and effort needed to become computer literate— and dismayed to realize that many students come to school far more tech savvy than their teachers. But as the technological revolution gains momentum, teachers will be expected to keep pace.

Each state and many school districts have technology plans that include standards for students and training and exams required of teachers. You should check with your individual state to see if you are up to speed, technologically speaking. As one example, to renew a teaching license in Virginia, you must be able to develop Web pages and create four lessons that integrate technology.[12]

The different attitudes and skills that teachers bring to using computers can make schoolwide implementation of new technology a challenge. Let's see how these concerns emerge in a fictitious faculty meeting, as principal Whyerd greets his staff:

PRINCIPAL WHYERD: Welcome back, although maybe welcome forward would be a better greeting. It's our first time to be together as the faculty of Bill Gates Middle School. With the new name and our new building, we have really opened up the latest window [he waits for a little laughter] on technology in education.

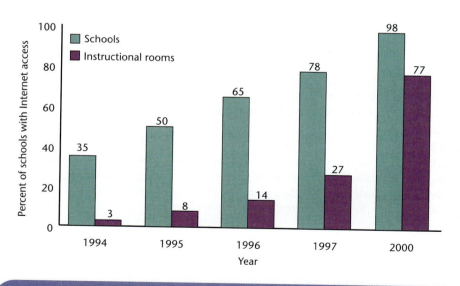

FIGURE 13.1
Going online. The percentage of public schools and classrooms with access to the Internet has been rising quickly, according to surveys of a nationally representative sample of schools between 1994 and 2000.

SOURCE: *Internet Access in Public Schools*, National Center for Education Statistics, U.S. Department of Education, 2001.

REFLECTION

Why have American schools responded so rapidly to the Internet? Has your schooling been influenced by this technology?

We have a spectacular computer lab; in every classroom, we have three online computers, video monitors, and we've hired a full-time technology resource instructor. Have you all met Pat Blizzard? [Pat stands confidently]. Okay? We also got the grant for the video production lab with computer hookups for editing and enhancement, so the project-based learning activities at the core of the social science program should really take off. Let's see . . . our Tech Task Force, eleven of you, from six departments, took advantage of the T3 (that's Teacher Tech Training) at the university. Anyone want to give us some quick feedback about those five days? Rafaela?

[As many eyes move to Rafaela Nueva, a few minds wander elsewhere.]

MR. POKEE: [with a slight eye roll] *Here we go again. If it's not one fad, it's another. I've been at this for years, and I can't fit one more thing on my plate. I don't have a computer at home, and I don't see why having one here is supposed to matter to me. Sure, if the kids want to use it, in their free time, to type—excuse me!—word process their papers, that's fine. But I am not about to waste another series of Saturdays on workshops that have nothing to do with my teaching style, my courses, and my students. My kids aren't sure which is bigger, our sun or our moon, but I suppose playing computer games will be more fun than learning.*

MS. HOPALONG: *Okay, okay, I've got it. We have all this new equipment and the kids probably know how to use it better than I do. At home my own kids taught me to do overheads for lessons and, now, if I don't get a handle on this Internet stuff, my students will be using the Web for who knows what. My daughters just laughed when I asked, "Where exactly is the Web?" (But I recognize that laugh. I'm not really sure they know.) When they hooked me into that chat room of teachers last night, it was weird but kind of fun. People were talking about tricks to learn students' names at the beginning of school. I got two good ideas that I'll try next week. Glad I learned how to type as a teenager. At least I could keep up with the conversation. Is that what they call it . . . conversation?*

MS. READDI: *This is so amazing. I'm student teaching and I'm totally nervous about the job. But these people are totally nervous about computers! The tech part is so easy! Even my college had what they've just purchased around here. I'll never forget my science methods course. We tested water samples from schools all over the country through a website. Most of my profs were using PowerPoint presentations when I started as an undergrad. Our dorm rooms were online . . . we used to see how much of a paper we could write without going to the library. Taking that Ed Tech course junior year may have been my best move. The faculty here see me as a resource.*

MR. APPLETOSS: *Funny how so many of the teachers are spooked by computers. I've always liked technology. Being the AV guy gave me a step up. From the stage crew in elementary school to the "AV Squad" in middle school, I have always been at home with machines. For the past eight years, teachers have come to me to solve their computer problems. Heck, I had my first computer when they were called by names, not numbers . . .*

MRS. GUDBRAKE: *I suspect it's going to be the same old, same old . . . but my kids lose, because they are the Title I pull-out crowd. Our rich kids, especially the boys, already have better equipment at home than we have in the "new" tech lab. They're using it for reports, term papers, college applications even their own Web pages. They've got access, opportunity, skills, equipment, summer computer camps, and the computer club. Too many of my Title I students have never touched a mouse, except when they try to corner one at home.*

While this faculty meeting reflects typical teacher attitudes toward technological change, it is atypical in at least one respect: In the scenario, funding and training appear readily available; in real life, this is not the case. More than four of every five computer dollars are spent on hardware and software, and less than one dollar on staff development.[13] The National Education Association (NEA) recommends beefing up the amount spent on training (more than doubling its share in technology spending, to 40 percent), and offers training and workshops across the nation (see www.nea.org/cet/indexeducator.html for technological strategies and resources for teachers). While university courses and school sponsored training programs abound, many teachers are most comfortable learning how to integrate technology in the classroom from other teachers. Then there are students, who are often far more skilled than their teachers. In a Colorado program, fourth- and fifth-grade students serve as technology mentors for teachers.[14] The average American student spends more than twice as much time on the computer at home than the ones at school, and has a home computer of higher quality than the one at school. One out of every five teenagers has a personal Web page.[15] (See Figure 13.2.)

Teachers approach technology with varying levels of confidence. Some are technological pathfinders, taking to computers with skill and excitement. Others adapt slowly, but with support and training, they do eventually adapt. Still others suffer from **technophobia**, an anxiety that renders all mechanical things foreign, alien, and frightening. Even answering machines and VCRs intimidate technophobes, who some authors are described by as digitally challenged.[16]

The Apple Classrooms of Tomorrow (ACOT) project followed teachers over several years as they learned to use computers and software. The researchers identified five stages of "instructional evolution" as shown in Figure 13.3[17]

As you sort out which of these stages might best describe your place in the cyber classroom, some perspective might be in order. One reason why so many teachers, especially older teachers, have been slow to take to the cyber classroom could be the long and unhappy history of hyped educational breakthroughs, breakthroughs that

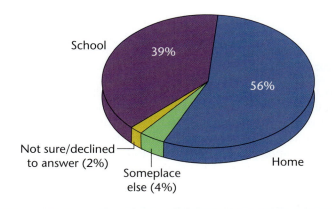

FIGURE 13.2
Where students learn about technology.

NOTE: Percentages do not add up to 100 because of rounding.

SOURCE: *Education Week*/MDR/Harris Interactive Poll of Students and Technology, 2001.

REFLECTION

Where have you learned the most about computers? How might economic class, culture, race, and gender influence student responses?

FIGURE 13.3
Five stages of instructional evoluation.

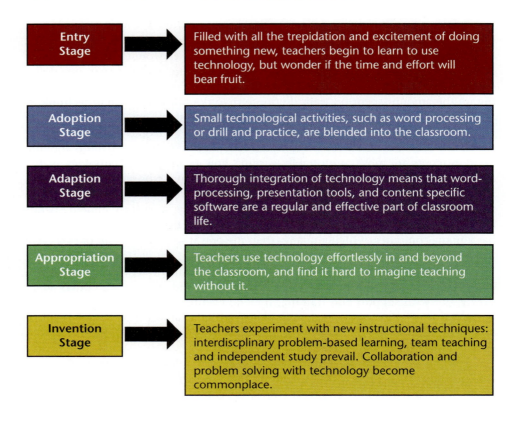

Entry Stage	→	Filled with all the trepidation and excitement of doing something new, teachers begin to learn to use technology, but wonder if the time and effort will bear fruit.
Adoption Stage	→	Small technological activities, such as word processing or drill and practice, are blended into the classroom.
Adaption Stage	→	Thorough integration of technology means that word-processing, presentation tools, and content specific software are a regular and effective part of classroom life.
Appropriation Stage	→	Teachers use technology effortlessly in and beyond the classroom, and find it hard to imagine teaching without it.
Invention Stage	→	Teachers experiment with new instructional techniques: interdiscplinary problem-based learning, team teaching and independent study prevail. Collaboration and problem solving with technology become commonplace.

delivered far less than promised. Television, open space classrooms, and teaching machines were all expected to revolutionize teaching in their day. None did. The jury is still out on the educational effectiveness or merit of computers and the Internet. People have invested far more energy and resources in placing computers in classrooms than in figuring out if all these computers will be worth the effort. And some teachers are sitting on the sidelines, waiting to see if this latest innovation will really make a difference.

It's the Teaching, Not the Technology

Perspective is too often lost in the glitz surrounding exciting new technologies. "New" can be exhilarating; "new" can also disappoint. Software developer and educator George Brackett reminds us, "Technologies do not change schools in any sense worth talking about. Thoughtful, caring, capable people change schools, sometimes with the help of technology, sometimes not, and sometimes even despite it. Too often we focus on the technology rather than the reform."[18]

Technology should be seen as a teacher's tool, and not the other way around. The first step is deciding how best to use that tool.[19] Here are some of the typical reasons educators give for using computers in school:

- *Increase basic skills* in math, reading and writing, as well as content areas, through sample quizzes, drill-and-practice, and additional course-related information. This reason becomes particularly attractive in this time of standardized testing.

- *Motivate students* through multimedia materials that capture their interest.
- *Promote higher order thinking* by introducing simulations, problem-based learning, Internet research, collaborative work, and student authoring programs.
- *Increase academic resources* by bringing the unlimited written and visual assets of the Internet into local schools.
- *Increase responsiveness to different learning styles* including special needs children, or students for whom the typical classroom culture means academic and/or social distress.
- *Improve workplace preparation* as students learn keyboarding skills, software applications, and technological operations common to future employment.
- *Save work for teachers* by creating a class Web page. A great deal of administrative time can be saved: Homework assignments, worksheets, notes, and exam dates can be posted on the Web page, and parent communication accomplished through e-mail. In fact, grading software can track attendance, average grades, and chart the results while even more cutting-edge programs use artificial intelligence, such as the Intelligent Essay Assessor (IEA), to grade essays.
- *Strengthen teacher performance* by adding resources, such as a PowerPoint presentation or a video clip, to create more dramatic and effective teacher presentations.
- *Modernize the school culture* by reshaping American education for the twenty-first century, moving beyond pencil and paper, chalk and chalkboards, into instant access to the world's digital resources.

Typically, computers have been used for drill and practice, simple programming, and educational games.

INTERACTIVE ACTIVITY
USING TECHNOLOGY IN EDUCATION. See examples of how technology is used in the classroom.

Goals for using technology vary, as does the effectiveness of technology as used in schools. The following descriptions offer specific examples of how technology can enhance effective teaching strategies (many effective strategies were discussed in Chapter 3). Since technology can also short-circuit learning, we note potential pitfalls as well.

MULTIPLE INTELLIGENCES Technologies open a wide door to Howard Gardner's world of multiple intelligences. For instance, authoring tools such as PowerPoint, Netscape Composer, TimeLiner, and Kid Pix Studio, enable students to create presentations and projects that incorporate text, animation, graphics, video, and sound, integrating several intelligence areas. The computer allows students to compose music, even if they are unable to read a note. In science and art classrooms, computer modeling programs teach and enhance spatial learning. A physical education or dance teacher could improve kinesthetic and visual learning through digital video recordings of student motion, enabling careful analysis of movement techniques. Gardner

WHAT IS THE INTERNET?

The **Internet** is the name given to the network of computers all over the world that are linked not only to each other but to a massive amount of information on an endless array of topics contained on many of those computers.

WHAT WILL I NEED TO GET CONNECTED?

For teachers, the key is learning how to access, view, and use this information, to broaden the classroom to include the resources provided by museums, libraries, news sources, and media outlets. The easiest way to access the Internet is through the **World Wide Web** (WWW). In order to see the Web, your computer needs an Internet connection, such as a modem, and Web browser software. Browser software tells the computer how to find and display WWW pages.

E-MAIL

One of the first Internet features was electronic mail (**e-mail** for short). As the name suggests, e-mail is similar to traditional mail service (haughtily called "snail mail" by Internet users) but usually takes just seconds or minutes to be delivered. One of the most significant advantages of e-mail (and many other Internet tools) is that it is basically free. Another benefit is that, unlike your postal address, which is tied to a fixed location, on the Internet your address "follows you." No matter where you are in the world, as long as you can find a client computer and access the Internet, you can receive or send mail.

THE WORLD WIDE WEB

Whenever you see an address that starts with "www" or "http://" (they often are advertised on television or radio and in newspapers or magazines) you are seeing a location on the World Wide Web.

Perhaps the most educationally exciting use for the WWW is the opportunity it affords students to connect with other users around the world. Students can write their own homepages that connect the outside world with their classrooms. Examples of such projects include:

- Students can create surveys for Internet users around the world to answer through a hyperlink connected to a class e-mail address.
- An ESL class might create a homepage celebrating each of their respective cultures, including links to homepages in their own countries.
- A reading and writing class could build a creative writing homepage filled with student work.
- Foreign language students can converse with native speakers on other continents by e-mail or by using advanced Internet tools that allow for the transmission of video and sound through the computers. Conversely, your class can help others touch up on their English.
- Students can participate in an online science fair, presenting science projects using text and graphics.
- Electronic student publications—school yearbooks, newspapers, and literary magazines—can be made accessible to the rest of the world.
- Students interested in science can browse pictures uploaded by NASA, along with resources from almost every major science or health organization.

REFLECTION

To some, this primer is "old news"; to others, it finally brings meaning to mysterious words and letters. Where are you on this continuum? Are there still words and letters that puzzle? Use our text website (www.mcgraw-hill.com/sadker) to see if others can answer your question.

NOTE: The primer on the Internet was written by Paul Degnan and was updated by Sara Kindler, both graduates of the School of Education at American University.

suggests still another use: "If, for example, we want students to be civil to one another, we need to develop their interpersonal skills. This could be done by recording tense interactions on video and having students choose the best human(e) means of reducing the tension; by involving students in chat rooms or discussion forums that include opportunities for helpfulness or deceit; or by creating cartoon simulations or virtual reality scenarios of human dilemmas where the student has options to interact in different ways."[20] While Howard Gardner is impressed with the potential marriage of technology with his multiple intelligences approach, he has also voiced concern about teachers who get enamored with the technological wizardry, and lose sight of the educational goal.

PROBLEM-BASED LEARNING David Williamson Schaffer, a lecturer at the Harvard Graduate School of Education, points out that the current information age brings us back to John Dewey. Thanks to technology, teachers can now guide students in real-world problem solving, often through collaborations with government or business.[21] The federally funded Challenge 2000 Multimedia Project has assisted many teachers in creating successful problem-based learning (PBL) experiences. For example, in Belmont, California, elementary school students produced a multimedia presentation that documented the 150-year history of their town. The students used HyperStudio, a student-authoring tool, to create an interactive history with video clips, digital pictures, and animated photographs. The students interviewed and videotaped members of the community, and conferred with the curator of a local museum. The "Belmont Then and Now Project" was not just a skill-building effort, for ultimately it taught the community and visitors about the area's history, and became an exhibit in the Belmont Historical Society.[22] (See also pblmm.k12.ca.us.)

The U.S. FIRST Robotics competition offers another example of problem-based learning. Nationally, hundreds of schools compete to create robots that perform tasks such as picking up balls and placing them in a trough. Upon entering the contest, each school receives a kit, which contains the control system, motors, and a number of other components. The students work together on building the robot for a period of six weeks, sacrificing many hours after school and weekends. (Much time is invested beforehand in the classroom preparing for the competition as well.) Students do the bulk of the planning and constructing themselves, but teachers and outside engineers provide guidance. (For a look at one of these projects, check out the entry of Montgomery Blair High School in Silver Spring, Maryland, at www.mbhs.edu/activities/robotics.)

Teachers need to be concerned about hazards associated with problem-based learning. Whenever students are involved with the real world, inappropriate comments or behaviors can be amplified and cause problems for students, teachers, and the school. Moreover, collaboration with private companies raises the specter of inappropriate commercialism and improper business influence in education. Both dangers call for careful planning and constant monitoring when using problem-based learning.

COOPERATIVE LEARNING AND SCAFFOLDING Educators get concerned when technology isolates and alienates students. Several software products are specifically designed to encourage student cooperation. "Knowledge Forum" is a website that promotes cooperative learning and guides individuals to deeper levels of thought. Participants share information on the Internet, consider questions and ideas, and work together to solve problems. For example, students who are trying to develop a theory enter information in appropriate stages of the Theory Building feature: "My Theory, I Need to Understand, New Information, This Theory Cannot Explain, Much Better Theory, Putting Our Knowledge Together." Students are able to comment on each other's findings and connect ideas graphically. (For more information, visit www.knowledgeforum.com.) As in any cooperative or independent learning activities, effective teachers monitor student work and interactions to insure that they are making progress and working well with one another.

MASTERY LEARNING Many software products and websites take advantage of the good fit between computer technology and the goal of mastery learning. Working at their own pace, students can master concepts about Newtonian mechanics (Thinker-Tools software) or develop mathematical skills (see www.renlearn.com/am). When mastery learning software is matched with traditional in-class learning, the result is called an **integrated learning system (ILS).** In Metrotech High School in Phoenix, Arizona, students attend classes to prepare for careers in areas as disparate as auto mechanics and television production, but they use software outside of class to refine their math and reading skills. The software diagnoses their levels of academic proficiency and then offers individualized programs designed to improve students' academic skills—all outside of class time, yet critical for in-class progress and success. Teachers need to carefully monitor all aspects of the ILS to verify that the program meets students' individual needs and that appropriate progress is being made, and to supply additional instruction as needed.

WAIT TIME AND TEACHER FEEDBACK The sometimes hectic pace of classroom interaction can make it difficult for teachers to patiently wait and offer each student specific and helpful suggestions. With technology, patience and precise reactions are easier to come by. The T-I Navigator, for example, enables each student to communicate instantly with the teacher through an individual wireless terminal. The teacher can ask a question and each student takes the time needed to punch in a private response. Students instantly learn whether their answers are correct, and teachers can adjust instruction accordingly. The T-I Navigator ensures that each student has time to respond, and that each student does in fact respond. Classroom interaction becomes both more thoughtful, and more equitable. What are the downsides? For one, a false sense of security may develop as teachers get to know the electronic student at the cost of personal connection. Students also need the opportunity to develop interpersonal skills, such as speaking and listening in public settings, skills that could be lost with an overreliance on this sort of technology (for more information on the T-I, visit education.ti.com/product/tech/tinav/overview/overview.html).

DEEP TEACHING Not long ago, the depth of curricular study was measured by the number of books in the school. Today's school library consists of tens of millions of articles, books, and media brought to the student's desk via the Internet. The key to deep teaching is no longer *finding* material; it is *choosing* material. Many professional organizations such as the National Council for the Social Studies (NCSS) list appropriate websites and online publications. TrackStar is a website where groups of teachers not only identify Internet resources by topic, but also include annotations, quizzes, sound bites, film clips, games, activities, and lesson plans (check out scrtec.org/track).

The Internet is an amazing source of wonderful—and awful—material. For the teacher, the major challenge is figuring out which is which, and helping students do the same. The dangers are not only the well-publicized Internet pornography and pedophilia websites, but also a minefield of misinformation, propaganda, and even hate, all parading as objective information. Groups with objective and even distinguished sounding names can be little more than "fronts" promoting a political or social position. Teachers are well-advised to check with librarians, professional associations, established government agencies, and watchdog groups that monitor hate organizations, to assess the quality and objectivity of Internet resources. Vigilance is not only the eternal price of democracy, it is the educator's entrance fee to the Internet.

DIRECT TEACHING   Traditional teacher-centered approaches can be enhanced by technology. Direct teaching and lecturing, for example, rely on effective presentations, and one of the more ubiquitous technological products in and beyond schools is the PowerPoint™ presentation. These computer-projected images are clear, organized, and appear like a "published" page for all the class to see. But savvy teachers tap other technology as well. Videotapes, computer graphics, and even digital microscopes can provide effective visuals. Even guest speakers can be transported to class via a Web camera. CUSeeMe can provide a camera for the speaker, and another in the class, facilitating a two-way exchange carried over the Internet. Videoconferencing and teleconferencing with other teachers and with subject matter experts is yet another possibility with CUSeeMe. (To find out more, visit www.fvc.com/attach/prod_videoware.pdf.)

SPECIAL POPULATIONS   For students with a variety of special needs or unique learning styles, technology can provide a real boost to teacher effectiveness. Several rich examples of this potential impact are technological devices designed for those with disabilities, called **assistive** or **adaptive technology**. Assistive technologies include wheelchairs, switches that respond to voice commands, and computer programs that read material for blind students. Students with visual motor problems can use voice-activated software or specialized touch screens to direct the computer's actions. Those with learning disabilities report that computers (especially handheld computers) are useful for taking notes in class and keeping their schedules organized. And learning disabled students especially benefit from such tools as Spellcheck. The list of adaptive technology devices promises to grow in the years ahead.[23]

The educational barriers facing poor students can be partially offset when schools offer take-home laptops. Schools provide training to both students and their parents in order to enrich the learning environment at home. The hope is that parental interest will not only result in helping their children with homework, but might extend to their attaining a General Equivalency Degree for themselves over the Internet, if they never completed high school. One such program is called ESTRELLA, and provides online curriculum in Spanish, aimed at migrant farm workers and their families.[24] (Visit www.estrella.org for more information.)

What are the pitfalls of such efforts, and can such "assistance" become too much? Some critics suggest that use of spelling and grammar tools for special education students (as well as others) can short-circuit learning, and that sending laptops home can lead to inappropriate use, from visiting pornography and hate groups websites to unsupervised Internet shopping excursions. (The *Frame of Reference* "A Teacher's Toolbox to Avoid E-Pitfalls" provides educators with suggestions on how to avoid some of the more common technological problems.)

The Global Curriculum

Teachers and students exploring the Internet's educational possibilities have been termed **Internauts**, trailblazers on this new educational frontier not limited by distance or national boundaries.[25] What are some of the options open to today's Internauts?

Unsound Software. Much of the software out there is made for profit, not children, and is not based on sound pedagogy. Seek endorsements and objective evaluations from respected colleagues. Often software developed in a university setting is more likely to be academically sound.

Stereotypes and Violence. The forms of bias discussed in Chapter 7 apply to technology as well. Stereotyping, omission, and un-reality, for example, thrive in software and on the Internet. And many computer games, even for the very young, are filled with violence. Evaluating materials for bias and violence is not only recommended, it is pretty much required.

Screen Potato Syndrome. Americans love technology, and have grown up in a media-rich environment, so it is not surprising that computer-generated images can mesmerize teachers and students, and lull them into an apathetic, nonactive learning role. Variety is still important, so get yourself and your students away from the computer screen and into role-plays, manipulatives, and "low-tech" learning options.

Information Overload. The wealth of technological imagery and video possibilities, not to mention overheads, slides, or simulations, can short-circuit learning. Make certain that students have enough time to digest and process what they have learned.

Internet Junk. While journals have editorial boards and libraries carefully evaluate acquisitions based on budgetary and other criteria, the Internet furnishes no such safeguards. Wonderful resources are provided along with propaganda, political advocacy, and hate literature. Most schools use filters to censor student access to inappropriate Internet material. Filters are not perfect, however, and teachers still should monitor what material students are accessing. You would be wise to teach your students how to evaluate Internet material. For example, have them ask: Who is providing this material? Is it an objective source? Does this group have a particular agenda? Is the material fact, or opinion? (Or opinion, disguised as fact?) Is the material current?

Internet Cheating. Nearly one in five students reports knowing someone who has used the Internet to cheat, but there are resources to detect cheating.[1] The Glatt Plagiarism Screening Program tests student's knowledge about information in the essays they have handed in. Check the Plagiarism Resource Center at The University of Virginia for free software and links to related sites at www.plagiarism.phys.virginia.edu. Working with students on their papers, from the draft stage to final product, will minimize plagiarism and the downloading of student papers provided on the Internet. By the way, there are also websites that provide answers to the problems or tests found in your students' textbooks, so you may want to supplement published homework activities and tests with your own.

[1]Joshua Benton, "For Some, Net Puts Library on Shelf," *DallasNews.com*, September 4, 2001.

REFLECTION

Which of these tech-tips do you find particularly helpful—or troubling? Can you add one of your own?

- **Virtual field trips** transport students to the National Zoo in Washington, D.C., where zookeepers share their knowledge of the animals and students can pose questions via a "chat interface." Similar virtual field trips take students to the ocean depths or to outer space on NASA's Shuttle site.

- **Distance learning** provides courses online that instantly cross national borders. Distance learning is today's "e-quivalent" of correspondence courses, providing educational options to home schooling families, those working unusual or unpredictable hours, commuters who would rather travel the Internet than the interstate, and individuals who simply like learning on their own time and in their own place.

- **Simulations** recreate events, such as elections, cross-cultural meetings, and historical events, to enhance realism and promote learning.

YOU BE THE JUDGE

COMPUTERS—EDUCATIONAL MARVEL OR MENACE?

Computers in Education *Enable* Us to . . .

TEACH MORE EFFECTIVELY

With computers we can individualize instruction, grant students autonomy, and empower students to learn at their own pace, rather than wait for the teacher's personal attention. Each learner benefits from having an omnipresent tutor to individually tailor schoolwork.

REACH AND TEACH MORE STUDENTS

Computers and Internet access can expand the educational horizons of children in isolated rural communities, children with limited community resources, or those children who are homebound because of disability or illness.

MAKE THE WORLD OUR CLASSROOM

Students with Internet access can directly tap resources in their communities or venture beyond their neighborhoods to other regions, nations, or cultures. Students can draw from limitless books, articles, pictures, and sound clips; follow links to experts or virtual field trips; and participate in real-time communications across the globe.

TURN LATCHKEY KIDS INTO CONNECTED KIDS

Too many youngsters have no one to talk to and are hesitant to ask questions of adults or teachers. The Internet offers a homework helper, a companion at the end of the school day, or a chat room of friends so that no one needs be home alone.

GET READY FOR THE FUTURE

Technology encourages interdisciplinary and collaborative work, facilitates problem-based learning, and provides an outlet for students to express their creativity. Students at ease with technology will be assets to future employers.

Computers in Education *Disable* Us Because . . .

EFFECTIVE TEACHING ALL BUT DISAPPEARS

Good teaching requires a personal connection. A teacher gazing at a student who is gazing at a computer screen is not teaching effectively. The Internet is unmonitored, filled with erroneous information, political propaganda, and phony research.

THE DIGITAL WORLD REMAINS DIVIDED

Technology amplifies economic disparities, awarding clear advantage to children from wealthy, high-tech homes attending wealthy, high-tech schools. Poor students soon discover technology's unwelcome mat tripping them up at the door of most career options.

STUDENTS RISK BECOMING ANTISOCIAL

Too many of today's youngsters can surf the Internet, but are unable to form personal connections. The Internet is home to countless narrow-interest groups that fragment society instead of unifying it. Technology can magnify antisocial behaviors, as children send destructive e-mails, organize sinister chat rooms, or create computer viruses.

COMPUTERS ARE A HEALTH RISK

Computer use is associated with increased eyestrain, repetitive motion injury, and the obesity that comes from a sedentary life style. Furthermore, how "healthy" is it for students to have easy access (via the Internet) to bomb-making information, or pornographic material?

FUNDAMENTAL SKILLS ARE SIDELINED

As spelling and grammar tools correct student writing, and computer screens replace engagement with books, real learning is compromised. Tomorrow's workers may become powerless automatons.

YOU BE THE JUDGE

Do you believe that computers are an educational asset or a liability? In what ways has your education been enriched—or diminished—by technology? How might you plan to safeguard your students against dangers listed above?

The "global village" created by the Internet is real, but the content of its curriculum is still being shaped. If you were to design a "Curriculum for the World," what issues, concepts, and skills would you include? Perhaps you might teach conflict-resolution strategies, to avoid a cataclysmic nuclear war. Problem-solving strategies could be useful in tackling ecological issues, such as global warming, deforestation, and toxic waste disposal. Maybe your curriculum would promote cross-cultural knowledge and communication skills to increase tolerance and understanding of the cultural, ethnic, and religious groups that share our planet. Educators investigating a world-based curriculum call their work **global education**.[26]

Author William Kniep suggests four domains for global inquiry:

1. *Human values*. The universal values shared by humanity, as well as the diverse values of various groups

2. *Global systems*. Emphasis on global systems and an interdependent world, including economy, ecology, politics, and technology

3. *Global issues and problems*. Worldwide concerns and challenges, including peace and security, environmental issues, and human rights

4. *Global history*. Including the evolution of universal and diverse human values, the history of global systems, and the roots of global problems.[27]

Schools around the country and the world are combining technology and global education. In Massachusetts, middle school students completed a unit on environmental science through a live teleconference with students from Karlsruhe, Germany,[28] while in another Massachusetts school students learned through direct computer discussion about the realities of life in another part of the globe from students in Kindersley, Saskatchewan.[29] Global educators, like technology advocates, emphasize the need to "educate children for the world they are entering rather than the world they are leaving behind."[30] (The U.S. Department of Education provides a useful portal for many of these projects: www.ed.gov/Technology/guide/international/socialstudies.html.)

- The First People's Project provides a site, in Spanish and English, for students from indigenous cultures. The goal is for students to learn about different cultures; students can also get involved in humanitarian efforts (see www.iearn.org.au/clp).

- Over six thousand schools from Mexico, the United States, and Canada participate in wildlife migration studies in the western hemisphere by recording sightings in their areas. "Journey North: A Global Study of Wildlife Migration" teaches students how they can protect wildlife by creating or protecting habitats (see www.learner.org/jnorth).

- At the Holocaust/Genocide Project, students produce a magazine called *An End to Intolerance* (see www.iearn.org/hgp/aeti/student-magazine.html).

- World Wise Schools is a Peace Corps project where classrooms can partner with a Peace Corps volunteer and follow them as they do their work during the course of a year (see www.peacecorps.gov/wws).

The rate of technological innovation is so fast that even as today's applications are being disseminated, newer ones are being tested. Will the next generation of computers continue the trend toward less expensive, smaller, yet more powerful machines, yielding pocket computers that outperform today's desktops? Will the next generation of computers converse with us, eliminating the need for keyboard skills and programming? Will we be able to print letters and papers by simply speaking, or will simply thinking our thoughts be enough to create computer commands? Will we still print papers, or will we be able to instruct our computer to transmit information, not only to other computers but also to people's minds? Will the next breakthrough be true artificial intelligence, computers that can counsel us on our professional and personal lives, becoming mechanical mentors? Or are these little more than fanciful illusions, examples of America's overconfidence in all things technological?

The Virtual Teacher

Picture this: You are a teacher in a very pleasant, comfortable, but small high school. You would love to offer a course about Native Americans, but your small school has only two students who want to enroll. During the year, you meet other students who express interest in many specialized courses, from marine biology and advanced physics to Latin American literature. Your Lilliputian school does not offer those courses either. Are you and your students out of options? Cheer up! All is not lost. You can join the Virtual High School, where you can teach your course, and your students can enroll in other specialized courses.

Started in 1997 by the Concord Consortium and the Public Schools in Hudson, Massachusetts, the **Virtual High School (VHS)** was the first large-scale project to create Internet-based courses at the high school level and has grown from thirty participating high schools and several hundred students to scores of schools and thousands of students. Most states now have their own virtual high schools, many serving thousands of students.[31] Now, a small town in Colorado can offer an anthropology course even after the anthropology teacher has left, and in Amman, Jordan, students can enroll in a geometry course never before offered at their school. Because the classes are offered over the Internet and are **asynchronous** (that is, people can join classroom activities at any time of the day or night), students from around the world can take the same course, regardless of time zones. Participating instructors are now able to offer special topics and unique courses which they were unable to teach in their own high school.

How does this Virtual High School work? Although virtual high schools differ from each other, the original VHS in Concord is basically a barter system, in which participating high schools contribute a teacher's time to develop and deliver one VHS netcourse. In return, the school is allowed to enroll twenty of its students in other netcourses offered by VHS. The courses offered do not compete with the regular offerings at each participating high school but are designed to augment local curricula. Each participating instructor receives training to become a VHS teacher, to learn how to teach on the Internet. Course offerings have included Bioethics Symposium; Earth 2525: A Time Traveler's Guide to Planet Earth; A Model United Nations Simulation Using the Internet; Business in the 21st Century; Folklore and Literature of Myth, Magic and Ritual; and Writing: From Inner Space to Cyberspace.

Some critics worry that the VHS isolates students from teachers, but many report that in fact VHS courses are more personal and individualized than typical classes. Recounts one new recruit to the Virtual High School, "In just two weeks, I feel like I know my Virtual High School teacher better than I ever knew any of my face-to-face teachers."[32]

Virtual high schools are being touted as an effective response to the teacher shortage, and the future may bring a dramatic increase in this new type of instruction. What is it like to teach in a virtual school? While many of the effective teaching practices that we discussed apply to virtual teaching, tasks do differ. As you read the following account of a virtual teacher's day, you may want to consider the differences and similarities between traditional and virtual teaching. (If you want to visit and

INTERACTIVE ACTIVITY
THE VIRTUAL HIGH SCHOOL. Click on the Virtual High School website to observe an online classroom.

CHRISTA MCAULIFFE AND SALLY RIDE—SISTERS IN THE SKY

Christa McAuliffe

Sally Ride

Christa McAuliffe's name is deeply etched in American history as the teacher who died in the *Challenger* explosion. Honest and direct, she did not hesitate to speak out on behalf of the constituency she represented: American public school teachers and students.

Astronaut Sally Ride had flown the *Challenger* just over a year earlier, but her world also exploded with the *Challenger's* final voyage in 1986. The astronauts who died were more than her friends; they were members of an intimate fraternity, tethered to one another for their very survival. Ride served on the Presidential team chosen to investigate the *Challenger* explosion, and then in 1987 she resigned from the NASA astronaut corps.

In her younger days, Sally Ride was a nationally ranked junior tennis player. She left the tour, however, because: "I couldn't always control the trajectory of the ball and this was unbearably frustrating. I need things to make sense."[1] Ride studied physics at Stanford University, reveling in science's precision and logic. After receiving her doctorate, she was one of more than eight thousand men and women who applied to become an astronaut. Thirty-five were accepted, six were women, and one of those women was Sally Ride. On June 18, 1983, she climbed into the flight engineer's seat of the *Challenger*, the first American woman in space. "The thing I'll remember most about the flight is that it was fun. It was the most fun I'll ever have in my life."[2]

Sally Ride's fascination with technology and exploration of the universe remains steadfast. "Science is fun. Science is curiosity. We all have natural curiosity. Science is a process of investigating, solving puzzles."[3] The college campus is now Ride's command center. A professor of physics at the University of California in San Diego, her academic reputation is

linked to science education and to service as a national policy advisor on space and disarmament issues. Her primary mission, like that of Christa McAuliffe before her, is to propel the study of science and technology in students of all ages and backgrounds. "Our future lies with today's kids and tomorrow's space exploration."[4] Adviser to two national science education programs, EarthKAM and Imaginary Lines, Ride designs lessons that extend far beyond the traditional classroom walls.

EarthKAM is an international program involving middle school students in the excitement of space exploration. The curriculum begins in classrooms, where students and teachers study a region or landmark on Earth to be photographed. They might elect to learn about deforestation in the Amazon, dust storms in Africa, or volcanoes in Hawaii. After calculating variables such as latitude and longitude, students send their data via the World Wide Web to EarthKAM at Mission Control in Houston where the coordinates are programmed into digital cameras on the Space Shuttle or International Space Station. Pictures from space are then transmitted back to the classroom. The photographs serve as tools through which students can study the planet in a variety of disciplines, such as geography, environmental studies, and the visual arts. Ride's hope is that the interactive nature of EarthKAM will do "nothing short of revolutionize science education in America."[5]

A pioneer in space travel, Sally Ride knows that young women are especially unlikely to take flight in science and technology careers. In elementary school, roughly the same numbers of girls and boys are interested in science and math. But beginning in about sixth grade, more girls than boys disengage from these subjects. Ride created Imaginary Lines to stop this leak in the pipeline. The program targets middle school girls interested in science and technology, and networks them through interactive projects and role modeling. At the heart of the program are Sally Ride and her message: "math and science will take you places." And her students are inspired. "She's a spectacular teacher. Dr. Ride's a hero at bringing the excitement of science into the classroom."[6]

[1]Janet Wiscombe, "Ask Sally Ride about Her Reasearch," *LA Times Magazine* (August 29, 1999).

[2]Carolyn Blacknall. *Sally Ride: First American Woman in Space* (Minneapolis: Dillon Press, 1984).

[3]Ibid.

[4]Ibid.

[5]Wiscome, "Ask Sally Ride about Her Research."

[6]Ibid.

REFLECTION

What evidence of cultural, socioeconomic, or gender gaps in science, math, and technology have you experienced in your education? As a teacher, how will you close these gaps? Visit EarthKAM at www.earthkam.ucsd.edu, Imaginary Lines at 207.110.50.133/ilines and McAuliffe/Challenger Center at www.christa.org. How might these resources support learning through technology? Would you use them in your classroom? Why or why not?

WRITE YOUR OWN *PROFILE IN EDUCATION*: Click on *Profiles in Education,* write a *Profile in Education* about an educator, and post it on the Online Learning Center. Check out *Profiles in Education* submitted by other future teachers.

To learn more about Christa McAuliffe and Sally Ride click on *Profiles in Education.*

take a tour of the Virtual High School in cyberspace, visit our online learning center to link to the Virtual High School. See Figure 13.4.)

A DAY IN THE LIFE OF A TEACHER: ANA'S STORY

Ana teaches in a small, rural school in Massachusetts. She started incorporating Internet research into her classes a couple of years ago but wondered how else she could use the Internet in her instruction. When her school was considering joining VHS, Ana applied to be one of the first VHS teachers. She enrolled in the Concord Consortium's graduate-level Teacher's Learning Conference (TLC), with about thirty other teachers from around the country, and began developing a netcourse, which she has delivered three times, to a total of sixty students in the VHS cooperative.

Part of what Ana loves about VHS is the way it has made her take a fresh look at her instructional methods after fifteen years of teaching. She has found that her evaluation is carrying over into her local classroom as well. She also loves being a "pioneer" and being connected to an intimate network of other teachers around the country.

8:00 A.M. TEACHERS' LOUNGE

Before her first local class of the day, Ana uses a phone line in her school's teachers' lounge to check in on her VHS course. She plugs in her laptop, connects to the phone line, and opens her Internet browser. She logs onto the VHS site, goes to the VHS Faculty Lounge to check for any new announcements, and then accesses her class over the Internet. This semester, Ana has students from eight states and fourteen high schools in her class. She wants to see if any new work assignments or discussion comments have come in from students over the weekend. She loves seeing work come in from her students at all hours of the day, sometimes seven days a week. She assigns work on a weekly basis, making it possible for all twenty students to contribute equally to the course, despite their varying schedules and time zones. After checking her course, Ana quickly peruses her e-mail to see if anyone has sent her a private message and then logs out to go teach her onsite classes.

FIGURE 13.4
Virtual High School Homepage.

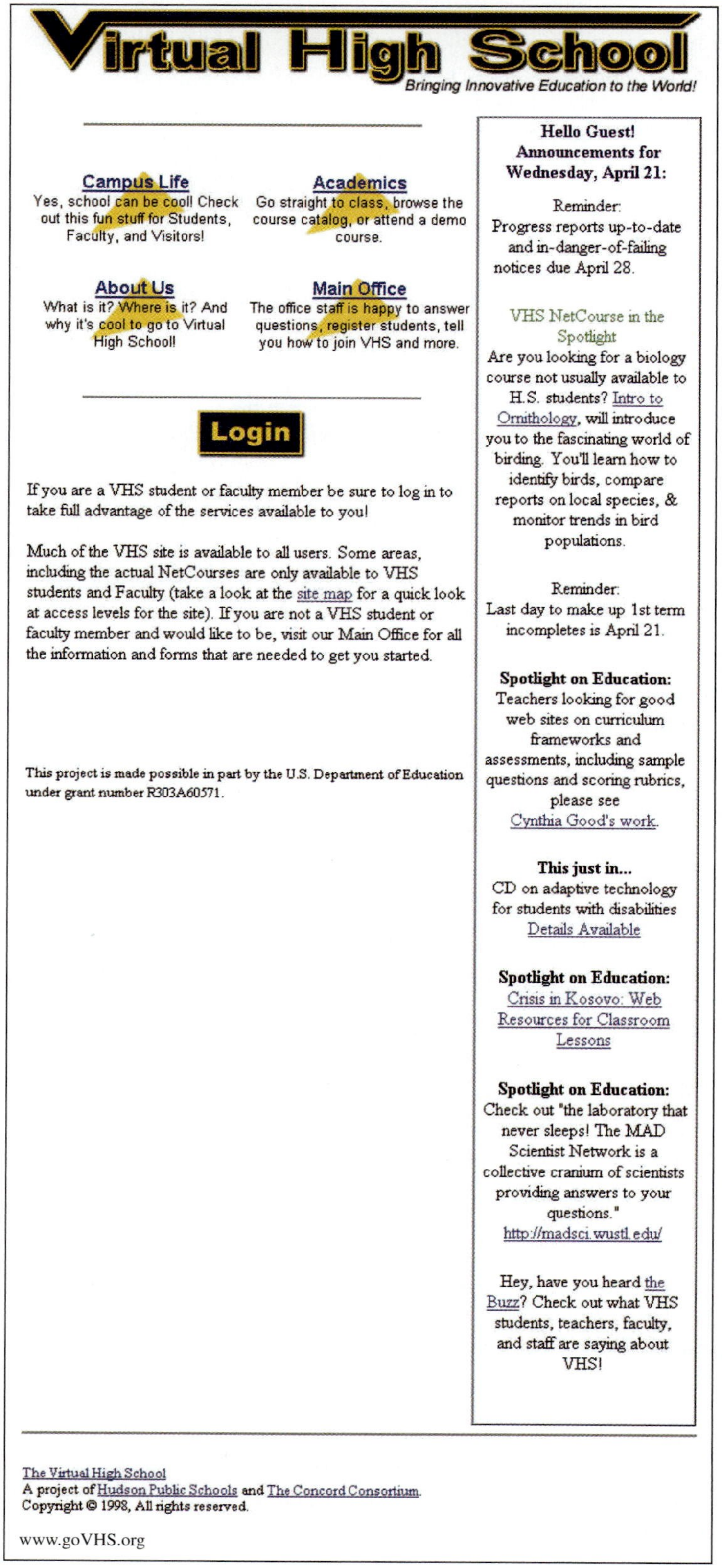

Virtual High School
Bringing Innovative Education to the World!

Campus Life
Yes, school can be cool! Check out this fun stuff for Students, Faculty, and Visitors!

Academics
Go straight to class, browse the course catalog, or attend a demo course.

About Us
What is it? Where is it? And why it's cool to go to Virtual High School!

Main Office
The office staff is happy to answer questions, register students, tell you how to join VHS and more.

Login

If you are a VHS student or faculty member be sure to log in to take full advantage of the services available to you!

Much of the VHS site is available to all users. Some areas, including the actual NetCourses are only available to VHS students and Faculty (take a look at the site map for a quick look at access levels for the site). If you are not a VHS student or faculty member and would like to be, visit our Main Office for all the information and forms that are needed to get you started.

This project is made possible in part by the U.S. Department of Education under grant number R303A60571.

Hello Guest!
Announcements for Wednesday, April 21:

Reminder:
Progress reports up-to-date and in-danger-of-failing notices due April 28.

VHS NetCourse in the Spotlight
Are you looking for a biology course not usually available to H.S. students? Intro to Ornithology, will introduce you to the fascinating world of birding. You'll learn how to identify birds, compare reports on local species, & monitor trends in bird populations.

Reminder:
Last day to make up 1st term incompletes is April 21.

Spotlight on Education:
Teachers looking for good web sites on curriculum frameworks and assessments, including sample questions and scoring rubrics, please see
Cynthia Good's work.

This just in...
CD on adaptive technology for students with disabilities
Details Available

Spotlight on Education:
Crisis in Kosovo: Web Resources for Classroom Lessons

Spotlight on Education:
Check out "the laboratory that never sleeps! The MAD Scientist Network is a collective cranium of scientists providing answers to your questions."
http://madsci.wustl.edu/

Hey, have you heard the Buzz? Check out what VHS students, teachers, faculty, and staff are saying about VHS!

The Virtual High School
A project of Hudson Public Schools and The Concord Consortium.
Copyright © 1998, All rights reserved.

www.goVHS.org

2:15 P.M. TEACHERS' LOUNGE

Ana has finished teaching her reduced load of onsite courses for the day and now switches gears to focus on her VHS course. Ana sets up her laptop and opens up Lotus Notes, so she can work on her course. Her students can access the class on any computer with an Internet browser, but she needs to use Lotus Notes software to make certain additions and changes to the course. Ana didn't know anything about using this software before she joined VHS, but the TLC professional development netcourse trained her to create and manage her course within Notes' LearningSpace environment.

First, Ana "replicates" her course locally; then she disconnects from the phoneline. When she is done making all the necessary changes, she'll "replicate" back. Offline, she can work more quickly and efficiently, and she doesn't have to tie up the phone line.

Creating a New Team Profile in the CourseRoom

Ana fine-tunes next week's assignment, which she will unlock soon for students who want to get an early start. She uses the instructor's tools in the CourseRoom to create student teams. Next week, she will ask the students to pair up and start working on a long-term project. The assignment centers around gathering and comparing regional information, so she partners students from different states when she creates the new teams. After she creates teams, the students will be able to create work documents that can be accessed and edited only by the two members of each team and the teacher.

Creating a New Discussion Topic in the CourseRoom

Next, Ana creates a new discussion topic to go along with the team assignments. She creates a link from the Schedule document, which describes the assignment, right to the new discussion thread where she wants students to post comments. Ana reads the new student comments and posts some responses to facilitate a deeper group discussion. A few new work assignments have been posted by students, marked "submitted for grading." Ana marks up the documents and resaves them in the CourseRoom. Her students will be able to open their graded work privately to read Ana's edits and comments. Finally, Ana enters her comments and grades in the student's online portfolios, located in the Profiles database.

She is impressed with one student's work in particular, and she sends an e-mail to the VHS staff, nominating the work for possible inclusion in the VHS showcase. She is worried about another student, who hasn't posted anything in a week, so she creates a private message for him in the CourseRoom and sends an e-mail to him and his site coordinator, both marked "urgent."

The Portfolio View in the Profiles Database

Ana connects to the Internet again and replicates all her changes back to the VHS server, so her students will see them. She packs up her laptop and heads for home.

After dinner, Ana sets up the laptop on her desk at home. Ana is one of TLC graduates asked to act as a mentor for the group of teachers currently in TLC training. Ana has been assigned as the "buddy" to a group of three teachers who are developing netcourses in a similar content area. The "newbies" in Ana's group are expected to comment and offer suggestions on each other's work. The latest assignment was to create and post a group activity for the proposed netcourse. Ana reads the three group activities created by her group members, smiling at their creativity. She posts a response to one of the activities, which she thinks is especially strong. (The teacher asks his students to do a hands-on experiment at home with their family and then to share their data with the class by posting their results in the CourseRoom. The students are asked to compare and contrast their findings with the rest of the class.) Ana writes some positive feedback to that assignment and tells the group that, in her experience, assignments are most successful when they balance work both on and off the computer. Ana is having a lot of fun sharing her expertise and experiences with this new group of teachers. It helps her feel connected to the project and keeps her from feeling isolated within her own course. Ana finishes and shuts down her computer for the night, the end of another VHS day.

Technology and Equity

Did you notice the combination of technology and sound teaching practice? Virtual teaching enabled Ana to take time and thoughtfully respond to each student, to get to know them as individuals (without ever really "meeting" them). She was able to have students from different areas share regional data, and display important issues and findings on the course website, activities she would be unable to do without the technology. Virtual teaching demands organization and good scheduling, and it is clear that this appeals to Ana. Looks like Ana is sold on the VHS process, but of course, being a fictional teacher, that was not much of a challenge. There are down-sides to virtual education, and not everybody thrives in this environment. How do you feel about virtual teaching?

The Digital Divide

While technology has many cheerleaders, not everyone gets to be a player. Wealth, race, and gender influence computer access, creating a **digital divide** both at school and at home.[33] White children are three times more likely to have computers at home than are black or Hispanic children, and they are three times as likely to have those computers connected to the Internet.[34] This early computer gap contributes to a later economic gap. African American men between the ages of 19 and 54 are the largest group not using computers, while college-educated Asian American males are the group most likely to use computers. Asian American men earn more than three times the salary earned by African American men.[35] Fewer than one in four children in households earning less than $20,000 have a computer at home, while over 90 percent of the children in households earning more than $75,000 per year have a home computer.[36] The same wealth gap exists between schools: Classrooms in wealthier communities are twice as likely to be connected to the Internet as those in poorer communities. Ironically, the Internet has the most positive impact on lower income students, the ones least likely to have it. (See Figures 13.5 and 13.6.) Yet just having the technology is not enough. As Professor Henry Hay Becker warns, "Efforts to ensure equal access to computer-related learning opportunities at school must move beyond a concern with the numbers of computers in different schools toward an emphasis on how well those computers are being used to help children develop intellectual competencies and technical skills."[37] In too many schools, especially rural and inner-city schools, computers are used solely for drill and practice, rather than more challenging and thoughtful applications. The lack of teacher training and the absence of a challenging curriculum can short-circuit even the most advanced technology.[38]

While race, class, and wealth create one technology gap, gender creates another. In the early years, girls are as interested in computers as boys are, but, as they grow older, this changes. By upper elementary school, as females' sex roles and sex identification strengthen, girls' computer usage declines. Video games and software help fan the flames of female disaffection, since they are computer games marketed for stereo-typical male interests, such as athletics and combat. (Particularly offensive software targets female characters for scorn, abuse, and even violence.) Schools contribute to sex-typing technology by placing computer courses in the math department. As one writer put it, "Women are not free to roam around computerland. This field has a

Percentage of Students with Access to Computer at Home

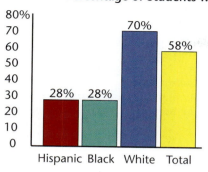
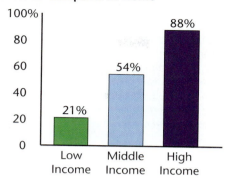

FIGURE 13.5
The digital divide on computers.

SOURCE: Condition of Education, National Center for Educational Statistics, 2001.

REFLECTION

What can schools do to close the digital divide?

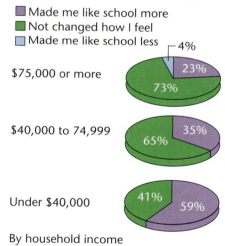

Using the Internet at School Has:

- Made me like school more
- Not changed how I feel
- Made me like school less

$75,000 or more — 4%, 23%, 73%

$40,000 to 74,999 — 35%, 65%

Under $40,000 — 41%, 59%

By household income

FIGURE 13.6
The digital divide on the Internet.

SOURCE: *The Washington Post*, April 4, 2000.

REFLECTION

How do you explain these differences? What are the academic implications of this data?

math and science image."[39] The maleness of technology is reinforced in literature, replete with the recurrent theme that technology was developed by men to serve their purposes. Boys flock to video arcades, computer summer camps, high school technology electives, and afterschool computer clubs. Males constitute over 80 percent of high school students taking advanced placement tests in computer science. Female enrollment is higher than male enrollment only in clerical and data entry classes, reminders of the secretarial careers of the past, and only one out of four computer science majors in college is female.[40]

Geography contributes to another digital divide. Running fiber optic cables to rural schools is often an expense that telecommunications companies avoid, a challenge that has been called the **last mile problem.**[41] The connections that are made are often slow, posing difficulties for students participating in online classes. Perhaps Internet connections via satellite or more advanced future technologies will resolve this problem, but for now, rural America is on the wrong side of the digital divide.[42] (See Figure 13.7.)

Before we leave this topic, we should reflect for a moment on the global divide as well. The language on most of the Internet is English, which disenfranchises most of the world's population. And where language does not disenfranchise, lack of finances does. The result is that the Internet is fundamentally a tool of western and high-tech nations. (See Figure 13.8.)

Is Computer Technology Worth the Effort?

To quote one educator, "If technology is the answer, what was the question?"[43] To evaluate the effectiveness of computers, we must first figure out what they are supposed to accomplish, and, according to University of California professor Henry Jay Becker, we have yet to identify clear goals for technology or to determine how to measure progress toward these goals.

> Traditional theory says that kids need to know discrete skills in computation or reading so that's what teachers teach . . . But most of the people who are excited about technology in schools . . . care more about having kids do sophisticated writing or engage in complex reasoning or learn to figure out things like adults do. And we don't have great ways of measuring such outcomes.[44]

Percent of Towns with Cable Modem Service

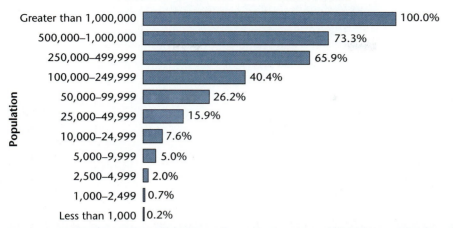

FIGURE 13.7
Rural America.

SOURCE: National Telecommunications and Information Administration, "Advanced Telecommunications in Rural America," 2000. An analysis of data from CED Magazine, "Cable Modem Deployment Update," March 2000, and U.S. Census Bureau, Census Gazetteer, 1990.

REFLECTION

How might technology change rural American schools and students?

Estimated Proportion of Population Using the Web

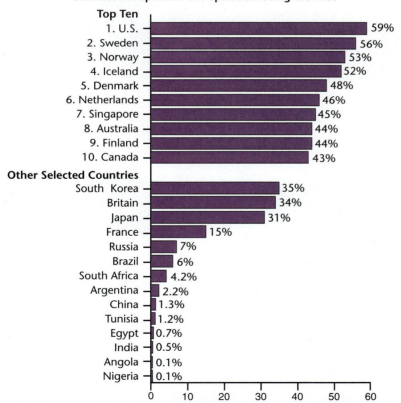

FIGURE 13.8
The international digital divide.

SOURCE: U.N. Human Development Report 2001, NUA Internet Surveys, Population Reference Bureau.

REFLECTION

How might wealth, population size, language, and type of government play a role in Web access?

While most American students have computer access at school, there are tremendous differences in how, when, and why they are used. Predict the use and impact of computers in each of these three school settings.

The bottom line is that the monumental investments in computer technology have not been matched by monumental gains in student achievement. In fact, researchers are divided on the academic benefits brought by computers. The *Secretary's Conference on Educational Technology* painted a rather positive picture and described a number of success stories.[45] One New Jersey school reported a five-fold increase in the number of students signing up for a chemistry course that had added new technologies; studies in Idaho and West Virginia indicated that technology increased student standardized test scores. A school in Juneau, Alaska, reported that interaction between the school and home increased dramatically through the use of online report cards. Evidence suggests that drill and practice done with a computer may help children develop basic skills. Computers make patient and diligent drill sergeants. Other studies indicate that students in classes with sizable numbers of computers do more writing than students in low-tech classrooms, but the research does not indicate whether more writing is better writing; for that to occur, teacher feedback is needed. Teachers report that some students, unmotivated by other instructional approaches, are enthusiastic when learning on the computer.

Then again, not everything done on the computer is educationally germane. The most prevalent uses of computers by fourth- and eighth-graders, for example, are playing games and word processing.[46] In a Brookings Institution study, fourth-grade

Here are a few suggestions for creating a more equitable technological society:

- Connect with one of the over 20,000 organizations that are helping to bridge the digital divide (such as PowerUP, www.powerup.org), or start your own.
- Explore partnerships with neighborhood businesses interested in supporting the school technology program.
- Recruit volunteers from the community to share their expertise in technology with the students at school.
- Help make technology available to at-risk groups after school, in public places and in clubs. Request that your school keep computer labs open after hours.
- Create a Student Tech Corps of savvy students to mentor less savvy students (and maybe you!).
- Bring role models to class to speak about women and people of color succeeding in technology careers.
- Encourage students to evaluate the school district's policy and practice on making computers and the Internet available to students in poorer schools in your community.
- Organize a "borrowing" program between wealthier schools with laptops and those with fewer resources.

REFLECTION

Can you add two more ideas to this list? Which are you most likely to implement?

students who used calculators everyday got the lowest scores on a national mathematics exam.[47] According to an *Education Week* survey, approximately 46 percent of teachers complain that they cannot find software appropriate for their curriculum. In addition, an overwhelming majority of teachers polled found the cost of software to be too high for their budgets.[48] While some studies suggest that technology can improve scores on standardized tests, most do not. Nor is there evidence linking technology to deeper student understanding of concepts and issues.

Though computers have little to show in the way of educational effectiveness, support for technology in schools remains high. Most parents, school board members, and business leaders believe that computers offer essential workplace skills—an important, if nonacademic goal. The public also believes that computers and the Internet provide a window on the latest information, and that somehow computers make education both more efficient and more enjoyable.

Stanford University professor Larry Cuban notes that when academic advances do not follow technological advances, we often blame teachers for not adequately embracing new technology. If teachers are not to blame, we place our criticism on the doorstep of an unresponsive school bureaucracy unable to manage change. If that does not work, then we explain failure in terms of insufficient resources, a public unwilling to fund costly technology. Rarely do Americans question the technology itself. He points out that we know little about using technology to enhance instruction, that the problem may not be teachers, administrators, or funding but, rather, America's unbridled faith in technology. Cuban believes that our technological expectations are unreasonably high.[49]

Teachers are caught in the middle. On the one hand, researchers can offer little in the way of strong evidence that computers significantly contribute to learning, yet public enthusiasm about technology is pushing schools and teachers into implementing computer education. What are educators to do?

It is helpful for teachers to maintain perspective when it comes to technology. While it is unlikely that education will be redefined completely in the near future, it is also clear that technology's influence is growing. Get comfortable with technology. Be open to learning new applications and approaches. Be willing to try out ideas. Consider technology mastery as part of your professional development. Attend relevant courses and workshops and observe colleagues applying technology.

Do not lose your skepticism, however. Be wary of "magic bullets," simple solutions to complex educational problems. The advocates of technology have yet to prove the educational effectiveness of computers. Even if their effectiveness does one day become evident to all, issues of inequity remain. Children of color, the poor, and females are too often left out of the technology picture. And they are the majority of the nation's children.

SUMMARY

1. Has technology changed schools?

- Technology has long been a part of life in schools. From chalkboards to duplicating machines to filmstrip projectors and videodisc players, a stream of technological innovations has made its way into the classroom.

- Although technology does influence schools, historically it has had only modest impact on education.

2. How does television affect children?

- While television holds great educational promise, with high-quality programming such as *Sesame Street*, much of television fare is, at best, unproductive and, at worst, damaging. The worldview presented through the TV lens is quite distorted, leaving viewers with an image of a society populated mostly by males, with few young children, and replete with ethnic and racial stereotypes.

- Violence, racism, and sexism on television send negative messages to children. Advertising, often targeted at young viewers, adversely influences children's behavior, including their diets and spending habits.

- While viewing television at home creates one set of questions, bringing television into the classroom raises other issues. How much television, and what kind of television, is worth class time?

- The growth of cable channels, such as C-SPAN, A&E, and The History Channel, offers new media learning opportunities. The growth of video libraries provides additional resources.

- The introduction of *Channel One*, a for-profit enterprise that brings current events and commercials into classrooms, raises questions about the role of commercial television in public schools.

3. Why is computer technology difficult to implement in schools?

- The latest technological innovation in education has been computers and Internet access. But implementation has been expensive. The costs of computer hardware and software purchases and the expense of wiring schools for Internet access have eaten into school budgets.

- By 2000, virtually all schools were connected to the Internet, although schools in poorer communities have fewer classrooms connected.

CHAPTER REVIEW

Go to the Online Learning Center to take a quiz, practice with key terms, and review key ideas from the chapter.

- Training teachers to use computers has also been challenging. While some teachers adapt easily to the new technology, others resist, and some suffer from technophobia, a fear of technology. Teachers go through several stages of "computer evolution," from entry level to invention, where they explore new and exciting computer uses.
- Contrast teacher fears with the computer knowledge and skills that many students bring to school, and a technological age gap is obvious. Some teachers still have a healthy distrust of whether computers will in fact make a difference.

4. How can teachers effectively use computers and the Internet?

- There are numerous educational applications of computers and the Internet, but these applications should be considered in light of our knowledge of effective teaching. Technology should be implemented with a clear purpose and in an appropriate context.
- Hardware, software, and websites can tie into many of the effective teaching strategies discussed in this text, including multiple intelligences, problem-based and cooperative learning, and direct and deep teaching, to name but a few.
- Virtual field trips take students around the world, online learning activities can create fascinating learning communities, simulations add increased realism, personal tutors diagnose learning needs, and distance learning brings education directly into the home, suggesting only a few of the advantages technology offers educators.
- Assistive or adaptive technology helps special needs students succeed in school.
- Technology raises some serious concerns for teachers, including monitoring the material that comes in on the Internet, avoiding some of the health risks of computers, and teaching students to detect and mediate the stereotypes and violence that are so much a part of software and Internet resources.

5. In what ways does global education refocus the curriculum?

- Global education investigates world topics that span national borders, including such issues as conflict reduction and ecology. Global education is a growing curricular phenomenon, thanks in part to the Internet.
- Websites now available to students focus on international issues from child labor and animal migration to confronting intolerance and racism.

6. How is teaching redefined in the virtual high school?

- The Virtual High School demonstrates the potential of technology to alter the way students learn and the way teachers teach. It enables students from around the nation, and around the world, to register for courses not available in their local high schools, and for teachers to teach a wider variety of courses.
- Through the use of the Internet, e-mail, and other technological tools, students and teachers in different geographic areas can work together in the same class.
- Virtual teaching uses many effective teaching practices, yet it is quite different from traditional classroom instruction. Virtual teaching offers tomorrow's teachers another type of instructional career, a role that may increase in the years ahead.

7. Does technology exacerbate racial, class, geographic, and gender divisions?

- Technology has not been an equal opportunity educational resource. Inequity continues to be a major problem as race, gender, and economic status influence access to computers and the Internet.
- Wealthier Americans, especially Asian and white males, are the most likely to use computers in school, and the most likely to realize salary benefits from that involvement after graduation.

- Rural America lags behind in getting connected to the Internet.
- On the world scene, non-English speaking nations, as well as poorer nations, also trail behind in technological connections and educational innovations in this computer age.

KEY TERMS AND PEOPLE

assistive (adaptive) technology, 529

asynchronous, 533

Channel One, 519

digital divide, 538

distance learning, 530

e-mail, 526

E-rate, 521

educational television programming, 519

global education, 532

integrated learning systems (ILS) , 528

Internauts, 529

Internet, 526

last mile problem, 540

Christa McAuliffe, 534

Sally Ride, 534

simulations, 530

technophobia, 523

virtual field trips, 530

Virtual High School (VHS) , 533

World Wide Web, 526

DISCUSSION QUESTIONS AND ACTIVITIES

1. Agree or disagree with each of the following:

   "Television viewing leads to misinformation."

   "Television viewing leads to unbridled capitalism, which often injures children."

   "Television viewing is a wasted educational resource."

   "Television viewing . . . " (You complete and support the sentence.)

2. How would you use television in your classroom? What rules might you establish for your students in relation to their viewing habits?

3. Will computer technology make a radical difference in America's schools? Support your position.

4. Why has technology not radically altered the way teachers teach and the way students learn? Can you envision a technological breakthrough that will revolutionize schools? Describe it.

5. Suggest six uses of the computer and the Internet in your classroom. Then identify six potential problems associated with computer and Internet use.

6. The Internet is filled with rich resources—and junk. Pornography topics are available on the Internet but are usually filtered out by schools. Other problems remain: political tracts couched as scholarship, hate information embedded in innocent-looking articles, inaccurate information presented as fact, and authors whose credentials are suspect. How would you prepare your students to handle the unreliable and unscholarly material found on the Internet?

7. Do you think it is important to include global education in the curriculum? Why or why not? What are some dangers inherent in a global education curriculum?

8. Describe the advantages and disadvantages of the Virtual High School or a similar program. Would you like to teach a virtual class? Why?

9. How can teachers work to overcome the way we are digitally divided by class, gender, and race in computer access?

547

WEB-*TIVITIES*

1. Television in Schools: *Channel One*

2. Wiring Up Schools, Charging Up Teachers

3. Computers in the Classroom: Virtual Field Trips and Global Education

4. The Virtual High School

5. Is Computer Technology Worth the Effort?

REEL TO REAL TEACHING

PAY IT FORWARD (2000)
Run Time: 123 minutes

Synopsis: Trevor McKinney, a twelve-year-old boy in a small California town, accepts a teacher's challenge: Earn extra credit by creating and putting into action a plan to change the world for the better.

Reflection:

1. What is the connection of *Pay It Forward* with technology? Visit the Pay It Forward Foundation at www.payitforwardfoundation.org to find out! As a teacher, how might you use this site? What knowledge, values, or skills would you want your students to learn from participating in the Pay It Forward project?

2. Video is a common form of technology often used in schools. Discuss the benefits and limitations of using this educational medium. In your answer, apply what you have learned about effective instruction, forces that shape the curriculum, and technology's impact on learning. Consider, too, how this book's *Reel to Real Teaching* feature has contributed to your learning.

3. *Pay It Forward* tackles issues that many of your future students will experience: student-on-student violence, family alcoholism, domestic abuse, and parental separation. Do you think film is a helpful tool to confront these issues? Describe the pros and cons as well as how you might use film in your classroom to confront social injustices.

Follow-up Activity: Take on Mr. Simonet's challenge: Create a project that makes our world a better place. Your project might improve your own local school or community. It may have a national or even international impact. Use technology (for example, television, film, the Internet) to implement your plan. Share your ideas on the Critics Corner, and invite your peers throughout the country to participate.

How do you rate this film? Click on *Reel to Real Teaching* to submit your review of this or another education-related film, and read reviews submitted by others.

FOR FURTHER READING

Breaking Down the Digital Walls: Learning to Teach in a Post-Modem World, by R. W. Burniske and Lowell Monke (2001). Examines what it means to be educated in our technological world. The authors wrestle with competing demands of developing students who are literate in technology, critical analysis, and social justice.

The Digital Classroom, by David Gordon (2000). Discusses the rewards and challenges of integrating technology into schools. Topics include equity, females and computers, and using computers across the curriculum.

Digital Divide: Computers and Our Children's Future, by David Bolt and Ray Crawford (2000). Explores the gap in technology access and achievement across racial, gender, and socioeconomic lines. Improved teacher training and curriculum are suggested as tools to close the divide.

Failure to Connect, by Jane Healy (1999). Debates the effectiveness of computers to improve the quality of education, concluding that technology leads to intellectual, emotional, and social disengagement and is not an educational panacea.

Student Cheating and Plagiarism in the Internet Era: A Wake-Up Call for Educators & Parents, by Ann Lathrop and Kathleen Foss (2000). Offers constructive school policies and teaching strategies to promote academic integrity as well as tips on how to identify material copied from the Internet.

14 Your First Classroom

FOCUS QUESTIONS

1. What are the stages of teacher development?
2. What resources do school districts provide for a teacher's first year in the classroom?
3. How can new teachers increase their chances of working in a school of their choice?
4. How do school districts, states, and the National Board for Professional Teaching Standards recognize and reward teachers?
5. What are the differences between the National Education Association and the American Federation of Teachers?
6. Are America's schools a secret success story, doing better than the press and the public believe?

WHAT DO YOU THINK? What Teaching Skills Are of Most Value? Check off the teaching skills you believe are most important. See how your criteria compare to those of your colleagues.

CHAPTER PREVIEW

It looks so small: the distance between the students' chairs and the teacher's desk. But traveling from a student's desk to a teacher's desk represents an enormous journey. This chapter is intended to prepare you for that transformation, from student to teacher.

As you enter your first classroom, chances are that you will focus on lesson planning, classroom management, and preparing for those visits by your supervisor. In short, you will be all about classroom survival. With time and experience, you will begin to refine your teaching strategies and focus less on survival skills and more on ways to enhance student learning. While we would love to serve up some ready-to-use answers to help you meet these first year classroom challenges, truth is, there are many questions that only you will be able to answer. Here are just a few for you to consider: Where should I teach? How can I win that ideal (at least satisfying) teaching position? What will my first year be like? Should I join a teachers' association? Should I stay in teaching long term? If so, what are the routes to advancement? And with all the negative press I read about schools, is this something that I want to do? This chapter provides you with some insights and practical advice about making that first year of teaching a successful one, and perhaps the beginning of many rewarding years.

Stages of Teacher Development

Will I be able to manage this class? Can I get through the curriculum? Do I know my subject well enough? Will the other teachers like me? Will the administrators rehire me? Am I going to be a good teacher? Will I like this life in the classroom?

When you begin teaching, the questions that occupy you are mostly about your ability, about visits by supervisors, and about control of the students. By the second year, teachers are more experienced (and confident), and they usually move beyond these questions, shifting the focus of their attention to student performance. For example, experienced teachers might spend time analyzing the needs of individual students, exploring a new curriculum strategy, and asking such questions as How can I help this shy child? and Why is this student encountering learning problems? If a colleague is achieving success using a new teaching strategy, an experienced teacher might observe, then adapt that strategy. As talented and experienced teachers mature, their interests and vision extend beyond their own classrooms. At this more advanced stage, they work to develop programs that could benefit large numbers of students. The chart in Figure 14.1 suggests stages that teachers pass through as they become more skilled in their craft.[1]

Attempts to reform education and improve student achievement are dependent on our ability to move teachers through these developmental stages. Although earlier studies by James Coleman and others seemed to call into question the educational impact of teachers, comprehensive studies in the 1990s found that teacher performance is critical. Every dollar spent to increase teacher qualifications (as measured by teacher test scores, number of graduate degrees, professional training, etc.) improves students' academic performance more than money invested in other areas. Although teachers applaud efforts to reduce class size or provide schools with up-to-date computer technology, research reveals that teacher expertise is more important. In fact, *teacher qualifications and skills are among the MOST important factors in improving student performance.*[2] (See Figure 14.2.)

What do we mean by a qualified and skillful teacher? The most effective teachers not only demonstrate mastery of the subjects they teach but also are adept in the methods of teaching and understand student development. Unfortunately many teachers receive little support, make little progress in their subject area or their teaching skills, and never grow to the more sophisticated levels of teaching. Some teachers struggle to master the initial survival level: Approximately one-third of all new teachers leave teaching within the first five years.[3]

Will you like teaching, be good at it, and advance through these developmental stages? The answer may be determined by your first impressions, your initial experiences as a teacher, and school districts know it. That is why a growing number of districts are investing resources to ensure that, when you step into your first classroom, you will not be alone.

While some teachers are "naturals," gifted classroom instructors from the first day they step foot in a classroom, most of us benefit from a support system that helps us refine our teaching skills. Ongoing support, in the form of professional development, is provided, not just for new teachers but for all teachers. States and school districts have long required continuous graduate training and credits for teachers in order to maintain their licenses. In recent years, many school districts have gone further, creating and implementing induction programs for beginning teachers.

FIGURE 14.1   Stages of teacher development.

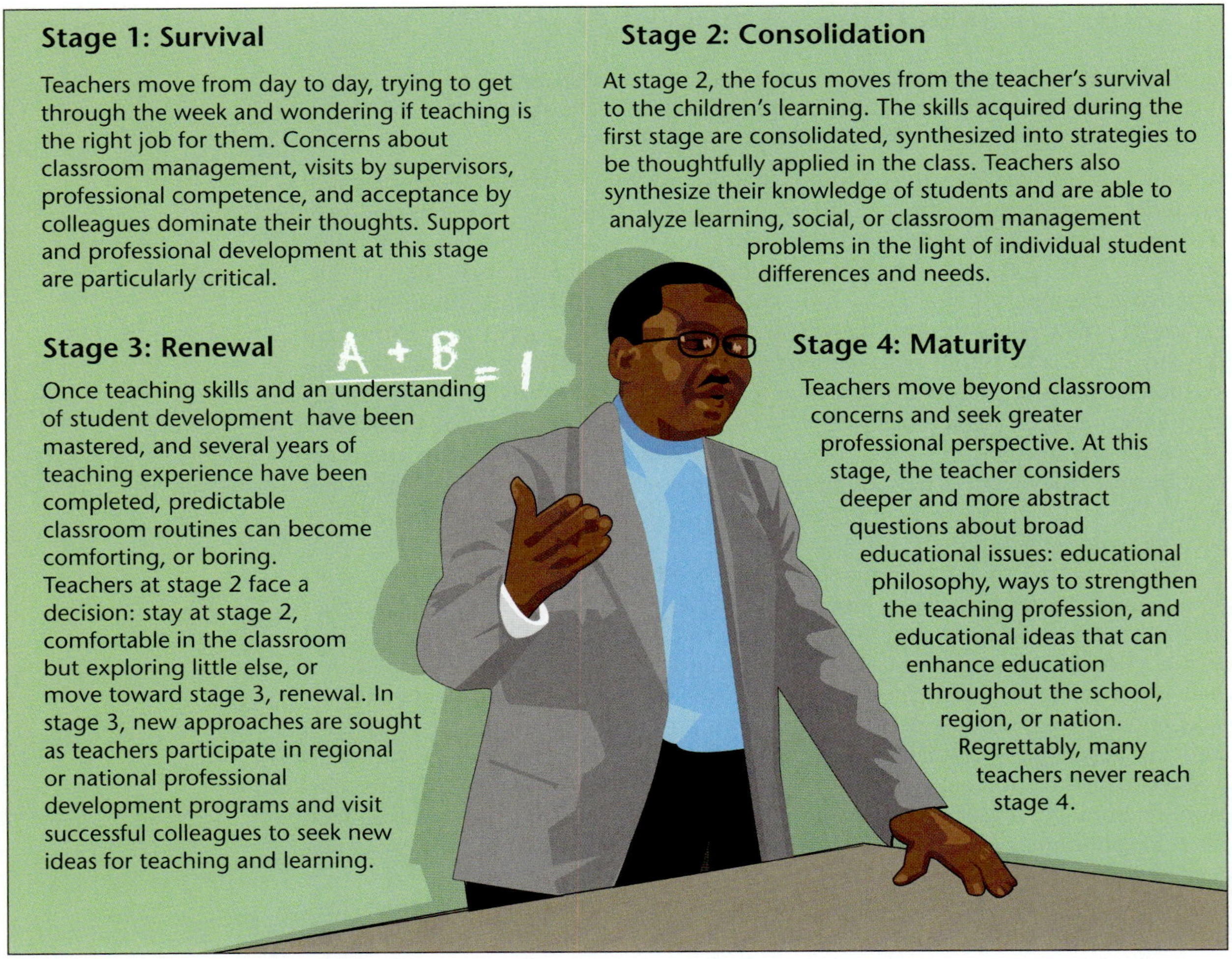

Stage 1: Survival

Teachers move from day to day, trying to get through the week and wondering if teaching is the right job for them. Concerns about classroom management, visits by supervisors, professional competence, and acceptance by colleagues dominate their thoughts. Support and professional development at this stage are particularly critical.

Stage 2: Consolidation

At stage 2, the focus moves from the teacher's survival to the children's learning. The skills acquired during the first stage are consolidated, synthesized into strategies to be thoughtfully applied in the class. Teachers also synthesize their knowledge of students and are able to analyze learning, social, or classroom management problems in the light of individual student differences and needs.

Stage 3: Renewal

$$A + B = 1$$

Once teaching skills and an understanding of student development have been mastered, and several years of teaching experience have been completed, predictable classroom routines can become comforting, or boring. Teachers at stage 2 face a decision: stay at stage 2, comfortable in the classroom but exploring little else, or move toward stage 3, renewal. In stage 3, new approaches are sought as teachers participate in regional or national professional development programs and visit successful colleagues to seek new ideas for teaching and learning.

Stage 4: Maturity

Teachers move beyond classroom concerns and seek greater professional perspective. At this stage, the teacher considers deeper and more abstract questions about broad educational issues: educational philosophy, ways to strengthen the teaching profession, and educational ideas that can enhance education throughout the school, region, or nation. Regrettably, many teachers never reach stage 4.

SOURCE: Based on the work of Lillian Katz.

REFLECTION

Have you been taught by teachers representing each of these four developmental stages? Describe their behaviors at each of the four levels. If you were to build in strategies to take you from Stage 1 to Stage 4, what might they be?

Your First Year: Induction into the Profession

Mentors

An **induction program** "provide(s) some systematic and sustained assistance to beginning teachers for at least one school year."[4] Induction programs promote a positive transition into the classroom by matching new teachers, called **intern**

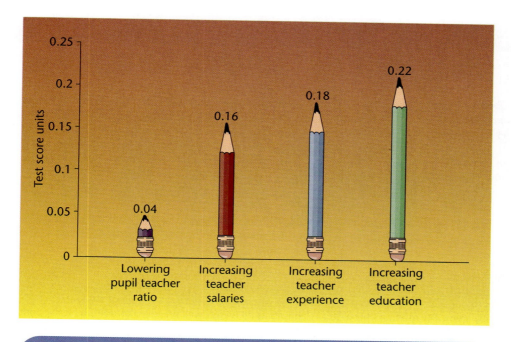

FIGURE 14.2
School resources and student achievement: size of increase in student achievement for every $500 spent on four areas.

SOURCE: Linda Darling-Hammond, "Teachers and Teaching: Testing Policy Hypothesis From a National Commission Report," *Educational Researcher* 27, no. 1, January–February 1998.

REFLECTION

Why do you suspect that so much attention has been given to reducing class size, and so little to demanding more rigorous teacher education?

teachers, with an experienced instructor, sometimes called a consulting teacher or mentor. Mentors may be assigned by the school administration, or by the local teachers' association, or by a combination of the two. **Mentors** guide intern teachers through the school culture and norms, shedding light on the "official" and "hidden" school governments (which memos need a quick response, which do not; who keeps the key to the supply room; where the best VCRs are hidden). Mentors can offer information about curricular materials, as well as observe a class to offer insights into teaching skills. In the best of circumstances, they help new teachers become skilled professionals. On a personal level, mentors can be valuable confidants, providing a friendly ear and helpful advice through new, and sometimes difficult, times. They may be able to help new teachers work out scheduling problems or smooth out stressful communication with a student, parent, administrator, or colleague (no minor feat during a year filled with new faces).

If having a mentor sounds appealing, and you find yourself in a school district that does not provide official mentors, you can certainly try to recruit an unofficial mentor to guide you through that first year. You might want to ask colleagues or administrators about teachers known for creative lessons or effective management or who generally might lend a helpful hand to a rookie such as yourself.

In many programs, mentors provide more than friendly support; they have an official responsibility to assess new teachers and to file reports to school supervisors. A poor performance report from a mentor can result in a recommendation for extra training for an intern teacher, which could be absolutely wonderful in solving a

A CLASSROOM CHALLENGE I JUST HAD TO TAKE
By Mathina Carkci

Mathina Carkci, who wrote about education as a reporter for suburban Maryland newspapers for three years, became a fourth-grade teacher at Bailey's Elementary School in Fairfax County.

The most surprising thing about being a teacher is how often I feel like a failure. I knew that teaching fourth grade would be hard, but I expected to be able to keep up with everything and to succeed. So it's disheartening, just two months into my first job, to feel the weight of things left undone, questionable decisions made and professional duties unmet.

My teacher friends say they used to feel the same way. Some admit they still do. My student-teaching supervisor sympathetically cautions that the first two years are so unlike the "real thing" that they don't count. The teacher across the hall reminds me to take baby steps. My mom, a university professor, promises it will get better. I'm too hard on myself, a former professor tells me; it takes time to grow into the teacher I want to be.

I take some comfort from the fact that friends who were in the same one-year master's certification program at the University of Maryland last year have found it hard from the word go. I called Natalie the evening of her first day, a week before I started.

"If you told me I didn't have to go tomorrow," she said, "I wouldn't."

I called Al on his second day. "After the kids left today, I shut the door and cried," he said.

My friends and family told me I'd be a great teacher. They said they imagined a group of children gazing up at me, accompanying me on exciting journeys that would fill their minds with wonder. "You're such a good person," my husband told me. "The kids are going to love you." It gave me the chills, the way good classical music does, to think of myself and my merry band of students, gallivanting through the curriculum.

So it's difficult to admit now how hard it is to be a first-year teacher: how every single day I feel as if I am drowning; how I spend 12 hours at school each day working and four hours at home worrying; how each evening as I leave school, I have to decide which of 100 equally important things I should leave undone; how I feel so far behind that I will never catch up until Christmas, when I have 10 days "off."

When I get to school, anywhere from an hour and a half to two hours before the kids, a list of tasks swims through my head, and, as the minutes tick away until 8:40 arrives, I run through my priorities. With any luck, I'll have put up the day's schedule, written the daily message to the students

and created the math warm-up exercise the night before. I might respond to kids' journals but change my mind when I realize the math lesson I had planned misses an important element. (Half my mind, all this time, is wondering what the best way is to teach kids to determine the volume of solid shapes.) I might walk to the copier, see the line of other teachers and decide instead to swing by the library to schedule a block of time for my students. Or I might run into the guidance counselor and discuss ways to help a student who's been misbehaving.

Then I notice a student's desk that seems to be exploding papers and books, and wonder how best to help the child get organized: Does she need me to go through the pile with her, paper by paper? (And when would I do that?) Or should I write her a note and carve out a chunk of the day for her to organize things herself? Or do I need to have a talk with the whole class about keeping things straight?

It isn't as if I wasn't well prepared or don't have support. My year-long internship, including 12 weeks of student teaching, gave me a taste of the challenges I'd face. A mentor at my school, Bailey's Elementary, meets with me regularly, and Fairfax County bends over backward to provide new teachers with help. Bailey's teems with kind, helpful colleagues. Volunteers, including my mom who comes in every Friday, offer assistance of all sorts. Short of having a personal assistant 12 hours a day, I don't think there's anything more anyone could do to ease my transition.

Idealistic grad school conversations about pedagogy and democracy in the classroom made me surer than ever that I was right to go into teaching, that here was where I would make my impact on a part of the world that mattered to me. The master's program helped me build a solid educational philosophy based on wanting children to discover for themselves how rewarding learning can be.

I never thought my career switch would be easy. I had covered education when I was a newspaper reporter, so I'd seen the kinds of tightropes that many teachers walk. But I wanted to do something more active than writing about them. As a teacher, I could be with students every day and show them in tangible ways that their ideas mattered.

I try to make this happen in the classroom, but as we all know, theory and practice don't always overlap. I spend more time thinking up ways to get students to hand in homework than I do thinking about how to help them to pursue their own questions, or promoting their curiosity. Despite having vowed not to use rewards and punishments as a method of controlling the class, I have found myself giving kids extra recess for walking quietly in line or sending them back to their seats if they seem disruptive. My interactions with kids are less positive than I once hoped they would be, and I say "No," without explanation, far more often than I would like. Instead of designing creative, hands-on lessons in every subject, I sometimes teach straight from the book in science and social studies classes.

But, in the end, I don't think I'm really a failure. We have meetings, where my whole class tries to solve problems anyone puts on the agenda. I play with the kids at recess, which might make me seem more like another kid than like a teacher, but I think it also helps them to see me as someone worth following. I've managed to avoid being ruled by the lesson plan. The other day, two boys invented their own way of conducting a science project that involved analyzing rocks, and, when I realized their way was better, I encouraged the rest of the class to go with it instead of following the instructions.

I may not be on the same social studies textbook chapter as the other fourth-grade teachers, and I'll probably be late returning standardized tests to the assistant principal, but I think my kids know they're important to me. I see it in tiny, fleeting moments. I see it when a student says, "Mrs. Carkci, I wish you could come to my house for the weekend. That would be fun." I see it when a boy writes to me to ask if I will take him to the movies, or when a girl gives me a goofy smile after I've led the class down the hall taking giant, silly steps. I'm proud that a girl believes it is okay to ask "Why in America do people speak lots of languages, while in Vietnam, they only speak one language?" Or that a boy knows I will encourage him to pursue his question, "Who invented the planets?"

Once or twice, early on, I considered quitting. But no longer. I like helping my 21 students learn about the four regions of Virginia; I enjoy encouraging them to write and to use new paragraphs for new ideas; and I thrive on watching them become mathematical thinkers. Just the other day a student told me, out of the blue, that he'd noticed how the desks in our classroom were like intersecting lines. It was our geometry unit made real.

I can't imagine what it will be like in two years, when I have figured out a good response to tattling and when I have prepared a classroom set of spelling games. I don't love teaching yet, but I am beginning to catch glimpses of what it will be like when I do.

REFLECTION

What insights and clues suggest that Mathina will succeed as a teacher? Do you share any of her attributes? Which teaching skills might you need to further refine?

---

persistent problem. If the problem is not resolved with additional resources and training, continuous negative classroom observations can lead to dismissal. Obviously, a mentor's evaluation responsibilities can inhibit open and effective communication, particularly if a new teacher is struggling and is concerned about being rehired.

Observation

Whether new teachers are assigned a mentor, find a mentor, or are mentorless, they are likely to have their classroom performance observed. It is not unusual for teachers to be observed three or four times in their first year and, in some districts, much more frequently. Observations come in two varieties: *diagnostic,* designed to help the teachers, and *evaluative,* intended to be used for employment decisions. Sometimes the same observation serves both purposes.

Observations may be conducted by your mentor, an administrator, or a veteran teacher. This last option, called **peer review,** has become popular in a number of school districts, including Minneapolis, Cincinnati, and Columbus, Ohio.[5] These districts, sometimes in cooperation with local teacher associations, identify their strongest teachers to evaluate and assist others, an approach that recognizes the movement toward greater teacher professionalism and autonomy.

What do observers look for during classroom observations of beginning teachers? It is wise for beginning teachers to ask a mentor or colleague about which skills and qualities are particularly valued in these observations. Some teachers find it useful (if a bit disconcerting) to arrange to be videotaped, so they can pinpoint strategies to improve their instruction. An evaluation framework, used by the Toledo Public Schools, offers insight into the typical skills and attributes considered worth evaluating. (See Figure 14.3.)

FIGURE 14.3
Intern assessment form.

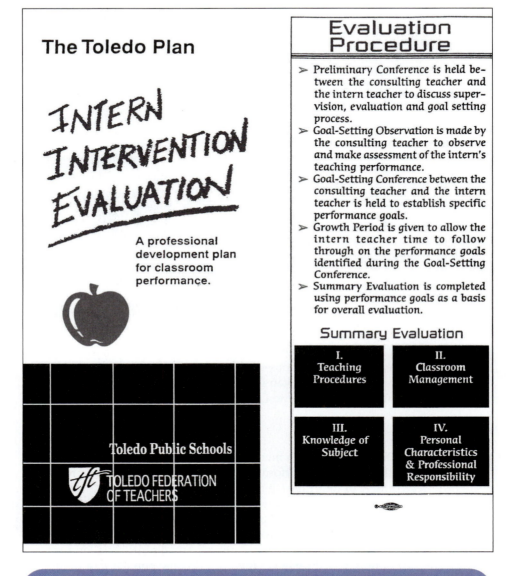

The Toledo Plan

INTERN INTERVENTION EVALUATION

A professional development plan for classroom performance.

Toledo Public Schools

tft TOLEDO FEDERATION OF TEACHERS

Evaluation Procedure

➤ Preliminary Conference is held between the consulting teacher and the intern teacher to discuss supervision, evaluation and goal setting process.
➤ Goal-Setting Observation is made by the consulting teacher to observe and make assessment of the intern's teaching performance.
➤ Goal-Setting Conference between the consulting teacher and the intern teacher is held to establish specific performance goals.
➤ Growth Period is given to allow the intern teacher time to follow through on the performance goals identified during the Goal-Setting Conference.
➤ Summary Evaluation is completed using performance goals as a basis for overall evaluation.

Summary Evaluation

I. Teaching Procedures	II. Classroom Management
III. Knowledge of Subject	IV. Personal Characteristics & Professional Responsibility

REFLECTION

The four evaluation areas on this form (I. Teaching Procedures, II. Classroom Management, III. Knowledge of Subject, IV. Personal Characteristics and Professional Responsibility) have been discussed in this text. As you glance over the form, which skills do you see as your strengths? Which ones need more study and practice? What specific steps in your teacher education program will prepare you to successfully pass this evaluation?

FIGURE 14.3 (concluded)

TEACHER SUMMARY EVALUATION REPORT

Name _____

College _____

School _____ Date _____

Grade or
Subject _____ Period of Sept.-Dec. ☐   Period of Jan.-March ☐   Period of Apr.-Dec. ☐

Certification _____

Number of Observations and Time _____ Conference Time _____

Intern semester completed _____

Check on March and Dec Report	Check on March Report Only	Contract Status
☐ Outstanding	☐ Recommended for first one-year contract	☐ First year contract
☐ Satisfactory		☐ Second year contract
☐ Unsatisfactory	☐ Recommended for a second one-year contract	☐ Four-year contract
☐ Written comment only		☐ One-year contract
☐ Irregular term	☐ Recommended for initial four-year contract	☐ Continuing contract
☐ Recommended for 2nd semester intern program	☐ Recommended for third one-year contract	☐ Long-term substitute (60 or more days)
	☐ Not recommended for reappointment	

* OUTSTANDING: Performance shows exceptional professional qualities and growth.
  SATISFACTORY: Performance at expected and desired professional qualities and growth.
* UNSATISFACTORY: Performance shows serious weaknesses or deficiencies.
* For more complete definition refer to page 10 in the Toledo Plan.
* Unsatisfactory and/or outstandings must have a written supportive statement.

	Out-standing	Satis-factory	Unsatis-factory
I. TEACHING PROCEDURES			
A. Skill in planning			
B. Skill in assessment and evaluation			
C. Skill in making assignments			
D. Skill in developing good work-study habits			
E. Resourceful use of instructional material			
F. Skill in using motivating techniques			
G. Skill in questioning techniques			
H. Ability to recognize and provide for individual differences			
I. Oral and written communication skills			
J. Speech, articulation and voice quality			
II. CLASSROOM MANAGEMENT			
A. Effective classroom facilitation and control			
B. Effective interaction with pupils			
C. Efficient classroom routine			
D. Instructional leadership			
E. Is reasonable, fair and impartial in dealing with students			
III. KNOWLEDGE OF SUBJECT–ACADEMIC PREPARATION			
IV. PERSONAL CHARACTERISTICS AND PROFESSIONAL RESPONSIBILITY			
A. Shows a genuine interest in teaching			
B. Personal appearance			
C. Skill in adapting to change			
D. Adheres to accepted policies and procedures of Toledo Public Schools			
E. Accepts responsibility both inside and outside the classroom			
F. Has a cooperative approach toward parents and school personnel			
G. Is punctual and regular in attendance			

Evaluator's Signature   Teacher's Signature   Principal's Signature
(when required)   (when required)

Evaluator's Position
                  Date of Conference _____

DIRECTIONS

1. Rate all categories, bold face and subcategories.
2. Attach all supporting documents that have been signed or initialed.

Observations, whether official or informal, are usually followed by a conference in which the mentor or supervisor shares the high points and "not-as-high-as-we-would-like" points of your teaching. Take notes and carefully consider these comments. You may find the comments to be useful, even insightful, offering you wise counsel on how to improve. Your attitude and openness in these conferences indicates your willingness to analyze your teaching and refine your teaching skills.

Professional Development Programs

School systems sponsor an amazing variety of professional training options, for new and veteran teachers, both during the summer and throughout the school year. Through these programs, teachers might satisfy state requirements for renewal of teacher licensure, work toward an endorsement or a license in a second teaching field, attend a summer institute to master new skills, obtain an advanced degree, or earn a higher salary.

Most teacher pay schedules are connected to professional development. Sometimes salaries are linked to the number of hours invested in courses and training programs, so that a teacher who takes thirty graduate credits at a college or thirty training hours offered by a school district would get a certain salary raise. In other districts, salary increases are tied to evaluations of teacher performance.

School districts vary greatly in their approaches to professional training. Sometimes districts identify a topic (e.g., student portfolio development or emotional intelligence), invite in one or more speakers to make a presentation on that topic, and require the whole faculty to participate. These professional development efforts are scheduled before, during, and at the end of the academic year. Teachers call them **in-service** days, while students are more likely to consider them vacation days. Many have criticized these one-time programs as "dog and pony" shows, charging that brief presentations given to a large group of educators lack long-term impact.

Other staff development strategies require more time and offer greater focus on a specific subject or skill area. Examples of this more in-depth approach include meetings and workshops over the course of a year to improve the science program and weekly sessions on relevant software. Recent research has underscored the value of teacher-designed programs, closely tied to practical classroom skills. Educational reformers suggest that the best **professional development** programs

- Connect directly to the teacher's work with students
- Link subject content with teaching skills
- Use a problem-solving approach
- Reflect research findings
- Are sustained and supported over time[6]

How can professional development programs incorporate these characteristics? One way is to ask teachers to prepare portfolios for board certification or merit review. Portfolio construction encourages teachers to develop insight and reflection about their instruction by creating tangible examples of their competence. Hopefully, over time, these examples will document their progress and development. Some school districts create a "teaching academy" that offers courses directly linked to particular teacher needs. Over the period of a semester, summer, or year, teachers might enroll in these courses to improve their questioning skills, create more equitable classroom participation, establish effective management strategies, or implement a

FIGURE 14.4 These announcements provide a taste of the continuous learning opportunities available to educators.

Professional Development
Once a Teacher, Always a Learner

Aesthetic Realism Teaching Method Explains the True Purpose of Education: for teachers and administrators, by Aesthetic Realism Foundation, NYC

Hands-on Science workshop by the American Association for the Advancement of Science, K–6, Washington, DC

Adult Education Always Traveling the Speed of Life, Sacramento, CA

Teacher Training Sessions: National Foundation for Teaching Entrepreneurship, San Francisco, CA

Annual Conference for Year-Round Education, K–12 teachers, principals superintendents, board members, parents, Waikiki, HI

Educational Theatre Association: Lighting for Musicals, Orlando, FL; **Disciplined-Based Theatre Education,** Austin, TX

Teachers' Symposium, American Montessori Society, Albuquerque, NM

Urban Education: Council of Urban Boards of Education and National School Boards of Education, Atlanta, GA

Learning Disabilities: Attention Deficit/Hyperactivity Disorder teachers grades 1–6, NYC

Six Traits, Methods of Assessing Student Writing, 2-day immersion, McCook, NE

School Facilities Annual Conference, Council of Educational Facilities Planners International for K–12 adminstrators and planners, architects, construction program managers, manufacturers, and suppliers and government representatives, Vancouver, British Columbia, Canada

Rap, Rhythm, and Rhyme, Transforming Teaching, KIPP Academy, Bronx, NY

Reaching all Students: Assessment in a Standards-Based Environment, Worcester, MA

Shape the Future of Technological Literacy by Opening Communication Lines Between Educators and Engineers, by the Institute of Electrical and Electronic Engineers, Baltimore, MD

The Nuts and Bolts of Operating a Local Teacher Organization by the National Association of Catholic School Teachers, Philadelphia, PA

Character Education Training and Information Conference, Baltimore, MD

Success, Standards, and Struggling Secondary Students: K–12 educators who work with at-risk youth, Renton, WA

National 1 Day Conference for Substitute Teachers, Petersburg, VA

Making Sense of Looping: Non-Graded Primary and Multi-age Classrooms, Cleveland, OH

Raising Standards in Rural Education, National Rural Education Association, Fort Collins, CO

International Conference on Computers in Education, Beijing, China

Integrating the Curriculum with Multiple Intelligences: The Balancing Act, Bloomington, IN

Council of School Attorneys' Advocacy Seminar and School Law Retreat, San Antonio, TX

Integrating the Arts with Literacy for teachers and administrators, Los Angeles, CA

SOURCE: Adapted from *Education Week on the Web*, 1998, 2001.

REFLECTION

Which of these opportunities do you find most interesting? Why? (You might need to consider numerous factors from geography to finances.)

new curriculum. Many programs tie course assignments to daily instructional activities, providing a useful link between professional development and real-world application.

Collaborative action research (CAR) also connects daily teaching responsibilities with professional growth, but in this case through the use of research. Typically, a group of teachers identifies a genuine problem in the school or classes, designs ways to address the problem, and then evaluates their success. If the teachers are concerned about the poor performance of girls in high school science courses, for example, they might decide to experiment with new methods to improve that performance. One teacher might try cooperative learning strategies in her science class, while a second teacher develops techniques to involve parents in their daughters' science work. A third teacher might initiate a new science curriculum designed to motivate female students. Each of these approaches would be evaluated and the most effective selected for use by all teachers. CAR encourages thoughtful, objective analysis of real teacher concerns.

Professional development takes many forms: graduate degree programs, collaborative action research projects, and teaching academies or inservice days. A quick glance at Figure 14.4 should convince you of the wide range of professional development programs. These descriptions are adapted from *Education Week,* a weekly newspaper and Internet publication that covers national education events, so they reflect realistic opportunities available to teachers.

Personalizing Schools

From a new teacher's perspective, what were once familiar school surroundings soon become strange. Teachers and students see school very differently. As a teacher, you will likely be shocked by the endless stream of paperwork that engulfs you, and you will struggle to learn the names of the students in your classes, as many as 150 students or more at the secondary level. You will work even harder getting to know the people behind the names. Typically, you will have only three to five scheduled hours a week to prepare your lessons or coordinate with your colleagues. You will find little time to meet with individual students, much less their parents. Much of your professional day will be spent trying to manage students in a world of adult isolation.[7] This school organization is at least a century old, and new teachers, as well as experienced ones, often find it both dehumanizing and inadequate.

It is not surprising, therefore, that educators are reconceptualizing schools in order to make them more responsive to the intellectual and emotional needs of both teachers and students. As you contemplate where you want to begin your teaching career, you may want to consider how school organization will affect your life in the classroom.

One major school reorganization effort is intended to nurture learning communities, an effort to create a more intimate and goal-oriented environment. When **learning communities** are established, students and teachers get to know each other both personally and intellectually as they develop shared academic goals and values. Reducing class size and lengthening school periods are two of several organizational changes that can reduce student alienation and build learning communities.

In other nations, teachers assume a greater number of responsibilities; as a result, they work more intensively with each student. In Japan, Germany, Switzerland, and Sweden, for example, teachers serve as counselors as well as instructors and have a greater range of interactions with their students. To meet their expanded responsibilities, teachers are given additional time to confer with their colleagues and plan their lessons. There are fewer support staff and administrators in these countries, and greater emphasis is placed on the teacher-student connection. While teachers constitute 60 to 80 percent of the school staff in European and Asian countries, they represent only 43 percent of the education staff in the United States. In fact, in the United States, the number of administrators and nonteaching staff members has more than doubled over the past three decades. Reformers believe student performance will not improve unless we reverse this trend.[8] (See Figure 14.5 for an international comparison of staffing patterns.)

Finding That First Teaching Position

The U.S. Department of Education projects that two million teachers will be needed over the next decade.[9] (See Figure 14.6 for the projected change in regional K–12 enrollments over the next few years.) With teachers in short supply, and many veteran teachers retiring, new teachers are in the driver's seat—sort of. If you are licensed or have an endorsement in certain fields, such as special education, bilingual education, chemistry, math, and physics, you are indeed in the driver's seat. You may find yourself courted by many school districts. (Isn't that nice!) Several districts now recruit teachers from abroad for these difficult-to-fill positions. As one Houston recruiter

FIGURE 14.5   International comparisons of teacher staffing patterns.

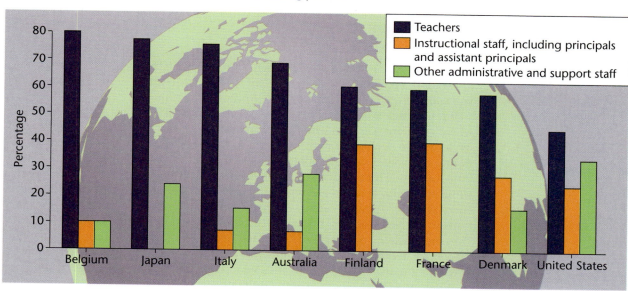

SOURCE: Organization for Economic Cooperation Development (OECD), Education at a Glance: OECD Indicators (Paris: OECD, 1995), Table 31, pp. 176–77.

REFLECTION

Why do you believe that U.S. schools are staffed so differently from other nations? Do you have a suggestion for an ideal or preferred teacher-staff ratio? In your years of schooling, have you been aware of the non-instructional staff and how they have contributed to your education? Explain.

FREE ADVICE FOR YOUR FIRST YEAR

Education World asked second-year teachers to reflect on their first year in the classroom, their successes and failures, and offer advice for new teachers:

- *Take charge.* Have a clear management plan, with well-defined rewards and consequences. Explain it to the students, send it home to the parents, and ask for signatures on the plan.
- *Keep students busy and engaged.* Have a number of potential class activities available. Bored kids get into trouble; busy kids stay out of trouble.
- *Get peer support.* If you are not assigned an official mentor, find an unofficial one.
- *Get parental support.* From extra supplies to celebration plans, parents are a hidden teacher resource, but only if they are pulled into class activities.
- *Organize yourself.* Develop a system that will keep you organized. There is a lot going on in teaching, grading, and monitoring dozens of children for hours each day.
- *Organize your students.* Teach students how to organize their homework, notebooks, etc.
- *Write and reflect.* Keep a journal to help you reflect on your first year, and become a stronger teacher your second year.
- *Have fun.* Teaching is not only stressful; it is joyful. Get into it and have fun!

SOURCE: *Education World* (www.educationworld.com/help/about.shtml).

REFLECTION

Compare this advice with the more formal areas of teacher effectiveness cited in the research and by the National Board for Professional Teacher Standards. What are the similarities and differences?

explained, "We saw more physics teachers in one week in Moscow than we see here in two or three years."[10] Also, if you want to teach in an urban or rural school district, you will most likely have an easy time finding a position.

But the teacher shortage is no guarantee that you will find a teaching position anywhere you want. Districts with high salary schedules and positive teacher morale, often located in popular locations with education-friendly communities, have little need to lure candidates. Since candidates flock to these districts, you will have a tougher time competing for one of these positions. And something else to keep in mind is that while many new teachers are fresh out of college, others are more mature and experienced workers. Termed "career switchers," these new recruits have left other occupations to become teachers, bringing years of skills and experiences to the classroom. They are changing our image of "new" teachers.[11] You can research the ever-changing market for teaching positions online, at websites such as Education Job Openings (www.nationjob.com/education) and Recruiting New Teachers (www.rnt.org).

When pondering where to apply for your first teaching position, the community and your colleagues are just some factors to consider. You may want to make a list of other issues that matter to you:

What subject or grade level do I prefer? What kind of community and students do I want to serve? What part of the country appeals to me? Is there a particular school organization I like? What educational philosophy and school culture am I most comfortable with? How important to me are incentives for superior teaching? What salary and benefits am I seeking? Am I more interested in a private or public school, or perhaps a charter or magnet school? Am I flexible and open to different options or focused in my preferences?

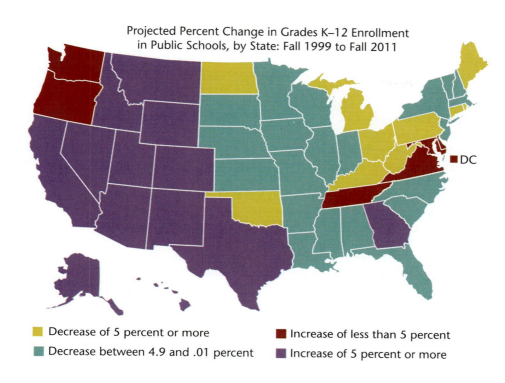

Projected Percent Change in Grades K–12 Enrollment
in Public Schools, by State: Fall 1999 to Fall 2011

■ Decrease of 5 percent or more   ■ Increase of less than 5 percent
■ Decrease between 4.9 and .01 percent   ■ Increase of 5 percent or more

FIGURE 14.6
Where the students are. As you consider where to teach, you may want to know where enrollments are likely to increase.

SOURCE: U.S. Department of Education, National Center for Education Statistics, Common Core of Data surveys; and State Public Elementary and Secondary Enrollment Model. Figure 7.

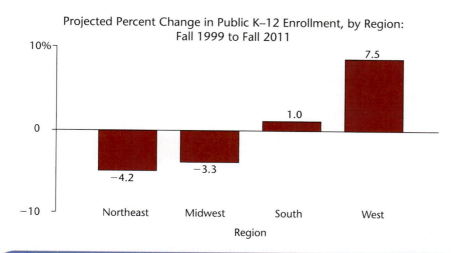

Projected Percent Change in Public K–12 Enrollment, by Region:
Fall 1999 to Fall 2011

SOURCE: U.S. Department of Education, National Center for Education Statistics, Common Core of Data surveys; and State Public Elementary and Secondary Enrollment Model. Figure 8.

REFLECTION

Do national trends like these influence your career decisions? Why or why not?

Many of the activities in this book, including the *You Be the Judge* in the first chapter, the inventory of your educational philosophy in Chapter 9, and the *Inter-missions,* will help you answer these questions. Once you sort out your priorities and identify the schools that are right for you, the next task is to get that first job.

Résumés, Portfolios, and Interviews

The most crucial documents in your job search may well be your résumé and your portfolio, if you have one. With these documents, you seek to convince potential employers that you are a great candidate for an interview. Both documents describe your background, interests and goals. A résumé presents a concise description of your strengths and competencies, while a portfolio offers a more comprehensive profile. Portfolios typically include videotapes of your teaching; sample lesson plans; journals; supervisor's observations; letters from parents, students, and administrators; and examples of student work. Many of the *Inter-mission* and other activities in this text have put you on the road to creating your own portfolio. (Portfolios and résumé building are described in greater detail in the next chapter, which is a "Question and Answer Guide to Entering the Teaching Profession.")

Interviews give employers the chance to see if someone who looks good on paper looks promising in real life as well. Some candidates who are portfolio superstars become interview "also-rans." Conversely, some candidates who have only mediocre credentials come out of an interview with a job offer, because they know how to diagnose and respond to the interviewer's needs. Interviews may be conducted by one or more administrators, a panel of teachers, or a combination of teachers and parents, and the average interview usually lasts thirty minutes to an hour.[12] So how do we make these interviews work for you?

INTERACTIVE ACTIVITY
YOUR PORTFOLIO. Visit the Online Portfolio section of the Online Learning Center to learn more about portfolios, and for guidance and resources to create your own portfolio.

Interviewing

The first thing that will strike an interviewer is appearance. Your prospective interviewer (or interview team) will be looking not only for appropriate professional attire, but also for such qualities as poise, enthusiasm, self-confidence, and an ability to think quickly and effectively on your feet. Appropriate grammar, a well-developed vocabulary, and clear speech and diction are important. You should be focused about your teaching philosophy and goals if you want to appear confident and purposeful in the interview. If you have developed a portfolio of teaching materials or other information that you are particularly proud of, you should take it to the interview. It cannot hurt to have it present, and it might help win the day.

Before interviewing with a school system, it is wise to find out as much as possible about both the particular school and the community. If you do not have friends in the community who can supply such information, you can try the local library, the Internet, or, better yet, stop by the school to talk with the students and others, scour the bulletin boards, and pick up available literature. Once you obtain information about a school or school system, you can begin matching your particular interests and skills with the school district's programs and needs.

As important as such preparatory work is, the most important way of learning what an interviewer is looking for is to listen. Sometimes interviewers state their needs openly, such as "We're looking for a teacher who is fluent in both Spanish and English." In other cases, interviewers merely imply their needs—for example, "Many of the children who attend our school are Hispanic." In this case, you have first to interpret the interviewer's remark and then to check your interpretation with a statement such as "Are you looking for someone who is fluent in both Spanish and English?" Or "Are you looking for someone who has experience in working with Spanish-speaking children?"

Once you have a clear understanding of the opening, it is your task to show that you have the interests, skills, and experience that are required. To continue with the previous example, you would now show, if you could, that you speak Spanish and that you have worked with Spanish-speaking children. If you do not possess these qualifications, the only thing you can do is to express an interest in working with Latino students and, in the process, learning their language and culture.

It is important to be prepared for some of the questions an interviewer is likely to ask. Common interview topics include strengths, weaknesses, personal philosophy of teaching, future plans, employment history, teaching style, and classroom management. Interviewers commonly look for: enthusiasm, warmth, caring, leadership skills, willingness to learn new things, and confidence.[13] You may also want to note what questions cannot legally be asked—for example, questions about your religion or marital or parental status. Such questions do not relate to your qualifications as a teacher. The Office for Civil Rights is one of several agencies that you can contact if you are victimized by such queries.

After interviewing, it is wise to send the interviewer a brief follow-up note, reminding her or him of how your qualifications meet the school system's needs. The interviewer may have talked with dozens of candidates, and under such circumstances it is easy to be forgotten in a sea of faces—your job is to make sure you stand out.

One word of caution: When a job offer comes your way, analyze the school system to make sure that you really want to teach there before signing on the dotted line. Try to find out

- If teachers in the district view it as a good place to work
- If there have been personnel problems recently and, if so, for what reasons
- What are the benefits and potential problems in the teachers' contract
- Typical class size
- What kind of support services are available
- If the school is adopting organizational changes to personalize the school climate.

Not all of these issues may be appropriate for discussion during an initial interview. However, once you have received an offer, you should find out the answers to these questions; if the answers do not please you, the job may not be right for you. It is unwise to accept a position with the notion that you will leave as soon as a better offer is made. That attitude can quickly lead to a job-hopping profile that may stigmatize you as someone who is either irresponsible or unable to work well with others. In short, do not simply jump at the first available job offer. If your credentials are good and you know how to market yourself, you will get other teaching offers.

Teacher Recognition

Project yourself into the future. You have worked hard in your school, and you are widely acclaimed as a terrific teacher (congratulations!). After some wonderful years in the classroom, you begin to think about what lies ahead. Having parents, students, and colleagues sing your praises is wonderful, but is there more than that? How are dedicated and excellent teachers recognized and rewarded? Without formal and meaningful recognition, frustration may well follow, a sentiment captured in all-too-typical teacher comments, such as the following:

Interview procedures vary by school and district—a meeting with the principal, a formal review by a panel of administrators, faculty and school parents, a round table discussion with potential colleagues—any or all could await you. How might you prepare for each of these situations? Would you be more comfortable in one rather than another setting? Why?

How would I describe my teaching? Well, let me put it this way—I work hard. Free time is a thing of the past. My students are really important to me, and I'm willing to go the extra mile to give them feedback, organize field trips and projects, meet with them or their parents, and give them a stimulating classroom. In fact, most Saturdays I'm working on grades or new projects. And I think it pays off—my kids are blossoming! That's a great feeling. But sometimes I wonder if it's all worth it. Is anyone ever going to notice my hard work? Brad down the hall just comes in and does his job without a second thought, and his paycheck looks just like mine. It doesn't seem fair. Teachers who deserve it should be able to earn something more—more money, more respect.

This view is held by thousands of teachers struggling for professional recognition. Working hard in a demanding profession, teachers often do not feel valued or appreciated, and many leave the field each year as a result.

While not a comprehensive solution to the problem, North Carolina has made a grand gesture in response to teacher burnout. The state opened a mountain lodge dedicated to pampering teachers. Over the course of a school year, nearly two thousand teachers, about 2 percent of the state's teachers, are invited to spend five days in the combination spa and mini-university. Sumptuous meals, outdoor walks, and quiet contemplation recharge a teacher's batteries, and are a way of saying thanks for their efforts. Although in-service courses are a part of the week's schedule, they are kept to a minimum and the focus is on relaxation. As one teacher remarked, "This is the closest teachers get to being treated like the corporate world."[14] Perhaps the future will bring more teacher spas, but for now, we will focus on three more common approaches to teacher recognition: board certification, merit pay, and career ladders.

The **National Board for Professional Teaching Standards (NBPTS)** is establishing higher standards for teaching and grants special certification to superior teachers. **Merit pay** is a plan to give additional financial compensation to teachers who demonstrate excellence, though different plans define excellence differently.

Career ladders allow teachers to take on additional responsibilities along with their teaching as a way of advancing in the field. Each of these solutions has drawbacks as well as advantages. Nevertheless, all three influence how teachers are recognized.

The National Board for Professional Teaching Standards

In 1987, the National Board for Professional Teaching Standards (NBPTS) was formed to promote teaching excellence through recognition of superior teachers. The NBPTS awards **board certification** to experienced teachers based on superior performance. It is available to all licensed teachers who hold a baccalaureate degree and have taught (in either public or private school) for a minimum of three years. In a few years, you may want to join the growing number of teachers participating in this effort. In January 1995, eighty-six National Board Certified Teachers were recognized; by 2000, almost ten thousand teachers had achieved board status. When the NBPTS was launched, former North Carolina governor James Hunt, Jr., proclaimed,

> For once in this country, we are working out standards for measuring excellence rather than minimum competency. The certification process has the potential to transform the current educational system, leverage current investment in teaching, and build a national consensus for increased support of schools.[15]

Part of the effort to assess, train, and reward qualified teachers involves direct observation of classroom teaching performance.

Deciding who will be board certified is the task of the sixty-three members of the independent, nonpartisan NBPTS. Most board members are classroom teachers, but others are school administrators, state political leaders, university officials, representatives from professional organizations, and business and community leaders.[16] Imagine yourself as a newly appointed board member responsible for determining what skills and behaviors identify truly excellent teachers, teachers who will be known as board certified. How would you begin? The board began by identifying five criteria: mastery of subject area, commitment to students, ability to effectively manage a classroom, continuous analysis of teaching performance, and a commitment to learning and self-improvement (see Chapter 3, "Teacher Effectiveness," for additional information about these five criteria).[17]

To demonstrate expertise to the NBPTS, teachers must complete a series of performance-based assessments, including written exercises that reflect mastery of their subject and understanding of the most effective teaching methods. Board candidates must also submit student work samples, videotapes of their teaching, and participate in simulations and interviews held at special assessment centers.[18]

Perhaps the biggest question is: What does board certification mean? Clearly, being recognized as exceptional is psychologically rewarding. Considering that there are literally millions of teachers in the United States, to be among a selected few is a major boost. Board certification has become a catalyst for rewarding superior teachers with salary increases and new job responsibilities. Several hundred local school districts and forty states provide some incentive for teachers who are board certified. However, such recognition is not universal. When funds are in short supply or a school district's organizational structure is inflexible, board-certified teachers may receive few tangible rewards or new responsibilities, despite their excellence. As you enter the teaching profession, you will want to stay abreast of the activities concerning the national board and determine if you want to work toward board certification. (For a current update of NBPTS activities, visit www.nbpts.org.)

Merit Pay

Merit pay plans attempt to make teaching more accountable, as well as more financially rewarding, by linking teacher performance and teacher salary. Many groups support this approach, including the National Science Board, the National Association of Secondary School Principals, the American Association of School Administrators, the National Association of Elementary School Principals, and the National Commission on Excellence in Education. But not all plans are acceptable to everyone, and the problems of bias and politics raise concerns, making teacher associations cautious.[19]

Why would merit pay raise teacher anxieties? Why are such plans controversial? Let's listen in on a faculty meeting to see what merit pay really involves for teachers.

Dr. Moore faced her staff and began, "You know the school board gave our district the go-ahead to develop a merit pay proposal. There are several different approaches. Just one example: Rochester, New York, awards merit pay for teachers who receive a second teaching license in reading; work in its professional development academy; accept teaching assignments in more challenging, low-achieving schools; or receive national board certification. To help us understand our options, I'd like to outline some of the different plans and then open the floor for your reactions." You watch intently as she clicks through a PowerPoint presentation to illustrate the different plans. "Basically, there are four different types of merit pay:

"Merit pay based on student performance. This rewards teachers whose students make gains on standardized tests. It implies that a good teacher will help students achieve in the content areas.

"Merit pay based on teacher performance. Under this program, the district would develop criteria to measure your teaching effectiveness, and you would receive raises based on evaluations by outside observers.

"Merit pay based on individualized productivity plans. Do you remember the personal goals each of you wrote for this school year? This plan would ask you to write more detailed goals for what you would like to accomplish this year. Once they are approved, you would receive financial bonuses based on how much you accomplish.

"Merit pay based on the teaching assignment. With this plan, you could receive compensation according to how difficult or how much in demand your teaching position is. Our math, science, and special education teachers would probably receive the greatest bonuses if we were to adopt this plan."

You think this sounds very interesting. There seem to be mixed feelings among the teachers, however. You overhear a number of different opinions:

"This sounds great! I can finally get that bonus I deserve for all my extra hours."

"I wonder how this can work. After all, does the teacher with all the smart kids really deserve a raise if they do well on tests?"

Teachers in Robbinsdale, Minnesota, have an important project due every five years. That's when they assemble their portfolios documenting their teaching skills. Teachers who do well on their portfolio assignments will be paid an additional $15,000 each year for five years. That amounts to $75,000 above their regular salary. The performance pay replaces automatic salary increments.

SOURCE: *Education Week on the Web,* February 1998.

REFLECTION

Do you agree with this approach? Why or why not? How might you design (or redesign) your portfolio if it were used to establish a starting salary?

 Click on *In the News* for recent *In the News* stories. Submit your own *In the News* summary to share with your colleagues.

"I don't think I'd feel comfortable if other people found out I was getting merit pay. Teaching is supposed to mean working as a team, not competing for bonuses."

"Only the people who are in good with the supervisors will get merit pay. How can that be fair?"

"I think we need some sort of merit pay system in teaching that will give all of us something to work for."

Obviously, there are many ways to look at merit pay. Many teachers fear the competition or the methods for judging who deserves merit pay, while others are excited about the possibility of a higher salary. Nevertheless, very few merit pay programs have succeeded in pleasing their districts. Merit and performance pay programs have been plagued by concerns about fairness, and states have been slow to adopt these measures.[20]

Career Ladder Programs

Career ladder programs offer another teacher recognition strategy. The career ladder is designed to create different levels for teachers by creating a "ladder" that one can climb to receive increased pay through increased work responsibility and status.[21] By the beginning of the 1990s, more than half the states had established a career ladder or an incentive program with state assistance. Some critics argue that career ladders have the same drawbacks as merit pay—a lack of clear standards or appropriate evaluation tools—but others claim that career ladders can be more effective because they are rooted in professionalism. The distinguishing characteristic of the career ladder is the increased responsibility given to the teacher. The Rochester, New York, *Career in Teaching* plan is a good example. Here, an outstanding teacher has the opportunity to become a "master" or "mentor teacher," write curricula, select textbooks, or plan staff development programs while continuing to teach in the classroom.[22] Thus, good teachers are not removed from the classroom, yet they earn increased responsibility and salary.

All teacher recognition plans share the goal of making the teaching profession more attractive and more rewarding, whether through official certification, financial compensation, or increased professional responsibility. In what other ways might teachers be able to earn more respect or more money? As you enter the teaching profession, you will want to be aware of the kinds of incentives available in different school districts and consider which incentives appeal to you.

Educational Associations

In colonial times, teachers typically were meek and quiet public servants. In fact, some of them actually were servants, since they had obtained the money to pay for their passage to America by indenturing themselves. Their pitiful wages were equivalent to those of a farmhand. In order to survive, many teachers were forced to board with a different family each week.[23] (Can you imagine eating dinner with a different student's family every week?) Low salaries were the rule through much of the nation's history. Even by 1874, in Massachusetts, male teachers were paid a monthly salary of $24.51. Women earned less than $8. This lowly status provided one motivation for teachers to organize.

In 1794, the Society of Associated Teachers of New York City became the first teacher association in this country. In 1857, this movement went national when the National Teachers' Association was formed, later to become the **National Education Association (NEA).** Half a century later, in 1916, the **American Federation of Teachers (AFT)** was created as a union of teachers affiliated with the American Federation of Labor. Through **collective bargaining** (that is, all the teachers in a school system bargaining as one group through a chosen representative), through

Often marked by acrimony and bitterness, strikes changed the traditional image of teachers as meek and passive public servants.

"America is on trial," declared Margaret Haley, standing before the National Education Association convention. Poor salaries, overcrowded classrooms, and the lack of teacher voice in school policy and curricular decisions, she argued, all undermine teachers' effectiveness.

Though Haley's charges sound disquietingly current, she was not critiquing today's curricular standards created by nonteachers, or the growing dependence on standardized tests to measure both students and teachers, or even the top-down management style of some current school administrators. In fact, Margaret Haley gave this speech a century ago. In 1904, she became the first woman and the first teacher to speak from the floor of an NEA convention. Her speech, "Why Teachers Should Organize," condemned as undemocratic the practice of treating a teacher as an "automaton, a mere factory hand whose duty it is to carry out mechanically and unquestioningly the ideas and orders of those clothed with the authority."[1]

Haley was born in 1851 in Joliet, Illinois, to Irish immigrant parents who valued education and fairness. Haley learned to read from her mother, who used the Bible and a pictorial history of Ireland to educate her daughter. Her father was an active member of local stone quarry and construction unions, who shared accounts of heated union rallies with young Margaret as bedtime stories. Her father also championed the rights and talents of women, and taught Margaret about suffragette Susan B. Anthony and America's first woman physician, Elizabeth Blackwell. Such lessons planted the seeds for Margaret Haley's later efforts to empower women teachers.

At Cook County Normal School, Haley eagerly studied the progressive ideas set forth by John Dewey, embracing the school as a democratic training ground for both students and teachers. But when she entered the classroom in Chicago's poor stockyard district, she encountered a vastly different reality. The curriculum she used was uninspiring and imposed by educational bureaucrats, and she was expected to teach it to fifty or sixty sixth graders. In the warm months, swarms of bugs visited her classroom, and in the winter, Haley shivered along with her students. Working in such deplorable conditions, she increasingly understood that teachers needed to fight the factory mentality of schools.

After twenty years of teaching in Chicago schools, Haley left the classroom to devote herself full-time to educational reform efforts through unions. As vice president and business agent for the Chicago Teachers' Federation (CTF), Haley transformed the fledgling organization into a national voice for teachers' rights. At the turn of the twentieth century, the CTF was the most powerful and militant of the teachers' organizations fighting for, in Haley's words, "the right for the teacher to call her soul her own."[2]

The earliest teachers' unions lacked any real legal authority. Without collective bargaining rights, the CTF relied on lawsuits and political campaigns to effect change. Haley's first action for the CTF was to force the Illinois Supreme Court to wrest unpaid taxes from five public utility companies—money that was earmarked for teachers' salaries. For Haley, now known as the "Lady Labor Slugger," the victory was one for both education and democracy: Teachers were given a raise and Chicago businesses were forced to uphold their civic responsibility to the public schools.

Unlike other teacher associations of the time, Haley deliberately limited the CTF to elementary school teachers. Women consequently dominated the organization, challenging the prevailing wisdom that women should remain quiet, confined to their classrooms. Through the CTF, teachers could become social activists. Under Haley's leadership, Chicago teachers won a tenure law, a pension plan, and were given power over curriculum and discipline. Haley also engineered a successful campaign to affiliate her union with the Chicago Federation of Labor. The status of teachers, in Haley's mind, was little more than that of a white-collar proletariat, strikingly similar to blue-collar manual workers. Although the CTF's alliance with labor shocked many teachers, the union ultimately helped the CTF gain political power. Though women could not yet vote, they worked with male labor workers to support a range of progressive issues: child labor laws, women's suffrage, and equal wages for men and women.

A century ago, Margaret Haley called for teachers "to save the schools for democracy and to save democracy in the schools."[3] Her tireless efforts and astute political skills helped create more humane schools for both teachers and students. Haley died in 1939.

[1]Nancy Hoffman, *Woman's "True" Profession: Voices from the History of Teaching* (Old Westbury, NY: The Feminist Press, 1981), p. 291.

[2]David Neiman (Producer), *Only a Teacher*, Part 2: *Those Who Can . . . Teach* (Princeton: Films for the Humanities and Sciences, 2000).

[3]Ibid.

WRITE YOUR OWN *PROFILE IN EDUCATION:* Click on *Profiles in Education,* write a *Profile in Education* about an educator, and post it on the Online Learning Center. Check out *Profiles in Education* submitted by other future teachers.

To learn more about Margaret Haley, click on *Profiles in Education.*

REFLECTION

Had you heard of Margaret Haley before reading this profile? If your answer is no, you are not alone. Why do we know so few of education's heroes, teachers whose efforts have improved the lives of teachers?

organized actions (including strikes), and through public relations efforts, the NEA and the AFT succeeded in improving both the salaries and the working conditions of teachers, and they continue to influence teachers' professional lives.

In your first few years as a teacher, you will find yourself in a new environment and without the protection of tenure. Teacher associations, such as the NEA and the AFT, can help alleviate that sense of vulnerability by providing you with collegial support, opportunities for professional growth, and the security that one derives from participating in a large and influential group. Today, teaching is one of the most organized occupations in the nation. Nine out of ten teachers belong to either the NEA or AFT. Six out of ten teachers are represented by one or the other in collective bargaining. It is not too early for you to start thinking about which one may best represent you.

Which Educational Association Speaks for You?

You have been a teacher in Mediumtown for all of two weeks, and you know about five faces and three names of other faculty members. You have just learned that your colleagues will be meeting to decide whether Mediumtown teachers should keep their affiliation with the Mediumtown Teachers' Association (a local chapter of the National Education Association), or create a new chapter associated with the American Federation of Teachers. You are not wild about attending another meeting, but it would be a chance to meet some of your new colleagues and a way to determine which organization speaks for you (and since the text is drawing to a close, this may be the last meeting you can eavesdrop on). So you decide to go.

At the meeting, NEA and AFT brochures are distributed, and speakers begin making their pitch. You flip through a brochure that gives you a bit of the NEA's long history. When the forty-three founders gathered in the mid-nineteenth century, they intended to form a broad organization that would encompass many different educational interests and groups. But school administrators and college professors dominated the NEA, and teachers had a limited role. During the 1960s and 1970s, the NEA became a stronger advocate of teachers' rights, and by the 1980s and 1990s, the association was also advocating various educational reforms.

The brochure describes the NEA as the largest professional and employee organization in the nation. It enrolls 2.6 million members, including elementary and secondary teachers, higher-education faculty, retired educators, and educational support personnel. It also offers many services, from journals such as *NEA Today* to training

INTERACTIVE ACTIVITY
WHO SAID WHAT? Match statements with the educational organizations they came from.

on issues like women's leadership, child abuse protections, technology and academic freedom, to legal services, if a teacher needs to be represented in court. The NEA members work to elect pro-education candidates and to promote legislation beneficial to teachers and students. (See www.nea.org.)

You are so impressed with the accomplishments and promise of the NEA and the local MEA that you're about ready to pay your membership dues. Just then, a teacher who has been sitting quietly next to you leans over and says, "I belong to the MFT, the Mediumtown Federation of Teachers. We're the local affiliate of the American Federation of Teachers. Don't sign anything until you've heard our side." He introduces himself with "just call me Al" and takes the floor.

"When John Dewey became our first member back in 1916, he recognized that teachers need their own organization. Teachers are the backbone of the educational system, and we must speak for ourselves. That is why the AFT will continue to be exclusively of teachers, by teachers, and for teachers.

"It was the AFT that backed school desegregation years before the 1954 Supreme Court decision that established the principle that separate is not equal. We ran freedom schools for Southern black students, and we have a strong record on academic freedom and civil rights.

"It was the AFT that demanded and fought for the teacher's right to bargain collectively. It was the AFT leaders who went to jail to show the nation their determination that teachers would no longer stand for second-class status. It was the AFT that won New York City teachers their pay increases and other benefits.

"And, as part of the great labor movement, the AFL-CIO, the AFT continues to show the nation that through the power of the union the voice of America's teachers will be heard."

You take a look at the AFT brochure. Even with only a million members, the AFT has significant influence. In 1961, the AFT strike in New York City gave it a national spotlight, and AFT membership began to grow in labor-oriented urban areas. Strikes increased, but so did salaries. In Washington, DC, Boston, Cleveland, Chicago, and other cities, teachers decided to join the AFT. Militancy brought the AFT both members and victories, usually confined in urban centers. The AFT's image as a streetwise, scrappy union has shifted since the 1970s. In fact, through the ideas and activities of its long-time president, Albert Shanker, the AFT took a leadership role in education reform. Shanker supported national exams for students as well as national standards for teachers and was a pioneer in the creation of charter schools. The AFT also supports induction programs that enable new teachers to work with master teachers and the active recruitment of people of color into the teaching profession.[24] The AFT provides services similar to the NEA, although on a smaller scale. (See www.aft.org.)

As you weigh the relative merits of the two organizations, you overhear some teachers muttering that they don't care to join either group and that in their opinion the NEA and AFT put the salaries of teachers above the needs of children. Listening more closely, you hear these teachers claim that teacher associations have pitted administrators against teachers, and teachers against the public, creating needless hostility. Even worse, these critics charge, unions too often protect incompetent teachers who should be removed from the classroom.

Still, you are intrigued by the promise of collective action. In fact, you cannot help but speculate about a merger of these two professional organizations, a merger that has in fact been under discussion for several years. A consolidation of the NEA and

Milestones in the birth and growth of teacher associations.

1794	The Society of Associated Teachers of New York City becomes the country's first teacher association.
1840–1861	Thirty state teacher associations form.
1857	The first National Teachers' Association is formed. In the late 1870s, this group merges with the National Association of School Superintendents and the American Normal School Association to become the National Education Association (NEA).
1902	A group of teachers from San Antonio, Texas, becomes the first to join a labor union, the American Federation of Labor (AFL).
1916	The American Federation of Teachers (AFT) is formed.
1920s	The AFT has more than 10,000 members.
1940s	More than 200,000 teachers belong to the NEA (up from about 7,000 in 1910). More than 30,000 teachers belong to the AFT.
1940s–1950s	More than 100 strike threats are carried out.
1960s–1970s	The AFT and then the NEA take up militant tactics, including even more frequent strikes.
1980s–1990s	Teacher organizations are involved in political action and show growing concern for increased professionalism.
1998	NEA members reject AFT merger plan. Talks for a future merger continue.

REFLECTION

Predict the future of teacher organizations and speculate when and what the next two or three entries might be.

AFT would form an incredibly powerful union of over three million teachers.[25] Such an organization could wield enormous national leverage, potentially gaining significant benefits for education in general and teachers in particular. And if they merged, you would not have to choose at all! But for right now, you have a decision to make. Does either the NEA or the AFT speak for you?

Professional Associations and Resources

In addition to the NEA and the AFT, you will find many resources that can help you in your professional development. Publications such as *Education Week* keep teachers abreast of educational developments. (The online version is available at www.edweek.org.) Journals, professional training, university courses, and professional associations can help you not only in those critical first few years, but throughout your teaching career as you refine your teaching techniques and adapt curricular resources. The Internet is a great source of classroom ideas and practical advice. Teacher-Zone (www.teacher-zone.com), The New Teacher page (www.geocities.com/Athens/Delphi/762), and Beginning Teacher's Tool Box (www.inspiringteachers.com), are typical of the online resources now available. And sometimes, just talking to others and learning about techniques for stress reduction can make all the difference in that first job, which is the idea behind Teachers Helping Teachers (www.pacificnet.net/~mandel).

Here are a few organizations that you may find helpful:

- *The Association for Supervision and Curriculum Development* is an international, nonprofit, nonpartisan association of professional educators whose jobs cross all grade levels and subject areas. (www.ascd.org)

- *National Middle School Association* works to improve the educational experiences afforded young adolescents, ages 10–15 years. (www.nmsa.org)

- *National Association for the Education of Young People* pulls together preschools, child care, primary schools, cooperatives, and kindergarten educators and parents in projects to improve the quality and certification of these schools. (www.naeyc.org)

- *National Association for Gifted Children* advances the opportunities and school programs for gifted students. (www.nagc.org)

- *The Council for Exceptional Children* is the largest international professional organization dedicated to improving educational outcomes for individuals with exceptionalities, students with disabilities, and the gifted. (www.cec.sped.org/ab-menu.html)

If you are interested in subject matter specialties, many organizations, journals, and websites can meet your needs. Here is a brief sample:

Bob Chase. In high school, his English teacher told Bob that he should become an educator and he did. Now Bob Chase finds himself the head of the National Education Association, the largest teachers' organization, trying to reform the profession.

Sandra Feldman. After three years of elementary school teaching, she became a field representative for the UFT (United Federation of Teachers), the New York chapter of the AFT. Now, as the first woman leader of the AFT since 1930, Feldman has several items on her agenda, including improving urban schools and reducing class size.

- *American Alliance for Health, Physical Education, Recreation and Dance* (www. aahperd.org)
- *National Council for Teachers of English* (www.ncte.org)
- *National Council for the Social Studies* (www.ncss.org)
- *National Science Teachers Association* (www.nsta.org)
- *Teachers of Speakers of Other Languages* (www.tesol.org)
- *National Council for the Teachers of Mathematics* (www.nctm.org)

As a teacher, you will find yourself in a learning community, not only teaching students, but continually improving your own knowledge and skills. We hope that these resources and others in this text will set you on that path of continuous learning and improvement. You may not have decided on whether teaching is right for you and you may still have a question or two left unanswered. That is what the final chapter is all about. In our last chapter, we share some of the frequent questions that students ask us about teaching. But before we get to that last chapter, there is one central (really irksome) question that we want to address now: Are America's schools failing? It is discouraging for teachers to invest their talent and energy only to be told by politicians and journalists that our schools are doing poorly. We would like to offer a platform to another side of the story, presenting a perspective we rarely hear.

American Schools: Better Than We Think?

School bashing is nothing new; it is as American as apple pie. In fact, some educators believe not only that the current wave of criticism is old hat, but that it is terribly misguided, because today's schools are doing as well as they ever have—maybe, just maybe, they are doing better.

Critics decry the low performance by U.S. students on international tests. But school advocates point out that test results may reflect cultural and curricular differences, not a failing educational system. Consider that Japanese middle school students score significantly higher that U.S. students on algebra tests, but most Japanese students take algebra a year or two earlier than U.S. students do. Moreover, most Japanese children attend private academies, called *Juku* schools, after school and on weekends. By 16 years of age, the typical Japanese student has attended at least two more years of classes than has a U.S. student. Yet because of the greater comparative effectiveness of U.S. colleges in relation to Japanese colleges, many of these differences evaporate on later tests. (Perhaps there are two lessons here: (1) U.S. students should spend more time in school and (2) the Japanese need to improve the quality of their colleges.)

Student selection also affects test scores. In other countries, students who do not speak the dominant language are routinely excluded. In some nations, only a small percentage of the most talented students are selected or encouraged to continue their education and go on to high school. As one might imagine, a highly selective population does quite well on international tests. In the United States, the full range of students is tested: strong and weak, English-speaking and non-English-speaking students. A larger number of American test-takers are likely to be poor. Comparing all of America's students with another nation's best is an unfair comparison.

Americans value a comprehensive education, one in which students are involved in a wide array of activities, from theater to sports to community service. The U.S. public typically values spontaneity, social responsibility, and independence in their

YOU BE THE JUDGE

HAVE PUBLIC SCHOOLS FAILED OR SERVED SOCIETY?

American Schools Have Failed Society Because . . .

INTERNATIONAL TESTS DOCUMENT POOR STUDENT PERFORMANCE

How embarrassing for the students in the richest, most powerful nation in the world to do so miserably on tests. Our students typically trail students in Korea, Japan, and most of Western Europe.

TOO MANY STUDENTS DROP OUT OR ACT OUT

The lack of discipline, decorum and control in America's schools is a sign that basic values are missing, poor management is commonplace, and school violence and dropouts are rampant.

WORKERS LACK BASIC SKILLS

America does not produce enough scientists, engineers, and mathematicians, and our workers lack not only key technical skills, but basic reading and writing competencies as well. American companies are now forced to provide remedial instruction to our ill-prepared workers.

SCHOOLS HAVE BECOME A MONOPOLY

The power of teacher unions and the inertia of the school bureaucracies have robbed schools of initiative and creativity. Competition through vouchers and charter schools is the answer.

American Schools Have Served Society Well Because . . .

INTERNATIONAL TEST SCORES MISS THE POINT

Americans value individuality and creativity, characteristics absent from these tests. Lower scores are due to the high number of American poor taking these tests, a sign of our society's failure, not school failure.

STUDENT SUCCESS IS REAL

Graduation rates are up for the poor, for non-English speakers, and for special education students. And incidences of violence have actually been reduced.

WORKERS ARE AMONG THE BEST IN THE WORLD

Many Americans are unaware of the fact that our colleges produce a higher percentage of engineers and scientists than any other nation in the world, and our workers are among the most educated and skilled in the world. America is an economic superpower because of our worker productivity.

THEY REPRESENT THE DEMOCRATIC IDEAL

Jefferson and Mann were right: The nation's future rests on public schools. Vouchers and privatization take money from already underfunded public schools and hurt free, democratic education.

YOU BE THE JUDGE

Why do Americans struggle over such a basic question? Do arguments about school effectiveness influence your decision to teach? Do school critics serve a useful purpose by prodding the public to create more effective schools, or are they more likely to mislead the public and discourage teachers?

children, values that are not assessed in international tests. Consider the way a South Korean teacher identifies the students selected for the International Assessment of Education Progress (IAEP).

> The math teacher . . . calls the names of the 13-year-olds in the room who have been selected as part of the IAEP sample. As each name is called, the student stands at attention at his or her desk until the list is complete. Then, to the supportive and encouraging applause of their colleagues, the chosen ones leave to [take the assessment test.][26]

U.S. students taking international exams do not engender cheers from their class-mates and do not view such tests as a matter of national honor, as do the South Korean students. Too often, our culture belittles intellectuals and mocks gifted students.

Despite these obstacles, on several key tests the nation's students are doing quite well. For example, by the mid-1990s, American students had achieved the second-highest average score among thirty-one nations on international comparisons of reading. The proportion of students scoring above 650 on the SAT mathematics tests had reached an all-time high. The number of students taking Advanced Placement (AP) tests soared, a sign that far more students are in the race for advanced college standing. Improvements have been documented on the California Achievement Test, the Iowa Test of Basic Skills, and the Metropolitan Achievement Test, tests used across the nation to measure student learning. One of the most encouraging signs has been the performance of students of color, whose scores have risen dramatically. Among 17-year-old African American students, average reading scores on the NAEP tests rose dramatically.[27] Decades ago, many of these students probably would not have even been in school, much less taking tests. In 1940, the overall high school graduation rate in the United States was only 38 percent; by the 1990s, it approached 90 percent. Other indicators reflect that students are not only staying in school longer but also are enrolling in more advanced math and science classes. U.S. schools are teaching more students, students are staying in school for longer periods of time, and children are studying more challenging courses than ever before.

Then why is there a national upheaval about education—why all the furor about our failing schools and why the demands for radical school reform? Educators have advanced a number of possible explanations:[28]

- Journalists and politicians have been critiquing schools since the founding of our nation.

- Adults tend to romanticize what schools were like when they attended as children, for they always studied harder and learned more than their children do (and when they went to school, they had to walk through four feet of snow, uphill, in both directions!).

- Americans hold unrealistic expectations. They want schools to conquer all sorts of social and academic ills, from illiteracy to teenage pregnancy, and to accomplish everything from teaching advanced math to preventing AIDS.

- Schools today work with tremendous numbers of poor students, non-English-speaking children, and special education students who just a few years ago would not be attending school as long or, in some cases, would not be attending school at all.

- In *The Manufactured Crisis,* David Berliner and Bruce Biddle put much of the blame for the current criticism on neoconservative policies of the 1990s supporting private schools, business interests, and vouchers. These policies marked the beginning of a major assault on public education, on federal involvement in schools, and on equal education programs targeting minority groups and women.

- Berliner and Biddle also finger the press, which has been all too willing to publish negative stories about schools—stories based on questionable sources. Sloppy, biased reporting has damaged the public's perception of schools.

It is helpful to remember two points. First, criticism can be fruitful. If additional attention and even criticism help shape stronger schools, then the current furor will have at least some positive impact. Second, there are countless students in all parts of the country who work diligently every day and perform with excellence. The United States continues to produce leaders in fields as diverse as medicine and sports, business and entertainment. To a great extent, these success stories are also the stories of talented and dedicated teachers. Although their quiet daily contributions rarely reach the headlines, teachers do make a difference. You represent the next generation of teachers who will, no doubt, weather difficult times and sometimes adverse circumstances to touch the lives of students and to shape a better America.

SUMMARY

1. What are the stages of teacher development?

   • Teachers provided with sufficient support can move through a series of stages: survival, consolidation, renewal, and maturity. Teachers become more effective as their focus moves from personal concerns (such as classroom management) to broader educational issues (school strategies that could enhance student learning).

   • Teachers make a difference. Studies underscore that, dollar for dollar, investments in teacher qualifications and training directly and substantially improve student achievement, even more than reduced class sizes and greater teaching experience do.

2. What resources do school districts provide for a teacher's first year in the classroom?

   • School districts are implementing a variety of induction programs designed to assist first-year teachers. Mentors, or consulting teachers, work with intern teachers to help them succeed in their new position. Mentors provide both personal and professional support, and sometimes are responsible for observing and evaluating new teachers' skills.

   • Classroom observations of teachers are done not only by mentors but also by supervisors or colleagues. When other teachers do the observation, the approach is called peer review.

   • Professional development is an integral part of a teacher's life, not just for new teachers but for all teachers. Effective professional development is directly related to a teacher's work, links subject content with teaching skills, uses problem solving, and is research-based and supported over time.

   • Collaborative action research connects daily teaching activities with professional growth. This is done as practicing teachers identify real classroom problems, then research the problem, and use that information to improve the quality of student learning.

3. How can new teachers increase their chances of working in a school of their choice?

   • Looking for a teaching position takes careful planning. Teaching candidates need to give careful consideration to questions such as: Do other teachers enjoy working in this school? Are benefits satisfactory? What are the children like? What kind of support do teachers receive? Does the community support its school system?

   • A strong résumé or portfolio may land you an interview. An effective interview is a critical arena for demonstrating your commitment, skills, and philosophy of education.

4. How do school districts, states, and the National Board for Professional Teaching Standards recognize and reward teachers?

- Established in 1987, the National Board for Professional Standards (NBPTS) seeks to identify and assess experienced teachers who are performing at a superior level. Candidates must take written tests, submit videotapes of their performance and samples of student work, and participate in simulations at assessment centers around the nation. Most states and many school districts offer additional incentives for board certification, including salary bonuses and supplementary responsibilities.

- Merit pay and career ladders are two other efforts aimed at professionalizing teaching.

- Merit pay offers teachers more money based on various criteria, including gains in student performance, typically measured by standardized tests; teacher performance, as measured by outside evaluators; individualized plans, in which teachers have a voice in setting their own goals; and the nature of the teaching assignment.

- Career ladders offer more systemic change. Teaching responsibilities increase, as does salary, as teachers move up a "ladder" to additional responsibilities and incentives. The intent is to reward superior performance with both increased salary and greater influence in the education of others.

- Merit pay and career ladders offer additional money for superior performance, but critics charge that these programs are compromised by unfair practices and do not improve education.

5. What are the differences between the National Education Association and the American Federation of Teachers?

- The National Education Association (NEA) is the largest professional and employee association in the nation. Formed during the second half of the 1800s, initially it was slow to work for the needs of its members, and was dominated by administrators and professors.

- During the 1960s and 1970s, the NEA became a stronger advocate of teachers' rights. In the 1980s and 1990s, the NEA refined its position on a variety of educational reform proposals while exploring merger possibilities with the AFT.

- When teacher unions from the Midwest affiliated with the American Federation of Labor in 1916, the American Federation of Teachers (AFT) was formed. While significantly smaller than the NEA, the AFT has historically taken a more militant position, demonstrated by its early support of teacher strikes.

- Under the longtime leadership of Albert Shanker, the AFT changed its image from that of a scrappy union to that of an important force in education reform.

- Today both the NEA and the AFT offer a range of services, including magazines, journals, and other professional communications; legal assistance; workshops and conferences; assistance in collective bargaining; and political activism.

- Other professional associations, journals, and websites offer new teachers resources and professional development opportunities throughout their teaching career.

6. Are America's schools a secret success story, doing better than the press and the public believe?

- The lower performance of American students on international tests may be attributed to curricular and cultural differences, not necessarily to educational deficiencies.

- Many indicators, from SAT scores to high school graduation rates, reflect an improvement in American schools.

- According to educators like Berliner and Biddle, school bashing reflects an old tradition of journalists and a popular activity of today's neoconservative politicians. We also have unrealistically high public expectations of what schools can do, yet schools confront significant challenges, including high levels of poverty and high numbers of non-English speakers.

- The bottom line is that despite the press and current perceptions, America's schools may be doing far better than we realize.

American Federation of
Teachers (AFT), 571

board certification, 568

career ladders, 568

collaborative action research
(CAR), 560

collective bargaining, 571

Margaret Haley, 572

induction program, 552

in-service, 558

intern teachers, 552

learning communities, 560

mentors, 553

merit pay, 567

National Board for Professional
Teaching Standards
(NBPTS), 567

National Education Association
(NEA), 571

peer review, 555

professional development, 558

stages of teacher
development, 552

DISCUSSION QUESTIONS AND ACTIVITIES

1. How might you redefine or modify any of the stages of teacher development? Can these stages be applied to other careers?

2. Visit a school and analyze the faculty in terms of the stages of development. What are the specific behaviors and skills that place a teacher at each of these stages?

3. Survey local school districts and analyze their first-year induction programs. What resources do they provide new teachers to assist them in making a successful transition into teaching? Will this affect your decision as to where to teach? You might want to research first-year teacher induction programs in the library or on the Internet to get a sense of the range of resources offered to first-year teachers.

4. Interview one or more first-year teachers. What are their biggest challenges? Where do they go to seek support? What lessons can they offer you?

5. Interview a mentor, a veteran teacher who has worked with new teachers during the induction period. What advice does the mentor have for you to help your first year be a success? Are there steps you can take now to build toward a successful first year?

6. What do you look for in a mentor? What strategies can you use to recruit such a mentor in your first teaching job?

7. In order to get a sense of the breadth of professional opportunities available to you, add to the list started in this book. Pull together notices of professional service courses, workshops, and other opportunities available to teachers. To do this, you may want to review professional journals and also contact local school districts, professional associations, state department of education, and colleges.

8. Develop some potential topics for a collaborative action research project. Consider undertaking this project as a research activity during your teaching education program.

9. What are the similarities and differences between the NEA and the AFT? Contact both organizations to find out more about them, or visit their Web pages. Which do you think will best meet your needs as a teacher?

10. Interview some practicing teachers to determine their opinions of the NEA and the AFT. Interview retired teachers for their reactions. Summarize your findings.

11. Research the historical development of these professional associations. Interview teachers who have participated in strikes. What are their opinions? Interview citizens, both those with and those without children in school. What are their opinions about teacher strikes?

12. Identify professional organizations that can be useful in your first-year teaching, and in all your teaching years. Share your list with others in the class.

13. Collect newspaper accounts of U.S. schools and student test performance. Research the accuracy of these stories. Do the same with statements made by political commentators on education in the United States today. Compare their statements with the issues raised by Berliner and Biddle. (Another good author for you to research is Gerald R. Bracey.)

WEB-*TIVITIES*

1. Observation: Peer Review
2. Finding That First Teaching Position
3. The National Board for Professional Teaching Standards
4. Teacher Recognition: Merit Pay
5. Teacher Associations: the NEA and AFT

REEL TO REAL TEACHING: IT'S YOUR TURN

You've been invited to watch films and reflect and respond to *Reel to Reals* throughout this book. It is now time to switch roles! As future teachers, you will be challenged to develop assignments that are clear and promote meaningful learning. It is also common to use media in the classroom to inspire and inform students who are accustomed to *edutainment*. So, we are inviting you to apply your skills and creativity to write this chapter's *Reel to Real Teaching*.

Activity: Choose a film or television show with an educational theme. Here are a few suggestions:

- A new film that has just burst onto the movie scene.
- A film about education that has not been reviewed in earlier chapters. Browse your favorite video stores, educational resource center or online listings for some ideas.
- A film suitable to your subject area and grade level. For example, the *Luzhin Defence* for mathematics, *Gandhi* for social studies, *Amadeus* for music, *Billy Elliot* for character education. Visit Teach with Movies at www.teachwithmovies.org for additional movie titles.
- A film mentioned in this text that you haven't yet seen.
- A television show, such as *The Education of Max Bickford* or *Boston Public*.

Now, design an original *Reel to Real Teaching,* using the template presented in previous chapters.

1. Write a brief synopsis of the film.
2. Develop three or four reflection questions that encourage readers to connect the film's story with chapter content and with personal experiences.
3. Create a follow-up activity that applies themes from the film to real first-year classroom experiences, effective teaching, or your teaching interests.

Reflection: Add a brief, special paragraph that examines your development of the Reel to Real. How did it feel to change roles and create an activity? What did you learn from the process? Were you able to integrate content from the textbook? Did you enjoy initiating an activity versus responding to someone else's assignment? Was creativity the toughest part? Did you struggle with clear and concise directions?

Click on *Reel to Real Teaching* to submit your own film activity. Be sure to include a synopsis, reflection questions, and a follow-up activity.

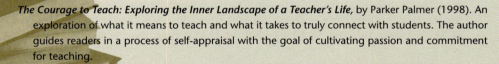

FOR FURTHER READING

The Courage to Teach: Exploring the Inner Landscape of a Teacher's Life, by Parker Palmer (1998). An exploration of what it means to teach and what it takes to truly connect with students. The author guides readers in a process of self-appraisal with the goal of cultivating passion and commitment for teaching.

Exploring the Moral Heart of Teaching: Toward a Teacher's Creed, by David Hansen (2001). Drawing on classroom observations, teacher testimony, and philosophical reflection, this book examines why teaching is essential in human life and why the most important factor in teaching is the *person* who teaches.

How to Develop a Professional Portfolio: A Manual for Teachers, by Dorothy Campbell (2000). Demonstrates how creating a professional portfolio allows teachers to play an active role in documenting their competence and achievements.

Reflections of First-Year Teachers on School Culture: Questions, Hope and Challenges, by Morgaen Donaldson and Brian Poon (1999). Thoughtful accounts of daily life in the classroom. Teachers reveal their expectations and experiences in educating the gifted, privileged, disadvantaged, and students with special needs.

Transforming Teacher Unions: Fighting for Better Schools and Social Justice, by Bob Peterson and Michael Charney (1999). An anthology of teacher union efforts from the local to the national level, weaving together issues of teachers as leaders, classroom reform, local community involvement, and social equity.

Why I Teach: Inspirational True Stories from Teachers Who Make a Difference, by Esther Wright (1999). A collection of true stories from teachers who have made profound differences in the lives of their students. Readers will meet teachers from small towns and large cities, from elementary schools through high schools, each with a story reflecting the magic of teaching.

FOCUS QUESTIONS

1. What does the education job market look like? (or, put another way, will I be able to find a satisfying teaching position?)
2. Can I make a decent salary as a teacher?
3. How do I use a résumé and a portfolio in applying for a teaching position?
4. What do I need in order to teach—a license or certification? (and how do I get one!)
5. What teacher competency tests do I need to take?
6. Why do teachers seek tenure? (and should I?)
7. Are there jobs in education outside of the classroom?

WHAT DO YOU THINK? What Questions Do You Have? Click on Ask the Author to submit any questions you still have. See what questions others have asked and the author's responses.

CHAPTER PREVIEW

Beyond questions concerning education as a field of study, students often have personal and practical questions about teaching, the kinds of questions that are more likely to be asked after class or during office hours. Students considering an education career want to know everything from where the jobs are to how to land a teaching position, from how teachers are licensed to what kinds of education careers are available beyond the classroom. We trust that this chapter will answer some of the questions you are asking, and even some you never thought to raise.

CHAPTER FOCUS
When students consider a career, they often bring more questions than can be answered during a semester's coursework. This chapter is intended to offer many answers and provide a change of pace in the textbook's structure. For a chapter outline, see the IM.

What Are My Chances of Finding a Teaching Position?

This is a practical and quite natural question for you to be asking right now. After all, you are thinking about investing time, energy, money, and talent in preparing yourself to become a teacher, so it makes sense to ask whether you will be able to land a position when you graduate. Here is a shortcut to sorting out your employment possibilities, the **"four Ws"**: *when, what, where,* and *who.* Let's begin with *when.*

Although you may not have planned when you would enter teaching, the good news is that this is a terrific time to be looking for a position in education. While there are few guarantees when it comes to predicting national labor needs, several factors suggest that there will be a significant number of teaching positions available into the next decade. Perhaps we can appreciate the current situation better if we take a look at "the bad old days."

Historically, the demand for new teachers has resembled a roller coaster ride. In the 1950s and 1960s, a teaching shortage meant virtually anyone would be hired as a teacher, with or without the proper credentials. Back then, new graduates of teacher education programs enjoyed the view from the roller coaster as it soared. By the 1970s, the teacher employment roller coaster had begun to descend. Shrinking school budgets and the end of the baby boom had led to far more teachers than there were positions; as more teachers were licensed than positions existed, **teacher oversupply** became part of the educational lexicon, and teacher unemployment was common. By the 1980s and 1990s, the roller coaster was back on the ascent, as teacher retirements increased and student enrollments began to climb.

Strong demand for new teachers continues into the twenty-first century.[1] An increasing student population, calls for smaller class sizes, ongoing teacher retirements, and the relative attractiveness of a teaching career have increased the demand for teachers.

Let's consider the second *W: what* subject and grade level you plan to teach. Teachers of certain subjects, such as science and math, are in short supply, and many school districts are being forced to hire science and math teachers who have not taken enough courses to qualify for a license in these fields. Science, computer science, and math are "hot" fields; in many districts, so are bilingual and special education.[2] One way to make yourself more marketable is to consider course work and school experiences in subjects and skills that are in demand.

Population shifts and political actions affect teacher demand, and they contribute to the third *w, where.* Recently, teacher shortages were felt in western and southwestern states (Arizona, California, Alaska, and Hawaii), while the need for new teachers was generally lower in the Northeast, Great Lakes, and Middle Atlantic areas.[3] But, despite these general trends, there are notable exceptions; for example, population increases in some communities in New Jersey and New Hampshire created local teacher shortages. Large cities, one of the more challenging classroom environs, also continue to experience a shortage of new teachers. In high-poverty urban and rural districts alone, more than 700,000 new teachers will be needed in the next decade.[4]

As we discussed earlier in the text, local and state governments are experimenting with new methods of school organization, changes that may impact the job market and go beyond the traditional four Ws. **Privatization** (the movement to turn over school management to private companies), voucher systems, and even charter schools challenge traditional employment practices by introducing productivity measures, individual school decision making, and the participation of parents and others in personnel actions. Many schools now monitor teacher competence through tests, and may even link pay increments to student achievement. These changes may affect teacher supply and demand in particular regions and schools in the years ahead.

States and local communities also differ in their resources and priorities. Wealthier districts are more likely to sponsor a greater variety of programs and course offerings and to establish smaller average class sizes, actions that translate into a need for more teachers, while many urban areas struggle to find qualified teachers and adequate resources. School districts from Dallas to Detroit to Washington, DC, offer an ever-increasing array of incentives, including thousands of dollars in signing bonuses. The federal government offers housing assistance and student loan forgiveness to recruit teachers to urban schools.[5]

Who Are My Teaching Colleagues? What Are the Demographics of Today's Teachers?

The typical teacher is a 44-year-old white woman who has been teaching for sixteen years. The average age of America's teachers is on the rise, a sign of growing retirements on the horizon and the burgeoning need for more teachers. Despite efforts to recruit people of color into teaching, most teachers are white and non-Hispanic. Although 17 percent of students are African American, only 9 percent of all teachers (and 7 percent of new teachers) are African American; while 16 percent of students are Hispanic, only 4 percent of teachers are Hispanic. About three out of four teachers are women. At the secondary level, 40 percent of teachers are men.

Many school districts are committed to hiring a diverse teaching staff. Such diversity provides students with a rich variety of role models, sending a clear message that the school district is not only teaching *about* democracy, but *practicing* it as well. To date, this effort has had only limited success, as relatively few people of color are becoming teachers. In recent years, only 7 percent of new teachers were African American and less than 4 percent were Hispanic, while nearly 85 percent were white.[6] (See Figure 15.1.) School administrators also would like to correct the gender imbalance among elementary school teachers. Because most elementary teachers are women, male elementary teachers are the focus of intense recruitment efforts. Here too, success has been minimal, and in fact there are fewer males in elementary teaching today (about 15 percent) than there were twenty-five years ago. Although more women today are school administrators than twenty-five years ago, gender imbalance prevails here as well. About 65 percent of school principals and 90 percent of superintendents are men.[7]

How many teachers are there? Nearly three-and-a-half million. About three million teachers work in public schools, and half a million work in private schools. There are about two million teachers at the elementary level and almost one-and-a-half million at the secondary level.[8]

What Are My Chances for Earning a Decent Salary?

The truth of the matter is that teaching offers incredible rewards, and these rewards go beyond salary. If you love teaching, as we do, it will be a joy to go to work. That joy, however, does not appear on your pay stub, and we are not alone in our belief that teachers are not paid what they deserve. The good news is that teachers' salaries have been improving in the last twenty years (although these increases have been more modest during the last ten years). When asked if teaching offers a decent salary, only 37 percent of the teachers surveyed in the mid-1980s said yes; but by the mid-1990s, 63 percent of teachers felt this way.[9] Consider the following:

FIGURE 15.1
New K–12 teachers by race/ethnicity and by gender.

SOURCE: National Education Association (NEA), *Fact Sheet on Teacher Shortages* (Washington, DC: NEA, 2001).

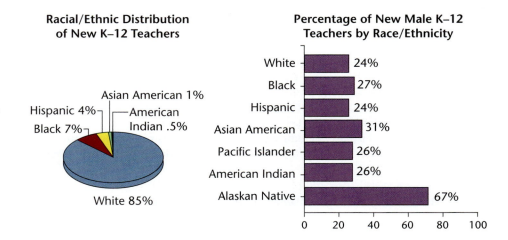

Racial/Ethnic Distribution of New K–12 Teachers

Asian American 1%
Hispanic 4%
American Indian .5%
Black 7%
White 85%

Percentage of New Male K–12 Teachers by Race/Ethnicity

White	24%
Black	27%
Hispanic	24%
Asian American	31%
Pacific Islander	26%
American Indian	26%
Alaskan Native	67%

REFLECTION

How can teacher education programs recruit more students of color? What might attract more men into elementary teaching?

- Between 1980 and 2000, the average public school teacher salary increased from $32,500 to $41,280 (in 2000 constant dollars) for an increase of almost 28 percent.

- The average beginning public school teacher salary increased nearly 30 percent between 1980 and 2000, from $21,600 to $28,800 (in 2000 constant dollars).[10]

Teacher salaries are greatly influenced by geographic location. Teachers in the Northeast receive the highest pay and those in the South the least. But even state salary scales can be misleading. Within each state, salaries between school districts vary, often dramatically. (You may want to contact specific school districts of interest to request a copy of their salary schedule.)

Do Private Schools Pay Less than Public Schools?

Yes. Private or independent schools generally pay teachers lower salaries. Although many extraordinary teachers work in private schools, private school teachers as a group have less schooling, less experience, and participate less in professional development than do public school teachers—differences that are used to explain their lower salaries. But, while the salaries are lower, many private schools offer teachers a different set of benefits—smaller classes, more motivated students, more supportive parents, a greater sense of community, a greater sense of teacher autonomy, a shorter school year, a more challenging curriculum, and sometimes, housing and meals. Private schools, like their public counterparts, vary significantly in their academic standing, salaries, and employment practices. If you are interested in teaching in this arena, remember that each school needs to be evaluated on an individual basis. While some private schools are quite competitive with local public school employment benefits and are academically demanding, others do not compare as well.[11]

How Do I Apply for a Teaching Job? Do I Need a Résumé or a Portfolio?

The first step is to prepare a résumé to submit to prospective employers. When your résumé is strong, school districts will want a closer look, and that's when a portfolio or an interview will be requested. Résumés and portfolios open doors, so let's take a closer look at how best to construct them.

At the top of your résumé, list your contact information: name, address, telephone, and e-mail address. But the heart of the **résumé** is your relevant education and experience. Indicate your formal education background—your college and university, your major and your minor (if you have one), and describe your student teaching experience, as well as other educational accomplishments. Summarize relevant work experiences. If you offered private instruction, worked as a camp counselor or at a religious school, or volunteered at a day care center or in a recreation program for the elderly, include these and note dates of employment, salient responsibilities, and accomplishments. Many candidates include professional objectives and a brief educational philosophy at the beginning of a résumé. If you take this approach, you might write an employment objective that details the type of teaching position you are seeking. You could also include some of the reasons that propel you to teach and perhaps a brief statement about your educational philosophy and beliefs. Your résumé should be typed in a clear and readable format; there are software templates available to help you. Check if the school districts you are interested in prefer hard copy or e-mail.

Employers rely on references and recommendations to get a clearer picture of applicants. Remember, as you list professors, supervisors, previous employers and cooperating teachers as references, you need to ask their permission and give them a "heads up" that they may be contacted. This is not only a basic courtesy, but also a way to measure their willingness to recommend you. Consider supplying them with "talking points" to aid them in preparing your recommendation.

Today, many school districts are going beyond résumés and recommendations, and are asking for a more in-depth view of you and your skills. A **portfolio** is a collection of materials that demonstrates your knowledge, competencies, and accomplishments as a teacher candidate. A portfolio does more than document your qualifications for a prospective teaching job (as a résumé does); it is a purposeful and reflective presentation of your professional development as a teacher.

People have different views concerning portfolios. Some see them as elaborate and lengthy presentations, while others consider an enhanced résumé with a few attachments to be a portfolio. Typically, portfolios include:[12]

I. Statement of Teaching Philosophy

II. Teaching Credentials
  A. Résumé
  B. Transcripts
  C. Letters of Reference
  D. Teaching Certificate/License
  E. Endorsement(s)

III. Teaching-Related Experiences
  A. Student Teaching
    1. Evaluations by University Supervisor
    2. Evaluations by Cooperating/Mentor Teacher
    3. Letters from Students and Parents

4. Sample Lesson Plans
5. Sample Classroom Floor Plans/Management Plans
6. Reflective Teaching Journal
7. Examples of Student Work
8. Photographs of Students/Classrooms
9. Videotape of Teaching
B. Employment in Child-Related Fields
C. Volunteer Work with Children

This text is designed to start you on the road to building a portfolio. The *Intermission* activities guide your portfolio development, differentiating between a working and a presentation portfolio (see page 000). The reflection questions and *You Be the Judge* features infused throughout the text are intended to help you consider relevant issues and form your own educational views and beliefs. In organizing the contents of your portfolio, consider using national standards (such as the INTASC standards identified in the *Inter-missions*) or the state or local standards of the school district to which you are applying for a job. Many teaching candidates rely on a loose-leaf type notebook to organize their portfolio work, allowing for flexibility incorporating and removing material. More recently, digital formats, such as a CD-ROM or a Web page, have become popular. With a digital or **e-portfolio,** you can simultaneously present your qualifications and demonstrate your technological proficiency. In developing your portfolio, ask for input from university supervisors and cooperating teachers; and it is a good idea to practice presenting your portfolio to them as well.

ELECTRONIC PORTFOLIO
Visit the Online Portfolio section for resources to build your own electronic portfolio.

 What Do I Need in Order to Teach—a License or Certification? By the Way, What's the Difference?

Project yourself a few years into the future. You have just completed your teacher preparation program. You stop by your local public school office and make a belated inquiry into teacher openings. The school secretary looks up from a cluttered desk, smiles kindly, and says, "We may have an opening this fall. Are you certified? Do you have a license?"

Oops! Certified? License? Now I remember. It's that paperwork thing. . . . I should have filled out that application back at school. I should have gone to that teacher licensure meeting. And I definitely should have read that Sadker textbook more carefully. I knew I forgot something. Now I'm in trouble. All that work and I will not be allowed to teach. What a nightmare!

And then you wake up.

 Many people use the terms *teacher certification* and *teaching license* interchangeably (as in "She has her teacher certification" while really meaning "She has her teaching license"). But it is important for you to be able to distinguish between a professional certification and a legal license, so we make the distinction in this book. **Teacher certification** confers professional standing; a **teacher's license** is a legal document. Teacher certification indicates that a professional group recognizes (certifies) that a teacher is competent and has met certain standards. A teacher's license, issued by the state government, grants the legal right to teach, not unlike a driver's license grants the legal right to drive. Both licenses mean that the "minimum" state requirements have been met. If you have been out on the roads recently, you know that meeting these minimum requirements to drive is not an indication that a person can, in fact, drive very well. It is the same with a teacher's license: Not all holders can teach well, especially if they are teaching a subject without adequate training in that field, a sad but not uncommon practice. Nevertheless, the intent of certification and licensure is to maintain high standards for teachers.

Who Awards Licenses, and How Do I Get One?

Teaching licenses are awarded by each of the fifty states and the District of Columbia. In a similar way, states are involved with the licensure of doctors, lawyers, and other professionals and nonprofessionals. When you meet the state's requirements, you can apply for and receive your teacher's license.

You should not assume that your teacher's license will automatically be issued to you when you graduate from your teacher education program, since state departments of education, not colleges and universities, issue teacher's licenses. Some colleges will apply to a designated state department in your name and request a license; others will not. In most states, filling out an application and passing the required national or state tests are all that is needed if you have graduated from an approved, accredited program. But not all teacher education programs are accredited (see the accreditation section of this chapter for more information). Regardless of your program, remember that you will probably need to apply to the state for a teacher's license. (See Appendix 1 for the contact information for the department of education in every state.)

You should also know that each state has its own requirements for teacher licensure. States have different policies concerning what courses teachers should take, what kinds of teacher's licenses should be offered, and even the length of time for which a teacher's license is valid. You may meet the standards in one state, but, if you decide to teach in another, you may find yourself unqualified for its license. Since the courses and experiences you need vary from state to state, it is useful to understand the major areas of preparation relevant to certification and licensure. Joseph Cronin, writing in the *Handbook of Teaching and Policy,* suggests three categories: knowledge of subject matter, knowledge of pedagogy, and practice teaching.[13] Chances are that your course work will fit within these categories.

When you have questions about obtaining a license, consult immediately with your college instructor, adviser, or teacher education placement office, or contact the appropriate state department of education. Do not depend on friends, whose well-intentioned advice may not be accurate.

What Type of License Do I Need? (You Mean, There's More than One?)

Most states issue more than one kind of license in order to differentiate among the applicants' qualifications and career goals. Although the specific names of these licenses (sometimes called certificates, now how's that for confusing!) vary from state to state, there are four common types:

1. An **initial,** or **provisional, license**—also called a *probationary certificate*—is the type frequently issued to beginning teachers and is generally nonrenewable. If you are awarded a provisional license, it means that you have completed most, but not all, of the state's legal requirements to teach. It may also mean that you need to complete some additional course work or that you need to teach for several years before you qualify for a higher or more permanent license. You may find yourself first getting a provisional license, giving you some breathing room as you work to complete all of the state's requirements for a standard, or professional, license.

Across the region and country, school districts are grappling with teacher shortages in areas such as math, science, special education, and foreign languages. More and more, school districts are looking abroad to fill the gaps. Houston has recruited 100 teachers from the Philippines and Spain. New York has hired 125 math and science teachers from Austria. Los Angeles now recruits in the Philippines, in addition to Canada, Mexico, and Spain, and Chicago gleaned 46 teachers from 25 countries in the last year.

SOURCE: Susan Snyder, "Philadelphia, Chester Upland Look Abroad for Teachers," *Philadelphia Inquirer*, March 26, 2001.

REFLECTION

How might such recruiting influence America's schools in the years ahead? Do you think that this is a productive strategy? Does it raise any concerns or other issues for you?

Click on *In the News* for recent *In the News* stories. Submit your Own *In the News* summary to share with your colleagues.

2. The **standard,** or **professional, license** is issued by the state after you have completed all the requirements to teach in that state. These requirements may include a specified number of courses beyond the bachelor's degree or one or more years of teaching experience.

3. A **special license** is a nonteaching license designed for specialized educational careers, including those in administration, counseling, library science, school social work, and school psychology. If after teaching for several years you decide that you want a career in school counseling (or administration, library science, and so forth), you will have to meet the requirements for this license.

4. A **conditional,** or **emergency, license** is a substandard license that is issued on a temporary basis to meet the needs of communities that do not have licensed teachers available. For example, a small high school in a rural community may not be able to attract a qualified teacher in physics. Faced with the unattractive prospect of not offering its students physics courses, the community may petition the state to award an emergency license to someone who does not meet current licensure standards.

Conditional licenses become commonplace when a shortage of teachers forces states to hire uncertified teachers. Historically, this has even included people who had never completed college. It is an unfortunate fact of life that, even today, when shortages in certain fields or geographic areas arise, substandard teaching licenses are issued.

What Is an Endorsement?

In some cases, a candidate may be licensed to teach in an additional area through what is termed an **endorsement.** For many teachers, especially those teaching in areas that have a large supply of candidates, endorsements can give you the edge over

592

other applicants. You may want to give some consideration to this option. Carefully planning your courses can help you get a second teaching area. So can practical experience. For instance, a teacher may have a standard or professional license in U.S. history but finds herself teaching biology courses as well. Or perhaps she has taken a number of college courses in biology and decides she wants to be recognized as a biology teacher as well as a history teacher. Since she already has a standard or professional license (in history), she need not apply for a new license. Instead, she applies to the state for an *endorsement* in biology. Although she did not take biology methods or student teach in biology, her teaching experience and background are considered for her endorsement in biology. The endorsement means that the state has approved her teaching both history and biology. Sometimes the subjects are more closely related than these. A teacher licensed in bilingual education, for example, with a number of courses in English as a Second Language (ESL), may seek an endorsement in ESL as well.

What Is Program Accreditation, and What Does It Mean in Terms of Getting a Teacher's License?

Some teacher preparation programs receive **accreditation** by an outside agency that ensures the institution meets accepted standards. Two such accrediting agencies are the **National Council for the Accreditation of Teacher Education (NCATE)** and the **National Association of State Directors of Teacher Education and Certification (NASDTEC).** If your teacher preparation program has been accredited, you will find that the process of becoming licensed in a number of states is facilitated. (See Figure 15.2.)

If your teacher education program has not been accredited by either NCATE or NASDTEC, your program may still be recognized in your state. State accreditation is fine if you plan to teach only in that state, but it is less than fine if you are considering other locations. You might want to check to see whether your state has made any **reciprocity agreements** with other states. A number of states have entered such agreements (sometimes referred to as *interstate reciprocity agreements*), in which one state agrees to recognize and license teachers from another state. Your state might have such an agreement or pact with other states, especially neighboring states; if so, this will increase your professional mobility. You should keep up to date with licensure requirements in states where you would like to teach. (See Appendix 1 for the addresses of the departments of education in every state.)

What Are "Alternative Routes" to Getting a Teacher's License?

Alternative licensing programs are gaining in popularity. Many of these programs enable college graduates to become teachers with less education training than required in traditional teacher education programs. In part, alternative licensure programs are popular due to teacher shortages, a desire to get candidates into teaching positions quickly, and a concern that traditional education programs too rarely attract teachers of color. Only eight states offered alternative routes to licensure in 1984, a movement that began in New Jersey. By 2001, forty-five states and the District of Columbia had implemented some form of alternative licensure option.[14]

How does alternative licensure work? Some states permit selective alternative licensing only, such as at the secondary but not the elementary level, or only in fields in which there are teacher shortages, such as math or science. Some states only allow

FIGURE 15.2
State participation with accrediting agencies. Accreditation of teacher education programs by an outside agency helps facilitate the certification process across states.

SOURCE: National Council for the Accreditation of Teacher Education (NCATE) and National Association of State Directors of Teacher Education and Certification (NASDTEC), 2001.

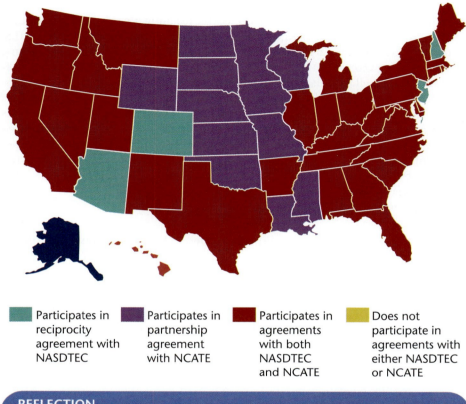

Participates in reciprocity agreement with NASDTEC

Participates in partnership agreement with NCATE

Participates in agreements with both NASDTEC and NCATE

Does not participate in agreements with either NASDTEC or NCATE

REFLECTION

Check out the accreditation status of the state where you might teach. Are you on track for licensure? Are there additional steps that you should be considering?

alternate routes that are designed by higher education institutions. Most alternative programs require a bachelor's degree, and some education course work, though usually far fewer education courses than are typically required. One of the best known of these alternative approaches is Teach for America.

Teach for America recruits applicants who have little if any education background but who are motivated to make a positive contribution by teaching in areas that suffer a teacher shortage, particularly inner-city and rural areas. This program has attracted individuals whose altruistic response is reminiscent of Peace Corps volunteers. Alternative programs like Troops to Teachers and Teach for America have drawn a higher percentage of mathematics and science applicants than have traditional programs, and have an impressive track record in recruiting applicants of color. Studies indicate that alternative programs have produced almost five times the proportion of teachers of color as traditional programs. For example, in Texas, 41 percent of the teachers entering the profession through the alternative teacher licensure program are from non-European ancestry, compared with only 9 percent of all the teachers in the state. Advocates of alternative approaches point to these statistics as proof that there is more than one way to prepare teachers.[15]

Not everyone views alternative routes to teacher preparation as terrific innovations. For one, the attrition rate for these programs is quite high: Many who volunteer to join also volunteer to leave, and no wonder. With limited preparation, these rookies wade into challenging teaching situations in some of the nation's most troubled and impoverished communities.

Studies of alternative licensure preparation have indicated that graduates of alternative programs represent more of an attempt at a "quick fix" for teacher shortages than a permanent solution. In many cases, their not-yet-honed teaching skills are unlikely to be improved, since graduates of alternative programs are less committed to staying in teaching or to pursuing graduate studies than are students from traditional teacher education programs. (In fact, about 2 percent of the alternative teachers report that they did not graduate from college.) Although alternative preparation programs try to attract older, more experienced Americans to a teaching career, more than half of those enrolled are fresh out of college. Many teacher educators are concerned that this approach is a step back to times past, when anyone who wanted to teach was hired. They fear that the alternative preparation of teachers signals a retreat from efforts toward full teacher professionalism. Some also worry about the elementary and secondary students who will be in classrooms with these new and not well-prepared teachers.

Despite the attention that alternative licensure programs have received in the press, relatively few teachers have moved through these programs and into the classroom. Since 1985, only 150,000 of the nation's teachers have been licensed through alternative programs. That's 150,000 out of 3.5 million, less than 5 percent. Alternative programs prepare relatively few teachers; their graduates typically stay in teaching for only a brief period of time; and, when competing for a position, alternative candidates seem to be at a disadvantage. As one dean of a school of education pointed out, very few alternatively prepared teachers get hired when there are well-qualified traditionally prepared teachers available.[16] Because these programs are relatively new, studies of their effectiveness will undoubtedly continue in the years ahead.

What Are Teacher Competency Tests?

Most states require teacher competency tests, and others are experimenting with additional forms of evaluation, such as supervised internships. Why are teachers facing new hurdles and higher standards? One reason is that, during the past few decades, the public became outraged about reports of students' declining standardized test scores and illiterate high school graduates. Between the 1960s and the 1980s, average SAT scores tumbled 42 points on the verbal and 26 points on the mathematical sections of the test. In 1983, the U.S. Department of Education published *A Nation at Risk,* highlighting these depressing test scores and calling for significant school changes, including fewer electives, an increase in core course requirements, more student testing, and better paid and more qualified teachers. In response, many states required elementary and secondary students, as well as teachers, to pass **minimum competency tests.** The movement for state-required competency tests spread—or raced—from a few states in the Southeast to the overwhelming majority of states across the nation. Since the early 1990s, most states have been using standardized tests for admission into teaching programs, for certification, and for licensure.[17] (See Appendix 2 for more information about state testing requirements.) Chances are strong that you will be tested, perhaps more than once, if you decide to enter teaching. Some of these tests are sponsored by states, and applicants have been required to

PROMISING PORTRAIT OF TODAY'S TEACHERS

According to a study released by the National Education Association, today's teachers have more academic training and classroom experience than their predecessors. About half of teachers (47%) have a master's degree or comparable course work, a rate almost twice as high as teachers in the 1970s. Eighty-five percent have participated in programs to improve their skills since last year.

SOURCE: Good News About America's Public Schools (2000). www.nea.org/publiced/goodnews/#quality.

REFLECTION

What changes in American society encourage greater academic preparation for teachers?

Click on *In the News* for recent *In the News* stories. Submit your own *In the News* summary to share with your colleagues.

write essays on topics related to education, as well as to pass basic skills tests of spelling, grammar, and punctuation. Some states also test mathematical skills. In other cases, states or local districts have developed more complex, competency-based evaluation systems. But many states now use a national exam.

The **National Teacher Examination (NTE),** initiated in 1940 under the auspices of the American Council on Education (ACE), came about when a group of superintendents asked for help in teacher selection. With a grant from the Carnegie Foundation, ACE and others formed the Educational Testing Services (ETS), and the exam became its responsibility. By the early 1990s, ETS determined that a new test was needed to replace the NTE.

That new test is the **Praxis Assessment for Beginning Teachers,** a three-part teacher assessment. The *Praxis I: Preprofessional Skills Test* consists of hour-long academic skills tests in reading, writing, and mathematics. These basic tests apply to prospective teachers in all fields and all grades, and are required in thirty states for admission into teacher education, or to obtain an initial teacher license.[18] *Praxis I* can be taken in the standard paper-and-pencil format on specified dates around the country or by means of a more costly computer version, with far more flexible timing, widespread availability, and immediate scoring.

The *Praxis II* assesses subject area, pedagogy, and professional education knowledge, offering more than 140 exams in subjects ranging from art to social studies. *Praxis II* exams are required in 29 states. *Praxis III* is a classroom performance assessment of teaching skills, covering classroom management, instructional planning, and assessment of student learning. While *Praxis III* is the most authentic assessment of beginning teachers, it is also the most challenging and costly test to implement, and it has not yet gained the widespread popularity of *Praxis I* and *II*.

Educators differ as to whether the Praxis series or other competency tests are necessary. Those who support competency exams maintain that the exams lend greater credibility and professionalism to the process of becoming a teacher. They claim that such tests identify well-educated applicants who can apply their knowledge in the classroom. They cite examples of teachers who cannot spell, write, or perform basic mathematical computations, and they plead persuasively that students must be protected from such incompetent teachers.

Some critics of the teacher exams argue that they are incredibly easy and not a real measure of competence. Other critics believe that such tests are more a political gesture than a way of improving education.[19] Part of the problem is the lack of evidence supporting the idea that teacher testing predicts teacher performance.[20] Some believe that the current process of state licensure and the period of assessment prior to tenure are sufficient to filter out incompetent teachers. Still others worry that we do not really know what makes good teachers, and we know even less about how to create tests to separate the good from the bad. We don't have tests that can measure enthusiasm, dedication, caring, and sensitivity—qualities that students associate with great teachers. Test makers are constantly working to respond to these charges, and to create more effective tests.

Another provocative and controversial problem is the impact of standardized competency tests on diversity. Historically, when African American teachers were systematically paid less, tests like the NTE were used as a vehicle for teachers of color to attain salary equity with whites. More recently, however, test results in states across the nation document the problems African American and Hispanic teacher candidates are having in passing such exams, problems that have been attributed to reasons ranging from test bias to social and educational differences. The continued use of such exams may detract people of color from becoming teachers. And the pipeline of nonwhite teaching candidates, already only a trickle, is in danger of dwindling further.[21] Nevertheless, the courts have ruled that such tests are an acceptable means of screening teacher candidates.[22] And with strong public sentiment favoring such tests, they are likely to be a part of the teacher education landscape for the foreseeable future.

How Do Teaching Contracts Work?

Congratulations! You have been hired by the school system of your choice, and a contract is placed before you. Before you sign it, there are a few things you should know about teacher contracts. This contract represents a binding agreement between you and the school district. It will be signed by you as the teacher being hired and by an agent of the board of education, often the superintendent. The contract usually sets the conditions of your work, perhaps including specific language detailing your instructional duties, and, of course, your salary.

If you do not have tenure, you will receive a new contract each year. Once you earn tenure, you will be working under a continuing contract and will probably be asked to notify the school district each year as to whether you plan to teach for the district the following year.

What Are Some Advantages of Tenure?

A teacher was once asked to leave his teaching position in Kentucky because he was leading an "un-Christian" personal life. He was Jewish.

A second-grade teacher was dismissed from her teaching assignment in Utah because of her dress. She wore miniskirts.

In Massachusetts, a teacher was fired because of his physical appearance. He had grown a beard.

Fortunately, these teachers all had one thing in common: **tenure.** And tenure prevented their school districts from following through on dismissal proceedings.

A vast majority of states currently have tenure laws. A newly hired teacher is considered to be in a probationary period. The **probationary teaching period** can be two, three, or even five years for public school teachers and about six years for college professors. After demonstrating teaching competence for the specific period, the teacher is awarded tenure, which provides a substantial degree of job security. Generally, a tenured teacher can be fired only for gross incompetence, insubordination, or immoral acts or because of budget cuts stemming from declining enrollments. In practice, public schools rarely fire a tenured teacher.

Since teachers have enjoyed the protection of tenure for many years, it is easy to forget how important this protection is. To get a fresh perspective on tenure, consider what life in schools might be like without it.

Without tenure, hundreds, perhaps thousands, of financially pressed school systems could respond to pressure from taxpayers by firing their experienced teachers and replacing them with lower-paid, less experienced teachers. This would significantly reduce school budgets, usually the largest cost item in the local tax structure. After two or three more years, these teachers would also face the financial ax. In short, teachers would once again become an itinerant, poorly paid profession. Would anyone really benefit?

Without tenure, the fear of dismissal would cause thousands of teachers to avoid controversial topics, large and small. Many teachers would simply become a mirror of their communities, fearing to stir intellectual debate or to teach unsettling ideas because job security had become their prime objective. Classrooms would become quiet and mundane places, devoid of the excitement that comes from open discussion of controversial ideas.

Without tenure, many teachers would have to modify their personal lifestyles. In some communities, they would have to avoid places where liquor is served; in others, their clothing or hairstyles would have to be altered. Any behavior that differed from the norms of the community would be potentially dangerous, for such behavior could provide the spark that would trigger public clamor for dismissal. A conformist philosophy would spread from the classroom to teachers' personal lives.

In short, without some protection such as tenure, teaching would take a giant step backward. Tenure provides teachers with the fundamental security that allows them to develop and practice their profession without fear of undue pressure or intimidation. Unfortunately, not all teachers have respected the academic freedom provided by tenure, as we shall see in the next section.

What Are Some Disadvantages of Tenure?

Over the years, it has become apparent that the protection of academic freedom through the tenure process has entailed serious drawbacks. One such drawback is the reality that ineffective teachers are protected from dismissal. Many of these ineffective teachers view tenure as a right to job security without acknowledging a corresponding responsibility to continue professional growth. Feeling that they are no longer subject to serious scrutiny, such teachers fail to keep up with new developments in their field, and each year they drag out old lesson plans and fading lecture notes for yet another outdated performance. Who pays the price for such ineffective teaching? The students, of course. Think back a moment. How many ineffective, tenure-protected teachers were you subjected to during your total school experience? How many do you face at present?

During the past few years, attempts to reform or dismantle tenure have gained momentum. Some school districts have extended the amount of time it takes to be awarded tenure. In Florida, a recent law reduced the time that poor-performing teachers are given to improve from one year to ninety days. New Hampshire's Republican lawmakers failed in their attempt to require teachers to pass tests and renew their licenses every three years, while a special Colorado task force has been formed to explore ways to limit tenure. One reason for these attempts is the cost involved in dismissing a tenured teacher. A New York School Boards Association Study showed that, in that state in the mid-1990s, it took an average of 455 days and $177,000 to dismiss a teacher. If the teacher appealed, the average price rose to $317,000.[23]

As you can see, tenure is a double-edged sword. It serves the extremely important function of preserving academic freedom and protecting teachers from arbitrary and unjust dismissal. But it also provides job security for ineffective teachers, bad news for the students of these teachers or for the new and more competent teachers trying to enter the profession.

Are Untenured Teachers Protected?

Many believe that, until tenure is granted, they are extremely vulnerable, virtually without security. This is not true. During the 1970s, in *Goldberg v. Kelly, Board of Regents v. Roth,* and *Perry v. Sinderman,* the United States Supreme Court outlined several of the rights that are enjoyed by nontenured teachers. In many circumstances, these rights include advance notice of the intention to dismiss a teacher, clearly stated reasons for termination, and a fair and open hearing. In addition, teacher organizations, such as the National Education Association (NEA) and the American Federation of Teachers (AFT), provide legal assistance for teachers who might be subjected to the arbitrary and unjust action of a school system. If the AFT and the NEA ever merge, one result may be even greater legal protection for teachers.

If, during your probationary years, you feel that you have been unfairly victimized by the school administration, you should seek legal advice. Even nontenured teachers possess rights, but these rights are effective only if they are exercised.

Can Principals Be Tenured?

Although about a dozen states still grant tenure or equivalent rights to principals, this protection has all but disappeared. Historically, a satisfactory probationary period of one to five years would result in principals earning tenure, as teachers do. Not anymore. Many of the same arguments used against granting teachers tenure (a shield for mediocrity or even incompetence, a lengthy process to remove poor performers, and so on) have been successfully used to rescind tenure for principals. The crux of the argument seems to be how one views principals. Those who see them as managers believe that, if they are not managing well, they should be fired. Others view principals as master teachers (from the term "principal teacher"), who should be afforded the same protections from arbitrary political pressures and inappropriate personnel decisions as other teachers. The management view is clearly winning out.[24]

What Kinds of Educational Careers Are Available Beyond Classroom Teaching?

The assumption that your education degree has prepared you only for a teaching career is a widespread myth. Actually, there are dozens of education-related careers,

You may find your education niche beyond the traditional classroom. Here are some authentic employment opportunities printed in the "want ads" of newspapers.

CAN YOU TEACH?

The largest computer software and network training company in the world is looking for additional full-time instructors to teach classes. Candidates must possess excellent presentation skills. Computer experience is helpful but not necessary; we will train you.

EDUCATIONAL CONSULTANT

We are seeking an experienced Education Consultant with classroom teaching background for per diem contracted and long-term assignments, with expertise in one or more of the following: dimensions of learning, performance assessments, state learning standards, early literacy, cooperative learning, differentiated instruction.

PRIVATE GIRLS' HIGH SCHOOL

seeks Director of Technology/ Computer Teacher, Classroom Experience Necessary.

ELEMENTARY ZOO INSTRUCTOR

The Education Department of the Zoo, one of the country's foremost institutions of informal science teaching, is seeking a dynamic instructor for its elementary-level programs. A highly interactive teaching approach, creativity, and a theatrical background will be helpful. This position involves program development for parents and teachers in addition to direct instruction of children ages 4–12. Excellent oral and written communication skills required.

EDITOR/WRITER

Familiar with higher edu. issues needed for Publications Dept. Will work with campus colleagues and assoc. staff to develop a natl. quarterly newsletter for faculty & administrators. Must know curriculum development, have solid editorial and publications mgmt. skills, research aptitude, & good writing skills.

Major nonprofit YOUTH SERVICE AGENCY seeks to fill the following positions (Bilingual, Spanish/English preferred): YOUTH COUNSELOR: B.A. 2 years experience in social service setting, PROGRAM COORDINATOR: B.A. 3–5 years experience, strong supervisory/communication skills necessary.

EDUCATIONAL RESEARCHER

Research and develop abstracts for www-based project about science and math education. Writing skills, attention to detail, ability to synthesize information quickly, and confident phone skills. Background in education helpful.

EDUCATIONAL COORDINATOR

The Historical Society seeks a creative, self-motivated team player to plan, implement, & promote educational programs for schools, families, & adults. Responsibilities incl.: organizing public programs & tours: coordinating National History Day, providing services for schools.

CHILD CARE DIRECTOR

Join our management team! Nonprofit corporate-sponsored child care management co., looking for a talented director to manage our state-of-the-art center. Must have ECE experience and have been through NAEYC accred. process.

LEARNING CENTERS offering individualized diagnostic and prescriptive programs are looking for dynamic PT cert. teachers to instruct students of all ages in reading, writing, math, and algebra.

SUBSTANCE ABUSE PREVENTION INTERVENTION SPECIALISTS

Seeking experienced professionals to provide services to students in substance abuse prevention and intervention. Will provide both group and individual counseling and conduct peer leadership groups for students at risk at various schools.

AMERICAN INTERNATIONAL SCHOOLS

Seeking excellent candidates. June interview in major cities. Two years of experience reqd.

WORKSITE TEACHER

Conduct worksite visits & act as liaison between worksite & classroom instruction, BA plus 2 yrs. teaching experience with adults req'd.

LOVE TO TEACH?

Are you considering a career change where you can continue to use your teaching ability? Call.

PROGRAM ASSISTANT

New vision in schools seeks a program assistant to provide support to a major school reform initiative. Must be meticulous with details & be able to write well, handle multiple projects, & and meet deadlines. Interest in public schools is preferred.

EDITOR

One of the most progressive and respected names in children's publishing is currently seeking an editor for a supplement on early childhood. In addition to a degree, editorial/publishing experience, and early childhood classroom experience, you must be highly creative and possess a strong knowledge of early childhood issues.

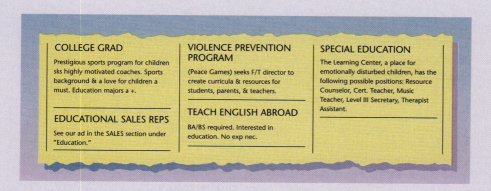

REFLECTION

Which of these careers do you find most appealing? Which is least appealing? Have you ever explored nonteaching education careers? Why or why not?

although tunnel vision often keeps them from view. (See *Frame of Reference: Education Want Ads.*) Obviously, if you are interested in school administration or a counseling career, starting as a classroom teacher makes a lot of sense and gives you an important perspective that will serve you well in these other school careers. But beyond administration and counseling lie many other options. The following list is intended to give you some idea of the less typical but potentially quite rewarding **nontraditional educational careers** available to you.[25]

Early Childhood Education. If you want to stay in touch with teaching but prefer a climate other than the typical classroom, you may want to explore such options as **day care centers.** Early childhood education is a vital component of the nation's educational system. Working parents seek quality options, not only for child care but for child education and development as well.

Although day care rarely offers much pay or status, a number of talented educators find early childhood education incredibly satisfying. If you are creative and flexible, you might even be able to develop your own facility. For example, some department stores advertise a day care service for shopping parents. You might consider opening a similar early childhood program and marketing your "children's center" to other stores, shopping malls, or businesses. (Check out your state's laws regarding operating standards, building restrictions, number of children permitted, and so on.) If you enjoy working with young children, you will find opportunities galore in this growing field.

Adult Education. If you prefer to work with a mature population, you might be attracted to **continuing** and **adult education** programs. These are offered through city and county governments, local school systems, and nearby colleges and universities. In addition, some private businesses now sponsor courses that are related to their products—recreation, crafts, cooking, technical training, and so forth. As the ranks of the retired swell with baby boomers, you can expect this field to grow rapidly. Older Americans often have the time, interest, and income to pursue education in topics, skills, and hobbies that have long eluded them. Elder hostels around the world are responding to the educational demand created by retirees. Researching available programs may take time, but you are apt to discover a variety of adult learning programs that can provide nontraditional teaching opportunities.

Pupil Service Professionals. Service professionals—school social workers, counselors, and psychologists—typically work as a team, assisting teachers in creating more effective learning environments. These professionals receive special training and education to meet the unique needs that frequently emerge in schools. Social workers, for example, work to improve the relationship between home and school. School psychologists, prepared in education and mental health, are responsible for coordinating and evaluating special learning and behavior problems.

Colleges and Universities. You will find many nonteaching, yet education-related, jobs in colleges and universities. To name a few, academic advisers work primarily on a one-to-one basis with students, discussing courses of study; admissions officers respond to the needs of students; alumni relations personnel conduct fundraising campaigns, organize alumni events, and maintain job placement services; and student services personnel do psychological and vocational counseling, advise international students, and administer residential programs. Most colleges offer their employees tuition benefits, so, if you want to pursue graduate studies, this may be a good way to gain both experience and an advanced degree.

Community Organizations. Think of a community group. Chances are, that group has an educational mission. Churches, synagogues, and nursing homes can use creative instructors and program planners. For example, a former English teacher, disturbed by the demeaning, artsy-craftsy programs in a local nursing home, inspired the residents to write their life histories, an experience they found very stimulating. Recreation and community centers hire instructors, program planners, and directors for their numerous programs. Hospitals and health clinics need people to plan and deliver training to their professional and administrative staffs. Some of the large municipal zoos conduct programs to protect endangered animal species and to interact with school groups. Libraries and media centers require personnel to maintain and catalog resources and equipment, as well as to train others in their use. Art galleries and museums hire staff to coordinate educational programs for school and civic groups and to conduct tours of their facilities.

The Media. The publishing and broadcasting industries hire people with education backgrounds to help write and promote their educational products. For example, large newspapers, such as *The Washington Post,* maintain staff writers whose job is to cover education, just as other reporters cover crime, politics, and finance. Some newspapers even publish a special edition of their paper for use in schools. Likewise, textbook publishers, educational journals, the Internet service providers, and television talk shows need people familiar with educational principles to help develop their programs.

Private Industry and Public Utilities. Large public and private corporations often rely on education graduates in their programs to train their staffs in areas such as organizational effectiveness, new technology training, civil rights and safety laws, and basic company policies and practices. Sometimes client needs come into play, as many of these firms need people with well-developed instructional skills to demonstrate the use of their sophisticated equipment or products to potential customers. Some education-related companies maintain permanent learning centers and seek persons with education backgrounds to plan and run them. If you like writing, you may want to work on pamphlets, brochures, curricula, and other materials describing a company's services and products, often written by education graduates.

Computer Software Development. With the dramatic increase in the use of educational software in the classroom, many companies are soliciting people with experience in education as consultants to help develop new programs. Creativity, familiarity with child psychology, and knowledge of the principles of learning are important resources for developing software that will appeal to a diverse and competitive market.

Technology. The blossoming of the computer age, with its software, email, websites, and Internet resources, has divided the population into those who are computer literate and those who are computer challenged (sometimes called technophobic). Those who are not yet citizens of cyberworld represent a ready population of potential students. If you enjoy programming, surfing the Net, or designing websites, you may want to become a tech-teacher, teaching these skills in either formal or informal settings. You may consider a position as a technology consultant for schools, helping design websites, create networks, or select software. You may choose to work outside a school organization, as a company representative providing educational services and equipment.

Educational Associations. National, state, and regional educational associations hire writers, editors, research specialists, administrators, lobbyists, and educators for a host of education-related jobs, from research and writing to public relations. There are hundreds of these associations, from the NEA to the American Association of Teachers of French. Check the *National Trade and Professional Associations of the United States and Canada* (Columbia Books, Inc.) for listings and descriptions of positions, or use the *Encyclopedia of Associations* (Gale Research) or the Internet to contact the associations directly.

Government Agencies. A host of local, state, and federal government agencies hire education graduates for training, policy planning, management, research, and so on. Various directories can help you through the maze of the federal bureaucracy. Among these is the *United States Government Manual* (Office of the Federal Register, National Archives and Records Service), which describes the various programs within the federal government, including their purposes and top-level staffs. The Internet is another useful source for exploring career opportunities in government-related education programs.

Global Opportunities. Want an international experience? Consider Department of Defense schools, private international schools, religious and international organizations, military bases offering high school and college courses to armed forces personnel, and the Peace Corps. A number of foreign companies now hire U.S. college graduates to teach English to their workers, positions that are sometimes very well paid. No matter the wages, high or low, the excitement of teaching in another culture (while learning about that culture) is hard to match.

As we indicated (more than once!), we love classroom teaching, but you should know there are many ways that you can serve society with an education background. You may want to explore one or more of these nonclassroom careers, even as an intern or volunteer at first, to see if these career paths appeal to you.

In this chapter—and in this text—we have tried to answer your questions about teaching. (If we missed one, we invite you to submit it to the website using the OLC Ask the Author button.) We hope that you have found this text chock-full of useful and interesting information, and that you have enjoyed reading this book. In fact, we hope that you enjoyed it so much that you choose to keep the book as a useful reference in the future (and do not resell it to the used bookstore!). But more than that, we hope that you are gaining greater clarity on your decision about whether teaching is for you, and whatever that decision turns out to be, we wish you the best of luck!

SUMMARY

CHAPTER REVIEW

Go to the Online Learning Center to take a quiz, practice with key terms, and review key ideas from the chapter.

1. What does the education job market look like? (or, put another way, will I be able to find a satisfying teaching position?)

   • Growth in the student population, efforts to reduce class size, and ongoing teacher retirements have increased the demand for teachers. As a result, it is predicted that more than two million teachers will be needed in the next decade.

   • Teachers are in short supply in subject areas such as math and science as well as in bilingual and special education.

   • The demand for teachers is critical in rural and urban areas. Urban school districts and the federal government are offering signing bonuses, housing assistance, and loan forgiveness to attract teachers.

   • More people of color are needed to join the teaching ranks. While students of color constitute nearly 40 percent of the school population, only about 15 percent of new teachers are of color.

2. Can I make a decent salary as a teacher?

   • Teacher salaries have steadily improved in the last twenty years, although increases have been more modest in the last ten years.

   • In 2000, the beginning teacher salary averaged $28,000 and the average teacher salary was $41,280.

   • Teacher salaries differ by state and region. In 2000, the beginning teacher salary was $32,000 in New York, but $20,000 in North Dakota. Teacher salaries also vary significantly between school districts in the same state.

3. How do I use a résumé and a portfolio in applying for a teaching position?

   • Strong résumés and portfolios provide prospective employers with critical information to decide whether an interview should be arranged.

   • While a standard résumé includes formal educational background, work experience, and other relevant information, a portfolio provides more depth and is assuming a greater role in the hiring process.

- A portfolio is a collection of materials that demonstrates your knowledge, skills, and accomplishments. A portfolio typically includes a statement of your teaching philosophy, a résumé, references, sample lesson plans, and perhaps videotapes of actual teaching. Some portfolios, called e-portfolios, can be constructed and transferred electronically.

4. What do I need in order to teach—a license or certification? (and how do I get one!)

- Teacher certification indicates that a professional group recognizes or certifies that a teacher is competent and has met certain standards. A teacher's license, issued by the state government, grants the legal right to teach. Teacher certification is a professional designation; a teacher's license is a legal document.

- Teaching licenses are awarded by state departments of education, not colleges and universities. Prospective teachers need to apply to their state to request a license.

- Requirements for teacher licensure differ from state to state. A teacher's license in one state may not be valid in another, unless the states have entered into a reciprocity agreement. Accreditation of college-level teacher education programs by NASDTEC and NCATE can facilitate new graduates becoming eligible for multistate teacher licenses.

- States issue various types of teaching licenses: an initial or probationary license to beginning teachers (generally nonrenewable), the standard or professional license to teachers who have completed a specified number of graduate-level courses and/or number of years teaching; a special license for educational careers in administration and counseling; and a temporary conditional or emergency license to fill teacher shortages in certain subject areas and geographic locations.

- Endorsements enable experienced teachers to gain additional licensure in a second subject area.

5. What teacher competency tests do I need to take?

- Teacher competency tests are used for admission into teacher education programs, for certification, and for licensure. Teacher competency tests are currently required in forty-two out of fifty states and the District of Columbia. (See Appendix 2 for more specific details.)

- *Praxis I* focuses on basic literacy, *Praxis II* on pedagogy and subject area competence, and the less used *Praxis III* on classroom performance. Many states have designed their own competency tests, which they require prospective teachers to take before being licensed.

- The use of teacher tests is intensely debated by educators and politicians. Supporters claim that competency testing lends greater credibility and professionalism. Critics claim that there is no evidence that teacher tests are related to teacher performance in the classroom. Moreover, such tests negatively impact teaching force diversity.

- Despite the controversies surrounding these tests, there is strong support from the public and from politicians for testing teachers and their students.

6. Why do teachers seek tenure? (and should I?)

- Most states currently have tenure laws. Under such laws, a new teacher is hired for a probationary period of 2–5 years. After demonstrating teaching competence for the specified period, the teacher is awarded tenure, which provides a substantial degree of job security.

- While tenure preserves academic freedom and protects teachers from arbitrary and unjust dismissal, it can also provide job security for ineffective teachers.

- For teachers, tenure—the right to job security—brings a corresponding responsibility to continue professional growth.

- Even before teachers earn tenure, they do enjoy certain legal protections.

- For the most part, states do not offer tenure to principals.

7. Are there jobs in education outside of the classroom?

   • An education degree prepares you not only for a teaching career, but for many education-related careers as well, in areas such as early childhood education, adult education, counseling and advising, and distance learning, and in organizations such as nonprofits, educational associations, private corporations, government agencies, and the media.

WEB-*TIVITIES*

1. Becoming Informed About the Job Market

2. Developing a Portfolio

3. Teacher Tenure

4. The Third W—Where?

KEY TERMS AND PEOPLE

accreditation, 593

adult education, 601

conditional (emergency) license, 592

continuing education, 601

day care centers, 601

e-portfolio, 590

endorsement, 592

four *Ws*, 586

initial (provisional) license, 591

minimum competency tests, 595

National Association of State Directors of Teacher Education and Certification (NASDTEC), 593

National Council for the Accreditation of Teacher Education (NCATE), 593

National Teacher Examination (NTE), 596

nontraditional educational careers, 601

portfolios, 589

Praxis Assessment for Beginning Teachers, 596

privatization, 586

probationary teaching period, 598

reciprocity agreements, 593

résumé, 589

special license, 592

standard (professional) license, 592

Teach for America, 594

teacher certification, 590

teacher oversupply, 586

teacher's license, 590

tenure, 597

PART 4: TOMORROW

Inter-mission

Here we are, at your final *Inter-mission.* These last applications and reflections are intended to get you ready for—tomorrow.

Applications and Reflections

4:1 ADD A NONTRADITIONAL HERO

Purpose: We know that students need inspiring figures—individuals who serve as role models and motivate students. Your subject matter expertise affords you knowledge of people who might motivate your future students. Although heroes come from all backgrounds, curricular materials do not always reflect diversity. The result is a "disconnect" between the growing diversity of America's students and the curriculum they study. You can tighten this connection by supplementing the curriculum. Can you add to the list of champions in their lives, especially nontraditional individuals (consider ethnicity, race, gender, age, class, lifestyle, and circumstances)? Identifying such heroes has the additional advantage of broadening your own scholarship.

> **INTASC PRINCIPLE 1**
> Knowledge of Subject Matter

Activity: In a subject area that you will be teaching, select a unique individual or hero who has *made a difference.* Create a billboard, poster, or computer graphic that captures the importance of this person. Make the language, content, and style relevant to the grade level you plan to teach, one that will attract and motivate your students.

Reflection: What has this activity taught you about nontraditional heroes? How might you plan to have your students seek out additional heroes? What criteria might you add to guarantee a good selection? What structure might produce informative research (questions to be covered, length and depth of coverage, assessment)? What format might you create for displaying your students' final products?

4:2 GETTING TO KNOW WHOM?

Purpose: Chapter 12, "The Struggle for Educational Opportunity," exposed some of life's heritage and happenings that influence who we are. Many of us have grown up in relatively homogeneous environments, knowing individuals of similar backgrounds and cultures. Meaningful conversations about how race, nationality, gender, substance abuse, and family crisis impact our own education are rare when diverse backgrounds are missing, yet such conversations could add essence and texture to your understanding of students.

> **INTASC PRINCIPLE 2**
> Knowledge of Human Development and Learning

Activity: Partner with a classmate, campus colleague, or friend who seems to come from a different background than you. Use the issues mentioned in the chapter to conduct an interview that will uncover information, stories, and perhaps feelings. Concentrate on being a good and an active listener. Some opening thoughts might include

- How do you identify your race or ethnicity?
- How would you describe your family heritage?
- How would you describe your family structure and patterns of daily life?
- Do you have memories of bias and discrimination?
- Do you have recollections about friends who struggled with substance abuse (drinking, drugs, and smoking), depression and suicide, or sexuality and teen pregnancy?
- What other concerns have you experienced or witnessed that denied or impeded educational opportunity?
- How has diversity influenced your own education or your commitment to teach?

Reflection: How are you and your interviewee different? How are you similar? How might this anecdotal information add to your understanding of child and human development? What aspects of your partner's cognitive, social, and emotional growth paralleled your own schooling? All in all, what words might describe your conversation: *insightful, laborious, superficial, intimate?* What words do you think your partner might use as a description?

4:3 A NOVEL READ

INTASC PRINCIPLE 3
Diversity in Learning

Purpose: Great teachers have an incredible ability to care, really deeply, about children. Such teachers learn about their students, hold high expectations for them, and fully appreciate their diverse cultural perspectives and learning styles. One marvelous way to understand youngsters is to read literature about the challenges they face. The right books will not only inspire you, but also will expand your awareness of diverse learners.

Activity: Maybe this is an *Inter-mission* activity you will save for summer vacation or a beach-based holiday. Or let this be a change of pace from your textbooks and research papers. Your education faculty will probably have additions to this book list. Pick a book and dig into it:

Teacher, Sylvia Ashton-Warner

Warriors Don't Cry: A Searing Memoir of the Battle to Integrate Little Rock's Central High, Melba Patillo Beals

Mentors, Masters and Mrs. MacGregor: Stories of Teachers Making a Difference, Jane Bluestein (Editor)

Bury My Heart at Wounded Knee, Dee Brown

America Is in the Heart, Carlos Bulosan

Family Values: A Lesbian Mother's Fight for Her Son, Phyllis Burke

Black Ice, Lorene Cary

House on Mango Street, Sandra Cisneros

The Water Is Wide, Patrick Conroy

Reflections of a Rock Lobster: A Story About Growing Up Gay, Aaron Fricke

One Child, Torey Hayden

Up the Down Staircase, Bel Kaufman

Among Schoolchildren, Tracy Kidder

Coming of Age in Mississippi, Ann Moody

The Bluest Eye, Toni Morrison

900 Shows a Year, Stuart Palonsky

The Education of a WASP, Lois Stalvey

Native Son, Richard Wright

Reflection: What did you learn from reading this book? Did you "unlearn" or abandon any misconceptions after your reading? Can you identify implications for your classroom? Would you assign this book to your students or suggest it for a faculty book club?

4:4 CYBERVISION

Purpose: For over a century, researchers have observed and analyzed classrooms. Now, technology is giving us another reason to examine teachers and student achievement. As Chapter 13, "Technology in Education," pointed out, the monumental investments in computer technology have not been matched by monumental gains in student achievement. Observing technology in the classroom will help you determine how best to use technology when you teach. What will your "cyber visitation" reveal in terms of technology's impact on instructional strategies?

Activity: Visit a high-tech educational site (a school with an established computer lab or a classroom that integrates technology). Take notes on what you see and hear. Focus on the teacher and the techniques that promote or inhibit learning.

Reflection: What do your notes reveal? Look for themes, concepts, and patterns. Given the teacher's instructional strategies (and your recall of Chapter 3, "Teacher Effectiveness"), what made the lesson successful? If you were going to coach the teacher, what skills might you suggest for his or her improvement? How will instructional strategies change as students huddle over isolated screens, work in global groups on the Internet, or e-mail homework from a holiday hideaway? What teaching techniques will look familiar? What new skills should be developed and practiced? What other questions and answers might you offer?

4:5 CLASS COMEDY CLUB

Purpose: Thank goodness! For all the crises in classrooms and children at risk, humor in the educational workplace survives and even thrives. Healthful humor (as opposed to targeted humor and sarcasm) can motivate students to participate and learn. Student humor, often unintentional, can be a major factor in keeping you happy and in the business of teaching. While you may never aspire to be a comic, sharing a funny teaching story will help you practice setting a positive and welcoming learning climate.

Activity: While there are books about kids who say and do the darnedest things, as well as e-mail and magazine features filled with funny stories, there is nothing like oral history and the stories of your peers to tickle a funny bone. Begin by freewriting answers to the following questions:

- The funniest teacher I recall from school . . .
- The funniest student happening was . . .

INTASC PRINCIPLE 4
Variety of Instructional Strategies

INTASC PRINCIPLE 5
Motivation and Management

- It sure was funny in school when . . . and she/he/they really did (or didn't) get in trouble . . .

Practice and dramatically deliver your funny stories. Encourage your peers to help you embroider them with colorful commentary, body language, and well-timed punchlines. Is there any chance that your class will finish the course with a post exam comedy club? If so, let your storytelling add to the performance.

Reflection: Are you ready for the stage? Even if you are not, what was the impact of hearing about the humorous escapades of students, teachers, and school life? What is your philosophy regarding the role of humor in education? How can you imagine using humor to motivate and manage students?

4:6 "DO IT YOURSELF" YOU BE THE JUDGE FEATURE

INTASC PRINCIPLE 6
Communication
Skills

Purpose: You certainly have your own experience, as a student, with computer technology. Are you wired into everything or stonewalling yourself away from it all? We want you to take both sides of the technology debate and fully develop two points of view: pro and con. Researching and refining polarized opinions is a communication challenge!

Activity: Consider what you have read about and explored in educational technology and generate a balance sheet that both supports and refutes the place of technology in education. (For a model, consider any of the *You Be the Judge* features throughout the textbook that take contrasting views on timely educational topics.) Select a very specific theme, especially one that is related to your subject area or grade level. Generate a title that polarizes opinions such as the following suggestions:

- Word Processing—Helping or Hurting Writing Skills
- Computers in Kindergarten—Absolutely Not or For Sure
- Our Technology Dollars—Classes For the Arts or For Computers
- Computers—One per Classroom or One per Child

For a more challenging activity, cite research studies to support both positions.

Reflection: By constructing both sides of an issue, what did you learn about balance and fairness in communication? What side of the sheet are you on? Could a reader detect that from your end product? Did you find that your views changed as you worked to present each side convincingly?

4:7 VIDEO VIEW

INTASC PRINCIPLE 7
Instructional
Planning Skills

Purpose: When the door between the hall and the classroom closes, the teacher is often the only adult in the room. Technological advances may open up tomorrow's classrooms, so that administrators, staff developers, mentor teachers, and even parents can observe your instruction through the magic of video. Can you imagine how being "on camera" might affect your teaching and students' learning? Try.

Activity: Write a 450- to 500-word essay about what's happening in your room, as if you were watching from the office video monitor. Remember, you are playing the role of teacher. Consider camera placement and room arrangement in your critique. Describe students who have starring or supporting roles. Detail the scene that is visible and suggest what might be happening off camera. Include an episode with a particular learner or lay out the entire lesson plan.

Reflection: What's happening in your room? Have you used the textbook's content to provide a firm and an informative foundation for your classroom? How do you feel about "seeing" yourself as the teacher in this video? This might be a worthwhile essay to retain in your portfolio, as it represents an overview of your classroom planning, philosophy, and accomplishments.

4:8 PRUNING YOUR PORTFOLIO

Purpose: Earlier *Inter-mission* activities, reflections, and artifacts helped you create a *working* portfolio. Now is the time to assess your portfolio and decide what is worth keeping or upgrading.

Activity: Consider, as a complete package, the quality of your *working* portfolio. Use the following rubric to chart the status of your collection. Score your portfolio according to how well it meets the criteria listed, on a scale of 1 to 5. Provide verbal or written evidence to support your position. Select a partner (or two) and set aside ten minutes to discuss and share your *working* portfolios and the assessment charts.

- Purposeful—with a structure that is sound, such as professional standards
- Selective—based on a specific purpose
- Diverse—representing a broad array of teaching talent beyond your transcript, student teacher critique, letters of recommendation, and philosophy statement

> **INTASC PRINCIPLE 8**
> Assessment

FORM: STATE OF THE PORTFOLIO

State of the Portfolio						
	Not at All				Very	Not Applicable
	1	2	3	4	5	
Item						
Purposeful:						
Selective:						
Diverse:						
Ongoing:						
Reflective:						
Collaborative:						
Other: _____						
Overall Appraisal:						

- Ongoing—relays learning incidents over time
- Reflective—both in process and product, should inspire thoughtfulness
- Collaborative—through conversations and interactions with others (peers, students, parents, professors, teachers, administrators, and others)

Reflection: What did you learn about your portfolio, including its strengths and weaknesses at this point? What did your discussion with your partners teach you? What are the next steps in selecting and organizing the materials that will become your *presentation* portfolio?

4:9 WEBSITE OF THE MONTH

INTASC PRINCIPLE 9
Reflection and
Responsibility

Purpose: Websites and Internet sources may prove to be of extraordinary benefit to your professional growth. However, quality control does not exist on the Internet, so, to be a reflective and responsible practitioner, you must learn to evaluate Internet sources.

Activity: Select three educational websites. (Links from our textbook site are certainly a good starting place.) Choose one that is relevant to a subject matter area; another that is interactive, featuring bulletin boards or opportunities to chat with colleagues; and a third that is monitored or sponsored by a professional organization such as the NEA or AFT.

Evaluate the sites by determining frequency of updates, investigating links, monitoring conversations, and assessing quality of content and graphics. Print out sample pages from the three sites and share your results informally with classmates.

Reflection: What other criteria can you use to decide which websites and Internet resources are reliable? Are there techniques and shortcuts to *surfing* educational sites? What addresses might offer lesson plans, emotional support for new teachers, factual materials for curriculum planning, and colleagues for an issue-based dialogue?

4:10 DO DROP IN

INTASC PRINCIPLE 10
Relationships and
Partnerships

Purpose: Many youths are served by agencies and support services beyond schools. Particularly when poverty threatens to limit children's potential, these community programs fill an important role. Your teaching can be more effective if you understand the contributions of those who work with children outside of schools. Or, you may find yourself drawn to youth service beyond the classroom setting.

Activity: Visit a community youth service agency, such as a Head Start center or one of the Boys and Girls Clubs of America. Request a tour of the facilities and try to arrange for a youth member or leader to spend some time with you. Use your questioning and interviewing skills (honed to a fine edge in previous *Inter-missions*) to find out about the impact of the organization on children and adolescents. Observe overt and subtle interactions between staff and members—watch procedures and rituals carefully.

Reflection: How does this agency serve youths in ways that support their education and achievement? How do issues of race, ethnicity, language, and class intersect in this nonschool environment? Do the children behave differently during the informal program than they do in school? Would you consider getting involved with this organization? What might you gain from working or volunteering in this nonschool setting? What formal connections exist between the schools and this agency?

Portfolio Artifact Collections

4:P6 NEWSWORTHY

Purpose: A brief and accurate declaration about you is an important introduction to your portfolio. As a template, you can use one of three formats sprinkled throughout the text: *Profiles in Education, Class Acts,* or an expanded *In the News* feature. These designs will set up a unique approach to describing you as a future teacher.

Activity: Write a brief personal statement (150 words) using one of the layouts, or create a design of your own. Whether your effort becomes the cover page to your presentation portfolio or an insert in your job application packet, this tight and compelling bio will be an invitation to read further.

4:P8 LETTERS, YOU'LL GET LETTERS

Purpose: Trying to keep your portfolio up-to-date is a long-term investment of your time and energy, and keeping letters of recommendation current is challenging. Former faculty, mentors, and employers can be tough to track down. This activity will keep your artifact collection contemporary.

Activity: Request a letter of recommendation from individuals who know the caliber of your work as a student, an employee, or a youth leader. Volunteer to help by providing a résumé, key points, or even a rough draft. Useful information includes

- Critical details (name, classes you have taken, your final grade, any special products or papers you submitted)
- Your specific job interest
- Personal and professional attributes that make you a good candidate for a position

Be sure to provide any necessary forms and envelopes with the correct address and postage. Filing a copy with the placement office at your university career center is advantageous. If your writers are willing, encourage them to provide extra copies, either open or signed and sealed, for your portfolio. This should be an ongoing activity to keep your file up-to-date. A handwritten thank-you note is always a courteous final step.

4:P9 STATE LICENSURE REQUIREMENTS

Purpose: Don't wait until the end of your program to explore licensure requirements. While predicting exactly what's ahead may be impossible, planning for it is not.

Activity: Meet with your program adviser. Discuss where you are considering applying for a teaching position. Your school may have an arrangement with one or more of the states that will facilitate your receiving a license. For instance, if your school is NASDTEC or NCATE accredited, or if there is an interstate reciprocity agreement, obtaining a license may be greatly facilitated. If your college does not have a special relationship with a state that you are considering, you may want to contact the state directly. In any case, start a folder for all this teacher's license information. Include information about state license requirements, such as required teacher competency tests. Don't forget to keep all relevant information and correspondence from your teacher education program, as well as from the state departments of education. It is important to remember to stay in touch with your teacher education program as you

> **INTASC PRINCIPLE 6**
> Communication Skills

> **INTASC PRINCIPLE 8**
> Assessment

> **INTASC PRINCIPLE 9**
> Reflection and Responsibility

go through this process and to plan your course work accordingly. Your college or university can be a big help, but the responsibility for getting the license is yours.

Finale

YOUR *INTER-MISSIONS* ARE OVER. THE ACTIVITIES, REFLECTIONS, AND ARTIFACT COLLECTION TASKS APPLIED THE MAJOR THEMES FOUND IN *TEACHERS, SCHOOLS, AND SOCIETY.* YOUR COMPLETED ASSIGNMENTS HAVE BECOME THE FOUNDATION OF YOUR *WORKING* PORTFOLIO. IT WILL TAKE FURTHER REFINING, CONSIDERABLE COURSE WORK, AND MANY HOURS OF PRACTICE TEACHING TO PRODUCE YOUR *PRESENTATION* PORTFOLIO. WE WISH YOU EVERY SUCCESS.

APPENDIX 1

STATE OFFICES FOR TEACHER CERTIFICATION AND LICENSURE

Alabama
Teacher Education and Certification
Alabama Department of Education
50 North Ripley Street
P.O. Box 302101
Montgomery, AL 36104
Phone: 334-242-9977
E-mail: tcert@alsde.edu
Homepage: www.alsde.edu

Alaska
Teacher Education and Certification
Alaska Department of Education
801 West 10th Street, Suite 200
Juneau, AK 99801-1894
Phone: 907-465-2831
E-mail: tcwebmail@eed.state.ak.us
Homepage: www.educ.state.ak.us/
TeacherCertification/home.html

Arizona
Teacher Certification
Arizona Department of Education
P.O. Box 6490
Phoenix, AZ 85005
Phone: 602-542-4367
Homepage: www.ade.state.az.us/
certification

Arkansas
Office of Professional Licensure
Arkansas Department of Education
4 State Capitol Mall,
Rooms 106B/107B
Little Rock, AR 72201
Phone: 501-682-4342
Homepage: www.arkedu.state.ar.
us/teacher.htm

California
California Commission on Teacher
Credentialing (CTC)
Information Services Unit
P.O. Box 944270
1900 Capitol Avenue
Sacramento, CA 94233-2700

Phone: 916-445-7254 or
888-921-2682
E-mail: credentials@ctc.ca.gov
Homepage: www.ctc.ca.gov

Colorado
Educator Licensing
Colorado Department of Education
201 East Colfax Avenue, Room 105
Denver, CO 80203
Phone: 303-866-6628
Homepage: www.cde.state.co.us/
index_license.htm

Connecticut
Bureau of Certification and Teacher
Preparation
Connecticut State Department of
Education
P.O. Box 150471, Room 243
Hartford, CT 06115-0471
Phone: 860-713-6969
E-mail: teacher.cert@po.state.ct.us
Homepage: www.state.ct.us/sde/
dtl/index.htm

Delaware
Delaware Department of Education
John G. Townsend Building
401 Federal Street
P.O. Box 1402
Dover, DE 19903-1402
Phone: 302-739-4601
Homepage:
www.deeds.doe.state.de.us

District of Columbia
Educational Credentialing and
Standards Branch
District of Columbia Public Schools
825 North Capitol Street, N.E.
6th Floor
Washington, DC 20002
Phone: 202-442-5377
Homepage: www.k12.dc.us/dcps/
home.html

Florida
Bureau of Educator Certification
Florida Department of Education
Suite 201, Turlington Building
325 West Gaines Street
Tallahassee, FL 32399-0400
Phone: (in-state toll-free number)
800-445-6739 or (out-of-state
number) 850-488-2317
E-mail: edcert@mail.doe.state.fl.us
Homepage: www.firn.edu/doe/
bin00022/home0022.htm

Georgia
The Georgia Professional Standards
Commission
1454 Twin Towers East
Atlanta, GA 30334
Phone: 404-657-9000 or
800-869-7775 (in Georgia)
Homepage: www.gapsc.com

Hawaii
Division of Administrative Services,
Personnel Services Branch
ATTN: Personnel Development and
Certification Section
Hawaii Department of Education
P.O. Box 2360
Honolulu, HI 96804
Phone: 808-586-3276
Homepage: www.doe.k12.hi.us

Idaho
Bureau of Certification and
Professional Standards
Idaho State Department of
Education
650 West State Street
P.O. Box 83720
Boise, ID 83720-0027
Phone: 208-332-6880
Homepage: www.sde.state.id.us/
certification

Illinois
Division of Professional Certification
Illinois State Board of Education
100 North First Street
Springfield, IL 62777
Phone: 800-845-8749
Homepage:
www.isbe.state.il.us/teachers/
teachers.htm

Indiana
Indiana Professional Standards
Board
251 East Ohio Street, Suite 201
Indianapolis, IN 46204-2133
Phone: 317-232-9010
Homepage: www.IN.gov/psb

Iowa
Iowa Board of Educational Examiners
Iowa Department of Education
Grimes State Office Building
Des Moines, IA 50319-0146
Phone: 515-281-3245
Homepage: www.state.ia.us/
educate/programs/boee/index.html

Kansas
Certification and Teacher Education
Kansas State Department of
Education
120 S.E. 10th Avenue
Topeka, KS 66612-1182
Phone: 785-291-3678
Homepage: www.ksbe.state.ks.us/
cert/cert.html

Kentucky
Education Professional Standards
Board
Division of Certification
Kentucky Department of Education
1024 Capital Center Drive,
Suite 225
Frankfort, KY 40601
Phone: 502-573-4606
Homepage: www.kde.state.ky.us/
otec/cert/default.asp

Louisiana
Teacher Certification and Higher
Education
Office of Quality Educators
Louisiana Department of Education
P.O. Box 94064
Baton Rouge, LA 70804-9064

Phone: 877-453-2721 or
225-342-3490
E-mail: customerservice@mail.state.
doe.la.us
Homepage: www.doe.state.la.us

Maine
Maine Department of Education
23 State House Station
Augusta, ME 04333
Phone: 207-624-6600
Homepage: www.state.me.us/
education

Maryland
Division of Certification &
Accreditation
Maryland State Department of
Education
200 W. Baltimore Street
Baltimore, MD 21201
Phone: 410-767-0412
Homepage: www.msde.state.md.
us/certification/index.htm

Massachusetts
Teacher Certification and
Credentialing Office
Massachusetts Department of
Education
350 Main Street, P.O. Box 9140
Malden, MA 02148-9140
Phone: 781-338-6600
E-mail: cert.inquiries@doe.mass.edu
Homepage: www.doe.mass.edu/
cert

Michigan
Office of Professional Preparation
Services
Michigan Department of Education
P.O. Box 30008
Lansing, MI 48909
Phone: 517-373-1925
Homepage:
www.state.mi.us/mde/off/ppc/
office.htm

Minnesota
Personnel Licensing Team
Minnesota Department of Children,
Families and Learning
1500 Highway 36 West
Roseville, MN 55113-4266
Phone: 651-582-8691

E-mail: Personnel.Licensing@state.
mn.us
Homepage: www.educ.state.mn.us/
licen/license.htm

Mississippi
Educator Licensure/Certification
Mississippi Department of Education
359 North West Street
Jackson, MS 39205
Phone: 601-359-3483
Homepage: www.mde.k12.ms.us/
license/index.html

Missouri
Teacher Certification
Division of Teacher Quality and
Urban Education
P.O. Box 480
Jefferson City, MO 65102-0480
Phone: 573-751-0051 or
573-751-3847
E-mail: webreplyteachcert@mail.
dese.state.mo.us
Homepage: www.dese.state.mo.us/
divteachqual/teachcert

Montana
Certification and Licensure
Montana Office of Public
Instruction
P.O. Box 202501
Helena, MT 59620-2501
Phone: 406-444-3150
E-mail: Cert@state.mt.us
Homepage: www.metnet.state.mt.
us/Cert/htm

Nebraska
Teacher Education and Certification
Nebraska Department of Education
301 Centennial Mall South
P.O. Box 94987
Lincoln, NE 68509
Phone: 402-471-2496
Homepage: www.nde.state.ne.us/
tcert/tcmain.html

Nevada
Teacher Licensure Office
Nevada Department of Education
1820 East Sahara, Suite 205
Las Vegas, NV 89104-3746
Phone: 775-486-6458
Homepage: www.ccsd.net/HRD/
NVDOE

New Hampshire
Bureau of Credentialing
New Hampshire Department of
Education
101 Pleasant Street
Concord, NH 03301-3860
Phone: 603-271-2408
Homepage: www.ed.state.nh.us/
Certification/teacher.htm

New Jersey
Office of Licensing and Credentials
New Jersey Department of
Education
CN 500
Trenton, NJ 08625-0500
Phone: 609-292-2070
Homepage: www.state.nj.us/njded/
educators/license

New Mexico
Professional Licensure Unit
New Mexico State Department of
Education
Education Building
Santa Fe, NM 87501-2786
Phone: 505-827-6587
Homepage: www.sde.state.nm.us/
divisions/ais/licensure/index.html

New York
Office of Teaching
New York State Education
Department
89 Washington Avenue
Albany, NY 12234
Phone: 518-474-3852
Homepage: www.highered.nysed.
gov/tcert

North Carolina
Licensure Section
Department of Public Instruction
301 North Wilmington Street
Raleigh, NC 27601-2825
Phone: 919-807-3310
Homepage: www.ncpublicschools.
org/employment.html

North Dakota
North Dakota Education Standards
and Practices Board
North Dakota Capitol Building
600 East Boulevard Avenue,
Department 202, 9th Floor

Bismarck, ND 58505-0080
Phone: 701-328-2264
Homepage: www.state.nd.us/espb

Ohio
Office of Certification/Licensure
Ohio Department of Education
25 South Front Street
Columbus, OH 43215-4183
Phone: 877-644-6338
Homepage: www.ode.state.oh.us/
tp/ctp

Oklahoma
Professional Standards Section
Oklahoma Department of Education
Hodge Education Building,
Room 211
2500 North Lincoln Boulevard
Oklahoma City, OK 73105
Phone: 405-521-3337
Homepage: www.sde.state.ok.us

Oregon
Teachers Standards and Practices
Commission
255 Capitol Street NE, Suite 105
Salem, OR 97310-1332
Phone: 503-378-3586
E-mail: contact.tspc.@state.or.us
Homepage: www.tspc.state.or.us

Pennsylvania
Bureau of Teacher Certification and
Preparation
Pennsylvania Department of
Education
333 Market Street
Harrisburg, PA 17126-0333
Phone: 717-787-3356
Homepage: www.teaching.state.pa.
us/teaching/site/default.asp

Rhode Island
Rhode Island Department of
Education
Shepard Building
255 Westminster Street
Providence, RI 02903
Phone: 401-222-4600
Homepage: www.ridoe.net/
teacher_cert/Default.htm

South Carolina
Division of Teacher Quality

South Carolina Department of
Education
1600 Gervais Street
Columbia, SC 29201
Phone: 877-885-5280 (in-state toll
free) or 803-734-8466 (out-of-state
and local callers)
E-mail: certification@scteachers.org
Homepage: www.scteachers.org/
scteachers/default.htm

South Dakota
Office of Policy and Accountability
Department of Education and
Cultural Affairs
700 Governors Drive
Pierre, SD 57501
Phone: 605-773-3553
Homepage: www.state.sd.us/deca/
account/certif.htm

Tennessee
State Department of Education
Office of Teacher Licensing
5th Floor, Andrew Johnson Tower
710 James Robertson Parkway
Nashville, TN 37243-0377
Phone: 615-532-4880
Homepage: www.state.tn.us/
education/lic_home.htm

Texas
State Board for Educator
Certification
1001 Trinity Street
Austin, TX 78701-2603
Phone: 512-469-3000
E-mail: sbec@mail.sbec.state.tx.us
Homepage: www.sbec.state.tx.us

Utah
Educator Licensing
Utah State Office of Education
250 East 500 South
Salt Lake City, UT 84111
Phone: 801-538-7740
Homepage: www.usoe.k12.ut.us/
cert

Vermont
Licensing Office
Vermont Department of Education
120 State Street
Montpelier, VT 05620-2501
Phone: 802-828-2445

E-mail: licensing@doe.state.vt.us
Homepage: www.state.vt.us/educ/
license/index.htm

Virginia
Division of Teacher Education and
Licensure
Virginia Department of Education
P.O. Box 2120
Richmond, VA 23218
Phone: 804-371-2522
Homepage: www.pen.k12.va.us/
VDOE/newvdoe/teached.html

Washington
Professional Certification
Office of Superintendent of Public
Instruction
Old Capitol Building
P.O. Box 47200

Olympia, WA 98504-7200
Phone: 360-753-6773
E-mail: cert@ospi.wednet.edu
Homepage: www.k12.wa.us/cert

West Virginia
Office of Professional Preparation
West Virginia Department of
Education
1900 Kanawha Boulevard
East Building 6, Room 252
Charleston, WV 25305-0330
Phone: 304-558-7826
Homepage: wvde.state.wv.us/
certification

Wisconsin
Bureau for Education, Licensing,
and Placement

Wisconsin Department of Public
Instruction
125 South Webster Street
P.O. Box 7841
Madison, WI 53707-7841
Phone: 608-266-1788
Homepage: www.dpi.state.wi.us/
dpi/dlsis/tel/licguide.html

Wyoming
Professional Teaching Standards
Board
Wyoming State Department of
Education
2300 Capitol Avenue
Hathaway Building, 2nd Floor
Cheyenne, WY 82002-0050
Phone: 307-777-7675
Homepage: www.k12.wy.us/ptsb

APPENDIX 2

INFORMATION ABOUT THE TEACHER COMPETENCY EXAMS (PRAXIS SERIES)

Educational Testing Service

The Praxis Series is an Educational Testing Service (ETS) program that provides tests and other services for states to use as part of their teacher licensure process. Some colleges and universities use these assessments to qualify individuals for entry into teacher education programs.

The Praxis Series is the choice of approximately forty states that include tests as part of their teacher licensure process. You will take The Praxis Series if you want to teach public school in one of these states or if you want to enter a teacher education program at a college or university that uses Praxis I: Academic Skills Assessments. Different states and institutions require different tests in the Praxis Series, so be sure you know which tests you need before you register.

The Praxis Series OnLine (www.teachingandlearning.org) provides useful information about the test series, how these assessments are used, how to register to take the tests, and how to get your scores. This online service lets you review and download specific teacher licensure policies and test requirements in each state that uses the Praxis Series program. You can get this information from the Praxis Series: Professional Assessments for Beginning Teachers, Registration Bulletin, available free from ETS or from your college or university. Still more is available from *The Praxis Series Tests at a Glance* booklets.

The three categories of assessments in the Praxis Series correspond to the three milestones in teacher development.

Praxis I: Academic Skills Assessment. These assessments are designed to be taken early in the student's college career to measure reading, writing, and mathematics skills vital to all teacher candidates. The assessments are available in two formats, paper-based and computer-based. Both measure similar academic skills, but the computer-based tests (CBTs) are tailored to each candidate's performance. CBTs also offer a wider range of question types, provide an immediate score in reading and math, and are available on demand throughout the year by appointment, eliminating the need to register in advance. The paper-based tests, called the PPST® or Pre-Professional Skills Tests, are given six times a year.

Praxis II: Subject Assessments. These assessments measure candidates' knowledge of the subjects they will teach, as well as how much they know about teaching that subject. More than 140 content tests are available. The tests are regularly updated, and several are available in each subject field, so a state can customize its program by selecting the assessments that best match its own licensure requirements. For added flexibility, each state can base its assessments on standard multiple-choice questions or incorporate new candidate-constructed-response modules. These performance-based items allow test-takers to demonstrate in-depth knowledge and reinforce the importance of writing in the teaching profession.

Praxis III: Classroom Performance Assessments. These assessments are used at the beginning teaching level to evaluate all aspects of a beginning teacher's classroom performance. Designed to assist in making licensure decisions, these comprehensive assessments are conducted in the classroom by trained local assessors who use a set of consistent, reliable, nationally validated criteria. Pathwise™, a companion product designed to be used in nonlicensing situations, is an in-class observation system created to guide preservice and inservice development activities for student and beginning teachers.

If you are planning to take one or more of these tests, you need a copy of *The Praxis Series: Professional Assessments for Beginning Teachers, Registration Bulletin.* The bulletin is free and provides complete test information plus test registration instructions. It's available at your college or university, or you can request one by calling 1-609-771-7395. You can also review and download the Registration Bulletin and Tests at a

Glance information instantly, from www.teaching andlearning.org, in the form of downloadable PDF files in Adobe® Acrobat® format. (In order to view and print these files, you may need information on down-loading Acrobat Reader software and configuring your browser.)

If you prefer to order your own free copy of any of the *Tests at a Glance* booklets, check with your college or university or call ETS at 1-609-771-7395.

The states and territories listed below use the Praxis Series tests as part of their teacher licensure process. You should check with each state to find out which tests are required, passing scores, and other information.

Alaska

Arkansas

California

Connecticut

Delaware

District of Columbia

Florida

Georgia

Hawaii

Indiana

Kansas

Kentucky

Louisiana

Maine

Maryland

Minnesota

Mississippi

Missouri

Montana

Nebraska

Nevada

New Hampshire

New Jersey

New Mexico

North Carolina

Ohio

Oklahoma

Oregon

Pennsylvania

Rhode Island

South Carolina

Tennessee

Texas

U.S. Virgin Islands

Vermont

Virginia

West Virginia

Wisconsin

National Evaluation Systems

While the Praxis assessments from ETS have received a great deal of attention, National Evaluation Systems, Inc. assesses almost as many prospective teachers, but is less well known. The Praxis series is administered to about 500,000 aspiring teachers; NES assesses just under 400,000. The reason is that NES customizes its exams for individual states. Some states use both NES and Praxis exams to assess their teachers. Specific information about NES-created tests is available directly from teacher licensure departments in:

Alaska

California

Colorado

Illinois

Massachusetts

Michigan

New Mexico

New York

Oklahoma

Texas

A SUMMARY OF SELECTED REPORTS ON EDUCATION REFORM

Title	Source	Data
The Paideia Proposal (1982)	Mortimer Adler for the Paideia Group	Twenty-two members contributed to a philosophical analysis of educational needs.
A Nation at Risk: The Imperative for Educational Reform (1983)	The National Commission on Excellence in Education—U.S. Department of Education	Eighteen political and educational leaders commissioned papers and reviewed available materials, including national and international test scores.
American's Competitive Challenge: The Need for a Response (1983)	Business—Higher Education Forum	Sixteen representatives of business and higher education reviewed expert opinions and past surveys.
Action for Excellence: A Comprehensive Plan to Improve Our Nation's Schools (1983)	Task Force of the Education Commission of the States, chaired by Governor James Hunt	Forty-one governors, legislators, labor leaders, business leaders, and school board members collected data and interpreted results.
Academic Preparation for College: What Students Need to Know and Be Able to Do (1983)	Education Equality Project—The College Board	Two hundred high school and college teachers and college board members collected and interpreted test results.
Making the Grade (1983)	Twentieth-Century Fund Task Force on Federal Elementary and Secondary Education Policy	Eleven members of state, local, and higher education organizations reviewed research studies.
Educating Americans for the 21st Century: A Report to the American People and the National Science Board (1983)	National Science Board Commission on Pre-College Education in Mathematics, Science and Technology	Commission members and others reviewed a number of professional association, business, and other education programs.
The Good High School: Portraits of Character and Culture (1983)	Sara Lawrence Lightfoot	Field study of six private and public schools
High School: A Report on Secondary Education in America (1983)	The Carnegie Foundation for the Advancement of Teaching	Ernest Boyer chaired a national panel of educators and citizens, which reviewed past research and undertook field studies in public high schools.
A Place Called School (1983)	John Goodlad	Presents observations of and responses to questionnaires administered in schools over an eight-year period

The book urges a radical reorganization to focus on three areas: (1) the development of personal, mental, moral, and spiritual growth; (2) citizenship; and (3) basic skills. Teaching methods and subject areas would be revised, and there would be a core curriculum for all students from elementary through secondary education.

The report's powerful rhetoric, such as the "rising tide of mediocrity" and "a nation at risk," galvanized public attention regarding school reform. The report suggests that poor school performance threatens our nation's economic health. It emphasizes rigorous courses, a core curriculum, the recruiting of talented teachers, and a thorough assessment of student and teacher competence.

The report indicates that a major reason for U.S. economic problems and falling productivity is the inadequate education of the nation's workers, who need more schooling in mathematics, science, critical-thinking skills, and verbal expression.

The report urges state leadership to develop action plans for improving education, including more community involvement, additional funds, better preparation and pay for teachers, stronger curricular offerings, greater accountability, more effective principals, and better programs for poorly achieving students.

More rigorous preparation for college is called for, including better-trained teachers, more demanding elementary and secondary curricula, and higher expectations of students. Colleges should also provide remedial help for ill-prepared students and should work more closely with high schools in preparing students for college.

The report states that the criticism of U.S. schools is exaggerated and that schools are fundamentally doing their job. Suggestions for improvement include federal aid for schools, a clearer focus on educational quality, a continued commitment to educational equity, and support for local decision making.

Emphasizing a strong mathematics and science curriculum, the report highlights the need to attract individuals with these skills into teaching.

Although this is not technically a reform report, the author's observations of four public and two private high schools provide valuable insights into effective and ineffective school practices.

The report recommends a heavy emphasis on English (particularly writing) and a strong academic core for all students. It suggests elimination of the vocational track and advocates a five-year teacher education program.

This report recommends making the principal a manager and creating a "head teacher" to focus on instructional improvement. Goodlad also calls for grouping students in clusters rather than by grade level. The book highlights the need for a greater variety of teaching methods to deal with student diversity.

Title	Source	Data
Horace's Compromise: The Dilemma of the American High School (1984)	Theodore Sizer	Interviews and observations in the fifteen schools in the report *A Study of High Schools*
The Shopping Mall High School (1985)	Arthur Powell, Eleanor Farrar, and David Cohen	One of three efforts in *A Study of High Schools,* this field analysis of fifteen schools used comprehensive interviews and classroom observation.
The Last Citadel (1986)	Robert Hempel	Four of the fifteen schools visited in *A Study of High Schools* were examined historically through oral histories, published and unpublished records, and historical files of a variety of educational institutions.
A Nation Prepared: Teachers for the 21st Century (1986)	Task Force on Teaching as a Profession, Carnegie Forum on Education and the Economy	Fourteen-member panel of educators, policy-makers, politicians, and others analyzed existing data.
Tomorrow's Teachers (Holmes Report, 1986)	Deans of selected teacher education colleges	Thirteen education deans and one college president formulate their professional and philosophical views.
Time for Results (1986)	National Governors Association	Lamar Alexander chaired the governor's task force that reviewed research and existing reports.
First Lessons (1986)	U.S. Department of Education	William Bennett and twenty-one other distinguished citizens summarize critical findings concerning more effective elementary education.
James Madison High (1986)	U.S. Department of Education	William Bennett provides his ideas for a high school curriculum, based on research and practice in secondary schools.
Turning Points: Preparing American Youth for the 21st Century (1989)	Carnegie Foundation Task Force on Education of Young Adolescents	David Hornbeck chaired the eighteen-member task force of educators, government officials, and others who, through analysis of interviews and commission studies, collected relevant data.
America 2000: An Education Strategy (1991) **Goals 2000: Educate America Act (1994)**	President Bush and governors; continued and modified by the Clinton administration	Administration-led political efforts to respond to educational needs cited in numerous reports, international test scores, etc.

Recommendations

Dramatizing the difficult working conditions facing teachers, Sizer emphasizes the need to develop close teacher-student relationships, high student motivation, and a less fragmented curriculum.

To ensure effective reform, the authors recommend an informed public, involved parents, high expectations and outstanding teachers, and more time in study and preparation of lessons, as well as greater standards of professionalism for teachers.

Hempel offers a study of the alteration of the U.S. high school since the 1940s, noting that academic subjects have remained intact and schedules and routines are virtually unchanged. The book highlights the need to deal sensitively with multiple priorities and recommends that more emphasis be place on orderly thinking than on orderly discipline.

The report called for the establishment of a National Board of Professional Teaching Standards to test and certify all teachers, as well as testing for and issuing an advanced teaching certificate. It recommends that all teachers take a five-year teacher education program, including four years of liberal arts and science.

Expressing their personal and professional views, these educators call for reforming teacher education by requiring that all teachers receive a bachelor's degree in an academic field and a master's degree in education. The report recommends greater recognition of teaching and improvement of teachers' working conditions.

The governors placed themselves on the cutting edge of school reform by producing numerous recommendations, including parental choice in school selection, career ladders, state takeovers of poorly performing school districts, programs to prevent students from dropping out, and emphasis on technology in teacher preparation.

The former Secretary of Education calls for elementary students to be taught a rigorous regime of reading and other basic skills, including foreign language and computer skills.

The former Secretary of Education recommends a traditional high school curriculum with few electives; four years of literature; a senior research paper; three years of math, science, and social studies with a U.S. and Western focus; and emphasis on foreign language.

This is an unusual report in that it focuses on the junior high, or middle school, a period of significant physical, social, and psychological change for young adolescents. Recommendations include the creation of small learning communities within large schools, a core curriculum that is academically demanding, the elimination of tracking, the empowerment of teachers and principals by giving them more authority, the improvement of school-community-parent relationships, and the promotion of student self-esteem.

A political consensus identified a number of national goals: among others, a 90 percent or higher high school graduation rate, number one ranking for U.S. students in math and science, 100 percent adult literacy, parental involvement, and teacher development.

OBSERVATION MANUAL

Many education courses now require or recommend field observation activities. This Appendix will help you sharpen and focus your field observation skills. Accurate data collection and thoughtful reflection about what you see can give you new insights into life in the classroom and the process of teaching.

General Observation Guidelines

While the field experience is an integral part of virtually all teacher preparation programs, the specific design and approach of school observation varies greatly. In some teacher education programs, the field experience is a component of the Introduction to Teaching Course or the Foundations of Education Course; in others, it is a separate course. In still others, it has become a continuous strand that links most, if not all, education courses.

Whatever approach your college or university provides, this experience, if used well, can offer rich insight into the real world of teaching and schools and can help answer your concerns and questions about teaching as a career. Unfortunately, poorly structured school visits quickly deteriorate into a vacuous waste of time. This Appendix, along with the *Inter-missions*, provide the structure and focus to ensure accurate observation and thoughtful reflection about the information you gather. But that is only half—perhaps less than half—of the formula needed for successful school observation. The other central ingredient is you. How you approach the experience, and what you do or do not do with the information you gather, ultimately will determine how well your field experience will work for you.

John Dewey, perhaps America's most famous educator, wrote extensively about *reflective thinking*, which he defined as avoiding routine and impulsive behaviors in favor of taking the time to give serious consideration to our actions. According to Dewey, the intelligent person thinks before he or she acts, and action becomes deliberate and intentional. If you want to glean knowledge and insight from your field experience, your observations must be careful, analytical, and deliberate. Once your observations have been made, you will need to consider carefully what you have seen before you formulate conclusions about life in schools.

Identifying Your Goals and Concerns

The reflective field experience structured in this Appendix and in the *Inter-missions* will encourage you not only to see what schools do but also to consider what they might do differently. Although each student approaches the field experience with a unique personal history and set of expectations, it is useful to think about and prioritize these perceptions and concerns before you begin. Take a minute and, on a separate sheet of paper or in your journal or notebook, write a brief list of your goals as you prepare for your field experience. In short, what information and insight do you want to get out of your field experience? After you have written down your goals, consider the following questions. Are your goals clear, or do you need to give them more thought? Are some of these goals more important than others? (You may want to rank them in order of priority.) Do your goals fall into one or two broad categories, or are they more diverse? This Appendix structures your field experiences into several categories: the setting, the teacher, the students, and the curriculum. Have you considered all these areas in your goals—or, like many beginning teachers, have you omitted one or more? Which areas have you omitted? Why? Since these are the key areas your field experience should emphasize, take a few moments before you arrive at your observation site and consider what you want to learn about the following components.

Setting. What is the socioeconomic status of the community? What are the community's values concerning education generally and the schools in particular? Are parents involved in the schools? What is the academic and social culture of the school? What is important in this community and in this school? How would you describe the physical environment of the community, the school, and the classroom? How are the classrooms organized to promote learning?

Teaching. Why do people enter teaching? What do they like about teaching? Why do people leave teaching? What are the responsibilities of teachers? How do you become an effective teacher? What successful teaching skills are used in this school? What needs to be improved? Do you like teaching? Are you good at it? How can you apply what you learn in your education courses to your own teaching?

Students. As you prepare for a teaching career, your concerns and interests are naturally focused on the teaching aspect of the classroom and whether you will like teaching and be good at it. But teaching does not exist in isolation; key to the context of teaching are the students. Who are the learners and what are their interests? What motivates students to learn? What are the barriers? How can work be individualized? How can discipline problems be handled? avoided? Which age group and which type of students do you prefer to work with?

Curriculum. Students spend approximately 90 percent of their academic time involved in reading textbooks and other curricular materials. Curricular issues that could be addressed in the field experience include the following: What is taught in your school? Is breadth or depth emphasized? Are students responsible for problem solving and critical thinking? Or are drill and rote memorization emphasized? Is adequate time provided for each subject? Is there bias in the curriculum? Which topics are emphasized? omitted? Is the curriculum interesting and motivating? What is the school's policy concerning a core curriculum? Has your college work prepared you to teach the curriculum? How might you present the curriculum differently?

This Appendix introduces each of these areas, providing you with a few sample activities. Working with your instructor and colleagues, you may want to develop and use other data collection activities as well.

Learning How to Observe

Students preparing to be teachers suffer from the handicap of too much familiarity with school. Consequently, they may block out valid and useful insights. Thousands of hours spent behind students' desks inure many to the subtle and not-so-subtle aspects of

schooling in the United States. In order to become an effective teacher, you need to erase this past conditioning and reawaken yourself to the realities of school and classroom life. Developing observation skills will sensitize you to these realities and enable you to judge the effectiveness of the various instructional and management practices that teachers and administrators use in dealing with them.

> I sat in class for days wondering what there was to observe. Teachers taught, reprimanded, rewarded while pupils sat at desks squirming, whispering, reading, writing, staring into space, as they had in my own grade school experience, in my practice teaching in a teacher training program, and in the two years of public school teaching I had done before World War II.[1]

So wrote George Spindler, the researcher who is credited with developing educational anthropology as a legitimate field of scholarship. His problem was one that faces any serious observer in an environment that is too familiar. Everything seems trivial and obvious. As Margaret Mead said, "If a fish were to become an anthropologist, the last thing that it would discover would be the water."[2]

Spindler became so frustrated with viewing the commonplace that he almost gave up his research. Education majors who are asked to observe in local elementary and secondary schools face similar problems. Because they find the environment as comfortable and everyday as a worn shoe, they often miss subtle incidents and the underlying significance of events.

Fortunately, Spindler did not give up school-based observations. He interviewed the target teacher he was observing, as well as supervisors and students. He collected autobiographical and psychological information from the teacher, analyzed the teacher's evaluations of his students, and conducted sociograms (i.e., recording popular and isolated students, as well as cliques) to determine students' attitudes toward one another. As a result of careful data collection, Spindler discovered that the target teacher, who at casual glance seemed to treat all students similarly, actually favored white middle- and upper-class students. The teacher was completely unaware of this differential treatment, but the students were readily able to identify the teacher's favorites. If the teacher had known how to observe subtle classroom dynamics, he would have been aware of this disparity. Without the skills of observation, interpretation, and reflection, the teacher remained ignorant of important elements of the classroom social structure.[3]

Classrooms and schools are complex intellectual, social, personal, and physical environments, where the average teacher has more than one thousand interactions a day, each with different levels and nuances of meaning. In this multifaceted, fast-paced, confusing culture called *school,* it is all too easy to miss much of what you think you "see." But, if you immerse yourself in this culture, observe and record your experiences systematically, then reflect on and interpret what you have seen, you can gain greater insight into how and why teachers and students behave the way they do.

There are many sources for collecting objective data. These include direct observation; document analysis of school mission statements, discipline codes, textbooks, student portfolios, and lesson plans; and interviews with key participants, such as teachers, students, administrators, and parents. Observation followed by reflection will provide crucial data about the realities, frustrations, and rewards of classroom life—information that will help you become a better teacher.

OBSERVATION TECHNIQUES

This Appendix provides you with a variety of *observation techniques* to collect information. You and your instructor may determine to use only a few of these methods—or all six.

Interviewing   Depending on the role they play in school, various participants may have different interpretations of and opinions about events. For example, a student's feelings about a pep rally may differ from those of the school principal. Interviews are an excellent method for bringing to light these different perspectives and points of view. Your interviewing protocol may consist of very specific questions ("How many years have you taught in this school?") or questions that are broad and open-ended ("How does this school differ from other elementary schools where you have taught?").

Asking questions that draw the subject out is a challenging skill to master. For example, during an interview you may ask, "Do you enjoy teaching?" If you get a simple "yes" or "no," you will need to ask follow-up, or probing, questions to get more detailed information. Assuring the interviewee that answers will be kept confidential may be helpful in obtaining frank and comprehensive responses.

Whenever possible, audio or video record or take notes during the interview, perhaps just jotting down key phrases if you do not have time to record complete sentences. Later you may find it difficult to remember exactly what the interviewee said, or you may inadvertently distort or rephrase what was said to fit your own preconceived notions of people and events. Although most of us like to think we are objective, our past experiences and our perspectives may cloud our vision.

Questionnaires   Interviews are a good strategy for gathering in-depth information, but time constraints will limit the number of people you can reach. Questionnaires provide the opportunity to gather information from a much larger sample of faculty, staff, or students. You will need to decide what you want to ask and how you want participants to respond. For example, you can ask an open-ended question:

How would you describe the audiovisual equipment in this school? _____

Or you might want to structure your questions so that a particular type of response is generated:

Audiovisual technology is used frequently.
Agree Strongly   Agree   Disagree   Disagree Strongly

You will also need to decide whether you wish respondents to identify themselves or whether questionnaires should be anonymous. Although questionnaires are not stressed in the data collection activities in this manual, they are a good source of information. If you are interested in this method of data collection, discuss how to develop and distribute questionnaires with your course instructor.

Observation Data   A much-used technique for capturing, comparing, and analyzing human behavior of all kinds is the *structured observation system.* Community life, school activities, and classroom behaviors can be recorded and evaluated through a coherent set of questions or more sophisticated coding techniques. In fact, a number of these structured observation systems were originally designed for educational research, but they have now found their way into everyday school practice. These instruments measure everything from the kinds of questions teachers ask to the nature of peer-group interaction. One of the earlier and more influential observation instruments is the Flanders Interaction Analysis, which is summarized briefly in Figure 1.

Originally developed as a research tool, Flanders Interaction Analysis became a widely used coding system to analyze and improve teaching skills. This observation system was designed to categorize the type and quantity of verbal dialogue in the classroom and to plot the information on a matrix so that it could be analyzed. The result gave a picture of who was talking in a classroom and the kind of talking that was taking place.

As a result of research with his coding instrument, Flanders uncovered the **two-thirds rule:** About two-thirds of classroom time is devoted to talking. About two-thirds of this time the person talking is the teacher, and two-thirds of the teacher's talk is "direct" (that is, lecturing, giving directions, and controlling students). The two-thirds rule is actually three related two-thirds rules and serves to substantiate that, typically, teachers verbally dominate classrooms.

Some people feel that Flanders' work has underscored the fact that a teacher's verbal domination of the classroom conditions students to become passive and to be dependent on the teacher. It is claimed that this dependency has an adverse effect on student attitudes toward school and student performance in school. Interestingly, Flanders found that when teachers are trained in his observation technique and become aware of the importance of language in the classroom, their verbal monopoly decreases.

To use the Flanders Interaction Analysis, one codes each verbal interaction as one of 10 categories, plots the coded data onto a matrix, and analyzes the matrix. Following are the 10 categories in the Flanders Interaction Analysis Coding Instrument.

Summary of Categories for Interaction Analysis

Indirect Teacher Talk

1. *Accepts feeling*
   Acknowledges student-expressed emotions (feelings) in a nonthreatening manner

2. *Praises or encourages*
   Provides positive reinforcement of student contributions

3. *Accepts or uses ideas of students*
   Clarifies, develops, or refers to student contribution, often nonevaluatively

4. *Asks questions*
   Solicits information or opinion (not rhetorically)

Direct Teacher Talk

5. *Lectures*
   Presents information, opinion, or orientation; perhaps includes rhetorical questions

6. *Gives directions*
   Supplies direction or suggestion with which a student is expected to comply

7. *Criticizes or justifies authority*
   Offers negative evaluation of student contributions or places emphasis on teacher's authoritative position

Student Talk

8. *Student talk—response*
   Gives a response to the teacher's question, usually a predictable answer

9. *Student talk—initiation*
   Initiates a response that is unpredictable or creative in content

10. *Silence or confusion*
    Leaves periods of silence or inaudible verbalization lasting more than 3 seconds

FIGURE 1

Flanders Interaction Analysis: an early and influential coding system.

Document Analysis By analyzing the documents, written records, and other classroom and school materials, you can gain important information about how the school works and what is emphasized. For example, does your school have a philosophy or mission statement in which goals are set forward? What policies govern staff and student behavior? Is there a disciplinary policy for students, and are they aware of it? What kinds of textbooks are used, and do teachers supplement texts with additional materials? What kind of report card or evaluation system is in use? What do newspapers and yearbooks tell you about the school's social system? The school's written records should provide an important complement to the data you collect from observing and interviewing.

Note Taking Note taking, a technique borrowed from cultural anthropologists, is one of the most commonly used methods for gathering data. When you first begin observing and taking notes on what you see, you may try to record everything. But, in the hectic, multifaceted school and classroom environment, you will soon discover that it is impossible to capture accurately so many different stimuli at one time. You will need to narrow your focus and target specific aspects of the environment for your data collection and note-taking activities. For example, you may choose to focus on how the curriculum is developed or the nature of leadership exerted by the principal. You may target your activities to record the frequency and quality of teacher questions or the way discipline is handled in the school. In order to select the most important information, you will need to go into the environment with a series of *focusing questions*.

Several focusing questions are included in the data collection activities in the next section, but you may wish to work with your peers and instructor on developing your own focusing questions. These will guide your observations and interviews and help you organize the field notes you record.

It is wise to keep your notes on your laptop or in a looseleaf notebook (such as the one you may have already begun using to record your observation goals and priorities). This gives you the advantage of being able to move and shift your notes around into different organizational formats. As you spend more time in field observation and collect increasing amounts of data, this ability to reorganize notes without losing them will be extremely helpful.

Sometimes it is impossible to take notes during observations and interviews. There may not be time, or you may sense that the interviewee will "clam up" if you whip out your notepad and pencil or laptop. In cases such as these, you will need to summarize your notes later. Whether you take notes during observations and interviews or make summary observations, you should record when and where each data collection activity took place. The more detailed dialogue and clearly defined images you include in your notes, the more useful they will be. Thorough and complete notes, filled with anecdotes and details, are called "rich data" and will help you reach the most insightful interpretations of events and behavior.

Logs and Journals Many teacher education programs require or recommend that you maintain a log or journal during your field experiences. Some programs specify a particular format, while others allow a more open-ended approach. In either case, the log or journal is intended to help you document and reflect on your observations. As you write your account, you will be giving thought both to the field experience and to its impact on you. Over time, you will detect growth and possibly significant change in what you believe about teaching and schools. When your field experiences are completed, you will have a written account of your activities and changing views during this formative period of your professional preparation.

In your log, you should also describe incidents observed or activities participated in as objectively as possible. This log should be kept on a daily basis, because time erases memories and feelings. Each day, your log should include one or two events that are particularly meaningful to you. An event may be significant because it impresses you (for example, a terrific teaching technique), because it is educationally important (such as a successful strategy for classroom management), because it disturbs you (for example, a poorly executed activity or a negative interaction you have), or because it challenges or confirms your beliefs and ideas. These events, whether positive or negative, should be selected and described because they are critical incidents for learning. The descriptions should be objective and detailed. Later you should set time aside, mull them over, and interpret what you learned. This part of the log is akin to a professional diary. If you have trouble analyzing any of these significant events, your instructor or other students may be able to assist. Identifying what events are most significant to you is a key step both in keeping a journal and in developing a reflective and professional approach to teaching. If your field experience does not have a specific log or journal format, here is one you may find useful:

Sample Log Format

Location: _____ Name: _____

Date: _____

Time: Activities:

————— ——————————
————— ——————————
————— ——————————
————— ——————————
————— ——————————
————— ——————————
————— ——————————
————— ——————————
————— ——————————

Significant event: _____

Description:

Analysis:

Other significant events, if appropriate:

In the log, as well as in your observation activities, it is useful to distinguish between description and judgment. It is also helpful to recognize some basic rules for observing. The next sections focus on these issues.

BECOMING ACCEPTED AS AN OBSERVER

A principal once told a story of an observer who became so involved in a teacher's lesson that he was soon raising his hand, responding to the teacher's questions, inserting personal anecdotes, and monopolizing classroom interaction. By the end of the class, the observer and the teacher were engaged in an animated dialogue, and the students had become passive onlookers. The observer had completely disrupted the classroom activities he was there to study. Such a complete role reversal is uncommon, but the following guidelines are offered as an antidote to the potentially disruptive effect posed by any classroom observer.

As an observer, you can generally avoid such direct verbal involvement as was described, but the more subtle challenge is to avoid nonverbal intrusion. What do you do when children engage you in nonverbal conversation consisting only of eye contact and facial expressions? Do you smile back, wink, and establish an unspoken kinship? Or, for fear of disturbing the class routine, do you ignore the students and possibly alienate them?

Although hard-and-fast rules are difficult to come by, it is clear that your presence in the classroom is not intended either to win friends and influence people or to alienate others. You must learn to accept students' nonverbal messages yet avoid prolonging these interactions. Ignoring all eye contact can be just as disruptive as encouraging such contact can be. With experience, you will be able to accept these subtle forms of communication without amplifying them. In this way, you can demonstrate that, although you are not insensitive to the interest and curiosity of students, your purpose in the classroom is to observe, not to alter, classroom life.

A primary goal is to observe the most and intrude the least. For most observations, this means positioning yourself as inconspicuously as possible, where you are behind the students but have a clear view of the teacher. It is also useful to conduct some observations from the side of the room, so that you can see the children's faces and nonverbal cues. The expressions, comments, and activities of the students will give valuable insights into student-teacher relationships and the nature of classroom life. In some cases, you may have to change your location while a lesson is in progress (for example, moving among various groups of students to observe their activities). Whatever your location, it is important to avoid coming between people who wish to communicate.

To some extent, our society consists of a series of minisocieties, each with its values and rules of order. Schools are examples of such minisocieties, with each level (elementary, secondary, college) having its own unique set of norms. As an observer in schools, you will be judged by students and staff alike on the basis of their norms, not on the basis of those you have become accustomed to in college or graduate school. You will probably be expected to dress rather formally, to arrive early or notify the school if you will be late, and to conform to the school's rules and regulations. Your instructor will probably inform you of the prevailing norms.

CONFIDENTIALITY OF RECORDS

As you observe and collect data, you must make certain that your actions do not invade the privacy of or in any other way harm those you are observing. Most schools require anonymity in your observations and confidentiality in the data you collect. Individual teachers, students, and others should not risk inconvenience, embarrassment, or harm as a result of your field experience.

Each school has its own norms and rules regarding what observers can and cannot do. Some require a signed release from school officials and/or from students (informed consent), while others are less formal. You should share your observation plan and data-gathering activities with your instructor to make certain that you are following the appropriate procedures. Your cooperating teacher and/or the principal in the school where you will be observing may also need to be informed. In cases where permission is not granted, you will need to find another setting.

All data that you collect should remain absolutely confidential. The importance of this point cannot be stressed too much. You may wish to use code names or numbers for people you describe, and you should never discuss observations with any members of the school community. For example, if you tell teachers some information you have learned about students, you run the risk of losing trust and credibility and possibly harming a member of the school community. Your records should be stored away from the field school, in a location that is both safe and private. In this way you can ensure that the confidentiality of your subjects will be protected.

DISTINGUISHING BETWEEN DESCRIPTION AND INTERPRETATION

As you collect data, your information should be recorded—at least initially—in a descriptive rather than a judgmental manner. As a student, your observations about school were probably casual, resulting in the formation of opinions, such as Teacher A is "interesting," School B is "the pits," or geometry is "hard." These interpretations, although colorful and useful, are personal and would have been likely to evoke disagreement from some of your fellow students.

A better approach for an observer is to gather descriptive data regarding an aspect of school or classroom life, interpret the data, and, when appropriate, form conclusions and judgments. Rather than saying that Teacher A is "good" (an interpretation), you might count the number of questions Teacher A asks, the amount of time Teacher A spends helping students, or even the number of advanced degrees Teacher A holds. All these findings provide objective,

descriptive data. Although some of your descriptive data may not be useful, other notes may be crucial to your final interpretations and insights.

Data collection activities presented in this manual frequently ask you to record descriptive details and, after reflection, to interpret the information. The following examples will help you distinguish between description and interpretation:

Description: The teacher asked twenty-three questions in seven minutes.

Interpretation: The teacher asked too many questions.

Description: The teacher scolded Henry ten times during the morning.

Interpretation: The teacher picked on Henry.

Description: The student yawned twice and spent eight minutes looking out the window.

Interpretation: The student was bored.

Description: The building was constructed in 1940.

Interpretation: The building is old.

Description: This school consists of 121 elementary school classrooms.

Interpretation: The school is too big.

Description: Twenty-five out of twenty-seven students volunteered answers during math class.

Interpretation: The students are interested in math.

This ability to separate fact from opinion is a crucial skill that can prevent you from jumping to erroneous conclusions. Most of us like to think that "seeing is believing," but sometimes "believing may be seeing." In other words, each of us brings to any observation a set of biases and perspectives through which events may be distorted. To guard against reaching inaccurate interpretations, make a careful record of what you see. Judgmental comments can also be made, but they should be kept separate from your descriptive observations. Some observers insert interpretations and questions into their records, but they separate them from their descriptive notes with parentheses.

INTERPRETING THE DATA

After you have collected your data, you will need to interpret and make sense of a vast amount of information. To do this, it will be helpful to look for words, patterns, phrases, and topics that keep recurring in your records. If competency testing is being used in your school, for example, you may find that the teachers talk about these exit exams in many classes and spend a great deal of time preparing students for them. After analyzing your notes from patterns, you may reach the conclusion that competency testing is exerting too great an influence on what is taught. As you form impressions and interpretations, it is a good idea to check these with participants in the environment. For example, you might ask the teachers, "I have noticed that your students will take competency exams this year. What influence do you think these exams have in the school?" You can also check your interpretations by searching for instances of contrary behavior. In this hypothetical situation, you have found that many teachers spend a great deal of time teaching for the competency tests. However, it is also important to look for counter instances, teachers who devote little time or attention to the competency tests. If you find several teachers in this category, your initial impressions may not be accurate. After all your notes have been recorded and analyzed, the final product is often an ethnographic report or case study. How insightful your report is will depend on the richness of detail in your notes and how thoughtfully you have interpreted the data. Typically, an ethnographic report comprises two sections: (1) a descriptive summary of the data you observed and (2) an interpretation or evaluation section that sets forth your conclusions. Your instructor can help you determine the particular form your final report should take.

DATA COLLECTION ACTIVITIES: THE SETTING

No student or teacher functions in isolation. As you think about your future life in the classroom, you must also consider the general community, the school building, and even the physical environment of the classroom. Students arrive at school after years of being taught the unofficial curriculum of parents, friends, and neighbors; their previously learned values and skills can help or hinder their efforts in the classroom. Understanding community attitudes and actions can be pivotal to enhancing your teaching effectiveness, as well as the classroom performance of your students. The physical qualities of the school building and the quantity and quality of classroom resources also will shape your life in the classroom.

Sample Activity 1: Local Newspaper Most communities have a local newspaper or are covered in a section of a large-circulation newspaper that focuses on community affairs. If your school library or the public library carries back issues of these publications, read those for the past several months. In addition, keep up with local news coverage for that community. From your analysis of the news stories, editorials, advertisements, and letters to the editor, how would you answer the following?

Guidelines: Local Newspaper

What are the major community concerns?

What are the school's major projects? Are there any school-community partnerships to accomplish education-related goals?

Which aspect of school life receives the most coverage (athletics, academics, cultural activities, and so on)?

How does the community react to standardized test scores, financial needs, new facilities, and other educational concerns?

Sample Activity 2: Unobtrusive Measures *Unobtrusive measurement* is a way of assessing a situation without altering it.[4] Obtrusive methods, such as asking questions directly, frequently contaminate the findings. For example, if you ask students what they think of a school, they may guard their comments and share only part of their real feelings. They do not know you or what you might do with the information.

As a student, you probably experience a similar phenomenon when you take exams. Before answering the questions, you may consider the attitudes and values of the teacher and tailor your responses accordingly. You may try to answer the questions not only correctly but also in a way that pleases the teacher. Have you ever changed the response you gave in order to fit your teacher's expectations? This strategy may improve your grade, but it denies the teacher an accurate insight into your attitudes and perspective.

One famous experiment in unobtrusive measures attempted to determine which exhibit in a museum was attracting the most visitors. An obtrusive measure (direct questioning) had previously indicated that a prestigious work of art was the most popular. However, an examination of the wear and tear on the floors, of the number of fingerprints on the protective glass, and of other unobtrusive data indicated that an incubator with hatching chickens was the most frequently visited exhibit. This contradiction between verbal and nonverbal responses was probably the result of the patrons' belief that visiting a work of art was more intellectually appropriate than watching chickens hatch. In short, the obtrusive interview technique distorted the responses and was, therefore, less effective than was the unobtrusive measure (that is, assessing the amount of dirt and the wear and tear on carpets and windows).

As these examples illustrate, unobtrusive measures are intentionally indirect in order to avoid contaminating the evidence. In the data collection activity that follows, you will be using unobtrusive procedures. Answer each question with descriptive data. Then think about the information you have gathered and consider what interpretations or judgments to make.

Guidelines: Unobtrusive Measures

Record the graffiti written on walls, desks, and, especially, in bathrooms.

Examine the exhibits and bulletin boards to determine if they are student-made, teacher-made, or commercially produced. Do they appear to have been there a long time, or do they seem to be changed regularly? As the students pass by, do they stop and look at them?

Ask the librarian if you may look at information about books that were checked out during the past two weeks. How many were checked out, and what were they about? Examine some books. Are they in good condition? Are they badly worn? defaced?

Check the lunchroom after lunch has been served. Are the trash cans filled with normal debris—or uneaten lunches?

Examine the floors for wear and tear. What floor spaces in the school and in the classrooms seem to be most worn? What is located in these areas? What areas of the school seem to be getting the least traffic? What is located in these areas?

Visit the main office and keep a tally of the conversations held by the school secretary. Who is scheduled to meet with the principal? How many of these visitors are students? faculty? parents? others?

Whom does the principal visit? How often does he or she leave the office to interact with teachers and students?

Data Collection Activities: The Teacher

As you approach your field experience, your primary concerns may be focused on teaching. Will you like it? Will you be good at it? Will the teacher you work with be helpful? What, precisely, is "good teaching"? During your teacher education program, and even during your initial years as a teacher, you will, in all likelihood, continue to focus on questions relating to teachers and teaching.

Many of these activities rely on a similar data collection approach and the use of a class seating chart. The research on teacher effectiveness discusses the importance of active student interaction in promoting learning and positive attitudes toward school. Unfortunately, teachers do not distribute their attention evenly; rather, they ask many questions of some students and none of others. Teachers may direct questions more to children of one gender or race than to those of another. Attention, questions, and praise may be distributed on the basis of which students the teacher likes, or even on the basis of where the students happen to be seated in the classroom. One very common form of bias is for teachers to direct most of their questions to the better students, because their replies are more likely to be on target and, therefore, satisfying. Both the quantity and quality of teacher attention have an impact on student achievement.

In the following activity, you will need to construct a seating chart. (Perhaps the teacher has one that you can use.) But, unlike the teacher's, your chart should include the name, gender, and, when possible, race or ethnicity of each student. (A sample seating chart is provided in Figure 2.)

To begin, on your seating chart you will record with whom the teacher interacts in the classroom. There are two types of teacher-student interactions to be recorded: (1) those that depend on voluntary responses offered by the students and (2) those that are involuntary. Voluntary student responses occur when students

- Raise their hands to respond
- Call out an answer
- Voluntarily respond to the teacher through any established classroom procedure

Involuntary student responses occur when the teacher requests a response from a student who has

FIGURE 2   **Sample seating chart 1.**

Teacher's name _____   Date _____

Observer's name _____   Time begin _____

Time end _____

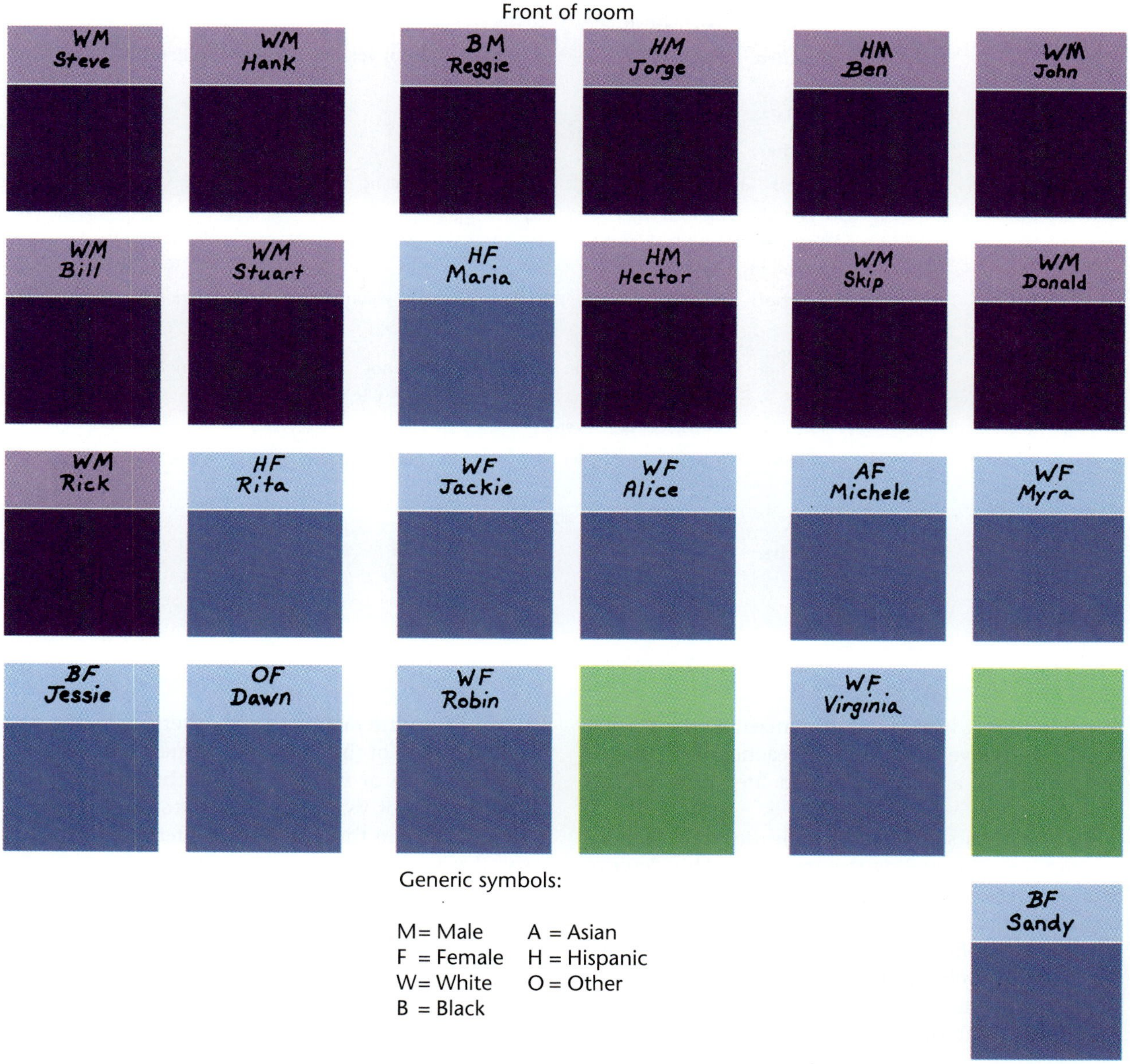

Front of room

WM Steve	WM Hank	BM Reggie	HM Jorge	HM Ben	WM John
WM Bill	WM Stuart	HF. Maria	HM Hector	WM Skip	WM Donald
WM Rick	HF Rita	WF Jackie	WF Alice	AF Michele	WF Myra
BF. Jessie	OF Dawn	WF Robin		WF. Virginia	

BF Sandy

Generic symbols:

M= Male   A = Asian
F = Female   H = Hispanic
W= White   O = Other
B = Black

not raised a hand, called out an answer, or in any other way indicated an interest in answering.

Each time a teacher elicits a response, the observer records a *V* or an *N* for that student directly on the classroom seating chart. *V*, representing a volunteer, indicates that the teacher is investing time in a student who is volunteering to respond. *N*, representing a nonvolunteer, indicates that the teacher is intentionally soliciting a response from a nonvolunteering student. (Note: a student calling out or in any other

FIGURE 3
Sample classroom dialogue.

	Dialogue	Action	Code
Teacher:	"Who can answer question number three?"	Hank raises a hand.	
Teacher:	"Hank."		Mark *V* for Hank.
Hank:	"Twenty-two."		
Teacher:	"No. That's not correct. Maria?"	Maria not volunteering.	Mark *N* for Maria.
Maria:	"Twenty."		
Teacher:	"Correct."		
Steve:	"I thought the answer was 18."	Steve calling out.	
Teacher:	"Let's look at the next question."		No mark. Steve was not recognized.
Teacher:	"Rita?"	Rita not volunteering.	Mark *N* for Rita.
Rita:	(*no response*)		
Teacher:	"Apply the formula, Rita."	Rita still not volunteering.	Mark *N* for Rita.
Rita:	"Oh, I see. Is it seven?"		
Teacher:	"Good. That's it. Why is it seven, Rita?"	Rita not volunteering.	Mark *N* for Rita.
Rita:	"You add the two sides."		
Teacher:	"Terrific."		

way responding who is not recognized by the teacher does not receive a code. The teacher has ignored this volunteer and not invested any time in this student.)

Figure 3 is a sample classroom dialogue, demonstrating how this coding system works. This description of classroom interaction is coded on the sample seating chart 2 in Figure 4.

Once you collect your observation data, several activities and levels of analysis are possible. Analyses such as those that follow provide important insights into the distribution of teacher attention.

Sample Activity 1: Classroom Geography Simply examining the pattern of teacher questions directly from the seating chart provides you with an immediate, visual impression of the areas in the classroom that receive a great deal of interaction, as well as the areas that are interaction-poor. Some students may be in-

volved in no interaction at all; others may take part in a number of interactions. Some students may only have one or two Ns, while others may have a great number of Vs. You may want to circle the areas of the classroom that are rich with teacher attention, as well as those areas that are interaction-poor.

Sample Activity 2: Detecting Racial Bias Although educators as a group are firmly committed to educational equity, subtle and often unintentional biases can emerge.[5] Teachers often unknowingly give more attention to students of one race than to those of another, or give different kinds of attention to one group than they give to another. You may be able to detect these subtle biases from data recorded on your seating chart. It is best to record several sessions of classroom interaction in order to obtain an accurate measure of potential racial or ethnic bias. The procedure then becomes one of simple mathematics. First, identify the

FIGURE 4 **Sample seating chart 2.**

Teacher's name _____   Date _____
Observer's name _____   Time begin _____
                                                              Time end _____

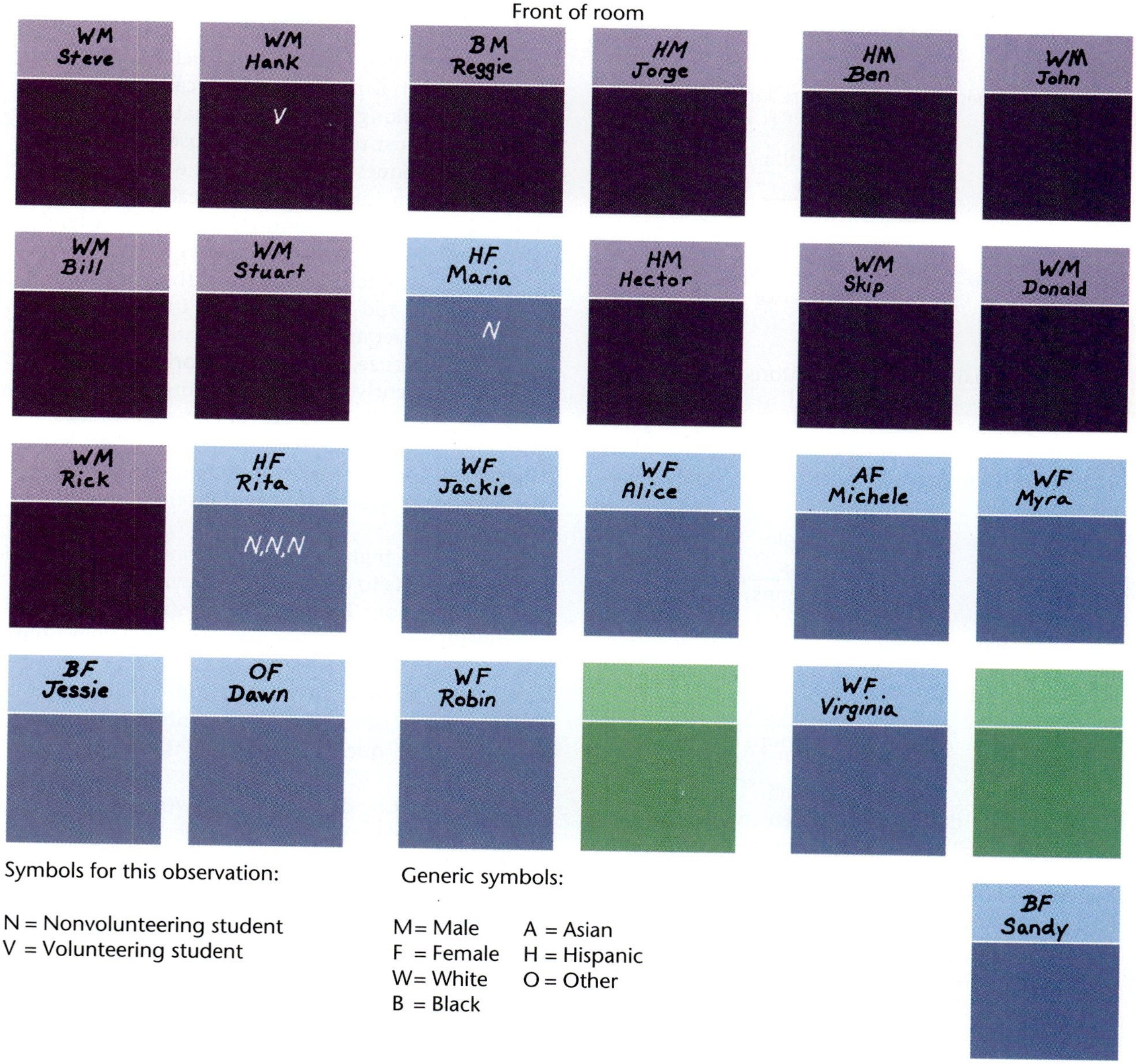

Front of room

| WM Steve | WM Hank | BM Reggie | HM Jorge | HM Ben | WM John |
| | V | | | | |

| WM Bill | WM Stuart | HF. Maria | HM Hector | WM Skip | WM Donald |
| | | N | | | |

| WM Rick | HF Rita | WF Jackie | WF Alice | AF Michele | WF Myra |
| | N,N,N | | | | |

| BF. Jessie | OF Dawn | WF Robin | | WF. Virginia | |

| | | | | | BF Sandy |

Symbols for this observation:

N = Nonvolunteering student
V = Volunteering student

Generic symbols:

M = Male   A = Asian
F = Female   H = Hispanic
W = White   O = Other
B = Black

expected number of interactions or questions (that is, a fair share) for each group. If, for instance, a class consists of 40 percent students of color, then a fair share would mean that students of color receive 40 percent of the teacher's questions. If the students of color receive fewer than 40 percent, they are not getting their fair share. For the second step, determine the actual number of interactions that each group receives. Finally, compare the figures. Here is how you would do the computations:

Sample Classroom Data

Class attendance
> 5 students of color
> 10 white students
> _____
> 15 total students in the class

Teacher questions
> 15 to students of color
> 45 to white students
> _____
> 60 total interactions

Step 1

Determine expected or fair share of questions, by race/ethnicity:

$$\text{Students of color fair share} = \frac{\text{Students of color attendance}}{\text{Total attendance}} = \frac{5}{15} = 33\%$$

$$\text{White fair share} = \frac{\text{White attendance}}{\text{Total attendance}} = \frac{10}{15} = 67\%$$

Step 2

Determine actual share of interactions, by race/ethnicity:

Percentage students of color interactions = Number of interactions with students of color ÷ Total interactions

$$= \frac{\text{Students of color interactions}}{\text{Total interactions}} = \frac{15}{60} = 25\%$$

Percentage white interactions = Number of interactions with white ÷ Total interactions

$$= \frac{\text{White interactions}}{\text{Total interactions}} = \frac{45}{60} = 75\%$$

Step 3

Determine the difference between expected (or fair share) and actual distribution of interactions:

Students of color actual share = 25%
Students of color fair share = 33%
> Difference = −8% (8% fewer interactions than a fair share)

White actual share = 75%
White fair share = 67%
> Difference = +8% (8% more interactions than a fair share)

Students of color received approximately 8 percent fewer questions than would be their fair share, or the amount that would be expected based on their representation in the class. White students received approximately 8 percent more than their fair share. Subtle bias exists in this sample classroom interaction.

Sample Activity 3: Questioning Level John Dewey was one of many noted educators who believed that questioning is central not only to education but to the process of thinking itself. Unfortunately, research indicates that most teachers do not use effective questioning techniques. Not only is the distribution of questions often inequitable, but teachers rarely use challenging classroom questions. Instead, they tend to rely on lower-order, or memory, questions.

Lower-order questions are those that deal with the memorization and recall of factual information. The student is not required to manipulate (that is, apply, analyze, synthesize, or evaluate) information. There is nothing inherently wrong with asking memory questions, such as "When did the American Revolution begin?" or "Identify one poem written by Robert Frost." However, a heavy reliance on such questions reduces the opportunity for students to develop higher-order thinking.

Conversely, higher-order questions are those that require students to apply, analyze, synthesize, or evaluate information. They encourage students to think creatively. When a teacher asks, "What is your opinion of this poem by Robert Frost, and what evidence can you cite to support your opinion?" that teacher is asking a higher-order question. Only 10 percent of most teachers' questions fall into this higher-order category.

To help you distinguish between lower-order (memory) questions and higher-order (thought) questions, here are some examples of each:

Lower-Order Questions

- Who founded abstract art?
- Name three Romantic authors.
- Whose signatures appear on the Declaration of Independence?
- In what year did the war begin?
- Who wrote your text?

Higher-Order Questions

- What conclusions can you reach concerning the images Shakespeare uses to portray death?

- What forces motivated Romantic authors?
- Why did no females or African Americans sign the Declaration of Independence?
- What does this poem mean to you?
- What would you say in a letter to the president of the United States?

Now, try coding the kinds of questions asked in a classroom. When a lower-order question is asked, record an *L* on your seating chart. When a higher-order question is asked, record an *H* on the seating chart. The sample coding form in Figure 5 illustrates the use of this approach. On Sample Seating Chart 3 in Figure 5, recording a hypothetical classroom discussion, the preponderance of lower-order questions is evident, as well as several patterns of bias. Can you detect some of these patterns? Take a minute to analyze the teacher's level and distribution of questions and jot down any problems you detect. Then compare your analysis to the one that follows.

Problems Reflected on Sample Seating Chart 3, Figure 5:

- Preponderance of lower-order questions
- Proportionately more questions asked to males
- Proportionately more questions asked to white students than students of color
- One side and back of the room ignored

Try this in a classroom that you are observing. After constructing a seating chart, choose a 20- or 30-minute segment of teacher-student interaction. Record the number of higher-order and lower-order questions asked of each student in the class by noting *H*s and *L*s, as called for, on your seating chart. Then analyze the questioning pattern, using the following questions as a guide.

Guidelines: Questioning Level and Race/Ethnicity and Gender Bias

How many questions were asked? What was the average number of questions per minute (total questions divided by minutes observed)?

What was the ratio of lower- to higher-order questions?

What were the areas of the class that received a greater number of higher-order questions?

Do you detect any patterns of racial, ethnic, or gender bias in the distribution of questions in general and of higher-order questions in particular?

Data Collection Activities: The Students

Although the students in any school constitute the reason for everything else—the building, the curriculum, the teachers—their interests are sometimes overlooked. You can learn a great deal about the school milieu, the community, and the kind of teaching students prefer by including an analysis of learners in your field experience. This section focuses on students and the social system in which they live and learn.

Many believe that schools are created and maintained by the larger society for the express purpose of socializing its young into the roles of the prevailing culture.[6] To the casual observer, this socializing function is not apparent. The school seems to be an isolated and self-contained subculture accountable to no one. Data on the school and classroom social system will show the links between school and society with great clarity, and you will be able to interpret their significance.

Most of us are so accustomed to the norms, values, and beliefs that constitute our culture, that we have difficulty detecting their influence all about us. We are much more alert to things that are new and different.

To gain new insights from the commonplace, researcher Seymour Saranson recommends that you take the perspective of a visitor from outer space, who will be more alert to both blatant and subtle patterns of the school as a social system.[7] For example, an important aspect of our schools, but one not usually thought about, is that they must provide custody and control of youngsters for a major part of the work week. Housing a large group of children and adolescents in a small space for many hours a day has a major impact on the classroom social system. "Only in school do thirty or more people spend several hours a day literally side by side. Once we leave the classroom, we seldom again are required to have contact with so many people for so long a time."[8] In these crowded conditions, students and teachers often clash, because their purposes may be vastly different. The teacher is there to socialize the young and to help them learn. Grade school students are often in class to play and have fun, whereas adolescents' goals may involve developing social and even intimate relationships.

In the densely populated classroom, the teacher functions as a supply sergeant (giving out paper, books, and so on), as a timekeeper (determining how long the class will spend on given activities), and as a

FIGURE 5   Sample seating chart 3.

Teacher's name _____   Date _____

Observer's name _____   Time begin _____

Time end _____

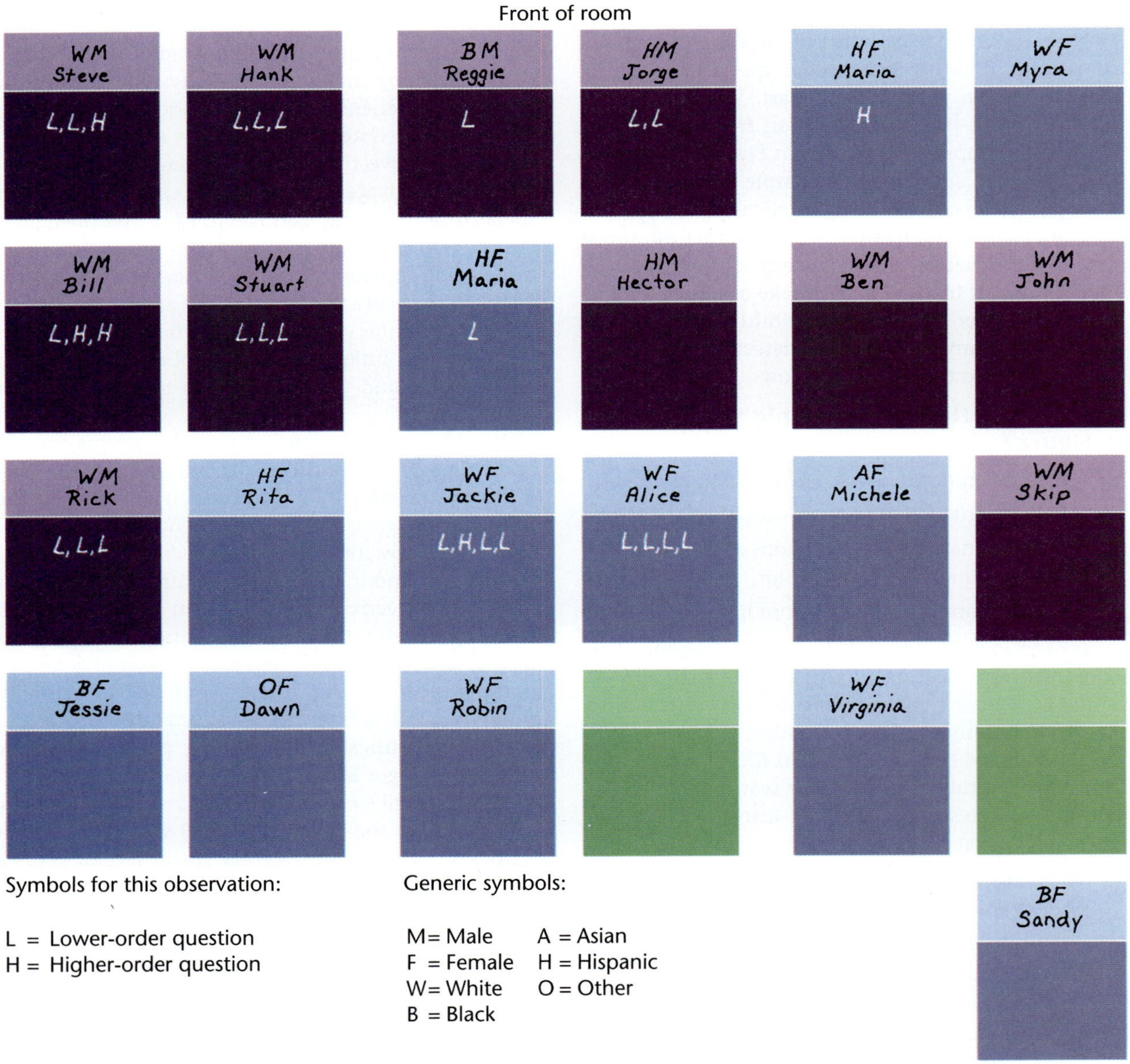

Front of room

WM Steve	WM Hank	BM Reggie	HM Jorge	HF Maria	WF Myra
L,L,H	L,L,L	L	L,L	H	

WM Bill	WM Stuart	HF Maria	HM Hector	WM Ben	WM John
L,H,H	L,L,L	L			

WM Rick	HF Rita	WF Jackie	WF Alice	AF Michele	WM Skip
L,L,L		L,H,L,L	L,L,L,L		

BF Jessie	OF Dawn	WF Robin		WF Virginia	

BF Sandy

Symbols for this observation:

L = Lower-order question
H = Higher-order question

Generic symbols:

M= Male   A = Asian
F = Female   H = Hispanic
W= White   O = Other
B = Black

gatekeeper to class discussion (deciding who will talk and for how long).[9] While the teacher is busy filling all these roles, students are left to wait and do nothing. They stand in lines, they sit with their hands raised, and they wait for other students to finish so that they can go on to other activities. Sitting still and remaining silent are denials of their natural instincts.

Frustrated by this densely populated and artificial situation, students often rebel, pitting their own group power against the authority of the teacher. Sometimes this power struggle is subtle, with the sizing up and testing of the teacher its only visible signs (for example, by not handing in homework on time or cajoling to get an assignment lessened or postponed). At other times, the power struggle erupts to the surface of the social system as students openly flout or disregard adult authority. Observing these overt signs of the power struggle is easy. Picking up the subtle rituals and patterns of the social system that underlie these disruptions is a more challenging task.

Sample Activity 1: Student Groups Social status is a powerful force in school, and groups and cliques are often officially or unofficially labeled. The race/ethnicity, gender, national origin, social class, or ability level of a group's members may affect how it is labeled. The following activity focuses on the treatment of these special groups. Some of these data can be collected through observation; in other cases, information can best be gathered through interviews. Answer as many of the following as you can to glean insight into the special world of students.

Guidelines: Student Groups

Do students form groups, or cliques, based on such characteristics as race/ethnicity, gender, religion, national origin, achievement level, or social class?

Do these groups occupy ("hang out" around) certain school areas? Do they sit together in class?

What are the values and priorities of such groups? How do they differ from other social groups?

Do school displays and classroom bulletin boards reflect all groups (females, students of color or with disabilities, and so on) or mainly white males? Do these displays promote stereotypic or nonstereotypic perceptions?

Do students from these different groups actively and equitably participate in classroom interaction? in extracurricular activities?

How does the school reflect community values in its treatment of females, students of color or with disabilities, and so on? How does the school environment differ from that of the community?

What special education needs are represented by exceptional children in the school? If physically disabled children are present, are there physical barriers within the school that restrict their access to facilities?

To what degree are students with special needs mainstreamed? To what degree are they provided with segregated special education?

Are students in the school "tracked"? If so, what generalizations can you make about the students in each track?

What provisions are made for students whose native language is not English? How does this affect their adjustment to the school?

Sample Activity 2: Teachers' Views of Students Try to talk to three or four teachers to assess their perceptions of the students who attend the school. The following teacher interview questions will enable you to learn about each teacher's perception of the students' social system, as well as the norms and rules they establish for classroom management.

Guidelines: Teachers' Views of Students

What are your classroom norms and rules for appropriate behavior?

What are the penalties for students who violate the rules?

What was the worst discipline problem you have ever had to handle?

What advice would you give a new teacher about classroom management?

How many cliques are there in your classroom? Are there isolates, students who do not seem to belong to any social group?

Is there race/ethnic or class segregation in work or play groups? Who does the segregating? Are there any penalties for students who try to integrate these groups?

How are the needs of special education students met? What is done to meet the needs of the gifted?

What social or interpersonal aspects of the class have given you the greatest pleasure during the past year? the greatest problem?

Data Collection Activities: The Curriculum

In the midst of a worldwide knowledge explosion, it has become impossible to teach or learn all the information and skills now known. Moreover, every year more and more knowledge becomes available. Clearly, decisions need to be made about what to teach and what to learn. Although states and local school districts are pivotal in shaping the curriculum you will be teaching, you have some decisions to make as well. You need to consider your own ability in the subject or subjects you are to teach. Do you need to take additional academic courses to improve your own preparation? Once assigned a curriculum, how do you decide what to emphasize? What are the most important things for your students to learn?

The nature and direction of the school curriculum are explored in several chapters in this text, but it is useful for you to consider these and other curricular issues during your field experience. The activities in this section will start you on a career-long investigation of what you should teach and what is worth knowing.

Sample Activity 1: People and Experiences Take a moment to think about how your individual experiences have led to your unique outlook on the curriculum. Next to the people and experiences listed below, indicate which have influenced your view of subject matter and the curriculum. (Note at least three people and three experiences and indicate how each has influenced your view.)

People
Family: _____

Relatives: _____

Teachers: _____

Friends: _____

Others: _____

Events
Trips: _____

Volunteer work: _____

Salaried employment: _____

Personal successes: _____

Personal failures: _____

Other: _____

Your personal life experiences, in conjunction with your school classes, have shaped and directed your view of subject matter and the curriculum. Your background also contributes to your philosophy of teaching and learning. Examine your answers to Sample Activity 1 and complete the following statement:

> I believe that some of the most important reasons to study my subject (or, if in elementary school, the subjects at my grade level) include
>
> _____
>
> _____.

Sample Activity 2: Textbook Analysis Review a textbook used in your school. In your analysis, look carefully at narrative and pictures. The following questions should guide your textbook review.

Guidelines: Textbook Analysis

How recent is the textbook edition? What is the copyright date?

How would you characterize the quality of the writing? Is it stilted and dull or rich and interesting? Give examples to support your point of view.

Is the textbook guilty of "mentioning"—providing facts and figures without adequate context and explanation? Give examples to support your point of view.

Does the text include an adequate representation of males and females from many diverse groups? Count the number of males, females, and their group membership in order to reach your conclusions.

What kind of supplementary materials accompany the textbook? Is there a workbook, a teacher's manual, a CD-ROM, a website, or other supplementary materials? Do these supplementary materials treat the teacher as a professional—or are the directions so specific that the teacher becomes little more than a technician?

Reflection: Looking Back on Your Field Observations

Your field experience is an exciting part of your professional preparation, bridging all your past experiences as a student with your future career as a teacher. The activities in this manual provide you with opportunities for experience and reflection. These forge a critical link between your current role as a student and your future role as a professional in the field of education. The more expert you become in observing and reflecting on school life, the more insight and understanding you will gain about the nature and challenges of teaching.

GLOSSARY

A

ability grouping The assignment of pupils to homogeneous groups according to intellectual ability or level for instructional purposes.

academic freedom The opportunity for teachers and students to learn, teach, study, research, and question without censorship, coercion, or external political and other restrictive influences.

academic learning time The time a student is actively engaged with the subject matter and experiencing a high success rate.

academies The private or semipublic secondary schools in the United States from 1830 through 1870 that stressed practical subjects.

accelerated program The more rapid promotion of gifted students through school.

accountability Holding schools and teachers responsible for student performance.

accreditation Certification of an education program or a school that has met professional standards of an outside agency.

achievement tests Examinations of the knowledge and skills acquired, usually as a result of specific instruction.

adequate education Provides a legal approach for ensuring educational opportunities for poorer students based on state constitution guarantees for an efficient, thorough, or uniform education. Calls for adequate education have replaced previous calls for equal educational expenditures.

adult education Courses and programs offered to high school graduates by colleges, business, industry, and governmental and private organizations that lead to academic degrees, occupational preparation, and the like.

advanced placement Courses and programs in which younger students can earn college credit.

aesthetics The branch of philosophy that examines the nature of beauty and judgments about it.

affective domain The area of learning that involves attitudes, values, and emotions.

affirmative action A plan by which personnel policies and hiring practices reflect positive steps in the recruiting and hiring of women and people of color.

allocated time The amount of time a school or an individual teacher schedules for a subject.

alternative families Family units that differ from the traditional image; examples include foster care children, single parents, central role of grandparents, and gay couples.

alternative school A private or public school that provides religious, academic, or other alternatives to the regular public school.

American Federation of Teachers (AFT) A national organization of teachers that is primarily concerned with improving educational conditions and protecting teachers' rights.

assertive discipline A behavior modification program developed by Lee and Marlene Canter designed to "catch" and reward students being good, while discouraging off-task and inappropriate behavior.

assistive (adaptive) technology Devices that help the disabled to perform and learn more effectively, from voice-activated keyboards and mechanical wheelchairs to laptops for class note taking and personal scheduling.

asynchronous Nonsimultaneous. Students enrolled in an Internet course need not participate at the same time, and may take the course although they live in different time zones.

authentic assessment A type of evaluation that represents actual performance, encourages students to reflect on their own work, and is integrated into the student's whole learning process. Such tests usually require that students synthesize knowledge from different areas and use that knowledge actively.

B

back to basics During the 1980s, a revival of the back-to-basics movement evolved out of concern for declining test scores in math, science, reading, and other areas. Although there is not a precise definition of back to basics, many consider it to include increased emphasis on reading, writing, and arithmetic, fewer electives, and more rigorous grading.

behavioral objective A specific statement of what a learner must accomplish in order to demonstrate mastery.

behaviorism A psychological theory that interprets human behavior in terms of stimuli-response.

behavior modification A strategy to alter behavior in a desired direction through the use of rewards.

bilingual education Educational programs in which students of limited or no English-speaking ability attend classes taught in English, as well as in their native language. There is great variability in these programs in terms of goals, instructional opportunity, and balance between English and a student's native language.

block grants Federal dollars provided to the states, with limited federal restrictions, for educational aid and program funding.

block scheduling Using longer "blocks" of time to schedule classes results in fewer but longer periods given to each subject. It is designed to promote greater in-depth study.

board certification Recognition of advanced teaching competence, awarded to teachers who demonstrate high levels of knowledge, commitment, and professionalism through a competitive review process administered by the National Board for Professional Teaching Standards.

board of education Constituted at the state and local levels, this agency is responsible for formulating educational policy. Members are sometimes appointed but, more frequently, are elected at the local level.

bond A certificate of debt issued by a government guaranteeing payment of the original investment plus interest by a specified future date. Bonds are used by local communities to raise the funds they need to build or repair schools.

Buckley Amendment The 1974 Family Educational Rights and Privacy Act granting parents of students under 18, and students 18 or over the right to examine their school records.

busing A method for remedying segregation by transporting students to create more ethnically or racially balanced schools. Before busing and desegregation were linked, busing was not a controversial issue, and, in fact, the vast majority of students riding school buses are not involved in desegregation programs.

C

canon The collection of literature and other works that typically reflects a white, Euro-centered view of the world.

career education (vocational education) A program to teach elementary and secondary students about the world of work by integrating career awareness and exploration across the school curriculum.

career ladder A system designed to create different status levels for teachers by developing steps one can climb to receive increased pay through increased responsibility or experience.

Carnegie unit A credit awarded to a student for successfully completing a high school course. It is used in determining graduation requirements and college admissions.

categorical grant Financial aid to local school districts from state or federal agencies for specific purposes.

certification State government or professional association's evaluation and approval of an applicant's competencies.

character education A model comprised of various strategies that promote a defined set of core values to students.

charter school A group of teachers, parents, and even businesses may petition a local school board, or state government, to form a charter school which is exempt from many state and local regulations. Designed to promote creative new schools, the charter represents legal permission to try new approaches to educate students. First charter legislation was passed in Minnesota in 1991.

chief state school officer The executive head of a state department of education. The chief state school officer is responsible for carrying out the mandates of the state board of education and enforcing educational laws and regulations. This position is also referred to as *state superintendent.*

child abuse Physical, sexual, or emotional violation of a child's health and well-being.

child advocacy movement A movement dedicated to defining and protecting the rights of children. Child advocates recognize that children are not yet ready to assume all the rights and privileges of adults, but they are firmly committed to expanding the rights currently enjoyed by children and to no longer treating children as objects or of the property of others.

child-centered instruction (individual instruction) Teaching that is designed to meet the interests and needs of individual students.

classroom climate The physical, emotional, and aesthetic characteristics, as well as the learning resources, of a school classroom.

cognitive domain The area of learning that involves knowledge, information, and intellectual skills.

Coleman report A study commissioned by President Johnson (1964) to analyze the factors that influence the academic achievement of students. One of the major findings of James Coleman's report was that schools in general have relatively little impact on learning. Family and peers were found to have more impact on a child's education than the school itself did.

collaborative action research Connects teaching and professional growth through the use of research relevant to classroom responsibilities.

collective bargaining A negotiating procedure between employer and employees for resolving disagreements on salaries, work schedules, and other conditions of employment. In collective bargaining, all teachers in a school system bargain as one group through chosen representatives.

Comer model James Comer of Yale has created and disseminated a program that incorporates a team of educational and mental health professionals to assist children at risk by working with their parents and attending to social, educational, and psychological needs.

Committee of Ten In 1892, the National Education Association formed the committee, influenced by college presidents, to reform the nation's high schools. The result was an academically oriented curriculum geared for colleges, and the creation of the Carnegie unit as a measure of progress through the high school curriculum.

common school A public, tax-supported school. First established in Massachusetts, the school's purpose was to create a common basis of knowledge for children. It usually refers to a public elementary school.

community schools Schools connected with a local community to provide for the educational needs of that community.

compensatory education Educational experiences and opportunities designed to overcome or compensate for difficulties associated with a student's disadvantaged background.

competency The ability to perform a particular skill or to demonstrate a specified level of knowledge.

comprehensive high school A public secondary school that offers a variety of curricula, including vocational, academic, and general education programs.

compulsory attendance A state law requiring that children and adolescents attend school until reaching a specified age.

computer-assisted instruction (CAI) Individualized instruction between a student and programmed instructional material stored in a computer.

computer-managed instruction (CMI) A recordkeeping procedure for tracking student performance using a computer.

conditional teacher's license Sometimes called an emergency license, a substandard license that is issued on a temporary basis to meet a pressing need.

consolidation The trend toward combining small or rural school districts into larger ones.

constructivism With roots in cognitive psychology, this educational approach is built on the idea that people construct their understanding of the world. Constructivist teachers gauge a student's prior knowledge, then carefully orchestrate cues, classroom activities, and penetrating questions to push students to higher levels of understanding.

content standards The knowledge, skills, and dispositions that students should master in each subject. These standards are often linked to broader themes and sometimes to testing programs.

cooperative learning In classrooms using cooperative learning, students work on activities in small groups, and they receive rewards based on the overall group performance.

core curriculum A central body of knowledge that schools require all students to study.

corporal punishment Disciplining students through physical punishment by a school employee.

critical pedagogy An education philosophy that unites the theory of critical thinking with actual practice in real-world settings. The purpose is to eliminate the cultural and educational control of the dominant group, to have students apply critical thinking skills to the real world and become agents for social change.

cultural difference theory This theory asserts that academic problems can be overcome if educators study and mediate the cultural gap separating school and home.

cultural literacy Knowledge of the people, places, events, and concepts central to the standard literate culture.

cultural pluralism Acceptance and encouragement of cultural diversity.

curriculum (formal, explicit) Planned content of instruction that enables the school to meet its aims.

curriculum development The processes of assessing needs, formulating objectives, and developing instructional opportunities and evaluation.

D

dame schools Primary schools in colonial and other early periods in which students were taught by untrained women in the women's own homes.

day care centers Facilities charged with caring for children. The quality of care varies dramatically and may range from well-planned educational programs to little more than custodial supervision.

decentralization The trend of dividing large school districts into smaller and, it is hoped, more responsive units.

deductive reasoning Working from a general rule to identify particular examples and applications to that rule.

de facto segregation The segregation of racial or other groups resulting from circumstances, such as housing patterns, rather than from official policy or law.

deficit theory A theory that asserts that the values, language patterns, and behaviors that children from certain racial and ethnic groups bring to school put them at an educational disadvantage.

de jure segregation The segregation of racial or other groups on the basis of law, policy, or a practice designed to accomplish such separation.

delegate representative Form of representative government in which the interests of a particular geographic region are represented through an individual or "delegate." Some school boards are organized so that members act as delegates of a neighborhood or region.

Department of Education U.S. cabinet-level department in charge of federal educational policy and the promotion of programs to carry out policies.

descriptive data Information that provides an objective depiction of various aspects of school or classroom life.

desegregation The process of correcting past practices of racial or other illegal segregation.

detrack The movement to eliminate school tracking practices, which often have racial, ethnic, and class implications.

differentiated instruction Instructional activities are organized in response to individual differences rather than content standards. Teachers are asked to carefully consider each student's needs, learning style, life experience, and readiness to learn.

digital divide A term used to describe the technological gap between the "haves" and "have nots." Race, gender, class, and geography are some of the demographic factors influencing technological access and achievement.

direct teaching A model of instruction in which the teacher is a strong leader who structures the classroom and sequences subject matter to reflect a clear academic focus. This model emphasizes the importance of a structured lesson in which presentation of new information is followed by student practice and teacher feedback.

disability A learning or physical condition, a behavior, or an emotional problem that impedes education. Educators now prefer to speak of "students with disabilities," not "handicapped students," emphasizing the person, not the disability.

distance learning Courses, programs, and training provided to students over long distances through television, the Internet, and other technologies.

dual-track system The European traditional practice of separate primary schools for most children and secondary schools for the upper class.

due process The procedural requirements that must be followed in such areas as student and teacher discipline and placement in special education programs. Due process exists to safeguard individuals from arbitrary, capricious, or unreasonable policies, practices, or actions. The essential elements of due process are (1) a notice of the charge or actions to be taken, (2) the opportunity to be heard, (3) and the right to a defense that reflects the particular circumstances and nature of the case.

E

early childhood education Learning undertaken by young children in the home, in nursery schools, preschools, and in kindergartens.

eclecticism In this text, the drawing on of elements from several educational philosophies or methods.

Edison Schools (Edison Project) An educational company that contracts with local school districts, promising to improve student achievement while making a profit in the process.

educable child A mentally retarded child who is capable of achieving only a limited basic learning and usually must be instructed in a special class.

educational malpractice A new experimental line of litigation similar to the concept of medical malpractice. Educational malpractice is concerned with assessing liability for students who graduate from school without fundamental skills. Unlike medical malpractice, many courts have rejected the notion that schools or educators be held liable for this problem.

educational park A large, campuslike facility often including many grade levels and several schools and often surrounded by a variety of cultural resources.

educational television programming Television programs that promote learning.

educational vouchers Flat grants or payments representing the cost of educating a student at a school. Awarded to the parent or child to enable free choice of a school—public or private—the voucher payment is made to the school that accepts the child.

Eight-Year Study Educator Ralph Tyler's study in the 1930s that indicated the effectiveness of progressive education.

elementary school An educational institution for children in grades 1 through 5, 6, or 8, often including kindergarten.

emergency license A substandard license that recognizes teachers who have not met all the requirements for licensure. It is issued on a temporary basis to meet the needs of communities that do not have licensed teachers available.

EMO (Educational Maintenance Organization) The term is borrowed from Health Maintenance Organizations (HMOs) and refers to the growing number of profit-driven companies in the business of public education.

emotional intelligence (EQ) Personality characteristics, such as persistence, can be measured as part of a new human dimension referred to as EQ. Some believe that EQ scores may be better predictors of future success than IQ scores.

empiricism The philosophy that maintains that sensory experiences, such as seeing, hearing, and touching, are the ultimate sources of all human knowledge. Empiricists believe that we experience the external world by sensory perception; then, through reflection, we conceptualize ideas that help us interpret the world.

enculturation The process of acquiring a culture; a child's acquisition of the cultural heritage through both formal and informal educational means.

endorsement Having a license extended through additional work to include a second teaching field.

engaged time The part of time that a teacher schedules for a subject in which the students are actively involved with academic subject matter. Listening to a lecture, participating in a class discussion, and working on math problems all constitute engaged time.

English grammar school The demand for a more practical education in eighteenth-century America led to the creation of these private schools that taught commerce, navigation, engineering, and other vocational skills.

environmental education The study and analysis of the conditions and causes of pollution, overpopulation, and waste of natural resources, and of the ways to preserve Earth's intricate ecology.

epistemology The branch of philosophy that examines the nature of knowledge and learning.

e-portfolio A digital version of the teacher's professional portfolio.

equal educational opportunity Refers to giving every student the educational opportunity to develop fully whatever talents, interests, and abilities he or she may have, without regard to race, color, national origin, sex, disability, or economic status.

equity Educational policy and practice that are just, fair, and free from bias and discrimination.

essentialism An educational philosophy that emphasizes basic skills of reading, writing, mathematics, science, history, geography, and language.

establishment clause A section of the First Amendment of the U.S. Constitution that says that Congress shall make no law respecting the establishment of religion. This clause prohibits nonparochial schools from teaching religion.

ethics The branch of philosophy that examines questions of right and wrong, good and bad.

ethnic group A group of people with a distinctive culture and history.

ethnocentrism The tendency to view one's own culture as superior to others, or to fail to consider other cultures in a fair or equitable manner.

evaluation Assessment of learning and instruction.

exceptional learners Students who require special education and related services in order to realize their full potential. Categories of exceptionality include retarded, gifted, learning disabled, emotionally disturbed, and physically disabled.

existentialism A philosophy that emphasizes the ability of an individual to determine the course and nature of his or her life and the importance of personal decision making.

expectation theory First made popular by Rosenthal and Jacobson, this theory holds that a student's academic performance can be improved if a teacher's attitudes and beliefs about that student's academic potential are modified.

expulsion Dismissal of a student from school for a lengthy period, ranging from one semester to permanently.

extracurriculum The part of school life that comprises activities, such as sports, academic and social clubs, band, chorus, orchestra, and theater. Many educators think that the extracurriculum develops important skills and values, including leadership, teamwork, creativity, and diligence.

F

failing school The term given to a school when a large proportion of its students do not do well on standardized tests or other academic measures. Critics charge that students attending such schools are not receiving their constitutionally guaranteed adequate education.

fair use A legal principle allowing limited use of copyrighted materials. Teachers must observe three criteria: brevity, spontaneity, and cumulative effect.

five factor theory School effectiveness research emphasizes five factors, including effective leadership, monitoring student progress, safety, a clear vision, and high expectations.

Flanders Interaction Analysis An instrument developed by Ned Flanders for categorizing student and teacher verbal behavior. It is used to interpret the nature of classroom verbal interaction.

flexible scheduling A technique for organizing time more effectively in order to meet the needs of instruction by dividing the school day into smaller time modules that can be combined to fit a task.

foundation program Program for distribution of state funds designed to guarantee a specified minimum level of educational support for each child.

Franklin Academy A colonial high school founded by Benjamin Franklin that accepted females as students and promoted a less classical, more practical curriculum.

full service school These schools provide a network of social services from nutrition and health care to parental education and transportation, all designed to support the comprehensive educational needs of children.

future shock Term coined by Alvin Toffler. It refers to the extraordinarily accelerated rate of change and the disorientation of those unable to adapt to rapidly altered norms, institutions, and values.

futurism The activity of forecasting and planning for future developments.

G

gender bias (see **sex discrimination**) The degree to which an individual's beliefs and behavior are unduly influenced on the basis of gender.

gendered career Is a term applied to the gender stereotyping of career and occupational fields. Teaching, for example, was initially gendered male, and today is gendered female, particularly at the elementary school level.

gifted learner There is great variance in definitions and categorizations of the "gifted." The term is most frequently applied to those with exceptional intellectual ability, but it may also refer to learners with outstanding ability in athletics, leadership, music, creativity, and so forth.

global education Because economics, politics, scientific innovation, and societal developments in different countries have an enormous impact on children in the United States, the goals of global education include increased knowledge about the peoples of the world, resolution of global problems, increased fluency in foreign languages, and the development of more tolerant attitudes toward other cultures and peoples.

guaranteed tax base program Adds state funds to local tax revenues, especially in poorer communities in order to enhance local educational expenditures.

Gun-free Schools Act Enacted in Congress in 1994, schools can lose federal funds if they do not have a zero-tolerance policy mandating one-year expulsions for students bringing firearms to schools. The vast majority of schools report zero-tolerance policies for firearms.

H

Head Start Federally funded pre-elementary school program to provide learning opportunities for disadvantaged students.

heterogeneous grouping A group or class consisting of students who show normal variation in ability or performance. It differs from homogeneous grouping, in which criteria, such as grades or scores on standardized tests, are used to group students similar in ability or achievement.

hidden (implicit) curriculum What students learn, other than academic content, from what they do or are expected to do in school; incidental learnings.

hidden government The unofficial power structure within a school. It cannot be identified by the official title, position, or functions of individuals. For example, it reflects the potential influence of a school secretary or custodian.

higher-order questions Questions that require students to go beyond memory in formulating a response. These questions require students to analyze, synthesize, evaluate, and so on.

home schooling A growing trend (but a longtime practice) of parents educating their children at home, for religious or philosophical reasons.

homogeneous grouping The classification of pupils for the purpose of forming instructional groups having a relatively high degree of intellectual similarity.

hornbook A single sheet of parchment containing the Lord's Prayer and letters of the alphabet. It was protected by a thin sheath from the flattened horn of a cow and fastened to a wooden board—hence, the name. It was used during the colonial era in primary schools.

humanistic education A curriculum that stresses personal student growth; self-actualizing, moral, and aesthetic issues are explored.

I

idealism A doctrine holding that knowledge is derived from ideas and emphasizing moral and spiritual reality as a preeminent source of explanation.

ideologues Home school advocates focused on avoiding public schools in order to impart their own set of values.

inclusion The practice of educating and integrating children with disabilities into regular classroom settings.

independent school A nonpublic school unaffiliated with any church or other agency.

individualized education program (IEP) The mechanism through which a disabled child's special needs are identified, objectives and services are described, and evaluation is designed.

individualized instruction Curriculum content and instructional materials, media, and activities designed for individual learning. The pace, interests, and abilities of the learner determine the curriculum.

Individuals with Disabilities in Education Act (IDEA) Federal law passed in 1990, which extends full education services and provisions to people identified with disabilities.

induction A formal program assisting new teachers to successfully adjust to their role in the classroom.

inductive reasoning Drawing generalizations based on the observation of specific examples.

informal education In many cultures, augments or takes the place of formal schooling as children learn adult roles through observation, conversation, assisting, and imitating.

infrastructure The basic installations and facilities on which the continuance and growth of a community depend.

in loco parentis Latin term meaning "in place of the parents"; that is, a teacher or school administrator assumes the duties and responsibilities of the parents during the hours the child attends school.

instruction The process of implementing a curriculum.

integrated curriculum (interdisciplinary curriculum) Subject matter from two or more areas combined into thematic units (i.e., literature and history resources to study civil rights laws).

integration The process of educating different racial and ethnic groups together, and developing positive interracial contacts.

interest centers Usually associated with an open classroom, such centers provide independent student activities related to a specific subject.

Internet The worldwide computer network that rapidly facilitates information dissemination.

J

junior high school A two- or three-year school between elementary and high school for students in their early adolescent years, commonly grades 7 and 8 or 7 through 9.

K

kindergarten A preschool, early childhood educational environment first designed by Froebel in the mid-nineteenth century.

L

labeling Categorizing or classifying students for the purposes of educational placement. One unfortunate consequence may be that of stigmatizing students and inhibiting them from reaching their full potential.

laboratory schools Schools often associated with a teacher preparation institution for practice teaching, demonstration, research, or innovation.

land grant colleges State colleges or universities offering agricultural and mechanical curricula, funded originally by the Morrill Act of 1862.

last mile problem Geography contributes to a digital divide, in part because running fiber optic cables to rural schools is often an expense that telecommunications companies avoid.

latchkey (self-care) kids A term used to describe children who go home after school to an empty house; their parents or guardians are usually working and not home.

Latin grammar school A classical secondary school with a Latin and Greek curriculum preparing students for college.

learning communities The creation of more personal collaboration between teachers and students to promote similar academic goals and values.

learning disability An educationally significant language and/or learning deficit.

least restrictive environment The program best suited to meeting a disabled student's special needs without segregating the student from the regular educational program.

license Official approval of a government agency for an individual to perform certain work, such as a teacher's license granted by a state.

limited English proficiency (LEP) A student who has a limited ability to understand, speak, or read English and who has a native language other than English.

logic The branch of philosophy that deals with reasoning. Logic defines the rules of reasoning, focuses on how to move from one set of assumptions to valid conclusions, and examines the rules of inference that enable us to frame our propositions and arguments.

looping The practice of teaching the same class for several years, over two or even more grades. The purpose is to build stronger teacher-student connections.

lower-order questions Questions that require the retrieval of memorized information and do not require more complex intellectual processes.

M

magnet school A specialized school open to all students in a district on a competitive or lottery basis. It provides a method of drawing children away from segregated neighborhood schools while affording unique educational specialties, such as science, math, and the performing arts.

mainstreaming The inclusion of special education students in the regular education program. The nature and extent of this inclusion should be based on meeting the special needs of the child.

malfeasance Deliberately acting improperly and causing harm to someone.

mastery learning An educational practice in which an individual demonstrates mastery of one task before moving on to the next.

McGuffey Reader For almost 100 years, this reading series promoted moral and patriotic messages and set the practice of reading levels leading toward graded elementary schools.

mentor A guide or an adviser, and a component of some first-year school induction programs designed to assist new teachers.

merit pay A salary system that periodically evaluates teacher performance and uses these evaluations in determining salary.

metacognition Self-awareness of our thinking process as we perform various tasks and operations. For example, when students articulate how they think about academic tasks, it enhances their thinking and enables teachers to target assistance and remediation.

metaphysics The area of philosophy that examines the nature of reality.

microteaching A clinical approach to teacher training in which the teacher candidate teaches a small group of students for a brief time while concentrating on a specific teaching skill.

middle schools Two- to four-year schools of the middle grades, often grades 6 through 8, between elementary school and high school.

minimum competency tests Exit-level tests designed to ascertain whether students have achieved basic levels of performance in such areas as reading, writing, and computation. Some states require that a secondary student pass a minimum competency test in order to receive a high school diploma.

misfeasance Failure to act in a proper manner to prevent harm.

moral stages Promoted by Lawrence Kohlberg as a model of moral development in which individuals progress from simple moral concerns, such as avoiding punishment, to more sophisticated ethical beliefs and actions.

Morrill Act Federal legislation (1862) granting federal lands to states to establish colleges to promote more effective and efficent agriculture and industry. A second Morrill Act, passed in 1890, provided federal support for "separate but equal" colleges for African Americans.

multicultural education Educational policies and practices that not only recognize but also affirm human differences and similarities associated with gender, race, ethnicity, nationality, disability, and class.

multiple intelligences A theory developed by Howard Gardner to expand the concept of human intelligence to include such areas as logical-mathematical, linguistic, bodily-kinesthetic, musical, spatial, interpersonal, intrapersonal, and naturalist.

N

National Assessment of Educational Progress (NAEP) Program to ascertain the effectiveness of U.S. schools and student achievement.

National Association of State Directors of Teacher Education and Certification (NASDTEC) An organization, comprising participating state departments of education, that evaluates teacher education programs in higher education.

National Board for Professional Teaching Standards (NBPTS) A professional organization charged with establishing voluntary standards for recognizing superior teachers as board certified.

National Council for the Accreditation of Teacher Education (NCATE) An organization that evaluates teacher education programs in many colleges and universities. Graduates of programs approved by the NCATE receive licenses in over half the states, pending the successful completion of required state exams.

national curricular standards Nationally prescribed or recommended standards, content skills, and testing.

National Defense Education Act Federally sponsored programs (1958) to improve science, math, and foreign language instruction in schools.

National Education Association (NEA) The largest organization of educators, the NEA is concerned with the overall improvement of education and of the conditions of educators. It is organized at the national, state, and local levels.

networking The term used to describe the intentional effort to develop personal connections with individuals who could be helpful in finding positions or gaining professional advancement.

New England Primer One of the first textbooks in colonial America, teaching reading and moral messages.

nonfeasance Failure to exercise appropriate responsibility that results in someone's being harmed.

nongraded school A school organization in which grade levels are eliminated for two or more years.

nonverbal communication The act of transmitting and/or receiving messages through means not having to do with oral or written language, such as eye contact, facial expressions, and body language.

normal school A two-year teacher education institution popular in the nineteenth century, many of which were expanded to become today's state colleges and universities.

norm-referenced tests Tests that compare individual students with others in a designated norm group.

Northwest Ordinance (1785, 1787) Provided for the sale of federal lands in the Northwest territory to support public schools.

O

objective The purpose of a lesson expressed in a statement.

objective-referenced tests Tests that measure whether students have mastered a designated body of knowledge rather than how they compare with other students in a norm group.

observation techniques Structured methods for observing various aspects of school or classroom activities.

Old Deluder Satan Law (1647) Massachusetts colony law requiring teachers in towns of fifty families or more and that schools be built in towns of one hundred families or more. Communities must teach children to read so that they can read the Bible and thwart Satan.

open classroom Based on the British model, it refers not only to an informal classroom environment but also to a philosophy of education. Students pursue individual interests with the guidance and support of the teacher; interest centers are created to promote this individualized instruction. Students may also have a significant influence in determining the nature and sequence of the curriculum. It is sometimes referred to as *open education.*

open enrollment The practice of permitting students to attend the school of their choice within their school system. It is sometimes associated with magnet schools and desegregation efforts.

open-space school A school building without interior walls. Although it may be designed to promote the concept of the open classroom, the open-space school is an architectural concept rather than an educational one.

opportunity to learn standards (also called **delivery standards**) These standards attempt to recognize and respond to individual differences and circumstances. Poorer students learning in schools with fewer resources should receive more appropriate and adequate learning opportunities, and if some students need more time to take tests, additional time should be provided.

oral tradition Spoken language is the primary method for instruction in several cultures around the world. Word problems are used to teach reasoning, proverbs to instill wisdom, and stories to teach lessons about nature, history, religion, and social customs.

outcome based education (OBE) An educational approach that emphasizes setting learning outcomes and assessing student progress toward attaining those goals, rather than focusing on curricular topics.

P

paraprofessional A lay person who serves as an aide, assisting the teacher in the classroom.

parochial school An institution operated and controlled by a religious denomination.

peace studies The study and analysis of the conditions of and need for peace, the causes of war, and the mechanisms for the nonviolent resolution of conflict. It is also referred to as *peace education.*

pedagogical cycle A system of teacher-student interaction that includes four steps: structure—teacher introduces the topic; question—teacher asks questions; respond—student answers or tries to answer questions; and react—teacher reacts to student's answers and provides feedback.

pedagogues Term given to home school advocates motivated by humanistic rather than religious goals.

pedagogy The science of teaching.

peer review The practice of having colleagues observe and assess teaching, as opposed to administrators.

perennialism The philosophy that emphasizes rationality as the major purpose of education. It asserts that the essential truths are recurring and universally true; it stresses Great Books.

performance standards Statements that describe what teachers or students should be able to do, and how well they should do it.

permanent license Although there is some variation from state to state, a permanent license is issued after a candidate has completed all the requirements for full recognition as a teacher. Requirements may include a specified number of courses beyond the bachelor's degree or a specified number of years of teaching.

philosophy The love of or search for wisdom; the quest to understand the meaning of life.

phonics An approach to reading instruction that emphasizes decoding words by sounding out letters and combinations of letters (as contrasted with the whole language approach).

political philosophy An approach to analyzing how past and present societies are arranged and governed and how better societies may be created in the future.

portfolio Compilations of work (such as papers, projects, videotapes) assembled to demonstrate growth, creativity, and competence. Often advocated as a more comprehensive assessment than test scores.

Praxis series of tests Developed by ETS to assess teachers' competence in various areas: reading, writing, math, professional and subject area knowledge. Praxis test requirements differ among states. (see Appendix 2)

primary school A separately organized and administered elementary school for students in the lower elementary grades, usually grades 1 through 3, and sometimes including preprimary years.

private school A school controlled by an individual or agency other than the government, usually supported by other than public funds. Most private schools are parochial.

privatization The movement toward increased private sector, for-profit involvement in the management of public agencies, including schools.

probationary teaching period A specified period of time in which a newly hired teacher must demonstrate teaching competence. This period is usually three years for public school teachers and six years for college professors. Generally, on satisfactory completion of the probationary period, a teacher is granted tenure.

problem-based learning An approach that builds a curriculum around intriguing real-life problems and asks students to work cooperatively to develop and demonstrate their solutions.

professional development School district efforts to improve knowledge, skills and performance of its professional staff.

progressive education An educational philosophy emphasizing democracy, student needs, practical activities, and school-community relationships.

property tax Local real estate taxes (also cars and personal property) historically used to fund local schools.

provisional license Also referred to as a *probationary license,* a provisional license is frequently issued to beginning teachers. It may mean that a person has completed most, but not all, of the state requirements for permanent licensure. Or it may mean that the state requires several years of teaching experience before it will qualify the teacher for permanent licensure.

R

racial discrimination Actions that limit or deny a person or group any privileges, roles, or rewards on the basis of race.

racism Attitudes, beliefs, and behavior based on the notion that one race is superior to other races.

rationalism The philosophy that emphasizes the power of reason and the principles of logic to derive statements about the world. Rationalists encourage schools to emphasize teaching mathematics, because mathematics involves reason and logic.

readability formulas Formulas that use objective, quantitative measures to determine the reading level of textbooks.

reciprocity States recognize and honor another state's actions, such as recognizing a teacher's license in one state as valid in another.

reconstructionism (reconstructionist) Also called social reconstructionism, this is a view of education as a way to improve the quality of life, to reduce the chances of conflict, and to create a more humane world.

reflective teaching Predicated on a broad and in-depth understanding of what is happening in the classroom, reflective teaching promotes thoughtful consideration and dialogue about classroom events.

résumé A summary of a person's education and experiences, often used for application to school or employment.

revenue sharing The distribution of federal money to state and local governments to use as they decide.

Robin Hood Laws As a result of court actions, many states are redistributing revenue from wealthier to poorer communities to equalize educational funding, a process not unlike the efforts of the hero of Sherwood Forest.

romantic critics Critics such as Paul Goodman, Herbert Kohl, and John Holt who believed that schools were stifling the cognitive and affective development of children. Individual critics stressed different problems or solutions, but they all agreed that schools were producing alienated, uncreative, and unfulfilled students.

rubric A scoring guide that describes what must be done, and often describes performance levels ranging from novice to expert, or from a failing grade to excellence.

S

sabbatical A leave usually granted with full or partial pay after a teacher has taught for a specified period of time (for example, six years). Typically, it is to encourage research and professional development. While common at the university level, it is rare for K–12 teachers.

scaffold Taking from the construction field, scaffolding provides support to help a student build understanding. The teacher might use cues or encouragement or well-formulated questions to assist a student in solving a problem or mastering a concept.

school-based management The recent trend in education reform that stresses decision making on the school level. In the past, school policies were set by the state and the districts. Now the trend is for individual schools to make their own decisions and policies.

school choice The name given to several programs in which parents choose what school their child will attend.

school financing Refers to the ways in which monies are raised and allocated to schools. The methods differ widely from state to state, and many challenges are being made in courts today because of the unequal distribution of funds within a state or among states.

school infrastructure The basic facilities and structures that underpin a school plant, such as plumbing, sewage, heat, electricity, roof, masonry, and carpentry.

school superintendent The chief administrator of a school system, responsible for implementing and enforcing the school board's policies, rules, and regulations, as well as state and federal requirements. The superintendent is directly responsible to the school board and is the formal representative of the school community to outside individuals and agencies.

School to Work Opportunities Act Programs that link school learning to job settings, often developed in partnerships between school and industry.

schools without walls An alternative education program that involves the total community as a learning resource.

second-generation segregation When a school's multiracial populations are separated through tracking, extracurricular activities, and even in informal social events, the school is considered to be in second-generation segregation.

secular humanism The belief that people can live ethically without faith in a supernatural or supreme being. Some critics have alleged that secular humanism is a form of religion and that publishers are promoting secular humanism in their books.

self-censorship (also called **stealth censorship**) In order to avoid possible problems and parental complaints, some educators quietly remove a book from a library shelf or a course of study. Teachers practice the same sort of self-censorship when they choose not to teach a topic or not to discuss a difficult issue.

separate but equal A legal doctrine that holds that equality of treatment is accorded when the races are provided substantially equal facilities, even though those facilities are separate. This doctrine was ruled unconstitutional in regard to race.

service credit By volunteering in a variety of community settings, from nursing homes to child care facilities, students are encouraged to develop a sense of community and meet what is now a high school graduation requirement in some states.

sex discrimination Any action that limits or denies a person or group of persons opportunities, privileges, roles, or rewards on the basis of sex.

sexism The collection of attitudes, beliefs, and behavior that results from the assumption that one sex is superior to the other.

sex-role stereotyping Attributing behavior, abilities, interests, values, and roles to a person or group of persons on the basis of sex. This process ignores individual differences.

sexual harassment Unwanted, repeated, and unreturned sexual words, behaviors, or gestures prohibited by federal and some state laws.

simulation A role-playing technique in which students take part in re-created life-like situations.

social reconstructionism (See Reconstructionism.)

sociogram A diagram that is constructed to record social interactions, such as which children interact frequently and which are isolates.

Socratic method An educational strategy attributed to Socrates in which a teacher encourages a student's discovery of truth by questions.

special education Programs and instruction for children with physical, mental, emotional, or learning disabilities or gifted students who need special educational services in order to achieve at their ability level.

special license A nonteaching license that is designed for specialized educational careers, such as counseling, library science, and administration.

state adoption The process by which members of a textbook adoption committee review and select the books used throughout a state. Advocates of this process say that it results in a common statewide curriculum that unites educators on similar issues and makes school life easier for students who move within the state. Critics charge that it gives too much influence to large states and results in a "dumbed down" curriculum.

state board of education The state education agency that regulates policies necessary to implement legislative acts related to education.

state department of education An agency that operates under the direction of the state board of education, accrediting schools, certifying teachers, appropriating state school funds, and so on.

stepfamilies These relationships are created when divorced or widowed parents remarry, creating a whole set of new relationships, including stepchildren, stepgrandparents, and stepparents.

street academies Alternative schools designed to bring dropouts and potential dropouts, often inner-city youths, back into the educational mainstream.

student-initiated questions These are content-related questions originating from the student, yet comprising only a small percentage of the questions asked in class.

superintendent of schools The executive officer of the local school district.

T

taxonomy A classification system of organizing information and translating aims into instructional objectives.

teacher centers Sites to provide training to improve teaching skills, inform teachers of current educational research, and develop new curricular programs.

teacher flexibility Adapting a variety of skills, abilities, characteristics, and approaches, according to the demands of each situation and the needs of each student.

Teach for America A program that places unlicensed college graduates in districts with critical teacher shortages as they work toward attaining a teacher license.

tenure A system of employment in which teachers, having served a probationary period, acquire an expectancy of continued employment. The majority of states have tenure laws.

Tesseract Formerly Educational Alternatives, this private company works in the public school sector, attempting to improve school efficiency and student achievement, while making a profit.

textbook adoption states States, most often those in the South and West, that have a formal process for assessing, choosing, and approving textbooks for school use.

Title I Section of the Elementary and Secondary Education Act that provides federal funds to supplement local education resources for students from low-income families.

tracking The method of placing students according to their ability level in homogeneous classes or learning experiences. Once a student is placed, it may be very difficult to move up from one track to another. The placements may reflect racism, classism, or sexism.

transitional bilingual education Teaching students in their primary language until they can learn in English.

trustee representatives This conception of a school board member's role differs from the delegate approach, as members are viewed as representatives of the entire community, rather than representing the narrower interests of a particular group or neighborhood.

tuition tax credits Tax reductions for parents or guardians of children attending public or private schools.

U

unobtrusive measurement A method of observing a situation without altering it.

unremarked revolution The unheralded but persistent move of schools away from formal tracking programs.

V

values clarification A model, comprising various strategies, that encourages students to express and clarify their values on different topics.

virtual field trip Visiting distant sites and events via the computer and the Internet.

vouchers A voucher is like a coupon, and it represents money targeted for schools. In a voucher system, parents use educational vouchers to "shop" for a school.

Schools receive part or all of their per-pupil funding from these vouchers. In theory, good schools would thrive and poor ones would close for lack of students.

W

wait time The amount of time a teacher waits for a student's response after a question is asked and the amount of time following a student's response before the teacher reacts.

whole language approach Teaching reading through an integration of language arts skills and knowledge, with a heavy emphasis on literature (as contrasted with a phonics approach).

women's studies Originally created during the 1970s to study the history, literature, psychology, and experiences of women, topics typically missing from the traditional curriculum.

World Wide Web Most common connection to the Internet; contains numerous sites which can be accessed by a Web browser.

Z

zero reject The principle that no child with disabilities may be denied a free and appropriate public education.

zero-tolerance policies Such rigorous rules offer schools little or no flexibility in responding to student infractions related to alcohol, drugs, tobacco, violence, and weapons. These policies have been developed by both local school districts and a number of state legislatures, and in most cases, students who violate such policies must be expelled.

zone of proximal development The area where students can move from what they know to new learning, a zone where real learning is possible.

NOTES

CHAPTER 1 Becoming a Teacher

1. Amy DePaul, *What to Expect Your First Year of Teaching* (Washington, DC: U.S. Department of Education, September 1998), p. 28.
2. Quoted in Ann Lieberman and Lynn Miller, *Teachers, Their World and Their Work* (Alexandria, VA: Association for Supervision and Curriculum Development, 1984), p. 22.
3. Louis Harris and Associates, *The Metropolitan Life Survey of the American Teacher 1996* (New York: Metropolitan Life Insurance Company, 1996).
4. Lieberman and Miller, *Teachers, Their World and Their Work,* p. 47.
5. William Lyon Phelps, quoted in Oliver Ikenberry, *American Education Foundations* (Columbus, OH: Merrill, 1974), p. 389.
6. Quoted in Myron Brenton, *What's Happened to Teacher?* (New York: Coward, McCann & Geoghegan, 1970), p. 164.
7. Quoted in Haim Ginott, *Teacher and Child* (New York: Macmillan, 1972), p. 315.
8. Steve Twomey and Richard Morin, "Teachers: Besieged, Delighted," *The Washington Post,* July 4, 1999, pp. A1, A12.
9. "Quality Counts, 2000, Who Should Teach," *Education Week* (Bethesda, MD: Editorial Projects) 19(18) pp. 8–9.
10. Quoted in Brenton, *What's Happened to Teacher?* p. 97.
11. Ibid., p. 94.
12. Anne Meek, "America's Teachers: Much to Celebrate," *Educational Leadership* 55, no. 5 (February 1998), pp. 12–16; National Education Association, *Status of the American Public School Teacher,* 1995–96 (Washington, DC: NEA, 1997).
13. Ellen Hogan Steele, "Reflections on a School Strike II," *Phi Delta Kappan* 57, no. 9 (May 1976), pp. 590–92; Carol Davis quote from "Are You Treated Like a Professional? Or a Tall Child?" *NEA Today,* December 1988, p. 4.
14. Jillian N. Lederhouse, "Show Me the Power" Education Week, June 13, 2001; *Teachers' Working Conditions: Findings from The Condition of Education 1996* (Washington, DC: National Center for Educational Research and Improvement, 1996), p. 12; see also NEA surveys, such as *The Conditions and Resources of Teaching.*
15. Ron Brandt, "On Teacher Empowerment: A Conversation with Ann Lieberman," *Educational Leadership* 46, no. 8 (May 1989), pp. 23–24.
16. Adopted from Robert Howsam et al., *Educating a Profession, Report on the Bicentennial Commission of Education for Profession of Teaching* (Washington, DC: American Association of Colleges for Teacher Education, 1976), pp. 6–7.
17. Ibid., pp. 8–9.
18. *Tomorrow's Teachers: A Report of the Holmes Group* (East Lansing, MI: Holmes Group, 1986).
19. Carnegie Forum on Education and the Economy, Task Force on Teaching as a Profession, *A Nation Prepared: Teachers for the Twenty-First Century* (New York: Forum, 1986).
20. John Goodlad, "A Study of the Education of Educators: One Year Later," *Phi Delta Kappan* 73, no. 4 (December 1991), pp. 311–16.
21. Michael Podgursky, "Should States Subsidize National Certification?" *Education Week on the Web,* April 11, 2001.
22. Ibid.; "Clinton Teacher Board Proposal Marks Milestone," *Education Week on the Web,* 1997; "Board Certification: Here at Last!" *American Teacher* 79 (March 1995), p. 3; Ann Bradley, "National Board Announces First Teacher Certificates," *Education Week* 11 (January 1995), p. 9.
23. Linda Darling-Hammond, "Who Will Speak for the Children?: How 'Teach for America' Hurts Urban Schools and Students," *Phi Delta Kappan* 76, no. 1 (September 1994), pp. 21–34; for the other side of this debate, see Wendy Kopp, "Ten Years of Teach for America" in *Education Week on the Web,* June 21, 2000.
24. Linda Darling-Hammond, "The Futures of Teaching," *Educational Leadership* 46, no. 3 (November 1988), p. 6.
25. *Different Drummers: How Teachers of Teachers View Public Education* (New York: Public Agenda, 1997).
26. David C. Berliner, "A Personal Response to Those Who Bash Teacher Education," *Journal of Teacher Education* 51, no. 5 (November/December 2000), pp. 358–71.
27. Ibid., p. 363. See also D. Gitomer, A. Latham, and R. Ziomek, *The Academic Quality of Prospective Teachers: The Impact of Admissions and Licensure Testing* (Princeton, NJ: Educational Testing Service, 1999); "Attracting the Best and the Brightest?" *Quality Counts 2000: Who Should Teach, Education Week on the Web.*
28. Carol Langdon, "The Fourth Phi Delta Kappa Poll of Teachers' Attitudes Toward the Public Schools," *Phi Delta Kappan* 79, no. 3 (November 1997), pp. 212–20; for other public reaction to education issues, follow the annual Kappan report on the Gallup Poll, such as Lowell C. Rose, Alee M. Gallup, and Stanley M. Elam, "The 29th Annual Phi Delta Kappa/Gallup Poll of the Public's Attitudes Toward Schools," *Phi Delta Kappan* 79, no. 1 (September 1997): pp. 41–56.
29. Andy Baumgartner, "A Teacher Speaks Out: Insights from the National Teacher of the Year," *The Washington Post,* March 26, 2000, p. B4.
30. Robert Gates, " Questions Every Teacher Should Answer," *Classroom Leadership,* (August 1999), pp. 1–3; Kevin and Jackie Freiberg, *Nuts!* (New York: Broadway Books, 1996), pp. 320–27.

CHAPTER 2 Student Diversity

1. *Do We Still Need Public Schools?* (Washington, DC: Center on National Educational Policy and Phi Delta Kappa, 1996), p. 14; Maxine Schwartz Seller, "Immigrants in the Schools—Again: Historical and Contemporary Perspectives on the Education of Post 1965 Immigrants in the

United States," *Educational Foundations* 3, no. 1 (spring 1989), pp. 53–75.

2. Kenneth Dunn and Rita Dunn, "Dispelling Outmoded Beliefs About Student Learning," *Educational Leadership* 45, no. 7 (March 1987), pp. 55–63.

3. James Keefe, *Learning Style Theory and Practice* (Reston, VA: National Association of Secondary School Principals, 1987); Paul Zielbauer, "Considering a Later Bell for Connecticut's Sleepy Children," *The New York Times*, February 20, 2001 (www.nytimes.com); Tamara Henry, "Open Up Schools, Let Sun Shine In: Creature Comforts Can Aid Learning," *USA Today*, 22 March 2001, p. 8D.

4. Dunn and Dunn, "Dispelling Outmoded Beliefs About Student Learning"; see also G. Price, "Which Learning Style Elements Are Stable and Which Tend to Change?" *Learning Styles Network Newsletter* 4, no. 2 (1980), pp. 38–40; J. Vitrostko, *An Analysis of the Relationship Among Academic Achievement in Mathematics and Reading, Assigned Instructional Schedules and the Learning Style Time Preferences of Third-, Fourth-, Fifth-, and Sixth-Grade Students*, unpublished doctoral dissertation, St. John's University, Jamaica, New York, 1983.

5. Howard Gardner and Thomas Hatch, "Multiple Intelligences Go to School: Educational Implications of the Theory of Multiple Intelligences," *Educational Researcher* 18, no. 8 (November 1989), p. 5.

6. Kathy Checkley, "The First Seven . . . and the Eighth: A Conversation with Howard Gardner," *Educational Leadership* 55, no. 1 (September 1997), pp. 8–13; Howard Gardner, "Beyond the I.Q.: Education and Human Development," *Harvard Educational Review* 57, no. 2 (spring 1987), pp. 187–93.

7. Thomas Armstrong, "Multiple Intelligences: Seven Ways to Approach Curriculum," *Educational Leadership* 52 (November 1994), pp. 26–28; see also Howard Gardner, *Intelligence Reframed: Multiple Intelligences for the 21st Century* (New York: Basic Books, 1999).

8. Howard Gardner, "Reflections on Multiple Intelligences: Myths and Messages," *Phi Delta Kappan* 77, no. 3 (November 1995), pp. 200–9; Veronica Borruso Emig, "A Multiple Intelligence Inventory," *Educational Leadership* 55, no. 1 (September 1997), pp. 47–50.

9. Thomas R. Hoerr, "How the New City School Applies the Multiple Intelligences," *Educational Leadership* 52 (November 1994), pp. 29–33.

10. Nancy Gibbs, "The E.Q. Factor," *Time* 146, no. 14 (October 2, 1995), pp. 60–68.

11. Ibid. See also Kevin R. Kelly and Sidney M. Moon, "Personal and Social Talents," *Phi Delta Kappan* 79, no. 10 (June 1998), pp. 743–46.

12. Daniel Goleman, "Emotional Intelligence: Why It Can Matter More Than IQ," *Learning* (May/June 1996), pp. 49–50; see a sample application of EQ in Emily Wax, "Educating More Than the Mind," *The Washington Post*, October 4, 2000, p. B3.

13. The demographic information in the following section is based on the following: "Overview of Race and Hispanic Origin," *Census 2000 Brief* (Washington, DC: U.S. Census Bureau, March 2001); "Projections of the Resident Population by Race, Hispanic Origin, and Nativity: 2025 to 2045," *Census 2000 Brief* (Washington, DC: U.S. Census Bureau, March 2001); "Profiles of General Demographic Characteristics," *Census 2000* (Washington, DC: U.S. Census Bureau, March 2001). William Branigin, "Nearly 1 in 10 in U.S. Is Foreign Born, Census Says," *The Washington Post*, April 9, 1997, p. A18; Jessica I. Sandham, "Graduates Growing More Diverse, Study Finds," *Education Week on the Web*, April 1, 1998; *Statistical Abstract of the United States, 1997* (Washington, DC: U.S. Department of Commerce, Bureau of the Census, 1996); *Youth Indicators* (Washington DC: National Center for Education Statistics, Department of Education, 1996).

14. S. D. McLemore and H. D. Romo, *Racial and Ethnic Relations in America* (Boston: Allyn & Bacon, 1998): John O'Neil, "Why Are the Black Kids Sitting Together?" *Educational Leadership* 55, no. 5 (December 1997/January 1998), pp. 12–17; Robert Slavin, "Research on Cooperative Learning: Consensus and Controversy," *Educational Leadership* 47, no. 4 (December 1989/ January 1990), pp. 52–54.

15. Slavin, "Research on Cooperative Learning"; McLemore and Romo, *Racial and Ethnic Relations in America;* see also James C. Hendrix, "Cooperative Learning: Building a Democratic Community," *Clearinghouse* 69, no. 6 (July–August 1996), pp. 333–36.

16. James Banks, "Multicultural Education: Characteristics and Goals," in James A. Banks and Cherry A. McGee Banks (eds.), *Multicultural Education: Issues and Perspectives* 4th ed. (Boston: Allyn & Bacon, 2001), pp. 3–30.

17. Carol Gilligan, *In a Different Voice: Psychological Theory and Women's Development* (Cambridge, MA: Harvard University Press, 1982). See also Mary Field Belenky, Blythe McVicker Clinchy, Nancy Rule Goldberger, and Jill Mattuck Tarule, *Women's Ways of Knowing: The Development of Self, Voice, and Mind* (New York: Basic Books, 1986).

18. Geneva Gay, "Achieving Educational Equality Through Curriculum Desegregation," *Phi Delta Kappan* 72, no. 1 (September 1990), pp. 56–62.

19. Peter Schmidt, "New Survey Discerns Deep Divisions Among U.S. Youths on Race Relations," *Education Week*, March 25, 1992, p. 5.

20. James Banks, "Approaches to Multicultural Curriculum Reform," in Banks and Banks, *Multicultural Education*, pp. 225–46.

21. James Crawford, ed., *Language Loyalties: A Source Book on the Official English Controversy* (Chicago: University of Chicago Press, 1992); see also Jonathon Zimmerman, "A Babel of Tongues," *U.S. News & World Report*, 24 November 1997, p. 39.

22. Diane Ravitch, "Politicization and the Schools: The Case of Bilingual Education," in *Taking Sides*, James W. Noll (ed.) (Guilford, CT: Dushkin, 1997), pp. 232–40.

23. Harold Hodgkinson, quoted in *Education Week*, May 14, 1986, pp. 14–40.

24. D. Hugo Lopez and Merle T. Mora, "Bilingual Education and the Labor Market Earnings Among Hispanics: Evidence Using High School and Beyond," *READ Perspectives* (Amherst, MA: Institute for Research in English Acquisition and Development), 1998.

25. Jorge Amselle, "Adios, Bilingual Ed," *Policy Review* no. 86, November 1997 (Washington, DC: Heritage Foundation), pp. 52–55.

26. Rene Sanchez and William Booth, "California Rejection: A Big Blow to Bilingualism: Decisive Vote Could Set Pace for Rest of Nation," *The Washington Post,* June 4, 1998, p. A16; Peter Baker, "Education Dept Faults Anti-Bilingual Measure," *The Washington Post,* April 28, 1998, p. A3; Lisa Anderson, "Bilingual Debate Reaches Boiling Point: Battle Wages with Ballots, Initiatives, Studies, Placards," *Tribune on the Web,* May 29, 2001.

27. "Bilingual Teachers: Shortage in High School," *The Washington Post,* January 31, 2001, p. 11; see also *The Condition of Education,* Indicator 23 (Washington, DC: U.S. Department of Education, 1999).

28. James Crawford, *Hold Your Tongue: Bilingualism and the Politics of "English Only"* (New York: Addison-Wesley, 1992), pp. 111–12.

29. Gary A. Cziko, "The Evaluation of Bilingual Education: From Necessity and Probability to Possibility," *Educational Researcher* 21, no. 2 (March 1992), p. 24; J. David Ramirez, "Executive Summary," *Bilingual Research Journal* 16 (Winter/Spring, 1992), pp. 1–245.

30. Rosalie Pedalino Porter, New York City Study. *READ Perspectives* 12 (2), 1995, quoted in Robert F. McNergney and Joanne M. Herbert, *Foundations of Education* (Needham Heights, MA: Allyn & Bacon, 1998), p. 311.

31. Peter Schmidt, "Three Types of Bilingual Education Effective, E.D. Study Concludes," *Education Week* February 20, 1991, pp. 1, 23.

32. Wayne Thomas and Virginia Collier, "Two Languages Are Better Than One," *Educational Leadership* 55, no. 4 (December 1997/ January 1998), pp. 23–26; Craig Donegan, "Debate over Bilingualism," *Congressional Quarterly Researcher* 6, no. 3 (January 19, 1996), pp. 51–59; Stephen Krashen, "Why Bilingual Education?" *ERIC Clearinghouse* (ED403101) (Washington, DC: OERI, U.S. Dept of Education, 1997); Kenneth J. Cooper, "Riley Endorses Two-Way Bilingual Education," *The Washington Post,* March 26, 2000, p. A2.

33. These categories build on the ones described by William Heward and Rodney A. Cavanaugh, "Educational Equality for Students with Disabilities," in James Banks and Cherry Banks (eds.), *Multicultural Education* (Boston: Allyn & Bacon, 1997), pp. 301–33; as well as William Heward and Michael Orlansky, "Educational Equality for Exceptional Students," in James Banks and Cherry Banks (eds.), *Multicultural Education* (Boston: Allyn & Bacon, 1989), pp. 231–50.

34. Findings from the *Condition of Education 1998* (Washington, DC: U.S. Department of Education, 1998) updated the original figures of Heward and Orlansky, "Educational Equality for Exceptional Students."

35. Susan DeFord, "Inclusive Classrooms," *Washington Post Magazine,* February 8, 1998, p. 8.

36. Marie Killilea, *Karen* (New York: Dell, 1952), p. 171.

37. Ed Martin, quoted in "PL 94-142," *Instructor* 87, no. 9 (1978), p. 63.

38. Michael D. Simpson, "Rights Watch: Who's Paying for Special Ed?" *NEA Today* 15, no. 9 (May 1997), p. 20.

39. Bridget Greenberg, "Study: More in College Have Learning Disabilities," *Austin American Statesman,* February 12, 2000, p. A21; *Eighteenth Annual Report to Congress on the Implementation of the Individuals with Disabilities Education Act* (Washington, DC: U.S. Department of Education, 1996); see also Martha McCarthy, "Severely Disabled Children: Who Pays?" *Phi Delta Kappan* 73, no. 1 (September 1991), pp. 66–71.

40. Jay Mathews, "Study Finds Racial Bias in Special Ed," *Washington Post,* 3 March 2001, p. A1; www.ed.gov/offices/OSERS/OSEP/OSEP2000AnlRpt/

41. U.S. Department of Education, *The Twenty-Second Annual Report to Congress on the Implementation of the Individuals with Disabilities Education Act,* Washington, D.C. (2000), p. 67.

42. Suzy Ruder, "We Teach All," *Educational Leadership* 58, no. 1 (September 2000), pp. 49–51; Mary Beth Doyle, "Transition Plans for Students with Disabilities," *Educational Leadership* 58, no. 1 (September 2000), pp. 46–48.

43. Quoted in David Milofsky, "Schooling the Kid No One Wants," *New York Times Magazine,* January 2, 1977, pp. 24–29.

44. The anecdotes and many of the quotations in this section were cited in Gene I. Maeroff, "The Unfavored Gifted Few," *New York Times Magazine,* August 21, 1977, reprinted in Celeste Toriero (ed.), *Readings in Education 78/79* (Guilford, CT: Dushkin, 1978).

45. Joseph S. Renzulli and C. H. Smith, "Two Approaches to Identification of Gifted Students," *Exceptional Children* 43 (1977).

46. Robert Sternberg, "Giftedness According to the Triarchic Theory of Human Intelligence," in Nicholas Congelo and Gary Davis (eds.), *Handbook of Gifted Education* (Boston: Allyn & Bacon, 1991).

47. John F. Feldhusen, "Programs for the Gifted Few or Talent Development for the Many?" *Phi Delta Kappan* 79, no. 10 (June 1998), pp. 735–38.

48. Judy Galbraith, "Gifted Youth and Self-Concept," *Gifted Education* 15, no. 2 (May 1989), pp. 15–17.

49. Ibid., p. 16.

50. Robert Morris, "Educating Gifted for the 1990s," *Gifted Education* 15, no. 2 (May 1989), pp. 50–52; for more information about gender bias, see *Gender Gaps: Where Schools Still Fail Our Children* (Washington, DC: American Association of University Women Educational Foundation, 1998).

51. Susan Winebrenner, "Gifted Students Need an Education, Too," *Educational Leadership* 58, no. 1 (September 2000), pp. 52–56.

52. John Feldhusen, "Synthesis of Research on Gifted Youth," *Educational Leadership* 46, no. 6 (March 1989), pp. 6–11.

53. Lisa Leff, "Gifted, Talented, and Under Siege," *Washington Post Educational Review,* April 5, 1992, p. 14.

54. Quoted in Galbraith, "Gifted Youth and Self-Concept," p. 17.

CHAPTER 3 Teacher Effectiveness

1. Among the resources on teacher effectiveness that you may want to consult are the *Journal of Teacher Education,*

Handbook of Research on Teaching, and *The Review of Research in Education.*

2. N. Filby Fisher, E. Marleave, L. Cahen, M. Dishaw, M. Moore, and D. Berliner, *Teaching Behaviors, Academic Learning Time, and Student Achievement: Final Report of Beginning Teacher Evaluation Study* (San Francisco: Far West Laboratory, 1978).

3. John Goodlad, *A Place Called School* (New York: McGraw-Hill, 1984).

4. Barbara M. Taylor, David P. Pearson, Kathleen F. Clark, and Sharon Walpole, "Effective Schools/Accomplished Teachers," *Reading Teacher* 53 (1999), pp. 156–59.

5. Herbert Walberg, Richard Niemiec, and Wayne Frederick, "Productive Curriculum Time," *The Peabody Journal of Education* 69, no. 3 (1994), pp. 86–100; Steve Nelson, *Instructional Time as a Factor in Increasing Student Achievement* (Portland, OR: Northwest Regional Lab, 1990); David Berliner, "The Half-Full Glass: A Review of Research on Teaching," in Philip Hosferd (ed.), *Using What We Know About Teaching* (Alexandria, VA: Association for Supervision and Curriculum Development, 1984).

6. C. M. Evertson, E. T. Emmer, B. S. Clements, J. P. Sanford, and M. E. Worsham, *Classroom Management for Elementary Teachers* (Englewood Cliffs, NJ: Prentice Hall, 1984). See also Carolyn Evertson and Alene Harris, "What We Know About Managing Classrooms," *Educational Leadership* 49, no. 7 (April 1992), pp. 74–78.

7. Robert Slavin, "Classroom Management and Discipline," in *Educational Psychology: Theory into Practice* (Englewood Cliffs, NJ: Prentice Hall, 1986); Vernon F. Jones and Louise S. Jones, *Comprehensive Classroom Management: Creating Communities of Support and Solving Problems* (Needham Heights, MA: Allyn & Bacon, 2001), pp. 251–55.

8. E. T. Emmer, C. M. Evertson, J. P. Sanford, B. S. Clements, and M. E. Worsham, *Classroom Management for Secondary Teachers* (Englewood Cliffs, NJ: Prentice Hall, 1984); B. Malone, D. Bonitz, and M. Rickett, "Teacher Perceptions of Disruptive Behavior: Maintaining Instructional Focus," *Educational Horizons* 76, no. 4 (1998), pp. 189–94.

9. Jacob Kounin, *Discipline and Group Management in Classrooms* (New York: Holt, Rinehart & Winston, 1970).

10. Jere E. Brophy, "Classroom Organization and Management," *The Elementary School Journal* 83, no. 4 (1983), pp. 265-85.

11. Thomas L. Good and Jere E. Brophy, *Looking in Classrooms* (New York: Longman, 2000), pp. 219–20.

12. Marilyn E. Gootman, *The Caring Teacher's Guide to Discipline: Helping Young Students Learn Self-Control, Responsibility, and Respect* (Thousand Oaks, CA: Corwin Press, 1997).

13. David Berliner, "What Do We Know About Well-Managed Classrooms? Putting Research to Work," *Instructor* 94, no. 6 (February 1985), p. 15; Carol Cummings, *Winning Strategies for Classroom Management* (Alexandria, VA: Association for Supervision and Curriculum Development, 2000).

14. Arno Bellack, *The Language of the Classroom* (New York: Teachers College Press, 1966).

15. Several of the sections on the pedagogical cycle are adopted from Myra and David Sadker, *Principal Effectiveness—Pupil Achievement (PEPA) Training Manual* (Washington, DC: American University, 1986).

16. Donald Cruickshank "Applying Research on Teacher Clarity," *Journal of Teacher Education* 36 (1985), pp. 44–48.

17. Myra Sadker and David Sadker, "Questioning Skills" in James M. Cooper (ed.), *Classroom Teaching Skills,* 7th ed. (Boston: Houghton Mifflin, 2003); P. Smagoinsky, "The Social Construction of Data: Methodological Problems of Investigation Learning in the Zone of Proximal Development," *Review of Educational Research* 65, no. 3 (1995), pp. 191–212.

18. Robert Slavin, "The Lesson," in *Educational Psychology: Theory into Practice.*

19. John Dewey, *How We Think,* rev. ed. (Boston: D. C. Heath, 1933), p. 266.

20. Myra Sadker and David Sadker, "Sexism in the Schoolroom of the 80s," *Psychology Today* 19 (March 1985), pp. 54–57.

21. Benjamin Bloom (ed.), *Taxonomy of Educational Objectives, Handbook I: Cognitive Domain* (New York: David McKay, 1956).

22. Myra Sadker and David Sadker, "Questioning Skills" in James Cooper (ed.), *Classroom Teaching Skills;* Trevor Kerry, "Classroom Questions in England," *Questioning Exchange* 1, no. 1, (1987), p. 33; Arthur C. Grassier and Natalie K Person, "Question Asking During Tutoring," *American Educational Research Journal* 31 (1994), pp. 104–37; William S. Carlsen, "Questioning in Classrooms: A Sociolinguistic Perspective," *Review of Educational Research* 61 (1991), pp. 157–78; Meredith D. Gall, "Synthesis of Research on Teacher's Questioning," *Educational Leadership* 42 (1984), pp. 40–47; David Berliner, "The Half-Full Glass: A Review of Research on Teaching," in Philip L. Hosford (ed.), *Using What We Know About Teaching,* pp. 51–84; L. M. Barden, "Effective Questions and the Ever-Elusive Higher-Order Question," *American Biology Teacher* 57, no. 7 (1995), pp. 423–26; Meredith D. Gall and T. Rhody, "Review of Research on Questioning Techniques," in William W. Wilen (ed.), *Questions, Questioning Techniques, and Effective Teaching* (Washington, DC: National Education Association, 1987), pp. 23–48; G. Brown and R. Edmondson, "Asking Questions," in E. C. Wragg (ed.), *Classroom Teaching Skills* (New York: Nichols, 1984), pp. 97–119; William W. Wilen and Ambrose A. Clegg, "Effective Questions and Questioning: A Research Review," *Theory and Research in Social Education,* 14, (1986), pp. 153–61.

23. Adapted from Myra Sadker and David Sadker, "Questioning Skills" in James M. Cooper (ed.), *Classroom Teaching Skills.*

24. Mary Budd Rowe, "Wait Time: Slowing Down May Be a Way of Speeding Up!" *Journal of Teacher Education* 37 (January/February 1986), pp. 43–50; Mary Budd Rowe, "Science, Silence, and Sanctions," *Science and Children* 34 (September 1996), pp. 35–37; Jim B. Mansfield, "The Effects of Wait-time on Issues of Gender Equity, Academic Achievement, and Attitude Toward a Course," *Teacher*

Education and Practice 12, no. 1 (Spring/Summer 1996), pp. 86–93.

25. D. Bridges, "A Philosophical Analysis of Discussion" in J. Dillion (ed.), *Questioning and Discussion: A Multidisciplinary Study* (Norwood, NJ: Alblex, 1988), p. 26; A. E. Edwards and D. G. P. Westgate, *Investigating Classroom Talk*, Social Research and Educational Studies Series: 4 (London and Philadelphia: Falmer, 1987), p. 170.

26. Myra Sadker, David Sadker, and Susan Klein, "The Issue of Gender in Elementary and Secondary Education," *Review of Research in Education* 17 (1991), pp. 269–334.

27. Goodlad, *A Place Called School.*

28. Jere E. Brophy, "Teacher Praise: A Functional Analysis," *Review of Educational Research* 51 (1981), pp. 5–32.

29. Gary Davis and Margaret Thomas, *Effective Schools and Effective Teachers* (Boston: Allyn & Bacon, 1989); Charles A. Dana Center, University of Texas at Austin, *Hope for Urban Education: A Study of Nine High-Performing, High-Poverty, Urban Elementary Schools* (Washington, DC: U.S. Department of Education, Planning and Evaluation Service, 1999). www.ed.gov./pubs/urbanhope/execsumm.html.

30. Susan Black, "Stretching Students Minds: Effective Teaching Is about What Students Will Learn, Not Just What They Will Do," *American School Board Journal* (June 2001). www.asbj.com/current/research.html.

31. Bruce R. Joyce and Emily F. Calhoun, *Learning Experiences: The Role of Instructional Theory and Research* (Alexandria, VA: Association for Curriculum and Supervision, 1996); Barak Rosenshine, "Synthesis of Research on Explicit Teaching," *Educational Leadership* 43, no. 4 (May 1986), pp. 60–69. See also Davis and Thomas, *Effective Schools and Effective Teachers.*

32. David Johnson, Roger Johnson, Edythe Johnson Holubee, and Patricia Roy, *Circles of Learning: Cooperation in the Classroom* (Alexandria, VA: Association of Supervision and Curriculum Development, 1984); Robert Slavin, "Research on Cooperative Learning: Consensus and Controversy," *Educational Leadership* 47, no. 4 (December 1989/January 1990), pp. 52–54.

33. Robert E. Slavin, "Cooperative Learning in Middle and Secondary Schools," *Clearinghouse* 69, no. 4 (March–April 1996), pp. 200–4; Robert E. Slavin, "Cooperative Learning," *Review of Educational Research* 50 (summer 1980), pp. 315–42. See also Robert Slavin, *Cooperative Learning: Student Teams* (Washington, DC: National Education Association, 1987).

34. Robert E. Slavin, *Cooperative Learning: Theory, Research, and Practice* (Boston: Allyn & Bacon, 1995); Roger Johnson and David Johnson, "Student Interaction: Ignored but Powerful." *Journal of Teacher Education* 36 (July–August 1985), p. 24. See also Robert Slavin, "Synthesis of Research on Cooperative Learning," *Educational Leadership* 48, no. 5 (February 1991), pp. 71–82; Susan Ellis and Susan Whalen, "Keys to Cooperative Learning, " *Instructor* 101, no. 6 (February 1992), pp. 34–37.

35. David Meichenbaum and Andrew Biemiller, *Nurturing Independent Learners: Helping Students Take Charge of Their Learning* (Cambridge, MA: Brookline Books, 1998); Joan S. Hyman and S. Alan Cohen, "Learning for Mastery: Ten Conclusions After 15 Years and 3000 Schools," *Educational Leadership* 36 (November 1979), pp. 104–9.

36. Glenn Hymel, "Harnessing the Mastery Learning Literature: Past Efforts, Current Status, and Future Directions," Paper presented at the annual meeting of the American Educational Research Association, Boston, MA, 1990; Thomas Guskey and Sally Gates, "Synthesis of Research on the Effects of Mastery Learning in Elementary and Secondary Classrooms," *Educational Leadership* 43 (May 1986), pp. 73–80.

37. Richard Arends, "Project Based Instruction," in *Classroom Instruction and Management* (New York: McGraw-Hill, 1997); Linda Torp and Sara Sage, *Problems as Possibilities: Problem-Based Learning for K–12 Education* (Alexandria, VA: Association for Supervision and Curriculum Development, 1998); Robert Delisle, *How to Use Problem-Based Learning in the Classroom* (Alexandria, VA: Association for Supervision and Curriculum Development, 1997).

38. Jere Brophy, "Probing the Subtleties of Subject-Matter Teaching," *Educational Leadership* 49, no. 7 (April 1992), pp. 4–8.

39. Carol Ann Tomlinson, "Reconcilable Differences? Standards-Based Teaching and Differentiation," *Educational Leadership* 58, no. 1 (September 2000), pp. 6–11.

40. Richard Prawat, "From Individual Differences to Learning Communities—Our Changing Focus," *Educational Leadership* 49, no. 7 (April 1992), pp. 9–13.

41. Joellen Killion and Guy Todnem, "A Process for Personal Theory Building," *Educational Leadership* 48, no. 6 (March 1991), pp. 14–16.

42. Bud Wellington, "The Promise of Reflective Practice," *Educational Leadership* 48, no. 6 (March 1991), pp. 4–5.

CHAPTER 4 Schools: Choices and Challenges

1. James Shaver and William Strong, *Facing Value Decisions: Rationale Building for Teachers* (Belmont, CA: Wadsworth, 1976).

2. Ernest L. Boyer, *High School: A Report on Secondary Education in America* (New York: Harper & Row, 1983), pp. 209–10.

3. Linda Perlstein, "'Serving' the Community Without Leaving School," *The Washington Post*, June 28, 1999, pp. A1, A6.

4. *The Condition of Education 2001*, U.S. Department of Education, NCES, Indicator 16: Social and Cultural Outcomes, Community Service Participation in Grades 6–12, p. 142. nces.ed.gov/pubs2001/2001072_2.pdf.

5. Bill Bigelow, "The Human Lives Behind the Labels: The Global Sweatshop, Nike, and the Race to the Bottom," *Phi Delta Kappan* 79, no. 2 (October 1997), pp. 112–19.

6. Paulo Freire, *The Pedagogy of the Oppressed* (New York: Herder & Herder, 1970).

7. John Goodlad, *A Place Called School* (New York: McGraw-Hill, 1984), pp. 35–39.

8. Arthur Eugene Bestor, *Educational Wastelands: The Retreat from Learning in Our Public Schools* (Urbana: University of Illinois Press, 1953), p. 75.

9. Boyer, *High School*, p. 5.

10. National Commission on Excellence in Education, *A Nation at Risk: The Imperative for Educational Reform* (Washington, DC: U.S. Government Printing Office, 1983), p. 1.
11. David Hill, "Fixing the System from the Top Down," *Teacher Magazine* (September/October 1989), pp. 50–55.
12. David L. Clark and Terry A. Astuto, "Reconstructing Reform: Challenges to Popular Perceptions About Teachers and Students," *Phi Delta Kappan* 75, no. 7 (March 1994), pp. 512–20.
13. Donald C. Ohlrich, "Education Reforms: Mistakes, Misconceptions, Miscues," *Phi Delta Kappan* 170, no. 7 (March 1989), pp. 512–17.
14. Valerie Strauss, "When Success Doesn't Add Up," *The Washington Post on the Web,* December 2000.
15. Clinton Boutwell, "People Without People," *Phi Delta Kappan* 79, no. 2 (October 1997), pp. 104–11.
16. Joy Dryfoos, "Full Service Schools," *Educational Leadership* 53, no. 7 (April 1996), pp. 18–23.
17. Henry J. Perkinson, *The Imperfect Panacea: American Faith in Education* (New York: McGraw-Hill, 1995), p. 191.
18. Debra Viadero, "Students Learn More in Magnets Than Other, Study Finds," *Education Week,* March 6, 1996, p. 6; Caroline Hendrie, "Magnets Value in Desegregating Schools Is Found to Be Limited," *Education Week on the Web,* November 13, 1996; "Research Notes," *Education Week on the Web,* September 16, 1998.
19. A. S. Byrk, Valerie Lee, and P. B. Holland, *Catholic Schools and the Common Good* (London: Harvard University Press, 1993).
20. "Another Round on Vouchers," *The Washington Post,* December 18, 2000, p. A26; Terry Moe, "The Public Revolution Private Money Might Bring," *The Washington Post,* May 9, 1999, p. B3. For more on the legal dispute, see *Jackson v. Benson* (1998), which held that vouchers used for religious school tuition did not violate the Wisconsin State Constitution. A Cleveland Scholarship and Tutoring Program, which uses vouchers for religious schools, was found to violate the First Amendment of Ohio's State Constitution, and is being appealed to the U.S. Supreme Court.
21. John E. Koppich, "Considering Nontraditional Alternatives: Charters, Private Contracts, and Vouchers," *The Future of Children* 7, no. 3 (winter 1997), pp. 96–111; Joseph P. Viteritti, "Stacking the Deck for the Poor: The New Politics of Schools Choice," *The Brookings Review* 14, no. 3 (summer 1996), pp. 10–13.
22. Majorie Coeyman, "Vouchers Get a Boost from Black Alliance," *The Christian Science Monitor on the Web,* July 10, 2001; Scott Stephens, "Support for School Vouchers a Struggle in Many States," *Plain Deal Reporter on the Web,* April 1, 2001.
23. Alex Molnar, "Charter Schools: The Smiling Face of Disinvestment," *Educational Leadership* 54, no. 2 (October 1996), pp. 9–15.
24. Joe Nathan, "Heat and Light in the Charter School Movement," *Phi Delta Kappan* 79, no. 7 (March 1998), pp. 499–505; Jessica Sandman, "Challenges to Charter Laws Mount," *Education Week,* May 2, 2001, pp. 1, 24, 25.
25. Bruno V. Manno, Chester E. Finn, Louann A. Bierlein, and Gregg Vanurek, "How Charter Schools Are Different: Lessons and Implications from a National Study," *Phi Delta Kappan* 79, no. 7 (March 1998), pp. 489–98.
26. Thomas L. Good and Jennifer Braden, "Charter Schools: Another Reform Failure or a Worthwhile Investment?" *Phi Delta Kappan* 81, no. 10, June 2000, pp. 745–750.
27. Molnar, "Charter Schools," p. 10.
28. Joel Spring, *American Education* (New York: McGraw-Hill, 1996), pp. 184–85.
29. Chuck Sudetic, "Reading, Writing and Revenue," *Mother Jones,* May–June 2001, pp. 84–95.
30. Peggy Farber, "The Edison Project Scores—and Stumbles—in Boston," *Phi Delta Kappan* 79, no. 7 (March 1998), pp. 506–11; Rene Sanchez, "Edison School Project Growing Slowly," *The Washington Post,* August 22, 1997, p. A3; Kevin Fedarko, "Starting from Scratch," *Time,* October 27, 1997, pp. 82–85; Jay Mathews, "For Profit School Firm Offers Teachers Stock," *The Washington Post,* October 22, 1998, pp. C-1, C-6.
31. Mike Hoffman, "Upstarts: Staking Out a Share of Public-School Gold," *Inc* (June 1998), pp. 25–27.
32. Mark Walsh, "Question[s?] About Finances Put Edison Project at Crossroad," *Education Week,* August 3, 1994, pp. 18–19; Walter Farrell, Jr., James Johnson, Cloyzelle Jones, and Marty Sapp, "Will Privatizing Schools Really Help Inner-City Students of Color?" *Educational Leadership* 52, no. 1 (September 1994), pp. 72–75.
33. Michael Winerip, "Schools for Sale," *New York Times Magazine,* June 14, 1998, pp. 42–49, 80, 86, 88–89; Mark Walsh, "Business," *Education Week on the Web,* March 4, 1998; Lynn Schnaiberg, "Seeking a Competitive Advantage," *Education Week on the Web,* December 8, 1999; Mark Walsh, "Report Card on For-Profit Industry Still Incomplete," *Education Week on the Web,* December 15, 1999.
34. Mark Walsh, "Disney Holds Up School as Model for Next Century," *Education Week,* June 22, 1994, pp. 1, 6.
35. Pedro Noguerar, "More Democracy Not Less: Confronting the Challenge of Privatization in Public Education," *Journal of Negro Education* 623, no. 2 (1994), p. 238.
36. Bruce Fuller, "Is School Choice Working?" *Educational Leadership* 54, no. 2 (October 1996), pp. 37–40; Lorna Jimerson, "Hidden Consequences of School Choice: Impact on Programs, Finances, and Accountability," paper presented at the American Educational Research Association annual meeting, San Diego, CA (1998); Steven Glazerman, "School Quality and Social Stratification: The Determinants and Consequences of Parental Choice," paper presented at the American Educational Research Association annual meeting, San Diego, CA (1998); Edd Doerr, "The Empty Promise of School Vouchers," *USA Today Magazine* 125, no. 2622 (New York: Society for the Advancement of Education), March 1997, pp. 89–90.
37. Spring, *American Education,* pp. 185–86.
38. Alex Molnar interviewed in "Giving Kids the Business, an Interview with Alex Molnar," *The Education Industry: The Corporate Takeover of Public Schools,* www.corpwatch.org/feature/education/; see also Alex Molnar, *Giving Kids the Business: The Commercialization of America's Schools* (Boulder, CO: Westview Press, 1996); see also Majorie Coeyman, "Vouchers Get a Boost from Black Alliance."

39. "Live and Learn," *Harper's Bazaar,* (September 1994), pp. 268–70.

40. Patricia Lines, "Educating a Minority: How Families, Policymakers, and Public Educators View Home Schooling," *Journal of Early Education and Family Review* 5, no. 3 (January/February 1998), pp. 25–28; Patricia Lines, "Home Schooling," *Eric Digest* 95 (1995), pp. 1–3; J. Natale, "Home, but Not Alone: Home Schoolers Are Linking up with E-mail and Online Classes," *The American School Board Journal* 182, no. 7, (July 1995), pp. 34–36; Home School Legal Defense Association, *Answers to Commonly Asked Questions About Home Schooling,* 1996, available from Home School Legal Defense Association, P.O. Box 159, Paeonian Springs, VA 22129.

41. M. Mayberry, "Characteristics and Attitudes of Families Who Home School," *Education and Urban Society* 21 (1988), pp. 32–41; M. Mayberry, "Home-based Education in the United States: Demographics, Motivations, and Educational Implications," *Educational Review* 41, no. 2 (1989), pp. 171–80.

42. J. A. Van Galen, "Schooling in Private: A Study of Home Education," doctoral dissertation, University of North Carolina, Chapel Hill, 1986.

43. Nancy Gibbs, *Time,* 31 October 1994, pp. 62–63; Jay Mathews, "A Home Run for Home Schooling," *The Washington Post,* March 24, 1999, p. A11.

44. "Home-Taught Students Miss School Activities," *The Washington Post,* November 26, 1995, pp. B-1, B-5; Chris Jeub, "Why Parents Choose Home Schooling," *Educational Leadership* 52, no.1 (September 1994), pp. 50–52.

45. Darwin L. Webb, "Homeschools and Interscholastic Sports: Denying Participation Violates United States Constitutional Due Process and Equal Protection Rights," *Journal of Law and Education* 26, no. 3 (July 1997), pp. 123–32; Gary Knowles, James A. Muchmore, and Holly W. Spaulding, "Home Education as an Alternative, to Institutionalized Education," *The Education Forum* 58 (spring 1994), pp. 238–43.

46. Barbara Kantrowitz and Pat Wingert, "Learning at Home: Does It Pass the Test?" *Newsweek,* October 5, 1998, pp. 64–71; "Charter 'Profit': Will Michigan Heap Money on an Electronic Charter School?" *The American School Board Journal* 181, no. 9 (September 1994), pp. 27–28; "The Dawn of Home Schooling," *Newsweek,* October 10, 1994, p. 67; see also, Nancy Trejos, "Home Schooling's Net Effect," *The Washington Post,* July 16, 2000, pp. C1, C9.

CHAPTER 5 Life in Schools

1. Philip W. Jackson, *Life in Classrooms* (New York: Holt, Rinehart & Winston, 1968).

2. Ibid.

3. Manuel Justiz, "It's Time to Make Every Minute Count," *Phi Delta Kappan* 65, no. 7 (March 1984), pp. 483–85; see also Herbert Walberg, "Families as Partners in Educational Productivity," *Phi Delta Kappan* 65, no. 6 (February 1984), pp. 397–400.

4. John Goodlad, *A Place Called School* (New York: McGraw-Hill, 1984).

5. Quoted in Ernest L. Boyer, *High School* (New York: Harper & Row, 1983); C. Fisher, N. Filby, E. Marliave, L. Cohen, M. Dishaw, J. Moore, and D. Berliner, *Teacher Behaviors, Academic Learning Time, and Student Achievement,* Final Report of Phase III-B, Beginning Teacher Evaluation Study (San Francisco: Far West Laboratory for Educational Research and Development, 1978).

6. G. Madaus et al., *School Effectiveness: A Reassessment of the Evidence* (New York: McGraw-Hill, 1980).

7. Jackson, *Life in Classrooms.*

8. Ned Flanders, "Intent, Action, and Feedback: A Preparation for Teaching," *Journal of Teacher Education* 14, no. 3 (September 1963), pp. 251–60.

9. Arno Bellack, *The Language of the Classroom* (New York: Teachers College Press, 1965).

10. Romiett Stevens, "The Question as a Measure of Classroom Practice," in *Teachers College Contributions to Education* (New York: Teachers College Press, 1912).

11. W. D. Floyd, *An Analysis of the Oral Questioning Activity in Selected Colorado Primary Classrooms.* Unpublished doctoral dissertation, Colorado State College, 1960.

12. Myra Sadker and David Sadker, "Questioning Skills," in James Cooper (ed.), *Classroom Teaching Skills,* 7th ed. (Boston: Houghton Mifflin, 2003).

13. Mary Budd Rowe, "Wait Time: Slowing Down May Be a Way of Speeding Up!" *Journal of Teacher Education* 37 (1986), pp. 43–50.

14. Goodlad, *A Place Called School.*

15. Talcott Parsons, "The School as a Social System: Some of Its Functions in Society," in Robert Havinghurst and Bernice Neugarten, (eds.), *Society and Education* (Boston: Allyn & Bacon, 1967), pp. 191–214.

16. Robert Lynd and Helen Lynd, *Middletown: A Study in American Culture* (New York: Harcourt Brace Jovanovich, 1929).

17. W. Lloyd Warner, Robert Havinghurst, and Martin Loeb, *Who Shall Be Educated?* (New York: Harper & Row, 1944).

18. August Hollingshead, *Elmtown's Youth* (New York: Wiley, 1949).

19. Robert Havinghurst et al., *Growing Up in River City* (New York: Wiley, 1962).

20. Ernest L. Boyer, *High Schools: A Report on Secondary Education in America* (New York: Harper & Row, 1983).

21. Shirl Gilbert and Geneva Gay, "Improving the Success in School of Poor Black Children," *Phi Delta Kappan* 67, no. 2 (October 1985), pp. 133–38.

22. Ray Rist, "Student Social Class and Teacher Expectations. The Self-Fulfilling Prophecy of Ghetto Education," *Harvard Education Review* 40, no. 3 (1970), pp. 411–51.

23. Jeannie Oakes, "Two Cities' Tracking and Within-School Segregation," *Teachers College Record* 96, no. 4 (summer 1995), pp. 681–90.

24. Jeannie Oakes and Martin Lipton, "Detracking Schools: Early Lessons from the Field," *Phi Delta Kappan* 73, no. 6 (February 1992), pp. 448–54.

25. James Rosenbaum, "If Tracking Is Bad, Is Detracking Better?", *American Educator.* Washington, DC: American Federation of Teachers (winter 1999–2000), pp. 24–29, 47.

26. Samuel Lucas, *Tracking Inequality: Stratification and Mobility in American High Schools* (New York: Teachers College Press, 1999).

27. Rebecca Gordon and Libero Della Piana, *Testing, Tracking, and Students of Color in U.S. Public Schools* (Oakland, CA: Applied Research Center, 1999).

28. Jeannie Oakes, *Multiplying Inequalities: The Effects of Race, Social Class, and Tracking on Opportunities to Learn Mathematics and Sciences* (Santa Monica, CA: RAND, 1990), (ED329615).

29. Carol Ascher, "Successful Detracking in Middle and Senior High Schools," *ERIC/CUE Digest* 82 (New York: ERIC Clearinghouse on Urban Education, October 10, 1992). (ED351426); Gary Burnett, "Alternatives to Ability Grouping: Still Unanswered Questions," *ERIC/CUE Digest* 111 (New York: ERIC Clearinghouse on Urban Education, December 1995), (ED390947).

30. Quoted in "Tracking," *Education Week on the Web,* October 14, 1998; see also Susan Allan, "Ability Grouping Research Reviews: What Do They Say About Grouping and the Gifted?" *Educational Leadership* 48, no. 6 (March 1991), pp. 60–65; Adam Gamoran, "Alternative Use of Ability Grouping in Secondary Schools: Can We Bring High-Quality Instruction to Low-Ability Classes?" *American Journal of Education* 102 (1993), pp. 1–22; Robert E. Slavin, "Achievement Effects of Ability Grouping in Secondary Schools: A Best-Evidence Synthesis," *Review of Educational Research* 60 (1990), pp. 471–99.

31. Quoted in Raphaela Best, *We've All Got Scars* (Bloomington: Indiana University Press, 1983), p. 9.

32. Ibid., p. 10.

33. Ibid., p. 162.

34. Steven Sher, "Some Kids Are Nobody's Best Friend," *Today's Education,* 71 no. 1. (February/March 1982), pp. 23–29.

35. "Unpopular Children," *The Harvard Education Letter,* Harvard Graduate School of Education in association with Harvard University Press, January/February 1989, pp. 1–3. See also Lisa Wolcott, "Relationships: The Fourth 'R,'" *Teacher* (April 1991), pp. 26–27.

36. Quoted from a student letter in the *Arlingtonian,* May 13, 1993.

37. Zappa, Coleman, Friedenberg, Vonnegut, and Ford are quoted in Ralph Keyes, *Is There Life After High School?* (Boston: Little, Brown, 1976).

38. James Coleman, *The Adolescent Society* (New York: Free Press, 1961).

39. Goodlad, *A Place Called School.*

40. Quoted in Boyer, *High School,* p. 202.

41. Ibid., p. 206.

42. Sara Lawrence Lightfoot, *The Good High School* (New York: Basic Books, 1983).

43. David Owen, *High School* (New York: Viking Press, 1981).

44. Keyes, *Is There Life After High School?*

45. Lloyd Temme, quoted in Keyes, *Is There Life After High School?*

46. Mel Brooks and Dustin Hoffman are quoted in Keyes, *Is There Life After High School?*

47. Quoted in Boyer, *High School.*

48. Patricia Hersch, *A Tribe Apart: A Journey Into the Heart of American Adolescence* (New York: Random House, 1999).

49. The Metropolitan Life Survey of the American Teacher 2000. *Are We Preparing Students for the 21st Century?* (New York: Harris Interactive, Inc., 2000).

50. *The Metropolitan Life Survey of the American Teacher, 1984–1995: Old Problems, New Challenges* (New York: Louis Harris and Associates, 1995).

51. Quoted in Ernest L. Boyer, "What Teachers Say About Children in America," *Educational Leadership* 46, no. 8 (May 1989), p. 73.

52. Ibid.

53. Ibid., p. 74.

54. Frances Ianni, "Providing a Structure for Adolescent Development," *Phi Delta Kappan* 70, no. 9 (May 1989), p. 677.

55. Patrick Welsh, *Tales Out of School* (New York: Viking, 1986), pp. 41–42.

56. Urie Bronfenbrenner, "Alienation and the Four Worlds of Childhood," *Phi Delta Kappan* 67, no. 6 (February 1986), pp. 430–35.

57. Lightfoot, *The Good High School.*

58. Quoted in Ianni, "Providing a Structure for Adolescent Development," p. 680.

59. Grace Pung Guthrie and Larry Guthrie, "Streamlining Interagency Collaboration for Youth At Risk," *Educational Leadership* 49, no. 1 (September 1991), pp. 17–22.

60. Alfie Kohn, "Caring Kids: The Role of Schools," *Phi Delta Kappan* 72, no. 7 (March 1991), pp. 496–506.

61. Carnegie Council on Adolescent Development, *Turning Points: Preparing American Youth for the 21st Century,* excerpted in "The American Adolescent: Facing a Vortex of New Risks," *Education Week,* June 21, 1989, p. 22.

62. Ibid.

63. Edward A. Wynne, "Looking at Schools," *Phi Delta Kappan* 62, no. 5 (January 1981), pp. 377–81.

64. George Weber, *Inner-City Children Can Be Taught to Read: Four Successful Schools* (Washington, DC: D.C. Council for Basic Books, 1971).

65. Ronald Edmonds, "Some Schools Work and More Can," *Social Policy* 9 (1979), pp. 28–32.

66. Barbara Taylor and Daniel Levine, "Effective Schools Projects and School-Based Management," *Phi Delta Kappan* 72, no. 5 (January 1991), pp. 394–97. See also Herman Meyers, "Roots, Trees, and the Forest: An Effective Schools Development Sequence." Paper delivered at the American Educational Research Association, San Francisco, April 1992.

67. Lightfoot, *The Good High School.*

68. Ibid., p. 67.

69. David Clark, Linda Lotto, and Mary McCarthy, "Factors Associated with Success in Urban Elementary Schools," *Phi Delta Kappan* 61, no. 7 (March 1980), pp. 467–70. See also David Gordon, "The Symbolic Dimension of Administration for Effective Schools." Paper delivered at the American Educational Research Association, San Francisco, April 1992.

70. William Rutherford, "School Principals as Effective Leaders," *Phi Delta Kappan* 67, no. 1 (September 1985), pp. 31–34. See also R. McClure, "Stages and Phases of School-Based Renewal Efforts." Paper presented at the

annual meeting of the American Educational Research Association, New Orleans, 1988.

71. *The Metropolitan Life Survey of the American Teacher 1999* (New York: Harris Interactive, Inc., 1999), p. 69.

72. Lowell C. Rose and Alec M. Gallup, "The 30th Annual Gallup Poll of the Public's Attitudes Toward the Public Schools," *Phi Delta Kappan* 80, no. 1 (September 1998), pp. 41–56.

73. Lightfoot, *The Good High School;* Kevin Dwyer and D. Osher, *Safeguarding Our Children: An Action Guide* (Washington, DC: U.S. Department of Education, August 2000).

74. Wilbur Brookover, Laurence Beamer, Helen Efthim, Douglas Hathaway, Lawrence Lezotte, Stephen Miller, Joseph Passalacqua, and Louis Tornatzky, *Creating Effective Schools* (Holmes Beach, FL: Learning Publications, 1982).

75. Herbert Walberg, Rosanne Paschal, and Thomas Weinstein, "Homework's Powerful Effects on Learning," *Educational Leadership* 42 (1985), pp. 76–79.

76. Robert Rosenthal and Lenore Jacobson, *Pygmalion in the Classroom* (New York: Holt, Rinehart & Winston, 1968).

77. Patrick Proctor, "Teacher Expectations: A Model for School Improvement," *Elementary School Journal* (March 1984), pp. 469–81; William Wayson, "The Politics of Violence in Schools: Double Speak and Disruptions in Public Confidence," *Phi Delta Kappan* 67, no. 2 (October 1985), pp. 127–32.

78. Larry Cuban, "Effective Schools: A Friendly but Cautionary Note," *Phi Delta Kappan* 64, no. 10 (June 1983), pp. 695–96; Daniel Levine, "Creating Effective Schools: Findings and Implications from Research and Practice," *Phi Delta Kappan* 72, no. 5 (January 1991), pp. 389–93.

79. Rebecca Jones, "What Works: Researchers Tell What Schools Must Do to Improve Student Achievement," *The American School Board Journal* 185, no. 4 (April 1998), pp. 28–32, 33; Mary Anne Raywid, "Synthesis of Research: Small Schools: A Reform That Works," *Educational Leadership* (December 1997/January 1998), pp. 34–39; Kenneth J. Cooper, "9 Schools Show How to Make the Grade," *The Washington Post,* January 13, 2000, p. A17.

CHAPTER 6 What Students Are Taught in School

1. Hilda Taba, *Curriculum Development: Theory and Practice* (New York: Harcourt Brace Jovanovich, 1962).

2. John Goodlad, *A Place Called School* (New York: McGraw-Hill, 1984).

3. National Center for Education Statistics, *The Condition of Education 1995.* Indicator 43, Extracurricular Activities (Washington, DC: U.S. Department of Education); Feminist Majority Foundation, *Empowering Women in Sports,* Washington, DC, 1995.

4. Allyce Holland and Thomas Andre, "Participation in Extracurricular Activities in Secondary School: What Is Known, What Needs to Be Known," *Review of Educational Research* 57, no. 4 (winter 1987), pp. 437–66.

5. National Center for Education Statistics, *Trends Among High School Seniors, 1972–1992* (Washington, DC: U.S.

Department of Education, 1995); American Association of University Women, *Gender Gaps: Where Schools Still Fail Our Children, (*Washington, DC: AAUW, 1998).

6. B. Bradford Brown, "The Vital Agenda for Research on Extracurricular Influences: A Reply to Holland and Andre," *Review of Educational Research* 58, no. 1 (spring 1988), pp. 107–11.

7. National Association of Secondary School Principals, *The Mood of American Youth* (Reston, VA: National Association of Secondary School Principals, 1984).

8. Data from *High School and Beyond* reported in "Extracurricular Activity Participants Outperform Other Students," *OERI Bulletin* (September 1986), p. 2.

9. Stephen Hamilton, "Synthesis of Research on the Social Side of Schooling," *Educational Leadership* 40, no. 5 (February 1983), pp. 65–72.

10. Jerome Bruner, *The Process of Education* (Cambridge, MA: Harvard University Press, 1960).

11. Donald Irish, "Death Education: Preparation for Living," in Betty Green and Donald Irish (eds.), *Death Education: Preparation for Living* (Cambridge, MA: Schenkman, 1971), pp. 45–68.

12. Ben Brodinsky, "Back to the Basics: The Movement and Its Meaning," *Phi Delta Kappan* 58, no. 7 (March 1977), pp. 522–27.

13. George Gallup, "Gallup Poll of the Public's Attitudes Toward the Public Schools," *Phi Delta Kappan* 64, no. 1 (September 1982), p. 39.

14. Philip Cusick, *The Egalitarian Ideal and the American High School* (New York: Longman, 1983).

15. Sara Lawrence Lightfoot, *The Good High School* (New York: Basic Books, 1983).

16. Ernest L. Boyer, *High School: A Report on Secondary Education in America,* The Carnegie Foundation for the Advancement of Teaching (New York: Harper & Row, 1983).

17. Goodlad, *A Place Called School,* p. 298.

18. Theodore Sizer, *Horace's Compromise: The Dilemma of the American High School* (Boston: Houghton Mifflin, 1984), p. 89.

19. Mortimer Adler, "The Paideia Proposal," *The Rotation,* September 1982.

20. E. D. Hirsch, Jr., *Cultural Literacy* (Boston: Houghton Mifflin, 1987).

21. E. D. Hirsch, Jr., "Cultural Literacy: Let's Get Specific," *NEA Today,* (January 1988), p. 18.

22. Jay Matthews, "Adult Illiteracy, Rewritten," *The Washington Post,* July 17, 2001, p. A9.

23. Carla Haymesfeld, "Filling the Hole in Whole Language," *Educational Leadership* 46, no. 6 (March 1989), pp. 65–68. James Collins, "How Johnny Should Read," *Time,* October 27, 1997, pp. 78–81.

24. Ibid; Collins, "How Johnny Should Read," pp. 78–81.

25. Mary Jordan, "Snapshot of Student Writing Finds Care Absent," *The Washington Post,* April 17, 1992, p. A-3.

26. Sandra Stotsky, "Whose Literature? America's!" *Educational Leadership* 49, no. 4 (December 1991/January 1992), pp. 53–56.

27. California Department of Education, *Recommended Literature: Kindergarten Through Grade Twelve* (July 15, 2001). www.cde.ca.gov/ci/literature.

28. David Barton, "Classic Debate!" *Sacramento Bee,* April 3, 1998, p. SC-1.

29. Philip Cohen, "Challenging History: The Past Remains a Battleground for Schools," *Association for Supervision and Curriculum Development Curriculum Update* (winter 1995), p. 2.

30. National Center for Educational Statistics, *National Center for Educational Progress: Civics,* 1998 National Test Questions and Performance Results. (Washington, DC: US Department of Education). nces.ed.gov/nationsreportcard/itmrls/ITMRLS.HTM.

31. John Fonte and Andre Ryerson (eds.), *Education for America's Role in World Affairs* (Lanham, MD: University Press of America, 1994), p. 44.

32. Diane Ravitch and Chester Finn, Jr., *What Do Our 17-Year-Olds Know?* (New York: Harper & Row, 1987).

33. Jennifer Lee, "Helping Teachers Get on Top of the World," *The Washington Post,* August 15, 1988, p. C-3.

34. David J. Hoff, "Math Council Again Mulling Its Standards," *Education Week on the Web,* November 4, 1998.

35. National Council of Teachers of Mathematics, *Principles and Standards for School Mathematics: An Overview (2000).* www.nctm.org/standards/principles.htm.

36. Eugene Owen (comp.), *Trends in Academic Progress* (Washington, DC: National Center for Educational Statistics, 1991); National Center for Education Statistics, *National Center for Educational Progress: 1996 Trends in Academic Progress* (Washington, DC: U.S. Department of Education, August 1997).

37. Ethan Bronner, "U.S. Trails the World in Math and Science," *New York Times,* February 25, 1998, p. 10.

38. National Council of Teachers of Mathematics, *Principles and Standards for School Mathematics: An Overview* (2000). www.nctm.org/standards/principles.htm.

39. National Research Council, *National Science Education Standards* (1996). www.books.nap.edu/html/nses/html/index.html.

40. National Center for Educational Statistics, National Assessment of Educational Progress, *Science Education Report Card* (1996). http://nces.ed.gov/nationsreportcard/science.

41. Annette Licitra, "Kids Start Strong in Science but Few Show Advanced Skills," *Education Daily,* March 26, 1992, p. 1; see also Owen (comp.), *Trends in Academic Progress.*

42. Steve Olson, "Science FRICTION." *Education Week on the Web,* September 30, 1998.

43. American Association for the Advancement of Science (AAAS), *Blueprints of Reform,* (Washington, DC, June 1998).

44. Steve Olson, "Science FRICTION."

45. Hugh McIntosh, "What Should Students Know? How Should Teachers Teach?" *National Research Council News Report* 43, no. 1 (winter 1993), pp. 2–6; Project 2061 (American Association for the Advancement of Science), *Benchmarks for Science Literacy* (New York: Oxford University Press, 1993).

46. National Center for Educational Statistics, *The Condition of Education 2001.* Indicator 35, Section 4, Quality of Elementary and Secondary School Environments. (Washington, DC: U.S. Department of Education), p. 61.

47. Sara Melendy, "A Nation of Monolinguals, a Multilingual World," *NEA Today* (January 1989), pp. 70–74.

48. Education Vital Signs, "Common Measures," *American School Board Journal Supplement* (December 1997).

49. National Center for Educational Statistics, *Internet Access in U.S. Public Schools and Classrooms: 1994–2000* (Washington, DC: U.S. Department of Education, May 2001). http://nces.ed.gov/pubs2001/internetaccess/2.asp.

50. Richard W. Riley, "Education First: Building America's Future," *Fifth Annual State of America Education,* February 17, 1998.

51. *Education Week on the Web, Dividing Lines* 20, no. 35 (May 10, 2001), pp. 12–13.

52. National Center for Educational Statistics, *Safeguarding Your Technology: Practical Guidelines for Electronic Educational Information Security* 297 (1998). http://nces.ed.gov/pubs98/safetech/execsum.html; National Center for Educational Statistics Task Force, *Technology @ Your Fingertips: A Guide to Implementing Technology Solutions for Education Agencies and Institutions* (January 2001). http://nces.ed.gov/pubsearch/pubsinfo.asp?pubid=98293.

53. Barb Albert, "Study Says Computer Use Raises Test Scores," *Indianapolis Star,* 4 October 1998, p. B-1.

54. National Center for Educational Statistics, NAEP Facts, *Frequency of Arts Instruction for Students,* 4, no 3 (Washington, DC: U.S. Department of Education, December 1999). http://nces.ed.gov/pubs2000/2000510.pdf

55. Debra Viadero, "38-Member Panel Adopts 81 Standards for the Arts," *Education Week,* February 9, 1994, p. 5.

56. Jane Bonbright, "Special Report: National Assessment of Educational Progress in the Arts," *JOPERD* 69, no. 8 (October 1998), pp. 28–33.

57. National Center for Health Statistics, National Health and Nutrition Examination Survey, *Prevalence of Overweight among Children and Adolescents: United States* (1999). www.cdc.gov/nchs/products/pubs/pubd/hestats/overwght99.htm.

58. National Association for Sport and Physical Education, *Shape of the Nation Report* (Reston, VA: National Association for Sport and Physical Education, 1997).

59. Ibid.

60. President's Council on Physical Fitness and Sports, *Research Digest* 3, no. 13 (March 2001), p. 9 www.fitness.gov/digest301.pdf.

61. "Issues: Should physical education classes return to teaching males and females separately?" *JOPERD* 70, no. 1 (January 1999), pp. 11–13; Linda Jean Carpenter and R. Vivian Costa, "Courtside: Coed Physical Education and the Law," *Strategies* 14, no. 6 (July/August 2001), pp. 5–8.

62. *Gender Gaps: Where Schools Still Fail Our Children* (Washington, DC: Commissioned by the American Association of University Women, 1998); President's Council on Physical Fitness and Sports, *Research Digest* 3, no. 13 (March 2001). www.fitness.gov/digest301.pdf.

63. National Center for Chronic Disease Prevention and Health Promotion, Comprehensive School Health Education, *School Health Policies and Program Study:*

Project Summary (2000). www.cdc.gov/nccdphp/dash/cshedef.htm.

64. Richard W. Riley and Donna E. Shalala, "Joint Statement of the Secretaries of Education and Health and Human Services," *Journal of School Health* 64, no. 4 (April 7, 1994), p. 136.

65. U.S. Newswire, *Highest-Ever Support for Sex Education* (June 2, 1999), www.feminist.org/news/newsbyte/newsnow.html.

66. National Center for Educational Statistics, *The Condition of Education 2001*. Indicator 35, Section 4, Quality of Elementary and Secondary School Environments (Washington, DC: U.S. Department of Education), p. 62.

67. John G. Wirt, "A New Federal Law on Vocational Education: Will Reform Follow?" *Phi Delta Kappan* 72, no. 6 (February 1991), pp. 425–33.

68. National Coalition for Women and Girls in Education, *Invisible Again: The Impact of Changes in Federal Funding on Vocational Programs for Women and Girls* (A Report from National Coalition for Women and Girls in Education, Washington, DC: October 2001).

69. T. Schmidt, *Inside the State House: The People and Ideas that Shaped School to Career Legislation,* National Conference of State Legislatures (2001); P. Hudis, *Making Schools Career-Focused: Final Report,* (US Department of Education, March 1, 2001). www.stw.ed.gov/products/download/3007.pdf.

70. Louis Raths, Selma Wasserman, Arthur Jones, and Arnold Rothstein, *Teaching for Thinking: Theory and Application* (Columbus, OH: Merrill, 1966.) See also Selma Wasserman, "Teaching for Thinking: Louis E. Raths Revisited," *Phi Delta Kappan* 68, no. 6 (February 1987), pp. 460–66.

71. Summaries of these approaches are found in Barbara Presseisen, *Thinking Skills: Research and Practice* (Washington, DC: National Education Association, 1986). See also R. Feuerstein, *Instrumental Enrichment An Intervention Program for Cognitive Modifiability* (Baltimore: University Park Press, 1980); A. H. Schoenfeld, "Measures of Problem-Solving Instruction," *Journal for Research in Mathematics Education* 13 (1962); E. de Bono, "The Cognitive Research Trust (CORT) Thinking Program," in W. Maxwell (ed.), *Thinking: The Expanding Frontier* (Hillsdale, NJ: Erlbaum, 1983); Joseph Hester, *Teaching for Thinking: A Program for School Improvement Through Teaching Critical Thinking Across the Curriculum* (Durham, NC: Carolina Academic Press, 1994), pp. 1–23.

72. J. Wink, *Critical Pedagogy: Notes from the Real World* (New York: Addison Wesley Longman, 1999), pp. 28–45.

73. Robert Slavin, "PET and the Pendulum: Faddism in Education and How to Stop It," *Phi Delta Kappan* 70, no. 6 (June 1989), p. 752.

CHAPTER 7 Controversy over Who Controls the Curriculum

1. Paul Barry, "Interview: A Talk with A. Bartlett Giamatti," *College Review Board* (spring 1982), p. 48.

2. John Merrow, "Undermining Standards," *Phi Delta Kappan* 82, no. 9 (May 2001), pp. 653–59.

3. John Elson, "History, the Sequel," *Time,* 7 November 1994, p. 53; see also Von Wiener, "History Lesson," *The New Republic,* January 2, 1995, pp. 9–11.

4. Joel Spring, *American Education* (New York: McGraw-Hill, 1996), pp. 237–41.

5. Lyn Nell Hancock with Nina Archer Biddle, "Red, White—and Blue," *Newsweek,* November 7, 1994, p. 54.

6. Christopher T. Cross, "The Standards Wars: Some Lessons Learned," *Education Week on the Web,* October 21, 1998, pp. 1–4.

7. "Seeking Stability for Standards Based Education," *Education Week on the Web,* Quality Counts 2001 Survey in 2001 Editorial Projects in Education 20, no. 17 (January 11, 2001), pp. 8, 9.

8. Merrow, "Undermining Standards," p. 655.

9. Kate Zernike, "Scarsdale Mothers Succeed in First Boycott of 8th-Grade Test," *New York Times on the Web,* May 4, 2001.

10. Michael A. Fletcher, "High Stakes Rise, School Group Put Exam to Test," *The Washington Post,* July 9, 2001, p. A1; "Seeking Stability for Standards Based Education," *Education Week on the Web.*

11. Linda McNeil, "Creating New Inequities: Contradictions of Reform," *Phi Delta Kappan* 81, no. 10, (June 2000), pp. 729–34.

12. Kathleen Kennedy Manzo, "Protests Over State Testing Widespread," *Education Week on the Web,* May 16, 2001.

13. Abby Goodnough, "Strains of Fourth-Grade Tests Drive Off Veteran Teachers," *New York Times on the Web,* June 14, 2001; Liz Seymour, "SOL Tests Create New Dropouts," *The Washington Post,* July 17, 2001, pp. A1, A8.

14. Diana B. Henriques and Jacques Steinberg, "Right Answer, Wrong Score: Test Flaws Take Toll," *New York Times on the Web,* May 20, 2001.

15. David Stratman, *New Democracy on the Web,* May 19, 2001.

16. Edward B. Fiske, *Smart Schools, Smart Kids: Why Do Some Schools Work?* (New York: Simon & Schuster, 1991), p. 122.

17. Ibid., p. 122.

18. Carin Rubenstein, "Surviving the Dreaded Kindergarten Exam," *Working Mother,* August 1989, p. 76.

19. Ibid., p. 75.

20. Grant Wiggins, "Teaching to the (Authentic) Test," *Educational Leadership* 46, no. 7 (April 1989), pp. 41–47. See also Rieneke Zessoules and Howard Gardner, "Authentic Assessment: Beyond the Buzzword and into the Classroom," in Vito Perrone (ed.) *Expanding Student Assessment* (Alexandria, VA: Association for Supervision and Curriculum Development, 1991).

21. Gene I. Maeroff, "Assessing Alternative Assessment," *Phi Delta Kappan* 73, no. 4 (December 1991), pp. 272–81.

22. Theodore Sizer, *Horace's School: Redesigning the American High School* (New York: Houghton Mifflin, 1992).

23. Rebecca Jones, "Textbook Troubles," *American School Board Journal,* December 2000, pp. 18–21.

24. Harriet Tyson Bernstein, *A Conspiracy of Good Intentions: America's Textbook Fiasco* (Washington, DC: The Council for Basic Education, 1988), p. 2.

25. Ibid., p. 20.

26. Rodger Farr and Michael Tulley, "Do Adoption Committees Perpetuate Mediocre Textbooks?" *Phi Delta Kappan* 66, no. 7 (March 1985), pp. 467–71.

27. Bonnie Ambruster, Jean Osborn, and Alice Davison, "Readability Formulas May Be Dangerous to Your Textbooks," *Educational Leadership* 42, no. 7 (April 1985), pp. 18–20.

28. Susan Ohanian, "Ruffles and Flourishes," *Atlantic Monthly,* September 1987, pp. 20–22.

29. Quoted in Bernstein, *A Conspiracy of Good Intentions,* p. 19.

30. Quoted in David Elliott, Kathleen Carter Nagel, and Arthur Woodward, "Do Textbooks Belong in Elementary School Studies?" *Educational Leadership* 42, no. 7 (April 1985), pp. 21–25; see also Rebecca Jones, "Textbook Troubles," *American School Board Journal,* V187 (December 2000).

31. Connie Muther, "What Every Textbook Evaluator Should Know," *Educational Leadership* 42, no. 7 (April 1985), p. 48.

32. Jean Osborn, Beau Fly Jones, and Marcy Stein, "The Case for Improving Textbooks," *Educational Leadership* 42, no. 7 (April 1985), pp. 9–16; see also Michael Apple, "Regulating the Text: The Social Historical Roots of State Control." Paper delivered at the American Educational Research Association, San Francisco, April 1992.

33. Howard Lyon, "Buyer Beware: Why We Must Hold Publishers Accountable for Textbook Mistakes," *American School Board Journal,* December 2000, pp. 22–24.

34. "Not Crystal Clear: Mistakes in Science Texts," *The Washington Post,* January 30, 2001, p. 11.

35. Rebecca Jones, "What Works: Researchers Tell What Schools Must Do to Improve Student Achievement," *American School Board Journal* 185, no. 4 (April 1998), pp. 32–33.

36. Eliot Eisner, "Should America Have a National Curriculum?" *Educational Leadership* 49, no. 4 (October 1991), pp. 76–81.

37. Michael Apple, "Curriculum in the Year 2000: Tensions and Possibilities," *Phi Delta Kappan* 64, no. 5 (January 1983), p. 323.

38. The forms of bias were developed by Myra Sadker and David Sadker for Title IX equity workshops.

39. Bernstein, *A Conspiracy of Good Intentions,* pp. 35–36.

40. Quoted in Edward B. Jenkinson, "The Significance of the Decision in 'Scopes II,'" *Phi Delta Kappan* 68, no. 6 (February 1987), p. 446.

41. Frances Goodrich and Albert Hackett, *The Diary of Anne Frank, In Great Waves Breaking,* Bernard J. Weiss (ed.) (New York: Holt, Rinehart & Winston, 1983), p. 387.

42. Transcripts of proceedings in *Mozert,* July 14, 1986, p. 24, as quoted in Jenkinson, *Scopes II.*

43. Robert Marzano and David Arredondo, *Tactics for Thinking—Teacher's Manual* (Alexandria, VA: Association for Supervision and Curriculum Development, 1986), p. 11; quoted in Edward Jenkinson, "The New Age of Schoolbook Protest," *Phi Delta Kappan* 10, no.1 (September 1988), p. 66.

44. Thomas McDaniel, "On Trial: The Right to Think," *Educational Leadership* 49, no. 4 (December 1991/January 1992), p. 85.

45. Perry Glanzer, "Religion in Public Schools," *Phi Delta Kappan* 80, no. 3 (October 1998), p. 220.

46. Craig Timberg, "Bible's Second Coming," *The Washington Post,* June 4, 2000, p. A1.

47. "Public School Drops Christian Textbooks," *The Washington Post,* September 17, 1999, p. 2.

48. Anthony Podesta, "For Full Discussion of Religion in the Schools," *The Wall Street Journal,* November 12, 1986, p. 32. See also Perry Glanzer, "Religion in Public Schools: In Search of Fairness," *Phi Delta Kappan* 80, no. 3 (November 1998), pp. 219–22.

49. "Religion in Class: More Needed, Report Says," *The Washington Post,* December 5, 2000, p. A-22.

50. Debra Viadero, "Christian Movement Seen Trying to Influence Schools," *Education Week,* April 15, 1992, p. 8.

51. Liz Leyden, "Story Hour Didn't Have a Happy Ending," *The Washington Post,* December 3, 1998, A3.

52. L. Adler, *Curriculum Challenges in California: Third statewide survey of challenges to curriculum materials and services* (Fullerton: California State University, ERIC Document Reproduction Service, 1993), (No. 375 475).

53. Myra Sadker and David Sadker, *Now upon a Time: A Contemporary View of Children's Literature* (New York: Harper & Row, 1977).

54. "Banned Books Week: Celebrate the Freedom To Read," American Library Association on the Web, March 30, 2000.

55. Suzanne Fisher Staples, "Why Johnny Can't Read: Censorship in American Libraries," *Digital Library and Archives,* Virginia Tech University on the Web (winter 1996).

56. *Attacks on the Freedom to Learn,* People for the American Way, 1995–1996 report.

57. "Ten Most Challenged Books in 2000," Office for Intellectual Freedom, American Library Association on the Web, 2001.

58. Kathleen Kennedy Manzo, "Despite Flap, Seattle to Keep Grant for Books About Homosexuality," *Education Week on the Web,* May 28, 1997.

59. Quoted in Lynne Cheney, *Humanities in America: A Report to the President, Congress and the American People* (Washington, DC: National Endowment for the Humanities, 1988), p. 17.

60. Quoted in William Bennett, *American Education: Making It Work* (Washington, DC: U.S. Department of Education, 1988).

61. Allan Bloom, *The Closing of the American Mind* (New York: Simon & Schuster, 1987), p. 63.

62. E. D. Hirsch, Jr., *What Your First Grader Needs to Know,* and *What Your Second Grader Needs to Know* (New York: Doubleday, 1991).

63. James Banks, "Multicultural Education: For Freedom's Sake," *Educational Leadership* 49, no. 4 (December 1991/January 1992), pp. 32–36.

64. Marge Scherer, "School Snapshot: Focus on African-American Culture," *Educational Leadership* 49, no. 4 (December 1991/January 1992), pp. 17–21.

65. Arthur Schlesinger, *The Disuniting of America,*(New York: Norton, 1992).

66. Michael Apple, "Curriculum in the Year 2000: Tensions and Possibilities," *Phi Delta Kappan* 64, no. 5 (January 1983), p. 323.

67. Abner Peddiwell (Harold Benjamin), *The Saber-Tooth Curriculum* (New York: McGraw-Hill, 1939).

CHAPTER 8 The History of American Education

1. Sheldon Cohen, *A History of Colonial Education, 1607–1776* (New York: Wiley, 1974).

2. Nathaniel Shurtlett, ed., *Records of the Governor and Company of the Massachusetts Bay in New England, II* (Boston: Order of the Legislature, 1853); see also H. Warren Button and Eugene F. Provenzo, Jr., *History of Education and Culture in America* (Englewood Cliffs, NJ: Prentice Hall, 1983).

3. James Hendricks, "Be Still and Know! Quaker Silence and Dissenting Educational Ideals, 1740–1812," *Journal of the Midwest History of Education Society,* Annual Proceedings, 1975; R. Freeman Butts and Lawrence A. Cremin, *A History of Education in American Culture* (New York: Holt, 1953).

4. Lawrence A. Cremin, *American Education: The Colonial Experience, 1607–1783* (New York: Harper & Row, 1970); see also Button and Provenzo, *History of Education and Culture in America.*

5. James C. Klotter, "The Black South and White Appalachia," *Journal of American History* (March 1980), pp. 832–49.

6. John H. Best, *Benjamin Franklin on Education* (New York: Teachers College Press, 1962).

7. Jonathon Messerli, *Horace Mann: A Biography* (New York: Alfred A. Knopf, 1972); Steven Tozer, Paul Violas, and Guy Senese, *School and Society* (Boston: McGraw-Hill, 1998).

8. Lawrence Cremin, *The Transformation of the School: Progressivism in American Education, 1876–1957* (New York: Alfred A. Knopf, 1961).

9. Jackie M. Blount, "Spinsters, Bachelors and Other Gender Transgressors in School Employment, 1850–1990," *Review of Educational Research* 70, no. 1, (spring 2000), pp. 83–101.

10. E. Marcus, *Making History: The Struggle for Gay and Lesbian Equal Rights, 1945–1990, An Oral History* (New York: Harper Collins Publishers, 1992).

11. Blount, "Spinsters, Bachelors and Other Gender Transgressors in School Employment, 1850–1990," p. 94.

12. Edward A. Krug, *The Shaping of the American High School, 1880–1920, I* (New York: Harper & Row, 1964); see also John D. Pulliam, *History of Education in America*, 4th ed. (Columbus, OH: Merrill, 1987); Joel Spring, *The American School, 1642–1985* (New York: Longman, 1986).

13. M. Lee Manning, "A Brief History of the Middle School," *The Clearing House* 73, no. 4, March–April 2000, p. 192.

14. National Education Association, *Report of the Committee on Secondary School Studies* (Washington, DC: U.S. Government Printing Office, 1893).

15. Gerald Grant, *The World We Created at Hamilton High* (Cambridge, MA: Harvard University Press, 1988).

16. Special thanks to Kate Volker for developing the Crandall and Ashton-Warner biographies.

CHAPTER 9 Philosophy of Education

1. William Bagley, "The Case for Essentialism in Education," *National Education Association Journal* 30, no. 7 (1941), pp. 202–20.

2. Robert M. Hutchins, *The Higher Learning in America* (New Haven, CT: Yale University Press, 1962), p. 78.

3. Mortimer Adler, *Reforming Education* (Boulder, CO: Westview Press, 1977), pp. 84–85.

4. John Dewey, *Experience and Education* (New York: Macmillan, 1963).

5. Larry Cuban, *How Teachers Taught*, 2nd edition (New York: Teachers College Press, 1993).

6. Paulo Freire, *Pedagogy of the Oppressed* (New York: Continuum Press, 1989).

7. Maxine Greene, *Landscapes of Learning* (New York: Teachers College Press, 1978); See also Maxine Greene, " Reflections on Teacher as Stranger" in C. Kridel (ed.) *Books of the Century Catalog* (Columbia, SC: University of South Carolina, Museum of Education, 2000).

8. Lee Canter, "Assertive Discipline: More Than Names on a Board and Marbles in a Jar," *Phi Delta Kappan,* 71, 1989, pp. 57–61.

9. Timothy Reagan, *Non-Western Educational Traditions: Alternative Approaches to Educational Thought and Practice* (Mahwah, NJ: Lawrence Earlbaum Associates, 1996).

10. *Aristotle, Politics*, trans. and intro. by T. A. Sinclair (Middlesex, England: Penguin, 1978).

CHAPTER 10 Financing and Governing America's Schools

1. Mark G. Yudof, David L. Kip, Betsy Levin, *Educational Policy and the Law,* 3rd ed. (St. Paul: West, 1992), p. 658; Betsy Levin, Thomas Muller, and Corazon Sandoval, *The High Cost of Education in Cities* (Washington, DC: The Urban Institute, 1973).

2. Barry Siegel, "Parents Get a Lesson in Equality," *Los Angeles Times* (Washington edition), April 13, 1992, pp. A-1, A-18–A-19.

3. *Robinson v. Cahill*, 69 N.J. 133 (1973); *Abbott v. Burke*, 119 N.J. 287 (1990) (known as *Abbott I*); *Abbott v. Burke*, 153 N. J. 480 (1998) (known *as Abbott V*).

4. Peter Enrich, "Leaving Equality Behind: New Directions in School Finance Reform," *Vanderbilt Law Review* 48(1995), pp. 101–194; for a description of this movement to adequacy arguments, visit http://nces.ed.gov/edfin/litigation/Contents.asp.

5. For a discussion of the impact in Wisconsin, see Daniel W. Hildebrand, "2000 Significant Court Decisions," *Wisconsin Lawyer* 74, no. 6 (June 2001). Similar analyses are available in other such law updates.

6. W. E. Thro, "The Third Wave: The Impact of the Montana, Kentucky and Texas Decisions on the Future of Public School Finance Reform Litigation," *Journal of Law and Education* 199, no. 2 (spring 1990), pp. 219–50; Robert F. McNergney and Joanne M. Herbert, *Foundations*

of Education: The Challenge of Professional Practice (Boston: Allyn & Bacon, 1995), pp. 475–78; Chris Pipho, "Stateline: The Scent of the Future," *Phi Delta Kappan* 76 (September 1994), pp. 10–11.

7. *Cited in Campaign for Fiscal Equality v. New York,* 86 N.Y. 2d 307 (1995); see also Bess Keller, "School Finance Case Draws to Close in N.Y.," *Education Week,* August 2, 2000.

8. Thomas Toch, "Separate but Not Equal," *Agenda* 1 (spring 1991), pp. 15–17.

9. Peter Keating, "How to Keep Your State and Local Taxes Down," *Money* 24, no. 1 (January 1995), pp. 86–92.

10. Bill Norris, "Losing Ticket in Lotteries," *Times Educational Supplement,* March 19, 1993, p. 17.

11. Joetta L. Sack, "Priorities Emerging for ESEA Reauthorization," *Education Week on the Web,* September 30, 1998; Anne C. Lewis, "Washington Report: House Democrats Criticize (in Unison) the Education Block Grant: Republicans Sing a Different Tune," *Phi Delta Kappan* 65, no. 6 (February 1984), pp. 379–80.

12. Jay Matthews, "More Public Schools Using Private Dollars," *The Washington Post,* August 28, 1995, pp. A-1, A-8; Justin Blum, "PTAs Give Some D.C. Schools an Edge," *The Washington Post,* April 17, 2000, p. B1; Nancy Trejos, "Schools Turning to No-Fuss Fundraising Online," *The Washington Post,* May 23, 2000, p. A1.

13. Anne Lewis, "Washington Seen: Buildings in Disrepair," *Education Digest* 60, no. 8 (April 1995); p. 71; Jacques Steinberg and John Sullivan, "In Disrepair for Years, Many Schools Pose a Risk," *New York Times,* February 2, 1998, p. A-21; "Educator's Wish List: Infrastructure Tops High-Tech," *The Washington Post,* October 24, 2000, p. A-13; "Fast Response Survey System, Survey on the Conditions of Public School Facilities," U.S. Department of Education, National Center for Education Statistics, Washington, DC, 1999.

14. For an insightful discussion of school boards, see Joel Spring, *American Education* (New York: McGraw-Hill, 2002), pp. 178–82.

15. Chester Finn, "Reinventing Local Control," in Patricia First and Herbert Walberg (eds.), *School Boards: Changing Local Control* (Berkeley: McCutchan, 1992); Emily Feistritzer, "A Profile of School Board Presidents," in *School Boards: Changing Local Control;* Neal Pierce, "School Boards Get Failing Grades, in Both the Cities and the Suburbs," *Philadelphia Inquirer,* April 27, 1992, p. 11; Mary Jordan, "School Boards Need Overhaul, Educators Say," *The Washington Post,* April 5, 1992, p. A-51.

16. Maria Newman, "These Days, Uneasy Lies the Head That Runs the Suburban School System," *New York Times,* May 12, 1998, p. A-21.

17. Cited in Joel Spring, *American Education* (New York: McGraw Hill, 2002), pp. 180–81.

18. Jay Mathews, "Nontraditional Thinking in Central Office," The School Administrator Web Edition, *The Washington Post,* June 2001; Tamar Lewin, "Leaders from Other Professions Reshape America's Schools, from Top to Bottom," *New York Times,* June 8, 2000; Nancy Mitchell, "Nontraditional School Bosses," *Denver Rocky Mountain News,* April 16, 2001.

19. Joanna Richardson, "Contracts Put Superintendents to Performance Test," *Education Week,* September 14, 1994, pp. 1, 12.

20. Vincent L. Ferrandino, "Challenges for 21st-Century Elementary School Principals," *Phi Delta Kappan* 82, no. 6 (February 2001), pp. 440–42; Linda Borg, "The Principal Dilemma Facing Schools in R.I.," *The Providence Journal,* projo.com/education (August 26, 2001).

21. "Seeing the Big Picture" in Education Vital Signs, *American School Board Journal,* December 1999.

22. Ferrandino, "Challenges for 21st-Century Elementary School Principals."

23. James G. Cibula, "Two Eras of Urban Schooling: The Decline of Law and Order and the Emergence of New Organizational Forms," *Education and Urban Society,* 29, no. 3 (May 1997), pp. 317–41.

24. Quoted in "Building Better Business Alliances," *Instructor* (winter 1986); (special issue), p. 21; see also Brian Dumaine, "Making Education Work," *Fortune,* spring 1990 (special issue), pp. 12–22.

25. Thomas Hatch, "How Community Action Contributes to Achievement," *Educational Leadership* 55, no. 8 (May 1998), pp. 16–19; Ron Lewis and John Morris, "Communities for Children," *Educational Leadership* 55, no. 8 (May 1998), pp. 34–36; Frank E. Nardine and Robert D. Morris, "Parent Involvement in the States," *Phi Delta Kappan* 72, no. 5 (January 1991), p. 365; Meg Sommerfeld, "National Commitment to Parent Role in School Sought," *Education Week,* April 15, 1992, p. 1;. See also Don Davies, "Schools Reaching Out: Family, School, and Community Partnerships for Student Success," *Phi Delta Kappan* 72, no. 5 (January 1991).

26. See Marianne Perle and David Baker, *Job Satisfaction Among America's Teachers: Effects of Workplace Conditions, Background Characteristics, and Teacher Compensation* (Washington, DC: National Center for Education Statistics, U.S. Department of Health, Education and Welfare, August 1997), pp. 41–42; See also John Lane and Edgar Epps (eds.), *Restructuring the Schools: Problems and Prospects* (Berkeley: McCutchan, 1992); Jeff Archer, "New Roles Tap Expertise of Teachers," *Education Week,* May 30, 2001.

27. Ann Bradley and Lynn Olson, "The Balance of Power: Shifting the Lines of Authority in an Effort to Improve Schools," *Education Week,* February 24, 1993, p. 10.

28. Fern Shen, "New Strategy for School Management," *The Washington Post,* February 17, 1998, pp. B-1, B-7.

29. Ann Bradley and Lynn Olson, "The Balance of Power."

30. For a good overview of school consolidation, see Karen Irmsher, "School Size." *ERIC Digest,* no. 113 (Eugene, OR: ERIC Clearinghouse on Educational Management, July 1997) (ED414615).

31. Catherine Gewertz, "The Breakup: Suburbs Try Smaller High Schools," *Education Week on the Web,* May 2, 2001; Craig Howley and Marty Strange and Robert Bickel, "Research about School Size and School Performance in Impoverished Communities," (Charleston, WV: ERIC Clearinghouse on Rural Education and Small Schools, December 2000); William Ayers, Gerald Bracey, and Greg

Smith, "The Ultimate Education Reform? Make Schools Smaller," (Milwaukee: Center for Education Research, Analysis, and Innovation, University of Wisconsin-Milwaukee, December 14, 2000).

CHAPTER 11 School Law and Ethics

1. Julius Menacker and Ernest Pascarella, "How Aware Are Educators of Supreme Court Decisions That Affect Them?" *Phi Delta Kappan* 64, no. 6 (February 1983), pp. 424–26; Louis Fischer, David Schimmel, and Cynthia Kelly, *Teachers and the Law* (New York: Longman, 1999).

2. Louis Fischer and David Schimmel, *The Civil Rights of Teachers* (New York: Harper & Row, 1973).

3. The legal situations and interpretations included in this text are adapted from a variety of sources, including Myra Sadker and David Sadker, *Sex Equity Handbook for Schools* (New York: Longman, 1982); Fischer and Schimmel, *The Civil Rights of Teachers*, and *Your Legal Rights and Responsibilities: A Guide for Public School Students* (Washington, DC: U.S. Department of Health, Education and Welfare, n.d.); Fischer, Schimmel, and Kelly, *Teachers and the Law*; Michael LaMorte, *School Law: Cases and Concepts* (Needham Heights, MA: Allyn & Bacon, 1999).

4. Sadker and Sadker, *Sex Equity Handbook for Schools.*

5. *Gebser v. Lago Vista Independent School District* (96 U.S. 1866 (1998); Greg Henderson, "Court Says Compensatory Damages Available Under Title IX," UPI, February 26, 1992; *North Haven Board of Education v. Bell,* 456 U.S. 512 (1982); *Franklin v. Gwinnett County Schools,* 503 U.S. 60 (1992).

6. *Thompson v. Southwest School District,* 483 F. Supp. 1170 (W.D.M.W. 1980). See also *Board of Trustees v. Stubblefield,* 94 Cal. Rptr. 318, 321 [1971]; *Morrison v. State Board of Education,* 461 P. 2d 375 [1969]; *Pettit v. State Board of Education,* 513 P. 2nd 889 [Cal. 1973]; *Blodgett v. Board of Trustees, Tamalpais Union High School District,* 97 Cal. Rptr. 406 (1970); Fischer, Schimmel, and Kelly, *Teachers and the Law.*

7. *Kingsville Independent School District v. Cooper,* 611 F. 2d 1109 (5th Cir. 1980); *Parducci v. Rutland,* 316 F. Supp. 352 (M.D. Ala. 1979); *Brubaker v. Board of Education, School District 149, Cook County, Illinois,* 502 F. 2d 973 (7th Cir. 1974). See also Martha McCarthy and Nelda Cambron, *Public School Law: Teachers' and Students' Rights* (Boston: Allyn & Bacon, 1997).

8. *Pickering v. Board of Education of Township High School District 205, Will County,* 391 U.S. 563 (1968); *Givhan v. Western Line Consolidated School District,* 439 U.S. 410 (1979); Nathan L. Essex, *School Law and the Public Schools: A Practical Guide for School Leaders* (Boston: Allyn & Bacon, 1999).

9. *Basic Books v. Kinko's Graphics Corp.,* 758 F. Supp. 1522 (S.D.N.Y.1991); Miriam R. Krasno, "Copyright and You," *Update,* winter 1983; Thomas J. Flygare, "Photocopying and Videotaping for Educational Purposes: The Doctrine of Fair Use," *Phi Delta Kappan* 65, no. 8 (April 1984), pp. 568–69; Gary Becker, "Copyright in a Digital Age: How to Comply with the Law and Set a Good Example for Students," *American School Board Journal* 187, no. 6 (June

2000), pp. 26–27; Constance S. Hawke, *Computer and Internet Use on Campus: A Legal Guide to Issues of Intellectual Property, Free Speech, and Privacy* (San Francisco: Jossey-Bass, 2001).

10. 115 ILCS 5/13 (1993 State Bar Edition); Ind. Code Ann 20-7.5-1-14 (West 1995); Nev. Rev. State 288.260 (1995); see also Michael La Morte, *School Law: Cases and Concepts* (Needham Heights, MA: Allyn & Bacon, 1999); *Hortonville Joint School District No. 1 v. Hortonville Education Association,* 426 U.S. 482 (1976).

11. Fisher, Schimmel, and Kelly, *Teachers and the Law,* p. 473; for privacy issues on the Internet, see Jeffrey T. Sultanik, "Legal Rights in Cyberspace," *School Business Affairs* 63, no. 5 (May 1997), pp. 25–33.

12. See Louis Fischer, David Schimmel, and Cynthia Kelly, *Teachers and the Law* (New York: Longman, 1999).

13. Sadker and Sadker, *Sex Equity Handbook for Schools;* Fischer, Schimmel, and Kelly, *Teachers and the Law.*

14. *Goss v. Lopez,* 419 U.S. 565 (1975); *Wood v. Strickland,* 420 U.S. 308 (1975); *Ingraham v. Wright,* 430 U.S. 651 (1977); Martha McCarthy and Dean Webb, "Balancing Duties and Rights," *Principal Leadership* 1, no. 1 (September 2000), pp. 16–21; Michael Martin, "Does Zero Mean Zero? Balancing Policy with Procedure in the Fight Against Weapons at School," *American School Board Journal* 187, no. 3 (March 2000), pp. 39–41; National Center for Education Statistics, *Indicators of School Crime and Safety, 2000* (Washington, DC, 2001); *James v. Unified School District No. 512,* 899 F. Supp. 530 (1995).

15. *Tinker v. Des Moines Independent Community School District,* 393 U.S. 503 (1969); *Beussink v. Woodland R-IV School District,* 30 F. Supp. 2d 1175 (1998); Jamin Raskin, *We the Students: Supreme Court Cases for and about Students* (Washington, DC: CQ Press, 2000).

16. *Bethel School District No. 403 v. Fraser,* 478 U.S. 675 (1986); *J. S. v. Bethlehem Area School District,* 757A. 2d 412 (2000); Kathleen Conn, "Offensive Student Web Sites: What Should Schools Do?" *Educational Leadership* 50, no. 5 (February 2001), pp. 74-77.

17. Benjamin Sendor, "Guidance on Graduation Prayer," *The American School Board Journal* (April 1997), pp. 17–18; Benjamin Sendor, "When May School Clubs Meet?" *The American School Board Journal* (August 1997), pp. 14–15; Ralph D. Mawdsley, "Religion in the Schools: Walking a Fine Legal Line," *School Business Affairs* 63, no. 5 (May 1997), pp. 5–10; *Engel v. Vitale,* 370 U.S. 421 (1962); *School District of Abington Township v. Schempp* and *Murray v. Curlett,* 373 U.S. 203 (1963); *Lee v. Weisman,* 112 U.S. 2649, (1992); *Good News Club v. Milford Central Schools,* 99 U.S. 2036 (2001); *Santa Fe Independent School District v. Doe,* 99 U.S. 62 (2000).

18. *Bellnier v. Lund,* 438 F. Supp. 47 (N.Y. 1977); *Doe v. Renfrou,* 635 F. 2d 582 (7th Cir. 1980), cert. denied, 101 S. Ct. 3015 (1981); *Veronia School District v. Acton,* 115 U.S. 2386 (1995); *New Jersey v. T.L.O.,* 105 U.S. 733 (1985).

19. *Hazelwood School District v. Kuhlmeier,* 108 S. Ct. 562 (1988); *Shanley v. Northeast Independent School District,* 462 F. 2d 960 (5th Cir. 1972); *Gambino v. Fairfax County School Board,* 564 F. 2d 157 (4th Cir. 1977).

20. Fischer, Schimmel, and Kelly, *Teachers and the Law.*
21. "U.S. Supreme Court Decision on Teacher-Student Sexual Harassment Changing Legal Landscape," *Educator's Guide to Controlling Sexual Harassment* 5, no. 12 (September 1998), pp. 1, 3, 4–5; Joel Spring, *American Education* (New York: McGraw-Hill, 1996), p. 276; *Davis v. Monroe County Board of Education,* 97 U.S. 843 (1999).
22. Harris Interactive Poll, *Hostile Hallways: Bullying, Teasing, and Sexual Harassment in School* (Washington, DC: American Association of University Women, 2001); Raskin, *We the Students: Supreme Court Cases for and about Students.*
23. Millicent Lawson, "False Accusations Turn Dream into Nightmare in Chicago," *Education Week,* August 2, 1994, p. 16; Harris Interactive Poll, *Hostile Hallways: Bullying, Teasing, and Sexual Harassment in School;* Mark Walsh, "High Court Addresses Harassment," *Education Week,* July 8, 1999, pp. 1, 30–31.
24. Fred Hechinger, *Fateful Choices: Healthy Youth for the 21st Century* (New York: Carnegie Council on Adolescent Development, 1992); Administration for Children and Families U.S. Department of Health and Human Services, ACF Press Room: HHS News, *HHS Reports New Child Abuse and Neglect Statistics* (Washington, DC: April 2, 2001).
25. Jan English and Anthony Papalia, "The Responsibility of Educators in Cases of Child Abuse and Neglect," *Chronicle Guidance* (January 1988), pp. 88–89; Carol K. Sigelman and David R. Shaffer, *Life-Span Human Development,* 3rd ed. (Pacific Grove, CA: Wadsworth Publishing, 1999).
26. Louis Harris and Associates, *The Metropolitan Life Survey of the American Teacher, Part III Students Voice Their Opinions on: Learning About Values and Principles in School* (New York: Louis Harris and Associates, 1996); Stephen Bates, "A Textbook of Virtues," *New York Times,* January 8, 1995, education supplement, p. EL-161.
27. Philip Cohen, "The Content of Their Character: Educators Find New Ways to Tackle Values and Morality," *Association for Supervision and Curriculum Development Curriculum Update,* spring 1995, p. 1; Character Education Partnership Online, "Public Support for Character Education," www.character.org (August 12, 2001).
28. Bates, "A Textbook of Virtues": Irene McHenry, "Conflict in Schools: Fertile Ground for Moral Growth," *Phi Delta Kappan* 82, no. 3 (November 2000), pp. 223–27; Meg Lundstrom, "Character Makes a Comeback," *Instructor* 109, no. 3 (October 1999), pp. 25–28.
29. David Carr, "Moral Formation, Cultural Attachment or Social Control: What's the Point of Values Education?" *Educational Theory* 50, no. 1 (winter 2000), pp. 49–62.
30. Thomas J. Lasley, "The Missing Ingredient in Character Education," *Phi Delta Kappan* 78, no. 8 (April 1997), pp. 654–55; Joan F. Goodman, "Objections (and Responses) to Moral Education," *Education Week* 20, no. 38 (May 30, 2001), pp. 32, 35.
31. Alfie Kohn, "How Not to Teach Values," *Phi Delta Kappan* 78, no. 8 (April 1997), pp. 428–37; Goodman, "Objections (and Responses) to Moral Education."
32. Howard Kirschenbaum, "A Comprehensive Model for Values Education and Moral Education," *Phi Delta Kappan* 73, no. 10 (June 1992), pp. 771–76.
33. Diane Berreth and Sheldon Berman, "The Moral Dimensions of Schools," *Educational Leadership* 54, no. 8 (May 1997), pp. 24–27; Merrill Harmin, "Value Clarity, High Morality: Let's Go for Both," *Educational Leadership* 45, no. 8 (May 1988), pp. 24–31; Kenneth R. Howe, "A Conceptual Basis for Ethics in Teacher Education," *Journal of Teacher Education* 37 (May/June 1986): p. 6; Karl Hostetler, *Ethical Judgment in Teaching* (Boston: Allyn & Bacon, 1997).

CHAPTER 12 The Struggle for Educational Opportunity

1. Andrew Hacker, *Two Nations: Black, White, Separate, Hostile, Unequal* (New York: Charles Scribner's, 1992), pp. 31–32.
2. Lowell C. Rose and Alec M. Gallup, "The 33rd Annual Phi Delta Kappa/Gallup Poll of the Public's Attitude Toward the Public Schools," *Phi Delta Kappan* 83, no. 1 (September 2001), pp. 41–58.
3. Ana Maria Villegas, "Culturally Responsive Pedagogy for the 1990s and Beyond," Washington, DC: ERIC Clearinghouse on Teacher Education, American Association of Colleges for Teacher Education, 1991.
4. Adapted from *The State of America's Children Yearbook 2001.* Children's Defense Fund (www.childrens defense.org/keyfacts.htm); *America's Children: Key National Indicators of Well-Being, 2001* (www.child stats.gov/ac2001/ac01.asp).
5. Much of the earlier educational history discussion of Native Americans, African Americans, and Latinos is based on Meyer Weinberg, *A Chance to Learn: A History of Race and Education in the United States* (New York: Cambridge University Press, 1977).
6. Robert S. Catterill, *The Southern Indians: The Story of the Civilized Tribes Before Removal* (1954; reprinted, Norman: University of Oklahoma Press, 1966).
7. William Denmert, "Indian Education: Where and Whither?" *Education Digest* 42 (December 1976). See also Ron Holt, "Fighting for Equality: Breaking with the Past," *NEA Today,* March 1989, pp. 10–11; NEA Ethnic Report, *Focus on American Indian/Alaska Natives,* October 1991.
8. Lee Little Soldier, "Is There an 'Indian' in Your Classroom?" *Phi Delta Kappan* 78, no. 8 (April 1997), pp. 650–53.
9. Susie King Taylor, *Reminiscences of My Life in Camp with the 33rd U.S. Colored Troop Late First S.C. Volunteers* (1902; reprinted, New York: Arno Press, 1968).
10. W. E. B. Du Bois, "The United States and the Negro," *Freedomways* (1971), quoted in Weinberg, *A Chance to Learn.*
11. Joel Spring, *American Education* (Boston: McGraw-Hill, 2002), p. 110.
12. National Advisory Commission on Civil Disorders, *Report of the National Advisory Commission on Civil Disorders* (Washington, DC: U.S. Government Printing Office, 1968), p. 369. See also Andrew Hacker, *Two*

Nations Black and White, Separate, Hostie, Unequal (New York: Charles Scribner's, 1992).

13. Louis Fischer, David Schimmel, and Cynthia Kelly, *Teachers and the Law* (New York: Addison Wesley Longman, 1999), p. 352.

14. Gary Orfield (with data analysis by Nora Gordon), "Schools More Separate: Consequences of a Decade of Resegregation" (Cambridge: Harvard University, July 2001).

15. Darryl Fears, "Schools Racial Isolation Growing," *The Washington Post*, July 18, 2001, p. A3; Richard Morin and Claudia Deane, "Defending Desegregation," *The Washington Post*, July 24, 2001, p. A19.

16. Kati Haycock, "Closing the Achievement Gap," *Educational Leadership* 58, no. 6, March 2001, pp. 6–11.

17. James Comer, "All Our Children," *School Safety*, winter 1989, p. 19.

18. Census, Population Project of the United States 1993–2050, CPS Report No. P25-1105, 1993; *Overview of Race and Hispanic Origins* (Washington, DC: U.S. Department of Commerce, Bureau of the Census, March 2001).

19. President's Advisory Commission on Educational Excellence for Hispanic Americans, *Our Nation on the Fault Line: Hispanic American Education* (Washington, DC, 1996).

20. Daniel Aragón Ulibarrì, "Hispanics Choose to Dropout Out of School?" *Santa Fe New Mexican*, March 2000 (www.ushispanic.net/USHisp/articles/HispDropouts.html); Anne Turnbaugh Lockwood and Patricia Anne DiCerbo, eds. "Transforming Education for Hispanic Youth: Broad Recommendations for Policy and Practice," *Issues Brief*, National Clearinghouse for Bilingual Education, no. 1 (January 2000).

21. The Handbook of Texas Online. *Crystal City Revolts* (The Texas State Historical Association, July 23, 2001). www.tsha.utexas.edu/handbook/online/articles/view/CC/wmc1.html

22. Quoted in Weinberg, *A Chance to Learn.*

23. Office of Migrant Education, State Migrant Education Program Directors Common Core of Data file, *Enrolling Migrant Children*, 1997.

24. *Puerto Rico Herald,* May 10, 2001. www.puertorico-herald.org/issues/2001/vol5n19/Media1-en.shtml.

25. President's Advisory Commission on Educational Excellence for Hispanic Americans, *Our Nation on the Fault Line: Hispanic American Education.*

26. Joan First, "Immigrant Students in U.S. Public Schools," *Phi Delta Kappan* 70, no. 3 (November 1988), p. 206.

27. Federal Interagency Forum on Child and Family Statistics, *America's Children: Key National Indicators of Well-Being* (Washington, DC, 1997).

28. Much of the information on the history of Asian Americans is adapted from James Banks, *Teaching Ethnic Studies* (Boston: Allyn & Bacon 1996).

29. National Center for Education Statistics, *Early Child Longitudinal Study, Kindergarten Class of 1998–99* (Washington, DC: U.S. Department of Education, 1999).

30. U.S. Department of Education, National Center for Education Statistics, Recent College Graduates Surveys (1977) and 1993 Baccalaureate and Beyond Longitudinal Study, First Follow-up (B&B: 93/94); *The Condition of Education 1996*, Supplemental Table 35–90; U.S. Bureau of the Census, Statistical Abstract of the United States (1998); findings from *Statistical Abstract of the United States*, (Washington, DC: U.S. Census Bureau, 2000).

31. Carlos Ovando, "Interrogating Stereotypes: The Case of the Asian 'Model Minority,' " *Newsletter of the Asian Culture Center* (Indiana University, Fall 2001). www.modelminority.com/academia/interrogating.htm.

32. Fred Cordova, *Filipinos: Forgotten Asian-Americans* (Dubuque, IA: Kendall/Hunt, 1983), pp. 9–57; Brian Ascalon Roley, "Filipinos—The Hidden Majority," *San Francisco Chronicles*, August 20, 2001, p. A-17.

33. Arthur W. Helweg and Usha M. Helweg, *Immigrant Success Story—East Indians in America* (Philadelphia, PA: University of Pennsylvania Press, 1990). See also Srirajasekhar Bobby Koritala, "A Historical Perspective of Americans of Asian India Origin, 1790–1997," www.tiac.net/users/koritala/india/history.htm.

34. Laurie Olsen, "Crossing the Schoolhouse Border: Immigrant Children in California," *Phi Delta Kappan* 70, no. 3 (November 1988), p. 213.

35. J. Shaheen, *The TV Arab* (Bowling Green, Ohio: Bowling Green State University, 1984).

36. For more information about Arab Americans, visit the website of the American-Arab Anti-Discrimination Committee at www.adc.org.

37. Patty Adeed and G. Pritchy Smith, "Arab Americans: Concepts and Materials," in James Banks (ed), *Teaching Ethnic Studies* (Boston: Allyn and Bacon, 1997), pp. 489–510.

38. Myra Sadker and David Sadker, "Sexism in the Classroom of the 80s," *Psychology Today* (March 1986). See also Myra Sadker, David Sadker, and Susan Klein, "The Issue of Gender in Elementary and Secondary Education," in Gerald Grant, ed., *Review of Research in Education* (Washington, DC: American Educational Research Association, 1991), pp. 269–334; American Association of University Women, *How Schools Shortchange Girls* (Washington, DC: American Association of University Women, 1992). See also Myra Sadker and David Sadker, *Failing at Fairness: How Our Schools Cheat Girls* (New York: Touchstone Press, 1995).

39. M. Carey Thomas, "Present Tendencies in Women's Education," *Education Review* 25 (1908), pp. 64–85. Quoted in David Tyack and Elisabeth Hansot, *Learning Together: A History of Coeducation in American Schools* (New Haven: Yale University Press, 1990), p. 68.

40. Adapted from "Through the Back Door: The History of Women's Education" and "Higher Education: Colder by Degrees," Myra Sadker and David Sadker, *Failing at Fairness: How Our Schools Cheat Girls*; Michael Kimmel, *The Gendered Society* (New York: Oxford University Press, 2000); Susan Faludi, *Stiffed: The Betrayal of American Men* (New York: William Morrow & Company, 2000); William Pollack, *Real Boys: Rescuing Our Sons from the Myths of Boyhood* (New York: Random House, 1998).

41. Quoted in John O'Neil, "A Generation Adrift?" *Educational Leadership* 49, no. 2 (September 1991), pp. 4–10.

42. Fred Hechinger, *Fateful Choices: Healthy Youth for the 21st Century* (New York: Carnegie Council on Adolescent Development, 1992), p. 2; Children's Defense Fund, *Key Facts: Children's Health Coverage in 1999* (www.childrens defense.org/healthy-start-chip-keyfacts.htm).

43. Barbara Vobejda, "Social Change Shows Signs of Slowing: Family Characteristics Appear More Stable," *The Washington Post*, November 11, 1996, p. A-3.

44. Pat Wingert, "I do, I do—Maybe," *Newsweek*, November 2, 1998; Karen S. Peterson, "Cohabitation Is Increasing, Census Data Confirm," *USA Today*, August 13, 2001 (www.usatoday.com/news/census/2001-05-15-cohabitate.htm).

45. Stanley D. Eitzen, "Problem Students: The Sociological Roots," *Phi Delta Kappan,* April 1992, p. 584; David Francis, "New Figures Show Wider Gap Between Rich and Poor," *Christian Science Monitor*, April 21, 1995 pp. 1, 8.

46. U.S. Department of Education, *Youth Indicators 1991: Trends in the Well-Being of American Youth* (Washington, DC: U.S. Department of Education, 1991); U.S. Department of Labor, Bureau of Labor Statistics, unpublished data, 1996; U.S. Department of Labor, *Employment Characteristics of Families in 1997*, 1998; Ken Bryson and Lynne M. Casper, *Household and Family Characteristics: March 1997*, P 20–509, Bureau of the Census, April 1998; Bureau of the Census, "Table F-7. Type of Family—Families (All Races) by Median and Mean Income: 1947 to 1996," www.census.gov/hhes/income/histinc/f07.html.

47. Phyllis Moen, "Couples and Careers Study," *Cornell Employment and Family Institute* (Cornell University Ithaca, NY: 1999). www.blcc.cornell.edu/cci/current.html.

48. Jerry Adler, "Tomorrow's Child," *Newsweek*, November 2, 1998.

49. The Annie E. Casey Foundation, *Kids Count Data Book* (Washington, DC: Center for the Study of Social Policy, 1992).

50. Candy Carlile, "Children of Divorce," *Childhood Education* 64, no. 4 (1991), pp. 232–34.

51. Beverly Bliss, *Step Families*, Parenthood in America Proceedings of the conference held in Madison, Wisconsin (1998). http://parenthood.library.wisc.edu/Bliss/Bliss.html.

52. Michael A. Fletcher, "Interracial Marriages Eroding Barriers," *The Washington Post*, December 29, 1998, p. A-1; Michael A. Fletcher, "The Myth of the Melting Pot, America's Racial and Ethnic Divide," *The Washington Post*, December 28, 1998, p. A1. www.washingtonpost.com/wpsrv/national/daily/ dec98/melt29.htm.

53. Eitzen, "Problem Students"; Lizette Peterson-Homer, "Latchkey Children," *Gale Encyclopedia of Childhood & Adolescence*. Gale Research, 1998; Sandra L. Hofferth and Zita Januniene, "Life After School," *Educational Leadership* 58, no. 7 (April 2001), pp. 10–23.

54. This anecdote is based on information in Children's Defense Fund, *A Vision for America's Future*, pp. 27–36. Washington, DC, 1989.

55. Rick Fantasia and Maurice Isserman, *Homelessness: A Sourcebook* (New York: Facts on File, 1994), pp. 113–14.

56. Samuel Peng, "High School Dropouts: Descriptive Information from High School and Beyond," *Bulletin*, National Center for Education Statistics, November 1983.

57. U.S. Department of Education, *Youth Indicators 1996: Trends in the Well-Being of American Youth* (Washington, DC: National Center for Education Statistics, 1996; National Center for Educational Statistics, *High School Completion Rates Dropout Rates in the United States* (Washington, DC: U.S. Department of Education, 1999). http://nces.ed.gov/pubs2002/dropout/figures3.asp; National Center for Educational Statistics, *Dropout Rates in the United States* (Washington, DC: U.S. Department of Education, 2000). http://nces.ed.gov/pubs2002/droppub_2001.

58. National Dropout Prevention Center Network, *Effective Strategies* (Clemson University, South Carolina, 2001). www.dropoutprevention.org/2levelpages/strategies.html.

59. Alan Guttmacher Institute, *Facts in Brief: Teenage Sexual and Reproductive Behavior* (New York: Alan Guttmacher Institute, 1991); Alan Guttmacher Institute, *Facts in Brief: Teen Sex and Pregnancy* (New York: AGI, Revised 1999). www.vix.comn/pub/men/index.html.

60. Alan Guttmacher Institute, *Teenage Pregnancy: Overall Trends and State-by State Information* (New York: AGI, 1999), Table 1; Stanley K. Henshaw, *U.S. Teenage Pregnancy Statistics with Comparative Statistics for Women Aged 20–24* (New York: AGI, 1999), p. 5.

61. Jamie Victoria Ward and Jill McLean Taylor, "Sexuality Education in a Multicultural Society," *Educational Leadership* 49, no. 1 (September 1991), pp. 62–64.

62. House Select Committee on Children, Youth, and Families, *A Decade of Denial: Teens and AIDS in America* (Washington, DC: U.S. Government Printing Office, 1992).

63. Centers for Disease Control and Prevention, "The HIV/AIDS Epidemic in the United States 1997–1998: Highlights from the Reports," *National Center for HIV, STD and TB Prevention* (Rockville, MD: Centers for Disease Control and Prevention, 1998); Centers for Disease Control and Prevention, *HIV Surveillance Supplemental Report* 5, no. 3 (Atlanta, GA: 1999), p. 8.

64. Center on Addiction and Substance Abuse, *Malignant Neglect: Substance Abuse and America's Schools* (Columbia University: New York, 2001). www.casacolumbia.org/newsletter1457/newsletter_show.htm?doc_id=80623.

65. Roberto Suro, "Study Finds Decline in Teen Substance Abuse," *The Washington Post*, December 19, 1998, p. A-3. Addiction Science Research and Education Center, *Alcohol Facts* (Austin, TX. 2000). www.utexas.edu/reserch/asrec/alcoholfacts.html.

66. Paul Taylor, "Surgeon General Links Teen Drinking to Crime, Injuries, Unsafe Sex," *The Washington Post*, April 14, 1992, p. A-1.

67. *Education Update* 9, no. 4 (fall 1986).
68. DeNeen Brown, "Fairfax Teenagers' LSD Arrests Send Parents a 'Wake-up Call,' " *The Washington Post*, April 27, 1992, p. B-1.
69. National Center on Addiction and Substance Abuse, *Teens Who Smoke Cigarettes Much Likelier to Try Pot* (New York: Columbia University Press, 1998); National Institute on Drug Abuse, "Use of Selected Substances by High School Seniors and Eighth-Graders, According to Sex and Race," *Monitoring the Future Study* (National Institutes of Health, Bethesda, MD: 2000), Table 63, pp. 240–241. www.cdc.gov/nchs/products/pubs/pubd/hus/tables/2000/00hus063.pdf.
70. John O'Neil, "A Generation Adrift?" See also Sidney Barish, "Responding to Adolescent Suicide: A MultiFaceted Plan," *NASSP Bulletin* 75, no. 538 (November 1991), pp. 98–103; Richard O'Connor, *Teen Suicide*, Focus Adolescent Services (Salisbury: MD 2000). www.focusas.com/Suicide.html; National Institute of Mental Health, *In Harm's Way: Suicide in America* (Bethesda, MD: 2001). www.nimh.nih.gov/pubicat/harmaway.cfm.
71. Jeanne Wright, "Treating the Depressed Child" *The Washington Post*, December 2, 1996, p. C-5.
72. Quoted in Paul Gibson, "Gay Male and Lesbian Youth Suicide," in Marcia Feinleib, ed., *Report of the Secretary's Task Force on Youth Suicide* (Washington, DC: U.S. Department of Health and Human Services, January 1989), pp. 3-110–3-142. See also James Sears, "Helping Students Understand and Accept Sexual Diversity," *Educational Leadership* 49, no. 1 (September 1991), pp. 54–56.
73. Jesse Green, "This School Is Out," *New York Times Magazine*, October 14, 1991, pp. 32–36, 59, 68.
74. Jessica Portner, "Districts Adopting Policies to Protect Gay Students' Rights," *Education Week*, October 5, 1994, p. 8; "More Inclusive Anti-Intimidation Policy Approved," *Cincinnati Enquirer*, August 28, 2001; Alan Horowitz, "Addressing Homophobic Behavior in the Classroom," *Online Resource Center* (Gay Lesbian and Straight Network: Washington, DC), June 5, 2001 (www.glsen.org/templates/resources/record.html?section=14&record=820).

Chapter 13 Technology in Education

1. Jeffrey Mortimer, "How TV Violence Hits Kids," *Education Digest* 60, no. 2 (October 1994), pp. 16–19.
2. *Balancing Acts: Work/Family Issues on Primetime TV Shows* (Washington, DC: The National Partnership for Women and Families, 1998); Jack Levin, "Mapping Social Geography," *Bostonia* (March/April 1989), pp. 64–65.
3. "Study Links TV, Music to Teen Drinking," *USA Today on the Web*, November 2, 1998; Annette Licitra, "Psychologists Spell Out Dangers of Unregulated TV Watching," *Education Daily*, February 26, 1992.
4. Richard P. Adler, "Children's Television Advertising: History of the Issue," in Edward Palmer and Aimee Dorr, eds., *Children and the Faces of Television* (New York: Academic Press, 1980), pp. 46–47.
5. Daniel Anderson and Patricia Collins, *The Impact on Children's Education: Television's Influence on Cognitive Development* (Washington, DC: U.S. Department of Education, April 1988).
6. Licitra, "Psychologists Spell Out Dangers."
7. Bruce Watkins, Althea Huston-Stein, and John Wright, "Effects of Planned Television Programming," in Edward Palmer and Aimee Dorr, eds., *Children and the Faces of Television* (New York: Academic Press, 1980), pp. 46–49.
8. Susan Herzog, "Selling Out Kids: Commercialism in Public Schools," *Our Children* 23, no. 3 (November 1997); pp. 6–10; Jason Vaughn, "Big Business and the Blackboard: A Winning Combination for the Classroom," *Journal of Law and Education* 26, no. 2 (April 1997), pp. 35–46; David Streitfeld, "Low Marks for Channel One," *The Washington Post*, May 2, 1992, p. C-5; Drew Tiene, "Channel One," *International Journal of Instructional Media* 21, no. 3 (1994): pp. 181–89; Drew Tiene, "Teens React to Channel One," *Tech Trends* 39 (April/May 1994), pp. 17–20.
9. For more information about Channel One and critics of commercialism in school, visit The Center for Commercial Free Public Education website at www.commercialfree.org/index.html.
10. Todd Oppenheimer, "The Computer Delusion," *The Atlantic Monthly* (July 1997), pp. 45–48, 50–56, 61–62.
11. Sara Dexter and Ron Anderson, "Teachers' Views of the Influence of Computers on Changes in Their Instructional Practice." Paper presented at the American Educational Research Association, April 1998; Bob Hoffman, "Integrating Technology into Schools," *NAASP Bulletin* (January 1997), pp. 51–55.
12. Emily Wax, "Teachers Confront Computer Fears," *The Washington Post*, June 29, 2000; p. B3; see also "Technology Counts, 2001: The New Divides," *Education Week* 20, no. 35, May 10, 2001.
13. Ibid. p. 52.
14. Clorinda Valenti, "Preparing Teachers for the High-Tech Classroom," in David T. Gordon, ed., *The Digital Classroom* (Cambridge: Harvard College, 2000), pp. 78–87.
15. Kathryn M. Doherty and Greg Orlofsky, "Student Survey Says," *Education Week on the Web*, May 10, 2001; Ariana Eunjung Cha, "Dear Web Diary, SO Much to Tell!", *The Washington Post*, September 2, 2001, p. A1.
16. Lyn Nell Hancock, Patricia Wingert, D. Rosenberg, and A. Samuels, "The Haves and the Have-Nots," *Newsweek*, February 27, 1995, p. 53.
17. Glenn Kleiman, "Myth and Realities about Technology in K–12 Schools," in David T. Gordon, ed., *The Digital Classroom* (Cambridge: Harvard College, 2000), pp. 7–15.
18. George Brackett, Technologies Don't Change Schools—Caring, Capable People Do," in David T. Gordon, ed., *The Digital Classroom* (Cambridge: Harvard College, 2000), pp. 29–30.
19. Peter W. Foltz, Darrel Laham, Thomas K. Landauer, "Automated Essay Scoring: Applications to Educational Technology." Paper presented at the ED-Media/ED-Telecom '99, World Conference on Educational

Multimedia/Hypermedia & Educational Telecommunications, Seattle, WA, 19–24 June 1999.

20. Howard Gardner, "Can Technology Exploit the Many Ways of Knowing?", in David T. Gordon, ed., *The Digital Classroom* (Cambridge: Harvard College, 2000), pp. 32–35.

21. David Williamson Schaffer, "This Is Dewey's Vision Revisited," in David T. Gordon, ed., *The Digital Classroom,* (Cambridge: Harvard College 2000), pp. 176–178.

22. William R. Penuel, Barbara Means, and Michael Simkins, "The Multimedia Challenge," *Educational Leadership* 58, no. 2 (October 2000), p. 34.

23. Charles A. MacArthur, "Using Technology to Enhance the Writing Processes of Students with Learning Disabilities," *Journal of Learning Disabilities* 29, no. 4 (1996), pp. 344–54; Debra K. Bauder, "Assistive Technology: Learning Devices for Special Needs Students," *Media & Methods* 32, no. 3 (1996), pp. 16, 18; Nancy Trejos, "Handheld PCs Put to the Test," *The Washington Post,* September 4, 2001, pp. B1, B2.

24. Jeri Kinser, Brenda Pessin, and Pat Meyertholen, "From the Fields to the Laptop," *Learning and Leading with Technology,* ISTE, February.

25. Carla Schutte, "Going Global," *Electronic School,* February 1995, pp. A39–A40; Elaine K. Bailey and Morton Cotlar, "Teaching via the Internet," *Communication Education* 43 (April 1994), pp. 184–93; Carol S. Holzberg, "Technology in Special Education," *Technology and Learning* 14 (April 7, 1994), pp. 18–21.

26. Barbara Benham Tye and Kenneth Tye, *Global Education: A Study of School Change* (Albany: State University of New York Press, 1992), pp. 1–13.

27. Andrew F. Smith, "A Brief History of Pre-collegiate Global and International Studies Education," in John Fonte and Andre Ryerson, eds. *Education for America's role in World Affairs* (New York: University Press of America, 1994), p. 15.

28. John LeBaron and Rebecca Warshawsky, "Satellite Teleconferencing Between Massachusetts and Germany," *Educational Leadership* 48, no. 7 (April 1991), pp. 61–64.

29. Bruce Watson, "The Wired Classroom: American Education Goes On-Line," *Phi Delta Kappan* 72, no. 2 (October 1990), pp. 109–12.

30. William Kniep, "Global Education as School Reform," *Educational Leadership* 47, no. 1 (September 1989), p. 45.

31. Rhea R. Borja, "Virtual High Schools Gain a Following," *Richmond Times Dispatch,* August 7, 2001; Rodney Thrash, "Virtual School Looks to Expand Base of Students," *Detroit Free Press on the Web,* September 5, 2001.

32. Mary Anne Mather, "Virtual Schooling: Going the Distance—Any Distance—to School," *Technology and Learning,* 1 April 1998; Mary Lord, "On Line Students E-mail Music to a Teacher's Ears," *U.S. News on Line,* December 28, 1998; Sandy Kleffman, Internet Creates a National Classroom," *The Atlanta Journal-The Atlanta Constitution,* July 27, 1997.

33. Andrew Trotter, "Closing the Digital Divide," *Education Week* 20, no. 35 (2001), pp. 37–38, 40; Maisie McAdoo, "The Real Digital Divide: Quality Not Quantity," in

David T. Gordon, ed., *The Digital Classroom* (Cambridge: Harvard College, 2000), pp. 143–51; American Association of University Women, *Gender Gaps: Where School Still Fails Our Children* (Washington, DC: American Association of University Women, 1998).

34. "Dividing Lines," *Education Week* 20, no. 35 (2001), p. 12.

35. Royce T. Hall, "Blacks, Hispanics, Still Behind Whites in Level of PC Ownership," *The Wall Street Journal on the Web,* August 3, 1998; Lyn Nell Hancock, Patricia Wingert, D. Rosenberg, and A. Samuels, "The Haves and the Have-Nots," *Newsweek,* February 27, 1995, p. 53, Richard Wolf, "Computers Should Be Made Available to Children of Low-Income Families," *USA Today,* September 18, 1997.

36. Robert C. Johnson, "Money Matters," *Education Week* 20, no. 35 (2001), p. 14; John Schwartz, "U.S. Cities Race Gap In Use of Internet," *The Washington Post,* July 9, 1999, p. A21.

37. Tamar Lewin, "Children's Computer Use Grows, but Gaps Persist, Study Says," *The New York Times,* January 22, 2001, p. A11.

38. Karla Scoon Reid, "Racial Disparities," *Education Week* 20, no. 35 (2001), p. 16.

39. A. Game and R. Pringle, *Gender at Work* (Boston: Allen & Unwin, 1983), p. 83.

40. American Association of University Women, *Gender Gaps: Where Schools Still Fail Our Children;* John Gehring, "Not Enough Girls," *Education Week* 10, no. 35 (2001), pp. 18–19; www.electronic-school.com, e-wire (June 1999); Margaret Riel, "A Title IX for the Technology Divide?" in David T. Gordon, ed., *The Digital Classroom* (Cambridge: Harvard College, 2000), pp. 161–170.

41. Mary Ann Zehr, "Rural Connections," *Education Week* 10, no. 35 (2001), pp. 24–25.

42. Ibid.

43. V. Robinson, "Methodology and Research-Practice Gap," *Educational Researcher* 27, no. 1 (1998): pp. 17–26.

44. J. Salpeter, "Taking Stock: What's the Research Saying?" *Technology and Learning* 18, no. 9 (1998); Mark Windschitl, "The WWW and Classroom Research: What Path Should We Take?" *Educational Researcher* 27, no. 1 (January/February 1998), pp. 28–32.

45. Mary McNabb, Mark Hawkes, and Üllik Rouk, "Critical Issues in Evaluating the Effectiveness of Technology," *The Secretary's Conference on Educational Technology,* 1999. www.ed.gov/Technology/TechConf/1999/confsum.html.

46. Patricia F. Campbell and S. S. Schwartz, "Microcomputers in the Preschool: Children, Parents, and Teachers," in Campbell & Greta G. Fein, eds., *Young Children and Microcomputers* (Englewood Cliffs, NJ: Prentice Hall, 1986), pp. 37–44.

47. Kevin Bushweller, "Beyond Machines," *Education Week* 20, no. 35 (2001), p. 34.

48. Edweek Survey, *Technology Counts 1999,* May 1999. www.edweek.org/sreports/tc99/articles/survey.htm.

49. Andrew Trotter, "A Question of Effectiveness," *Education Week on the Web,* October 1, 1998; Larry Cuban, *Teachers and Machines: The Classroom Use of Technology since 1920* (New York: Teachers College Press, 1986).

CHAPTER 14 Your First Classroom

1. Lilian Katz, "The Development of Preschool Teachers," *The Elementary School Journal* 73, no. 1 (October 1972), pp. 50–54.
2. Linda Darling-Hammond, "Teachers and Teaching: Testing Policy Hypothesis from a National Commission Report," *Educational Researcher* 27, no. 1 (January/February 1998), pp. 5–15; "Teachers Are the Key," *Reading Today* 14, no. 4 (February/March 1997), pp. 3–4.
3. National Center for Educational Statistics, *Characteristics of Stayers, Movers, and Leavers: Results from the Teacher Followup Survey, 1994–1995* (Washington, DC: U.S. Department of Education, 1997).
4. L. Huling-Austin, "Research on Learning to Teach: Implications for Teacher Induction and Mentoring," *Journal of Teacher Education* 43, no. 3 (May/June 1992), pp. 173–78.
5. Ellen Nakashima, "Montgomery Teachers May Face Peer Review," *The Washington Post,* January 2, 1999, pp. B-1, B-6.
6. Judith W. Little, "Teachers' Professional Development in a Climate of Educational Reform," *Educational Evaluation and Policy Analysis* 15 (1993), pp. 129–51; Linda Darling-Hammond and Milbrey W. McLaughlin, "Policies That Support Professional Development in an Era of Reform," in Milbrey W. McLaughlin and Ida Oberman, eds., *Teaching and Learning: New Policies, New Practices* (New York: Teachers College Press, 1996), pp. 208–18.
7. National Education Association, *Status of the American Public School Teacher, 1995–1996* (Washington, DC: National Education Association, 1997).
8. Organization for Economic Cooperation and Development (OECD), *Education at a Glance, OECD Indicators* (Paris: OECD, 1995), pp. 176–77.
9. Julie Blair, "Lawmakers Plunge into Teacher Pay," *Education Week* 20, no. 23 (February 21, 2001), pp. 1, 16.
10. Jeff Archer, "Recruitment Pinch Fuels Global Trade in K–12 Teachers," *Education Week* 20, no. 22 (February 14, 2001), p. 8; Lynette Holloway, "Foreign Teachers Receive a Short Course on the City," *The New York Times on the Web,* August 14, 2001.
11. Susan Moore Johnson, Susan Kardos, and Christine Sanni, "Research on New Teaching Shows a Changing Profession: 43% of New Teachers in New Jersey Plan to Leave Classroom Teaching; Nearly Half Are Mid-Career Entrants," *Harvard Graduate School of Education on the Web,* August 27, 2001; Lee Foster, "New Teachers Relish Mid-Life Career Change," *The Hartford Courant on the Web,* October 23, 2000.
12. Maria Mihalik, "Thirty Minutes to Sell Yourself," *Teacher,* April 1991, p. 32d.
13. Ibid., p. 32e.
14. Jacques Steinberg, "Giving the Teacher Balm for Burnout," *The New York Times on the Web,* January 7, 2001.
15. Quoted in "Forging a Profession," *Teacher* (September/October 1989), pp. 12, 16.
16. National Board for Professional Teaching Standards website (www.nbpts.org).
17. "National Certification Picks Up Steam," *American Teacher* 76, no. 6 (May/June 1992), p. 3.
18. National Board for Professional Teaching Standards website (www.nbpts.org).
19. Briant Farnsworth, Jerry Debenham, and Gerald Smith, "Designing and Implementing a Successful Merit Pay Program for Teachers," *Phi Delta Kappan* 73, no. 4 (December 1991), pp. 320–25.
20. Kenneth J. Cooper, "Performance Pay for Teachers Catches On," *The Washington Post,* February 26, 2000, p. A4.
21. *Is "Paying for Performance" Changing Schools?* The SREB Career Ladder Clearinghouse Report 1988 (Atlanta: Southern Regional Education Board), p. 8.
22. Adam Urbanski, "The Rochester Contract: A Status Report," *Educational Leadership* 46, no. 3 (November 1988), pp. 48–52.
23. Much of the information in this section was drawn from Marshall O. Donley, Jr.'s excellent article, "The American School Teacher: From Obedient Servant to Militant Professional," *Phi Delta Kappan* 58, no. 1 (September 1976), pp. 112–17.
24. Albert Shanker, "Where We Stand: Is It Time for National Standards and Exams?" *American Teacher* 76, no. 6 (May/June 1992), p. 5.
25. Jeff Archer, "NEA Board Approves AFT 'Partnership' Pact," *Education Week on the Web,* February 21, 2001.
26. Lapointe quoted in Gerald W. Bracey, "The Second Bracey Report on the Condition of Public Education," *Phi Delta Kappan* (October 1992), pp. 104–17, cited in David C. Berliner and Bruce J. Biddle, *The Manufactured Crisis,* (Reading, MA: Addison Wesley, 1995), p. 54.
27. Gerald W. Bracey, "U.S. Students: Better Than Ever," *The Washington Post,* December 22, 1995, p. A-9; and Robert J. Samuelson, "Three Cheers for Schools," *Newsweek,* December 4, 1995, p. 61. See also Berliner and Biddle, *The Manufactured Crisis,* pp. 13–64.
28. Berliner and Biddle, *The Manufactured Crisis,* p. 146; see also Richard Rothstein, *The Way We Were? The Myths and Realities of America's Student Achievement* (Washington, DC: Century Fund, 1998).

Chapter 15 Q and A Guide to Entering the Teaching Profession

1. National Center for Education Statistics (NCES), *Projections of Education Statistics to 2011.* Washington, DC: U.S. Department of Education, 2001; National Center for Education Statistics (NCES), *Predicting the Need for Newly Hired Teachers in the United States to 2008–2009* (Washington, DC: U.S. Department of Education, 1999).
2. Ibid.
3. American Association for Employment in Education, *Educator Supply and Demand in the United States, 1999* (Columbus, OH: AAEE, 2001).
4. National Education Association (NEA), *Fact Sheet on Teacher Shortages* (Washington, DC: NEA, 2001).
5. Barbara Kantrowitz and Pat Wingert, "Teachers Wanted," *Newsweek,* October 2000, pp. 37–42; Julie Blair, "Districts Wooing Teachers with Bonuses, Incentives" in *Education Week on the Web,* August 2, 2000.
6. National Education Association (NEA), *American Education Statistics at a Glance* (Washington, DC: NEA, 2000).

7. National Center for Education Statistics (NCES), *Digest of Education Statistics, 2000* (Washington, DC: U.S. Department of Education, 2000).

8. National Center for Education Statistics (NCES), *Digest of Education Statistics, 2000* (Washington, DC: U.S. Department of Education, 2000); National Center for Education Statistics (NCES), *Condition of Education, 2001* (Washington, DC: U.S. Department of Education, 2001); National Education Association (NEA), *Estimate of School Statistics, 2001* (Washington, DC: NEA, 2001); Kantrowitz and Wingert, "Teachers Wanted;" National Education Association (NEA), *Fact Sheet on Teacher Shortages* (Washington, DC: NEA, 2001); National Center for Education Statistics (NCES), *America's Teachers: Profile of a Profession, 1993–1994* (Washington DC: U.S. Department of Education, 1997).

9. Louis Harris and Associates, *The Metropolitan Life Survey of the American Teacher, 1984–1995; Old Problems, New Challenges* (New York: Louis Harris and Associates, 1995), p. 15.

10. American Federation of Teachers (AFT), *Survey and Analysis of Teacher Salary Trends, 2000* (Washington, DC: AFT, 2000).

11. National Center for Education Statistics (NCES), *Job Satisfaction among America's Teachers: Effects of Workplace Conditions, Background Characteristics, and Teacher Compensation* (Washington, DC: U.S. Department of Education, 1997); National Center for Education Statistics (NCES), *Public and Private Schools: How Do They Differ? Findings from the Condition of Education, 1997* (Washington, DC: U.S. Department of Education, 1997).

12. Patricia L. Rieman, *Teaching Portfolios: Presenting Your Professional Best* (New York: McGraw-Hill Companies, 2000).

13. Joseph Cronin, "State Regulations of Teacher Preparation," in Lee Shulman and Gary Sykes (eds.), *Handbook of Teaching and Policy* (New York: Longman, 1983), p. 174.

14. C. Emily Feistrizter and David T. Chester, *Alternative Teacher Certification: A State by State Analysis, 2001* (Washington, DC: National Center for Educational Information, 2001).

15. Ibid.

16. Jessica Sandman, "Study Finds Alternative Teachers Less Qualified, But Meeting Needs," *Education Week on the Web,* September 10, 1997.

17. Brenda Freeman and Ann Schopen, "Quality Reform in Teacher Education: A Brief Look at the Admissions Testing Movement," *Contemporary Education,* 62(4), p. 279; Educational Testing Service (ETS), *The Praxis Exam: State by State Requirements.*

18. Educational Testing Service (ETS), *The Praxis Exam: State by State Requirements* (Princeton, NJ: ETS, 2001).

19. Thomas Toch, *In the Name of Excellence* (New York: Oxford University Press, 1991), p. 164.

20. National Research Council, *Testing Teacher Candidates: The Role of Licensure Tests in Improving Teacher Quality* (Washington, DC: National Academy Press, 2001).

21. National Center for Education Statistics (NCES), *Condition of Education, 2001* (Washington, DC: U.S. Department of Education, 2001); National Center for Education Statistics (NCES), *America's Teachers: Profile of a Profession, 1993–1994* (Washington, DC: U.S. Department of Education, 1997).

22. Freeman and Schopen, "Quality Reform in Teacher Education: A Brief Look at the Admissions Testing Movement"; National Research Council, *Testing Teacher Candidates: The Role of Licensure Tests in Improving Teacher Quality* (Washington, DC: National Academy Press, 2001).

23. Kerry White, "In a Push for Accountability, Tenure Becomes a Target," *Education Week on the Web,* June 25, 1997.

24. Caroline Hendrie, "Principals Losing Tenure," *Teacher Magazine on the Web,* April 1998.

25. Special thanks to Diana Coleman, Kevin Dwyer, Phyllis Lerner, and Kathryn McNerney for their assistance in preparing this section.

APPENDIX 4 Observation Manual

1. George Spindler, *Doing the Ethnography of Schooling: Educational Anthropology in Action* (New York: Holt, Rinehart & Winston, 1982), p. 24.

2. Quoted in Spindler, *Doing the Ethnography of Schooling,* p. 24.

3. Marilyn Cohn, Robert Kottkamp, and Eugene Provanzo, Jr., *To Be a Teacher: Cases, Concepts, Observation Guides* (New York: Random House, 1987).

4. Eugene J. Webb, Donald Campbell, Richard Schwartz, and Lee Sechrest, *Unobtrusive Measures* (Skokie, IL: Rand McNally, 1966).

5. Hugh B. Price, "Multiculturalism: Myths and Realities," *Phi Delta Kappan* 74, no. 3 (November 1992), pp. 208–13.

6. Joseph Grannis, "The School as a Model of Society," *Harvard Graduate School of Education Association Bulletin* 21 (1967). See also Jules Henry, *Culture Against Man* (New York: Random House, 1963); Seymour Sarason, *The Culture of the School and the Problem of Change* (Boston: Allyn & Bacon, 1971); George D. Spindler, ed., *Education and Culture: Anthropological Approaches* (New York: Holt, Rinehart & Winston, 1963); Talcott Parsons, "The School as a Social System: Some of Its Functions in American Society," in Robert J. Havinghurst, Bernice L. Neugarten, and Jacqueline M. Falk, eds., *Society and Education* (Boston: Allyn & Bacon, 1967).

7. Sarason, *The Culture of the School and the Problem of Change.*

8. Philip Jackson, *Life in Classrooms* (New York: Holt, Rinehart & Winston, 1968).

9. Jackson, *Life in Classrooms.*

PHOTO CREDITS

PART 1

2 © Dick Clintsman/Stone

CHAPTER 1

11 © Bonnie Kamin Photography; 19 © Butch Martin Inc./Image Bank; 28 © AP/Wide World Photos

CHAPTER 2

42 © Bonnie Kamin/PhotoEdit; 43 © Michael Newman/PhotoEdit; 50 (top) © Bettmann/Corbis; 50 (bottom) © Rhoda Sidney/PhotoEdit; 52 © Ellen Sinisi/The Image Works, Inc.; 56 © Ian Shaw/Stone; 57 © Woodfin Camp/Woodfin Camp & Associates; 63 © Florida State Archive; 67 © Bill Bachmann/PhotoEdit; 71 © David Young-Wolff/PhotoEdit

CHAPTER 3

83 © Jeff Greenberg/Unicorn Stock Photos; 87 © Mary Kate Denny/PhotoEdit; 88 © MacDonald Photography/Index Stock Imagery; 91 (top left) © Bob Daemmrich/The Image Works, Inc.; 91 (bottom left) © Mark Richards/PhotoEdit; 91 (right) © Richard Hutchings/Photo Researchers, Inc.; 97 © Mary Kate Denny/PhotoEdit; 103 © Bill Cramer/Getty Images; 104 © Gabe Palmer/Corbis/Stock Market; 106 © Mugshots/Corbis/Stock Market; 107 © Stanford University; 111 © Mugshots/Corbis/Stock Market

PART 2

132 © Will & Deni McIntyre/Photo Researchers

CHAPTER 4

135 © Dana White/PhotoEdit; 139 © Spencer Grant/Photo Researchers, Inc.; 151 © George Zimbel; 156 © James Wilson/Woodfin Camp & Associates; 158 © AP/Wide World Photos; 164 (top left) © Macduff Everton/Corbis; 164 (top right) © Michael Newman/PhotoEdit; 164 (bottom) © Kim Kraichely; 165 (top) © Joseph Sohm; ChromoSohm Inc/Corbis; 165 (bottom) © N. R. Rowan/ Stock, Boston

CHAPTER 5

177 © Jeff Greenberg/Unicorn Stock Photos; 181 © Frank Siteman/Stock Boston; 183 © Grant LeDuc; 188 © UCLA/ GSE; 190 © Jeff Greenberg/Photo Researchers, Inc.; 196 © Tom Pollack; 202 © Jim Pickerell/ Stock Connection; 204 © Ulrike Welsch Photography; 208 (top) © David Young-Wolff/PhotoEdit; 208 (bottom) © Mary Kate Denny/PhotoEdit; 209 (top) © Ian Shaw/Stone; 209 (bottom) © Hulton Archive/Getty Images

CHAPTER 6

221 © Tony Freeman/PhotoEdit; 229 © Culver Pictures; 231 © Robert E. Daemmrich/Stone; 236 © Adam Taylor—Photographer/Georgia State University; 238 © David Young-Wolff/PhotoEdit; 248 © Lawrence Migdale/Photo Researchers, Inc.; 244 (top) © Bob Daemmrich/Stock Boston; 244 (bottom) © Michael Pole/Corbis; 245 (top) © Aneal Vohra/Index Stock Imagery; 245 (bottom) © Owen Franken/Corbis

CHAPTER 7

265 (left) © Republished with permission of Globe Newspaper Company Inc/The Boston Globe; 265 (right) © AP/Wide World Photos; 266 © Alfie Kohn; 277 © Michael Newman/PhotoEdit; 280 © Jim Pozarik/Getty Images; 283 © AP/Wide World Photos; 286 © Jeffry W. Myers/Corbis/Stock Market

PART 3

302 © John Wezenbach/Corbis/Stock Market

CHAPTER 8

306 © Culver Pictures; 308 © North Wind Picture Archives; 310 © Bettmann/Corbis; 312 © Bettmann/Corbis; 315 © Bettmann/Corbis; 319 © Peter Chartrand/Getty Images; 322 © Bob Daemmrich/The Image Works, Inc.; 324 (top) © H. Schmeiser/Unicorn Stock Photos; 324 (bottom) © Rick Stiller/Getty Images; 325 © J. Shive/ H. Armstrong Roberts; 330 © Stock Montage; 330 © Culver Pictures ; 331 Johann Heinrich Pestalozzi © New York Public Library Picture Collection; 331 © New York Public Library Picture Collection; 332 © New York Public Library Picture Collection; 332 © Culver Pictures; 333 © Culver Pictures; 334 © AP/Wide World Photos; 335 © Topham/The Image Works, Inc.; 335 © Bettmann/Corbis; 336 © Bettmann/Corbis; 337 © Bettmann/Corbis; 337 © Bendo; 338 © Wallace Britton/Black Star; 339 © Raimondo Borea & Associates; 339 © New School for Social Research; 340 © Jeremy Bigwood/Getty Images

CHAPTER 9

366 © Columbia University Teacher's College; 366 © University of Chicago-News & Info Office; 366 © Special Collections, Morris Library, Southern Illinois University, Carbondale, IL/Morris Library Special Collections; 366 © Routledge & Kegan Paul Publishers; 367 © The Core Knowledge Foundation; 367 © Bettmann/Corbis; 367 © Nel Noddings; 367 © South End Press; 367 © Special Collections, Milbank Memorial Library, Teachers College, Columbia University; 370 (top) © Andy Sacks/Stone; 370 (bottom) © Dennis MacDonald/PhotoEdit; 371 (top) © Michelle Bridwell/PhotoEdit; 371 (bottom) © Bill Aron/PhotoEdit; 371 (right) © David Young-Wolff/PhotoEdit

CHAPTER 10

387 © Bob Daemmrich/The Image Works, Inc.; 392 © AP/Wide World Photos; 396 (top) © Yvonne Hemsey/Getty/Liaison Agency; 396 (bottom) © Robert Frerck/Woodfin Camp & Associates; 405 © Kolvoord/The Image Works, Inc.; 406 © National School Boards Association; 410 © Tony Freeman/PhotoEdit; 412 (top) © AP/Wide World Photos; 412 (bottom) © Laura Dwight/PhotoEdit; 414 © Lori Grinker/Woodfin Camp & Associates

CHAPTER 11

428 © James Wilson/Woodfin Camp & Associates; 432 © Renato Rotolo/Getty Images; 435 © Acey Harper/TimePix; 439 © AP/Wide World Photos; 441 © David Young-Wolff/PhotoEdit

PART 4

470 © James Wilson/Woodfin Camp & Associates

CHAPTER 12

476 © Bettmann/Corbis; 478 © Library of Congress; 479 © Ellis Herwig/Stock Boston; 480 © A. Ramey/PhotoEdit; 482 © Jonathon Nourok/PhotoEdit; 483 © Bettmann/Corbis; 487 © Bonnie Kamin/PhotoEdit; 491 © Brown Brothers; 493 (top) © Grant LeDuc; 493 (bottom) © Leif Skoogfors/Woodfin Camp & Associates; 494 (top) © Lambert/Hulton Archive/Getty Images; 494 (bottom) © American Stock/Hulton Archive/Getty Images; 495 (left) © William R. Sallaz/Duomo Photography Inc.; 495 (right) © William R. Sallaz/Duomo Photography Inc.; 498 © Hulton Archive/Getty Images; 500 © Tony Freeman/PhotoEdit; 502 © AP/Wide World Photos; 503 © Will & Deni McIntyre/Photo Researchers, Inc.; 505 (top) © UPI/Corbis

CHAPTER 13

520 © Contact Press Images/Woodfin/Alon Reininger/Woodfin Camp & Associates; 525 © Lawrence Migdale; 534 (left and right) © TimePix; 542 (top) © Paul Conklin/PhotoEdit; 542 (bottom) © Jonathan Nourok/PhotoEdit

CHAPTER 14

566 (top) © Michael Newman/PhotoEdit; 566 (bottom) © Michael Newman/PhotoEdit; 567 © Michael Newman/PhotoEdit; 571 © AP/Wide World Photos; 572 © Chicago Historical Society; 576 (left) © AP/Wide World Photos; 576 (right) © American Federation of Teachers

INDEX

A

Abbott v. Burke, 390
Ability grouping, 186–187
Academic damage, 429
Academic freedom, 428–429
Academic goals, 144
Academic learning time, 83–84
    teacher effectiveness and, 83–84
Academic structure, 92–93
    clarification, 93
    closure, 93
    directions, 93
    enthusiasm, 93
    examples, 93
    motivation and, 92
    objectives of, 92
    review and, 92
    scaffold, 93
    transition and, 92
Academies, 228, 310, 317
The Academy, 374
Accelerated programs, 73
Acceptance, 100
Accountability, 395
Accreditation, 593
Acculturation, 147
Active learning, 103
Active teaching, 104
Adaptation stage, 524
Adaptive technology, 529
Additive approach, to multicultural education, 55
Adequate education, 390, 396
Adler, Mortimer, 233, 356, 364, 367, A–8
Administrators; *see also* Principals
    curriculum control and, 258
    effective, 201–202
The Adolescent Society (Coleman), 193
Adoption stage, 524
Adult education, 601
Advanced Placement (AP) exams, 73, 187, 238, 579
Aesthetics, 378
Affective domain, 39
Affective student needs, 197–200
African Americans, 50, 54, 68, 163, 185, 223, 518; *see also* Racial bias
    educational opportunity for, 477–480
    exclusion from school, 307
Afrocentrists, 286
AIDS, 503–504
Alborn, Mitch, 378
Alcohol abuse, 505

Alexander, Lamar, A–10
Allocated time, 83
Alternative families, 498
American Alliance for Health, Physical Education, Recreation and Dance, 577
American Association for the Advancement of Science (AAAS), 239
American Association of Colleges for Teacher Education (AACTE), 12
American Association of School Administrators, 569
American Association of University Women (AAUW), 406
American Bar Association (ABA), 438
American Council on Education (ACE), 596
American education, history of; *see* History of American education
American Federation of Teachers (AFT), 155, 161, 166, 432, 571–575, 599
    Bill of Rights, 454–455
    curriculum control and, 259
Americanization, 147
American Library Association, 283
American Psychological Association (APA), 518–519
American Spelling Book, 311
Anchored instruction, 109
Anderson, David, 518
Andre, Thomas, 221
Apple, Michael, 287
Apple Classrooms of Tomorrow (ACOT), 523
Applications, 119
Apprenticeship, 306
Appropriate education, 66
Appropriation stage, 524
Arab Americans, 488–489
Aristotle, 374, 376, 378
Artifacts, 109, 131
Arts education, 243
Arts Education Consensus Project, 243
Ashton-Warner, Sylvia, 338–339
Asian Americans, 484, 518
Asian Indian Americans, 486
Assertive discipline, 372
Assessment, 212
Assistive technology, 529
Association for Supervision and Curriculum, 576
Asynchronous, 533
Athletic participation, 221–222

At-risk children, 501–507
    abused children, 447, 450
    AIDS and HIV, 503–504
    dropping out, 501–503
    gays, lesbians, and bisexuals, 507
    poverty and, 493, 495
    sexuality and teenage pregnancy, 503–504
    substance abuse, 504–507
    youth suicide, 507
Attention deficit hyperactivity disorder, 64
Auditory learners, 41
    teaching tips for, 41
Authentic assessment, 269–270
Authentic learning, 109

B

Backlash (Faludi), 492
Back to basics movement, 232–233, 354
Bagley, William, 354, 364, 366
Banks, James, 54–55, 285
Bank's approach to multicultural education, 55
Barnard, Henry, 312
Barth, John, 284
Basal readers, 234
Baumgartner, Andy, 24
Becker, Henry Jay, 538, 540
Beecher, Catherine, 314, 490
Behavioral objective, 106
Behavior disorders, 64
Behaviorism, 337, 371–372
Behavior modification, 372
Bellack, Arno, 90
Benjamin, Harold, 287
Bennett, William, 356, 364, A-10
Berliner, David, 89, 579
Bernstein, Harriet Tyson, 271
Bersin, Alan, 408
Bestor, Arthur, 144, 320
Best, Raphaela, 187–189
Bethel School District v. *Fraser,* 439, 449
Bethune, Mary McLeod, 336
Bias; *see also* Gender bias; Racial bias
    in computer technology, 530
    cosmetic bias, 279
    imbalance and selectivity as, 278
    interaction bias, 52, 93
    invisibility, 277
    linguistic bias, 278–280
    seven forms of, 276–279
    stereotyping, 277
    in testing, 264

Bias—*Cont.*
     in textbooks, 276–279
Bible fundamentalists, 279
Biddle, Bruce, 579
Bilingual education, 56–63
     backlash against, 61–62
     Bilingual Education Act, 57, 323
     court cases on, 57–58, 60–61
     defined, 57
     English as a Second Language
          (ESL), 58–59
     history of, 56–57, 59
     language submersion/immersion, 59
     LEP students, 58, 60
     maintenance (or developmental)
          approach, 58
     political issues of, 59, 62
     transitional approach to, 58
Bilingual Education Act (1968), 57, 323
Bisexuals, 507
Bissinger, H. G., 223
Black Alliance for Education, 155
Black Americans; *see* African Americans
Blacknall, Carolyn, 535
Bliss, Traci, 286
Block grants, 393
Block scheduling, 111
Bloom, Alan, 284
Bloom, Benjamin, 94, 106
Bloom's taxonomy, 94–95, 106
Blueprints of Reform (AAAS), 239
Board certification, 15–18, 567–569
*Board of Education, Island Trees Union
     Free School District No. 26 v.
     Pico*, 449
*Board of Education of the Westside
     Community Schools v.
     Mergens*, 448
Board of Regents v. Roth, 599
Boat people, 488
Bodily-kinesthetic skills, 43
Bond, 398
Bonus play, 413
Book banning, 285
Books; *see* Textbooks
Book of Virtues (Bennett), 356
Boston Latin Grammar School, 307
Boutwell, Clinton, 149–150
Boyer, Ernest, 145, 150, 233, A–8
Bracey, Gerald W., 270
Brackett, George, 524
Brameld, John, 365
Brandsford, John D., 249
Brookings Institution, 543
Brophy, Jere, 101
Brown, Ann L., 249
Brown, B. Bradford, 185, 222
Brown v. Board of Education of Topeka
     (1954), 65, 322, 325, 327,
     435, 479

Bruner, Jerome, 230, 339–340
Bryant, Anne, 406
Buckley Amendment, 434
Bureau of Indian Affairs (BIA), 477
Busing, 480

C
Cafeteria-style curriculum, 148
Canon, 235
Canter, Lee, 372
Canter, Marlene, 372
*Cardinal Principles of Secondary
     Education*, 318
Career education, 246–248
Career ladder programs, 567–568,
     570–571
Career opportunities; *see also*
     Employment
     nontraditional, 599–604
Career preparation; *see* Teacher
     education
Career switchers, 562
Carkci, Mathina, 554–555
Carlson, Kenneth, 70, 113
Carnegie Council on Adolescent
     Development, 199–200
Carnegie Forum, 16–17, A–10
Carnegie Foundation for the
     Advancement of Teaching,
     142, A–8
Carnegie unit, 318
Carter, Jimmy, 393
Cartesian dualism, 377
Categorical grants, 322, 393
Censor, 282
Censorship, 438
     of books, 279–284
     the curriculum and, 281–284
     the Internet and, 433–434
     stealth censorship, 283
     of student publications,
          442–443, 449
Center for Commercial-Free Public
     Education, 235
Certification, 29–30
     board-certified, 17
     state offices for, A-1–A-4
Challenge 2000 Multimedia Project, 527
Channel One, 519
Character education, 451
Charter schools, 155–160
Chase, Bob, 576
Chavez, Cesar, 483
Cheating, 450
Cheney, Lynne, 262
Chief state school officer, 401–402
Child abuse, 447
     warning signs of, 450
Child-centered approach, 232
Children, poverty and, 493, 495

Children's boards, 151
Children's Defense Fund (CDF), 502
Children's policy, 151
Children's Television Workshop
     (CTW), 519
Chinese Americans, 485
Choice programs, 395
Christian fundamentalists, 279
Chubb, John, 157
Cigarette smoking, 506
Civics, 237
Civil Rights Act of 1964, 57, 322,
     425, 479
Clarification, 93
Clarity, 92–93
Clarke, Edward, 490
Clark, Kenneth, 339
Classroom climate, 54
Classroom environment
     cooperative education and, 496
     displays, 496
     mobility in, 496
     for nonsexist, nonracist teaching,
          496–497
     as safe and orderly, 202–203
     segregated seating patterns,
          496, 509
Classroom interaction, 182; *see also*
     Questioning
     gender bias and, 52, 93
     interaction bias and, 52
     racial bias and, 52
Classroom law, 424
Classroom management, 84–90
     cultural diversity and, 51–54
     fragmentation problem, 89
     group alerting, 87–88
     high-traffic areas, 86
     instructional presentations, 86
     listening skills, 89
     overlapping, 88
     planning and, 85
     principle of least intervention, 88
     procedures and routines, 86
     providing student choice, 89
     questioning and, 93–99
     room arrangement and, 85
     rules in, 84–95
     setting expectations, 85
     strategies and techniques in, 85–87
     student anger and aggression, 89
     student participation, 85
     student responsibility and, 89
     teaching materials and supplies, 86
     transitions and, 89–90
Classroom transitions, 89–90
     dangles, 90
     flip-flops, 90
     fragmentation, 90
     overdwelling, 90

Classroom transitions—*Cont.*
    thrusts, 90
Class size, 211
Clinton, William J., 426, A-10
Clock watching, 180–181
Closed social system, 192
The Closing of the American Mind
        (Bloom), 284
Closure, 93
Coalition of Essential Schools, 270, 355
Cocking, Rodney R., 249
Cocurriculum, 221
Codell, E. R., 560
Cognitive domain, 39
    affective domain and, 39
    learning styles and, 39
Coleman, James, 153, 192–193, 551
Colfax, Grant, 167
Collaborative action research (CAR), 560
Collaborative decision making, 415
Collaborative learning, 109
Collective bargaining, 571
College Board, 49
Colleges and universities, 602
    curriculum control and, 259
    nonteaching jobs in, 602
    teacher education in; *see* Teacher
        education
Collier, Virginia P., 62–63
Collins, Patricia, 518
Comenius, 330
Committee of Ten, 317–318
Common schools, 310, 312, 317
Communications Decency Act, 434
Community organizations, 602
    curriculum control and, 257
Community partnership, 199
Competition, 20–21
Comprehensive values education,
        452–453
Compulsory education, 309
Computer literacy, 149
Computer software development, 603
    nonteaching careers in, 603
Computer technology, 520
    Apple Classrooms of Tomorrow
        (ACOT), 523
    basics of, 526
    cooperative learning and, 527
    digital divide, 241, 538–541, 544
    direct teaching, 529
    distance learning, 530
    e-rate (education rate), 521
    gender bias and, 530
    global curriculum, 529–533
    global education and, 532
    goals of, 525
    identification of goals for, 540–545
    impact of, 212
    in instruction, 241–242

Computer technology—*Cont.*
    the Internet and, 520–521
    mastery learning, 528
    mathematical instruction and,
        239, 242
    problem-based learning and, 527
    pros vs. cons of, 531
    reasons for school use, 524–527
    scaffolding and, 527
    science education and, 240
    simulations, 530
    special populations and, 525, 529
    stereotypes and violence, 530
    technology revolution, 517–520
    technophobia, 523
    virtual field trips, 530
    writing skills and, 235, 242
Conditional license, 592
Confidentiality, A-17–A-18
Connors, Neila E., 407
Consolidation, 415–416
Constitution, 425
Constructivism, 369–370
Content standards, 261
Continuing education, 601
Contributions approach, to multicultural
        education, 54
Cooperative education, 496
Cooperative groups, 192
Cooperative learning, 53, 105–106,
        199, 527
Copying published material, 430–432
Copyright Act, 431–432
Copyrighted materials
    brevity, 431
    copying published material,
        430–432
    cumulative effect, 431
    spontaneity, 431
Core curriculum, 199, 232–233, 355
Core knowledge, 284
Corporal punishment, 232,
        437–438, 449
Corrective feedback, 102
Cortés, Carlos, 518
Cosmetic bias, 279
Cottle, Thomas J., 443
Council for Exceptional Children, 576
Counts, George S., 361, 365–366
Court cases; *see* Legal cases; Supreme
        Court
Court system, 425
Covert power, 409–411
Crandall, Prudence, 334–335
Crawford, James, 62
Cremin, Lawrence, 313
Critical pedagogy, 249
Critical thinking skills, 248
Criticism, 101
Cross-disciplinary work, 109

Cruz-Jansen, M. I., 133
Cuban, Larry, 107–108, 544
Cuban Americans, 484
Cultural clues, 496
    touching and personal space, 496
Cultural difference theory, 475
Cultural diversity, 47–63
    bias and; *see* Bias
    bilingual education and, 56–63
    classroom management and, 51–54
    demographic forecasting, 48
    education and, 51–54
    immigration trends, 47
    influences on education, 372–373
    learning styles and, 52, 54
    multicultural education and, 54–56
    sensitivity to, 51–52
    stereotyping vs. generalizations, 51
    television's portrayals, 518
Cultural imperialism, 284–286
Cultural literacy, 284–286, 355
*Cultural Literacy: What Every American
        Needs to Know* (Hirsch), 233,
        285, 355
Cultural values, transmission of,
        140–141
Culture
    peer groups and, 187–197
    of schools; *see* School culture
Curriculum, 219–249
    back to basics movement, 232–233
    bias in, 276–279
    cafeteria-style curriculum, 148
    core curriculum, 199, 232–233
    cosmetic bias in, 279
    in eighteenth century, 228
    environmental education, 231
    explicit, 220
    extracurriculum, 221–224
    formal, 220, 226
    global curriculum, 529–533
    hidden (implicit) curriculum,
        225–226
    historical perspective on, 228–233
    implicit (hidden), 220
    life-adjustment education, 230
    multicultural approach, 231
    new directions for, 248–249
    in nineteenth century, 228–229
    open classroom, 232
    peace studies, 231
    progressive education, 229
    reform of, 148–149
    service credits, 142–143
    in seventeenth century, 228
    social action curriculum, 141–142
    social relevance and, 230–232
    standards movements, 233; *see also*
        Standards movement
    subjects of; *see* Formal curriculum

Curriculum—*Cont.*
  twentieth century, 229–233
  women's studies, 231
Curriculum canon, 284
Curriculum control, 256–288
  administrators and, 258
  Afrocentrists and, 286
  alternatives to high-risk testing, 267–270
  censorship and, 281–284
  colleges and universities, 259
  as cultural imperialism, 284–286
  cultural literacy debate, 284–286
  education commissions and committees, 259
  federal government and, 258
  local government, 259
  parental and community groups, 257
  professional organizations, 259–260
  publishers, 260
  religious fundamentalists and, 279–281
  The Saber-Tooth Curriculum, 287–288
  special interest groups, 260
  standardized tests and, 259
  standards movement and, 260–270
  state government, 258
  students and, 257
  subject area associations, 259–260
  teachers and, 257
  textbooks and, 270–276
Cusick, Philip, 232

D

Dame schools, 306, 314, 317
Dance, 243
Danforth Foundation, 404
Dangles, 90
Dare the Schools Build a New Social Order? (Counts), 361
Darling-Hammond, Linda, 19, 212, 553
Data collection
  sample activities, A-20–A-28
  setting for, A-19–A-20
  unobtrusive measures, A-20
Davis, Carol, 12
Davis, Jim, 413
Davis v. *Monroe County Board of Education,* 444, 449
Day care centers, 601
Death at an Early Age (Kozol), 156
Decaying infrastructure, 398
Decentralization, 415
Deductive reasoning, 378
Deep teaching, 110, 528
Dees, Morris, 435
De facto tracking, 186
De facto (unofficial) segregation, 479
Deficit theory, 474

De jure segregation, 478–479
Delegate representatives, 403
Delpit, Lisa, 236–237
Demographic forecasting, 48
Dengan, Paul, 526
Dependability, 21
Descartes, René, 377
Deschooling Society (Illich), 169
Description vs. interpretation, A-18
Desegregation, 479
Detracking, 184–185
Developmental approach, 58
Dewey, John, 93, 157, 229, 319–321, 335–336, 359–361, 365–366, 527, A-12
The Diary of Anne Frank, 279–280
Dietz, Mary, 120
Differentiated instruction, 110
Digital divide, 241, 538–540, 544
Digital Millennium Copyright Act, 432
Direct instruction, 161
Directions, 93
Direct teaching, 104–105, 529
  daily review, 104
  guided practice, 105
  independent practice, 105
  new material, 105
  principles of, 104–105
  specific feedback, 105
  weekly/monthly reviews, 105
Disabled students, cooperative learning and, 53
Discipline, 20, 436, 497
Discovery method, 230
Disney, 161
Displays, 496
Distance learning, 530
Diversity; *see also* Cultural diversity; Student diversity
  cultural values and, 140
  curriculum demands for, 236
  sexual diversity, 508
Divorce, 498
Document analysis, A-16
Dominant male peer group, 189
Drill, 232
DuBois, W. E. B., 479
Due process, 436
Dumbing down, 274

E

Early childhood education, 601
  academic achievement and, 210
Economic issues, 9; *see also* School financing
Economic reconstructionists, 142–143
Edelman, Marian Wright, 502
Edgewood v. *Kirby,* 388
Edison, Thomas, 519
Edison Schools, 160–161

Edmonds, Ronald, 201
Educating a Profession (AACTE), 12
Education 2000, 260
Education
  academic goals of, 144
  as acculturation/ Americanization, 147
  bilingual; *see* Bilingual education
  career education, 247–248
  cultural influences on, 372–373
  as dynamic field, 27
  early childhood, 210, 601
  effective schools, characteristics of, 201–207, 210–212
  environmental education, 231
  history of; *see* History of American education
  multicultural, 54–56
  nontraditional careers in, 599–604
  personal goals of, 144
  philosophy of; *see* Philosophy of education
  progressive, 319–320
  psychological influences on, 369–372
  purpose of school and schooling, 140–147
  resistance to change in, 107–108
  social and civic goals of, 144
  to transmit knowledge and values, 140–141
  vocational education and goals, 144, 247–248
Education for All Handicapped Children Act, 66
Educational Alternatives Incorporated (EAI), 161
Educational associations, 571–577, 603; *see also* American Federation of Teachers (AFT); National Education Association (NEA)
  nonteaching careers in, 603
Educational isolationism, 228
Educational malpractice, 429
Educational opportunity, 472–509
  Arab Americans, 488–489
  Asian Americans, 484–485
  Asian Indian Americans, 486
  Black Americans, 477–480
  Chinese Americans, 485
  Cuban Americans, 484
  equity and excellence, 508–509
  Filipino Americans, 485–486
  for Hispanics, 481–484
  Japanese Americans, 486–487
  Mexican Americans, 483
  Native Americans, 476–477
  new Latin American immigrants, 484
  Pacific Islanders, 484–485
  Puerto Ricans, 483

Educational opportunity—*Cont.*
  segregated setting, 509
  Southeast Asian Americans, 487–488
  Title IX impact, 492
  tracking and, 182–185
  women and, 490–492
Educational outcomes, 390
Educational partnerships, 411–413
Educational records, 434
Educational television
    programming, 519
Educational Testing Service (ETS), 28,
    596, A-5
Educational vouchers, 154–157
Education commissions and committees,
    curriculum control and, 259
Education Job Openings, 562
Education maintenance organizations
    (EMOs), 160–163
Education reform, 148–151
  charter schools, 155–160
  children's boards, 151
  children's policy, 151
  choice concept, 153
  comprehensive services, 150
  EMOs (educational maintenance
      organizations), 160–163
  full service schools, 151
  home schooling, 166–169
  magnet schools, 153
  open enrollment, 153–154
  privatization of public schools, 161
  for profit schools, 160–163
  school choice debate, 163–166
  school restructuring, 150
  standards and, 149–150
  standards movements, 233
  summary of selected reports,
      A-8–A-11
  three waves of, 149–150
  vouchers, 154
Eight-Year Study, 320
Elementary schools, 312, 317
  common school movement and,
      310–313
  peer culture in, 187–191
Elementary and Secondary Education
    Act (ESEA) of 1965, 258, 323
Eliot, Charles, 317
E-mail, 526
Emergency license, 592
EMOs (educational maintenance
    organizations), 160–163
Emotional intelligence, 45–47
  elements of, 46
  empathy, 46
  managing emotions, 46
  motivation and focus, 46
  relationships, 46
  self-awareness, 46

Emotional intelligence—*Cont.*
  as social intelligence, 47
Emotional intelligence quotient (EQ), 45
Emotionally disturbed students, 64
Empathy, 46
Empiricism, 377
Employment
  applying for a job, 589–590
  finding first position, 561–563
  international, 603
  nontraditional opportunities,
      599–604
  preparation for, 564–565
  résumés, portfolios, and interviews,
      564–566
  tips on obtaining, 586–587
Empowering teachers, 151
Enculturation, 54
Endorsements, 592–593
Engaged pedagogy, 367
Engaged time, 83
Engel v. *Vitale*, 448
English, as subject area, 234–235
English Classical School, 315
English grammar school, 228, 317
English-only movement, 61–62
English as a Second Language (ESL),
    58–59
Enthusiasm, 93
Entrepreneurs, 160
Entry stage, 524
Environmental education, 231
Epistemology, 376
E-portfolio, 590
EQ (emotional intelligence quotient),
    45–47
Equal Educational Opportunities Act
    (EEOA), 58
E-rate (education rate), 521
Escalante, Jaime, 28
Essentialism, 354–355
Establishment clause, 425, 448
Estate (or gift) tax, 392
Ethical issues, 378, 445–456
  AFT Bill of Rights, 454–455
  character education, 451
  cheating, 450
  child abuse, 450
  in the classroom, 453–456
  comprehensive values education,
      452–453
  moral education and, 447–453
  moral stages of development, 452
  NEA code, 454
  values clarification, 451
Ethnicity; *see* Cultural diversity;
    Educational opportunity; Racial
    bias
Ethnocentrism, 372
Examples, 93

Exceptional learners, 64–74
  appropriate education, 66
  categories of, 64
  court decisions and federal law,
      65–66
  critical principles of, 65–66
  gifted and talented students, 68–74
  historical context of, 65
  identifying learning-disabled (LD)
      students, 67
  individualized education program
      (IEP), 66–67
  least-restrictive environment, 66
  mainstreaming debate, 70
  nondiscriminatory education, 66
  procedural due process, 66
  Public Law 94-142, 66
  struggle for educational rights of,
      64–65
  zero reject principle, 65
Excise taxes, 392
Exeter, 310
Exhibits, 109
Existential intelligence, 43
Existentialism, 364–369
Expectations, 206–207
Expectation theory, 474
Experience-based education, 109
Experimentalism, 336
Explicit curriculum, 220, 226; *see also*
    Formal curriculum
Explicit teaching, 104
Extracurricular activities, 30
Extracurriculum, 221–224
  controversial issues of, 223–225
  pay to play regulations, 223
  value of, 221
Eye contact, 496

F
Faculty-led renewal, 415
Failing schools, 390
Fair use, 431
Faludi, Susan, 492
Family patterns, 495–501
  alternative families, 498
  at-risk children, 501–507
  divorce, 498
  homeless families, 500–501
  interracial marriages, 498
  latchkey kids, 498–499
  stepfamilies, 498
  wage earners and parenting,
      497–499
Family Rights and Privacy Act, 434
Fast track training programs, 18
Federal government
  careers in, 603
  curriculum control and, 258
  educational policies of, 321–324

Federal government—*Cont.*
    federal legislation, 323
    school financing and, 393–394
Federal grants
    block, 393
    categorical grants, 393
Federal laws, 425–426
Federal legislation, 323
Feedback, 528
    corrective feedback, 102
    productive feedback, 101
    specific, 105
Feistritzer, C. Emily, 404
Feldman, Sandra, 576
Females; *see also* Gender bias
    educational opportunity and,
        490–492
    exclusion from school, 307, 490–491
Feminism, 362
Fernald, Grace, 65
Field-based training, 113
Filipino Americans, 485–486
Financial input, 390
Financing; *see* School financing
First Amendment, 154, 425, 434,
    439–440, 448–449
First, Patricia, 404
Fischer, Louis, 446
Fiske, Edward B., 267
Five-factor theory of effective schools,
    201–207
Flag salute, 448
Flanders Interaction Analysis, A-14–A-15
Flip-flops, 90
Fordham, Signithia, 185
Foreign languages, 240–241
Foreign language speakers; *see* Bilingual
    education
Formal curriculum, 220, 226
    the arts, 243
    foreign languages, 240–241
    health, 247
    language arts and English, 234–236
    mathematics, 238–239
    physical education, 243–246
    science, 239–240
    social studies, 236–238
    subjects of, 234–248
    technology, 241–243
    vocational and career education,
        247–248
For-profit schools, 160–163
    pros and cons of, 162
Fortune, Jim C., 404
Foundation program, 389
Four States Effect, 273
Fourteenth Amendment, 425, 436
Fourth Amendment, 425
Four Ws, 586

Fragmentation, 89–90, 278
Franklin Academy, 310
Franklin, Benjamin, 56, 62, 310
Franklin v. *Gwinnett County Public
    Schools,* 444, 449
Freedom of access to printed word, 449
Freedom of association, 448
Freedom of the press, 442–443, 449
Freedom of speech, 430, 438–439, 448
    students, 438–439, 448–449
    of teachers, 430
    teachers, 448
Freeman, Jesse L., 404
Freire, Paulo, 143, 340, 363–364
Frieberg, Jackie, 24
Frieberg, Kevin, 24
Friedman, Milton, 153–154, 156
Friendless children, 191
Friendship relationships
    in elementary school, 191
    in high school, 192–197
Froebel, Friedrich, 331
Frostig, Marianne, 65
Fulghum, Robert, 44
Full service schools, 151

G

G.I. Bill of Rights, 323
Gaines, Ernest J., 322
Gamoran, Adam, 186
Gardner, Howard, 43–45, 52, 71,
    525, 527
Gardner's theory of multiple
    intelligences, 43–45
Gaskins, Pearl Fuyo, 498
Gatekeeping, 182
Gay and lesbian individuals, 314–315,
    427, 507
Gebsner v. *Lago Vista Independent School
    District,* 444, 449
Gender bias, 362
    classroom interaction and, 52, 93
    digital divide, 538–541
    in hiring, 425–426
    historical perspective on, 490–491
    in physical education, 246
    in scholarships and awards, 436
    test bias and, 264
    in textbooks, 276–279
Gendered career, 313–314
Gender wall, 189
Generalizations, 51
Geography studies, 238
Gerstner, Louis, 411
Giamatti, Bartlett, 259
Giftedness
    analytic, 71
    definition of, 71–72
    practical, 71

Giftedness—*Cont.*
    synthetic, 71
Gifted students, 64, 68–74
    accelerated programs, 73
    feelings of isolation of, 72
    inclusion of, 73
    minority and females, 73
    special needs of, 73–74
Gift tax, 392
Gilligan, Carol, 54, 452
Glass wall, 492
Global curriculum, 529–533
Global education, 532
Global opportunities, 603
Global village, 532
Goldberg v. *Kelly,* 599
Golden Mean, 375–376
Goleman, Daniel, 45–47, 71
Goodbye, Mr. Chips (Hilton), 11–12
The Good High School (Lightfoot), 201,
    233, A-8
Goodlad, John, 83, 101, 144, 150–151,
    180–181, 183, 188, 193, 220,
    233, A-8–A-9
Good News Club v. *Milford Central
    Schools,* 448
Gorenberg, Nancy, 449
Goss v. *Lopez,* 436, 449
Government; *see also* Federal
    government; Local government;
    State government
    careers in, 603
    curriculum control and, 258–259
Graduation requirements, 149
Graeber, Laurel, 205
Grant, Gerald, 150, 325
Great Books, 356–357
Greene, Maxine, 365, 367–368
Group alerting, 87
Groups, 106, 109
Guaranteed tax base program, 389
Guided practice, 105
Gun-Free Schools Act, 437

H

Hacker, Andrew, 473–474
Haley, Margaret, 572
Hall, G. Stanley, 314
Hall, Reverend Samuel, 15
Hands-on learning, 103
Hardware, 527
Harvard College, 307
Havinghurst, Robert, 184
Hazelwood School District v. *Kuhlmeir,*
    442, 449
Head Start, 323, 327
Health, 246–247
Health and physical impairments, 64
Hearing impaired students, 64

Heiferman, Marvin, 326
Heins, Marjorie, 283
Heller, Rafael, 28
Henry, Jules, 226
Herbart, Johann, 332
Herron, Carolivia, 282
Hersch, Patricia, 197
Heterogeneous (mixed ability)
    classes, 184
Hidden curriculum; see Implicit
    curriculum
Hidden government, 410
Higher-order questions, 94
High-stakes testing, alternatives to,
    267–270
High School (Boyer), 233
High School and Beyond, 223
High schools, 317
    Cardinal Principles goals, 318
    case study of, 326–329
    as closed social systems, 192
    establishment of, 315–316
High-stakes testing, 267–270
High-traffic area, 86
Hill, Anita, 426
Hilton, James, 11
Hiring, legal issues, 425–426
Hirsch, E. D., Jr., 233, 285, 355, 364, 367
Hispanics, 481–484
History of American education, 304–340
    apprenticeship programs, 306
    case study of, 326–329
    in colonial period, 305–309
    common school movement, 310–313
    dame schools, 306
    in early 19th century, 311–312
    in early New England, 306–309
    educational milestones, 327
    federal government in, 321–324
    federal legislation, 323
    gender barriers in, 313–315
    influential figures in, 330–340
    in late 19th century, 316
    Latin grammar school, 307
    in mid- to late 20th century,
        326–329
    overview of, 317
    progressive education, 319–320
    religious influences and, 306–309
    school reform efforts, 316–319
    secondary school movement,
        315–316
    Supreme Court, 322, 325, 327
    textbooks and, 311
HIV-infected students, 443, 503–504
Hofferth, Sandra, 190
Hoffman, Nancy, 573
Holland, Allyce, 221
Hollingshead, August, 184

Holmes, Henry H., 16
Holmes Group, 16
Holt, John, 166
Homeless families, 500–501
Home schooling, 166–169, 306
    ideologues, 167
    the Internet and, 169
    pedagogues, 167
Homework, 205–206, 232
Homogeneous classes, 182
Homophobia, 315, 507
Honesty, 21
Hooks, bell, 367
Hopwood v. State of Texas, 480
Horace's Compromise (Sizer),
    233, A-10
Hornbeck, David, A-10
Hornbook, 228, 311
How Schools Short-Change Girls
    (AAUW), 406
Hunt, James, Jr., 568
Husen, T., 186
Hutchins, Robert M., 356, 364, 366

I

Ianni, Frances, 198–199
Idealism, 376
Ideologues, 167
Illich, Ivan, 166, 169
Imbalance, 278
Immersion, 59
Immigration trends, 47
Implicit curriculum, 220, 225–226
Incentives, 18, 212
Inclusion, 68, 70
Independent practice, 105
Individual analysis, 451
Individualized education program (IEP),
    66, 231
Individuals with Disabilities Education
    Act (IDEA), 66–67, 231, 323, 443
Induction program, 552
Inductive reasoning, 378
Informal education, 373
Information overload, 530
Ingraham v. Wright, 438, 449
Initial license, 591
In loco parentis, 306, 441
In-service days, 558
Instructional alignment, 108
Instructional materials, bias in, 54
Instructional presentations, 86
Instructional time, 180–181
Integrated learning system (ILS), 528
Intelligence
    assessment of, 42–45
    cultural diversity and, 43–44
    defined, 43
    emotional intelligence, 43–47

Intelligence—Cont.
    emotional intelligence quotient (EQ),
        45–47
    existential intelligence, 43
    multiple intelligences, 43–47
    portfolio assessment, 45
    social intelligence, 47
Interaction analysis, A-14–A-15
Interaction bias, 52
    gender, 52, 93
    racial, 52–53
Interaction strategies, 496–497
Interest centers, 232
Inter-mission
    applications and reflections,
        607–614
    foundations, 462–469
    portfolios, 119–122
    schools and curriculum, 294–301
Intern assessment form, 557
International Assessment of Education
    Progress (IAEP), 578
International Baccalaureate (IB)
    program, 73
Internauts, 529–533
Internet, 520–521
    access to, 526
    censorship and, 433–434
    cheating by, 530
    deep teaching and, 528
    defined, 526
    e-mail, 526
    e-rate (education rate), 521
    global village of, 532
    home schooling and, 169
    inappropriate material, 530
    problems to avoid, 530
    use of, 242–242
    virtual teacher, 533–538
    web pages, 523
    World Wide Web, 526
Internment camps, 487
Intern teachers, 552–553
Interpersonal skills, 43
Interracial marriage, 498
Interstate New Teacher Assessment and
    Support Consortium (INTASC),
        121–123
Interstate reciprocity agreements, 593
Interviews, 564–566, A-14
    applying for a position, 425–426
    employment, 425–426
    gender bias in, 425–426
    with teachers, 123–124, 127–128
Intrapersonal skills, 43
Invention stage, 524
Invisibility, 277
IQ score, 42–43, 71, 210, 474
Isolation, 278

Is There Life After High School?
    (Keyes), 192
Itinerant schools, 317

J

Jackson, Andrew, 311
Jackson, Philip W., 179, 182, 186
Jacobson, Lenore, 207, 474
Japanese Americans, 486–487
Jefferson, Thomas, 166, 310
Job interviews
    gender bias in, 425–426
    questions in, 425–426
Job market
    finding a position, 586–587
    nontraditional careers in, 599–604
Juku schools, 577
Junior high schools, 229, 316–317

K

Kalamazoo, Michigan, case, 316, 327
Katz, J., 538
Katz, Lillian, 552
*Keeping Track: How Schools Structure
    Inequality* (Oakes), 184, 188
Kelly, Cynthia, 446
Kerner Commission, 480
Keyes, Ralph, 192
Kin, Kwan Weng, 141
Kindergarten, 331
Kindler, Sara, 526
Kinesthetic learners, 41, 103
    teaching tips for, 41
King, Edward, 327
Kirschenbaum, Howard, 452
Kirst, Michael, 492
Kismaric, Carole, 326
Kniep, William, 532
Knowledge explosion, 275
Kohlberg, Lawrence, 452
Kohn, Alfie, 199, 266
Kounin, Jacob, 88, 90
Kozol, Jonathan, 156–157, 166

L

Labeling, 185
Laboratory school, 319, 360–361
Labor rights, 432–433
Ladson-Billings, Gloria, 563
Lamb, Christopher, 305–306
LaMorte, Michael, 425
Land-Grant College Acts, 323
Land Ordinance Act, 321, 323
Landsman, Julie, 484
Langdon, Carol, 23
Language arts, 234–235
Language impaired students, 64
Language submersion, 57
Last mile problem, 540–541
Latchkey (self-care) kids, 498–499, 531

Latin grammar schools, 228, 307, 317
Latino students, 223, 484
Lau v. *Nichols,* 57–58
Leadership, 201
Learning
    authentic, 109
    cooperative, 105–106
    mastery learning, 106–108
Learning centers, 232
Learning communities, 110–111, 560
Learning disabilities, 68
Learning-disabled (LD) students, 64
    identification of, 67
Learning divide, 241
Learning styles, 38–42
    affective domain and, 39
    auditory learners, 41
    cultural diversity and, 52, 54
    definition of, 38
    factors of, 39–40
    kinesthetic learners, 41
    locus of control and, 39
    myths about, 40
    physiological factors in, 40
    preferred styles, 41
    teaching tips for, 41
    visual learners, 41
Learning time, 212
Least intervention, 88
Least-restrictive environment, 66
Lee v. *Weisman,* 448
Lefkowitz, Bernard, 196
Legal cases
    Abbott v. *Burke,* 390
    Bethel School District v. *Fraser,*
        439, 449
    *Board of Education, Island Trees Union
        Free School District No. 26* v. *Pico,*
        449
    *Board of Education of the Westside
        Community Schools* v. *Mergens,*
        448
    Board of Regents v. *Roth,* 599
    Brown v. *Board of Education of Topeka*
        (1954), 65, 322, 325, 327, 435,
        479
    Davis v. *Monroe County Board of
        Education,* 444, 449
    Edgewood v. *Kirby,* 388
    Engel v. *Vitale,* 448
    Franklin v. *Gwinnett County Public
        Schools,* 444, 449
    Gebsner v. *Lago Vista Independent
        School District,* 444, 449
    Goldberg v. *Kelly,* 599
    Good News Club v. *Milford Central
        Schools,* 448
    Goss v. *Lopez,* 436, 449
    Hazelwood School District v. *Kuhlmeir,*
        442, 449

Legal cases—*Cont.*
    Hopwood v. *State of Texas,* 480
    Ingraham v. *Wright,* 438, 449
    Lau v. *Nichols,* 57–58
    Lee v. *Weisman,* 448
    Lemon v. *Kurtzman,* 154, 448
    McCollum v. *Board of Education,* 448
    Meyer v. *State of Nebraska,* 57
    Mill v. *D.C. Board of Education,* 65
    *Pennsylvania Association for Retarded
        Children* v. *Commonwealth,* 65
    Perry v. *Sinderman,* 599
    Pickering v. *Board of Education,* 448
    Plessy v. *Ferguson,* 327, 478
    San Antonio v. *Rodriguez,* 388
    Santa Fe Independent School District v.
        Doe, 449
    Serrano v. *Priest,* 388
    Shelton v. *Tucker,* 448
    Smith v. *YMCA,* 435
    Stone v. *Graham,* 448
    Thompson v. *Southwest School
        District,* 427
    Tinker v. *Des Moines Independent
        Community School District,*
        438–439, 448
    Wallace v. *Jaffree,* 448
    West Virginia State Board of Education
        v. *Barnette,* 448
    Wood v. *Strickland,* 437
Legal issues
    academic freedom, 428–429
    applying for a position, 425–426
    censorship, 438
    child abuse, 447, 450
    copying published material,
        430–432
    corporal punishment, 437–438, 449
    distribution of scholarships, 436
    educational records, 434
    fair use, 431
    flag salute, 448
    freedom of the press, 442–443
    freedom of speech, 430, 438–439
    HIV-infected students, 443
    Internet censorship, 433–434
    job interview questions, 425–426
    labor rights, 432–433
    legal liability, 429–430
    obscene speech, 439
    personal lifestyle, 427
    school prayer, 440, 448–449
    search-and-seizure activities, 441
    sexual harassment, 426,
        443–445, 449
    students' rights and responsibilities,
        434–445
    suspension and discipline, 436–438
    teachers' rights and responsibilities,
        425–434

Legal liability, 429–430
Lemon v. Kurtzman, 154, 448
Lerner, Phyllis, 119
Lesbians, 507
Levenson, William, 519
Levy, Harold, 408
Lewis, Michael, 533
Licenses, 29–30
    alternative routes to, 593–595
    conditional (emergency), 592
    endorsements, 592–593
    initial (provisional), 591
    portfolios and, 120
    program accreditation and, 593
    reciprocity for, 593
    standard (professional), 121, 592
    state offices for, A-1–A-4
Life-adjustment education, 230
Life in Classrooms (Jackson), 179
Lightfoot, Sara Lawrence, 201, 233, A-8
Limited English proficiency (LEP), 58, 60
Linguistic bias, 278–279
Linguistic skills, 43
Llewellyn, Grace, 167
Local control, 387
Local fundraising, 395
Local government, curriculum control
    and, 259
Local laws, 425
Local private schools, 317
Local school districts, 403
Locus of control, 39
Logic, 378
Logic-mathematical skills, 43
Logs and journals, A-16
Looping, 111
Lower-order questions, 94
Lyceum, 374
Lynd, Helen, 183
Lynd, Robert, 183
Lyon, Mary, 490

M

McAuliffe, Christa, 534–535
McCarthy, Donald, 408
McCarthy, Joseph, 320
McCollum v. Board of Education, 448
McDaniel, Thomas, 280
McGuffey Readers, 229, 311
McKinney Homeless Assistance Act, 500
Magnet schools, 153
Mainstreaming (inclusion), 53, 65, 68,
    70, 231
Maintenance (developmental)
    approach, 58
Malfeasance, 429
Maloney, Karen, 362
Mann, Horace, 15, 166, 312–313, 315,
    317, 327, 333–334

The Manufactured Crisis (Berliner and
    Biddle), 579
Martin, Jane Roland, 362, 365
Marzano, Robert, 249, 280
Massachusetts Law of 1647, 307
Master teacher, 570
Mastery learning, 106–108, 528
    instructional alignment and, 108
Mastruzzi, Robert, 201
Materialism, 376
Matero, Dary, 452
Mathematics, 238–239
Matthews, Jay, 266
Mazur, Joan, 286
Media, 602
    nonteaching careers in, 602
Mental retardation, 64
Mentioning phenomenon, 275
Mentors, 552–555
Merit pay, 567, 569–570
    individualized productivity plans, 569
    student performance and, 569
    teacher performance and, 569
    teaching assignment, 569
Metacognition, 249
Metaphysics, 376
Mexican Americans, 483
Meyer v. State of Nebraska, 57
Middle schools, 316–317
Mildly handicapped students, 64
Mill v. D.C. Board of Education, 65
Miner, Myrtilla, 490
Minimum competency tests, 595
Misfeasance, 429
Mission, 202
Mixed ability classes, 184
Mobility, 496
Model minority, 485
Molnar, Alex, 166
Montessori, Maria, 335
Montessori schools, 335
Moore, D. N., 168
Moore, R. S., 168
Moral education, 447–453
Moral stages of development, 452
Morrill Land Grant College Acts, 323
Motivation, 46
Motor vehicle license fee, 392
Multicultural approach, 231
Multicultural education, 54–56,
    285–286
    additive approach to, 55
    Bank's approach to, 55
    contributions approach to, 54
    goal of, 54
    social action and, 56
    transformation approach to, 55
Multiple intelligences (MI), 43, 124
Municipal overburden, 388
Murphy, Joseph, 150

Music, 243
Musical ability, 43

N

National Assessment of Educational
    Progress (NAEP), 235, 238–239
National Association for the
    Advancement of Colored People
    (NAACP), 155, 502
National Association for the Education
    of Young Children (NAEYC),
    259, 576
National Association of Elementary
    School Principals, 569
National Association for Gifted
    Children, 576
National Association of Secondary
    School Principals, 569
National Association of State Directors
    of Teacher Education and
    Certification (NASDTEC), 593
National Board for Professional Teaching
    Standards (NBPTS), 17, 112, 120,
    567–569, A-11
National Center for Educational
    Statistics (NCES), 9, 521
National Commission on Excellence in
    Education, 148, 233, 318,
    569, A-8
National Commission on Testing and
    Public Policy, 267
National Council for the Accreditation of
    Teacher Education (NCATE), 593
National Council for the Social
    Studies, 577
National Council for Teachers of
    English, 577
National Council of Teachers of
    Mathematics (NCTM), 238, 577
National Defense Education Act (NDEA),
    230, 321, 323
National Education Association (NEA), 9,
    161, 166, 314, 432–433, 507,
    523, 571–575, 599
    Code of Ethics, 454
    Committee of Ten, 317–318
    curriculum control and, 259
    school reform and, 317–318
National Education Resource
    Center, 148
National Education Standards and
    Improvement Council, 261
National Education Summit, 259–261
National evaluation systems, A-6
National Geographic Society, 238
National Middle School
    Association, 576
National School Board Association
    (NSBA), 406
National Science Board, 569

National Science Teachers Association, 577
National Teacher Examination (NTE), 259, 596
A Nation at Risk: The Imperative for Educational Reform, 148–149, 233, 259, 261, 318, 354, 595, A-8
A Nation Prepared (Carnegie Forum), 16, A-10
Native Americans, 47, 51, 55, 278, 322, 518
  educational opportunity for, 476–477
  exclusion from school, 307
Naturalistic ability, 43
Negligence, 429–430
Neill, A. S., 365–366, 368
Neiman, David, 573
Nelson, Jack L., 70
Nelson, L., 113
Neoessentialism, 354
Networking, 30
New Age movement, 281
New England Primer, 228–229, 311
Noddings, Nel, 365, 367
Nolan, Virginia, 53
Nondiscriminatory education, 66
Nonfeasance, 429
Nonteachers, 372–373
Nontenured teachers, 599
Nontraditional careers, 601–604
Normal schools, 15, 313
Norm-referenced tests, 205
Northwest Ordinance, 321, 323
Note taking, A-16
Noverbal signs, 207
Nuts (Frieberg and Frieberg), 24
Nyquist case, 154

O

Oakes, Jeannie, 184, 186, 188–189
Objective, 92
Objective-referenced tests, 205
Obscene speech, 439
Observation, 555–559
Observation manual, A-12–A-28
  curriculum, A-13
  general guidelines, A-12
  identifying goals and concerns, A-12–A-13
  learning how to observe, A-13–A-20
  setting, A-12
  students, A-13
  teaching, A-13
  techniques for, A-14
Observation techniques
  becoming accepted as observer, A-17
  confidentiality and, A-17–A-18
  description vs. interpretation, A-18
  document analysis, A-16

Observation techniques—*Cont.*
  Flanders Interaction Analysis, A-14–A-15
  interviewing, A-14
  logs and journals, A-16
  note taking, A-16
  observation data, A-14
  questionnaires, A-14
Odden, Allan, 276
Office for Civil Rights, 426
Ogbu, John, 185
Old Deluder Satan Law, 307
O'Neill, Grace, 560
O'Neill, John, 189
Open classroom, 232
Open enrollment, 153–154
Opportunity-to-learn standard, 264
Oral tradition, 373
Orfield, Gary, 480
Other People's Children (Delpit), 237
Ovando, Carlos J., 58, 63
Overdwelling, 90
Overlapping, 88
Owen, David, 194

P

Pacific Islanders, 484
Page, Reba, 186
The Paideia Proposal (Adler), 233, 356, A-8
Palonsky, Stuart B., 70, 113
Parents, 9, 409, 411; *see also* Family patterns
  curriculum control and, 257
  divorced, 498
  working, 497–499
Parent Teacher Associations, 395
Parker, Francis, 319
Parker, Palmer, 378
Parsons, Talcott, 183
Participatory management, 415
Pay, 9–11, 14, 587–588
  bonuses/incentives, 18
  merit pay, 569–570
  private vs. public schools, 588
Pay to play regulations, 223
Peace studies, 231
Pedagogical cycle, 90–93, 182
  academic structure in, 92–93
  questioning in, 91
  reaction in, 91, 99–102
  responding in, 91
  sample classroom dialogue, 92
  structure in, 90–91
Pedagogues, 167
Pedagogy, 21
The Pedagogy of the Oppressed (Freire), 143, 340
Peer culture
  in elementary school, 187–191

Peer culture—*Cont.*
  in high school, 192–197
Peer review, 555
Pennsylvania Association for Retarded Children v. *Commonwealth,* 65
Perennialism, 355–357
Perennialists, 356
Performance-based testing, 267
Performance standards, 263
Perkins, David, 249
Perkins (Carl D.) Vocational and Applied Technology Act, 248
Perry v. *Sinderman,* 599
Personal goals, 144
Personal income tax, 392
Personalizing schools, 560–561
Personal lifestyle, 427
Personal space, 496
Pestalozzi, Johann Heinrich, 331
Phillips Academy, 310
Phillips Exeter Academy, 310
Philosophy
  aesthetics, 378
  basic issues and concepts of, 376–378
  branches of, 377
  classical Greek, 374
  deductive reasoning, 378
  epistemology and, 376–377
  ethics, 378
  inductive reasoning, 378
  logic, 378
  metaphysics and, 376–377
  political philosophy, 378
Philosophy of education, 347–379
  classical western philosophy, 374–375
  cultural influences, 372–373
  essentialism, 354–355, 364
  existentialism, 364–369
  five philosophies of, 353–369
  perennialism, 355–357, 364
  progressivism, 359–361
  psychological influences, 369–372
  self-test for, 348–353
  social reconstructionism, 361–364
  student-centered philosophies, 359–369
  teacher-centered philosophies, 354–359
Phonics, 234
Physical abuse, 450
Physical education, 243–246
Physiological factors, learning and, 40
Piaget, Jean, 337, 369, 452
Pickering, Marvin, 430
Pickering v. *Board of Education,* 448
A Place Called School (Goodlad), 83, 101, 144, 220, 233, A-8
Placement folder, 31

Plato, 374, 376
Plessy v. *Ferguson,* 327, 478
Political philosophy, 378
Pollack, David C., 475
Portfolios, 31, 45, 269, 564–565, 589
    artifact collection, 131
    building of, 120
    introduction to, 119–122
    objectives for, 120
    presentation portfolio, 120
    starting on, 120
    working portfolio, 120
Postlethwaite, T. Neville, 186
Postman, Neil, 284
Poussaint, Alvin, 518
Pragmatism, 336, 359
Praise, 100–102
Praxis Assessment for Beginning
        Teachers, 364, 596, A-5
Presentation portfolio, 120
President's Council on Physical Fitness
        and Sports, 246
Principals, 407–409
    curriculum control and, 258
    effective, 201–202
    tenure of, 599
Privacy rights, 425
Private industry, 602
    nonteaching careers in, 602–603
Private schools, 317
    in colonial America, 307, 317
    pay scale for, 588
    school choice and, 153
Privatization, 161, 586
Probationary teaching period, 598
Problem-based learning (PBL),
        108–109, 527
Procedural due process, 66
Procedures, 86
The Process of Education (Bruner),
        230, 340
Productive feedback, 101
Profession, criteria for, 12
Professional associations and resources,
        575–577
Professional development, 559
    collaborative action research
        (CAR), 560
    educational associations, 571–577
    professional associations and
        resources, 575–577
    programs for, 558–560
Professionalism
    board-certified teachers, 15–18
    new version of, 15–18
Professional license, 592
Professional organizations, curriculum
        control and, 259–260
Progressive education, 229, 319–321
    criticism of, 320

Progressive Education Association
        (PEA), 318
Progressive schools, as working model
        of democracy, 360
Progressivism, 359–361
Project-based instruction, 109
Project Head Start, 323, 327
Property taxes, 387–388
Proposition 13, 389
Provisional license, 591
PSAT, 264
Psychological influences on education,
        369–372
    behaviorism, 371–372
    constructivism, 369–370
Public Agenda, 20
Public Law 94-142, 66
Public utilities, nonteaching careers in,
        602–603
Publishers, curriculum control and, 260
Puerto Ricans, 483–484
Pupil service professionals, 602
Pygmalion in the Classroom (Rosenthal
        and Jacobson), 207

Q
Questioning
    Bloom's taxonomy for, 94–95
    by teacher, 93–99
    higher-order question, 94–96
    lower-order question, 94–96
    productive feedback, 99–102
    reaction and, 99–102
    student-initiated questions, 99
    student response to, 96–99
    teacher echo, 98
    wait time and, 98–99
Questionnaires, A-14

R
Rabey, Steve, 602
Racial bias
    anti-achievement climate, 185, 187
    in educational materials, 54
    interaction, 52–53
    peer culture and, 191–192
    school achievement and, 184
    segregation and, 322, 325, 327,
        479–480
    in standardized testing, 49
    teacher competency tests and, 597
    in textbooks, 276–279
    tracking and, 184–187
Racism, 314
Raloff, J., 222
Ramsey, Charles, 408
Rand, Ayn, 143
Raney, Mardell, 157
Rationalism, 377

Reaction, 99–102
    acceptance response, 100–101
    criticism as, 101
    praise response, 100
    remediation and, 100
Readability formulas, 274
Reasoning
    deductive, 378
    inductive, 378
Reciprocity agreements, 593
Reconstructionists, 141
Reflective teaching, 111, A-12
Reformers, 160
Regular education initiative, 68
Religion, 306–309
    in school, 440
Religious education, 154–155, 448
Religious fundamentalism, 279–281
Religious Right, 279
Remediation, 100
Renzulli, Joseph, 71
The Republic, 374
Résumés, 31, 564–565, 589
Reviews, 105
Rickover, Hyman, 320
Ride, Sally, 534–535
Right to due process, 425, 449
Riley, Richard, 508
Rist, Ray, 184
Robb, Daniel, 492
Robin Hood reformers, 389, 395
Romantic critics, 230
Romer, Roy, 408
Room arrangement, 85; *see also*
        Classroom environment
Roosevelt, Franklin D., 479, 487
Roosevelt, Theodore, 314
Rose, Christine, 328
Rosenthal, Robert, 207, 474
Rothstein, Richard, 59
Rousseau, Jean-Jacques, 330–331, 362
Routines, 86
Rowe, Mary Budd, 98–99

S
The Saber-Tooth Curriculum, 287–288
Sadker, David, 490
Sadker, Myra, 490
St. John's College, 356–357
Salaries, 9–11, 14, 587–588
    merit pay and, 569–570
    private vs. public schools, 588
Sales tax, 392
Salovey, Peter, 46
San Antonio v. *Rodriguez,* 388
Sanford, John, 408
Santa Fe Independent School District v.
        Doe, 449
Sartre, Jean-Paul, 364
SATs, 259, 264, 579

Savage Inequalities (Kozol), 156
Scaffold, 93
Scaffolding, 369, 527
Schaffer, David Williamson, 527
Schimmel, David, 446
Schlesinger, Arthur, 286
Schmidt, Benno, 160
Scholarships, 436
Scholastic Assessment Test (SAT), 259,
    264, 579
School-based management, 415
School boards, 151, 401, 404–405
School choice, 153, 395
    pros and cons of, 163–164
School culture, 175–212
    ability grouping, 186–187
    affective side of school reform,
        197–200
    classroom interaction and, 182
    clear mission, 202
    clock watching and, 180–181
    delay and social distraction in,
        179–180
    detracking and, 184–185
    effective schools, characteristics of,
        201–207, 210–212
    emotional tone in, 183
    expectations and, 206–207
    five-factor theory of effective schools,
        201–207
    gatekeeping in, 182
    homogeneous classes vs. tracking,
        182–185
    leadership and, 201
    mission and, 202
    monitoring of student progress,
        203–206
    rules, rituals and routines, 176–179
    safe and orderly climate, 202–203
    socioeconomic bias in, 183–184
    strong leadership and, 201
School environment, as safe and orderly,
    202–203
School financing, 386–415
    accountability and, 395
    block grants, 393
    bonds in, 398
    categorical grants, 393
    choice programs, 395
    decaying infrastructure, 398
    equity vs. adequacy, 391
    federal government's role, 393–394
    financial input vs. educational
        outcome, 390
    future trends and issues, 393–398
    importance of, 386–387
    local fundraising, 395–396
    move toward adequacy, 389–390
    personal income tax, 392
    property taxes in, 387–388

School financing—*Cont.*
    public opinion on spending, 398
    reforming of, 388–389
    Robin Hood reformers and, 389
    sales tax in, 392
    sources and uses of funds, 389
    state actions and, 389–393
    state lotteries, 392
    Supreme court cases on, 388
School governance
    chief state school officer, 401–402
    covert power in, 409–411
    educational partnerships, 411–413
    legal control of schools, 400
    local level, 401
    making schools responsive, 413–415
    parents and, 409, 411
    principal, 407–409
    quiz on, 399–400
    school-based management, 415
    school boards, 404–405
    school superintendent, 407–409
    state department of education,
        401–402
    state influence, 403–407
    state level, 401
    superintendent, 401–402
    teacher empowerment and, 415
    top-down decision making, 415
School law, 424–445
    basics of, 425
    classroom law, 424
    Constitution, 425
    court system, 425
    federal laws, 425–426
    rights quotient (RQ), 424, 445
    state and local laws, 425–426
    students' rights and responsibilities,
        434–445
    teachers' rights and responsibilities,
        425–434
*The School Managers: Power and Conflict
    in American Public Education*
    (McCarty and Ramsey), 408
School mascots, 328
Schoolography, 325
School prayer, 440, 448
School reform, 148–151, 317–318; *see
    also* Education reform
    affective side of, 197–200
    five-factor theory of effective schools,
        201–207
    limitations of research, 207–210
    three waves of, 149–150
School-related violence, 202–203
School(s)
    academies, 317
    acculturation/Americanization
        by, 147
    charter schools, 155–160

School(s)—*Cont.*
    common schools, 312, 317
    criticism of, 577–580
    dame schools, 306, 317
    decaying infrastructure of, 398
    effectiveness factors, 200–207
    elementary schools, 312, 317
    English grammar schools, 228, 317
    evaluation of, 577–580
    five-factor theory of effective schools,
        201–207
    for-profit schools, 160–163
    full service schools, 151
    goals of, 144–147
    high schools, 317
    home schooling, 166–169
    itinerant schools, 317
    junior high schools, 317
    laboratory school, 319, 360–361
    Latin grammar schools, 228,
        307, 317
    local private, 317
    magnet schools, 153
    middle schools, 317
    Montessori, 335
    names of, 148
    normal, 313
    performance of, 577–580
    personalizing, 560–561
    private schools; *see* Private schools
    privatization of, 161
    property taxes and, 387–388
    public demands for, 144–145
    purpose of, 140–143
    research problems of, 207–210
    secondary schools, 317
    segregation in, 479–480
    size of, 210
    as tools for change, 141–143
    as transmitters of culture and
        knowledge, 140–141
School secretary, 409–410
School size, 210
*Schools More Separate: Consequences
    of a Decade of Resegregation*
    (Orfield), 480
School superintendent, 407–409
*The Schools We Need and Why We Don't
    Have Them* (Hirsch), 355
School time, 180–181
School uniforms, 204, 208
Science, 239–240
Scientific method, 360
Scott, Darrell, 602
Screen potato syndrome, 530
Search-and-seizure activities, 441
Secondary school movement, 315–317
Second-generation segregation, 480
*Secretary's Conference on Educational
    Technology*, 543

Secular humanism, 281
Segregated seating patterns, 496, 509
Selectivity, 278
Self-awareness, 46
Self-care kids, 499
Self-censorship, 283
Self-fulfilling prophecy, 207
Semiprofession, criteria for, 13
Senge, Peter M., 410
Separate but equal, 65, 478
Separation of church and state,
    448–449
Sequoyah, 477
Serrano v. Priest, 388
Service credit, 142–143
Servicemen's Readjustment Act
    (1944), 323
Sesame Street, 519
Seven forms of bias, 276
Severance tax, 392
Sex in Education (Clarke), 490
Sexism, 490–492
Sex-role stereotyping, 492
Sexual abuse, 450
Sexual diversity, 508
Sexual harassment, 426, 443–445, 449
Sexuality, 503
Shanker, Albert, 155
Shared leadership, 415
Shell Game: Corporate America's Agenda
    for Schools (Boutwell), 149
Shelton v. Tucker, 448
Sherman, Ruth, 281–282
Shreve, Porter, 493
Shreve, Susan Richards, 493
Sigford, Jane L., 409
Signing bonuses, 18
Simulations, 530
Sin tax, 392
Site-based (school-based)
    management, 415
Sizer, Theodore, 109–110, 150, 233,
    270, 355, A-10–A-11
Skinner, B. F., 337–338, 372, 520
Slavin, Robert, 106, 249
Smith, C. H., 71
Smith-Hughes Act (1917), 323
Smith v. YMCA, 435
Snook, Pamela A., 438
Social action approach, to multicultural
    education, 56
Social action curriculum, 141
Social/civic goals, 144
Social Darwinism, 363
Social exclusion, 190
Social intelligence, 47
Social reconstructionism, 361–364
Social status
    in elementary school, 191
    in high school, 192–197

Social studies, 236–238
Sociograms, 191–192
Socrates, 374, 376
Socratic method, 374–375
Southeast Asian Americans, 487–488
Southwest Airlines (case example),
    24–27
Spatial ability, 43
Special education, 65
Special high schools, 73
Special interest groups
    curriculum control and, 260
    religious fundamentalists, 279–281
    secular humanism as, 281
Special license, 592
Special needs students, mainstreaming
    of, 70
Specific feedback, 105
Spindler, George, A-13
Spinsters, 314
Sputnik, 230, 320, 323, 327, 354
Staff development; see Teacher
    development
Stages of teacher development,
    551–552
Standardized testing, 109, 151
    alternatives to high-risk testing,
        267–270
    authentic assessment, 269
    curriculum control and, 259,
        263–264
    learning vs. test learning, 264,
        266–267
    performance on, 579–580
    racial bias and, 597
    racial-ethnic groups and, 49
    for teacher competency, 595–597
    to monitor student progress, 205
Standard license, 592
Standards, 20, 149, 268, 309
    state standards and tests, 272
Standards movement, 233
    alternatives to high-risk testing,
        267–270
    content standards, 261–262
    curriculum control and, 260–270
    history content debate, 262–263
    opportunity-to-learn standards, 264
    performance standards, 263
    testing and, 263–267
State board of education, 401
State department of education, 402
State government, 403
    curriculum control and, 258
State laws, 425–426
State lotteries, 392
State offices, for certification and
    licensure, A-1–A-4
Status
    social, 191

Status—Cont.
    of teaching, 9–15
Statutes, 425
Stealth censorship, 283
Steele, Ellen Hogan, 11–12
Steinberg, Laurence, 185
Steindam, Sharon, 107
Stepfamilies, 498
Stereotyping, 51, 277; see also Bias
Sternberg, Robert, 71
Stewart, Potter, 387
Stone v. Graham, 448
Stowe, Harriet Beecher, 490
Student backpacks, 246
Student-centered philosophies, 320
    existentialism, 364–369
    progressivism, 359–361
    social reconstructionism, 361–364
    summary of, 365
    vs. teacher-centered approaches,
        358–359
Student diversity, 37–74; see also
    Cultural diversity; Educational
    opportunity
    bilingual education and, 62
    exceptional learners and, 64–68
    learning styles and, 38–42
    standardized testing and, 49
Student-initiated questions, 99
Student learning styles, 38
Student-led prayer, 449
Student participation, rules in, 85
Student performance
    homework, 205–206
    monitoring of, 203–206
    norm-referenced tests, 205
    objective-referenced tests, 205
    teacher expectations and, 206–207
    technology and, 212
Student publications, censorship of,
    442–443
Student response, 96–99
Student(s); see also At-risk children
    adolescent angst, 197
    anger and aggression of, 89
    commercial marketing to, 235
    community service by, 142–143
    curriculum control and, 257–258
    digital divide, 538–540
    discipline of, 436–438
    freedom of speech of, 438–439
    misbehavior of, 89
    peer culture of, 192–197
    rights and responsibilities of,
        434–445, 448–449
    sexual harassment of, 443–445
    social and emotional needs of,
        197–200
    teacher expectations and, 206–207
    teacher's impact on, 8

Students' rights and responsibilities,
      434–445, 448–449
   distribution of scholarships, 436
   freedom of the press, 442–443
   freedom of speech, 438–439, 448
   HIV-infected students, 443
   school prayer, 440
   search and seizure, 441
   sexual harassment, 443–445
   students records, 434–436
   suspension and discipline, 436–438
Substance abuse, 504–507
Summer, S. G., 372
Superintendent, 401–402
Supreme Court, 322, 325, 327, 388,
      393, 444, 478–479
   First Amendment, 154, 425, 434,
      439–440, 448–449
   Fourteenth Amendment, 425, 436
   Fourth Amendment, 425
   freedom of access to printed
      word, 449
   freedom of association, 448
   freedom of the press, 442–443, 449
   freedom of speech, 430, 438–439,
      448–449
   privacy rights, 425
   right to due process, 425, 449
   Tenth Amendment, 321, 400
Suspension, 436
Susskind, Ron, 480
Swaden, Martin, 264
Systematic teaching, 104

T
Taba, Hilda, 220
Tactics for Thinking (Marzano), 280
Tatum, Beverly D., 184
Taxes
   estate tax, 392
   excise tax, 392
   gift tax, 392
   personal income tax, 392
   property taxes, 387–388
   sales tax, 392
   severance tax, 392
   sin tax, 392
Taylor, Suzie King, 478
Teach for America, 18–19, 594
Teacher associations, 575–577; see also
      American Federation of Teachers
      (AFT); National Education
      Association (NEA)
Teacher bashing, 149
Teacher-centered philosophies, 354–358
   essentialism, 354–355, 364
   perennialism, 355–357, 364
   vs. student-centered approaches,
      358–359
   summary of, 364

Teacher certification, 15–18, 590
   board-certified, 17
Teacher competency exams, 595–597,
      A-5–A-6
Teacher contracts, 597
Teacher development
   consolidation stage, 552
   evaluation in, 555–557
   in first year, 552–563
   maturity stage, 552
   mentors and, 552–555
   observation in, 555–559
   peer review, 555
   personalizing schools, 560–561
   professional development programs
      for, 558–560
   renewal stage, 552
   stages of, 551–552
Teacher echo, 98
Teacher education, 199, 212
   certification and licensure, 29–30
   classroom management, 20
   current status of, 18–20
   fast track training programs, 18
   normal schools in, 313
   on-the-job-training, 18
   policy-making and, 24
   preparation for employment, 29–32
   resistance to change, 107–108
   university vs. field-based
      training, 113
Teacher effectiveness, 80–113; see also
      Classroom management
   academic learning time and, 83–84
   academic structure and, 92–93
   clarity and, 92–93
   classroom interaction, 182
   classroom management and, 84–90
   cooperative learning, 105–106
   direct teaching, 104–105
   lesson pattern, 103
   mastery learning, 106–108
   models for, 104–109
   new directions in, 109–113
   pedagogical cycle and, 90–93
   planning and, 85
   problem-based learning (PBL),
      108–109
   professional standards, 112
   questioning and, 93–99
   reflective teaching, 111
   room arrangement, 85
   setting expectations, 85
   student anger and aggression, 89
   transitions, 90
   variety in process/content, 102–104
   wait time and, 98
   withitness, 88
Teacher empowerment, 415
Teacher expectations, 206–207

Teacher-family relationships, 496
Teacher interviews, 123–124, 127–128
Teacher oversupply, 586
Teacher preparation, alternative routes
      to, 594–595
Teacher recognition, 565–568
   board certification, 567–569
   career ladders, 567–568
   merit pay, 567, 569–570
Teacher(s)
   applying for a job, 589–590
   board-certified teachers, 15–18
   as committed, 112
   curriculum control and, 257
   demographics of, 587
   development of, 551–552; see also
      Teacher development
   empowerment of, 151
   expectations of, 206–207
   experience and, 112
   first-year, 52–563
   freedom of speech of, 430
   as gatekeepers, 182
   impact of on students' lives, 8
   intern, 552–553
   interpersonal skills of, 26
   job satisfaction of, 9, 14
   learning community and, 112
   liability of, 429–430
   license vs. certification, 590–591
   mentoring of, 552–555
   myths of, 21–22
   oversupply of, 586
   personal qualities of, 22–23
   private lives of, 427, 446
   professionalism of, 9–15
   professional standards, 112
   qualifications and standards, 149
   responsibility for
      managing/monitoring
      learning, 112
   salaries of, 8–11, 14
   shortage of, 562, 595
   standardized testing of, 267
   subject knowledge, 112
   traditional values and, 21
   women as, 313–314
Teacher shortages, 562, 595
Teacher's license, 590
Teachers' rights and responsibilities,
      425–434, 448
   academic freedom, 428–429
   applying for a position, 425–426
   copying published material,
      430–432
   freedom of association, 448
   freedom of speech, 430, 448
   Internet censorship, 433–434
   labor rights, 432–433
   legal liability, 429–430

Teachers' rights—*Cont.*
  personal lifestyle, 427
  sexual harassment, 426
Teachers of Speakers of Other
    Languages, 577
Teaching
  advantages and disadvantages of,
    5–9
  as art vs. skill, 81–83
  as career option, 5
  creativity in, 6–7
  deep teaching, 110
  direct, 104–105
  efficient use of time and, 180–181
  as a gendered career, 313–314
  intellectual stimulation in, 7–8
  intrinsic rewards of, 9
  job market for, 29–30
  mainstreamed classrooms, 68
  prestige of, 9
  professionalization of, 9–15
  reflective teaching, 109–113
  resistance to change, 107–108
  as semiprofession, 13
  social impact of, 8–9
  status and recognition for, 6–7
  student diversity and, 48–51
  working with others, 6
Teaching materials and supplies, 86
*Teaching for Thinking: Theory and
    Application*, 248–249
Technology, 241–243, 603; *see also*
    Computer technology
  adaptation stage, 524
  adoption stage, 524
  appropriation stage, 524
  assistive (adaptive), 529
  careers in, 603
  computer revolution, 517–520
  digital divide, 538–541, 544
  entry stage, 524
  global curriculum, 529–533
  identification of goals for, 540–545
  impact on curriculum, 212, 248–249
  instructional evolution, 524
  invention stage, 524
  nonteaching careers in, 603
  special populations and, 529
  as teacher's tool, 524–527
  technophobia, 523
  television's influence, 517–518
Technophobia, 523
Teenage pregnancy, 503–504
Telecommunications Reform Act,
    520–521
Television
  Channel One, 519
  educational television
    programming, 519
  influence of, 517–518

Television—*Cont.*
  as part of school life, 519
Tenth Amendment, 321, 400
Tenure, 597–99
  advantages of, 597
  disadvantages of, 598–599
  nontenured teachers, 599
  principals and, 599
Tesseract (Educational Alternatives
    Incorporated), 161
Test bias, 264
Tests, 232; *see also* Standardized testing
  alternatives to high-risk
    testing, 267–270
  norm-referenced tests, 205
  objective-referenced tests, 205
  state standards and, 272
  teacher competency, 595–597
Texas and California effect, 273
Textbook adoption states, 271–273
Textbooks
  adoption states of, 271–273
  bias in, 276–279
  current trends in, 275–276
  curriculum control and, 270–276
  dumbing down of, 274
  gender bias in, 276–279
  history of, 311
  lack of depth in, 275
  mentioning phenomenon, 275
  process of development, 271
  racial bias in, 54, 276–279
  readability formulas, 274
  religious fundamentalists and,
    279–280
Theater, 243
Thinking operations, 248
Thomas, Clarence, 426
Thomas, M. Carey, 491
Thomas, Wayne, 62
Thompson, Michael, 560
Thompson v. *Southwest School
    District*, 427
Thomson, Tana, 269
Three waves of reform, 149–150
Thrusts, 90
Tinker v. *Des Moines Independent
    Community School District*,
    438–439, 448
Title IV of the Civil Rights Act, 479
Title VI of the Civil Rights Act, 479
Title VII of the Civil Rights Act, 426
Title IX of the Education Amendments
    Act, 246, 323, 425–426, 436,
    444–445, 449, 492
Titone, Connie, 362
Tomorrow's Teachers (Holmes), 16
Top-down decision making, 415
Torres, Carlos Alberto, 189
Touching, 496

Tracking, 182–183, 199
Traditional inculcation, 447
The Transformation of the School
    (Cremin), 313
Transformative approach, to
    multicultural education, 55
Transition, 90
Transitional approach, 58
Trevino Hart, Elva, 483
*A Tribe Apart: A Journey Into the Heart of
    American Adolescence* (Hersch),
    197
Trustee representatives, 403
*Turning Points: Preparing American Youth
    for the 21st Century*,
    199–200, A-10
Tutors, 357
Twentieth Century Fund, 404, A-8
*Two Nations: Black, White, Separate,
    Hostile, Unequal* (Hacker),
    473–474
Two Rs curriculum, 228

U

Underwood, Kenneth E., 404
Uniforms, 204, 208
United Federation of Teachers
    (UFT), 576
United States Department of Education,
    9, 233, 393, 532, A-10
U.S. FIRST Robotics competition, 527
Unreality, 278
Unremarked revolution, 185

V

Values clarification, 451
Van Galen, J. A., 167
Van Reken, Ruth E., 475
Variety, 103
Varsity sports, 223
Videoconferencing, 529
Virtual field trips, 530
Virtual High School (VHS), 533–538
Virtual teacher, 533–538
Visual arts, 243
Visual learners, 41
  teaching tips for, 41
Visually impaired students, 64
Vocational education, 246–248
Vocational goals, 144
Volunteerism, 142–143, 233
Vouchers, 154
Vygotsky, Lev, 369

W

Wage earners, 497–498
Wait time, 98–99, 497, 528
  student behavior and, 98
  teacher behavior and, 98
Walberg, Herbert, 205, 404

Walker case, 264
Wallace v. *Jaffree,* 448
Walton, John, 161
Warner, W. Lloyd, 183
Watkins, Tom, 160
The Way We Were? (Rothstein), 59
Weber, George, 200
Webster, Noah, 311, 327
Werner, Heinz, 65
West Virginia State Board of Education v.
    Barnette, 448
Whittle, Chris, 160

Whole language movement, 235
Willard, Emma Hart, 327, 332–333, 490
Wiscombe, Janet, 535
Withitness, 88
Wolf, Kenneth, 120
Women's studies, 231
Wood v. *Strickland,* 437
Working portfolio, 120
World Wide Web, 526

X

Xenophobia, 57

Y

Youth charter, 199
Youth suicide, 507

Z

Zealots, 160
Zero reject, 65
Zero-tolerance policy, 437–438
Zittleman, Karen, 449